The Handbook of Experimental Economics

The Handbook of Experimental Economics

John H. Kagel and
Alvin E. Roth

Editors

PRINCETON UNIVERSITY PRESS

PRINCETON · NEW JERSEY

Copyright © 1995 by Princeton University Press
Published by Princeton University Press, 41 William Street,
Princeton, New Jersey 08540
In the United Kingdom: Princeton University Press, Chichester, West Sussex

All Rights Reserved

Library of Congress Cataloging-in-Publication Data

The handbook of experimental economics / John H. Kagel and
Alvin E. Roth, editors.
p.   cm.
Includes bibliographical references and index.
ISBN 0–691–04290–X
1. Economics—Methodology. I. Kagel, John H. (John Henry), 1942–
II. Roth, Alvin E., 1951–   .
HB131.H355   1995
330′.0724—dc20   94–42500

This book has been composed in Times Roman

Princeton University Press books are printed on acid-free paper
and meet the guidelines for permanence and durability of the
Committee on Production Guidelines for Book Longevity of the
Council on Library Resources

Printed in the United States of America

1 3 5 7 9 10 8 6 4 2

Designed by Laury A. Egan

Contents

7. Auctions: A Survey of Experimental Research
John H. Kagel

8. Individual Decision Making
Colin Camerer

Preface

The impetus for *The Handbook of Experimental Economics* came from the great growth of interest in the results and methods of laboratory experiments in economics. This created a growing feeling, both inside and outside the experimental community, that it would be useful to have an overview of the field in order to lower the barriers to entry facing potential experimenters, as well as those facing economists and others who wish to have a critical understanding of what experiments accomplish in economics. The charge to the author of each chapter was therefore both to provide a survey for specialists that could help set an agenda for future research and to provide the nonspecialist with a critical review of work completed to date, with the aim of elucidating the role of experimental studies as a progressive research tool. For this reason, authors were asked where possible to concentrate on series of experiments, not merely single experiments in isolation, in order to demonstrate the way that experiments build on one another to more clearly delineate observed phenomena and to narrow their possible causes.[1]

This handbook is the work not only of many years, but also of many people besides the authors of the chapters. In order to invite the maximum amount of feedback to the author of each chapter, a three-day conference was convened in Pittsburgh in June 1990, at which each author presented an extended outline of his proposed chapter. Investigators from every major center of experimental economics at the time were invited to attend, and most of these centers were in fact represented.[2] The discussions were lively, sometimes even heated. Each author subsequently circulated the various versions of his chapter widely to both experimenters and others interested in the particular topic area and received many comments and suggestions. Indeed, the pace of experimentation was so rapid during the writing of the book that revisions were often required to take account of recent developments that had been initiated by the earlier discussions.

The capstone of this effort came in January 1994, when the (virtually) final chapters were presented at the meeting of the American Economic Association, in Boston.

This handbook has eight chapters. Every one except the first surveys an area of economics in which there has been a concentration of experiments. The first chapter, in contrast, is meant to serve as an introduction to experimental economics as a whole. In our editorial discussions with the chapter authors, they were told that they were free to write each chapter under the assumption that readers would have read the introduction. Thus each author was free to focus each chapter as sharply as seemed appropriate.

One suggestion that we received more than once during the course of this project was that the handbook should include a chapter on methodology, which would tell people how to do experiments. We have not done this. Our view is that a better way to learn how to design and conduct experiments is to consider how good experiments grow organically out of the issues they are designed to investigate and the hypotheses among which they are designed to distinguish. For this reason, we asked each author to address methodological issues that are important for the experiments being discussed.[3]

One of the pleasures of participating in this project has been that it has afforded us the best seats from which to observe one of the most exciting games in town. New centers of experimental economics have sprung up continually while this work was under way, and the interaction between theorists and experimenters has increased apace. Indeed, one of the special pleasures of finally finishing this project is that it is clear that in only a few more years, a single volume will no longer be able to do even the rough justice that we manage here to such a rapidly growing area of economic research.

March 1994
Pittsburgh

Notes

1. This volume thus has a very different, although complementary purpose to the earlier volume *Laboratory Experimentation in Economics: Six Points of View* (Alvin E. Roth, ed., [Cambridge University Press, 1987]). In that volume, six investigators with different approaches to experimentation (John Kagel, Charles Plott, Alvin Roth, Reinhard Selten, Vernon Smith, and Richard Thaler) were each asked to describe work that illustrated their own approach. In this handbook, in contrast, the authors were asked to describe how series of experiments are mediated by and mediate the different approaches of different investigators.

2. Although we failed to preserve a complete list of attendees, some of whom attended only for a day, the following list is nearly complete: Colin Camerer (University of Pennsylvania, now at California Institute of Technology), Robin Dawes (Carnegie-Mellon University), Robert Forsythe (University of Iowa), Glen Harrison (University of South Carolina), John Hey (University of York), Elizabeth Hoffman (University of Arizona, now at Iowa State University), Charles Holt (University of Virginia), John Kennan (University of Iowa, now at University of Wisconsin), John Ledyard (California Institute of Technology), Dan Levin (University of Houston), Graham Loomes (University of York), John O'Brien (Carnegie-Mellon University), Jack Ochs (University of Pittsburgh), Vesna Prasnikar (University of Pittsburgh, now at Ljubljana and Northwestern University), Tatsuyoshi Saijo (University of Tsukuba), Andrew Schotter (New York University), Leo Simon (University of California at Berkeley), Vernon Smith (University of Arizona), Sanjay Srivastava (Carnegie-Mellon University, Richard Thaler (Cornell University), John Van Huyck (Texas A&M University), and James Walker (University of Indiana). Regrettably, no one from the active German (then West German) group of experimenters was able to accept our invitation.

3. Readers with a methodological inclination might keep an eye out for the following kinds of issues: the role of monetary incentives on behavior, demand-induced effects, subject pool effects, inducing risk preferences (the binary lottery technique), techniques for inducing infinite horizon games, effects of subject experience, within versus between group designs, and abstract versus concrete problem representation (to name some of the issues that appear in more than one chapter).

Contributors

Colin Camerer is the Rea A. and Lela G. Axline Professor of Business Economics at the California Institute of Technology.

Charles A. Holt is Professor of Economics at the University of Virginia.

John H. Kagel is Professor of Economics at the University of Pittsburgh.

John O. Ledyard is Professor of Economics and Social Sciences at the California Institute of Technology.

Jack Ochs is Professor of Economics at the University of Pittsburgh.

Alvin E. Roth is A. W. Mellon Professor of Economics at the University of Pittsburgh.

Shyam Sunder is Richard M. Cyert Professor of Management and Economics at the Graduate School of Industrial Administration at Carnegie-Mellon University.

The Handbook of Experimental Economics

1

Introduction to Experimental Economics

Alvin E. Roth

Over thirty years ago, one of the first reviews of experimental economics began by noting that "[experimental] research is rapidly becoming voluminous, but an overview of it can still be crammed into one article" (Rapoport and Orwant 1962, 1). The task facing contemporary reviewers is orders of magnitude larger, and in the general overview of the literature presented in this chapter, and even in the more focused chapters that follow, a good deal of selection has been required.

Nevertheless, as this multiyear task nears completion, I find myself feeling about experimental economics as a distinct enterprise much as I felt about game theory in the late 1970s. At that time there was already a very considerable body of game theoretic work, but the revolution that has today made game theory an important part of most areas of economic theory was still in its early stages. And in the late '70s it was still—just barely—possible to know, or at least know *of*, everyone who had done important work in game theory.

Today, as we approach the midpoint of the 1990s, experimental economics looks much the same way. Quite a substantial body of replicable experimental evidence has been gathered on a growing number of topics, in an increasingly cumulative way, as different groups of experimenters build upon one another's work. Experimental evidence appears regularly in the major economics journals, and it has begun to be reflected in the work of economists who do not themselves do experiments—both in research and in teaching. And with the ever growing numbers of economists who conduct experiments as at least a part of their research, it is fast becoming impossible to keep abreast of all the important new work.

In short, it is both an exhilarating time to do experimental economics and an excellent time to take stock of the experimental enterprise.

I begin this task at the beginning, with a brief history. My historical description, in section I of this chapter, concentrates mostly on the pioneering work done in the 1930s, '40s, and '50s, during which time a number of themes emerged that are still important in contemporary experimental economics. I content myself with painting the more recent history only in the broadest strokes, as this more recent work will provide the substance both of section III of this chapter and of the other chapters in the handbook.

Section II is also an attempt to set the stage for what follows, but in a different way. It describes some of the different uses to which experimentation has been and can be put in economics. I argue that there are few if any areas of economics in which experimental methods do not have the potential to complement, at least indirectly, more traditional methods of investigation. And experimentation gives us a way to attack many important questions that do not yield easily if at all to other methods.

Section III begins to follow series of experiments, in each of the general areas covered by the handbook chapters. I take the *series* of experiments (rather than single experiments) to be the unit around which the discussion is organized, because series of experiments allow the full power of the experimental method to be displayed best.

I. A Brief History of Experimental Economics

In the course of coediting this handbook, it became clear to me that many contemporary experimental economists carry around with them different and very partial accounts of the history of the field. The account that follows began as an attempt to merge these "folk histories."[1]

I won't try to pin down the *first* economic experiment, although I am partial to Bernoulli (1738) on the St. Petersburg paradox. The Bernoullis (Daniel and Nicholas) were not content to rely solely on their own intuitions and resorted to the practice of asking other famous scholars for their opinions on that difficult choice problem. Allowing for their rather informal report, this is not so different from the practice of using hypothetical choice problems to generate hypotheses about individual choice behavior, which has been used to good effect in much more modern research on individual choice.

But I think that searching for scientific "firsts" is often less illuminating than it is sometimes thought to be. In connection with the history of an entirely different subject, I once had occasion to draw the following analogy (Roth and Sotomayor 1990, 170):

> Columbus is viewed as the discoverer of America, even though every school child knows that the Americas were inhabited when he arrived, and that he was not even the first to have made a round trip, having been preceded by Vikings and perhaps by others. What is important about Columbus' discovery of America is not that it was the first, but that it was the *last*. After Columbus, America was never lost again.

That being the case, I will try to identify the historical context out of which contemporary experimental economics has grown, by identifying early experiments that have initiated streams of experimental investigation that continue to the present. For this purpose, I begin in the 1930s. Starting from a low level of activity, the literature of experimental economics has experienced exponential growth in every decade since, which has yet to level off.[2]

I will concentrate on three strands of the early experimental literature, each of which have left both substantive and methodological trails in the modern literature.

The first strand concerns experiments designed to test theories of individual choice. I will focus on an experiment reported by Thurstone (1931), concerned with ordinal utility theory, on an influential critique of this experiment by Wallis and Friedman (1942), and on subsequent experiments taking account of this critique by Rousseas and Hart (1951) and Mosteller and Nogee (1951), as well as on the celebrated work of Allais (1953).

The second strand I will concentrate on concerns tests of game-theoretic hypotheses. I will start with the experiment performed by Dresher and Flood in 1950, which formulated the now famous Prisoner's Dilemma game (Flood 1952, 1958), and continue with the work of Kalisch, Milnor, Nash, and Nering (1954), and Schelling (1957). And I will discuss the work of Suppes and Atkinson in the late 1950s, which investigated learning in game environments.

The third strand I will concentrate on concerns early investigations in Industrial Organization. I will focus on the work of Chamberlin (1948) and Siegel and Fouraker (1960).[3]

One of the methodological themes that can be traced in all three of these strands is how economists have come to rely today primarily on experiments in which subjects' behavior determines how much money they earn.

Finally, each of these strands of experimental economics was profoundly influenced by the publication in 1944 of von Neumann and Morgenstern's *Theory of Games and Economic Behavior,* and I shall try to follow this connection also.

A. Early Experiments: 1930–1960

1. Individual Choice and the Wallis-Friedman Critique

An early formal experiment on individual choice, whose direct descendants in the economics literature are easy to follow, was reported by L. L. Thurstone (1931), who considered the problem of experimentally determining an individual's indifference curves.[4] Thurstone was concerned with testing the indifference curve representation of preferences and with the practicality of obtaining consistent choice data of the sort needed to estimate indifference curves. To this end he reported an experiment in which each subject was asked to make a large number of hypothetical choices between commodity bundles consisting of hats and coats, hats and shoes, or shoes and coats. (For example, the questions about hats and shoes would involve expressing a preference between a bundle consisting of eight hats and eight shoes and one consisting of six hats and nine shoes, and so on for many such pairs of bundles.) He reported the detailed data for one subject and found that, after estimating from the data the relative trade-offs the subject was prepared to make between hats and shoes and between hats and coats (under the assumption that the indifference curves were hyperbolic), it was possible to estimate a curve that fit fairly closely the data collected for choices involving shoes and coats. Thurstone concluded that this kind of choice data could be adequately represented by indifference curves and that it was practical to estimate them in this way.

A lengthy and critical review of Thurstone's experiment was given by W. Allen Wallis and Milton Friedman (1942, particularly 177–83). One of their lines of criticism was that the experiment involved ill specified and hypothetical choices. They summarized their position as follows (179, 180):

> It is questionable whether a subject in so artificial an experimental situation could know what choices he would make in an economic situation; not knowing, it is almost inevitable that he would, in entire good faith, systematize his answers in such a way as to produce plausible but spurious results.

> For a satisfactory experiment it is essential that the subject give actual reactions to actual stimuli. . . . Questionnaires or other devices based on conjectural responses to hypothetical stimuli do not satisfy this requirement. The responses are valueless because the subject cannot know how he would react.[5]

Rousseas and Hart (1951) reported a subsequent experiment on indifference curves designed in reply to Wallis and Friedman and as a follow-up to Thurstone. They constructed what they viewed as a more concrete and realistic choice situation by having subjects choose from different possible breakfast menus, with each potential breakfast consisting of a specified number of eggs and strips of bacon. For added concreteness they specified that "each individual was obliged to eat all of what he chose—i.e. he could not save any part of the offerings for a future time" (p. 291).[6] In this experiment individual subjects made only a single choice (repeated subsequently a month later) and also were asked to state their ideal combination of bacon and eggs. While this had the advantage of avoiding the artificiality of having subjects make many choices of the same type, it left Rousseas and Hart with the problem of trying to combine individual choice data collected from multiple individuals. They adopted the approach of seeing whether choices made by individuals with similar ideal combinations could be pieced together to form consistent indifference curves. Although they pronounced themselves satisfied with the results, we will see that the practice of testing theories of *individual* choice primarily on data from *groups* of subjects was regarded as questionable by subsequent experimenters.[7]

To put subsequent experiments in perspective, however, it is important to note that 1944 was the year in which von Neumann and Morgenstern's *Theory of Games and Economic Behavior* appeared. This presented and brought to wide attention both a more powerful theory of individual choice and a new theory of interactive behavior, and both had a profound influence not only on economic theory but also on experimental economics. The predictions of expected utility theory gave a new focus to experiments concerned with individual choice, and the predictions of game theory—and its concern with precisely specified "rules of the game"—sparked a new wave of experimental tests of interactive behavior.[8]

Starting with the individual choice experiments, various aspects of expected utility theory were soon subjected to experimental investigation—see, for example, Preston and Baratta (1948), Mosteller and Nogee (1951), Allais (1953), Edwards (1953a, 1953b), May (1954), Davidson, Suppes, and Siegel (1957), and Davidson and Marschak (1959), to name only a few.[9] Of these, the most closely connected to that of Thurstone (1931) is the experiment of Mosteller and Nogee (1951), who essentially sought to test expected utility theory in much the same spirit that Thurstone had examined ordinal utility theory. (Mosteller and Nogee were also well aware of the Wallis-Friedman critique of Thurstone's experiment.)[10]

Mosteller and Nogee (1951) began their paper thus (371):

> The purpose of this paper is to report a laboratory experiment that measured in a restricted manner the value to individuals of additional money income. Although the notion of utility has long been incorporated in the thinking of economic theoreticians in the form of a hypothetical construct, efforts to test the validity of the construct have mostly—and in many cases necessarily— been limited to observations of the behavior of *groups* of people in situations where utility was but one of many variables.

Their point was that von Neumann-Morgenstern expected utility functions are derived from assumptions about *individual* choice behavior and that laboratory experimentation provides an opportunity to look at this behavior unconfounded by other considerations. Their general plan of attack had four main steps (372–3):

> (a) to have subjects participate in a game with opportunities to take or refuse certain gambles or risks entailing use of *real money*; (b) from behavior in the game to construct a utility curve for each subject; (c) to make predictions from the utility curves about future individual behavior toward other and more complicated risks; and (d) to test the predictions by examining subsequent behavior toward more complex risks.

The method underlying their construction of the utility curves involved observing whether subjects would accept lotteries with given stakes as the probabilities varied. (They also devoted some attention to arguing that the size of the payoffs could be regarded as significant in terms of alternative employment opportunities available to their subjects.) Their general conclusions (399) were that it was possible to construct subjects' utility functions experimentally and that the predictions derived from these utility functions "are not so good as might be hoped, but their general direction is correct." And with differences of emphasis, I think that this is a conclusion with which many experimental economists would still agree in the light of much subsequent work.

However, much more is now known about various systematic violations of expected utility theory that can be observed in the lab. Perhaps the most famous of these is the "Allais paradox." (Allais suggested, incidentally, that experiments could be used not only to test the predictions of particular theories of rational choice, but also to *define* rational behavior.)[11] Allais asked subjects to make two hypothetical choices. The first choice was between alternatives A and B defined (Allais 1953, 527) as

> A: Certainty of receiving 100 million (francs)

and

> B: Probability .1 of receiving 500 million
> Probability .89 of receiving 100 million
> Probability .01 of receiving zero

and the second choice was between alternatives C and D defined as

> C: Probability .11 of earning 100 million
> Probability .89 of earning zero

and

> D: Probability .1 of earning 500 million
> Probability .9 of earning zero.

It is not difficult to show that an expected utility maximizer who prefers A to B must also prefer C to D. However, Allais reported that a common pattern of preference was that A was preferred to B but D was preferred to C. Note that although Allais's choices were hypothetical, the phenomenon he reported has subsequently been reproduced with real choices (involving much smaller amounts of money). Camerer discusses these matters in some detail in chapter 8.

It is worth noting that not all of the individual choice experiments motivated by von Neumann-Morgenstern expected utility theory in fact depended in any critical way upon the novel parts of that theory. For example, May (1954) reported that it was possible to elicit intransitive preferences in choices involving no uncertainty. His results thus show a violation of even ordinal utility theory, and his experiment could in principle have been conducted as a test of the earlier theory. However (as has often seemed to be the case since), the further development of the theory may have clarified the role that experiments could play.

2. Game-Theoretic Hypotheses

As mentioned earlier, following von Neumann and Morgenstern (1944), there also began to be considerable attention paid to experiments involving interactive behavior. We turn next to some of these.

In January of 1950, Melvin Dresher and Merrill Flood conducted at the Rand Corporation an experiment which has had an enormous if indirect influence, since it introduced the game that has subsequently come to be known as the prisoner's dilemma.[12] The game they studied was the hundred-fold repetition of the matrix game given below, between a fixed pair of subjects who communicated only their choices of row (1 or 2) or column (1 or 2).

$$-1, 2 \qquad 1/2, 1$$
$$0, 1/2 \qquad 1, -1$$

Payoffs were in pennies, with each player receiving the sum, over the one hundred plays of the game, of his payoffs in each play. The unique Nash equilibrium prediction is that the players should choose (2,1)—the second row and the first column—at each of the hundred repetitions. Thus the predicted earnings of the players are 0 for the row player (henceforth "Row") and $0.50 for the column player (henceforth "Column").[13] Of course this is inefficient, since if the players instead played (1,2) at every period, for example, their earnings would be $0.50 for Row and $1.00 for Column—i.e., they would both earn more. But this is not equilibrium behavior. The fact that equilibrium play is substantially less profitable than cooperative play made Dresher and Flood anticipate—correctly, as it turns out—that this game would present a difficult test of the equilibrium predictions.

The observed payoffs, for a pair of players whose play was reported in detail in Flood (1952, 1958) were $0.40 for Row and $0.65 for Column. This outcome is far from the equilibrium outcome, although it also falls considerably short of perfect cooperation. (As will be discussed in section III.A of this chapter, this observation has since been replicated many times.) Dresher and Flood interpreted this as evidence against the general hypothesis that players tend to choose Nash equilibrium strategies, and in favor of the hypothesis that a cooperative "split the difference" principle would be more powerful in organizing the data from games of this kind.

Despite their own interpretation of the data, Dresher and Flood included in their report of the experiment the following passage, describing an alternative interpretation given by John Nash (Flood 1958, 16):

Dr. Nash makes the following comment (private communication) on this experiment:

"The flaw in this experiment as a test of equilibrium point theory is that the experiment really amounts to having the players play one large multi-move game. One cannot just as well think of the thing as a sequence of independent games as one can in zero-sum cases. There is much too much interaction, which is obvious in the results of the experiment.

"Viewing it as a multimove game a strategy is a complete program of action, including reactions to what the other player had done. In this view it is still true the only real absolute equilibrium point is for [Row] always to play 2, [Column] always 1.

"However, the strategies:

[Row] plays 1 'til [Column] plays 1, then 2 ever after,
[Column] plays 2 'til [Row] plays 2, then 1 ever after,

are very nearly at equilibrium and in a game with an indeterminate stop point or an infinite game with interest on utility it *is* an equilibrium point.

"Since 100 trials are so long that the Hangman's Paradox cannot possibly be well reasoned through on it, it's fairly clear that one should expect an approximation to this behavior which is most appropriate for indeterminate end games with a little flurry of aggressiveness at the end and perhaps a few sallies, to test the opponent's mettle during the game.

"It is really striking, however, how inefficient [Row] and [Column] were in obtaining the rewards. One would have thought them more rational.

"If this experiment were conducted with various different players rotating the competition and with *no information given to a player of what choices the others have been making until the end* of all the trials, then the experimental results would have been quite different, for this modification of procedure would remove the interaction between the trials."

Dr. Dresher and I were glad to receive these comments, and to include them here, even though we would not change our interpretation of the experiment along the lines indicated by Dr. Nash.

Despite the limitations of this very exploratory, preliminary experiment,[14] there are many ways in which it foreshadows some of the best of experimental economics. It tests the clear predictions of a general theory, on a difficult test case. And the results allow alternative hypotheses to be developed. When they are as clearly stated as Nash's comments, they suggest further experiments. We will return to some of the more modern of these subsequent experiments in section III.A.[15] And as the quoted passage makes clear, some of the most interesting outcomes of an experiment may be the manner in which its results pit alternative interpretations against each other.

Note that in choosing a difficult test case, Dresher and Flood formulated a game that has since engaged both theorists and experimenters in a number of disciplines, as a large literature has developed around the prisoner's dilemma, which has been used as a metaphor for problems from arms races to the provision of public goods.[16] This too is one of the indirect virtues of experimentation. The design of an experiment to test a particular theory often forces the experimenter to focus on specific aspects of the theory other than those that naturally come to the fore in the theoretical literature. The insights gained from designing an experiment are, as in this case, often of value even apart from the actual conduct of the experiment. Thus there is an interplay, on many levels, between theory and experiment.

In 1952 the Ford Foundation and the University of Michigan sponsored a conference on "The Design of Experiments in Decision Processes," which was held in Santa Monica (in order to accommodate the game theorists and experimenters associated with the Rand Corporation). Some of the experimental papers from this conference appear in Thrall, Coombs, and Davis (1954).[17] The paper by Kalisch, Milnor, Nash, and Nering, which reported a small-scale experiment involving several different n-person games, anticipates some issues of experimental design that have played important roles in the subsequent literature. Some of the games they looked at were constructed to allow particular theoretical predictions to be tested on a domain on which the theories in question would make unambiguous predictions. They write as follows:

> The negotiation procedures were formalized (e.g., the identities of a player's opponents were concealed from him and he was allowed to bid, accept, decline, or counter-bid in a very limited number of ways . . .). The construction of a theory to deal with an unlimited or very large number of negotiation possibilities is as yet so difficult that it seems desirable to restrict and severely formalize the negotiation procedure to the point where a meaningful theory can be constructed. (302)

The choices the players made were not hypothetical, rather the profits they would take home from the experimental session were proportional to their payoffs in the experimental games. And (after finding mixed support for various game-theoretic hypotheses) the authors concluded with a discussion of design features that might make it easier to interpret future experiments, saying (326):

> The same set of players should not be together repeatedly since there is too much of a tendency to regard a run of plays as a single play of a more complicated game.

> It would be better to play an unsymmetrical game so that there would be no obviously fair method of arbitrating the game and avoiding competition.

These two bits of advice are very different from one another, but are each representative of what have proved to be important aspects of the design of economic experiments.

The first bit of advice is solidly grounded in theory. If the same players play a game more than once, their behavior even the first time they play may be different than if they were going to play only once, since in the repeated case they can anticipate that actions in the first period may affect the outcome in future periods.[18]

The second bit of advice was grounded not in theory, but in a clearly observed experimental regularity: in symmetric situations players often agreed on equal divisions. By suggesting that this is because equal division in symmetric games is a "fair" method of division and that experimenters should seek to avoid such situations, the authors seem to have been suggesting that subjects are sometimes motivated by considerations that the experimenter can only imperfectly control. In this view, the demands of fairness in situations that seem to subjects to call for fair behavior may sometimes overwhelm the motivations that the experimenters are trying to induce (via the monetary rewards), so that the game being played is different than the one intended by the experimenter.

Another hypothesis about why equal divisions are so often observed in symmetric situations was offered by Thomas Schelling. He proposed that in many situations the problem facing economic agents is predominantly one of coordination, and that by focusing on outcomes that might be "prominent," some of the costs of coordination failure could be avoided. Schelling (1957) reported an experiment in which he confronted "an unscientific sample of respondents" with a variety of (hypothetical) problems. The following are two examples:[19]

> You and your partner (rival) are to be given $100 if you can agree on how to divide it without communicating. Each of you is to write the amount of his claim on a sheet of paper; and if the two claims add to no more than $100, each gets exactly what he claimed. If the two claims exceed $100, neither of you gets anything. (24)

> You and your two partners (or rivals) each have one of the letters A, B, and C. Each of you is to write these three letters, A, B, C, in any order. If the order is the same on all three of your lists, you get prizes totaling $6, of which $3 goes to the one whose letter is first on all three lists, $2 to the one whose letter is second, and $1 to the person whose letter is third. If the letters are not in identical order on all three lists, none of you gets anything. (23)

Schelling reports that in the first of these problems, thirty-six out of forty subjects chose $50. Of course, since this yields an equal division, it could have been caused by a desire to be fair, instead of because it is a "prominent" outcome.[20] But it is harder to explain the results of the next problem as a result of anything but the prominence of alphabetical order: 9 out of 12 As, 10 out of 12 Bs, and 14 out of 16 Cs chose the order ABC. This illustrates the power of experiments to test a hypothesis in different ways, the better to distinguish it from alternative hypotheses that might yield similar predictions on some domains.[21]

Schelling's point was that a wide variety of cues could serve to make an outcome prominent and facilitate coordination. His comments were directed primarily at game theorists, the point being that highly abstract models might exclude factors that play an essential role in facilitating coordination. But there is a lesson for experimenters too, which is that details of how experiments are conducted may be of considerable importance, even if they concern features of the environment not addressed by existing theories. Sometimes these details will be worth study in their own right, and sometimes the experimenter will wish to avoid constructing the environment in a way that introduces unwanted influences (e.g., think how the results for the second problem would differ if the players were identified by colors instead of letters). The considerable influence of Schelling's experiments was for many years felt mostly indirectly, through the ways in which various kinds of phenomena were interpreted by subsequent authors.[22] Recently, however, there has been a renewed interest in coordination experiments, motivated in part by macroeconomic questions, and these are discussed by Jack Ochs in chapter 3.

A final set of studies worth mentioning here were not designed to test game-theoretic hypotheses directly, but nevertheless involved careful study of strategic environments. Suppes and Atkinson (1960) reported an extensive series of experiments (involving more than 1,000 subjects) designed to investigate the predictive power of simple learning theories in game situations (see also Atkinson and Suppes 1958, 1959). They started by reporting experimental sessions in which subjects didn't even know that they were playing a game, but were simply asked to make a sequence of choices, after each of which they were told what outcome had resulted, without being told that the outcome was determined in part by the actions of another subject in the experiment, with whom they were in fact playing a game. They then reported sessions in which subjects were increasingly informed about the game. In these sessions, subjects either knew they were playing a game, but did not see the payoff matrix, or else knew both that they were playing a game and how the outcomes were determined through the actions of the players. All of these sessions were conducted with hypothetical payoffs, and a final set of experimental sessions were conducted in which subjects were fully informed about the game and earned actual payoffs based on their performance.

In general, Suppes and Atkinson found that their results corresponded better to the predictions of learning theories than to those of game theory. They took care to emphasize that they found this unsurprising in view of the fact that in most cases their subjects did not know what game they were playing. However, when they reported experimental sessions in which subjects were fully informed about the game and rewarded for the outcomes, their results were somewhat different. In particular, when they considered (in chap. 10) the effects of monetary payoffs, they observed significant effects due to the presence and size of monetary payoffs on subject behavior, which they summarized as follows.

> In the present study the subjects tended to approach an optimal game strategy as the monetary reward increased, and it may well be that this result can be directly generalized to more complex reinforcement schedules. However, results of the type described in Chapter 9 (where subjects were shown the payoff matrix and deviated from learning-theory predictions, but not in the direction predicted by game theory) leave the issue open to further analysis. (198)

Because Suppes and Atkinson used different games (zero and nonzero sum, two and three person, and with mixed and pure strategy equilibria) in their different information and payoff conditions, no general conclusion about how the conditions affect the accuracy of the game theoretic predictions can be drawn. (Recall that their experiments were designed primarily to test predictions of their learning theory.) However, their work foreshadows some contemporary experimental work that has developed in conjunction with a growing interest among game theorists in models of learning and adaptation.[23]

3. Industrial Organization

Turning now to the organization of markets, one early experiment that has exerted a major, if delayed, influence on modern experimentation was reported in 1948 by Edward Hastings Chamberlin. Chamberlin prefaced his article with an explanation of what he thought laboratory experiments might bring to economics, beginning with a description of what he took to be the conventional wisdom on the subject. He wrote as follows:

> It is a commonplace that, in its choice of method, economics is limited by the fact that resort cannot be had to the laboratory techniques of the natural sciences. On the one hand, the data of real life are necessarily the product of many influences other than those which it is desired to isolate—a difficulty which the most refined statistical methods can overcome only in small part. On the other hand, the unwanted variables cannot be held constant or eliminated in an economic "laboratory" because the real world of human beings, firms, markets, and governments cannot be reproduced artificially and controlled. The social scientist who would like to study in isolation and under known conditions the effects of particular forces is, for the most part, obliged to conduct his "experiment" by the application of general reasoning to *abstract* "models." He cannot observe the actual operation of a *real* model under controlled conditions.
>
> The purpose of this article is to make a very tiny breach in this position: to describe an actual experiment with a "market" under laboratory conditions and to set forth some of the conclusions indicated by it. (1948, 95)

Chamberlin went on to describe the hypothesis motivating his experiment, which was that—contrary to the prevailing orthodoxy—market outcomes would often differ from competitive equilibrium "under conditions (as in real life) in which the actual prices . . . are not subject to 'recontract' (thus perfecting the market), but remain final" (95).

Chamberlin created an experimental market by informing each buyer and seller of his reservation price for a single unit of an indivisible commodity (i.e., for each buyer the price below which he could profitably buy, and for each seller the price above which he could profitably sell), and he reported the transactions that resulted when buyers and sellers were then free to negotiate with one another in a decentralized market. He noted that the reservation prices of the buyers, in aggregate, determined the market's demand curve, while the reservation prices of the sellers determined the supply curve, so that the competitive equilibrium (price and volume) could be established unambiguously and controlled by the experimenter (under only the assumption that buyers and sellers were willing to trade at the reservation prices established for them in this way).

The experiment he reported involved forty-six markets, with slightly varying equilibrium prices. He observed that the number of units transacted was greater than the competitive volume in forty-two of these markets and equal to the competitive volume in the remaining four markets, while the average price was below the competitive price in thirty-nine of these markets and higher in the rest.[24] Chamberlin interpreted the systematic differences he observed between actual transaction prices and volumes and those predicted by the competitive equilibrium as supporting his hypothesis. At the same time, he noted that the results he observed caused him to correct an erroneous assertion he had made in Chamberlin

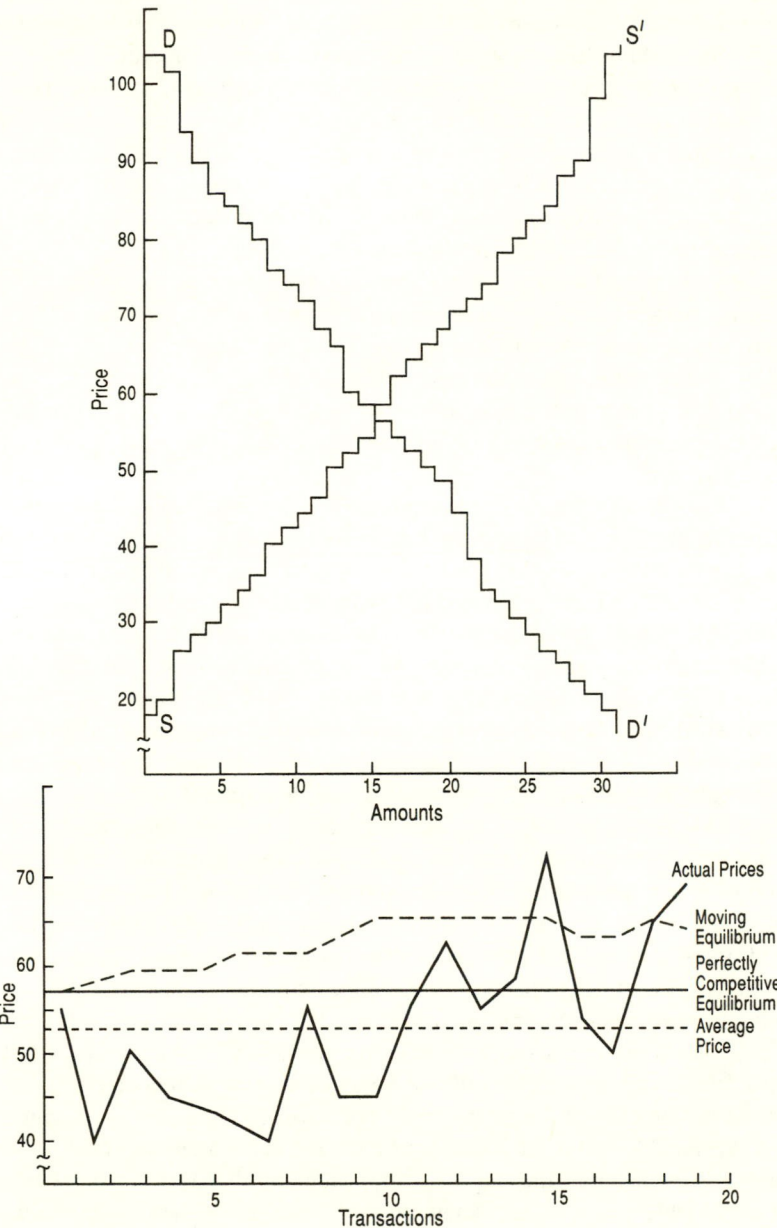

Figure 1.1. The induced supply and demand curves (top) and the observed prices compared to the equilibrium predictions. *Source:* Chamberlain 1948.

(1933, 27) that none of the "normally included buyers and sellers" (i.e., those who would transact at equilibrium) could fail to transact even when the market did not achieve equilibrium. In fact, what he observed was that sometimes a buyer, for example, might find that all of those sellers from whom he could afford to buy had already sold their unit to some other buyer, at a price below the equilibrium price.[25] Figure 1.1 records the path of transactions over time in one of his markets.[26] Chamberlin closed by cautioning that his results should be regarded as preliminary and noted that some of the regularities he observed might be sensitive to the shape of the supply and demand curves.

In the years since Chamberlin's experiment, his technique for constructing experimental markets with known supply and demand curves has been widely employed, and we shall return to it in section III of this chapter, and in the chapters by Holt, Kagel, and Sunder. More generally, Chamberlin's experiment illustrates the empirical power that comes from being able to create an environment in which the predictions of a theory (in this case competitive equilibrium) can be precisely known.

Like May's experiment on intransitivities in individual choice, Chamberlin's is an experiment that could have been done before von Neumann and Morgenstern, since it tested hypotheses that predated their work. Also, it should be noted that Chamberlin's experiment employed only hypothetical payoffs.

The end of the decade of the 1950s, and the beginning of the next, was marked by experiments concerning duopoly and oligopoly behavior, in the work of Hoggatt (1959), Sauermann and Selten (1959, 1960), and Siegel and Fouraker (1960) (which won the 1959 Monograph Prize of the American Academy of Arts and Sciences). The work of Siegel and Fouraker was perhaps the most extended experimental economics study reported up until that time.[27]

Siegel and Fouraker (1960) reported a series of experiments in which subjects bargained in pairs until they reached agreement over a price and quantity, which served to determine their profits (each subject was given a payoff table that informed him of his own profits for each possible price and quantity). They designed a series of careful experiments to distinguish among a large variety of hypotheses concerning bilateral monopoly; hypotheses drawn from diverse sources in classical economic theory, game theory, psychology, and from the earlier game theory experiments of Schelling (1957). (They concluded [69] that "consideration of traditional economic forces cannot be depended on to yield an adequate explanation of the prices arrived at in bilateral monopoly bargaining.") One of the notable features of their experiments was the attention they paid to the information available to the subjects about each other's payoffs. They compared the case in which each subject knew only his own payoff table with the case in which one subject knew both payoff tables and the case in which both subjects knew both payoff tables. They found that, as the information increased in this way for the game they considered, the frequency with which subjects chose the Pareto optimal quantity increased, as did the frequency with which they chose a price that gave them equal payoffs.

Two methodological aspects of Siegel and Fouraker's work are especially notable. First, they took pains to insure that their subjects interacted anonymously, in order to avoid introducing into their experiment uncontrolled "social" phenomena. This is a subject to which I will return in chapter 4. Second, not only did they follow the increasingly common practice of motivating subjects with monetary payoffs, but they investigated the effect of changing the incentives by changing the size of the payoff differences that resulted from different decisions. That is, they were not content to observe that subjects could make substantial profits from choosing, for example, the Pareto optimal quantity. They also considered how much of a difference it made if the quantity chosen was only a little more or a little less than the Pareto optimum. They noted that in the first of the payoff tables they used this difference was small and conjectured that the variance they observed around the Pareto optimal quantity might be due to the fact that the subjects felt that the potential payoff difference was not worth the hazards of continued bargaining. They say (34):

> If this reasoning is correct, then increasing the difference in payoff to each bargainer between contracts at the Paretian optima and contracts at quantities adjacent to the optima should lead to the negotiation of a higher percentage of contracts on the optima.

They then went on to present results obtained from payoff tables that increased the size of these differences and reported that they did indeed observe much less variance around the Pareto optimal quantity.

Siegel and Fouraker used their results to motivate a theory based on the "level of aspiration" of the subjects, which they proposed was the variable effected by the differing amounts of information. They went on to explore this hypothesis in oligopoly models as well (Fouraker and Siegel 1963). Independently, Sauermann and Selten (1959, 1960) formed related hypotheses on the basis of rather different oligopoly experiments.[28]

I think Siegel and Fouraker's views on the place of experimentation in economics have stood the test of time. They said (1960, 72–3):

> Our data have been observations made specifically to meet the purposes of this research. We have not turned to preexisting data. In the specific case of bilateral monopoly, it would be extremely unlikely that appropriate naturalistic data could be collected to test the theoretical models. . . . Although exchanges under bilateral monopoly conditions are common, such . . . descriptions as may be available will not generally be in an appropriate form for testing theoretical models. Following Boulding [unpublished speech], we may say that in science the shift from relying on existing information collected for other purposes to using information collected specifically for research purposes is analogous to primitive man's shift from food collecting to agriculture, and "provides the same kind of stimulus to development and accumulation. It is when a science starts to go out to ask exactly what it wants to know, rather than relying on information collected for other purposes, that it begins to obtain control of its own growth."

We have made our observations under controlled conditions. We have not only collected observations especially for this research, but we have also done so under conditions which make the observations relevant to the research purposes. In using the laboratory rather than the field, we have been able to isolate the phenomena of interest to the research. . . .

We have used the experimental method. That is, we have manipulated certain variables and observed the effects of variations in these upon certain other variables. By so doing, we have demonstrated that the amount of information available to a bargainer and his level of aspiration are significant determinants of the price-quantity contracts which will be reached. We aver that only the experimental method could have demonstrated the influence and importance of these determinants.

Note that, in analyzing their experimental results, Siegel and Fouraker sought to develop game theory in new directions; that is, they sought not merely to test game theoretic predictions, but to develop new theories better able to predict the outcome of games such as those they studied.[29] Schelling (1958; see also Schelling 1960) further proposed that the relationship between game theory and experimentation *must* be two way in this sense. In a section of his paper entitled "Game Theory and Experimental Research" he wrote (1958, 257):

some *essential* part of the study of mixed-motive games is necessarily empirical. This is not to say just that it is an empirical question how people do actually perform. . . . It is a stronger statement: that the principles relevant to *successful* play, the *strategic* principles, the propositions of a *normative* theory, cannot be derived by purely analytic means from a priori considerations.

It is striking to note a number of distinguished game theorists among the earliest experimenters (Nash, Schelling, Selten, and Shubik, for example, set a high standard of distinction by any measure). I have already indicated that I think this is no accident. Rather, game theory brought to economics a kind of theory that lent itself to experimental investigation, and in some cases demanded it. The reason is that it seeks to provide precise models of both individual behavior (in von Neumann–Morgenstern utility functions) and of economic environments. This concern with the "rules of the game," the institutions and mechanisms by which transactions were made, together with precise assumptions about the behavior of individuals and the information available to them, gave rise to theories that could be tested in the laboratory.

Before moving on to more modern experiments, it should be noted that by the end of the 1950s two of the features that have come to distinguish experimental economics were already clearly in evidence. The first of these, just referred to, is the concern for testing theories of great potential generality (such as theories of equilibrium) on specific, controlled environments and the consequent attention to rules of play. The second is the fact that many of the experiments attempted to gain control of subjects' motivations by paying the subjects based on their performance so that subjects' performance could be analyzed under the assumption that they were seeking to maximize the utility (or sometimes simply, the expected value) of the money earned. That is, by this time the reaction of experimental economists to the Wallis-Friedman critique of hypothetical choices was already beginning to take shape in a tendency to rely primarily on experiments in which subjects' behavior determined their *monetary* payoffs.[30]

And although the end of the 1950s marks a time that is still quite early in the development of experimental economics, a number of the experiments that were completed well before then have continued to exert a powerful influence on modern research, in ways that will be covered at greater length in both the other sections of this chapter and the other chapters of this volume. Individual choice experiments in the spirit of Allais (1953) have inspired the search for other systematic violations of expected utility theory, and these are surveyed by Camerer in chapter 8. Prisoner's dilemma experiments in the spirit of Dresher and Flood (Flood 1952, 1958) became a small cottage industry by themselves, and also influenced game theory in ways that make their full effect hard to grasp, but they are very close kin to the public goods experiments described by Ledyard in chapter 2. And the basic design of Chamberlin (1948) for inducing individual reservation prices and aggregate supply and demand curves has become one of the most widely used techniques in experimental economics, and plays a role in many of the chapters of this volume, as do the methodological considerations raised by Siegel and Fouraker (1960). Finally, the theoretical work of the early game theorists, especially of von Neumann and Morgenstern and of Nash, have had such profound effects on both modern economic theory and on experimental economics that it is fair to say that their influence is pervasive in every chapter of this volume.

B. The 1960s to the Present

The 1960s were a decade of steady growth for experimental economics, and the first *reviews* of economics experiments began to appear (see Rapoport and Orwant 1962; Cyert and Lave 1965; and Friedman 1969).[31] Rapoport and Chammah (1965) compiled a considerable body of work associated with the prisoner's dilemma, and a set of German experiments is reported in Sauermann (1967) (who may have coined the term "experimental economics").[32] Well over a hundred experimental economics papers were published in the 1960s.[33] By the end of the decade a good deal of thought had begun to be given to questions of experimental methodology as such (see, for example, the description of a computerized laboratory by Hogatt, Esherich, and Wheeler 1969).

An important methodological advance, which illustrates the close connection between economic theory and experimental design, came in the work of Becker, DeGroot, and Marschak (1964). They conducted an experiment to measure individuals' expected utility functions and were concerned with the problem of how to motivate experimental subjects to reveal their "true" reservation prices for lotteries. The solution they hit upon was that each subject was endowed with a lottery and then asked to name the amount of money for which he would be willing to sell it. Each subject was told that the selling price he named would be compared with a price to be determined randomly. If the randomly determined price (the offer price) was higher than the named selling price, then the experimenter would buy the lottery from the subject for the randomly determined *offer* price (*not* for the named selling price); otherwise the subject would keep and play the lottery and earn its random outcome. It is not hard to see that the dominant strategy for a utility maximizer faced with such a mechanism is to state his true selling price, (i.e., the price that makes him indifferent between selling the lottery or keeping it).[34] Because many modern economic theories are based on the assumption that agents are expected utility maximizers, so that it is frequently the case that the predictions of the theory can only be known if the utility functions of the subjects can be accurately estimated, this technique has found wide application even in experiments whose primary purpose is not to estimate utility functions.

Note that if the subjects are not expected utility maximizers, the selling price elicited in this way may not have all the properties that it would for utility maximizers. But to test the predictions of a theory that assumes the subjects are utility maximizers one first needs to know what the theory predicts, and the BDM procedure just described gives experimenters one way of knowing precisely what are the predictions of the theory they are testing, for the subjects they are examining, in the environment they have created. The ability to test the predictions of a theory when they are precisely known in this way is one of the principle attractions of controlled experimentation in the laboratory.

An important experiment from this period that established another way in which individuals may systematically deviate from being perfect *subjective* expected utility maximizers was Ellsberg (1961), who showed that Bayesian probability assessments are not always descriptive of observed behavior. Camerer will report on some of the many followups to this line of investigation in chapter 8. Another influential experiment from this period, which employed, to quite different effect, the basic design of Chamberlin's (1948) experiment, was reported by Vernon Smith (1962), and this is discussed at greater length in section III.D of this chapter and by Holt in chapter 5. Smith (1992) reports that his first experiment (Smith 1962) was motivated by a desire to see if competitive outcomes could be observed using Chamberlin's basic design but with different pricemaking rules and with repetition using constant parameters.[35]

The 1970s brought further growth, including growth of research support.[36] In this latter regard, the fact that the National Science Foundation began providing sustained support to a number of different laboratories had a significant impact on the development of experimental economics. Jim Blackmun and Dan Newlon are the NSF officials who came to be most closely associated with this critical support. The 1970s were also marked by a number of conferences, in (then West) Germany and in the United States, that began to bring different groups of experimenters into contact (see Sauermann 1972, 1978a, 1978b, for collections of papers from the German conferences). Experimenters who played a leading role in these activities include Heinz Sauermann, Reinhard Selten, and Reinhard Tietz in Germany, and Charles Plott and Vernon Smith in the United States. During this time, the experimental economics literature became increasingly distinct from experimental psychology, although the two literatures retain many points of overlap.[37]

In the 1980s and early '90s the growth of experimental economics became explosive, and with this growth came the accompanying signs of having become a "mainstream" subject.[38] An early experimenter—Maurice Allais—even won the 1988 Nobel Memorial Prize in Economics.[39] The vastly increased numbers of experiments and experimenters also instigated a sea change in the way experimental economics is done. For the first time, there began to be a wide variety of areas in which different groups of experimenters began to study the same issues from different points of view. This meant that there began to be *series* of experiments in which investigators with different hypotheses responded to one anothers' experiments, critically examining earlier conclusions. It is this process, in which experimental results suggest new experiments and in which different theoretical points of view suggest different experiments to different groups of experimenters, that allows us to begin to look back on experimental economics as a cumulative process. This kind of dialogue is one of the great sources of strength of the experimental method, a sentiment which has been expressed somewhat jocularly by the experimental psychologist Georg von Bekesy:

> Another way of dealing with [experimental research] errors is to have friends who are willing to spend the time necessary to carry out a critical examination of the experimental design beforehand and the results after the experiments have been completed. An even better way is to have an enemy. An enemy is willing to devote a vast amount of time and brain power to ferreting out errors both large and small, and this without any compensation. The trouble is that really capable enemies are scarce; most of them are only ordinary. Another trouble with enemies is that they sometimes develop into friends and lose a good deal of their zeal. It was in this way that the writer lost his three best enemies. (1960, 8–9)

It is the development of experimental economics into this kind of cumulative, progressive dialogue that makes this handbook possible today, when not many years ago it would have been premature.

II. The Uses of Experimentation

Experiments can be done for different reasons, and in reading about the series of experiments described in the remainder of this chapter and of this volume, it may help to keep some of them in mind. In the summer of 1985, in a symposium on experimental economics at the Fifth World Congress of the Econometric Society, I suggested that experiments might be loosely classified according to how they were motivated and to whom they were intended to be persuasive, that is, according to the dialogues they were part of.[40] I referred to these different kinds of dialogues as "Speaking to Theorists," "Searching for Facts" (and, closely related, "Searching for Meaning"), and "Whispering in the Ears of Princes." To the extent that these categories have since gained wider currency, it is perhaps because they can be used as a metaphor for what economists do generally.[41] For the purpose of looking at experiments, they help to focus attention on how different kinds of experiments emphasize different aspects of experimental design. Most series of economics experiments, and even many individual experiments, have elements of more than one of these motivations.

The category "Speaking to Theorists" includes experiments designed to test the predictions of well articulated formal theories, and to observe unpredicted regularities, in a controlled environment that allows these observations to be unambiguously interpreted in relationship to the theory. Such experiments are intended to feed back into the theoretical literature—i.e., they are part of a dialogue between experimenters and theorists.

The category "Searching for Facts" includes experiments studying the effects of variables about which existing theory may have little to say. Often these experiments are motivated by earlier experiments and are designed to isolate the cause of some observed regularity, by varying details of the way the experiments were conducted. Such experiments are part of the dialogue that experimenters carry on with one another. And as these facts begin to accumulate, "Searching for Meaning" becomes possible, as theories of the observed behavior can be proposed and then tested. So this kind of work contributes also to the dialogue between theorists and experimenters.

The category "Whispering in the Ears of Princes" deals with the dialogue between experimenters and policymakers. These experiments might be motivated, for example, by the kind of question raised by regulatory agencies, about the effect of changes in the way some market is organized. Their characteristic feature is that the experimental environment is designed to closely resemble, in certain respects, the naturally occurring environment that is the focus of interest for the policy purposes at hand. This category of experiments has so far not given rise to any extended series of experiments by different investigators but offers the possibility of bringing scientific methods to bear on one of the traditional responsibilities of economists, to formulate advice on questions of policy whose answers lie beyond the reliable scientific knowledge of the profession.[42]

What this classification should suggest is that experiments may potentially play a role in most of the things that economists do. Since many economists find (or used to find) this a surprising idea, it may be helpful to point out, by way of a loose analogy, that experiments play a role in most of the things that biologists do, and, like economists, biologists have a lot of ground to cover, from molecular biology to evolution, to medicine. Experiments can obviously play a very direct role in testing and refining theories of molecular biology, since the phenomena in question can be brought entirely into the laboratory. But although experiments cannot be conducted on the fossil record, evolutionary biologists nevertheless obtain much of their understanding of selection and evolution from experiments in microbiology, genetics, and plant breeding. And while physicians are often called upon to treat diseases that are beyond the reliable scientific knowledge of their profession, clinical trials help them to discern the effects of different drugs even when the mechanism by which they work is still obscure. In the same way, economic experiments may play a role not only in testing and refining theories concerned with individuals or small groups, but also concerning questions about large markets, industrial organization, and macroeconomics.

The remainder of this chapter, and of this volume, aims to show how economists can use the tools they find in the laboratory to make steady, incremental progress on answering questions that might otherwise be intractable. We focus on *series* of experiments, which together tell us more than any one of them. By "more" I do not mean that these series of experiments necessarily permit us to draw *broader* conclusions than might have seemed warranted on the basis of one experiment alone. While this will sometimes be so, subsequent experiments sometimes define more narrowly the conditions under which some initially observed phenomenon occurs and sometimes cause the results of an earlier experiment to be entirely reinterpreted and initial conclusions to be rejected. What I hope this volume will illustrate is how series of experiments can be constructed to allow us to draw more *reliable* conclusions, both about what we know and about what we know we don't know.

This process is particularly informative when different groups of investigators with different theoretical points of view conduct experiments intended to test each others' conclusions. Series of experiments arising in this way may still leave room for experts to differ, but they narrow the room for disagreement and clarify the nature of the remaining disagreement by forcing investigators to refine their hypotheses. And, long after many of the particular experiments so far conducted have receded to no more than historical importance, it is this that is likely to be the chief contribution of controlled experimentation to economics.

III. Some Series of Experiments[43]

My aim in this section is to introduce some topics of contemporary interest to experimenters and in doing so to introduce and provide some context for the specialized chapters of this volume.

Chapter 2, by Ledyard, deals with the problems associated with providing public goods, and the incentives that agents have to "free ride" and enjoy the goods that may be produced by others without contributing to their production. As in the prisoner's dilemma, if no one cooperates to produce the public good, everyone is worse off than if they had cooperated. Ledyard proposes that public goods provision games in which the equilibrium behavior is for no one to contribute to the production of public goods can best be thought of as prisoners' dilemmas, while those games in which the equilibria call for some players to contribute and others to free ride are like the game of "chicken" (see Table 2.11).[44] I will accordingly start my discussion in section III.A with some prisoner's dilemma experiments, before moving on to series of experiments dealing with more traditional formulations of public goods provision. This is an area in which experimental results have led to new directions of theoretical investigation, including various ways of considering whether players may have motivations not well captured by the payoffs in the game, such as altruism, or other kinds of preferences concerning more than one's own's welfare.

Chapter 3, by Ochs, considers problems of coordination. Coordination problems arise in a fundamental way in games with multiple equilibria, since in general if the players fail to coordinate their expectations and actions on a single equilibrium, the outcome is inefficient. The frequency of inefficient outcomes and the conditions which make them more or less likely to occur, are a theme that this area shares with the study of public goods provision, which is one of the very many domains in which coordination problems arise. Schelling's work in the 1950s poses some of the problems still being investigated today. Compared to other chapters in this volume, however, there are relatively few extended *series* of experiments in this area, and so my introduction in section III.B will be relatively brief and will concentrate on the way in which coordination experiments cast light on the manner in which equilibrium is reached. Data from coordination games suggest that models of learning and adaptive behavior will be important in understanding which (if any) equilibria are reached as players gain experience in a game.

Bargaining is the subject of chapter 4, and, since I am its author, I won't try in this introduction to discuss the same material from a different point of view. Instead, I concentrate in chapter 4 on experiments concerning models of bargaining with highly structured rules for exchanging offers. A very active interchange among experimenters has developed in the last ten years on this subject. I will lay the groundwork for this in section III.C of this chapter by discussing a largely earlier (but somewhat overlapping) series of experiments concerned with unstructured bargaining, in which many of the same issues arise. (And as I was a principal investigator in those earlier experiments, this will also serve to indicate the point of view that I brought to the dialogue among many experimenters, which is the subject of chapter 4.) Like the two chapters that precede it, chapter 4 is concerned with inefficient outcomes, which in bargaining take the form of disagreements and delays. As in the case of public goods problems, theories of other-regarding preferences have been proposed and tested to explain deviations from received theory (with "fairness" playing the role in bargaining that "altruism" plays in the discussion of public goods). And bargaining has some resemblance to the coordination problems of chapter 3, with bargainers needing to coordinate their expectations to reach an agreement.

Chapter 5, by Holt, and chapter 6, by Sunder, both consider series of experiments that arise out of the vibrant tradition whose origins are in Chamberlin's (1948) experiment. Like Chamberlin's experiment, the experiments in these two chapters seek to test theories of exchange that can be formulated in terms of the aggregate supply and demand curves of the market, and these are induced in the laboratory using Chamberlin's technique of giving each buyer and seller a reservation price for each unit they demand or supply. The two chapters between them study a variety of different forms by which market exchange can be organized, as well as differences due to the kind of commodity being traded. (Sunder considers trading in financial assets, which may have different value to different participants depending on the state of the world, about which different participants may have different information.) One important form of market organization is the double auction market, first experimentally studied by Smith (1962), who observed rapid convergence to competitive equilibrium when the market was repeated several times with stationary parameters. Subsequent investigators have made substantial progress in understanding this phenomenon, and this is one thread of the literature that I consider in this introduction.

Chapter 7, by Kagel, concerns a variety of markets organized as auctions and focuses primarily on tests of game-theoretic hypotheses about the effect of different auction rules and different kinds of commodities. One important distinction among commodities is whether their value to each bidder is known or unknown, and, if unknown, whether or not the value to each bidder is independent of the value to other bidders. In many cases of interest the value of the object being auctioned is unknown to the bidders, but is essentially the same for all of them. (Consider, for example, the auction of the right to drill for oil at a given location—the value of this right is highly dependent on the unknown amount of recoverable oil beneath the surface.) One question that arose in the trade literature, and has been addressed in the experimental literature, was whether there might be a tendency for the winning bidder in such a "common value" auction to be a bidder who overestimated the value. This is the theme I concentrate on in my introduction, as it forms a good bridge between the equilibrium considerations of the preceding chapters and the errors and choice anomalies that are the focus of chapter 8.

Chapter 8 is concerned primarily with experimental observations of individual choice behavior that are at odds with the view of decision makers as idealized rational information processors and (expected utility) maximizers. The work in this chapter, more than any other in the volume, represents an interaction between experimental economists and psychologists, and as such it gives a view not only of the substantive issues involved in various particular debates, but also of how these are played out across a disciplinary boundary that sometimes divides a common subject matter. By way of introduction, I concentrate on a phenomenon called preference reversal, in which subjects can sometimes be observed to choose one of a pair of lotteries when faced with a choice between the two, but to name a higher price for the other lottery when asked to specify a price for which they would be prepared to sell the right to participate in the lotteries. This is a phenomenon that has raised both questions of experimental procedure, and, once its robustness was established, questions about its implications for economic theory. In this respect, the phenomenon of preference reversal is similar to many of the phenomena discussed by Camerer in chapter 8.

A. Prisoners' Dilemmas and Public Goods

1. The Prisoner's Dilemma

Variations on the prisoner's dilemma have been the subject of virtually continuous experimental interest since the 1950 experiment of Dresher and Flood was reported in Flood (1952, 1958). But whereas they deliberately chose an asymmetric form of the game, much of the subsequent literature has focused on the symmetric game, corresponding to the story of the two prisoners formulated by Tucker (1950). He referred to a game we can represent by the following matrix, with $b > a > c > d$.

	confess	not confess
confess	(c,c)	(b,d)
not confess	(d,b)	(a,a)

The "dilemma," of course is that it is a dominant strategy for each prisoner to confess, since $c > d$ and $b > a$, but that both of them would be better off if neither confessed, since a > c. So the only equilibrium of this game is the dominant strategy equilibrium at which both prisoners confess and receive the (non–Pareto optimal) payoff of c each. (In much of the literature the strategy "not confess" is called "cooperate," and "confess" is called "defect.")

The observation that equilibria could be inefficient did not strike game theorists as odd (always assuming, of course, that the situation facing the players, and their preferences over the outcomes, are accurately modeled by the above matrix); rather it served to emphasize the usefulness of being able to write binding contracts. However to many social scientists this conclusion seemed to represent an error in analysis, their feeling being that when players properly understood the game, they would choose to cooperate with one another and not confess.

A related observation, however, struck (even) game theorists as symptomatic of problems with the notion of equilibrium. If a prisoner's dilemma game is repeated finitely many times, say 100, and if the payoffs to the players are the sum of their payoffs in each game, then it can be seen by backwards induction starting from the last period that no equilibrium of the game yields cooperation at *any* period. That is, the unique equilibrium behavior involves confessing at every period, even though confessing is no longer a dominant strategy (recall the discussion in section I). Not only did this seem contrary to intuition, it was also disturbing to note that the equilibrium prediction was unchanged no matter how many times the game was repeated. So even as the number of repetitions increases, the finitely repeated game does not approach the infinitely repeated game (or the game played in continuous time) in which cooperation is (also) an equilibrium behavior. For these reasons the finitely repeated game received special note in the game theory literature.

The prisoner's dilemma has motivated literally hundreds of experiments, and so I will not even attempt to review them individually. (Representative examples of early work are Lave 1962, and Rapoport and Chammah 1965.) Typical experiments concerning the one-period game reported a level of cooperation that responded readily to various kinds of experimental manipulation but that was bounded well away from either zero or 100 percent. A number of experiments were conducted to isolate various factors[45] contributing to the level of cooperation.[46]

However many experiments which were analyzed as one period games were in fact conducted on various kinds of repeated games, using rules that made it difficult to determine precisely what the equilibria were. In a paper about designing prisoner's dilemma experiments Roth and Murnighan (1978) wrote:

> It is often contended in the literature that if subjects are not informed of the number of periods to be played, the resulting game yields the same equilibria as the infinite game, since no period is known to be the last. However, this is a considerable oversimplification. Since it is apparent that the game must eventually terminate, subjects must form subjective probabilities greater than zero that a given period might be the last. Although such probabilities have neither been observed nor controlled by experimenters, we shall see that they play a critical role in determining the nature of equilibrium outcomes. (191)

The paper goes on to derive the conditions for equilibrium in the repeated game with a fixed probability p of continuing after each play: cooperation can be achieved at equilibrium only if the probability of continuing is sufficiently large.[47]

A pilot experiment was then conducted, in large part to show that the design was feasible.[48] The payoff matrix was chosen so that cooperation was consistent with equilibrium if and only if $p \geq 1/3$, and subjects played three games, with probabilities of continuing of .1, .5, and .9. (Half the players played in that order, half the players in the opposite order.) The results of the experiment were that significantly more cooperative choices were made in the two higher probability conditions (in which these are equilibrium choices) than in the low probability condition. However, even in the high probability condition, only 36 percent of first period choices were cooperative, while in the low probability condition 19 percent of the first period choices were (nevertheless) cooperative. So the results remain equivocal.

Similarly equivocal results seem to be typical. A recent experiment, whose results help crystallize a lot of what I think has been observed piecemeal in previous experiments, is reported by Selten and Stoecker (1986). In their experiment, subjects played twenty-five "supergames," each of which was a (ten-period) repeated prisoner's dilemma.[49] So this experiment looked at repeated play of the *repeated* game and thus gave subjects the opportunity to gain experience with the ten-period game.

By far the most common pattern of observed play was initial periods of mutual cooperation (at least four), followed by an initial defection, followed by noncooperation in the remaining periods. After about round 16 almost all of the plays exhibit this pattern in each round. (A round is a play of the supergame; that is, round 22 is the twenty-second repetition of the ten-period repeated game.) Even more common is the pattern of "end-effect play," which the authors define to be at least four consecutive rounds of mutual cooperation (not necessarily starting from period 1), with no further cooperation following the first defection. (Notice that this pattern includes the previous one.)

The most striking results concerns the progress in the observed (and "intended") period of first defection. Having learned to cooperate, players start to defect earlier and earlier in subsequent supergames—i.e., the cooperation starts to unravel from the end.[50]

The paper then develops a learning theory model in which each player is represented by the period in which he intends to defect, and updates this, via three probabilities, depending on whether he defects first, simultaneously, or last. Steady state probability distributions are computed for various parameter configurations: It appears that in the typical stable distribution, cooperation either breaks down very early or very late. Monte Carlo simulations based on parameters estimated for each subject based on the first twenty rounds are then made for the pairings in the last five rounds. Like the observed behavior, these predictions have cooperation unravelling from round 20 to round 25.

I think it is fair to summarize these observations as follows: in the initial rounds players learned to cooperate (and consequently exhibited more periods of mutual cooperation starting from the very beginning and breaking down only near the end). In the later rounds, players learned about the dangers of not defecting first, and cooperation began to unravel. There is a sense in which this observed behavior mirrors the game-theoretic observation that the equilibrium recommendation never to cooperate isn't a good one, but that all other patterns of play are unstable.

These observations are consistent with many earlier observations of finitely repeated games in which cooperation is observed for some periods, but breaks down near the end. A number of new theories have been motivated by such experimental observations. For example Kreps, Milgrom, Roberts, and Wilson (1982) propose a model in which players may entertain certain slight doubts about the nature of their opponent, who may not after all be the sort of player to whom the backward induction logic applies (either because of limitations on what strategies he may play, or because he may in fact have some inclination to cooperate not captured by the standard payoffs of the game). They show that at equilibrium of such a model in which the uncertainties are of the right sort, there will be cooperation until near the end, because players will have a motive to engage in building reputations as the kind of players who will continue to cooperate when faced with cooperation. Andreoni and Miller (1993) report an experiment motivated by this model and observe both that some players in their subject pool apparently do have some inclination to cooperate not captured by the monetary payoffs and that the observed rates of cooperation are consistent with a model of reputation building on the part of the other players.[51]

In summary, interest over the course of many experiments has shifted from the one-time game to the repeated game. The contemporary discussion proceeds on both theoretical and experimental lines.

a. Experiments versus Simulations: A Methodological Digression

There was a time when computer simulations, and the kinds of investigations one can do with them, were sometimes confused with experiments involving the observation of real people in controlled environments. Selten and Stoecker's use of both technologies makes the distinction clear. Computer simulations are useful for creating and exploring theoretical models, while experiments are useful for observing behavior.

Recently, however, there have been a growing number of investigations that combine experimentation and computer simulation. For example, an interesting set of computer simulations that have an unusually experimental flavor are reported in Axelrod (1980a, 1980b, 1984). These have their origin in a pair of computer "tournaments." In the first of these, the author elicited, from fourteen scholars in several disciplines who had written on the prisoner's dilemma, short computer programs encoding a strategy to play the repeated game. Each of the programs played each of the others, as well as a copy of itself and a program that generated random choices, in a 200-play repeated prisoner's dilemma. The strategy with the highest cumulative score was "tit for tat," which starts with cooperation and then echoes the other program's previous move. It and all of the other highest scoring rules were "nice" in the sense that they never defected first.[52] Some programs got into sequences of alternating moves with tit for tat, with one program defecting on the odd numbered moves and cooperating on the even numbered moves and tit for tat doing the opposite, which for the parameters used in the tournament was not nearly as profitable as steady cooperation.[53] This is a pattern you might expect humans would be able to avoid, although it is easy to see how short computer programs could fall into it.

Axelrod (1980b) presented a second round of the tournament, with new entries, in which the game was repeated with a fixed probability of continuation after each round (with $p = .99$ so that now cooperation is an equilibrium strategy), as discussed above in connection with Roth and Murnighan (1978). Again, tit for tat was the winner. Some simulations of different possible tournaments were presented to show that there are some senses in which this result is robust, but other results were reported to show that this is not an entirely simple matter: "Had only the entries which actually ranked in the top half been present, then TIT FOR TAT would have come in fourth after the ones which actually came in 25th, 16th, and 8th" (402).

These computer tournaments thus suggest that behavior will eventually converge to cooperation. This conclusion is at odds with experimental results such as Selten and Stoecker's. I suspect that the difference in results has a great deal to do with the learning that goes on when experimental subjects are allowed to adapt their strategies as they gain experience with the game and with the behavior of the rest of the subject pool.[54]

Apart from the use of simulation, there are also interesting questions raised by eliciting from the subjects in an experiment a complete strategy—i.e., a rule of action that determines in advance their decision at each of their information sets in the game—instead of having them make only those decisions that arise in the course of the play of the game, as they arise. Experimental designs using this feature may first have been explored by Selten (1967c). I discuss such designs, in chapter 4, in the methodological digression on the "strategy method."

I turn now from the experiments motivated directly by the prisoner's dilemma to those motivated by the provision of public goods.[55]

2. The Free Rider Problem in Public Goods Provision

The free rider problem in the provision of public goods was noted in connection with the debate among nineteenth-century economists about whether taxation for public goods should be related to the benefit each agent derived from those goods. The nature of a public good is that once it has been created everyone may use it, and so if each individual is to be taxed in proportion to the profit he derives from the public good, there will be an incentive for individuals to claim that these profits are small, since small contributors will derive the same benefit from the good as if they had been large contributors. The potential for under-contribution to a public good is particularly clear when contributions are voluntary. (American listeners to National Public Radio will immediately recognize the problem.)

The first clear formulation of the free rider problem is generally attributed to an essay written at the end of the last century by the Swedish economist Knut Wicksell, who also anticipated the direction of much subsequent theoretical research by suggesting that the mechanism by which public projects were decided upon would be important. (He suggested that a way to deal with the problem would be to require that proposals for public projects be considered together with proposals to raise the necessary revenue and that the whole package should be subject to [close to] unanimous approval.) For references and an introduction to much of the subsequent theory focusing on the role of the decision mechanism, see Green and Laffont (1979).

Because it is readily apparent that some more-or-less public goods are in fact produced even though they depend on voluntary contributions, the focus of debate shifted both to assessing how serious the free rider problem might be and what circumstances or mechanisms might ameliorate it. So at the same time as a good deal of theoretical progress was being made in "solving" the free rider problem (e.g., Groves and Ledyard 1977), skepticism was being voiced about the importance of the problem and the quality of the empirical evidence in support of it (e.g., Johansen 1977). Since it is difficult to collect field data to determine, for example, how close to the optimum amount of some public good is being supplied, this problem presented a natural opportunity for laboratory experiments. In addition, since some of the mechanisms proposed for solving or ameliorating the free rider problem had no counterpart in existing institutions, some of the questions that presented themselves could not be addressed except by experimentation.

An early public goods experiment, by Bohm (1972), was sponsored by the Swedish Radio-TV broadcasting company. A sample of adult residents of Stockholm was invited to come to the broadcasting company for an interview and asked to state how much (of their interview fee) it would be worth to them to see a half-hour program by two well-known comedians. They were told they would see the program only if the sum of the amounts stated (by their group and others) exceeded the cost of showing it. The experimental variable consisted of five different rules for how they would in fact be charged on the basis of their stated amounts, ranging from the full amount to some percentage of that amount, to a lottery related to the amount, to a small fixed fee, to nothing.

The responses of the different groups of subjects given these different instructions were found not to vary significantly. Bohm argues that the first payment mechanism (everyone pays their stated amount) gives no incentive to overstate willingness to pay, and the last (no actual payment required) gives no incentive to understate willingness to pay, so the similarity of the responses under the two conditions suggests there may not in fact be much of a practical problem in estimating people's demands for a public good.[56] In short, these results suggest that free riding may not be a big problem.

Several other experiments employed what I will loosely call the same general design, of presenting subjects with some public good whose value to them was unknown to the experimenter and of comparing the results of different methods of eliciting their willingness to pay. Sweeney (1973) considered the willingness of subjects to power an electric light by pedaling an exercise bicycle (free "riding" indeed) and found that this responded to whether they perceived themselves as being in a small or large group (a perception he manipulated by controlling the brightness of the light with a rheostat). The public good was if they would all receive credit for participating in the experiment, which depended on how brightly the light remained lit. Scherr and Babb (1975) compared voluntary contributions with those elicited in pricing schemes proposed for public goods by Clarke (1971) and by Loehman and Whinston (1972) and found no significant differences in the amount of public goods (in this case concert tickets and books donated to the library) provided under the three schemes. In general, the experiments using this design support the proposition that at least some public good can be supplied even by voluntary contribution. But it is much more difficult to interpret how much (if any) free riding is being observed, since the true value of the public good to each subject is unknown.

In order not to miss the opportunity to tell a colorful story, let me describe one more experiment of this general type, which was conducted by Schneider and Pommerehne (1981) at the University of Zurich and which would be unlikely, I think, to have been permitted at an American university.[57] The subjects for their experiment were a group of economics students preparing for their comprehensive examinations. Without knowing that they were the object of an experiment, these students were approached by a confederate of the experimenters posing as the representative of a publishing company. She informed them that their professor (who, I surmise, would write the comprehensive exam) was writing a book on the subject of the exam, which would not be available until after the exam. However, the publishing company was interested in getting feedback on the book, and for this purpose might be willing to make specimen copies available, *before* the exam. (The authors remark that the students "had a strong incentive to try to obtain the book beforehand" [694–695]) The students were then told they could submit written bids of how much they were willing to pay to get an advance copy, with copies going to the ten highest bidders from both this group and two other groups from which bids had supposedly already been solicited. After these bids were collected the two highest bidders were told that they were among the ten winners. The remaining students were then told that there was another way in which they could obtain the book before the exam: if together with the two other groups they could raise SFr4,200, they would each get a copy. Again, written bids for the now public good were collected, and the heart of the analysis is the comparison of the two bids.[58] The authors note that the second bids were less than the first, but not by much.[59] They conclude (702) that "there is only modest evidence for free riding as compared with the importance attributed to it in the literature."

A different kind of experimental design, in which the public good is an artificial one, makes it possible to employ an experimental strategy of trying to control each subject's value for the good, rather than trying to measure it. The idea is that if the experimenter assigns to each agent a payment depending on the quantity of the public good, then so long as the public good is not one that itself induces strong preferences among the agents, their preferences can be assumed to correspond to their monetary payoffs.[60] In this way the payments of the agents for the public good and the amount of public good provided under a given decision mechanism can be compared not only with the amounts under another decision mechanism, but also with a priori notions about the optimal amount, such as the Lindahl equilibrium.

Smith (1979a, 1979b, 1980) reports three such experiments.[61] In the first, he compared a version of a mechanism proposed by Groves and Ledyard (1977), designed to eliminate incentives to free ride by disentangling the price each agent pays from the price he states, with a procedure in which each agent pays his stated willingness to pay. Both procedures were implemented in an iterative manner that allowed agents to revise their statements in light of those of the others. Smith observed that, under some settings of the experimental parameters determining agents' demands, the Groves-Ledyard mechanism resulted in decisions at the Lindahl equilibrium, while the other mechanism exhibited substantial free riding, sometimes to the point that no public good was produced. A third iterative mechanism was then investigated, which Smith (1979a) called the auction mechanism and which incorporates the features suggested by Wicksell, in that the quantity of the public good and the amount to be contributed by each agent must be unanimously agreed to before the agreement is effective. (In the absence of agreement, no public good is produced.) The theoretical properties of this mechanism are somewhat unclear since it has many Nash equilibria. However under this mechanism too, Smith reports that Lindahl prices and quantities were good predictors for the market parameters considered.

In the light of these results, Smith suggests that the results of Bohm's (1972) experiment might be reinterpreted, since the mechanism he considered to have the most probability of producing free riding (everyone pays their stated amount) resembled the auction mechanism in the sense that if too much free riding took place, no public good would be produced. That is, Smith suggests that the similarity of the bids in all of Bohm's procedures may merely reflect that the situation he considered (inadvertently) gave subjects good incentives *not* to free ride, because of the fear that no public good would be provided. In this spirit, Smith (1979b) reports an experiment designed to determine which aspects of the auction mechanism may have contributed to its apparent success. He compares the auction mechanism, in which agents propose both a contribution and a quantity of the public good, with a "free rider mechanism" in which each agent simply states his contribution and the quantity of the public good is whatever the summed contributions will buy. (A mechanism intermediate between the two was also considered.) All mechanisms were implemented with a unanimity rule that gave agents a chance to examine (and accept or reject) the outcome before it was implemented. Although the auction mechanism provided an amount of the public good nearer to the Lindahl quantity than the other mechanisms when it reached agreement, its frequency of agreement was sufficiently less than that of the other two mechanisms to make the overall quantity of public good similar under all mechanisms. Smith concludes by noting that under none of the mechanisms was a very strong free rider effect observed and conjectures that this may be due to the rule of unanimous approval. However, as Ledyard emphasizes in chapter 2 (see Table 2.18), subsequent experimenters have reached sharply different conclusions about the benign role of a unanimity rule.

Of course, different theoretical dispositions suggest different regularities in the data. For example, Smith (1980) reports in connection with another experiment that (597) "on average subjects contribute approximately one-half their endowments to the public good and retain one-half for private use." Marwell and Ames (1981), drawing primarily on a series of their own studies that also use a controlled, artificial public good, suggest that this may be an important kind of regularity. Noting that previous studies examined fairly small groups (mostly of fewer than ten individuals), they conducted a study in which both small and large groups could be examined. In a series of studies in which subjects were mostly high school students, subjects were told that they were part of a group and that each member of the group had an endowment of tokens to invest in either a public or private good. The public good had the higher return, but its proceeds were distributed equally to all group members. Over a number of conditions, Marwell and Ames report that on average the percentage of resources invested in the public good was surprisingly regular, in the range of 40 to 60 percent, with some indication of a decrease when the stakes were raised.[62] Among the few exceptions they noted was that a group of first semester economics graduate students only invested 20 percent in the public good, leading them to suggest that economists may be different from everyone else (and hence the title of their paper).[63]

The remaining experiments I will discuss differ from these previous ones in that they investigate how some of these mechanisms behave when they are used repeatedly, instead of just once. Thus each of these experiments, by Kim and Walker (1984), Isaac, McCue, and Plott (1985), and Banks, Plott, and Porter (1988) give subjects the chance to gain some experience with how the mechanisms work.

Isaac, McCue, and Plott (1985) seek to show that the free rider problem is alive and well, by examining a mechanism already suspected of being favorable to free riding and letting repetition have what effect it would. The mechanism chosen was that of direct contribution: each agent stated his contribution, and the amount of public good the summed contributions would buy was produced. (There was no requirement that the allocation be unanimously approved.) After all agents were informed of how much public good had been produced and had computed their payoff for that period, the process was repeated, with the same individuals and the same demand parameters. The results from a number of trials involving groups of ten subjects were that positive levels of the public good were produced in initial periods, but by around the fifth period these levels declined to near zero. The authors write, "Our results unambiguously demonstrate the existence of the under-provision of public goods and related 'free riding' phenomenon and thereby discredit the claims of those who assert as a general proposition that the phenomenon does not or cannot exist" (51–52). (They also note in reply to Marwell and Ames [who are sociologists] that their experiment included a group of undergraduate sociology students as well as groups of undergraduate economics students, and no differences were found.)

Kim and Walker (1984) report a similarly motivated experiment with similar results, using a much larger (simulated) group size. In their experiment subjects were instructed that they were part of a group of 100, and given a payoff table indicating how much each would be paid as a function of the total contributions made that day to a "common fund." (For example, if the fund received $100 [e.g., from $1 per person], each person would be paid $2.) Each day each subject phoned in his contribution, and had his earnings for the day delivered to him that evening.[64] The results of the experiment, like that of Isaac, McCue, and Plott, were that positive initial contributions sharply diminished in succeeding days, so that substantial free riding was observed.

That results from repeated trials may differ from those in a single trial was confirmed by Banks, Plott, and Porter (1988), who examined both the direct contribution mechanism and Smith's auction mechanism, both with and without the rule of unanimous consent. Although they observed that the auction mechanisms outperformed the direct contribution mechanisms as producers of the public good, they found that the unanimity rule *decreased* efficiency in the repeated setting. They note that (319) "this result is directly counter to expectations formed from data and conjectures found in the literature." They also found that efficiency decreased over time, suggesting that more free riding occurs with increased experience with these mechanisms. They conclude, "A more reliable process must be found before we proceed with an application at the practical/political level of analysis."

In summary, the experiments discussed here began with studies of one-shot decisions about various kinds of public goods, in which different decision mechanisms were compared. These experiments often reported little or no free riding. These were followed by experiments in which the public good was artificial and, therefore, more easily controllable. These experiments began to detect some degree of free riding and differences among mechanisms and environments. The most recent experiments introduced repetition and reported results at odds with the experiments preceding them. Since the theoretical properties of these mechanisms under repeated play are not well understood, it would be premature to confidently attribute these results merely to increased experience with the mechanisms.[65] So the experimental results suggest a further theoretical agenda, as well as a continued experimental examination of other mechanisms. In the course of these experiments, the debate has thus shifted from whether or not free riding occurs, to how much and under what conditions it occurs, to what mechanisms and environments may be most vulnerable and most invulnerable to its effects. At this stage there still remains a considerable gap between the experimental results and related questions about the free rider problem in natural environments. (But, as we will see in section III.E in connection with the auction phenomenon of the "winner's curse," such gaps between experimental and field data need not remain unbridgeable.)

B. Coordination

A fundamental problem for players in a game with multiple equilibria (and for theories of equilibrium in such environments) is how to coordinate on a particular equilibrium. This kind of problem shows up clearly in macroeconomic theories of rational expectations, where players' expectations about future events need to become coordinated for equilibrium to be achieved. The theory of rational expectations has thus led to several experimental studies, which Jack Ochs discusses in chapter 3. However, the problems of coordination become apparent even in very much simpler environments.

As Schelling showed in his experiments in the 1950s, players are sometimes able to achieve coordination by focusing on aspects of their environment that are often left out of abstract models. (Recall the experiment in which players were identified by letters of the alphabet and were able to achieve a substantial rate of successful coordination by focusing on alphabetical order.) More recent work has shown that, not only is coordination on a particular equilibrium influenced by features of the environment that are ignored in economic models, but also that features of a game that some theories explicitly assume are irrelevant are not.

For example, a very carefully conducted set of experiments by Cooper,

DeJong, Forsythe, and Ross (1990) considered two-person games in which each player had three strategies. In any play of the game, the players each chose one of their strategies without knowing the choice of the other player. In the games they used to study coordination, there were two strict, pure strategy equilibria, which arose when the players coordinated either on their first pure strategy or the second. (That is, when either player employed one of her first two strategies, the other player maximized her own payoff by choosing the same strategy.) In each game, the third strategy of each player was a strictly dominated strategy—i.e., it gave a strictly lower payoff than one of the first two strategies, for every possible action of the other player. Cooper et al. found that, although the dominated strategy was seldom played, especially after the players had gained a little experience with the game, its presence had a profound effect on which of the two equilibria the players tended to reach after acquiring some experience with the game. Players apparently were influenced in their choice between their first and second strategies by what their payoffs would be in each case in the (unlikely) event that the other player chose his dominated third strategy.

The effect that Cooper et al. noticed was made even more dramatic because the equilibria in their games were Pareto ranked—i.e., both players did better at one of the equilibria than at the other. Nevertheless, sometimes the dominated strategy made it easier for them to coordinate on the less desirable equilibrium. An even clearer example of how coordination can fail to produce socially optimal results comes from an experiment reported by Van Huyck, Battalio, and Beil (1990), who considered a family of *pure coordination games*, or games in which there is no conflict of interest at all among the players.

Van Huyck et al. considered a game played by groups of around fifteen players, each of whom simultaneously had to choose an integer from 1 to 7. The payoff to any player i depended on both the integer e_i chosen by that player and the *minimum* $m = \min\{e_j\}$ chosen by any of the players (including player i himself). In the version of their game which I will speak of here (which was their "condition A"), the payoff to player i was equal to $\$0.60 + [\$0.20(m) - \$0.10(e_i)]$. (See the payoff table at the top of Figure 1.2.) Thus all the players had a common interest in a high value of m, but there was a penalty for stating a number higher than the minimum chosen by the other players. In particular, this game has seven strict, pure strategy equilibria, at each of which every player chooses the same integer. However, the equilibrium at which all the players choose 7 (and all earn $1.30) gives a higher payoff to every player than any other equilibrium (or any other outcome of the game), while the equilibrium at which all the players choose 1 gives each player the lowest payoff ($0.70) of any equilibrium. (Of course, the lowest payoff that a player can possibly get is when he chooses 7 and at least one other player chooses 1, in which case he earns only $0.10 for that round.)

Van Huyck et al. observed that when the game was played repeatedly, with the outcome made public after each play of the game, the minimum quickly converged to 1 in each group they examined. For nine groups of subjects who played the game ten times each, a diffuse distribution of choices in the first period quickly evolved into a very high concentration of 1's in each group.[66] (In no group was the minimum choice higher than 1 in any period after the third.) Thus, despite the common interest of all the players in the equilibrium outcome at which each player chooses a 7, this never occurred. To the contrary, behavior in this game quickly evolved in the direction of the least profitable equilibrium. Because it is clear that players learn from their experience in these games, it is natural to look to models of learning and adaptation to begin to explain the observed behavior.

In this spirit, a theoretical model to help explain these observations was put forward by Crawford (1991), who proposed to adapt game-theoretic models of the kind considered by evolutionary biologists. In evolutionary games (see Maynard Smith 1982), an outcome is considered to be an evolutionarily stable equilibrium if, in addition to being a strategic (i.e., a Nash) equilibrium, it is stable against "invasion" by strategies that are not present in the population at equilibrium, but may be introduced at low levels by mutation. In order to be stable against this kind of invasion, it must be the case that when the equilibrium population of strategies is perturbed by the introduction of a non-equilibrium strategy, the strategies present at the equilibrium must do better in this new population than the strategies introduced by mutation. (If not, the mutation strategies would thrive and increase their presence in the population.)

Crawford observed that all but the minimum equilibrium in Van Huyck et al.'s "minimum" game were in fact quite unstable to this kind of invasion. Consider an equilibrium at which all players choose the same integer greater than 1. If some player were now to choose a smaller number, that player would have the highest payoff in the population. To the extent that high payoff strategies are more likely to "reproduce" themselves in the next period, as in the evolutionary model, this induces a dynamic process that tends towards the lowest number chosen. And if new strategies occasionally appear by some sort of mutation, then the dynamic will lead to the lowest feasible number, as was observed in the experiment.

As Crawford is careful to note, while evolutionary dynamics provide a very suggestive model of the observed behavior in this game, we cannot suppose that the dynamics actually being observed in the experiment are evolutionary in nature. Rather than natural selection from a variable population, we are witnessing some kind of learning and adaptation. In this vein, a very simple model of learning is explored by Roth and Erev (1995) in connection with some of the bargaining games to be discussed in chapter 4, and the contrast between the games studied there and the coordination games considered here is instructive.

Roth and Erev considered a family of adaptive models designed to be consistent with two of the most robust properties observed in the large experimental psychology literature on both human and animal learning, namely that choices that have led to good outcomes in the past are more likely to be repeated in the future[67] and that learning curves tend to be steep initially, and then flatter.[68] The models they considered are all variations on the following basic model.[69]

At time $t = 1$ (before any experience has been acquired) each player n has an initial propensity to play his kth pure strategy, given by some real number $q_{nk}(1)$. If player n plays his kth pure strategy at time t and receives a payoff of x, then the propensity to play strategy k is updated by setting

(1) $$q_{nk}(t + 1) = q_{nk}(t) + x$$

where player n just played strategy k and earned x, while for all other pure strategies j,

(2) $$q_{nj}(t + 1) = q_{nj}(t).$$

The probability $p_{nk}(t)$ that player n plays his kth pure strategy at time t is

(3) $$p_{nk}(t) = q_{nk}(t)/\Sigma q_{nj}(t),$$

where the sum is over all of player n's pure strategies j.

So pure strategies that have been played and have met with success tend over time to be played with greater frequency than those that have met with less success, and the learning curve will be steeper in early periods and flatter later (because $\Sigma q_{nj}(t)$ is an increasing function of t, so a payoff of x from playing pure strategy k at time t has a bigger effect on $p_{nk}(t)$ when t is small than when t is large).

It turns out that this simple model captures quite well the dynamics observed in certain two-person bargaining games to be discussed in chapter 4. However the modification required for it to capture the results observed by Van Huyck et al. (1990) is illuminating. Instead of having players learn from their own experience only, we can consider the otherwise identical model in which equation (1) is replaced by one in which the strategy that is updated at each period is the strategy that was most successful in the previous period, regardless of which player chose it. That is, in the model with imitation (or common learning), equation (1) is replaced by

(1′) $$q_{nk}(t + 1) = q_{nk}(t) + x$$

where strategy k was the most successful strategy used the previous period and earned x.

The first column of Figure 1.2, from Erev and Roth (in preparation), shows the data of Van Huyck et al. displayed so as to indicate the period-by-period evolution of the probabilities of each number being chosen. (So, we observe that the highest frequency choice in period 1 was a 7, but that the frequency of 1's—i.e., the probability that a 1 will be chosen by a given player—rises steadily from one period to the next.) Column two shows these probabilities as simulated by the learning rule with equation (1′), and column three shows the simulations by the learning rule with equation (1). In each simulation the initial propensities (i.e., the period 1 propensities) are taken to be those observed by Van Huyck et al., with the learning rule determining the subsequent probabilities of play. (The graphs in the latter two columns each represent the average of ten simulations.)

Payoff Table A

		Smallest Value of X						
		7	6	5	4	3	2	1
	7	1.30	1.10	0.90	0.70	0.50	0.30	0.10
Your	6	–	1.20	1.00	0.80	0.60	0.40	0.20
Choice	5	–	–	1.10	0.90	0.70	0.50	0.30
	4	–	–	–	1.00	0.80	0.60	0.40
of	3	–	–	–	–	0.90	0.70	0.50
X	2	–	–	–	–	–	0.80	0.60
	1	–	–	–	–	–	–	0.70

$$T = 0 - 10$$
$$S(1) = 2, \ \varepsilon = 0, \mu = 0.1, \varphi = 0$$

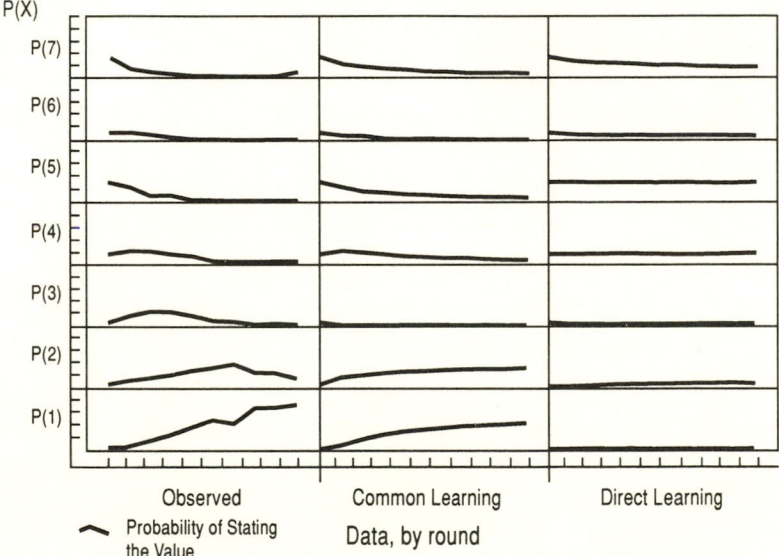

Figure 1.2. The data of Van Huyck et al. (column 1) and the predictions of the Roth-Erev learning model with imitation (common learning) and without imitation (direct learning). *Sources:* Van Huyck, Battalio, and Beil 1990; Erev and Roth, in preparation.

Looking first at the last column, we see that the learning model in which each player learns only from his own experience fails to capture the rise in choices of "1" from periods 1 to 10. However, the model in which players learn from the common experience of the previous period does a much better job. Thus it appears plausible that some of the role played by natural selection in evolutionary models may be played by imitation in the learning dynamics we are witnessing in this experiment.[70]

In summary, the coordination problems facing players in games with multiple equilibria provide a clear lens through which to view the process of equilibration. Because it is clear that players learn from their experience in these games, it is natural to look to models of learning and adaptation to begin to explain what is being observed. More generally, experiments with coordination games have shown that factors that many traditional economic models suggest should be irrelevant (like the presence of strictly dominated strategies) may play a decisive role in determining the outcome of a game, while factors that many traditional models suggest should be of great importance (like Pareto dominance) may fail to overcome other influences on which equilibria will be observed. We will see that some of these issues come to the fore in the study of bargaining games as well, which also have a multiplicity of equilibria.

C. Bargaining Behavior

Theories of bargaining that depend on purely ordinal descriptions of bargainers' preferences tend to predict large sets of outcomes, and for this reason many economists (at least since Edgeworth 1881) have argued that bargaining is fundamentally indeterminate. In the language of cooperative game theory, the difficulty is associated with the fact that the core corresponds to the entire set of individually rational Pareto optimal outcomes. Similarly, in strategic models the problem is that all of this typically large set of outcomes can be achieved as equilibria of the game. Theories of bargaining that seek to make stronger predictions have attempted to distinguish among this multiplicity of equilibria by making use of more detailed information about bargainers' preferences or strategic options.

Since this kind of information is hard to observe in uncontrolled environments, these theories have been notoriously difficult to test with field data. Although there have been some attempts to explain observed bargaining outcomes by inferring what the utility functions of the bargainers would have to have been in order to be consistent with the prediction of some particular theory (i.e., with the prediction that could have been made had these utility functions been observable), such exercises cannot serve to provide any sort of direct test of the theory itself. Similarly, the detailed procedural information required to specify a strategic model of bargaining is mostly unobservable in field environments. Consequently, for tests of such theories it is natural to look to the kind of controlled environment and relatively unlimited access to the bargainers that can be obtained in the laboratory.

Although there has been some convergence between the theoretical literature concerned with strategic and cooperative models of bargaining (see, e.g., Osborne and Rubinstein 1990), the bargaining environments for which their predictions can be most clearly derived are rather different. This section will therefore be concerned with experimental tests of cooperative models, and chapter 4 will take up a more recent experimental literature concerned with strategic models. One of the interesting things to note in comparing the series of experiments discussed here with those in chapter 4 is how much experimental designs are shaped by the hypotheses among which they are intended to distinguish. Another thing to note is that the experiments in chapter 4, which were largely conducted in the latter part of the 1980s and early 1990s, are conducted by a much more diverse group of experimenters than those covered in this section, which were conducted in the late 1970s and early 1980s by a single group of researchers.[71] In this respect, bargaining experiments reflect the change that has occurred in experimental economics generally in recent years.

One of the best known family of game-theoretic models of bargaining arises from the work of John Nash (1950). Because of the way he specified his assumptions, these models are referred to as "axiomatic," and many specific models other than the one originally proposed by Nash have entered the literature (see Roth 1979).

Nash considered the "pure bargaining problem," in which two bargainers must agree on one alternative from a set A of feasible alternatives over which they have different preferences. If they fail to reach agreement, some fixed disagreement alternative δ results. Nash modeled such a problem by a pair (S, d), where S is a subset of the plane, and d a point in S. The set S represents the feasible expected utility payoffs to the bargainers—i.e., each point $x = (x_1, x_2)$ in S corresponds to the expected utility payoffs to players 1 and 2, respectively, from some alternative α in A, and $d = (d_1, d_2)$ corresponds to the utility payoffs to the players from the disagreement alternative δ. The theory of bargaining he proposed and the other theories that have followed in this tradition take as their data the set (S, d) and thus represent the feasible outcomes (solely) in terms of the expected utility functions of the bargainers. So such theories predict that the outcome of bargaining will be determined by the preferences of the bargainers over the set of feasible alternatives, together with their willingness to tolerate risk.

Because of the difficulty of attempting to capture the information contained in bargainers' expected utility functions, there were sometimes claims in the experimental literature that the theory was essentially untestable.[72] To get around the difficulty, the earliest experiments designed to test Nash's theory assumed, for the purpose of making predictions about the outcome, that the utility of each bargainer was equal to his monetary payoff. That is, they assumed that the preferences of all bargainers were identical and risk neutral.[73]

Important aspects of the predictions of the theory obtained in this way were inconsistent with the experimental evidence. This disconfirming evidence, however, was almost uniformly discounted by economists, who felt that the results simply reflected the failure to measure the relevant parameters. Nash's theory, after all, is a theory that predicts that the preferences and risk aversion of the bargainers exercise a decisive influence on the outcome of bargaining (and, furthermore, that these are the only personal attributes that can influence the outcome when bargainers are adequately informed). If the predictions made by Nash's theory *under the assumption* that bargainers had identical risk neutral preferences were disconfirmed, this merely cast doubt on the assumption. The theory itself had yet to be tested.[74]

It was, therefore, clear that, in order to provide a test of the theory that would withstand the scrutiny of theorists, an experiment would have to either measure or control for the expected utility of the bargainers.

A class of games that control for the bargainers' utilities was introduced in the experiment of Roth and Malouf (1979). In these *binary lottery games*, each agent i can eventually win only one of two monetary prizes, a large prize λ_i or a small prize σ_i (with $\lambda_i > \sigma_i$). The players bargain over the distribution of "lottery tickets" that determine the probability of receiving the large prize: for example, an agent i who receives 40 percent of the lottery tickets has a 40 percent chance of receiving λ_i and a 60 percent chance of receiving σ_i. Players who do not reach agreement in the allotted time each receive σ_i. Since the information about preferences conveyed by an expected utility function is meaningfully represented only up to the arbitrary choice of origin and scale (and since Nash's theory of bargaining is explicitly constructed to be independent of such choices), there is no loss of generality in normalizing each agent's utility so that $u_i(\lambda_i) = 1$ and $u_i(\sigma_i) = 0$. The utility of agent i for any agreement is then precisely equal to his probability of receiving his large prize λ_i—i.e., equal to the percentage of lottery tickets he has received. Thus in a binary lottery game, the pair (S,d) that determines the prediction of Nash's theory is precisely equal to the set of feasible divisions of the lottery tickets.

Note that no assumptions have been made here about the behavior of the experimental subjects themselves in binary lottery games. (That is, the subjects might not be utility maximizers [see section III.F and chapter 8], or they might have preferences over distributions of payoffs to both players, rather than over their own monetary payoffs [see chapter 4].) What binary lottery games do allow us to know is the utility of utility maximizers who are concerned with their own payoffs. Since this is the kind of data required by Nash's theory, experiments using binary lottery games allow us to use the theory to make precise predictions. It is this which was missing from earlier experiments and from efforts to analyze bargaining data by inferring ex post what the utility of the bargainers might have been.

Under the assumptions of the theory, the set of relevant outcomes—i.e., of expected utility payoffs to the players—of a binary lottery game is insensitive to the magnitudes of λ_i and σ_i for each agent i. Furthermore, the bargainers have what the game theory literature calls "complete" information whether or not they know the value of one another's prizes, since knowing a bargainer's probability of winning his prize is equivalent to knowing his utility. Thus a theory of bargaining under conditions of complete information, which depends only on the utility payoffs to the bargainers, predicts that the outcome of the game will depend neither on the size of the prizes, nor on whether the bargainers know the monetary value of one another's prizes.

The experiment of Roth and Malouf (1979) was designed in part to test this prediction and to determine whether or not changes in the size of the prizes, and if the bargainers knew one anothers' prizes, influenced the outcome. In this experiment (and in the other binary lottery experiments described in this section) the small prizes of both bargainers were always equal to $0.00. In this experiment the large prizes of the two bargainers were equal in some games, while in others they were in a ratio of 1 to 3 ($1.25 to $3.75). All games were played by bargainers seated at separated computer terminals, who could send text messages to each other, but who were prevented from identifying themselves to one another or from otherwise determining who they were bargaining with. Each bargainer played games with different prizes against different opponents in one of two information conditions. In the "full information" condition, each bargainer knew both his own prize and his counterpart's, while bargainers in the "partial information" condition each knew only their own prize value. (In each of these games, under both information conditions the prediction of Nash's theory is that the bargainers would each receive 50% of the lottery tickets.)

The results were that, in the partial information condition and also in those games of the full information condition in which the two bargainers had equal prizes, observed agreements clustered very tightly around the "equal probability" agreement that gives each bargainer 50 percent of the lottery tickets. In the full information condition, in those games in which the bargainers' prizes were unequal, agreements fell between two "focal points": the equal probability agreement and the "equal expected value" agreement (75%,25%) that gives each bargainer the same expected value. The mean agreement in these games fell approximately half way between the equal probability and equal expected value agreements. That is, in these games the bargainer with the lower prize tended to receive a higher share of the lottery tickets. Thus, contrary to the prediction of the theory, the monetary values of the bargainers' prizes were clearly observed to influence the agreements reached when the bargainers knew each other's prizes.[75]

One difference between the two information conditions of the Roth and Malouf (1979) experiment, which might account for the different outcomes observed, has to do with the messages the players could formulate. The transcripts of the messages show that comparisons of the two bargainers' prizes played a considerable part in the negotiations in the full information condition, in which both players knew each others' prize values. The equal probability (50%,50%) proposal and the (75%,25%) equal expected value proposal occupied prominent places in these negotiations. Although notions of "fairness" were mentioned by both parties, there was clearly a strategic aspect to how these notions of fairness were employed, since the player advancing the (50%,50%) outcome as fair could be reliably counted on to be the player with the larger prize.[76] One natural question is whether the different agreements reached in the two conditions might be entirely due to the different messages possible when prizes could be compared, or whether some sociological factors relating to commonly held notions of equity might be an essential ingredient in the effectiveness of the strategic appeals to "fairness."

The experiment of Roth, Malouf, and Murnighan (1981) was therefore designed to see whether *arbitrary* focal points could be created. It employed binary lottery games with prizes stated in terms of an intermediate commodity, "chips," having monetary value. Each player always knew the number and value of chips in his own prize, but a player's information about his opponent's prize was an experimental variable. The conditions of the previous experiment were essentially replicated with "low information" and "high information" conditions, and in addition there was an "intermediate information" condition, in which each player knew the number of chips in his opponent's prize, but not their value.

The observed results were that the low and high information conditions replicated the partial and full information conditions of the previous experiment, but the outcomes observed in the intermediate information conditions did *not* differ significantly from those in the low information condition: the observed agreements tended to give both players equal probabilities, regardless of the size of their prize in chips.[77] Thus, the ability to compare prizes in terms of the artificial commodity, chips, did not affect the outcomes in the same way as did equivalent information about money. This supports the hypothesis that there is a "social" aspect to the focal point phenomenon, that depends on something like the players' shared perceptions of the credibility of any bargaining position.

Given the robustness of the observed (but unpredicted) effect of information about the size of the prizes on the outcome of bargaining, a subsequent experiment (Roth and Murnighan 1982) was designed to separate the observed effect of information into components that could be attributed to the possession of specific information by specific individuals. Each game of that experiment was a binary lottery game in which one player had a $20 prize and the other a $5 prize. In all eight conditions of the experiment, each player knew at least his own prize. The experiment used a 4 (information) x 2 (common knowledge) factorial design. The information conditions were as follows: 1) *neither knows* his opponent's prize; 2) the *$20 player knows* both prizes, but the $5 player knows only his own prize; 3) the *$5 player knows* both prizes, but the $20 player knows only his own prize; and 4) *both players know* both prizes. The second factor made this information common knowledge for half the bargaining pairs, but not common knowledge for the other half. For example, when the $20 player is the only one who knows both prizes, then the (common) instructions to both players in the common knowledge condition reveal that both players are reading the same instructions, and that, after the instructions are presented, one player will be informed of only his own prize and that the other will be informed of both prizes. In the not-common knowledge condition, the instructions simply state that each player will be informed of his own prize and may or may not be informed of the other prize.[78]

The results of this experiment permitted three principal conclusions. First, the equal expected value agreement becomes a focal point if and only if the player with the smaller prize knows both prizes. When the $5 player knew that the other player's prize was $20, this was reflected not only in his messages and proposals, but also in the mean agreements (when agreement was reached) and in the shape of the distribution of agreements (see Figure 1.3). And the mean agreements reached when neither player knows both prizes and when both players know both prizes replicate the results of Roth and Malouf (1979), both in direction and magnitude.

Second, the frequency of disagreement depends on whether it is common knowledge what information the bargainers possess. The frequency of disagreement in the two not-common knowledge conditions in which the $5 player knew

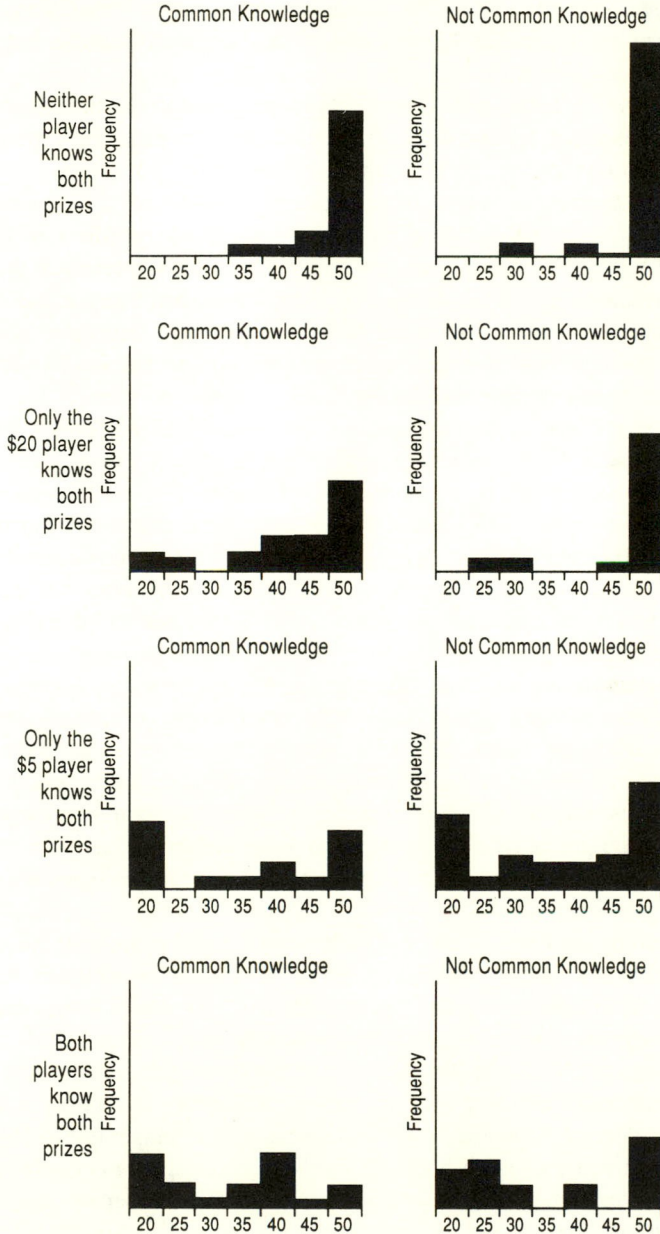

Figure 1.3. Distribution of payoffs obtained by the player with the $20 prize when agreement was reached (frequency of agreements in terms of the percentage of lottery tickets obtained by the $20 player). *Source:* Roth and Murnighan 1982.

both prizes is significantly higher than in the other conditions. The highest frequency of disagreement (33%) occurs when the $5 player knows both prizes, the $20 player does not, but the $5 player doesn't *know* that the $20 player doesn't know both prizes. (In this situation the $5 player cannot accurately assess whether or not the $20 player's [honest] skepticism that his opponent's prize is only $5 is just a bargaining ploy.)

Third, the regularities among these unpredicted effects of information make it unlikely that they can be attributed primarily to mistaken or irrational behavior on the parts of the bargainers. For example, in the four cells in which the bargainers do not know what information their counterpart has, the tradeoffs between the higher payoffs demanded by the $5 player when he knows both prizes and the correspondingly increased frequency of disagreements is just what would be expected at equilibrium, in that the increase in the number of disagreements just offsets the increased share obtained by the $5 player when agreements are reached.

A subsequent experiment (Roth and Schoumaker 1983) lends support to the hypothesis that the effect of information about the cash value of prizes is attributable to its effect on the *expectations* of the bargainers about what constitutes a credible bargaining position. Such information may help bargainers (and theorists) to select from among the multiplicity of equilibria that are found in bargaining games.

The bargaining experiments discussed above all involved variables which the theories in question predict will not influence the outcome of bargaining. They revealed ways in which the theories systematically fail to be descriptive of observed behavior. As such, the experimental results demonstrate serious shortcomings of the theories. However, in order to fully evaluate a theory, we also need to test the predictions it makes about those variables it predicts *are* important. For theories based on bargainers' expected utilities, risk posture is such a variable.

The predictions of these theories concerning the risk posture of the bargainers were developed in a way that lent itself to experimental test in Roth (1979), Kihlstrom, Roth, and Schmeidler (1981), and Roth and Rothblum (1982).[79] (One indirect virtue of experimentation is that it can provide a discipline to theoretical work and suggest directions in which theory ought to be explored.) A broad class of apparently quite different models, including all the standard axiomatic models,[80] yield a common prediction regarding risk aversion. Loosely speaking, they all predict that risk aversion is disadvantageous in bargaining, except when the bargaining concerns potential agreements that have a positive probability of yielding an outcome worse than disagreement.

Three closely related experimental studies exploring the predicted effects of risk aversion on the outcome of bargaining are reported in Murnighan, Roth, and Schoumaker (1988). Whereas binary lottery games were employed in the earlier experiments precisely in order to control out the individual variation due to differences in risk posture, these studies employed *ternary* lottery games having three possible payoffs for each bargainer i. These are large and small prizes λ_i and σ_i

obtained by lottery when agreement is reached, and a disagreement prize δ_i obtained when no agreement is reached in the allotted time. (In binary lottery games, $\sigma_i = \delta_i$.)

The bargainers' risk postures were first measured by having them make a set of risky choices. (Note that, in contrast to the experiments just discussed, the strategy in this experiment was to *measure* preferences rather than to control them.) Statistically significant differences in risk aversion were found among the population of participants, even on the relatively modest range of prizes available in these studies (in which typical choices involved choosing between receiving \$5 for certain or participating in a lottery with prizes of $\lambda_i = \$16$ and $\sigma_i = \$4$).

Those bargainers with relatively high risk aversion bargained against those with relatively low risk aversion in pairs of games such that the disagreement prizes were larger than the small prizes in one game and smaller in the other. The prediction of game-theoretic models such as Nash's is that agreements reached in the first game should be more favorable to the more risk averse of the two bargainers than agreements reached in the second game.

Let me be precise. The theory actually makes a stronger prediction, but only the weaker form is confirmed by the experiments, and the reasons for this illuminate not only the design and analysis of these experiments, but of many experiments designed to test economic theories. When the prizes of both bargainers are all equal (i.e., $\lambda_1 = \lambda_2 = \lambda$, $\sigma_1 = \sigma_2 = \sigma$, and $\delta_1 = \delta_2 = \delta$) the theories in question predict that the more risk averse player will get more than 50 percent of the lottery tickets when $\delta > \sigma$, and less than 50 percent of the lottery tickets when $\delta < \sigma$. Thus the prediction is not only that the more risk averse player should do better in the first game than he does in the second, but that he should do better than the less risk averse player in the first game, and worse in the second.

Now, as had already been established by the earlier experiments, these axiomatic theories fail to predict the effects of the bargainers' information about one anothers' prizes. Among the earlier observations was the very high concentration of (50%,50%) agreements in games with equal prizes or in which bargainers know only their own prizes, and a shift in the direction of equal expected values in games with unequal prizes known to both bargainers. The strongest form of the predictions about risk aversion concern games in which the bargainers have equal prizes, and so the first experiment of Murnighan, Roth, and Schoumaker (1988) used such a symmetric game. However a test of the predictions requires data from pairs of agreements between the same subjects, and it was quickly observed that a high percentage of pairs reached (50%,50%) agreements in the game with $\delta < \sigma$, and ended in disagreement in the game with $\delta > \sigma$. Although there was a weak effect of risk aversion in the predicted direction, it was not significant. One way to read this, of course, is as a rejection of the prediction, but in view of the relatively small scale of the prizes it was thought that any effect of risk aversion might simply be overpowered by the "focal point" effect already observed in connection with the equal probability agreement. So it was decided to run a subsequent experiment in which the prizes were unequal, in order to give any effect of risk aversion a wider range on which to be observed.[81] But, as had already been noted, this meant that the player with the smaller prize could be expected to receive the higher percentage of lottery tickets, irrespective of the relative risk aversion of the two bargainers. Consequently only the weaker form of the risk aversion prediction could be tested on such a game, and it is this prediction that was ultimately confirmed by the data. That is, the results of these experiments support the predictions of the game-theoretic models that more risk averse bargainers do better when the disagreement prize is high than when it is low.[82]

But these results also suggest that, in the (relatively modest) range of payoffs studied here, the effects due to risk aversion may be much smaller than some of the effects due to changes in information observed in previous experiments. How much this has to do with the size of the payoffs remains to be determined.[83]

So one lesson that can be drawn from all this is that it is possible to design experiments to investigate the qualitative predictions of theories that may already be known not to be good point predictors. Because of the relative complexity of economic phenomena compared to the relative simplicity of economic theories intended to account for them, this is frequently the problem facing economic experimenters, one they have in common with econometricians studying field data.

The results also illustrate a frequent and perplexing problem in interpreting experimental work: how should one assess the "size" (or relative importance) of effects observed in the laboratory, particularly when these may be sensitive to the size of the payoffs to the subjects? Since it has so far proved far easier to observe the unpredicted effects of information than the predicted effects of risk aversion on the outcome of bargaining, can we conclude that the former are more important than the latter? I do not think that the available evidence fully justifies this conclusion. The problem is that there is reason to believe that risk aversion is a phenomenon many of whose consequences are easiest to observe when decisions involve very large gambles. In principle this presents no obstacle to experimental investigation (just conduct experiments with very large prizes). But in practice, experimental budgets always make it likely that payoffs in the laboratory will be smaller than those in many situations to which economic theories are naturally applied. Not being able to compare the significance of these unpredicted and predicted effects means that, on the evidence so far available, we cannot deliver a conclusive verdict on the overall health of every aspect of theories of bargaining such as Nash's.

In looking over this whole series of experiments, two other phenomena stand out. First, there was a non-negligible frequency of disagreements. Second, there was a clear "deadline effect." Across all experiments, which varied considerably in the terms and distribution of agreements, the data reveal that a high proportion of agreements were reached in the very final seconds before the deadline. As these observations are closely related to the results observed in the experiments that will be discussed in chapter 4, they will be discussed there.

In summary, the series of experiments discussed here shows several things. First, it disconfirms some important aspects of the received theory of bargaining, chief among which is what constitutes a "complete" specification of the information available to bargainers. This is particularly notable in light of the fact that much of the theoretical criticism of the complete information assumption is founded on the assumption that bargaining is better modeled by assuming that the bargainers have strictly *less* than complete information. The experimental evidence suggests that, although bargainers may certainly be expected in general to have less of *some kinds* of information, the outcome of bargaining is also highly sensitive to information the bargainers may have about each other *in addition* to what is included in "complete" information about utility functions. These experiments also provide preliminary support for some of the subtle but robust predictions of these bargaining theories about the effect of risk aversion.

D. Market Organization and Competitive Equilibrium

Both chapter 5 by Holt and chapter 6 by Sunder review experiments that primarily involve markets created using the basic design of Chamberlin's 1948 experiment for motivating subjects' supply and demand behavior. That is, each potential buyer of an artificial commodity is told an amount that the experimenters will pay him if he purchases the commodity (so that a buyer's total profit will be this amount minus the price he paid for the purchase), and each seller is told an amount that will be subtracted from the sale price if he sells a unit of the commodity. The assumption that subjects treat these amounts as their reservation prices then permits the experiment to be analyzed in terms of the resulting aggregate supply and demand curves, from which predictions or benchmarks such as competitive equilibria, consumer surplus, etc. can be computed.[84]

However in most of the markets reviewed in those chapters, the pricemaking mechanism differs from the bilateral negotiations employed by Chamberlin. (And indeed one focus of Holt's chapter is on the effect of different pricemaking mechanisms.) One of the frequently explored pricemaking mechanisms is the "double auction," in which sellers may make offers and buyers may make bids. Sellers and buyers may make new offers and bids whenever they like; the lowest outstanding offer is the "market asked price," and the highest outstanding bid is the "market bid price." If any seller offers the market bid price or if any buyer bids the market asked price, a transaction is consummated between the seller and buyer whose prices coincide.

In the first part of this section I will concentrate on a series of experiments that study the behavior of double auction markets when the market is repeated several times with identical parameters. In the second part of the section I will discuss experiments that compare different forms of market organization. Both of these sets of experiments, and chapters 5 and 6, testify to the continuing importance of Chamberlin's 1948 experimental design. In the final part of this section I will describe some experiments underway at the University of Iowa, which use double auction markets without seeking to control supply and demand behavior, but which use the laboratory environment to allow such behavior to be carefully observed and measured.

1. Repeated Double Auctions with Stationary Parameters

Smith (1962) employed a double auction procedure in which all payoffs were hypothetical, and once all transactions had been made, subjects repeated the process, with the same reservation prices, several times. He describes the differences between his experiment and Chamberlin's as follows (Smith 1962, 114):

> The design of my experiments differs from that of Chamberlin in several ways. In Chamberlin's experiment the buyers and sellers simply circulate and engage in bilateral higgling and bargaining until they make a contract or the trading period ends. As contracts are made the transaction price is recorded on the blackboard. . . . Each trader's attention is directed to the one person with whom he is bargaining, whereas in my experiments each trader's quotation is addressed to the entire trading group one quotation at a time. Also Chamberlin's experiment constitutes a pure exchange market operated for a single trading period. There is, therefore, less opportunity for traders to gain experience and to modify their subsequent behavior in the light of such experience. It is only through some learning mechanism of this kind that I can imagine the possibility of equilibrium being approached in any real market.

About this latter difference Smith further notes (115):

> One important condition operating in our experimental markets is not likely to prevail in real markets. The experimental conditions of supply and demand are held constant over several successive trading periods in order to give any equilibrating mechanisms an opportunity to establish an equilibrium over time. Real markets are likely to be continually subjected to changing conditions of supply and demand.

Thus the focus of this experiment was on producing conditions under which competitive equilibrium might be observed, and in this respect it succeeded—the repeated double auction markets that Smith reports all show convergence of transaction prices towards the competitive price in the course of only a small number of repetitions of the market. In subsequent experiments Smith reproduced this phenomenon with real monetary payoffs, rather than the hypothetical payoffs employed in Smith (1962).[85] These and other experiments confirmed a tendency for transactions to converge towards competitive equilibrium in repeated double auction markets. (The behavior of repeated double auction markets is thus one of the phenomena to have been first observed with hypothetical payments, and later confirmed with real payments, a point that I do not recall seeing mentioned in the debate about the role that experiments with hypothetical payments might continue to play in experimental economics.)

In the ensuing years, Smith and his students and colleagues replicated this result many times, further demonstrating convergence to competitive outcomes in repeated double auctions. However, as the attention of other experimenters was drawn to the repeated double auction, experiments were designed both to explore conditions under which competitive outcomes would or would not be observed in double auctions, and to explain the convergence that was often observed. Two experiments that are especially worth mentioning are those reported by Holt, Langan, and Villamil (1986), and by Gode and Sunder (1993).

Holt, Langan, and Villamil (1986) considered whether or not convergence to competitive equilibrium in double auctions might be influenced by the parameters determining the supply and demand curves. They considered, for example, a double auction examined by Smith, which he reported (Smith 1982a, 172), "provides the most stringent of all reported tests of the equilibrating tendency in double auction trading," since the competitive equilibrium gave all of the exchange surplus[86] to one side of the market. Holt et al. observed that, while in this dimension the test is indeed stringent, nevertheless the supply and demand is such that (112) "the lack of market power is so severe in this design that even if one buyer unilaterally withholds demand for all four of his units, he has no effect on market price."

They proposed to examine double auction markets that differed from those previously examined in that agents on one side of the market had market power, in the sense that, by foregoing some trades, they could move the competitive price sufficiently in their favor so that they would earn a larger profit on their remaining transactions than if they had made all the trades that would be profitable for them. Holt et al. note that this is a natural place to begin an investigation aimed at finding nonconvergence to competitive equilibrium, since the hypothesis that this kind of market power may lead to noncompetitive outcomes goes back as far as Cournot (1838). Holt (1989, S108) further notes that this definition of market power is embodied in the Department of Justice horizontal merger guidelines.

Holt et al. first replicated the results of the double auction discussed by Smith, confirming the tendency of the market to converge to competitive equilibrium (see, e.g., Figure 5.4 for the graph of a similar market). They then conducted seven multiperiod double auctions each involving five buyers and five sellers, using the procedures of previously published experiments, but with parameters that gave market power either to some of the buyers or to some of the sellers. Three of their double auctions used experienced subjects. Contrary to the convergence to competitive equilibrium uniformly observed in earlier experiments (Smith 1982b), four of the seven auctions observed here, including all of those with experienced subjects, failed to converge to the competitive price and converged instead to a price reflecting the distribution of market power (see, e.g., Figure 5.7).

The results of this experiment thus support the hypothesis that the parameters of the market may influence the convergence to competitive equilibrium previously observed in double auction markets, particularly when experienced subjects are involved. And subsequent experiments have also shown that the high efficiency observed in early double auction experiments may also depend on the market parameters employed (see Banks, Ledyard, and Porter 1989; Van Boening and Wilcox 1993[87]). However, as Holt notes in chapter 5, the significance and implications of such results are still a matter of lively controversy.

One conclusion that can clearly be drawn from the many repeated double auction experiments is that it is possible for competitive equilibrium outcomes to be observed with very few buyers and sellers. This simple fact provides a powerful challenge and stimulus to developing new theories of competitive behavior. One of the most interesting of these is developed by Gode and Sunder (1993), who compare experimentally observed (human) behavior with the simulated behavior of what they call "zero-intelligence traders."

Gode and Sunder report an experiment in which they used Chamberlin's procedure to construct four sets of supply and demand curves that past experience suggested would reliably lead to competitive equilibrium in a repeated double auction, and one that might not. (In this latter case, the reservation prices of some buyers and sellers would prevent them from trading at the equilibrium price, so they had strong incentives to try to transact trades at other prices.) Gode and Sunder compared the behavior of human subjects in six repetitions for each set of parameters with the behavior of a simulated market in which the traders were represented by simple computer programs.

Two kinds of programmed traders were considered, each of which generated *random* bid or asked prices (depending on whether it was a buyer or a seller). The first kind of programmed trader generated bid or asked prices from a uniform distribution on the integer prices from 1 to 200, a range that defined the feasible range of trading prices. The second kind of programmed trader only was able to generate random bid or asked prices that would not yield a negative profit if accepted; that is, these traders were constrained by their reservation prices (and thus, although still random, could be viewed as having a *little* intelligence). The first kind of programmed trader was called a ZI-U (zero intelligence, unconstrained) trader, while the second was called a ZI-C (constrained) trader.

Gode and Sunder simulated double auction markets consisting of six buyers and six sellers, all of the same type, i.e., all ZI-U or all ZI-C. The rules of the market were that a transaction occurred whenever any bid or asked crossed (i.e., if some bid price was at least as high as some asked price), with the transaction price equal to whichever of the two prices had been posted earlier. Each transaction was for a single unit.

As expected, the human subjects converged fairly smoothly to the competitive equilibrium in the markets with the first four sets of parameters, with prices near competitive prices, and efficiency (percentage of feasible buyer plus seller profits) near 100 percent after the first few periods. Also as conjectured, the fifth set of parameters was further from the competitive outcome, with a lower efficiency, as some of the "wrong" units were traded away from the equilibrium price.

In contrast, the simulated markets with the ZI-U traders exhibited no trend— transaction prices were distributed with high variance, and efficiency was dimin-

ished by the fact that the maximum feasible number of units (equal to the smaller of the total units sellers were allowed to sell or the buyers were allowed to buy) were always traded, regardless of whether these trades were profitable.

However, the results of the simulated markets with the ZI-C traders are in some important ways much closer to that of the human traders than to the ZI-U traders. First, the transaction prices are much closer to the equilibrium price than those of the ZI-U traders, although not as close to equilibrium as those of the human traders. Second, the efficiency achieved by the ZI traders, while it falls short of the 100% seen in many periods with the human traders, is very high (and in fact higher than the efficiency of the human traders under the fifth parameter set). Third, and to my mind most striking, *there is a tendency for the prices of transactions reached later in a given market period to be nearer to the competitive price than are the prices of early transactions*. That is, although the ZI-C traders cannot learn and although (in contrast to the human subjects) their transactions in any period therefore look exactly like the transactions in any other period, their transactions within a period exhibit a trend towards competitive prices. This is seen most clearly in their fourth parameter set, shown in Figure 1.4.

Gode and Sunder explain that this trend

> . . . is caused solely by the progressive narrowing of the opportunity sets of ZI-C traders. The left end of the market demand function represents units with higher redemption values. Expected values of the bids generated for these units by ZI-C traders are also higher. Therefore, these units are likely to be traded earlier than units further down the market demand function. As the higher-value units are traded, the upper end of the support of ZI-C bids shifts down. Similarly, as the lower-cost units are sold earlier in a period, the lower end of the support of ZI-C offers moves up.
>
> This means that the feasible range of transactions prices narrows as more units are traded. Though individual units may not be traded in the order in which they appear in the market demand and supply functions, there is a greater probability that the last transaction represents an exchange between the marginal buyer and the marginal seller. (129)

Thus Gode and Sunder have identified a feature of the double auction trading rules that, when combined with very minimal trader intelligence (just enough to know not to buy or sell at a loss), produces high levels of efficiency and exhibits a tendency towards equilibrium prices. And, although the simulated ZI-C traders cannot learn as human subjects do, these results suggest why human subjects are able to learn so quickly to make equilibrium-price transactions when the market is repeated with the same parameters. Because the repeated parameter design makes the supply and demand conditions identical from one period to the next (so that past consumption does not influence future demand, but instead the market "starts over" at each period) the information obtained in the latter part of one period is of very high relevance for the next period.[88]

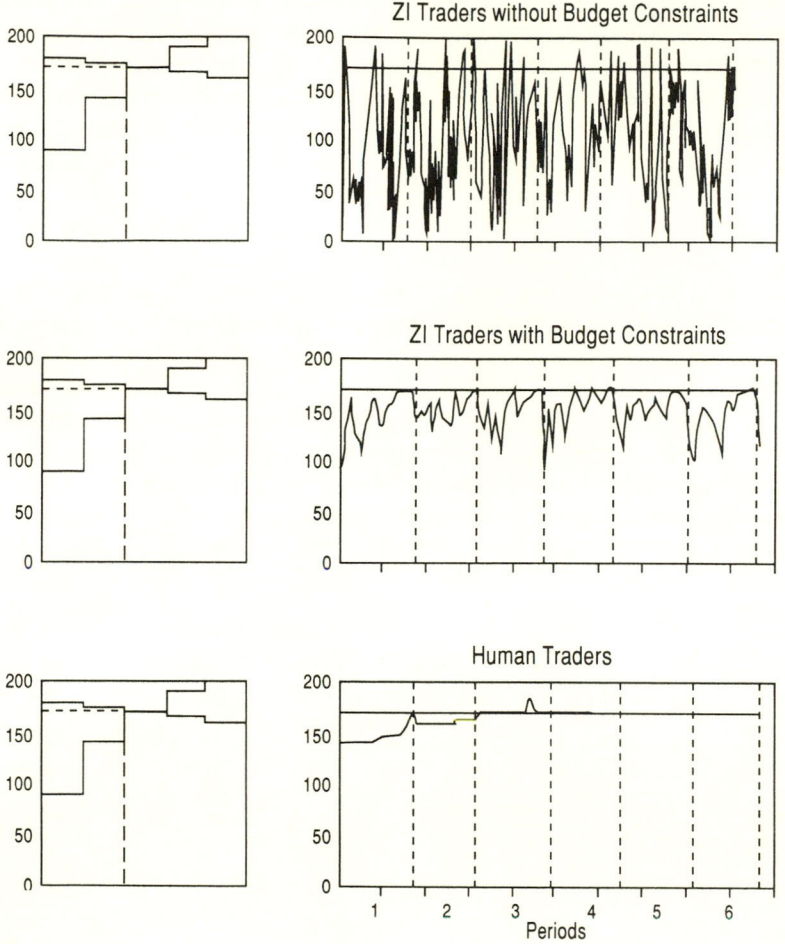

Figure 1.4. Demand and supply functions and transaction price time series (market 4). *Source:* Gode and Sunder 1993.

Thus, over a long period of time, we see a series of experiments that begin with a demonstration that competitive equilibrium outcomes can be observed in markets even with relatively few buyers and sellers and that eventually move from demonstrations to investigations of the causes and conditions under which this occurs. As can be expected of such a productive series of experiments, the latter experiments raise as many issues as they settle and suggest new hypotheses and further experiments. For example, the results of both Holt et al. (1986) and Gode and Sunder (1993) suggest that further exploration of the sensitivity of double auction outcomes to supply and demand parameters is well justified. And the

results of Gode and Sunder help explain observed convergence results in double auction markets and suggest how some of the properties of these markets may interact with the experimental repetition of a stationary set of parameters. This suggests that the exploration of markets without stationary repetition of parameters may be called for, particularly when it is desirable to compare the performance of different forms of market organization.

2. Some Policy-Oriented Comparisons of Market Rules

The next set of experiments I will discuss have been motivated by questions of policy, of the kind raised by government regulatory agencies, typically about the effect of changes in the rules by which some market is organized. These investigations bring scientific methods to bear on one of the traditional *non*scientific vocations of economists, which is whispering in the ears of princes who require advice about pressing practical questions about which little is known.

One of the studies I will speak about (Hong and Plott 1982) arose in a matter of concern to the Interstate Commerce Commission; the other (Grether and Plott 1984) in a case before the Federal Trade Commission. Both cases had to do with complex posted price markets, and in both cases an attempt was made to mirror as closely as possible in the laboratory the industrial structure of the market in question.

The ICC case concerned whether or not barge operators should be required by the ICC to post their prices and announce price changes in advance. The existing market allowed rates to be set by individual negotiations between barge operators and their customers, so that the terms of each contract were private information. Plott (1986) reports that the question arose because railroad companies were lobbying to require such price posting. The reasons offered by the railroads were that (735) "public information on prices would make prices more competitive and protect small barge owners from large barge owners, who were allegedly making secret price concessions."

In their introductory comments, Hong and Plott (1982) say the following about their use of laboratory experimentation to illuminate the issues raised by the proposed change (1):

> The full consequences of a rate filing policy are unknown. Plausible theoretical arguments can be made on both sides of the policy argument. When existing theory does not yield a definitive answer, one can usually turn to previous experiences with policies, but in this case we are aware of no industrial case study that would provide direct evidence on either side of the controversy.

They go on to note that it would be difficult to draw any compelling policy conclusions regarding the barge industry from previous laboratory experiments concerning posted price markets (in particular those of Williams 1973 and Plott and Smith 1978), since (2)

Any extrapolation from published experimental results to the barge industry itself is open to two potential criticisms, the reasonableness of which this study was designed to assess. First, the barge industry has several prominent economic features that are not incorporated in existing laboratory market studies. Examples include the relative sizes of buyers and sellers, the demand and supply elasticities, and the cyclical nature of demand. Naturally, we can never be certain that all the important features have been included in the present design. If something important has been misspecified or omitted, then the observed behavior of the laboratory market may not extend to the barge industry, and additional appropriately modified experiments can be conducted as checks on our conclusions. The second potential criticism is that the effects of price posting in laboratory studies have only been measured relative to the performance of oral auction markets. Since auction markets differ from the negotiated price markets of the industry, the relevance of the comparison can be questioned.

Hong and Plott proceeded to design their experiment around a laboratory market scaled to resemble, in the features mentioned above, the market for transporting grain along the upper Mississippi River and Illinois Waterway during the Fall of 1970. (This market was chosen because it was believed to be representative of a significant portion of the dry bulk barge traffic in the United States and because adequate data about the market parameters were available.) Aggregate supply and demand functions for the laboratory market were scaled to estimates available for the target market, as was the distribution of large and small firms on each side of the market. The laboratory market was divided into periods representing two weeks of the target market, and the seasonal aspects of the target market were modeled by having demand in the laboratory market scaled to resemble two months of normal demand followed by two months of high demand, followed by two months of normal demand. The experimental design involved running the market under both posted price and negotiated price policies.

In presenting the data from this experiment, Hong and Plott report that (10–1)

> The results are easy to summarize. The posted price policy causes higher prices, reduced volume, and efficiency losses. Furthermore, the posted price policy works to the disadvantage of most market participants, especially the small ones, and helps only the large sellers.

They also conclude that the posted price markets react more slowly to the seasonal change in demand than do the negotiated price markets. Plott (1986) reports that this experimental evidence helped to deter the lobbying of the railroads on this matter, and that the price posting policy that they had advocated was not pursued.

We will consider the relationship of these experimental results to policy conclusions after briefly considering the experiment of Grether and Plott, which was motivated by an FTC complaint that also involving posted prices, among other things.

The FTC case involved a complaint by the FTC against the pricing practices of the Ethyl Corporation, E.I. du Pont de Nemours and Company, PPG Industries, Inc., and Nalco Chemical Corporation, the four domestic producers of tetraethyl and tetramethyl lead, the additives in "leaded" gasoline that raise its octane level. The FTC sought to have the producers cease and desist from a number of unusual pricing practices used for these additives, that, according to the FTC theory, had the effect of reducing price competition.

One of these pricing practices was that suppliers agreed to give at least a thirty-day notice of all proposed price increases, and usually such announcements were made with even more than the contractual thirty-day warning. Another practice was that "most favored nation" clauses were commonly included in contracts, by which a buyer was assured that he would receive the best terms being offered by the seller to any customer. (Apparently "meet or release" clauses were sometimes also used, which assured a buyer that the seller would meet the price offered by any other seller, or else release the buyer from any contractual obligation to buy from that seller.) In addition, all prices were quoted in terms of "delivered prices," for goods delivered to the purchaser regardless of his location.

Some of these practices might appear to favor the buyers, but the FTC theory was that, together, they worked to allow the producers to cooperate in raising prices. One way to explain this idea is as follows. If a producer thought that a price increase was desirable, he could announce, with somewhat more than the required thirty-days warning, his intention to raise his price. This wouldn't cause a customer with a "meet or release" clause to start searching for a supplier with a better price, because such a customer is assured that, in any event, he will only be charged the lowest price. (The lowest price is known, since prices are announced, and it is unambiguously defined, since only delivered prices are quoted, so there can be no hidden discounts in transportation costs.) If the other producers agree that this price increase is desirable, they can also announce it; otherwise, it will be rescinded by the initial producer. So a producer faces little cost in exploring the possibility of a price rise, while at the same time has little incentive to explore a price cut, since he will not be able to increase his market share (again, because of advance announcements, and "meet or release" clauses).

In its defense, the industry advanced the competing theory that price levels were determined entirely by the concentrated structure of the industry, and that, in such a concentrated industry, prices were unaffected by the pricing practices described.

Expert testimony by economists was available in support of both positions. The experiment of Grether and Plott was intended to be a possible source of evidence for rebuttal of the industry theory that the indicated pricing policies could not be affecting the price in such a concentrated industry. A scaled-down model of the industry was implemented in the laboratory, with careful attention paid to preserving the relative costs, capacities, and numbers of participants. The experimental design involved a number of multiperiod repeated markets, each of which would be examined both with and without (some or all of) the pricing practices in question. The results were fairly clear—when all the practices were in force, the observed prices were above those that are observed when none of the practices were employed.[89]

Looking at these two experiments together, it is apparent that one of the differences between these experiments and those described in the previous sections has to do with the complexity of the economic environment being studied. There is some tension between the goal of designing an experimental market to resemble a particular naturally occurring market and the goal of designing an experiment whose results will be likely to support some fairly general conclusion.

On the other hand, it should also be apparent that these "policy-oriented" experiments have something in common with "theory-testing" experiments, since both involve the testing of hypotheses, whether those hypotheses arise from formal economic theories or from the arguments of lawyers, lobbyists, and expert witnesses. However, in contrast to hypotheses drawn from general economic theories, which are presumably applicable to any market in which the conditions of the theory are met, the hypotheses of interest in this case are explicitly concerned with the target market and not with the experimental market. Therefore, the bearing that the experimental evidence has on the hypotheses is different in these policy-oriented experiments than in the theory-testing experiments.

Hong and Plott aptly describe the role of experimental evidence in policy debates of this kind as serving to *shift the burden of proof*. Speaking of the experiments modeled on the barge industry, they put it this way (16–8):

> From a scientific point of view, we have solid evidence only that price posting markets do not necessarily operate better than negotiated price markets under the parametric conditions we considered. From a policy point of view, this evidence presumably shifts the burden of proof to the price posting advocates, who must now identify the specific features of the barge industry which, if incorporated in the experiment, would reverse the conclusions.

Plott (1986) closes by noting (737–8) that this research "demonstrates that laboratory experimental methods can be used in economics for basic, applied, and policy research. Such a demonstration presents a real challenge to the commonly held belief that economics is not a laboratory science as a matter of principle."

3. Information Aggregation: Markets as Forecasters

While I am on the subject of the range of uses to which economic experiments can be applied, I would be remiss not to at least mention a fascinating set of ongoing experiments at the University of Iowa, one piece of which is reported in Forsythe, Nelson, Neumann, and Wright (1992).[90] What Forsythe and his colleagues have done is create and operate a variety of double auction markets in which, over a period of months, participants can buy and sell assets whose ultimate value depends on some future event, which occurs after the close of the market. The extent to which market prices at the close can be used to predict the future event can then be examined, the larger aim being to understand better the ways in which markets can aggregate information.

Forsythe et al. (1992) report the results of a market that opened for trading on June 1, 1988, in which the ultimate value of the assets traded would be determined by the proportion of votes received by each candidate in the election in November of that year for the Presidency of the United States. They describe the market as follows (1143–4):

> Aspiring traders were sold portfolios of shares in candidates at $2.50 each, with each basic portfolio consisting of one share in each major candidate in the campaign. The slate of candidates included George Bush, Michael Dukakis, Jesse Jackson, and a candidate labeled "Rest-of-Field." Shares were given value by the dividends paid after the election, with the dividend on each share determined as the candidate's fraction of the popular vote times $2.50. Since Rest-of-Field covered all third-party candidates who earned votes in the election, the vote shares summed to 1 across the four candidates, and the total dividend paid on a basic portfolio of one share in each candidate just matched the fee charged for that portfolio. This investment/payoff rule was adopted . . . because it provides a direct translation of market prices into estimates of vote shares,
>
> $$\text{expected vote share} = \text{price}/\$2.50$$
>
> and thus offers a prediction of not only the election winner, but also the margin of victory.

Traders in this electronic market also maintained cash accounts from which they could finance additional purchases and could log on at any time to post bids or offers for shares in a particular candidate. So the full record of the market allows conclusions to be drawn not only about closing prices, but also about the reaction of the market to particular events during the course of the election campaign, and not only about aggregate results, but also about the behavior of particular traders. The experimenters also conducted regular surveys of the traders and so were able to identify supporters of the different candidates.

Forsythe et al. (1992) conclude, on the basis of over 16,000 transactions observed over the course of the market, that although there is evidence that individual traders exhibited biases related to their political opinions, the market as a whole, as measured by the prices on November 7, was a very good predictor of the November 8 election results and was at least comparable to the major national opinion polls. (In particular, they report that the vote share forecast by the November 7 market prices were 53.2 percent for Bush, 45.2 percent for Dukakis, and 2 percent for any other candidate, while the actual vote shares were 53.2 percent, 45.4 percent, and 1.4 percent respectively, and major opinion polls in that week forecast the Bush vote in a range from 48 to 54 percent.) So although the average trader is not free of biases, the fact that the transaction prices are determined by the traders on the margin reduces the influence such biases play on the market price of each candidate's shares.

Similar political stock markets have since been conducted at Iowa and elsewhere, and, since January of 1993, two financial futures markets have been initiated at Iowa (the Iowa Earnings Market and the Iowa Economic Indicators Market), open to traders with appropriate electronic access from around the world.[91] The contracts initially offered on the Iowa Earnings market were based on the earnings per share (EPS) of five companies—three in the airline industry (American, Delta, and United) and two in the computer industry (Apple and IBM). Each company had a separate set of contracts for reported EPS in the first and second quarters of 1993. The Iowa Economic Indicators Market initially offered two types of contracts: inflation rate contracts whose liquidation values are determined by the monthly change in the Consumer Price Index, and currency contracts in the Mexican peso whose liquidation values are determined by the end-of-month exchange rate between the dollar and the peso.

The detailed scrutiny available in experimental markets in contrast to field markets (e.g., concerning the behavior of individual traders) promises to make these markets a unique resource for studying how the market aggregates information across traders. This is a topic that has attracted the attention of experimenters using more traditional laboratory based techniques, and Sunder surveys much of this work in chapter 6.

We turn next to consideration of another class of markets in which we can consider the relationship of experimental and field data and in which aggregation of different information held by different traders is a crucial issue.

E. Auction Markets and Disequilibrium Behavior

1. The Winner's Curse

My topic in this section is in some ways the reverse of the discussion of free riding in public goods provision. Instead of discussing a theoretical prediction that seemed difficult to investigate with field data and initially proved difficult to detect experimentally, this section discusses an *un*predicted effect that was initially postulated on the basis of field data, whose existence was debated, and which proved to be easy to observe in the laboratory. Of course, questions remain about how the experimental evidence applies to assessing the importance of this phenomenon in field data. Experience and motivation (of the experimental subjects in comparison with agents in the natural markets), the usual suspects, play a role here too. But in this case some ingenious comparisons between experimental and field data have been suggested, which I think have promise of furthering this part of the debate.

The story begins with a 1971 article by Capen, Clapp, and Campbell, three petroleum engineers employed by the Atlantic Richfield Company. They claimed that oil leases won by competitive bidding yield unexpectedly low rates of return, "year after year," and that this has to do with the fact that the winning bidder is typically the one with the highest estimate of the value of the recoverable oil and that the highest estimate is often an overestimate.

The important feature of this kind of auction is that all the bidders are trying to estimate a common value, in this case the value of the oil in a given tract. So even if all bidders have unbiased estimates of the true value, one bidder's estimate would convey valuable information to other bidders: the expected true value given a single estimate is higher than the expected true value given the information that the estimate is the highest of n, where n is the number of bidders. The hypothesis behind the "winner's curse" is that winning bidders must frequently have the highest estimate but fail to take this into account.

Now, the idea that bidders persistently make mistakes flies in the face of standard notions of equilibrium, and so this thesis was greeted with skepticism by many economic theorists, particularly as the details of equilibrium behavior in auctions became increasingly well understood (in which regard see particularly Wilson 1977 and Milgrom and Weber 1982). It seemed likely to many that a simpler explanation of why oil company engineers might urge others to lower their bids could be found in cartel theory rather than bidding theory.

Nevertheless, evidence from field data drawn from common value auctions of other kinds was increasingly cited in support of the thesis that this winner's curse might frequently account for low or negative returns to the winners. But such field data as is available is sufficiently complex and incomplete so as to allow many interpretations. The profitability of an oil field, for example, cannot be known for years after the auction of drilling rights, and so the auction price is only one of many determinants of the rate of return. So the debate continued much as before.

Laboratory experiments provide an opportunity to investigate at least the basic questions associated with whether or not the winner's curse is a robust phenomenon, and to what features in the auction environment it might respond. As we will see, they also reveal patterns in the data, associated with the presence or absence of a winner's curse, that suggest directions in which the field data can be further investigated.

Bazerman and Samuelson (1983) reported an experiment designed to see not merely if the winner's curse could be observed in the laboratory, but to explore how it might be related to the bidders' uncertainty about the value of the object being auctioned. The basic idea of their experiment was the following: subjects were asked to estimate the number of coins in a jar that in fact contained 800 pennies. (To motivate the subjects to be accurate in this part of the task, a small prize was given for the closest estimate.) Subjects were then asked to bid for the jar, with the understanding that the highest bidder would pay the amount of his bid and receive in return the value of the coins in the jar.[92] Subjects were also asked to write down their 90 percent confidence interval around their estimated value and to bid on other similar objects (e.g., a jar of nickels) also worth $8.

The main results were that a clear winner's curse was observed in the data, with average winning bids around $10, which is $2 more than the value of the objects being auctioned. This is in contrast to the average estimated value, which at around $5 underestimates the number of coins in the jar. So auctions were mostly being won by bidders with high estimates, and these were overestimates often enough to make the average winning bid higher than the true value. Analysis of various factors contributing to the level of bids suggested that, when the reported valuations were more uncertain, a winner's curse would start to appear among smaller numbers of bidders. (The amount that the highest value estimate must be discounted is greater when it is the highest of twenty than when it is the highest of four, so it is unsurprising that the winner's curse should be more readily observable among larger numbers of bidders.)

While the results show that the winner's curse is not hard to observe, the subjects in this experiment had no prior experience, and so the results could be attributed to the mistakes of novice bidders. Also, there was a wide range of bidding behavior, so the results could potentially be attributed to the mistakes of just a few bidders. (Bazerman and Samuelson report that the average winning bid is sensitive to [629] "a handful of grossly inflated bids.") One might suppose that in the natural economic environments in which questions about the winner's curse arose, bidders would have some opportunity to learn from their mistakes, and those who did not might be driven from the market by their losses. It is therefore still a reasonable question if the phenomenon observed in this experiment could occur in environments in which experience could be gained and in which bankruptcy could occur.

The experiment of Kagel and Levin (1986) was designed to address these issues and also to control (rather than simply to measure) the uncertainty surrounding the value of the object being auctioned. Their experiment involved auctions in which a value x_0 was chosen from a known uniform distribution, and each bidder was given a private information signal x_i drawn from a uniform distribution on $[x_0 - \epsilon, x_0 + \epsilon]$, for known ϵ (which was one of the experimental variables, varying from \$12 to \$30).[93] If the high bid is b, the high bidder earns $x_0 - b$ and everyone else earns 0. Subjects were given an initial cash endowment, and the opportunity to bid in a series of auctions. Subjects whose losses exhausted their initial endowments were declared bankrupt and were no longer allowed to bid. In addition, after each auction, the subjects were all given substantial feedback about the results: not only was the winning bid announced, but all bids were posted next to the signal that had been received by that bidder, and the true value x_0 was announced. Thus bidders not only had an opportunity to learn from their own experience, but also from the experience of others. In particular, all bidders had an opportunity to observe the actual earnings of the high bidder. In addition, all subjects in this experiment had some prior experience in experimental auctions.[94]

The main results for this part of the experiment are that bids were observed to be above the (risk neutral) Nash equilibrium bids. Profits were generally positive for groups of three or four bidders (at around 65 percent of the equilibrium profits) and negative for groups of six or seven bidders.[95] Overall, the data are consistent with the conclusion that the winner's curse diminishes with experience, but that changes in the environment (particularly in the number of bidders) require some readjustment during which profits are lower than they are after some additional experience has been accumulated.

Although a winner's curse was clearly observed in this experiment, there is still room to question the relevance of the findings for the kinds of field data that motivated the initial questions. After all, the results do suggest that the phenomenon might eventually disappear as bidders become more experienced. One might suppose that professional bidders for, say, oil companies would have far more experience than can be obtained in a series of laboratory auctions. This may be so, but it should be noted that the argument can also be made the other way: in this experiment, bidders received immediate feedback on the true value of the object and the profit made by the winning bidder. The field data on, say, drilling rights in the Gulf of Mexico, come from bids most of which were made before good information on the value of oil fields ultimately became available. And in many cases, only the winning bidder knows this information in any detail, so, unlike in the experimental environment, it might be that the only bidders to have experience with the winner's curse are its victims. Under this point of view, the bidders in the experimental environment might be thought to have more relevant experience than do bidders in natural environments.

Another line of attack concerns the subject pool itself: maybe the students who were the subjects in this experiment have not been selected for the kind of judgement that successful bidders may possess. Dyer, Kagel, and Levin (1989) address this question in a subsequent experiment, in which the behavior of student subjects was compared with that of construction industry executives and found to be qualitatively similar.[96]

Of course, there are always going to be differences between laboratory and field environments that make judgments such as these partly matters of taste. However, the second part of the experiment reported by Kagel and Levin (1986) suggests a way to make a direct connection between the experimental and field data. That part of the experiment concerned the effect of introducing public information.

To understand what is at issue here, first note that the equilibrium prediction is that as public information about the value of the object being auctioned is increased, winning bids will rise. The reason is that, at equilibrium, agents must discount their private information about the value, in order to avoid the winner's curse. The more uncertainty there is about the value, the more they must discount their private information. So *in a market at equilibrium*, additional public information, which reduces uncertainty about the true value, will cause agents (particularly those whose private estimates are low) to discount their private information less, and this should in turn, on average, cause winning bids to *rise* (as even bidders with high estimates have to bid higher to account for the reduced discounting of other bidders). However the winner's curse occurs when winning bidders overestimate the true value. To the extent that increased public information reduces the uncertainty about the value, it should help bidders with high private signals to correct their overestimates. So, *in a market in which the winner's curse is present*, additional public information should on average cause winning bids to *fall*.

Kagel and Levin's experimental results are that in auctions with small numbers of bidders and positive profits, introducing public information (e.g., by announcing the lowest signal value publicly) does cause the winning bids to rise, but in auctions with large numbers of bidders and negative profits the public information causes winning bids to fall.

So, when the effect of public information can be observed, this suggests a test of field data for whether the winner's curse is present. In fact, some data about the effects of information are available for oil auctions, from the work of Mead, Moseidjord, and Sorensen (1983, 1984), who compare differential rates of return between *wildcat* and *drainage* tracts. A wildcat tract is one for which no positive drilling data are available, while a drainage tract is one in which hydrocarbons have been located on an adjacent tract. The neighbors of a drainage tract are the companies who lease the adjacent tract(s). They have some private information unavailable to other bidders. There is also a public component to this information. Kagel and Levin argue that (915)

> If the information available on drainage leases were purely public, it should, according to Nash equilibrium bidding theory, raise average seller's revenues, hence reducing bidder's profits. . . . If the information were purely private, under Nash equilibrium bidding theory it would increase the rate of return for insiders (neighbors) relative to outsiders (nonneighbors) *and* reduce the average rate of return for nonneighbors. . . . If the added information on drainage leases contains both public and private information elements, rates of return for neighbors should be greater than for nonneighbors, but with nonneighbor returns definitely less than in the absence of the additional information (both the public and private information components push in this direction for nonneighbors)."

What Mead et al. found were higher rates of return on drainage compared to wildcat leases for *both* neighbors (88.6% higher) *and* nonneighbors (56.2% higher). Further, nonneighbors won 43.2 percent of all drainage leases. While the higher rate of return for neighbors compared with nonneighbors can be explained by the presence of insider information (the explanation Mead et al. offer, 1983, 1984), the substantially higher rates of return for nonneighbors remains puzzling within the context of Nash equilibrium bidding theory. However, the higher rate of return for *both* neighbors and nonneighbors on drainage leases is perfectly consistent with our experimental findings, given the existence of a winner's curse in bidding on wildcat leases. According to this explanation, the additional information available from neighbor tracts served to correct for the overly optimistic estimate of lease value recorded in the average winning bid on wildcat tracts, thereby raising average profits for both neighbors and nonneighbors alike. In this respect the OCS lease data parallel our experimental results with public information in the presence of a winner's curse.

Although this argument may go somewhat beyond the available mathematical theory and although Kagel and Levin are careful to note that there are alternative explanations for why both nonneighbors and neighbors do better on drainage leases, the experimental results establish a qualitative relationship among the data that are associated with the presence of the winner's curse, and this relationship opens new avenues for the investigation of field data.[97]

2. Some Other Auction Results

Two papers that offer some interesting comparisons with those just discussed are by Kagel, Harstad, and Levin (1987), and Kagel, Levin, and Harstad (1988).

Kagel, Levin, and Harstad (1988) study *second price* common value auctions. In a second price auction, the high bidder wins but the price he pays is the second highest bid. Vickery (1961) noted that it is a dominant strategy in private value auctions conducted in this way to bid one's true willingness to pay (and second price auctions are sometimes called "Vickery auctions"). In a common value auction it is still necessary for bidders to discount their private sample in order to arrive at an unbiased estimate of the value (in order to take into account that the winning bidder is the one with the highest of n samples), but no essentially strategic considerations influence the optimum bid. Thus, in contrast to the first price auctions considered earlier (in which the price is equal to the highest bid and in which there is a strategic incentive to underbid), second price auctions disentangle the issue of evaluating how much an object is worth from strategic questions about how much to bid. Nevertheless, the authors report similar behavior as was observed by Kagel and Levin (1986): positive profits were earned in small groups of bidders, and negative profits in larger groups. Thus these results support the hypothesis that the winner's curse derives primarily from errors in judgement about the value of the object.

Kagel, Harstad, and Levin (1987) study a number of issues concerned with *private value* auctions, in which each agent knows with certainty the value to him of the object being auctioned, but has only probabilistic information about the value of the object to other agents. So in private value auctions there is no problem of evaluating how much the object is worth; the problem of choosing a bid is all strategic. Nevertheless, the authors observed that in the second price auctions, bidders had a persistent tendency to bid somewhat above their true values and that the bids did not exhibit any tendency to converge to the true values over time. (Recall that it is a dominant strategy to bid true values in such an auction.) Because the winning bidder does not pay his bid, but only the amount of the next highest bid, this tendency to overbid had only a small effect on the (positive) expected payoffs to the bidders.[98] The authors conjecture that the overbidding is due to (1299) "the illusion that it improves the probability of winning with no real cost to the bidder. . . ."

A striking feature of this result is that it is just the opposite of some previously reported results about second price auctions, which had concluded that bids tended to be *below* true values. However upon inquiry Kagel et al. learned that (1286) "in these earlier private value auction experiments subjects were *not permitted* to bid in excess of their private values."

They go on to remark (1298):

> This persistent excess of market price above the dominant strategy price stands in marked contrast to reports of second price sealed bid auctions with independent private values (Coppinger, Smith and Titus, 1980; Cox, Roberson and Smith, 1982). Results from those experiments show average market price consistently below the dominant strategy price. . . . The key institutional feature responsible for these different outcomes is, we believe, that those earlier second-price auction experiments did not permit bidding in excess of private valuations.[99]

Notice what this illustrates about the power of experimental methods. As economists, we have become accustomed to the fact that, because field data is noisy and incomplete, apparently similar data sets may yield different conclusions. With experimental data, however, since the collection of the data is fully under the control of the researchers, we can hope to be able to identify the causes of such differences. In this case, by inquiring of the authors, Kagel et al. were able to learn that the earlier experiments had a restriction that bids in excess of a bidder's private value were not allowed. Once this point had been clarified, the differences between the two data sets also became rather clear.

Kagel, Harstad, and Levin (1987) also consider the effect of public information on bids in first price private value auctions with affiliated values. Here, there is a closer correspondence between the equilibrium predictions and the observed outcomes than there was in the case of common value auctions discussed earlier. This adds some weight to the conclusion of Kagel and Levin (1986) that the contrary information effects they observed for common value auctions were due to the presence of the winner's curse.

a. Controlling Incentives: A Methodological Digression

One topic I should mention in passing concerns the recurring methodological theme that it is difficult to control subjects' preferences. Recall from section I.A that, in this regard, Siegel and Fouraker (1960) investigated the effects not only of the total payoffs available to bargainers in their experiments, but also of the effect of increasing the difference in payoffs available at different contracts. A closely related question is raised in a critique by Harrison (1989), who reanalyzes the conclusions reached by Cox, Roberson, and Smith (1982), and Cox, Smith, and Walker (1983, 1988) in a series of experiments concerned with first price private value auctions. In those experiments, subjects' ordinal preferences were taken to be equivalent to their monetary payoffs, and the authors estimated the expected utilities of the bidders, under the assumption that each of the experimental data points that they observe represents a Nash equilibrium that is reached immediately and is constant over time, and that the utility functions are of a certain functional form. Their analysis of the bid data under this assumption led them to reject the hypothesis that all the bidders have identical and risk neutral preferences. However, they observed that the bidding data conforms well to the equilibrium hypothesis once different, unobserved risk aversion parameters have been estimated for each bidder.

Harrison concludes that the control of the bidders' ordinal preferences via their monetary payoffs in these experiments was insufficient to reach even this conclusion. His point, like that of Siegal and Fouraker (1960), is that it is not the total payoff to the bidders that is relevant, but the difference in payoffs that bidders get corresponding to different bids they might make. Harrison's key observation is that when one examines the expected payoffs to the bidders, the bids that appear to be significantly different from the risk neutral equilibrium bids differ only by pennies in expected payoff.[100]

The methodological thrust of the argument is that the whole point of paying subjects in experiments is to gain control of their incentives, that is, to create an environment in which their incentives are known. But if the observed bids frequently differ from the equilibrium bid by only pennies of expected income, other (uncontrolled) incentives that the bidders might have may be stronger than the effective monetary incentive.

I think that there is an even more general point involved here, which is that the difficulty of indirectly inferring an unobserved or uncontrolled variable may be as great in experimental data as in other kinds of data.[101] This will be discussed at greater length in chapter 7. But this "marginal payoff critique" is of special importance in investigations of equilibrium phenomena, precisely because many equilibrium phenomena are predicted to happen on the margin, where agents may be more or less indifferent between a number of choices, regardless of the total payoffs available.[102]

F. Individual Choice Behavior

Almost simultaneously with the rise of expected utility theory to pride of place among economists' models of individual choice behavior, early experiments began to establish that there are at least some situations in which a substantial percentage of experimental subjects can be observed to exhibit systematic patterns of choice that violate predictions of the theory. The best known of these is due to Allais (1953), who, as discussed in section I.A, observed that certain kinds of risky choices could not be squared with utility theory. Around the same time, May (1954) observed that intransitive choices could be systematically elicited over multidimensional alternatives that did not even involve risk.

These observations did not materially impede the adoption of utility maximization as the primary vehicle for modeling individuals in economic theory. To the extent that utility theory is in part viewed as a prescriptive theory of rational choice, this is unsurprising, since it is unclear how experimental evidence of this kind can, or should, be incorporated into a theory of "ideally rational" behavior. But even when utility theory is viewed as an approximately descriptive theory of actual choice behavior, this is not too surprising, since the nature of the regular violations of the theory were still unclear, no powerful alternative theories had been proposed, and there was ample room to question the importance for economic applications of the reported violations.

In the intervening years, the nature of these and many other reliable "anomalies" in choice behavior have started to be much more thoroughly explored in experiments by both psychologists and economists, and in the last few years these have prompted the proposal of several interesting alternative theories of choice. There still remains ample room to question the importance of these anomalies for economics, but of necessity these questions must now be more pointed and specific and, hence, seem more likely to be answerable.

1. Preference Reversals

The anomaly I will consider in detail here is the discovery that it is possible to construct pairs of lotteries with the property that many people, when asked at what price they would be willing to sell (or buy) the lotteries, put a higher price on one, but when asked to choose which they would prefer to participate in, choose the other.

Investigation of this phenomenon, called "preference reversal," had its roots in a paper by Slovic and Lichtenstein (1968) that considered how different ways of assessing lotteries were differently influenced by the lotteries' prizes and probabilities. On the set of (hypothetical) lotteries they examined, how much subjects were willing to pay to play a given lottery was correlated more highly with the amount of the potential loss than with any other dimension, while the stated "attractiveness" of the lottery correlated most highly with the probability of winning. They argued that this difference was evidence that subjects considered different kinds of information when asked to choose between lotteries than when asked to price them. They conjectured that being asked to bid (an amount of money) for the right to participate in a lottery caused subjects to concentrate on the monetary values of the prizes, in a way that choosing between lotteries did not.

This motivated a subsequent study (Lichtenstein and Slovic 1971), in which preference reversals were first reported. In that paper they wrote (47):

> The notion that the information describing a gamble is processed differently for bids than for choices suggested that it might be possible to construct a pair of gambles such that S[ubjects] would choose one of them but bid more for the other. For example, consider the pair consisting of Bet P (.99 to win $4 and .01 to lose $1) and Bet $ (.33 to win $16 and .67 to lose $2). Bet P has a much better probability of winning but Bet $ offers more to win. If choices tend to be determined by probabilities, while bids are most influenced by payoffs, one might expect that S[ubject]s would choose Bet P over Bet $, but bid more for Bet $.

To test this conjecture, three experiments were performed. In the first, subjects were presented with matched pairs of P and $ bets with positive expected values, and asked to pick the bet they would prefer. Later, subjects were presented with the bets singly, and asked to name the minimum price for which they would be willing to sell each bet rather than play it. Subjects were told that all lotteries were hypothetical and would not actually be played or sold.

The results were that, although subjects preferred the P bets to the $ bets only about half the time, they put a higher price on the $ bet far more often. In fact, 73 percent of the subjects were observed to always make the predicted reversal (p48): "For every pair in which the P bet was chosen, the $ bet later received a higher bid." In contrast the unpredicted reversal (choosing the $ bet but putting a higher price on the P bet) was much less frequent, and only 17 percent of the subjects ever made this kind of reversal.

The second experiment was much like the first except that, instead of being asked at what price they would be willing to sell each bet, subjects were asked at what price they would be willing to *buy* it. The prices thus elicited were lower than the corresponding selling prices in the first experiment, and this decrease in price was substantially more pronounced for the $ bets than for the P bets. This decreased the number of predicted reversals and increased the number of unpredicted reversals.

In the third experiment, which was intended (51) "to maximize motivation and minimize indifference and carelessness," transactions were actually carried out. All outcomes were stated in "points," which would be converted into cash at the end of the experiment. (However, subjects were not informed of the rates at which they would be paid.) The data again yielded a high proportion of predicted reversals and a low proportion of unpredicted reversals. One feature of this third experiment worth mentioning is that care was taken to motivate the subjects to reveal their "true" selling prices for each lottery. The technique employed was proposed for this purpose by Becker, DeGroot, and Marschak (1964). (Recall the description of the BDM technique in section I.B.)

Based on these three experiments, the authors concluded that the preference reversal effect is robust, that it is inconsistent with not only utility theory but with "every existing theory of decision making," and that it gives strong support to the view that subjects process information differently in making choices and in stating prices. They favor the view that subjects employ what has come to be called an "anchoring and adjustment" heuristic in stating prices, in which they first "anchor" on the amount of money to be won and then "adjust" their price to reflect that a win is not certain. In this view, preference reversals arise because subjects fail to adjust sufficiently. (For an account of other decision heuristics considered in the psychology literature, see Kahneman, Slovic, and Tversky 1982.)

A similar experiment by Lindman (1971) found qualitatively similar results over a set of hypothetical lotteries that included some with negative expected values. Shortly thereafter, Lichtenstein and Slovic (1973) sought to replicate the basic results using potentially significant amounts of money and a different subject pool. (In the previous studies, subjects had been college students.) In the new experiment, subjects were volunteer participants in a Las Vegas casino. Lichtenstein and Slovic describe the environment as follows (17):

The game was located in the balcony of the Four Queens Casino. . . . The game was operated by a professional dealer. . . . The S[ubject]s were volunteers who understood that the game was part of a research project. Only 1 S[ubject] could play the game at a time. Anyone could play the game, and the player could stop playing at any time (the dealer politely discouraged those who wanted to play for just a few minutes; a single complete game took 1–4 hr.). . . . At the start of the game, S was asked to choose the value of his chips. Each chip could represent 5¢, 10¢, 25¢, $1, or $5, and the value chosen remained unchanged throughout the game. The player was asked to buy 250 chips; if, during the game, more chips were needed, the dealer sold him more. At the end of the game (or whenever the player quit), the player's chips were exchanged for money.

In the choice part of the experiment, each subject was faced with four bets at a time, all with the same absolute expected value, two positive and two negative. Subjects were instructed to choose one of the positive and one of the negative expected value bets, and these were played with the aid of a roulette wheel. In the pricing part of the experiment, subjects were presented with the lotteries, one at a time, and told to state a price such that either "I will pay the dealer — chips to get rid of this bet" or "The dealer must pay me — chips to buy this bet." The Becker, DeGroot, and Marschak (1964) procedure was used to determine transaction prices, with the dealer's offer being determined by the roulette wheel, so it was a dominant strategy for utility maximizers to state their true reservation price. Again, predicted reversals were frequent and unpredicted reversals rare.[103] The authors conclude that (20)

> The widespread belief that decision makers can behave optimally when it is worthwhile for them to do so gains no support from this study. The source of the observed information-processing bias appears to be cognitive, not motivational.

These results, which all appeared in the psychology literature, were viewed with suspicion by many economists. This is well expressed in the report of a subsequent experiment by Grether and Plott (1979), who were concerned that the earlier experiments (and also Slovic 1975) either did not use real payoffs or did not control for income effects. (That is, in the course of choosing between real lotteries the subjects become richer, which might change their preferences sufficiently to produce the reported reversals.) They also expressed concerns related to the fact that most of the experimental subjects were psychology undergraduates (629) "one would be hesitant to generalize from such very special populations") and that the experimenters were psychologists (629) ("Subjects nearly always speculate about the purposes of experiments and psychologists have the reputation for deceiving subjects"). They therefore proposed experiments to address these questions, designed, in their words (623), "to discredit the psychologists' works as applied to economics."

They employed the same gambles as in the third experiment of Lichtenstein and Slovic (1971), using subjects recruited from economics and political science classes. In the first experiment, subjects were divided into two groups. Subjects in the first group were paid a flat rate of $7 for participating and made only hypothetical choices, while subjects in the second group were told they had a credit of $7, with their final payment being the sum of the initial $7 and any gains or losses they might get from the lotteries. They were told that, at the end of the experiment, *one* of their decisions would be chosen at random to be actually played. (The authors remark that this procedure, rather than one in which all lotteries are played, should reduce any income effect.) Finally, the design of the experiment counterbalanced the two tasks so that subjects first chose between lottery pairs, then priced lotteries, then chose between the remaining lottery pairs. Prices were elicited as selling prices using the Becker, DeGroot, and Marschak (1964) procedure. (In a second experiment, all mention of "selling" was suppressed, in case this should be a reason why subjects might overstate their reservation prices.)

The chief result was that preference reversals persisted. There were observable differences between the data from hypothetical and from real lotteries, with a *higher* percentage of reversals arising from the real lotteries. The propensity to reverse was the same for lottery choices made before the pricing task as for those made after it. As before, prices for $ bets were generally higher than those for P bets, and higher than their expected values, so the data remains consistent with the hypothesis that pricing decisions are reached by "anchoring" and (insufficient) "adjustment."

These results did not settle the matter. Two subsequent studies, by Pommerehne, Schneider, and Zweifel (1982) and Reilly (1982), were motivated by concern that the experiment of Grether and Plott had not been effective in giving the subjects substantial motivation, because the amounts involved were not large. Pommerehne et al. conducted an experiment with higher payoffs and reported a frequency of reversals that is still substantial, but lower than that observed by Grether and Plott.[104] Reilly's experiment provides a within experiment comparison that supports the conclusion that increased payoffs do reduce the rate of reversals. But in his experiment also, substantial percentages of reversals were observed. Thus this series of experiments supports the notion that preference reversals are not simply an artifact of certain narrow experimental procedures.[105]

Reilly's results suggest that the rate of reversals does decrease as financial motivation increases (at least for some range of payoffs, since Grether and Plott report the reverse effect in moving from hypothetical lotteries to small payoffs), so it is reasonable to ask whether the rate of reversals might decline to insignificance if the subjects were sufficiently well motivated. This kind of question remains after many experimental studies. However, the following experiment of Berg, Dickhaut, and O'Brien (1985) shows that such questions can sometimes be addressed by means other than simple extrapolation.

Briefly, their experiment was designed to assess the effect of making subjects pay for every preference reversal they stated, by running them around a "money pump." Using a pricing task in which subjects were required to state, for each lottery, a single price at which they would be willing either to buy *or* sell it, they extracted a fine from subjects who stated preference reversals in a first set of choices by first selling them the high price lottery (the $ bet) for the indicated price, then trading it for the low price lottery (the preferred P bet) and then buying back that lottery at its (lower) price. (Note that at this point these transactions were not voluntary: subjects had been told that they would be obliged to honor their stated preferences and prices, for either buying or selling.) Comparing those conditions of their experiment that do not extract this fine with those that do, they found no significant differences in the *number* of reversals, but a significant decrease in the dollar *value* of the reversals (i.e., the difference in prices between the two bets). As subjects gained more experience, the dollar value of the reversals declined, but reversals did not disappear. Thus the evidence suggests that subjects tried to eliminate reversals but were unable fully to do so.

This lends some indirect support, I think, to the view among psychologists that preference reversal may reflect a "cognitive illusion" in the pricing task, similar in some ways to familiar optical illusions. By analogy, consider an experiment where the paired comparison task is to estimate the length of two horizontal lines each of which is "framed" with sideways Vs facing either out or in to make them look longer or shorter, respectively. The "pricing" part of the experiment is to look at lots of horizontal lines, framed one way or the other, in random order, and estimate their length in inches. Even after you know that outward Vs make the lines look longer, it might remain hard to estimate them in inches, and increasing your motivation would not be expected to solve the problem.

a. Alternative Theoretical Directions

But this is not the only way to view the evidence, and here the different theoretical points of view of psychology and economics suggest different directions in which it might be fruitful to proceed. This is a subject I will only introduce here, as it is elaborated on in chapter 8.

Loosely speaking, much of the work by psychologists on this and related subjects has been motivated by the point of view that people make choices in a manner analogous to interrogating a data base, and that how questions are asked therefore makes a difference in what answers will be obtained. In contrast, economists (who are generally interested in choice behavior at a somewhat different level of detail, and are therefore typically more willing to sacrifice some accuracy for some generality) have viewed choice behavior as reflecting underlying, already existing, and reasonably stable preferences. The assumptions about such preferences embodied in standard expected utility theory are of course not the only ones imaginable, and one way of seeking to capture the kinds of behavior discussed here is by relaxing such assumptions, while preserving the idea that at some useful level of approximation agents do indeed have preferences. A number of such theories have now been proposed (for a good introductory survey, see Machina 1987).

Loomes and Sugden (1983) discuss how preference reversals are consistent with a theory of choice, called "regret theory," which they earlier proposed in a 1982 paper, in which choices between risky alternatives reflect not only some underlying "choiceless" utility, but also comparisons ("regret" or "rejoicing") with what might have been. These comparisons depend on the subsequent realization of the underlying random events. Different comparisons are involved in choosing between two bets than are involved in choosing between each of them and a selling price, and the previous experiments allowed subjects to make some of these comparisons. That is, a subject might choose the P bet over the $ bet in part because of the regret he would feel if he chose the $ bet and the random device (e.g., roulette wheel) subsequently produced a number that meant a loss in the $ bet but would have meant a win in the P bet. But the same subject, with appropriately specified regret function, might still set a higher price on the $ bet, because the pricing task involves different comparisons between the random outcome of each lottery and the selling price.

Another hypothesis to account for preference reversals has been suggested independently by Holt (1986) and Karni and Safra (1987). This is that individuals may possess preferences that violate the "independence" assumption of expected utility theory, but not necessarily the transitivity assumption. (Following Machina [1982] a number of choice theories without independence have been proposed.) Independence is the assumption that says an outcome A is weakly preferred to B if and only if a lottery between A and C is weakly preferred to a lottery with the same probabilities between B and C, for any outcome C. It is this assumption that makes the utility of a lottery a linear function of the probabilities, so that compound lotteries may be decomposed in the standard way. And it is this that implies that the price a utility maximizer will state in the Becker, DeGroot, and Marschak (1964) elicitation procedure can be interpreted as his reservation price: that is, it implies he is indifferent between a lottery A and a selling price p if and only if p is the price that maximizes the utility of the compound lottery between A and prices greater than p that he faces after stating a price.[106] To emphasize that preference reversals may be compatible with transitive preferences over lotteries, Karni and Safra (1987) couch their discussion in terms of such a family of generalizations of utility theory proposed by Quiggin (1982) and Yaari (1987).

Holt (1986) further notes that the procedure of paying subjects for only one of their decisions, randomly chosen after all decisions are made, which was employed by Grether and Plott (1979) to control for income effects, only can be interpreted as having that effect if the independence assumption is satisfied. That is, the assumption is that the optimal choice in each decision evaluated separately is also the optimal choice when each decision is evaluated as part of the compound lottery consisting of the whole experiment; but without independence this may not be the case. And Karni and Safra note that the direct elicitation of preferences may present difficulties if preferences do not satisfy independence. So there is ample room for further experiments exploring these hypotheses.[107]

It should be emphasized that the Becker, DeGroot, and Marschak (1964) elicitation procedure allows us to predict what prices *utility maximizers* would state. That non-utility-maximizers may have incentives to respond differently is in no way a criticism of the experimental designs that incorporate this procedure. On the contrary, the virtue of those experimental designs is that they allow us to test predictions made in terms of utility theory, by permitting unambiguous predictions about what utility maximizers would do. In the absence of such a design, we would be unable to conclude that the observed phenomenon constituted a violation of the theory.[108] This is a point worth repeating: one of the major virtues of laboratory experiments well designed to test theoretical predictions is that they allow us to make observations in theoretically unambiguous circumstances. To appreciate the power of this, consider the difficulty presented by any attempt to obtain unambiguous *field* observations concerning preference reversals. (In this connection, see the interesting experiment of Bohm [1994], which reports a lack of preference reversal observations in an experiment in which subjects purchased a used car. See also Bohm and Lind, forthcoming.)

b. Market Behavior

The very difficulty of making such observations in the field raises again the question of what is the importance of such phenomena for economics. I think it is fair to say that quite a broad range of opinions have been expressed on this point, with some economists taking the view that choice anomalies have not yet been shown to occur in typical economic environments such as markets.

To give a brief account of how that discussion has begun to be pursued by experimental means, it will be helpful to consider not only preference reversals, but the related phenomenon that stated buying prices have been observed to be substantially below stated selling prices (more than can be accounted for by income effects) in a number of studies of hypothetical choice (recall experiment 2 of Lichtenstein and Slovic 1971). Knetsch and Sinden (1984) review these results from hypothetical choice experiments and report an experiment showing this disparity between buying and selling prices persists for real transactions.

In a reply to Knetsch and Sinden, Coursey, Hovis, and Schulze (1987) propose to test what I will call the *market hypothesis*, which is that agents in a market environment will behave like utility maximizers: that is, experimental subjects in a market will receive feedback and experience of a kind that will extinguish such anomalies as the buying and selling price disparity.[109] The market environment in their experiment is a second price auction, so that it will be a dominant strategy for utility maximizers to state their true reservation prices. (Buying and selling auctions were conducted separately: what is being bought and sold is the right not to taste, a "bitter . . . non-toxic . . . very unpleasant" substance called SOA.) In addition, the auction result would only be considered final if it was unanimously agreed to; otherwise another trial would be conducted to determine which (four out of eight) subjects would taste the SOA. The authors report that, although initial trials yielded the familiar disparity between buying and selling prices, and although the auction results continued to show some continued disparity, this diminished over auction periods, and by the final period the remaining gap between the two prices was no longer statistically significant. (Most of the movement came in subjects' declining prices for agreeing to taste the SOA.) They conclude that "the divergence obtained in early trials of the experiment . . . may result mainly from lack of a market experience."[110]

In their rejoinder, Knetsch and Sinden (1987) decline to attribute the same significance to the diminution of the buying and selling price disparity in the above experiment. Apart from critiquing aspects of the experiment (they are not persuaded that tastes of SOA are a typical economic commodity), they also cite some stylized facts about market behavior that they think may reflect choice anomalies similar to this price disparity.

Kahneman, Knetsch, and Thaler (1990) present some evidence in support of this view, from a market experiment in which half the subjects have been endowed with a small consumer good (e.g. mugs, pens). In these experiments subjects who wished to buy or sell a good (with their own money) were free to do so, and the authors report that substantially fewer trades were transacted than would be expected in the absence of an endowment effect, i.e. without an unexplained tendency of subjects to prefer what they already have.[111] This experiment thus lends support to the view that observed anomalies in choice behavior do not vanish simply because the environment in which they might arise is a market.

2. Other Choice Phenomena

I have concentrated on preference reversals here because they have been the subject of a long series of experimental investigations, from different points of view, which serve well to illustrate some ways in which experimental investigations may proceed. There are other individual choice "anomalies" with equal (and equally contested) claims to importance. For a discussion of some of these, see Thaler (1987), who particularly concentrates on what in his view is the importance of these phenomena for economics. As Camerer discusses in chapter 8, these other choice phenomena offer other possibilities to design experiments by which various generalizations of expected utility theory may be tested. Battalio, Kagel, and Jiranyakul (1990) succinctly summarize the state of theoretical affairs by stating (46): "None of the alternatives to expected utility theory considered here consistently organize the data, so we have a long way to go before having a complete descriptive model of choice under uncertainty." In fact, even laboratory animals have been observed to exhibit some choice anomalies of this kind (see Battalio, Kagel, and McDonald 1985; Kagel 1987), so experiments on these matters need not be confined to humans.

Before leaving the subject of individual choice behavior, I will mention one more experiment, that differs from those so far discussed in the scale of rewards that were offered. Binswanger (1980) reports the results of an experiment carried out among village farmers in areas of India, where (397) "the average physical wealth of the households . . . is very low by international standards." Villagers from a sample with substantial variations in wealth were repeatedly given the opportunity to choose among a set of gambles that could be ranked in order of riskiness (395–396). ("To overcome moral problems confronting low income people involved in gambling, the gambling was limited so that the worst possible outcome was a zero gain.") First, relatively small gambles were offered, with the prizes eventually increasing to levels (405) "commensurate with monthly wage rates or small agricultural investments." Subjects considered their choices for several days.

The chief results were that, at very low payoff levels, there was a wide distribution of observed levels of risk aversion, but at higher payoff levels there was much less variance, with most responses concentrated in an "intermediate to moderate" level of risk aversion. Furthermore, subjects' risk aversion at these high payoff levels did not appear to be significantly influenced by their wealth.[112] Binswanger also observed that these results obtained from actual gambles varied in important ways from the answers initially obtained from hypothetical questions about high stakes gambles. The hypothetical results showed both many more severely risk averse choices, and more risk neutral or risk preferring choices, than did the comparable data from actual choices.

In summary, in the series of experiments reported here the focus of debate was initially on if certain kinds of anomalous choice behavior were artifacts of the experimental procedure, and in particular if they would persist in nonhypothetical choice situations. In the case of preference reversals, the phenomenon survived both the change from hypothetical to real choices and increases in the payoff level. (However, questions about the reliability of hypothetical choices are not always resolved in this way, as is shown by the results of Binswanger.) The debate has now shifted to the underlying causes of the phenomena and if market environments will moderate the observed effects. Some of the various theories that have been advanced as possible explanations of certain kinds of choice behavior not only suggest new experiments, but new directions for pursuing traditional kinds of economic theory (see, e.g., Crawford 1990). It is clear that the degree of success such theories achieve in organizing and explaining phenomena in domains other than individual choice behavior itself will be important. At the same time, the question of whether or not individual choices in market and other economic environments are systematically different from what can be observed in various unstructured environments (either because certain kinds of choices do not arise in markets or because markets provide a certain kind of feedback) will undoubtedly require proponents of different points of view to sharpen their hypotheses about market phenomena.

3. Why Haven't These Demonstrated Anomalies Swept Away Utility Theory?

As the number of replicable violations of utility theory, and of even more basic models of rational choice, has grown, a question we frequently hear from some of our psychologist colleagues, and one that we can reasonably ask ourselves, is "what accounts for economists' reluctance to abandon the rationality model, despite considerable contradictory evidence?"

In a handbook of this sort, this question deserves to be addressed at at least two levels. The first, which I shall attempt in this section, concerns the implications of these "anomalous" experimental results for economic *theory*, and the second, which I'll address in the next section, concerns the implications for experimental economics per se.

Regarding economic theory, I'll argue that

1. There are quite defensible reasons for a reluctance to abandon theories of rationality in favor of nonrational theories (and, in view of this, some kinds of evidence and theories are likely to be more successful in attacking these defenses than others), and
2. There is (nevertheless) a considerable and growing attempt by economic theorists to respond to experimental evidence by moving away from an overdependence on idealized models of hyper-rationality.

Regarding the first point, to the extent that economists view expected utility maximization (merely) as a useful approximation of human behavior and not as a precisely true description in all cases, then to attack the central role it plays in economic theory, it isn't sufficient to show counterexamples, even many counterexamples.

Notice in this regard that even the simpler model of expected *value* maximization (i.e., risk neutral expected utility maximization for monetary rewards) remains a useful, and much used, approximation, although economists must universally agree that it does not provide a precise description of human behavior. But the reason utility theory at least partially replaced expected value theory as economists' "typical" approximation was because economists became convinced that the phenomena that couldn't be explained by the approximation that individuals maximize expected value were of central importance, and justified a model with unobservable parameters of risk aversion. (The phenomena that could only be captured this way include whole industries, such as the insurance industry.) I very much doubt that expected utility theory would have made such inroads into economics only on the strength of anomalies (from the expected value point of view) like the St. Petersburg paradox (for which Bernoulli proposed a kind of expected utility theory as a resolution.)

In this respect, I think that economists are likely to find most persuasive those attacks on rational models of choice that produce (more) examples of how not fully rational phenomena (such as framing effects) are reflected and exploited in important economic activities (e.g., in marketing and advertising and retailing) in ways that cannot be accounted for by rational models of individual choice.

There is also increasing attention being paid in the economics literature to alternatives to expected utility maximization as a model of individual behavior. One approach is to consider theories that are "plug compatible" with utility theory, in the sense that they are meant to replace it but to do the same job, and fit into strategic and market theories in the same way. Some of these are reviewed by Camerer in chapter 8 and are typically generalizations of expected utility theory, which relax some of its assumptions and which thus yield theories with more unobserved personal parameters (much as the replacement of expected value with expected utility introduced personal parameters of risk aversion). Many of these are motivated by particular experimental anomalies (the Allais paradox has played an unusually large motivating role in this connection). By introducing additional parameters they are able to provide a better fit to the motivating data. But it remains an open question whether any of these theories organizes all of the data in a way that is clearly superior to utility theory, particularly when the costs (in diminished predictive power) of adding unobserved parameters are counted in.

Another approach involves the exploration of nonrational or boundedly rational foundations for economic phenomena involving collective choice—e.g., for theories of equilibrium and market behavior. The evolutionary and adaptive learning models I have discussed are good examples of these. The object of the theoretical work on these models is to understand the extent to which equilibrium phenomena, of the kind which economists have traditionally motivated with models of very rational economic agents, might also arise from more bounded sorts of rationality. To the extent that the reason economists don't dispense with hyperrational models of choice is that their primary interest lies in strategic and market phenomena (rather than in individual choice per se) this second approach may be even more important than the first. If important economic phenomena can be explained without reliance on rational models (or if the uses to which economists put rational models can be shown not to depend on them), the apparent gap between economists and psychologists in their models of individual behavior may diminish in importance.[113]

In summary, there exists a substantial body of experimental evidence that shows that individuals are not ideally rational utility maximizers; on the contrary, there are a growing number of systematic violations of utility theory that can be robustly demonstrated and reliably replicated in the laboratory. Nevertheless, even a brief review of the contemporary economic literature reveals that economists remain by and large quite content to model individuals as utility maximizers. What can account for this?

I've argued here that, to the extent that utility maximization is viewed as a useful approximation of behavior, it can't easily be displaced by counterexamples, since approximations always admit counterexamples. The experimental evidence is nevertheless very valuable—it is of the utmost importance to know where approximations break down. But in order to inspire theorists to *replace* a model that is regarded as a useful approximation, it is probably necessary to show that it is not useful for the purposes that it is being used. Some of the debate among experimenters about whether or not choice anomalies persist in market environments is addressed to this issue, and I expect that this debate will continue and become more specific about the types of market environments in which particular choice anomalies may or may not persist. And the usefulness of an approximation depends on what other approximations are available, and the further development of boundedly rational models of strategic and market behavior (also a response to the experimental evidence) may reduce the weight placed on rational models of individual choice by economists primarily interested in studying collective behavior.

Of course even an approximation that is adequate for many purposes may sometimes fail to provide the precise control desired in experimental design. We turn next to consider some of the implications of experimental results on individual choice for the design of economic experiments generally.

4. Experimental Control of Individual Preferences

Laboratory experiments make available a high degree of control of the environment, which makes possible two strategies for experimental design when the incentives facing participants in an experiment must be known: the experimenter can try to control the preferences of the subjects, or try to measure them. And because the theories being tested in an economic experiment are often phrased in terms of utility maximizing economic agents and also because the techniques of measurement and control often posit utility maximizing subjects, experimenters have to be alert to deviations from utility maximizing *behavior* on the part of experimental subjects.

In this section I will briefly discuss, from this point of view, some of the techniques for control and measurement of preferences that I have already mentioned in this chapter. But before discussing particular features of experimental design, there is one result of the experimental investigations of individual choice that has quite general implications. This is that the choice an individual makes is sometimes sensitive to the way it is presented, or "framed," in the sense that even theoretically equivalent choices may elicit different responses when presented differently (as in the case of preference reversals when comparisons are made by choosing between two lotteries or by stating a reservation price for each). This reinforces the general conclusion that the most reliable comparisons will be "within experiment" comparisons, in which the effect of a single variable can be assessed within an otherwise constant environment and "frame." For this reason also, economic experiments can rarely be interpreted to yield "constants" (e.g., the percentage of altruists in the population or the percentage of disagreements in bargaining), since the precise values observed in any experiment may be sensitive in unexpected ways to details of the experimental environment.

We turn next to specific concerns, related to utility maximization, which arise in connection with particular experimental procedures.

a. The BDM Procedure for Measuring Reservation Prices

As already noted, the Becker, DeGroot, and Marschak (1964) procedure has the property that it gives utility maximizers the incentive to reveal their true reservation price for an object, that is, the price at which they would just be indifferent between selling it and not selling it (or buying it and not buying it). The chief role it plays in experimental designs, therefore, is to allow the experimenter to determine unambiguously what are the predictions of theories that assume (among other things) that the subjects are utility maximizers and that their choices depend on their reservation prices. The substantial use (and usefulness) of the technique arises from the fact that so much of economic theory is of precisely this sort.

However, what if the subjects are not behaving as utility maximizers? This is a question that could in principle arise even when the predictions of a theory that assumes utility maximization are supported by the observed behavior (since many different theories may yield the same predictions in any given case). In practice, the question is raised most often when the results of an experiment violate the predictions of the theory, as was the case in the preference reversal literature. We saw there that when subjects' violation of utility theory is of the right sort (i.e., violation of the independence axiom) then the BDM procedure loses its "truth revealing" properties. Indeed, when subjects are not utility maximizers, the whole idea that they have a single reservation price, or that it is an indicator of their choice behavior, may be on shaky ground—this is after all the phenomenon that preference reversals explore. Consequently different designs may be required to test some of the generalized utility theories for which the information obtained by the BDM procedure is not germane.

b. Controlling Preferences with Monetary Payoffs

The same issues arise with experimental designs intended to control subjects' preferences, starting with the simplest designs in which subjects are paid in money and the predictions of the theories being tested are formulated as if subjects were interested only in maximizing their own income. As I discussed in the context of both public goods and bargaining, there is abundant experimental evidence that these designs may sometimes fail to control subjects' preferences, because subjects may in fact also be concerned with the payoffs of other subjects. Chapters 2 and 4 both discuss experiments designed to test such hypotheses, that is, experiments in which it is not assumed that subjects' preferences are successfully controlled and can be equated with their payoffs in this way. Note, however, that to design an experiment that allows one to contrast a more complex theory of preferences with a theory based on simple income maximization, it is nevertheless necessary to know what the income maximization theory predicts, so that it remains necessary to control for the predictions of the simpler theory even when more complex theories of behavior are being examined.

Even when the experimenter only wishes to control subjects' reservation prices, as in the Chamberlin design for implementing markets with given supply and demand curves, there remains a question of whether subjects will in fact buy and sell at the prices the experimenter wishes. For example, Gode and Sunder (1993) express a good deal of skepticism that the Chamberlin procedure for inducing supply and demand behavior in fact delivers the intended experimental control. In motivating their study of programmed traders (discussed in section III.D), they say:

> It is not possible to control the trading behavior of individuals. Human traders differ in their expectations, attitudes toward risk, preferences for money versus enjoyment of trading as a game, and many other respects. The problem of separating the joint effects of these variations, unobservable to

the researcher, can be mitigated by studying market outcomes with participants who follow specified rules of behavior. We therefore replaced human traders by computer programs. (Gode and Sunder 1993, 120)

As their programmed traders show, the nature of the individual behavior of the traders cannot be inferred from the fact that for some market structures and parameters the results may reliably approach equilibrium, and so the extent to which the Chamberlin procedure controls the preferences of the traders is a subject yet to be fully explored.

c. Controlling for Unobserved Risk Preferences with Binary Lottery Payoffs

One technique for controlling preferences that has not only been very widely used, but has also been the object of a good deal of experimental study designed to assess its effect, is the binary lottery procedure of Roth and Malouf (1979) for controlling risk preferences. The primary use for this technique has been for introducing a medium in which utility maximizers will be risk neutral, regardless of their (unobserved) natural risk postures. However, the technique also allows artificial intermediate commodities to be created in which utility maximizers can be induced to have arbitrary risk postures, and a number of experiments have begun to employ binary lotteries this way also, following the work of Berg, Daley, Dickhaut, and O'Brien (1986). They introduced a set of procedures by which subjects could be introduced to the notion that their payoffs would be computed in "points," and that their probability of winning the binary lottery would be a function of the points they received. Since the expected utility of a utility maximizing subject is precisely equal to his probability of winning the binary lottery, if the function f converts points into probability, then the subject's utility function *for points* should be precisely the function f. Since f can be chosen by the experimenter, the idea is that any utility function can be induced. This extended notion of binary lottery control of preferences thus gives considerable scope for tests of whether the procedure in fact induces actual experimental subjects to behave in accordance with the predictions for utility maximizers.

The most comprehensive test to date of the binary lottery procedure, both in its risk neutral and in its arbitrary utility function forms, is by Prasnikar (1993). She presented subjects with a large number of individual decision tasks in the form of choices between lotteries, after first attempting to endow each subject with one of five expected utility functions (whose functional forms were risk neutral, constant relative risk averse, constant relative risk preferring, and constant absolute risk averse and risk preferring). She could then test both if the aggregate responses deviated detectably from the precise coefficient of risk aversion she had attempted to induce in each group of subjects, and also if and how each individual subject might deviate from the choices that would be made by an ideal utility maximizer. An ingenious feature of Prasnikar's experiment was that after completing all choices each subject was tested to see if he understood how to calculate the probability of winning the binary lottery resulting from a compound lottery, with prizes in points, using the induced utility function he had been endowed with. (This information had not been included in the instructions, which had simply presented, in tabular form, the probability of winning the binary lottery corresponding to each number of points.) This questionnaire thus allowed those subjects who had a good understanding of the binary lottery procedure to be distinguished from those who did not.

Prasnikar's main results were as follows. First, there were no substantial differences between subjects who knew how to quantitatively decompose compound lotteries and those who did not, indicating that even those subjects who knew how to do so apparently did not make their choices by conducting precise arithmetic computations. Second, the coefficients of risk aversion estimated from the observed data for each group of subjects (i.e., for all subjects endowed with the same utility function) did not differ significantly from those that had been induced. However, the data were quite noisy; individuals frequently deviated from the choices that would have been made by ideal utility maximizers. Prasnikar then sought to detect whether there were any systematic components to the deviations from the choices predicted for ideal utility maximizers. She found that the choices of the subjects who did not understand how to decompose compound lotteries were somewhat correlated with their natural risk aversion (which had been tested before each subject was introduced to the binary lotteries). However, no such correlation was detected among those subjects who had understood how the binary lotteries worked.

Prasnikar concludes that "the gross features of risk preference can be reliably implemented, albeit with a non-negligible amount of error." In particular, her results suggest that whether the amount of control of subjects' choice behavior achieved by the binary lottery technique is adequate for particular experimental purposes depends on both what those purposes are, and how carefully the binary lotteries are introduced to the subjects. If the design requires that each individual invariably perform as an ideal utility maximizer, it is unlikely that this technique delivers the desired control. However if the design requires that the aggregate risk posture of the subjects should be controlled, or that the unobserved natural risk aversion that subjects bring to the experiment should be neutralized, then the technique, carefully implemented, performs largely as expected.

Similar conclusions are reached by Rietz (1993), who tests, in a very different way, the ability of the binary lottery procedure to produce risk neutral behavior. Unlike Prasnikar (1993), who conducts a direct test of the induced individual choice behavior, Rietz explores the effect of the binary lottery procedure in an indirect manner, by considering its effect on bidding behavior in auctions. The equilibrium predictions for the first price auctions he considers are that risk averse players should bid higher than risk neutral players. Rietz therefore compares auctions with monetary payoffs to those with binary lottery payoffs to see if the attempt to induce risk neutral behavior via the binary lottery design will cause observed bids to decline. Of course, this is a test of the joint hypothesis that the players are utility maximizers (in the sense required for the binary lottery procedure to control their risk aversion) and that they are making equilibrium bids. As Kagel discusses in chapter 7, there is good reason to believe that players may have a tendency to bid higher than the equilibrium predictions (for reasons other than risk aversion) so that even a completely successful attempt to render the players risk neutral would not be expected to cause them to reach equilibrium. However, the power of Rietz's test comes from the ability to see whether the introduction of binary lottery payoffs has a substantial effect on the players' behavior in a situation in which a change in their risk aversion is predicted to have such an effect.[114] Rietz concludes that

> . . . [binary lottery] procedures can perform well in complex market environments such as sealed-bid auctions. However, they should be implemented carefully. The implementation should fit the environment, and the procedures should be simple enough for subjects to understand procedural implications completely. (212).

Thus the results of both Prasnikar (1993) and Rietz (1993) indicate that binary lotteries are not a magic wand, which can be waved over subjects to change their behavior. But carefully used, it appears that binary lottery payoffs can give experimenters a substantial measure of control over subject behavior, by neutralizing the unobserved natural risk postures that subjects bring with them into the laboratory.

Note again that, because the binary lottery procedure controls for the risk aversion of (ideal) utility maximizers, it allows experimental environments to be created in which the predictions of theories which depend on expected utility maximization can be known. This is what makes the technique so useful. However, in interpreting the results of an experiment which uses binary lottery payoffs, it is helpful to know the extent to which the procedure successfully controls the unobserved risk posture of experimental subjects who are not ideal utility maximizers. The evidence to date suggests that here too a substantial, although far from perfect degree of control can be achieved by careful application of binary lottery procedures.

(1) Preferences and Probabilities: A Historical Digression on
Binary Lotteries and Related Experimental Designs

If I can end this chapter as I began it, with a foray into the history of thought, I recently became aware of an interesting precursor to the introduction of the binary lottery technique into experimental economics by the paper of Roth and Malouf (1979), in a 1961 paper by Cedric A. B. Smith. Smith's paper was on the foundations of subjective expected utility theory, and he was interested in exploring the ways in which subjects' assessments of probabilities could be separated from their preferences over outcomes. That is, if one individual can offer a bet to another who is willing to accept it, the problem is how to distinguish between the case in which the individuals have different subjective probabilities about the outcome, and the case in which they have different risk preferences, that is, different expected utility functions on the payoffs. Although Smith's paper was purely theoretical, his approach to this problem actually took the form of an experimental design (albeit not a completely practical one) as follows (1961, 13):

> To avoid these difficulties [differences in risk aversion between individuals] it is helpful to use the following device, adapted from Savage (1954). Instead of presenting cash to Bob and Charles, the Umpire takes 1 kilogram of beeswax (of negligible value) and hides within it at random a very small but valuable diamond. He divides the wax into two parts, presenting one to each player, and instructs them to use it for stakes. After all bets have been settled, the wax is melted down and whoever has the diamond keeps it.
>
> Effectively this means that if, say, Bob gives Charles y grams of wax, he increases Charles's chance of winning the diamond by $y/1000$.
>
> ... Hence using the beeswax or "probability currency" the acceptability of a bet depends only on the odds ... and not on the stake. . . .

Smith goes on to outline how, "by using this currency, Bob and Charles can bet together; and from these bets we can construct a system of 'personal odds,' i.e. sets of lower and upper odds ... for pairs of propositions . . ." (14).

Note that Smith's proposed use for his two outcome [diamond/no diamond] probability currency was just the opposite of the use for which the binary lottery technique was eventually introduced into experimentation in Roth and Malouf (1979). Whereas Smith was interested in establishing a method of determining probability assessments, the standard use of binary lotteries in the experimental literature has been for determining the expected utility to experimental subjects of risky outcomes with known probabilities. In this respect, it is interesting to compare binary lottery designs with the Becker, DeGroot, and Marschak (1964) procedure for determining subjects' values for objects, independently of their probability assessments. Their paper, which introduced the technique by reporting an actual experiment, was immediately incorporated into the experimental economics literature. In contrast, although Smith's paper was referred to in discussions of the axiomatization of subjective expected utility, his probability currency idea was before its time and appears not to have entered the discussions among economists until binary lotteries were already a standard procedure among experimenters. (Although I have been able to check the citation indexes going back only to 1967, it appears that Smith's 1961 paper was *never* cited in an economics journal before 1988, when it was referred to in a paper by Page [1988], concerned with a broad class of mechanisms for eliciting truthful probability revelation.[115])

It is interesting to speculate why Smith's binary lottery idea, and certainly its practical implications, were lost for eighteen years and had to be independently rediscovered, while its contemporary, the BDM procedure, was quickly adopted as a practical feature of experimental design. It would be discouraging (but possibly not unrealistic) to conclude that this reflects the impermeability of the scientific literature, so that a practical idea that is first floated in a theoretical discussion in one discipline can take years to find its way to its natural users in another. More optimistically, the reason may be instead that there are other, simpler ways for experimenters to control probabilities, since probabilities can often be made objective by conducting lotteries in the presence of subjects, with verifiable probabilities (e.g., by spinning a roulette wheel or a bingo cage). In contrast, preferences are more inherently individual and subjective, and therefore experimenters have more need of techniques to control or measure them.[116] The fact that when binary lottery designs finally did become a standard technique it was to control preferences rather than probabilities provides some support for this more optimistic view, that Smith's binary lottery proposal may have gotten temporarily lost merely because he proposed to use binary lotteries to measure subjects' probability assessments and that in many cases experimenters preferred to deal with probability assessments more directly.

This brings me to my final point, which is that there are both costs and benefits associated with adopting possibly cumbersome elements of experimental design in order to better control the experimental environment.

d. To Control or Not to Control? Costs and Benefits

As long as utility based hypotheses are being tested, it is desirable to control for the preferences of utility maximizers in the design of experiments. (Failure to do so might mean that there would be room to dispute what the standard theory was supposed to predict, so that it would be unclear ex post whether the observed behavior supported the theory.) But there are costs to controlling preferences, from the direct cost of making subjects' decisions have nontrivial monetary consequences, to the indirect cost of adding complexity to an experiment (if only because each additional feature of the design must be explained to subjects and has the potential of being misunderstood so that additional complexity can translate into additional variance). And, as the discussion of the previous sections indicates, some of the benefit from particular experimental technologies may be reduced if their effect on subject behavior is unclear, or high variance. So in designing any particular experiment, it is reasonable to try to balance these costs and benefits.

Consider, for example, the binary lottery procedure for controlling risk preferences. The benefits of the control it offers are greatest when the theories being tested are sensitive to the risk posture of the subjects or when risk posture is being offered as a primary explanatory variable of observed behavior, and it is for this kind of experiment that the technique has become fairly standard. In other experiments, in which the theory being tested is relatively insensitive to the unobserved risk aversion of the players and in which this risk aversion does not play a primary role in the hypotheses being offered to explain the data, it is probably a reasonable first approximation to assume that players are risk neutral in monetary payoffs, particularly when the range of feasible payoffs is relatively small. And in experiments in which risk aversion is thought to play no role, nothing is gained by controlling for it.

Much the same could be said for the BDM procedure, and many of the same arguments apply as well to the general question of whether (and on what scale) monetary payoffs should be the primary means by which an experimenter attempts to control the ordinal preferences of subjects. It is important, I think, to avoid establishing rigid orthodoxies on questions of methodology.

Notes

1. I first circulated a draft of this history at the Handbook Conference in 1990, and it has been substantially revised since then in response to the many comments I received. A slightly shortened version of my account of the period 1930–1960 appears in the *Journal of the History of Economic Thought*, under the title "On the Early History of Experimental Economics" (Roth 1993).
2. In a prescient speculation about experiments (and perhaps with mostly field experiments in mind) Wesley C. Mitchell in his 1924 presidential address to the American Economic Association said:

   The work of experimenting in the social sciences requires a technique different from that of the natural sciences. The experimenter must rely far more upon statistical considerations and precautions. The ideal of a single crucial experiment cannot be followed. The experiments must be repeated upon numerous individuals or groups; the varieties of reactions to the stimuli must be recorded and analyzed; the representative character of the samples must be known before generalizations can be established. . . . But whatever approaches are made toward controlling the conditions under which groups act will be eagerly seized upon and developed with results which we cannot yet foresee.
   In collecting and analyzing such experimental data as they can obtain, the quantitative workers will find their finest, but most exacting opportunities for developing statistical technique—opportunities even finer than are offered by the recurrent phenomena of business cycles. It is conceivable that the tentative experimenting of the present may develop into the most absorbing activity of economists in the future. (1925, 9)

3. Of course there is something artificial about dividing up the work in this way, and there are other ways in which it could be connected. For example, Siegel and Fouraker's work is in the game-theoretic tradition as well and influenced not only subsequent experiments in industrial organization but also in bargaining.
4. Thurstone (1931, 139) remarks:

   "The formulation of this problem is due to numerous conversations about psychophysics with my friend Professor Henry Schultz of the University of Chicago. It was at his suggestion that experimental methods were applied to this problem in economic theory. According to Professor Schultz, it has probably never before been subjected to experimental study."

5. We will see in what follows that, while this line of criticism is by no means uncontroversial, the question of actual versus hypothetical choices has become one of the fault lines that have come to distinguish experiments published in economics journals from those published in psychology journals. Of course, laboratory animals in psychology experiments face very well motivated choices, and Wallis and Friedman expressed some optimism about economic experiments using animal subjects as well and cite Wolfe (1936) and Cowles (1937) as interesting examples. And in fact a modern body of economic experiments has been developed using laboratory animals; see, for example, Kagel (1987) and Kagel, Battalio, and Green (1994).
6. However, this stipulation may have been addressed more at the first of Wallis and Friedman's criticisms (concreteness) than at the second (real payoffs). Although Rousseas and Hart's description of their experiment is somewhat ambiguous on this score (a situation that would

not be seen in a contemporary report of an economic experiment) it appears to me that the choices were still hypothetical and that no breakfasts were in fact cooked and consumed in response to the choices made (although for additional concreteness it was nevertheless specified that all eggs would be scrambled). However MacCrimmon and Toda (1969, 435) read Rousseas and Hart's account differently and conclude that their subjects were indeed required to eat their most preferred choice. MacCrimmon and Toda conducted an experiment themselves in which subjects did eat their choices; see the next note also.

7. See for example MacCrimmon and Toda (1969) who follow up on Thurstone and Rousseas and Hart with a similarly designed experiment that addresses the previous criticisms by using well-motivated individual choice data. In one part of MacCrimmon and Toda's experiment, the choices were among bundles involving combinations of cash and French pastries, "with the stipulation that the pastries had to be consumed in the laboratory, before the subject received any other payoff" (441). (Subjects made multiple choices, and the determination of which bundle they would actually receive was made by the Becker, DeGroot, Marschak (1964) elicitation technique, which will be discussed shortly, in the discussion of the 1960s.) MacCrimmon and Toda argue that this procedure squarely addresses the Wallis-Friedman critique of Thurstone's experiment.

8. Expected utility theory had its predecessors in the work of Bernoulli and Ramsey, and there were predecessors of parts of game theory as well (see Weintraub 1992), but recall my earlier comments about scientific "firsts."

9. I make no attempt to include a full list, particularly since many early utility theorists employed an informal, but nevertheless, revealing style of casual experimentation, casually reported. For example, Markowitz (1952) gives a qualitative account of the responses "of my middle-income acquaintances" to hypothetical questions about lotteries involving gains and losses. More formal reports of experiments involving hypothetical choices still play an important role in this literature.

10. They report (372) that "plans for this experiment grew directly out of discussions with [Milton] Friedman and [L. J.] Savage at the time they were writing their [1948] paper. W. Allen Wallis also contributed to the discussions." The Friedman Savage (1948) paper contains a conceptual experiment along these lines, and I think the two papers taken together make a fine illustration of the great distance between the first conception of an experiment and its careful implementation and realization.

11. "[R]ationality can [also] be defined experimentally by observing the actions of people who can be regarded as acting in a rational manner" (Allais 1953, 504).

12. The famous story of the two prisoners each of whose dominant strategy is to confess, even though both do better if neither confesses, is due to Tucker (1950). Straffin (1980) recounts how Tucker came across the game on Dresher's blackboard and composed the story that has given the game its name. Apparently Howard Raiffa independently conducted experiments with a prisoner's dilemma game in 1950, but did not publish them (see Raiffa 1992).

13. Note that, if the game were played only once, it would in fact be a dominant strategy for Row to play row 2, and for Column to play column 1. In the repeated game these are no longer dominant strategies. That (nevertheless) no other actions occur at any period of the equilibrium of the repeated game follows by backward induction from the now familiar observation that on the *last* play of the game no player can do better than to play his one period equilibrium strategy, and so for the purpose of calculating the equilibrium we can now treat the game as a ninety-nine period repeated game and repeat the argument.

14. Limitations of which the very first paragraph of Flood (1958) makes clear the investigators were aware.

15. But note that Flood's 1952 report led quickly to follow-up experiments. Two that were funded by the Air Force and conducted at Ohio State University were reported by Scodel, Minas, Ratoosh, and Lipetz (1959) and Minas, Scodel, Marlowe, and Rawson (1960). Like Dresher and Flood's experiment, these used monetary payoffs to avoid hypothetical choices. However, some of the phenomena the authors observed made them question if very small payoffs were significantly different from hypothetical payoffs.

16. See, for example, Poundstone (1992) for a popular biography of von Neumann and his times, which focuses on the prisoner's dilemma. Poundstone devotes a good deal of attention to the early prisoner's dilemma experiments.

17. Specifically Coombs and Beardslee (1954), Estes (1954), Flood (1954a, 1954b), Hoffman, Festinger, and Lawrence (1954), and Kalisch, Milnor, Nash, and Nering (1954). And see Simon (1956) for some reinterpretation of the results of Estes. Oskar Morgenstern gave a talk at that conference, later published as Morgenstern (1954), in which he applauded the appearance of "strictly planned experiments" and anticipated a large future role for economic experiments of various kinds.

18. Recall Nash's comments about the prisoner's dilemma experiment.

19. Schelling's paper and these examples were also reprinted in his influential 1960 book *The Strategy of Conflict*.

20. See Stone (1958) for a related bargaining experiment with more complicated sets of feasible agreements.

21. Of course, it might still be that the equal division in the first problem is prominent *because* it is fair, so Schelling's prominence hypothesis does not necessarily contradict the fairness hypothesis implicit in the advice of Nash and his colleagues. In fact, hypotheses about fairness play a lively role in the contemporary exchange among experimenters, and we will see in section III and in chapter 4 how experiments have served to advance and to focus the debate.

22. This is not to say that there were not contemporary follow-ups to his experiments: see, for example, Willis and Joseph (1959).

23. Ledyard touches on models of learning in chapter 2 when he discusses the effects of repetition and experience in public goods experiments, and I will discuss in chapter 4 how simple models of learning track the data of repeated play in certain kinds of bargaining experiments. In section III.B of this chapter I discuss learning models of behavior in coordination games.

24. He cautions that there were some accounting differences between different trials (cf. footnote 2, page 98), as well as some differences between how completed transactions were reported to the participants in the different markets.

25. Chamberlin notes that in fact he observed this happen "ten to twelve times out of the forty-six trials" (98).

26. The "moving equilibrium" line in Chamberlin's figure graphs the price determined after each transaction by the intersection of the aggregate supply and demand curves of the agents still in the market.

27. Especially when viewed in the light of their immediate follow-ups to that work, in collaboration with Donald Harnett and Martin Shubik, in Fouraker, Shubik, and Siegel (1961), Fouraker, Siegel, and Harnett (1962), and Fouraker and Siegel (1963).

28. Interestingly, the aspiration hypothesis has attracted different amounts of attention on different sides of the ocean. American experimenters and theorists have subsequently come to regard aspirations as, at most, an intermediate variable, rather than as a primary explanatory variable. Our German counterparts have been more inclined to regard aspirations as a primary explanatory variable (although the two sides do not divide up quite so neatly: see, e.g., the edited volume on "Aspiration Levels in Bargaining and Economic Decision Making" [Tietz 1983]). For other early thoughts on aspirations and expectations, see Simon (1959). The work of Sauermann and Selten in these early papers, and subsequently, has other things in common with the work of Simon, such as their common interests in decision making *process* (see, e.g., Cyert, Simon, and Trow [1956] for a nonlaboratory study).

29. And although these directions involved "non standard" game-theoretic considerations such as aspirations, Siegel and Fouraker saw both the origins of their experiments and their outcome as squarely in the game-theoretic tradition. Speaking of von Neumann and Morgenstern's *Theory of Games and Economic Behavior*, Fouraker and Siegel say (1963, 6): "The reinforcement of economic theory with the mathematics and general methodology of that magnificent work has provided the impetus for a broad front of new research; we hope this book is a proper element of that movement."

30. It has today become extremely rare to see an experiment that does not use real payments published in an economics journal. However, the relative efficacy (and cost efficiency) of the two kinds of experiments remains a subject of lively debate (particularly when the real payments may be small, or not very sensitive to players' behavior), and the debate is fueled by the fact that a number of individual choice phenomena, which were first identified with (inexpensive) experiments using hypothetical rewards, have subsequently been robustly reproduced with real payments. (See, e.g., Thaler [1987], who after reviewing a number of studies in which the difference between real and hypothetical payments did not yield important differences in results notes that [120]: "Asking purely hypothetical questions is inexpensive, fast, and convenient. This means that many more experiments can be run with much larger samples than is possible in a monetary-incentives methodology.") This debate will show up in several chapters, including chapters 7 and 8 by Kagel and Camerer.

31. Friedman (1969) appeared in a special "Symposium on Experimental Economics" that also included reports of experiments by Carlson and O'Keefe (1969), Cummings and Harnett (1969), Hogatt (1969), MacCrimmon and Toda (1969), and Sherman (1969).

32. The experimental papers included in Sauermann (1967) are Sauermann and Selten (1967a,1967b), Selten (1967a,1967b,1967c), Tietz (1967), and Becker (1967). The volume also includes English summaries of these papers and a bibliography of experimental literature compiled by Volker Haselbarth.

33. See, for example, the extensive bibliographies for this period in Sauermann (1967) and Shubik (1975). Some of the other notable experimenters and experiments from this period are Becker, DeGroot, and Marschak (1963a,1963b,1964); Bower (1965); Contini (1968); Dolbear, Lave, Bowman, Lieberman, Prescott, Rueter, and Sherman (1968); Ellsberg (1961); Friedman (1963); Lave (1962); Lieberman (1960); Maschler (1965); Rapoport and Cole (1968); Shubik (1962); Smith (1962, 1964); and Yaari (1965). Rapoport, Guyer, and Gordon (1976, 423) present a graph of the "number of articles, books, memoranda, etc., published from 1952 to 1971, on various aspects of game experiments," which shows a fairly steady rise from about thirty papers published in 1960 to between ninety and a hundred papers in each of 1967, 1968, and 1969, many by social psychologists.

34. The argument is the same as the argument of Vickery (1961) that it is a dominant strategy to bid your true value in a second price auction. (Smith [1979a, footnote 1] recounts how he heard this kind of procedure described by Jacob Marschak in 1953.) Becker, DeGroot, and Marschak (1964) report that they used this technique to repeatedly estimate the utility functions of two experimental subjects. They concluded that their subjects' responses were not consistent with utility maximization, although their behavior became more consistent with repeated exposure to the problem.

35. Smith (1992) writes of his early involvement in experimental economics and notes that his first exposure came as a graduate student at Harvard in 1952, when he attended a class taught by Chamberlin in which Chamberlin's 1948 experiment was conducted as a classroom exercise. (As such he may be the first "second generation" experimental economist. He reports that among his contemporaries Jim Friedman also learned of experiments as a graduate student, from Martin Shubik at Yale. Perhaps more common at that time was the experience of Reinhard Selten, whose experimental work Smith reports was inspired by the 1954 experiment of Kalish, Milnor, Nash, and Nering. I suspect that certainly until very recently, and perhaps in many cases still, economists have often ventured into experimentation without having had any direct contact with experimenters as part of their formal education.) Smith notes that he was not active in experiments for a period from the late 1960s through the early 1970s and that his collaboration with Charles Plott played an important role in his reemergence as an active experimenter. Their first paper, Plott and Smith (1978), made an important contribution to the experimental industrial organization literature and will be discussed at greater length by Holt in chapter 5.

36. It was in this period that the editors of the present volume each published their first experimental work.

37. A notable contributor to experimental economics from the psychology side of the divide is Amnon Rapoport, a collection of whose papers, from the 1960s through 1990, are contained in Rapoport (1990). In his introduction he characterizes with regret the separateness of the two literatures, saying in part (ix):

> The history of experimentation in psychology is rich and old. It would have been quite natural and highly desirable for psychologists to extend their scope of research and assume a major role in the study of economic decision behavior. Psychology professes to be the general study of human behavior. Most psychologists are trained to regard their discipline as an observational science; they do not have to overcome the conditioning of many economists who think of economics as an *a priori* science. Psychologists' knowledge of experimental techniques is comprehensive, and their experience in conducting experiments, analyzing data, and discovering empirical regularities exceeds that of most economists. However, with the exception of research on individual choice behavior—where psychologists like Tversky, Kahneman, and Slovic have played a major role—psychologists have not contributed in any significant way to the growing research in experimental economics.

More recently there have been indications that this divide is being closed, and important experimental contributions by psychologists to the investigation of economic phenomena have been made in recent years. Many of these, made by students and associates of Rapoport (such as Bornstein, Budescu, Erev, Suleiman, Weg, and Zwick), by Robyn Dawes and his colleagues, and by Keith Murnighan and his colleagues, will be encountered in the chapters of this volume. As Ledyard points out in chapter 2, the interaction between disciplines has been particularly productive in experimental studies of the provision of public goods, with contributions not only in the economics and psychology literatures, but also in sociology and political science. (For a collection of papers representing the growing use of experiments in political science, see Palfrey [1991]. In this connection, see also McKelvey and Ordeshook [1990].)

38. For example, in the middle of the decade the *Journal of Economic Literature* initiated a separate bibliographic category for "Experimental Economic Methods," and by the end of the decade experiments were beginning to become standard fare in introductory economics courses (see, e.g., the excellent graduate textbook by David Kreps [1990], which pays particular attention to bargaining experiments, but also to experiments concerning individual choice and market behavior). Among undergraduate texts, the instructor's manual of Varian's intermediate microeconomics text (Varian 1990) contains a section written by Glenn Harrison (87–116) on running classroom market experiments (and the new text by Stiglitz comes with software for that purpose). (The use of experiments in the classroom as a teaching tool is showing signs of becoming a subject in its own right: see, e.g., the special issue of the *Journal of Economic Education* devoted to Classroom Experimental Economics, containing articles by Williams and Walker [1993], Bell [1993], Williams [1993], DeYoung [1993], Leuthold [1993], and Fels [1993]. There is also a small newsletter devoted to the subject, called *Classroom Expernomics*, edited and published by Greg Delemeester at Marietta College in Ohio and John Neral at Frostburg State University in Maryland.) We have even started to see texts devoted to experimental economics—see Hey (1991), Davis and Holt (1993), and Friedman and Sunder (1994). Finally, we have seen the establishment of laboratories that plant the seeds of experimental economics in new communities of economists (e.g., in England, France, the Netherlands, Spain, and Japan).

39. Although Allais was cited for his work in general equilibrium theory, the statement from the Royal Swedish Academy of Sciences referred to his experimental work by noting (1989, 3) that "he is perhaps best known for his studies of risk theory and the so-called Allais paradox." In his summary of Allais' career contributions on the occasion of the Nobel Prize, Grandmont (1989, 23–4) writes: "Another of Allais' outstanding contributions—this time one which is well known—concerns the theory of decision-making among risky prospects. . . . Allais' attitude towards the [expected utility hypothesis] has been characteristic of his constant view that theory should be confronted with facts. At a meeting that he organized on this topic in

1952, Allais conducted a series of experiments in order to test the empirical relevance of the hypothesis, the results of which were partially reported in [Allais, 1953]. These experiments showed that actual behavior violated systematically the expected utility hypothesis. This fact, which is known to economists as the *Allais paradox*, has generated an increasing amount of research work, both empirical and theoretical, especially in recent years." This work is discussed by Camerer in chapter 8.

40. A somewhat reorganized version of that talk appeared as Roth (1987a). While the contents of the present chapter are substantially different from that earlier survey, I have felt free to borrow from it where appropriate and also from my subsequent survey of different experimental topics in Roth (1988).

41. They are used in just this way in Michael Bruno's 1986 presidential address to the Econometric Society, which appears as Bruno (1989) (see particularly 300–1).

42. In this respect, these kinds of laboratory experiments are close kin to field experiments of the kind surveyed by Ferber and Hirsch (1982) or Hausman and Wise (1985), as well as to the analysis of complex special situations, such as the cigarette economies that arose in POW camps (see, e.g., Radford 1945).

43. I will try to use the singular term "experiment" to cover an entire experimental design, which may consist of many observations, each one a potentially complex interaction among many participants. I have elsewhere (Roth 1994) argued against the practice in some experimental economic literature (now much less common than it once was) of regarding each trial as a separate experiment. When combined with a tendency to report only "successful" experiments, this practice raises the risk of introducing a misleading element into experimental reports, similar to that facing econometricians who conduct many regressions and report only those that appear significant (cf. Leamer 1983).

44. "Chicken" takes its name from the story of two drivers (presumably adolescent, presumably male) who play a game of nerves by driving their cars directly at one another at high speed. Each player's preferred outcome is that the other will "chicken out" at the last minute and swerve to avoid a collision, while the player who did not swerve is rewarded with a (good) reputation for reckless disregard for his own safety. To swerve earns a less favorable reputation, but the worst outcome occurs when neither player swerves, and the game ends in a fatal collision. So the game has two equilibria, in each of which exactly one of the two players swerves. (What makes the game exciting is the problem of equilibrium selection.)

45. From payoffs and number of trials to personality differences: see, for example, Lave (1965) and Terhune (1968).

46. The nonnegligible observed rates of cooperation have caused many investigators to entertain hypotheses concerning the altruism of the participants. However, a recent experiment by Shafir and Tversky (1992) suggests that the reasons why cooperation is so often observed in the one period game may be complex. They compare rates of cooperation in a conventional one period prisoner's dilemma with rates of cooperation observed in a one period game in which a subject is first told what the other player has done. Somewhat surprisingly they observe lower rates of cooperation in the modified game than in the conventional prisoners dilemma, not only when subjects are told that the other player defected, but also when they are told that the other player cooperated. Shafir and Tversky therefore attribute some of the cooperation observed in the conventional prisoner's dilemma not to altruism (which should cause subjects who know that the other player has cooperated to also cooperate), but to the difficulty of evaluating choices when their consequences are not clear (i.e., to the difficulty of evaluating whether to cooperate or defect when the consequent outcome of the game will depend on the still uncertain action of the other player, in comparison to the simpler problem faced by subjects in their modified game). A related experiment with a very different design has led Andreoni (1993) to somewhat similar conclusions about the causes of the nonnegligible rates of contribution observed in public goods provision games whose equilibria call for no contributions.

47. Cooperation can be achieved by some equilibrium if and only if $p \geq (b - a)/(b - c)$, and it can be achieved "easily," by the "tit for tat" strategy of first cooperating and then doing whatever the other player did in the previous period, if and only if $p \geq (b - a)/(a - d)$ also.

48. Subjects played against a programmed strategy (without knowing what it was). In fact the programmed opponent always played the "tit for tat" strategy. And the players' incentives were only loosely controlled. Note that, since the equilibrium calculations depend on expected values, it would have been necessary to control for expected utility, not just ordinal utility, in order to do a proper job of controlling the equilibrium predictions. The experimental tools for doing that (via binary lottery games, as will be discussed in sections III.C and III.F) weren't introduced until the paper of Roth and Malouf (1979).

49. The payoffs were $b = 1.45$ German marks, $a = 0.6$, $c = 0.1$, and $d = -0.5$. The choices were phrased as setting a high price (cooperation) or a low price. (For early discussions of the prisoner's dilemma as a model for cooperation among oligopolists, see Shubik [1955]. An early experiment on collusion among several oligopolists that refers to the prisoner's dilemma as such a model is Dolbear, Lave, Bowman, Lieberman, Prescott, Rueter, and Sherman [1968]. [I have always suspected that so many authors may indicate a predisposition to collusion].)

50. The authors caution, however (54), "Even if it is very clear from the data that there is a tendency of the end-effect to shift to earlier periods, it is not clear whether in a much longer sequence of supergames this trend would continue until finally cooperation is completely eliminated."

51. Other theoretical attempts have been directed at changing the notion of equilibrium entirely (see, e.g., Rosenthal 1980) or at studying closely related problems (see, e.g., Selten's [1978] chain store paradox and the papers by Kreps and Wilson [1982] and Milgrom and Roberts [1982]). An experimental study motivated in turn by this literature is reported in Camerer and Weigelt (1988), who interpreted their results as supporting the predictions of models in which a small amount of incomplete information is introduced. Subsequent experiments, by Neral and Ochs (1992) and by Jung, Kagel, and Levin (1994), suggest however that this interpretation may have been premature. Orbell and Dawes (1993) point out that allowing players to exit from games if they wish also produces changes in both predicted and observed behavior. In the repeated prisoner's dilemma, this can increase efficiency by making it possible for players faced with noncooperation to exit rather than retaliate.

52. It turns out that there were two "kingmakers," that is, two programs that largely determined how the other programs did.

53. Of course, the results are also sensitive to the payoff matrix, which in this tournament had payoffs of $b = 5$, $a = 3$, $c = 1$, and $d = 0$, so that this kind of alternation gives up a half point each period in comparison to steady cooperation.

54. Another way of combining simulation with experimentation is explored by Roth and Erev (1994), who simulate via simple learning rules how the behavior of game players evolves as they gain experience. When the initial behavior in the simulations is estimated from the initial behavior observed experimentally, Roth and Erev report that, for a variety of games, the behavior predicted by the simulations for experienced players resembles the experimentally observed behavior. I discuss this at greater length in chapter 4 and some related work in section III.B of this chapter.

55. Although public goods provision is a subject older and larger than the prisoner's dilemma, the role of game theory in the foundations of experimental economics is reflected in the much longer history of prisoner's dilemma experiments than other kinds of public goods experiments. That is not to say by any means that the division between the two is clear. For a particularly interesting set of experiments in which prisoner's dilemma considerations are inextricably entwined with some of the larger issues of public goods, see for example, Bornstein and Ben-Yossef (1993) and Bornstein and Hurwitz (1993), which consider prisoner's dilemmas played by teams, in which the issue of free riding enters not only between teams but within teams. Bornstein, Erev, and Goren (1994) study learning in repeated play of these games, using the learning model of Roth and Erev (1994).

56. However, he notes that a sixth group of subjects who were asked in a purely hypothetical way how much such a program would be worth to them gave significantly different responses from the other five groups. He says (125): "This result may be seen as still another reason to doubt the usefulness of responses to hypothetical questions. . . ."

57. Experiments with human subjects in the United States are now regulated by state and federal laws that require that universities maintain review boards to determine in advance that experiments do not violate certain guidelines. These laws were passed in response to some hair-raising abuses, with notable contributions from both psychologists and biomedical researchers.

58. However, the experiment did not end here. The students were told that they had failed to reach the required sum, so only the two original high bidders would get the book, although the offer would remain (696) "open for a few days should the students still want to try to bring the money together." The (now surely desperate?) students were then presented with a third scheme, in which they were told essentially that any bids they submitted would be sufficient. These bids provided a third comparison, and, while they were significantly less than the previous two bids, they were significantly greater than the minimum bid required to be included among those who would (supposedly) receive the books before the exam. (Unfortunately we do not learn how the students did on the exam, or if their bids were good predictors of their grades.)

59. There are some complexities in the data, since ten students bid zero in the first auction, but contributed positive amounts when the book was offered as a public good. The authors consider the possibility that this was a result of coalition formation in the auction.

60. However, Palfrey and Rosenthal (1987) speculate that in a number of these experiments the monetary payoffs cannot simply be taken as equivalent to the utility of the agents, because there may be an unobserved "altruistic" component to agents' preferences. They go on to study the effect that this could have in a strategic situation in which being able to estimate how much others will contribute is important.

61. Another interesting experiment using this general design is that of Ferejohn, Forsythe, and Noll (1979). They examined a public goods provision mechanism abstracted from one used by station managers in the (American) Public Broadcasting Service to decide on what shows to collectively purchase.

62. One feature of the procedures in this study that differed from the studies so far discussed is that subjects knew they would be required to explain their decisions to the experimenter.

63. However, they attribute this to selection rather than training, noting that few of the economics graduate students "could specifically identify the theory on which this study was based." In view of the fact that there were other obvious differences between the subject pools (e.g., graduate students versus high school students), I suspect that the authors do not take this result as seriously as some of the others they report. However, the point that different subject pools may behave differently is always a matter of potential concern, and one which can be addressed empirically.

64. Since in fact there were only five subjects, payoffs were based on calculating the total contributions to the fund as if each subject represented twenty, with some modifications designed to conceal from the subjects how few of them there were. In chapter 2 John Ledyard takes strong exception to designs that involve any deception of the subjects; however, his view is not universally shared.

65. But see Isaac, Walker, and Thomas (1984), who observe some related results in a design that helps separate experience from repetition among a fixed group.

66. In seven of these groups, only the minimum choice was publicly reported, while in two groups the whole distribution of choices was made public after each period of play.

67. This result, known as the "Law of Effect," has been observed in a very wide variety of environments at least since Thorndike (1898).

68. This observation is known as the "Power Law of Practice" and dates back at least to Blackburn (1936).

69. This basic model was proposed as an approximation of evolutionary dynamics by Harley (1981).

70. In the same way, the role of mutation in evolutionary models may be played by experimentation and error in models of learning. For some recent theoretical work in this direction, see Fudenberg and Kreps (1988) for a model of persistent experimentation in extensive form games.

71. For a more detailed survey of this material, see Roth (1987b).
72. For example, Morley and Stephenson (1977) state that "these theories . . . do not have any obvious behavioral implications" (86).
73. These experiments are reviewed in Roth and Malouf (1979).
74. Of course, it is commonplace in interpreting field data in economics that one is often obliged to accept or reject joint hypotheses, which cannot be separated from one another. Much of the power of experimental methods comes from the fact that they often allow us to test such hypotheses separately.
75. The appearance from the results of Roth and Malouf (1979) that Nash's theory was a good point predictor of agreements in the partial information condition did not survive examination of a wider class of games. The robust feature of those results, rather, was that when players did not know one another's monetary value for agreements, there was a tendency to reach agreements that gave each bargainer an equal share of the commodity being divided, whether this was lottery tickets or some more usual medium (see Roth and Malouf 1982).
76. For a further exploration of self-serving assessments of fairness, see Babcock, Loewenstein, Issacharoff, and Camerer (forthcoming).
77. The means in each game do reflect a small tendency for the player with the smaller number of chips in his prize to receive a higher percentage of the lottery tickets; however, this effect is approximately an order of magnitude smaller than the difference between the prizes of the players with low and high *monetary* values in either the full information condition of the previous experiment or the high information condition of this one.
78. It is hard to even imagine any field data that might allow the effect of this kind of information difference to be observed. But, in view of the importance of notions such as "common knowledge" in contemporary game theory, differences of precisely this kind are increasingly encountered in the theoretical literature. Laboratory experiments give us a way to investigate them.
79. For related theoretical work, see Tijs and Peters (1985) for risk aversion in axiomatic models; Roth (1985, 1989) for work on risk aversion in strategic models; Safra, Zhou, and Zilcha (1990) for extension and generalization of the results of Roth and Rothblum (1982) on games with risky outcomes, and the important early paper by Kannai (1977).
80. Including those of Nash (1950), Kalai and Smorodinsky (1975), and Perles and Maschler (1982).
81. That is, it was thought that the high concentration of agreements around a focal point such as (50%,50%) might reflect forces at work that made it unprofitable for bargainers to try to achieve small deviations from equal division, but that, once the bargaining had shifted away from such a compelling focal point (into a region in which previous experiments had shown agreements would have greater variance), the influence of risk aversion on the precise terms of agreement might be greater.
82. Note that this is an experimental design that depended critically on the theoretical demonstration, in Roth and Rothblum (1982), that there are situations in which theories of bargaining like Nash's predict that risk aversion will be advantageous to a bargainer. Prior to that demonstration it had not been clear how to design an experiment that would separate the predicted (*dis*advantageous) effects of risk aversion from the possible effects of other personal attributes that might be correlated with risk aversion. If risk aversion were predicted to be disadvantageous in all the bargaining situations under examination and if an experiment were conducted in which it was observed that more risk averse bargainers do worse than less risk averse bargainers in these situations, then it might still be the case that risk aversion was correlated with, say, a lack of aggressiveness and that it is aggressiveness that accounted for the results.
83. When prizes are small, the relatively small effect of risk aversion observed here suggests that it may not be critical to always control for unobserved effects of risk aversion by employing binary lottery games in an experimental design, particularly when risk aversion is not a primary cause of concern for the phenomenon being investigated. Roth and Malouf (1982) report experiments similar to those of Roth and Malouf (1979), but in which players are paid

in money rather than in lottery tickets, and observe that the qualitative effects of information are very similar. Harrison and McCabe (1992), Radner and Schotter (1989), Cox, Smith, and Walker (1985), and Walker, Smith, and Cox (1990) also observe only small differences between certain observations made with and without binary lottery games. (However, Rietz, [1993] reports a very careful replication and extension of the experiment reported in Cox, Smith, and Walker and Walker, Smith, and Cox, and concludes that their results, which concern an environment in which risk aversion may play a role, are primarily due to artifacts of their experimental procedure. This will be discussed further in section III.F, when we discuss tests of the effects of binary lottery designs on subject behavior.)

84. In experiments in which multiple units of a commodity, or of different commodities, are available, subjects can be given separate reservation prices for each unit (e.g., to induce increasing or decreasing costs of "production" among sellers).

85. Smith (1962) acknowledged that using hypothetical payoffs amounted to swimming against the prevailing methodological tide among experimental economists, by noting before beginning (in a footnote to the title) that "the next phase is to include experimentation with monetary payoffs and more complicated experimental designs to which passing references are made here and there in the present report."

86. Except for 5¢ "commissions" that were paid for each transaction in that experiment, in order to encourage players to make trades at the margin.

87. Van Boening and Wilcox (1993) summarize their conclusions as follows (i):

> Thirty years of experiments show that the double auction trading institution achieves nearly maximal efficiency across a wide variety of market structures. Accordingly the contemporary consensus is that the performance of the institution is virtually independent of market structure and the strategies of agents. We show that this is not so: (1) Large avoidable costs can undermine both the efficiency and stability of the double auction; (2) Certain sellers who must produce for full efficiency in such markets earn negative profits, on average, when they do produce; and (3) Price dynamics in such markets are described well by recent theory meant to explain price dynamics of ordinary marginal cost double auctions. We conclude that double auctions are neither as robust, nor well understood, as currently thought; and that the performance of the double auction *does* depend on market structure, and through it on rationality and strategy as well.

88. For example, if prices start high in the first period and trend downward, then everyone learns from the last transactions in the period that there are sellers willing to trade at below the average price for the period. Because all parameters are the same in the next period, buyers can start the next period by trying to buy at those prices, etc. This can be seen in the transaction paths of many repeated double auction experiments, in which, for example, prices of the first transactions in the second period begin at those of the last transactions in the first.

89. Plott (1986) reports that this experimental evidence was ultimately not used in the court testimony. The government won the case, but was reversed on appeal. For some subsequent theoretical work that supports the general conclusions of this experiment, see Holt and Scheffman (1987).

90. See also Forsythe et al. (1991a,1991b).

91. These markets fall under the regulatory purview of the Commodity Futures Trading Commission, which has issued a "no action" letter, stating that no adverse regulatory action will be taken so long as the market maintains a limit on the size of the initial capital investment in each account ($500), does not engage in paid advertising, and remains non-profit.

92. Not the coins themselves (to control for "penny aversion").

93. Thus private signals are "positively affiliated" in the sense of Milgrom and Weber (1982).

94. For a similar experiment with previously inexperienced subjects, see Kagel, Levin, Battalio, and Meyer (1989), who report similar results.

95. It is a little difficult separating group size from experience and selection in these results, since although group size was one of the design variables, some of the small groups are the result of bankruptcies by overbidders in early periods.

96. The authors remark: "We believe that the executives have learned a set of situation specific rules of thumb which permit them to avoid the winner's curse in the field but which could not be applied in the lab." (It is, of course, also possible that the bidding environment encountered in the field is not well represented by the one created for the experiment. For example, in a field study of machine tool auctions, Graham and Marshall [1987] and Graham, Marshall, and Richard [1990] found that collusion among bidders was pervasive.)
97. For another analysis of the field data, see Hendricks, Porter, and Boudreau (1987).
98. The authors report that the probability of losing money based on the observed amount of overbidding averaged only .06.
99. The "we believe" is due to the fact that the values here aren't *independent*, but rather affiliated. However, they note (footnote 22):

> It is unlikely that positive affiliation is responsible for these differences. We have conducted one second-price experiment with independent private values which showed average market prices in excess of the predicted dominant strategy price. Further, recently published nondiscriminatory, multiple unit sealed bid auctions with independent private values, where the dominant strategy is to bid one's value, show a substantial (and persistent) percentage of all bids in excess of private values. (Cox, Smith, and Walker 1985b)

And in a subsequent experiment, Kagel and Levin (1993) replicate the overbidding in second price single object auctions with independent private values, as part of a very interesting experiment designed to investigate the qualitative differences predicted to hold for first, second, and *third* price auctions.
100. Deviations in expected payoffs from the equilibrium payoff will differ less than the deviation of the bids from the predicted bid, since the former is the latter times the probability that the bid will be the winning bid. So, particularly for low bids, which have low probability of winning, substantial changes in the bid can have very small consequences for the payoff.
101. In this connection, the assumptions involved in introducing unobserved parameters always deserve careful, skeptical examination. For example, in the papers of Cox et al., which Harrison critiques, the fundamental assumption is that all observations are at equilibrium. This certainly flies in the face of much of the auction data, which suggests that a great deal of learning takes place in early periods of play. Indeed, learning is one of the ubiquitous phenomena observed in experiments, as will be seen in nearly all of the chapters of this volume.
102. Note the relationship to other phenomena, such as the observation of Kagel, Harstad, and Levin (1987) of overbidding in second price private value auctions. There (and also in the "disadvantageous counteroffers" observed in bargaining experiments and discussed in chapter 4), actions that would be "irrational" if expected monetary income could be equated with utility result in only small expected monetary losses, and so cannot be regarded as strong evidence of irrational behavior. They may simply be evidence that small monetary differences may be insufficient to override nonmonetary elements in subjects' utility or that negative feedback that occurs with only small probability may be insufficient to correct misconceptions. See Fudenberg and Levine (1993) for a reexamination of several experiments along these lines.
103. For the pairs of negative expected value bets, the prediction is (since subjects are predicted to focus in the pricing task on the size of the potential loss) that they will be willing to pay more to avoid playing the $ bet, with its large potential loss, than they are to avoid playing the P bet. The "predicted reversal" thus occurs when the bets are priced in this way, but the $ bet is chosen over the P bet. For these bets also, the predicted reversals outnumbered the unpredicted reversals. The authors note that, by including negative expected value bets in the design, they are able to rule out one alternative hypothesis for the results in the positive expected value case, namely that subjects price the $ bets in such a way as to increase the likelihood that they will retain them (either out of a strategic impulse to state high selling prices or out of a preference for playing out gambles). Such a strategy for negative expected

value gambles would involve stating a less negative price, and this would have diminished the number of predicted reversals.

104. In their reply, Grether and Plott (1982) note that Pommerehne et al. did not replicate the earlier experiment so that it is premature to attribute the lower rate of reversals to the higher payoffs, since the experiments differed in other ways as well.

105. In a comment on these experiments, Slovic and Lichtenstein (1983) urge economists to view such reversals not as an isolated phenomenon, but as part of a family of choice anomalies that may arise from information processing considerations.

106. As noted above, the argument for the Becker, DeGroot, and Marschak procedure is the same as that for second price auctions, and so violations of independence have the same implications there when outcomes are uncertain. See Karni and Safra (1985).

107. An initial experiment in this direction is that of Loomes, Starmer, and Sugden (1989).

108. Note the parallel to the use of binary lottery games discussed in section III.C.

109. A similarly motivated experiment concerned with anomalies in the perception of probabilities is reported in Camerer (1987).

110. In a related experiment, Brookshire and Coursey (1987) go on to compare different methods of eliciting values for public goods and report a similar decrease in price discrepancies elicited from a repeated market-like elicitation procedure as compared to data elicited in a hypothetical survey.

111. Interestingly, Marshall, Knetsch, and Sinden (1986) report that individuals exhibit a much smaller buying/selling price disparity when they are asked to act as an agent for someone else than when they are acting on their own behalf.

112. In Binswanger (1981) and Quizon, Binswanger, and Machina (1984), this is interpreted as reflecting utility functions defined in terms of changes in wealth, rather than in terms of net wealth (cf. Markowitz 1952; Kahneman and Tversky 1979), or else as reflecting some deviation from expected utility maximization such as those involving failures of the independence assumption.

113. The gap is not really between the disciplines of psychology and economics, but between what levels of approximation seem to be useful for addressing what kinds of problems. The cognitive psychologist John Anderson has written persuasively of the need to look at optimizing models: he argues that if you want to know how people solve problems, you can often get good predictions by assuming they find optimal solutions. For example, he says (1990, 22):

> So far, I have discussed three levels of analysis: a biological level, which is real but almost inaccessible to cognitive theorizing, the approximate but essential implementation level, and the real and accessible algorithmic level. . . .
>
> The rational level of analysis offers a different cut at human behavior. . . . It is not "psychologically real", in the sense that it does not assert that any specific computation is occurring in the human head. Rather, it is an attempt to do an analysis of the criteria that these computations must achieve. . . . This turns out to be an important level at which to develop psychological theory. . . . This level of analysis . . . can tell us a lot about human behavior and the mechanisms of the mind. The function of this book is to demonstrate the usefulness of the rational level of analysis.

114. An interesting feature of Rietz's analysis is that he compares experimental procedures that he finds successfully use binary lotteries to control risk aversion with the procedures that an earlier experiment (reported in Walker, Smith, and Cox 1990) had reported did not have much effect. Rietz attributes the difference to the fact that Walker et al. had first trained their subjects with ordinary monetary payoffs, and then simply switched to binary lottery payoffs, with what he regards as insufficient explanation. He concludes that "hysteresis resulting from switching between monetary payoffs and lottery procedures . . . hinders success"(199).

115. Such mechanisms, which go by the name of *proper scoring rules*, form a literature that goes back at least as far as Brier (1950), on weather forecasters (see also Savage 1971) and has attracted the attention of experimenters testing theories that require them to assess sub-

jects' subjective probability estimates. Some experiments of this kind are discussed by Camerer in chapter 8.

116. Of course, not all probabilities can be made objective—e.g., players' subjective assessments of how other players will react, and it is for this reason that some experiments employ proper scoring rules and other devices to elicit probability estimates. And not all preferences are entirely subjective—it is for this reason that a considerable measure of control can be obtained by paying subjects in money.

Bibliography

Allais, Maurice. 1953. Le comportement de l'homme rationnel devant le risque: Critique des postulats et axiomes de l'ecole americane. *Econometrica* 21:503–46.

Anderson, John R. 1990. *The adaptive character of thought.* Hillsdale, N.J.: Lawrence Erlbaum Associates.

Andreoni, James. 1993. Cooperation in public goods experiments: Kindness or confusion? Working paper, Department of Economics, University of Wisconsin.

Andreoni, James, and John H. Miller. 1993. Rational cooperation in the finitely repeated prisoner's dilemma: Experimental evidence. *Economic Journal* 103:570–85.

Atkinson, Richard C., and Patrick Suppes. 1958. An analysis of two-person game situations in terms of statistical learning theory. *Journal of Experimental Psychology* 55:369–78.

———. 1959. Applications of a Markov model to two-person noncooperative games. Chap. 3 in *Studies in mathematical learning theory,* R. R. Bush and W. K. Estes, editors. Stanford, Calif. Stanford University Press.

Axelrod, Robert. 1980a. Effective choice in the iterated prisoner's dilemma. *Journal of Conflict Resolution* 24:3–25.

———. More effective choice in the prisoner's dilemma. *Journal of Conflict Resolution* 24:379–403.

———. 1984. *The evolution of cooperation.* New York: Basic Books.

Babcock, Linda, George Loewenstein, Samuel Issacharoff, and Colin Camerer. Forthcoming. Biased judgments of fairness in bargaining. *American Economic Review.*

Banks, Jeffrey S., John O. Ledyard, and David P. Porter. 1989. Allocating uncertain and unresponsive resources: An experimental approach. *RAND Journal of Economics* 20 (Spring): 1–25.

Banks, Jeffrey S., Charles R. Plott, and David P. Porter. 1988. An experimental analysis of unanimity in public goods provision mechanisms. *Review of Economic Studies* 55: 301–22.

Battalio, Raymond C., John H. Kagel, and Komain Jiranyakul 1990. Testing between alternative models of choice under uncertainty: Some initial results. *Journal of Risk and Uncertainty* 3:25–50.

Battalio, Raymond C., John H. Kagel, and Don N. McDonald. 1985. Animals' choices over uncertain outcomes: Some initial experimental results. *American Economic Review* 75:597–613.

Bazerman, Max H., and William F. Samuelson. 1983. I won the auction but don't want the prize. *Journal of Conflict Resolution* 27:618–34.

Becker, Gordon M., Morris H. DeGroot, and Jacob Marschak 1963a. An experimental study of some stochastic models for wagers. *Behavioral Science* 8:199–202.

———. 1963b. Probabilities of choices among very similar objects: An experiment to decide between two models. *Behavioral Science* 8:306–11.

———. 1964. Measuring utility by a single-response sequential method. *Behavioral Science* 9:226–32.

Becker, Otwin. 1967. Experimentelle Untersuchung der Erwartungsbildung fur eine Zeitreihe." In Sauermann, 1967, 226–254.

Bell, Christopher R. 1993. A noncomputerized version of the Williams and Walker stock market experiment in a finance course. *Journal of Economic Education*, Special Issue on Classroom Experimental Economics, 24:317–23.

Berg, Joyce E., Lane A. Daley, John W. Dickhaut, and John R. O'Brien. 1986. Controlling preferences for lotteries on units of experimental exchange. *Quarterly Journal of Economics* 2:282–306.

Berg, Joyce E., John W. Dickhaut, and John R. O'Brien. 1985. Preference reversal and arbitrage. In *Research in experimental economics*, Vol. 3, V. Smith, editor, Greenwich, Conn.: JAI Press, 31–72.

Bernoulli, Daniel. 1738. Specimen theoriae novae de mensura sortis. *Commentarii Academiae Scientiarum Imperialis Petropolitanae* 5:175–92. English translation in *Econometrica* 22 (1954): 23–36.

Binswanger, Hans P. 1980. Attitudes toward risk: Experimental measurement in rural India. *American Journal of Agricultural Economics* 62:395–407.

Binswanger, Hans P. 1981. Attitudes toward risk: Theoretical implications of an experiment in rural India. *Economic Journal* 91:867–90.

Blackburn, J. M. 1936. Acquisition of skill: An analysis of learning curves. IHRB Report No. 73.

Bohm, Peter. 1972. Estimating demand for public goods: An experiment. *European Economic Review* 3:111–30.

———. 1994. Behavior under uncertainty without preference reversal: A field experiment. *Empirical Economics*, Special Issue on Experimental Economics, 19:185–200.

Bohm, Peter, and Hans Lind. Forthcoming. Preference reversal, real-world lotteries, and lottery-interested subjects. *Journal of Economic Behavior and Organization*.

Bornstein, Gary, and Meyrav Ben-Yossef. Forthcoming. Cooperation in inter-group and single-group social dilemmas. *Journal of Experimental Social Psychology*.

Bornstein, Gary, and Roger Hurwitz, 1993. Team games as models of intergroup conflicts. Discussion Paper, Center for Rationality and Interactive Decision Theory, Hebrew University of Jerusalem.

Bornstein, Gary, Ido Erev, and Harel Goren. 1994. The effect of repeated play in the IPG and IPD team games. *Journal of Conflict Resolution*, forthcoming.

Bower, Joseph L. 1965. The role of conflict in economic decision-making groups: Some empirical results. *Quarterly Journal of Economics* 79:263–77.

Brier, G. 1950. Verification of forecasts expressed in terms of probability. *Monthly Weather Review.* 78:1–3.

Brookshire, David S., and Don L. Coursey. 1987. Measuring the value of a public good: An empirical comparison of elicitation procedures. *American Economic Review* 77: 554–66.

Bruno, Michael. 1989. Econometrics and the design of economic reform. *Econometrica* 57:275–306.

Camerer, Colin F. 1987. Do biases in probability judgment matter in markets? Experimental evidence. *American Economic Review* 77:981–97.

Camerer, Colin, and Keith Weigelt. 1988. Experimental tests of a sequential equilibrium remutation model. *Econometrica* 56:1–36.

Capen, E. C., R. V. Clapp, and W. M. Campbell. 1971. Competitive bidding in high-risk situations. *Journal of Petroleum Technology* 23:641–53.

Carlson, John A., and Terrence B. O'Keefe. 1969. Buffer stocks and reaction coefficients: An experiment with decision making under risk. *Review of Economic Studies* 36: 467–84.

Chamberlin, Edward H. 1933. *The theory of monopolistic competition*. Cambridge: Harvard University Press.

Chamberlin, Edward H. 1948. An experimental imperfect market. *Journal of Political Economy* 56(2):95–108.

Clarke, Edward H. 1971. Multipart pricing of public goods. *Public Choice* 11:17–33.

Contini, Bruno. 1968. The value of time in bargaining negotiations: Some experimental evidence. *American Economic Review* 58:374–93.

Coombs, C. H. and David Beardslee. 1954. On decision-making under uncertainty. In R. M. Thrall et al., 1954, 255–285.

Cooper, Russel W., Douglas V. DeJong, Robert Forsythe, and Thomas W. Ross. 1990. Selection criteria in coordination games: Some experimental results. *American Economic Review* 80:218–33.

Coppinger, Vicki M., Vernon L. Smith, and Jon A. Titus. 1980. Incentives and behavior in English, Dutch and sealed-bid auctions. *Economic Inquiry* 18:1–22.

Cournot, Antoine Augustine. 1838. *Recherches sur les principes mathematiques de la theorie des richesses*. Paris: Librairie des Sciences Politiques et Sociales.

Coursey, Don L., John L. Hovis, and William D. Schulze. 1987. The disparity between willingness to accept and willingness to pay measures of value. *Quarterly Journal of Economics* 102:679–90.

Cowles, John T. 1937. *Food-tokens as incentives for learning by chimpanzees*. Comparative Psychology Monographs, 14:5, Baltimore: Williams and Wilkens.

Cox, James C., Bruce Roberson, and Vernon L. Smith. 1982. Theory and behavior of single object auctions. In *Research in experimental economics, vol. 2*, V. L. Smith, editor, Greenwich,, Conn.: JAI Press, 1–43.

Cox, James C., Vernon L. Smith, and James M. Walker. 1983. Tests of a heterogeneous bidders theory of first price auctions. *Economics Letters* 12:207–12.

———. 1985a. Experimental development of sealed-bid auction theory: Calibrating controls for risk aversion. *American Economic Review Papers and Proceedings* 75:160–65.

———. 1985b. Expected revenue in discriminative and uniform price sealed-bid auctions. In *Research in experimental economics, vol. 3*, V. L. Smith, editor, Greenwich, Conn.: JAI Press. 183–232.

———. 1988. Theory and individual behavior of first-price auctions. *Journal of Risk and Uncertainty* 1:61–99.

Crawford, Vincent P. 1990. Equilibrium without Independence. *Journal of Economic Theory* 50:127–154.

———. 1991. An 'evolutionary' interpretation of Van Huyck, Battalio, and Beil's experimental results on coordination. *Games and Economic Behavior* 3:25–59.

———. 1992. Adaptive dynamics in coordination games. Working paper, University of California, San Diego.

Cummings, L. L., and D. L. Harnett. 1969. Bargaining behaviour in a symmetric bargaining triad: The impact of risk-taking propensity, information, communication and terminal bid. *Review of Economic Studies* 36:485–501.

Cyert, Richard M., and Lester B. Lave. 1965. Collusion, conflit et science economique. *Economie Appliquee* 18:385–406.

Cyert, Richard M., Herbert A. Simon, and Donald B. Trow. 1956. Observation of a business decision. *Journal of Business* 29:237–48.

Davidson, Donald, and Jacob Marschak. 1959. Experimental tests of a stochastic decision theory. In *Measurement: Definitions and theories*, C. West Churchman and Philburn Ratoosh, editors, New York: Wiley. 233–69.

Davidson, Donald, and Patrick Suppes, in collaboration with Sidney Siegel. 1957. *Decision making: An experimental approach*. Stanford, Calif.: Stanford University Press.

Davis, Douglas D., and Charles A. Holt. 1993. *Experimental economics*. Princeton: Princeton University Press.

DeYoung, Robert 1993. Market experiments: The laboratory versus the classroom. *Journal of Economic Education*, Special Issue on Classroom Experimental Economics, 24: 335–51.

Dolbear, F. T., L. B. Lave, G. Bowman, A. Lieberman, E. Prescott, F. Rueter, and R. Sherman. 1968. Collusion in oligopoly: An experiment on the effect of numbers and information. *Quarterly Journal of Economics* 82:240–59.

Dyer, Douglas, John H. Kagel, and Dan Levin. 1989. A comparison of naive and experienced bidders in common value offer auctions: A laboratory analysis. *Economic Journal* 99: 108–15.

Edgeworth, F. Y. 1881. *Mathematical psychics*. London: Kegan Paul.

Edwards, Ward. 1953a. Experiments on economic decision-making in gambling situations. Abstract. *Econometrica* 21:349–50.

———. 1953b. Probability-preferences in gambling. *American Journal of Psychology* 66: 349–64.

Ellsberg, Daniel. 1961. Risk, ambiguity and the savage axioms. *Quarterly Journal of Economics* 75:643–69.

Erev, Ido, and Alvin E. Roth. In preparation. Adaptation and imitation in experimental games.

Estes, W. K. 1954. Individual behavior in uncertain situations: An interpretation in terms of statistical association theory. In R. M. Thrall et al., 1954. 127–37.

Fels, Rendigs. 1993. This is what I do, and I like it. *Journal of Economic Education*. Special Issue on Classroom Experimental Economics, 24:365–70.

Ferber, Robert, and Werner Z. Hirsch. 1982. *Social experimentation and economic policy*. Cambridge Surveys of Economic Literature, Cambridge: Cambridge University Press.

Ferejohn, John, Robert Forsythe, and Roger Noll. 1979. An experimental analysis of decision making procedures for discrete public goods: A case study of a problem in institutional design. In *Research in experimental economics: Vol. 1*, V. L. Smith, editor, Greenwich, Conn.: JAI Press. 1–58.

Flood, Merrill M. 1952. Some experimental games. Research Memorandum RM-789, RAND Corporation, June.

———. 1954a. On game-learning theory and some decision-making experiments. In R. M. Thrall et al., 1954. 139–58.

———. 1954b. Environmental non-stationarity in a sequential decision-making experiment. In R. M. Thrall et al., 1954. 287–99.

———. 1958. Some experimental games. *Management Science* 5:5–26.

Forsythe, Robert, Forrest Nelson, George R. Neumann, and Jack Wright. 1991a. Forecasting the 1988 presidential election: A field experiment. In *Research in experimental economics vol. 4*, R. Mark Isaac, editor, Greenwich, Conn.: JAI Press. 1–44.

———. 1991b. Forecasting elections: A market alternative to polls. In *Contemporary Laboratory Experiments in Political Economy*, Thomas R. Palfrey, editor, Ann Arbor: University of Michigan Press. 69–111.

———. 1992. Anatomy of an experimental political stock market. *American Economic Review* 82:1142–61.

Fouraker, Lawrence E., Martin Shubik, and Sidney Siegel. 1961. Oligopoly bargaining: The quantity adjuster models. Research Bulletin 20, Pennsylvania State University, Department of Psychology.

Fouraker, Lawrence E., Sidney Siegel, and Donald L. Harnett. 1962. An Experimental disposition of alternative bilateral monopoly models under conditions of price leadership. *Operations Research* 10:41–50.

Fouraker, Lawrence E., and Sidney Siegel. 1963. *Bargaining behavior*. New York: McGraw Hill.

Friedman and Sunder 1994. *Experimental methods: A primer for Economists*, Cambridge University Press.

Friedman, James W. 1963. Individual behaviour in oligopolistic markets: An experimental study. *Yale Economic Essays* 3:359–417.

———. 1969. On experimental research in oligopoly. *Review of Economic Studies* 36: 399–415.

Friedman, Milton, and L. J. Savage. 1948. The utility analysis of choices involving risk. *Journal of Political Economy* 56:279–304.

Fudenberg, Drew, and David M. Kreps. 1988. A theory of learning, experimentation, and equilibrium in games. Draft 0.11, mimeo.

Fudenberg, Drew, and David K. Levine. 1993. How irrational are subjects in extensive-form games? Mimeo, Harvard Institute of Economic Research.

Gode, Dhananjay K., and Shyam Sunder. 1993. Allocative efficiency of markets with zero-intelligence traders: Market as a partial substitute for individual rationality. *Journal of Political Economy* 101:119–37.

Graham, Daniel A., and Robert C. Marshall. 1987. Collusive bidder behavior at single object second price and english auctions. *Journal of Political Economy* 95:1217–39.

Graham, Daniel A., Robert C. Marshall, and Jean-Francois Richard. 1990. Differential payments within a bidder coalition and the Shapley value. *American Economic Review* 80:493–510.

Grandmont, Jean-Michel. 1989. Report on Maurice Allais' scientific work. *Scandinavian Journal of Economics* 91:17–28.

Green, Jerry R., and Jean-Jacques Laffont. 1979. *Incentives in public decision-making*. Amsterdam: North-Holland.

Grether, David M., and Charles R. Plott. 1979. Economic Theory of Choice and the Preference Reversal Phenomenon. *American Economic Review*. 69:623–638.

———. 1982. Economic theory of choice and the preference reversal phenomenon: Reply. *American Economic Review* 72:575.

———. The effects of market practices in oligopolistic markets: An experimental examination of the Ethyl case. *Economic Inquiry* 22:479–507.

Groves, Theodore, and John Ledyard. 1977. Optimal allocation of public goods: A solution to the "free rider" Problem. *Econometrica* 45:783–809.

Harley, C. B. 1981. Learning the evolutionarily stable strategy. *Journal of Theoretical Biology* 89:611–33.

Harrison, Glenn W. 1989. Theory and misbehavior of first-price auctions. *American Economic Review* 79:749–62.

Harrison, Glenn W. and Kevin A. McCabe. 1992. Testing non-cooperative bargaining theory in experiments. In *Research in Experimental Economics*, vol. 5, R. Mark Isaac, editor, Greenwich, Conn.: JAI Press.

Hausman, Jerry A., and David A. Wise, editors. 1985. *Social experimentation*. National Bureau of Economic Research.

Hendricks, K., R. H. Porter, and B. Boudreau. 1987. Information, returns, and bidding behavior in OCS auctions: 1954–1969. *Journal of Industrial Economics* 35:517–42.

Hey, John Denis. 1991. *Experiments in Economics*. Oxford: Blackwell.

Hoffman, Paul J., Leon Festinger, and Douglas H. Lawrence. 1954. Tendencies toward group comparability in competitive bargaining. In R. M. Thrall et al., 1954. 231–253.

Hoggatt, Austin C. 1959. An experimental business game. *Behavioral Science* 4:192–203.

Hoggatt, Austin C. 1969. Response of paid student subjects to differential behaviour of robots in bifurcated duopoly games. *Review of Economic Studies* 36:417–32.

Hoggatt, Austin C., J. Esherich, and J. T. Wheeler. 1969. A laboratory to facilitate computer-controlled behavioral experiments. *Admininistrative Science Quarterly* 14:202–7.

Holt, Charles A. 1986. Preference reversals and the independence axiom. *American Economic Review* 76:508–15.

———. 1989. The exercise of market power in laboratory experiments. *Journal of Law and Economics*, Special Issue on Empirical Approaches to Market Power, 32. 2:S107–31.

Holt, Charles A., Lorin Langan, and Anne Villamil. 1986. Market power in oral double auctions. *Economic Inquiry* 24:107–23.

Holt, Charles A., and David Scheffman. 1987. Facilitating practices: The effects of advance notice and best-price policies. *Rand Journal of Economics* 18:187–97.

Hong, James T., and Charles R. Plott. 1982. Rate filing policies for inland water transportation: An experimental approach. *Bell Journal of Economics* 13:1–19.

Isaac, R. Mark, Kenneth F. McCue, and Charles R. Plott. 1985. Public goods provision in an experimental environment. *Journal of Public Economics* 26:51–74.

Isaac, R. Mark, James M. Walker, and Susan H. Thomas. 1984. Divergent evidence on free riding: An experimental examination of possible explanations. *Public Choice* 43: 113–49.

Johansen, Lief. 1977. The theory of public goods: Misplaced emphasis? *Journal of Public Economics* 7:147–52.

Jung, Yun Joo, John H. Kagel, and Dan Levin. 1994. On the existence of predatory pricing: An experimental study of reputation and entry deterrence in the chain-store game. *RAND Journal of Economics*, 25:72–93.

Kagel, John H. 1987. Economics according to the rats (and pigeons too): What have we learned and what can we hope to learn? In *Laboratory experimentation in economics: Six points of view*, Alvin E. Roth, editor, Cambridge: Cambridge University Press. 155–92.

Kagel, John H., Raymond C. Battalio, and Leonard Green. Forthcoming. *Economic choice theory: An experimental analysis.* Cambridge: Cambridge University Press.

Kagel, John H., Ronald M. Harstad, and Dan Levin. 1987. Information impact and allocation rules in auctions with affiliated private values: A laboratory study. *Econometrica* 55:1275–1304.

Kagel, John H., and Dan Levin. 1986. The winner's curse and public information in common value auctions. *American Economic Review* 76:894–920.

———. 1993. Independent private value auctions: Bidder behavior in first, second and third-price auctions with varying numbers of bidders. *Economic Journal* 103:868–79.

Kagel, John H., Dan Levin, Raymond C. Battalio, and Donald J. Meyer. 1989. First-price common value auctions: Bidder behavior and the "winner's curse." *Economic Inquiry* 27:241–58.

Kagel, John H., Dan Levin, and Ronald M. Harstad. 1988. Judgment, evaluation and information processing in second-price common value auctions. Mimeo.

Kahneman, Daniel, Jack L. Knetsch, and Richard Thaler. 1990. Experimental tests of the endowment effect and the Coase theorem. *Journal of Political Economy* 98:1325–48.

Kahneman, Daniel, Paul Slovic, and Amos Tversky, editors. 1982. *Judgment under uncertainty: Heuristics and biases.* Cambridge: Cambridge University Press.

Kahneman, Daniel, and Amos Tversky. 1979. Prospect theory: An analysis of decision under risk. *Econometrica* 47:263–91.

Kalai, Ehud, and Meir Smorodinsky. 1975. Other solutions to Nash's bargaining problem. *Econometrica* 43:513–18.

Kalisch, Gerhard K., J. W. Milnor, John F. Nash, and E. D. Nering. 1954. Some experimental n-person games. In R. M. Thrall et al., 1954. 301–27.

Kannai, Yakar. 1977. Concavifiability and constructions of concave utility functions. *Journal of Mathematical Economics* 4:1–56.

Karni, Edi, and Zvi Safra. 1985. Vickrey auctions in the theory of expected utility with Rank dependent probability. *Economics Letters* 20:15–8.

———. 1987. "Preference reversal" and the observability of preferences by experimental methods. *Econometrica* 55:675–85.

Kihlstrom, Richard, Alvin E. Roth, and David Schmeidler. 1981. Risk aversion and solutions to Nash's bargaining problem. In *Game theory and mathematical economics*, O. Moeschlin and D. Pallaschke, editor, Amsterdam: North-Holland. 65–71.

Kim, Oliver, and Mark Walker. 1984. The free rider problem: Experimental evidence. *Public Choice* 43:3–24.

Knetsch, Jack L., and J. A. Sinden. 1984. Willingness to pay and compensation demanded: Experimental evidence of an unexpected disparity in measures of value. *Quarterly Journal of Economics* 99:507–21.

Knetsch, Jack L., and J. A. Sinden. 1987. The persistence of evaluation disparities. *Quarterly Journal of Economics* 102:691–95.

Kreps, David M. 1990. *A course in microeconomic theory.* Princeton: Princeton University Press.

Kreps, David M., and Robert B. Wilson. 1982. Reputation and imperfect information. *Journal of Economic Theory* 27:253–79.

Kreps, David M., Paul Milgrom, John Roberts, and Robert Wilson. 1982. Rational cooperation in the finitely repeated prisoner's dilemma. *Journal of Economic Theory* 27:245–52.

Lave, Lester B. 1962. An empirical approach to the prisoner's dilemma game. *Quarterly Journal of Economics* 76:424–36.

Lave, Lester B. 1965. Factors affecting co-operation in the prisoner's dilemma. *Behavioral Science* 10:26–38.

Leamer, Edward E. 1983. Let's take the con out of econometrics. *American Economic Review* 73:31–43.

Leuthold, Jane H. 1993. A free rider experiment for the large class. *Journal of Economic Education*, Special Issue on Classroom Experimental Economics, 24:353–63.

Lichtenstein, Sarah, and Paul Slovic. 1971. Reversal of preferences between bids and choices in gambling decisions. *Journal of Experimental Psychology* 89:46–55.

———. 1973. Response-induced reversals of preference in gambling: An extended replication in Las Vegas. *Journal of Experimental Psychology* 101:16–20.

Lieberman, Bernhardt. 1960. Human behavior in a strictly determined 3x3 game. *Behavioral Science* 5:317–22.

Lindman, Harold R. 1971. Inconsistent preferences among gambles. *Journal of Experimental Psychology* 89:390–97.

Loehman, Edna, and Andrew Whinston. 1972. A new theory of pricing and decision-making for public investment. *The Bell Journal of Economics and Management Science* 2:606–25.

Loomes, Graham, Chris Starmer, and Robert Sugden. 1989. Preference reversal: Information-processing effect or rational non-transitive choice? *Economic Journal* 99:140–51.

Loomes, Graham, and Robert Sugden. 1982. Regret theory: An alternative theory of rational choice under uncertainty. *Economic Journal* 92:805–24.

———. 1983. A rationale for preference reversal. *American Economic Review* 73:428–32.

MacCrimmon, K. R., and M. Toda. 1969. The experimental determination of indifference curves. *Review of Economic Studies* 36:433–51.

Machina, Mark J. 1982. "Expected utility" analysis without the independence axiom. *Econometrica.* 50:277–323.

———. 1987. Choice under uncertainty: Problems solved and unsolved. *Economic Perspectives* 1:121–54.

Markowitz, Harry. 1952. The utility of wealth. *Journal of Political Economy* 60:151–158.

Marshall, J. D., J. L. Knetsch, and J. A. Sinden. 1986. Agents' evaluations and the disparity in measures of economic loss. *Journal of Economic Behavior and Organization* 7: 115–27.

Marwell, Gerald, and Ruth E. Ames. 1981. Economists free ride, does anyone else? Experiments on the provision of public goods, IV. *Journal of Public Economics* 15:295–310.

Maschler, Michael 1965. Playing an n-person game: An experiment. Econometric Research Program Memorandum No. 73, Princeton University, 109pp. Reprinted in Sauermann, 1978b. 283–328.

May, Kenneth O. 1954. Intransitivity, utility, and the aggregation of preference patterns. *Econometrica* 22:1–13.

Maynard Smith, John 1982. *Evolution and the theory of games.* Cambridge: Cambridge University Press.

Mead, Walter J., Asbjorn Moseidjord, and Philip E. Sorensen. 1983. The rate of return earned by leases under cash bonus bidding in OCS oil and gas leases. *Energy Journal* 4:37–52.

———. 1984. Competitive bidding under asymmetrical information: Behavior and performance in Gulf of Mexico drainage lease sales, 1959–1969. *Review of Economics and Statistics* 66:505–8.

McKelvey, Richard D., and Peter C. Ordeshook. 1990. A decade of experimental research on spatial models of elections and committees. In *Advances in the Spatial Theory of Voting,* J. M. Enelow and M. J. Hinisch, editors, Cambridge, Eng.: Cambridge University Press.

Milgrom, Paul R., and John Roberts. 1982. Predation, reputation, and entry deterrence. *Journal of Economic Theory* 27:280–312.

Milgrom, Paul R., and Robert J. Weber. 1982. A theory of auctions and competitive bidding. *Econometrica* 50:1089–1122.

Minas, J. Sayer, Alvin Scodel, David Marlowe, and Harve Rawson. 1960. Some descriptive aspects of two-person non zero sum games II. *Journal of Conflict Resolution* 4: 193–97.

Mitchell, Wesley C. 1925. Quantitative analysis in economic theory (Presidential address delivered at the 37th Annual Meeting of the American Economic Association, 1924). *American Economic Review*, 15:1–12.

Morgenstern, Oskar. 1954. Experiment and large scale computation in economics. In *Economic Activity Analysis*, O. Morgenstern, editor, New York: Wiley. 484–549.

Morley, I., and G. Stephenson. 1977. *The social psychology of bargaining*. London: Allen and Unwin.

Mosteller, F., and Nogee, P. 1951. An experimental measurement of utility. *Journal of Political Economy* 59:371–404.

Murnighan, J. Keith, Alvin E. Roth, and Francoise Schoumaker. 1988. Risk aversion in bargaining: An experimental study. *Journal of Risk and Uncertainty* 1:101–24.

Nash, John 1950. The bargaining problem. *Econometrica* 28:155–62.

Neral, John, and Jack Ochs. 1992. The sequential equilibrium theory of reputation building: A further test. *Econometrica* 60:1151–69.

Orbell, John M., and Robyn M. Dawes. Forthcoming. Social welfare, cooperators' advantage, and the option of not playing the game. *American Sociological Review*.

Osborne, Martin J., and Ariel Rubinstein. 1990. *Bargaining and markets*. New York: Academic Press.

Page, Talbot. 1988. Pivot mechanisms as a link between probability and preference revelation. *Journal of Economic Theory* 44:43–62.

Palfrey, Thomas R., editor. 1991. *Laboratory research in political economy*. Ann Arbor: University of Michigan Press.

Palfrey, Thomas R., and Howard Rosenthal. 1987. Private incentives in social dilemmas: The effects of incomplete information and altruism. Social Science Working Paper 659. California Institute of Technology.

Perles, M. A., and M. Maschler. 1981. The super-additive solution for the Nash bargaining game. *International Journal of Game Theory* 10:163–93.

Plott, Charles R. 1986. Laboratory experiments in economics: The implications of posted-price institutions. *Science* 232:732–38.

Plott, Charles R., and Vernon L. Smith. 1978. An experimental examination of two exchange institutions. *Review of Economic Studies* 45:133–53.

Pommerehne, Werner W., Friedrich Schneider, and Peter Zweifel. 1982. Economic theory of choice and the preference reversal phenomenon: A reexamination. *American Economic Review* 72:569–74.

Poundstone, William. 1992. *Prisoner's dilemma*. New York: Doubleday.

Prasnikar, Vesna. 1993. Binary lottery payoffs: Do they control risk aversion? Discussion paper 1059, Center for Mathematical Studies in Economics and Management Science, Northwestern University.

Preston, M. G., and P. Baratta. 1948. An experimental study of the auction value of an uncertain outcome. *American Journal of Psychology* 61:183–93.

Quiggan, J. 1982. A theory of anticipated utility. *Journal of Economic Behavior and Organization* 3:225–43.

Quizon, Jaime B., Hans P. Binswanger, and Mark J. Machina. 1984. Attitudes toward risk: Further remarks. *Economic Journal* 94:144–48.

Radford, R. A. 1945. The economic organization of a P.O.W. camp. *Economica* 12:189–201.

Radner, Roy, and Andrew Schotter. 1989. The sealed bid mechanism: An experimental study. *Journal of Economic Theory* 48:179–220.

Raiffa, Howard. 1992. Game theory at the University of Michigan, 1948–1952. In Weintraub, 1992. 165–75.

Rapoport, Amnon. 1990. *Experimental studies of interactive decisions.* Dordrecht: Kluwer Academic Publishers.

Rapoport, Amnon, and Nancy S. Cole. 1968. Experimental studies of independent mixed-motive games. *Behavioral Science* 13:189–204.

Rapoport, Anatol, and Albert M. Chammah. 1965. *Prisoner's dilemma: A study in conflict and cooperation.* Ann Arbor: University of Michigan Press.

Rapoport, Anatol, Melvin J. Guyer, and David G. Gordon. 1976. *The 2x2 game.* Ann Arbor: University of Michigan Press.

Rapoport, Anatol, and Carol Orwant. 1962. Experimental games: A review. *Behavioral Science* 7:1–37.

Reilly, Robert J. 1982. Preference reversal: Further evidence and some suggested modifications in experimental design. *American Economic Review* 72:576–84.

Rietz, Thomas A. 1993. Implementing and testing risk-preference-induction mechanisms in experimental sealed-bid auctions. *Journal of Risk and Uncertainty* 7:199–213.

Rosenthal, Robert. 1980. New equilibria for noncooperative two-person games. *Journal of Mathematical Sociology* 7:15–26.

Roth, Alvin E. 1979. *Axiomatic models of bargaining.* Lecture Notes in Economics and Mathematical Systems no. 170, Springer Verlag.

———. 1985. A note on risk aversion in a perfect equilibrium model of bargaining. *Econometrica* 53:207–11.

———. 1987a. Laboratory experimentation in economics. In *Advances in economic theory, Fifth World Congress,* Truman Bewley, editor, Cambridge, Eng.: Cambridge University Press. 269–99.

———. 1987b. Bargaining phenomena and bargaining theory. In *Laboratory experimentation in Economics: Six points of view,* A. E. Roth, edited, Cambridge, Eng.: Cambridge University Press. 14–41.

———. 1988. Laboratory experimentation in economics: A methodological overview. *Economic Journal* 98:974–1031.

———. 1989. Risk aversion and the relationship between Nash's solution and subgame perfect equilibrium of sequential bargaining. *Journal of Risk and Uncertainty* 2:353–65.

———. 1993. On the early history of experimental economics. *Journal of the History of Economic Thought* 15:184–209.

———. 1994. Let's keep the con out of experimental economics. *Empirical Economics,* Special Issue on Experimental Economics 19:279–89.

Roth, Alvin E., and Ido Erev. 1995. Learning in extensive-form games: Experimental data and simple dynamic models in the intermediate term. *Games and Economic Behavior* 8 (January):164–212. (Special Issue on the Nobel Symposium on Game Theory, June 18–20, Bjorkborn, Sweden.)

Roth, Alvin E., and Michael W. K. Malouf. 1979. Game-theoretic models and the role of information in bargaining. *Psychological Review* 574–94.

———. 1982. Scale changes and shared information in bargaining: An experimental study. *Mathematical Social Sciences* 3:157–77.

Roth, Alvin E., Michael W. K. Malouf, and J. Keith Murnighan. 1981. Sociological versus strategic factors in bargaining. *Journal of Economic Behavior and Organization* 2: 153–77.

Roth, Alvin E., and J. Keith Murnighan. 1978. Equilibrium behavior and repeated play of the prisoner's dilemma. *Journal of Mathematical Psychology* 17:189–98.

———. 1982. The role of information in bargaining: An experimental study. *Econometrica.* 50:1123–42.

Roth, Alvin E., and Uriel G. Rothblum. 1982. Risk aversion and Nash's solution for bargaining games with risky outcomes. *Econometrica* 50:639–47.

Roth, Alvin E., and Francoise Schoumaker. 1983. Expectations and reputations in bargaining: An experimental study. *American Economic Review* 73:362–72.

Roth, Alvin E. and Marilda Sotomayor. 1990. *Two-sided matching: A study in game-theoretic modeling and analysis*. Econometric Society Monograph Series, Cambridge, Eng.: Cambridge University Press.

Rousseas, Stephen W., and Albert G. Hart. 1951. Experimental verification of a composite indifference map. *Journal of Political Economy* 59:288–318.

Royal Swedish Academy of Sciences. 1989. The Nobel Memorial Prize in Economics, 1988. *Scandinavian Journal of Economics* 91:1–4.

Safra, Zvi, Lin Zhou, and Itzhak Zilcha. 1990. Risk aversion in the Nash bargaining problem with risky outcomes and risky disagreement points. *Econometrica* 58:961–65.

Sauermann, Heinz, editor. 1967. *Contributions to experimental economics* (Beitrage zur Experimentellen Wirtschaftsforschung, vol. 1, Tubingen: J.C.B. Mohr.

———. editor. 1972. *Contributions to experimental economics vol. 2*, Tubingen: J.C.B. Mohr.

———, editor. 1978a. *Bargaining behavior*. Contributions to Experimental Economics, vol. 7, Tubingen: J.C.B. Mohr.

———, editor. 1978b. *Coalition forming behavior*. Contributions to Experimental Economics, vol. 8, Tubingen: J.C.B. Mohr.

Sauermann, Heinz, and Reinhard Selten. 1959. Ein oligolpolexperiment. *Zeitschrift fur die Gesamte Staatswissenschaft* 115:427–71. See also Sauermann and Selten 1967a, in Sauermann, 1967. 9–59.

———. 1960. An experiment in oligopoly. *General Systems*. Yearbook of the Society for General Research. 5 (1960): 85–114.

———. 1967b. Zur Entwicklung der experimentellen Wirtschaftsforschung. In Sauermann, 1967. 1–8.

Savage, L. J. 1954. *The foundations of statistics*. New York: Wiley.

———. 1971. Elicitation of personal probabilities and expectations. *Journal of the American Statistical Association* 46:783–801.

Schelling, Thomas C. 1957. Bargaining, communication, and limited war. *Journal of Conflict Resolution* 1:19–36.

———. 1958. The strategy of conflict: Prospectus for a reorientation of game theory. *Journal of Conflict Resolution* 2:203–64.

———. 1960. *The strategy of conflict*. Cambridge: Harvard University Press.

Scherr, Bruce A., and Emerson M. Babb. 1975. Pricing public goods: An experiment with two proposed pricing systems. *Public Choice* 23:35–48.

Schneider, Friedrich, and Werner W. Pommerehne. 1981. Free riding and collective action: An experiment in public microeconomics. *Quarterly Journal of Economics* 96: 689–704.

Scodel, Alvin, J. Sayer Minas, Philburn Ratoosh, and Milton Lipetz. 1959. Some descriptive aspects of two-person non zero sum games. *Journal of Conflict Resolution* 3:114–9.

Selten, Reinhard. 1967a. Investitionsverhalten im oligopolexperiment. In Sauermann, 1967. 60–102.

———. 1967b. Ein oligopolexperiment mit preisvariation und investition. In Sauermann, 1967. 103–35.

———. 1967c. Die Strategiemethode zur Erforschung des eingeschrankt rationalen Verhaltens im Rahmen eines Oligopolexperimentes. In Sauermann, 1967. 136–68.

———. 1978. The chain-store paradox. *Theory and Decision* 9:127–59.

Selten, Reinhard, and Rolf Stoecker. 1986. End behavior in sequences of finite prisoner's dilemma supergames: A learning theory approach. *Journal of Economic Behavior and Organization* 7:47–70.

Shafir, Eldar, and Amos Tversky. 1992. Thinking through uncertainty: Nonconsequential reasoning and choice. *Cognitive Psychology* 24:449–74.

Sherman, Roger. 1969. Risk attitude and cost variability in a capacity choice experiment. *Review of Economic Studies* 36:453–66.

Shubik, Martin. 1955. *Strategy and market structure*. New York: Wiley.
————. 1962. Some experimental non-zero-sum games with lack of information about the rules. *Management Science* 8:215–34.
————. 1975. *The uses and methods of gaming*. New York: Elsevier. (See particularly chapter 9, Experimental gaming: A literature guide, 144–165.)
Siegel Sidney, and Lawrence E. Fouraker. 1960. *Bargaining and group decision making: Experiments in bilateral monopoly*. New York: McGraw-Hill.
Simon, Herbert A. 1956. A comparison of game theory and learning theory. *Psychometrika*, 21:267–72.
————. 1959. Theories of decision-making in economics and behavioral science. *American Economic Review* 49:253–283.
Slovic, Paul. 1975. Choice between equally valued alternatives. *Journal of Experimental Psychology: Human Perception and Performance* 1:280–87.
Slovic, Paul, and Sarah Lichtenstein. 1968. Relative importance of probabilities and payoffs in risk taking. *Journal of Experimental Psychology Monograph Supplement* 78 (no. 3, pt. 2):1–18.
————. 1983. Preference reversals: A broader perspective. *American Economic Review* 73:596–605.
Smith, Cedric A. B. 1961. Consistency in statistical inference and decision. *Journal of the Royal Statistical Society* Series B. 23:1–25.
Smith, Vernon L. 1962. An experimental study of competitive market behavior. *Journal of Political Economy* 70:111–37.
————. 1964. Effect of market organization on competitive equilibrium. *Quarterly Journal of Economics* 78:181–201.
————. 1979a. Incentive compatible experimental processes for the provision of public goods. In *Research in experimental economics: Vol. 1*, V. L. Smith, editor, Greenwich, Conn.: JAI Press. 59–168.
————. 1979b. An experimental comparison of three public good decision mechanisms. *Scandinavian Journal of Economics* 81:198–215.
————. 1980. Experiments with a decentralized mechanism for public good decisions. *American Economic Review* 70:584–99.
————. 1982a. Markets as economizers of information: Experimental examination of the "Hayek hypothesis." *Economic Inquiry* 20:165–79.
————. 1982b. Microeconomic systems as an experimental science. *American Economic Review* 72 (December): 923–55.
————. 1992. Game theory and experimental economics: Beginnings and early influences. In E. Roy Weintraub, 1992. 241–82.
Stiglitz, Joseph. 1993. *Principles of microeconomics*, New York: W.W. Norton.
Stone, Jeremy J. 1958. An experiment in bargaining games. *Econometrica* 26:286–97.
Straffin, Philip D., Jr. 1980. The prisoner's dilemma. *UMAP Journal*. 1:102–3.
Suppes, Patrick, and Richard C. Atkinson. 1960. *Markov learning models for multiperson interactions*. Stanford, CA: Stanford University Press.
Sweeney, John W., Jr. 1973. An experimental investigation of the free-rider problem. *Social Science Research* 2:277–92.
Teitz, Reinhard. 1967. Simulation eingeschrankt rationaler Investitionsstrategien in einer dynamischen Oligopolsituation. In Sauermann, 1967. 169–225.
Terhune, K. W. 1968. Motives, situations, and interpersonal conflict within prisoner's dilemma. *Journal of Personality and Social Psychology Monograph Supplement* 8:1–24.
Thaler, Richard. 1987. The psychology of choice and the assumptions of economics. In *Laboratory experimentation in economics: Six points of view*, Alvin E. Roth, editor, Cambridge, Eng.: Cambridge University Press. 99–130.
Thorndike, E. L. 1898. *Animal intelligence: An experimental study of the associative processes in animals*. Psychological Monographs, 2.

Thrall, R. M., C. H. Coombs, and R. L. Davis, editors. 1954. *Decision processes*. New York: Wiley.

Thurstone, L. L. 1931. The indifference function. *Journal of Social Psychology* 2:139–67.

Tijs, Stef, and Hans Peters. 1985. Risk sensitivity and related properties for bargaining solutions, *Game-theoretic models of bargaining*, A. E. Roth, editor, Cambridge: Cambridge University Press. 215–31.

Tucker, A. W. 1950. A two-person dilemma. Mimeo, Stanford University. Published under the heading On jargon: The prisoner's dilemma. *UMAP Journal*, 1 (1980): 101.

Van Boening, Mark V., and Nathaniel T. Wilcox. 1993. Avoidable cost: Ride a double auction roller coaster. Mimeo, University of Houston.

Van Huyck, John B., Raymond C. Battalio, and Richard O. Beil. 1990. Tacit coordination games, strategic uncertainty, and coordination failure. *American Economic Review* 80:234–48.

Varian, Hal R. 1990. *Intermediate microeconomics instructor's manual*. New York: W.W. Norton.

Vickrey, W. 1961. Counterspeculation, auctions, and competitive sealed tenders. *Journal of Finance* 16:8–37.

von Bekesy, Georg. 1960. *Experiments in hearing*. New York: McGraw-Hill.

von Neumann, John, and Oskar Morgenstern. 1944. *Theory of games and economic behavior*. Princeton: Princeton University Press.

Walker, James M., Vernon L. Smith, and James C. Cox. 1990. Inducing risk neutral preferences: An examination in a controlled market environment. *Journal of Risk and Uncertainty* 3:5–24.

Wallis, W. Allen, and Milton Friedman. 1942. The empirical derivation of indifference functions. In *Studies in mathematical economics and econometrics in memory of Henry Schultz*, O. Lange, F. McIntyre, and T. O. Yntema, editors, Chicago: University of Chicago Press. 175–89.

Weintraub, E. Roy, editor. 1992. *Toward a history of game theory*, Annual Supplement to Volume 24, History of Political Economy, Durham, N.C.: Duke University Press.

Williams, Arlington W., and James M. Walker. 1993. Computerized laboratory exercises for microeconomics education: Three applications motivated by experimental economics. *Journal of Economic Education*. Special Issue on Classroom Experimental Economics, 24:291–315.

Williams, F. 1973. Effect of market organization on competitive equilibrium: The multiunit case. *Review of Economic Studies* 40:97–113.

Williams, Robert B. 1993. Market exchange and wealth distribution: A classroom simulation. *Journal of Economic Education*. Special Issue on Classroom Experimental Economics, 24:325–34.

Willis, Richard H., and Myron L. Joseph. 1959. Bargaining behavior I: "Prominence" as a predictor of the outcomes of games of agreement. *Journal of Conflict Resolution* 3:102–13.

Wilson, Robert 1977. A bidding model of perfect competition. *Review of Economic Studies* 4:511–18.

Wolfe, John B. 1936. *Effectiveness of token-rewards for chimpanzees*, Comparative Psychology Monographs, vol. 12, no. 5. Baltimore: Williams and Wilkens.

Yaari, Menahem E. 1965. Convexity in the theory of choice under risk. *Quarterly Journal of Economics* 79:278–90.

———. 1987. The dual theory of choice under risk. *Econometrica* 55:95–115.

2

Public Goods: A Survey of Experimental Research

John O. Ledyard

Environments with public goods are a wonderful playground for those interested in delicate experimental problems, serious theoretical challenges, and difficult mechanism design issues. In this chapter I will look at one small but fundamental part of the rapidly expanding experimental research. In section I, I describe a very simple public good experiment—what it is, what some theories predict, what usually happens, and why we should care—and then provide a methodological and theoretical background for the rest of the chapter. In section II, I look at the fundamental question: are people selfish or cooperative in volunteering to contribute to public good production? We look at five important early experiments that have laid the foundations for much that has followed. In section III, I look at the range of experimental research which tries to identify and study those factors which increase cooperation. In order to help those new to experimental work I have tried to focus on specific experimental designs in section II and on general results and knowledge in section III. The reader will find that the public goods environment is a very sensitive one. Many factors interact with each other in unknown ways. Nothing is known for sure. Environments with public goods present a serious challenge even to skilled experimentalists, and they offer many opportunities for imaginative work.

I. Introduction

Some of the most fundamental questions about the organization of society center around issues raised by the presence of public goods. Can markets provide optimal allocations of public goods such as air pollution or public health? How well do current political institutions perform in the production and funding of public goods such as space exploration or national defense? How far can volunteerism take us in attempts to solve world environmental problems? If existing institutions, thrown up in the natural evolutionary process of history, do not produce desirable results in the presence of public goods, can we discover other organizational arrangements that would better serve the interests of society? At an even more basic level, public goods raise issues about the very nature of humans. Are people cooperative or selfish? Do they behave differently when confronting public goods decisions than when making private goods decisions? Are altruism or fairness concepts that a social scientist must come to terms with before solving the organizational problems or can these phenomena be safely ignored? Such questions have been argued throughout history on the basis of much introspection and little evidence. With the development of an experimental methodology for economics, we now enter a new era in the debates.

A. A Simple Public Goods Experiment

Perhaps more than in any other area covered by this handbook, it is difficult to identify a typical public goods experiment. As we will see, there are as many variations in procedures and treatments as there are research groups. For now, let us look at a design that has some of the basic features of many and is easy to describe and understand.

What does a public goods experiment look like? Four male undergraduates from a sociology course are brought to a room and seated at a table. They are each given an endowment of $5. They are then told that each can choose to invest some or all of their $5 in a group project. In particular, each will simultaneously and without discussion put an amount between $0 and $5 in an envelope. The experimenter will collect the "contributions," total them up, double the amount, and then divide this money among the group. The private benefit from the public goods, in this case, is one half the total contributions, which is what each receives from the group project. No one, except the experimenter, knows others' contributions, but all know the total. The procedure is implemented and the subjects are paid. The data collected, beyond the description of the experimental parameters, is simply the amount contributed by each individual.

What should one expect to happen in this public goods experiment? There are many theories. One, the economic/game-theoretic prediction, is that no one will ever contribute anything. Each potential contributor will try to "free ride" on the others. In this theory it is a dominant strategy to choose $0 in the experiment because each $1 contributed yields only $.50 to its contributor, *no matter what the others do*. This is called a public goods problem or a social dilemma because the group would be best off in some sense (taking home $10 each) if all contributed $5. Each $1 contributed yields $1.50 to the others at no cost to them. From the point of view of this theory, individual self-interest is at odds with group interest.

Another theory, which I will call the sociologic-psychologic prediction, is that each subject will contribute something. Although it is hard to find precise statements, it is sometimes claimed that altruism, social norms or group identification will lead each to contribute $5, the group optimal outcome. From the point of view of this theory, there is no conflict between individual and group interests.

What does happen in a public goods experiment? Examination of the data reveals that neither theory is right. In many cases, some contribute $0, some contribute $5 and some choose a middle course and contribute something less than $5. Generally, total contributions can be expected to lie between $8 and $12, or 40 percent to 60 percent of the group optimum. Dawes and Thaler (1988) state: "It is certainly true that there is a 'free rider problem.' . . . On the other hand, the strong free rider prediction is clearly wrong." This lack of precision is disconcerting. They seem to claim that a full range of behavior exists from fully selfish to fully altruistic. If so, outcomes in public goods environments can be almost anything depending on which subjects walk into the room, and we can learn no more from further experiments. More likely, the imprecision of results is due to the fact that we have simply not yet achieved sufficient control in our public goods experiments to be able to identify what is really happening. It is only recently that careful experimental work has begun to uncover how changes in payoff parameters and in institutional features can change the amounts contributed for the production of public goods. Being able to change amounts contributed by changing treatments means some measure of control can be achieved. We are thus beginning to understand behavior through better control and a growing accumulation of evidence.

Why should we care about public goods experiments? Both economists and sociologists recognize that the desired outcome is for all to contribute $5. The experimental evidence suggests that voluntary contributions will not produce that desired outcome. Economic theory suggests that it may be possible to change the institutions by which group choices are made in a way that causes the outcome to be closer to the group optimum.[1] To know how to do that, however, requires anticipating how individual choices will change as the institutions change. Since both the economic/game-theoretic and sociopsychologic theoretical predictions are wrong, we need to discover more about behavior not only in the context of voluntary contributions but also in the presence of many institutional designs. Experiments are the only way to do so.

B. The Art of Experiment: Sensitivity and Control

The research problem underlying this survey, then, is to understand behavior in the presence of public goods and in the context of many institutions. Once that understanding is achieved, all the other questions we have raised can be answered in a relatively straight-forward manner. On a broader level, we are really searching for useful principles of behavior that apply across all environments and institutions. If we are successful as social scientists, we should be able to model behavior in the same way, whether there are private or public goods and whether there are markets or committees. On the surface, this statement is simply a tautology; on deeper examination, it is the heart of what a theorist tries to do. To illustrate, suppose it were shown experimentally that subjects behaved differently when instructions were on green paper than when they were on white paper. To explain this phenomenon, we could add a parameter to our model of behavior, called, for example, "the color of the paper on which instructions are written."

Suppose our original model of behavior is $\mu(e)$; that is, if the experiment is e we will observe $\mu(e)$, and if the experiment is e' we will observe $\mu(e')$. If behavior is μ_g when green paper is used and μ_w when white is used, the new theory is $\mu(e; x)$ where $\mu(e; g) = \mu_g$ and $\mu(e; w) = \mu_w$. This does not, of course, allow us to predict what will happen when red is used; $\mu(e; r) = ?$. For that we need a set of principles, a set which allows us to say something about behavior for any color. We would ultimately like to be able to say: you give me the details of the environment and a complete description of an institution, then my model of behavior will predict what will happen. Thus, the study of behavior in the presence of public goods should be viewed simply as an extension of the more general study of behavior in groups, examples of which are covered throughout this book. Experimentalists must believe this, if the results of the lab are to tell us anything about behavior in the field. Theorists must believe this, if they are to be able to predict the implications of changes in institutional designs.

One might take this view, that principles of behavior exist independent of environment and institution, to imply that there is nothing special about studying behavior in public goods or dilemma environments.[2] That would be an incorrect inference. In fact, I think these are exactly the right environments for one simple reason: aggregate results and measurable aspects of behavior seem to be very sensitive to variations in parameters and other treatments. For example, experiments in private good environments, such as the work with Double Auctions (see chapter 6) and bargaining (see chapter 4), seem to produce similar predictable results independent of the experimenter, subject pool, and parameters. Demand-supply equilibria arise in simple markets in spite of subject "mistakes" or other characteristics. When one subject errs in a Double Auction with private goods,[3] another will immediately adjust and take advantage of the mistake but the rest of the group will not be too severely affected. A buyer may take advantage of a seller's error, but the group still achieves near 100 percent efficiencies. Subtleties in behavior are difficult to identify and measure. In public goods environments this "averaging" or "smoothing" phenomenon can not happen. A misstep by one is felt by all and cannot be easily corrected. Subtleties in behavior are not only identifiable and measurable, they are endemic. Public goods and dilemma experiments appear to be the simplest environment within which to uncover variations in behavior in groups.[4]

Of course the sensitivity of the experimental medium is a double-edged sword. Control is made more difficult. Let me illustrate what I mean. When I was taking freshman physics, I was required to perform a sequence of rather dull laboratory exercises (which may be one reason I became an economic theorist). One standard experiment involved rolling a steel ball down a ramp with a ski jump at the end. The trajectory followed by the ball was to be filmed, using a strobe camera, so we could plot the parabolic arc of the ball and confirm that Newton's laws were indeed consistent with experimental evidence. In an effort to enliven the proceedings, my lab partner and I substituted a table-tennis ball we had painted silver, and during its trajectory, we gently blew on it. The resulting experimental evidence captured on film, that Newton's laws appeared to be rejected, was indisputable.

Nevertheless, the lab instructor rejected the data as inconsistent with the theory. More correctly, he did not believe they were replicable with the original equipment. Table-tennis balls enable the experimenter to display effects hidden by the insensitivity of metal balls, but they also allow unintended and uncontrolled intrusions to contaminate and mislead.[5]

Public goods and dilemma experiments are like using table-tennis balls; sensitive enough to be really informative but only with adequate control. For example, the experiment we described in section I.A is neither particularly elegant nor carefully controlled. Even so, at least twelve major choices have been made in creating this design: (1) the number, (2) gender, and (3) education of the subjects, (4) whether they are face to face or acting through computer terminals or in isolated rooms, (5) how much endowment to give to each and in what form (cash, tokens, promises, . . .), (6) whether discussion is allowed and in what form, (7) whether contributions are private or public, (8) by how much to increase the total contributions, (9) how to divide up the larger pie (for example, in proportion to contribution or to number), (10) whether or when to announce the results, (11) whether to pay subjects publicly or privately, and finally (12) whether to run the procedure once or, say, 10 times. Each of these choices represents a potential treatment or control. Each treatment has been shown by at least one experimenter to have a significant effect on the rate of contribution.[6] This means that there are more than 2^{12} possible designs.[7] Further, there still remain uncontrolled phenomena which might affect behavior in the experiment, such as the experience of the subjects, whether they are roommates or not, the beliefs and risk-attitudes of the subjects, and the willingness of a subject to trade decision-making effort and precision for the dollars to be made in the experiment. In many Double Oral Auction experiments this lack of control does not seem to be a problem.[8] But, as we will see, it causes serious difficulties in the voluntary provision of public goods.

Experiments with Double Oral Auctions and private goods yield precise replicable patterns of data on exchange prices and quantities: markets are easy to control but provide little insight into individual behavior.[9] Experiments with voluntary contribution mechanisms and public goods yield imprecise patterns of data on contributions: volunteerism is not very easy to control but, perhaps, yields some insight into individual behavior. This delicate balance between sensitivity and control is a constant challenge to experimentalists. Sometimes the language and theory can be a guide.

C. The Language of Experiment:
Mechanisms and Environments

Modern developments in theory and experimental methods have created a framework and a language within which to study systematically the questions raised at the beginning of this chapter. This new framework, called mechanism design,[10] also provides an outline within which to organize what we know about public goods experiments. The main components featured are *environments, outcomes, performance criteria, institutions* and *models of behavior.* To see how these fit together into a coherent and useful framework, let us look at them one at a time.

An *environment* describes the details of the situation that the analyst takes as given and the experimentalist manipulates: the exogenous variables. Included in the environment are the number of people, or agents, their preferences and endowments, the physical constraints on behavior (biological and physical laws), those aspects of the legal structure (such as property rights) that will be taken as fixed, the structure of information (who knows what, and to what extent that might be common knowledge), the technical details and possibilities for production, and so forth. Also included in the environment is a description of the range of possible outcomes of interest to agents.

Outcomes are what the furor is all about. An outcome describes the final distribution of resources and payoffs. How each individual feels about the outcome will depend on the particular environment since an individual's preferences for outcomes are part of the description of an environment. Similarly whether a particular outcome might be good for the group will depend on the details of the environment.

A *performance criterion* determines, for each environment, a ranking over outcomes. The idea is that in each environment the best outcome is the one which is ranked highest by the performance criterion. A standard performance criterion used in experimental work is a cost/benefit measure, which computes the sum of payoffs received as a percent of the maximum attainable.[11] From a mechanism design point of view, if someone knew all the details of the environment (and were benevolent) we could simply ask them to announce the best outcome for that environment. One problem that might arise would be the difficulty in communicating all relevant details and the complexities in computing it. But one of the main contributions of modern economics is the recognition that information about the environment is dispersed and that individuals may have incentives not to provide the requested information. Further, even if the information is correctly known, self-interested agents may be unwilling to follow the suggested actions. Enforcement is, thus, another possible problem. We cannot readily rely on beneficent omniscience.

Instead, *institutions* arise to aggregate information and coordinate activities. An institution specifies who should communicate with whom and how, as well as who should take various actions and when. An example of a very simple institution designed to deal with public goods production is the *voluntary contribution mechanism* (without communication) in which each individual is told to contribute an amount of a private good privately and without any information about what others are doing, as in section I.A. The level of public goods provided then equals that producible with the total private goods contributed. The outcome describes the amount of public goods produced and the amount of each contribution. Given a set of individuals, their preferences and their endowments, the outcome we observe is the result of both the mechanism rules and the choices made by the agents. Another more complicated institution is the modified *Lindahl mechanism,*

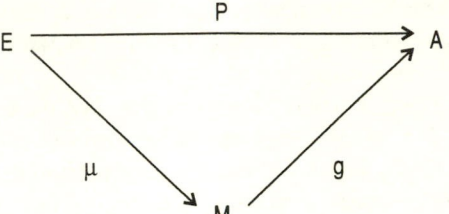

Figure 2.1.

in which all agents write down a schedule of their willingness-to-pay (in private goods) for various amounts of a public good. The level of public goods is chosen to maximize the sum of the willingness-to-pay minus the production cost. Each individual is required to contribute (pay) an amount equal to his or her *marginal* willingness to pay (for that amount of the public goods) times the amount of the public goods. The outcome describes the amount of the public goods produced and the amount of each contribution. The possible outcomes for the Lindahl mechanism are exactly the same as those for the voluntary contribution mechanism. But the actual values achieved may be very different because the choices of the agents may differ in the context of different mechanisms.

A particularly interesting question is whether the individuals would be better off with the voluntary contribution mechanism or with the modified Lindahl mechanism. To answer this we must be able to evaluate the performance of these institutions. To evaluate how well an institution performs (according to a particular performance criterion) we need to be able to predict what outcomes will occur in each environment when that institution is used. To do that we need a *model of behavior*; that is, we need a theory of how individuals respond in each environment to requests for information and action by an institution. In general, the model will predict different responses in different environments to the same institution as well as different responses in the same environment to different institutions.

Figure 2.1, from Mount and Reiter 1974, captures all the components of the framework. E is a set of environments and A is a set of outcomes. $P: E \rightarrow A$ is the performance criterion where $P(e) = \{a\}$ is a (possibly set-valued) function which identifies the best outcomes for each environment e. The institution is (M, g) where M is the language of communication,[12] and g $(m^1, \ldots, m^N)$ specifies the outcomes which are chosen if each individual i responds to the institution with m^i. The behavioral model is μ where μ $(e, (M, g)) = (m^1, \ldots, m^N)$ specifies how each individual will actually respond if the environment is e and the institution is (M, g).

This structure makes it easy to recast our earlier questions in a more precise form and to identify a variety of other interesting questions. Let us look at three. (1) How does a given institution (M, g) perform, and does it perform optimally over a range of environments; that is, what is μ $[e, (M, g)]$ and does μ $(e, (M, g))$ $\in P$ (e) for all $e \in E$? Examples of this type of question are: do markets efficiently allocate resources in private goods economies, and how efficient is the allocation of resources in a public goods environment if we rely on voluntary contributions? (2) Is μ a good theory; that is, do we observe μ $(e, (M, g))$ as we vary both e and (M, g)? Examples of these types of questions are: do buyers in a first-price sealed bid auction follow Bayes-Nash strategies, and are agents in a public goods situation selfish or altruistic? (3) Can we design an optimal mechanism for a class of environments; that is, given (E, P) can we find (M, g) such that μ $(e, (M, g)) = P$ (e) for all $e \in E$? Examples of this type of question are: how can we fix up problems caused by market failure, such as air pollution, how should we organize a firm, and how should we make decisions about public goods so that desirable outcomes occur? If we can simultaneously observe the details of the environment, e, the mechanism, (M, g), and the outcome for a wide variety of environments and mechanisms, we have a chance to answer these questions without making arbitrary assumptions about behavior. Experiments provide the opportunity.

D. The Range of Public Goods Environments

The range of experiments which have a public goods structure is more extensive than most realize. To see why, let me describe some very simple environments with public goods. There are two goods, one private and one public, and N individuals. Each individual $i = 1, \ldots, N$ is endowed with some amount of the private good, z_i. The public good is produced from the private according to the production function $y = g$ (t) where t is the amount of private good used to produce y. An outcome is a level of public good, y, and an allocation of the private good for each agent $x^1, \ldots, x^N$. Each agent values outcomes according to the utility function U^i (x^i, y).[13] Feasible outcomes are $a = (y, x^1, \ldots, x^N)$ such that $y = g [\Sigma^N_{i=1}(z^i - x^i)]$. We will call $t^i = z^i - x^i$ the amount of i's payment for the public good and occasionally restrict the range of possible t^i. For example, sometimes it is required that $t^i \in [0, z^i]$, the endowment is divisible but no one can contribute more than z^i, nor can they repeat compensation, and sometimes it is required that $t^i \in \{0, z^i\}$, either z^i is contributed or nothing is contributed. We can summarize the environment as $e = \; < g, U^1, \ldots, U^N, z^1, \ldots, z^N >$.

Virtually any public good or social dilemma experimental environment is a special case of e in which specific forms for $(g, U^1, \ldots, U^N)$ and specific values for $z^1, \ldots, z^N$ are chosen.[14] U^i is then paid to i based on the choices of $x_1, \ldots, x_n$. One special case, called the *linear symmetric variable contribution environment*, has been used extensively in experimental research[15] and is described by g $(t) =$ at/N and U^i $(x^i, y) = px^i + y$. It is called linear because of the assumption that all U^i and g are linear functions. It is called symmetric because a renumbering of the agents should change nothing. It is called variable contribution because x^i can be any real number. Another environment, called the *linear symmetric threshold environment*,[16] is described by g $(t) = 1$ if $t \geq \bar{t}$ and g $(t) = 0$ otherwise, and U^i $(x^i, y) = px^i + y$. It is called threshold because of the form of g.

There are many other classes of experimental environments which also have the public goods structure. For one example, consider the common property resource problem of Walker, Gardner, and Ostrom (1990). They study problems "that potentially arise whenever multiple appropriators withdraw resource units from a common-pool resource (CPR)." In their experiments, individuals are endowed with T tokens and choose to invest t_i tokens. Each i is then paid $h_i(t)$ where

$$h_i(t) = 5(T - t_i) + (t_i / \Sigma t_k)(23 \Sigma t_k - .25(\Sigma t_k)^2).$$

The idea is that the investment of t_i creates a negative externality and lowers the marginal physical product of others' individual investments, t_j. To see why this can be thought of as a public goods environment, let $z_i = T$, $g(t) = 23 - .25t$, and $U^i(x^i, y) = (z_i - x_i)y + 5x_i$. Here, $x^i = z_i - t_i$ is the amount of the private good endowment z^i which i chooses to retain for consumption.[17] The fact that $dg/dt < 0$ should not deter one from recognizing the public good nature of this environment. We can further transform variables to make the point. Let $y^* = g^*(t) = .25t$. Then $dg^*/dy^* > 0$. Let $z_i = T$. Let $x^i = T - t_i = z_i - t_i$. Let $U^{*i}(x^i, y^*) = 5x_i + 23(z_i - x_i) - (z_i - x_i)y^*$. (In the investment space, one would have $U^{*i}(t^i, y^*) = 5z^i + 18t_i - t^i y^*$.) Here one might be tempted to call y^* a public bad because increases in y^* yield decreases in U^{*i}. Also there are income effects since

$$\frac{d}{dx^i}\left[\frac{dU^{*i}/dy}{dU^{*i}/dx^i}\right] = \frac{1}{y^* - 18} \neq 0.$$

Nevertheless, the fundamental public good structure is revealed by the careful description of the environment. This also illustrates that the same economic environment can be presented to subjects in many apparently unrelated formats. One hopes that behavior would be the same whether $h_i(t)$, $U^i(x_i, y)$, or $U^{*i}(t_i, y^*)$ is used, but this is rarely checked.

Another example arises in a totally different context. In Cournot oligopoly models, (see chapter 5) firms choose quantities q_i, the market price which depends on the total amount brought to market is $P(\Sigma q_i)$, and firms are paid $\pi_i = P(\Sigma q_i) q_i - C^i(q_i)$ where $C^i(\cdot)$ is i's cost function. Let $g(t) = P(t)$ and $U^i(x_i, y) = x^i y - C^i(x^i)$ to see why this is a public good environment.

I have listed many of the examples I am aware of[18] and the appropriate references in Appendix A. One may think it is stretching a bit to include all of these as public goods environments, but the advantage gained by recognizing that these are all the same structure is that it brings more experimental data to bear on the really difficult question: what is behavior in the presence of public goods?

E. What Is and Is Not to Be Surveyed

The contents of a complete survey on public goods experiments would include material from four main categories: (1) experiments with voluntary contribution mechanism over a wide range of environments, (2) experiments with a wide range of mechanisms over a limited class of economic environments, (3) experiments with mechanisms in political environments, and (4) experiments with applications or policy problems as the focus.

Category (1) includes work by sociologists, social psychologists, political scientists, and economists intended to isolate fundamental aspects of group behavior when voluntary contributions are socially desirable but individually bad. In this paper we will concentrate on this category of work.[19]

Category (2) includes work primarily by economists aimed at identifying those aspects of mechanisms which might lead to socially optimal outcomes even if basic individual incentives operate to foil such goals. Much of this work is motivated by the theoretical findings of Hurwicz (1972) and others.[20] A good example of early work in this area is found in Smith (1979a, 1979b, 1980). A follow-up study to Smith's research can be found in Ferejohn, Forsythe, Noll, and Palfrey (1982). An example of more recent work is found in Banks, Plott, and Porter (1988). Work from psychology would include Shepperd (1993).

Research in Category (3) has been predominantly generated, as one might expect, by political scientists. In political environments, no compensation is available to ease the group decision making process. As opposed to economic environments in which transfers of the private goods from winners can be used to compensate losers, in political environments there is more of a flavor of multilateral bargaining. A classic example of this type of research, focusing on the institution of committees, is found in Fiorina and Plott (1978). A survey of more recent work, including institutions based on elections, can be found in McKelvey and Ordeshook (1990).

The research in Category (4) has more of an applied flavor than that in (1)–(3). Here, the experimental lab serves the mechanism designer in the same way the wind-tunnel does the aeronautical engineer and the towing tank does the naval architect.[21] Mechanisms which are created from the imagination of designers can be tested in a controlled environment. We need no longer be restricted to studying only those organizations thrown up by the slow evolution of naturally occurring institutions. An early example of this work is Ferejohn and Noll (1976) and Ferejohn, Forsythe, and Noll (1979). A more modern example is Banks, Ledyard, and Porter (1989). Here the basic research in mechanism design meets the world of everyday problems. Airport slot allocation (Grether, Isaac, and Plott 1989, Rassenti, Smith, and Bulfin 1982), coordinating the use of shared facilities (Banks, Ledyard, and Porter 1989), managing the development and operations of deep space missions (Olson and Porter 1994), environmental control through markets (Franciosi et al. 1991, Ledyard and Szakaly 1992) and siting noxious facilities (Brookshire, Coursey, and Kunreuther [forthcoming], Kunreuther et al. 1986) are just a few of the complex organizational problems being attacked. Although this is an infant science, I believe that mechanism design and testbedding will ultimately become the foundation of policy analysis.

I do not have space to survey all research across (1)–(4). I have chosen to cover only (1)—behavior in voluntary contribution mechanisms in public goods environments—for two main reasons. First, the research, development, and application of mechanisms in (2), (3), and (4) requires a basic understanding of behavior in group situations. The research on voluntary contribution mechanism is one of the simplest ways to develop that understanding. The experiments are difficult to control but are sensitive revealers of behavior. Second, the research on behavior with public goods has been aggressively multi-disciplinary with excellent programs maintained by economists, political scientists, psychologists, and sociologists.[22] Many experiments have been created in response to work of others. Several labs have long running programs in which data have been generated by systematically varying environments and institutions. The best results do seem to come from the more systematic efforts. Perhaps more often than in any other area trod by experimental economists,[23] research on voluntary contributions has brought the fundamental beliefs and hypotheses of economics into conflict with those of other fields. The debate has been joined: the resolution, as we will see, remains in doubt.

II. Are People Selfish or Cooperative?

Research on the voluntary provision of public goods must come to grips with this simple but still unanswered question about the fundamental nature of humankind. The debate has been long-standing with much heat and little light.[24] Economists and game-theorists argue that the hypothesis of selfish behavior is the only viable one as an organizing principle, yet they also contribute to public television and vote in elections. Sociologists and political scientists argue that societies are naturally cooperative through the evolution of social norms or altruism. Preconceived notions bordering on the theological have sometimes been rejected by data. But those who are reluctant to part with cherished theories have in turn rejected the data. Disciplinary boundaries have been drawn, breached, and redrawn. It is into this fray that experimentalists have come, trying to generate light where previously there was little.

Although many have contributed to the development of our knowledge, the systematic experimental effort of three research groups has been fundamental. Marwell in Sociology at Wisconsin,[25] Dawes in Psychology at Oregon and then at Carnegie-Mellon University, and Orbell in Political Science at Oregon,[26] and Isaac and Walker in Economics at Arizona and Indiana[27] have all carried out sustained efforts to understand whether and why cooperation might occur in public goods problems. Many of these still continue the study. The result of this effort and the sometimes heated interaction has been just what one might hope for; a slowly emerging consensus, which would have been impossible without carefully controlled experiments. Let us see how this has happened by trying to discover what we know now and why.

A reasonable reading of the literature[28] on voluntary contribution mechanisms and social dilemmas would probably lead one to conclude that the major findings to date are:

1. In one-shot trials and in the initial stages of finitely repeated trials, subjects generally provide contributions halfway between the Pareto-efficient level and the free riding level,
2. Contributions decline with repetition, and
3. Face to face communication improves the rate of contribution.

The first finding suggests the public goods problem is not as bad as some economists make it out to be, but that there is still room for improvement. For those interested in creating more desirable outcomes, the second is bad news and the third is good news. But, although these are generally acknowledged stylized facts, they should be viewed with some skepticism. And, perhaps, others should be added. To see why, let us dig deeper.

The public goods problem, that individual incentives are at odds with group interest, has long been recognized at the theoretical level by economists. Lindahl discussed it as early as 1919,[29] Samuelson (1954) conjectured it, and Ledyard and Roberts provided a proof in 1974. (See Groves and Ledyard 1987 for details). At the same time political scientists recognized it as a problem of collective action (Olson 1971) and as the tragedy of the commons (Hardin 1968), while social psychologists called it a social dilemma (Dawes 1980). But, even though the problem was widely recognized there were few data. This allowed wide disagreement about whether there really was a problem. Lindahl (1919), not recognizing the incentives for misrepresentation, suggested that a bargaining equilibrium would arise that was optimal. For a modern version of the argument that the public goods problem is over-exaggerated see Johansen (1977). Most economists believed there was a free rider problem and that voluntary contribution mechanisms would provide very little public goods. Other organizations would be needed. Eventually data were brought to bear on the debate, but that is a relatively recent occurrence. For example, Marwell and Ames (1979, 11336) note at the time of their work that "no body of experimental research asks explicitly what level of self-denial on behalf of achieving collective goods may be expected from some population, and under what conditions this self-denial may vary." The earliest experiment they acknowledge was reported by Bohm (1972).[30] We start there.

A. Bohm: Estimating Demand

In one of the earliest attempts to discover experimentally whether there is a public goods problem, Bohm (1972) set up a well-thought-out test "involving five different approaches to estimating demand for a public good." His conclusion after the data were analyzed was that "the well-known risk for misrepresentation of preferences in this context may have been exaggerated" and people may be willing to contribute to the public good even if their own self-interest runs counter. What did Bohm do, and was his conclusion correct?

1. Procedures

Let me first describe Bohm's experimental procedures and then explain why his study raised more questions than it answered. In his own words:

> The test was carried out by the Research Department of the Swedish Radio-TV broadcasting company (SR) in November, 1969. A random sample of 605 persons was drawn from the age group 20 to 70 of the population of

Stockholm. They were asked to come to the premises of the broadcasting company to answer some questions about TV programs and were promised a fee of Kr.50 ($10) for a one-hour "interview." Normally, some 35–50% show up in tests of this kind. (Bohm 1972, 118)[31]

After dividing the sample,

The persons in each subgroup were placed into a room with two TV-sets and were, for allegedly "practical reasons," immediately given the fees promised them in four ten-Crown bills, one five-Crown bill and small change to make Kr.50. The administrator gave an oral presentation of the test which involved a half-hour program by Hasse Alfredsson and Tage Danielsson,[32] not yet shown to the public. The subjects were given the impression that there were many groups of the same size simultaneously being asked the same questions in other rooms elsewhere in the broadcasting company. The responses, given in writing by the persons in each subgroup, were taken away and said to be added to the statements from other groups. . . . The main part of the instructions given to groups I to V was as follows: Try to estimate in money terms how much you find it worth at a maximum to watch this half-hour program in this room in a little while, i.e., what is the largest sum you are willing to pay to watch it. If the sum of the stated amounts of all the participants covers the costs (Kr. 500) of showing the program on closed-circuit TV, the program will be shown; and you will have to pay

(to group I)	the amount you have stated,
(to group II)	some percentage (as explained) of the amount you have stated,
(to group III)	either the amount you have stated or a percentage (as explained) of this amount, or Kr.5 or nothing, to be determined later by a lottery you can witness,
(to group IV)	Kr.5,
(to group V)	nothing. In this case the participants were informed that the costs were to be paid by the SR, i.e., the taxpayers in general.

"Counter-strategic" arguments (see below in section II.A.3) were added to instructions I, II, IV and V.

The subjects in group VI, who received instructions which differed from the instructions to the first five groups, were simply asked how much they found the program to be worth at a maximum. In a second round, these people were asked to give their highest bids for a seat to watch the program and were told that the 10 highest bidders out of an alleged group of some 100 persons were to pay the amount they had bid and see the program. (Bohm 1972, 118–119)

The design of the experiment was intended to test whether, as economists might have predicted, group I would understate their willingness to pay and groups IV and V would overstate.

2. Results

The data Bohm found are summarized in Table 2.1: They imply that no significant differences (at the 5% level) could be found between any pair of instructions I to IV. (Bohm 1972, 120).

3. Comments

There are three aspects of the design which deserve mention because they suggest a lack of control. First, Bohm does not know and cannot directly measure the true willingness-to-pay of his subjects to see a specific television show. Since he did not control this variable (subjects were not paid but would get to watch the show) he is forced to make probabilistic statements across groups.[33] Further, it is impossible for him to distinguish between two key hypotheses: no misrepresentation of preferences and simple irresponsible responses. He notes that "the reactions received from different groups are compatible with the possibility of getting *identical* responses to instructions I to V" (Bohm 1972, 124; emphasis is his). He also remarks, in discussing group VI but with relevance to group V, that "the results are of course compatible with the general view that, when no payments and/or formal decisions are involved, people respond in an 'irresponsible' fashion. In other words, this result may be seen as still another reason to doubt the usefulness of responses to hypothetical questions." (125). The lack of direct control over the fundamental parameter, willingness-to-pay, creates a serious difficulty in knowing what to conclude without a significantly large number of experiments with randomly assigned subjects so that statistical procedures can substitute for direct control.[34]

Second, because he wanted to study the effect of large groups and because he did not have much money, Bohm misrepresented the true situation to the subjects. There were no other "groups of the same size simultaneously being asked the same questions," and in fact the program was always shown no matter what the answers were. The experimenter may hope the subjects believe that the group is large, but control may have been lost. Bohm is not the only one to adapt this strategy in order to save money. In section III.C.2 I will discuss the problems of doing experiments with large numbers and one of the creative attempts at solution. The problem remains open.

Third, "the use of counter-strategic" arguments in experiments is clearly controversial. Instructions IV and V say

> It is easy to see that it would pay for any one of you who really wanted to watch this program to state a much higher amount than he actually would be willing to pay. In this way the total sum of the amounts stated would increase and so would the chances of having the program shown here. But this would of course make it impossible for us to find out just how much you really think watching this program is worth to you. It could also be said that such an overstatement would indicate a lack of solidarity or respect for the views of your neighbors, who may be called upon to pay for something that is not really desired by all of you together. In other words, it should be seen as

Table 2.1. Amounts Stated at Instructions I–VI: 2.

Kr.	I	II	III	IV	V	VI:1	VI:2
0–0.50				1	1	2	5
0.60–2.5	2	2		4	3	4	4
2.60–4.50	4	5	2	1	4	4	
4.60–6.50[a]	8	6	15	13	8	10	10
6.60–8.50	4	3	2	6	7	3	3
8.60–10.50[b]	1	7	9	4	8	13	12
10.60–12.50		1		1	1	3	1
12.60–17.50[c]	3	1		6	3	11	12
17.60–22.50[d]		3		1	1	1	4
22.60–27.50[e]		1	1		3	2	2
27.60–32.50[f]	1						1
50						1	
Number	23	29	29	37	39	54	54
Mean	7.61	8.84	7.29	7.73	8.78	10.19	10.33
Standard deviation	6.11	5.84	4.11	4.68	6.24	7.79	6.84
Median	5	7	5	6.5	7	10	10

[a] 55 out of 70 stating Kr. 5.
[b] All 54 stating Kr. 10
[c] 35 out of 36 stating Kr. 15
[d] All 10 stating Kr. 20
[e] 8 out of 9 stating Kr. 25
[f] Both stating Kr. 30

something of a "duty" to state the amount you actually find it worth to see the program. (128–129)

Instructions I and II say,

> . . . it could pay for you to give an understatement of your maximum willingness to pay. But, if *all* or *many* of you behave in this way, the sum won't reach Kr.500 and the program won't be shown to you. (128)

It is well known now that subjects may actually be trying to do what they think the experimentalist thinks they should be doing. Even subtle cues in the instructions can cause subjects' decisions to vary. Strong moral imperatives such as those used by Bohm are equivalent to blowing on table-tennis balls. There may be economic principles involved, but we will never find them this way. We might, however, find out whether such mechanisms can increase contributions. I will take up a discussion about the role of moral suasion in section III.E.

Bohm's imaginative study was, for its time, a major advance in the attempt to identify the extent of voluntary behavior in the presence of public goods. Although he tentatively concluded that that misrepresentation of preferences was less a problem than believed by economists, his experiment was seriously flawed in at least three ways. As a result, the data were not convincing and he was forced to conclude correctly that "the test would seem to encourage further work in the field of experimental economics." The question of cooperative vs. selfish behavior remained open.

B. Dawes et al.: Social Dilemmas

While economists were struggling to get their experiments under control, social psychologists were independently studying a phenomenon which, I would argue, is a special case of public goods—social dilemmas. One of the best and most persistent groups has included Robyn Dawes and John Orbell. Let us look at Dawes, McTavish, and Shaklee (1977) for an example of this type of work that avoids many of the flaws of Bohm.

1. Procedures

The experiment is simple.[35] Eight–person groups were created, although sometimes less showed up. A total of 284 subjects were used in 40 groups. Each individual in each group marked an X or an O on a card in private. They were told[36]

> If you choose an O, you will earn $2.50 minus a $1.50 fine for every person who chooses X. If you choose X, you will earn $2.50 plus $9.50 minus $1.50 fine for each person, including yourself, who chooses X. (Dawes, McTavish, and Shaklee 1977, pp. 4–5)[37]

Subjects were also presented the payoffs in the form of one half of Table 2.2. Some groups faced the loss condition; some groups faced the no-loss condition.

Four communication conditions were tried, the details on which can be found in section III.C.3. After discussions, subjects made a single choice, received nominal payoffs in private (but, as shown below, dollar payoffs were determined on the basis of total earnings from their friendship group), and were dismissed separately.

A peculiar aspect of the experimental design is centered around trying not to force subjects to take a loss while at the same time maintaining the standard social dilemma structure. Students were recruited in (friendship) groups of four. This worked as follows:

> Friendship groups met initially with an experimenter who informed them that each person would go to a different decision group where she or he would make a decision with seven other people. The four friends would then return to their friendship group, pool their earnings, and divide them equally among themselves. If the total were negative, no member of the friendship group would receive anything (although people who did not win at least

Table 2.2. Payoff Matrix

Loss Condition				No-Loss Condition			
Payoff to X	Number Choosing		Payoff to O	Payoff to X	Number Choosing		Payoff to O
	X	O			X	O	
—	0	8	2.50	—	0	8	2.50
10.50	1	7	1.00	10.50	1	7	1.00
9.00	2	6	−.50	9.00	2	6	0
7.50	3	5	−2.00	7.50	3	5	0
6.00	4	4	−3.50	6.00	4	4	0
4.50	5	3	−5.00	4.50	5	3	0
3.00	6	2	−6.50	3.00	6	2	0
1.50	7	1	−8.00	1.50	7	1	0
0.00	8	0	—	0.00	8	0	—

$2.00 were contacted later and paid from $1.00 to $2.50 depending on their initial earnings). One member from each friendship group was sent to each of the four communication conditions. Two went to groups in which it was possible to lose money (the loss condition), two to groups in which negative payoffs were truncated at zero (the no-loss condition). Thus the eight groups of four friends separated and formed four groups of eight strangers to play the commons dilemma game. (Dawes, McTavish, and Shaklee 1977, 4)

The design was intended to identify, among other things, the effect of communication on contributions.

2. Results

The data on non-contributions (X) is displayed in Table 2.3.

The main result appears to be (see Dawes 1980) that only 31 percent contribute without communication or with irrelevant communication while 72 percent contribute when relevant communication occurs. A secondary but puzzling result is that the no-loss treatment had apparently no effect.

3. Comments

The first thing to notice is that this really is a public goods environment as described in Section I.D. Let z_i, the initial endowment, be 0. Require that $t_i \in \{0, 9.50\}$. Let $g(t) = [(12/9.5) t]/8$. Finally, let $U^i(t_i, y) = z_i - t_i + g(t)$. For example, if two individuals contribute (their $t = 9.50$) and six do not (their $t = 0$), then

Table 2.3. Non-Contribution (frequency of choosing X)

	Condition			
Condition	No Communication	Irrelevant Communication	Unrestricted Communication	Communication Plus Vote
Loss	.73	.65	.26	.16
No Loss	.67	.70	.30	.42

Source: Dawes, McTavish, and Shaklee 1977, 5.

contributers receive $U^i = 0 - 9.50 + [(12/9.5)(2 \times 9.50)/8] = -6.50$ and non-contributers receive $U^i = 0 - 0 + (12/9.50)(2 \times 9.50)/8 = 3.00$. Compare this to Table 2.2 under the loss condition.

A second observation concerns the lack of impact of the no-loss treatment. Let us look first at the structure of the problem. In the loss condition (ignoring for now the complication created by membership in a friendship group), a decision to defect gains a subject $8 and costs everyone else $1.50. Alternatively spending $9.50 by cooperating generates $1.50/person, no matter what others decide to do. In the no-loss condition, the situation is very different. The marginal cost and gain of a decision to defect by choosing X now depends on the number of other defectors choosing X. This is calculated in Table 2.4.

Thus in the no-loss condition the marginal cost a subject imposes on others by defecting is no larger than in the loss condition and is much less on cooperators. One should expect this to induce more defection *ceteris paribus*. But the marginal benefit to a subject from defecting is also reduced if at least two others defect. This would induce, perhaps, less defection *ceteris paribus*. One way to understand the puzzling fact that the no-loss treatment had no effect is to realize that for the subjects in these experiments the two countervailing effects could easily have cancelled each other.

Another way to measure the tension between the selfish gain from defecting and the public gain from contributing is to calculate the per subject return from switching $1 to contributions.[38] For these experiments this is simply $\partial u^i / \partial t_i$ or, in the loss condition, 1.5/9.5. In the no-loss condition the algebra is somewhat different. If there are, say, five other defectors, then if I contribute I lose $3 and those five gain 1.5 each. Other contributors gain nothing. Therefore the per capita gain per $ is $[(5 \cdot 1 \cdot 5)/8] \cdot (1/3)$. These calculations are made in Table 2.5.

Thus if the subject expects the other defectors to be fewer than four, the no-loss condition should raise the incentive to defect by lowering the marginal gain from cooperating. Similarly, if the subject expects more than three other defectors, the no-loss condition should lower the incentive to defect by raising the marginal benefit of contributing.[39] As can be seen, the incentive effects of the no-loss treatment are complex and out of control. This should give experimentalists reason to

Table 2.4.

Number of Defectors Other Than You	Marginal Cost to Other Defectors	Marginal Cost to Other Cooperators	Marginal Gain to You
0	1.50	1.50	8.00
1	1.50	1.00	8.00
2	1.50	0	7.50
3	1.50	0	6.00
4	1.50	0	4.50
5	1.50	0	3.00
6	1.50	0	1.50
7	1.50	0	0

pause. A relatively simple appearing alteration in the payoff structure, replacing negative numbers with zeros, creates a very complex change in the incentive structure because the direction of the effect depends on the subjects' expectations, which are not controlled by the experimenter.[40]

A third observation is that the fear of losses on the part of the experimenters that led them to create friendship groups and no-loss conditions could have been avoided by recognizing that the experiment is almost identical to that described in section I.A if an initial endowment of \$9.50/subject had been provided. Of course that would have cost an additional \$9.50 × 284, or about \$2,700. An alternative way to save money and to avoid forcing subjects into losses would have been to add \$9.50 to each entry (so all payoffs are non-negative) and then divide all entries by some number to lower the total paid out.[41] A modicum of salience is lost, but one avoids the lack of control from treatments such as the no-loss payoff table or the use of friendship groups to "average" payoffs across trials. Budget constraints force experimentalists to make these choices all the time, and the ability to control payoffs allows one to analyze the potential impact of the choices.

The last observation concerns the most obvious and least informative result: relevant talking matters a lot, but although four different types of communication were tried the data provide little information as to why. Just letting subjects talk in an uncontrolled framework opens up the chances for all sorts of contamination and unintended effects. Are facial expressions important? Which ones? Would one get the same effect if each subject just could say "zero" or "one" once and simultaneously? Would it matter if "zero" were changed to "I won't contribute" and "one" were changed to "I will contribute"? If we are to understand the role of communication in encouraging voluntary contributions, we need better control and precision in our experimental designs. This remains an open problem. The state of the art is described in section III.C.3.

Table 2.5.

Number of Other Defectors	Loss (return on $1)	No Loss (return on $1)
0	.158	.158
1	.158	.12
2	.158	.05
3	.158	.093
4	.158	.16
5	.158	.3
6	.158	.75
7	.158	∞

C. Marwell et al.: The Free-Rider Problem

During the same time as and independently from Dawes, McTavish, and Shaklee (1977), Gerald Marwell was initiating the first systematic experimental research program on the determinants of the voluntary provision of public goods—or, as he put it, on "a fundamental sociological question: when will a collectivity act to maximize its collective interest even though such behavior conflicts with a course of action that would maximize the short-term interests of each individual separately" (Marwell and Ames, 1979). Not just trying to demonstrate that "the effects of free-riding were much weaker than would be predicted from most economic theory," the Marwell group tried to determine what affects the rate of contribution. In the process, they tested the distribution of resources, group size, heterogeneity of benefits, provision points, strength of induced preferences, experience of subjects, the divisibility of the public good, and the economics training of the subjects. This was a carefully thought out research program focused on an important phenomenon. The data generated could not be ignored. In fact it was in response to this study (Marwell and Ames, 1981) that experimental economists finally began laying the groundwork needed to study free riding. No longer would provision of public goods be just a theoretical debate.

1. Procedures

High school students were contacted by telephone and given tokens which could be invested in a private exchange yielding 1¢/token or in a public exchange yielding an amount depending on the total contribution to the public exchange. In the words of the experimenters:

> The experiment was conducted during a single summer and fall using 256 high school students between the ages of 15 and 17. Subjects were divided into 64 four-person groups, resulting in eight groups assigned to each treat-

ment condition. . . . Since each group contained two female and two male subjects, each cell contained 16 males and 16 females.[42] High school-age subjects were selected for study because we felt that the amount of money at stake in their decision (about \$5.00) would be most meaningful to young people and that at the same time these subjects would be old enough to understand the investment decision they had to make. (Marwell and Ames 1979, 1341)[43]

The study was performed in a "natural" setting, in that all interaction with the subjects was by telephone and mail, with subjects remaining in their normal environments throughout the course of the research.

After willingness to participate had been established by phone, the subject was mailed a set of instructions appropriate to the experimental condition to which he or she was assigned. . . .

Within a few days an experimenter telephoned the subject to go over each point in the mailed instructions. This discussion usually lasted 15–20 minutes. . . . An appointment was then made for another telephone conversation the next day (or as soon as possible), in which the subject could invest the study tokens.

In this next telephone call the subject invested the tokens in either of two exchanges (which are explained below) or split them between the two. (1342–43)

The payoff table, given to the subjects, for a large group of eighty with unequal benefits (designated blue and green) and unequal resources is provided in Table 2.6.[44]

One unusual feature (corrected and tested in Marwell and Ames [1980]) about this induced valuation structure is the peak at 7,999 total tokens. At all other levels the marginal benefit from contributing one more token (worth 1¢) is less than 1¢ whereas at 7,999 the marginal benefit is about 6¢. This means there are multiple Nash equilibria: one at which no one contributes (the strong free-rider hypothesis), and a bunch where everyone contributes partially. For example, if all contribute 4/9 of their tokens, then a total of 8,000 from 18,000 is contributed. If the initial endowment is equally distributed, then each begins with 225 tokens, so each is contributing 100 tokens at a cost of \$1 and receiving a marginal return \$5.98. Because of this feature, which Marwell and Ames call a provision point, not contributing is no longer a dominant strategy and, at least in the equal distribution case, contributing 44 percent on average is an obvious focal point.

Group size was varied between four and eighty. In small groups there were a total of 900 tokens and in large groups there were a total of 18,000 tokens. In some small groups one individual might have as many tokens as the provision point, and everyone knew this.[45] But as in the Bohm experiments some of this was a fiction.

Group size was specified as "small" when there were four members in the group and "large" when there were 80 members. However, no individual

Table 2.6. Payoff from Group Exchange in Large, Unequal-Interest, Unequal-Resource Groups

Total Number of Tokens Invested in the Group Exchange by All Group Members	Total Money Earned by the Group ($)	How Much Money You Get	
		Blue ($2^1/4$¢ of each group dollar)	Green ($^9/_{10}$¢ of each group dollar)
0–1,999	0	0	0
2,000–3,999	14.00	0.32	0.13
4,000–5,999	32.00	0.72	0.29
6,000–7,999	54.00	1.22	0.49
8,000–9,999	320.00	7.20	2.93
10,000–11,999	350.00	7.88	3.21
12,000–13,999	390.00	8.78	3.57
14,000–15,999	420.00	9.45	3.85
16,000–17,999	440.00	9.90	4.03
18,000	450.00	10.13	4.12

was actually a member of a group of 80 persons. All groups contained just four real subjects. Because group members never interacted with one another it was possible to tell them that there were any number of members in their group and have them make their investment decisions in terms of this assumption. Telling half our subjects that they were in large, 80-person groups was the only element of deception in this experiment. (Marwell and Ames 1979, 1345)

2. Results

The finding claimed by Marwell and Ames was "a lack of support for . . . the strong free rider."[46] Approximately 57 percent of available resources are invested in the public good. If those subjects whose endowments are greater than the provision point are excluded, then the contribution rate is 41 percent.

In all, tests of the hypotheses derived more or less directly from the economic theory support a *very* weak free-rider hypothesis, with the proviso that groups containing a member whose interest is greater than the cost of provision invest substantially more in public goods than do other groups. No other hypothesized process demonstrated a substantial effect on group investment. (Marwell and Ames 1979, 1352)

A second finding which we will examine more closely in section III.D.1. was that the rate of contribution was less if initial endowments were unequal.

Table 2.7. Payoffs from Group Exchange

Total Number of Tokens Invested in the Group Exchange by All Group Members	Previous Study: Provision Point		Present Study: No Provision Point	
	Total Money Earned by the Group	How Much Money You Get (1¼¢ of each group dollar)	Total Money Earned by the Group	How Much Money You Get (1¼¢ of each group dollar)
0–1,999	0	0	0	0
2,000–3,999	14.00	0.18	44.00	0.55
4,000–5,999	32.00	0.40	88.00	1.10
6,000–7,999	54.00	0.68	132.00	1.65
8,000–9,999	320.00	4.00	176.00	2.20
10,000–11,999	350.00	4.38	220.00	2.75
12,000–13,999	390.00	4.88	264.00	3.30
14,000–15,999	420.00	5.25	308.00	3.85
16,000–17,999	440.00	5.50	352.00	4.40
18,000	450.00	5.63	396.00	4.95

Source: Marwell and Ames 1980, 931.

3. Comments

A number of issues are raised by this study. Many have since been addressed either by Marwell's group (see Marwell and Ames 1980, Alfano and Marwell 1980, and Marwell and Ames 1981) or by the economists who initially thought something must be wrong if there was so much contribution.

The existence of a provision point could quite obviously have increased contributions to 44 percent. But in a later study by Marwell and Ames (1980) the provision point was removed, as in Table 2.7.

The result reported after the change was that "the subjects averaged 113 tokens invested in the group exchange or approximately 51% of the tokens they had available" (932). This would seem to blunt the criticism that subjects were focused on a focal point equilibrium. However, notice that multiple Nash equilibria still exist at positive levels of contribution. For example at 1,999, 3,999, etc., a 1¢ contribution yields a personal return of 55¢. So if the others contribute some amount between 1,946 and 1,999 or 3,946 and 3,999, etc., it pays one to contribute up to 54 tokens. That means there can be many equilibria. Of course, this still does not explain why individuals are contributing 113 on average instead of something between 1 and 54.

A smoother, more continuous payoff schedule would not have this property but would, perhaps, be harder to explain to the subjects. An extremely important methodological question for experimentalists concerns the presentation of the payoffs to the subjects. Does the form matter? Are tables better than graphical presentation? Are functions impossible to use? What if there are four dimensions and graphs and tables become unwieldy? I do not know of any systematic study of these issues,[47] although it is widely recognized, for example, that changes in the placement of information on a computer screen, the amount and form of feedback, and the complexity of instructions all can lead to changes in behavior. It is vitally important to understand these effects if one wants to control induced valuations. The sensitivity of the public goods environment strongly highlights these presentation effects.

A second observation echoes one I made in section II.A on Bohm's research. Even though groups were actually of size 4, half of the subjects were told they were in a group of 80. Since all of the experimental interaction was over a phone, no subject could know for sure what the group size was other than relying on the veracity of the experimenter. How do we know for sure what the subject believed? Since the experimenter was deceptive about $N = 80$, why not about $N = 4$? It is believed by many undergraduates that psychologists are intentionally deceptive in most experiments. If undergraduates believe the same about economists, we have lost control. It is for this reason that modern experimental economists have been carefully nurturing a reputation for absolute honesty in *all* their experiments. This may require costlier experiments where not just 4 subjects but 80 are paid. It may require more clever procedures to get 80 subjects together at one time. But if the data are to be valid, honesty in procedures is absolutely crucial. Any deception can be discovered and contaminate a subject pool not only for that experimenter but for others. Honesty is a methodological public good and deception is equivalent to not contributing. It is important for the profession to remember this, especially since, as John Kagel pointed out to me, it is conventional wisdom that economists free ride.

D. Economists Begin to React

The work of Marwell and Ames described in section II.C provided stark and clean evidence against the standard economic predictions: data confirmed that subjects contribute and do not all free ride. The research caught the attention of the new economic experimentalists who had been focusing on markets and who felt sure that the study by sociologists must be flawed. Theory could not be that wrong, could it?

In this section we will look at two studies which were created in direct response to Marwell and Ames. Indeed the purpose of both Kim and Walker (1984) and Isaac, McCue, and Plott (1985) was to show that Marwell and Ames were wrong and "to explore the behavior of groups within a set of conditions where we expected the traditional model would work with reasonable accuracy" (Isaac, McCue, and Plott 1985, 51). By this they mean they expected to find free-riding and underprovision of the public good, a finding that would be at odds with Marwell and Ames (1979, 1980) and Dawes, McTavish, and Shaklee (1977).

1. Procedures

The main divergence of both Isaac, McCue, and Plott and Kim and Walker from Marwell and Ames was the introduction of repetition; that is, subjects faced the same decision process for a series of periods rather than just making their decisions once. We will describe the Isaac, McCue, and Plott experiment.[48]

> A total of nine experiments were conducted. . . .
>
> Subjects were guaranteed a minimum of $5.00 for participating. Before the instructions were read, subjects were endowed with the $5.00 and told that all earnings in the experiment would be paid in addition to that initial amount. . . . Each subject was assigned one of the two payoff conditions . . . called "high" and "low" payoff condition. . . . The earnings of a subject in a period was the individual's payoff as determined by the level of public good provided that period and the individual's payoff chart minus the amount the individual contributed toward the provision of the public good that period. Thus, the total earnings of an individual during the experiment was the initial payment guarantee plus the sum over all periods of the earnings for each period.
>
> . . . there were ten subjects in each experiment (except experiments 4 and 9) half of which had the high payoff condition and the other half had the low payoff condition. the public good was supplied at a constant marginal cost of $1.30. (Isaac, McCue, and Plott 1985, 53)[49]

Subjects were given a table which indicated both their marginal payoff and total payoff at each level of the public good from 0 to 40. The functions which generated these marginal payoffs, where q is the amount of the public good actually chosen, were $\$.44 - 0.011q$ for the high types and $\$.276 - 0.008q$ for the low types. Given this environment the optimal group allocation, which maximizes total payoff, is at $q = 23$ or 24. The Nash equilibrium is $q = 0$, and it is a single-period dominant strategy for both types not to contribute.

> The decision process for the primary voluntary contributions process proceeds as follows. At the beginning of a period each subject privately wrote on a slip of paper the amount (s)he wished to contribute to the jointly provided public good that period. The paper was collected by the experimenter. The sum of these contributions by the subjects was calculated by the experimenter and was divided by the (constant) cost of the units to obtain the level of the project funded. The level of the project thus funded was announced and used to determine each individual subject's monetary payoff from the payoff chart. This payoff determination was made privately by each individual. The subjects recorded the payoff amount on a form provided as a part of the instructions. The earnings for a subject were calculated as the difference between the monetary payoff determined by the level of the public good and the contribution made by the subject for the provision of the good. A brief period was allowed for the computation of this profit before the next period began.

There were two standard rules regarding the information of participants: first, the subjects were not allowed to communicate with one another during the experiment. Secondly, the individuals had no knowledge about the nature of any payoff charts other than their own. In a technical sense it was *public* information that no one had information about other subject preferences. Furthermore, it was public information that the final period was known with certainty to no one. (Isaac, McCue, and Plott 1985, 57)

2. Results

Did Isaac et al. find evidence that contradicts the Marwell and Ames results? The answer is yes and no. In the first period decisions, contributions strongly resemble those observed by Marwell and Ames. On average, first period contributions yield a public goods level of 8.8, which yields a group payoff of 50 percent of the maximum possible. So the first decisions of subjects are similar in both studies. However, by the fifth period the average number of units provided has dropped to 2.1 for a group payoff, which is 9 percent of the maximum. So, after repetition, one can observe significant underprovision and the free-riding phenomenon.

3. Comments

The relatively high initial contribution rate which declines with repetition has been found by others and is discussed in more detail in section III.B. Kim and Walker (1984) with a similar design found contributions provided 41 percent of the maximal group payoff in the first period and declined to 11 percent by the third period. I have not emphasized their study more because, although they were extremely careful to try to eliminate nine experimental design features of earlier studies which they argued might be invalidating factors,[50] they misled their 5 subjects hoping they would think there were actually 100 subjects.[51] Whether the subjects believed that or not is unknowable.

An innovative feature of both the Isaac, McCue, and Plott and the Kim and Walker experiments was the use of a declining marginal payoff curve (in the public good) for each subject and no constraint on contributions within a period imposed by an initial endowment of tokens (just a total capital constraint across all periods). Such a payoff structure means that the private incentives not to contribute increase as the others' contributions increase. Let us look at that incentive. For the high types, contributing one dollar more to public good provision yields $1/1.30$ units of the good which yields an extra benefit, to that individual, of $m = [.44 - .011q] \, 1/1.30$. When $q = 0$, $m = .3385$; when $q = 10$, $m = .25$; and when $q = 24$ (the group maximal amount), $m = .13$. For low types we have $m = 0.2123$ when $q = 0$, $m = 0.158$ when $q = 10$, and $m = 0.0646$ at $q = 24$. Since $m < 1$ for all q it is a dominant strategy not to contribute. $m - 1$ measures the marginal gain from contributing \$1, $1 - m$ measures the marginal gain from withholding \$1. We will see in the next section that m is an important variable in determining the extent of contributions.[52] To see whether 0.34 is large, let us compute the similar statistic for Dawes et al. (in section II.B).[53] Under the loss condition (see Table 2.2), contributing by choosing O instead of X is equivalent to spending \$9.50 privately to gain an extra \$1.50/person. Thus, $m = 1.5/9.5 = 0.158$. Equivalent numbers are computed for the no-loss condition in Table 2.5. Isaac, McCue, and Plott do not seem to have chosen parameters with incentives not to contribute any stronger than Dawes et al. One might, therefore, conclude that the low contribution rate is attributable to repetition.

That leads to a final comment. The fact that repetition is an important treatment is good to know, but there is no way to know why it is from this paper.[54] Are subjects learning? If so, are they learning how to compute dominant strategies or how to interpret the payoff tables or whether the others are "fair" or . . . ? Maybe the decline in contributions is simply the result of complicated strategic decisions and/or attempts at signaling.[55] Repetition confounds the one-period gains from contribution with the multiple-period gains from communicating. Controls must be created to disentangle strategic and learning effects from each other. Finally, one might wonder whether the decline in contributions is an attempt to punish "unfair" behavior by others, but one must also then wonder how that could be proven. We will take up some of these issues in section III.B.

E. Isaac et al.: Systematic Study by Economists

By 1981, the results of Dawes et al., Marwell and Ames, Kim and Walker, and Isaac, McCue and Plott were fairly well known. The work of the first two groups suggested that free riding was at best a weak phenon.enon in single decision situations; the work of the last two groups seemed to suggest that free riding was an important and strong phenomenon in repeated situations. It was time to try to figure out what was really happening. One of the first systematic studies truly designed to reconcile and understand the reasons for the range of seemingly divergent experimental results was that of Isaac, Walker, and Thomas (1984). Isaac and Walker continue today in systematic efforts to understand behavior in voluntary contribution situations. I include a description of their first work here because of the craftsmanship with which it was designed. But even with a careful design they were left with many unanswered questions. In particular they conclude that "free riding is neither absolutely all pervasive nor always nonexistent . . . . The extremes of strong free riding and near-Lindahl optimal behavior can and do occur" (140). So we still do not know what to expect— anything can happen.

Nevertheless because of the care taken, we do learn something about the existence of

> . . . systematic effects of attributes of the decision setting upon the existence of free riding . . . . General theories about the importance of free riding are not failing because of some inexplicable randomness in previous experiments. (Isaac, Walker, and Thomas 1984, 125)[56]

1. Procedures

Four undergraduate students at the University of Arizona were brought into a room and each was assigned to a PLATO computer terminal. All communication, including instructions to the subjects, was done through the terminals. As they indicate

> One feature of this set of experiments that differs from the previously cited experiments is the use of the Plato computer system for conducting the experiments. This system allows for minimal experimenter-subject interaction during experimental sessions as well as insuring that all subjects see identical programmed instructions and examples for a given experimental design. The use of the computer system also facilitates the accounting process that occurs in each decision period and minimizes subject's transactions costs in making decisions and recalling information from previous decisions. (Isaac, Walker, and Thomas 1984, 116)

Continuing the description:

> The programmed instructions described to the participants the following decision problem: given a specific endowment of resources (tokens), participants faced the decision of allocating them between an individual exchange (private good) and a group exchange (public good). The individual exchange was described as an investment which paid to the investor $.01 for each token invested. . . . The group exchange was explained to the participants as an investment which yielded a specific return per token to the individual as well as the same return to all other participants. . . . The payoff from the group exchange was reported to each participant in the form of a table which gave group and individual returns from the group exchange for various investment levels (from zero up to the total tokens owned by the group.)
>   The information position of each participant can be described as follows: First, each participant knew his own endowment of tokens for each decision trial and the total tokens for the group. He did not know the specific allocation of tokens to other participants. Second, participants knew the exact size of the group and that each participant return from the group exchange was identical. Each participant knew with certainty his own return from the private exchange. Participants were not informed that all other participants received the same return per token from their contributions to the private exchange. Third, each participant knew there would be 10 decision trials and his endowment for each trial would be equal. Finally, it was explained that the monetary gains from each trial were binding and total payments to the participant equaled the sum of his return for the group and individual exchanges totaled over all ten trials. At the end of each trial the participant received information on his return from the individual and group exchange. They were also told the total number of tokens contributed by the group to

the group exchange. Before making an investment decision in any one trial, a participant could obtain this same information for all previous trials. (Isaac, Walker, and Thomas 1984, 117)

Isaac, Walker, and Thomas were interested in identifying factors which increased or decreased free riding and they chose four particular ones: repetition, group size, marginal payoff, and experience. They, of course, hoped to control for all else.

Here each participant knew there would be exactly ten periods and the participants' endowments and payoffs would remain constant across the repetitions. Group size was easy to control: they chose $N = 4$ and $N = 10$. But keeping all other possible effects constant proved more challenging. In particular, they discovered that keeping the marginal individual payoff (a measure of selfish gain) constant and simultaneously keeping the marginal group payoff (a measure of altruistic gain) constant was impossible. Algebraically, the payoffs in this experiment were $u^i = p\,(z - c_i) + a\,(\Sigma c^k)/N$. The marginal individual gain from contributing a token is a/N. Normalize by the cost, p and get $a/pN = M$. This is simply the marginal rate of substitution of the private for the public good, $y = \Sigma c^k$. That is, $M = -\,(\partial u^i/\partial y)\,/\,(\partial u^i/\partial c_i)$. Isaac and Walker call this the marginal per capita return.[57] The marginal group return, computed from $\Sigma u^i = p\,(Nz - \Sigma c^i) + a(\Sigma c^i)$ is a/p. If we increase N and change nothing else then the incentives for individual interest increase relative to the incentives for the group interest. If we increase N but keep M constant by increasing a then the incentives for the group interest increase relative to the incentives for individual interest. It does not seem possible to change N without changing the incentives between group and self interest. Isaac, Walker, and Thomas deal cleverly with this by considering a 2×2 design with $N = 4$ or 10 and $M = 0.3$ or 0.75. Always $p = 1$. Then, since $a = NM$, we have four parameter choices (N, M, a):(4, 0.3, 1.2), (4, 0.75, 3), (10, 0.3, 3), and (10, 0.75, 7.5). These allow comparing a change in N keeping M constant (for both $M = 0.3$ and $M = 0.75$) and comparing a change in N keeping $a = 3$ constant.

Finally, experience is measured as previous participation in similar experimental sessions.

2. Results

The only extant formal theory at the time of these experiments predicts no contributions. That is clearly false as can be seen in Table 2.8 and Figure 2.2.

The average percentage contribution across all treatments is 42 percent, and the average across first periods is 51 percent. These look very much like Dawes et al. and Marwell and Ames. But the variance is high, with contributions ranging from 0 percent (period 8 with $M = 0.3$, $N = 4$, experienced subjects) to 83 percent (period 5 with $M = 0.75$, $N = 4$, and inexperienced subjects). So something more than just 40–60 percent contribution is going on. There are three obvious conclusions. First, increasing M from 0.3 to 0.75 increases the rate of contribution in all cases. The effect is dramatic and strong and in the direction one should expect

Ave. % contributions for

		M =	
		.3	.75
N =	4	19	57
	10	33	59

Figure 2.2.

when the strength of the private (selfish) incentive is reduced relative to the public (altruistic) incentive. Second, experience matters with inexperienced subjects contributing more. This suggests that some form of learning may be occurring. Finally, repetition decreases and group size increases contributions for low $M = 0.3$ but neither seem to have any effect if $M = 0.75$.

3. Comments

This experiment epitomizes the difficulties in doing experimental research in public goods. One can identify general effects which cause free riding, but there are always cases which contradict the general finding. For example, the strongest effect seen in this experiment was that a decrease in M will cause contributions to drop, but in the first period of $N = 10$, $M = 0.3$, and experienced subjects there were 46 percent contributions, whereas in the first period of $N = 10$, $M = 0.75$, and experienced subjects there were only 44 percent contributions. The change in M had no effect. This may say more about the random nature of first period play than it does about the systematic effect of M, but we do not have enough evidence to know for sure. The experimental design, one of the best, is really carefully thought out, and an attempt is made to control the obvious confounding variables. Yet the data are not that precise, and conclusions are hard to draw out. The lack of any helpful theory beyond calculation of marginal rates of substitution prevents a precise analysis of the obvious interaction effects between variables. One experiment will not be enough; a history of comparable efforts may be needed before we fully understand what helps or hinders volunteerism.

A second comment foreshadows the rest of this chapter. The fact that repetition and group size have a noticeable effect when $M = 0.3$ but not when $M = 0.75$ signals a real difficulty with public goods experiments and our ability as economists to extract useful information from these experiments. To see why, let me try to summarize what we know to here.

4. A Summary to This Point

We have looked at six major experiments that have studied behavior in public goods environments. Three claim to have established that selfishness is not as rampant as we might have expected,[58] while three claim to have established that altruism has no staying power.[59] It seems pretty easy to demonstrate that subjects

Table 2.8. Percentage Contribution Data for IWT (1984)

	Period										Average
	1	2	3	4	5	6	7	8	9	10	
All	51.1	47.2	44.1	47.4	46.7	38.1	40.6	35.2	35.8	37.3	42.4
$M = 0.3$	43	35	28	32	26	25	20	17	20	17	26
$M = 0.75$	60	59	60	63	67	51	61	53	52	57	58
Inexperienced	53	53	45	50	55	43	50	41	39	44	47
Experienced	49	41	43	45	38	33	31	30	33	30	37
$N = 4$	50	50	38	40	38	30	36	32	38	30	38
$N = 10$	56	50	40	41	41	34	32	33	37	35	40

contribute. All experiments have periods with at least 40 percent contributions. But determined experimenters also seem to be easily able to extinguish most but not all of the altruistic impulse (if that is what it is) through low marginal payoffs and repetition. We need to understand the causes of these observations better. But none of these experiments is truly comparable with any of the others. Look at the summary of the designs and results in Table 2.9. At least two features, sometimes more, change between any two experiments.

The two closest designs may be Marwell and Ames (1979) and Isaac, Walker, and Thomas (1984), but even they differ in marginal payoff, provision point, and repetition. The difference in designs implies that sometimes subjects contribute and sometimes they do not. The research problem is to discover when and why. I suppose that if one had all the data from these six studies one could do some complex multivariate statistical analysis, but experiments are supposed to free economists from that necessity.[60]

Our task would be easier if there were significant comparability across experiments and experimenters. However, as we will see in section III, there is precious little comparability, and perhaps as a result a lot of uncertainty still remains about behavior in public goods environments.

III. What Improves Cooperation?

In section II we looked at some of the pioneering efforts in the experimental analysis of behavior in the presence of public goods. We found that not everyone free-rides all the time. That subjects would voluntarily provide public goods in some situations is amply demonstrated by Dawes et al., Marwell et al., and the early periods of Isaac et al. This early work also identified two factors which seemed to improve cooperation: relevant communication (by Dawes et al.) and increases in the marginal payoff for contributing (by Isaac et al.). One factor which seemed to decrease cooperation, repetition, was also identified (by Isaac,

Table 2.9. Summary of Designs and Results

	B	DMS	MA	IMP	KW	IWT
Numbers	?[a]	8	4,80[a]	10	100[a]	4,10
Marginal payoff	?	0.16, 0.16–0.75	Nonlinear	0.34[b]–0.06	0.02[b], 0.05, 0.07	0.3, 0.75
Repetition	No	No	No	Yes[c]	Yes[c]	Yes
Provision point	Yes	No	Yes	No	No	No
Tokens	No	1 per person	Yes	No	No	Yes
Heterogeneity	?	No	No, yes	Yes	No	No
Experience	No	No	No	No	No	Yes, no
Communication	No	Yes, no	No	No	No	No
Moral suasion	Yes	No	No	No	No	No
Contributions						
Initial period	N.A.	31%[d]	41%	50%	68%	51%
Last period	N.A.	N.A.	N.A.	9%	8%	19%

Sources and notes: B = Bohm (1972); DMS = Dawes, McTavish, and Shaklee (1977); MA = Marwell and Ames (1979); IMP = Isaac, McCue, and Plott (1985); KW = Kim and Walker (1984); IWT = Isaac, Walker, and Thomas (1984). Question mark indicates uncontrolled design. Two entries mean both treatments were tried.

[a] Deception played a role.

[b] Declines as q increases.

[c] Subjects did not know number of repetitions.

[d] Without communication (it was 71% with communication).

McCue, and Plott). As one can see from Table 2.9 in section II, there were at least six other factors which were deemed potential influences on behavior: numbers, provision points, number of tokens, heterogeneity of payoffs and endowments, experience, and moral suasion. Of course one might think of many other factors, and the next cohort of experimentalists have done just that. It is time now to try to understand the state of the art today. I tried in section II to give the reader an idea about how experiments with public goods have been conducted; in this section I am going to concentrate on what modern experimental research has discovered and, therefore, where the next work might begin.[61] The reader is strongly encouraged to consult the original papers for details of the experimental designs.

One of the major goals of research on public goods is to discover the nature of the relationship $\mu\ (e,\ (M,\ g)) = \{a\}$: that is, contributions $= \mu$ (environment, mechanism). The issue is not so much honest revelation of preferences as it is what level of public goods will be provided by subjects and how that is affected by environment and mechanism. In Table 2.10, I have listed 19 variables various

Table 2.10. Stylized Facts

	Effect on Percentage Contributions	Section
I. Environment—easy to control		
MPCR (marginal per capita return)	++	III.C
Numbers	00	III.C
Repetition	−−	III.B
Common knowledge	+	III.D
Gender	0	III.D
Homogeneity (symmetry)	+	III.D
Thresholds	+	III.A
II. Systemic—difficult to control		
Beliefs	+	III.D
Economics training	−−	III.D
Experience	−−	III.B
Friendship/Group identification	+	III.D
Learning	0	III.B
Altruism, fairness	?	III.E
Effort	?	III.E
Risk aversion	?	III.E
III. Design variables		
Communication	++	III.C
Rebates	+	III.C
Unanimity	−	III.D
Moral suasion	?	III.E

Note: + means increase, 0 means no effect, − means decrease, and ? means that I do not believe these have been measured yet. A double symbol means the effect is strong and apparently replicable. A single symbol, other than ?, means the effect is apparently there but weak and difficult to replicate.

researchers have identified as having an effect on the level of contributions. I have found it useful to group the variables identified by existing research into three main categories: the *environment* (numbers, strength of incentives, extent of homogeneity, thresholds imposed by the production technology, initial information structure, gender, . . .), *systemic variables* (fairness concepts, altruism, risk attitudes, beliefs, . . .), and *design variables* (such as unanimity rules, structured communication, and moral suasion). The variables in the first two categories are aspects of what I have called the environment: I have split them into two parts to emphasize that some are more easily controllable with current experimental technologies. In particular, those identified as environmental are relatively straightforward to control, while those listed as systemic are currently more difficult. The variables in the category, labeled design variables, are factors identified by experimentalists which should be more properly thought of as aspects of institutional design. These variables are amenable to change and the mechanism designer can use them to improve solutions to the free-rider problem.

In Table 2.10, I summarize what seems to be the consensus of experimentalists about the effect of a change in one of these variables on the change in total contributions as a percent of the efficient level. Some effects are more certain than others, in that replication has confirmed initial findings. Understanding behavior would be easier if each of these variables had a separable and identifiable effect on contributions.[62] Unfortunately that is not true: the details of the environment seem to matter. Left unexplained in the table are what I call cross-effects. The latter are very important and not well tracked in the literature.[63] In some cases, cross-effects may even reverse the direction of effect of a variable. We will see this below.

I organize the rest of this chapter as follows. In section III.A, I describe a very important structural feature in environments with public goods which must be tracked in order to make comparisons across experiments. In section III.B, I take up results dealing with repetition and the related issues of learning and experience. In section III.C, I cover the strong effects of marginal payoff (and its related problem of numbers) and communication. In III.D, I turn to weak effects. In III.E, I discuss some of the factors which may be important but of which little is known primarily because of an inability to control their impact on an experiment. In section IV, I conclude with some final thoughts on what we really know and where we might go.

A. Thresholds and Provision Points

To compare data across experiments one must recognize that there is a fundamental difference in the structure of incentives when a threshold or provision point exists from when it does not. Without a threshold the voluntary contributions mechanism is usually a prisoners' dilemma game; with a threshold it becomes a game of chicken.[64] See Table 2.11. In the former it is a dominant strategy not to cooperate, and there is (usually) a unique noncooperative equilibrium which is not Pareto-optimal.[65] In the game of chicken there are generally many noncooperative equilibria, each of which may be optimal and none of which is dominant, and the task of the players is to coordinate their actions to select one. The environments of Dawes et al. (1977) and of Isaac and Walker (1988b) are of the prisoners' dilemma variety. The environment of Marwell and Ames (1979) is more like a game of chicken. It is not surprising that we see different results in these two types of environments. For example, if the players can talk, one might suspect that in the game of chicken they would correlate their strategies. This is even easier in repeated play because they can then try to equalize sacrifice. But one might expect that communication would have a lesser effect in dilemma games since there is no problem of coordination.

Table 2.11. Prisoner's Dilemma and Chicken

	Prisoner's Dilemma (MPCR = 0.75)		Chicken (Require 1C)	
	D	C	D	C
D	(4, 4)	(7, 3)	(4, 4)	(10, 6)
C	(3, 7)	(6, 6)	(6, 10)	(6, 6)

Note: payoffs = (row player, column player); D = do not contribute, defect;
   C = contribute, cooperate.

For now let us address the simpler problem: do thresholds cause contributions to increase, *ceteris paribus*. One often sees campaign targets set when raising funds for charities or university endowments. Do these work? We do not have much evidence but what there is seems to suggest that increases in thresholds increase contributions but also increase the probability the target will not be reached.[66] There are many papers reporting on experiments with thresholds, but six actually vary the threshold to determine its effect.[67] Marwell and Ames (1980) actually compare contributions with and without the provision point discussed in section II.C. They found no significant difference. However, as mentioned in section II.C.3, there remained a problem: while they did eliminate the major jump in payoff at 8,000 tokens, in their no-provision point design there are still actually nine provision points since the payoff is constant across 2,000 token intervals (see Table 2.7, in section II.C). What changed was marginal payoff at each provision point: some increased and some decreased. So it is not obvious in what direction the provision points are moving. Isaac, Schmidtz, and Walker (1988) provide a better study of this problem in the context of the Isaac, Walker, and Thomas (1984) design described in section II.E. They consider three different provision point levels and keep all else constant, such as repetition and marginal pay-off. This is done by paying subjects $p^i(z^i - c^i) + A \cdot a(\Sigma\ c^j)/N$ where $A = 0$ if $\Sigma c^i < T$, and $A = 1$ if $\Sigma c^i \geq T$, where T is the threshold or provision point. They find that increases in T increase contributions but also increase the proportion of times that $\Sigma c^i < T$. They also find that the increase in contributions disappears with repetition, so the failure of provision is because $\Sigma c_i < T$ eventually dominates. Suleiman and Rapoport (1992) confirm this with a similar study. The main difference is that they provide a payoff of $u^i = p_i\ (z_i - c_i) + Ar$; that is, the return from the public good is independent of the total contributions.[68] They also found contributions increased with T, and the probability of provision decreased.[69] The numbers are reported in Table 2.12. It is not obvious from these data what the efficiency, $\Sigma\ u^i$ divided by the max possible, levels were. Dawes, Orbell, Simmons, and van de Kragt (1986) report similar results when subjects make an all or none contribution one time only.[70] Here everyone could contribute $5 or $0. If at least K of 7 contributed, everyone got $10: contributors end up with $10, non-

Table 2.12.

Threshold	Average Contributions (%)	Provision (%)
10	53	85
15	66	80
20	73	39

contributors receive $15. They find that for $K = 3$, 51 percent contribute, and for $K = 5$, 64 percent contribute. I could not calculate the provision proportions from the data reported.

So increases in thresholds seem to increase the percent contributed and lower the probability of provision. But in a followup study Rapoport and Suleiman 1993 report results that could cause one to worry about accepting this proposition too quickly. Changing the experiment by randomly assigning the endowments z_i to be 3, 4, 5, 6, and 7, they found that changes in the threshold had no significant effect on the percent contributed. With $N = 5$, the average individual contributions were 54 percent, 63 percent, and 60 percent for $T = 10$, 15, and 20, respectively.[71] The provision percentages were 80 percent, 65 percent, and 12 percent respectively. Palfrey and Rosenthal 1991a find similar ambiguities in a heterogeneous environment. There $N = 3$, marginal payoffs are heterogeneous, and each agent has one token. The threshold is K of N. They find that percentage contributions increase as K is increased from 1 to 2 but decrease as K is increased from 2 to 3.

In the Palfrey and Rosenthal 1991a framework, pure strategy Bayesian equilibrium theory predicts a decrease from $K = 1$ to 2 and from $K = 2$ to 3 for their parameters. However, a careful look at mixed strategy equilibria for these environments with thresholds suggests that game theory would predict that changes in the threshold can have an ambiguous effect on changes in contributions (see, e.g., Palfrey and Rosenthal 1988). The ambiguity is resolved only when specific parameters are known. The theory is telling us we should not expect a definitive answer to the question,"does an increase in threshold increase contributions," which is independent of other factors. The data are supporting that view.

B. Experience, Repetition, and Learning

A natural explanation for the large rate of contribution in many voluntary contribution experiments can be found in the inexperience of the subjects. Perhaps a 40 to 60% contribution rate occurs simply because if one must contribute a number between 0 and Z and does not understand the implications of the act, then a natural choice is somewhere in the middle.[72] This would be especially true of experiments such as Isaac and Walker in which payoffs are linear. Clearly it is important to be able to discover whether the data are simply the result of confusion and inexperience or the result of some more purposeful behavior. One way to do this is to create payoffs such that the two key points of interest, the dominant strategy contribution and the group optimum contribution are moved to the interior of [0, 100]. That is discussed in section IV. We explore another way here.

Repetition (not replication) has become a common feature of much research in experimental economics[73] in an effort to eliminate or control for at least two types of experience effects: learning how to play the particular class of games, such as what keys to press in a computerized continuous auction or how to read a particular payoff schedule, and learning about the specific game one is in, such as what the environment is and what the other subjects are like. One can easily control for the first type of experience by simply bringing back subjects who have previously participated in similar experiments. This has not been done as often as one might suspect. The data from Isaac, Walker, and Thomas (1984) and Palfrey and Prisbrey (1993) suggest that subjects who have previously been in a voluntary contribution experiment contribute less than those who are first-timers but still more than zero. Palfrey and Prisbrey (1993) suggest that experience does not actually have a significant effect on the percentage of contributions, because, although experienced subjects contribute less, they also make fewer errors. They also find that experienced subjects are more responsive to MPCR. Two other studies which control for experience this way (Marwell and Ames 1980 and Isaac, Schmidtz, and Walker 1988), however, find no significant effect. There was a threshold in the latter two and not in the former. Does that explain the different data? We do not know.[74]

Significant decreases from repetition in non-threshold environments are reported by Isaac, Walker, and Thomas (1984), Isaac, McCue, and Plott (1985), Isaac, Walker, and Williams (1990) for $N = 4$ and $N = 10$, Brookshire, Coursey, and Redington (1989a), Kim and Walker (1984), Brown-Kruse and Hummels (1992), Banks, Plott, and Porter (1988), Sell and Wilson (1990), Andreoni (1988b), and Isaac and Walker (1987). Experiments in which repetition had no effect[75] and in which there was no threshold are reported by Isaac, Walker, and Williams (1990) for $N = 40$ and $N = 100$ and by Palfrey and Prisbrey (1993). In experiments with thresholds the results are considerably more mixed. Bagnoli and McKee (1991) report a positive effect on contributions, Palfrey and Rosenthal (1991a) report a small drift towards Nash equilibrium, and Suleiman and Rapoport (1992) and Isaac, Schmidtz, and Walker (1988) report a negative effect. From a theoretical perspective the natural question is not whether contributions decline but rather whether convergence to Bayes-Nash equilibrium is occurring. With no threshold, the equilibrium is zero contribution and convergence seems to be empirically verified (at least for small N). With a threshold, there are usually multiple Nash equilibria, so the convergence question is more clouded: we need to look at details other than simple increases or decreases. Since the data and theory for the no threshold environments are more straightforward, let us concentrate on those for now.

The data suggest there is a deterioration in contributions after some number of iterations. Is this due to strategy or experience? From a theoretical point of view, one must consider significantly different models depending on which is really happening. It is possible to construct a model in which there is a very small probability that some subjects are not fully rational (i.e., they use dominated strategies) and in which even fully rational selfishly maximizing subjects, even perhaps economists, would contribute all or most tokens—at least in the early periods. Towards the last iteration, the rational players will not contribute. Thus, one should observe the development of a bimodal distribution in contributions as iteration continues. Isaac, Walker, and Williams (1990) have data somewhat like this in large groups of 100. Such a theory can be found in Kreps et al. (1982) and McKelvey and Palfrey (1992). If, on the other hand, subjects are simply trying to learn (by some suitable groping process) what the appropriate one-trial strategy is, given this environment and this collection of subjects, then a better model would be something like a learning algorithm found in Miller and Andreoni (1991), Boylan (1990), Crawford and Haller (1990), or Kalai and Lehrer (1990). If everyone learns, then one should observe the contributions converge to the non-cooperative equilibrium after enough periods. This seems to happen after 10 iterations in small groups. We do not know how long it would take in large groups.[76]

The experimental puzzle is to develop designs which allow separation of these two types of temporal phenomena and help us identify those aspects of the institution which speed learning or channel strategy when that is desirable. Andreoni (1988b) represents a good start on this complicated problem. In a unique design he compared two treatments called Strangers and Partners in an Isaac and Walker environment with $p = 1$, $a/N = .5$, $N = 5$, and $z_i = 50$, all of which were known to everyone. The Partners played repeatedly 10 times just as in Isaac, Walker, and Thomas (1984). The Strangers were 20 subjects randomly reassigned by computer to groups of 5 after each repetition. The idea was to separate strategic play by Partners from no strategic play with Strangers. Thus one should see only learning in the Strangers condition but see learning and strategy in the Partners condition. The data are in Table 2.13 (Andreoni 1988b).[77]

Surprisingly, contrary to received strategic theory, Partners contribute less than Strangers and the difference increases over time. Andreoni further argues that since there is no reason Strangers should learn slower than Partners, learning alone is not responsible for the observed decay in contributions. But strangers are in a noisier environment and, therefore, may indeed learn more slowly. A strategic hypothesis, that giving occurs early because it generates more later, appears to be inconsistent with the data. A learning hypothesis might be consistent. That decay in contributions occurs with repetition in environments with a zero dominant strategy is indisputable. What explains the phenomenon remains to be found. Follow up research is needed.

Table 2.13. Average Investment in Public Good per Subject

	Round										All Rounds
	1	2	3	4	5	6	7	8	9	10	
Partners	24.1	22.9	21.5	18.8	18.4	16.8	12.8	11.2	13.7	5.8	16.6
Strangers	25.4	26.6	24.3	22.2	23.1	21.9	17.8	19.7	14.0	12.2	20.7
Difference	−1.3	−3.7	−2.8	−3.4	−4.7	−5.1	−5.0	−8.5	−0.3	−6.4	−4.1

C. Strong Effects

In this section I want to concentrate on identifying those factors which, like repetition, have a well-documented effect on contributions in the voluntary provision of public goods. There are really just two factors that fall into this category: one environmental, marginal payoffs; and one institutional, communication. I will, however, include a discussion of numbers and rebates since their effects are virtually impossible to disentangle from those of marginal payoffs.

1. Marginal Payoffs and Rebates

Two of the variables most easily controlled in public goods experiments are the marginal benefit of the public good relative to the private and the number of subjects in a group. In terms of our general model, an agent's payoff is $u^i(w^i - t^i, g(\Sigma t_j))$. To see the incentives for contributing, differentiate with respect to t^i, and get $-u^i_x + u^i_y g_z$. Normalizing by u^i_x yields $-1 + (u^i_y/u^i_x)g_z$. It is the product of the marginal rate of substitution, (u^i_y/u^i_x), and the marginal rate of transformation, g_z, which determines the marginal incentive to contribute. Isaac, Walker, and Thomas (1984) called this product the marginal per capita return, MPCR. For their environment, $u = p(w - t) + y$ and $g(\Sigma t_j) = a/N(\Sigma t_j)$ and, therefore, MPCR = $(1/p)(a/N)$. Isaac, Walker, and Thomas (1984) and Isaac and Walker (1988b) began a systematic exploration of the effect of changes in MPCR on rates of contribution. As was evident from the data presented earlier in section II.D, Table 2.8, increasing the MPCR from 0.3 to 0.75 increases the rate of contribution independent of N for $N = 4$ or $N = 10$. Thus, although the strong game-theoretic prediction of free riding is false, subjects do appear to respond to incentives in a predictable and systematic fashion. Does other research confirm this? Unfortunately not very many other experimenters have controlled the marginal payoff (MPCR) to assess its effect on contributions. But those that have generally find observations consistent with the hypothesis that marginal incentives matter.[78] Kim and Walker (1984) increase marginal payoffs, in the midst of their experiment, after repetitions 3 and 11. Their MPCR changes from 0.02 to 0.05 to 0.07. Each change is accompanied by a significant increase in contributions. Brown-

Table 2.14. Percentage Contributing

	$K = 3$ of 7	$K = 5$ of 7
Baseline	51	64
No fear	61	65
No greed	86	93

Kruse and Hummels (1992) confirm the effect for MPCR = 0.5 and 0.3. Saijo and Yamaguchi (1992) confirm the effect for MPCR = 0.7 and 1.43.[79]

We can also get some indirect evidence on the effect of marginal payoffs from two other sources: experiments with asymmetric payoffs and experiments with rebates. An example of the former can be found in section II.D, where Isaac, McCue, and Plott (1985) found (conclusion 7) that "individuals in the high payoff condition contribute more than individuals in the low payoff condition"(64). Marwell and Ames (1979) also report more contributions from "high interest" (blue) subjects (see Figure 2.6 in section II.C for the payoffs) than "low interest" (green) subjects. Other confirming evidence with asymmetric payoffs can be found in Brookshire, Coursey, and Redington (1989a), Fisher, Isaac, Schatzberg, and Walker (1988), Palfrey and Rosenthal (1991a), and Rapoport and Suleiman (1993). One of the more powerful sets of supporting data is in Palfrey and Prisbrey (1993), who mimic the Isaac and Walker framework but allow the private value to be asymmetric across subjects. In particular $u^i = P_i (z - c_i) + a\Sigma c_i$ where P_i is private information, drawn randomly and uniformly from the set $\{1, 2, \ldots, 20\}$. Here it is a dominant strategy to contribute if $P_i < a$ and to not contribute if $P_i > a$. They used a total of 64 subjects in four different experimental sessions involving 4-person groups. A very simple probit model, Probability (contribute) = f (constant + α (a/p)) is able to predict correctly 83 percent of the observations.[80]

Clearly, the marginal payoff a/p is an important effect.[81] This is true whether thresholds are present or not. Indeed one other source of confirming data comes from the analysis of rebates in threshold situations. Dawes, Orbell, Simmons, and van de Kragt (1986) study two changes in their simple payoff structure, both of which increase the marginal payoff to contributing *ceteris paribus*. In their baseline condition each subject could contribute or keep $5. If at least K of N contribute, then all get $10. In a "no fear" condition all contributors get their $5 back if less than K contribute. In a "no greed" condition subjects who do not contribute only get $5 more if at least K contribute. The data are in Table 2.14. In another study with thresholds, Isaac, Schmidtz, and Walker (1988) also find a significant effect for rebates.

The only report which might cast any doubts on the strong effect of increasing marginal payoffs can be found in Isaac, Walker, and Williams (1990). Here they begin to explore the effect of large numbers ($N = 40$ and 100) without the deception which characterized others' earlier attempts. They found, with these large numbers, that varying MPCR between 0.3 and 0.75 had no significant effect on percentage contributions. In fact, it was not until MPCR dropped from 0.3 to 0.03 that any significant decline in contributions occurred. Either increasing numbers has a dampening second order effect on the effect of marginal payoffs or there was something else in their experimental design which caused the effect to be eliminated. Let us see what we can find out about numbers.

2. Numbers

The second variable that is most easy to control is the number of subjects. One of the longest running debates among theorists, other than whether contributions will occur at all, is whether contributions increase or decrease with group size.[82] Those arguing for a decrease in Σt_i as N increases generally believe that, in larger groups, non-cooperative behavior is more difficult to detect and, therefore, self-interested subjects will be more willing not to contribute. The argument that an increase in Σt_i will occur as N increases usually relies on the fact that the marginal effect on $\Sigma_i u^i$ with respect to t_i increases as N increases and, therefore, any tendency toward altruism should be reinforced as N increases. In the Isaac and Walker environments $u^i = p_i(z_i - c_i) + a/N (\Sigma_j > c_j)$. The marginal (selfish) incentive to contribute is $a/p_i N = \text{MPCR}$. The marginal (selfish) incentive not to contribute is $p_i N/a$. The group benefit if $p_i = p$ for all i is $\Sigma u^i = p (\Sigma z_i - \Sigma c_i) + a(\Sigma_j c_j)$, so the marginal (altruistic) incentive to cooperate is a/p. If we keep a and p constant but increase group size, we increase the marginal selfish incentive not to contribute relative to the marginal altruistic incentive to contribute; causing contributions to decrease with N. If we keep a/N and p constant and increase N, we cause the marginal altruistic incentive to contribute to increase relative to the marginal selfish incentive not to contribute and cause contributions to increase. Does that happen? What do the data say?

While there are many experiments with different numbers, and different MPCRs, there are only a small number which systematically vary N as one of the treatments. Of those, only Isaac and Walker's group recognized the intimate relationship between MPCR and N. Three studies by Marwell and Ames (1979), Chamberlin (1978), and Bagnoli and McKee (1991) involved provision points. Marwell and Ames (1979) (see section II.C) found no effect from varying numbers. They did, however, adjust payoffs between large and small groups.

> Keeping the situations of subjects in large and small groups otherwise comparable also required keeping mean interest (^-V_i) and resources constant over groups. This meant that for large groups the total resources and interest had to be 20 times as large as in small groups. For this reason cutting points for changes in payoffs were also kept proportionate, so that, for example, 20 times as many tokens had to be invested by the large group before the payoffs became larger than one cent per token. Thus, the mean contributions were required to be identical for identical effects. (Marwell and Ames 1979, 1346)

I think this means that a/N was held constant as N increased, but I cannot really tell from their description. Chamberlin (1978) found a negative effect on contributions as N increased. Bagnoli and McKee (1991) also found a negative effect particularly in early periods. They conjecture that "individuals in a larger group may find it more difficult to focus on a particular equilibrium vector of contributions."[83]

I find the Isaac and Walker experiments without thresholds most revealing because they attempt to control for the purely private incentives (measured by MPCR) in order to isolate the effect of numbers, and they have tried large numbers without deception. Initially they used groups of 4 and 10 and MPCRs of 0.3 and 0.75. Those data were displayed in section II.D in Table 2.8. They found that MPCR mattered and N did not. The only way N mattered was if a were held constant causing a crowding effect where MPCR $= a/(pN)$ declines as N increases. Believing they had discovered a systemic relation between contribution and numbers, they then designed with Williams an experiment for $N = 40$ and $N = 100$. In doing so they had to overcome several methodological difficulties. To avoid the extremely high cost of such experiments, they developed a new method for rewarding their subjects. In their own words:

> As explained in the class handout, subject i's experimental dollar earnings were converted into the following "performance index" prior to being converted into extra-credit points:
>
> $$\frac{i\text{'s Actual Earnings} - i\text{'s Minimum Possible Earnings}}{i\text{'s Maximum Possible Earnings} - i\text{'s Minimum Possible Earnings}}$$
>
> which can range from 0 to 1 for each individual. At the end of the final round, this fraction was computed for each individual (based on earnings in all rounds), multiplied by 3, and added to the subject's final grade average. Thus, the range of possible extra-credit points was [0, 3]. The performance index was used so that the maximum and minimum possible extra-credit earnings did not depend upon the design cell assignment. All classes from which subjects were drawn utilized a 100-point scale and, with minor modifications, used a standard mapping of point totals into letter grades (A = 90's, B = 80's, etc.). Furthermore, Indiana University allows + and − letter grades, so a unique letter grade typically comprised a 3 to 4 point interval.
>
> We have spent a great deal of time considering questions of practicability and fairness in the use of extra-credit points as a motivator. On the issue of fairness, we can report that of the hundreds of subjects who participated in the VCM-MS-XC experiments,[84] we do not know of a single grade appeal in which these extra credit points were an issue. (Isaac, Walker, and Williams 1990, 6–7).[85]

A second methodological innovation for $N = 40$ and $N = 100$ involved a technique which allowed subjects to make decisions when not all 100 were in the same room at the same time. In particular, each decision-making round lasted several days, rather than a few minutes, so students could access the experiment on a network and make their decisions. This contrasts with the typical single session which usually lasts only an hour or two. As they note:

> The experimental procedures outlined above represent a logical link between standard single-session laboratory experiments and actual field experiments. Certainly some experimental control is lost relative to a strictly controlled laboratory setting, however, the gain in feasible group sizes, the real time between allocation decisions, and the more "natural" communication opportunities available in this environment add an element of parallelism with non-experimental settings that could have important methodological and behavioral ramifications. (Isaac, Walker, and Williams 1990, 6)

Both innovations are clever and important advances in the methodology of experimental economics, and if their innovations are valid, Isaac, Walker, and Williams have found a very inexpensive way to do experimental economics. They did run control sessions in order to check validity. In a comparison to their earlier results with cash payments they claim that "for a specific group size and MPCR, the aggregate pattern of token allocations ... [is] very similar." A significant difference (through a t-test) in the percentage of tokens contributed is found in only one round.

Contrary to most economists' expectations, not only were contributions higher with large N, but the effect of MPCR was significantly diluted. In particular they make three observations based on their data with large N.

> First, the impact from variations in the magnitude of the marginal per-capita return from the public good (MPCR) appears to vanish over the range [0.30, 0.75]. Second, with an MPCR of 0.30, groups of size 40 and 100 provide the public good at higher levels of efficiency than groups of size 4 and 10. Third, with an MPCR of 0.75, there is no significant difference in efficiency due to group size. (Isaac, Walker, and Williams 1990, 13)

Finally, in an attempt to rescue the "MPCR effect" they ran three single session 40 person experiments with money (at a cost of about $900 each) and an MPCR = 0.3. They found no deterioration in contributions but, in fact, a slight increase over the "no money" experiments. Continuing their rescue attempt they ran 4 experimental sessions with $N = 40$ but MPCR = 0.03, three with credit points and multiple sessions and one with money and a single session. Here they finally found contribution rates that looked more like the $N = 4$, MPCR = 0.3 experiments. Instead of using large numbers to hide one's selfishness, subjects actually seem to become more cooperative in the larger groups. This would be consistent with the existence of the selfish vs. altruistic tradeoff described earlier where holding $a/(Np)$ constant and increasing N increases contributions. But another possible implication of all this is that voluntary contributions experiments with public goods, as many do them, are yielding data which are not very sensitive to the incentives provided by the experimentalists.

What do we now know and what do we need to find out? Clearly, subjects appear to respond positively to increases in their MPCR although the effect is diluted in large groups. To really pin down the relationship between contributions, MPCR, and N will cost a lot of money and effort since we need to fill in data between $N = 10$, 40, and 100. We also need observations for more values of MPCR than just 0.03, 0.3, and 0.75. There are many other observations on various pairs of MPCR and N in the literature, but they need to be extracted and tabulated.[86] This would be, to me, a very interesting subject for a dissertation.

Also, can we now conclude altruism is at work? Rather than running a very large number of experiments, one could try to leap to an understanding by creating a new theory which explains or predicts a relationship $(\Sigma t_i/N) = f$ [MPCR, N, α] where Σt_i is total contributions, N is the number of subjects, and α represents parameters, perhaps uncontrolled and unobserved. The development of such a theory would also point to new experiments which might require new theory, and so forth. Let us see how this might work.

Standard game theory predicts, for the Isaac and Walker environment that

$$\frac{(\Sigma t_i)}{N} = 0 = f(M, N, \alpha)$$

for all $M < 1$ where $M = \text{MPCR} = a/(pN)$. Try as they might, however, experimental economists have been unable to support that theory in the lab. Based on their own experiments, Isaac, Walker, and Williams (1990) suggest a theory based on the concept of a successful group effort.[87] The idea is that those who contribute are happy to do so if at least those who do are better off than at the initial endowment. This will be true if and only if $[(\Sigma t_i)/N] a > p$. This means there is a minimally sized successful group $S = 1/(\text{MPCR})$ so that if at least S contribute, then those who do are satisfied. This effectively creates a threshold payoff in utility as opposed to dollars. Keeping MPCR fixed as N grows, S becomes a smaller percentage and, presumably, more likely to occur, so agents are more likely to risk contributing. One can formalize this and generate an equation for the expected percentage contribution

$$E\left[\frac{(\Sigma t_i)}{N}\right] = \Pi\, [pZ, \text{MPCR}, N]$$

where the form of Π depends on the unknown and uncontrolled distribution of the subjects' tastes for success. But $\Pi(\cdot)$ is estimable from enough data. It can be shown that $\partial\Pi/\partial M > 0$, $\partial\Pi/\partial p < 0$, and $\partial\Pi/\partial z < 0$, independently of that distribution. One other implication is that if payoffs are increased, that is if $u = \lambda\,[p(z - t) + a/N \Sigma t]$ where $\lambda > 1$, then (since this does not change the MPCR but does increase pz) we should see contributions decline. All implications are testable in the lab.

Another theory, based on the idea that subjects trade off selfish payments against altruism would suggest a personal utility payoff of $V^i[u^i, \Sigma u^k]$ where u^i is paid to i and Σu^k is the total paid to all subjects. Approximating V^i linearly yields $u^i + \beta\Sigma_k u^k$. For the Isaac and Walker environment

$$V^i = [p(z - t^i) + \frac{a}{N} \Sigma\, t^k] + \beta\, [p\, (Nz - \Sigma\, t^n) + a\Sigma t^k].$$

Thus, i will contribute if and only if $\beta \geq (1 - M)/NM - 1)$. For this theory, the distribution of β is uncontrolled and unobservable, but the predictions are that[88]

$$E\, [(\Sigma t_i)\, /N] = \gamma\, \left[\, \frac{1 - M}{NM - 1}\, \right]$$

where $\gamma' < 0$. Thus $\partial\gamma/\partial N > 0$, $\partial\gamma/\partial pz = 0$, and $\partial\gamma/\partial M > 0$. As opposed to the model based on minimally sized successful groups, this model predicts no change in percentage contribution if payoffs are increased since M will not change.

A third theory, based on the idea that subjects care about fairness or equality, would have $V^i = u^i + \delta\, (1/N)\, [\Sigma_j\, (u_j - \bar{u})^2]$ where $\bar{u} = (1/N)\, \Sigma_j\, u^j$, and $\delta < 0$. When $u^i = p\, (z - t^i) + (a/N)\, \Sigma_j\, t_j$ then

$$V^i = p\, (z - t^i) + a\bar{t} + \frac{\delta}{N} \Sigma_j\, [\, p^2(\bar{t} - t^j)^2\,]$$

where $\bar{t} = (1/N)\, \Sigma_j\, t_j$. Differentiate V^i with respect to t_i, set it equal to zero and get

$$-p + \frac{a}{N} - 2\frac{\delta}{N}\, p^2\, (\bar{t} - t_i) = 0$$

or

$$t_i = \bar{t} + \frac{N(1 - M)}{2\delta p}\, .$$

The expected percentage contribution is therefore

$$E\, [\%C] = E\, \left(\frac{\Sigma t_i}{N}\right) = \frac{\Sigma_j\, \bar{t}^j}{N} + \frac{N(M - 1)}{2p}\, E\left(\frac{-1}{\delta}\right)$$

where $\bar{t}^j$ is j's belief about others' expected contributions.[89] Therefore

$$E(\%C) = \sigma\, \left[\, E\, (\bar{t}),\, \frac{N(M - 1)}{p}\, E\left(\frac{-1}{2\delta}\right)\right]$$

where $\partial\sigma/\partial p > 0$ and $\partial\sigma/\partial N < 0$ since $M < 1$. If payoffs are increased then $E(\%C)$ decreases since N, M stay constant but p increases.

We now have three theories based on three different uncontrollable and unobservable parameters. Each is consistent with the finding that increases in M increase contributions. Each yields different predictions for the comparative statics of N, P, and z and they can, therefore in principle, be separated in the lab even if full control is not possible. At least two should be demonstrably incorrect based on data. Maybe the third is also.[90] The next round belongs to the experimentalists.

3. Communication

In section II.B we saw that Dawes, McTavish, and Shaklee (1977) were able to demonstrate that relevant communication increased contributions in N-person dilemma experiments. This seems to be a consistent, replicable, and strong finding, especially for environments without thresholds. What does theory say? As it turns out, not much. Preplay communication, however structured, in the language of modern game theory is simply cheap talk. If there is a unique dominant strategy equilibrium, as is true of most experiments without thresholds, then talking should have no effect on rates of contribution: we should see none. If there are multiple Nash equilibria, as is often the case with thresholds, cheap talk generally expands the number of equilibria but might lead to better coordination by subjects. This might raise the efficiency of the voluntary contributions mechanisms.

What do the data say? Let us look first at non-threshold environments. At least nine papers report an obvious and significant increase in group payoffs when communication is allowed prior to play. Dawes, McTavish, and Shaklee (1977) report an increase in payoffs from 31 to 72 percent when *relevant* communication occurs (see Table 2.3 in section II.B). Isaac, McCue, and Plott (1985, 67) report that "communication increases the level of contribution (and efficiencies). The increase is small but it appears to be stable."[91] Isaac and Walker (1988a) report "Our results document the significant impact of group communication in the reduction of free riding behavior."[92] Their four groups average greater than 80 percent contributions. In a follow-up study Isaac and Walker (1991) designed an experiment to make communication costly. In fact it was made a threshold public good.[93] In spite of the cost of communication the groups still achieved an efficiency level higher than 91 percent in six of ten periods.

One interesting aspect of these results is that repetition seems to increase the rate of contribution with communication rather than inhibit it. The Dawes et al. results are for one-shot decisions and yield 70 percent levels, while the Isaac and Walker results are for 10 or more periods and yield 90 percent. There are of course other differences in their experiments, so the comparison is somewhat tenuous. But Sell and Wilson (1990) have tested this comparison directly. Groups of 6 subjects with 40 tokens each contributed to an Isaac and Walker type public good with MPCR = 0.3 under a 2 × 2 treatment design. What was varied was (a) whether subjects were told what others did in past decisions and (b) whether subjects could announce whether they intended to contribute in the next decision. The idea is that no information–no announcement is like a one-shot experiment, information–no announcement is like the Isaac, Walker, and Thomas experiments without communication and information–announcement is like Isaac and Walker with very limited communication. The results are given in Table 2.15. I am not sure what to make of this. Communication without verification (announcement only) seems to reduce contributions. With verification it helps (59.3 versus 46.0%). But no information or communication, the one-shot equivalent, yields

Table 2.15. Duncan's Multiple-Range Test for Contributions

Treatment	Mean	N	Duncan Grouping
No information, no announcement	60.3	72	A
Information, announcement	59.3	72	A
Information only	46.0	72	B
Announcement only	34.0	72	C

Source: Sell and Wilson 1990, 23. I would like to thank J. Sell for permission to quote from this report.

Note: Means with the same letter are not significantly different at 0.05

the same rate of contribution as information and communication, the repetition and communication equivalent. Sell and Wilson state:

> Our results are consistent with other reported results using a voluntary contribution mechanism. Everywhere we observe a consistent decay in provisioning that extends over the periods. . . . Where individuals are able to make announcements and check on one another's behavior, they are somewhat less likely to lie in their announcements (the Pearson's correlation coefficient between one's announcement and contribution is .34, compared with .10 under the *Announcement Only* condition).

But they also admit that they are "far from capturing the essence of communication."

Dawes and Orbell have been studying communication in dilemmas systematically, trying to identify that essence. Experiments without thresholds are reported in Dawes, van de Kragt, and Orbell (1987), Orbell, van de Kragt, and Dawes (1988), and Orbell, Dawes, and van de Kragt (1990). Their present position seems to be that communication "works either because it provides an occasion for (multilateral) promises or because it generates group identity—or, possibly some combination of those two hypotheses" (Orbell, Dawes, and van de Kragt 1990, 619, footnote 7). They also note that multilateral promising only goes so far. In their words

> Perhaps the psychology of multilateral promising reduces to the psychology of a set of bilateral promises—perhaps, that is, people in our experiment felt they were making promises, as Hobbes put it, "every one apart, and Man by Man." But the straightforward interpretation of our data is that people do revert to what we have called multilateral promising and that, when they do, it can work. As this article has suggested, the interesting problem is that when people do revert to multilateral promising, there is no fully satisfactory rule for specifying when one's announced willingness to accept the proposed

terms of multilateral exchange becomes an ethical obligation to do so. Our data are consistent with their adopting in practice a rule saying that promises are not ethically binding until everyone in the group has promised. This rule is as simple as the analogous rule that works nicely in the bilateral case and is attractive to that extent. But the conditions under which it can produce satisfactory multilateral exchanges are quite restrictive. It only requires a single individual to withhold a promise for whatever reason, and the effort at multilateral promising collapses. We note that, for many N-person prisoner's dilemma configurations, losses from such a failure could be quite substantial.

Short of further empirical investigation, we do not know whether the unanimity requirement is progressively relaxed as size increases so that some proportion or number less than everyone promising is sufficient to trigger ethical obligation. It is, nevertheless, instructive that, among our relatively small fourteen-person groups, only about half managed to meet the obligation-invoking unanimity criterion—and to capture the benefits that came with that. (Orbell, Dawes, and van de Kragt 1990, 627)[94]

We see that communication increases contributions in no-threshold environments with small ($N < 15$) groups. We do not know why. We also do not know what would happen in large groups.

For completeness we should consider environments with thresholds. Here the evidence is mixed, although the theory suggests that there should be even more group gains from communication than in the dilemma environment. Whereas van de Kragt, Orbell, and Dawes (1983) report that communication increases efficiency and contribution, Chamberlin (1978) and Palfrey and Rosenthal (1991b) report no discernible effect. This needs more study.

D. Weak Effects

In this section I will briefly identify and describe a variety of additional phenomena to which experimentalists have pointed as possible explanations for behavior observed in voluntary contribution games. I separate these into environmental, systemic, and institutional effects, as was done in Table 2.10. Each effect has some evidence supporting its importance, but I have called these weak effects because there does not yet appear to me to be enough evidence for acceptance. In many cases there is apparently conflicting evidence. Future research will determine whether any one of these effects should be included among those in section III.C.

1. Environment

Homogeneity and Information

In many of the early experiments with voluntary contributions, all subjects were given the same preferences and endowments.[95] There is now reason to believe that such homogeneity in the environment has a positive effect on contributions.

Table 2.16.

	Threshold	Repetition	Complete Information[a]	More Heterogeneity Implies Percentage Contribution
Bagnoli and McKee (1991)	Y	Y	Y	Decrease
Brookshire et al. (1989a)	N	Y	Y and N	Decrease
Fisher et al. (1988)	N	Y	N[b]	Decrease in first ten periods
Marwell and Ames (1979, 1980)	Y	N	N	No effect
Rapoport and Suleiman (1993)	Y	Y[c]	Y	Decrease only at high threshold

[a] Complete information means that subjects know the *ex ante* distribution of possible types.
[b] All values were changed at period 10; and subjects were told that values "might not be the same."
[c] Repetition occurred, but no information about previous contributions of others was provided.

Isaac, McCue, and Plott (1985) conjectured this in their attempt to reduce contributions and included asymmetries in payoffs. But they did not control for the effect by also studying their environment without asymmetries.

We have already seen that contribution rates are responsive to marginal payoffs (see section III.B). What is at issue here is whether there is an additional effect due to heterogeneity in payoffs or endowments. For example, suppose if everyone is the same, contributions are 60 percent with MPCR = 0.75 and 30 percent with MPCR = 0.3. Now suppose we have an environment with half MPCR's equal to 0.75 and half equal to 0.3. Is the aggregate contribution rate 45 percent? Or are the contribution rates of the high-MPCR types now less than 60 percent since they can safely mimic the behavior of the low-MPCR types? Theory is no help since it predicts contributions of 0 no matter what. What do the data say?

Table 2.16 provides a summary of five papers which compare *ceteris paribus* contributions in homogeneous environments to contributions in heterogeneous environments. Looking only at the last column would lead one to conclude that heterogeneity lowers contributions. But the effect can clearly be dampened by a lack of information and/or a lack of repetition (or repetition without reports of previous outcomes). Can we separate these effects? Let us look at the role and impact of alternative information structures.

An important environmental treatment which can be controlled by the experimentalist is what subjects know about the environment and about the actions of others. As early as Fouraker and Siegel (1963) it was recognized by experimentalists that this information structure was important. Even the usually predictable behavior of subjects in Double Oral Auction Markets becomes more volatile and less responsive to the Law of Supply and Demand if subjects know each other's payoffs (see Smith and Williams 1990). Unfortunately, however, there have been only two studies of this easily controlled effect. Brookshire et al. (1989a) provide two information structures—one (called incomplete) in which each subject knows only her own payoff and endowment and another (called complete) in which each subject knows the list of others' payoffs and endowments but does not know who has which one.[96] They check five different payoff structures and find that contributions tend to be less under complete information than under incomplete information in all environments except the one in which all subjects were identical. In that homogeneous case information had no effect. Isaac and Walker (1989) studied only the homogeneous case and found no effect on contributions from changing the information conditions. So the studies are consistent but hardly conclusive, and it is not easy to find other experimental evidence to provide support. For example, although the evidence from experiments with asymmetric payoffs and common knowledge of the possible types that Palfrey and Rosenthal (1991b) and Palfrey and Prisbrey (1993) conducted suggest lower contributions than those of Dawes, McTavish, and Shaklee (1977) and Isaac, Walker, and Thomas (1984), it is only a suggestion and not a controlled experiment. We can make several tentative conjectures, but nonetheless they need considerably more testing before they become "stylized facts."[97] First, heterogeneity lowers the rate of contribution—unless there is incomplete information and no repetition. Second, complete information leads to less contribution than with incomplete information—unless there is homogeneity. The existence of a threshold does not seem to play an interactive role with heterogeneity (see Chan et al. 1993 for additional work with heterogeneous endowments).

Gender

One of the most obvious but easiest to control aspects of the environment is gender.[98] The question is simple: does gender affect the rate of contribution and how? There are five relevant studies, but the evidence is nevertheless still inconclusive. On the one side, there are two studies which purport to find that females tend to contribute more than males. Dawes, McTavish, and Shaklee (1977, 10) find this in one experiment but are quick to point out that it occurred only in the relevant communication condition and that "we have never been able to replicate the sex effect"(their footnote 5). Mason, Phillips, and Redington (1991) find, for two-person games, that "at the beginning of experiments women tend to be more cooperative than men and have a higher variance of choices." But they also note that "after 25 periods these differences vanish." In the middle, finding no effect, are Isaac, McCue, and Plott (1985), Poppe and Utens (1986), and Orbell, Schwartz-Shea, Dawes, and Elvin (1992). On the other side, there is the only experiment designed specifically to isolate and identify a gender effect in a public goods experiment with more than two players, Brown-Kruse and Hummels (1992). They used an Isaac and Walker design with $N = 4$ and MPCR's of 0.3 and 0.5. They also varied a condition they called "community," a group identity phenomena discussed further in section III.D.2. They found first that there were no significant differences either in the way men and women responded to the community or multiplier (MPCR) treatments, or in the way they contributed by period. But they also found significant gender differences in contribution rates: "males contributed at higher rates than did women" (12). Men's initial contribution rates are higher but their comparative statics are the same. So are there gender differences? I think the question remains open.[99]

2. Systemic

In this section I consider three explanatory variables that may be important determinants of cooperative behavior but which are difficult to measure and control.

Economics Training

In Marwell and Ames (1981), a tongue-in-cheek but still provocative question was raised: are economists the only free riders? They reported finding that contributions were significantly lower if and only if the subjects were graduate students in economics at Wisconsin. Isaac, McCue, and Plott (1985) took exception to this and used students in an undergraduate sociology course at Pasadena City College and students from undergraduate economics courses at Caltech. They found, under repetition, that "the tendency for erosion of contributions is not unique to societies populated by economists.... Our single experiment with sociology subjects yielded substantially the same results as other subject pools, including economists." I find neither set of data particularly convincing. It is not obvious what is being measured by participation in a class: experience, training, self-selection, or propensity to contribute? Are high school, two-year college, four-year college, and graduate classes different? Is the effect large enough (if it exists at all) to be found across a large number of very sensitive environments? The effect of training and/or self-selection on cooperation remains a wide-open problem.[100]

Beliefs

It is not surprising that some researchers have tried to explain contributions, when not contributing is a dominant strategy, as mistakes. One systematic way to do this is by assuming subjects arrive in the lab with beliefs about the world, that these beliefs affect their behavior, and that these are not controlled in the experiments. Indeed not only are they not controlled, they may also be only indirectly measurable. Three approaches have been taken: two with thresholds, one without. Let us look at the threshold environments first. Rapoport (1985) introduced the notion of strategic uncertainty or a subject's probability belief that the sum of contributions of other players is less than or equal to X, call it $F_j(X)$. So when j's payoff is

$$\begin{cases} r + z_j - t_j \text{ if } \sum t_i \geq T \\ z_j - t_j \text{ if } \sum t_i < T \end{cases}$$

and j maximizes expected payoff, j will choose t_j to

$$\max (r + z_j - t_j)(1 - F_j (T - t_j)) + (z_j - t_j) F_j (T - t_j)$$

or

$$\max r [1 - F_j (T - t_j)] + z_j - t_j.$$

From a theorist's point of view this is very straightforward. From an experimentalist's point of view the problem is that the subject brings the function $F_j (\cdot)$ to the lab. Suleiman and Rapoport (1992) try to discover what F_j is by asking questions of the subjects. No payments were made contingent on their answers.[101] Using the estimated F_j Suleiman and Rapoport can predict t_j from the maximization problem and then compare it to the actual contributions. Although this approach seems to have some explanatory power,[102] in their most recent paper Rapoport and Suleiman (1993, 30) conclude, "Although we have achieved limited success in accounting for the contribution decisions of some of the subjects, our results show that neither the cooperative nor the expected utility model account for the behavior of the majority of the subjects." I would suggest that perhaps the (survey) data on beliefs and risk attitudes are unreliable and that before one rejects those models one should try to find better ways to measure what is needed. Perhaps some of the techniques discussed in chapter 8 would be of help.

An alternative approach is devised by Palfrey and Rosenthal (1991a), who consider misspecified priors in a more complete game-theoretic framework. This allows a much clearer test of the expected utility approach using only the actual decisions of the subjects (for which they were paid). By changing the experiment so that (1) contributions are all or none, and (2) the public good is provided if at least K of N contribute, it is easy to show that a subject contributes if and only if $rP_j^{K-1} \geq z^j$ where P_j^{K-1} is j's belief (probability) that exactly $K - 1$ others will contribute. If z^j is randomly chosen from a cdf $G (\cdot)$ then at a Bayes equilibrium[103] each expected payoff maximizing subject contributes if and only if $z_i \leq z^*$, the probability any one subject contributes is $G (z^*)$, and z^* satisfies

$$\frac{1}{r} z^* = \binom{N - 1}{k - 1} G (z^*)^{K - 1} (1 - G (z^*))^{N - K}.$$

Palfrey and Rosenthal carefully induce the payoffs and G. In their words:

> At the beginning of each experiment, subjects were told K, N, r in "francs,"
> . . . and all other relevant information about the experimental procedures.
> They were also told how many cents per franc they would receive at the
> conclusion of the session. These values were held constant throughout an
> experiment. Subjects earned between \$10 and \$20 during each session. Sessions lasted between forty-five minutes and an hour and a half.
>
> In each round, subjects were each given a single indivisible "token" (endowment). Token values in franc increments between 1 and either 90 or 204

were independently drawn with replacement from identical uniform distributions and randomly assigned to subjects, and this was carefully explained to the subjects in the instructions. . . . Then each subject was told the value of his or her token, but not told the values of the tokens of other subjects. Subjects were then asked to enter their decisions (spend or not spend the token).

The results were very striking. First using the predicted z^* (K, N) and varying K and N ($N = 3$ and 4, $K = 1$, 2, and 3), one can get a prediction of subjects' earnings in the Bayes equilibrium. The regression of predicted on actual yields

actual earnings $= -0.054 + 1.045z^*$ predicted with $n = 33$ and $R^2 = 0.95$.

The intercept is not statistically different from 0, and the slope is not different from 1. But individual behavior differs substantially from that predicted by the model: contribute when $z^i \leq z^*$ (K, N). Palfrey and Rosenthal consider four alternative models: biased probabilities, risk aversion, other nonlinear utility forms including altruism and the Rapoport model, and cooperation. They show that these yield different predictions about how contributions change with K and N. They then proceed to show that the data support only the hypothesis that subjects' priors about G $(z^*$ $(K, N))$ are biased upward—that is, subjects expect a slightly higher rate of contribution than is consistent with an unbiased Bayes-Nash equilibrium. Whether this methodological approach would yield similar results for the complete information world of Dawes, Orbell, Simmons, and van de Kragt (1986) remains an open question.

It is important to recognize the methodological differences between Rapoport and Palfrey and Rosenthal. The latter use a standard economic approach to data analysis computing comparative statics predictions from theory and then comparing those predictions to the data using standard hypothesis tests. In many cases this circumvents the need to measure utility functions and/or priors directly because the indirect predictions are independent of the precise details of those functions. Survey data in an experimental context are unreliable so it is important to find ways to avoid their use.[104] Indeed, that is the purpose of the lab. Theory, comparative statics, and statistical procedures can allow us to test and identify, using indirect evidence, the existence of effects which are otherwise unmeasurable and, perhaps, uncontrollable.

Beliefs have also been used as an explanation for contributions in experiments without thresholds. The data can be found as early as Dawes, McTavish, and Shaklee (1977); a theory for two–person dilemmas can be found in Orbell and Dawes (1991).[105] In their N-person dilemma experiments, described earlier in section II.B, they also asked subjects about their expectations of others' behavior. They report that

One of our most consistent findings throughout these studies—a finding replicated by others' work—is that cooperators expect significantly more cooperation than do defectors. This result has been found both when payoffs are "step-level" (when contributions from a subset of K subjects ensure provision of a benefit to all) and when they are "symmetric" (when all contributions ensure a constant benefit to all). (Orbell and Dawes 1991, 518)[106]

The data on beliefs are the results of surveys, but there does seem to be something systematic; subjects with a propensity to cooperate (for whatever reason) also tend to believe others are more likely to cooperate. Dawes, McTavish, and Shaklee (1977) go farther and claim that it is choice causing beliefs, and not vice versa.[107] In Orbell and Dawes (1981) they use this as one assumption in a model which purports to explain the evolution of cooperation and, presumably therefore, the tendency to cooperate in the one-shot experiments. I think these ideas deserve to be explored further, especially in a way that provides more reliability in the responses to questions about beliefs. Scoring rules or payments to the subject whose predicted percentage cooperation is closest to the actual percentage might tighten up the data. It would also be interesting to see how repetition affects predictions and how prediction affects behavior.[108]

Friends, Group Solidarity

Two experimentalists have tried to discover whether some form of group identity might cause contributions to increase. Both have indicated the answer is yes. Orbell, van de Kragt, and Dawes (1988) report the results of an experiment similar to the Dawes, McTavish, and Shaklee (1977) experiments described in section II.B. One difference was that some groups were told their contributions would provide a public good, not for those in their own room, but for a similar group in another room. Although the payoff structure is identical in both treatments, cooperation is significantly higher (almost twice as high) when the public good accrues to subjects in one's own room. The data are in Table 2.17. The effect is magnified by discussion although, somewhat surprisingly to me, discussion increases contributions even when the benefits go to others.[109]

Brown-Kruse and Hummels (1992) also try to control for group identity by using a community versus noncommunity treatment. In their words:

> In the community v. noncommunity treatment, we controlled the nature of pre-experiment communication. By filling out a required questionnaire, subjects in the community setting were encouraged to meet, talk, and learn something about each other. Our goal was to arouse a sense of membership in a group. (Brown-Kruse and Hummels 1992, 6)[110]

This is very similar to the irrelevant communications treatment of Dawes, McTavish, and Shaklee (1977). Although only a small direct effect was found for community, the hypothesis of no effect can be rejected with only about 80 percent probability. A significant interaction was found with marginal payoffs. When the MPCR was high, contribution rates did not depend at all on the community treatment; when the MPCR was low, contribution rates depended strongly on the presence of the community treatment. Brown-Kruse and Hummels explain this

Table 2.17. Percentage Contributions

	Give to	
	Own Group	Other Group
No discussion	37.5	19.6
Discussion	78.6	30.4

using the concepts of trust and risk. Higher MPCRs mean lower risk, more community means more trust, and low risk means trust is unimportant while high risk means trust is important.

We are left with the undefined and unmeasured concepts of discussion induced group solidarity (Orbell, van de Kragt, and Dawes 1988) and trust (Brown-Kruse and Hummels 1992) to explain part of the rate of contribution. There may be something here, but it has not yet been isolated, measured, and controlled.

3. Institutional

Unanimity

Building on an idea from Wicksell (1958), Smith (1977, 1979a) identifies unanimity as a potentially important driving principle in generating contributions toward public goods.[111] The idea is that after contributions are proposed, a vote is taken. A single no vote means contributions are returned and no public good is provided. These votes are more than just talk since they change the Nash equilibrium of the game. The hope is that this raises contributions since one can potentially contribute a lot but then veto if others do not contribute enough and so get one's money back. Banks, Plott, and Porter (1988) subjected these ideas to a very rigorous test in response to a proposal to use a mechanism like Smith's public goods auction to allocate resources on Space Station Freedom. This research is a nice example of the use of experiments to test the limits of a potentially useful idea for a new institution in a way that would be difficult if one were only able to use field data. Using the Isaac, McCue, and Plott environment, described earlier in section II.D, Banks, Plott, and Porter generated the data in Table 2.18. The effect of unanimity is large and apparently obvious; efficiencies are way down and the effect of repetition disappears. A closer examination of the data reveals some clues. From the data in Table 2.19 we see that unanimity does increase contributions if there are no vetos, but there are so few success periods (13 percent) that the gain in potential contributions is outweighed by the failures. This effect is very similar to the effect of increases in thresholds observed in section III.A. Since there is only this one study,[112] one must be careful about leaping to conclusions, but it seems likely that unanimity is not desirable as an institutional device to increase contributions, a fact that would have been impossible to discover with theory or field data.

Table 2.18. Average Efficiencies (percent)

	For All Periods	For Early Periods	For Later Periods
With unanimity	8	7	8
Without unanimity	32	53	21

Source: With unanimity data from Banks, Plott, and Porter (1988). Without-unanimity data are from Isaac, McCue, and Plott (1985).
Note: Early periods are periods 1 and 2. Later periods are period 3 and subsequent periods.

Table 2.19.

	Efficiencies in Success Periods (%)	% Successful Periods
With unanimity	57.5	13%
Without unanimity	32	100%

Source: All data from Banks, Plott, and Porter (1988).
Note: A success period is one in which no veto occurs.

Revision and Sequence

Two other institutional variations may have a more positive effect on cooperation than unanimity. One, sequencing, has been tested in a threshold environment,[113] and one, revision, has been tested across different environments including an Isaac and Walker environment and a threshold environment. They each deserve further exploration.

The idea of sequencing is not new,[114] but one of the first studies of its properties in public goods environments seems to be in Erev and Rapoport (1990). Sequencing allows or requires participants to make their decisions sequentially with complete information about previous decisions in the sequence. When there is a threshold this significantly changes the theoretical properties of the game. If one applies the modern notions of sub-game perfection to a game in which the monetary public good is provided if and only if K of N contribute, then the theory predicts the last K in the sequence will contribute and the good will always be provided efficiently. The data lend limited support to this conclusion. Using an environment similar to van de Kragt, Orbell, and Dawes (1983) requiring three of five contributors, Erev and Rapoport found that the percentage of cooperation was essentially the same whether decisions were sequential (45.3 percent) or simultaneous (42.9 percent). However, under the sequential protocol the public good was provided 66.7 percent of the time, whereas it was provided only 14 percent under the simultaneous protocol.[115] A sequential choice mechanism does not increase cooperation in this threshold environment, but it does solve some of the coordination problem. Of 75 subject choices in the sequential mechanism, 20, or 27 percent, violated the predictions of game theory.[116] No one knows why, although the fact that most errors occurred in the early decisions (75 percent of the decisions which violate the theory were made by the first three movers) suggests that backward induction may be difficult for the subjects.[117] Other possibilities are that early movers may anticipate mistakes by later movers, or late movers may be spiteful. The explanation here must be somehow related to that of behavior in centipede games (see McKelvey and Palfrey 1992). Sequential protocols are a possible solution to coordination problems with small numbers. They should be studied more.

The idea of revision is also not new since it can be found in one of the oldest market institutions, the English Auction. Dorsey (1992), using the Isaac, Walker, and Thomas (1984) design, with MPCR = 0.3 and N = 4, made one change and allowed subjects to adjust their planned contributions in real time. Only the final contribution levels were binding. He found 11.5 percent contribution rates when allowing both increases and decreases (compared to Isaac, Walker, and Thomas, who found 26 percent). Allowing increases only—a form of partial commitment—Dorsey found contribution rates of 23 percent. It is not obvious that revisions are helping in this public goods environment.[118] In fact, they seem to give subjects an opportunity to discover others' less than fully cooperative behavior and to lower contributions upon that discovery. But more needs to be done before definite conclusions are possible.

E. Unknown Effects

There are a number of other possible treatments or phenomena which might affect contributions or cooperation and which, as far as I know, have not been fully tested. Three of these are decision costs, attitudes of fairness, and moral suasion. Each is usually presented as a motivation beyond monetary gain which might cause the decisions of subjects to be different from those predicted by reward maximizing models.

Decision Costs

Decision costs are related to bounded rationality and computational and informational complexity. Generally the idea is that precise optimization carries cognitive processing costs which are traded off by subjects against rewards: the lower the rewards the more errors in computation. While Smith and Walker (1992) address some of the issues in the context of private goods, it is difficult to identify any systematic study in the context of public goods. Two papers are vaguely related. Dawes and Orbell (1982) report the results of an experiment using one of their standard dilemma designs with no threshold, with no communication, and with losses truncated at zero, in which they tried to check whether communication causes increases in contributions because it facilitates thinking. They allowed some subjects only 5 minutes to think about their choice and allowed others 24 hours. The results were clear and unequivocal: cooperation rates were 35.6 percent for 5 minutes and 35.9 percent for 24 hours. "Thinking time per se does not help" (172). In a second study related to decision costs, Saijo and Yamaguchi (1992) compare rates of contribution in an Isaac and Walker type design with MPCR = 0.7 and 1/0.7 and with $N = 7$. They provide two different payoff tables to different subjects. The one they call *rough*, similar to that provided by Isaac and Walker, provides two columns of data: "total contributions" in increments of 10 and "your (public good) payoff." In the format they call *detailed*, they provide a 61×11 matrix whose rows are the "sum of others' contributions," including all integers ranging from 0 to 60, and "your contribution," ranging from 0 to 10. The entries are "your (total) payoff." They obtain considerably different results with the detailed table than with the rough. Using the rough table and MPCR = 0.7, the rates of contribution and the decline with repetition mimic those in Isaac, Walker, and Thomas (1984) (see section II.E): more than 30 percent contribution early with decay towards 10 percent. With the detailed table "the mean investment for all ten periods is significantly less (19.6% vs. 34.1%) than the previous experiments and no specific decay toward period 10 is observed" (10). It seems from Saijo and Yamaguchi (1992) that reducing cognitive processing costs by providing the detailed table reduces contributions and eliminates the decline with repetition.[119] This is consistent with a hypothesis that some subjects make errors (which are one-sided at 0) that they correct with repetition or with detail. This is a wide open area of research at the edge between psychology and economics. It is related to the issue of presentation raised in footnote 17. It certainly seems to me to be worth a lot more careful research.

Fairness

It is often claimed that non–reward maximizing behavior arises because of subjects' concerns for fairness. There has been a lot of study or at least claims of this in bargaining experiments (see chapter 4) but very little has been done in the context of public goods. Marwell and Ames (1979) administered a survey as part of their experiment (see section II.C), and they propose that the answers to that "suggests one major theme—the consideration of 'fairness' as a mediating factor in investment decisions" (1357). However, they also recognize that "investment in the public good did not vary with definitions of fairness" (1357), where *definition* means what is a fair percentage of contribution. However, contributions did vary with a "concern for fairness."

> Those who were not so concerned were markedly concentrated in the lowest levels of investment. For these people, at least, "being fair" may be driven out by greed. If the stakes are high enough, almost everyone may opt for profit over fairness. But this would still deny the strong free-rider hypothesis for a large range of meaningful economic conditions.

So here again is a possible explanation for contributions above those maximizing personal payoff. I am uncomfortable with the use of survey data and the fact that "concern for fairness" is not measurable, but nevertheless I think there is something which deserves to be followed up. One way would follow up on the theory presented in section III.C.2.

Moral Suasion

I include a final class of phenomena which are possible explanations for non–maximizing behavior under a general heading of moral suasion. We have already seen, in section II.A, how instructions in Bohm's experiments included what he called "counter-strategic arguments." These are simply an extreme form of an effect which may lead subjects to make decisions as they think the experimenter wants them to. The existence of such an effect has seemingly been demonstrated weakly by Hoffman and Spitzer (1985) and by Hoffman, McCabe, Shachat, and Smith (1992) in the context of two-person bargaining experiments.[120] The latter state in their abstract, "We conducted dictator experiments in which individual subject decisions could not be known either by the experimenter or by anyone else except the decision maker. The results yielded by far our largest observed proportion of self-regarding offers."[121] The conjecture is that even if the experimenter can prevent subjects from knowing what each other do, the fact that the experimenter knows can still lead subjects to entertain other-regarding behavior. It would be interesting to know whether such protection from the experimenter (and not just from each other) is really important, and whether it would significantly reduce contributions in any of the public goods situations we have described in this paper.

Finally, one should notice that each of the three phenomena mentioned (decision costs, fairness, moral suasion) trades off against the private stakes. All experimenters, including psychologists like Dawes and sociologists like Marwell, recognize that "if the stakes are high enough almost everyone may opt for profit." It is indeed a systematic if not often replicated fact in experimental data that increasing the stakes (that is, for example, doubling the value of each unit of endowment and doubling the value of each unit of the public good) reduces the contribution rate in dilemmas.[122] This is a matter of control.

It is obvious that subjects bring motivations, beliefs, and capabilities to the lab that may be vastly different from those assumed in standard game-theoretic models. Some experimental situations such as Double Oral Auctions appear to be very robust against such variations. No control is needed. Some experimental situations such as voluntary contribution mechanisms with public goods are very sensitive to such variations. That sensitivity can be controlled with high payoffs, but little is learned. The hard problem is to isolate and measure the effects of the variations. This will keep experimentalists busy for a long time.

IV. Final Thoughts

What do we know about behavior in public goods environments? In particular, *are subjects naturally cooperative, contributors, and altruistic?* Conventional wisdom is based on the data generated by Marwell and Ames, Dawes and Orbell, Isaac and Walker, and others in environments without thresholds. These suggest that in public goods experiments where the dominant payoff maximizing strategy is to give nothing and where the group optimum is to give everything, in one-shot decisions or in the early rounds of repetitive decisions contributions from 30 percent to 70 percent occur.[123] There are at least two explanations for the data: (a) subjects trade off altruistic and cooperative responses against personal payoffs, or (b) subjects make mistakes, do not care, are bored, and choose their allocations randomly. How can we tell the difference? Let us look at four recent papers which, I think, provide a clue. Two use environments which retain a dominant strategy feature but test the hypothesis of natural cooperation by eliminating the conflict between group and self-interest.[124] Two others study an environment with an interior Nash and interior social optimum so mistakes can be made by both contributing too much and contributing too little.[125]

In Palfrey and Prisbrey (1993) and Saijo and Yamaguchi (1992), each subject faces an Isaac-Walker type payoff of $u^i = p^i(z - t_i) + b^i(\Sigma_j t_j)$. Sometimes $b^i < p^i < N b^i$, so self-interest suggests $t_i = 0$ and group interest suggests $t_i = z$. But sometimes $p^i < b^i$, so both group and self regarding behavior would suggest $t_i = z$. Palfrey and Prisbrey use an asymmetric information environment in which each subject has a different value of b/p but each knows the common distribution that generates these values. Saijo and Yamaguchi use a complete information homogeneous environment where all subjects have the same b/p, all know it, and all are provided very detailed information on payoffs. The results, nevertheless, are remarkably similar. If we classify subjects as Nash players (a Palfrey and Prisbrey approach) if they contribute when $b^i > p^i$ and do not contribute when $p^i > b^i$ and if we allow some error, then Palfrey and Prisbrey find 49 percent Nash players.[126] In Saijo and Yamaguchi in the first period of play 50 percent of the decisions (in the detailed treatment) are Nash. This increases to 62 percent by the last period.[127] *At least half the subjects are very close to behaving as self-payoff maximizing game theory would predict.*

What about the others? Are they cooperative? Again Saijo and Yamaguchi (1992) provides some clues. They used homogeneous groups of 7 with MPCR of 0.7 sometimes and 1.4 other times. They also used a rough payoff table (similar to that of Isaac and Walker) and a very detailed table. The rates of contribution are listed in Table 2.20. The rough payoff data with MPCR = 0.7 are similar to previous data of Isaac and Walker and others. What is surprising is the rough payoff data for MPCR = 1.4. If one wants to interpret the 40 percent contribution with MPCR = 0.7 as contributory and the result of natural altruism or some other group-regarding behavior, then one must also interpret the 50 percent lack of contribution with MPCR = 1.4 as noncontributory and the result of natural spitefulness. The alternative, that there are a lot of mistakes and inattention to payoff detail, seems more plausible to me. The 20 percent and 75 percent early rates of contribution, when payoffs are better explained to the subjects, support that view but still leave about 20 to 25% of the aggregate contributions unexplained.[128] What has not been controlled?

Another approach to separating errors from altruism places the non-cooperative equilibrium in the interior of $[0, z]$ and separates that equilibrium from the group optimum. Both Andreoni (1993) and Walker, Gardner, and Ostrom (1990) do this by introducing income effects.[129] Andreoni (1993) wanted to study

Table 2.20. Approximate Percentage Contributions:
First Period, Tenth Period, Average

MPCR	Rough Payoff Table	Detailed Payoff Table
1.4	50,45,50	75,70,72
0.7	40,25,35	20,16,18

whether government funding of the public good would crowd out private contributions. He recognized that to do so required an environment with an interior noncooperative equilibrium. He created an environment in which an individual's payoff is $u = \alpha \ln (z - t_i) + (1 - \alpha) \ln (y)$, $y = \Sigma_i t_i$, and $0 \le t_i \le z_i$. The first thing to note about this world is that the noncooperative equilibrium (that generated by perfectly selfish game-theoretic behavior) is

$$t^* = \frac{(1 - \alpha)}{1 + \alpha(N - 1)} z$$

so that for $0 < \alpha < 1, 0 < t^* < z$. The second thing to notice is that the marginal per capita return (MPCR) to contributing is

$$\frac{u_y^i}{u_x^i} = \frac{1 - \alpha}{\alpha} \cdot \frac{x}{y} = \frac{1 - \alpha}{\alpha} \frac{z - t}{y}$$

which is not constant in z. This is what is meant by income effects. At the noncooperative equilibrium,[130] t^*, MPCR = 1, so if the subjects' cooperative nature is similar to that in the linear world of Isaac and Walker, we should expect to see contributions greater than t^*. If everyone is symmetric, we can identify a group optimum as that $\hat{t}$ which maximizes $\alpha \ln (z - t) + (1 - \alpha) \ln Nt$. Thus $\hat{t} = (1 - \alpha)z$.[131] Notice that, for $0 < \alpha < 1$ and $N > 1$, $0 < t^* < \hat{t} < z$, and the MPCR at $\hat{t}$ is $1/N$ for all subjects.[132] With this design it is possible for an experimenter to manipulate t^* and $\hat{t}$ to see whether subjects respond or not. Andreoni's data suggest that they do. Although he only used one set of parameters with $z = 7$, $t^* = 3$, and $\hat{t} = 6$, contributions averaged 2.84 over a number of periods and were bounded between 2.11 and 3.33 in each period. This is clearly near the noncooperative equilibrium, is less than altruism would suggest, and is nowhere near the optimum. Although I have not analyzed these data to separate out the percentage of Nash players, this is certainly additional evidence supporting the conventional wisdom that average rates of contribution are 50 percent may be the unintended result of a corner noncooperative equilibrium and not altruism.[133]

Another study that, serendipitously, was based on an environment with an interior noncooperative equilibrium is that by Walker, Gardner, and Ostrom (1990). In their attempt to understand common property management problems they created a public good world where $u^i = x^i y + px^i$, $g(\Sigma x_j) = F(\Sigma x_j)/(\Sigma x_j)$, and imposed the constraint $0 \le x^i \le z$. The particular $F(x)$ they used was $23x - 0.25 x^2$ with $p = 5$. One can do the same analysis here as we did above to Andreoni's environment to find that t^* is 8 and $\hat{t}$ is 4. One very interesting feature here is that t^* and $\hat{t}$ are reversed so that $0 < \hat{t} < t^* < z$. Ostrom, Walker, and Gardner found that contributions tended to be around t^*, the Nash equilibrium, providing more evidence against the simple altruism model of behavior.

Although no one has yet created an experimental study which would more closely compare the data from environments with interior noncooperative equilibria to those without,[134] the above experiments suggest that it would be worth the effort. If, as I suspect, the data in environments with interior Nash equilibria continues to be close to that predicted by noncooperative behavior, and if that is true for $N = 4, 10, 40, 100$, then we would certainly need a close reexamination of the stylized fact that subjects contribute 40 to 60 percent of the optimal level because they are naturally group-regarding.

Let me conclude with some personal conjectures and beliefs arrived at while writing this survey. (1) *Hard-nosed game theory cannot explain the data.* Subjects contribute even though noncontribution is a dominant strategy. Even the most fervent economic experimentalist cannot force rates of contribution much below 10 percent (see Isaac, McCue, and Plott 1985). If these experiments are viewed solely as tests of game theory, that theory has failed. (2) *Contributions are however certainly responsive to marginal selfish payoffs* (see Isaac, Walker, and Thomas 1984 and Palfrey and Prisbrey 1993). Most of the 50 percent who are not Nash players seem to respond on average to selfish incentives. This is certainly consistent with the view that altruism, self-interest, decision costs, and fairness (among other possibilities) are all competing with each other in a subject's true preferences. A task facing experimentalists is to separate the effect of these forces from each other. (3) *Altruism or group-regarding preferences cannot explain the data.* When the conflict between group interest and self-interest is removed, subjects still contribute in ways that are counter to both their self-interest and their group interest (see Saijo and Yamaguchi 1992). Up to 50 percent of the subjects appear to be solely self-interested when they understand the experimental situation[135] (see Palfrey and Prisbrey 1993). Further, experience, repetition, better detail in payoffs, and information about heterogeneity reduce the apparent altruistic instinct of 30 to 40 percent of other subjects. (4) *It is possible to provide an environment in which at least 90% of subjects will become selfish Nash players.* Heterogeneous payoffs and resources, complete and detailed information particularly about the heterogeneity, anonymity from others and the experimenter, repetition and experience, and low marginal payoffs will all cause a reduction in rates of contribution, especially with small numbers. Add unanimity to the mechanism and rates will go to zero (see Banks, Plott, and Porter 1988). It is possible to extinguish any trace of "altruism" in the lab. (5) *It is possible to provide an environment in which almost all of the subjects contribute toward the group interest.* Homogeneous interest, little or rough information, face-to-face discussions in small groups,[136] no experience, small numbers and high marginal payoffs from contributing will all cause an increase in contributions. Why and how often this all works remains a mystery. (6) *There appear to be three types of players*: dedicated Nash players who act pretty much as predicted by game theory with possibly a small number of mistakes, a group of subjects who will respond to self-interest as will Nash players if the incentives are high enough but who also make mistakes and respond to decision costs, fairness, altruism, etc., and a group of subjects who behave in an inexplicable (irrational?) manner. Casual observation suggests that the proportions are 50 percent, 40 percent, 10 percent in many subject pools. Of course, we need a lot more data before my outrageous conjectures can be tested.

Let me add one pessimistic and one optimistic observation from the point of view of the mechanism designer. My pessimistic remark is that although inexperienced subjects can be led to provide large contributions in one-time decisions with the use of relevant discussions, one cannot rely on these approaches as a permanent organizing feature without expecting an eventual decline to self-interested behavior. Thus, for example, techniques such as TQM (total quality management), political orations, and half-time speeches can have at best a transitory effect in calling upon the altruistic impulses of some. Ultimately self-interest takes over. My optimistic remark is that since 90 percent of subjects seem to be responsive to private incentives, it will be possible to create new mechanisms which focus that self-interest toward the group interest. We need not rely on voluntary contribution approaches but can instead use new organizations such as those found in Smith (1979a), Groves and Ledyard (1977), or Ledyard and Palfrey (1992). Experiments will provide the basic empirical description of behavior which must be understood by the mechanism designer, and experiments will provide the test-bed in which the new organizations will be tested before implementation. But that is another paper.

Appendix

Table A.1. Examples of Public Goods Environments

Utility, U^i	Endow-ment	Production $G(t_s)$	Feasible Contributions	Sample Reference
$y + px^i$	z	$\frac{a}{N}t_s$	$0 \le t^i \le z$	Isaac, Walker, and Thomas (1984)
$y + px^i$	1	$\frac{a}{N}t_s$	$t^i \in \{0, 1\}$	Dawes, McTavish, and Shaklee (1977)
$ry + v_i x^i$	1	1 if $t_s \ge \frac{K}{N}$ 0 else	$t^i \in \{0, 1\}$	Palfrey and Rosenthal (1984)
$y + px^i$	z	y' if $a_1 < t_s \le a_2$ y'' if $a_2 < t_s \le a_3$ $\vdots$	$a \le t^i \le z$	Marwell and Ames (1979)
$-\|y - \mu_i\|$	0	$y \in Y$	$t^i = 0$	Fiorina and Plott (1978)
$R^i(y) + x^i$	z	$\frac{1}{C}t_s$	$0 \le t^i \le z$	Isaac, McCue, and Plott (1985)
yx^i	z	$\frac{1}{C}t_s$	$0 \le t^i \le z$	Shenker (1990c)
$yx^i + px^i$	z	$F(t_s)/t_s$	$0 \le t^i \le z$	Walker, Gardner, and Ostrom (1990)
$yx^i - c^i(x^i)$		$D^{-1}(x_s)$	$0 \le x^i$	Chapter Holt (1994)
$R^i(x^i) - W^i - E(y)$		$y = x_s$	$x^i \in \{0, 1\}$	Plott (1983)
$w^j - c^j(x^j) - E(y)$		$\Sigma_j - \omega^j = \Sigma_i \omega^i$		

Notes

I thank the Flight Projects Office of the Jet Propulsion Laboratory of NASA for their financial support. For their intellectual help and advice, I thank Peter Bohm, Don Coursey, Robyn Dawes, Roy Gardner, Mark Johnson, John Kagel, Jamie Brown-Kruse, Susan Laury, Gerald Marwell, Rosemarie Nagel, John Orbell, Elinor Ostrom, Tom Palfrey, Charles Plott, Amnon Rapoport, Al Roth, Tatsuyoshi Saijo, Steve Slutsky, Richard Thaler, James Walker, most of the participants in the Conference on Experimental Research on the Provision of Public Goods and Common-Property Resources at the Workshop in Political Theory and Policy Analysis at Indiana University, and especially Mark Isaac, without whom I would not have gotten even this far. Some of these strongly disagree with parts of my commentary. They may be justified.

1. See, for example, Groves and Ledyard (1977) or Ledyard and Palfrey (1992).
2. There would be something special about studying institutions, though.
3. It is not always obvious what is an error and what is some subtle form of sophisticated play but for purposes of this example suppose a seller offers to sell a unit at less than her marginal cost. This is either an error (a loss will be incurred) or an altruistic act. We generally treat it as a mistake.
4. I emphasize groups here since single person decision experiments lack the ability to examine complicated feedback effects from interpersonal interactions.
5. Using steel balls allows control but is not very illuminating.
6. In fact, for most of these variables it is possible to find experimental evidence suggesting a positive effect, evidence suggesting no effect, and evidence suggesting a negative effect. See section III.
7. Variables such as number of subjects and the conversion rate of contributions into public goods make the possibilities infinite.
8. See chapter 6.
9. See Easley and Ledyard (1992) for the extensive range of behaviors consistent with the data.
10. This structure has been developed over many years by many researchers. Examples can be found in d'Aspremont and Gerard-Varet (1979), Groves and Ledyard (1987), Hurwicz (1972), Myerson (1991), Kiser and Ostrom (1982), Radner (1987), and Smith (1982a). A complete exposition would require another book.
11. This is sometimes incorrectly identified as efficiency or Pareto-optimality in environments with income effects.
12. This can include iterative procedures, bids and offers, votes, oratory, etc.
13. This assumes that i is "selfish." We will see later why one might want to relax this assumption. In fact, we will need to go further and distinguish the payoff to subjects, say $p^i (x^i, y)$, from the utility they get, $V^i = V^i (p^i, \beta^i)$ where β^i may be a collection of variables which are difficult to observe or control or β^i may include the payoffs to others. If we knew β^i, then $U^i (x^i, y) = V^i (p^i (x^i, y), \beta^i)$.
14. This point is also made, with graph in Dawes (1975)
15. This is the basis of Isaac, Walker and Thomas (1984), among others.
16. See Dawes, Orbell, Simmons, and van de Kragt (1986)
17. An equivalent theoretical representation in the space of investments would yield $U^i (t^i, y) = t^i y - 5t^i + 5z^i$. In each case the initial endowment is a parameter in the utility function but it is exogenous, fixed and known so that it creates no theoretical problems under standard economic and game theories. There may, of course, still be differences in subject behavior when payoffs are presented in the different forms $h_i(t)$, $U^i(t_i, y)$, and $U^i(x_i, y)$. See section IV for more on this problem of presentation.
18. See Schram and Sonnemans (1992) for another involving voter turnout.
19. I will, however, not survey two-person games.
20. For a recent survey of the theoretical literature see Groves and Ledyard (1987).

21. In an early work (1984) for the Jet Propulsion Lab of NASA on space station allocation, I adopted the phrase "testbedding," used by their engineers to describe one phase of spacecraft development, to identify this type of experimental organizational analysis.

22. Listed alphabetically.

23. The exception might be in research on decisions under uncertainty (see chapter 8).

24. For an example of the often silly rhetoric of the debate see Mansbridge (1990).

25. Work from this group includes Marwell and Ames (1979, 1980, 1981), Alfano and Marwell (1980), and Marwell (1982).

26. Work from this group includes Dawes, McTavish, and Shaklee (1977), Dawes (1980), Orbell and Dawes (1981), Dawes and Orbell (1982), van de Kragt, Orbell, and Dawes (1983), Dawes, Orbell, and van de Kragt (1985), Orbell, van de Kragt, and Dawes (1988), Dawes, Orbell, Simmons, and van de Kragt (1986), Dawes, van de Kragt, and Orbell (1987), Orbell, Dawes, and van de Kragt (1990), Orbell and Dawes (1991).

27. Work from this group includes Isaac and Walker (1983), Isaac, Walker, and Thomas (1984), Isaac, McCue, and Plott (1985), Isaac and Walker (1987), Isaac, Schmidtz, and Walker (1988), Isaac and Walker (1988a, 1988b), Fisher, Isaac, Schatzberg, and Walker (1988), Isaac and Walker (1989, 1991), Isaac, Walker, and Williams (1990), Walker, Gardner, and Ostrom 1990.

28. Andreoni (1988b, 291). See also Isaac and Walker (1987), Mansbridge (1990), p. 17, and Dawes and Thaler (1988), p. 189, for examples of these claims.

29. See Bohm (1987).

30. They identified it as related but not focused on their question of interest.

31. I would like to thank Elsevier Science Publishers for permission to quote from this report.

32. Well-known Swedish comedians.

33. We need to develop an econometrics of experiments to deal with the estimation and identification of uncontrolled variables.

34. Other early experiments also had this problem. For example, Schneider and Pommerehne (1981b) used students as subjects and the public good was the purchase of the professor's forthcoming book: see the discussion of this experiment in Chapter 1.

35. Simplicity is a good feature of experiments. You are more likely to understand what you have learned.

36. The subjects were also asked to indicate beliefs about others' choices. I will comment on this aspect of their experiments later in section III.D.2.

37. I would like to thank the American Psychological Association for permission to quote from this report.

38. Isaac, Walker, and Thomas (1984) call this the marginal per capita return (MPCR) and were the first to identify this very important parameter. More on this later in section III.C.1.

39. In the extreme case, if seven others plan to defect then each subject faces no cost from contributing but can provide 1.50 to the others by doing so.

40. I have not had the time to figure out in what way this might explain the data on predictions of others' behavior. Dawes, McTavish, and Shaklee (1977) claim that defectors expected more defection than cooperators. But the incentive structure suggests that the no-loss incentives would lead those who expect defection by others to defect less often than those who expect more cooperation. Dawes, McTavish, and Shaklee further claim that "the possible loss manipulation was not only ineffective in eliciting differential cooperation, it was ineffective in eliciting differential predictions about others' behavior as well" (Dawes, McTavish, and Shaklee 1977, p. 5). I remain suspicious and believe this needs more investigation.

41. For example, a rough calculation for these Dawes experiments suggests a payoff of $3.75 to 5.5 defectors and −$5.75 to 2.5 (= 0.3 × 8) contributors for a total of $52.50. A similar calculation for communication suggests $1.25 to 5.5 (= 0.7 × 8) contributors and $8.25 to 2.5 defectors for a total of $137.50. Adding $9.50 to each of 8 payoffs would yield a cost for each trial of 76 + 137.50 = $223.50. Dividing by 2 would then have cost on average $111.75 for

communication trials and $64.25 for noncommunication trials. The total for each pair would then be $176, a saving as opposed to the original $190. Table 2.2 would then have entries such as a payoff to $X = 7.25$ and a payoff to $O = 3.00$ if $X = 4$ and $O = 4$.

42. This is a Marwell and Ames footnote: "One male subject named Chris was inadvertently classified as female and the mistake was not discovered until long after completion of the experiment. Thus, one group was composed of three males and one female. Deletion of this group or this subject makes no meaningful change in the results."

43. I would like to thank the University of Chicago Press for permission to quote from this report.

44. How a group of 4 becomes a group of 80 is discussed below.

45. Theory suggests in this case that one Nash equilibrium involves only that person contributing.

46. The strong free-rider hypothesis is that everyone contributes zero to the public good

47. One study that suggests this is important is Saijo and Yamaguchi (1992) which is discussed in more detail in section IV. I have also learned recently of the work of Schwartz-Shea and Simmons (1987), but have not had time to incorporate it into this paper.

48. Kim and Walker is covered in section II.D.3.

49. I would like to thank Elsevier Science Publishers for permission to quote from this report.

50. "Factors which, if they intrude into the experimental situation, will render the theory . . . inapplicable" (p. 11). Such factors involve a loss of control by the experimenter.

51. I have indicated in section II.C.3 how I feel about this design to save money.

52. Isaac, Walker, and Thomas (1984) were the first to identify and study this effect systematically. Their work is described in section II.E.

53. In Marwell and Ames (1980) there is not a smooth marginal contribution function, so it is not obvious what the appropriate m would be. One might compute an average where every 2,000 tokens yields 0.55/person so $m = 0.0275$. This seems very small but it did not deter contributions.

54. A similar comment applies to communication in the Dawes et al. experiment described in section II.B.

55. Isaac, McCue, and Plott point to a phenomenon they call "pulsing"—a contribution larger than in a previous period—and conjecture it may be an attempt to get others to cooperate. No one knows for sure as "pulsing" has never been systematically isolated and studied.

56. I would like to thank Kluwer Academic Publishers for permission to quote from this report.

57. We saw this variable in section II.D.3.

58. Bohm (1972), Dawes, McTavish, and Shaklee (1977), and Marwell and Ames (1979).

59. Isaac, McCue, and Plott (1985), Kim and Walker (1984), and Isaac, Walker, and Thomas (1984).

60. In an extremely interesting paper, Sally (1992) took 130 treatments from 37 studies and ran a regression with percentage contribution as the dependent variable. He found significant positive coefficients for moral suasion, frequency of discussion, solicitation of promises by the experimenter, and (perhaps surprisingly) whether players earned money. He found a significant negative effect for marginal payoffs. His R^2 were about 0.7 to 0.8. However, I think he missed some interesting experiments and variables.

61. I cover about 40 papers in this section. I apologize to the authors I leave out. I just ran out of time and space.

62. I have in mind here something like the robustness of the supply-demand equilibrium with private goods. See chapter 5.

63. For example, the effects of changes in the marginal per capita return seem to vary depending on group size. See Isaac and Walker (1988b) and Isaac, Walker, and Williams (1990).

64. In the Prisoners' dilemma, each player's dominant strategy is D. There is one Nash equilibrium: (D, D). In Chicken, there are two Nash equilibria: (D, C) and (C, D). There are no dominant strategies. See Chapter 1 for an early history of these experiments.

65. A strategy is dominant if it maximizes the return to an individual no matter what his oppo-

nents do. That is, if player i's strategy is s and the others' strategies are x and i's payoff is $u(s, x)$, then the strategy c is dominant if and only if c solves max $u(c, s)$ for all possible s.

66. So if you are running a campaign you want a high enough target to encourage contribution increases but low enough to prevent failure to attain the goal. This is the fund-raiser's art.

67. These are Marwell and Ames (1980), Dawes, Orbell, Simmons, and van de Kragt (1986), Isaac, Schmidtz, and Walker (1988), Rapoport and Suleiman (1993), Suleiman and Rapoport (1992), and Palfrey and Rosenthal (1991a).

68. In the experiments reported $r = 10$, $z_i = 5$, and $T = 10$, 15, or 20. $N = 5$.

69. They also had repetitive trials, but since no information or feedback was provided between trials, the repetition had no apparent effect.

70. Suleiman and Rapoport (1992) actually test whether requiring an all or none payment affects the rate of contribution. They find that contributions increase if c_i is not restricted to be all or none. Palfrey and Prisbrey (1993) have a similar finding for a non-threshold environment.

71. What did have an effect on the average contributed was the introduction of heterogeneity. More on this in section III.D.

72. An alternative yielding the same data would be to randomize between contributing 0 and contributing z. This, however, does not appear to be supported by individual data. But I am not sure whether a more diffuse contribution strategy based on random behavior can be rejected since one only sees realizations and not the strategy itself.

73. At least 25 of the 40 or so papers reported here have used this technique.

74. In another attempt to control for inexperience, Dawes and Orbell (1982) let some subjects think about the problem for a day. It did not matter. There was no threshold. See section III.E.

75. Saijo and Yamaguchi (1992) report both decreases and no effect depending on the details of the payoff schedules. More on this in section IV.

76. Isaac, Walker, and Williams are apparently now running some experiments for up to 60 decision rounds, which may provide some answers.

77. I would like to thank Elsevier Science Publishers for permission to quote from this report.

78. I use marginal incentives here in contrast with what has been called the strength or salience of payoffs. That would mean increasing the rate at which subjects are paid while keeping the marginal payoffs constant. For the Isaac and Walker environments this would mean increasing a and p while keeping a/p constant.

79. At 0.7 it is a dominant strategy to contribute nothing. At 1.43 it is a dominant strategy to contribute everything. Neither happens in this experiment, but an increase in contributions (on average from 27 percent to 40 percent) does occur with the increase in MPCR. These puzzling data will be discussed in more detail in section 4 below.

80. The t statistic on the estimated coefficient α is 86.358.

81. For additional work see Carter et al. (1992).

82. Olson (1971) is usually cited as arguing for the decrease. Chamberlin (1974) provides conditions under which there might be an increase.

83. One other interesting set of experiments with Cournot oligopoly, reported in Morrison and Kamarei (1990), finds no effect from numbers. As with thresholds there is an interior equilibrium, but unlike with thresholds it is unique.

84. My footnote: VCM-MS-XC means "voluntary contribution mechanism–multiple session–extra credit."

85. I would like to thank R. M. Isaac for permission to quote from this report.

86. One of the problems a theorist faces in trying to decide what we know is the fact that many experimentalists make very little effort to relate their results to others.

87. They have since provided some detail based on expectations about the effects of signaling. Their model predicts that contributions will decrease with $(1 - M)/[M (N - 1)]$ and will not change with a multiplicative increase in payoffs.

88. γ is $1 - F(\cdot)$ where F is the population cumulative distribution function of β, a sample of which appears in the lab. Under the maintained hypothesis that the theory is correct, γ can be estimated from the data.

89. Since $M < 1$, $t_i < \bar{t}^i$ so, strictly speaking, $t_i = 0$ if $\bar{t}^i + N(M-1)/(2\,\delta^i p) \leq 0$. Thus $E\,(\%C)$ is an overestimate of the correct number. This does not affect the comparative statics below. Also it does provide a somewhat ad hoc explanation for a decline in contributions with repetition since if subjects use last periods contributions to estimate this periods $\bar{t}^i$ then contributions will follow the time path given by

$$\%C_\tau = \%C_{\tau-1} + k\left(\frac{N(M-1)}{p}\right)$$

where k is a subject pool specific constant.

90. Since none predicts splitting of tokens, a well-known fact, all are technically deficient. See Chen (1993) for a theory which might explain splitting.

91. See section II.D for a description of their experimental design.

92. Their environment is described in section II.D. Here they used an MPCR of 0.3.

93. If at least four of six contributed 10¢, all could talk. There were no rebates.

94. I would like to thank the University of Chicago Press for permission to quote from this report.

95. This is true of Dawes, McTavish, and Shaklee (1977), Isaac, Walker, and Thomas (1984), and some of Marwell and Ames (1979).

96. In the language of modern game theory, the distribution of types is common knowledge. Information is complete but imperfect.

97. For example Brookshire et al. (1989a) suggest that the effect of heterogeneity depends on the range of alternative types—how many and how different. This needs more exploration.

98. This is still not perfectly controlled always. See, for example, footnote 42 in section II.C for a problem encountered by Marwell and Ames.

99. Robyn Dawes has suggested to me that a "wild speculation would be that men cooperate more when the experimenter is female," and vice versa. This can be tested.

100. In research on ultimatum games, a two-person situation, Carter and Irons (1991) find that economists are more selfish. Frank, Gilovich, and Regan (1993) have a similar finding for two-person prisoner dilemmas. Kagel, Kim, and Moser (1992) do not support the Carter and Irons result. I know of no other work specifically designed to isolate an "economist" effect than these three, but see Schram and Sonnemans (1992) for additional work in this area.

101. This yields a rather peculiar juxtaposition of strong control of payoffs and absolutely no control over the data on beliefs.

102. The interested reader can check the data analysis in Suleiman and Rapoport (1992) and Rapoport and Suleiman (1993). They also generalize the model above by assuming subjects have expected utility functions of the form $u(x) = kx^c$. They estimate c by fitting kx^c to nine responses of each subject about two alternative gambles and their certainty equivalents. No payments were contingent on the responses, so one must be careful about the quality of these data.

103. See Palfrey and Rosenthal (1991a) for the details.

104. I use the term survey data to identify data collected by asking subjects questions for which there is nothing at stake. This includes standard debriefing such as "What were you doing?" As a classroom exercise, I have often asked students to describe their strategy after an experiment. In the overwhelming majority of cases the data generated in that experiment reject the subjects' own hypotheses about their own behavior. I now tend to ignore any *ex post* anecdotal evidence from surveys.

105. A critique and response can be found in McLean, Orbell, and Dawes (1991).

106. I would like to thank the American Political Science Association for permission to quote from this report.

107. They survey both subjects who were decision makers and subjects who were (unseen) observers. The variance of responses of the former was larger suggesting that choice affected beliefs.

108. That is, does the mere act of asking for predictions affect the rate of contribution?

109. They provide a second set of data, which shows that the opportunity of promising may be an important part in explaining the effect of discussion. This is further discussed in Orbell, Dawes, and van de Kragt (1990).

110. I would like to thank J. Brown-Kruse for permission to quote from this report.

111. A recent theoretical analysis is Bigman (1992).

112. There have been other mechanisms tested with unanimity. Banks et al. (1988) also test Smith's auction process and obtain data similar to that in Tables 2.18 and 2.19. Smith et al. (1982) tested Oral Double Auctions with unanimity and found that the extramarginal units which were rationed out by the price system—as they should be—tended to veto the allocations and significantly reduce efficiencies.

113. This variation, sequencing, is clearly related to sequential protocols in bargaining such as ultimatum games. See chapter 4.

114. See, for example, the work of Harstad and Marrese (1978, 1981, 1982) or Cremer and Riordan (1982).

115. Notice that the average (or percentage of) cooperation will not be the same as the percentage of time the good is provided. If cooperation is efficient and exactly three of five contribute each time, then $(3/2)(\%\ cooperation) = \%\ provision$.

116. E.g., if exactly two of five have cooperated and you are the fifth to move, you should cooperate.

117. John Kagel points out that "these results contrast to sequential games requiring 1 out of 2 to contribute to the public good—where, with experience, subgame perfection works almost perfectly. This supports the notion of the failure of backward induction argument, as these games involve only two moves compared to 5."

118. Banks, Ledyard, and Porter (1989) found revisions very helpful in a private good, coordination problem.

119. The detail table eliminates computation and interpolation but increases informational size from 2×11 entries to 61×11 entries. Does this increase or decrease decision costs?

120. These are discussed in chapter 4.

121. Dictator experiments allow a subject to divide $10 between themselves and another. The other must accept the division.

122. See, for example, Marwell and Ames (1980), Palfrey and Prisbrey (1993), and McKelvey and Palfrey (1992), who test this hypothesis directly.

123. See, for example, Table 2.9.

124. See Andreoni (1993a) and (1993b) for additional work like this.

125. In Dawes et al., Marwell et al., and Isaac et al., etc. the dominant strategy was $t = 0$. Only mistakes such that $t > 0$ are possible.

126. Palfrey and Prisbrey use a score maximizing procedure to do this. In Saijo and Yamaguchi, $z = 10$, and I have arbitrarily allowed errors of 1; that is, $t_i = 0$ or 1 is not giving and $t_i = 9$ or 10 is giving.

127. Two other interesting observations can also be made. First, initially there are 33 percentage more Nash responses when MPCR = 0.7 and Nash is antigroup behavior than when MPCR = 1/0.7 and Nash is exactly progroup behavior. This suggests to me that the explanation for contributions in one-shot experiments with MPCR < 1 is not altruism. Second, classifying 10 and 9 when MPCR = 0.7 and 0 and 1 when MPCR = 1/0.7 as *absolutely not Nash*, we see 12 percent responses, with no decline, which are of this type, evenly distributed between both values of MPCR. This suggests to me that, on average, about 10 percent of laboratory subjects may be simply immune to the control that experimenters try to exert by paying them.

128. As I indicated in section III.C.1, Palfrey and Prisbrey (1993) provide a probit estimation of individual decisions and suggest that 80 percent of the decisions can be explained by expected contribution $= f [\alpha_o + \alpha_1 (MPCR)]$. This also leaves about 20 percent unexplained.

129. A simple theoretical exercise which would provide an interesting environment for an experiment is to determine an environment where every subject has a dominant strategy to contribute t_i^* where $0 < t_i^* < z$ and where the group optimum t^o is such that $t^o \neq \Sigma_{i=N}^N t_i^*$.

130. For any utility/payoff functions the MPCR, for all players, will equal 1 at an interior Nash equilibrium.

131. If there are asymmetries and either $x^i \neq x^j$ or $z^i \neq z^j$, it is not clear what a group optimum is. Instead, there are many Pareto optima. If the subjects are maximizing their total take, then the best function to maximize is $\Sigma_i u^i$. But this may leave some subjects very badly off.

132. As N grows, t goes to zero while $\hat{t}$ stays constant and the MPCR at $\hat{t}$ goes to 0. To get some idea of the strength of the incentives consider $\alpha = \frac{2}{3}$ and $N = 10$. Then $t^*/z \cong 5$ percent, $\hat{t}/z = 33$ percent, and MPCR$(\hat{t}) = 0.10$. To make it possible to keep MPCR at $\hat{t}$ constant in N one must use a CES utility function.

133. A methodological point to Andreoni's study must be noted with respect to the inducement of preferences, u^i. Rather than tell them the function—which they might not understand—he gave them a matrix; their t^i as the column, the sum of others t^i's as the row and the entries were $u^i = \alpha \ln (z - t^i) + (1 - \alpha) \ln t^i + \Sigma_{j \neq i} t^i$. As with Saijo and Yamaguchi, this presentation of the data seems to provide subjects with computational help that leads them to choose more self-interestedly. The fact that the form of the payoff table affects behavior confirms the very delicate and sensitive nature of public goods experiments and the need for better control if data are to be accepted.

An experimental design problem, as we move to more complicated environments, will be how to induce very complicated nonlinear preferences with income effects and substitution among many (more than two) dimensions. At some point experimentalists must let go of their simple world in which marginal willingness to pay schedules are the same as demand functions. Of course that is harder to control and will require new procedures.

134. Isaac and Walker have responded to an early version of this paper by doing so, but I have not yet seen the full set of data and analysis.

135. Even Isaac, Walker, and Williams find 38 percent Nash behavior in their large group–no money experiments by round 10.

136. One unanswered question is how or whether this works in large ($N \geq 40$) groups.

Bibliography

Abdalla, A., R. Cooper, D.V. DeJong, R. Forsythe, and T. W. Ross. 1989. Forward induction in coordination and battle of the sexes games: Some experimental results. Discussion paper, Dept. of Economics, Illinois State University, Normal, Ill.

Admati, A. and M. Perry. 1991. Joint projects without commitment. *Review of Economic Studies* 58:259–76.

Alfano, G. and G. Marwell. 1980. Experiments on the provision of public goods by groups III: Nondivisibility and free riding in "read" groups. *Social Psychology Quarterly* 43:300–309.

Andreoni, J. 1988a. Privately provided public goods in a large economy: The limits of altruism. *Journal of Public Economics* 35:57–73.

———1988b. Why free ride? Strategies and learning in public goods experiments. *Journal of Public Economics* 37:291–304.

———1989. Giving with impure altruism: applications to charity and Ricardian equivalence. *Journal of Political Economy* 97(6):1447–58.

———. 1993a. Cooperation in public goods experiments: Kindness or confusion? Technical Report 9309, University of Wisconsin, Madison, Wis.

———1993b. An experimental test of the public goods crowding-out hypothesis. *American Economic Review* 83:1317–27.

———1993c. Warm–glow versus cold–prickly: The effects of positive and negative framing on cooperation. Technical report, University of Wisconsin, Madison, Wis.

Andreoni, J., and J. Miller. 1993. Rational cooperation in the finitely repeated prisoner's dilemma: Experimental evidence. *Economic Journal* 103:570–85.

Andreoni, J., and H. Varian. 1992. Pre-play contracts in the prisoner's dilemma. Technical report, CREST Working Paper, University of Michigan.

Arrow, K. 1969. The organization of economic activity: Issues pertinent to the choice of market versus non–market allocation. In *Public expenditure and policy analysis*, R. Haveman and J. Margolis, editors, Chicago: Markham. 67–81.

Arrow, K. J. 1979. The property rights doctrine and demand revelation under incomplete information. In *Economics and human welfare*, M. Boskin, editor, New York: Academic Press. 23–39.

Austen-Smith, D. 1980. Individual contribution to public goods. *Economic Letters* 5:359–61.

Bagnoli, M., and B. Lipman. 1989. Provision of public goods: Fully implementing the core through private contributions. *Review of Economic Studies* 56:583–601.

Bagnoli, M., and M. McKee. 1991. Voluntary contribution games: Efficient private provision of public goods. *Economic Inquiry* 29:351–66.

Banks, J. S., and R. L. Calvert. 1989. Communication and efficiency in coordination games. Working Paper 196, Dept. of Political Science, University of Rochester, Rochester, N.Y.

———1992. A battle-of-the-sexes game with incomplete information. *Games and Economic Behavior* 4(3):347–72.

Banks, J., J. Ledyard, and D. Porter. 1989. Allocating uncertain and unresponsive resources: An experimental approach. *RAND Journal of Economics* 20(1):1–25.

Banks, J., C. Plott, and D. Porter. 1988. An experimental analysis of unanimity in public goods provision mechanisms. *Review of Economic Studies* 55(182):301–22.

Bergstrom, T., L. Blume, and H. Varian. 1986. On the private provision of public goods. *Journal of Public Economics* 29:25–49.

Berman, S., and A. Schotter. 1982. When is the incentive problem real? *Games, Economic Dynamics, and Time Series Analysis*, M. Deistler, E. Furst, and G. Schwodiauer, editors, Wurzburg: Physica-Verlag. 127–40.

Bernheim, D. 1986. On the voluntary and involuntary provision of public goods. *American Economic Review* 75:789–93.

Bigman, D. 1992. Unanimity and exclusion as mechanisms to eliminate free riding in public goods. *Journal of Economic Behavior and Organization* 19:101–17.

Binger, B., E. Hoffman, and A. Williams. 1985. Implementing a Lindahl equilibrium with a modified tatonnement mechanism: Some preliminary experimental results. Discussion paper, Purdue Unviersity.

Bliss, C., and B. Nalebuff. 1984. Dragonslaying and ballroom dancing: The private supply of a public good. Discussion Paper 1038, Harvard University.

Bohm, P. 1972. Estimating demand for public goods: An experiment. *European Economic Review* 3:111–30.

———1983. Revealing demand for an actual public good. *Journal of Public Economics* 24:135–51.

———1987. Lindahl on public finance. In *The new Palgrave: A dictionary of economics*, J. Eatwell, M. Millgate, and P. Newman, editors, London: Macmillan.

Bolle, F., and P. Ockenfels. 1990. Prisoners' dilemma as a game with incomplete information. *Journal of Economic Psychology* 11:69–84.

Bornstein, G., and A. Rapoport. 1988. Intergroup competition for the provision of step-level public goods: Effects of preplay communication. *European Journal of Social Psychology* 18:125–42.

Bornstein, G., A. Rapoport, L. Kerpel, and T. Katz. 1989. Within- and between-group communication in intergroup competition for public goods. *Journal of Experimental Social Psychology* 25:422–36.

Boylan, R. T. 1990. Equilibria resistant to mutation. Social Science Working Paper 691, California Institute of Technology.

Boylan, R.T., and M. A. El-Gamal. 1990. Fictitious play: A statistical study of multiple economic experiments. Discussion paper, California Institute of Technology.

Brewer, M. 1985. Choice behavior in social dilemmas: Effects of social identity, group size, and decision framing. Discussion paper, University of California, Los Angeles.

Brookshire, D., and D. Coursey. 1987. Measuring the value of a public good: An empirical comparison of elicitation procedures. *American Economic Review* 77(4):554–66.

Brookshire, D., D. Coursey, M. Dickie, S. G. A. Fisher, and W. Schulze. 1985. Tests of parallelism between laboratory and the field. Discussion paper, University of Wyoming, Laramie.

Brookshire, D., D. Coursey, and H. Kunreuther. 1991. Compensation schemes in the presence of negative externalities: A field experiment. In *Research in experimental economics*, vol. 4, R. M. Isaac, editor, Greenwich, Conn.: JAI Press. 81–106.

Brookshire, D., D. Coursey, and D. Redington. 1989a. Special interests and the voluntary provision of public goods. Discussion Paper, Washington University, St. Louis.

————1989b. Equity and the incentive compatible provision of public goods. Discussion paper, Dept. of Economics, University of Wyoming, Laramie, Wyo.

Brookshire, D., and W. Schulze. 1985. Experiments in the solicitation of private and public values: An overview. Discussion Paper, University of Wisconsin.

Brown, P. 1992. An experimental examination of voluntary compliance. Technical report, University of Massachusetts, Boston, Mass.

Brown-Kruse, J., and D. Hummels. 1993. Gender effects in laboratory public goods contribution: Do individuals put their money where their mouth is? *Journal of Economic Behavior and Organization*. 22:255–67.

Brubaker, E., and D. Gumucio. 1982. Sixty-eight percent free revelation and thirty-two percent free ride? Demand disclosures under varying conditions on exclusion. In *Research in experimental economics*, vol. 2 V. Smith, editor, Greenwich, Conn.: JAI Press, 151–66.

Budescu, D., A. Rapoport, and R. Suleiman. 1990. Resource dilemmas with environmental uncertainty and asymmetric players. IPDM Report 83, Institute of Information Processing and Decision Making, University of Haifa.

Caldwell, M. D., 1976. Communication and sex effects in a five-person and prisoner's dilemma game. *Journal of Personality and Social Psychology* 33:273–80.

Calvert, R., and R. Wilson. 1984. Comment on van de Kragt, Orbell, and Dawes. *The American Political Science Review* 78:496–7.

Camerer, C. 1995. Individual decisionmaking. In *The handbook of experimental economics*, J. Kagel and A. Roth, editors, Princeton, N.J.: Princeton University Press.

Carter, J., B. Drainville, and R. Poulin. 1992. A test for rational altruism in a public goods experiment. Technical report, College of the Holy Cross, Worcester, Mass.

Carter, J. R., and M. D. Irons. 1991. Are economists different, and if so, why? *Journal of Economic Perspectives* 5:171–7.

Castore, C., and J. Murningham. 1978. Determinants of support for group decisions. *Organizational Behavior and Human Performance* 22:75–92.

Chamberlin, J. 1974. Provision of collective goods as a function of group size. *American Political Science Review* 68:707–16.

————1978. The logic of collective action: some experimental results. *Behavioral Science* 23:441–5.

Champsaur, P., D. J. Roberts, and R. W. Rosenthal. 1975. On cores in economies with public goods. *International Economic Review* 16:751–64.

Chan, K., S. Mestelman, R. Moir, and R. Muller. 1993. The voluntary provision of public goods under varying endowment distributions. Technical Report Working Paper No. 93-02, McMaster University, Hamilton, Ontario, Canada.

Chander, P. 1988. Incentives and a process converging to the core of a public goods economy. Social Science Working Paper 677, California Institute of Technology, Pasadena, Cal.

Chari, V. V., and L. E. Jones. 1988. A reconsideration of the problem of social cost: free riders and monopolists. Working Paper 324, Research Department, Federal Reserve Bank of Minneapolis, Minneapolis.

Chen, K.-Y. 1993. Subrational equilibria in voluntary contribution games. Technical report, California Institute of Technology.

Clarke, E. H. 1971. Multipart pricing of public goods. *Public Choice* 8:19–33.

Cohen, S., and M. Loeb. 1984. Theory and experiments in decentralized organization. Paper presented at TIMS XXVI, Copenhagen.

Cooper, R., D. V. DeJong, R. Forsythe, and T. Ross. 1987. Selection criteria in coordination games: Some experimental results. Department of Economics Working Paper 87-20, University of Iowa, Iowa City.

——— 1989. Communication in coordination games. Department of Economics Working Paper 89-16, University of Iowa, Iowa City.

——— 1990. Cooperation without reputation. Discussion paper, College of Business Administration, University of Iowa, Iowa City.

Cornes, R., and T. Sandler. 1985. The simple analytics of pure public good provision.*Economica* 52:103–116.

——— 1986. *The theory of externalities, public goods, and club goods*. Cambridge, England: Cambridge University Press.

Coursey, D., and W. Schulze. 1986. The application of laboratory experimental economics to the contingent valuation of public goods. *Public Choice* 49:47–68.

Coursey, D., and V. L. Smith. 1984. Experimental tests of an allocation mechanism for private, public or externality goods. *Scandinavian Journal of Economics* 86(4):468–84.

Cowen, T., ed. 1988. *The theory of market failure, a critical examination*. Fairfax, Va: George Mason University Press.

Cox, J., B. Roberson, and V. L. Smith. 1982. Theory and behavior in single object auctions. In Smith (1982c).

Crawford, V. P. 1990. Thomas Schelling and the analysis of strategic behavior. Discussion Paper 90-11, Dept. of Economics, University of California, San Diego.

Crawford, V. P., and H. Haller. 1990. Learning how to cooperate: Optimal play in repeated coordination games. *Econometrica* 58(3):571–5.

Cremer, J., and M. Riordan. 1982. A Stackelberg solution to the public goods problem. CARESS working paper, University of Pennsylvania.

Cremer, J., and M. Riordan. 1985. A sequential solution to the public goods problem. *Econometrica* 53:77–84.

Danzinger, L., and A. Schnytzer. 1991. Implementing the Lindahl voluntary-exchange mechanism. *European Journal of Political Economy* 7:55–64.

Darley, J., and B. Latane. 1968. Bystander intervention in emergencies: diffusion of responsibility. *Journal of Personality and Social Psychology* 8:377–83.

d'Aspremont, C., and L. A. Gerard-Varet. 1979. On Bayesian incentive compatible mechanisms. In Laffont (1979, 269–88).

Daughety, A. F., and R. Forsythe. 1987. Complete information outcomes without common knowledge. Working Paper Series 87-24, Dept. of Economics and Management Sciences, College of Business Administration, University of Iowa, Iowa City.

Dawes, R. 1975. Formal models of dilemmas in social decision-making. In *Human judgment and decision processes*, M. Kaplan and S. Schwartz, editors, New York: Academic Press. 87–107.

Dawes, R. 1980. Social dilemmas. *Annual Review of Psychology* 31:169–93.

Dawes, R. J. McTavish, and H. Shaklee. 1977. Behavior, communication, and assumptions about other people's behavior in a commons dilemma situation. *Journal of Personality and Social Psychology* 35(1):1–11.

Dawes, R., and J. Orbell. 1982. Cooperation in social dilemma situations: Thinking about it doesn't help. In Smith (1982c), 167–73.

Dawes, R., J. Orbell, R. Simmons, and A. van de Kragt. 1986. Organizing groups for collective action. *American Political Science Review* 8:1171–85.

Dawes, R., J. Orbell, and A. van de Kragt. 1985. A 'great society' or a 'small society'?: The threshold-of-the-room effect in social dilemmas. Prepared for the Public Choice Society Meetings, New Orleans, February 1985.

Dawes, R., and R. Thaler. 1988. Cooperation. *Journal of Economic Perspectives* 2(3):187–97.

Dawes, R., A. van de Kragt, and J. Orbell. 1987. Not me or thee but we: The importance of group identity in eliciting cooperation in dilemma situations: Experimental manipulations. Carnegie Mellon University. Presented at the Public Choice Meeting, Tucson, Ariz., March 28, 1987, and the Midwestern Psychological Association Meeting (invited address), Chicago, May 8, 1987.

Dorsey, R. 1992. The voluntary contributions mechanism with real time revisions. *Public Choice* 73:261–82.

Downs, A. 1957. *An economic theory of democracy.* New York: Harper and Row.

Dreze, J., and D. de la Vallee-Poussin. 1971. A tatonnement process for public goods. *Review of Economic Studies* 38:133–50.

Dutta, P. K., and R. K. Sundaram. 1989. The tragedy of the commons? A complete characterization of stationary equilibria in dynamic resource games. Discussion paper, Department of Economics, Columbia University, New York.

Easley, D., and J. Ledyard. 1992. Theories of price formation and exchange in double oral auctions. In *The Double Auction Market*, vol. 15, D. Friedman, J. Geanakoplos, D. Lane, and J. Rust, editors, Addison-Wesley. Proceedings of the Santa Fe Institute Studies in the Sciences of Complexity.

Edney, J., and C. Harper. 1978. Profile: The commons dilemma. *Environmental Management* 2(6):491–507.

Edwards, J. H. Y. 1990. Indivisibility and private preference for collective provision. Discussion paper, Department of Economics, Tulane University, New Orleans, La.

El-Gamal, M. A., R. D. McKelvey, and T. R. Palfrey. 1991. A Bayesian sequential experimental study of myopia and strategic learning in the centipede game. Social Science Working paper, California Institute of Technology.

Erev, I., and A. Rapoport. 1990. Provision of step-level public goods, the sequential contribution mechanism. *Journal of Conflict Resolution* 34(3):401–25.

Evans., R., and F. Harris. 1982. A Bayesian analysis of free rider metagames. *Southern Economic Journal* 49(1):137–49.

Ferejohn, J., R. Forsythe, and R. Noll. 1979. Practical aspects of the construction of decentralized decisionmaking systems for public goods. In *Collective decision making: Applications from public choice theory*, C. S. Russell, editor, Baltimore, Md: Johns Hopkins University Press.

Ferejohn, J., R. Forsythe, R. Noll, and T. Palfrey. 1982. An experimental examination of auction mechanisms for discrete public goods. In Smith (1982c).

Ferejohn, J., and R. Noll. 1976. An experimental market for public goods: The PBS station program cooperative. *American Economic Review* 66:267–73.

Fernadez-Arias, E., and A. Kofman. 1989. Equilibrium characterization in finite-horizon games of reputation. Discussion paper, Dept. of Economics, University of California, Berkeley.

Fiorina, M. P., and C. R. Plott. 1978. Committee decisions under majority rule: An experimental study. *American Political Science Review* 72:575–98.

Fisher, J., R. Isaac, J. Schatzberg, and J. Walker. 1994. Heterogeneous demand for public goods: Effects on the voluntary contributions mechanism. To appear in *Public Choice*.

Foley, D. 1967. Resource allocation and the public sector. *Yale Economic Essays* 7:45.

Fouraker, L., and S. Siegel. 1963. *Bargaining behavior.* New York: McGraw-Hill.

Franciosi, R., R. Isaac, D. Pingry, and S. Reynolds. 1993. An experimental investigation of the Hahn-Noll revenue neutral auction for emission licenses. *Journal of Environmental Economics and Management* 24:1–24.

Frank, R. 1985. If *Homo economicus* could choose his own utility function, would he want one with a conscience? Liberty Fund Symposium.

Frank, R., T. Gilovich, and D. Regan. 1993. Does studying economics inhibit cooperation? *Journal of Economic Perspectives* 7(2):159–71.

Frohlich, N., T. Hunt, J. Oppenheimer, and R. H. Wagner. 1975. Individual contributions for collective goods. *Journal of Conflict Resolution* 19(2):310–29.

Fudenberg, D., and E. Maskin. 1990. Evolution and cooperation in noisy repeated games. *American Economic Review* 80(2):274–79.

Gardner, R., and E. Ostrom. 1989. Rules and games. *Public Choice* 70:121–49.

Gradstein, M. 1991. Time dynamics and incomplete information in the private provision of public goods. Technical report, Ben-Gurion University, Beer Sheva, Israel.

Gradstein, M., and S. Nitzan. 1990. Binary participation and incremental provision of public goods. *Social Choice and Welfare* 7:171–92.

Gradstein, M., S. Nitzan, and S. Slutsky. 1991a. Neutrality and the private provision of public goods with incomplete information. Mimeo. University of Toronto and Ben-Gurion University of the Negev, Israel.

———— 1991b. Private provision of public goods under price uncertainty. Mimeo. University of Toronto and Ben-Gurion University of the Negev, Israel.

Green, J., and J. J. Laffont. 1977. Characterization of satisfactory mechanisms for the revelation of preferences for public goods. *Econometrica* 45:427–38.

————1978. *Incentives in public decision making*. Amsterdam: North Holland.

Grether, D., M. Isaac, and C. Plott. 1989. *The allocation of scarce resources: Experimental economics and the problem of allocating airport slots*. Boulder, Col.: Westview Press.

Groves, T. 1970. *The allocation of resources under uncertainty*. Dissertation. University of California, Berkeley.

————1973. Incentives in teams. *Econometrica* 41:617–63.

————1976. Information,incentives, and the internalization of production externalities. In *Theory and Measurement of Economic Externalities*, S. Lin, editor, New York: Academic Press.

————1979a. Efficient collective choice when compensation is possible. *Review of Economic Studies* 46:227–41.

————1979b. Efficient collective choice with compensation. In Laffont (1979), 37–59.

Groves, T., and J. Ledyard. 1977. Optimal allocation of public goods: A solution to the 'free rider' problem. *Econometrica* 45:783–809.

————1987. Incentive compatibility since 1972. In *Information, Incentives, & Economic Mechanisms: Essays in Honor of Leonid Hurwicz*, T., Groves, R. Radner, and S. Reiter, editors, Minneapolis: University of Minnesota Press. 48–111.

Guler, K., C. Plott, and Q. Vuong. 1987. A study of zero-out auctions: Experimental analysis of a process of allocating private rights to the use of public property. Social Science Working Paper 650, California Institute of Technology.

Guttman, J. 1978. Understanding collective action: Matching behavior. *American Economic Review* 68:251–5.

————1987. A non-Cournot model of voluntary collective action. *Economica* 54:1–19.

Hardin, R. 1968. The tragedy of the commons. *Science* 162:1243–8.

————1976. Group provision of step goods. *Behavioral Science* 21:101–6.

Harris, R. J. 1988. The altruism modification model (AMM). Presented at a colloquium at UGA, October 7, 1988; also, informal paper at University of Wisconsin (SESP).

Harrison, G. and J. Hirshleifer. 1989. An experimental evaluation of weakest link/best shot models of public goods. *Journal of Political Economy* 97(1):201–25.

Harstad, R., and M. Marrese. 1978. Experimentation on the effects of decision processes on public good allocations. Discussion Paper 78-50, University of British Columbia.

————1981. Implementation of mechanisms by processes: Public good allocation experiments. *Journal of Economic Behavior and Organization* 2:129–51.

————1982. Behavioral explanations of efficient public good allocations. *Journal of Public Economics* 19:367–83.

Hirshleifer, D., and E. Rasmusen. 1989. Cooperation in a repeated prisoners' dilemma with ostracism. *Journal of Economic Behavior and Organization* 12:87–106.

Hirshleifer, J. 1983. From weakest-link to best-shot: The voluntary provision of public goods. *Public Choice* 41:371–86.

Hoffman, E., K. McCabe, K. Shachat, and V. Smith. 1994. Preferences, property rights and anonymity in bargaining games. *Games and Economic Behavior* 7(3):346–380.

Hoffman, E., and M. Spitzer. 1985. Entitlements, rights and fairness: An experimental examination of subjects' concepts of distributive justice. *Journal of Legal Studies* 15:254–97.

Holmstrom, B. 1979. Groves schemes on restricted domains. *Econometrica* 47:1137–44.

Holt, C. 1995. Industrial organization: A survey of laboratory research. In *The Handbook of Experimental Economics*, J. Kagel and A. Roth, editors, Princeton: Princeton University Press.

Huberman, B., and N. Glance. 1992. Diversity and collective action. Technical report, Dynamics of Computation Group, Xerox Palo Alto Research Center.

Hurwicz, L. 1972. On informationally decentralized systems. In *Decision and organization: A volume in honor of Jacob Marschak*, R. Radner and C. B. McGuire, editors, Amsterdam: North Holland. 297–336.

———1973. The design of mechanisms for resource allocation. *American Economic Review* 63:1–30.

———1979a. On allocations attainable through Nash-equilibria. In Laffont (1979), 397–419.

———1979b. Outcome functions yielding Walrasian and Lindahl allocations at Nash equilibrium points. *Review of Economic Studies* 46:217–25.

Hurwicz, L., and M. Walker. 1990. On the generic nonoptimality of dominant-strategy allocation mechanism: A general theorem that includes pure exchange economies. *Econometrica* 58(3):683–704.

Hylland, A., and R. Zeckhauser. 1979. A mechanism for selecting public goods when preferences must be elicted. Discussion Paper 70D, Harvard University.

Isaac, R., D. Schmidtz, and J. Walker. 1988. The assurance problem in a laboratory market. *Public Choice* 62(3):217–36.

Isacc, R. M. 1991. *Research in experimental economics*, vol. 4. Greenwich, Conn: JAI Press.

Isaac, R. M., K. McCue, and C. Plott. 1985. Public goods provision in an experimental environment. *Journal of Public Economics* 26:51–74.

Isaac, R. M., and J. Walker. 1983. Marginal private returns and public goods provision. Mimeo. University of Arizona, Tucson.

———1984. The effects of communication on free riding behavior. Discussion paper, University of Arizona, Tucson.

———1987. Success and failure of the voluntary contributions process: Some evidence from experimental economics. Discussion Paper 87-1, University of Arizona, Tuscon.

———1988a. Communication and free riding behavior: The voluntary contribution mechanism. *Economic Inquiry* 26(2):585–608.

———1988b. Group size effects in public goods provision: The voluntary contributions mechanism. *Quarterly Journal of Economics*, 103 (Feb. 1988): 179–99.

———1989. Complete information and the provision of public goods. Discussion Paper 89-18, University of Arizona, Tuscon.

———1991. Costly communication: An experiment in a nested public goods problem. In *Laboratory research in political economy*, T. Palfrey, editor, Ann Arbor: University of Michigan Press. 269-86.

Isaac, R. M., J. Walker, and S. Thomas. 1984. Divergent evidence on free riding: An experimental examination of possible explanations. *Public Choice* 43(1):113–49.

Isaac, R. M., J. Walker, and A. Williams. 1990. Group size and the voluntary provision of public goods: Experimental evidence utilizing very large groups. Working papers in economics, Indiana University.

Jackson, M., and H. Moulin. 1992. Implementing a public project and distributing its cost. *Journal of Economic Theory* 57(1):125–40.

Johansen, L. 1977. The theory of public goods: misplaced emphasis? *Journal of Public Economics* 7:147–52.

———1982. On the status of the Nash type of non-cooperative equilibrium in economic theory. *Scandinavian Journal of Economics* 84(3):421–41.

Kagel, J., C. Kim, and D. Moser. 1992. "Fairness" in ultimatum games with asymmetric information and asymmetric payoffs. Technical report, University of Pittsburgh.

Kalai, E., and E. Lehrer. 1990. Rational learning leads to Nash equilibrium. Discussion Paper 895, Center for Mathematical Studies in Economics and Management Science, Northwestern University, Evanston, Ill.

Kim, O., and M. Walker. 1984. The free rider problem: Experimental evidence. *Public Choice* 43:3–24.

Kiser, L., and E. Ostrom. 1982. The three worlds of action: A metatheoretical synthesis of institutional approaches. In *Strategies of Political Inquiry*, E. Ostrom, editor, Beverly Hills: Sage Publications.

Kolm, S.-C. 1989. Cooperative-game properties of international coordination. Technical report, Paris.

Kreps, D., P. Milgrom, J. Roberts, and R. Wilson. 1982. Rational cooperation in the finitely repeated prisoners' dilemma. *Journal of Economic Theory* 27:245–52.

Kunreuther, H., P. Kleindorfer, P. Knez, and R. Yaksick. 1987. A compensation mechanism for siting noxious facilities: Theory and experimental design. *Journal of Environmental Economics and Management* 14:371–83.

Laffont, J., ed. 1979. *Aggregation and revelation of preferences*. Amsterdam: North Holland.

Laffont, J. and E. Maskin. 1982. The theory of incentives: An overview. In *Advances in economic theory: Invited papers for the fourth world congress of the econometric society 1980, Aix-en-Provence*, W. Hildebrand, editor, Cambridge, England: Cambridge University Press, 31–94.

———1983. A characterization of strongly locally incentive compatible planning procedures with public goods. *Review of Economic Studies* L (1), no. 160: 171–86.

Ledyard, J., and T. Palfrey. 1992. Voting and lottery drafts as efficient public goods mechanisms. Social Science Working Paper 717, California Institute of Technology, Pasadena.

Ledyard, J. and J. Roberts. 1974. On the incentive problem with public goods. Discussion Paper 116, Center for Mathematical Studies in Economics and Management Science, Northwestern University, Evanston, Ill.

Ledyard, J., and K. Szakaly. 1992. Designing organizations for trading in permit rights. Mimeo. California Institute of Technology, Pasadena.

Li, Q., S. Nakamura, and G. Tian. 1989. Nash-implementation of the Lindahl correspondence with decreasing returns to scale technology. Discussion paper, Dept. of Economics, Texas A&M University, College Station.

Lindahl, E. 1958 (1919). Die Gerechtigkeit der Besteuerung. Lund, Greerup. Part I, ch. 4, "Positive Lösung," translated by E. Henderson and reprinted as "Just taxation—a positive solution." In *Classics in the Theory of Public Finance*, R. Musgrave and A. Peacock, editors, London: Macmillan.

Lipnowski, I., and S. Maital. 1983. Voluntary provision of a pure public good as the game of chicken. *Journal of Public Economics* 20:381–6.

MacCrimmon, K., and D. Messick. 1976. A framework for social motives. *Behavioral Science* 21:86–100.

Mailath, G., and A. Postlewaite. 1990. Asymmetric information bargaining problems with many agents. *Review of Economic Studies* 57(3):351–67.

Makowski, L., and J. Ostroy. 1987. Vickrey-Clarke-Groves mechanisms and perfect competition. *Journal of Economic Theory* 42(2):244–61.

Malinvaud, E. 1967. Decentralized procedures for planning. In *Activity analysis in the theory of growth and planning*, E. Malinvaud and M.O.L. Bacharach, editors, London: Macmillan. 170–208.

————1971. A planning approach to the public goods problem. *Swedish Journal of Economics* 1:96–111.

Mansbridge, J. J. 1990. *Beyond self-interest*. Chicago: University of Chicago Press.

Martin, F. 1989. Common pool resources and collective action: a bibliography. Discussion paper, Workshop in Political Theory and Policy Analysis, Indiana University, Bloomington.

Marwell, G. 1982. Altruism and the problem of collective action. In *Cooperation and helping behavior: theories and research*, V. Derlega and J. Grzelak, editors, New York: Academic Press.

Marwell, G. and R. Ames. 1979. Experiments on the provision of public goods I: Resources, interest, group size, and the free-rider problem. *American Journal of Sociology* 84(6):1335–60.

————1980. Experiments on the provision of public goods II: Provision points, stakes, experience, and the free-rider problem. *American Journal of Sociology* 85(4):926–37.

————1981. Economists free ride, does anyone else? Experiments on the provision of public goods, IV. *Journal of Public Economics* 15:295–310.

Mason, C. F., O. R. Phillips, and D. B. Redington. 1991. The role of gender in a non-cooperative game. *Journal of Economic Behavior and Organization* 15:215–35.

McGuire. 1974. Group homogeneity and aggregate provision of a pure public good under Cournot behavior. *Public Choice* 18:107–26.

McKelvey, R., and T. Palfrey. 1992. An experimental study of the centipede game. *Econometrica* 60(4):803–36.

McKelvey, R. D., and P. C. Ordeshook. 1990. A decade of experimental research on spatial models of elections and committees. In *Advances in spatial theory of voting*, M. Hinich and J. Enelow, editors, Cambridge, England: Cambridge University Press.

McLean, I., J. Orbell, and R. Dawes. 1991. What should rational cognitive misers do? *American Political Science Review* 85(4):1417–26.

McMillan, J. 1978. The efficient supply of public inputs. Research Report 7805, Dept. of Economics, University of Western Ontario.

Merlo, A., and A. Schotter. 1990. Experimentation and learning in laboratory experiments: Harrison's criticism revisited. Discussion Paper 90-23, Department of Economics, New York University, New York.

Messick, D., and M. Brewer. 1983. Solving social dilemmas, a review. In *Review of personality and social psychology*, vol. 4, L. Wheeler and P. Shaver, editors, Beverly Hills: Sage. 11–44.

Meyer, R., and C. Plott. 1975. The technology of public goods, externalities and the exclusion principle. In *Economics analysis of environmental problems*, E. Mills, editor, New York: Columbia University Press. 65–94.

Miller, J., and J. Andreoni. 1991. Can evolutionary dynamics explain free riding in experiments? *Economics Letters* 36:9–15.

Monderer, D., and D. Samet. 1989. Approximating common knowledge with common beliefs. Technical Report 545, Institute for Mathematical Studies in the Social Sciences, Stanford University.

Morrison, C. C., and H. Kamarei. 1990. Some experimental testing of the Cournot-Nash hypothesis in small group rivalry situations. *Journal of Economic Behavior and Organization* 13:213–31.

Mount, K. and S. Reiter. 1974. The informational size of message spaces. *Journal of Economic Theory* 8:161–91.

Muench, T., and M. Walker. 1979. Identifying the free rider problem. In Laffont (1979), 61–90.

————1983. Are Groves-Ledyard equilibria attainable? *Review of Economic Studies* 50:393–6.

Murnighan, J., T. King, and F. Schoumaker. 1987. The dynamics of cooperation in asymmetric dilemmas. Discussion paper, University of Illinois.

Myerson, R. 1991. *Game theory analysis of conflict*. Cambridge, Mass.: Harvard University Press.

Nitzan, S., and E. Ostrom. 1990. The nature and severity of collective action problems—the voluntary provision of mixed public goods approach. Discussion paper, Workshop in Political Theory and Policy Analysis, Indiana University.

Nitzan, S., and S. Slutsky. More on free riding and uncertainty. Discussion paper, Department of Economics, University of Florida.

Olson, M. 1971. *The logic of collective action*, vol. 124, Cambridge, Mass.: Harvard University Press.

Olson, M., and D. Porter. 1994. An experimental examination into the design of decentralized methods to solve the assignment problem with and without money. *Economic Theory* 4:11–40.

Orbell, J., and R. Dawes. 1981. Social dilemmas. In *Progress in applied social psychology*, vol. 1, New York: John Wiley and Sons. 117–33.

———1991. A 'cognitive miser' theory of cooperators' advantage. *American Political Science Review* 85:515–28.

———1993. Social welfare, cooperators' advantage, and the option of not playing the game. *American Sociological Review* 58:787–800.

Orbell, J., R. Dawes, and P. Schwartz-Shea. 1993. Trust, social categories, and individuals: The case of gender. Technical report, University of Oregon. Submitted to *Ethics*.

Orbell, J., R. Dawes, and A. van de Kragt. 1990. The limits of multilateral promising. *Ethics* 100:616–27.

Orbell, J., P. Schwartz-Shea, R. Dawes, and D. Elvin. 1992. Gender as a basis for choosing partners in prisoners' dilemma games. Technical report, University of Oregon. Presented at the American Political Science Association Annual Meeting in Chicago, 1992.

Orbell, J., P. Schwartz-Shea, and R. Simmons. 1984. Do cooperators exit more readily than defectors. *American Political Science Review* 78(1):147–62.

Orbell, J., A. van de Kragt, and R. Dawes. 1988. Explaining discussion-induced cooperation. *Journal of Personality and Social Psychology* 54(5):811–19.

Orbell, J., and L. Wilson. 1978. Institutional solutions to the N-Prisoners' Dilemma. *American Political Science Review* 72:411–21.

Ostrom, E. 1992. *Governing the commons. The evolution of institutions for collective action.* Cambridge, England: Cambridge University Press.

Ostrom, E., J. Walker, and R. Gardner. 1990. Sanctioning by participants in collective action problems. Discussion paper, Indiana University. Presented at the Conference on Experimental Research on the Provision of Public Goods and Common-Pool Resources.

———1992. Covenants with and without a sword: Self-governance is possible. *American Political Science Review* 86(2):404–17.

Ostrom, E., and J. M. Walker. 1991. Communication in a commons: Cooperation without external enforcement. In *Laboratory Research in Political Economy*, T. Palfrey, editor, Ann Arbor: University of Michigan Press. 287–322.

Palfrey, T., and J. Prisbrey. 1993. Anomalous behavior in linear public goods experiments: How much and why? Social Science Working Paper 833, California Institute of Technology.

Palfrey, T., and H. Rosenthal. 1984. Participation and the provision of discrete public goods: A strategic analysis. *Journal of Public Economics* 24:171–93.

———1988. Private incentives in social dilemmas: The effects of incomplete information and altruism. *Journal of Public Economics* 28:309–32.

———1991a. Testing game-theoretic models of free riding: New evidence on probability bias and learning. In *Laboratory Research in Political Economy*, T. Palfrey, editor, Ann Arbor: University of Michigan Press.

———1991b. Testing for effects of cheap talk in a public goods game with private information *Games and Economic Behavior* 3:183–220.

———1992. Repeated play, cooperation and coordination: An experimental study. Social Science Working Paper 785, California Institute of Technology.

Plott, C. 1979. The application of laboratory experimental methods to public choice. In *Collective decision making: Applications from public choice theory*, C. Russell, editor, Washington, D.C.: Resources for the Future. 137–60.

————1983. Externalities and corrective policies in experimental markets. *Economic Journal* 93:106–27.

————1990. Will economics become an experimental science? Social Science working paper 758, California Institute of Technology, Pasadena.

Poppe, M., and L. Utens. 1986. Effects of greed and fear of being gypped in a social dilemma situation with changing pool size. *Journal of Economic Psychology* 7:61–73.

Pratt, J. W., and R. Zeckhauser. 1980. Incentive-based decentralization: Expected externality payments induce efficient behavior in groups. Discussion Paper Series 83D, John Fitzgerald Kennedy School of Government, Harvard University.

Prisbrey, J. 1990. An experimental study of equilibrium selection in a public goods setting. Social Science Working Paper, California Institute of Technology.

Radner, R. 1987. Decentralization and incentives. In *Information, incentives, & economic mechanisms. Essays in honor of Leonid Hurwicz*, T. Groves, R. Radner, and S. Reiter, editors, Minneapolis: University of Minnesota Press. 48–111.

Rapoport, A. 1985. Public goods and the MCS experimental paradigm. *American Political Science Review* 79:148–55.

————1987. Research paradigms and expected utility models for the provision of step-level public goods. *Psychological Review* 94(1):74–83.

————1988. Provision of step-level public goods: Effects of inequality in resources. *Journal of Personality and Social Psychology* 54(3):432–40.

Rapoport, A., and G. Bornstein. 1987. Intergroup competition for the provision of binary public goods. *Psychological Review* 94(3):291–9.

Rapoport, A., G. Bornstein, and I. Erev. 1989. Intergroup competition for public goods: Effects of unequal resources and relative group size. *Journal of Personality and Social Psychology* 56(5):748–56.

Rapoport, A., D. Budescu, and R. Suleiman. 1993. Sequential requests from randomly distributed shared resources. *Journal of Mathematical Psychology* 37:241–65.

Rapoport, A., D. Budescu, R. Suleiman, and E. Weg. 1992. Social dilemmas with uniformly distributed resources. In *Social Dilemmas: Theoretical Issues and Research Findings*, W. Liebrand, D. Messick, and H. Wilke, editors, New York: Pergamon Press. 43–57.

Rapoport, A., and A. M. Chammah. 1965. Sex differences in factors contributing to the level of cooperation in a prisoners' dilemma game. *Journal of Personality and Social Psychology* 2:831–8.

Rapoport, A., and D. Eshed-Levy. 1989. Provision of step-level public goods: Effects of greed and fear of being gypped. *Organizational Behavior and Human Decision Processes* 44:325–44.

Rapoport, A., and R. Suleiman. 1992. Equilibrium solutions for resource dilemmas. *Group decision making and negotiation.* 1:269–94.

————1993. Incremental contribution in step-level public goods games with asymmetric players. *Organizational behavior and human decision processes.* 55:171–94.

Rassenti, S., V. L. Smith, and R. Bulfin. 1982. A combinatorial auction mechanism for airport time slot allocation. *Bell Journal of Economics* 13:402–17.

Reiter, S., ed 1986 *Studies in mathematical economics*, vol. 25, Washington, D.C.: Mathematical Association of America.

Rob, R. 1989. Pollution claim settlements under private information. *Journal of Economic Theory* 47:307–33.

Roberts, D. J. 1972. Notes on the existence of Lindahl equilibrium with a measure space of consumers. Working paper, Graduate School of Management, Northwestern University.

————1976. The incentives for the correct revelation of preferences and the number of consumers. *Journal of Public Economics* 6:359–74.

————1979. Strategic behavior in the MDP planning procedure. In Laffont (1979), 353–62.

————1987. Lindahl equilibrium. In *The new Palgrave: A dictionary of economics*, J. Eatwell, M. Millgate, and P. Newman, editors, London: Macmillan.

Roberts, J. and A. Postlewaite. 1976. The incentives for price-taking behavior in large economies. *Econometrica* 44:115–28.

Roberts, R. 1984. A positive model of private charity and public transfers. *Journal of Political Economy* 92(1):136–48.

———1985. A taxonomy of public provision. *Public Choice* 47:267–303.

———1987. Financing public goods. *Journal of Political Economy* 95:420–37.

Roberts, R. D. 1990. The tragicomedy of the commons: Why communities rationally choose 'inefficient' allocations of shared resources. Political Economy Working Paper 140, School of Business and Center in Political Economy, Washington University, St. Louis.

Romer, T., and H. Rosenthal. 1983. A constitution for solving the asymmetric n-prisoners' dilemma. *American Journal of Political Science* 27:1–26.

Roth, A. 1988. Laboratory experimentation in economics: A methodological overview. *Economic Journal* 98:974–1031.

———1995. Bargaining experiments. In *The handbook of experimental economics*, J. Kagel and A. Roth, editors, Princeton: Princeton University Press.

Saijo, T., and Y. Tatamitani. 1991. Characterizing neutrality in the voluntary contribution mechanism. Working Paper, Institute of Socio-Economic Planning, University of Tsukuba, Japan.

Saijo, T., and H. Yamaguchi. 1992. The "spite" dilemma in voluntary contribution mechanism experiments. Technical Report, University of Tsukuba, Japan.

Sally, D. 1992. Conversation and cooperation in social dilemmas: Experimental evidence from 1958 to 1992. Technical Report, University of Chicago.

Samuelson, C. D., and S. T. Allison. 1990. Social decision heuristics, role schemas, and the consumption of shared resources. Discussion paper, Workshop in Political Theory and Policy Analysis, Indiana University. Conference on Experimental Research on the Provision of Public Goods and Common-Pool Resources.

Samuelson, P. A. 1954. The pure theory of public expenditure. *Review of Economics and Statistics* 387–9.

———1975. Diagrammatic exposition of a theory of public expenditures. *Review of Economic Theory* 10:187–217.

Sandler, T., F. P. Sterbenz, and J. Posnett. 1987. Free riding and uncertainty. *European Economic Review* 31:1605–17.

Sarkar, A. 1990. Joint provision of public goods with incomplete information about costs. BEBR Faculty Working Paper 90-1657, University of Illinois.

Satterthwaite, M. 1975. Strategy-proofness and Arrow's conditions: Existence and correspondence theorems for voting procedures and social welfare functions. *Journal of Economic Theory* 10:187–217.

Scherr, B., and E. Bab. 1975. Pricing public goods: An experiment with two proposed pricing systems. *Public Choice* 23:35–48.

Schmidtz, D. 1991. *The limits of government, and essay on the public goods argument.* Boulder: Westview Press.

Schneider, F., and W. Pommerehne. 1981. Free riding and collective action: An experiment in public microeconomics. *Quarterly Journal of Economics* 96(4):689–704.

Schram, A., and J. Sonnemans. 1992. Voter turnout and the role of groups: Participation game experiments. Technical report, University of Amsterdam, the Netherlands.

Schwartz-Shea, P., and R. Simmons. 1987. Social dilemmas and perceptions: Experiments on framing and inconsequentiality. Forthcoming in *Social Dilemmas*, D. Schroeder, editor, New York: Praeger. 1995.

Sell, J., and R. K. Wilson. 1990. The effects of signalling on the provisioning of public goods. Discussion paper, Workshop in Political Theory and Policy Analysis, Indiana University.

Selten, R., and R. Stoecker. 1986. End behavior in sequences of finite prisoner's dilemma supergames. *Journal of Economic Behavior and Organization* 7:47–70.

Shenker, S. 1990a. A brief overview of congestion control in computer networks from a mechanism design view point. Technical report, Xerox Palo Alto Research Center.

———1990b. Efficient network allocations with selfish users. Technical report, Xerox Palo Alto Research Center.

————1990c. Making greed work in networks: A game-theoretic anaysis of gateway service disciplines. Technical report, Xerox Palo Alto Research Center.

Shepperd, J. 1993. Productivity loss in performance groups: A motivation analysis. *Psychological Bulletin* 113(1):67–81.

Shotter, A., K. Weigelt, and C. Wilson. 1990. A laboratory investigation of multi-person rationality and presentation effects. Economic research report 90-24, Department of Economics, New York University.

Smith, V., A. Williams, W. Bratton, and M. Vannoni. 1982. Competitive market institutions: Double auctions vs. sealed bid-offer auctions. *American Economic Review* 72(1):58–77.

Smith, V. L. 1976. Mechanisms for the optimal provision of public goods. Conference on American Re-evolution, Tucson. 19–21.

————1977. The principle of unanimity and voluntary consent in social choice. *Journal of Political Economy* 85(6):1125–39.

————1978. Experimental mechanisms for public choice. In *Game theory and political science*, P. Ordeshook, editor, New York: New York University Press. 323–55.

————1979a. An experimental comparison of three public good decision mechanisms. *Scandinavian Journal of Economics* 81:198–215.

————1979b. Incentive compatible experimental processes for the provision of public goods. In Smith (1979c), 59–168.

————1979c. *Research in experimental economics*, vol. 1. Greenwich, Conn.: JAI Press.

————1980. Experiments with a decentralized mechanism for public goods decision. *American Economic Review* 70(1):584–99.

————1982a. Microeconomic systems as an experimental science. *American Economic Review* 72(5):923–55.

————1982b. Reflections on some experimental mechanisms for classical environments. In *Research in marketing, supplement 1: Choice models for buyer behavior*, L. McAlister, editor, Greenwich, Conn.: JAI Press.

————1982c. *Research in experimental economics*, vol. 2. Greenwich, Conn.: JAI Press.

————1990. Experimental economics: Behavioral lesson for microeconomic theory and policy. Discussion Paper 90-14, Dept. of Economics, University of Arizona. Nancy L. Schwartz Memorial Lecture, Northwestern University.

Smith, V. L., and J. M. Walker. 1993. Monetary rewards and decision cost in experimental economics. *Economic Inquiry* 31(April 1993):245–61.

Smith, V. L., and A. W. Williams. 1990. Experimental market economics. Discussion Paper 90-7, Department of Economics, University of Arizona.

Stark, O. 1985. On private charity and altruism. *Public Choice* 46:325–32.

Sugden, R. 1985. Consistent conjectures and voluntary contributions to public goods: Why the conventional theory does not work. *Journal of Public Economics* 27:117–24.

Suleiman, R., and A. Rapoport. 1988. Environmental and social uncertainty in single-trial resource dilemmas. *Acta Psychologica* 68:99–112.

————1992. Provision of step-level public goods with continuous contribution. *Journal of Behavioral Decision Making* 5:133–53.

Sunder, S. 1987. Structure of organizations for production of public and private goods. Mimeo, Carnegie Mellon University.

Sunder, S. 1995. Experimental asset markets: A survey. In *The handbook of experimental economics*, J. Kagel and A. Roth, editors, Princeton: Princeton University Press.

Taylor, M., and H. Ward. 1982. Chickens, whales, and lumpy goods: Alternative models of public goods provision. *Political Studies* 30(3):350–70.

Thomson, W. 1987. Monotonic allocation mechanisms in economies with public goods. Working paper 117, University of Rochester.

Tian, G. 1989. Implementation of the Lindahl correspondence by a single-valued, feasible and continuous mechanism. *Review of Economic Studies* 56:613–21.

Tian, G. and Q. Li. 1990. Implementation of the ratio-balanced cost share correspondence viewed as a state-ownership system with the general variable returns in production. Discussion paper, Department of Economics, Texas A&M University.

Tian, G., Q. Li, and S. Nakamura. 1990. Nash-implementation of the Lindahl correspondence with decreasing returns to scale technology. Working Paper 90-17, Dept. of Economics, Texas A&M University.

Truchon, M. 1984. Non-myopic strategic behavior in the MDP planning procedure. *Econometrica* 52:1179–90.

van de Kragt, A. 1984. Experimental N-person dilemmas and group size: An elaboration. Presented at the Meeting of the Public Choice Society, March 1984, Phoenix.

van de Kragt, A., J. Orbell, and R. Dawes. 1983. The minimal contributing set as a solution to public goods problems. *American Political Science Review* 77:112–22.

Varian, H. R. 1990a. Sequential provision of public goods. Discussion paper, University of Michigan.

———1990b. A solution to the problem of externalities and public goods when agents are well-informed. Discussion paper, Dept. of Economics, University of Michigan.

Vega-Redondo, F. 1989. Public projects and private contributions. Discussion paper, Instituto de Análisis Económico, Universitat Autonoma de Barcelona.

Vickrey, W. 1961. Counterspeculation, auctions, and competitive sealed tenders. *Journal of Finance* 16:8–37.

Walker, J. M., R. Gardner, and E. Ostrom. 1990. Rent dissipation in limited access common-pool resource environments: Experimental evidence. *Journal of Environmental Economics and Management* 19:203–11.

Walker, M. 1978. A note on the characterization of mechanisms for the revelation of preferences. *Econometrica* 46:147–52.

———1980. A simple incentive compatible scheme for attaining Lindahl allocations. *Econometrica* 48:1521–40.

Warr, P. 1982. Pareto optimal redistribution and private charity. *Journal of Public Economics* 19:131–8.

———1983. The private provision of a public good independent of the distribution of income. *Economics Letters* 13:207–11.

Wicksell, K. 1958. A new principle of just taxation. In *Classics in the theory of public finance*, R. Musgrave and A. Peacock, editors, London: Macmillan.

Young, D. J. 1989. A "fair share" model of public good provision. *Journal of Economic Behavior and Organization* 11:137–47.

3
Coordination Problems

Jack Ochs

Introduction

More than thirty years ago, Thomas Schelling (1960, 162) forcefully argued that "some *essential* part of the study of mixed motive (non-zero-sum) games is necessarily empirical." His point was that the notion of an equilibrium in such games, entailing consistent expectations, leads us naturally to ask how people achieve this "meeting of the minds." This question becomes unavoidable when we study games with multiple equilibria, each of which could be supported by some set of mutually consistent beliefs. A good theory of such games should tell us not merely whether or not *an* equilibrium will be observed, but *which* equilibrium will be observed. Consequently, it was natural for Schelling to develop his thesis around a discussion of various games with multiple equilibria.

One response to the problem of sorting amongst equilibria has been to develop various "refinement" criteria. These criteria are meant to eliminate from further consideration equilibria that would, to a "rational" player, appear to rest upon incredible beliefs. However, even if one accepts the empirical significance of these refinement criteria—a matter that is still open to dispute[1]—we are still left with a plethora of games in which many Nash equilibria still remain after "refinement."

The fundamental problem is that focal points around which people coordinate cannot, generally, be found by simply contemplating what the purely rational player or a set of purely rational players would do, absent empirical knowledge of how people who find themselves in a particular game with multiple equilibria actually behave. In games with multiple equilibria the required rationality is, as Arrow (1986) points out, a *social* phenomenon, rather than a characteristic of individuals that can be defined without reference to their common understanding. An equilibrium is focal because a group of people have come to believe that members of this group will expect play consistent with this equilibrium. When an equilibrium is known to be focal then it becomes "rational" for each player to expect that all other players will expect play consistent with this equilibrium and to act on that expectation. Conversely, whatever the abstract properties of a particular equilibrium in a game, if it is known that this equilibrium is one upon which players generally do not focus, then it is not "rational" for any given player to act on the expectation that the strategies of other players will be consistent with this particular equilibrium. Schelling's point was that we simply cannot know what makes an equilibrium focal without studying how individuals actually behave.

While Schelling himself conducted a number of informal experiments with coordination games, interest of other economists in the experimental study of games with multiple equilibria has been stimulated recently, in part, by theoretical developments in macroeconomics that have been directed at establishing a microeconomic foundation for macroeconomics.[2]

One line of theoretical inquiry that has stimulated experimental study is the development of overlapping generations models.[3] In these models a given individual will participate in a sequence of spot markets but not all traders are present at any given time. As a consequence, every individual must condition his actions at any given moment on forecasts of future spot market prices. But these future spot prices will themselves necessarily reflect the expectations of a different set of individuals about the actions of still other agents. In the early development of these models no attention was given to the process by which expectations are formed. Instead, the theoretical work was carried out under the assumption that an equilibrium would be supported by *rational expectations*, whatever might be the nature of the process of expectation formation. Assuming rational expectations in these models is, as Gale (1982) points out, a shortcut to the problem of building a closed and consistent model of expectation formation. It allows the theorist to bypass the question of how people come to have such expectations. The theorist is then left free to explore the implications of the assumption that, in equilibrium, expectations will be such that no one has any reason to revise them as they observe the realizations of the variables upon whose forecasted values they had predicated their actions. The usefulness of this shortcut in studying problems within the overlapping generations paradigm is, however, diminished by the fact that such models have a continuum of rational expectations equilibria.[4] In such circumstances, one cannot draw sharp comparative static predictions without having a theory of which equilibrium from the continuum organizes the data under a given set of parameter values. As Lucas (1986) noted,

> The issue involves a question of how collections of people will behave in a specific situation. Economic theory (i.e., equilibrium theory) does not resolve the question. One can imagine other principles that would, but this cannot rule out the possibility that still other principles might resolve it quite differently. It is hard to see what can advance the discussion short of assembling a collection of people, putting them in the situation of interest, and observing what they do.

Just as Lucas was calling for experiments to study the way people behave when placed in an experimental overlapping generations economy, Lim, Prescott and Sunder (1988) were conducting this type of experiment. I will discuss their experiment together with a sequence of additional experiments conducted by Sunder and various associates in the next section.

A second line of theoretical development in macroeconomics that has sparked experimental studies has been the explicit treatment of decentralized processes by which buyers and sellers are matched.[5] The decentralization of trading creates at least two different types of coordination games. First, there are models that treat the matching process as a predetermined stochastic process. The focus of these models is on the coordination of production decisions when production must take place before trade. Because the expected profitability of production for any agent depends on the probability that he will meet another agent who has inventory to trade, there is a production externality in these models. This externality gives rise to a multiplicity of rational expectations equilibria. Furthermore, these equilibria can be Pareto ranked. This has stimulated interest in studying games with Pareto ranked equilibria experimentally. I discuss several such experiments in section II.

Second, in a decentralized market model the matching process itself may be modelled as a non-cooperative game.[6] Such games also have multiple equilibria, but the set of equilibria cannot be ordered by the Pareto criterion. In section III I discuss two experiments that study the behavior of agents who, in choosing strategies for distributing themselves over a set of trading locations, are playing this type of coordination game.

I. Experiments Using Overlapping Generations Environments

A. Adaptive Learning Processes and Rational Expectations Equilibria

In a nonstochastic environment where each agent's best current action must be conditioned on that agent's expectation of future spot prices, a rational expectations equilibrium implies that the agent has perfect foresight. Theorists who use the concept of rational expectations to close their models are not committed to the premise that people are actually endowed with perfect foresight. Instead, as Lucas (1986, 218) argues, the concept is used to model situations that can be thought of as ". . . steady states of some adaptive process (where) decision rules (have been) found to work over a range of situations and hence are no longer revised appreciably as more experience accumulates."

Monetary theorists have been interested in overlapping generations models in which money is the only asset that can be carried forward in time. These models focus upon money's role as a store of value. The value of money as an asset depends, of course, upon future prices at which goods will be exchanged for money. In these models, there will generally be a multiplicity of equilibria, each supported by self-confirming beliefs as to future prices. Lucas suggested that considerations of the stability of adaptive learning processes might serve as a criterion for identifying which equilibrium is most likely to be observed when agents have acquired sufficient experience operating under a given set of parameters so that they may be assumed to be fully adapted to that environment. In particular, he discussed an overlapping generations environment with money as the sole store of value in which there were only two stationary rational expectations equilibria. At one stationary equilibrium money had positive value, at the other it was worthless.

An example of such an economy is one where all individuals are identical. Each agent born in generation t lives two consecutive periods $(t, t + 1)$, consumes y_t units at the end of the first period and z_{t+1} units at the end of the second period. Each agent is endowed with e_y units of the consumption good in the first period of life and e_z units of the consumption good in the second period of life, where $e_z < e_y$. There are n persons per generation and mn units of fiat money in the economy which the old can use to buy units of the consumption good from the young each period. Each agent's preferences are defined over the agent's lifetime consumption profile (y_t, z_{t+1}) and are represented by the utility function $U = y_t z_{t+1}$. In equilibrium, individuals hold money only at the end of the first period of their lives. An individual's money holdings, $m = P_t(e_y - y)$, are just sufficient to finance $P_{t+1}(z_{t+1} - e_z)$ and all individuals are maximizing utility subject to their lifetime budget constraint. The first order condition for the agent's constrained maximization problem implies that in equilibrium the following first-order difference equation relating next period's price of consumption good to this period's price must be satisfied:

(1)
$$P_{t+1} = \frac{e_y}{e_z} P_t - \frac{2m}{e_z}$$

Any evolution of prices which satisfies equation 1 is a rational expectations equilibrium path. However, equation (1) has only one stationary solution with a positive real value of money:

$$P^s = \frac{2m}{e_y - e_z}$$

Given that $(e_y/e_z) > 1$, if $P_t > P^s$ then $p_{t+1} > p_t$. Therefore, the zero inflation stationary solution is not stable under rational expectations, and all rational expectations equilibria other than the zero inflation stationary equilibrium have the commodity price growing without bound so that, in the limit, money is worthless. However, if expectations are formed adaptively, i.e., by looking backward, then the zero inflation stationary equilibrium is stable under adaptive expectations. This is because the dynamics are reversed if expectations are *adaptive* instead of rational. Under adaptive expectations, P^*_{t+1} is interpreted as the forecast at the beginning of period t of the price that will be realized in period $t + 1$. Equation (1) then defines the momentary equilibrium between the price in period t and the forecast in t of the price in $t + 1$, or

$$P_t = \frac{e_z}{e_y} P^*_{t+1} + \frac{2m}{e_y}$$

Under adaptive expectations, forecasts of the price next period are updated each period by taking a weighted average of the past realizations and the past forecasts. If, for example, expectations adapt according to the rule,

$$P^*_{t+1} = aP_{t-1} + (1-a) P^*_{t-1}$$

then the momentary equilibrium price path follows the equation

$$P_t = \frac{e_z}{e_y} \{aP_{t-1} + (1-a) P^*_{t-1}\} + \frac{2m}{e_y}$$

Therefore, under adaptive expectations, if the forecast is above P^s, the realization in period t will be below the weighted average of P_{t-1} and P^*_{t-1}. Declining prices induce a downward revision in the forecast price, P^*_{t+1}, which in turn leads to a lower realized price, P_t. This interaction between declining realized prices and decreasing forecast prices moves the system towards the zero inflation stationary equilibrium, P^s.[7]

Lucas's conjecture was that in an experimentally controlled environment corresponding to this simple model one should expect to see prices converging to a constant value consistent with the zero inflation stationary, rational expectations equilibrium. This hypothesis is, of course, consistent with a broader hypothesis that inflation is inherently associated with growth in the money supply and that, absent such growth, inflation cannot be sustained.

B. The Path of Prices When the Rate of Growth of the Money Stock Is Zero: Lim, Prescott, and Sunder (1988)

This paper presents a first, exploratory experiment conducted in an environment designed to match the specification of the above example. Lim, Prescott, and Sunder had to address two design issues in achieving this matching. First, in the theoretical model there are an infinite number of generations, and each generation participates in a market with members of another generation only once in its lifetime. In an experimental session only a finite number of subjects are available. Therefore, if a large sequence of market periods are to be observed, each subject would have to be a member of several "generations." This called for creating a form of "re–incarnation" of individuals without having individual "generations" or well-defined groups of individuals having more than one "life." Lim, Prescott, and Sunder met this problem by creating an overlapping generations environment the following way: They recruit $N > 3n$ subjects to participate in an experimental session, where n is the number of individuals in each generation. In any market period during the session, two generations of subjects participate in a spot market, with the old generation using "francs" (fiat money) to buy chips (the consumption good) from the young. The remaining $N - 2n$ subjects sit on the sidelines as onlookers. At the end of a market period, n of the onlookers are selected at random to take the role of the next young generation and given an initial endowment of chips, the current young generation moves to the role of the current old generation, carrying its franc holdings forward, and is given an additional number of chips, and the current old generation subjects join the ranks of the onlookers. The random selection of the next generation from the group of onlookers is intended to impede the formation of a supergame.[8]

The second design problem they faced was that in the theoretical model there is no last period and therefore nothing in the formal structure of the model to determine the value of francs at the end of the game. However, the actual session has a finite number of periods, and in the last period of the experimental session some subjects will be holding francs. Since subjects knew that an experimental session had a definite time limit, if the price at which francs would be converted into chips (the objects on which payoffs depended) at the end of the session were known, then they could apply backward induction to determine that such a price was *the* equilibrium price throughout the session. Lim, Prescott, and Sunder solved this problem by giving the onlookers each period the task of forecasting the price at which chips will exchange for francs. Each period, the subject with the most accurate forecast won a prize. They made it public knowledge that the price at which franc holdings would be converted into chips in the last period of the session would be determined by the average of the forecast prices made that period by that period's onlookers. In this way, the price path would be entirely conditioned by the nature of the expectations each subject formed about how other subjects would behave.[9]

At the end of each period the old generation were paid off according to a function of the number of chips they held at the end of each of the two periods of their "lives." The payoff function was structured so that there were only two stationary rational expectations equilibria in the infinite generation game, a constant price equilibrium where the young sold chips for francs, and an equilibrium where francs were worthless and no trade took place between generations.

Table 3.1 presents the design of this experiment. Notice that none of the four sessions (called "experiments" in the table) were exact replications. Each session differed from the others in one or more of the following variables: the payoff function, the initial endowment of francs, the trading institution through which francs were exchanged for chips and an equilibrium spot market price was determined,[10] the level of experience of subjects, and the number of subjects per generation. Because more than one variable changes from session to session, it is not possible to analyze how differences in experimental conditions may have affected outcomes. Instead, the emphasis is on similarities of behavior across conditions.

Figure 3.1 presents the history of both actual market prices and the mean of the actual forecast prices made by the onlookers in the third session. Notice that the actual price starts out above the stationary Nash equilibrium and then converges towards that equilibrium. In spite of the variation in experimental variables, these two aspects of price dynamics were common to all four sessions. These dynamics are contrary to rational expectations dynamics since, if the initial price were on a rational expectations equilibrium path, prices should have moved away from the

Table 3.1. Design of Lim, Prescott, and Sunder's Experiments

Experiment	Market Type	Experience	Number of Subjects in the Experiment and in Each Generation	Chip Endowment		Money Endowment (francs)[a]		Expected Payoff Function	Double Prize Wheel
				Entry	Exit	Entry	Exit		
1	Double oral	Inexperienced	14/4	7	1	1,000	0	$\dfrac{\$6 \log(y_t z_{t+1})}{\log 30}$	Yes
2	Double oral	Experienced	14/4	7	1	250	0	$\dfrac{\$6 \log(y_t z_{t+1})}{\log 30}$	Yes
3	Shubik	Inexperienced	14/4	7	1	1,000	0	$\$1.20(y_t z_{t+1})^{1/2}$	No
4	Shubik	Experienced	11/3	7	1	250	0	$\$0.75(y_t z_{t+1})^{1/2}$	No

Source: Lim, Prescott, and Sunder 1988, table 2.

[a] Money endowment was given only in the first period. No further money was injected into the economy.

constant price equilibrium. The observed dynamics are, however, consistent with adaptive expectations, both in the approach of market price to the adaptive expectations equilibrium and in the mean forecast adjusting in the direction of the deviation of last period's realization from last period's mean forecast.[11]

In the game used in this experiment by Lim, Prescott, and Sunder (1988), the constant price rational expectations equilibrium supports a Pareto optimal pattern of resource allocation while all of the other rational expectations equilibria produce much lower payoffs. Does adaptive behavior account for the observations, or do the data reflect some type of implicit, cooperative play among the subjects? Or is the fact that one of the equilibria implied a constant price responsible for their findings?

C. Price Inflation with a Growing Money Stock

In response to these questions, Marimon and Sunder (1988) designed another experiment with the same type of overlapping generations environment. In this second experiment, the amount of francs in the economy grows from period to period. This comes about by having the experimenter purchase a fixed number, d, of chips (corresponding to the financing of a constant real deficit) with francs at the price that cleared the market for chips when the experimenter's constant demand was added to the demand of the older generation. It was common knowledge that the experimenter would always take d chips from the market, and that

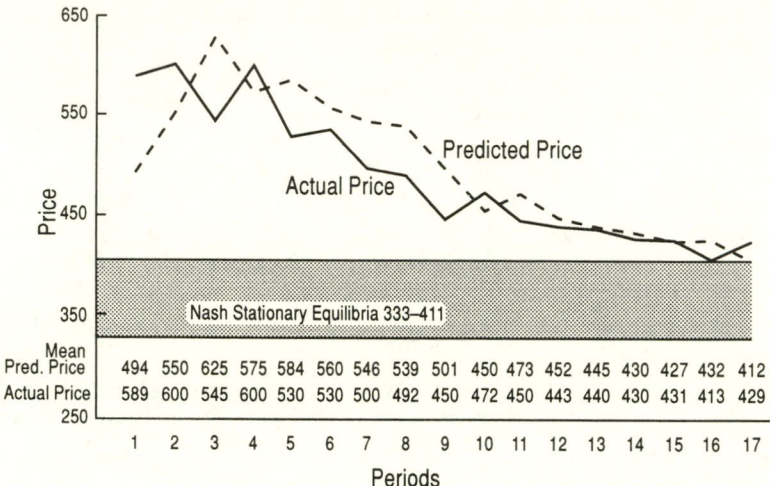

Figure 3.1. Transaction prices: Market no. 3. *Source*: Lim, Prescott, and Sunder (1988), figure 3.

as a consequence the stock of francs in the economy would always be growing. In this inflationary environment there were two stationary, rational expectations equilibria, a low constant inflation rate equilibrium and a high constant rate of inflation equilibrium. All of the nonstationary rational expectations equilibrium paths converge to the high inflation rate stationary equilibrium. However, a least squares adaptive learning path will tend toward the low level stationary equilibrium.[12] Furthermore, with the introduction of a constant deficit the pattern of trade that maximizes per-capita payoff is different from the pattern of trade in any of the rational expectations equilibria.

Table 3.2 presents the design of this experiment. As in the Lim, Prescott, and Sunder experiment, in this design each session is conducted under different experimental conditions. Since there is no replication within a given set of conditions, this experiment should also be viewed as exploratory in nature.

Figure 3.2 shows the actual time paths of inflation (measured in percent/period). The line labelled AE (for Adaptive Expectations) shows the low stationary rational expectations equilibrium rate of inflation to which adaptive expectations paths converge under a least squares learning rule. The line labelled PO (for Pareto Optimality) shows the inflation path consistent with smoothing consumption per period, as required for maximizing per-capita payoff, with the payoff function used in the experiment. The line labelled RE (for Rational Expectations) is the high stationary rational expectations equilibrium path to which all nonstationary rational expectations equilibria converge. Notice that in three of the four plots RE is not shown. This is because the actual inflation rates were always below RE by a wide margin. In the plot of Economy 3, neither AE (whose value was 100 percent) nor RE (whose value was 250 percent) are shown. In Economy 4, a parameter change is introduced in period 8, which reduces RE from 250 percent per period (not shown) to 100 percent per period from period 8 onward,

Table 3.2. Design of Experimental Overlapping-Generations Economies

Economy	Number of Subjects in Economy (N) and Generation (n)	Prior Experience	Endowment Chips Young (ω_1)	Old (ω_2)	Money (h_0)	Government Deficit per Capita d	Periods T	Theoretical Low Inflationary Steady State (%)	Inflation High Inflationary Steady State (%)	Constraint Consumption (%)
1	(14, 4)	None	7	1	10	0.05	1–19	21	479	18
2[a]	(13, 4)	Economy 1	7	1	10	0.25	1–17	9	541	9
						1.25	18–33	100	250	53
3[b]	9% (12, 3)	Three inexperienced; nine from Economy 1 or 2	7	1	3,722	1.25	1–17	100	250	53
4[c]	(12, 3)	Economy 3	7	1	3,722	1.25	1–7	100	250	53
			3	1		0.25	8–20	50	100	29

Source: Marimon and Sunder 1988, tables 1 and 2.

[a] Deficit change announced at end of period 13 is to be effective in period 18.

[b] At outset subjects were informed that parameters would not change.

[c] At outset subjects were informed that parameters would change in period 8. They were also informed of what the parameters, values would be and that they would not change again.

while simultaneously reducing AE from 100 percent per period to 50 percent per period. As the plots indicate, the actual path of inflation in these sessions not only stayed far below the high stationary equilibrium path, but also tended to fall below the low level stationary equilibrium inflation path. This indicates a strong bias towards patterns of trade that smoothed consumption in a way which maximized per-capita payoff.

The design of Economy 4 is especially interesting. In that session it was announced at the beginning of the session that in the eighth period endowments and deficit parameters would change, and what these parameter values would be. The parameters for the first seven periods were set at the same values as in Economy 3 (and the second half of Economy 2). Since rates of inflation in the neighborhood of 50 percent per period were observed in these prior sessions under these parameters, it was expected that subjects in Economy 4 would also acquire experience with a similar inflation rate. The parameter values for the remainder of Economy 4, beginning with period 8, were selected so that the high level inflation stationary equilibrium under these new parameters would equal the low level stationary equilibrium under the initial parameters, *while the new value of the low level stationary equilibrium fell from 100 percent to 50 percent and the level which sustained constant consumption per period fell below 50 percent.* In this

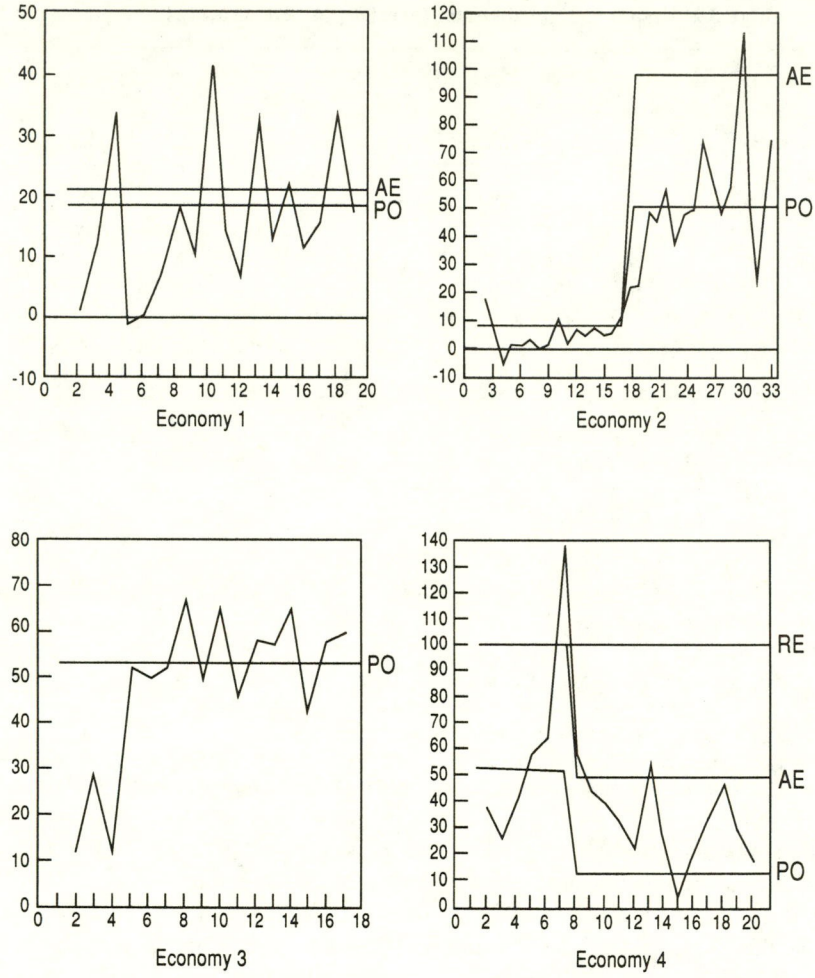

Figure 3.2. Inflationary Paths. *Source*: Marimon and Sunder (1988), figure 2.

way, Marimon and Sunder hoped to give subjects prior experience with an inflation rate that could be sustained as an equilibrium when the parameters changed. What they observed, however, was that in the early periods price (and trading volumes) were in the vicinity of the PO path and, while the approach of the parameter change triggered an unexplained one period jump in inflation, following the parameter changes trading volumes and inflation rates fell below the new AE inflation rate towards the new rate consistent with Pareto optimality. This provides strong evidence of a bias away from equilibrium.

In the design used by Marimon and Sunder, as well as that used in Lim, Prescott, and Sunder, subjects are asked to submit a supply schedule for chips. The submitted supply schedules are then aggregated and the market clearing price determined. If subjects were adopting strategies designed to equalize their holdings of chips across both periods of a given "life," they would submit a schedule which was perfectly price inelastic. However, this is not what subjects do. Instead, most subjects submit supply schedules where the quantity of chips offered is an increasing function of price. Therefore, the bias away from equilibrium observed by Marimon and Sunder in the market data evidently reflects the apparent inability of subjects to derive a supply schedule from their underlying payoff function that corresponds to the "competitive" supply schedule, conditional on their forecast of next period's prices. This raises the obvious question as to whether the supply schedules submitted by individuals would come closer to the schedules that would support an equilibrium if the rewards for coming closer to the equilibrium were greater.[13]

I have called the experiments of Lim, Prescott, and Sunder and of Marimon and Sunder, "exploratory," because each of their sessions constitutes a single observation under fixed parameters, and they have varied a large number of parameters from session to session. As a result, one can only form conjectures as to what does, and what does not, systematically influence the dynamics of behavior observed in these nonstochastic overlapping generations environments. There is, however, one characteristic common to all of these sessions that is of direct interest to monetary economists. In none of these sessions is there any evidence that individuals have the "foresight" to follow rational expectations equilibrium paths that generate hyperinflation. In this sense, the experiment lends support to the hypothesis that hyperinflation cannot be generated without an acceleration in the rate of growth of the money supply. Of course, this evidence would be even stronger if there were a treatment under which the rate of growth of the money supply were accelerating for some period of time, and it was observed that this built expectations to sustain a hyperinflation.[14]

D. "Sunspots"

The multiplicity of equilibria in an overlapping generations model with fiat money gives rise to the possibility that individuals will learn to coordinate their beliefs about future prices by conditioning their expectations on a purely extrinsic random variable. If this occurs, then the equilibrium path of the economy will reflect the volatility of this "sunspot."[15] Woodford (1990) proposed an adaptive learning dynamic, which has the property that individuals who, observing an apparent correlation between a sunspot variable and an independent endowment shock, forecast next period's price level on the basis of the realization of the sunspot will find their expectations converging over time to a "sunspot rational expectations equilibrium." While a demonstration that there is an adaptive learning rule that would lead agents to converge to a sunspot equilibrium is interesting in its own right, the principal "lesson" to be gleaned from Woodford's paper is that different adaptive learning processes will lead to different equilibria, so that one cannot make an a priori argument that one equilibrium is more likely to be focal than another by a simple appeal to stability under adaptive expectations. This leaves open the empirical question, therefore, as to *which* adaptive learning process, if any, best characterizes the behavior of individuals when different adaptive learning rules lead to different rational expectations equilibria.

Marimon, Spear, and Sunder (1991)

Marimon, Spear, and Sunder have devised an overlapping generations experiment whose basic innovation is the introduction of a payoff function that yields both a perfect foresight stationary equilibrium, where price is constant, and a perfect foresight cyclic equilibrium, where price cycles between two values. In their experiment, under both perfect foresight and first order adaptive expectations, the stationary equilibrium is stable and the cyclic equilibrium is unstable. Under second order adaptive expectations, the stationary equilibrium is unstable and the cyclic equilibrium is stable.[16] This design allows a clearer determination of whether behavior follows a simple adaptive process and, assuming it does, whether that process is better characterized as a first or a second order adaptive process.

A second feature of their design was to attempt to "train" their subjects to condition their forecasts of future prices on observed realizations of a purely extrinsic two-state variable, or "sun spot." The state of the "sun spot" was signified by a color on the subject's computer screen. The value of this state regularly alternated from period to period. During the "training periods" the value of the "sunspot" was perfectly correlated with an intrinsically important variable whose value subjects could not observe: the number of subjects who were in the position of the "young" generation. Since the larger the number of "young" people the greater the demand for money, during this training period subjects observed a correlation between the realized market price of a chip and the state of the sunspot, although they were not aware of the change in the parameter, which was in fact responsible for the change in market demand. At the conclusion of the training period, the intrinsically important but unobservable variable (the size of the young generation) took on a constant value, but the value of the "sunspot" continued to change regularly from period to period. Since the "sunspot" alternated with perfect regularity, if subjects learned to believe that prices would be correlated with the sunspot state they would generate a cyclic pattern of demand for money. Furthermore, the rational expectations sunspot equilibrium supported by such beliefs corresponds to the rational expectations cyclic equilibrium.

A third noteworthy feature of the design used in this experiment is that the task of generating an individual subject's optimal money demand schedule for period t, conditional on that individual's forecast of the money price of chips in period $t + 1$, is assigned to a computer program rather than to the subject. In this design, the subject simply submits a forecast of $P(t + 1)$, and the program generates the subject's demand schedule for chips. These individual demands are then aggregated and the market clearing price for that period is calculated and

Table 3.3. Parameters and Equilibria for Experimental Economics

						Equilibrium Prices	
	Number of		Genera-	Total		Cyclic	
	Subjects (N)		tion	Money	Steady		
Economy	(and Experience)	Period	Size	Supply	State	p	q
1	14	1–16	4–3	100	N.A.	2.50	35.18
	(1 Trial Economy)	17–46	4	100	5.00	2.56	14.75
2	10	1–16	3–2	75	N.A.	2.50	49.62
	(None)	17–27	3	75	5.00	2.56	14.75
3	10	1–10	3–2	75	N.A.	2.50	49.62
	(Economy 2)	11–30	3	75	5.00	2.56	14.75
4	13	1–20	4–3	100	N.A.	2.50	35.18
	(None)	21–50	4	100	5.00	2.56	14.75
5	15	1–14	4	100	5.00	2.56	14.75
	(None)	15–36	5–4	100	N.A.	2.00	29.13
		37–67	4	100	5.00	2.56	14.75

Source: Marimon, Spear, and Sunder 1993, table 1.

Notes: The following parameters remained unchanged through all five economies: money endowment of the old in period 1 = 25 per capita; chip endowment of the young (ω_1) = 10; chip endowment of the old (ω_2) = 0; prize for best price prediction each period = 5; and probability of transition for sunspot variable = 1.

Generation size alternated in consecutive periods.

reported to the subjects. This feature reduces the "noise" that might otherwise be generated by the limited abilities of subjects to solve the appropriate optimization problem.

Table 3.3 above describes the design features and equilibrium predictions of the sessions they conducted.

A common characteristic of observed prices in all of these sessions was that the fluctuations in price induced by variations in the size of the young generation persisted after the size of the young generation stopped fluctuating. Figures 3.3 and 3.4 show the sequence of realized temporary equilibrium prices in Economy 1 and Economy 5 of this experiment. In Economy 1 the variations in size took place over the first 16 periods, while in Economy 5 these variations started in period 15 and continued through period 36.

Note that in Economy 5 realized price tended to hover in the neighborhood of the steady state equilibrium for the first 14 periods. Therefore, absent correlated real shocks, the sunspot variable played no systematic role in coordinating beliefs. Furthermore, the pattern of prices over this interval indicates that initially subjects did not make their forecasts on the basis of a second order adaptive process, while the persistence of the fluctuations in price after period 37 indicates

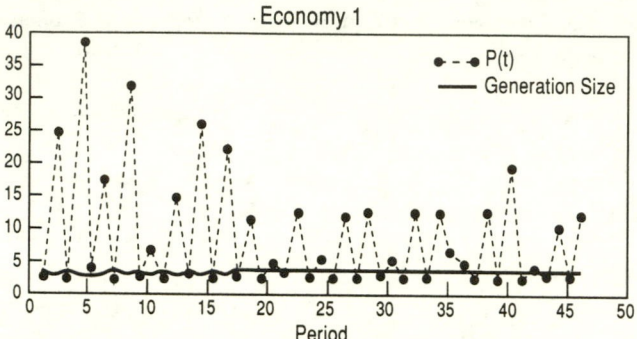

Figure 3.3. Economy 1. *Source*: Marimon, Spear, and Sunder (1991), figure 4.

that the experience with price fluctuations caused subjects to change the basis of their forecasts. Note further that while fluctuations persist after the training period there is not any obvious convergence to the cyclic equilibrium.

Did the observed correlation of realized price with the "sunspot" state during the "training period" cause subjects to learn to condition their forecasts on the sunspot? Or did the subjects simply come to believe that there would be a regular pattern of fluctuating prices? Because of the perfect regularity of the alternation in the state of the sunspot variable, it is not possible to disentangle the role of the sunspot per se in conditioning beliefs from the effect of having experienced a sequence of periods over which realized price regularly fluctuated. To distinguish the role of the sunspot from the role of a historical experience with cyclic movement in observed prices the design could be altered in two ways. First, observations could be taken in sessions in which there was an initial training with unobserved, regular real shocks but no sunspot variable. If one observed the same persistence in price fluctuations after the training period as were observed in the last 30 periods of Economy 5, then this would count against the hypothesis that beliefs were conditioned on the sunspot. Second, the state of the sunspot variable could be determined by a Markovian stochastic process, so that during the training period there was not a perfect correlation between the alternation in the size of the young generation and the sunspot variable. In this way, an equilibrium in which beliefs were conditioned on the observed value of the sunspot could be distinguished from a pure cyclic equilibrium that was supported by subjects who learned to forecast that prices would regularly fluctuate.

What can the macrotheorist learn from the results of these overlapping generations experiments of Sunder and his associates? Inevitably, the reading of the evidence will depend upon the methodological predisposition of the theorist. In the earlier experiments of Sunder, Lim, and Prescott and of Marimon and Sunder there is a clear bias towards equal consumption, even when this is not consistent with any rational expectations equilibrium. If one chose to disregard this bias, perhaps on the grounds that there was not sufficient reward for subjects to make the "optimal" supply decisions, then these experiments might

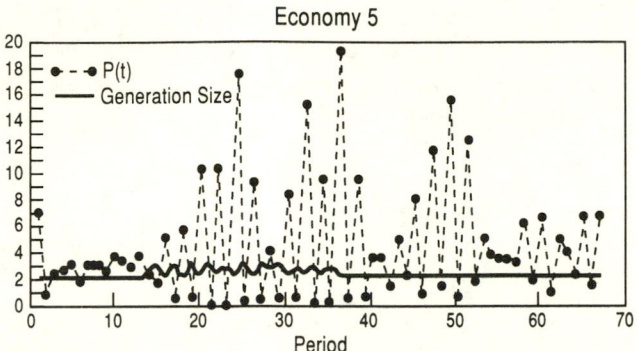

Figure 3.4. Economy 5. *Source*: Marimon, Spear, and Sunder (1991), figure 8.

be read by macrotheorists as evidence in favor of the methodological position that the use of the rational expectations assumption to close models will do little violence to reality—provided that one is only interested in steady states and not the process by which they are reached. However, the evidence from the Marimon, Spear, and Sunder experiment suggests that a transitory unobserved variation in a "fundamental" variable such as the size of the market may have permanent effects via its influence on expectations. Therefore, macrotheorists who are partial to nonequilibrium models may wish to read this evidence as supporting the methodological position that one cannot avoid the problem of modelling the process of expectations formation and hope to have an empirically valid model.

II. Coordination Games with Pareto Ranked Equilibria

When production decisions are decentralized, but the profitability to any single producer of producing at a particular rate depends on the production rates chosen by others, then there may exist multiple equilibria that are Pareto ranked. In games having such equilibria there are two possible types of coordination failure. First, facing a multiplicity of equilibria, players may fail to achieve any of them. Second, even if coordination is achieved on some equilibrium, players may not coordinate on the Pareto optimal equilibrium. This possible failure to coordinate on the Pareto optimal equilibrium is emphasized in the recent literature on macroeconomic coordination games.[17]

A. *Payoff Dominance, Security and Historical Precedent*

Van Huyck, Battalio, and Beil have conducted a series of experiments using coordination games with strict equilibria that are Pareto ranked. In these experiments subjects play a number of repetitions of one or more such games. By allowing a given group of subjects to play the same game repeatedly, they are able to observe whether individuals immediately coordinate on a particular equilibrium or, in the event that they do not achieve an equilibrium outcome immediately, whether they eventually coordinate on one. If equilibrium is observed, then they wish to know the properties of the equilibrium.

Van Huyck, Battalio, and Beil (1990)

In this experiment, the coordination game involves a group of n players. Each player, i, must select an integer, e_i, between 1 and 7, and will receive a payoff according to the function:

$$\pi(e_i, \underline{e}) = a\underline{e} - be_i,$$

where $\underline{e}$ is the *minimum* of the numbers selected by all players and $a > b \geq 0$. Each player selects his or her action privately, with no communication allowed between players. After all players have made their selection, the minimum of the numbers selected is publicly posted, and the game is repeated. In this class of games, any n-tuple of choices in which all individuals select the same integer is an equilibrium. All of these equilibria are Pareto ordered by the value of the integer.

Table 3.4 displays the design of this experiment. Seven sessions were conducted, each with a different group of subjects. In these sessions the entire group first played 10 repetitions of a game with $b > 0$ (Treatment A), then 5 repetitions of a game with $b = 0$ (Treatment B), and then another 5 to 7 repetitions of the game with b set at its original value (Treatment A').

The payoff tables for these two treatments that were presented to the students are displayed below. Notice that in Treatment A, a player is penalized for selecting a number which exceeds the minimum of the numbers selected.[18] This creates a conflict between a desire to encourage others to select a high number (because the game will be repeated) and a desire to protect oneself against the possibility that others will not select a high number in the current game. No such conflict between seeking the payoff-dominant equilibrium and individual security exists in Treatment B were $b = 0$. In Treatment B the choice of 7 is a dominant strategy for each player. The insertion of Treatment B, where each player has a dominant strategy, serves two purposes. First, it is a diagnostic. If one were to observe a significant number of individuals failing to play a dominant strategy, then this would signal that the experimenters have lost experimental control. Either subjects are insufficiently motivated or they don't understand the game or both. Second, if everyone repeatedly plays the dominant strategy in this game, then the sequence would possibly serve to create a historically determined focal point for players when Treatment A' is introduced.

There were some problems in using the same treatment as both a diagnostic and as a device to induce a focal point. Only 76 of the 91 subjects who were given Treatment B played the dominant strategy the first period that game was played. However, the number who played the dominant strategy tended to increase with repetition of the game. In the fifth, and last, repetition 87 of the 91 subjects played the dominant strategy. Interpreting this as a diagnostic, one might say that almost

Table 3.4. Tacit Coordination Games Experimental Design

Experiment	Size	A Payoff A Full Size	B Payoff B Full Size	A′ Payoff A Full Size	C Payoff A Size Two[a]
1	16	1^p, 2,..., 10	—	—	—
2	16	1^p, 2,..., 10^p	11,..., 15	16^p,..., 20	—
3	14	1^p, 2,..., 10^p	11,..., 15	16^p,..., 20	—
4	15	1^p, 2^p,..., 10^p	11^p,..., 15	16,..., 20	21,..., 27
5	16	1^p, 2^p,..., 10^p	11^p,..., 15	16,..., 20	21,..., 27
6	16	1^p, 2^p,..., 10^p	11^p,..., 15	16,..., 20	21,..., 25
7	14	1^p, 2^p,..., 10^p	11^p,..., 15	16,..., 22	21,..., 25

Source: Van Hyuck, Battalio, and Beil 1990, table 1.
Note: Superscript "p" indicates a period in which subjects made predictions.
[a] In experiments 4 and 5 pairings were fixed, while in experiments 6 and 7 pairings were random.

Table 3.5. Payoff Tables for Treatments A and B

Your Choice of X	Smallest Value of X Chosen					
	7	6	5	4	3	2
7	1.30	1.10	0.90	0.70	0.50	0.30
6	—	1.20	1.00	0.80	0.60	0.40
5	—	—	1.10	0.90	0.70	0.50
4	—	—	—	1.00	0.80	0.60
3	—	—	—	—	0.90	0.70
2	—	—	—	—	—	0.30
1	—	—	—	—	—	—

Your Choice of X	Smallest Vaue of X Chosen					
	7	6	5	4	3	2
7	1.30	1.20	1.10	1.00	0.90	0.80
6	—	1.20	1.10	1.00	0.90	0.80
5	—	—	1.10	1.00	0.90	0.80
4	—	—	—	1.00	0.90	0.80
3	—	—	—	—	0.90	0.80
2	—	—	—	—	—	0.80
1	—	—	—	—	—	—

Source: Van Huyck, Battalio, and Beil: 1990, payoff tables A (top) and B (bottom).

all subjects seemed to be well motivated and understood the game. However, none of these groups experienced much coordination on the selection of the pay-off-dominant equilibrium. Indeed, most of their experience during these treatments was experience of coordination failure. Therefore, the treatment could not reasonably be interpreted as providing a strong focal point for the play in the follow-up sequence in Treatment A'.

In all seven sessions there was a consistent pattern of behavior observed over the course of Treatment A. In the first period the choices of subjects tended to be relatively dispersed. Only 2 out of 107 subjects selected 1 in the first period of this treatment. However, by the tenth period under this treatment, the choices were always heavily concentrated, with 77 of the 107 subjects selecting 1. That is, while repetition of the game induced a pattern of learning that improved the degree to which individuals coordinated their behavior, in this game the cost of being "optimistic" when others were "pessimistic" was evidently too high to allow a group that was not initially well coordinated to achieve a collectively desirable equilibrium.

Table 3.6 shows how experience with Treatment B affected how subjects played when Treatment A', which used the same game parameters as Treatment A, was introduced. Rather than going back to the security equilibrium[19] of 1, upon which the groups had settled prior to Treatment B, most of the groups displayed a significant dispersion of choices in the first period of Treatment A'. However, they all quickly converged back towards the security equilibrium. We cannot be sure that the structure of Treatment B had this effect since there is the possibility that *any* break in the repeated play of the game in Treatment A would have produced the same effect.

Group size was a second treatment variable in this experiment. This treatment variable was used to manipulate the influence of "security" considerations on individual behavior. Specifically, if each subject initially places small subjective probability on anyone choosing less than 7, then the smaller the size of the group the smaller the probability that at least one person will choose a number less than 7 and the smaller the "security" motivation to choose a number below 7. Van Huyck, Battalio, and Beil had two treatments where the size of the group was reduced to two. In sessions 4 through 7, after the entire group had completed between 20 to 22 periods of play, subjects were divided into pairs. In sessions 4 and 5 each pair then played several additional periods, while in sessions 6 and 7 random pairings were made each period.

Under the fixed pairings of sessions 4 and 5, most pairs converged to the *Pareto dominant* equilibrium although only one pair started there. Forty-two percent of subjects selected 7 in the first stage of this treatment even though the treatment was given to individuals who in larger groups had experienced equilibrium at 1. Reducing group size may have either changed the subjects' assessment of the risk of choosing 7 or induced them to think in terms of signalling a long term strategy for the repeated game. Whatever the correct explanation for the remarkable difference in behavior between the large size group and the behavior of the pairs, the observed difference clearly suggests that group size can be an important determinant of the dynamics of the equilibrium selection process.

With random pairings in sessions 6 and 7, the initial period of play was not very different from that observed in the initial period with the fixed pairings of sessions 4 and 5. However, under random pairings no equilibrium evolved as a focal point as more periods were played. This highlights the role of the repeated game properties of an environment in the evolution of play.

The clearest result of this experiment is that payoff dominance is not so strong a focal principle that one can be confident that a group that has achieved equilibrium in a game where equilibria are strictly Pareto ordered will have achieved the Pareto Optimal equilibrium. This contradicts the hypothesis of some theorists that if there is a payoff-dominant equilibrium, that equilibrium will necessarily be focal.[20] In addition, this experiment indicates that in at least some environments people can learn to coordinate on a strict equilibrium even when there is not any initially focal equilibrium. Further, the apparent role that considerations of security played in the dynamics of this experiment suggests that its power to influence dynamics should be explored in other environments.

Van Huyck, Battalio, and Beil (1991)

This experiment follows up on the one described above.

Table 3.7 displays its design. The experiment involves three different games. All of these games have the same set of pure strategy equilibria. In each session a different group of nine subjects played several repetitions of two of these three games. The order in which the sequence of games was presented was varied across sessions so that experimenters could test for the effect of the order in which the game sequences were presented.[21]

In the baseline game, Γ, the payoff function for subject i is

$$\pi = aM - b\,[M - e_i]^2 + c$$
$$a > 0,\ b \ge 0$$

where M is the median of the integers selected and e_i is the integer selected by subject i. (Table 3.8a is the payoff table used in the instructions.) Notice that the set of pure strategy equilibria is the same as Treatment A of the first experiment. However, by punishing deviations from the median rather than from the minimum of the values selected by the group, the payoff function in Γ might be expected to create different learning dynamics than was observed in the first experiment. Van Huyck et al. were interested in determining whether the dynamic would be different and, in particular, whether the payoff-dominant equilibrium would be focal under this treatment.

In the game Ω, $b = 0$ and $\pi = 0$ if $e_i \ne M$. The actual payoff table for this treatment is reproduced in Table 3.8b. In this game all equilibria are equally secure. Therefore, the use of Ω allows the study of the development of focal behavior in a setting in which considerations of security are irrelevant.

Table 3.6. Experimental Results for Treatment B and Treatment A′

	Treament B					Treatment A′				
	11	12	13	14	15	16	17	18	19	20
Experiment 2										
No. of 7's	13	15	16	16	16	8	2	0	0	0
No. of 6's	1	0	0	0	0	0	0	0	0	0
No. of 5's	0	1	0	0	0	1	0	0	0	0
No. of 4's	1	0	0	0	0	1	2	0	0	0
No. of 3's	1	0	0	0	0	1	1	1	1	0
No. of 2's	0	0	0	0	0	3	3	4	2	0
No. of 1's	0	0	0	0	0	2	8	11	13	16
	3	5	7*	7*	7*	1	1	1	1	1*
Minimum										
Experiment 3										
No. of 7's	13	13	12	13	14	6	2	2	1	1
No. of 6's	0	0	1	1	0	1	0	0	0	0
No. of 5's	0	0	1	0	0	0	2	1	0	0
No. of 4's	1	0	0	0	0	1	0	0	0	1
No. of 3's	0	1	0	0	0	0	0	0	0	0
No. of 2's	0	0	0	0	0	2	4	2	3	0
No. of 1's	0	0	0	0	0	4	6	9	10	12
	4	3	5	6	7*	1	1	1	1	1
Minimum										
Experiment 4										
No. of 7's	12	13	14	14	15	3	1	0	0	0
No. of 6's	0	0	0	0	0	0	0	0	0	0
No. of 5's	1	0	0	1	0	0	0	0	0	0
No. of 4's	0	1	1	0	0	2	0	0	0	0
No. of 3's	0	1	0	0	0	2	0	0	0	0
No. of 2's	0	0	0	0	0	2	1	2	0	0
No. of 1's	2	0	0	0	0	6	13	13	15	15
	1	3	4	5	7*	1	1	1	1*	1*
Minimum										
Experiment 5										
No. of 7's	13	13	15	15	15	1	0	0	0	0
No. of 6's	0	0	0	0	0	0	0	0	0	0
No. of 5's	1	1	0	0	0	0	0	0	0	0
No. of 4's	1	1	0	0	0	0	0	0	0	0
No. of 3's	0	0	0	0	0	1	1	0	0	0
No. of 2's	0	0	0	0	0	3	4	2	2	3
No. of 1's	1	1	1	1	1	11	11	14	14	13
	1	1	1	1	1	1	1	1	1	1

Table 3.6. Continued

	Treament B					Treatment A'				
	11	12	13	14	15	16	17	18	19	20
Minimum										
Experiment 6										
No. of 7's	13	13	12	12	13	2	2	2	2	2
No. of 6's	0	1	1	1	0	0	0	0	0	0
No. of 5's	0	1	1	0	1	0	0	0	0	0
No. of 4's	1	0	1	1	0	1	0	0	0	0
No. of 3's	0	1	0	1	0	1	0	0	0	0
No. of 2's	1	0	0	0	1	5	6	7	6	5
No. of 1's	1	0	1	1	1	7	8	7	8	9
	1	3	1	1	1	1	1	1	1	1
Minimum										
Experiment 7										
No. of 7's	12	14	13	13	14	3	4	2	2	2
No. of 6's	0	0	1	0	0	0	0	0	0	0
No. of 5's	0	0	0	0	0	1	0	0	0	0
No. of 4's	1	0	0	0	0	2	0	0	0	0
No. of 3's	0	0	0	1	0	2	0	0	0	0
No. of 2's	0	0	0	0	0	2	4	2	2	1
No. of 1's	1	0	0	0	0	4	6	10	10	11
Minimum	1	7*	6	3	7*	1	1	1	1	1

Source: Van Huyck, Battalio, and Beil 1990, table 3.
Note: Asterisk indicates a mutual best response outcome.

In game Φ, $a = 0$ and $c > 2bk$, where k is a positive integer. Table 3.8c reproduces the actual table used in the experiment. The use of game Φ in the design of this second experiment is intended to further distinguish between the emergence of a focal point as a pure consequence of the evolution of experience and the security properties of an equilibrium. In this game, the equilibria all yield the same payoff, but there is a unique equilibrium supported by the maximin strategy. If a focal point emerges which is not the maximin strategy equilibrium then this would be clear evidence that a concern for security does not always have a predominant influence on the evolution of a focal point.

The results of this experiment have two points in common with the results of the first experiment:(1) In none of these twelve sessions was an equilibrium observed in the first period of a sequence of play of *any* game. (2) In all of the sequences there was convergence toward an equilibrium. Indeed, in all but two cases equilibrium was observed in the last period of the sequence under every treatment. The principal difference between the behavior observed in this experi-

Table 3.7. Experimental Design Matrix Treatment

Experiment	Gamma Table Γ	Omega Table Ω	Phi Table Φ	Gamma Table Γ
1	1^p,2, ..., 10	11^p, ..., 18	—	19^p, 10
2	1^p,2, ..., 10	11^p, ..., 18	—	19^p,20
3	1^p,2, ..., 10	11^p, ..., 18	—	19,20
4*	1^p,2, ..., 10	11^p, ..., 15	—	—
5*	1^p,2, ..., 10	11^p, ..., 15	—	—
6*	1^p,2, ..., 10	11^p, ..., 15	—	—
7	—	1^p,2, ..., 10	—	11^p, ..., 15
8	—	1^p,2, ..., 10	—	11^p, ..., 15
9	—	1^p,2, ..., 10	—	11^p, ..., 15
10	—	—	1^p,2, ..., 10	11^p, ..., 15
11	—	—	1^p,2, ..., 10	11^p, ..., 15
12	—	—	1^p,2, ..., 10	11^p, ..., 15

Source: Van Huyck, Battalio, and Beil 1991, table 1.
Notes: Superscript "p" indicates a period in which subjects made predictions. Asterisk indicates dual market treatment.

Table 3.8a. Payoff Table Γ

Your Choice of χ	Median Value of χ Chosen						
	7	6	5	4	3	2	1
7	1.30	1.15	0.90	0.55	0.10	−0.45	−1.10
6	1.25	1.20	1.05	0.80	0.45	0.00	0.55
5	1.10	1.15	1.10	0.95	0.70	0.35	−0.10
4	0.85	1.00	1.05	1.00	0.85	0.60	0.25
3	0.50	0.75	0.90	0.95	0.90	0.75	0.50
2	0.05	0.40	0.65	0.80	0.85	0.80	0.65
1	−0.50	−0.05	0.30	0.55	0.70	0.75	0.70

Source: Van Huyck, Battalio, and Beil 1991.

ment and the behavior observed in Van Huyck et al's first experiment is that in this second experiment the equilibrium observed at the end of a sequence of play of any given game was *always equal to the median of the distribution of values chosen in the first period of that sequence* whereas this was *never* true in their first experiment.

Table 3.9 shows the distribution of actions chosen in the initial play under each treatment. Notice the difference in distributions under the baseline treatment

Table 3.8b. Payoff Table Ω

Your Choice	Median Value of χ Chosen						
of χ	7	6	5	4	3	2	1
7	1.30	0	0	0	0	0	0
6	0	1.20	0	0	0	0	0
5	0	0	1.10	0	0	0	0
4	0	0	0	1.00	0	0	0
3	0	0	0	0	0.90	0	0
2	0	0	0	0	0	0.80	0
1	0	0	0	0	0	0	0.70

Source: Van Huyck, Battalio, and Beil 1991.

Table 3.8c. Payoff Table Φ

Your Choice	Median Value of χ Chosen						
of χ	7	6	5	4	3	2	1
7	0.70	0.65	0.50	0.25	−0.10	−0.55	−1.10
6	0.65	0.70	0.65	0.50	0.25	−0.10	−0.55
5	0.50	0.65	0.70	0.65	0.50	0.25	−0.10
4	0.25	0.60	0.65	0.70	0.65	0.50	0.25
3	−0.10	0.25	0.50	0.65	0.70	0.65	0.50
2	−0.55	−0.10	0.25	0.50	0.65	0.70	0.65
1	−1.10	−0.55	−0.10	0.25	0.50	0.65	0.70

Source: Van Huyck, Battalio, and Beil 1991.

game Γ, where the secure action is action 3, and under treatment Ω, where all equilibria were equally (in)secure. This suggests that players who face strategic uncertainty at the start and consequently have diffuse priors as to how other players will act tend to give weight to considerations of security in their initial play of a game. A comparison of initial play under treatment Φ and treatment Ω provides another way of examining the role considerations of security may have in shaping initial play of coordination games. In treatment Ω the secure action is 4, and all equilibria yield the same payoff. The action, 4, did draw a somewhat larger initial response in Ω, where it is the secure play, than in baseline treatment Γ, where 3 is the secure action. However, the distribution of choices is not statistically different between the two treatments. Therefore, the role of secu-

Table 3.9. Distribution of Choices in Period 1

	Treatment								
	GAMMA		GAMMADM		Combined (Baseline)		OMEGA		IOTA	
Action	Number	%	Number	%	Number	%	Number	%	Number	%
7	5	18	3	11	8	15	14	52	2	7.5
6	3	11	1	14	4	7	1	4	3	11
5	8	30	7	25	15	28	9	33	9	33
4	8	30	11	41	19	35	3	11	11	41
3	3	11	5	18	8	15	0	0	2	7.5
2	0	0	0	0	0	0	0	0	0	0
1	0	0	0	0	0	0	0	0	0	0
Total	27	100	27	100	54	100	27	100	27	100

Source: Van Huyck, Battalio, and Beil 1991, table 2.

rity in influencing the starting point (and therefore the equilibrium eventually reached) of the dynamic processes created by these coordination games remains in doubt.

Taken together, these first two experiments of Van Huyck, Battalio, and Beil demonstrate that the dynamics of the process by which a group comes to focus on an equilibrium is apparently quite sensitive to the nature of the penalty a player incurs for deviating from equilibrium. This suggests an obvious area for further systematic experimental investigation.[22]

B. The Relevance of Dominated Strategies

A third study using a game with multiple Pareto-ranked equilibria is reported by Cooper, DeJong, Forsythe, and Ross (1990). Figure 3.5 presents the payoff tables for the row player for the various two-person 3×3 symmetric games used in this experiment. All of these games have the same two Pareto ordered Nash equilibria (1,1), (2,2). Furthermore, strategy 3 is strictly dominated in all of the games. Note further that in Games 3 through 6 the nonequilibrium strategy vector (3,3) yields the largest sum of payoffs to the two players.

The objectives of Cooper et al. were somewhat different from those of Van Huyck and his associates. In the designs of Van Huyck et al., each possible one play strategy was consistent with some equilibrium. The question Van Huyck and his associates were interested in studying was how the dynamics of a process by which a given group came to focus upon a particular equilibrium would be influenced by the payoff function. The experiment of Cooper et al. is not designed to

Game 3
Row Player's Payoff Matrix

		Column Player		
		1	2	3
Row	1	350	350	1000
	2	250	550	0
Player	3	0	0	600

Nash Equilibria at (1,1) and (2,2)

Game 4
Row Player's Payoff Matrix

		Column Player		
		1	2	3
Row	1	350	350	700
	2	250	550	0
Player	3	0	0	600

Nash Equilibria at (1,1) and (2,2)

Game 5
Row Player's Payoff Matrix

		Column Player		
		1	2	3
Row	1	350	350	700
	2	250	550	1000
Player	3	0	0	600

Nash Equilibria at (1,1) and (2,2)

Game 6
Row Player's Payoff Matrix

		Column Player		
		1	2	3
Row	1	350	350	700
	2	250	550	650
Player	3	0	0	600

Nash Equilibria at (1,1) and (2,2)

Game 7
Row Player's Payoff Matrix

		Column Player		
		1	2	3
Row	1	350	350	700
	2	250	550	0
Player	3	0	0	500

Nash Equilibria at (1,1) and (2,2)

Game 8
Row Player's Payoff Matrix

		Column Player		
		1	2	3
Row	1	350	350	1000
	2	250	550	0
Player	3	0	0	500

Nash Equilibria at (1,1) and (2,2)

Figure 3.5. Multiple Nash equilibrium game. *Source*: Cooper, DeJong, Forsythe, and Ross (1990), figure 4.

study the dynamics of evolution to a particular equilibrium. Rather it is designed to study how the focal power of an equilibrium in a one play game is influenced by payoffs to strategies that are not played in any equilibrium.

In this experiment each subject played twenty repetitions of the same game with a series of anonymous opponents. Each subject was paired with another subject for only two repetitions, alternating roles of column and row player. In this way, Cooper et al. were able to give subjects experience with a given game without creating a supergame for which repeated play of (3,3) might be considered part of an equilibrium trigger strategy. By using the payoffs for strategy 3 as

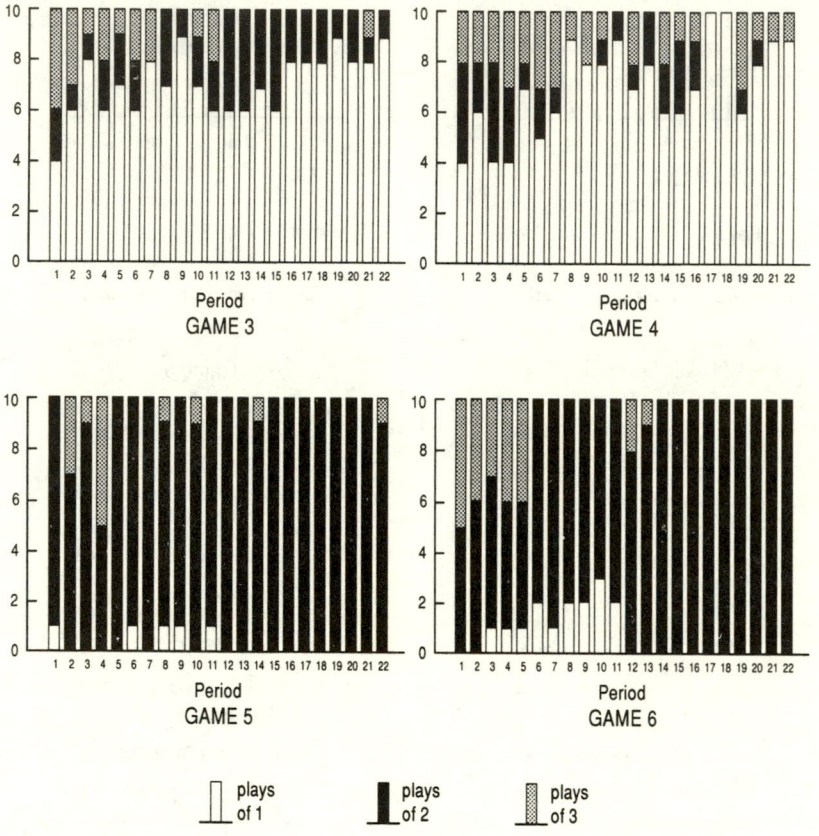

Figure 3.6. Games 3, 4, 5, and 6. *Source*: Cooper, DeJong, Forsythe, and Ross (1990), figure 8.

treatment variables, they could examine how variations in payoffs out of equilibrium would affect both the likelihood of observing equilibrium play and the relative frequency with which the two pure strategy equilibria were played.

Figure 3.6 shows how the relative frequency of choice of strategy evolved as players gained experience in Games 3 through 6. As the figure shows, after subjects have accumulated experience in any one game they tend to concentrate on one of the pure strategy equilibria of that game. That is, with experience, subjects do not have difficulty coordinating even if they do not have a common history. However, the play of Games 3 and 4 clearly shows that Pareto dominance is not a selection criterion, since (2,2) Pareto dominates (1,1). Furthermore, the striking difference in play between Games 3 and 4 on the one hand, and Games 5 and 6 on the other, provides strong evidence that the nature of play can be affected by the payoffs that are associated with the play of a dominated strategy. That is, dominated strategies, that are not themselves played in equilibrium are, nevertheless, relevant for determination of the equilibrium that is eventually selected.

Why does the nature of the payoff function conditional on selecting a dominated strategy influence the selection of the equilibrium? Cooper et al. suggest two possible hypotheses. First, individuals may be uncertain as to the rationality of their opponent. In that case, each individual should give greater weight to selecting a given undominated strategy when that strategy is a best response to strategy 3 (the dominated strategy) than when it is not a best response to strategy 3. The second hypothesis they entertained was that each individual may believe that the experimenters have not achieved full control over the payoffs and that a subject has a positive probability of encountering an opponent who always selects the strategy for which the joint payoff is maximal. (Cooper et al. label individuals who always select the strategy that is consistent with maximal joint payoff "altruists.") Under the first hypothesis, the relative frequency of selection of strategy 3, and of the best response to strategy 3, should be independent of whether or not strategy 3 allows the maximal joint payoff. Under the second hypothesis, the relative frequency of these choices should be dependent on this condition. The purpose of Games 7 and 8 in their design was to sort out between these competing hypotheses. Except for the payoff for the outcome (3,3) the payoff matrix for these games corresponds to Games 3 and 4 respectively. In both of these games, as in Games 3 and 4, strategy 1 is a best response to a play of strategy 3 by the other person. Therefore, if it is merely the possibility of an opponent irrationally playing a dominated strategy that affects a (rational) player's choice of strategy, the pattern of play in Games 7 and 8 should correspond to those observed in Games 3 and 4. However, the maximal joint payoff in the Games 7 and 8 is associated with the play of the strategy pair (2,2), while in Games 3 and 4 the maximal joint payoff is associated with (3,3). Therefore, under the second (presence of "altruist") hypothesis, play should evolve to (2,2) in Games 7 and 8. As figure 3.7 shows, in these games play was concentrated on the payoff dominant equilibrium (2,2), whereas in Games 3 and 4 play was concentrated on (1,1).

Cooper et al. conclude that play in the initial rounds of a game must reflect players' assessments of the likelihood of playing against an individual who is an "altruist," that is, someone who is motivated by an experimentally uncontrolled interest in cooperation, rather than reflect players' assessments of running into an opponent who simply cannot recognize a dominated strategy. While this conclusion is plausible, it is not the only possible interpretation of their data. Players may have *any* variety of initial beliefs about the character of other players. Since these initial priors are unobservable, one is free to assume that there are as many different types (however specified) of players in a session as there are players in the session.[23] Indeed, it doesn't matter how many types there "really" are in the session, since a person's type is private information. In principle, we can build a model which assumes a particular distribution of types and then treat the entire session as a game of incomplete information. However, unless the experimenter can set up experimental controls which make this distribution *common knowledge*, it is difficult to see how we can produce experimental tests of any theoretical predictions of such a model.

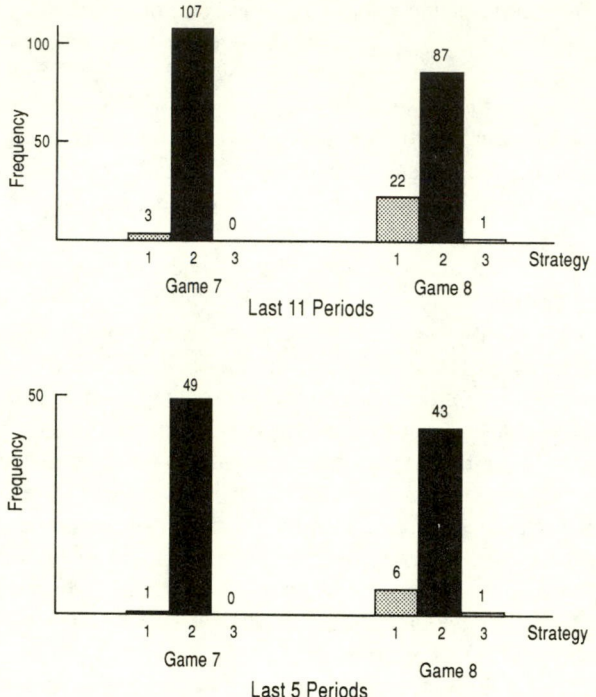

Figure 3.7. Games (a) last 11 periods; (b) last 5 periods. *Source*: Cooper, DeJong, Forsythe, and Ross (1990), figure 7a.

There is another, and to me, a more natural approach to understanding the dynamics of this type of experiment. As long as people have diffuse priors we cannot expect them to focus immediately on an equilibrium. Certainly, in this experiment equilibria were not frequently observed in early rounds of play of any game. In my view, the empirically most relevant question therefore is not about the nature of unobservable and experimentally uncontrolled beliefs. Rather, the fundamental question is how the starting point of a social process interacts with the structure of the payoff function to effect the selection of the equilibrium that eventually emerges when a group of people, all of whom have experienced repetitions of the same game but none of whom have exactly common experience, acquire sufficient experience to reach an equilibrium.[24]

C. Influencing Equilibrium Selection

One way of manipulating the starting point of such a learning process is to introduce a pregame. What happens to the play of a coordination game when it is preceded by some form of pregame communication? Both Van Huyck et al. and Cooper et al. have extended their work by conducting experiments to address this question.

Column Player's Strategy

		1	2	3
Row Player's Strategy	1	350,350	350,250	1000,0
	2	250,350	550,550	0,0
	3	0,1000	0,0	600,600

Figure 3.8. *Source*: Cooper, DeJong, Forsythe, and Ross (1989b), figure 1.

1. Pregame Communication: Cheap Talk

Cooper, DeJong, Forsythe, and Ross (1989b)

In this experiment subjects were asked to play the coordination game shown in Figure 3.8. Play of this game was preceded by structured pregame communication in which either one player (one-way treatment) or both (two-way treatment) were allowed to announce via their computer terminal the action which that player planned to make in the following coordination game. There was no payoff for any announcement, and players were specifically instructed that they were not required to choose in the coordination game the action they announced in the pregame.

From a formal point of view, the two-stage game is much more complicated than the one-stage game since a strategy in this game includes both a message and an action. An equilibrium in the two-stage game must be supported by beliefs as to how messages are being interpreted. However, if one applies Farrell's (1987) credibility criterion that a message of one player is credible if it would be optimal for the player to do what he announces given that the other player makes a best response to the announced action, then in the one-way communication treatment only announcements consistent with equilibria (1 or 2) are credible. Considerations of "credibility" in the one-way treatment should therefore reduce the frequency of play of strategy 3. Furthermore, since the equilibria are Pareto rankable, in the one-way communication treatment one should observe a much higher frequency of selection of the Pareto dominant equilibrium than in the play of the game with no communication at all.

The two-way communication treatment opens the possibility that both players do not send the same message. If this were to occur, then a player's best response, conditional on his own message being believed, is different from his best response, conditional on his believing the message of the other player. Farrell assumes that the messages have no effect on the second-stage game when the first-stage game generates this type of noise.

Table 3.10 displays the frequencies with which both players selected various pairs of strategies under different treatment conditions.[25] As the table shows, the play of the coordination game was dramatically affected by the one-way communication treatment relative to no pregame communication treatment. The frequency with which both parties selected an equilibrium (1,1) or (2,2) was higher with one-way communication than with no communication. More dramatically,

Table 3.10. Frequency of Equilibrium Play

Treatment	N	1.1	2.2	1 & 3	3.3
None	165	103 (62.4%)	5 (3.0%)	6 (3.61%)	
One-way	165	25 (15.2%)	111 (67.3%)	12 (7.3%)	3 (1.8%)
Two-way					
Rep. 1	55	35 (63.6%)	3 (5.5%)	7 (12.7%)	1 (1.8%)
Rep. 2	55	19 (34.5%)	6 (10.9%)	12 (21.8%)	1 (1.8%)
Rep. 3	55	6 (10.9%)	39 (70.9%)		

Source: Cooper, DeJong, Forsthye, and Ross 1989b, table 1.

Table 3.11. Mapping of Announcements to Actions, One-Way Communications

Announcements (row)	Actions (row, column)									Total
	(2,2)	(3,3)	(1,1)	(1,3)	(3,1)	(2,3)	(3,2)	(1,2)	(2,1)	
1			1	8		1		2		12
2	111								7	118
3		2	17	6	5		1	3	1	35
Total	111	3	25	6	6		1	5	8	165

Source: Cooper, DeJong, Forsythe, and Ross 1989b, table 2.

while the Pareto dominant equilibrium (2,2) was the equilibrium observed in less than 5 percent of all of the equilibrium outcomes with no pregame communication, it was the equilibrium observed in more than 67 percent of the cases with one-way pregame communication.

The two-way communication treatment did not consistently increase the relative frequency of equilibria observed relative to the no communication treatment. Moreover, conditional on an equilibrium being observed, the relative frequency with which the Pareto dominant equilibrium occurred was not consistently higher in the two-way communication treatment sessions than in the no communication sessions.

As Table 3.11 shows, even though the announcement of an intention to play strategy 3 is not credible, it was the second most frequent announcement made in the one-way communication treatment (35 of 165 announcements), and in 8 of the cases in which it was announced it was actually played by the person making the

Table 3.12. Mapping of Announcements to Actions, Two-Way Communication

Announce-ments (row, column)	(1,1)	(1,2)	(1,3)	(2,1)	(2,2)	(2,3)	(3,1)	(3,2)	(3,3)	Total
	\multicolumn{9}{c}{Actions (row, column)}									
(2,2)		1			38					39
(3,3)	11	1	2	1			3		1	19
(1,1)	6		1	1			2			10
(1,3)	19	2	1				1			23
(3,1)	11		1				2			14
(2,3)	6	2		5		1	3	2		19
(3,2)	2	2	1	5	5	1			1	17
(1,2)	3	2	1	1	1		1			9
(2,1)	2	1		8	4					15
Total	60	11	7	21	48	2	12	2	2	165

Source: Cooper, DeJong, Forsythe, and Ross 1989b, table 3.

announcement. In the two-way communication treatment at least one of the two players announced the intention to play strategy 3 in 92 of 165 cases (see Table 3.12). In only 6 of these cases did the player making the announcement actually play strategy 3 in the second stage game. The frequency of incredible announcements casts some doubt upon the usefulness of the Farrell credibility criterion to account for the effects of "cheap talk."

A comparison of the frequency with which the announcement of the intention to play the dominated strategy, 3, was made relative to the frequency of observing the payoff-dominant equilibrium (2,2) in the second stage game across different replications of the two-way communication treatment suggests that the higher the frequency of the announcement of 3, the less likely (2,2) will be observed. In this sense, the experiment suggests that two-way communication can sometimes produce worse outcomes than no communication at all.[26]

2. Forward Induction

Van Huyck, Battalio, and Beil (1993)

In this experiment Van Huyck and his associates construct a two-stage game in which the baseline median-opinion game, Γ, used in Van Huyck, Battalio, and Beil (1991) is the second-stage game while the first-stage game consists of an auction for the right to be a participant in the second-stage, median-opinion game. The basic idea behind this design is that the equilibrium price in the first-stage auction must reflect what participants in that auction believe they will be able to earn in the second-stage, average-opinion game. Given the results of the auction, this price might then be commonly expected to put a lower bound on the action that will be taken by all participants in the median-opinion game, thereby reducing the set of possible equilibria in the second-stage game. That is, each participant in the second stage, knowing the price every participant paid to be in the second stage and assuming the rationality of the participants in the first stage, may reason as follows: "Surely, anyone who submitted a bid greater than or equal to the market-clearing price, P, must believe that they can earn back in the second stage at least this amount of money. To earn this amount, they must believe that the median of the actions taken in the second stage will be at least $\underline{e}$, since a lower median will not allow them to recover P. The best response of anyone who believes that the median will be at least $\underline{e}$, is at least $\underline{e}$. Therefore, the smallest action I should observe others taking in the second-stage game is $\underline{e}$." If this type of forward induction occurs, then subjects who play the second stage are updating their priors as to the distribution of actions that will be observed, based on the market-clearing price observed in the first-stage auction. Further, the expressions of opinion embodied in the price of the first stage auction will be positively correlated with the observed median of the distribution of choices in the second stage game.

Van Huyck et al. find very strong evidence of this correlation. The first period price of the right to participate varied across sessions. The lower bound for the actions in the second-stage game implied by the forward induction hypothesis was almost never violated, and the median of the actions in the second-stage game was positively correlated with the observed price in the first-stage game. Moreover, the dynamics observed with repetitions of this two-stage game was quite different from that observed when only the median-opinion game was played. In the two-stage game sessions, there was *always* convergence towards the payoff-dominant equilibrium of the median-opinion game. This was *never* observed when this game was not preceded by the auction of the right to play.

Van Huyck et al. interpret their results as indicating that subjects use forward induction to infer that everyone who is playing the second stage, median-opinion game will choose an action at or above the level consistent with nonnegative profits from the entire game. While plausible, this is not the only possible interpretation. Not everyone gets to play the second-stage game. Only those who are willing to pay at least the market price play. Therefore, the first stage game may simply filter out those individuals who are most concerned with security or who have the lowest priors as to where the median action in the second-stage game might be, without having any influence on the priors held by anyone who actually plays the second stage game. In order to distinguish between these possible explanations one would have to have an independent measure of the priors with respect to the median action in the second-stage game of all of the participants in the first-stage auction.

Cachon and Camerer (1991)

Cachon and Camerer note that when players must pay an entry fee for the right to play a median effort coordination game, that fact raises the median action necessary for the player to recoup the cost or earn a positive return. A second way of raising the median action necessary to earn a positive amount is simply to subtract a positive constant amount from all entries in a player's payoff table. The difference between these two methods is that in the first subjects are actually playing a two-stage game where the payment of the fee in the first stage might be interpreted as a signal of intention to take an action in the second stage, while a simple transformation of the payoff function still leaves the game as a one-stage game in which there is no room for forward induction.

Cachon and Camerer study the difference in subject responses to these two methods of raising the median action necessary to earn positive amounts. In their design all subjects play three rounds of the median effort game of Van Huyck, Battalio, and Beil (1991), described earlier in section II.C.2, and, as in Van Huyck, Battalio, and Beil (1991), they observe that the median action is either 4 or 5 in all of their sessions. Starting in round four of each session, players under the one-stage game (Must Pay) treatment face a payoff function that is modified by the subtraction of a constant amount regardless of outcome, such that if a player makes a best response to a median action of at least 4, that player will have a positive net payoff. In the seventh round of play this constant is increased so that the median action must be at least 6 in order for the player's best response to produce a positive payoff. Under the two-stage game (Opt Out) condition, starting in round four, at the beginning of each round each player had to choose whether or not to play that round. A player who opted out received zero payoff. A player who opted in faced the same payoff function as that faced by subjects in the Must Play condition for that round. Figure 3.9 reproduces Figure 2 of Cachon and Camerer. The label "sunk cost" in the figure represents the value of the constant subtracted from all entries in the median value game payoff table.

As Figure 3.9 shows, under both treatments the change in the payoff function beginning in round seven—a change that left the previously achieved median action unprofitable in all but one session—induced similar reactions under both treatment conditions. Under both conditions the median action increased sufficiently to be profitable for those who played it. However, the most notable difference between the two treatments is, of course, the fact that in round seven 15 of 36 subjects chose the Opt Out option. If forward induction "worked," we would not expect such a high percentage of people to choose that option.

A common characteristic of both of the treatments described above is that it was common knowledge that the payoff function in the median value game was being transformed for everyone in the same way. Cachon and Camerer investigate what happens when the payoff function of the median value game is transformed, but this knowledge is private to each player. They find that the median action is *not* displaced in this case. This suggests that the common knowledge of a payoff transformation is more important than whether the transformation is or is not accompanied by adding on a first, option selection, stage to the game.

Abdalla, Cooper, DeJong, Forsythe, and Ross (1989)

This experiment is also designed to assess the power of the ideas behind forward induction to influence play in a game with multiple equilibria. One game used in this experiment as the second stage of a two-stage game is the same coordination game used in Cooper, DeJong, Forsythe, and Ross (1989b). The first stage of the game consists of giving one of the players the right to choose not to play the

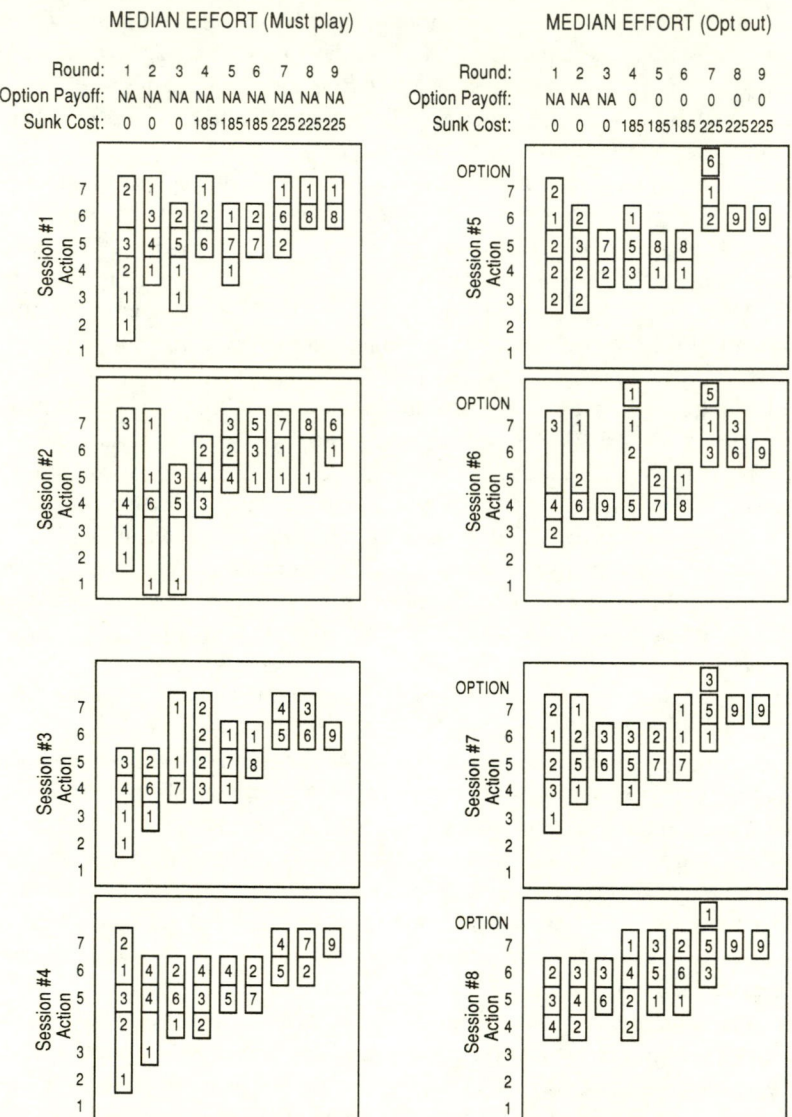

Figure 3.9. Choices in median effort sessions. *Source*: Cachon and Camerer (1991), figure 2.

second stage. If this right is exercised, then both players get a payoff equal to the average of the two equilibrium payoffs in the coordination game. If this option is not exercised, then the second stage coordination game is played. (See Table 3.13.) A forward induction argument for equilibrium selection implies that rejecting the outside option signals that the person who forgoes the option will select the strategy that is his component of the higher equilibrium payoff vector and that he expects the other player to do likewise.

Table 3.13.

		Column Player's Strategy		
		1	2	3
Row	1	(350,350)	(350,250)	(1000,0)
Player's	2	(250,350)	(550,550)	(0,0)
Strategy	3	(0,1000)	(0,0)	(600,600)

Source: Cooper, DeJong, Forsythe, and Ross 1989b, figure 1.

Table 3.14. Coordination Games: Frequency of Outcomes in Last Eleven Periods

	(1,1)	(2,2)	Frequency of Nonequilibrium Second-Stage Pairs	Frequency of Selection of Outside Option	Total
Coordination game	116 (70%)	4 (2%)	45 (27%)	—	165 (100%)
Coordination game with outside option	14 (8%)	5 (3%)	26 (16%)	120 (73%)	165 (100%)

Source: Abdalla, Cooper, DeJong, Forsythe, and Ross 1989, table 2.

Abdalla et al. observe that *when the outside option is not taken*, forward induction "works" in the sense that this equilibrium, (2,2), is observed 11.1 percent of the time in the continuation coordination games while it is observed only 2 percent of the time when the coordination game is not preceded by this first-stage game. (See Table 3.14.) However, subjects who have had no previous experience with the coordination game chose the outside option 73 percent of the time. Moreover, when one player declines to take the outside option, this signal is evidently not as easily interpretable by the other player as when the first player simply states his intention to take action 2, since (2,2) was observed with a much higher relative frequency (67.3 percent) under one-way communication in Cooper et al. (1989b).

A second game used in this experiment is the 2×2 Battle of the Sexes game, illustrated in Table 3.15. In this game the Row Player has available an outside option that yields the payoff (300,300). Refusal of that option therefore signals that the Row Player intends to play Strategy 2. As seen in Table 3.15, only 20 percent of the subjects selected the outside option, and conditional on the op-

Table 3.15. Battle of the Sexes Game

		Column Player's Strategy	
		1	2
Row	1	(0,0)	(200,600)
Player's	2	(600,200)	(0,0)
Strategy			

Source: Abdalla, Cooper, DeJong, Forsythe, and Ross 1989,
figure 2.

Table 3.16. Battle of the Sexes 3 × 3 Game

		Column Player's Strategy		
		1	2	3
Row	1	(0,0)	(200,600)	(1000,0)
Player's	2	(600,200)	(0,0)	(0,0)
Strategy	3	(0,0)	(0,1000)	(800,800)

Source: Abdalla, Cooper, DeJong, Forsythe, and Ross 1989, figure 3.
Note: Row player's outside option is (300,300).

tion being refused, in 118 of 132 cases the subsequent play was the equilibrium favored by the person who had refused the outside option. Clearly, the forward induction implication of rejecting the outside option in this game is a much more salient equilibrium selection principle than it is in the 3 × 3 coordination game.

Abdalla et al. note that the forward induction implications of a one-way announcement by the row player was also more powerful in the Battle of the Sexes game than in their coordination game.[27] This leads them to conjecture that it is the possibility of encountering an "altruist" who would play the "cooperative" strategy which reduces the power of forward induction in the coordination game.

To test this conjecture, they conducted a Battle of the Sexes game to which a third strategy was added for each player. Table 3.16 is the payoff table for this game. The third strategy has the "cooperative strategy" property of being payoff dominated for each player by other strategies available to the player, but yielding

**Table 3.17. Battle of the Sexes Game: Frequency of Outcomes
in Last Eleven Periods**

Game	(2,1)	(1,2)	Frequency of Nonequilibrium Second-Stage Pairs	Frequency of Selection of Outside Option	Total
2 × 2 Battle of the Sexes game with outside option	118 (72%)	0 (0%)	14 (8%)	33 (20%)	165 (100%)
3 × 3 Battle of the Sexes game	0 (0%)	65 (39%)	40 (24%)	60 (36%)	165 (100%)

Source: Abdalla, Cooper, DeJong, Forsythe, and Ross 1989, table 3.

the highest joint payoff to both players if both players play it. The refusal of the outside option may either signal that the Row player is an "altruist" who intends to play the "cooperative" strategy, 3, or that he intends to play 2. If each player selected his best response to the other player's "cooperative" strategy, then the observed outcome would be the equilibrium favored by the Column Player. However, if the Row Player refuses the outside option and plays 2, then the Column Player who correctly reads the signal that the Row Player intends to select 2 will play 1, and the observed outcome would be the equilibrium favored by the Row Player.

Table 3.17 displays the outcomes from the 2 × 2 Battle of the Sexes Game and from the game with the cooperative strategy added (3 × 3). The outcome (2,1) is the row player's favored equilibrium while the outcome (1,2) is the column player's favored equilibrium. The next column displays the frequency with which the second-stage strategy pairs were other than equilibrium pairs. The second-last column shows the frequency with which the outside option was exercised.

As Table 3.17 indicates, the inclusion of this third strategy had a dramatic effect on observed behavior. The power of the signal implied by foregoing the outside option simply vanished. The row player rejected the outside option in 105 cases. In 62 percent of these cases *both players* chose *that strategy which was a best response to the other player's choosing the "cooperative" strategy*, while the equilibrium favored by the row player was *never observed*.

An anticipation that the other player would chose the "cooperative" strategy was not completely unfounded. Of the 210 strategy choices made in the last 11 periods by players in both roles, 40 (19 percent) were the "cooperative" strategy.

Why did the introduction of a cooperative, dominated strategy reduce the power of the row player to get the equilibrium he desired? In particular, does this failure to observe the Row player's favored equilibrium mean that the introduction of the cooperative strategy reduces the power of forward induction to serve as an equilibrium selection principle, as Abdalla et al. suggest in their concluding remarks?[28] Not necessarily. We may interpret the fact that strategy 3 was played as an indication either that there were some subjects who did not recognize it as a dominated strategy or that there were some subjects who secured some extra, uncontrolled utility from playing a cooperative strategy, or both. Call this group "altruists." Suppose that all nonaltruists believed that there were some altruists in the group who would always play the cooperative strategy. A nonaltruistic column player always either plays 2 (his best response to the "cooperative" strategy of the row player) or plays 1 (the strategy that is his component of the equilibrium vector preferred by the row player). A player who assigns a probability of $\frac{1}{6}$ or more to the event that the other player will play the cooperative strategy would maximize his expected payoff by always playing his best response to the "cooperative" strategy. Otherwise, the nonaltruistic column player should play 1, on the assumption that if the row player who refused the outside option is nonaltruistic, then the row player will play 2. Nonaltruistic row players, observing that column players have a probability of .19 of facing a row player who plays the cooperative strategy, will then infer that with probability .81 they will be facing a nonaltruistic column player who will play strategy 2 (the column player's best response to an altruist row player.) The row player would maximize his expected payoff, therefore, by playing his strategy 1. Furthermore, with a probability of .19 of encountering a column player who plays the altruist's strategy 3, the nonaltruistic row player has a higher expected payoff (352) from the second stage game than from exercising the outside option (300). Therefore, the observed pattern of play is consistent with the hypothesis that adding a cooperative, dominated strategy to the game which allowed "altruists" to play this third strategy will have an effect on the equilibrium selected when nonaltruists *correctly* infer from the refusal of the outside option exactly what to expect from one another. Under this interpretation, forward induction remains as strong an equilibrium selection principle in the 3×3 Battle of the Sexes game as it was in the 2×2 game. It simply selects a different equilibrium.

The addition of the "cooperative" strategy to the Battle of the Sexes game had a large effect on the frequency with which the outside option was selected. While Row players selected the outside option only 20 percent of the time in the 2×2 Battle of the Sexes game, the outside option was selected 36 percent of the time in the 3×3 game. Why do so many subjects take the outside option in both the Battle of the Sexes game and in the coordination game (73 percent) when this "cooperative," dominated strategy is present? I believe that the most plausible explanation lies in the fact that the likelihood of a row player being an "altruist" is *not common knowledge*. Recall that the best action for a nonaltruistic row player to take if he does not exercise this option depends on his estimate of the column player's estimate of the likelihood that the row player is an "altruist." Since there is no objective basis for making this estimate prior to experience with this game, the row player who forgoes the outside option is placing himself in a game whose outcome cannot be inferred by any purely rational analysis. For many people, opting out of a game with inherent strategic uncertainty must be more attractive than the possible rewards available to playing such a game.

In summary, the results of Van Huyck et al. (1993) suggest that forward induction *can* serve as a device for getting coordination on a Pareto optimal equilibrium in a game of pure coordination. The results of Abdalla et al. (1989) suggest that forward induction can serve to focus play on the equilibrium desired by the player who has the power to signal his intended strategy choice, *provided there is common knowledge of the likelihood of a given signal being associated with a given strategy.* The results of Abdalla et al. also suggest that unless this common knowledge condition is met, forward induction will not have much power to serve as a coordinating device.

III. Experiments in Decentralized Matching Environments: Games with Multiple Optimal Equilibria

A decentralized market consists of several locations at which trades can take place and a set of agents, each of whom must decide at which location to attempt to trade without having the benefit of prior information on where other agents are going. This gives rise to an obvious coordination problem. There have been two responses to this problem in the theoretical literature. One response has been to ignore it and work with representative agent, market clearing models.[29] Implicit in this approach is an assumption that any failures to coordinate are transitory in nature. That is, if one were to observe a system with a stationary set of agents who had the opportunity to adapt to one another, over time a stationary state would be achieved in which there would not be any missed trading opportunities because of coordination failures. A second response has been to assume that this type of coordination failure is a central feature of the steady state of a decentralized market economy and to characterize the process of matching buyers and sellers as a stochastic process.[30] One rationalization for this second perspective is that important markets do not have a stationary set of agents who can adapt to one another over time but are, instead, characterized by high turnover.

These two theoretical responses give rise in turn to two empirical questions that can be studied experimentally. First, while in natural markets the set of players is never completely stationary, in a laboratory we can create and observe an environment where the same set of agents repeatedly play a coordination game. Under such conditions, will coordination failures be transitory? Second, suppose that we can observe the sequence of play of a coordination game by a nonstationary set of agents, such as exists in labor markets in which individuals who are successfully matched to jobs are continually replaced by new entrants. Such a setting does not give agents the opportunity to adapt to each other's past play. While there is no external mechanism producing any given match with any given probability, if players achieve the same mixed strategy equilibrium at each point in the sequence, then the resulting sequence will look as though it were generated by a stationary stochastic process. Does the sequence of plays of a coordination game generated by a nonstationary set of players exhibit the characteristics of a mixed strategy Nash equilibrium of the one-play game?

In Ochs (1990) a first pass was made at addressing these questions. This experiment used the following market coordination game: a market consisted of a set of locations at which units of stock were available and a set of agents, each of whom had to select a single location. At the beginning of a market period nine units of stock were distributed over the locations, and the distribution was publicly posted. Nine agents from the set of subjects participating in the experiment were assigned to this market. All of these agents simultaneously made their respective choice of locations without any prior conversation. The payoff associated with an agent's choice of location i in a given play of the game depended on the number r_i of agents who chose location i and the units of stock posted at that location that period, s_i. If $r_i \leq s_i$, then each agent who selected i was successful. If $r_i > s_i$, then s_i successful agents were selected at random from the r_i agents. A success was worth x cents, and a failure was worth y, where $x > y$ and x and y were themselves treatment variables which varied across some experimental sessions.

Any allocation of the agents over the locations that assigns each location just as many agents as there are units of stock posted at that location is an equilibrium. But all of these "market clearing" equilibria in pure strategies are asymmetric. They require not only that agents with identical information choose different pure strategies, but also that each pure strategy be chosen in the proper proportion. In addition to the multiplicity of pure strategy equilibria there is a unique, symmetric Nash equilibrium in mixed strategies to each specific game. (There are also many equilibria in asymmetric mixed strategies.) There is no compelling reason to believe, a priori, that people who have no common history on which to condition their choices will be able to achieve perfect coordination in this game. Will people choose mixed strategies in playing this game, and if they do, will observed behavior be consistent with equilibrium? These questions motivated one part of this experiment. Formally, the hypothesis tested was that individuals tend to adopt mixed strategies in the one-play version of this game and that this behavior exhibits the properties of a symmetric Nash equilibrium.

To study behavior in a market where the set of participants was not stationary from period to period the following design was employed. In a given experimental session three market games of the type described above operated simultaneously for a number of periods. The markets differed from one another in the distribution of stock over the locations, and each market was identified by a particular color. In a given period the 27 subjects participating in a session were partitioned into 3 groups of 9, with each group assigned to a different market. Each subject knew the market to which s/he was assigned in a given period by the color of the response form the subject was to use that period to communicate his/her choice of location to the experimenter. The market assignments changed from period to period in such a way that no pair of subjects had the same sequence of market assignments. This fact was stressed in the instructions and could be observed by subjects if they noted the differences among subjects in their respective sequences of color coded response forms. In this sense, nonstationarity of the set of participants in a given market was common knowledge.

There is little sense in testing a hypothesis against its logical complement since we can never expect to observe data that *exactly* conform to our theoretical prediction. Therefore the experiment was designed to test qualitative predictions of the theory. In particular, the design allows the behavior of the same subjects across markets with different stock distributions to be compared with the variation in symmetric equilibrium predictions across these same distributions.

Table 3.18 displays both the theoretical Nash Equilibrium probability weights and the observed relative frequency of choices in the various market games used in this part of the experiment. The responsiveness of the distribution of choices to variations in the distribution of stock both within and across markets is remarkably consistent with the symmetric Nash equilibrium hypothesis. The location in each market that had the largest volume of stock tended to draw a percentage of the choices that consistently exceeded the percentage of the total stock in the market posted at that location.[31]

A further test of the power of the symmetric Nash equilibrium to organize the data is whether the time series on the failure rates generated in these markets had the properties of a stationary stochastic process. Such tests, not formally reported in the published version of the paper, did not give strong reasons to reject the stationarity hypothesis.

While the general pattern of behavior in these market coordination games is qualitatively consistent with important implications of the symmetric Nash equilibrium hypothesis, the actual pattern of behavior was not fully consistent with the best response property of a Nash equilibrium. In particular, given the observed relative frequency of choices of the location with the most stock, any one subject could increase his expected payoff by concentrating exclusively on that location. However, given the small amount of money at stake, the difference adopting this strategy would make in his expected success rate necessarily makes a small difference in expected payoff. Given the possible lack of saliency of small payoff differences, it is difficult to interpret this deviation from equilibrium as counting against the equilibrium hypothesis.

The second hypothesis tested in Ochs (1990) is that when the same market coordination game is played repeatedly by a *stationary set of players*, an adaptive process will develop which leads to an absorbing state of perfect coordination.[32] Since the symmetric Nash equilibrium of the one play game remains an equilibrium for every stage of this supergame, one natural null hypothesis is that there is no systematic difference between behavior when the set of players is stationary and when the set of players is nonstationary. Table 3.19 shows the failure rates in both the high-turnover markets (i.e., markets where $\frac{2}{3}$ of subjects assigned to a particular market in period t are assigned to a different market in period $t + 1$) and zero-turnover markets (i.e, a market in which the same subjects were always assigned to a given market). In Table 3.19 the failures per period value is the aver-

Table 3.18. Symmetric Nash Equilibrium Probability Weights
and Observed Distribution Choices

Stock Distribution	Equilibrium Probablity Weights	
	Probability Weights[a]	Expectation of Success[a]
(6,1,1,1)	(0.835,0.055,0.055,0.055)	.79
(5,2,1,1)	(0.683,0.2,0.0585,0.0585)	.79
(4,3,1,1)	(0.517,0.367,0.058,0.058)	.79
(6,2,1)	(0.783,0.167,0.05)	.83
(5,3,1)	(0.63,0.32,0.05)	.825
(3,3,3)	(0.333,0.333,0.333)	.818

Experiment	Actual Distribution of Choices

Experiment 1

Stock distribution	(1, 1, 2, 5)	(1, 1, 1, 6)	(1, 1, 3, 4)
Frequency of choice	(0.101, 0.111, 0.222, 0.566)	(0.111, 0.111, 0.091, 0.687)	(0.101, 0.081, 0.323, 0.495)
Stock distribution	(1, 1, 5, 2)	(1, 1, 6, 1)	(1, 1, 4, 3)
Frequency of choice	(0.056, 0.078, 0.689, 0.177)	(0.111, 0.067, 0.072, 0.1)	(0.089, 0.133, 0.467, 0.311)
Stock distribution	(2, 5, 1, 1)	(1, 6, 1, 1)	(3, 4, 1, 1)
Frequency of choice	(0.156, 0.644, 0.100, 0.100)	(0.122, 0.756, 0.089, 0.033)	(0.444, 0.289, 0.167, 0.100)
Stock distribution	(5, 2, 1, 1)	(6, 1, 1, 1)	(4, 3, 1, 1)
Frequency of choice	(0.667, 0.192, 0.061, 0.08)	(0.657, 0.121, 0.101, 0.121)	(0.485, 0.283, 0.141, 0.091)

Experiment 2

Stock distribution	(1, 1, 2, 5)	(1, 1, 1, 6)	(1, 1, 3, 4)
Frequency of choice	(0.113, 0.087, 0.225, 0.575)	(0.086, 0.099, 0.160, 0.655)	(0.136, 0.136, 0.345, 0.383)
Stock distribution	(1, 1, 5, 2)	(1, 1, 6, 1)	(1, 1, 4, 3)
Frequency of choice	(0.125, 0.056, 0.667, 0.152)	(0.125, 0.125, 0.667, 0.683)	(0.097, 0.083, 0.569, 0.251)
Stock distribution	(2, 5, 1, 1)	(1, 6, 1, 1)	(3, 4, 1, 1)
Frequency of choice	(0.194, 0.625, 0.097, 0.084)	(0.111, 0.764, 0.042, 0.083)	(0.319, 0.444, 0.139, 0.098)
Stock distribution	(5, 2, 1, 1)	(6, 1, 1, 1)	(4, 3, 1, 1)
Frequency of choice	(0.543, 0.321, 0.074, 0.062)	(0.716, 0.098, 0.088, 0.098)	(0.395, 0.222, 0.222, 0.161)

Experiment 5

Stock distribution	(2, 5, 1, 1)	(1, 1, 6, 1)	(1, 3, 1, 4)
Frequency of choice	(0.209, 0.575, 0.101, 0.115)	(0.101, 0.105, 0.712, 0.082)	(0.111, 0.284, 0.105, 0.500)

Experiment 11

Stock distribution	(6, 2, 1)	(5, 3, 1)	(3, 3, 3)
Frequency of choice	(0.707, 0.173, 0.120)	(0.549, 0.340, 0.111)	(0.321, 0.327, 0.352)

Source: Ochs 1990, table 4.

[a] Approximate.

Table 3.19.

Experiment	Turnover Rate	Failure Rates Stock Distribution	Failures per Period
1	0.667	6,1,1,1	1.3778
2	0.667	6,1,1,1	1.5278
5	0.667	6,1,1,1	1.5676
12	0	6,1,1,1	0.6786
1	0.667	6,1,1,1	0.667
2	0.667	6,1,1,1	0.667
5	0.667	5,2,1,1	1.8378
12	0	5,2,1,1	0.8214
1	0.667	4,3,1,1	1.9778
2	0.667	4,3,1,1	2.1111
5	0.667	4,3,1,1	2.1892
12	0	4,3,1,1	0.3929
11	0.667	6,2,1	1.2973
3	0	6,2,1	1.0400
4	0	6,2,1	0.9565
6	0	6,2,1	0.4318
7	0	6,2,1	0.5800
8	0	6,2,1	0.5135
11	0.667	3,3,3	1.6216
3	0	3,3,3	0.5200
4	0	3,3,3	0.3913

Source: Ochs, 1990, table 3.

age number of subjects per period, out of nine assigned to the market, who failed to be matched up with stock available in that market.

Given the strong incentives to coordinate, it is not surprising that the observed matching processes in games with a stationary set of participants were significantly different from those observed with high turnover rates. Somewhat more surprisingly, the incentives to achieve perfect coordination did not produce perfect coordination as an absorbing state in most of the zero turnover markets. A group of subjects would often achieve perfect coordination. However, while most people would continue to make the choice of location at which they were successful the previous period, some people sometimes changed location even though they had been successful at that location in the immediately preceding period. Once someone moved, these markets did tend to adapt again to generate another episode of perfect coordination.

What accounts for this episodic behavior in the zero turnover market environment? There was one market in which perfect coordination was never sustained simply because one person *always* selected a different location than the one she selected the previous period. When queried afterwards, she remarked that she simply wanted to see what would happen. Such behavior can never be completely controlled, and the pattern of episodic spells of coordination failure observed in other sessions might simply have reflected a lack of adequate reward for repeating the same choice period after period, given the possibility of boredom. The design of the experiment incorporated a variation in rewards and punishments. If boredom was a factor, then we might expect its effect to be offset by an increase in reward. The reward varied from $.25/success in Experiment 6 to $1.00/success in Experiment 8. Notice that the failure rate was higher in Experiment 8 than in Experiment 6. This counts against the hypothesis that boredom was a contributing factor in the inability of the markets to sustain perfect coordination. An alternative explanation is that individuals change location because they do not have confidence that other individuals will stay put. In other words, belief that others will continue to stay put may be fragile and easily upset by any transient shock. Once the belief that others will stay put in their current positions is overturned, the group has to go through a new adaptive process which may or may not converge to sustained perfect coordination.

This fragility hypothesis was explored in Ochs (1990) in three different ways. First, a market was run in which the size distribution of the stock was changed twice without prior notification. While the group immediately adapted to the first perturbation and sustained perfect coordination until the second perturbation, after the second perturbation perfect coordination was observed only episodically. Second, three markets were run in which the size distribution of the stock remained unchanged but where the distribution of stock over locations in the market was perturbed twice without prior notification of the subjects. All of these markets had sustained perfect coordination for at least eleven periods prior to the first perturbation, and all of them achieved perfect coordination within two periods of the first perturbation. However, only one of these three markets was able to sustain perfect coordination until the next perturbation, which occurred nine periods later. Furthermore, after the second shock the other two markets exhibited episodes of perfect coordination interrupted by someone moving.

Third, a market was run in which the size distribution was perturbed several times in a way which presented the same distribution (3,3,3) three different times. Subjects kept a running history of the distribution of stock, the distribution of choices, and their own choice, and they were encouraged to refer to these histories before making any choice. A switch from one distribution to another distribution was always made after a period in which the group had achieved perfect coordination. Therefore, if they referred to their prior experience with the (3,3,3) market and were confident that everyone was doing so, they could have achieved perfect coordination as soon as they were presented with that distribution for the second and the third time. This did not occur.

In sum, these tests give some credence to the hypothesis that confidence in the belief that others will not move once equilibrium has been achieved is itself quite fragile.

Meyer, Van Huyck, Battalio, and Saving (1992)

Is the difficulty subjects experienced in sustaining perfect coordination in the repeated game environment of the experiment conducted by Ochs (1990) an artifact of some details of that environment? An experiment conducted by Meyer, Van Huyck, Battalio, and Saving indicates that coordination failures can be observed in other repeated coordination games. The game used in their experiment consists of two markets and N players, each of whom must make a binary choice of market. The payoff to a player who chooses a market is a decreasing function of the number of individuals who choose the same market. Each market has the same payoff function so that a pure strategy equilibrium is characterized by equality of payoff and of numbers of individual choices across both markets. There are $N!/\{(N - 2)!2!\}$ (asymmetric) pure strategy equilibria to this stage game. In addition, there is a unique, symmetric, mixed strategy equilibrium in which the expected payoff is equal across both markets. (There are also many asymmetric, mixed strategy equilibria.) In a given session, a game of this form with fixed parameters is played repeatedly by the same set of subjects. The history of the number of individuals who chose each market and the payoff/subject (price) at each market in every prior period of a session are common knowledge. The object of this experiment was to determine whether (a) subjects would, once they achieved an equal distribution over markets, use that particular distribution to continue to coordinate by simply repeating their respective choices, or (b) ignore precedent and fail to achieve perfect coordination. In the event that perfect coordination was not an absorbing state, they were then interested in determining whether the pattern of fluctuations was consistent with a mixed strategy equilibrium or with some nonequilibrium dynamic. A mixed strategy equilibrium implies that there will be zero serial correlation in the number of individuals who choose a given location. By contrast, cobweb dynamics imply negative serial correlation while hesitant nonresponsiveness to possible profitable moves will produce positive serial correlation.

Table 3.20 describes their design. The three treatments of particular interest to us are (1) the number of periods the stage game is repeated, (2) the payoff schedule, and (3) the experience of subjects. Figure 3.10 (see page 241) shows the number of individuals who choose market A each period and the number of people who change location from the previous period for the first 15 repetitions of the game. In these sessions subjects had no prior experience with the game. As the figure indicates, when inexperienced subjects play a relatively small number of repetitions of a given stage game there is no tendency to use any given pattern of choices that produced equality of payoff across the markets (payoffs were equal across markets when there were three people in each market) as a precedent.

Table 3.21 displays the transition frequencies in prices generated by switches of players from one market to the other from repetition to repetition. The table reveals a positive serial correlation in the relative frequency with which a given market was selected, indicating that the markets had not achieved a mixed strategy equilibrium.

Table 3.20. Meyer et al.'s Experimental Design

Experiment	Treatment	Periods	Demand Curve	Comments
1,2	E(i5)	1–15	Iso-elastic	
	RE(10)	16–25	Iso-elastic	Recontracting
3–7	E(i5)	1–15	Iso-elastic	
3–11	W(60)	1–60	Iso-elastic	
12–15	L(60)	1–60	Linear	
15–19	EE(15)	1–15	Iso-elastic	Experienced subjects

Source: Meyer, Van Huyck, Battalio, and Saving 1992, table 2.

Table 3.21. Transition Frequencies, Iso-Elastic Demand: Experiments 1–11, Periods 2–15, Price in Market A

	$P_t > P^*$	$P_t = P^*$	$P_t < P^*$	Sum	Row χ_2^2
$P_{t-1} > P^*$	22 (42%)	23 (43%)	8 (15%)	53	9.02*
$P_{t-1} = P^*$	17 (37%)	15 (33%)	14 (30%)	46	0.32%
$P_{t-1} < P^*$	13 (24%)	12 (22%)	30 (55%)	55	9.92**
Sum	52 (34%)	50 (32%)	52 (34%)	154	
		$\chi_8^2 = 23.38**$			

Source: Meyer, Van Huyck, Battalio, and Saving 1992, table 4.
* 5 percent level of statistical significance.
** 1 percent level of statistical significance.

In experimental sessions 8–11 subjects played for 60 periods. The additional experience induces some learning but not convergence on a precedent. Instead, the correlation observed in the early periods does not persist over a larger number of periods of play, and the relative frequencies with which the number of choices of a particular market are above, equal, and below the mixed strategy equilibrium frequencies seem to converge to the mixed strategy equilibrium frequencies.

Two payoff schedules were used, a linear schedule, $P_i = \$.7 - 0.117Q_i$, and an iso-elastic schedule, $P_i + \$1.05/Q_i$. The iso-elastic schedule is tangent to the linear schedule at the pure strategy equilibrium quantity, $Q_i = 3$. There was some difference in behavior observed across sessions with different payoff functions. In particular, in one of the four sessions run with the linear payoff function, the last 13 periods sustained perfect coordination with no one switching markets from period to period. One possible explanation is that relative to the iso-elastic payoff function, under the linear payoff function there is a larger difference between the expected payoff from a mixed strategy equilibrium and the payoff from the pure strategy equilibria, providing a stronger incentive to use precedent. However, there also appears to be a smaller number of individuals switching their

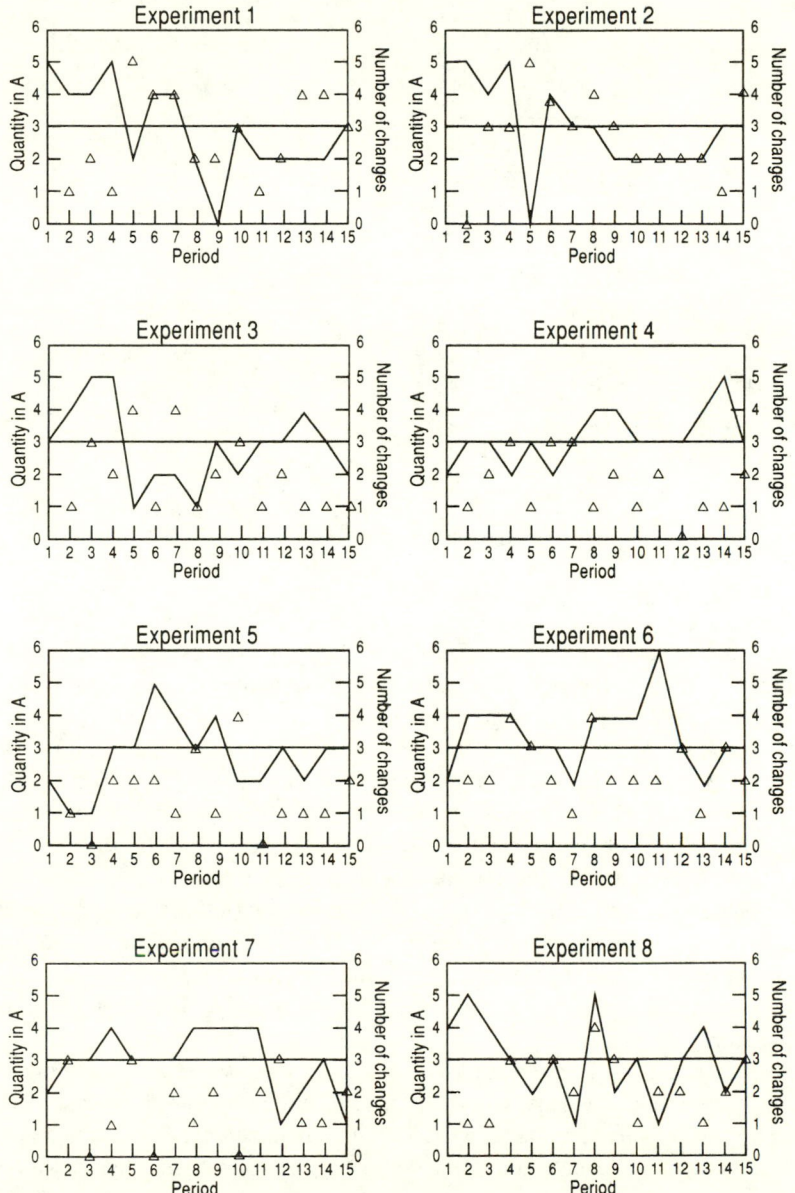

Figure 3.10. Iso-elastic demand. *Source*: Meyer et al. (1992), figure 2.

choices when the payoffs are unequal across markets in the linear case than in the iso-elastic case, suggesting that the inertia in a set of markets may be influenced by the structure of the payoff function, independently of any incentive to achieve and sustain a pure strategy equilibrium rather than a mixed strategy equilibrium.

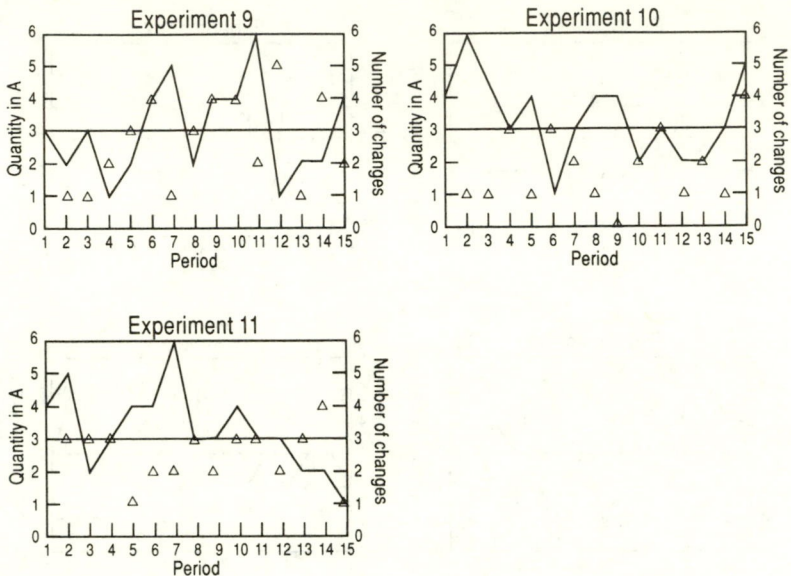

Figure 3.10. *continued.*

The most striking treatment effect observed by Meyer et al. is the effect of bringing back subjects who had previously participated in sessions with 15 repetitions. Figure 3.11 (see page 243) displays the number of experienced subjects who chose Market A in sessions 16–19. In three of the four sessions with subjects who were called back from earlier sessions with only 15 periods, perfect coordination was achieved in the very first period. In one of these three sessions, the same distribution was repeatedly observed for 10 periods, someone then moved, but the group quickly returned to an equilibrium. In the other two sessions, someone moved in the second period, but in both of these sessions equilibrium was quickly reestablished and sustained. That is, in three of the four sessions with experienced subjects, precedence provided a strong focal point. (The fourth session looks remarkably like sessions played by individuals with no previous experience.)

The experiments of Ochs and of Meyer et al. are suggestive about what one can expect to observe in markets with decentralized matching, but they are far from definitive. Both Ochs's results with games with a nonstationary set of players and the observation of Meyer et al. with a stationary set of inexperienced players in their game point to the potential power of a mixed strategy Nash equilibrium to organize the data generated in at least some games. However, neither of the designs in these experiments compels one to accept this interpretation of the data. In the Ochs experiment, one might as reasonably interpret the data from the sessions with a nonstationary set of players as being consistent with the hypothesis that the probability of an individual selecting a location is equal to the proportion of all of the market's stock available at that location (i.e., each unit of stock has equal attractiveness) as with the equilibrium hypothesis (which implies that dispropor-

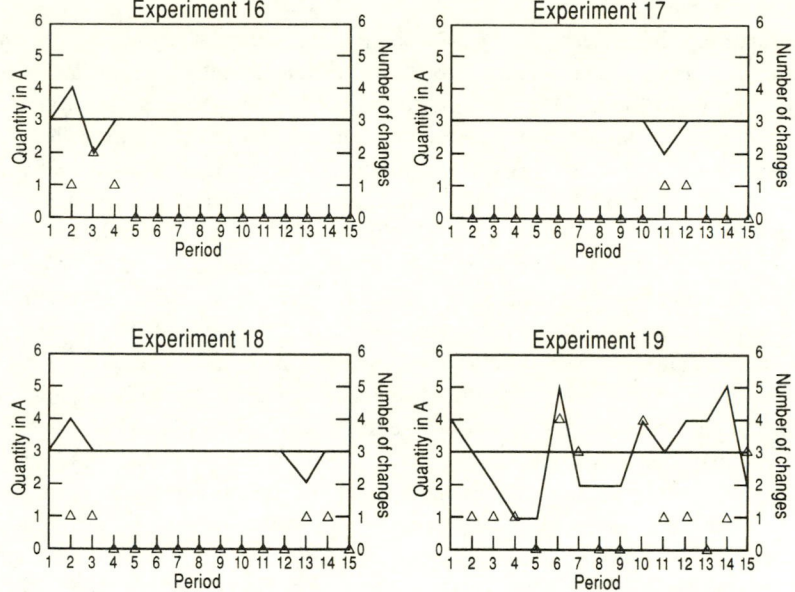

Figure 3.11. Experienced subjects: Iso-elastic demand. *Source*: Meyer et al. (1992), figure 5.

tionate weight be given to the location with the most stock). In the Meyer et al. experiment, the mixed strategy equilibrium interpretation is based upon the inability to *reject* that hypothesis with a high degree of confidence in interpreting the time series data generated under fixed conditions. Furthermore, the observations under a linear payoff condition are inconsistent with a mixed strategy equilibrium hypothesis. This might reduce one's confidence that one was observing a mixed strategy equilibrium in the isoelastic demand case.

The common finding of both of these experiments is that a distribution consistent with a pure strategy equilibrium is not an absorbing state in repeated games with a stationary set of inexperienced subjects. This raises a number of questions as to whether this finding is an artifact of experimental design or something we should expect in a wide variety of coordination games, both experimental and naturally occurring. First, in these experiments inexperienced subjects are asked to make a series of decisions with little time to be reflective between decisions. The fact that Meyer et al. observe such a significant difference between the behavior of experienced and inexperienced groups suggests that the way individuals interact in an experimental environment will depend on their frequency of interaction. More systematic observation of the variation in behavior as this aspect of the design is varied is surely called for. A second possible interpretation of the difference Meyer et al. observe in sessions with experienced subjects from sessions with inexperienced subjects is that experience per se had no effect, but that the difference simply reflected the fact that in those sessions where a precedent emerged it emerged because perfect coordination was achieved in the very first period of the session. To explore this hypothesis one could consider a design in which the early experience of the subjects was manipulated to secure perfect coordination. Third, when the hypothesis of interest is that people will learn to coordinate, one must be sensitive to the potential disruptiveness of any single subject who may be insufficiently motivated or lack the capacity to understand the benefits of sustaining a pattern of coordination to focus upon a precedent. The experiments reviewed here involved small groups of people (six or nine subjects) in any one set of decentralized market observations. Obviously, the potential for any one person to induce other persons in the market to give up on the attempt to focus on precedent is much smaller the larger the number of players in the market. Before too much weight is placed upon the "fragility of beliefs" interpretation of the observed failures to coordinate, prudence requires that additional sessions with substantially larger numbers of subjects per market be conducted. Fourth, the cost to an individual of switching locations once the group had achieved a pattern of perfect coordination is not large in these experiments (as compared, say with the expected cost to a person in the United States who deviates from the custom of driving on the right hand side of the road). One must always ask whether the behavior of subjects is sensitive to variations in the difference in payoffs between possible courses of action. In studies that are looking for coordination failures, this issue must be taken even more seriously than in the typical experiment, and these studies have not systematically explored the effect of variation in payoffs to any significant degree.

While the experiments reviewed are far from the last word, they are suggestive. In particular, since a perfectly stationary state is never observed in natural environments, the behaviors observed in these experiments cast at least some doubt over the methodological presumption that the coordination problem is insignificant when our observations come from environments that are only approximately stationary. At the same time, the experimentalist has an obligation to explore thoroughly the robustness of a finding that is, at least to me, so surprising.

IV. Concluding Remarks

This chapter has focused upon the experimental study of games with multiple equilibria. While most of the experiments discussed were motivated by macroeconomic models, games with multiple equilibria arise in very many different contexts. As a result, interest in experiments of the type discussed in this chapter should be quite general.

The empirical content of game theory rests fundamentally upon the proposition that when a particular game is played the play will be focused around *some* Nash equilibrium of that game. This principle is put to a stern test in the empirical study of coordination games since players in these games face a problem of strategic uncertainty that cannot be resolved by appeal to decision-theoretic arguments. Does this strategic uncertainty prevent agents from achieving *any* Nash equilibrium? Or, as Schelling believed, will agents overcome this problem and focus on a particular equilibrium? Further, if agents do come to focus upon a particular equilibrium, can that equilibrium be identified simply by knowing the logical structure of the game? These are the general questions to which the experiments reviewed in this chapter are addressed.

Game theory, as it has developed to date, is a theory of *equilibrium*. It does not give an account of out of equilibrium play. But all experimenters know that the initial strategy choices subjects make in a given environment are unlikely to be equilibrium choices. Instead, the strategies chosen tend to change as subjects acquire experience. As a result, when testing a hypothesis about the equilibrium to be observed in a given environment it is common practice to give the same subjects a sequence of replications of that environment. The equilibrium hypothesis is then tested by asking whether the data generated over this sequence are converging to the hypothesized equilibrium rather than by asking whether all of the data are consistent with the particular hypothesis of interest.[33]

Using this kind of convergence test, in most, but not all, of the experiments reviewed in this chapter the data seemed to converge to *a* Nash equilibrium. The strategic uncertainty inherent in games with multiple equilibria apparently does not often prevent subjects with *sufficient experience* from coordinating on *some* equilibrium when the environment is *sufficiently stationary*. This is encouraging. However, we obviously know very little about how much experience, and about the nature of the experience subjects must have before convergence is observed in any well defined class of games with multiple equilibria. Similarly, to date there has not been any systematic study of how shocks and other elements of nonstationarity in the environment affect the likelihood of observing convergence to an equilibrium, let alone a specific equilibrium.

Moreover, even in perfectly stationary environments convergence to an equilibrium is only the beginning of the story. What remains to be told is how a group of subjects tend to converge on a particular equilibrium. We are far from being able to give a full account of the equilibrium selection process. But the experiments reviewed do mark out some important facets of this story. First, the pattern of play of coordination games is not generally group specific. When different groups play the same game, the same equilibrium often emerged. Therefore, the dynamics of play were evidently related to the structure of the game. However, the experiment by Van Huyck, Battalio, and Beil (1991) shows that in at least some games the equilibrium selected can be powerfully affected by a group's first experience with the game and that this experience may vary from group to group in an uncontrolled and unpredictable way. Consequently, while it is unlikely that a general theory based entirely on the structure of a game will ever give a complete account of equilibrium selection, any satisfactory theory of equilibrium selection will undoubtedly have to be grounded in elements of a game's structure. Second, failure to coordinate on the Pareto dominant equilibrium was observed in several of these experiments. Therefore, Pareto dominance does not necessarily make a given equilibrium focal. Third, these experiments show that changes in the out of equilibrium payoffs can have a powerful effect on the equilibrium toward which a group converges. Therefore, a satisfactory theory of equilibrium selection must account for how out of equilibrium payoffs shape the dynamics which lead to a particular equilibrium.[34]

To date, we have an insufficient base of data from controlled experiments to give any hint to theorists as to the more detailed structure of behavior that a theory of equilibrium selection must capture. Furthermore, it seems to me to be quite likely that no general theory of equilibrium selection will be possible. Instead, the best we can probably hope for is to find a classification system that will allow us to identify types of coordination games within which the selection process is the same, but between which different processes are at work. The challenge to experimentalists is to explore systematically how people deal with the strategic uncertainty inherent in coordination games in a way that may eventually allow the development of a taxonomy of such games.

Notes

1. See, for example, Brandts and Holt (1992), Banks, Camerer and Porter (1994) for experimental tests of refinements in signalling games that yield mixed results. The power of sequential equilibrium to account for reputational phenomena is studied in Camerer and Weigelt (1989) and Neral and Ochs (1992). These studies also report conflicting results. The subgame perfection refinement hypothesis is examined in McKelvey and Palfrey (1992) and in the sequential bargaining experiments reviewed in chapter 4. The data from these latter experiments can only be reconciled with the refinement prediction if one postulates that some experimentally uncontrolled element of payoffs has a systematic effect on behavior. This reconciliation of the observations with the theory further requires that subjects somehow come to have a common understanding of these uncontrolled payoffs.
2. While the discussion in this chapter is principally organized around coordination problems which arise in macroeconomic contexts, multiplicity of equilibria is characteristic of a very broad range of economic settings, and discussions of relevant experiments with games which have a multiplicity of equilibria can be found throughout this text. For a discussion of focal points in bargaining experiments see chapter 4. The problem of getting a minimum number of contributors toward the provision of a public good is another game with a multiplicity of equilibria which has been the subject of experimental investigation. For a discussion of this literature see section III, of chapter 2.
3. The earliest overlapping generations model was Samuelson's (1958). Lucas (1972) and Wallace (1980), among others, study monetary phenomena within this framework.
4. See Calvo (1978). The source of the multiplicity of equilibria in these models is that agents must act with incomplete information. There are many different types of models in which agents must act with incomplete information which have multiple equilibria.
5. See, for example, Diamond (1981, 1982, 1984).
6. See Mortensen (1973, 1982).
7. For a discussion of the convergence of adaptive learning processes to rational expectations equilibria see Blume and Easley (1982) and Bray (1982).
8. The problem of giving subjects relevant experience without creating a supergame is a quite general one in the design of experiments. Aliprantis and Plott (1990) use the Lim, Prescott, and Sunder design to study whether auction markets for a perishable commodity, such as those studied by Smith (1962), would converge to the competitive equilibrium when the set of agents in the market was not stationary from period to period. See Ochs (1990) for another rotation design that addresses the problem of studying behavior with a non–stationary set of agents in a different context.
9. The problem of designing an experiment which must end in finite time to test a theory in which the theoretical environment is of infinite duration is quite general. While the device

used by Lim, Prescott, and Sunder to make the final price endogenous is quite natural for their specific environment, it is not clear how it could be adapted to use in other environments. An early use of a probabilistic device to deal with infinite horizon effects can be found in Roth and Murnighan (1978). See also Camerer and Weigelt (1989).

10. "Money" has no payoff value to a member of the old generation. Therefore, the demand for the consumption good on the part of the old generation is simply $n*m/p$. In the "Shubik" auction, each seller submitted a supply schedule of the consumption good. These individual supply schedules were then aggregated, and the market clearing price of the consumption good was determined by the "auctioneer." This price was announced, and the individual transactions consistent with this price were credited to the various subjects according to their sumitted supply schedules and their actual money holdings.

11. See chapter 8 of this volume for a review of price forecasting experiments in different contexts.

12. See Marcet and Sargent (1989) for a description of the properties of least squares learning.

13. Alternatively, if the bias is simply a reflection of the inability of individuals to determine optimal supply schedules, conditional on their respective forecasts of next period's price, then we should expect to observe equilibrium price paths if individuals were simply asked to submit their forecasts of next period's price and have their supply schedules generated by a computer algorithm. This procedure is used in the next set of experiments I will discuss. In Marimon and Sunder (1993) a report is presented of a more extensive set of these experiments with a greater variety of payoffs and experience than in the initial set presented in the working paper I have been discussing. In describing these more extensive results they note that "subjects tend to behave more competitively when incentives to do so are greater." They also note that more experienced subjects "learn to submit competitive supplies."

14. A second common characteristic of these sessions is that the dynamics consistently exhibit a tendency to move toward a Pareto optimal pattern of trade, even though such a pattern is inconsistent with the individual best response properties of a Nash equilibrium. This is a phenomenon which deserves systematic exploration. Is this an artifact of the design of these environments, such as the fact that all subjects had the same payoff function, or the fact that the payoff function was symmetric in chips held at the end of each period? Or did it simply reflect that there might not have been enough periods of experience, or time to reflect between periods for any subject to recognize that the realized pattern of inflation, if sustained, would present him with opportunities to earn more by selling more chips when he was young?

15. Azariadis(1982) developed the first model with stationary sunspot equilibria. See also Cass and Shell (1983) and Spear (1984).

16. A first-order learning scheme is of the form

$$P^e(t + 1) - \alpha\, P^e(t) + (1 - \alpha)\, P(t)$$

And a second-order scheme is of the form

$$P^e\,(t + 1) - \alpha\, P^e\,(t - 1) + (1 - \alpha)\, P(t - 1)$$

where P^e is the forecast made at the beginning of the period and P is the actual price realized in the period.

17. See e.g., Bryant (1983), Diamond (1984), Cooper and John (1988).

18. This game corresponds to an example discussed by Bryant (1983).

19. I.e., the equilibrium that is achieved when every player chooses the strategy that maximizes his minimum payoff.

20. For example, the equilibrium selection theory of Harsayni and Selten (1988) implies that when there is a payoff-dominant equilibrium it will be selected.

21. In sessions four, five, and six subjects participated simultaneously in two games, one with a group size nine and the other with a group size of 27. Only the results from group size nine are discussed in detail. The authors note that the mean difference in actions was not significantly different between group sizes although there was a marked difference in the relationship between an agent's predictions and that agent's behavior in the two environments.

22. Crawford (1989) presents an extensive discussion of the results of the Van Huyck, Battalio, and Beil experiments. He provides an analysis of the minimum game in terms of an adaptive learning model patterned on notions of evolutionary dynamics and shows that the equilibrium observed is the unique evolutionarily stable equilibrium of this game. However, the concept of evolutionary stability does not, in general, yield a unique equilibrium. In particular, as Crawford notes, in the median game all of the equilibria are evolutionarily stable.

   An appeal to evolutionary stability considerations cannot account for the observed median of the distribution of choices in the first stage game played by a given group of subjects, although it may account for the extreme dependence of the equilibrium eventually achieved on this first realization. There is an apparent order effect in the experiment of Van Huyck, Battalio, and Beil (1991). The equilibrium achieved by the end of the second treatment in a session always has at least as high and, generally, a higher payoff than the equilibrium achieved by the end of the first treatment in the same session. Crawford suggests that this might represent the phenomenon of learning from imperfect analogies. However, this phenomenon was not observed in Van Huyck, Battalio, and Beil's first experiment. Furthermore, systematic exploration of learning from imperfect analogies will require an operational way of measuring the degree to which games are analogous.

23. Holt (1990) proposes a method by which all of the data from a given experimental session can be used to estimate the percentage of prespecified "types" of individuals who could have been participating in the experiment, under the maintained hypothesis that the entire session constitutes a Bayesian game of incomplete information and that each period is a Nash equilibrium of this game.

24. It is, of course, possible that what one is observing in these sessions is not a learning phenomenon, as I believe it to be, but rather the outcome of strategic play of a supergame of incomplete information. We cannot settle this question of how best to interpret the time series generated by observations of play by the same group of individuals without designing experiments specifically to test well-articulated theories of such dynamic processes. I do believe that if such well-articulated theories were available and an experiment was designed to discriminate among them, a "learning" theory would outperform a "strategic" theory. Others would place their bets in the other way. I advocate the systematic exploration of how steady states are related to starting points and payoff structures, even without having a well-articulated general theory to test.

25. The authors do not report the frequencies with which one individual selected 2 and the other selected 1 or 3.

26. Cooper, DeJong, Forsythe, and Ross (1989) report the results of allowing pregame communication in a 2×2 Battle of the Sexes experiment. They found in that game that preplay communication unambiguously increased the relative frequency with which equilibrium play was observed and that the relationship of actual play to preplay announcements was consistent with Farrell's theory.

27. The effect of preplay communication in the Battle of the Sexes game is studied in Cooper et al. (1989a).

28. In their conclusion, Abdalla et al. remark, "The results . . . show that forward induction coordinates actions in some environments but not in others. . . . In the coordination game and 3×3 battle of the sexes game . . . there is the possibility that altruistic players passing on the outside option could be trying to send a message different from that sent by egoists. Our results indicate that in these games forward inductions is unsuccessful at coordinating actions."

29. See, for example, Lucas and Sargent (1981).

30. See Diamond (1984) for a spirited defense of this approach.

31. Locations within a market game were identified by letter (A,B,C,D), and subjects were asked to respond by choosing a letter. Since there was some possibility of subjects exhibiting a bias towards a particular letter, in sessions (labelled "experiments") 1 and 2 the location where the greatest volume of stock was posted in a given market game was varied from period to period. There is no evident letter bias in the data.

32. One such possible process would be for individuals who were successful last period to make the same choice of location this period while individuals who were unsuccessful to adopt a mixed strategy this period that is a best response, given the pattern of distribution of those who were successful last period.
33. See, however, Holt (1990).
34. See Roth, chapter 4 in this volume, for further discussion of evidence that out of equilibrium payoffs shape the dynamics that lead to a particular equilibrium.

Bibliography

Abdalla, A. R., D. Cooper, D. DeJong, R. Forsythe, and T. Ross. 1989. "Forward induction in coordination and battle of the sexes games: Some experimental results." Manuscript.

Aliprantis, C., and C. Plott. 1992. Competitive equilibria in overlapping generations experiments. *Economic Theory* 2: 389–426.

Arrow, Kenneth J. 1986. Rationality of self and others in an economic system. In *Rational choice. The contrast between economics and psychology*, R. Hogarth and M. Reder, editors, Chicago: University of Chicago Press. 201–16.

Azariadis, C. 1982. Self-fulfilling prophecies. *Journal of Economic Theory* 25: 380–96.

Banks, J., C. Camerer, and D. Porter. 1988. An experimental analysis of Nash refinements in signalling games. *Games and Economic Behavior* 2: 389–426.

———. 1994. An experimental analysis of Nash refinements in signaling games. *Games and Economic Behavior* 6: 1–31.

Blume, L. E., and D. Easley. 1982. Learning to be rational. *Journal of Economic Theory* 26: 340–51.

Brandts, J., and C. Holt. 1992. An experimental test of equilibrium dominance in signalling games. *American Economic Review* 82: 1350–65.

Bray, Margaret. 1982. Learning, estimation and the stability of rational expectations. *Journal of Economic Theory* 26: 318–39.

Bryant, J. 1983. A simple rational expectations Keynes-type model. *Quarterly Journal of Economics* 98: 525–29.

Calvo, Guillermo. 1978. On the indeterminacy of interest rates and wages with perfect foresight. *Journal of Economic Theory* 19: 321–37.

Cachon, Gérard, and Colin Camerer. 1991. The sunk cost fallacy, forward induction, and behavior in coordination games. Mimeo.

Camerer, Colin, and Keith Weigelt. 1988. Experimental tests of a sequential equilibrium reputation model. *Econometrica* 56: 1–36.

———. 1989. A test of a probabilistic mechanism for inducing infinite horizons in experiments. Mimeo.

Cass, David, and Karl Shell. 1983. Do sunspots matter? *Journal of Political Economy* 91: 193–227.

Cooper, R., D. DeJong, R. Forsythe, and T. Ross. 1989a. Communication in the battle of the sexes game: Some experimental results. *Rand Journal of Economics* 20: 568–87.

———. 1989b. Communication in coordination games. Working Paper Series 89–16. College of Business Administration, University of Iowa.

———. 1990. Selection criteria in coordination games: Some experimental results. *American Economic Review* 80: 218–33.

Cooper, R., and A. John. 1988. Coordinating coordination failures in Keynesian models. *Quarterly Journal of Economics* 103: 441–63.

Crawford, Vincent. 1989. An "Evolutionary" explanation of the Van Huyck, Battalio, and Beil's experimental results on coordination. Manuscript.

Diamond, Peter. 1981. Mobility costs, frictional unemployment, and efficiency. *Journal of Political Economy* 90: 798–812.

Diamond, Peter. 1982. Aggregate demand management in search equilibrium. *Journal of Political Economy* 90: 881–94.

———. 1984. *A search-equilibrium approach to the micro foundations of macroeconomics.* Cambridge, Mass.: MIT Press.

Farrell, J. 1987. "Cheap talk, coordination, and entry. *Rand Journal of Economics* 18: 34–39.

Gale, Douglas. 1982. *Money: In equilibrium.* Cambridge, Eng.: Cambridge University Press.

Harsanyi, J., and R. Selten. 1988. *A general theory of equilibrium selection in games.* Cambridge, Mass.: M.I.T. Press.

Holt, Debra. 1990. "An empirical model of strategy choices in coordination games. Manuscript. Carnegie Mellon University.

Lim, S., E. Prescott, and S. Sunder. 1988. Stationary solution to the overlapping generations model of fiat money: Experimental evidence. Manuscript. University of Minnesota. Reprinted in *Empirical economics*, J. D. Hey, editor. Forthcoming.

Lucas, Robert E., Jr. 1972. Expectations and the neutrality of money. *Journal of Economic Theory* 4: 103–24.

———. 1986. Adaptive behavior and economic theory. In *Rational choice: The contrast between economics and psychology*, R. Hogarth and M. Reder, editors, Chicago: University of Chicago Press. 217–42.

Lucas, Robert E., Jr. and T. Sargent. 1981. *Rational expectations and econometric practice.* Minnesota: University of Minnesota Press.

Marcet, A., and T. Sargent. 1989. Convergence of least squares learning mechanisms in self referential linear stochastic models. *Journal of Economic Theory* 48: 337–68.

Marimon, Ramon, and S. Sunder. 1988. Rational expectations vs. adaptive behavior in a hyperinflationary world: Experimental evidence. Discussion Paper 247. Center for Economic Research, University of Minnesota.

———. 1993. Indeterminancy of equilibria in a hyperinflationary world: Experimental evidence. *Econometrica* 61: 1073–1107.

Marimon, R., S. Spear, and S. Sunder. 1991. Expectationally-driven market volatility: An experimental study. Manuscript Published as "Expectationally-driven market volatility: An experimental study. *Journal of Economic Theory* 61: 74–103.

McKelvey, R., and T. Palfrey. 1992. An experimental study of the centipede game. *Econometrica* 60; 803–37.

Meyer, D., J. Van Huyck, R. Battalio, and T. Saving. 1992. History's role in coordinating decentralized allocation decisions: Laboratory evidence on repeated binary allocation games. *Journal of Political Economy* 100: 292–316.

Mortensen, Dale. 1973. Search equilibrium in a simple multi-market economy. Discussion Paper No. 54. Northwestern University Center for Mathematical Studies in Economics and Management Science.

———. 1982. "The matching process as a noncooperative bargaining game. In *The economics of information and uncertainty*, J. J. McCall, editor, Chicago: University of Chicago Press.

Neral, J., and J. Ochs. 1992. The sequential equilibrium theory of reputation building: A further test. *Econometrica* 60: 1151–69.

Ochs, Jack. 1990. The coordination problem in decentralized markets: An experiment. *Quarterly Journal of Economics* 105: 545–59.

Samuelson, Paul A. 1958. An exact consumption—loan model of interest with or without the social contrivance of money. *Journal of Political Economy* 66: 467–82.

Schelling, Thomas C. 1960. *The strategy of conflict.* Cambridge, Mass.: Harvard University Press.

Spear, Steven. 1984. "Sufficient conditions for the existence of sunspot equilibria. *Journal of Economic Theory* 34: 360–70.

Van Huyck, J., R. Battalio, and R. Beil. 1993. Asset markets as an equilibrium selection mechanism. Forthcoming in *Games and Economic Behavior* 5: 485–504.

———. 1990. Tacit coordination games, strategic uncertainty, and coordination failure. *American Economic Review* 80: 234–48.

————. 1991. Strategic uncertainty, equilibrium selection principles, and coordination failure in average opinion games. *Quarterly Journal of Economics* 106: 885–911.

Wallace, Neil. 1980. The overlapping generations model of fiat money. In *Models of monetary economics*, John Kareken and Neil Wallace, editors, Minneapolis: Federal Reserve Bank of Minneapolis. 49–82.

Woodford, Michael. 1990. Learning to believe in sunspots. *Econometrica* 58: 227–307.

4

Bargaining Experiments

Alvin E. Roth

This chapter is divided into two major sections, the better to focus on particular organizing themes that emerge in the literature.*

Section I concerns the terms of agreement observed in bargaining experiments and the factors that cause these to vary. An important debate among bargaining experimenters focuses on the relative roles played by strategic considerations of the kind captured by game-theoretic models compared to sociological or cultural factors which may cause bargainers to focus on certain kinds of agreements in ways that are less sensitive to the strategic features of the bargaining situation. Early experiments uncovered a range of phenomena that were interpreted in almost contradictory ways by different experimenters. As more comprehensive experimental evidence accumulated, there was increasing agreement on the nature of the phenomena to be explained, and new phenomena emerged with wider implications. Some of these implications concern how completely it is possible to observe and control even experimental environments, while others concern the kind of learning that goes on as subjects gain experience in different strategic environments.

Section II concerns disagreements and costly delays, and the factors that lead to inefficiency in bargaining. One of the clearest experimental results, which also accords well with field data, is that a nonnegligible frequency of disagreements is a characteristic of bargaining in virtually all kinds of environments. An opportunity to explore this phenomenon further is presented by the fact that an exception to this generalization is observed in a set of experiments in which subjects interact face to face. A new experiment is discussed, whose results suggest that the cause of this anomaly lies in the special problems of experimental control that arise in relatively uncontrolled face to face encounters. This brief experiment was presented at the 1990 Handbook Workshop in Pittsburgh and has since sparked related experiments that together help illustrate how experiments can be used to test, refine, and/or reject alternative hypotheses. Section II then proceeds to survey the variety of experiments that have been conducted to explore the causes of disagreements and other forms of inefficiency in bargaining. The hypotheses that these experiments test span a wide range of game-theoretic models, and so the results also speak to the larger question of the status of game theory as a descriptive theory of observable behavior. Section II concludes with a discussion of the distribution of agreements over time in bargaining situations in which there is a deadline. This is a subject about which it had proved difficult to gather reliable field data. However, a very clear "deadline effect" was observed in a number of experiments, and this has helped to stimulate theoretical work that in turn suggests directions for further experiments.

Section III concludes with reflections on some of the things these several series of experiments suggest about bargaining, about game theory, about the relationship between observations in the laboratory and in the field, and about the relationship between theory and experiment.

I. Agreements

Different hypotheses about the roles of strategic and cultural factors have been advanced to explain the results of the unstructured bargaining experiments discussed in chapter 1. However, the debate has been brought into clearer focus with experiments designed around more highly structured bargaining. So, after setting the stage with a brief account of how these competing hypotheses have been applied to the unstructured bargaining experiments, I will turn to the main topic of this section, which concerns experiments in which communication between bargainers is limited to making offers, and accepting or rejecting them, with precise rules governing these exchanges.

There is a certain kind of quiet, unfinished drama that plays itself out as this series of experiments unfolds, because many of the investigators approach this subject from almost opposite points of view. To oversimplify a bit, there are the "game theory purists," who seek to test game-theoretic models, and refine them if necessary, and who see this as the best approach for understanding the choices bargainers make in the course of negotiations. And there are the "social norm purists," who seek to describe and understand what they see as binding social constraints that effectively determine bargainers' behavior. (Of course, many investigators are not purists of either sort, but lean towards one of these two very different points of view while being willing to incorporate elements of the other to improve the descriptive power of their hypotheses. And there are bounded rationality versions of these two approaches, as well as other points of view.) We will see how initial experiments in this series gave a common focus to the investigations conducted by these differently inclined investigators, and how subsequent experiments caused them to refine and modify hypotheses. When we get to the present, we will see that these hypotheses show signs of moving towards each other (albeit slowly) and that the nature of the remaining disagreements has been substantially clarified. This is, I think, typical of what we can expect of experiments.

A. Unstructured Bargaining Experiments

The experiments discussed in chapter 1, in which bargaining was conducted in relatively unstructured environments (e.g., with relatively free communication between bargainers) were initially designed to test a particular family of bargaining theories, and went on to investigate the nature of the unpredicted phenomena observed in the initial experiments. It is useful to begin our discussion here by considering some of the alternative hypotheses put forward to explain these phenomena, in order to see why it was natural to pursue the investigation of these hypotheses by turning to experiments in which the individual choices of the bargainers (and not just the outcome of their mutual interaction) could be more clearly observed.

Recall from section III.C of chapter 1 that in the binary lottery game experiments of Roth and Malouf (1979), it was observed that bargainers who were uninformed about the cash value of one anothers' prizes tended to reach agreements in which lottery tickets were divided evenly, while bargainers who were both informed about one anothers' prizes tended to reach agreements in which the bargainer with the smaller prize obtained a higher percentage of the lottery tickets. While the experiment of Roth, Malouf, and Murnighan (1981) supported the view that this shift could not be accounted for entirely in terms of the strategic features of the game, the subsequent experiment of Roth and Murnighan (1982) suggested that the phenomenon was something the bargainers themselves were able to take account of in a strategic way, since the tradeoff between terms of agreement and rates of disagreement in that experiment were observed to coincide closely with what would be expected at a strategic equilibrium.

My colleagues and I tentatively interpreted the data as suggesting that certain agreements became "focal" for reasons that might not be captured by the game-theoretic models (recall the early experiments of Schelling [1957] discussed in chapter 1), but that the existence of these focal agreements was recognized by the bargainers, who incorporated them into their behavior in a strategic, game-theoretic manner. The experiment of Roth and Schoumaker (1983), which showed that the choice of equilibrium could be influenced by manipulating subjects' expectations, provided indirect support for the hypothesis that the effect of the different information conditions on the outcomes observed in Roth and Murnighan (1982) could be accounted for by the way such information changed subjects' expectations. And in Roth (1985) I suggested that parts of the data appeared similar to equilibrium behavior in a coordination game in which the focal points were taken as given. (I will return to this latter study in section II.C.)

A related focal point hypothesis has recently been tested by Mehta, Starmer, and Sugden (1990), who constructed an experiment in which focal points could be manipulated.[1] They observed bargaining situations in which two subjects had to agree on how to divide £10 between them, with each bargainer receiving zero if no agreement were reached. Before the bargaining began, the subjects were dealt four playing cards each, from a deck consisting of eight cards, four aces and four deuces. The subjects were told that all four aces were worth £10, and in order to be paid they must agree to pool their aces and agree how to divide the £10. Since the agreement of both players is required for any money to be received, conventional game-theoretic models treat this as a completely symmetric problem (since only situations in which neither player held all four aces were considered). Yet, although Mehta et al. observed that equal divisions were the modal proposal by holders of one, two, or three aces, they noted that deviations were in the direction of giving more to the bargainer with more aces, with a second mode being a demand of only £2.50 by holders of only a single ace. Their interpretation is that the bargainers use the cards dealt to them as cues to help solve the coordination problem embedded in any bargaining problem, in a manner that causes divisions proportional to cardholdings to join the equal division as a focal agreement.

Other experimenters have interpreted those earlier "focal point" experiments differently. For example, two views that are also very different from each other are expressed by Harrison (1990) and Guth (1988), both of whom consider the experiments of Roth et al. discussed above. Harrison suggests that the appearance of focal points can be explained in entirely game-theoretic terms, since all agreements can arise as strategic equilibria in such games. Guth, on the other hand, proposes that the data is best explained in entirely *non*-game-theoretic terms. He outlines a "behavioral theory of distributive justice," according to which bargainers conclude agreements at what they perceive to be a fair distribution, with information about each others' prizes allowing them to utilize more fundamental notions of fairness. A similar interpretation of these experiments is independently proposed by Foddy (1989). Both Guth and Foddy can be interpreted as proposing that a descriptive theory of bargaining behavior must essentially *be* a theory of what constitute fair distributions of income.[2]

Thus a number of quite different hypotheses about bargaining behavior have been used to organize the data from these unstructured bargaining experiments. Since these hypotheses concern the choices facing the bargainers in the course of negotiations, the experiments that have been conducted to directly investigate them have tended to focus on more structured bargaining situations, in which these choices can be directly observed, and about which these hypotheses therefore make more pointed predictions.[3] We turn now to consider these more structured bargaining experiments.

B. Sequential Bargaining Experiments

There has been a good deal of attention, both theoretical and experimental, given to models of two-party bargaining in which time is divided into periods and the opportunity to make an offer alternates between the bargainers. The basic model motivating most of the experiments to be discussed is the following: two bargainers, 1 and 2, alternate making offers over how to divide some amount k of money.

In odd numbered periods t (starting at an initial period $t = 1$) player 1 may propose to player 2 any division $(x_1, x_2) = (x, k - x)$. If player 2 accepts this proposal then the game ends and player 1 receives a utility of $(\delta_1)^{(t-1)} x$ and 2 receives a utility $(\delta_2)^{(t-1)}(k - x)$, where δ_i is a number between 0 and 1 reflecting player i's cost of delay. (That is, a payoff of y dollars to player i at period t gives him the same utility as a payoff of $\delta_i y$ dollars at period $t - 1$.) If player 2 does not accept the offer and if period t is not the final period of the game, then the game proceeds to period $t + 1$, and the roles of the two players are reversed. If an offer made in the last period of the game is refused, then the game ends with each player receiving 0. A game with a maximum number of periods T will be called a T-period game.[4] An observer of such a game will see not only the final outcome, but a sequence of individual choices concerning what offers to make and whether to accept or reject them.

Such a game has many strategic equilibria, but most of these can be thought of as involving an attempt by one of the bargainers to threaten a course of action he would not wish to carry out if his bluff were called. For example, in a two-period game, the player who makes the offer in the first period, player 1, might demand 99 percent of the gains from trade for himself, and threaten that, if player 2 refuses to accept this offer, then in the second period he (player 1) will refuse *any* offer, so that disagreement will result and each player will receive nothing. If this threat is believed, player 2's best response is to accept the 1 percent she is offered in the first period. But the threat implies that, if player 2 rejects the offer in the first period, player 1 will reject offers in the next period that he would then prefer to accept. For this reason such threats may not be credible. The class of equilibria that do not involve such threats are called *subgame perfect*.

A subgame perfect equilibrium can be computed by working backward from the last period. An offer made in period T is an ultimatum, and so at such an equilibrium player i (who will receive 0 if he rejects the offer) will accept any nonnegative offer when payoffs are continuously divisible.[5] So at a subgame perfect equilibrium, player j, who gets to make the proposal in period T, will receive 100 percent of the amount k to be divided, if the game continues to period T. Consequently at period $T - 1$ player j will refuse any offer of less than $(\delta_j)k$ (the present value of what she will get if the game continues to the next period) but accept any offer of more, so that at equilibrium player i receives the share $k - (\delta_j)k$ if the game goes to period $T - 1$, and so at period $T - 2$ he must be offered $(\delta_i)(k - [\delta_j]k)$, and so forth. Working back to period 1 in this way, we can compute the equilibrium division: that is, the amount that the theory predicts player 1 should offer to player 2 at period 1, and player 2 should accept.[6]

The earliest experimental studies of this kind of bargaining reported markedly different results. Their authors drew different conclusions, along the lines of the various hypotheses discussed in section I.A, about the predictive value of perfect equilibrium models of bargaining and about the role that experience, limited foresight, or bargainers' beliefs about fairness might play in explaining their observations. (Questions of fairness arise because in some of these experiments, as in the unstructured bargaining experiments, many observed agreements give both bargainers 50 percent of the available money.) Subsequent experiments brought more agreement on the description of the phenomena to be explained, and the most recent experiments have started to narrow some of the differences in interpreting these phenomena.

1. An Initial Exchange of Views

In each of the following experiments, the predictions tested involved only the ordinal utilities of the bargainers, not their risk posture. Following standard practice in the experimental literature when only ordinal utilities are of concern, in the initial experiments the utility of the bargainers was assumed to be measured by the amount of money they receive (a point I will discuss in detail later).

Guth, Schmittberger, and Schwarz (1982) examined one-period ("ultimatum") bargaining games. Player 1 could propose dividing a fixed sum of k deutsche marks any way he chose, by filling out a form saying "I demand DM x." Player 2 could either accept, in which case player 1 received x and player 2 got $k - x$, or she could reject, in which case each player received 0 for that game. (The subjects were divided into two groups of equal size, with the offer of each player 1 being assigned at random to one of the player 2's, so that no bargainer knew with whom he was bargaining in the other group.)

The perfect equilibrium prediction for such games is that player 1 will ask for and get (essentially) 100 percent of k. However the average demand that players 1 were observed to make was for under 70 percent, both for players playing the game for the first time and for those repeating the game a week later.[7] About 20 percent of offers were rejected. The authors conclude that

> . . . subjects often rely on what they consider a fair or justified result. Furthermore, the ultimatum aspect cannot be completely exploited since subjects do not hesitate to punish if their opponent asks for "too much."[8] (384)

A different conclusion is reached by Binmore, Shaked, and Sutton (1985), who write:

> The work of Guth et al. seems to preclude a predictive role for game theory insofar as bargaining behavior is concerned. Our purpose in this note is to report briefly on an experiment that shows that this conclusion is unwarranted. . . .[9] (1178)

Their experiment studied a two-period bargaining game, in which player 1 makes a proposal of the form $(x, 100 - x)$ to divide 100 pence. If player 2 accepts, this is the result. Otherwise, 2 makes a proposal $(x', 25 - x')$ to divide 25 pence. If player 1 accepts, this is the result; otherwise, each player receives 0. Thus in this game $\delta_1 = \delta_2 = 0.25$, and (since proposals are constrained to be an integer number of pence) at any subgame perfect equilibrium player 1 makes an opening demand x in the range 74–76 pence, and player 2 accepts any opening demand of 74 pence or less. Subjects played a single game, after which player 2 was invited to play the game again, as player 1. In fact, there was no player 2 in this second game, so only the opening demand was observed.[10]

The modal first demand in the first game was 50 pence, and 15 percent of the first offers were rejected. In the second game (in which only first demands were observed), there was a mode around a first demand near 75 pence. There was thus a clear shift between the two distributions of first demands, in the direction of the equilibrium demand. The authors conclude,

> Our suspicion is that the one-stage ultimatum game is a rather special case, from which it is dangerous to draw general conclusions. In the ultimatum game, the first player might be dissuaded from making an opening demand at, or close to, the "optimum" level, because his opponent would then incur a negligible cost in making an "irrational" rejection. In the two-stage game, these considerations are postponed to the second stage, and so their impact is attenuated. (1180)

Guth and Tietz (1988) responded with an experiment examining two two-stage games with discount factors of 0.9 and 0.1, respectively. So the subgame perfect equilibrium predictions (in percentage terms) for the two cases are (10%, 90%) and (90%, 10%), respectively. They say:

> Our hypothesis is that the consistency of experimental observations and game theoretic predictions observed by Binmore et al. as well as by Fouraker and Siegel is solely due to the moderate relation of equilibrium payoffs which makes the game theoretic solution socially more acceptable.

Subjects played one of the two games twice, each with a randomly chosen other bargainer. Subjects who played the first game as player 1 played the second game as player 2. One difference from the sequential bargaining games discussed above was that disagreement automatically resulted if player 2 rejected an offer from player 1 but made a counterproposal that would give her (player 2) less than player 1 had offered her.[11]

In the first game, the average first demand in games with a discount factor of .1 was 76 percent, and in the second game 67 percent (compared with a perfect equilibrium prediction of 90 percent). For games with a discount factor of 0.9, the average first demand in the first game was 70 percent, and in the second game 59 percent (compared to a predicted first demand of 10 percent).[12] The authors conclude:

> Our main result is that contrary to Binmore, Shaked and Sutton "gamesmen-ship" is clearly rejected, i.e., the game theoretic solution has nearly no pre-dictive power.

Neelin, Sonnenschein, and Spiegel (1988) also responded to Binmore, Shaked, and Sutton (1985). They reported two experiments involving two-period, three-period, and five-period bargaining games. Neelin et al. observe that the data for all their (2, 3, and 5 period) games are near the perfect equilibrium prediction for two period games. They conclude:

The strong regularity of the behavior we observed is one of the most note-worthy aspects of our results and lends power to our rejection of both the Stahl/Rubinstein theory and the equal-split model. (829)

In a reply, Binmore, Shaked, and Sutton (1988) declined to attribute the same significance to these results and conjectured that the differences described among these experiments may be due to the differences in experimental procedures employed.

Thus different experimenters reached markedly different conclusions, based on experiments with different parameters and using different procedures.

2. A Larger Experimental Design

Following most of this exchange, Ochs and Roth (1989) conducted an experiment utilizing a larger experimental design, which allowed games with different pa-rameters to be compared under a common set of procedures. They noted that the prior analyses had focused on the accuracy of the perfect equilibrium as a point predictor, that is, on whether the observed outcomes were distributed around the perfect equilibrium division or around some other division of the available money. Their experiment was designed to test the predictive accuracy of some of the *qualitative* predictions of the perfect equilibrium in sequential bargaining, and to detect if changes in the parameters of the game influence the observed out-comes in the predicted direction, even in the case that there might be a systematic error in the point predictions.[13] To this end the experiment was implemented in a way that allowed the discount factors of the two bargainers to be varied indepen-dently.[14] In order to compare games like those considered in the earlier experi-ments, the experimental design allowed comparisons between different combina-tions of discount factors for games of fixed length, as well as between games of different length for given discount factors. The eight cells of the experiment compare two and three period games using all four combinations of discount factors (δ_1, δ_2), with δ_i equal to 0.4 or 0.6 (see Figure 4.1). The bargainers sat in two rooms and conveyed their offers and responses by filling out a written form. Each bargainer participated in ten bargaining encounters, against a different (anonymous) partner in each round. At the conclusion of each experimental ses-sion, one round was chosen at random to be the payoff round, and each bargainer was paid his earnings for that round.[15]

Figure 4.2 displays the following data for each cell of the experiment: (1) the number of bargaining pairs per round; (2) the mean of the observed first period offers to player 2 in each of the ten rounds; (3) the maximum and minimum first period offers in each round; (4) plus and minus two standard errors from the mean offer in each round; (5) the number of first period offers that were rejected in each round. In addition to the data, the perfect equilibrium offer and the equal division offer (which is always $15) are displayed. The offers made in round 10 of each cell represent the behavior of the most experienced bargainers. As Figure 4.2 shows, the subgame perfect equilibrium offer was generally a very poor point

	Two Period		Three Period	
	Chips	Money	Chips	Money
$\delta_1=.4, \delta_2=.4$	**Cell 1:** (59,41) to (61,39)	($17.70, $12.30) to ($18.30,$11.70)	**Cell 5:** (76,24)	($22.80,$7.20)
$\delta_1=.6, \delta_2=.4$	**Cell 2:** (59,41) to (61,39)	($17.70, $12.30) to ($18.30,$11.70)	**Cell 6:** (84,16)	($25.20,$4.80)
$\delta_1=.6, \delta_2=.6$	**Cell 3:** (39,61) to (41,59)	($11.70, $18.30) to ($12.30,$17.70)	**Cell 7:** (77,23) to (76,24)	($23.10,$6.90) to ($22.80,$7.20)
$\delta_1=.4, \delta_2=.6$	**Cell 4:** (39,61) to (41,59)	($11.70, $18.30) to ($12.30,$17.70)	**Cell 8:** (65,35)	($19.50,$10.50)

Figure 4.1. Experimental design and range of equilibrium predictions. *Source:* Ochs and Roth, 1989.

predictor of the observed outcomes. Cell 1 is the only cell in which the perfect equilibrium offer is within two standard errors of the observed mean. In no other cell does the perfect equilibrium offer fall within plus or minus two standard errors of the estimated population mean.

The perfect equilibrium not only fails as a point predictor of observed behavior, it also fails to account for observed qualitative differences between cells, such as mean first period offers. (As a predictor of the direction of differences in pairwise comparisons of means, the theory does little better than coin flipping.) And while parts of the data appear to be consistent with similar observations made in the earlier experiments, the larger experimental design allows more comparisons to be made, so that observations which, piecewise, appear contradictory, emerge as part of a larger picture. In this regard, the paper notes (379):

> If we had looked only at Cell 1 our conclusions might have been similar to those of Binmore et al., since the data for that cell looks as if after one or two periods of experience, the players settle down to perfect equilibrium proposals. . . . And if we had looked only at Cells 1 and 5, our conclusions might have been similar to those of Neelin et al., since in those two cells both the two and three period games yield observations near the two period predictions. . . . And if we had looked only at cells 5 and 6, we might have concluded, like Guth and Teitz, that the phenomena observed here was closely related to the relatively extreme equilibrium predictions in those cells.

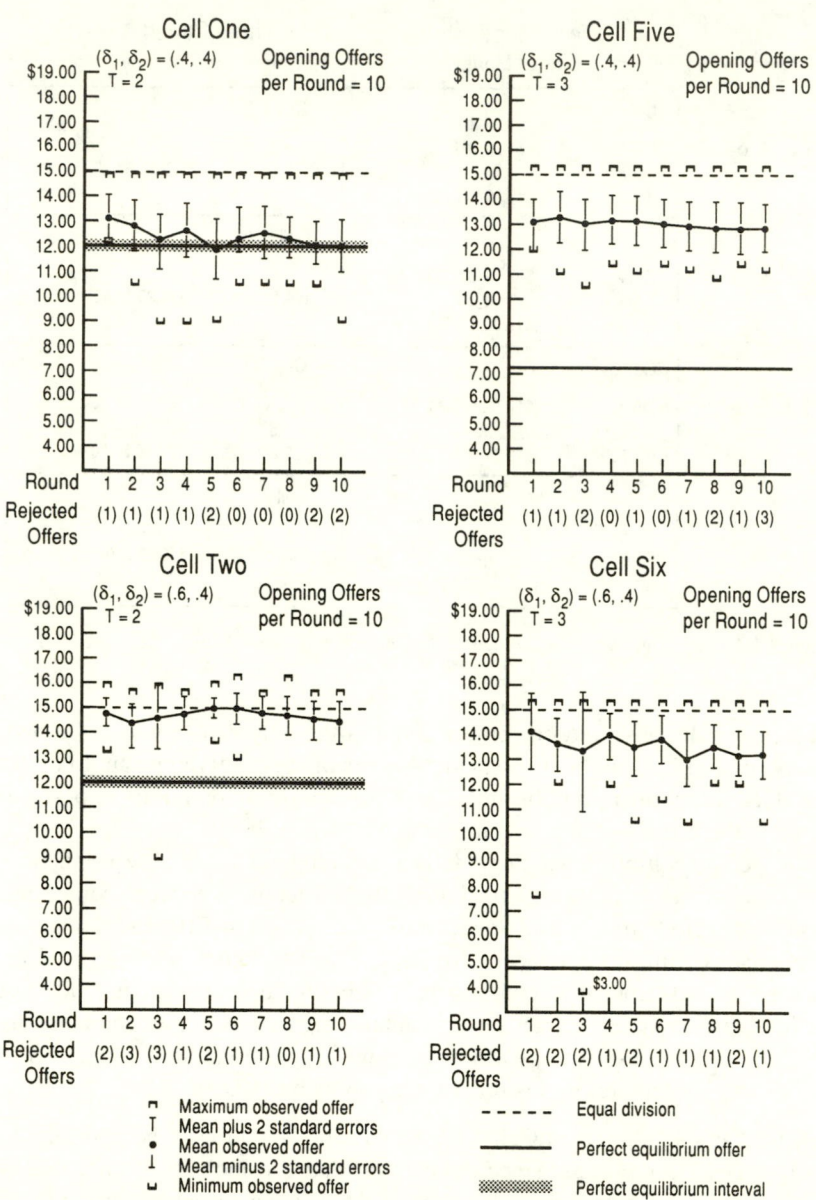

Figure 4.2a. Opening offers to Player 2. *Source:* Ochs and Roth 1989.

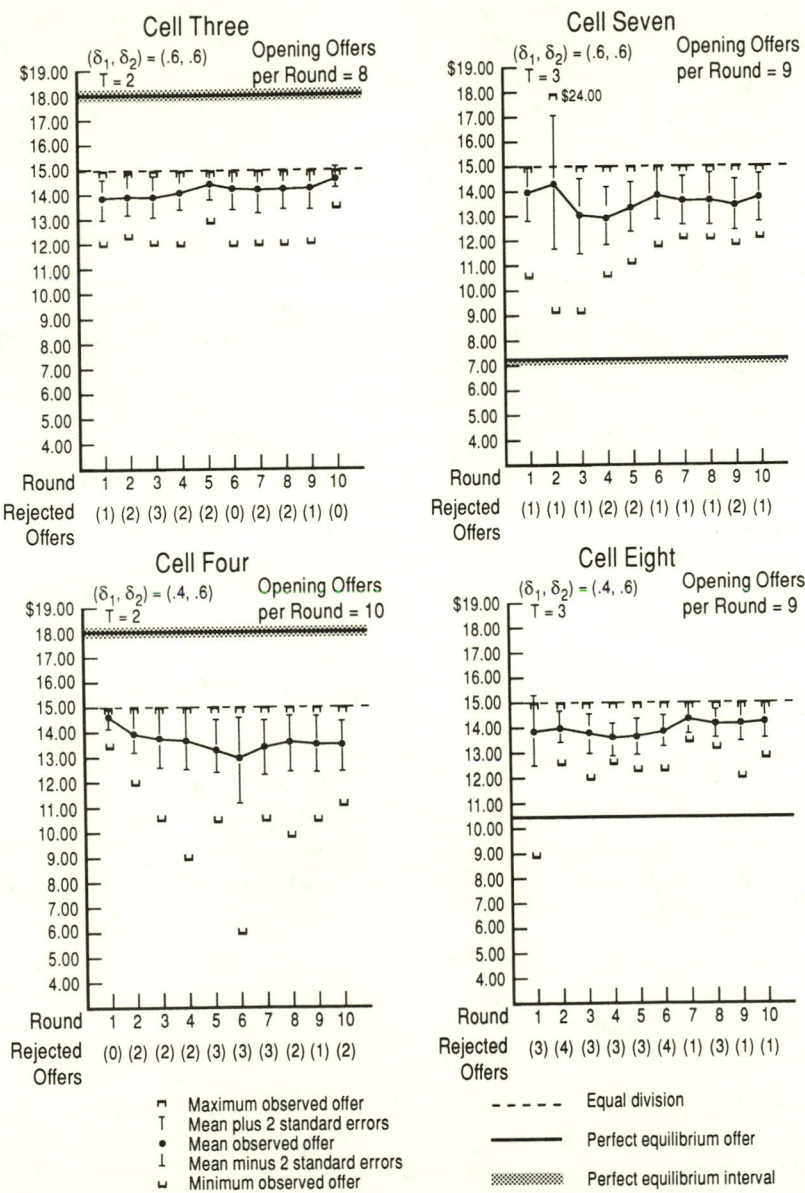

Figure 4.2b. Opening offers to Player 2. *Source:* Ochs and Roth 1989.

Perhaps the most interesting observed regularity for our present purposes concerns what happens when first period offers are rejected, both in this experiment and, as it turns out, in the previous experiments. Approximately 15 percent of first offers met with rejection (including those in games with experienced subjects who had played ten games against different opponents), and of these well over half were followed by counterproposals in which player 2 demanded *less* cash than she had been offered. A significant number of player 2s were rejecting small shares of the relatively large gains available in the first period in favor of large shares of the much smaller gains available in the second period. Since, after player 1 has made a proposal, player 2 is faced with an individual choice problem, we can conclude by revealed preference that these player 2s' utility is *not* measured by their monetary payoff, but must include some nonmonetary component. That is, a player 2 who has made this kind of disadvantageous counteroffer has chosen to make it rather than accepting the offer player 1 had already made, which would have given her (player 2) a higher monetary payoff than she would receive (even) if her own counteroffer is accepted.

Perhaps the most significant observation, though, in view of the diverse results reported in previous experiments, was that when the data of the previous experiments were reanalyzed with this in mind, it turned out that this pattern of rejections and disadvantageous counterproposals was strikingly similar in all of these experiments.[16] Thus the single-period, ultimatum games (in which subjects were observed to reject positive offers) were not a special case in this respect. Table 4.1 summarizes the data.

Ochs and Roth (1989) go on to argue that this and other patterns in the data can plausibly be explained if the unobserved and uncontrolled components of utility in these experiments have to do with subjects' perceptions of "fairness," which involve comparing their share of the available wealth to that of the other bargainer. They note that in most cases agents propose divisions that give them more than half of the proceeds, and say:

> We do not conclude that players "try to be fair." It is enough to suppose that they try to estimate the utilities of the player they are bargaining with, and ... at least some agents incorporate distributional considerations in their utility functions.

That is, if agents' preferences are such that they will refuse "insultingly low" offers, then this must be taken into account in making offers.[17]

Note that uncontrolled elements in the bargainers' utility in these experiments suggests that none of them can be easily interpreted as tests of perfect equilibrium per se, since to compute a perfect equilibrium we need to know the preferences of the players (and so do they).[18] But the uniformity with which disadvantageous counterproposals have appeared, in contrast to the otherwise quite varied results of these experiments, suggests that bargaining may be an activity that systematically gives bargainers motivations distinct from simple income maximization.

Table 4.1. Disadvantageous Responses

Study	Number of Observations	First-Offer Rejections (%)	Disadvantageous Responses (%)
Guth et al. (1982)	42	19 (8/42)	88 (7/8)[a]
Binmore et al. (1985)	81	15 (12/81)	75 (9/12)
Neelin et al. (1988)	165	14 (23/165)	65 (15/23)
Ochs and Roth (1989)	760	16 (125/760)	81 (101/125)

Source: Ochs and Roth 1989.
[a] One of the rejections was of a (100,0) division, and so was not disadvantageous.

In summary, while many regularities were observed and while the rather different results of previous experiments were mirrored in this experiment as pieces of a larger pattern, the disadvantageous counteroffers observed in this experiment, and then found in previous experiments, suggest that the phenomena being studied have elements that have so far eluded experimental control.

That being the case, it is not surprising that this experiment also has been subject to different interpretations by investigators with different points of view. For example, Thaler (1988), who agrees that this and other evidence suggest that "subjects' utility functions have arguments other than money," writes:

We have seen that game theory is unsatisfactory as a positive model of behavior. It is also lacking as a prescriptive tool. While none of the subjects in Ochs and Roth's experiments came very close to using the game-theoretic strategies, those who most closely approximated this strategy did not make the most money. (202)

Guth and Tietz (1990) suggest that even less of the traditional apparatus of economic theory can be saved. They write that they "strictly reject" the conclusion of Ochs and Roth that there are uncontrolled elements in the utility functions of the bargainers, since this implies that the bargainers engage in tradeoffs between underlying preferences and strategic considerations. Rather, they favor modeling players as shifting between strategic and equitable considerations in a hierarchical way so that at any point in time players are primarily concerned with one aspect of the problem.

Kennan and Wilson (1993), on the other hand, focusing on the disadvantageous counteroffers, argue that, since bargainers' preferences were not completely controlled in any of the experiments in which Ochs and Roth found disadvantageous counteroffers, the bargainers themselves could not have had common knowledge of one anothers' preferences, and so the most promising models of these phenomena are models of games of incomplete information—i.e., game-theoretic models in which players' uncertainty about one anothers' preferences is explicitly modeled.

Thus this experiment, while it brings some unity to the phenomena that investigators of various persuasions wish to explain, continues to permit quite different interpretations. And it raises new questions. We turn next to consider recent experiments that address some of these.

3. Investigating Observed Regularities

Before trying to explain the pattern of results observed in Ochs and Roth (1989), it is natural to first ask whether this pattern is robust, and which if any aspects of it are sensitive to the particular parameters chosen in that experiment. Several studies address this question.

Weg, Rapoport, and Felsenthal (1990) consider alternating offer bargaining games in which the subjects were not informed precisely how many periods would be allowed, but were given to understand that there would be many. (In fact, bargaining was terminated after twenty periods, and Weg et al. report that only a small fraction of the games they observed went this long.) They first looked at games with discount factors (δ_1, δ_2) of (.9,.5), (.67,.67), and (.5,.9), and then in a second experiment with lower discount factors, of (.5,.17), (.17,.17), and (.17,.5). Of the unpredicted regularities reported by Ochs and Roth (1989), they focused on the frequency of disadvantageous counteroffers, and of offers of equal monetary payoffs and of equal divisions of chips.[19] They report that their results are entirely consistent with the previous observations that the perfect equilibrium is a poor predictor, that there are many offers of equal divisions (predominantly equal monetary divisions), and that many rejections are followed by disadvantageous counteroffers. They do note that the percentage of disadvantageous counteroffers declines as player 2's discount factor rises. This seems natural, since the range of nondisadvantageous counteroffers available to player 2 increases as his discount factor increases.

In another experiment, Rapoport, Weg, and Felsenthal (1990) report a different kind of alternating offer game, in which each player pays a fixed fee for continuing the bargaining another period, rather than having the value of his payoffs diminish by a fixed percentage. They find that the perfect equilibrium predictions perform much better in this kind of game, an observation I shall return to later, in section B.4.[20]

Bolton (1991) reports a comprehensive investigation that begins by considering the replicability of four of the observed regularities enumerated by Ochs and Roth (1989). These are that there was a consistent first mover advantage, that observed mean offers deviated from the perfect equilibrium prediction in the direction of equal division, that a substantial proportion of first period offers were rejected, and that a substantial proportion of rejections were followed by disadvantageous counteroffers. He begins by replicating these observations (see Figure 4.3a,b, cells 1 and 2) for two-period games using discount factors (δ_1, δ_2) of (1/3, 2/3) and (2/3, 1/3), and an initial pie of \$12. Like Weg et al. (1990), he observes that the rate of disadvantageous counteroffers is sensitive to the discount factors.[21] He then considers whether these features of the data might be due to the inexperience of the subjects, but finds that when experienced subjects (with experience from earlier sessions) play the game, the observed outcomes exhibit the same phenomena (see Figure 4.3a, cell 4)[22]: the observed agreements have the same means as those of inexperienced subjects, with lower variance, and "the aggregate data on rejections and disadvantageous counteroffers is very similar."

Bolton also tests whether bargainers might be influenced by the fact that they keep the same role from round to round, or that these roles were assigned randomly, by conducting a trial in which bargainers alternate between being player 1 and player 2 for 12 rounds. He finds that the mean agreements observed under these procedures do not differ from those in which bargainers retained the same (randomly assigned) role for all trials.

Having satisfied himself as to the robustness of these observed regularities, Bolton then turns his attention to explaining them, together with the additional regularity noted by Ochs and Roth, that even in two-period games the discount factor of player 1 influences the outcome (in contradiction to the perfect equilibrium prediction when players are simple income maximizers). He proposes a theory of bargainer preferences in which bargainers care not only how much they earn, but what share of the pie they receive. That is, he proposes that bargainers be modeled as having utility functions with two arguments, income and relative share. The idea is that this latter argument is what causes bargaining to deviate from the perfect equilibrium predictions for bargainers who are concerned only with their own income, particularly insofar as it causes bargainers to make rejections and counteroffers that are disadvantageous in terms of income but not in terms of relative share. Bolton further postulates that a bargainer will compare his payoff to that of the person he is bargaining with only when they "share the same pie." In particular, he predicts that when players are paid tournament-style, based on how well they do in comparison with other players in the same position (i.e., other player 2s for a player 2 and other player 1s for a player 1), observed agreements will conform more closely to the perfect equilibrium prediction.

The extent to which this treatment has the predicted effect can be assessed by examining Figures 4.3a and b (cells 5–8), which allow the results of bargaining under a tournament compensation scheme to be compared with those observed when the bargainers are paid in proportion to their share of any agreement reached. Cells 5 and 6 show little evidence of difference (from cells 1 and 2, respectively) when the bargainers are inexperienced, but this changes when experienced bargainers are observed. Comparing cells 7 and 4 we see that when the discount factors are (2/3, 1/3) the observed agreements converge to the perfect equilibrium prediction in the tournament condition, but not in the ordinary payoff condition. However, this seems to be sensitive to the discount factors, as the agreements reached by experienced bargainers in the tournament condition of the (1/3, 2/3) game (cell 8) show no sign of converging to the predicted agreement. So these experiments provide some support for the hypothesis that there are uncontrolled factors in the bargainers' preferences, but leave open many questions about the nature of these factors.

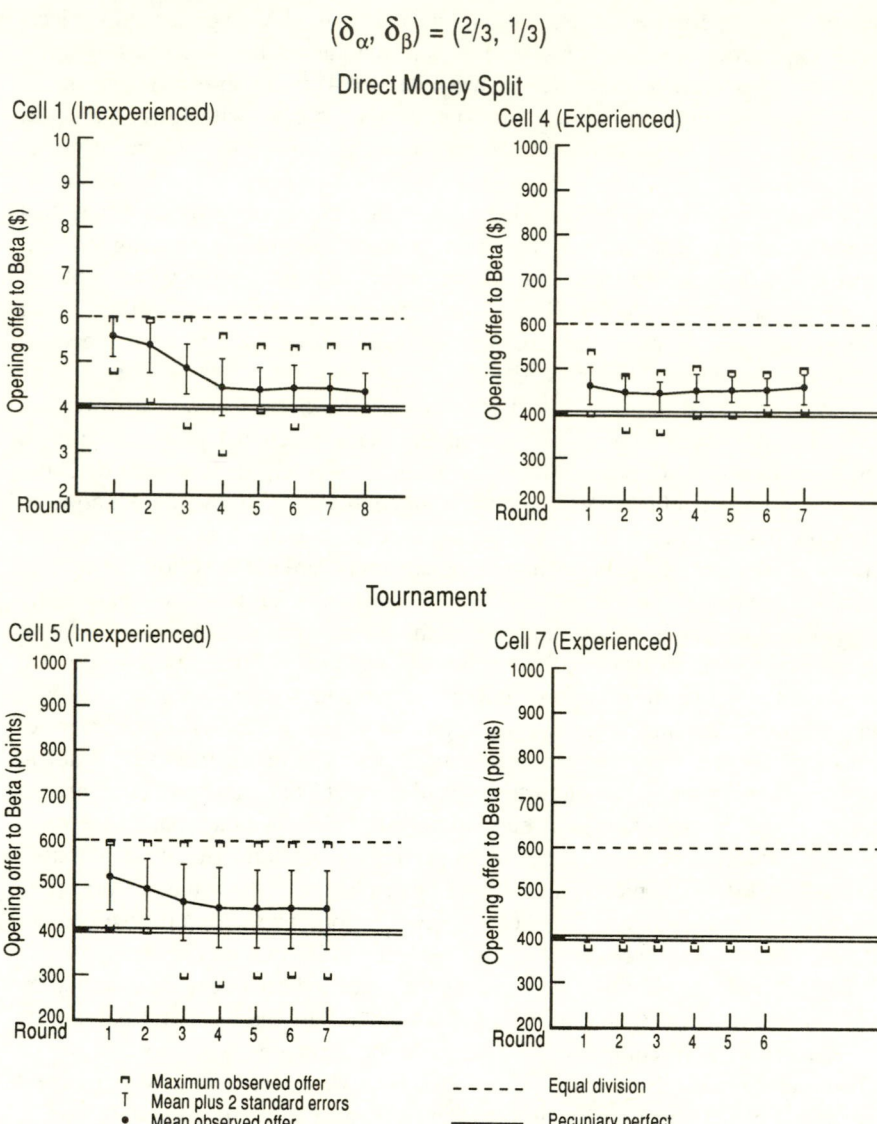

Figure 4.3a. Opening offers with $(\delta_\alpha, \delta_\beta) = (2/3, 1/3)$. *Source:* Bolton 1991.

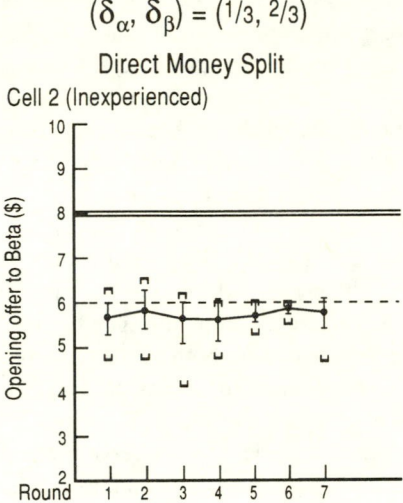

$$(\delta_\alpha, \delta_\beta) = (1/3, 2/3)$$

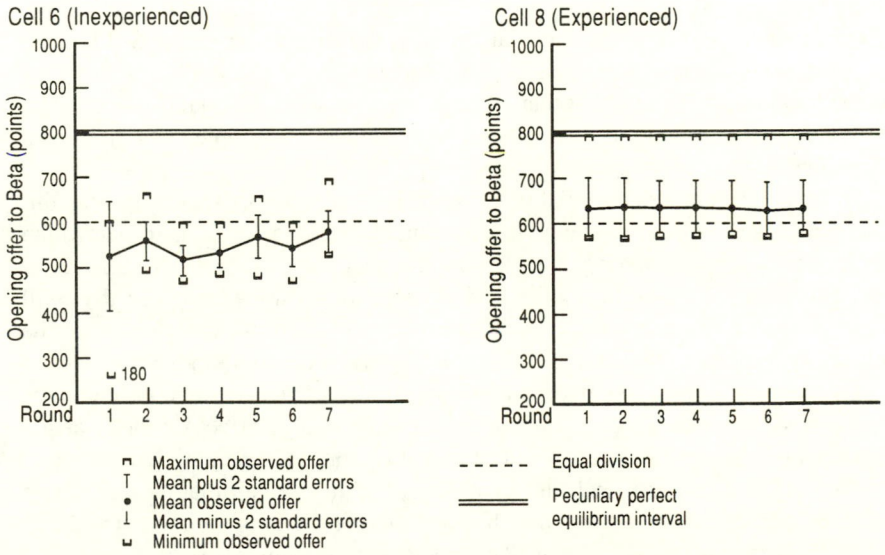

Figure 4.3b. Opening offers with $(\delta_\alpha, \delta_\beta) = (1/3, 2/3)$. *Source:* Bolton 1991.

a. Are Players "Trying to Be Fair"?

One hypothesis about bargainers' preferences that has received some attention is the possibility that they may behave altruistically, at least to the extent that they "try to be fair." This hypothesis cannot be directly tested on data from bargaining games of the kind discussed above, because a player who offers an equal division, for example, may be doing so in order to avoid a negative reaction by the other bargainer.

To explore this hypothesis, Forsythe, Horowitz, Savin, and Sefton (1994) compared ultimatum and "dictator" games. Like an ultimatum game, a dictator game is a two-player game in which player 1 proposes a division of some resource between the two. However, unlike an ultimatum game, in a dictator game player 2 may not reject this proposal (and cause both players to receive zero); the players receive whatever player 1 (the dictator) proposes. So in a dictator game player 1's proposal can be interpreted as a pure expression of his preferences. In the dictator game, but not in the ultimatum game, they observe that the modal offer is the equilibrium offer, at which player 1 offers zero to player 2 (see Figure 4.4, which graphs proposed divisions of $5). Forsythe et al. conclude that "players are more generous in the ultimatum game than in the dictator game," and so they reject the "fairness hypothesis" as the primary explanation for the generous offers observed. But Forsythe et al. also observe a concentration of offers of equal division in the dictator game, and this is the modal result in the ultimatum game. So the data support the hypothesis that *some* of the subjects may be primarily motivated by considerations of fairness, but that the high concentration of equal division offers observed in the ultimatum game cannot be attributed to a simple desire for equal divisions on the part of players 1.

Bolton (1991) makes a similar observation in the context of sequential bargaining games with more than one period, by considering two period games in which the last period is a dictator game. He observes that player 1s in such games offer more than they do in ordinary two period bargaining games (in which they will have a chance to reject player 2s counteroffer). Thus, in these games also, the player 1s respond to the strategic difference between the two kinds of games.

Of course, if even a few players are substantially influenced by considerations of fairness, this may in some circumstances have a large effect on the strategic environment in which the other players must operate. Kahneman, Knetsch, and Thaler (1986a) created such an environment. After an ultimatum game was played, subjects were told that they had a choice of dividing some money either with another subject, U, who in the previous ultimatum game had chosen to offer an unequal division, or with a subject, E, who had previously chosen to offer an equal division. If they chose U, then the two of them (the chooser and subject U) would each receive $6, and subject E would receive zero. If they chose E, then the two of them would each receive $5, and subject U would receive zero. A majority chose E, thus exhibiting a willingness to sacrifice a dollar in order that E rather than U should be paid. (However, among subjects who had themselves made unequal offers in the previous ultimatum game, only a minority chose E.)

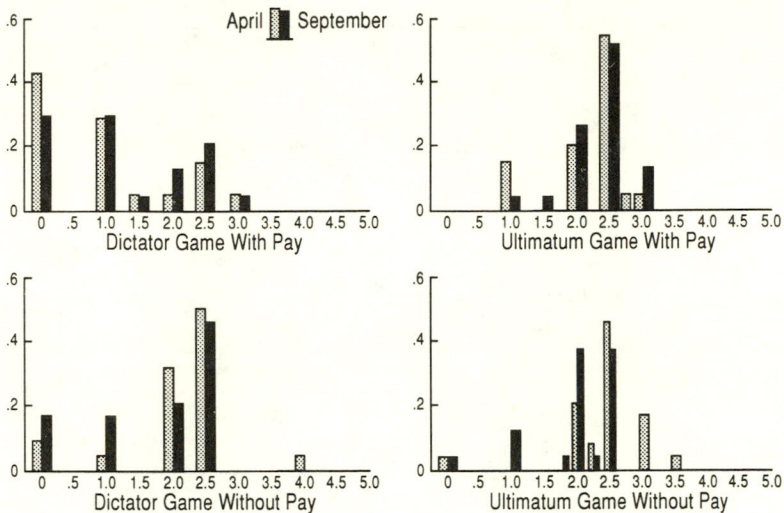

Figure 4.4. Offers in dictator and ultimatum games. *Source:* Forsythe, Horowitz, Savin, and Sefton 1994.

To the extent that some subjects are willing to punish past behavior that they see as unfair (even to others) one can easily imagine how social norms could be created and enforced. For some theoretical literature on the evolution of social norms in environments in which deviators can be punished, see Guth and Yaari (1990a,1990b), Okuno-Fujiwara and Postlewaite (1990), and Kandori (1992). Bolton (1993) and Van Huyck et al. (1992) describe the evolution of social norms in a more biological sense.

But there is a chicken and egg problem here. Although subjects may have clear ideas about what is fair in a variety of circumstances,[23] and although these ideas about fairness may influence the strategic environment, the evidence suggests that subjects adapt their ideas about what is fair in response to their experience, in ways that may be heavily influenced by strategic considerations. That is, although the strategic environment is influenced by ideas about fairness, ideas about fairness are influenced by the strategic environment.

For example, Binmore, Morgan, Shaked, and Sutton (1991) studied two closely related alternating offer sequential bargaining games, which differed only in a relatively subtle way, concerning how the games ended. In "optional breakdown games," players who did not reach agreement in a given period could continue to the next period with the size of the pie reduced by a discount factor δ, unless one of them chose to end the game. If either player chose to end the game, players 1 and 2 received "breakdown" payments α and β respectively, where α is a small fixed percentage of the pie, and β is a larger percentage that changed between games as one of the experimental variables. In "forced breakdown games," players who did not reach agreement in a given period could continue to the next period with probability δ, but with probability $1-\delta$ the game would end and the players would receive their breakdown payments. In each game, the

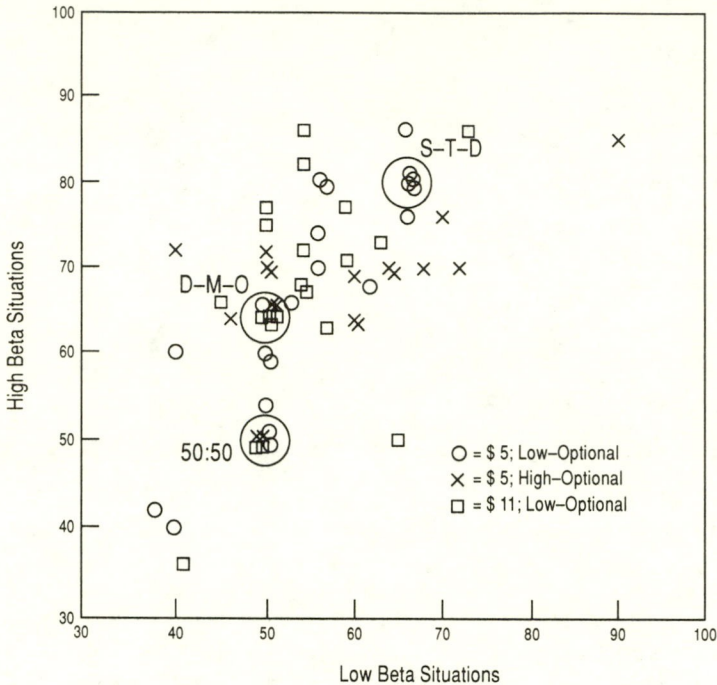

This figure shows the share of the cake for player II proposed as "fair" for low and high
β situations by subjects who had experienced *optional* breakdown games.

Figure 4.5a. "Fair" divisions. *Source:* Binmore, Morgan, Shaked, and Sutton 1991.

amount the players could divide by reaching agreement was greater than the sum
of their breakdown payments, and β was set to be either 36 percent or 64 percent
of the total available pie, while α was equal to 4 percent.

The subgame perfect equilibrium prediction for the optional breakdown game
is that the relative sizes of the breakdown payments will not influence the outcome of negotiations unless the breakdown payment of one of the players is larger
than his share of the pie at equilibrium of the game in which players' breakdown
payments are zero. (The reason is that at a perfect equilibrium in this case no
player would choose at any subgame to end the game and receive a payment
smaller than his equilibrium payment from continuing, so the breakdown payments are irrelevant.) But the prediction for the forced breakdown game is that
agreements should be reached that give a larger share of the pie to the player with
the larger breakdown payment, even when that payment is relatively small. (The
reason is that in any subgame in which agreement has not been reached, the player
with the higher breakdown payment has a higher expected payoff, since there is
a positive probability of breakdown.)

With these parameters, the predictions are approximately that player 2's
share will be 50 percent in the "low beta" (β = 36 percent) optional breakdown
game and 64 percent in the "high beta" optional breakdown game, a pattern

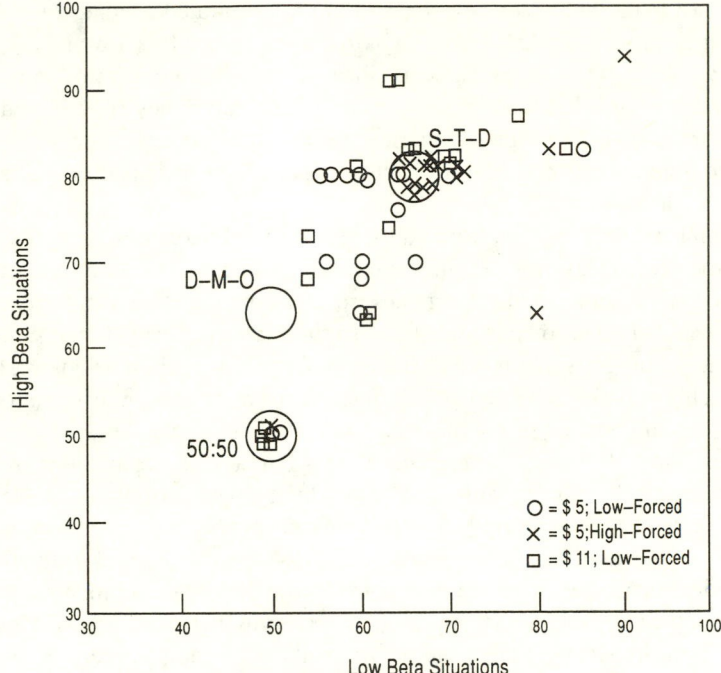

This figure shows the share of the cake for player II proposed as "fair" for low and high β situations by subjects who had experienced *forced* breakdown games.

Figure 4.5b. "Fair" divisions. *Source:* Binmore, Morgan, Shaked, and Sutton 1991.

that Binmore et al. call "deal me out." In the forced breakdown game, the prediction is that the players will each get their breakdown payment plus half the surplus $1 - (\alpha + \beta)$, so that player 2 will receive 66 percent in the low beta game and 80 percent in the high beta game, a pattern that Binmore et al. call "split the difference."

Following several plays of each game in which each subject participated as both player 1 and player 2 in one of these games, Binmore et al. presented subjects with a questionnaire asking them to indicate what they thought was a "fair" offer to player 2 for each configuration of breakdown payoffs. (Everyone agreed that 50 percent was fair when breakdown payoffs were equal.) The responses for low and high values of β are graphed in Figure 4.5a for players who experienced the optional breakdown games, and in Figure 4.5b for players who had experienced the forced breakdown games.

It is the difference between the two figures that is especially notable. While some subjects in each kind of game propose that a fair outcome gives player 2 only 50 percent for both low and high beta situations, most subjects think it fair that player 2 should get more than 50 percent in both situations. But while the responses from subjects who had experienced the optional breakdown game are diffuse (Figure 4.5a), the responses of those who had experienced the forced breakdown game are much less so, and are concentrated around the split-the-difference numbers, that give 66 percent to player 2 when β is low and 80 percent when β is high. Thus many subjects' ideas about what constitute "fair" agreements have been influenced by the version of the game they played, and in the forced breakdown game their experience of a strategic environment in which split-the-difference is equilibrium behavior has led to their adopting it as their idea of a fair outcome.[24]

In summary, the evidence from all these sequential bargaining games suggests that some of the away-from-equilibrium behavior (e.g., disadvantageous counteroffers, equal divisions in dictator games) results from bargainers' preferences that concern not only their own income but also their relative share. At the same time, the evidence suggests that much of the away-from-equilibrium behavior does not have such a simple cause, but results instead from strategic considerations (including the anticipation that some offers may not be accepted because of fairness considerations). Despite the heterogeneity of bargainers' motivations, much of the observed behavior contains clear, reproducible regularities (as in Ochs and Roth [1989], Weg et al. [1990], and Bolton [1991]), which indicate that the deviations from the equilibrium predictions reflect systematic features of the bargaining environment. Yet there are also some anomalies (e.g., similar games with different observed behavior) that present the opportunity to design experiments to test different hypotheses about the nature of these systematic features. Some of these are considered next.

4. Pursuing Anomalies

In concentrating on sequential bargaining games in which the players take turns making offers of how to divide a diminishing pie, we have considered a family of games in which the perfect equilibrium and its usual auxiliary assumptions (e.g., that the bargainers are motivated by simple income maximization) yield notably poor predictions. Yet there are other, related games in which the perfect equilibrium predictions perform much better, such as the fixed-cost sequential bargaining games reported by Rapoport et al. (1990). These particular games are difficult to compare with the other sequential bargaining games so far studied, because of the different cost structure they employ, the much greater number of periods they were allowed to run, and the different equilibrium predictions. Yet the similarities between these games are sufficient so that the different success of the equilibrium predictions demands further investigation. We turn next to consider this kind of anomaly.

The simplest of the sequential bargaining games is the ultimatum game, in which each player makes only one decision. The results of the ultimatum game experiments are clear: observed behavior is far from the equilibrium prediction. One way to explore this phenomenon more fully would be to identify a game with closely parallel structure and equilibrium predictions, but in which observed behavior would conform to the equilibrium prediction. Prasnikar and Roth (1989,

1992) identified such a game and conducted an experiment designed to compare it with the ultimatum game.

The game in question was earlier studied by Harrison and Hirshleifer (1989), as one of several games in an experiment concerned with different mechanisms for the provision of public goods. In one of the games, player 1 first proposed a quantity q_1 that he would provide, then player 2 (after being informed of q_1) proposed a quantity q_2 that he would provide, with the quantity q of public good provided being the *maximum* of q_1 and q_2 (the "best shot"). Both players were then paid a "redemption value" based on the quantity q provided; however each player i was charged for the quantity q_i that *he* had provided, at a flat rate of 82¢ per unit (see Table 4.2).

The perfect equilibrium predictions are that player 1 will choose $q_1 = 0$ and player 2 will choose $q_2 = 4$, giving player 1 a profit of \$3.70 and player 2 a profit of \$3.70 − \$3.28 = \$0.42. Harrison and Hirshleifer (1989) conducted an experiment in which best shot games were played under conditions of partial information, in which each player was unaware that his counterpart had the same costs and redemption values. They observed results that were strikingly close to the perfect equilibrium predictions.

One hypothesis is that players' lack of information about each others' payoffs may have disabled whatever countervailing force in favor of more equal distributions of payoffs was at work in the bargaining games reported above. That is, perhaps the reason subjects in the role of player 2 were willing to accept a payoff of \$0.42 was because they were unaware (or unsure) that player 1 was receiving \$3.70, in contrast to the case of ultimatum bargaining games in which such extreme payoff disparities proved to be unacceptable. (Guth's [1988] theory of hierarchical social norms, accessed according to the information available, would presumably account for the results in this way.) This could potentially explain why such a relatively extreme distribution of payoffs was observed in this data, but virtually never in the data from ultimatum games for comparable amounts of money.[25]

The experiment of Prasnikar and Roth (1989, 1992) was designed to investigate both this hypothesis and the hypothesis that the difference between observed behavior in best shot and ultimatum games (despite their similar equilibrium predictions) was due to the different incentives these games gave to players *off* the equilibrium path. To this end, best shot games were examined both under partial information, as in Harrison and Hirshleifer, and under full information, with both players knowing each other's payoffs. In addition, in order that other details of procedure should not complicate the comparisons, a set of ultimatum games were conducted using the same detailed procedures (of recruiting subjects, of transmitting messages, etc.). The best shot games under partial and full information conditions provide a test of the hypothesis that the extreme equilibrium payoffs will only be observed when subjects cannot compare their payoffs, while the comparison of the full information best shot game with the ultimatum game run under the same conditions provides a test of the hypothesis that the structural

Table 4.2. Redemption Values and Expenditure Values for the Best-Shot Games

	Redemption Values		Expenditure Values	
Project Level (Units)	Redemption Value of Specifiic Units	Total Redemption Value of All Units	Number of Units You Provide	Cost to You of the Number Units You Provide
0	$0.00	$0.00	0	$0.00
1	1.00	1.00	1	0.82
2	0.95	1.95	2	1.64
3	0.90	2.85	3	2.46
4	0.85	3.70	4	3.28
5	0.80	4.50	5	4.10
6	0.75	5.25	6	4.92
7	0.70	5.95	7	5.74
8	0.65	6.60	8	6.56
9	0.60	7.20	9	7.38
10	0.55	7.75	10	8.20
11	0.50	8.25	11	9.02
12	0.45	8.70	12	9.84
13	0.40	9.10	13	10.66
14	0.35	9.45	14	11.48
15	0.30	9.75	15	12.30
16	0.25	10.00	16	13.12
17	0.20	10.25	17	13.94
18	0.15	10.35	18	14.76
19	0.10	10.45	19	15.58
20	0.05	10.50	20	16.40
21	0.00	10.50	21	21.22

differences in the games make the extreme equilibrium payoffs more likely to be observed in one than in the other. Each subject played only one of the three games, but played it ten times, against a different anonymous opponent in each round. So the experiment also allows the learning that goes on in each game to be compared.

Table 4.3 reports the mean offers x_2 in the ultimatum game, as well as the mean quantities q_1 provided in the sequential best shot games under full and partial information. Recall that the perfect equilibrium prediction is that all these quantities will be zero. The observed means are reported round by round for each game.[26]

In the sequential best shot game under full information the observed means clearly have converged to the equilibrium quantity by the seventh round, after

Table 4.3. Mean Offers by Periods

Periods	Ultimatum Game (mean x_2)[a]	Best Shot, full information game (mean q_1)[b]	Best Shot, partial information game (mean q_1)[c]
1	4.188 (0.329)	1.625 (0.610)	2.700 (0.617)
2	3.825 (0.530)	0.875 (0.482)	2.900 (0.994)
3	3.725 (0.480)	1.125 (0.597)	3.000 (0.848)
4	3.581 (0.438)	0.125 (0.116)	2.100 (0.793)
5	4.231 (0.276)	0.125 (0.116)	2.700 (0.906)
6	4.418 (0.234)	0.125 (0.116)	1.250 (0.605)
7	4.294 (0.166)	0.000 (0.000)	1.100 (0.537)
8	4.531 (0.155)	0.000 (0.000)	0.800 (0.505)
9	4.325 (0.232)	0.000 (0.000)	0.950 (0.567)
10	4.531 (0.155)	0.000 (0.000)	0.700 (0.401)

Source: Prasnikar and Roth 1992.
Note: Values in parentheses are standard errors.
[a] Perfect equilibrium prediction: $x_2 = 0$.
[b] Perfect equilibrium prediction: $q_1 = 0$.
[c] Perfect equilibrium prediction: $q_1 = 0$.

which no player 1 is observed to provide any positive quantity. (And the modal response of players 2 is the equilibrium response of $q_2 = 4$, with 41% of offers $q_1 = 0$ receiving this response overall.) Although the results in the partial information best shot games are significantly different from those in the full information games, the observed means in both best shot games are clearly much closer to zero than are the observed means in the ultimatum games, which are quite similar to the observations for ultimatum games previously reported in the literature. So the best shot game is one in which, even when the players can compare their payoffs, equilibrium payoffs can be observed even though they are extreme.

An indication of how the best shot games are different from the ultimatum games comes from examining the learning that took place over the course of the

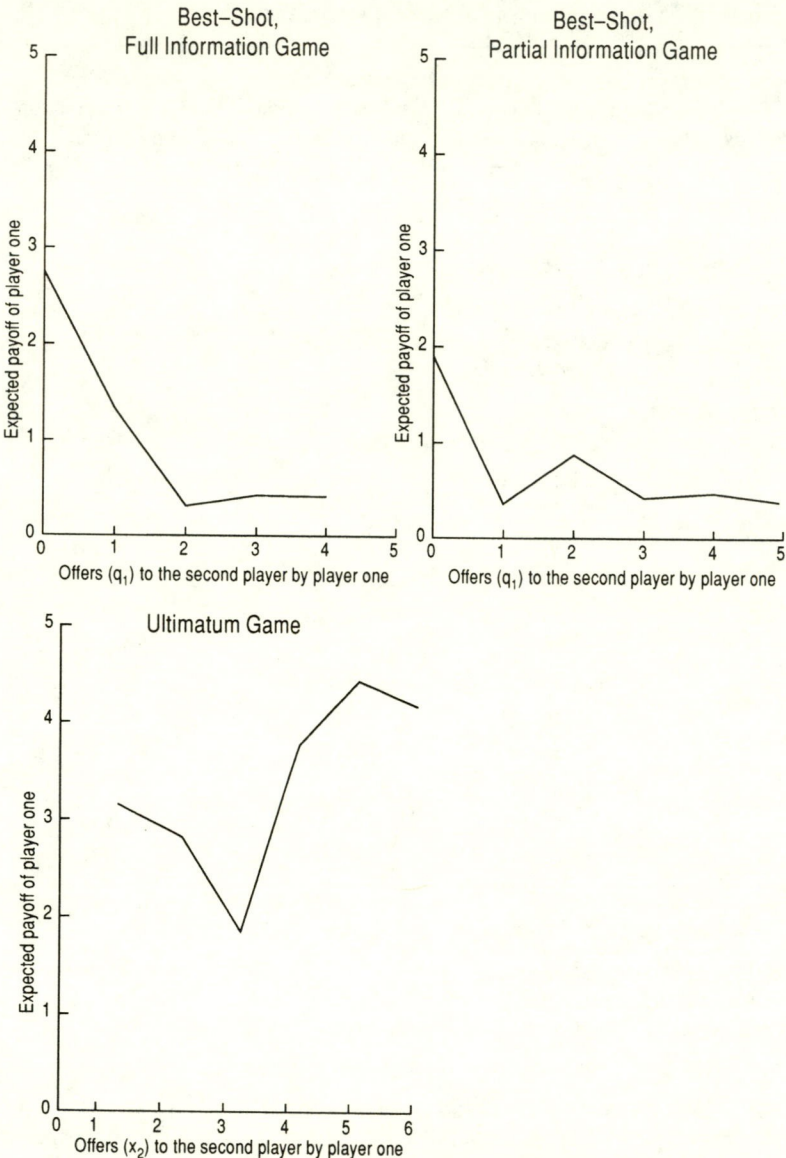

Figure 4.6. Expected payoff of each offer. *Source:* Prasnikar and Roth 1992.

ten rounds each game was played. In the best shot games, half the player 1s in the full information condition and nine out of ten of the player 1s in the partial information condition began by offering positive quantities, but in the face of consistent lack of a positive reply by the player 2s, the number of player 1s offering positive quantities steadily diminished. In contrast, in the ultimatum game, offers by the first player were closest to the equilibrium prediction in the first four rounds, but in the face of steady rejections of low offers, the lowest offer x_2 steadily climbed.

Prasnikar and Roth concluded that the difference between the observed behavior in best shot and ultimatum games, despite the similarity of their equilibrium predictions, is in the off the equilibrium path behavior. This can be assessed by considering how player 2s react when player 1s deviate from the equilibrium prediction—i.e., when they offer $q_1 > 0$ in the best shot games or $x_2 > 0$ in the ultimatum games. The prediction of subgame perfect equilibrium is in all cases that player 1 will maximize his payoff by making the equilibrium offer—i.e., at perfect equilibrium; the predicted response of player 2 is such that a positive offer will yield player 1 a lower payoff than an offer of zero. However, as the graphs in Figures 4.6a, b, and c make clear the best shot games exhibit different behavior in this regard than the ultimatum games. In the best shot games, under both information conditions, the average payoff of player 1s who contributed the equilibrium quantity $q_1 = 0$ is greater than that of player 1s who contributed positive quantities. However, in the ultimatum game, the average payoff to a player 1 who offers player 2 an amount x_2 rises to a maximum for x_2 between 4 and 5 (which is where we observe the mean offer). So in the ultimatum games a player 1 does better as he deviates further from equilibrium, but not in the best shot games. This behavior is comprehensible in both games: in the best shot games, the more player 1 provides, the less incentive player 2 has to provide anything (see Table 4.2), while in the ultimatum games, the more player 1 offers to player 2, the greater his incentive to accept the offer.

To the extent that this explanation identifies the important difference between best shot and ultimatum games, it suggests that whatever role considerations of fairness may play in such games, it is mediated by considerations of strategy of the kind that game theorists are accustomed to studying. But quite a different hypothesis has also been proposed.

a. Distinguishing between Alternative Hypotheses

After an early version of these results was circulated (Prasnikar and Roth 1989), Guth and Tietz (1990) suggested an alternative hypothesis to explain them. They say:

> [E]qual positive contributions in best shot games are obviously inefficient since one of the two contributions is completely useless. If sharing the burden of providing the public good is impossible, fairness considerations cannot be applied. (428)

These comments refine Guth and Tietz's (1988) hypothesis concerning the role played by extreme payoff distributions (recall footnote 25), by adding considerations of convexity and efficiency. In doing so, they raise a clear counterhypothesis to the interpretation given above to the observed differences between best shot and ultimatum games. According to our interpretation, the different off-the-equilibrium-path properties of the two games is responsible for the different observed behavior, despite the comparably unequal payoff distribution at equilibrium. The contrary hypothesis suggested by Guth and Tietz (1990) is that the different observed behavior in the two games is due to the fact that players are concerned with fairness only in the ultimatum games, and that no comparable considerations arise in the best shot games because in those games equality and efficiency are incompatible.

To examine these competing hypotheses, Prasnikar and Roth examined a sequential market game, consisting of one seller and nine buyers. As in the ultimatum games, each buyer offered a price, which if accepted determined the division of $10 between the successful buyer and the seller. (If the seller accepts an offer p from buyer 1, then that buyer earns $10 - p$, the seller earns p, and all other buyers earn $0. If the seller rejects all offers, then all players in the market receive $0.)[27] Since the smallest unit in which prices could be quoted was $0.05, there are two subgame perfect equilibrium prices, $9.95 and $10.00. Thus any subgame perfect equilibrium gives (virtually) all the wealth to the seller.[28]

In this game all transactions, not merely equilibrium transactions, are efficient. Thus this game has equilibrium payoff distributions that are as extreme as those of the ultimatum or best shot games, but (like the ultimatum game and unlike the best shot game) it has efficient equal-payoff outcomes.[29] It therefore presents an opportunity to test the conjecture that the observed outcomes of the best shot games were intimately related to the fact that equal payoffs in that game can only be achieved inefficiently.

The observed results do not support this hypothesis. By the fifth round, prices had converged to equilibrium, and all subsequent transactions were at the equilibrium price of $10.[30] (See Table 4.4.) Table 4.4 also makes clear that (except in round 7 in market B) from round 5 on no buyer could have increased his payoff by more than $0.05 by changing his bid. The high bidders in these rounds (who always received zero) were always competing either with another bidder who made the same bid, or one who made a bid that was only $0.05 less.[31] Thus in this game, as in the best shot game and in contrast to the ultimatum game (recall Figures 4.6 a–c), the observed pattern of play is such that agents could not increase their payoff by deviating from the equilibrium prediction. This lends further support to the hypothesis that the off the equilibrium path behavior is of critical importance in understanding the observed behavior in these games. (This hypothesis is also supported by the data from the "infinite horizon" bargaining games of Rapoport, Weg, and Felsenthal [1990] and Weg and Zwick [1991], in which equally extreme equilibrium predictions were achieved with some regularity.) Note that this certainly does not mean that considerations of fairness do not play a role in determining the outcome of the game, but rather that such considerations interact with the strategic features of the game.[32]

Table 4.4. The Highest and Second-Highest Prices in Each of the Markets and the Basic Descriptive Statistics

Period	Market	Highest Price (\$)[a]	Second-Highest Price (\$)[a]	Mean and SD[b]	Mode[c]	Median	N[d]
1	A	8.90 (1)	8.25 (1)	6.48 (2.52)	8.05	8.05	9
	B	9.90 (1)	8.95 (1)	6.76 (1.84)	5.00	6.50	9
2	A	9.60 (1)	9.00 (1)	6.57 (3.07)	5.00	8.05	9
	B	9.90 (1)	9.00 (2)	6.69 (3.26)	x	8.00	9
3	A	9.85 (1)	9.65 (1)	7.24 (3.24)	x	9.00	9
	B	10.00 (1)	9.95 (1)	8.08 (2.31)	x	9.00	9
4	A	10.00 (2)	9.95 (2)	7.32 (4.00)	x	9.90	9
	B	9.95 (1)	9.90 (1)	7.31 (2.67)	9.00	9.00	9
5	A	10.00 (2)	9.95 (2)	9.14 (1.61)	x	9.90	9
	B	10.00 (2)	9.95 (2)	7.93 (2.76)	x	8.50	9
6	A	10.00 (3)	9.95 (1)	7.21 (3.69)	10.00	9.00	9
	B	10.00 (1)	9.95 (4)	7.81 (3.32)	9.95	9.95	9
7	A	10.00 (1)	9.95 (2)	6.43 (3.28)	x	7.00	9
	B	10.00 (1)	9.60 (1)	5.23 3.07	5.00	5.00	9
8	A	10.00 (2)	9.85 (1)	5.76 (3.74)	x	5.00	9
	B	10.00 (2)	9.85 (1)	5.72 (4.31)	x	7.00	9
9	A	10.00 (1)	9.95 (1)	4.73 (4.11)	x	5.00	9
	B	10.00 (1)	9.95 (1)	5.98 (3.72)	x	5.00	9
10	A	10.00 (2)	9.95 (1)	6.22 (4.23)	x	9.00	9
	B	10.00 (2)	9.95 (1)	6.47 (3.32)	5.00	5.00	9

Source: Prasnikar and Roth 1992.

[a] The number in parentheses is the number of buyers who bid that price.
[b] Numbers in parentheses are standard deviations.
[c] An "x" in the mode column means that there were fewer than three observations at any one price.
[d] N represents the number of buyers in each of the markets.

b. A Cross-Cultural Experiment

It turns out that this behavior is quite robust to changes in subject pools. Roth, Prasnikar, Okuno-Fujiwara, and Zamir (1991) conducted an experiment in which this kind of market game was examined, together with an ultimatum bargaining game, in Jerusalem, Ljubljana, Pittsburgh, and Tokyo.[33] (In each environment, subjects gained experience in ten consecutive transactions with different players, as in Prasnikar and Roth [1992].) Outcomes in the market game converged to equilibrium in all four locations, while outcomes in the ultimatum game remained far from the equilibrium prediction, although there were differences between the bargaining outcomes in different countries. Before discussing these results, it is worth spending a moment on some of the problems of experimental design that arise in conducting an experiment in four countries, namely the problems of controlling for the effects of different experimenters, languages, and currencies. The discussion of these aspects of the experimental design will be organized as a statement of a particular problem, followed by the element of the design that addressed this problem.

Problem 1   *Experimenter effects:* Since the experiment involved several experimenters in different locations, between-country differences might arise because of uncontrolled procedural differences or uncontrolled personal differences among the experimenters.

Design solution   Each experimenter came to Pittsburgh and ran (at least) a bargaining session and a market session. The Pittsburgh data were thus gathered by all of the experimenters before they returned to their home countries to gather the data there. In this way we were able to coordinate the detailed operational procedures among the different experimenters. And the Pittsburgh data can be used to detect any effect due to purely personal characteristics of the experimenters, since if these effects were present they would have shown up not only in the comparisons between countries, but in comparisons of the Pittsburgh sessions conducted by the different experimenters.

Problem 2   *Language effects*: Because the instructions for the experiment were presented in English, Hebrew, Japanese, and Slovenian, systematic differences between countries might be observed because of the way the instructions are translated. (Consider, for example, the English words "bargaining," "negotiating," and "haggling," which are all approximate synonyms, but whose different connotations might possibly elicit differences in behavior.)[34]

Design solutions   The problem of language effects was addressed both through the way in which the translations were made and, more formally, in the way the instructions for the bargaining and market environments were related.

1. *Translations*: The experimenter responsible for each translation was a national of the country in question who is both linguistically and culturally fluent in American English. Efforts were made to phrase the English instructions in

terms that could be faithfully translated into each of the languages. Aside from avoiding terms with heavy or ambiguous connotations either in English or in translation, this also led to phrasing in less abstract terms than are sometimes used in single-culture experiments. (For example, subjects in bargaining experiments are sometimes instructed that they will be in the position of "player 1" or "player 2," but this turns out to be difficult to translate into Slovenian without sounding frivolous.)

2. *Control for translation differences*: The instructions for the bargaining and market environments were written in parallel, using the same vocabulary. (For example, in both environments, subjects who made proposals were referred to as "buyers," while those who made acceptances or rejections were termed "sellers.") So if a translation difference is responsible for an observed behavior difference between countries, it should show up in both the market and bargaining data. In particular, the pattern of results that we observed—no between-country differences in the market behavior, but differences in the bargaining behavior—at least put an upper bound on the effect of the translation and establish that it is not large enough to cause the markets to yield different results in the different countries. This supports the hypothesis that the translation is not the cause of the observed difference in the bargaining.

Problem 3 *Currency effects*: Because the subjects were paid in dinars, dollars, shekels, and yen, systematic differences between countries might be observed because of the different incentives that the potential payments give to subjects, or because of the different numerical scale on which payments are made. (That is, subjects in experiments often tend to choose round numbers [see, e.g., Albers and Albers 1983], and these may depend on the units involved so that subjects proposing prices in dollars might choose different numbers than those dealing in thousands of yen, or hundreds of thousands of dinars.[35])

Design solutions First, to assess the extent to which between-country differences might be due to differences in purchasing power, the Pittsburgh data establish a baseline by including sessions in which the potential payoff ranged from $10 to $30. In each country the size of the payoffs was then chosen to give a purchasing power on the high side of $10. So if observed differences between countries fall outside the range of differences due to payoffs observed in Pittsburgh, they are likely to be due to other factors. Second, to control for differences in units, proposed prices in all countries were made in terms of 1,000 tokens, with increments being made in units of 5 tokens.

Of course, there remain many uncontrolled differences between subject pools. For example, in Israel and Slovenia a much higher percentage of the sample of subjects were army veterans than in the United States or Japan. So any conclusions about the *causes* of between-country differences have to be circumspect.

Figure 4.7a summarizes the market results from Slovenia, Japan, and Israel, and shows that they are quite similar to those observed in the United States: offers

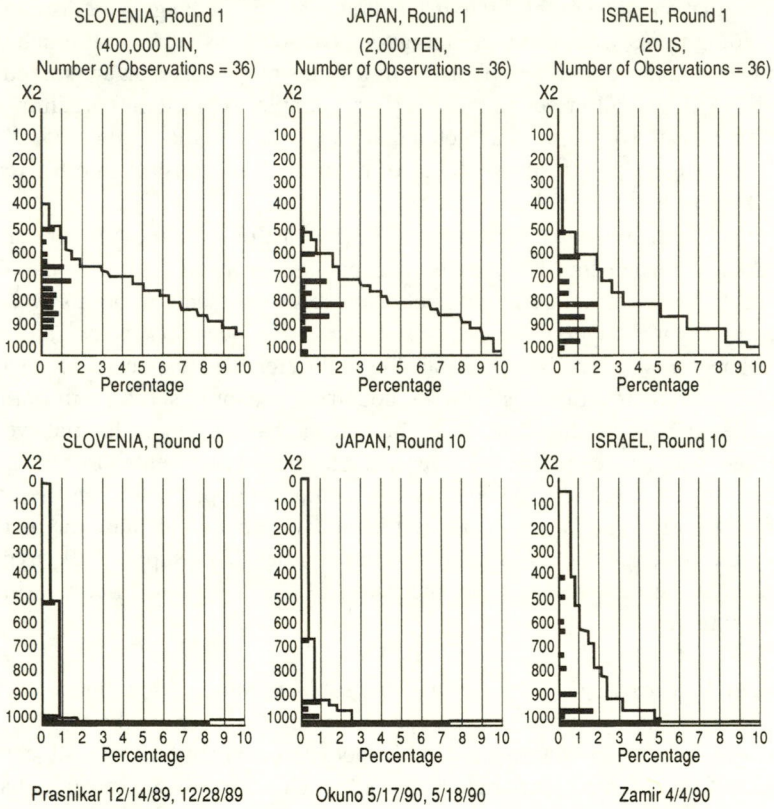

Figure 4.7a. Distribution of market offers in Slovenia, Japan, and Israel. *Source:* Roth, Prasnikar, Okuno-Fujiwara, and Zamir 1991.

in round 1 are diffuse, but by round 10 there is a concentration of offers at the equilibrium prices. So by the tenth round there were no payoff relevant between-country differences observed in these markets.

The situation is different for the ultimatum bargaining game. In each of the countries the modal offer in the first round is the equal division offer of 500. And in none of the countries do the tenth round offers approach the equilibrium prediction of zero. But by the tenth round the distributions of offers are significantly different in different countries. In the United States and Slovenia the modal offer in the tenth round remains at 500, as in the first round. But in Japan, the tenth-round offers exhibit modes at 450 and 400, and in Israel the mode is at 400.[36] Figure 4.7b shows the first- and tenth-round distributions for Slovenia, Japan, and Israel (the distribution observed in the U.S. is similar to that of Slovenia).

These between-country differences offer the opportunity to examine what other features of the bargaining outcomes vary together with the distribution of offers. We can anticipate section II of this chapter by considering how the rate of acceptances and rejections varied between countries. Such a comparison can be made by considering how often the proposal of a given price is accepted. These compar-

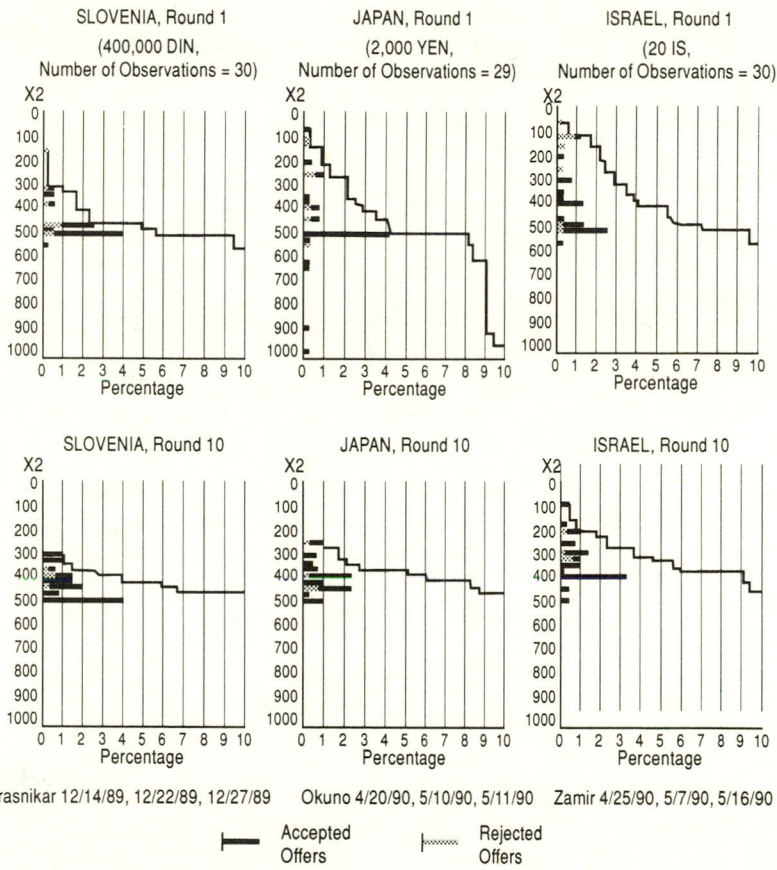

Figure 4.7b. Distribution of bargaining offers in Slovenia, Japan, and Israel. *Source:* Roth, Prasnikar, Okuno-Fujiwara, and Zamir 1991.

isons are slightly complicated by the fact that the number of proposals of a given price is different in different countries, and that observed rates of acceptance fluctuate widely for offers that were observed only rarely. However, the underlying pattern is clear, as is demonstrated by Figure 4.7c. The curves for each country represent the percentage of acceptances for each price that was proposed at least ten times (over all rounds). Each cell of Figure 4.7c compares the resulting curves for a pair of countries, and these comparisons mirror those concerning the distribution of proposals. In each case, the country with the lower distribution of offered prices has a higher rate of acceptance for each proposed price. Thus we see that the acceptance rate in Israel for each offer is higher than that in the United States, Slovenia, and Japan, respectively, while the acceptance rates in Japan are higher than those in the United States and Slovenia. Only in the comparison of the United States and Slovenia (whose distributions of observed offers did not differ significantly) do we have two acceptance rate curves such that one is not higher than the other.

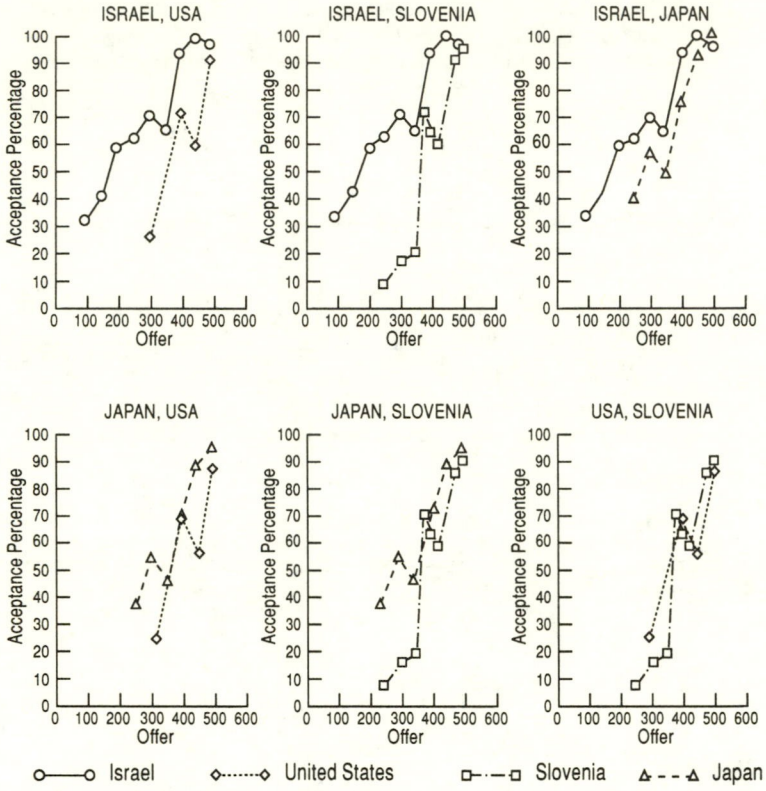

Figure 4.7c. Pairwise comparisons of acceptance rates in bargaining. *Source:* Roth, Prasnikar, Okuno-Fujiwara, and Zamir 1991.

Given that different offers are accepted with different probabilities, it is natural to ask, for each country, what is the expected payoff to a buyer from making a particular offer? Since the behavior of the bargainers is changing from round to round, this is something of a moving target. But Figure 4.7d presents the curves based on the pooled data from all rounds in each country, for all offers that were made at least ten times. Thus, for example, if a buyer proposes a price of 300 he will earn 700 if it is accepted and 0 if it is rejected. In the United States the price 300 was proposed fifteen times and accepted four times (26.7 percent), so on average the proposal earned $(700 \times .267) = 186.9$, which can be read from the graph for the United States in Figure 4.7d. It is instructive to compare these graphs to the modal offers observed in round 10 in each country. The modal offer in the final round in both the United States and Slovenia is 500, and looking at Figure 4.7d we see that 500 is also the proposed price that maximizes a buyer's average earnings in the United States and Slovenia. The modal offer in the final round in Israel is 400, and we see in Figure 4.7d that here too this is the price that maximizes a buyer's average earnings. And in Japan there are two modal offers in round 10, at 400 and 450, and the latter maximizes a buyer's

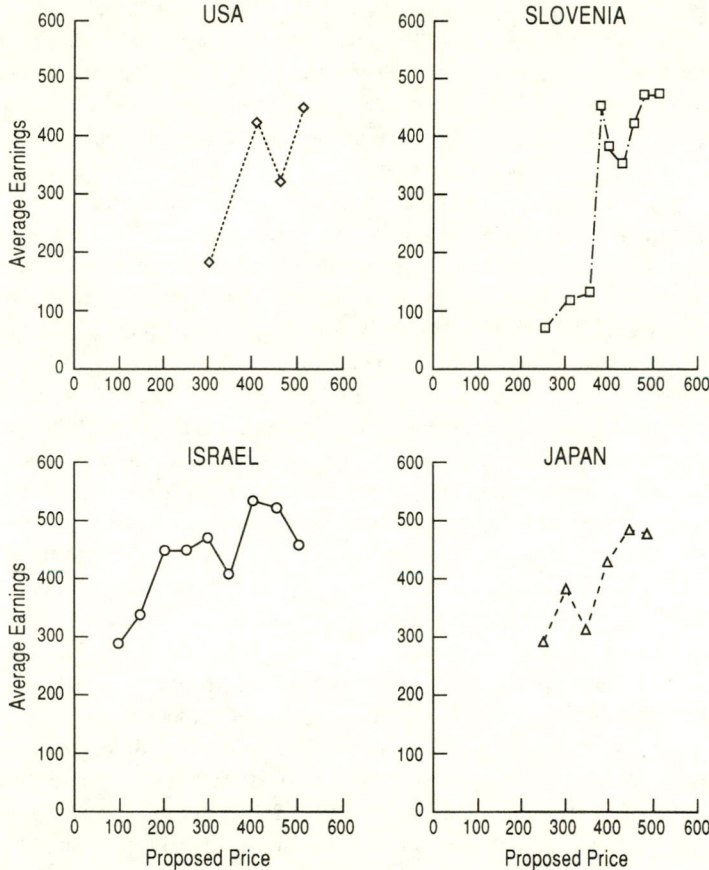

Figure 4.7d. Buyers' earnings in bargaining, by Proposed Price. *Source:* Roth, Prasnikar, Okuno-Fujiwara, and Zamir 1991.

average earnings. Thus by round 10 the buyers seem to be adapting to the experience of the prior rounds in a manner roughly consistent with simple income maximization. (The same cannot be said of the sellers, who continue to reject low positive offers.)

These results bring us back to the question of the previous section, "Are players trying to be fair?" Taken together, Figures 4.7b and 4.7d suggest that in the ultimatum games the behavior of the player 1s, at least, may be well accounted for by simple income maximization. But the fact that the modal offer in round 10 was in each case the income maximizing offer means that player 1s are able to take into account the behavior of the player 2s, which included (non-income-maximizing) rejections of positive offers even in the final round.

Thus the evidence provides some support for the conjecture that, while efforts to *be* fair do not play a large role in the observed behavior, efforts to avoid being *treated* unfairly oneself may influence the data: that is, the player 2s who reject low positive offers apparently prefer to do so rather than accept an offer that seems to them unreasonably low. To the extent that this is the case, the relationship observed in this experiment between offers and acceptance rates in different subject pools can help distinguish between alternative hypotheses about how ideas about the fairness, or "reasonableness," of different proposals might account for these subject pool differences.

One hypothesis is that the different subject pools share a common idea about what constitutes a fair, or reasonable, proposal (an obvious candidate is the fifty-fifty proposal of 500), and that the difference among subject pools is in something like their aggressiveness, or "toughness." In this view, buyers in more aggressive subject pools would be more inclined to take advantage of their first mover position to try to obtain more for themselves than might be considered fair. That is, such a buyer would recognize that a fifty-fifty split is "fair," but would seek to take more. However, if aggressiveness is a property of the subject pool, the sellers would share it and would presumably be less inclined to accept unfair offers than less aggressive sellers in other subject pools. So under this hypothesis, high rates of disagreement would be associated with subject pools in which offers are low. This is *not* what we observe.[37] (Another way to make the point is to note that the question of in which country the bargainers proved to be the toughest is not a well posed question, in the sense that the "toughest" buyers are found in the same place as the least tough sellers.)

Instead, the subject pools where offers are low (Japan and Israel) do not exhibit any higher rates of disagreement than the high-offer subject pools. This suggests that what varies between subject pools is not a property like aggressiveness, or toughness, but rather the perception of what constitutes a reasonable offer under the circumstances. That is, suppose that in all subject pools it seems reasonable for the first mover to ask for more than half the profit from the transaction, and what varies between subject pools is how much more seems reasonable. To the extent that offers tend towards what is commonly regarded as reasonable and that offers regarded as reasonable are accepted, there would be no reason to expect disagreement rates to vary between subject pools, even when offers do. Our data thus lends some support to the hypothesis that the subject pool differences observed in this experiment are related to different expectations about what constitutes an acceptable offer, rather than different propensities to trespass on a shared notion of what constitutes such an offer.

5. Learning and the Role of Experience

Tables 4.3 and 4.4 illustrate that experience plays an important role and that its effect may be different in different games. In the best shot and market games, experience brings the outcome more in line with the equilibrium predictions, but this is not at all the case in the ultimatum games, any more than it was in the two and three period sequential bargaining games studied by Ochs and Roth and summarized in Figure 4.2. And in the four country experiment just discussed, experience brought the market behavior in different countries closer together, while the bargaining behavior became more distinct as the players gained experience (Figures 4.7a,b).

A number of other experiments speak to the role of experience and also to how the process of accumulating experimental evidence allows simple hypotheses to be reformulated and refined. Recall from section I.B.1 that Binmore, Shaked, and Sutton (1985) found that the modal first-period offers in a two-period game were equal divisions the first time the game was played, but that when players 2 were told that they would be players 1 in a second game, their modal first-period offers were at the perfect equilibrium division. They summarized their views at the time as follows (1180):

> While we have considered various possible explanations, the interpretation that we favor is this: subjects, faced with a new problem, simply choose "equal division" as an "obvious" and "acceptable" compromise—an idea familiar from the seminal work of Thomas Schelling (1960). We suspect, on the basis of the present experiments, that such considerations are easily displaced by calculations of strategic advantage, once players fully appreciate the structure of the game.

More recently, the study of Binmore et al. (1991), discussed in section I.B., allowed optional breakdown games played by subjects with several periods of experience to be compared with optional breakdown games played by subjects with only a single period of experience (but with different breakdown payments) reported in Binmore et al. (1989). Binmore et al. (1991) note that this is a case in which the increased experience seems to *decrease* the ability of the equilibrium prediction to organize the data, a phenomenon they characterize as "unlearning." They state (311):

> For the moment, the only safe conclusion would seem to be that, if people are indeed "natural gamesmen" (a view that has been wrongly attributed to us in the past), then experience in this context would appear to lead to some "unlearning" of their game-playing skills.

Of course, different kinds of experience might produce different effects. For example, Binmore et al. (1985) already observed that the simple opportunity to play a game a second time would not be sufficient to cause offers to converge to the equilibrium prediction, since (recall from section I.B.1) Guth et al. (1982) had observed ultimatum games played by players who had experienced a previous game, without finding any difference between the two plays analogous to that observed by Binmore et al. This suggested that perhaps Binmore et al.'s (1985) procedure of having players 2 in the first game become players 1 in the second game gave them an especially appropriate kind of experience for the task of anticipating the strategic situation facing the second player. But recall that when this hypothesis was tested (e.g., by Guth and Tietz [1987], and Bolton [1990]) it was found that reversal of roles in this way did not generally promote convergence to the equilibrium predictions.

Harrison and McCabe (1991) report an experiment designed to help reconsider the question of whether "appropriate" experience might promote convergence to equilibrium behavior. In their experiment, bargainers play a sequence of alternating offer sequential bargaining games, switching back and forth between a three-period game and a two-period game. In the three-period game, the amounts to be divided in the three periods are in the proportions 100, 50, and 25, while in the two-period game the amounts are 50 and 25, so the two-period game is the subgame of the three-period game that arises if the first proposal is rejected. The perfect equilibrium proposal in the two-period game is the equal division (25, 25), so the perfect equilibrium in the three-period game calls for player 1 to propose the division (75, 25). Harrison and McCabe observe that equal divisions are observed immediately in the two-period games, and that in the three-period games average initial proposals move from near (50,50) in the direction of the perfect equilibrium proposal, approaching (70, 30) by the end of fifteen rounds of alternating between the two games.

In interpreting their results, Harrison and McCabe say (13–4):

> Our experiments and those of OR [Ochs and Roth] are the only ones to give subjects any length of experience in terms of more than two repetitions of the game. OR focus on the pure role of experience, and find that the evidence is mixed for two-round games and decidedly negative for game theory in three-round games. . . . In other words, experience *per se* does not appear to be a reliable basis for the formation of common expectations [of achieving the perfect equilibrium].

But they go on to say:

> When one combines experience *and* sequencing the conclusion is a simple one and is perfectly consistent with the predictions of game theory.

Spiegel, Currie, Sonnenschein, and Sen (1990), however, report a related experiment in which subjects play a sequence of five alternating offer sequential bargaining games against different opponents, starting with a one period (ultimatum) game and working their way up to a five-period game. The games have the property that if the first proposal is rejected in any game, the subgame that arises is the game that was played just previously. Thus prior to playing the five-period game players have the experience of playing each of its subgames. Spiegel et al. observe no tendency for proposals in any of their games to approach the perfect equilibrium prediction. This is not too surprising in view of the fact that, as each game is begun, the experience that subjects have of its subgames (starting with the ultimatum game) is different from the perfect equilibrium prediction. But it serves to emphasize that prior experience of a game's subgames does not necessarily promote equilibrium behavior. And the comparison with the experiment of Harrison and McCabe (1991) is illuminating, since in Harrison and McCabe's experiment the two period subgame had a subgame perfect equilibrium that coincides with the "equal split" solution seen so often in experimental data for reasons having nothing to do with subgame perfection. So the different results of the two experiments suggest that it may be necessary to experiment with a range of parameter values before attempting to draw firm conclusions.

In a subsequent experiment with a game derived from the ultimatum game, Harrison and McCabe (1992b) had subjects each simultaneously submit both offers and acceptance/rejection strategies for an ultimatum game, knowing only that they had an equal chance of being assigned the role of player 1 or player 2. (Notice that under this design, *any* symmetric behavior gives both players an equal expected payoff.) In two of the cells of their experiment they attempted to condition the expectations of their subjects with a design loosely modeled on that of Roth and Schoumaker (1983), by exposing the subjects to the play of automated robots playing near equilibrium strategies, and/or by making available other subjects' past histories (including the history of their strategy choices).[38] They report that in the cells in which expectations were conditioned (but not in the unconditioned control condition) the strategies evolve in the direction of the perfect equilibrium.

Overall, the data suggest that both the kind of prior experience and the kind of game that is experienced influence the way in which behavior changes with experience. While different investigators still maintain different points of view on these matters, in the course of these experiments these differences have been substantially narrowed. In this respect, the progress that has been made in experiments concerned with experience and learning reflects the progress that has been made on understanding other aspects of bargaining behavior, in the course of interchange among experimenters with varying points of view.

This is also a case in which some of the questions left open by the experimental evidence suggest further theoretical work. In this vein, Roth and Erev (1995) explore a family of simple models of adaptive learning (recall the discussion in section III.B of chapter 1).[39] A free variable in this kind of model is the choice of initial conditions, which determine the probabilities with which strategies are played the first time that the game is played, before players have had a chance to start accumulating experience. Roth and Erev find that the learning behavior in the ultimatum game is much more sensitive to the initial conditions than is the behavior in the best shot or market games studied in Prasnikar and Roth (1992) and Roth, Prasnikar, Okuno-Fujiwara, and Zamir (1991). For a wide range of initial conditions, behavior predicted by this model in the best shot and market games converges to the perfect equilibrium prediction. However, this is not the case with the ultimatum game, which over most of this range converges to equilibria at which player 1 offers a nonnegligible percentage of the pie to player 2.[40] Only when the initial conditions are relatively close to the perfect equilibrium does the behavior converge to perfect equilibrium in the ultimatum game.[41]

Roth and Erev go further and simulate the four-country experiment of Roth et al. (1991) using this kind of learning rule. When the initial conditions are as observed in the experiments, the qualitative results of the simulation track those of the experiment. That is, when the initial propensities to play each strategy are estimated from the data observed in the first-period play in Jerusalem, Ljubljana, Pittsburgh, and Tokyo, then the simulated behavior converges to what was observed in the tenth period of the experiment. The market game results quickly approach perfect equilibrium for all four simulations, while in the simulated ultimatum game offers remain at 50 percent when begun with the initial propensities observed in Ljubljana and Pittsburgh, while offers move to 40 percent when begun with the initial propensities observed in Tokyo and Jerusalem. These results thus suggest the conjecture that the differences in ultimatum game results observed in those places may be due primarily to the different behavior of the subjects in the first period. Similarly, when the best-shot game is simulated, starting with the initial propensities observed in the full and partial information conditions of Prasnikar and Roth (1992), the full information simulation approaches perfect equilibrium faster than the partial information simulation, as in the experiment. That is, the simulations suggest that the experimental results are consistent with the hypothesis that subjects used essentially the same learning rules in all games in all locations and that the observed differences in bargaining behavior reflect different initial expectations.[42]

Of course, theoretical results do not begin to prove that this was the case, but they do suggest further experiments to distinguish between this and competing hypotheses. This is what we should expect from the interaction between theory and experiment.[43]

In closing, one aspect of a bargainer's experience that obviously has the potential to affect his future behavior is his experience with rejected proposals and other forms of disagreements and costly delays in reaching agreement. The second part of this chapter concerns such disagreements and delays.

II. Disagreements and Delays

A. The Frequency of Disagreements and Delays

One of the facts about bargaining that has struck empirical investigators of all sorts is that a nonnegligible frequency of disagreements and costly delays seems to be ubiquitous. While this would be unsurprising if it occurred only in situations that presented the bargainers with no mutually profitable agreements, most of the evidence suggests that disagreements and costly delays are pervasive even when it is evident that there are gains to be had from agreement. Kennan and Wilson (1990a) summarize this by observing that an element of regret is characteristic of bargaining: they note that most strikes, for example, are eventually settled on terms that could have been reached earlier, without incurring the costs that the strike imposes on all parties.

The game-theoretic models most often used to explain an irreducible frequency of disagreements and delays are models of incomplete information. In these models, bargainers are uncertain about some important features of one anothers' situations, which, if known, would influence the distribution of profits between the parties. The bargainers in these models convey information to one another about

Table 4.5a. Frequency of Disagreements and Delays

Study	Frequency of Inefficient Outcomes (%)
Malouf and Roth (1981)	0–37
Roth and Murnighan (1982)	8–33
Guth, Schmittberger, and Schwarze (1982)	10–29
Binmore, Shaked, and Sutton (1985)	19–42
Neelin, Sonnenschein, and Spiegel (1988)	5–35
Ochs and Roth (1989)	10–29
Forsythe, Kennan, and Sopher (1990a)	19–67

Source: Forsythe, Kennan, and Sopher 1991, 267.

Table 4.5b. Reported Dispute Rates

Study	Data	Rate (%)
Collective Bargaining: Strikes		
Card (1988)	Canadian private sector contracts	22
McConnell (1989)	U.S. private sector contracts	17
Currie and McConnell (1989)	Canadian public sector contracts	13
Collective Bargaining: Arbitrations		
Currie and McConnell (1989)	Canadian public sector contracts	32
Currie (1989)	British Columbia teachers	33
Ashenfelter and Bloom (1984)	New Jersey police	30–49
Ashenfelter et al. (1992)	Arbitration experiments	28–43
Boden (1989)	Worker's compensation	43
Other Types of Negotiations		
Ochs and Roth (1989)	Two-person bargaining games	15
Mnookin et al. (1989)	California child custody	22[a]
White (1989)	Medical malpractice	11[a]

Source: Ashenfelter and Currie 1990, 416.
[a] Percentage of cases that go to court.

their situations by their willingness to risk disagreement or to tolerate delay, in order to influence how the profits are divided.

While these models have much to recommend them, experimental evidence suggests that disagreements are pervasive even in situations (such as those discussed in the first part of this chapter: recall Table 4.1) that eliminate the most obvious potential sources of incomplete information. Forsythe, Kennan, and Sopher (1991), for example, tabulate the data from the different conditions in a number of such experiments as in Table 4.5a.

The frequencies of disagreement and costly delays observed in these experiments are not so different from those observed in a variety of field studies. Ashenfelter and Currie[44] summarize the situation as in Table 4.5b, which includes both field studies and experiments.

Other researchers agree with the rough magnitudes of the figures for field studies.[45]

The frequency of disagreement in "complete information" experiments, and the similar rates of disagreement found in other experiments and in field studies, raises some question about whether the incomplete information models are focusing on the underlying causes of disagreement. There are various approaches to answering this, and we will come back to these models in section IIC. However, before discussing the various experiments that have been conducted to explicitly examine the causes of disagreement and the effects of incomplete information, there is an empirical issue that remains to be settled, since reviewing the literature reveals an anomaly that has as yet been only incompletely explored.

While the experiments referred to above consistently report a nonnegligible frequency of disagreement and delay in the same rough range as do various field studies, these experiments have all been conducted so that the bargainers interact anonymously. In contrast, a number of bargaining experiments have been reported in which the bargainers deal with one another face to face, and these tend to report a much lower rate of disagreement. That is, the frequency of disagreements observed under face-to-face bargaining is substantially lower than that observed under anonymous bargaining, and investigators have tended to generalize from these different bodies of data in quite different directions. We consider this anomaly next.

B. Anonymous versus Face-to-Face Bargaining

In the various face-to-face bargaining experiments discussed here, each pair of bargainers engaged in unrestricted conversation over how to divide an available sum of money. In some cases the experimenter sat with the bargainers to monitor the conversation. In some cases there were restrictions on how the money could be divided. With some notable exceptions, these experiments report that observed outcomes are Pareto optimal in almost all cases.[46]

For example, Nydegger and Owen (1975) observed thirty pairs of subjects each play one of three games, in which agreement was required to divide an available pot of money. (In the absence of agreement each bargainer would receive zero.) In each of these games, every pair reached agreement on the outcome that gave the two bargainers equal monetary payoffs.

Similar results were observed in a somewhat different bargaining environment in experiments conducted by Hoffman and Spitzer (1982, 1985). In one of the conditions in their 1982 paper, pairs of subjects were asked to agree on how to divide up to $14, in face-to-face negotiations. However, if no agreement was reached one of them (the "controller," chosen just before negotiations began by the toss of a coin) could simply choose an outcome that would give her up to $12 and the other bargainer nothing. When bargainers negotiated with each other twice under these conditions, twelve out of twelve agreed to split the $14 equally (i.e., each bargainer received $7), so that the controller settled for a smaller cash payoff than she could have obtained unilaterally. In Hoffman and Spitzer's other observations of two person bargaining, only two out of thirty-two outcomes failed to maximize joint profits (and 14 of these 32 also were equal divisions, giving the controller less than he could obtain unilaterally).[47]

Of course, we have to exercise caution in interpreting these data: since these experiments are different in other ways from the anonymous experiments discussed above, it might be that the much higher levels of efficiency (and equal divisions) are due to something other than the face-to-face conduct of the bargaining.[48] However, in an experiment involving bargaining with incomplete information, Radner and Schotter (1989) reported a careful comparison of face-to-face and anonymous bargaining. They found that face-to-face bargaining captured over 99 percent of the gains from trade in an environment in which anonymous bargaining captured only 92 percent.[49]

In what follows, we consider two very different hypotheses about the causes of these differences and a new experiment to help distinguish between them.

1. Two Hypotheses

a. The Uncontrolled Social Utility Hypothesis

The hypothesis that has motivated many experimenters to conduct experiments under anonymous conditions is that face-to-face interactions call into play all of the social training we are endowed with, and may make it unusually difficult to control preferences. (Ask yourself if you would agree to be very rude to a stranger if I offer to pay you $5.) Under this interpretation, it is difficult to interpret face-to-face bargaining experiments because of the possibility that powerful social motivations that may have little to do with bargaining may be responsible for the observed behavior.[50]

Siegel and Fouraker (1960, 22–3) explained their decision to conduct anonymous bargaining experiments in this way:

> This procedure eliminates certain variables which may well be important in bargaining—variables connected with interpersonal perceptions, prejudices, incompatibilities, etc. It is our belief that such variables should either be systematically studied or controlled in experimentation on bargaining. It cannot be assumed, as has often been done, that such variables may simply be neglected. We have chosen to control these variables at this stage of our research program, with the intention of manipulating and studying them systematically in future studies.

Fouraker and Siegel never did get to the future studies: Their 1963 monograph, published after Siegel's death, also studied anonymous bargaining. But while I am not aware of any subsequent bargaining experiments directed at dissecting the components of face-to-face interaction that contribute to the low incidence of disagreement, there is abundant experimental evidence in the social psychology literature that small differences in the social environment can cause large differences in behavior. For example, Dawes (1990) summarizes a variety of experiments on public goods provision in which manipulations designed to alter individuals' feelings of group identity have substantial effects on the amount of public goods provided. Thus there is indirect evidence that makes plausible the hypothesis that the results of face-to-face bargaining experiments may reflect motivations deriving primarily from uncontrolled aspects of the social environment.

b. The Communication Hypothesis

The counterhypothesis that I think is at least implicit in the work of many experimenters who have focused on face-to-face bargaining is that there are many channels of communication available to face-to-face bargainers that are inevitably eliminated by any procedures that secure anonymity, even if those procedures otherwise allow fairly extensive communication. For example, Radner and Schotter (1989) compared anonymous bargaining in which only numerical bids and offers could be exchanged with face-to-face bargaining in which there was unrestricted verbal communication. They note that they cannot conclude that the high levels of efficiency in face-to-face bargaining were due simply to the fact that the bargainers could talk to each other, since the levels of efficiency they obtain also exceed those reported in Roth and Murnighan (1982), in which bargaining was conducted anonymously via computer terminals, and bargainers could freely exchange typed messages (recall the discussion of this experiment in chapter 1). They raise the question of whether the high levels of efficiency might arise from the channels of communication that face-to-face bargaining makes available *in addition* to the purely linguistic channel.

While I am not aware of any experiments designed to explore this hypothesis in the context of bargaining, there is ample evidence from the large literature on nonverbal communication generally that face-to-face communication employs many channels of communication, including tone of voice, body language, and facial expression. (For example, Grammer et al. [1988] study the "eyebrow flash," which they find serves in a variety of cultures as "a 'social marking tool' which emphasizes the meaning of other facial cues, head movements and even verbal statements.") Thus there is indirect evidence that makes plausible the hypothesis that the low observed levels of disagreement and inefficient agreements in face-to-face bargaining are due to the communication opportunities that such bargaining provides, and that the higher levels of disagreement in anonymous bargaining are due to the restricted channels of communication that are available to anonymous bargainers even when messages are allowed.

2. A New Experiment

Plausible conflicting hypotheses are what the experimental method thrives on, and I take the opportunity here to report briefly a small experiment that takes a step towards investigating the hypotheses just described. Bargaining in an ultimatum game (to divide $10) is compared under three conditions. In the first, baseline condition, bargaining is anonymous, with no communication other than written

Table 4.6. Comparisons of Ultimatum Games Played Anonymously

Condition	Disagreement Frequency (%)	Mean Offers (x_2)	Standard Error	Number of Observations	Percentage of Offers with $x_2 = 5.00$	Percentage of Offers with $x_2 = 5 \pm 0.50$
No communication	33	4.27	1.17	189	31	50
Unrestricted face-to-face communication	4	4.85	0.73	49	75	83
Social face-to-face communication only	6	4.70	0.46	49	39	82

Notes: In order to be comparable to the data in the next two rows, all data in the first row are for the first seven (out of ten) rounds of bargaining. For all ten rounds the corresponding figures are as follows: disagreement frequency is 28%, mean x_2 is 4.30, standard error is 1.05, number of observations is 270, percentage of offers with $x_2 = 5.00$ is 33%, and percentage of offers with $x_2 = 5 \pm 0.50$ is 51%.

offers and acceptances-rejections. In the second condition, there is unrestricted face-to-face communication: prior to making an offer, the buyer and seller have two minutes to discuss the game (or anything else). In the third condition, the buyer and seller have two minutes to converse, but are restricted to "social" conversation; they are required to learn each others' first name and year in school and are *not* allowed to discuss the bargaining game.[51]

If prior observations that face-to-face bargaining yields few disagreements are well founded, the unrestricted face-to-face communication condition should yield fewer disagreements than the anonymous bargaining condition. The comparison of the unrestricted and social communication conditions will then provide a test of the two hypotheses discussed above. If the lower disagreement frequency in the unrestricted communication condition is due to the increased communication, then the substantial decrease in the amount of communication allowed in the social communication condition, which eliminates the most germane verbal communication, should cause the disagreement frequency in that condition to be substantially higher than in the unrestricted communication condition. But if the lower disagreement frequency is due to social pressures arising directly from the face-to-face encounter and unrelated to what the bargainers say to each other about the bargaining, then the disagreement frequency in the social communication condition should be comparable to that in the unrestricted communication condition.

The results are summarized in Table 4.6. The disagreement rate declines from 33 percent in the anonymous condition to 4 percent in the face-to-face with unrestricted communication condition, which conforms with the frequencies of disagreements obtained under those conditions in earlier experiments. But the

ALVIN E. ROTH

disagreement frequency when only social communication is allowed is only 6 percent: that is, it does *not* rise appreciably (or significantly).[52] Thus the results cast doubt on the communication hypothesis and support the uncontrolled social utility hypothesis as an explanation of disagreement frequency.

Note that the data suggest that the presence or absence of unrestricted verbal communication may have influenced the distribution of agreements in the two face-to-face conditions, even though it did not influence the disagreement frequency. The percentages of precisely equal divisions in the anonymous and social communication conditions are much lower than in the unrestricted communication condition.[53] But this data set is not large enough to know if this difference is important, especially since when we look at offers that are within fifty cents of an equal division, the two face-to-face conditions resemble each other more than the anonymous condition.

3. Some Further Experiments

After these results were presented at the Handbook Workshop, several of the experimenters who participated conducted follow-up experiments. The first of these to be reported was by Hoffman, McCabe, Shachat, and Smith (1991), at the annual convention of the American Economic Association. They proposed that, since face-to-face interaction among bargainers had such a pronounced effect compared to anonymous bargaining, perhaps a similar effect might be traced to the fact that subjects in these experiments are known to the experimenter. In particular, they proposed to compare games in which (following the usual practice) the experimenters could identify how each subject had behaved with games in which the experimenters would know only how a group of subjects had behaved, and would not know precisely what each subject had done. Their hypothesis was that the failure to observe perfect equilibrium in ultimatum games might be due to the fact that subjects felt they were being observed by the experimenter (e.g., player 1s might feel embarrassed to demand too much for fear of appearing greedy to the experimenter), and that extreme offers, as predicted by the perfect equilibrium, might therefore be forthcoming if experimenters only observed the actions of anonymous subjects.

To test this hypothesis they designed an experiment that examined both ultimatum games and dictator games,[54] and that included an anonymity condition for dictator games in which subjects passed sealed envelopes in which they received their pay without being directly observed by the experimenter.

Hoffman et al. reported that for dictator games conducted under non-anonymity conditions and using the instructions of Forsythe et al (1994), the distribution of offers was similar to that observed by Forsythe et al. (with a mode at the equilibrium offer), while the dictator games in the anonymity condition with the new instructions yielded an even larger mode at the equilibrium offer, although nonequilibrium offers were not extinguished. Their reported ultimatum game results concerned games run under nonanonymity conditions with different instructions. Offers were lower in cells in which the instructions gave the player 1s the "moral authority" to make low offers, but in no cells did offers approach the perfect equilibrium prediction of zero.[55]

On the basis of these results Hoffman et al. concluded that when bargainers were anonymous not only to each other but also to the experimenter, perfect equilibrium offers would more likely be observed. In general, they concluded (Hoffman et al. 1991, 1992):

> The results also emphasize that the argument for the use of anonymity in bargaining experiments as a means of controlling for social influences on preferences has not gone far enough. The presence of the experimenter, as one who knows subjects' bargaining outcomes, is one of the most significant of all treatments for reducing the incidence of self-regarding behavior.

There were a number of reasons to treat these conclusions cautiously, however, in part because of the way the experiment had been conducted and reported. In particular, the results Hoffman et al. attributed to their anonymity condition appeared to be confounded with other possible causes, because the instructions to subjects were radically different in their anonymity and nonanonymity conditions, and because different experimenters conducted the anonymity and nonanonymity conditions. Furthermore, results run under the anonymity condition were reported only for the dictator game and not for the ultimatum game. Thus the conclusions about anonymity rested on differences observed in offers made in dictator games under their anonymity and nonanonymity conditions. The ultimatum games they reported were run under nonanonymity conditions only, and only the proposals made by player 1s were reported—whether they were accepted or rejected by player 2s was not reported. In addition, no hypothesis was offered as to why the lack of subject-experimenter anonymity might inhibit players from making or accepting extreme demands in ultimatum games given that extreme payoffs are not inhibited in other games, such as the best shot games or sequential market games discussed earlier.

To address these concerns, Bolton and Zwick (1992) conducted an experiment that attempted to see whether the conclusions of Hoffman et al. about anonymity could be supported in an experiment that would not be subject to such criticisms. Regarding the difficulty of drawing conclusions about ultimatum games from dictator games (and the importance of reporting disagreement frequencies in ultimatum games) they note:

> Recall that lab ultimatum game investigators consistently report that second movers reject money. It is a key observation. In particular, even if first movers do act to maximize their personal earnings, they will not want to make the perfect equilibrium offer if a large enough proportion of second movers are going to reject it.

And regarding the importance of uniform instructions across cells of the experiment, they note:

Because the control of information passing between experimenter and subject is crucial, we conducted the entire experiment from a script, referred to as the Experimental Protocol. It provides a thorough description of all remarks made by the experimenter during the experimental session.

The use of a uniform script also reduces most of the potential for introducing uncontrolled variation in conditions when different experimenters conduct different cells of the experiment, but Bolton and Zwick apparently also used the same personnel for each cell of their experiment.

In addition to comparing ultimatum games under anonymous and nonanonymous play, Bolton and Zwick examine a game that has the same move sequence as the ultimatum game and the same incentive structure as the dictator game, which they call the "impunity" game (since player 1s may make low offers "with impunity"). In the impunity game player 1 proposes how to split the pie, and player 2 may accept or reject, but player 1 receives the share he proposed for himself even if player 2 rejects—player 2's acceptance or rejection determines only if player 2 receives the share that player 1 allocated to her. Because ultimatum and impunity games have the same structure, the three cells of their experiment (anonymous and nonanonymous ultimatum games and nonanonymous impunity games) could be conducted from the same script with only very minor modifications.[56]

In examining their data, Bolton and Zwick propose to test two competing hypotheses, which they call the anonymity and punishment hypotheses. By the anonymity hypothesis they mean the conclusion of Hoffman et al. that an important determinant of observed behavior will be whether or not the experimenter can observe the actions chosen by individual subjects in the experiment. In contrast, the punishment hypothesis, motivated by the earlier experimental findings for bargaining games, is that an important determinant of player 2's behavior will be a desire to "punish" player 1 when he makes offers that are "too low" and that the behavior of player 2s will be an important determinant of the behavior of player 1s, who will attempt to maximize their earnings while taking the anticipated response of player 2 into account.

What Bolton and Zwick found is that anonymity made little difference—in the first five rounds of their ultimatum games, offers by player 1s were slightly lower in the nonanonymous condition, and in the last five rounds they were slightly lower in the anonymous condition, and in both conditions behavior was comparable to that observed in previous (nonanonymous) ultimatum game experiments. In contrast, the absence of punishment opportunities had a dramatic effect—in the impunity game virtually 100 percent of the plays in the last five rounds were perfect equilibrium plays, with player 2 receiving the smallest feasible payoff. They conclude that "the punishment hypothesis strongly outperforms the anonymity hypothesis. . . ."[57]

Notice that Bolton and Zwick's impunity game joins a growing list of games—including the best shot and market games discussed earlier—in which experiments have shown that extreme perfect equilibria can be descriptive of observed behavior. As Bolton and Zwick note, this "provides evidence that first movers act in a self-interested manner even if the experimenter can observe their actions." That is, not only did Bolton and Zwick observe directly that the presence or absence of subject-experimenter anonymity did not influence the frequency of extreme demands, they also observed that extreme demands could be observed with very high frequency even without subject-experimenter anonymity.

Bolton, Katok, and Zwick (forthcoming) conducted a subsequent experiment concerned with dictator games, in order to better analyze whether the effect observed for those games by Hoffman et al. might nevertheless be due to subject-experimenter anonymity or if it was more likely due to the other uncontrolled differences between cells in that experiment. To this end, Bolton, Katok, and Zwick conducted an experiment in which dictator games were examined under different presentation conditions, and with and without anonymity under one of the presentation conditions. They observed that the game was sensitive to presentation effects, and in one of their (nonanonymous) conditions they observed a very large mode at the perfect equilibrium offer. However, they observed essentially no effect due to subject-experimenter anonymity, when games in which the experimenter could not observe which subjects made which offers were compared with other games, presented in the same way, in which the experimenter could make these observations. They conclude (27):

> We find no evidence for the anonymity hypothesis. . . . Comparison of our data with that of previous studies suggests that differences in the context of the game, affected by differences in written directions and independent of experimenter observation, account for the observed differences across dictator studies.

Thus there is no evidence that observation by the experimenter inhibits player 1 in ultimatum games, nor that it is the cause of extreme demands in dictator and impunity games. Rather, the evidence supports the view that the different behavior observed in games with similar perfect equilibrium predictions is due to differences in the games, off the equilibrium path. (The off the equilibrium path difference between ultimatum games and dictator or impunity games is particularly clear, since on the equilibrium path no offer is rejected in any of the games, but only in the ultimatum game is there an off-the-equilibrium-path possibility that an offer will be rejected). The evidence further suggests that the results of ultimatum game experiments show some sensitivity to how the games are presented to the subjects, but that this sensitivity is insufficient to overcome the robust observation that outcomes remain far from the perfect equilibrium prediction.

Two further studies round out the tale. Berg, Dickhaut, and McCabe (1993), in a paper presented at a conference on experimental economics in Amsterdam in 1993, reported an experiment in which a subject decided how much (x) of his \$10 show up fee to send to another (anonymous) subject in another room, who would receive three times the amount of money sent by the first subject. The second subject would then decide how much of this amount (\$3x) to return to the first.

Perfect equilibrium in this game predicts that no money is sent in either direction. However, the authors found that, under conditions of subject-experimenter anonymity similar to those developed by Bolton and Zwick, nonnegligible sums are sent in both directions. Thus the results of this experiment further disconfirm the conjecture of Hoffman, McCabe, Shachat, and Smith (1991, 1992) that subject-experimenter anonymity would promote perfect equilibrium play.[58]

Finally, Hoffman, McCabe, and Smith (1993), in a paper presented at the Southern Economic Association meetings in November, reported an ultimatum game experiment conducted in the usual way (i.e. without subject-experimenter anonymity), whose chief aim was to see whether a large increase in the monetary incentives would move the results closer to the perfect equilibrium prediction. To this end, they compared ultimatum games played one time where the amount to be divided was either $10 or $100, in units of either $1 or $10, respectively. In addition, they again compared the effects of presenting the game to the subjects by means of different sets of instructions. In this experiment they compared each of two sets of instructions both with $10 games and $100 games so that the separate effects of instructions and monetary incentives could be reliably assessed.

Their experiment confirmed that different sets of instructions could influence the distribution of offers, although in no case did they observe any substantial frequency of perfect equilibrium offers (of $0 or $1 in the $10 games, or of $0 or $10 in the $100 games). Rather, under both sets of instructions, for both $10 and $100 games, offers were predominantly much higher, ranging up to $5 in the $10 games and $50 in the $100 games, and consistent with distributions observed previously.

As to the effect of changing the stakes from $10 to $100, they write that, under both sets of instructions (6), "We cannot reject the hypothesis that the offers are identical with $10 stakes and with $100 stakes."

Thus we see here a series of experiments. one of whose results seems to be that even initially very skeptical investigators are becoming persuaded that the experimental results observed in ultimatum games are not easily displaced artifacts of the experimental methods, but rather represent a very robust phenomenon.

4. Recapitulation of the Methodological Issues

The methodological issues raised by the experiments considered in this section can usefully be thought of at three different levels of generality, concerning the design of individual experiments, concerning the issues of experimental control raised by this whole series of experiments, and concerning the role that series of experiments play in revising hypotheses and resolving discrepancies.

At the level of the individual experiment, it is a familiar observation that it is easiest to reliably observe the effect of a particular variable by changing only that variable. Designing appropriate experiments may require considerable ingenuity, but, as the experiment of Bolton and Zwick shows, a really well-designed experiment can eliminate a great deal of potential confusion.

Notice that the design questions associated with attributing an observed effect to a particular cause may be more complex. For example, while I do not think that anyone can reasonably dispute that subject-experimenter anonymity had at most a negligible effect on the ultimatum games in Bolton and Zwick's experiment (or on dictator games in Bolton, Katok, and Zwick [1993]), it is easy to imagine that some investigator will come up with an alternative explanation of the big difference they observed between ultimatum and impunity games. The reason is that an experimental design intended to distinguish between alternative hypotheses controls for the variables that are relevant for those hypotheses (in this case, the structure of the two games), but may not have controlled for variables relevant to some other (perhaps as yet unstated) hypothesis. Thus there is a strong sense in which "appropriate" experimental designs are creatures of their time—they depend not only on what is being tested, but on what are the most plausible hypotheses at the time they are being tested.

Concerning the issues of experimental control raised by this series of experiments, an analogy may be useful. Chemical reactions are studied in glass vessels rather than in pots made of metal, or even clay, because glass is more inert, less volatile. Before chemists figured this out, they often must have had to deal with anomalous results coming from investigators who used different kinds of pots. Of course, there are materials that are even less volatile than glass, and these may be required to effectively control certain kinds of experiments, but for most purposes glass seems to do fine. In a similar way, face-to-face interaction is a volatile environment in which to conduct economics experiments, and most investigators have followed Siegal and Fouraker in avoiding it and conducting experiments in environments that preserve between-subject anonymity. We have reconfirmed that there is good reason for this. And the experiments of Bolton and Zwick and Bolton, Katok, and Zwick strongly suggest that between-subject anonymity is enough for most purposes, since little if any additional effect was observed due to subject-experimenter anonymity. And just as face-to-face interaction is volatile, so too may be instructions that try to give players the "moral authority" to take certain actions or that in other ways may induce experimenter-demand effects by too clearly indicating the goals of the experimenters.

But while there is ample reason for preferring glass to clay for conducting most experiments, this certainly does not mean that it is not interesting to study the chemistry of clays. Even if the phenomena observed in face-to-face bargaining experiments largely reflect uncontrolled aspects of social interaction, these are worth studying, not only as a means of learning which laboratory procedures are especially volatile, but also as a means of understanding subjects' social perceptions.[59] For example, Burrows and Loomes (1990) use Hoffman and Spitzer's (1985) observation that observed agreements were sensitive to noneconomic aspects of the instructions to motivate an investigation aimed primarily at elucidating subjects' notions of fairness.[60]

Furthermore, the fact that face-to-face bargaining may be difficult to study does not mean that it is unimportant or that its presence or absence may not alter the course of negotiations (even) over stakes much larger than can be studied in the laboratory. Newspaper accounts of bilateral meetings between American presidents and their foreign counterparts are full of analyses of the personal relationships established or not established between the leaders, and there is much anecdotal testimony that such face-to-face meetings may influence negotiations (although not always in the direction of efficiency).[61] Similarly, the fact that many negotiations are conducted through intermediaries (such as lawyers or real estate agents) suggests that many people are prepared to go to considerable expense to avoid face-to-face negotiations, perhaps because they feel the outcome will be different (and more profitable) if the social pressures arising from face-to-face negotiations between principals are avoided.[62] Of course, these phenomena can be explained in other ways as well, which is why it would be useful to study them under controlled conditions.

Finally, since most of the material in this handbook addresses the role that series of experiments play in refining hypotheses and resolving different points of view, let me focus here simply on the *speed* with which this process has proceeded in the present case, in comparison to what we might expect if we had to rely exclusively on field data. In a relatively short period of time, a consensus seems to have (re)emerged about the role played by anonymity between subjects (versus face-to-face interaction); an experiment was reported that suggested to its authors that a similar role might be played by subject-experimenter anonymity; and new experiments were conducted and showed that this was unlikely to be the case. What makes this a relatively fast process is not merely that experimental data can often be gathered more quickly than field data, but that experimental data can be gathered to fit precisely the question of interest (e.g., hypotheses about ultimatum games can be tested on ultimatum games). Furthermore, although investigators with different hypotheses may be inclined to collect different data, and even report different aspects of it, the fact that experimenters all have access to essentially the same data universe, since they can conduct their own experiments, means that investigators are much less dependent on obtaining access to data than in situations where access is limited either by expense or the uniqueness of the field situations being studied.

Returning to substantive matters, the material in this section reconfirms the importance of disagreements in determining the nature of agreements, and the next section considers experiments designed to investigate the causes of disagreements.

C. Tests of Hypotheses about the Causes of Disagreements and Costly Delays

The main approaches to modeling disagreements and delays in bargaining can be ordered by how much information they include about the environment, and in how much detail they model the behavior of the bargainers. The simplest models attempt to relate disagreement frequency to features of the bargaining situation such as the shape of the set of possible agreements (and the consequent divergence of interest between the bargainers) or the value of potential agreements and the costliness of delays in reaching agreements. These models are nonstrategic, in that they do not attempt to model the detailed behavior of the bargainers. A more detailed approach seeks to model the bargaining as a game of complete information, in which the same kinds of features of the bargaining situation, together with rules of bargaining, produce equilibrium behavior on the part of the bargainers that in turn determines the frequency of disagreement. And the most detailed attempts involve modeling bargaining as a game of incomplete information, in which each bargainer takes into account different kinds of private information in determining his own (equilibrium) behavior and in forming his expectations about the behavior of the other bargainer.

Experimental investigations of each of these classes of models are only in their earliest stages so that there are as yet no extended series of closely connected experiments to report. However, in reviewing some of the initial steps that have been taken, it is easy to see how even initial experiments raise questions that suggest further experiments.

1. Nonstrategic Models

A nonstrategic model proposed by Axelrod (1970) was tested in an experiment reported by Malouf and Roth (1981). Axelrod had proposed a measure of what he called "conflict of interest" inherent in a bargaining situation, based (like Nash's solution[63]) on the set of feasible expected utility payoffs available to the bargainers, together with their utilities in the event that no agreement is reached. The idea is that when the set of Pareto optimal agreements consists of a unique point at which both players receive their maximum payoff, as in game 1 of Figure 4.8, there is no conflict of interest between the players. But when the maximum individually rational payoffs of the players are incompatible, some conflict of interest exists. (Because this is a theory based on the independently measured expected utilities of the bargainers, the origin and scale of the units in Figure 4.8 are not important for determining the conflict of interest. Here we take the utilities in case of disagreement to be normalized to (0,0): the experimental implementation of the games will be discussed in a moment.) More formally, consider the rectangle formed by the players' disagreement payoffs and their maximum individually rational payoffs. For the games in Figure 4.8, these are the rectangles whose lower left corner is (0,0), and whose upper right corners are (60, 30) in game 1, (90, 40) in game 2, (90, 50) in game 3, and (90, 90) in game 4. Axelrod proposed that conflict of interest for each game could be measured by the proportion of the associated rectangle that is not in the set of feasible agreements. By this measure, the conflict of interest is 0 for game 1, and it rises to its maximum of .5 for game 4, with games 2 and 3 having intermediate values (of .22 and .27, respectively).

Malouf and Roth (1981) reported an experiment involving the four games in Figure 4.8, to test the hypothesis that the frequency of disagreements would be greater in games with a higher conflict of interest as measured in this way. Since Axelrod's measure was defined in terms of the bargainers' expected utilities, the

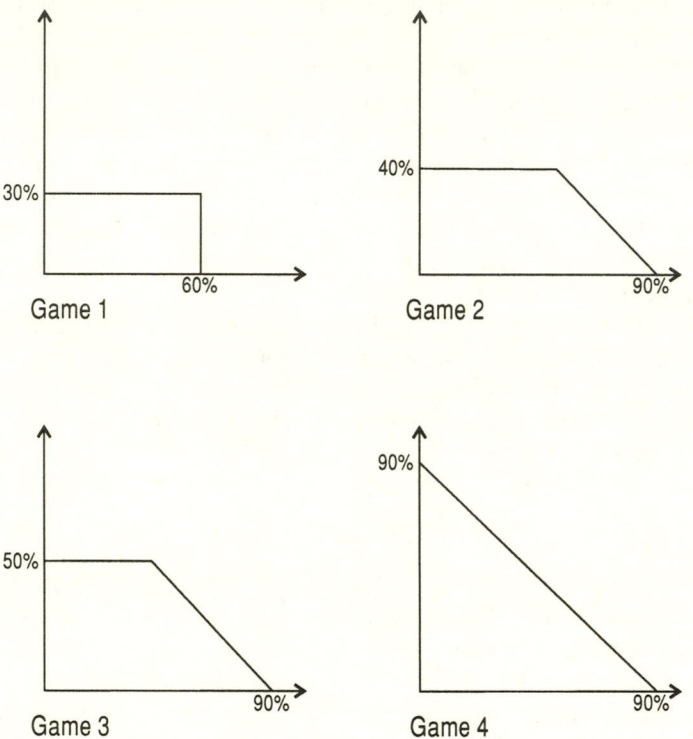

Figure 4.8. Four games with increasing "conflict of interest." *Source:* Roth and Malouf 1981.

games were implemented as binary lottery games with large and small prizes of $10 and $5, respectively.[64] In each game, players divided lottery tickets subject to a restriction on the maximum percentage each player was allowed to receive. (As indicated in Figure 4.8, this maximum was 60 percent for player 1 in game 1 and 90 percent in games 2, 3, and 4, while for player 2 it was 30, 40, 50, and 90% in games 1 through 4.) The principal variables of interest were the mean time to agreement in each game and the percentage of disagreements.

Although the mean times to reach agreement were roughly consistent with the ordering of the games by the conflict of interest measure,[65] the frequencies of disagreement were not. The observed frequencies of disagreement for the four games were 0, 21, 37, and 0 percent, respectively. That is, in game 4 as well as game 1, no disagreements were observed.

Looking at the agreements reached in the four games, an explanation immediately suggests itself. While in games 2 and 3 there is some variance in how the lottery tickets were divided between the two bargainers when agreement was reached, in game 1 almost all of the agreements were for a (60, 30) division, and in game 4 almost all of the agreements were for a (45, 45) division. Thus, despite the incompatibility in the maximum payoffs to the two players in game 4, captured by the high value of the conflict of interest measure for that game, the symmetry of the game serves to focus the attention of the players on the equal division agreement, just as the lack of conflict of interest in game 1 concentrates the agreements on the unique Pareto optimal agreement. To put it another way, these results suggest that the frequency of disagreements increases with dispersion in the terms of observed agreements. This should not be surprising insofar as the failure to reach agreement presumably reflects that the two bargainers have different expectations about the terms of agreement, and such different expectations are easier to maintain in an environment in which observed agreements are more diverse.

We turn next to examine the experimental evidence in the context of a nonstrategic model that relates the frequency of disagreement to its cost.

Two closely related experiments, by Sopher (1990), and by Forsythe, Kennan, and Sopher (forthcoming), were conducted to test an appealingly simple hypothesis about disagreements formulated by Kennan (1980). Kennan's hypothesis, which was formulated to explain the rate of strikes and settlements in labor management negotiations, is that the incidence and duration of strikes will be a decreasing function of the marginal cost of a strike and an increasing function of the total size of the pie to be divided. Forsythe et al. used a four-cell factorial design in which the pie size ($4.00 and $8.00) and marginal cost ($1.00 and $.50) were varied,[66] in a manner made clear by their description of one cell of their experiment (12):

> Games in this cell consisted of Years which were 8 Months long. In each Year, a "Pot" of $9.60 was available for division between the two bargaining partners. If no agreement was reached in a given Month, the pot was reduced by $9.60/8 = $1.20, and the bargainers received their threat points of $.70 and 0, respectively. Thus, the marginal strike cost is 1.20 − .70 − 0 = $.50, and the total pie size is $.50 × 8 = $4.00."

Bargainers negotiated anonymously via written messages and proposals.

Although both experiments observe a substantial number of periods in which agreement is not reached, the results of these experiments yield little support, on the range of costs studied, for the prediction that strike activity (i.e., periods in which bargainers fail to reach agreement) falls as marginal costs rise. But both experiments report weak support for the proposition that strike activity increases as the size of the pie increases.

Clearly these results suggest directions for future work. The hypothesis that periods of disagreement will decline as the costs of disagreement rise is an appealing one, and it certainly still seems possible that a differently designed experiment (perhaps with larger costs, or with out of pocket costs charged against an initial endowment) might detect such an effect. In the other direction, because of the way the size of the pie was increased, an alternative hypothesis about the increased disagreement frequency observed in the cells with larger pie size is that this increase is related to the larger number of periods over which bargaining took place (e.g., because of the increased incentive in longer games to build a reputation in the early periods as a tough bargainer). The size of the pie and the length of the bargaining horizon are matters that cannot always be distinguished in field studies, but could be varied independently in the laboratory.

An experiment in which the frequency of disagreements *was* observed to be inversely correlated with the cost of disagreement is reported by Ashenfelter, Currie, Farber, and Spiegel (1992), who considered bargaining followed by binding arbitration in the case of disagreements. In the labor relations literature, the hypothesis that reducing the cost of disagreement (by imposing binding arbitration) will increase the frequency of disagreement is referred to as the "chilling effect" of arbitration. It has furthermore been hypothesized that disagreements will be more frequent under conventional arbitration (in which the arbitrator chooses the final outcome if the parties fail to agree) than under final offer arbitration (in which the arbitrator must choose the final offer proposed by one of the two parties to the dispute if they fail to agree).

A major problem in the design of any experimental test of bargaining in which arbitration plays a role is that arbitration is (at least) a three-party activity, involving two bargainers and an arbitrator. If the arbitrator is to be one of the subjects in the experiment, a critical design feature will be how to design the incentives for the arbitrator, which will influence not only his behavior, but also, therefore, the behavior of the bargainers. Ashenfelter et al. find an elegant solution to this design problem, by incorporating results from the field studies of Ashenfelter and Bloom (1984) and Ashenfelter (1987). These studies suggest that the selection process for arbitrators causes them to behave in such a way that one arbitrator is statistically exchangeable for another. The idea is that, since arbitrators must be acceptable to both parties, arbitrators who are known to favor one side or the other are eliminated. Consequently in Ashenfelter et al.'s experiment, the arbitrator is represented as a random draw from a fixed distribution. The outcome over which the bargainers negotiate is a number between 100 to 500, with one bargainer profiting from higher numbers and the other from lower numbers. (Players had symmetric payoff schedules, but each player knew only his own payoffs.) When bargaining is to be followed by conventional arbitration, the outcome in the case of disagreement is simply the number drawn by the arbitrator. When bargaining is followed by final offer arbitration, the outcome in the case of disagreement is whichever of the bargainers' final offers is closer to the number drawn by the arbitrator.

Data were gathered from fixed pairs of subjects who negotiated with each other for twenty periods. In the first ten periods there was no arbitration; failure to reach agreement resulted in a zero distribution for that period to both parties. Prior to the second ten periods, the bargainers were informed that either conventional or final offer arbitration would determine the outcome in each remaining period, in case no agreement was reached by the bargainers themselves. The bargainers were not informed that the arbitrator was a random distribution, but were given a list, generated from the arbitrator's distribution, of what they were told were the arbitrator's last one hundred decisions. Aside from varying the form of arbitration, the experiment also varied the variance of the arbitrator's distribution in the conventional arbitration conditions.

In all of the experimental conditions, Ashenfelter et al. observed a higher rate of disagreements in the second ten rounds, when disagreement resulted in arbitration, than in the first ten rounds, when disagreement resulted in zero payoffs to both bargainers. They also observed that the frequency of disagreements in the conventional arbitration condition declined as the variance of the arbitrator's distribution increased. Both of these observations are consistent with the hypothesis that disagreement frequency is inversely related to the cost of disagreement, the idea being that higher arbitrator variance increases the cost of arbitration to risk averse bargainers. However, contrary to the hypothesis that final offer arbitration has less of a chilling effect than conventional arbitration, Ashenfelter et al. observed that the dispute rate under final offer arbitration was no lower than under conventional arbitration.

Ashenfelter et al. are careful to note that an alternative explanation of the higher dispute rates observed when arbitration was present is possible, due to a feature of their experimental design that confounds two effects. The source of this confound is that in the first ten periods the bargaining situation was symmetric, with the symmetric agreement being 300 (recall that one party prefers higher numbers, the other lower numbers). However, the second ten periods (the arbitration periods) were not symmetric, since the mean of the arbitrator's distribution was 350, that is, since the arbitrated solutions tended to favor one of the bargainers in case no agreement was reached. Recall from the discussion of Malouf and Roth (1981), earlier in this section, that negotiations in nonsymmetric situations had more disputes than negotiations in symmetric situations. Ashenfelter et al. therefore point out that the asymmetry introduced in their arbitration periods may also account for some of the increase in disagreement frequency that they observe.

Taken together, the work of Malouf and Roth (1981), Sopher (1990), Forsythe et al. (1991), and Ashenfelter et al. (1992) suggest that there may be considerable progress to be made by considering theories of bargaining that depend (only) on the gross features of the bargaining problem. We turn next to consider some experiments motivated by theories that depend on the more detailed strategic structure of the bargaining game.

2. Strategic Models

a. Complete Information Models

Recall that, in the binary lottery bargaining games reviewed in chapter 1, agreements were often bimodal, with one mode at the equal division of lottery tickets and the other at the division yielding equal expected payoffs. Two questions arise in considering how one might try to incorporate this observation into a theory of bargaining. The first is, what causes some potential agreements and not others to become focal points in this way? The second is, given that the bargainers recognize that (for whatever reason) certain potential agreements are especially credible bargaining positions, how will this affect aspects of the bargaining such as the frequency of disagreements? In Roth (1985) I undertook to look at this latter question and to test the predictions of a very simple strategic model.

Table 4.7. A Coordination Model of Disagreement

(50, 50)	$(\frac{1}{2}(50 - h), (\frac{1}{2}(150 - h))$	$h \geq 50 \geq d_1$
(d_1, d_2)	$(h, 100 - h)$	$50 \geq 100 - h \geq d_2$

Source: Roth 1985.

In particular, consider a highly structured model of a binary lottery bargaining situation in which two credible bargaining positions are recognized, the (50, 50) division of lottery tickets and another division $(h, 100 - h)$ where $h \geq 50$. If both players agree on one of these two divisions then it is the outcome of the game. If each player holds out for the division more favorable to him, then disagreement results, and if each player is willing to accept the division more favorable to the other, then a compromise agreement is reached whose expected value is the average of the two credible divisions. This game is represented as a two-by-two matrix game in Table 4.7, in which the strategies of the players are simply which of the two divisions to demand, and the disagreement utilities of the players are given by (d_1, d_2).

There are two pure strategy equilibria of this game, each of which results in one of the two credible divisions. There is also a mixed strategy equilibrium, which can be taken as a simple model of disagreement frequency as a function of the distance between the two focal divisions. That is, at the mixed strategy equilibrium, disagreements occur because of coordination failure of the kind proposed by Schelling (1960), and discussed in other contexts in chapter 3. In particular, a disagreement occurs whenever player 1 demands h and player 2 demands 50. At the mixed strategy equilibrium, the probability that 1 demands h is $p = (h - 50)/(150 - h - 2d_2)$ and the probability that player 2 demands 50 is $q = (h - 50)/(h + 50 - 2d_1)$, so the probability of disagreement, pq, is an increasing function of h. That is, as the second focal point becomes more distant from (50, 50), the predicted frequency of disagreement increases. (This hypothesis is, of course, consistent with the more general notion discussed above, in connection with the experiment of Malouf and Roth [1981] that the disagreement frequency is positively associated with the observed dispersion of agreements.)

Table 4.8 considers the disagreement frequency of three earlier experiments that allow a rough test of this prediction, in that they include games with values of h of 50, 75, and 80.[67] The prediction of the mixed strategy equilibrium is that disagreements should be observed with frequencies of 0 percent, 7 percent, and 10 percent respectively for these values of h, and overall the observed frequencies of disagreement are 7 percent, 18 percent, and 25 percent. Thus the observed frequencies of disagreement on this data set move in the direction predicted by this simple coordination model.

Of course, the data in Table 4.8 was assembled from experiments designed for other purposes. It thus seemed worthwhile to conduct an experiment to more specifically test this prediction of the mixed strategy equilibrium model of disagreement frequency. Such an experiment was reported in Roth, Murnighan, and

Table 4.8. Frequency of Disagreement

Experiment	(50, 50)	(75, 25)	(80, 20)
		$(h, 100 - h)$	
Roth and Malouf (1979)	2% (1/54)[a]	14% (3/21)[b]	
Roth, Malouf, and Murnighan (1981)	6% (2/32)[c]	20% (6/30)[d]	24% (7/29)[e]
Roth and Murnighan (1982)	11% (7/63)[f]		25% (37/146)[g]
All experiments combined	7% (10/149)	18% (9/51)	25% (44/175)
Prediction of the coordination model (mixed-strategy equilibrium)	0%	7%	10%

Source: Roth 1985.

[a] Games with only a (50,50) focal point in this experiment are all those in the partial-information condition, and games with equal prizes for both bargainers in the full-information condition.

[b] Games with a (75, 25) focal point in this experiment are games 3 and 4 in the full-information condition.

[c] Games with only a (50, 50) focal point in this experiment are all games in the low-information condition.

[d] Games with a (75, 25) focal point in this experiment are games 1 and 3 in the high-information condition.

[e] Games with an (80, 20) focal point in this experiment are games 2 and 4 in the high-information condition.

[f] Games with only a (50, 50) focal point in this experiment are those in which neither player knows both prizes, in the common- and non-common-knowledge conditions.

[g] Games with an (80,20) focal point in this experiment are all those in conditions in which $5 player knows both prizes.

Schoumaker (1988). It involved binary lottery games in which both bargainers had the same low prize (i.e., their payoff in the event of disagreement, or if they lost the lottery resulting from an agreement) of 0, but different high prizes. Games were examined with high prizes for the two bargainers of $10 and $15, $6 and $14, $5 and $20, and $4 and $36. Thus the equal expected value agreements in these four conditions were (60, 40), (70, 30), (80, 20), and (90, 10), respectively. That is, in terms of the model of Roth (1985) the values of h were 60, 70, 80, and 90.

As in the previous binary lottery bargaining experiments the greater the difference between the prizes of the two bargainers, the higher the mean percentage of lottery tickets received by the bargainer with the smaller prize. However, unlike some of the previous experiments, the distribution of agreements was approximately normal rather than bimodal. And, contrary to the predictions of the mixed strategy equilibrium of the coordination game (and contrary to my expectations), the disagreement frequency stayed approximately constant as h varied from 60 to 90. Thus the simple coordination model seems *too* simple to organize the data on disagreement frequencies in this case.

b. Incomplete Information Models

A class of more complex models are models of incomplete information, in which each player may have some private information about his own situation that is unavailable to the other players, while having only probabilistic information about the private information of other players. Following Harsanyi (1967, 1968), models of games of incomplete information proceed by adopting the assumption that (other) players all start with the same prior probability distribution on this private information (which they may update on the basis of their own private information) and that these priors are common knowledge. This is modeled by having the game begin with a probability distribution, known to all the players, which determines each player's private information.[68] Thus players not only have priors over other players' private information, they also know what priors the other players have over their own private information. Strategic models of incomplete information thus include an extra level of detail, since they specify not only the actions and information available to the players in the course of the game, but also their prior probability distributions and information prior to the start of the game.

Experiments seeking to test formal theories of incomplete information must be carefully constructed if they are to meet the assumptions of the theory while controlling for the information and beliefs of the players. The experimental designs discussed below all deal with this by beginning the game with an objective probability distribution known to all of the players, so that the analysis of the experiment can proceed by taking each player's prior probability distribution to be equal to this objective distribution.[69]

Despite these common features of design, the experiments discussed below reflect an interesting diversity of experimental philosophy and theoretical disposition. We will see this both in the design of the experiments—which differ in how closely the experimental environments are related to the models whose predictions are being tested—and in the conclusions drawn from them. I will return to this point later.

Hoggatt and Selten et al. (1978) tested an incomplete information model of bargaining studied by Harsanyi and Selten (1972) and Selten (1975). The game in question involves bargaining over the division of twenty money units with each bargainer having private information about his own cost of reaching agreement, which is either zero or nine units, chosen with equal probability. A bargainer's cost is deducted from his payoff (only) in the event that an agreement is reached. In each of these experiments a money unit was worth ten cents. Some of the flavor of the experiment, and of how the common prior probability distributions of the players were induced, can be given by quoting from the instructions (131–2):

> There are six persons participating in this session and you will play the same bargaining game once against each of the others. In any game two players may divide 20 money units between themselves if they reach agreement. If they reach conflict neither receives any money units. At the beginning of a bargaining game it is decided by a separate random experiment for each player by drawing an "H" or "L" from the bag [which contains two

balls, one of each kind] whether he has high or low cost. High cost = 9 money units, and low cost = 0 money units. These costs are deducted from the payments in the event that agreement is reached. . . . You will not know the cost of the other player but you will know your own cost and you also know that the cost of the other player was chosen high or low with equal probability independently from the selection of your costs. In any one game you will not know against which of the other participants you are playing. The other player will find himself in exactly the same general situation.

The bargaining is done via teletype and proceeds in discrete stages. At the first stage the teletype will accept your demand for a share which must be an integer no lower than your cost and not higher than 20. In succeeding stages your demand must not be higher than the demand in the previous stage and no lower than your cost. . . . If a player's move is not completed within [2 minutes] the computer will take the demand of that player in the previous stage. . . .

Conflict occurs at any stage for which neither player makes a concession, i.e. both demands remain at the levels set in the previous stage. . . . In case of conflict . . . both players have a net payoff of zero.

Agreement is reached should a stage occur in which the sum of both demands is at most 20 money units . . . [in which case] each player gets his demand and then the amount by which the sum of demands falls short of 20 is split evenly.

The authors focus on the predictions of one of the multiple equilibria of the model, which they call the "main representation." Among the predictions at this equilibrium is that whenever two players with high costs play each other (a HH pair) disagreement will result, while for every other combination (HL, LH, and LL pairs) no disagreements will result. The observed results of the experiment were that the disagreement frequency was .729 for HH pairs, .471 for LH and HL pairs, and .097 for LL pairs (compared with predictions of 1.00 for HH and 0 otherwise), so the frequencies have a tendency in the direction of the theory. The authors say (143–144), "This weak tendency in the direction of the theory is not trivial, since a superficial analysis of the game may easily come to the conclusion that there should be no conflict at all, since mutually profitable agreements are possible for each of the type combinations."

However, the authors are less sanguine about the ability of the theory to organize other aspects of the data. For example, agreements are predicted to give the players equal gross payoffs only in the case of two low cost bargainers, while the data shows that for all kinds of bargaining pairs (HH, LH or HL, and LL) the modal agreement gave the players equal gross payoffs of ten money units each (i.e., equal payoffs before the private information bargaining cost was deducted).[70]

An interesting unpredicted feature of the data concerns the effects of the bargainers' risk aversion on the frequency of conflict. (Although the authors assume that the players are all risk neutral in order to simplify their theoretical analysis, they also collect data on the risk aversion of their subjects, by having them choose from a set of lotteries prior to the bargaining experiment.[71] In this preliminary experiment, a subject makes a sequence of A or B choices, with a higher number of A choices signifying a greater propensity to take risks.) A small but significant effect of risk aversion on disagreement frequency appears in the data of the main experiment, with a curious pattern. In the data for LL pairs and LH or HL pairs, an increase in the bargainers' propensity to take risks results in an increased frequency of conflict. However, the data for HH pairs reveals the reverse correlation: an increased propensity to take risks is associated with a reduced frequency of conflict. The authors go on to examine the correlation between risk taking propensity and the number of times bargainers repeat their demands in the course of a bargaining session. (Recall that a bargainer faces a risk that the game will end with disagreement on the next period only if he repeats his previous demand.) What they find is that for LL pairs (in which the stakes are high, since the bargaining costs are low) increased propensity to take risk leads to an increase in repeated demands. But for HH pairs (in which the stakes are lower, since most of the wealth will be consumed by the bargaining costs) the reverse is true. They conclude (158):

> With this result we can now understand the reversal. . . . Risk-takers are attracted by large payoffs and they are more likely to repeat a demand if there is a possibility of a large net payoff. A small additional net payoff does not induce them in the same way to take the risk of losing a small net payoff.
>
> This result illustrates the value of sequential analysis on a large data base. Given the anomaly [of reversals] we were led to search for an explanation by making a finer breakdown of the data.

In an effort to integrate both the predicted and unpredicted results of their experiment, the authors conclude their paper by presenting a "behavioral robot" in order "to produce a complete behavioral representation of modal behavior for the game."[72] Thus while the paper begins with a set of detailed game theoretic predictions about the play of the game, and a careful implementation of experimental conditions corresponding to the model for which the prediction was made, it ends with a non-game-theoretic model of player behavior.

A rather different approach is taken by Forsythe, Kennan, and Sopher (1991), who consider a bargaining game in which only one bargainer is informed about the size of the pie to be divided, while the other bargainer knows only the probability distribution that determines the size of the pie. In particular, the pie can take on one of two values, H ("the good state") and L ("bad state"), with $H > L$, and it takes on the high value H with a known probability p. They write that (253) "a particular goal of this work is to identify predictions that are robust with respect to the simplifying assumptions used in theoretical modeling." To this end, they use as the basis for their theoretical analysis two games—an ultimatum game and a "random dictator" game—which are highly structured and easy to analyze, and then seek to experimentally test the predictions derived from that analysis in a bargaining environment that is much more unstructured and complex, since it involves the free exchange of messages.

In their ultimatum game, the *un*informed player must propose a division of the pie (by specifying how much he demands for himself), which the informed player then accepts or rejects. At a subgame perfect equilibrium the informed player will reject any demand larger than the actual size of the pie (since by doing so he secures a payoff of zero instead of a negative payoff) and accept any demand that is not larger than the pie. So a risk-neutral uninformed player will demand H (i.e., all of the large pie) if $pH > L$, since this gives him an expected payoff of pH. And he will demand L if $pH < L$, which gives him an expected payoff of L.

In the random dictator game both the informed and the uninformed player submit a nonnegative proposal of how much the uninformed player should receive. One of these proposals is then chosen at random and implemented if it is feasible (i.e., if the amount does not exceed the size of the pie). Here also, the strategy of a risk-neutral uninformed player is to demand H if $pH > L$ and to demand L otherwise.

Thus a prediction of both simple models is that there will be disagreement— i.e., both players will receive 0—if and only if $pH > L$ and the pie size is L. The prediction implies that there will never be disagreement in the good state—i.e., when the pie is large, regardless of the probability p.

Forsythe et al. proceeded to test this prediction experimentally, both on a random dictator game of the kind just described and on an unstructured bargaining game in which the subjects were free to exchange written messages as well as offers and acceptances and rejections for ten minutes. They found that in the unstructured bargaining environment the prediction about disagreements was weakly supported, in the sense that disagreements were most frequent in games in which $pH > L$ and the size of the pie was L. But, as in Hoggatt and Selten et al. (1978), the support for the prediction was only weak, in the sense that there were substantial numbers of agreements in this case also, as well as disagreements when the pie size was H.[73] And the division of the pie when agreements were reached did not always conform to the predicted values.

In comparing the behavior observed in the unstructured bargaining with that observed in the random dictator game, Forsythe et al. observe similar behavior in many respects, with the notable exception that disagreements never occurred in the random dictator game when the pie was large, since no player ever demanded more than H. They summarize this comparison as follows (264–5):

> Our results show that the general pattern of the outcomes in the [unstructured] bargaining games was very similar to that of the R[andom] D[ictator] games. Communication did not substantially affect the incidence of strikes in the bad state; however, in the good state, strikes occurred only in the bargaining games, where the informed player could insist that the pie was small and the uninformed player had the right to insist that it was not.

Thus in this experiment increased opportunities for (anonymous written) communication *increased* the frequency of disagreement.[74] Since the random dictator games can be viewed as individual decision problems, the authors analyzed the individual data to see if the subjects are expected income maximizers, as assumed. They conclude that the formal predictions for the random dictator game (and therefore perhaps also for the unstructured bargaining game) failed to be fully descriptive (271) "because there was considerable heterogeneity among our subjects, including sizeable minorities of both risk-averse and risk-loving types, and another minority of altruists."[75] They conclude as follows (271):

> Although we have some encouraging results on the predictive power of the [predictions about disagreement], the results on heterogeneity of preferences and on inconsistency of decisions indicate that much caution is needed in drawing conclusions from behavior in bargaining (and other) experiments. In any game in which the players interact strategically, the theoretical analysis should not begin (as ours did) with the assumption that the players' objective functions are common knowledge.[76]

The next experiment I will discuss, by Radner and Schotter (1989; see also Schotter 1990) reports an incomplete information experiment, using a highly structured sealed bid mechanism. Buyers and sellers would each simultaneously submit a proposed (bid or asked) price, and no trade would result if the buyer's bid was lower than the seller's asked; otherwise the transaction price would be the average of the two. Buyers and sellers had private reservation values drawn from the same distribution.

The single play version of this game, in which the buyer and seller meet only once, has received a good deal of theoretical attention. Chatterjee and Samuelson (1983) studied an equilibrium of the game in which the players' bids are a linear function of their private values. Myerson and Satterthwaite (1983) observed that no equilibrium of the game can achieve one hundred percent efficiency (by achieving trades whenever the buyer's value is higher than the seller's), but that the linear equilibrium studied by Chatterjee and Samuelson achieves maximal efficiency on the set of equilibria.[77] And Leininger, Linhard, and Radner (1989) observed that there are a multitude of other equilibria, with widely varying efficiency. Radner and Schotter write that it is this multiplicity of equilibria ("this theoretical morass") that motivated their experiment. Their idea is that the negative implications of the theoretical multiplicity of equilibria may be tempered, for practical purposes, if subjects can in practice achieve the efficiency of the most efficient, linear equilibrium.

Radner and Schotter adopt an experimental strategy somewhere between that of Hoggatt and Selten et al. (1978) and Forsythe et al. (1991) in terms of how closely the experimental environment they construct conforms to the theoretical model whose predictions are to be tested. In particular, the information and communication available to the players are structured to conform precisely to the model being tested. But whereas the model describes a one-period game, the experiment studies a multiperiod repeated game. They describe their experimental environment as follows (182–3):

> Each seller/buyer drew 15 envelopes from a pile of 500. Each envelope contained a slip of paper with a number written on it. The numbers were generated randomly according to a commonly known probability distribu-

tion. If the subject was a buyer, then this random number indicated the value to him of the good being sold in that round. If the subject was a seller, the number represented the cost of producing the good in that round. After observing the realization in the envelope and recording it in their work sheets, subjects then wrote their bids on pieces of paper and handed them to a set of experimental administrators who collected them. When the slips of the buyers and sellers were brought to the front of the room, they were randomly sorted into pairs, each containing the bid of one buyer and one seller. These bids were then compared, and, using the rules of the sealed bid mechanism . . . prices and payoffs were determined. The price and trade results of these transactions were then distributed back to the subjects, and the next round began, which was conducted in an identical manner. In subsequent rounds subjects were paired against the same pair member. . . . Despite the danger of introducing repeated-game elements into what is intended to be a test of a static theory, we felt that this design feature was necessary if the subjects were to successfully select one equilibrium from the multitude defined by the mechanism.

The danger to which Radner and Schotter refer has to do with the fact that the multiperiod game that the subjects in the experiment actually play (since each buyer remains paired with the same seller throughout) has more equilibria than the one-period game, including equilibria which achieve a higher degree of efficiency than any in the one-period game.[78] This presents a special complication in the interpretation of their results, since it turns out that, rather than observing lower efficiency than at the linear equilibrium, they observed *higher* efficiency. That is, when the buyer's value is higher than the seller's, so that trade is profitable, agreements were observed more often than predicted. In the static, one-period case for which the theory was developed, this would be clear indication of non-equilibrium behavior, since the linear equilibrium is maximally efficient on the set of equilibria. However, since this is not the case in the repeated game actually played, the observed behavior could nevertheless be consistent with equilibrium play.

The questions of experimental design that this raises are worth a digression. Although economic theories of equilibrium so far have little to say about *equilibration*—i.e. about how equilibrium might be achieved—experimenters still have to think about it. (For example, few people would be persuaded to reject an otherwise plausible theory of equilibrium on the basis of a single play of a game by inexperienced subjects.) For this reason it is increasingly common in experimental tests of equilibrium predictions to give the subjects an opportunity to gain some experience with the game. The most common way to handle this is to have the subjects play the game many times, but against different opponents each time, to preserve the one-period nature of the games being played.[79] (In the present case, such a design would have avoided the difficulties in interpreting the observed efficiency of the bargaining results.) But when there are multiple equilibria it might be that different groups of subjects will drift to different equilibria, and that the ability of the experimenter to observe this would be sacrificed if each subject gains his experience from the whole subject pool. It was apparently an hypothesis of this sort that led Radner and Schotter to their repeated game design. The implications of this for interpreting the results would have been different had the results been different or had the issue of the maximum efficiency achievable at equilibrium not been at the center of the hypotheses to be tested.

Returning to the behavior observed by Radner and Schotter, much of it appeared to be linear; that is, subjects' prices were linear functions of their private values in each period. But there was less "shading" of buyers' bids than predicted at the linear equilibrium, and consequently more agreements were reached than predicted. (This linearity appeared to diminish as subjects gained experience, however.) The experiment also included several cells with different rules. In one of these, payoffs were by binary lotteries, to control for unobserved risk aversion that might be a factor in causing buyers to shade their bids less than the equilibrium prediction. If so, the prediction for the binary lottery games is that the "correct" amount of shading would be observed. The results were not consistent with this hypothesis. Similarly, the one-period equilibrium prediction that efficiency would be lower if an ultimatum game replaced the split-the-difference mechanism was not confirmed in a cell in which the ultimatum game was played. But in these games also, the fact that repeated games rather than single-period games were observed suggests that further experimentation might clarify what was observed.

Another experiment in which greater efficiency was observed than was predicted is reported by Rapoport, Erev, and Zwick (forthcoming). They studied a multiperiod game in which a seller negotiates with a buyer over the price of an indivisible good. It is common knowledge that the good has zero value to the seller, but its value to the buyer, v, is known only to the buyer: the seller knows only that v was drawn from a deck of 101 cards numbered 0 through 100. In each period $t = 0, 1, \ldots$, the seller (the uninformed player) sets a price, which the buyer accepts or rejects. If the buyer accepts price p in period t, then the game ends and the seller's payoff is $\delta^t p$ and the buyer's payoff is $\delta^t(v - p)$, where δ is a (common) discount factor between 0 and 1. If the buyer rejects, the game continues to the next period, and the seller again sets a price, unless the quantity $\delta^t(v - p)$ has become smaller than \$1, in which case the game is terminated by the experimenter.[80] Subjects played the game eighteen times, against changing opponents, as both buyers and sellers. Each subject played under three different discount factors δ; 0.9, 0.66, and 0.33.

This game is modeled on the infinite horizon game examined by Fudenberg, Levine, and Tirole (1985), who identified a generically unique sequential equilibrium path when the (continuous) distribution from which the buyer's value is drawn has a support that strictly exceeds the seller's value.[81] In this equilibrium, the price set by the seller declines in each period, in a nonlinear way, from the initial price that the seller chooses. And this initial price is highest when the discount factor is lowest. At equilibrium the game ends with agreement in finitely many periods, but not generally in the first period. Thus agreements are predicted to be inefficient, in the sense that costly delays are a part of the equilibrium.

Rapoport et al. observed that prices did decline monotonically, as predicted, but found the other aspects of the equilibrium predictions to be less descriptive. First, the initial prices set by sellers increased as the discount factor increased, contrary to prediction. Second, as sellers gained experience, they adopted a strategy of setting linearly declining prices. Finally, buyers tended to accept sooner than predicted. As in the experiment of Radner and Schotter, the deviations from equilibrium resulted in a higher than predicted efficiency of bargaining, which in this case means that agreements were reached sooner than predicted, and so suffered less discounting.

The final incomplete information experiment I will discuss, by Mitzkewitz and Nagel (1993), uses an innovative design to explore ultimatum games in a manner that also sheds some light on the behavior observed in complete information ultimatum games. They explored two different kinds of ultimatum games. In each of them, the amount to be divided (the "size of the cake") was first determined by the roll of a die to be an integer amount between 1 and 6. (All payoffs were counted in an artificial currency called "thalers," with one thaler worth 1.20 DM. Proposals could only be made in units of 0.5 thalers, which the authors remark was the price of a cup of coffee in the student cafeteria at the University of Bonn.) Only the proposer (player A) was informed of the size of the cake, while the accepter/rejecter, player B, knew only that the probabilities of each size from 1 to 6 were equal. Subjects played one of two different ultimatum games, an "offer game" or a "demand game," eight times against a different, anonymous other player each time. A given subject always played the same game and was always in the same position (A or B).

In the "offer game," after the die is thrown and player A is informed of the result, he makes an offer to player B. An offer may be any multiple of 0.5 that does not exceed the size of the cake: for example, if the die comes up 2, there are five feasible offers: 0, 0.5, 1, 1.5, and 2. If player B rejects the offer, both players receive zero. If player B accepts, then she (player B) earns the amount offered, while A earns the actual value of the cake minus the amount offered. So after player B hears the offer, she knows precisely what she will earn if she accepts, but she does not know what player A will earn (except if she is offered 5.5 or 6.0, in which case she can deduce that the cake was of size 6).

The demand game proceeds like the offer game, except that after player A is informed of the size of the cake, he communicates to player B a demand (of what he, player A, will receive) rather than an offer. If B rejects the demand, both players receive zero. If she accepts the demand, then player A earns what he demanded, while B earns the actual value of the cake minus what A demanded. So after player B hears the demand, she knows what player A will earn if she accepts his proposal, but she doesn't know what she will earn herself (unless the demand is 5.5 or 6.0, in which case she can deduce that she will receive 0.5 or 0.0, respectively).

While these two games each have numerous equilibria, the sequential equilibria all involve player B receiving either 0.0 or 0.5, that is, either zero or the smallest monetary unit. The equilibria at which B receives 0.0 are weak, in the sense that B is indifferent between accepting and rejecting the proposal at those equilibria, so the authors concentrate on the sequential equilibria that are strict on the equilibrium path—i.e., which give both players a positive incentive not to deviate. In both games, therefore, the prediction is that player B will receive 0.5, the smallest monetary unit, regardless of the size of the cake, and that player A will receive the rest. Note that *no* disagreements are predicted (unlike the ultimatum game whose equilibrium predictions were studied by Forsythe et al., in which the *un*informed player made the proposal).

The prediction that player B will receive no more than the smallest unit (and that no disagreements will occur) is of course familiar from the case of ultimatum games with complete information, where we have observed that the experimental results are far from the equilibrium prediction. Mitzkewitz and Nagel point out that if simple envy is the reason small positive offers are rejected in complete information games, then we might expect different behavior in these incomplete information games, in which player B cannot directly compare the payoffs to the two players. This is particularly so in the offer game, in which player B never learns the payoff of player A.

Following Selten (1967), the authors employ the "strategy method" in their experimental design. Both players are required to submit complete *strategies* for the game, *before* the die is thrown and player A is informed of the size of the cake. That is, player A is required to submit in advance the offer or demand he will make, depending on the size of the cake, for each of the six possible outcomes of the toss of the die. And player B is required to indicate whether she will accept or reject each of the thirteen possible offers or demands from 0.0 to 6.0.

While the data that they gather in this way is quite complex, a sense of the behavior of player As can be gotten from considering the modal offer for each possible cake size (pooled over all eight rounds). In the offer game, for cake sizes (1, 2, 3, 4, 5, 6), the modal *offers* are (0.5, 1, 1.5, 2, 2, 2).

That is, the modal behavior in the offer game is for player As to offer half the cake until it gets to be size 4, and to continue offering 2 for cakes of size 5 and 6. The mean percentage of the cake which player A proposes to keep for himself rises as the cake size increases. The authors note that in this weak sense, the data conforms to the prediction of the strict sequential equilibrium.

By contrast in the demand game, the modal *demands* for cake sizes 1 to 6 are (1, 2, 3, 3, 3, 3). That is, the modal behavior in the demand game is for player As to demand all of the cake until it reaches size 3, and to offer the remainder to player B for cakes of size 4, 5, and 6.

A sense of the player B's behavior can be gotten from considering the mean frequencies with which different offers or demands were accepted. A particularly illuminating comparison is between offers of 0.5 in the offer game and demands of 5.5 in the demand game, since in both cases player B is sure to receive 0.5. In the offer game, this is accepted 51 percent of the time, while in the demand game (when it means player A will get 5.5) it is accepted only 24 percent of the time—i.e. less than half as often. (The authors characterize this as "resistance to visible unfairness" on the part of players B in the demand game.) In the offer game, the rate of acceptance rises to 96 percent with offers of 2, and 99 percent with offers of 2.5, while in the demand game the acceptance rate does not rise to over 90 percent until the demand drops to 1.5, and it does not reach 99 percent until the demand is only 0.5. So here also there is a considerable difference between the two games. But in both games there is a substantial frequency of disagreement, contrary to the prediction.

In analyzing the data round by round, the authors observe another difference between the offer and demand games. In the demand games, but not in the offer games, it may happen that a player B accepts a proposal, expecting to receive a positive payoff, but instead receives zero. The authors observe that, following such a "failure by accepting," player Bs are more inclined to reject subsequent demands, but that no parallel pattern is present in the offer games.

Thus in the offer game, player As seem reluctant to offer too little, while in the demand game they hesitate to demand too much. Since player B's judgment of what is "too little" or "too much" must be made in ignorance of the actual size of the cake, the difference between the offer game and the demand game is marked.[82] The differences observed between the offer and demand games, which both have the same strict sequential equilibrium predictions when subjects are assumed to care only about their own payoffs, provide further support for the proposition that a descriptive theory of bargaining behavior will need to take account of more complex kinds of preferences.

In summary, these experiments suggest that there remains considerable room for improvement in our understanding of the causes of disagreement and delay. Even in this group of experiments designed to test the most complex and subtle of the strategic theories of bargaining, rates of disagreement are observed that are both higher and lower than predicted in various circumstances. More generally, in each of these five incomplete information experiments, the equilibrium predictions capture at least some of the qualitative features of the data, but fall considerably short of being perfect predictors. Speaking of the "weak tendency towards the equilibrium outcome" observed in their offer games, Mitzkewitz and Nagel write (42), "We are curious whether believers in the descriptive relevance of game theory find this result encouraging or disappointing. . . ." The same could be asked about the results of each of these incomplete information experiments and, indeed, of many of the experiments discussed in this volume.

In this regard, while I have focused more on the results of these experiments than on the broadest conclusions their authors draw from them about the status of game theory as a descriptive theory, I would be remiss not to mention that these experimenters too express the full range of opinions on this subject. (Among these incomplete information experimenters, Radner and Schotter have been the most optimistic in their conclusions about the extent to which the data they observe conforms to equilibrium predictions for the game they studied, and, based on qualitatively similar evidence, Rapoport, Erev, and Zwick have been perhaps the least optimistic.) While all of these experiments have shown the predictive value of some of the qualitative predictions of some equilibria of the game (or of a closely related game), and the failure of others, different investigators assign these different importance. In this respect the situation in the emerging experimental study of bargaining under incomplete information mirrors the tests of game theoretic models generally.

There is, however, something special about theories of incomplete information that may continue to make their experimental evaluation not only especially difficult, but also especially susceptible to controversy. I have already referred to the fact that theories of incomplete information present special problems of experimental control, since they depend on the beliefs that players maintain. These problems of control are complicated by the fact that very small changes in beliefs—sometimes even arbitrarily small changes in beliefs about events that are predicted not to occur—can support very different equilibria. Part of the appeal of such models in the theoretical literature is precisely that they can be used to account for some observed behavior in terms of essentially unobservable parameters. But to the extent that the predictions derived from these models depend on those aspects of the experimental environment that are hardest to control or to observe, tests of these models will present continuing challenges to experimental design. And the interpretation of experimental tests will likely leave room for differences of opinion about whether or not the relevant features have been adequately controlled.

c. A Digression on the Strategy Method

This is a good place to pause and consider some of the advantages and disadvantages of the strategy method—i.e. of simultaneously asking all players for strategies (decisions at every information set) rather than observing each player's choices only at those information sets that arise in the course of a play of the game.[83] The obvious disadvantage is that it removes from experimental observation the possible effects of the timing of decisions in the course of the game. Thus, for example, in ultimatum games played by the strategy method, it will not be possible to observe any effects that may be due to the accepter/rejecter making her decision *after* the proposer has made his decision, knowing what has been proposed.[84]

The equally obvious advantage to collecting full strategies from the participants is that it allows the experimenter to acquire data on all information sets of the game, not just those that are actually reached in the course of the game. Thus, for example, in the experiment of Mitzkewitz and Nagel discussed above, it was possible to observe acceptance and rejection decisions for all offers, not merely those that were actually made. (In comparison, recall Figure 4.7c, discussed earlier in connection with Roth et al. [1991], in which reliable data on acceptances and rejections could only be gathered from offers that had been made sufficiently often.) Furthermore, as Mitzkewitz and Nagel note, observing subjects' entire strategies, rather than just the moves that occur in the game, may give insight into their motivation. Thus a subject in their offer game who offers half of a small cake might be thought to be "trying to be fair," but if we observe that the same subject would have offered less than half of a large cake, we may have reason to reconsider this hypothesis.

Finally, a difference that is not obviously either an advantage or a disadvantage, but which may be a cause of different outcomes for games played by the strategy method versus those played in the ordinary manner, is that having to submit entire strategies forces subjects to think about each information set in a different way than if they could primarily concentrate on those information sets that arise in the course of the game. This is a similar point to that raised in the debate about why certain sorts of "structured" experience may have different effects than simple experience with the ordinary play of a game, as discussed earlier.

In summary, if a game has many information sets, then changing from ordinary play of the game, in which subjects may make decisions at different times and with varying information, to having subjects simultaneously make all potential decisions at the same time, amounts to a significant change in the game itself. Formally, a game that has many information sets when played in the ordinary manner is transformed by the strategy method to a game in which each player has only a single information set. However, this is a change that leaves many game theoretic predictions unchanged, since it is equivalent to going from the game represented by the extensive form to the game represented by the strategic ("normal") form. There is thus room for experiments focused on determining for which kinds of games there may be significant differences in observed behavior when the strategy method is used. The results of such experiments have the potential not only to illuminate an important issue of experimental methodology, but also to point to domains in which the transformation from the extensive to the strategic form representations of a game may conceal important features of the game.

D. Deadlines

The previous section discussed experiments designed to test the predictions of particular theories. The present section discusses a class of phenomena in which experimental observation preceded the theories that have now been proposed. The phenomena in question concern the distribution of agreements over time in bargaining environments in which there is a deadline. This is a topic that has been widely discussed in an anecdotal way, but which turns out not to have been subjected to a great deal of systematic study.

Roth, Murnighan, and Schoumaker (1988) analyzed the distribution of agreements over time from four bargaining experiments, three of which were previously published experiments designed to test hypotheses unrelated to the timing of agreements.[85] In each of these experiments, unstructured anonymous bargaining was permitted to proceed between nine and twelve minutes, via terminals in a computer laboratory that automatically recorded the time of each agreement. Players could transmit English language messages to each other via terminals, monitored to prevent violations of anonymity, and sometimes subject to other restrictions. If agreement was not reached in the specified time, each player received zero. The last three minutes of bargaining were marked by a "time remaining" clock on the screen.

Although these experiments displayed considerable variation in the terms of agreements that were reached, and in the frequency of disagreements, there were substantial similarities in their distribution of agreements over time. In all experiments there was a high concentration of agreements near the deadline.

Overall, slightly less than half of all agreements were observed in the final thirty seconds of bargaining. Of those agreements reached in the final thirty seconds, approximately half were reached in the final five seconds. And of those agreements reached in the final five seconds, approximately half were reached in the final second.

Figures 4.9a and 4.9b display the distribution of agreements over time in all observations from the fourth new experiment reported in Roth et al. (1988).[86] The figures are typical of the distributions observed in all four experiments. In this experiment, bargainers engaged in binary lottery games in which the two bargainers had different prizes.[87] In the four experimental conditions, the prizes were $10 and $15; $6 and $14; $5 and $20; and $4 and $36. (So the distributions of lottery tickets that would equalize bargainers' expected incomes were (60 percent, 40 percent); (70 percent, 30 percent); (80 percent, 20 percent); and (90 percent, 10 percent) respectively.) Both bargainers were informed about the value of both prizes, and this was common knowledge. As in previous experiments of this kind, the percentage of lottery tickets obtained by the bargainer with the lower prize was observed to increase significantly across conditions as the low prize decreased. But although the observed agreements were different, neither the timing of agreements nor the variance of agreement times responded to the differences in the bargainers' prize values. That is, the distribution of agreements over time varied much less than the agreements themselves, and showed high concentrations of agreements near the deadline in all four conditions.

Roth et al. summarize the role of laboratory experimentation in this exploratory way as follows (806):

Since last-minute agreements are widely believed to occur frequently in naturally occurring negotiations, it may be helpful to state clearly just what it is that laboratory investigations have to contribute to the study of deadline phenomena. First, while there is a great deal of anecdotal information about the frequency of "eleventh hour" agreements in naturally occurring negotiations, it has proved difficult to collect reliable data. Second, being able to study deadline phenomena in the laboratory will enable us to distinguish between alternative hypotheses in a way that the study of field data does not permit.[88] Third, while the distribution of agreements over time is one of the clearest phenomena observed in bargaining experiments to date, none of the presently available theoretical models of bargaining is able to account simultaneously for the distribution of agreements over time together with the observed patterns of agreements and substantial observed frequency of disagreements, so these results suggest clear directions for further theoretical work.

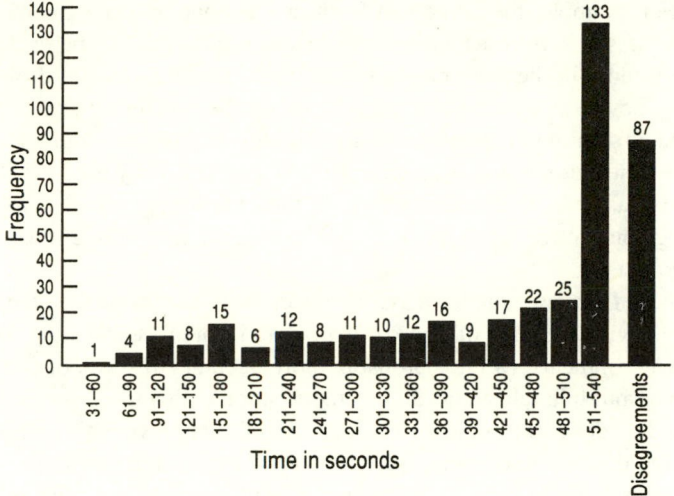

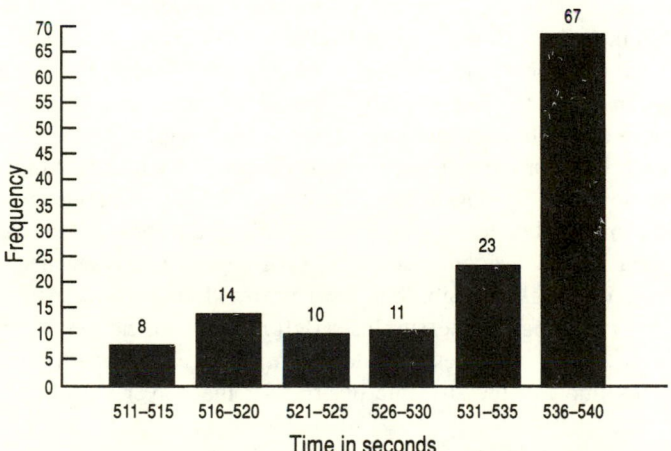

Figure 4.9. (a) Frequency of agreements and disagreements. (b) Frequency of agreements received in the last 30 seconds of bargaining. *Source:* Roth, Murnighan, and Schoumaker, 1988.

The deadline effect has indeed subsequently proved to be a fruitful subject for theoretical models. Regarding the description of the deadline effect itself, Kennan and Wilson (1993) observe that the data reported in Roth et al. (1988) can be roughly described with an "accelerated failure time model." That is, the increasing agreement rate as time expires has the property that whatever the rate is during the first x percent of the available time is roughly the same as the rate during the first x percent of the remaining $(1 - x)$ percent of the time. In such a model the time remaining can be thought of as a rescaling of the whole bargaining interval. For example, they note that Roth et al. reported 621 agreements from bargaining sessions with a nine-minute deadline, and that 11 percent of these agreements came in the first three minutes, that is, in the first third of the time available. They then observe that 13 percent of the remaining 552 agreements came in the first third of the remaining six minutes, and that the figure for the first third of the last four minutes is again around 11 percent. They note (95) that "this does not explain why the agreement rate in the initial three minutes was 11 percent, but given any initial agreement rate, the rescaling argument explains the deadline effect."

A number of strategic models have also been proposed to explain the deadline effect, in varying degrees of approximation and completeness, and in several different environments. (So it is probably more accurate to speak of these papers as exploring multiple related deadline effects, some with a more stylized relation to empirical evidence than others.) These models fall into two main categories. As in the earlier discussion of game-theoretic models of disagreement, these can be usefully separated into models with complete information and with incomplete information. The two classes of models suggest two distinct causes of deadline effects and thus suggest avenues for further experimentation.

In particular, two of the complete information models can be thought of as stylized "timing models," in which a deadline effect arises as bargainers jockey to get into the position of the proposer in an ultimatum game, by trying to delay until they can make the last effective offer. Fershtman and Seidmann (1993) model deadline effects in a multiperiod sequential bargaining model in which the player who will propose in each period is chosen by lottery. In their model, bargainers can make "endogenous commitments": once a bargainer rejects an offer he is committed never to take a worse offer. Equilibrium behavior in their model depends on the discount factor: if it is low, agreement is reached in the first period, but if it is high enough, then the game will end in the last period with the proposer receiving all the surplus. (Before the end, no serious offers are made in this case, since these would be rejected and—via the endogenous commitment—improve the strategic position of the player who had rejected a positive offer.)

Ma and Manove (1993) look at a complete information model in which time is continuous and in which there are random delays in transmitting and responding to offers. Players alternate offers in their model, and a player whose turn it is to make an offer can prevent the other player from taking the initiative by delaying his offer. At equilibrium player 1 waits until a critical moment near the end before making an offer, which is accepted if it arrives near enough to the deadline, but rejected if it arrives too early, in which case a counteroffer is made.

In contrast, incomplete information models such as those by Hart (1989), Ponsati-Obiols (1989), Cramton and Tracy (1992), and Spier (1992) present deadline effects as arising from attempts by bargainers to show that their private information puts them in a powerful position. Only by engaging in costly delays can they distinguish themselves from bargainers in weaker positions. Ponsati-Obiols and Spier model deadlines after which no further bargaining can take place, while Hart and Cramton and Tracy consider models in which bargaining may proceed after the deadline, but becomes significantly more costly. All of these models yield equilibria in which a substantial concentration of agreements occur around the deadline.[89]

Each of these strategic models generates testable hypotheses. Because each of the models is formulated for a different environment, tests of their precise predictions would involve an array of experimental environments as well. However, to the extent that each model is meant to identify features of bargaining that contribute to deadline effects in a variety of bargaining environments, it becomes possible to contemplate experimental tests designed to better discern and compare the extent of such contributions. In particular, theories of incomplete information suggest that deadline effects are associated with the efforts of some players to distinguish themselves on the basis of their private information, while timing models suggest that the detailed mechanics of sending and receiving offers may play a large role. Both of these effects are predicted to occur in ways that will make them hard to control (even) in the laboratory, but because the effects are different it should be possible to design experiments that help to distinguish between them.

Deadline effects also offer a window through which to examine the effect of the bargaining that takes place well before the deadline. That is to say, even if the majority of agreements take place in the final minute of a ten-minute bargaining session, for example, presumably the bargaining that occurs before the final minute influences those agreements that are reached very near the deadline. It thus seems plausible to expect a different pattern of agreements and disagreements in the final minute of a two-minute bargaining session than of a ten-minute session.[90] The nature of this difference would shed some light on the effect of the bargaining that takes place long before the deadline.

III. Concluding Remarks

We did not need experiments to tell us that bargaining is subtle and complex, but experiments have given us insights into these subtleties and complexities that would have been difficult to obtain in any other way. In these concluding remarks I will not try to comprehensively summarize the experimental results presented in this chapter; they defy easy summary, since they deal with many issues and suggest further experiments in many directions. Instead, I will try to select a few results to illustrate the kinds of things we have learned from these series of experiments. First I will consider what kinds of things we have learned about bargaining and about game-theoretic models of bargaining. Then I will briefly reflect on what we have learned about experiments more generally and about the relationship between theory and experiment.

One of the most general things that experiments demonstrate is that subjects adjust their behavior as they gain experience and learn about the game they are playing and the behavior of other subjects. This is an observation that is certainly not confined to bargaining experiments and suggests that theoretical work on learning and dynamic adjustment and adaptation may eventually prove very fruitful.

One of the particular things bargaining experiments suggest is that bargainers may be concerned with more than their own payoffs in evaluating the outcome of bargaining. On a purely methodological level, this illustrates how difficult it is, even in the laboratory, to gain complete control over the experimental environment. This means that experimental tests of some kinds of theories may require considerable perseverance and ingenuity. And this will become more relevant the more the theories being tested rely on features of the environment that are difficult to control, or on observations that are difficult to make. (The incomplete information theories of disagreement frequency come immediately to mind.)

At the same time, the degree of control available in the laboratory makes possible observations that could not be made as clearly, if at all, in field data. Experiments have proved in this way to be a powerful instrument for bringing to light overlooked regularities and for investigating hypotheses about their causes. For example, the prevalence of equal divisions in the experimental data led naturally to hypotheses that these might be intimately related to notions of fairness. Further evidence, however, made clear that whatever the extent to which notions of fairness may play a role in determining the outcome of bargaining, it is not the case that bargainers are primarily trying to *be* fair. (If they were, they would not have produced the consistent first mover advantages observed in Figure 4.2, or the difference between ultimatum games and dictator games observed in Figure 4.4, or the modal offers consistent with income maximization observed when the tenth round offers in Figure 4.7b are compared with the revenue curves in Figure 4.7d.)

This is not to say that some notions of fairness may not play an important role—recall the frequency with which disadvantageous responses are observed (e.g., in Table 4.1) when bargainers are offered what they may regard as inequitable divisions. But notions of fairness are labile and appear to respond to strategic considerations (recall Figures 4.5a and 4.5b comparing players' assessments of fair outcomes after playing optional or forced breakdown games, and recall the extreme payoff disparities that proved to be acceptable in best-shot and market games, e.g., in Table 4.3 and Table 4.4 or Figure 4.7a).

What does this tell us about the game-theoretic models that the sequential bargaining experiments I concentrated on in this chapter were primarily designed to test? If we take the position that the assumption that players are concerned only with their own payoffs is a critical part of these models, then the evidence provides little support for their general predictive power (although in some games, such as the best shot, market, and impunity games, they work just fine, an observation that raises theoretical questions of its own). But if we take the position that the models only yield predictions after we have accurately determined the preferences of the players, then we have to be more cautious. It is in just this sense that I would not want to claim that the results for ultimatum games provide a test of subgame perfectness per se.

On the one hand, the frequent observation of disagreements and disadvantageous responses generally is consistent with the hypothesis that, although bargainers are concerned primarily with their own payoffs, a wider range of threats are credible than are captured in refinements such as subgame perfection. Under this interpretation, less emphasis on equilibrium refinement and more emphasis on the effects of multiple equilibria might be a productive direction in which to look for theories with descriptive power. On the other hand, the observation that we see the simple equilibrium predictions supported in some games but not in others is consistent with the hypothesis that players have more complex preferences and that the outcome of a game is not only influenced by the preferences of the players, but also influences them. Under this interpretation, it would be productive to redirect some of the theoretical effort now spent on solving games and spend relatively more time on learning how to model as games the situations we wish to study. These two approaches are not mutually exclusive of course, but they illustrate how different hypotheses suggest different theoretical directions, just as they suggest different additional experiments.

Because these experiments have been designed to test particular theories, it is natural to evaluate them in terms of those theories. But (particularly because the experiments have uncovered unpredicted phenomena) it is also natural to ask to what extent the phenomena observed in the laboratory are likely to generalize to the wider world. It seems to me that there are two different reasons to entertain some healthy skepticism. The first reason is that the environments we explore in the laboratory are quite simple and artificial, precisely because they are designed to provide controlled tests of particular hypotheses. So bargaining outside of the laboratory virtually always takes place in more complex environments. Consequently, some of the phenomena that appear important in the laboratory may have much diminished importance in naturally occurring negotiations, and phenomena that have no opportunity to emerge in the laboratory may assume much more importance.

But there is also cause for optimism that many of the phenomena that appear important in laboratory negotiations are also important outside of the laboratory. To mention just a few reasons, consider that the ubiquity of disagreements is reflected in both experimental and field data (recall Table 4.5), as is the deadline effect (recall Figure 4.9 and the deadline effect in contract renegotiations noted in field data by Cramton and Tracy). Similarly, a concern for equity certainly appears to play a role in many large negotiations, such as when executive bonuses become an issue in salary negotiations with unionized manufacturing workers.

The second cause for skepticism about the generalizability of experimental results has to do with the scale of rewards that it is feasible to offer in most experiments. For example, what can we conclude from the results of ultimatum bargaining games for thirty dollars, about the likely results if the same games were played for a million dollars? In particular, how much would *you* offer if given the opportunity to propose an ultimatum division to an anonymous person picked at random from some well specified population? Let me suggest that the answer would likely depend on the population and might be different if your opposite number is picked from a group of business tycoons than from a group of manual laborers. Right away, this suggests a departure from the simple predictions of the theory, which is that you should make the same offer—of no more than a penny—regardless of the amount you are dividing and who you are dividing it with. And suppose it should turn out (perhaps because you are risk averse) that the utility maximizing offer when dividing a million dollars is in the neighborhood of a hundred thousand dollars, while the utility maximizing offer when dividing a billion dollars is only a million dollars. Should we draw much comfort from the fact that, in percentage terms, we are approaching the simple predictions of the theory? I think there would not be much comfort to draw if that is how the data from these immensely costly experiments turned out, since the fact that the percentage offered moves towards zero does not negate the fact that, contrary to the simple prediction, the amount it is sensible to offer is not negligible.

That is, while there is no reason to think that the percentages we see in the laboratory when the stakes are small are universal constants that will be observed for stakes of any size, neither is there any reason to suppose that the unpredicted phenomena uncovered in the laboratory would disappear as the stakes surpassed some threshold. Comparing the results of existing experiments already allows us to observe similar phenomena as the scale of rewards changes.

But it goes without saying that, in speculating about the outcomes of experiments that have not been conducted, I am just speculating. In this respect the situation may resemble that which faces chemists and chemical engineers. While the basic theories of chemistry apply to reactions across an enormous range of scales and while the phenomena observed in test tubes allow these theories to be tested and refined, and provide the basis for our understanding of most chemical phenomena, it is nevertheless true that new phenomena emerge as reactions are scaled up from the lab bench to the pilot plant, and from the pilot plant to commercial production. So, while I think there is every reason to believe that the phenomena that appear to be important in the economics laboratory will remain important outside of the laboratory, I do not doubt that some laboratory observations will prove of more general importance than others. To distinguish among them will require other kinds of empirical work as well.

Aside from what we have learned about bargaining and bargaining theory, the series of experiments discussed in this chapter also say something about the relationship of experiments and theory. One of the first things that strikes me, which may be a reflection of how early in the history of experimental economics we still are, is that the boundaries between experimental and other kinds of work are still very permeable. One measure of this is how often in the present chapter I have had the occasion to refer to experimental work by famous economists who are far better known for their nonexperimental work. (For example, from A to Z—Orley Ashenfelter, Ken Binmore, Roy Radner, Reinhard Selten, Hugo Sonnenschein, Manny Yaari, and Shmuel Zamir—are all Fellows of the Econometric Society who fall into this category.) This reflects the naturally close relationship between theory and experiment, particularly when the object of the experiment is to test a well-formulated theoretical proposition.

That being the case, it is worthwhile to note that there is also a certain degree of natural *separation* between theory and experiment. Although some experimental results lead quickly to new theory (recall the discussion of the deadline effect), it is perhaps more common to see experiments lead first to other experiments. For example, the ultimatum results of Guth et al. (1982) led to a series of experiments intended to test the robustness of the unpredicted phenomena they observed. Only when a clear pattern of related regularities was observed (recall the experiment of Ochs and Roth [1989]) did we start to see new game-theoretic models proposed and tested, as in the work of Bolton (1991, 1993).[91] Because the tasks of elucidating regularities and explaining them involve different kinds of effort, it should come as no surprise that the theoretical and experimental literatures will often proceed with their own agendas, on separate but intersecting paths, particularly when the object of the experiments is to explore unpredicted regularities.

Notes

*This chapter has been revised in response to comments from the participants in the 1990 Handbook Workshop in Pittsburgh and from readers of subsequent versions including particularly Gary Bolton, Ido Erev, Bob Forsythe, Werner Guth, Glenn Harrison, Charlie Holt, John Kagel, Michael Mitzkewitz, Rosemarie Nagel, Jack Ochs, Vesna Prasnikar, and Rami Zwick.

1. They write: "This experiment is complementary with experiments by Roth and Malouf (1979) and Roth and Murnighan (1982), and addresses the same basic issue."

2. Guth highlights the differences in our interpretations as follows (1988, 709–10):

   > The experimental results of Roth and Malouf show that expected monetary payoffs dominate winning probabilities as a reward standard. But since expected monetary payoffs can only be equilibrated if both prizes are known, the dominant reward standard cannot be used if this prerequisite is not given. . . . This interpretation is supported by another study (Roth and Murnighan, 1982) showing that the shift toward equal expected monetary rewards is mainly caused by the fact that the player with the smaller prize is informed about both prizes. . . .
   >
   > "It seems justified to say that the behavioral theory of distributive justice offers an intuitively convincing and straightforward explanation for the experimental results of Roth and Malouf contradicting the most fundamental game theoretic axioms. In our view this explanation is more convincing than the approach of Roth and Schoumaker (1983). . . .
   >
   > "What Roth (1985) calls the focal point phenomenon is in our view just the problem of deciding between two reward standards differing in their prerequisites. One can only wonder why Roth and his coauthors do not even consider the explanation offered by the behavioral theory of distributive justice (the first version of this paper, finished in 1983, was strongly influenced by discussions with Alvin E. Roth). Probably the main reason is that this would mean to finally give up the illusion that people can meet the requirements of normative decision theory.

3. Since this is a handbook, let me emphasize the methodological point. The design of an experiment is intimately related to the kinds of hypotheses it is intended to test. The unstructured binary lottery experiments were designed to test hypotheses generated by theories

phrased in terms of bargainers' risk aversion. The more structured experiments discussed next are designed to investigate hypotheses concerning individual behavior in the course of bargaining.

4. Much of the recent theoretical work using this kind of model follows the treatment by Ariel Rubinstein (1982) of the infinite horizon case. An exploration of various aspects of the finite horizon case is given by Ingolf Stahl (1972). For a survey, see Osborne and Rubinstein (1990).

5. If payoffs are discrete so that offers can only be made to the nearest penny, for example, then there are subgame perfect equilibria at which i refuses to take 0 but accepts the smallest positive offer—e.g., one cent.

6. When payoffs are continuous this equilibrium division is unique, so perfect equilibrium in a two-period game calls for player 1 to offer player 2 the amount $\delta_2 k$ in the first period (and demand $k - \delta_2 k$ for himself), while in a three-period game player 1 offers player 2 the amount $\delta_2(k - \delta_1 k)$ in the first period, and demands $k - \delta_2(k - \delta_1 k)$ for himself.

7. Each subject played a single game in each session.

8. Kahneman, Knetsch, and Thaler (1986a) report an ultimatum game experiment that focuses more precisely on subjects' willingness to "punish" what they perceive as unfair behavior. This experiment will be discussed in section B.3.

9. They add: "This does not mean that our results are inconsistent with those of Guth et al. Under similar conditions, we obtain similar results. Moreover our full results would seem to refute the more obvious rationalizations of the behavior observed by Guth et al. as 'optimising with complex motivations.' Instead, our results indicate that this behavior is not stable in the sense that it can be easily displaced by simple optimizing behavior, once small changes are made in the playing conditions."

10. In the second game the subject now in the role of player 1 had no opportunity to observe that no player 2 was present, since in this experiment the two bargainers sat at computer terminals in different rooms.

11. Note that this rule makes the games more like ultimatum games, since some demands of player 1 (e.g., demands of less than 90 percent in games with discount factor of .1) can only be rejected at the cost of disagreement.

12. Similar results are observed in two period games with even more extreme equilibrium predictions by Weg and Smith (1992).

13. Recall that the unstructured bargaining experiments discussed in chapter 1 found support for the qualitative predictions about risk aversion made by theories whose point predictions were systematically in error.

14. Each of the earlier experiments was designed to correspond to the case that the players have equal discount factors, i.e., $\delta_1 = \delta_2 = \delta$, with the costliness of delay implemented by making the amount of money being divided in period $t + 1$ equal to δ times the amount available at period t. Since half the cells of the experimental design of Ochs and Roth require different discount rates for the two bargainers, the discounting could not be implemented in this way. Instead, in each period, the commodity to be divided consisted of 100 "chips." In period 1 of each game, each chip was worth \$0.30 to each bargainer. In period 2, each chip was worth $\delta_1(\$0.30)$ to player 1 and $\delta_2(\$0.30)$ to player 2, and in period 3 of the three period games each chip was worth $(\delta_1)^2(\$0.30)$ and $(\delta_2)^2(\$0.30)$ respectively. That is, the rate at which subjects were paid for each of the 100 chips that they might receive depended on their discount rate and the period in which agreement was reached.

15. Having only one payoff round helps control for income effects.

16. When the necessary data from these earlier experiments were not contained in published accounts, they were readily available from the working papers circulated by the authors. That this is a good experimental practice cannot be overemphasized, since the easy availability of data permits just these sorts of comparisons. And there is a special place in heaven for any journal editor who permits unaggregated data to be published. (Of course, most of these places remain vacant.)

17. Kravitz and Gunto (1992) investigate this hypothesis by conducting an ultimatum game experiment in which insulting or accommodating messages (prepared by the experimenters) are presented along with the offers (which are also prepared by the experimenters, although subjects are led to believe that other subjects have sent the offers). Holding offers constant, they observe a higher rate of rejection of offers accompanied by insulting messages. They remark (80) that "the effects of [the messages] illustrate the importance of nonstrategic factors in economic behavior." They also report a roleplaying experiment (in which all prizes are hypothetical) and a questionnaire study in which subjects are asked to estimate the rejection rates for various offers. From these they conclude that the primary motivation leading to offers of equal division is the fear that lower offers are likely to be rejected. Apart from its bearing on the matter at hand, this experiment also allows me to note that experiments like this one, which are primarily addressed to an audience of psychologists, often tend to have a different style from those in the economics literature, even when they build upon the same prior experiments and explore similar hypotheses. In this connection, see also Loewenstein, Thompson, and Bazerman (1989), who estimate a utility function for distributions of income in bargaining outcomes, based on data in which subjects rate how satisfied they would be with various outcomes to a hypothetical bargaining situation. They reach the conclusion, similar to that reached on the basis of some of the quite different experiments surveyed in this chapter, that subjects dislike inequalities in which they receive the smaller share much more than they dislike inequalities as such; that is, their concerns seem to focus more on not being at a disadvantage than on being fair. Although I cannot begin to explore it here, it is interesting to note how different, although complementary, styles of research may develop in different disciplines for reasons that are dictated not merely by different choices of problems or even different theoretical dispositions, but also by the history and sociology of the disciplines.

18. However, Ochs and Roth (1989) do report consistency across subgames; for example, the pattern of offers and responses observed in the second period of those three period games in which the first offer is rejected resembles the pattern observed in the first period offers and responses. This could be interpreted as indirect evidence supporting the subgame perfectness hypothesis with respect to the unobserved preferences.

19. These latter two kinds of equal divisions were different from each other even in the first round of their experiment because (92) "in contrast to the procedure used by Ochs and Roth, in the present study discounting commenced on round 1," so that bargainers who split the chips equally nevertheless have different earnings if they have different discount factors.

20. Similar results are found in a subsequent study by Weg and Zwick (1991). An earlier study using this kind of cost structure viewed from a different theoretical framework is reported in Contini (1968).

21. For both sets of discount factors he observes that about 20% of the first offers are rejected, with about 85% of these rejections followed by disadvantageous counterproposals when the discount factors were (2/3, 1/3), and about 20% when the discount factors were (1/3, 2/3). (Daughety [1993] presents a model of utilities in which envy plays a role, in which disadvantageous offers are predicted to occur more often when player 2's discount factor is low.) Zwick, Rapoport, and Howard (1992) make the related observation that the rate of disadvantageous counteroffers is sensitive to the probability of termination.

22. Garcia and Roth (in preparation) get similar replication for both inexperienced and experienced Ss in two period games with discount factors (.4,.4) and (.6,.6) with a $10 initial pie.

23. See Yaari and Bar Hillel (1984), Kahneman, Knetsch, and Thaler (1986b), and Blinder and Choi (1990) for studies that emphasize this point in nonbargaining contexts.

24. For related experiments, see Zwick, Rapoport, and Howard (1992), Weg, Zwick, and Rapoport (forthcoming), and Kahn and Murnighan (1993). Kahn and Murnighan look at a large experimental design, varying the existence of an outside option, its size, the probability of termination following a rejection, the discount factor, and which player is the first mover. (They refer to the resulting experiment as a "Noah's ark $2 \times 2 \times 2 \times 2 \times 2$ design") They find

some qualitative support for game-theoretic predictions, but only weakly, and observe that, contrary to the equilibrium prediction, players often exercised their outside option. In summation, they state "Previous demand and ultimatum game research . . . also contributes to the idea that game theory does not predict at all well in these situations. But these studies often concluded that concerns for fairness or altruism might explain the results. . . . But the data here find no support for fairness or altruism either. Instead, these data make a strong case for Ochs and Roth's (1989) hypothesis that players focus on a minimally acceptable offer. . . ." Weg et al. (1992) interpret their results as being more favorable to game-theoretic predictions, although they surmise on the basis of their results that some of Binmore et al.'s (1991) observations may be sensitive to the choice of parameters.

25. Guth and Tietz (1988) write (113): "Our hypothesis is that the consistency of experimental observations and game theoretic predictions observed by Binmore et al . . . is solely due to the moderate relation of equilibrium payoffs which makes the game theoretic solution socially more acceptable." They note that Binmore et al. (1985) examined two-period bargaining games whose equilibrium prediction was for payoffs in the ratio 3:1. In their own experiment, Guth and Tietz employed equilibrium payoff ratios of 9:1. So the equilibrium payoff ratio in these best shot games is virtually identical to those in the bargaining games discussed by Guth and Tietz, since \$3.70/\$0.42 = 8.8.

26. It is worth pausing to consider some of the statistical issues that arise in formally analyzing this kind of experimental data. The fact that each subject played ten consecutive games means that the data from different periods of the same game cannot be assumed to be independent. And not only autocorrelation, but also potential learning effects (diminishing variance by periods) raise questions that need to be addressed in analyzing the data. There remains considerable room for improvement in econometric methods and tests to address these issues. In Prasnikar and Roth (1992), we approached them as follows. Let $y_{it} = \mu_t + \epsilon_{it}$, where i indexes individuals and t indexes periods. Consider the following error structure:

$$(*) \quad \epsilon_{it} = \rho \, \epsilon_{it-1} + u_{it}, \qquad E(u^2_{it}) = \sigma^2_t$$

and $E(\epsilon_{it}, \epsilon_{jt}') = 0$ if $i \neq j$. To test whether σ^2_t is constant across t, we used the Breusch-Pagan (score) test. The test statistics are 87.59 for the full information game, 17.95 for the partial information game, and 27.48 for the ultimatum game. Since the critical value is $\chi^2(0.95; 9) = 16.90$, this indicates the presence of heteroscedasticity. We corrected for the presence of heteroscedasticity using White's (1980) consistent estimator of Σ. To test for autocorrelation, we estimated ρ in the above equation while imposing the constraint $\sigma^2_t = \sigma^2$. The estimates of ρ are 0.247 (standard error = 0.109) for the full information game, 0.644 (standard error = 0.076) for the partial information game, and 0.694 (standard error = 0.081) for the ultimatum game. Thus we also found evidence of positive autocorrelation. A test of the joint null hypothesis of no heteroscedasticity and no autocorrelation produced a test statistics of 21.43 which is greater then the critical $\chi^2(0.95; 10) = 18.30)$.

27. Twenty subjects participated, each playing ten rounds. In each round two markets, A and B, operated simultaneously, and buyers were switched between the markets from round to round so that the composition of the markets was not the same in any two rounds. In each round every buyer submitted a price, and the maximum price in each market was reported to the seller in that market, who could accept or reject it. The transactions were then made public (by being recorded on a blackboard). Successful buyers were identified only by anonymous identification numbers. If more than one buyer offered the maximum price (and it was accepted) then one of those buyers would be chosen at random to complete the transaction.

28. The computation of pure strategy perfect equilibria is straightforward. The assumption of subgame perfectness means that the seller never rejects the maximum bid when it is positive. Because any buyer who does not submit the maximum bid earns zero with certainty, there cannot be any equilibria at which the high bidder makes a positive profit (by bidding \$9.95 or less) and some other bidder submits a lower bid, since a low bidder could do better by raising his bid to the high bid, which would then give him a positive expected payoff. So if

the high bid is no greater than $9.95, all bids must be equal. But if all bids are equal, they cannot be less than $9.95, since if they were then a bidder who raised his bid by $0.05 would increase his expected payoff since he would win with certainty instead of with probability 1/9. So the only perfect equilibrium at which the maximum bid is not $10.00 has all bids equal to $9.95, so that the seller earns virtually all of the profit. There are also equilibria at which the maximum bid is $10.00. In fact, *any* distribution of bids at which two or more buyers bid $10.00 is an equilibrium, since in this case no buyer can earn a positive payoff (even) by changing his bid. So there are many equilibria, but only two equilibrium prices, $10.00 and $9.95. And the situation is the same when we consider perfect equilibria in mixed strategies.

29. There are two kinds of equal-payoff outcomes: if all buyers offer a price of $1, every player has an expected payoff of $1, and if all buyers offer a price of $5, the successful buyer will have the same payoff as the seller.

30. In the subsequent experiments with this game discussed next, the transaction price has sometimes settled down at $9.95 (i.e., at the other equilibrium price).

31. It is noteworthy that the high bids were not submitted by a small proportion of the buyers (in which case we might have supposed that the high bidders were unrepresentative of the buyer population). *Half* of the buyers (9 out of 18) submitted at least one bid of $10, and in the last period 6 out of 18 buyers submitted bids of $9.95 or $10.00.

32. Regarding the sequential market game, Prasnikar and Roth (1992, 885) emphasize this point as follows:

> Note that we are not claiming that the dynamics that led to equilibrium in the later rounds of this game are necessarily due to simple income maximization, although it would be surprising if this did not play some role. To be clear about what we mean, it may be useful to speculate a little, beyond the evidence, about buyers' motivations. Consider a hypothetical buyer whose preference for equality is such that his very first choice outcome would be to have all buyers submit identical bids of $5 (or $1), and who bids accordingly in the first two rounds. When he sees how high the actual transaction price is he becomes annoyed with the other buyers and (with the same motivation that would have caused him to express his displeasure by rejecting too small an offer if he were a seller in the ultimatum game) he decides to become the high bidder in round 3, in order to deprive other buyers of the benefits of what he sees as their unreasonable behavior. The point in considering such a hypothetical buyer is to observe that in *this* game his non-monetary preferences cause him to behave in a manner indistinguishable from an income maximizer, while in the ultimatum game his preferences lead away from the equilibrium predicted for income maximizers.

33. At the time the experiment was conducted, Ljubljana, which is the capital of Slovenia, was a part of Yugoslavia.

34. This problem could not have been avoided by presenting the identical instructions in English to English-speaking subjects in each of the countries. Aside from the selection effects of choosing only English speakers, there is no way to control the different connotations that various English terms and phrases might have to nonnative English speakers in different countries.

35. After the Ljubljana data were collected, a devaluation reduced Yugoslav currency units by a factor of 10,000.

36. The observed distributions are significantly different for every pair of countries except the United States and Slovenia, and the between country differences are larger than the differences between groups within a given country. (Because the distributions are highly asymmetric, the statistical test used is the Mann-Whitney U test, which is based on the rank of each observation in the sample distribution.) Other observations of bargaining behavior in different subject pools are found in Spiegel, Currie, Sonnenschein, and Sen (1990), Carter and Irons (1991), Kagel, Kim, and Moser (1992), and Eckel and Grossman (1992a,1992b). Carter and Irons report some subject pool differences between economics and psychology students in

one period play, while Kagel, Kim, and Moser find no such differences in an experiment with repeated play against different opponents (although the experiment of Kagel et al. is primarily designed to investigate the effects of information differences in bargaining, so there are respects in which it and the experiment of Carter and Irons are difficult to compare). Eckel and Grossman report gender differences.

37. In the tenth round, 19 percent of offers were rejected in the United States, 23 percent in Slovenia, 14 percent in Japan, and 13 percent in Israel.

38. Note how the formal structure of this game is very different from that of an ultimatum game, in which players know which role they will play, and move sequentially, rather than simultaneously. For example, because players move simultaneously, this game has no subgames, unlike the ultimatum game. This difference is magnified in the repeated game: in a repeated ultimatum game, players can receive experience on past plays of the game, for example, on how player 2's reacted to offers which were made, but not on how they would have reacted to other offers that were not made. That players have this information in the present design vastly increases the number of information sets, and thus the strategy sets, of the players. How issues like these influence the design of experiments will be briefly discussed later, in the section on the strategy method. The experiments referred to in that section share with this one the feature that subjects simultaneously select entire strategies. But Harrison and McCabe's design differs from the typical "strategy method" experiment in which subjects only get feedback on the actual play of the game, rather than on the entire strategies chosen by other subjects. Thus the change in the repeated game under Harrison and McCabe's design is more substantial than that discussed later.

39. In this family of models, which can be applied to games with finite pure strategy sets, each player initially has some propensity to play his ith pure strategy, given by some real number q_i, and the probability that he plays his ith pure strategy the first time he plays the game is $q_i/\Sigma q_j$, where the sum is over all his pure strategies j. If the ith pure strategy is played at stage k and the player receives a payoff of x, then the propensity to play strategy i is updated according to the payoff received (e.g., by replacing q_i with $q_i + x$), so that pure strategies that have been played and have met with success tend over time to be played with greater frequency than those that have met with less success.

40. The reason is that the propensity to make very low offers falls more quickly than the propensity to accept very low offers rises. This is because the difference between accepting and rejecting a very low offer is small and thus has only modest impact on the propensities of player 2 to reject small offers, while the difference for player 1 between having a very low offer rejected, and earning zero, or having a moderately low offer accepted, and consequently earning more than half the pie, is much larger, and more quickly encourages player 1 to abandon very low offers in favor of somewhat larger ones. Once player 1 makes very low offers less often, there is even less pressure on player 2s to learn not to reject them, and so on.

41. See also Gale, Binmore, and Samuelson (forthcoming) for some simulations of ultimatum game play using replicator dynamics motivated by biological evolution.

42. Let me hasten to add that there is no reason to think that subjects use the particular simple learning rule just described. In fact, there are good reasons to think that they do not, for example, the convergence observed in the simulations takes many more iterations than the ten iterations needed to produce the same behavior in the experiments. The fact that the simple simulated learning rule may be very different from those used by the experimental subjects, but both sets of rules produce similar intermediate term outcomes, suggests that the phenomena discussed here may be quite robust—i.e., that very different learning rules will converge to perfect equilibrium in the best shot and market games, but will not converge to perfect equilibrium in the ultimatum game.

43. And of course, different theoretical developments suggest different ways to analyze experimental data. In just such a way, Fudenberg and Levine (1993c) reanalyze the best shot data of Prasnikar and Roth (1992) and the ultimatum data of Roth et al. (1991), based on the learning-based equilibrium notions set out in Fudenberg and Levine (1993a,1993b).

44. A bio/bibliographic note: Janet Currie is the former Janet Neelin of Neelin et al. (1988).
45. See, e.g., Kennan and Wilson (1990b), and Card (1990) on labor disputes. And in a study of legal disputes arising from private antitrust litigation, Salop and White (1988, Table 1.9) report a disagreement rate (interpreted as a lack of either a settlement or a dismissal) of about 25 percent, on a sample of almost 2,000 cases, and they cite other studies that find comparable rates. Kennan and Wilson (1993) further observe that disagreement rates in legal disputes substantially underestimate the inefficiencies associated with such disputes, and they cite studies indicating that the sum of the attorneys' fees often exceed the amount collected by successful plaintiffs. And Salop and White (1988, 43) estimate that in their sample "the litigation costs of settled cases were 70 to 80 percent of those of fully litigated cases." A similar argument can be made about the level of inefficiency in labor agreements. (At the Summer School on Bargaining held by the Institute for Advanced Studies of the Hebrew University of Jerusalem in June, 1990, Ken Arrow cited featherbedding agreements reached in the transportation and printing industries as examples of how disagreement rates in labor negotiations underestimate the inefficiency rate.) Of course, in contrast to experiments, in field studies it may be difficult to determine the set of efficient agreements.
46. One exception is Rapoport, Frenkel, and Perner (1977), who employed bargaining games presented in a matrix format in which Pareto optimal mixtures were not transparent and who observed significant departures from Pareto optimality.
47. Harrison and McKee (1985) argue that it is difficult to interpret the experiment of Hoffman and Spitzer (1982) as they intended, since the fact that controllers settled for a smaller payoff than they could have taken for themselves indicates that their monetary payoffs did not serve to experimentally control their preferences, which were therefore uncontrolled. Using somewhat larger payoffs, Harrison and McKee report a lower frequency of equal divisions, but the percentage of Pareto optimal agreements remained comparably high.
    In their 1985 paper, Hoffman and Spitzer report that in similar experiments in which the position of "controller" was allocated to the winner of a simple game and in which the instructions to the participants gave the controller "moral authority" to claim his prize unilaterally, the frequency of equal splits was reduced, while the frequency of Pareto optimal agreements remained high (91 percent overall). See Shogren (1992) for a related experiment using binary lottery games.
48. For example, Harrison (1992), in discussing a subsequent paper (Harrison, Hoffman, Rutstrom, and Spitzer 1987) in this stream of work, notes that the subjects had a special motivation to reach what they regarded as the "right" answer. He says (13), "In this case there was something other than financial motivation at work; it should be noted that their Professor, the experimenter, was present in the room, albeit silent and impassive." Precisely to avoid such uncontrolled sources of motivation, many experimenters routinely exclude their own students from participating in the experiments they conduct.
49. And there are a number of fairly close "between experiment" comparisons that support this conclusion. For example, Binmore, Shaked, and Sutton (1989) report an experiment in which, as in Hoffman and Spitzer (1982), one of the bargainers can unilaterally give himself a certain minimum payoff. In their experiment, in which bargaining is conducted anonymously, the player with the outside option receives no less than his outside option, and there are significant numbers of rejected offers, in sharp contrast to the results of Hoffman and Spitzer. And in another pair of closely parallel experiments, Roth and Malouf (1982) observed fewer equal splits and more disagreements in anonymous bargaining than were observed by Nydegger and Owen (1975) in face-to-face bargaining.
50. In the introduction to their 1950 study "Social Pressures in Informal Groups," Festinger, Schachter, and Back note (4) that "much of the pressure to conformity undoubtedly comes from the smaller groups within a society to which individuals belong. These pressures exist as group standards of the face-to-face group and are only sometimes formalized and made very explicit. Their enforcement depends more on relatively subtle influences and indirect pressures although these are frequently very powerful."

51. The data for the anonymous bargaining condition were collected as part of the Prasnikar and Roth (1992) study already discussed in section I.B.4. The data for the two face-to-face conditions were also collected by Prasnikar and Roth, from the same subject pool, using the same instructions modified only to accommodate the new rules of communication. Twenty-eight subjects were recruited and randomly divided into the buyer/seller positions in the two conditions so that there were seven buyers and seven sellers in each of the two conditions. In each condition, each buyer bargained once with each seller over the division of $10. One of the seven bargaining rounds was then chosen at random to be the payoff round.

52. But note again the statistical problems that arise even in the analysis of such a small data set as this, because of the lack of independence between different rounds of the same game. Recall the discussion in footnote 26 of statistics in connection with the similar experimental design of Prasnikar and Roth (1992).

53. In the unrestricted communication condition, bargainers could (and did) sometimes state that they would not accept anything less than an equal share. Formal theoretical models of how such "cheap talk" (i.e., not backed up by any formal method of commitment) might influence behavior are beginning to appear in the literature (see, e.g., Crawford 1990 or Farrell 1987). For an experiment directly motivated by such models, see Cooper, DeJong, Forsythe, and Ross (1989) (and cf. chapter 3).

54. Recall from our discussion of the experiment of Forsythe et al. (1994) that a dictator game differs from an ultimatum game in that player 2 may not accept or reject player 1's offer— whatever division player 1 proposes is the outcome of the game. So in a dictator game, unlike an ultimatum game, player 1 need not be concerned with the possibility that player 2 will reject his proposal.

55. The modal offer in a cell with Forsythe et al.'s ultimatum instructions was 50 percent, while in various cells in which the instructions sought to encourage low offers the mode was 40 percent, with a second mode at 30 percent in one cell.

56. A particularly elegant feature of Bolton and Zwick's design is the way in which the anonymous and nonanonymous conditions and the ultimatum game and impunity game conditions were made closely comparable. In the anonymity condition, player 1 began the game by putting a box, corresponding to one of the feasible (discrete) offers, in a mailbag for transmittal to player 2. Player 2 began the game with a *pair* of boxes corresponding to each possible offer, one corresponding to rejection of the offer, and one corresponding to acceptance. Player 2's boxes contained envelopes with the payoffs, and player 2 responded to player 1's offer by unsealing one of the two boxes, taking out his own envelope, and putting the box and player 1's payoff in the mailbag to be transmitted to player 1. At the end of this process player 2 once again had in his possession a pair of boxes corresponding to each possible offer (since the one sent to him by player 1 substituted for the one he opened and sent back) so that the experimenter could verify that only one box had been opened (the boxes all had seals) without knowing what offer had been sent or whether it had been accepted or rejected. At the end of a round, all remaining boxes were put in a trash bag, and it is by examining the discarded boxes after the experiment that the experimenters were able to know what offers and acceptance/rejections had been made during the round, without knowing which subjects had made them. For the nonanonymity conditions, the only difference was that instead of boxes filled with cash, the players received cards and, to be paid, had to turn in the cards to the experimenter, who would therefore know (from their cards) what had transpired.

57. Both Bolton and Zwick's and Hoffman et al.'s results were presented together at a conference on experimental economics conducted at the University of Amsterdam in September 1992. Hoffman et al. (1992) responded to the earlier criticism by including the disagreement data from the nonanonymous ultimatum games reported. The disagreement data did not support the conclusion that behavior in the "moral entitlement" conditions was moving in the direction of perfect equilibrium play, because a nonnegligible percentage of the lower offers that were elicited in these conditions had in fact been rejected. Thus the results of these two investigations are not in fact quite as different as they seemed when the disagreement data were not available.

58. Two interesting experiments that show that similar kinds of "reciprocal fairness" are not extinguished by market environments are reported in Fehr, Kirchsteiger, and Riedl (1993a,1993b).

59. Questions about volatile laboratory environments are an area in which it may be profitable for experimental economists to examine the psychology literature: the earlier mentioned work of Robyn Dawes on public goods comes to mind in this regard, as does the bargaining experiment of Deutsch and Kotik (1978). For a review of the social psychology literature on negotiation, see Thompson (1990), for the organizational behavior literature, see Neale and Bazerman (1991).

60. Marwell and Schmitt (1968), in a paper titled "Are 'Trivial' Games the Most Interesting Psychologically?" argued that laboratory games in which the underlying economic motivations are small relative to other motivations may be especially good instruments for studying these other motivations.

61. For example, the origins of the Cuban missile crisis have sometimes been attributed to Nikita Kruschev's impression in his first face-to-face summit meeting with John Kennedy that Kennedy was indecisive and would not respond to the stationing of missiles.

62. And there is experimental evidence that negotiators who are acting as agents behave differently than when they are acting as principals: see, for example, Lamm (1978) and the references he cites. (Lamm finds that negotiators elected to be representatives of groups have more disagreements than those bargaining on their own behalf.) Similarly, Shogren (1989) reports that face-to-face negotiations proceed differently when subjects are acting as part of a team rather than as individuals, and Schotter, Snyder, and Zheng (1992) report that principals act somewhat as if they are submitting sealed bids when they give instructions to agents who will bargain on their behalf (with a consequent loss of efficiency). Of course, different kinds of inefficiencies (from the point of view of the principals) are introduced when both sides hire agents: see Ashenfelter and Bloom (1990) for some estimates of the extent to which the decision to hire lawyers in certain kinds of negotiations constitutes a prisoner's dilemma.

63. Recall the discussion of bargaining in chapter 1.

64. Recall the discussion of binary lottery games in sections II.C.2 and II.F.4 of chapter 1. In a binary lottery game, subjects are paid in lottery tickets which determine their probability of winning one of two monetary prizes, so that each subject's expected utility can be taken to be his probability of winning the larger of his two prizes.

65. Because of the high variance in the time taken to reach agreement in the cases in which agreement was reached, the only significant differences were between game 1, which had the shortest mean time to agreement, and game 4, which had the longest.

66. The doubling of pie size was achieved by doubling the number of periods of the game. Forsythe et al. also consider the effect of negotiations over long-term versus short-term contracts.

67. In games in which players knew the value of one another's prizes, the potentially focal division $(h, 100 - h)$ was taken to be the equal expected value division, while (50,50) was taken to be the only focal agreement for games in which the bargainers had equal prizes, and for games in which they did not know one another's prizes. Since each of the experiments summarized in the table was a binary lottery game, in the event of disagreement each bargainer had a probability of 0 of winning his prize, so $(d_1, d_2) = (0,0)$.

68. In game-theoretic terminology, this means that the game of incomplete information (in which some aspects of the game tree are not common knowledge) is *modeled* as a game of *imperfect* information, in which the game tree is common knowledge, but players have different information about an initial chance move.

69. That is, the experiments are designed to implement the games of imperfect information used to model situations of incomplete information.

70. This mode was most pronounced for the HH pairs, where 12 out of 13 observed agreements gave each player a gross payoff of 10 (and the other agreement had gross payoffs of 9.5 and 10.5). And although equal agreements were the mode in the LL case, where equal agreements

are predicted (14 out of 56 LL agreements were (10,10) splits, with the next most commonly observed agreement, a (9,11) split, being observed 7 times), 75 percent of the observations (42 out of 56) were *not* equal splits. About these, the authors say (145):

> It is interesting to look at the reasons for the occurrence of so many cases of LL-agreements where one player received more than the other. One may be tempted to think that the player with the higher payoff achieves this result by some kind of bluffing behavior which involves repetitions of demand in order to convey the impression that he is a type H player. Actually in 25 of the 42 cases of LL-agreements with unequal payoffs the player with the higher agreement payoff did not repeat his demand even once. Obviously in these cases the other player either had a lower initial demand or he lowered his demand more quickly. The player with the higher agreement payoff did not have to do anything special in order to get the higher payoff. It just happened to him that the other behaved in a "soft" way.

71. Recall that the method of controlling for risk aversion via binary lottery games had not yet been introduced at the time this experiment was conducted.
72. In a subsequent paper, Hoggatt, Brandstatter, and Blatman (1978) refer to such robots as *"Selten* robots." (See also Hoggatt [1969] for an earlier exploration of robots in experimental work.)
73. Like Hoggatt and Selten et al. (1978), Forsythe et al. conclude that the predictions of the incomplete information model about the frequency of disagreements capture important features of the observed behavior, particularly in view of the base level rate of disagreements observed even in complete information experiments (recall Table 4.5a).
74. Recall our discussion of the communication hypothesis versus the uncontrolled social utility hypothesis in connection with the *lower* frequency of disagreement observed by Radner and Schotter (1989) when increased communication was also accompanied by face-to-face interaction in the environment they studied. (Radner and Schotter's environment is further discussed next.)
75. The conclusions about risk aversion are only indirect inferences, because, as the authors note, they have attempted to neither measure nor control for risk aversion. In this respect they note (268):

> If the subjects were all selfish expected-utility maximizers . . . the heterogeneity in risk attitudes could be eliminated by using the ingenious binary lottery procedure introduced by Roth and Malouf (1979). We chose not to use this procedure, mainly because it introduces considerable additional complexity in an already complicated experimental environment. In addition, the procedure works only under assumptions which are implausible in our context: that each subject acts selfishly and obeys the compound lottery axiom.

> In this regard, Forsythe and his colleagues seem to be conforming to an increasingly common practice in experimental work by attempting to introduce careful and elaborate controls for risk aversion only in experiments in which risk aversion is thought (at the outset) to be a major factor influencing behavior. (See in this connection the papers by Cooper, DeJong, Forsythe, and Ross [1989, 1990], both of which use the binary lottery procedure.) In the context of the present experiment Forsythe et al. are also careful to warn of the problems associated with subjects who may be concerned about the distribution of payoffs rather than merely with their own payoffs, since for such subjects the outcomes will no longer be binary even when binary lottery games are employed. (Recall the discussion of binary lottery games in chapter 1.)

76. Note the similarity to the conclusions of Kennan and Wilson (1993) discussed in the beginning of this chapter in connection with the "complete information" environments considered by Ochs and Roth (1989).
77. A pair of strategies that would achieve 100 percent efficiency would be for each player to state his reservation price. But this would not be an equilibrium, since when there are substan-

tial gains from trade (i.e., when the buyer's reservation price is substantially higher than the seller's) then the buyer could have increased his profit by stating a lower price, and the seller could have increased his profit by stating a higher price. But when both players "shade" their bids in this way, they will miss those trades that could have occurred, for small profit, when the buyer's reservation price is only slightly higher than the seller's. So there is a tradeoff between efficiency and the maximization of expected profit that occurs at equilibrium.

78. The theoretical argument is roughly that high degrees of efficiency can be achieved in the many period game via an equilibrium in which deviation is deterred by the threat of adopting a highly inefficient equilibrium in the final periods. Precisely the degree of efficiency that can be achieved depends on both the length of the game and the distribution from which values are drawn, since the players can only detect deviations statistically.

79. Recall the discussion of learning in section I.

80. Subjects were not informed of the termination rule in case the payoffs became too small, and the authors report that fewer than 6 percent of the games were terminated for this reason.

81. Thus the experimental game approximates the game from which the predictions are derived, but differs in having a finite stopping rule, a discrete distribution of buyer values, and a positive probability that the buyer's value equals the seller's.

82. A similarly designed incomplete information experiment that focuses on the effect of varying the uncertainty about the amount available to be divided is reported by Rapoport, Sundali, and Potter (1992). Some related observations are made by Straub and Murnighan (1992) and by Croson (1992), who conduct ultimatum game experiments in which the amount to be divided may be either known or unknown by player 2 (but in which no attempt was made to induce a probability distribution on the unknown amount).

83. In much of the German experimental literature following Selten (1967) the term "strategy method" is reserved for a set of procedures in which subjects first gain experience playing the game in the usual way, before being asked to submit strategies, and have the opportunity to revise those strategies based on further experience.

84. Since both players know the timing structure of the game, this could have an effect not only on the accepter/rejecter but also on the proposer. This might be true for purely behavioral reasons not captured in formal game-theoretic models of idealized rationality (e.g., if subjects are unable to adhere to commitments they would wish to make before knowing what proposal will be made), but also for reasons reflected in formal game-theoretic models. For example, the notion of subgame perfect equilibrium is lost in the transition from the extensive to the strategic form of the game, since there are no subgames in a game in which players state their strategies simultaneously.

85. The previously published experiments were Roth, Malouf, and Murnighan (1981), Roth and Murnighan (1982), and Murnighan, Roth, and Schoumaker (1988), all of which are briefly described in chapter 1. Roth et al. (1988, 808) caution that "although all this data comes from laboratory experiments, there is a sense in which it is not all fully 'experimental data,' since the experiments were mostly designed for purposes other than to test specific hypotheses about agreement times."

86. This experiment was briefly discussed above as a test of the complete information model of disagreement frequency proposed in Roth (1985).

87. The general procedures were the same as those in Roth and Murnighan (1982), discussed in chapter 1.

88. "For example, labor negotiators often attribute a tendency to reach agreements just before contracts expire to the difficulty of selling any agreement to a diverse constituency if there is still time for continuing negotiations. However the deadline effect observed in our laboratory environment cannot be attributed to this, since each bargainer is bargaining strictly on his own behalf."

89. Cramton and Tracy (1992) also present new empirical evidence from field data concerning deadline effects. In data concerning 5,002 contracts culled from publications of the Bureau of Labor Statistics and the Bureau of National Affairs, they observe a sharp peak in settlement rates just *after* the deadline created by the expiration of the existing contract.

90. I don't know of any experiments that directly address this point. However, Coursey (1982) compared single play bargaining with a 1 hour deadline to repeated bargaining with a 128 second deadline and found more disagreements in the latter condition. Since most disagreements were observed in early periods of the repeated bargaining, when bargainers have the most incentives to engage in reputation building (since they bargain repeatedly with the same partner), it would be premature to draw any conclusions about the influence of the deadlines in this experiment.

91. See also Rabin (1993) for some theoretical work on fairness motivated by experimental results.

Bibliography

Albers, Wulf, and Gisela Albers. 1983. On the prominence structure of the decimal system. In *Decision making under uncertainty*, R.W. Scholz, editor. Amsterdam: Elsevier. 271–87.

Ashenfelter, Orley. 1987. A model of arbitral behavior. *American Economic Review*, 77: 342–46.

Ashenfelter, Orley, and David Bloom. 1984. Models of arbitrator behavior: Theory and evidence. *American Economic Review* 74:111–25.

———. 1990. Lawyers as agents of the devil in a prisoner's dilemma game. Mimeo.

Ashenfelter, Orley, and Janet Currie. 1990. Negotiator behavior and the occurrence of disputes. *American Economic Review, Papers and Proceedings* 80:416–20.

Ashenfelter, Orley, Janet Currie, Henry S. Farber, and Matthew Spiegel. 1992. An experimental comparison of dispute rates in alternative arbitration systems. *Econometrica* 60: 1407–33.

Axelrod, Robert. 1970. *Conflict of interest*. Chicago: Markham.

Berg, Joyce, John Dickhaut, and Kevin McCabe. 1993. Trust, reciprocity, and social Norms. Mimeo. University of Minnesota.

Binmore, Ken, Peter Morgan, Avner Shaked, and John Sutton. 1991. Do people exploit their bargaining power?: An experimental study. *Games and Economic Behavior* 3:295–322.

Binmore, Ken, Avner Shaked, and John Sutton. 1985. Testing noncooperative bargaining theory: A preliminary study. *American Economic Review* 75:1178–80.

———. 1988. A further test of noncooperative bargaining theory: Reply. *American Economic Review* 78:837–9.

———. 1989. An outside option experiment. *Quarterly Journal of Economics* 104:753–70.

Blinder, Alan S., and Don H. Choi. 1990. A shred of evidence on theories of wage stickiness. *Quarterly Journal of Economics* 1003–15.

Boden, Leslie. 1989. Dispute resolution in worker's compensation: The role of adversarial experts. Mimeo. Boston University.

Bolton, Gary. 1991. A comparative model of bargaining: Theory and evidence. *American Economic Review* 81:1096–1136.

Bolton, Gary E. 1993. The rationality of splitting equally. Working Paper. Penn State University.

Bolton, Gary E., Elena Katok, and Rami Zwick. Forthcoming. Dictator game giving: Rules of fairness versus random acts of kindness. *International Journal of Game Theory*.

Bolton, Gary E., and Rami Zwick. Forthcoming. Anonymity versus punishment in ultimatum bargaining. *Games and economic behavior*.

Burrows, Paul, and Graham Loomes. 1990. The impact of fairness on bargaining behavior. Mimeo. Center for Experimental Economics. University of York.

Card, David. 1988. Strikes and wages: A test of a signalling model. Mimeo. Princeton University.

Card, David. 1990. Strikes and bargaining: A survey of the recent empirical literature. *American Economic Review* 80:410–15.

Carter, John R., and Michael D. Irons. 1991. Are economists different, and if so, why? *Journal of Economic Perspectives* 5:171–77.

Chatterjee, Kalyan, and William Samuelson. 1983. Bargaining under incomplete information. *Operations Research* 31:835–51.

Contini, Bruno. 1968. The value of time in bargaining negotiations: Some experimental evidence. *American Economic Review* 58:374–93.

Cooper, Russell, Douglas V. DeJong, Robert Forsythe, and Thomas W. Ross. 1989. Communication in the battle of the sexes game: Some experimental results. *RAND Journal of Economics* 20:568–87.

———. 1990. Selection criteria in coordination games: Some experimental results. *American Economic Review* 80:218–33.

Coursey, Don L. 1982. Bilateral bargaining, Pareto optimality, and the empirical frequency of impasse. *Journal of Economic Behavior and Organization* 3:243–59.

Cramton, Peter C., and Joseph S. Tracy. 1992. Strikes and delays in wage bargaining: Theory and data. *American Economic Review* 82:100–21.

Crawford, Vincent P. 1990. Explicit communication and bargaining outcomes. *American Economic Review, Papers and Proceedings* 80:213–19.

Croson, Rachel T. A. 1992. Information in ultimatum games: An experimental study. Mimeo. Department of Economics. Harvard University.

Currie, Janet. 1989. Who uses interest arbitration? The case of British Columbia's teachers 1947–1981. *Industrial and Labor Relations Review* 42:363–79.

Currie, Janet, and Sheena McConnell. 1989. Strikes and arbitration in the public sector: Can legislation reduce dispute costs? Mimeo. UCLA.

Daughety, Andrew F. 1993. Socially-influenced choice: Equity considerations in models of consumer choice and in games. Working paper #93–01. Department of Economics, University of Iowa.

Dawes, Robyn M. 1991. Social dilemmas, economic self-interest, and evolutionary theory. In *Recent research in psychology: Frontiers of Mathematical Psychology: essays in honor of Clyde Coombs*, D. R. Brown and J.E.K. Smith, editors, New York: Springer-Verlag.

Deutsch, Morton, and Paul Kotik. 1978. Altruism and bargaining. In *Bargaining Behavior*, Contributions to Experimental Economics 7, Heinz Sauermann, editor, Tubingen: J.C.B. Mohr. 20–40.

Eckel, Catherine C., and Philip Grossman. 1992a. Chivalry and solidarity in ultimatum games. Working paper. Virginia Polytechnic Institute.

———. 1992b. The Price of Fairness: Gender Differences in Punishment Games. Working paper. Virginia Polytechnic Institute.

Farrell, Joseph. 1987. Cheap talk, coordination, and entry. *RAND Journal of Economics* 18: 34–9.

Fehr, Ernst, Georg Kirchsteiger, and Arno Riedl. 1993a. Does fairness prevent market clearing? An experimental investigation. *Quarterly Journal of Economics* 108:437–59.

———. 1993b. Gift exchange and ultimatums in experimental markets. Mimeo. University of Technology. Austria.

Fershtman, Chaim, and Daniel J. Seidmann. Forthcoming. Deadline effects and inefficient delay in bargaining with endogenous commitment. *Journal of Economic Theory*.

Festinger, Leon, Stanley Schachter, and Kurt Back. 1950. *Social pressures in informal groups: A study of human factors in housing*. Stanford, Calif.: Stanford University Press.

Foddy, Margaret. 1989. Information control as a bargaining tactic in social exchange. *Advances in Group Processes* 6:139–78.

Forsythe, Robert, John Kennan, and Barry Sopher. Forthcoming. Dividing a shrinking pie: An experimental study of strikes in bargaining games with complete information. In *Research in experimental economics*, R. Mark Issac (editor). Greenwich, Conn.: JAI Press.

———. 1991. An experimental analysis of bargaining and strikes with one sided private information. *American Economic Review*. 81:253–78.

Forsythe, Robert, Joel L. Horowitz, N. E. Savin, and Martin Sefton. 1994. Fairness in simple bargaining experiments. *Games and economic behavior*.6:347–69.

Fouraker, Lawrence E., and Sidney Siegel. 1963. *Bargaining behavior*. New York: McGraw Hill.

Fudenberg, Drew, and David K. Levine. 1993a. Self-confirming equilibrium. *Econometrica* 61:523–46.

———. 1993b. Steady state learning and Nash equilibrium. *Econometrica* 61:547–73.

———. 1993c. How irrational are subjects In extensive-form games? Discussion paper 14. Harvard Institute of Economic Research, November.

Fudenberg, Drew, David K. Levine, and Jean Tirole. 1985. Infinite-horizon models of bargaining with one-sided incomplete information. In *Game-theoretic models of bargaining*, A. E. Roth, editor, Cambridge: Cambridge University Press. 73–98.

Gale, John, Kenneth G. Binmore, and Larry Samuelson. Forthcoming. Learning to be imperfect: The ultimatum game. *Games and economic behavior*.

Grammer, Karl, Wulf Schiefenhovel, Margret Schleidt, Beatrice Lorenz, and Irenaus Eibl-Eibesfeldt. 1988. Patterns on the face: The eyebrow flash in crosscultural comparison. *Ethology* 77:279–99.

Guth, Werner. 1988. On the behavioral approach to distributive justice: A theoretical and experimental investigation. In *Applied Behavioral Economics*, S. Maital, editor, New York: New York University Press, 2:703–17.

Guth, Werner, R. Schmittberger, and B. Schwarz. 1982. An experimental analysis of ultimatum bargaining. *Journal of Economic Behavior and Organization* 3:367–88.

Guth, Werner, and Reinhard Tietz. 1988. Ultimatum bargaining for a shrinking cake—An experimental analysis. In *Bounded Rational Behavior in Experimental Games and Markets*, R. Tietz, W. Albers, R. Selten, editors, Springer: Berlin.

———. 1990. Ultimatum bargaining behavior: A survey and comparison of experimental results. *Journal of Economic Psychology* 11:417–49.

Guth, Werner, and Menahem Yaari. 1990a. An evolutionary approach to explaining reciprocal behavior in a simple strategic game. Mimeo.

———. 1990b. Incomplete information about reciprocal incentives: An evolutionary approach to explaining cooperative behavior. Mimeo.

Harrison, Glenn W. 1990. Rational expectations and experimental methods. In *Rational Expectations and Efficiency in Futures Markets*, B. A. Goss, editor, London: Routledge.

Harrison, Glenn W. 1992. Flat payoff functions and the experimentalists: Reply to the critics, Mss., February, University of South Carolina.

Harrison, Glenn W., and J. Hirshleifer. 1989. An Experimental Evaluation of Weakest Link/Best Shot Models of Public Goods. *Journal of Political Economy*. 97:201–225.

Harrison, Glenn W., Elizabeth Hoffman, E. E. Rustrom, and Matthew L. Spitzer. 1987. Coasian solutions to the externality problem in experimental markets. *Economic Journal* 97: 388–402.

Harrison, Glenn W, and Kevin A. McCabe. 1991. Testing non-cooperative bargaining theory in experiments. Working paper B-91–03. College of Business Administration, University of South Carolina. Forthcoming in *Research in Experimental Economics*, *vol. 5*, R. Mark Isaac, editor, Greenwich, Conn.: JAI Press.

———.1992b. Expectations and fairness in a simple bargaining experiment. Working paper B-92–10. September, University of South Carolina.

Harrison, Glenn W. and Michael McKee. 1985. Experimental evaluation of the Coase theorem. *Journal of Law and Economics* 28:653–70.

Harsanyi, John C. 1967–1968. Games with incomplete information played by 'Bayesian' players. Parts I-III. *Management Science* 14:159–82, 320–34, 486–502.

Harsanyi, John C., and Reinhard Selten. 1972. A generalized Nash solution for two-person bargaining games with incomplete information. *Management Science* 18:80–106.

Hart, Oliver. 1989. Bargaining and strikes. *Quarterly Journal of Economics* 104:25–44.

Hoffman, Elizabeth, Kevin McCabe, Keith Shachat, and Vernon L. Smith. 1991. Preferences, property rights and anonymity in bargaining games. Mimeo. December, University of Arizona. rev. June 1992.

Hoffman, Elizabeth, Kevin McCabe, and Vernon L. Smith. 1993. On property rights and the monetary stakes in ultimatum game bargaining. Mimeo. University of Arizona.

Hoffman, E., and M. L. Spitzer. 1982. The Coase theorem: Some experimental tests. *Journal of Law and Economics* 25:73–98.

———. 1985. Entitlements, rights, and fairness: An experimental examination of subjects' concepts of distributive justice. *Journal of Legal Studies* 14. 2:259–97.

Hoggatt, Austin C. 1969. Response of paid student subjects to differential behaviour of robots in bifurcated duopoly games. *Review of Economic Studies* 36:417–32.

Hoggatt, Austin C., Hermann Brandstatter, and Peter Blatman. 1978. Robots as instrumental functions in the study of bargaining behavior. In *Bargaining Behavior*, Contributions to Experimental Economics 7, H. Sauermann, editor, Tubingen: J.C.B. Mohr. 179–210.

Hoggatt, Austin C., Reinhard Selten, David Crockett, Shlomo Gill, and Jeff Moore. 1978. Bargaining experiments with incomplete information. In *Bargaining Behavior*, Contributions to Experimental Economics 7, H. Sauermann, editor, Tubingen: J.C.B. Mohr. 127–78.

Kagel, John H., Chung Kim, and Donald Moser. 1992. Ultimatum games with asymmetric information and asymmetric payoffs. Mimeo. University of Pittsburgh.

Kahn, Lawrence M., and J. Keith Murnighan. 1993. A general experiment on bargaining in demand games with outside options. *American Economic Review* 83:1260–80.

Kahneman, Daniel, Jack L. Knetsch, and Richard H. Thaler. 1986a. Fairness and the assumptions of economics. *Journal of Business* 59, no. 4, pt. 2:S285–S300.

———. 1986b. Fairness as a constraint on profit seeking: Entitlements in the market. *American Economic Review* 76:728–41.

Kandori, Michihiro. 1992. Social norms and community enforcement. *Review of Economic Studies* 59:63–80.

Kennan, John. 1980. Pareto optimality and the economics of strike duration. *Journal of Labor Research* 1:77–93.

Kennan, John, and Robert Wilson. 1990a. Theories of bargaining delays. *Science* 7 September, vol. 249: 1124–8.

———. 1990b. Can strategic bargaining models explain collective bargaining data? *American Economic Review, Papers and Proceedings*. May vol. 80: 405–09.

———. 1993. Bargaining with private information. *Journal of Economic Literature* 31:45–104.

Kravitz, David A., and Samuel Gunto. 1992. Decisions and perceptions of recipients in ultimatum bargaining games. *Journal of Socio-Economics* 21:65–84.

Lamm, Helmut. 1978. Group-related influences on negotiation behavior: Two-person negotiation as a function of representation and election. In *Bargaining Behavior*. Contributions to Experimental Economics 7, Heinz Sauermann, editor, Tubingen: J.C.B. Mohr. 284–309.

Leininger, W., P. Linhard, and R. Radner 1989. Equilibria of the sealed-bid mechanism for bargaining with incomplete information. *Journal of Economic Theory* 48:63–106.

Loewenstein, George F., Leigh Thompson, and Max H. Bazerman. 1989. Social utility and decision making in interpersonal contexts. *Journal of Personality and Social Psychology* 57:426–41.

Ma, Ching-to Albert, and Michael Manove. 1993. Bargaining with deadlines and imperfect player control. *Econometrica* 61:1313–39.

Malouf, Michael W. K., and Alvin E. Roth. 1981. Disagreement in bargaining: An experimental study. *Journal of Conflict Resolution* 25:329–48.

Marwell, Gerald, and David R. Schmitt. 1968. Are "trivial" games the most interesting psychologically? *Behavioral Science* 13:125–8.

McConnell, Sheena. 1989. Strikes, wages and private information. *American Economic Review* 79:801–15.

Mehta, Judith, Chris Starmer, and Robert Sugden. 1990. Focal points in bargaining: An experimental investigation. Mimeo. Economics Research Centre, University of East Anglia.

Mitzkewitz, Michael, and Rosemarie Nagel. 1993. Envy, greed and anticipation in ultimatum games with incomplete information: An experimental study. Discussion paper B-181. March. Universitat Bonn. *International Journal of Game Theory* 22:171–98.

Mnookin, Robert et al. 1989. Private ordering revisited: What custodial arrangements are parents negotiating? Mimeo. Stanford University.

Murnighan, J. Keith, Alvin E. Roth, and Francoise Schoumaker. 1988. Risk aversion in bargaining: An experimental study. *Journal of Risk and Uncertainty* 1:101–24.

Myerson, Roger, and Mark Satterthwaite. 1983. Efficient mechanisms for bilateral trading. *Journal of Economic Theory* 29:265–81.

Neale, Margaret A., and Max H. Bazerman. 1991. *Cognition and rationality in negotiation.* New York: The Free Press.

Neelin, Janet, Hugo Sonnenschein, and Matthew Spiegel. 1988. A further test of noncooperative bargaining theory: Comment. *American Economic Review* 78:824–36.

Nydegger, Rudy V., and Guillermo Owen. 1975. Two person bargaining: An experimental test of the Nash axioms. *International Journal of Game Theory* 3:239–349.

Ochs, Jack, and Alvin E. Roth. 1989. An experimental study of sequential bargaining. *American Economic Review* 79:355–84.

Okuno-Fujiwara, Masahiro, and Andrew Postlewaite. 1990. Social norm in random matching games. Mimeo.

Osborne, Martin J., and Ariel Rubinstein. 1990. *Bargaining and markets.* San Diego: Academic Press.

Ponsati-Obiols, Clara. 1989. The deadline effect in bargaining: A theoretical note. Mimeo. Bellcore.

Prasnikar, Vesna, and Alvin E. Roth. 1989. Perceptions of fairness and considerations of strategy in bargaining: Some Experimental Data. Preliminary draft.

———. 1992. Considerations of fairness and strategy: Experimental data from sequential games. *Quarterly Journal of Economics* August:865–88.

Rabin, Matthew. 1993. Incorporating fairness into game theory and economics. *American Economic Review* 83:1281–1302.

Radner, Roy, and Andrew Schotter. 1989. The sealed bid mechanism: An experimental study. *Journal of Economic Theory* 48:179–220.

Rapoport, Amnon, Ido Erev, and Rami Zwick. Forthcoming. An experimental study of buyer-seller negotiation with one-sided incomplete information and time discounting. *Management Science.*

Rapoport, Amnon, James A. Sundali, and Richard E. Potter. 1992. Ultimatum games with incomplete information: Effects of the variability of the pie size. Mimeo. University of Arizona.

Rapoport, Amnon, Eythan Weg, and Dan S. Felsenthal. 1990. Effects of fixed costs in two-person sequential bargaining. *Theory and Decision* 28:47–72.

Rapoport, Anatol, Oded Frenkel, and Josef Perner. 1977. Experiments with cooperative 2×2 games. *Theory and Decision* 8:67–92.

Roth, Alvin E. 1985. Toward a focal-point theory of bargaining. In *Game-theoretic models of bargaining*, A. E. Roth, editor, Cambridge: Cambridge University Press. 259–68.

Roth, Alvin E., and Ido Erev. Learning in extensive-form games: Experimental data and simple dynamic models in the intermediate term. *Games and Economic Behavior* 8 (January): 164–212. (Special Issue on the Nobel Symposium on Game Theory, June 18–20, Bjorkborn, Sweden.)

Roth, Alvin E., and Michael W. K. Malouf. 1979. Game-theoretic models and the role of information in bargaining. *Psychological Review* 86:574–94.

———. 1982. Scale changes and shared information in bargaining: An experimental study. *Mathematical Social Sciences* 3:157–77.

Roth, Alvin E., Michael W. K. Malouf, and J. Keith Murnighan. 1981. Sociological versus strategic factors in bargaining. *Journal of Economic Behavior and Organization* 2: 153–77.

Roth, Alvin E., and J. Keith Murnighan. 1982. The role of information in bargaining: An experimental study. *Econometrica* 50:1123–42.

Roth, Alvin E., J. Keith Murnighan, and Francoise Schoumaker. 1988. The deadline effect in bargaining: Some experimental evidence. *American Economic Review* 78:806–23.

Roth, Alvin E., Vesna Prasnikar, Masahiro Okuno-Fujiwara, and Shmuel Zamir. 1991. Bargaining and market behavior in Jerusalem, Ljubljana, Pittsburgh, and Tokyo: An experimental study. *American Economic Review* 81:1068–95.

Roth, Alvin E., and Francoise Schoumaker. 1983. Expectations and reputations in bargaining: An experimental study. *American Economic Review* 73:362–72.

Rubinstein, Ariel. 1982. Perfect equilibrium in a bargaining model. *Econometrica* 50:97–109.

Salop, Steven C., and Lawrence J. White. 1988. Private antitrust litigation: An introduction and framework. In *Private antitrust litigation*, L. J. White, editor, Cambridge: MIT Press.

Schelling, Thomas C. 1957. Bargaining, communication, and limited war. *Journal of Conflict Resolution* 1:19–36.

Schelling, Thomas C. 1960. *The strategy of conflict*. Cambridge: Harvard University Press.

Schotter, Andrew. 1990. Bad and good news about the sealed-bid mechanism: Some experimental results. *American Economic Review, Papers and Proceedings* 80:220–26.

Schotter, Andrew, Blaine Snyder, and Wei Zheng. 1992. Bargaining through agents: An experimental Study. Mimeo. New York University. October.

Selten, Reinhard. 1967. Die strategiemethode zur erforschung des eigeschrankt rationalen verhaltens im rahmen eines oligopolexperiments. In *Beitrage zur experimentellen wirtschaftsforschung*, H. Sauermann, editor, Tubingen: J.C.B. Mohr. 136–68.

Selten, Reinhard. 1975. Bargaining under incomplete information: A numerical example. In *Dynamische wirtschaftsanalyse*, O. Becker and R. Richter, editors, Tubingen: J.C.B. Mohr. 203–32.

Shogren, Jason F. 1989. Fairness in bargaining requires a context: An experimental examination of loyalty. *Economics Letters* 31:319–23.

Shogren, Jason F. 1992. An experiment on Coasian bargaining over ex ante lotteries and ex post rewards. *Journal of Economic Behavior and Organization*, Special Issue on Experimental Economics, 17:153–69.

Siegel, Sidney, and Lawrence E. Fouraker. 1960. *Bargaining and group decision making: Experiments in bilateral monopoly*. New York: McGraw-Hill.

Sopher, Barry. 1990. Bargaining and the joint-cost theory of strikes: An experimental study. *Journal of Labour Economics* 8:48–74.

Spiegel, Matthew, Janet Currie, Hugo Sonnenschein, and Arunava Sen. 1990. First-mover advantage and the division of surplus in two-person, alternating-offer games: Results from bargaining experiments. Mimeo.

Spier, Kathryn. 1992. The dynamics of pretrial negotiations. *Review of Economic Studies* 59: 93–108.

Stahl, Ingolf. 1972. *Bargaining theory*. Stockholm: Economic Research Institute.

Straub, Paul G., and J. Keith Murnighan. 1992. An experimental investigation of ultimatum games: Information, fairness, expectations, and lowest acceptable offers. Mimeo. December 28, University of Illinois.

Thaler, Richard H. 1988. The ultimatum game. *Journal of Economic Perspectives* 2: 195–206.

Thompson, Leigh. 1990. Negotiation behavior and outcomes: Empirical evidence and theoretical Issues. *Psychological Bulletin* 3:515–32.

Van Huyck, John, Raymond Battalio, Sondip Mathur, Andreas Ortmann, and Patsy Van Huyck. 1992. On the origin of convention: Evidence from symmetric bargaining games. Working paper. Department of Economics. Texas A&M University.

Weg, Eythan, Amnon Rapoport, and Dan S. Felsenthal. 1990. Two-person bargaining behavior in fixed discounting factors games with infinite horizon. *Games and Economic Behavior* 2:76–95.

Weg, Eythan, and Vernon Smith. 1993. On the failure to induce meager offers in ultimatum games. *Journal of Economic Psychology* 14:17–32.

Weg, Eythan, and Rami Zwick. 1991. On the robustness of perfect equilibrium in fixed cost sequential bargaining under an isomorphic transformation. *Economics Letters* 36:21–4.

Weg, Eythan, Rami Zwick, and Amnon Rapoport. Forthcoming. Bargaining in uncertain environments: A systematic distortion of perfect equilibrium demands. *Games and economic behavior.*

White, Michelle. 1989. Dispute prevention and dispute resolution in medical malpractice. Mimeo. University of Michigan.

Yaari, Menahem E., and Maya Bar-Hillel. 1984. On dividing justly. *Social Choice and Welfare* 1:1–24.

Zwick, Rami, Amnon Rapoport, and John C. Howard. 1992. Two person sequential bargaining behavior with exogenous breakdown. *Theory and Decision* 32:241–68.

5

Industrial Organization: A Survey of Laboratory Research

Charles A. Holt

I. Overview

Despite the contrast between the relative simplicity of the laboratory and the complexity of most naturally occurring markets, there is a well-established tradition of experimental research in the field of industrial organization (IO).* Indeed, the first market experiment resulted from Edward Chamberlin's conjectures about the imperfect nature of competition. This chapter will survey the extensive experimental literature that is motivated by IO issues, beginning in sections II and III with the story of how economists initially became interested in experimentation, and with a discussion of the potential usefulness of laboratory techniques in this area. Section IV contains a review of some procedural issues that arise in the conduct of market experiments. One pervasive theme is the importance of the rules and informational conditions of the laboratory *market institution*. Section V contains descriptions and comparisons of the trading institutions that are used in the study of industrial organization issues. The four substantive sections that follow are organized around traditional topics: monopoly regulation and potential entry, concentration and market power, conditions that facilitate cooperation, and product differentiation.

One set of issues to be considered is the extent to which a monopoly seller can exercise market power in the laboratory, if this power can be protected with predatory pricing, and whether contestability and decentralized regulatory mechanisms mitigate this power. A second set of issues is based on the usefulness of simple concentration measures: do they predict supra-competitive pricing, or it is necessary to consider more subtle notions of market power? Contracts, trading rules, communications, and other factors that do and do not seem to facilitate cooperation in laboratory situations are discussed. In experiments with interrelated markets, the discussion covers failures (due to asymmetric quality information) and successes (where competition generates efficient coordination across markets).

II. Beginnings

Chamberlin, like many other economists, observed behavior in naturally occurring contexts and formulated theories to organize and explain these observations. *The Theory of Monopolistic Competition (A Re-orientation of the Theory of Value)*, which appeared in 1933, was inspired by the failure of markets to adjust to the shocks of the Depression. What differentiated Chamberlin from his predecessors is that he then set up an experiment to evaluate his theoretical work. He *induced* the structure of the laboratory market by handing out cards with value and cost information to students in his class.[1] For example, a student receiving a seller card with a cost of $1 would have the capacity to sell one unit, and the profit on this unit would be the difference between the sale price and the cost of $1. This seller would have an inelastic supply function with a step at $1. Similarly, a subject receiving a buyer card with a value of $2 would have the ability to purchase a unit, and the profit on the unit would be the difference between the value of $2 and the price paid for the unit. This buyer would have a perfectly inelastic demand for one unit of the commodity at any price below $2. If this seller and buyer were to arrange a contract for a price of $1.50, each would earn 50¢ from the trade. Other buyers and sellers can have different values and costs. The market demand and supply functions result from a horizontal summation of the individual buyers' and sellers' demand and supply functions. Students were allowed to circulate around the room and arrange trades in a decentralized manner. Chamberlin's (1948) experiment, to be discussed in more detail in the next section, provided some support for his conjecture that actual markets would not generate the efficient outcomes predicted by the intersection of market demand and supply.

Chamberlin's paper was initially ignored in the literature.[2] Vernon Smith, who was a student participant in Chamberlin's trading sessions, was also skeptical at first. But later, as an assistant professor at Purdue, Smith decided that the decentralized trading institution used in Chamberlin's sessions would not create an environment likely to be consistent with received theories of perfect competition. Smith (1962, 1964) developed a laboratory double auction institution in which all bids, offers, and transactions prices are publicly observed. In a double auction, buyers may start bidding at a low level and raise each other's bids as in a familiar auction for art or antiques. At the same time, sellers may start with high asking prices and begin a second, reversed auction process of price cutting. A contract occurs when the bid-ask spread narrows and a buyer accepts a seller's ask or a seller accepts a buyer's bid. A laboratory double auction can be a noisy process in which traders raise their hands frantically to get the attention of the auctioneer, who recognizes them one at a time and has their bids or asks recorded publicly on the blackboard, as only officially recorded bids and asks can be accepted by another trader.

Smith was motivated by observations of efficient, centralized stock exchanges in which the best standing price quotes at any instant determine a bid-ask spread that is observed by all, unlike the Chamberlinian markets in which buyers' bids in one part of the room, for example, could be much higher than sellers' asking prices in another location. Smith demonstrated that double auctions could converge to efficient, competitive outcomes, even with a small number of traders who initially knew nothing about market conditions. Smith's early experimental work was also largely ignored, presumably because it was consistent with widely held beliefs. His intense interest in the mechanics of how markets function has led to a large number of subsequent papers, and many of his colleagues, students, and coauthors have become significant contributors.[3]

Charles Plott, who had been an assistant professor at Purdue, saw Smith's early work and realized that it could be applied to the study of public choice. Plott began doing voting and committee-choice experiments at Cal Tech in the early 1970s, and he taught a seminar with Vernon Smith during Smith's visit to Cal Tech in 1974. A particularly significant outcome of this collaboration was the Plott and Smith (1978) comparison of trading institutions, which reveals the inefficiencies that can result from a rule that limits the ability of traders to deviate from posted prices.

There is a separate and largely unrelated group of experimental studies done by psychologists, game theorists, and business school economists in the 1950s and 1960s.[4] Much of this work was stimulated by early interest in computerized business games with teaching objectives (Bellman et al. 1957). The first oligopoly experiment to be reported is Hoggatt (1959), who used Berkeley faculty colleagues in a relatively uncontrolled setting with no financial incentives.[5] At about the same time, classic studies of cooperation and competition in oligopoly situations were conducted by Sauermann and Selten (1959), Siegel and Fouraker (1960), and Fouraker and Siegel (1963). The care with which Fouraker and Siegel (a psychologist) treated the laboratory environment and the financial incentives is particularly notable. These early researchers were intrigued by the structure of prisoner's dilemma duopoly games in which each of two matched participants would make a price or quantity decision and record it on a piece of paper, which would then be collected and used to calculate each person's earnings from a payoff matrix. The noncooperative equilibrium typically involves a low-profit outcome with low prices (or high quantities in a Cournot quantity-choice setting). In such an equilibrium, neither person has an incentive to raise price unilaterally, but both can increase their earnings considerably if they raise prices (cut quantities) at the same time. One effect of this work was to extend the psychologists' and economists' interest in prisoner's dilemma games (Rapoport and Chammah 1965; Lave 1962 and 1965) to the study of more complex bargaining and pricing interactions in market environments (e.g., Dolbear et al. 1968; Friedman 1963, 1967, and 1969). The interdisciplinary approach at professional business schools such as Carnegie Mellon's Graduate School of Industrial Administration led to a series of experimental papers, including an early survey paper (Cyert and Lave 1965) and an experimental thesis on behavior in oligopoly situations (Sherman 1966).[6]

Early laboratory results, however, were overshadowed by the outpouring of regression studies of structure-performance relationships that followed the advent of inexpensive computing. Indeed, the first edition of Scherer's (1970) textbook, which dominated the field for more than a decade, only contained a brief mention of prisoner's dilemma experiments and no mention of Vernon Smith's experimental research.[7, 8] Most of the econometric analysis of IO issues in the 1970s was only loosely related to economic models, and the ensuing reaction stimulated an interest in theoretical foundations that is reflected in the heavy game-theoretic content of the Tirole (1988) book, which has replaced Scherer in graduate IO courses. It is only a slight exaggeration to say that all of the action in theoretical IO now involves applied game theory, and that very little of the new theory has been subjected to empirical testing.[9] Many of these new theories have subtle and important implications that are ideally suited for laboratory testing.

Summary. Most of the initial work in experimental economics was motivated by the study of issues central to industrial organization: competition, collusion, and market efficiency. Recent applications of game theory in industrial organization provide a rich agenda for laboratory research.

III. The Relevance of Experiments to the Study of IO

There is an important distinction between markets that occur naturally in society, that is, natural markets, and laboratory markets in which the structure is determined by instructions and payment procedures specified by the experimenter. Natural markets are so complex that much of the empirical work in industrial organization is based on one or more convenient simplifications, for example, perfect product homogeneity, which are violated in natural markets, often to an unknown extent. In contrast, laboratory markets are typically less complex; the procedures must be simple enough for subjects to understand and gain experience in the trading environment within the two- to three-hour time frame of most laboratory sessions.

Considering the complex workings of consumer and producer goods markets that have been the focus of antitrust cases, a skeptical reader must wonder whether effective simplification is possible, that is, if laboratory experiments will yield *any* useful insights for IO economists. Although this issue will be addressed in the context of specific examples in subsequent sections, it is instructive to begin here with a discussion of three basic purposes of laboratory experimentation in IO contexts.[10]

A. *Experiments That Evaluate Behavioral Assumptions*

It is difficult to falsify a theory with data from naturally occurring markets, since the simplifying assumptions of theories are rarely, if ever, satisfied in the field. Experiments do permit one to subject a theory to a minimal test, that is, that it provide reasonably good predictions in special cases in which its basic assumptions are satisfied. A theorist may argue that this is the only appropriate test of a theory, since the theory does not predict anything if the assumptions are not satisfied. If this extreme position is accepted, then most theories in IO have no empirical implications for naturally occurring markets and can only be tested in the laboratory.

It is useful to highlight the distinction between the structural and behavioral assumptions of a theory to be tested. In game-theoretic terms, structural assumptions determine the extensive form, and behavioral assumptions pertain to the equilibrium concept. Experimentalists are usually not interested in trying to impose or induce key behavioral assumptions, for example, a belief that one's purchases have no effect on the market price. But by controlling traders' incentives and information, the laboratory environment can be made to correspond quite closely to the structural assumptions of a specific theory. In this way, it is possible to evaluate the internal workings of a theory, for example, behavioral assumptions such as noncooperative behavior and rational forecasting. This type of evaluation is important in oligopoly theory, where the word "equilibrium" frequently follows one or more juicy adjectives. Even if we restrict attention to noncooperative game theory, there are many equilibria, some of which are thought to be "unintuitive" and not "perfect," and others of which are termed "divine," "universally divine," or "strategically stable." Many of the theoretical issues here involve very subtle points, such as the nature of beliefs off the equilibrium path, and there is little hope that such issues can be evaluated with nonexperimental data.

It is, however, more difficult to use experimentation to evaluate the usefulness of simplifying assumptions about the structure of the market environment. For example, consider a test of the contestable markets hypothesis in which the incumbent must make a binding, public price decision before the entrant. This timing assumption, which could be *imposed* as a part of the structure of the experiment, is precisely the main point of contention in some of the critical reviews of market contestability theory, and, therefore, the experiment would not resolve this particular controversy.[11] Even though it is possible to elicit some preference information from financially motivated subjects, experiments will never be very useful in settling important empirical disputes about the actual structure of the economy.

One argument against laboratory experimentation is summarized by Werden (1991, 18): Experimental conditions can never be very realistic. The subjects in the experiments are not experienced businessmen; they are not playing for serious sums of money; and they are not accountable to shareholders. The complex dynamics of real firms and markets, involving long-term investments and commitments also are not likely to be captured by an experiment. This comment raises an interesting question: which, if any, of the parameters and structural elements of the *formal theory* are not present in the laboratory? Most theories that pertain to industrial organization are cast at a level of generality that applies to laboratory settings. The best response to the argument that experiments are not realistic is given by Plott (1989, 1165): [L]aboratory markets are 'real' markets in the sense that principles of economics apply there as well as elsewhere. . . . General theories and models should be expected to work in the special cases of laboratory markets.[12] Moreover, it is possible to use businessmen as subjects, and studies that have done this have not reported major differences in the rationality of decisions made by students and those made by professionals.[13] But the Werden critique should not be dismissed too casually. The possibility of subject pool effects is more of a worry for industrial organization experiments than for other types of experiments that parallel natural situations in which students have experience (e.g., shopping, bargaining, and choices in risky situations).

In antitrust analysis, the effectiveness of a policy may hinge on behavioral assumptions, and it is risky to impose an antitrust or regulatory remedy that back-fires under ideal laboratory conditions. For example, Hong and Plott (1982) conducted experiments with a proposed rate filing policy that would have re-quired shippers on U.S. inland water routes to post prices with a regulatory agency. The effect of this proposal was to raise prices and reduce efficiency in the laboratory, as will be explained in section VIII. If the behavioral assumptions fail under ideal conditions, the burden of explanation should be shifted to the advo-cates of a policy.

B. Tests for Sensitivity to Violations of Structural Assumptions

It is important to know whether the power of a theory (or the effectiveness of a policy) is sensitive to violations of obviously unrealistic structural assumptions.[14] For example, theories of perfect competition and perfect contestability would be of limited practical value if they were unable to accommodate finite numbers of agents or small, positive entry costs. By altering the treatment conditions of an experiment, these simplifying assumptions can be evaluated one at a time in a manner that is usually not possible with an analysis of data from naturally occur-ring markets. Another example involves information: most game-theoretic mod-els specify complete information or incomplete information in a carefully limited dimension. Game theory, which is the dominant approach to modeling in indus-trial organization at present,[15] is being applied too simplistically if the accuracy of its predictions is sensitive to small amounts of uncertainty, either about structural parameters or about the distributions that generate these parameters. There is some evidence that noncooperative equilibrium predictions are at least as accu-rate under conditions of incomplete information as they are under complete information.[16] This may be because subjects do not have to calculate the non-cooperative equilibrium strategies in the way that a theorist would, all they have to do is to use the best response to the observed distribution of others' decisions. Moreover, with complete information, subjects may take other's earn-ings more seriously, which can generate the confounding effects of jealousy and altruism.

C. Searching for Empirical Regularities

It is often very difficult to evaluate theoretical propositions with firm-level or industry-level data, since the key cost and value parameters of most theories, such as marginal costs, are unobserved and must be estimated. Therefore, nonexperi-mental tests of theories are really joint tests involving many auxiliary assump-tions. In contrast, a particularly valuable type of empirical research in industrial organization has been the discovery of regularities in relationships between observable variables. For example, the effect of cumulative production experience on unit costs has led to a large theoretical and empirical literature on "learning curves."

Experimentation can also be used to discover and document such stylized facts.[17] This search is facilitated in laboratory markets in which there are no measurement errors and in which the basic underlying demand, supply, and informational conditions are induced, and hence known. For example, it would be difficult to conclude that prices in a particular industry or trading institution are perfectly competitive if marginal costs or (discounted) transactions prices could not be measured very well, as is usually the case. Moreover, any student who has tried to make sense of the many interindustry, concentration-profits studies can appreciate the attractiveness of learning something from market experiments, even if the conclusions must be interpreted in the context of the specific parametric structure of the experimental markets. One potential problem with the search for stylized facts in the laboratory is that the choice of design parameters becomes more subjective when the work is not guided by a specific theory or a specific fact situation of an antitrust case. Porter (1991, 566) is skeptical of the use of experiments to search for stylized facts: "In my view, experimental outcomes are of most interest when they are couched as tests of theories, rather than as data-generating exercises."

Summary. Experiments are usually not suited to address empirical issues about the underlying structure of industrial markets. An experiment can be used to test the behavioral assumptions of a theory that relates structure to performance, to stress-test a theory by introducing small violations of its structural assumptions, and to search for stylized facts or patterns in laboratory markets. The particular objective affects the degree of parallelism between the experimental design and the motivating theories or natural markets.

IV. Design and Procedural Issues

My colleague Roger Sherman once remarked that the process of establishing the procedures for a laboratory market is a little like computer programming: a seemingly small error can render the data useless or difficult to interpret. This section deals with some preliminary procedural issues that come up in experiments motivated by IO issues; a more comprehensive discussion can be found in chapter 1 of Davis and Holt (1993).

A. Instructions

When I read an experimental paper, I often look at the instructions appendix first; this permits me to obtain a feel for the environment before reading the authors' interpretations. Instructions that are complete and clear will facilitate interpretation and replication of the data. The instructions and appended descriptions of procedures are inadequate if the author would not accept the validity of replication by a third party using these instructions.

Although simple tests of game-theoretic concepts can be (and usually should be) conducted without giving economic names to the decision variables, in other, more complicated trading institutions the use of market terminology is valuable in communicating the structure of the payoff functions effectively. In principle, it would have been possible to conduct Chamberlin's market experiments without ever using the words "buyer," "seller," "price," etc., but it would be very difficult to explain the structure to the subjects. The use of more complicated economic terminology, however, increases the risk that subjects' beliefs and decisions will be affected by the terminology and not by the underlying incentives.

The wording of instructions is very important; I generally begin with standard, commonly used instructions, and modify them as needed. For example, consider an excerpt of general instructions, loosely adapted from Plott and Smith (1978, 150):

Instructions—General

This is an experiment in the economics of market decision making. Various foundations have provided funds for this research. The instructions are simple, and if you follow them carefully and make good decisions, you may earn money, which will be paid to you in cash, privately, immediately after the session ends today.

In this experiment, we are going to set up a market in which some of you will be buyers and some of you will be sellers in a sequence of "trading periods." Attached to these instructions you will find a sheet, labeled Buyer or Seller, which describes the value to you of any decisions you might make. *You are not to reveal this information to any other participant.* It is your own private information.

Notice that there is no statement that can be interpreted as a suggestion of the type of behavior expected by the experimenter. In contrast, the instructions published in a recent issue of a major journal began: "This is an experiment funded by a government agency to study the operation of a competitive market. . . . The objective will be for buyers and sellers to make a contract." The explicit statement of an objective introduces an unnecessary nuisance factor into the incentive structure. Pilot experiments and individual "debriefing" sessions are essential in spotting and correcting problems with the instructions.[18] For example, a student subject once told me that the word "oligopoly" on a receipt form "gave away" the purpose of the experiment, since he remembered from his introductory economics class that oligopolists should collude. This person was unusually successful at cooperating to earn higher profits in a duopoly market session, and, therefore, I changed the wording and discarded the data that had already been collected.

Numerical examples in the instructions can be avoided in simple setups, but in complex institutions they are important. One approach is to use symbols such as "p" instead of actual numerical price examples. A computerized posted-price program, written by Doug Davis, solves this problem by having the computer program generate random numbers that are used for the values, costs, and prices that are used in the instructions. Subjects are told that the numbers are randomly generated and that they differ from subject to subject.[19] Perhaps the most common approach is to use obviously unrealistic, large dollar figures, as do the buyer's instructions that follow, again adapted loosely from Plott and Smith (1978):

Specific Instructions to Buyers

During each market period you are free to purchase from any seller or sellers as many units as you might want. For the first unit that you buy *during a trading period* you will receive the amount listed in row (1) of your decision sheet, marked *value of 1st unit*. If you buy a second unit you will receive the amount listed in row (4) marked *value of 2nd unit*, etc. (For illustrative purposes, we only consider the two-unit case.) The earnings on each purchase, which are yours to keep, are computed by taking the difference between the unit value and the purchase price of the unit bought.

Suppose, for example, that the value of your 1st unit is $200, as shown in row (1) [in Fig. 5.1], and the value of your 2nd unit is $180, as shown in row (4). If you pay $150 for your 1st unit, you would enter this amount in row (2), and your earnings would be $200 - 150 = 50$ on the 1st unit, as shown by the entry in row (3). Similarly, suppose that you buy a second unit and pay $160, which is recorded in row (5). Then your earnings for this unit would be $180 - 160 = 20$, as shown by the entry in row (6). Your total earnings for the period would be 50 (on the first unit) + 20 (on the second unit), which equals 70, to be entered in row (7).

row		period 0
1	value of 1st unit	200.00
2	− purchase price	−150.00
3	= earnings on 1st unit	= 50.00
4	value of 2nd unit	180.00
5	− purchase price	−160.00
6	= earnings on 2nd unit	= 20.00
7	total earnings for period	70.00
8	cumulative earnings	0.00 (practice)

Figure 5.1. Decision sheet for buyer.

The blanks in the table will help you keep track of your earnings. Regardless of whether or not others have already purchased units during the period, the purchase price for the first unit that *you* purchase *in a trading period* should be entered in row (2) at the time of purchase. You should then record the earnings on this purchase, as directed in row (3). The purchase of your 2nd unit during the period would be recorded similarly in rows (4)–(6), of the column for the period. At the end of the period, record the total earnings on all units for the period in row (7). Subsequent periods will be recorded similarly, but at the beginning of each new period, you will start at the top of the column for that period and work downward. You cannot start purchasing units in the next column until that period begins. You may keep track of your cumulative earnings in the bottom row of the table.

In this modification of the Plott and Smith (1978) instructions, I removed (1) the prohibition against trades that generate a loss, and (2) the payment of a $.05 "commission" on each unit traded.[20] Specific instructions to sellers are similar, except that the sellers' costs are subtracted from the sale prices.[21]

B. Design Considerations

It is easy to lose ultimate research perspectives in the mechanical processes of generating and reporting data. Given the relative simplicity of laboratory markets, it is tempting to add complexity to an experiment, but this often results in situations that are difficult to analyze in theory and difficult for subjects to comprehend quickly. It is also tempting to err in the other direction; a researcher with a primary interest in theory may select a very sparse environment in which to consider policy issues that are more marketable with granting agencies. Another prisoner's dilemma experiment is not going to reveal much useful information about subtle issues in antitrust or macroeconomics, regardless of tantalizing interpretations and labels of players' decisions. One key to good experimental work on IO issues is to introduce the right simplifying conditions, without losing the essential features of the market environment.

Besides the choice of trading institution, discussed in the next section, the selection of a cost and demand structure is critical. The values and costs presented in the instructions determine the structure of the market. The example in Figure 5.2 serves to introduce the simple mechanics of induced values. In the figure, the six buyers are indicated by the numbers B1 to B6, and the six sellers are numbered S1 to S6. Each step in the figure is a single unit. For example, B6 has a unit with a reservation value of $1.90 and a second unit at $.90. An important detail is that the *first* unit purchased by a buyer is required to be the one with the higher reservation value, which implements an assumption that individual demand is downward sloping. Similarly, it is typically the case that a seller is required to sell the unit with the lowest cost first.[22]

Figure 5.2 also illustrates the way in which the efficiency of a laboratory market outcome is usually measured. In the absence of externalities, the perfectly competitive outcome will maximize the total surplus, which equals the total combined earnings of all buyers and sellers in the market. Using this as the standard, one measures efficiency as the percentage of maximum earnings that is obtained. For example, the competitive outcome that results from matching B6 with S6, B5 with S5, etc., generates earnings of $1.10 on the trade between B6 and S6, $.90 on the next trade, etc., for a total of $3.60 on the six units traded. This allocation maximizes earnings and yields an efficiency of 100 percent. Efficiency is reduced by the failure to trade infra-marginal units or the trading of extra-marginal units. The design obviously affects the interpretation of the absolute levels of the effi-

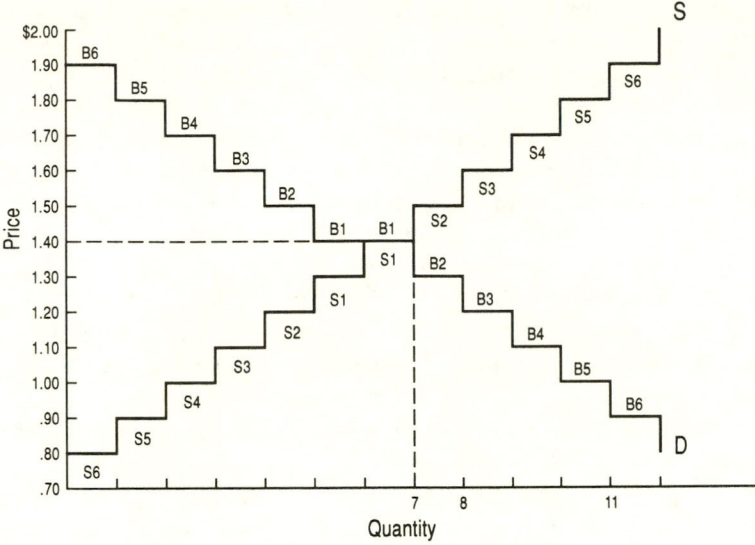

Figure 5.2. Induced supply and demand structure for a market experiment.

ciency measure. For example, a large increase in the value of the first unit for B6 will increase total earnings in a session, since this unit is very likely to be purchased. The simultaneous increase in actual and potential earnings will raise efficiency in a somewhat artificial manner.

Value and cost parameters should be selected carefully, to simplify and separate the predictions of alternative theories. Since subjects expect to earn money, earnings should be adequate for all alternative outcomes under serious consideration. For example, Holt (1985) added $.45 to all entries in a payoff table so that the competitive outcome where price equals (constant) marginal cost would generate positive earnings. Subjects expect to make money during the experiment, and behavior may become erratic if earnings are zero or negative for several stages or market periods. Therefore, it is important to have alternative equilibrium predictions provide a positive reinforcement at each stage. A related consideration is that earnings should be adequate for the session as a whole. The general feeling is that, for student subjects, payments should not fall below going alternative wage levels, say $7 to $10 per hour in the United States. Game-theoretic equilibria can be difficult to calculate for the step-function structures that result from the trade of discrete units, and, therefore, it is essential to work on applying the relevant theories so that the design can be simplified as necessary before generating the data. Incredible as it may seem, authors sometimes overlook the most obvious alternative theories. For example, I know of at least five experiments in which sellers select quantities prior to market trading activity, but in no case did the authors calculate the noncooperative (Cournot) equilibrium for the quantity-choice game.

Obviously, the choice of treatments depends on which experimental objective is relevant. For example, a minimal test of the behavioral assumptions of an oligopoly or game theory should reproduce the informational environment that is assumed in the theory. Experiments in which traders do not know each others' costs and values, such as Smith's (1962) initial market experiments, can be appropriately viewed as both sensitivity tests and as efforts to discover stylized facts in realistic environments. Before proceeding, it will be useful to clarify some terminology used to describe information conditions. With *complete information*, participants know all features of the extensive-form game and, in particular, each participant knows the payoff functions of all others.[23] A common practice is to provide participants with only the relevant aspects of their own payoff functions. For example, Fouraker and Siegel (1963) gave subjects a table showing their own monetary earnings as a function of their decision and of the other seller's decision, but they were given no information about the other's payoff table. Fouraker and Siegel and others have called this "incomplete information," but I will refer to it as *private incomplete information* in order to distinguish it from a case in which subjects are given specific probabilistic information about others' payoff functions.[24] I will reserve the term *probabilistic incomplete information* for the approach, first taken by Vickrey (1961), in which the parameters of each subject's payoff function are drawn from a distribution that is known to all subjects.[25] For example, the unknown parameter could be the monetary value of a prize in an auction, and each subject knows his or her own value and knows the population distribution(s) from which others' values are drawn. The advantage of using probabilistic incomplete information in the laboratory is that initial beliefs are directly induced, giving the experimenter greater control. Murphy (1966, 298) notes that some subjects in incomplete-information duopoly sessions took it for granted that their partners had the same payoff table, and others expressed "wonder and surprise" when they realized that this was the case.

Finally, the order and nature of structural and institutional treatments can be important. In many market trading institutions, there may be large differences from one group of participants to another. If substantial "group" effects are anticipated, it is sometimes useful to apply different treatment conditions to the same group of participants, and alternate the treatment order in a "blocked" design.[26]

Summary. Attention to detail is critical; a procedural flaw can invalidate an extensive laboratory study. Instructions should be clear and complete enough to permit replication by a disinterested third party. There is no substitute for analysis of substantive theoretical and design issues before the data are generated.

V. Trading Institutions

Before conducting an experiment, many choices must be made about the exact nature and timing of subjects' decisions, for example, who posts prices and in which order, whether and when discounts can be offered, and whether communications are allowed. Although the rules of trading institutions are rarely discussed in the IO literature, seemingly small variations in the market institution can have large effects, both on the relevant game-theoretic predictions and, as we shall see, on the observed behavior of subjects.[27] For this reason, issues of institutional design have been the focus of much experimental work. It is useful to begin with a description of some of the commonly used laboratory trading institutions before turning to more traditional IO topics. The emphasis in this section is on trading institutions that have direct applications in the study of IO issues; in each case the institution will be described, and representative results will usually be presented. One can think of institutions as spanning the range from highly structured two-person bargaining games (with a single price offer and a yes or no response) to large, complex double auctions (with no restrictions on the timing and order of price messages and responses). Most markets of interest to industrial organization economists have more structure than a double auction, and, therefore, much of the discussion that follows can be thought of as a categorization of restrictions on the price posting process in different types of auction markets.

The primary differences between the initially bewildering array of laboratory market institutions to be considered in this section are presented in Table 5.1, which will serve as a reference point. The institutions are listed in the first column on the left. The second column indicates the numbers of buyers and sellers, where a "-" indicates one or more, and the number of sellers (buyers) is listed to the left (right) of the "/" mark. For example, an auction institution with a single seller would be represented: "1 / -." The third column shows whether buyers or sellers send price messages: "bids" for buyers and "offers" or "asks" for sellers. The fourth column indicates whether the price messages are selected independently (and in this sense simultaneously) or sequentially. The final column on the right shows how trades are confirmed. The footnotes to the table describe special cases: auctions with a single prize and bargaining games with one buyer and one seller. These bargaining and auction games are treated in Roth (chapter 4) and Kagel (chapter 7), respectively.

A. Posted Prices

Publicly posted "list" prices are especially common in developed economies: sellers quote prices on a take-it-or-leave-it basis in many retail and mail-order situations, for example. Posted prices became common in the last century in large stores in which the owner/managers had to rely on numerous sales clerks.[28] In addition, government regulation in industries such as shipping and alcoholic beverages sometimes requires that prices be posted with the regulatory agency and that discounts not be granted.[29]

In theory, markets with independently selected, nonnegotiable prices are analyzed as a Bertrand game. In the laboratory, this institution is called a *posted offer* (PO) auction, but the laboratory implementation differs from the standard Bertrand model without capacity constraints, in that sellers are almost always given a limited number of "units" that can be sold. The posted-offer auction is summarized in row 1 of Table 5.1. Each seller independently selects a price, and buyers are called on in a random order and allowed to make purchase decisions. Buyers can be simulated.[30] The trading rules of a posted-offer market are de-

Table 5.1. Laboratory Market Trading Institutions

		No. of Sellers/ No. of Buyers	Who Makes Price Proposals	Decisions Sequential or Simultaneous	How Contracts Are Confirmed
(1)	Posted offer auction[a]	— / —	Sellers	Offers posted simultaneously	Buyers shop in sequence
(2)	Posted bid auction[a]	— / —	Buyers	Bids posted simultaneously	Sellers shop in sequence
(3)	Discriminative auction[b]	1 / —	Buyers	Bids posted simultaneously	Highest N bidders pay own bid prices
(4)	Competitive auction[c]	1 / —	Buyers	Bids posted simultaneously	Highest N bidders pay $N + 1$st price
(5)	Clearinghouse auction	— / —	Buyers and sellers	Bids and offers simultaneously	Intersection of bid and offer arrays
(6)	Cournot quantity choice	— / —	Endogenous price	Seller quantities simultaneously	Intersection of total quantity and demand
(7)	Walrasian auction	— / —	Auctioneer	Price adjusted sequentially	Confirmation when excess demand is 0
(8)	Dutch auction	1 / —	Seller clock	Price lowered sequentially	Buyer confirmation stops clock
(9)	English auction	1 / —	Buyers	Price raised sequentially	Sale to highest bidder
(10)	Bid auction	— / —	Buyers	Prices raised sequentially	Sellers
(11)	Offer auction	— / —	Sellers	Prices lowered sequentially	Buyers
(12)	Double auction	— / —	Both types	Bids raised and offers lowered sequentially	Both types
(13)	Decentralized negotiation[d]	— / —	Both types	Sequential but decentralized	Both types
(14)	List/discount	— / —	Sellers	Simultaneous (list), sequential (discounts)	Buyers

[a] With one prize, one buyer and one seller, this is an ultimatum bargaining game.
[b] With one prize, this is a "first-price auction," since the winning bidder pays the highest (first) price.
[c] With one prize, this is a "second-price auction," since the winning bidder pays the second highest price.
[d] With one buyer and one seller, this is a bilateral bargaining game.

scribed in the excerpt reproduced below, which is adapted from Plott and Smith (1978, 152).[31] This excerpt can be combined with the instructions components given above (general and specific for buyers and sellers) to obtain a complete set of instructions for a posted offer.

Market Organization (posted offer):

The market for this commodity is organized as follows: we open the market for each trading period. Each seller decides on a price offer, which he or she will write on one of the cards provided. The sellers will be given two minutes to submit their prices. After all sellers have chosen prices, the cards will be collected and the prices written on the blackboard.

Buyers will then be free to make bids to purchase whatever quantities they desire and to specify the seller from whom they wish to buy. Bids will be made as follows: a buyer will be chosen using random numbers, and will indicate the seller and a desired purchase quantity. The designated seller will then accept any part of the buyer's bid by stating the quantity he or she wishes to sell. However, a seller who posts a price must be prepared to sell at least one unit at that price. If the first seller selected will not sell all units the buyer wants to purchase, the buyer is free to choose a second seller, and so on.

When the first buyer has made all desired purchases, another buyer will be selected at random and will make bids in the same manner. The process will be continued until all buyers have had a chance to make purchases. This completes the trading period. We will reopen the market for a new trading period by having sellers submit new prices, and the process will be repeated. Except for the bids and their acceptance, you are not to speak to any other subject. Are there any questions?

When I used to conduct posted-offer markets orally, I would assign a color to each buyer, and I would draw colored marbles out of an urn to determine the shopping sequence. There can be a lot of interest and anxiety at this point, since buyers are looking at the sellers' prices on the blackboard, and they will want to be able to go to low-priced sellers before these sellers run out of stock.

When posted offers are run by computer programs, the seller typically is prompted to choose both a price and a maximum quantity to be sold at the price selected, perhaps subject to some restrictions, for example, on not selling below cost. After prices and quantity limits have been selected independently, the prices (but not quantity limits) are displayed on all traders' computer screens. Then buyers (simulated or human) are chosen randomly from a waiting mode. The quantity limits preclude the necessity of asking the seller about a sale each time that a buyer wishes to make a purchase.

In order to understand the effects of the posted-offer institution, consider the simplest bilateral monopoly, with one seller, one buyer, and a single unit. Suppose that the seller has a cost of $1 for one unit and the buyer has a value of $2 for one unit. With unstructured bilateral bargaining, one would expect the traders to reach a price agreement somewhere in the middle. But if the trading institution

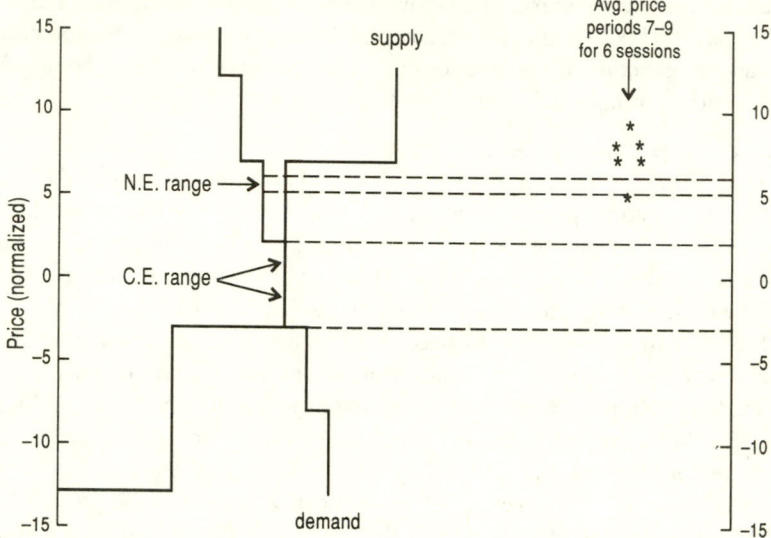

Figure 5.3. Average prices for six posted-offer sessions. *Source:* Ketcham, Smith, and Williams
(1984) data for design 2.

enables the seller to post a take-it-or-leave-it price offer, then this institutional
asymmetry would benefit the seller. In theory, the seller could sell one unit at a
price of $1.99, but such extreme price demands often result in refusal to purchase
and a zero efficiency.[32]

If the intuition provided by the bilateral monopoly case carries over somewhat
to oligopoly cases, then one would expect posted-offer auctions to result in prices
that are higher than those observed in more symmetric trading institutions. Although the theory and observed behavior in posted-offer markets will be discussed in the next sections, it can be said here that the overall effect of requiring
the sellers to post prices is to raise prices and reduce market efficiency, especially
when limitations on sellers' capacities create market power. The price-increasing
effect of this institution is illustrated by data from Ketcham, Smith, and Williams
(1984), summarized in Figure 5.3. Each of three sellers in this design has five
units of capacity; seller one has the units on the lowest supply step on the left side
of the figure, seller 2 has the units in the middle step, and seller 3 has the extra-
marginal units to the right of the CE price, on the upper step. In a competitive
equilibrium, the ten units of sellers 1 and 2 sell at a price in the range of (normalized) prices from −3¢ to 2¢. The price of 7¢ is a limit price in the sense that it
precludes the third seller, but demand is only nine units here, and sellers 1 and 2
have an incentive to cut price to try to sell their fifth units. Seller 1, with the lowest
costs, has the strongest incentive to cut price, and the authors show that a noncooperative Nash equilibrium for the market period game is for sellers 1, 2, and
3, to post prices of 5, 6, and 8, respectively.[33] In equilibrium, all units are sold at
prices of 5 or 6, so these prices delimit the "N.E. range" on the left side of the
figure. Six sessions are reported, and the average price for periods 7–9 of each

session is represented as an asterisk next to the vertical price scale on the right side of the figure. Average prices are at or above the Nash range in the posted-offer markets. In contrast, all but one of the six parallel double auction sessions (not shown) were in the competitive range. This paper is notable in that, unlike other posted offer studies before (and many since), the noncooperative equilibrium price is calculated explicitly, which makes the deviation from competitive prices easier to interpret.

Since the posted-price institution is similar to the rate-posting procedures that have been imposed by government regulators in several industries, the relative inefficiency of the posted price institution has important policy implications (e.g., see Hong and Plott 1982, discussed in section VIII below). The inefficiency that can result from high posted prices may be mitigated by the fact that the posted offer institution reduces negotiation costs. In particular, haggling over price is not allowed, and search is simplified by the public nature of pricing. Indeed, I would not be surprised if the public, centralized nature of the posted-offer institution even enhances efficiency in some environments, as compared with a case in vhich buyers must incur a cost to travel to each seller to find out about that eller's price. Notice that the comparison here is not with a centralized double auction, but with costly decentralized negotiation. The point is that it is important to be specific about the standard of comparison when discussing the efficiency of a trading institution.

There are many variations and special cases of posted-offer auctions. When the roles of buyers and sellers are reversed—i.e., when buyers post bids and sellers are selected in a random order to make sales decisions—the institution is called a *posted-bid auction* (second row of Table 5.1). The posted-bid auction is most commonly encountered in the special case of a single seller. With multiple buyers submitting posted bids to a seller with N units, or "prizes," the result is essentially a *discriminative auction* in which the highest N bidders obtain the prizes at their own bid prices (third row of Table 5.1).[34] A variant of the discriminative auction is used in the weekly sale of U.S. Treasury bills to major buyers.

B. Uniform Prices

Uniform Price Auctions

The price discrimination that occurs in a discriminative auction can cause a sense of regret among buyers, and the sale of all prizes at a uniform price, in contrast, can create an appearance of fairness. A *competitive auction* (row 4) is a uniform price auction in which all N prizes are sold at the market-clearing price determined by the highest rejected bid, the $N + 1$st price.[35] Grether, Isaac, and Plott (1981 and forthcoming) proposed a variation of a competitive auction as a way of allocating landing time "slots" at congested airports in the United States. The auction allocation procedure was compared with a committee-consensus allocation process in a parallel series of laboratory sessions. The auction was much more efficient at reallocating slots from low-value owners to high-value users.[36]

A *call market*, or *clearinghouse, auction* is another uniform-price auction, but it differs in that both buyers and sellers submit price bids, offers, and quantity limits in a symmetric manner. The market-clearing price is determined by the intersection of the demand and supply functions obtained by arraying the bids and offers in order, as summarized in the fifth row of Table 5.1. A call market procedure is used to provide the daily opening price on the New York Stock Exchange. Call markets are also used in some of the new electronic trading exchanges in the United States and abroad, and, therefore, this institution is a candidate for computerized implementations of asset trading. The strong competitive tendencies of call markets are discussed in Smith, Williams, Bratton, and Vannoni (1982), who find that this institution, which they call "$P(Q)$," is not quite as efficient as the double auction but is more efficient than the other uniform price auctions considered.[37, 38]

1. Cournot Games

The Cournot model is probably the most commonly used theoretical apparatus among IO economists; this model is tractable even in general settings, and the results are often (but not always) intuitive. In a Cournot market game, the sellers select output quantities simultaneously, which determine the market price at which all units are sold. It is sometimes useful to think of a Cournot game as a variation of a clearinghouse auction, with simulated buyers and with sellers being forced to offer a price minimum of zero for each unit of output that they decide to offer. Then the aggregate output of all sellers determines the uniform price at which there is no excess demand for the simulated buyers. This institution is summarized in row 6 of Table 5.1.

In a quantity-choice duopoly experiment, the earnings for each seller can be determined by a payoff matrix, where the sellers' decisions determine a row and column. With matrix payoffs, the buyer side of the market is simulated and is built into the payoff matrix, which typically has a prisoner's dilemma structure that arises from the incentives sellers have to defect unilaterally from a joint-profit-maximizing outcome. Some of the first Cournot quantity-choice sessions were reported in a classic study by Fouraker and Siegel (1963), which will be discussed in section VIII below.

A Cournot quantity-choice market can be explained without the use of a payoff matrix by providing subjects with the demand and cost functions, perhaps in tabular form. Subjects choose quantities simultaneously at the start of each period, and the aggregate quantity determines price according to a simulated-buyer inverse demand schedule. Subjects are always given their own marginal cost information, and they may or may not have complete information about demand and others' costs. The key feature is that quantity decisions are simultaneous, and all sales are at the uniform price at which the aggregate quantity intersects the simulated demand. This institution is sometimes called a "posted price" institution, which is very misleading terminology, especially for theorists who are unfamiliar with the experimental literature.[39]

Various applications of simultaneous-quantity-choice institution include the following: the Carlson (1967) and Johnson and Plott (1989) studies of adjustment and stability; the Wellford (1990) study of horizontal mergers; the Mason and Phillips (1991) study of vertical integration; the Binger, Hoffman, and Libecap (1988) study of cartel quotas; the Binger et al. (1990) study of communication; and the Beil (1988) study of factors, such as monitoring and punishments, that facilitate collusion. The main results from some of these papers will be reviewed in section VIII, but one significant pattern can be summarized here: the outcome in multiperiod, quantity-choice experiments with more than two sellers is usually *more competitive* than the Cournot prediction. In multiperiod Cournot duopolies, the outcomes fall on both sides of the Cournot prediction and may range from perfectly collusive to relatively competitive.

2. Tatonnement Processes

Perhaps the most familiar uniform price auction for economists is the *Walrasian mechanism* in which the auctioneer calls out a price and agents submit proposed purchase or sales quantities. As indicated in the right-hand column of row 7 in Table 5.1, the price is adjusted systematically until the reported excess demand is zero, at which time all trades are finalized. Notice that this is the first mechanism encountered in the table with a sequential timing element. A full description of a Walrasian trading institution requires a specification of the (real-time) rule that the auctioneer uses to adjust the called price, whether or not this rule is known by the traders. The Walrasian institution was first used in the laboratory by Joyce (1984).

C. One-Sided Sequential Auctions

Consider a special case of a Walrasian auction with a single seller of a single unit. If the auctioneer starts with a relatively high price, excess supply is positive. As the price is lowered, the first buyer who indicates a willingness to purchase will cause excess demand to be zero, which stops the process. When the lowering of the price is done mechanically—e.g., with a pointer that falls over a price scale on a "clock" visible to all bidders—this is known as a *Dutch auction* (row 8), which derives its name from its long use in the sale of flowers in Holland. On the other hand, suppose that the Walrasian auctioneer starts with a low price, that is, with excess demand for the seller's single unit, and raises the price until only one interested bidder remains. This is called an *English auction* (row 9). As Ashenfelter (1989) notes, the seller often uses a reserve price; if the bidding does not reach the reserve price level the auctioneer will "knock down" the item as if a sale occurred, but only later will bidders realize that it was "bought in" by the current owner.

Two other one-sided, sequential auctions are listed in rows 10 and 11 of Table 5.1. A (one-sided) *offer auction* is an institution in which sellers can make price offers at any time, and buyers are able to accept any offer, but not to make counter-offers (bids). This process is similar to what happens as airlines post fares sequentially in real time through a computerized reservation service, and travel agents and their customers make purchases at the best current rates.[40] Conversely, a (one-sided) *bid auction* refers to the opposite case in which buyers can make bids, but sellers can only indicate that a bid is accepted.[41]

D. Double Auctions

Smith's (1962, 1964) *double auction* (DA) is symmetric in that both buyers and sellers can actively post and accept prices in a public manner, as summarized in row 12 of Table 5.1.[42, 43] A market period usually lasts from three to ten minutes, depending on the numbers of traders and units being traded. The following instructions component, again loosely adapted from Plott and Smith (1978), describes the trading process.[44]

Market Organization (double auction):
The market for this commodity is organized as follows: we open the market for each trading period, which lasts for __ minutes. Any buyer is free at any time during the period to raise his or her hand, and when recognized by the auctioneer, to make a verbal bid to buy one unit of the commodity at a specified price. Always state your buyer ID number first, and then the price: "Buyer __ bids $__." Any seller is free at any time to raise his or her hand to state an asking price for one unit of the commodity at a specified price: "Seller __ asks $__." Any bid or asking price will remain on the blackboard until it is either accepted or improved (replaced by a higher bid or a lower asking price). Any buyer is free at any time to accept or not accept the asking price of any seller, and any seller is free at any time to accept or not accept the bid of any buyer. If a bid or ask is accepted, a binding contract has been closed for a single unit, and the buyer and seller should record the contract price to be used in their earnings calculations. An acceptance cancels all outstanding bids and asks. Any ties in bids, asks, or their acceptance will be resolved by random choice of buyer or seller. Except for bids, asks, and their acceptance, you are not to speak to any other participant. There are likely to be many bids and asks that are not accepted, but you are free to keep trying. Are there any questions? . . . The market is now open for bids and asks; please raise your hands and do not speak until recognized by the auctioneer.
(to be read after the first contract in the first period):
The contract is: Buyer __, Seller __, at a price of $__. This buyer and seller should record their earnings for their 1st unit at this time. Then this buyer and seller will be considering a second unit. All other traders' bids and asks still pertain to their first unit until it is bought or sold.

Traders are typically given no information about the values and costs of other traders (private incomplete information). Smith (1976) recalls that he "did not seriously expect competitive price theory to be supported," but that the double auction would give the theory its best chance. Smith's sessions produced prices

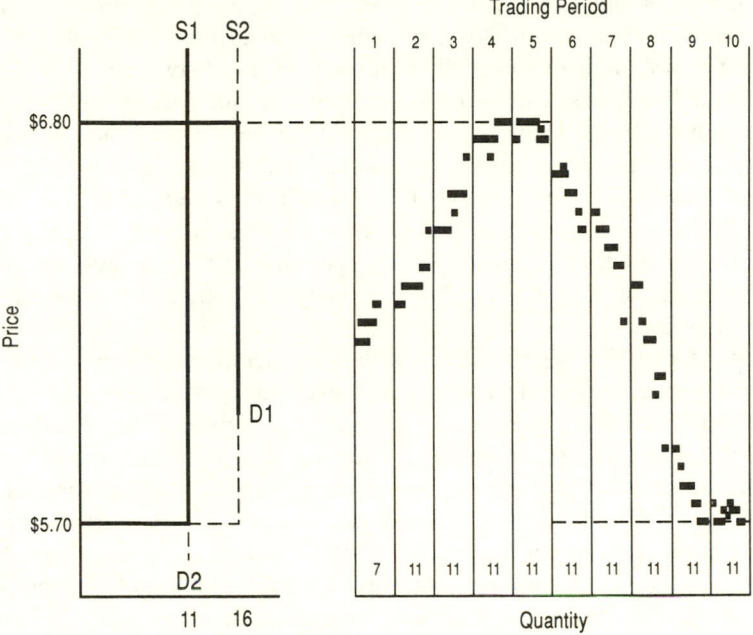

Figure 5.4. A rectangular design. *Source:* Holt, Langan, and Villamil 1986.

and quantities that were surprisingly near the competitive levels, although some marginally profitable units did not always trade, for example, the units of traders B1 and S1 in Figure 5.2.[45]

Due to its impressively robust performance, the double auction is probably the most commonly used laboratory trading mechanism. Such auctions are often conducted on a computer network, either a mainframe network or a network of personal computers.[46] In particular, there is typically an "improvement rule," which specifies that bids (offers) must be successively higher (lower), and a "rank queue," which stores ranked bids that are below the highest outstanding bid (or inversely ranked offers that are above the lowest outstanding offer).[47] Computerization greatly facilitates the bookkeeping associated with queues, but outrageous errors are more common in computerized markets, for example, entering a price of $10.30 instead of a price of $1.30.

Figure 5.4 presents the structure and data for a simple double auction market from Holt, Langan, and Villamil (1986), which replicates a session reported in an earlier version of Smith and Williams (1989).[48] There are four buyers and four sellers in this market. In each of the first five periods, each buyer has four units with values of $6.80, so the market demand, represented by the dark line labeled D_1 in Figure 5.4, is perfectly inelastic at a quantity of 16 for all prices below $6.80. Three of the sellers have three units and one seller has two units, all with costs at $5.70, so market supply at higher prices is vertical at a quantity of 11, as shown by dark line labeled S_1 in the figure. These functions intersect at a quantity of 11 and a price of $6.80, in each of the first five periods.[49] No trader knew the costs or values of any of the other traders. The transactions prices for each period are plotted sequentially as a series of dots between the two vertical lines that fall on each side of the period number. The initial prices in period 1 were about midway between the sellers' costs and buyers' values, and prices rose slightly during the period, with seven units being traded, as indicated by the number above the horizontal axis. There is an excess demand of five units at prices in this range, and, therefore, the upward trend in prices continued until prices reached the level of buyers' values in period four. Even though buyers were earning very little in period 5, trading efficiency was 100 percent at the competitive equilibrium.

At the beginning of period 6, all sellers' capacities were increased to four units at the same cost level as before, and buyers' units were reduced so that the new demand curve, D_2, intersected the supply S_2 at a price of $5.70 and a quantity of 11. Since subjects received new decision sheets with their own costs or values at the start of each period, no subject had any way of knowing whether or not others' unit allocations had changed. But surely the sellers, who were earning about a dollar per unit in period five, would have been delighted with additional unit(s), and, conversely, the buyers would have been frustrated. These emotions were short-lived, since prices began an immediate decline in period 6 and fell to the competitive level in period 10. Although trading eleven units at any price between $5.70 and $6.80 would yield 100 percent efficiency, the actual prices converge to the competitive levels, despite the resulting inequality in earnings.

The striking competitive tendency of the double auction institution, which has been confirmed by at least a thousand market sessions in a variety of designs, indicates that neither complete information nor large numbers of traders is a *necessary* condition for convergence to competitive equilibrium outcomes. Gode and Sunder (1989, 1991) have also observed very high efficiencies in double auctions involving simulated traders with "zero intelligence," that is, traders who use pre-programmed trading rules.[50] Smith (1976, 57) concludes:

> There are no experimental results more important or more significant than that the information specifications of traditional competitive price theory are grossly overstated. The experimental facts are that no double auction trader needs to know *anything* about the valuation conditions of other traders, or have *any* understanding or knowledge of market supply and demand conditions, or have *any* trading experience (although experience may speed convergence) or satisfy the quaint and irrelevant requirement of being a price "taker" (every trader is a price *maker* in the double auction).

Whether or not these conditions are sufficient for convergence is an issue to be considered in section VI.

The double auction yields higher market efficiencies than institutions with which it has been compared. Some representative comparisons are summarized in

Table 5.2. Comparisons of Market Efficiency across Trading Institutions (percent)

	Trading Institution[a]				
	Double Auction	Posted Offer	Clearing-house	Negoti-ated Prices	Posted Price with Subsequent Negotiations
(1) Davis and Williams (1986)[b]	96	82			
(2) Ketcham, Smith, and Williams (1984)[c]	97	94			
(3) Davis, Harrison, and Williams (1993)[d]	97	66[e]			
(4) Davis and Williams (1991)	98	92[f]			
(5) Smith, Williams, Bratton, and Vannoni (1982)	95		89		
(6) Friedman and Ostroy (1989)[g]	96		90		
(7) Hong and Plott (1982)		87		92	
(8) Davis and Holt (1994a)		94			83

[a] Efficiencies are average of the overall (all periods) efficiencies for all sessions in a treatment, except as noted below.

[b] Efficiencies are an average for periods 1–8 for both designs 1 and 2. The double auctions used for comparison were originally reported in Smith and Williams (1982).

[c] Efficiencies are for periods 7–9.

[d] The efficiency listed is an average of the efficiency for "cyclical" and "trend" treatments.

[e] Buyers in the posted-offer sessions were simulated.

[f] Buyers were simulated in half of the PO sessions.

[g] The comparison involves the sessions: "ODD1," "ODD2," "CH2," and "CH3." Under each institution, fractional units could be traded.

Table 5.2.[51] Row 1 shows the Davis and Williams (1986) comparison of their posted offer sessions (82 percent efficiency) and the parallel series of double auction sessions (96 percent efficiency) done earlier by Smith and Williams (1982). Both studies used the same pair of designs in which ⅔ of the trading surplus goes to either the buyers or sellers and in which supply and demand schedules that did not shift between trading periods. Ketcham, Smith, and Williams (1984) made a similar comparison of double auctions and posted-offer auctions using the PLATO computer network. Davis, Harrison, and Williams (1993) compare the institutions under conditions of shifting and cycling supply and demand. The PO efficiency is only 66 percent on average, because there is less information transmitted during posted-offer trading, and, as a result, the posted prices do not track the changes in competitive equilibrium prices very well.[52] Finally, note that the double auction has also performed better than the clearinghouse mechanism in the two studies listed in rows 5 and 6 of the table.

The superior performance of the double auction probably has a lot to do with its sequential nature, which provides a strong temptation to make price concessions at the end of the period in order to make sales or purchases of marginal units. The importance of this sequential property is also suggested by the classic Plott and Smith (1978) comparison of sequential, one-sided bid auctions (99 percent efficiency) and a parallel series of nonsequential, posted-bid auctions (95 percent efficiency). The importance of sequential price reductions is also indicated by the effect of the possibility of a "clearance sale" in a posted-offer market with advance production (Mestelman and Welland 1992). The sale is a second simultaneous price posting at the end of the period that allows sellers to unload unsold units and avoid inventory carryover charges. There is no additional production at the time of this second sale, but this chance to offer a nonselective, public discount increases the efficiencies of posted-offer markets. For the advance production setup used by Mestelman and Welland (1992), there is very little difference between efficiencies in double auctions and those in posted-offer markets with the clearance sale. Finally, it should be noted that double auction efficiencies can be degraded by the introduction of seller fixed costs that preclude the existence of a competitive equilibrium (Van Boening and Wilcox 1992).

A second stylized fact that emerged from double auction experiments (Smith 1962) is that the price tends to converge to the competitive level from below if producer surplus exceeds consumer surplus at the competitive price, and from above in the reverse situation.[53] This convergence pattern is necessarily observed in the design in Figure 5.4, but it also shows up with other, less extreme imbalances in trading surplus. Holt and Villamil (1990) argue that the direction of convergence in double auctions can also be affected by an extreme asymmetry of market power, as is the case in Figure 5.5. (Market power is discussed in section VII below.) Moreover, the initial prices in early trading periods seem to be pulled away from the competitive equilibrium towards the average of the lowest costs and highest values, that is, the costs and values of the first several units on the left sides of the supply and demand functions. Finally, the division of the surplus at the competitive price does not affect the direction of convergence in posted-offer markets, where prices tend to exceed competitive levels in most designs.[54]

Note that Table 5.2 contains no comparisons between double and one-sided sequential auctions. Smith (1964) initially observed a consistent ranking: bid auction prices > double auction prices > offer auction prices. Roth (1986) noted that there is no theoretical basis for expecting such a ranking, and, therefore, in the absence of additional studies, the ranking should not be regarded as an established pattern. Interestingly, the pattern observed by Smith did not appear in another series of experiments with a different parameterization (Walker and Williams 1988). This episode is important because it illustrates the importance of (1) evaluating results in the context of theory, and (2) verifying results through a series of related experiments.

E. Decentralized Negotiations

The simplest symmetric two-sided institution with a sequential dimension involves unstructured, decentralized negotiations. Recall that Chamberlin's (1948) subjects were allowed to roam freely around the room and negotiate contracts, which were reported to the front desk. The most striking departure from the competitive outcome predicted by the intersection of the induced (step-function) supply and demand curves was the tendency for quantity exchanged to be too high.

Chamberlin attributed the high sales quantity to the decentralized nature of the bargaining process, and he supported this conjecture with a *simulation* in which he first constructed a series of submarkets by randomly drawing three buyer cards and three seller cards from a deck of cost and value cards and by enacting all trades that would occur in a competitive equilibrium for the submarket.[55] Untraded cards were returned to the deck, and the process was repeated many times. This simulation generated transactions quantities that exceeded the competitive level, and the excess quantity declined as the size of the submarkets was increased.

To understand how decentralized negotiations can generate high trading volume, the reader may wish to calculate the maximum number of units that can be traded (at a positive profit from each agent) for the market depicted in Figure 5.2. In determining the trade pattern that maximizes the number of (individually profitable) transactions, the reader should specify the exact order in which all trades occur and the total earnings that result from the allocation. Notice that the number of units traded can exceed the competitive quantity of six or seven, but that price has to be quite variable to generate (inefficient) trades of extra-marginal units with high costs or low values. This is the way that price variability, which goes with decentralized trade, can generate the inefficient trade of extra-marginal units. If eleven units trade, for example, total earnings are reduced by $2 to a level of $1.60, for an efficiency of 44 percent. This excess-quantity result is discussed in more detail in section VIII.

F. Discounting

Both in a Bertrand game and in the corresponding posted-offer auction, sellers are not able to discount from the posted list price. But buyers are in fact able to solicit and obtain price concessions in many markets for producer goods and consumer durables. Note that sellers in a double auction are able to reduce price at any time during a market period in response to the reductions of rivals, but such reductions are public and nonselective in the sense that the price reduction is offered to all buyers. Price reductions are also public and nonselective in the interesting "clearance sale" structure of the Mestelman and Welland (1992) posted-offer markets, described above. One striking regularity about many producer goods markets is the prevalence of discounts that are selective and private. Indeed, the apparent absence of secret discounts from list prices was one of the factors that triggered the Federal Trade Commission investigation of contractual practices of lead-based gasoline additive producers (the *Ethyl* case).[56]

Experiments with discounts from posted list prices are relatively rare. Grether and Plott (1984), motivated by the *Ethyl* case, conducted sessions in which one of the treatments involved the electronic communication of sellers' list prices to buyers and sellers in individual rooms. Then buyers could contact sellers by telephone to seek discounts, subject to contractual constraints that were the target of the FTC litigation. More recently, Davis and Holt (1994a) used a "list/discount" institution in which sellers post prices at their computer terminals, and buyers are selected from a waiting queue in a random sequence as in a posted-offer auction (see row 14 of Table 5.1). Once selected, a buyer can request a private discount, and the seller may or may not respond with a price reduction for that particular buyer.[57] One significant result is that sellers will offer discounts if given the opportunity, at least in the market structure used by Davis and Holt (1994a). This propensity to discount highlights the importance of the restriction to a nonnegotiable price in the commonly used posted-offer institution. In particular, the results of posted-offer experiments should not be invoked casually when considering policies in markets where discounts are common.

When discounts are permitted, it may not be as unfortunate for a seller to post the highest price, since buyers may come anyway in search of large discounts. This observation may help explain the high list prices reported by Davis and Holt (1994a) for some of the sessions with discount possibilities, which in turn reduced efficiencies (see the bottom row of Table 5.2).[58] In other sessions, sellers seemed to compete on the basis of list prices, which generated very competitive outcomes. The inefficiencies in sessions with high list prices is interesting. When list prices are high and deep discounts are common, there can be a considerable variation in transaction prices. The extent of this variability depends on the costs that buyers face in their price search process. When inflated list prices lose their informational value, market efficiency suffers.

G. Other Institutions

There are many ways to alter the posted-offer and double auction institutions described in this section. These alternatives deserve serious consideration for several reasons. Discounts from posted prices are pervasive in many markets of interest to industrial organization economists, such as producer goods markets; indeed, the absence of discounts (in combination with other factors) can raise antitrust scrutiny. And while the double auction approximates the structure of many asset markets, there are few (if any) producer and consumer goods markets in which bids and offers are displayed publicly in continuous time. Given the documented importance of the rules of the trading institution, it is important to use institutions carefully, with an eye to parallel naturally occurring markets. Hong and Plott (1982) and Grether and Plott (1984) are particularly good examples of studies in which the alternative trading institutions were carefully de-

signed to address relevant antitrust and regulatory issues. One interesting variation is the introduction of continuous trading in a continuous-time context.
Millner, Pratt, and Reilly (1990a,1990b) have developed a flow-market version
of the posted-offer institution. Sellers can alter prices at any instant, and the
simulated demand determines sales flows per unit of time as a function of the
prices. Although flow markets have not been analyzed theoretically, they introduce an element of realism that, as we shall see, is useful in the analysis of "hit-
and-run" entry.

H. Disadvantages of the Cournot Quantity-Choice Institution

After reviewing the differences between diverse pricing mechanisms, the market
clearing assumption of the Cournot model appears to be quite mechanical. The
Cournot model is much more commonly used in theory than it is in experiments,
and, in this case, it is the experimentalists who are right, in my opinion. One
disadvantage of this quantity-choice institution is that behavioral assumptions
are built into the market institution; the implicit assumption is that, after having
produced their output quantities, competition will drive price down to the level at
which there is no excess demand. One defense of the Cournot assumption is
that it is thought to be a reasonable predictor of the result of *price competition*
with small numbers of sellers. For example, Spence (1976, 235) remarks, "The
quantity version captures a part of the tacit coordination to avoid all-out price
competition, that I believe characterizes most industries." Hart (1979, 28) makes
a similar argument: "We reject the Bertrand approach because it has the implausi-
ble implication that perfect competition is established even under duopoly."
These arguments cannot be used to justify the exogenous imposition of the
Cournot institution in laboratory markets. Indeed the arguments suggest the opposite approach: that is, the use of a price-choice institution to see whether the
prices that result approximate the level determined by a Cournot equilibrium.

   A second, more persuasive defense of the Cournot assumption has been provided by Kreps and Scheinkman (1983), who analyzed theoretical models in
which firms simultaneously choose capacity in the first stage, and after capacity
decisions are observed, choose prices in the second stage. Noncooperative behavior in the Kreps and Scheinkman two-stage game generates the Cournot price and
quantity outcome. But for most purposes, it is a large leap to "hard-wire" the price
determination into the mechanics of the experimental institution exogenously,
especially since the Kreps and Scheinkman result is sensitive to the rationing rule
used to allocate excess demand.[59]

   From a game-theoretic point of view, the relevant issue to be decided is, what
is it that firms choose independently? If firms make key input purchases that
limit their quantity decisions before learning others' decisions, then it would be
appropriate to implement some variant of the Kreps and Scheinkman model
with second-stage price competition. But if firms set prices independently, with
sales quantities being determined jointly by buyers' responses to all prices,
then a price-choice model is appropriate. In either case, there are many possi-

ble institutional arrangements under which actual transactions prices can be negotiated.

Many results in the theoretical IO literature are reversed when one switches between Bertrand price-choice and Cournot quantity-choice assumptions.[60] The same issue arises in antitrust policy, where one would take a much more tolerant view of horizontal mergers if the industry is characterized by price rather than quantity competition. Experiments cannot settle the issue of whether firms do or do not make key, independent input decisions that precommit them to quantity decisions. In contrast, experiments can indicate whether the Cournot outcomes are observed if the trading rules impose quantity precommitment prior to the market trading that determines prices. I know of no study that directly addresses this issue.[61] Mestelman and Welland (1987, 1988), Mestelman, Welland, and Welland (1987), and Johnson and Plott (1989) report prices that converge to competitive levels when quantity precommitment decisions are followed by auctions (double or posted-offer) that determine prices. These experiments, however, involve four to six sellers, so the Cournot prediction (which is not provided) may be close to competitive levels. For the design used by Mestelman and Welland (1987, 1988) and by Mestelman, Welland, and Welland (1987), I calculate that the Cournot equilibrium involves a one unit restriction of output by the seller with the marginal units (number 2), which would raise price about six cents and raise this seller's profit by about four cents.[62] Therefore, the design does not distinguish between the Cournot and competitive outcomes very well, but the clearly competitive outcomes for this design do not provide support for the Cournot model.

The sections that follow describe how these laboratory trading institutions have been used in the reexamination of traditional IO issues, beginning with the exercise of monopoly power. Before proceeding, it is useful to summarize.

Summary. Trading institutions are characterized in Table 5.1, with posted-price auctions in rows 1–3, uniform price institutions in rows 4–7, one-sided sequential auctions in rows 6–11, and double, sequential institutions in 12–14. The more structured, simultaneous-choice institutions at the top of the table are generally those for which it is easiest to derive the implications of relevant theories. More complicated institutions, especially those that allow discounting and active buyer shopping for discounts, are difficult to analyze but provide rich environments that are appropriate for the study of markets with large buyers, such as producer goods markets.

Double auctions, which mimic markets with organized exchanges, such as, securities, do not implement the message structure of markets of most interest to IO economists. The double auction tends to yield efficient outcomes, as indicated by the comparisons in Table 5.3. Prices can be higher, and efficiencies lower, in the posted-offer institution, however. This institution seems to be a good approximation of the pricing process in retail situations in which sellers price on a take-it-or-leave-it basis, perhaps because buyers are small and relatively insignificant. But sellers in typical posted-offer designs will offer private, selective discounts to human buyers if such discounts are permitted, so the results of PO markets with a single-price restriction should be interpreted with caution. The simultaneous nature of PO price competition implements a situation in which sellers make price decisions at discrete intervals. In contrast, the newly developed flow-market version of the posted-offer institution may prove to be useful in the analysis of markets with more-or-less continuous opportunities to monitor and adjust price and quantity decisions.

Despite its prominence in the theoretical literature, the Cournot model is deficient for the experimental study of many IO issues because the essential mechanics of price determination are simulated. One open question, taken from Kreps and Scheinkman (1983), is whether quantity precommitment and Bertrand competition yield Cournot outcomes (in the laboratory).

VI. Monopoly Regulation and Potential Entry

Two aspects of monopoly performance that receive the most attention are the welfare loss due to prices that exceed marginal cost and the presence of supra-competitive profits.[63] Most economists, however, are more worried about the traditional cure, regulation, than the monopoly problem itself, especially since many monopoly positions are obtained and protected by regulation. The standard, decreasing-cost rationale for regulation has been questioned by the proponents of the "contestable markets hypothesis," who argue that potential competition, under some conditions, is as effective as actual competition in constraining market power. The first part of this section is a review of monopoly experiments, which is necessary to evaluate the extent of the monopoly problem in laboratory markets, for purposes of later comparison with decentralized regulatory schemes that are discussed in the second part. The third part of the section summarizes experiments in which one seller's monopoly position can be contested by equally efficient potential competitors. Experiments discussed in the final part pertain to an incumbent seller's ability to price in a predatory manner in an effort to secure a monopoly position.

Before proceeding, it will be useful to clarify the terminology that will be used to describe subject experience. By common usage, "experienced" means that all subjects in a session have participated in at least one previous session using the same trading institution, but possibly with different market parameters and role assignments, for example, as buyers or sellers. The terminology to be used here is as follows: *inexperienced*: have not participated with the same institution; *experienced*: have participated at least once with the same institution; *design experience*: have participated with the same institution and parameters; *role experience*: have participated with the same institution and role.

A. Monopoly

Smith (1981a) reports the results of several posted-offer sessions that illustrate the effect of the type of trading institution on a monopolist's ability to exercise market power. Figure 5.5 shows two sessions with identical cost and demand conditions; in each case the monopolist has increasing marginal costs for twelve units, and the five buyers have two units each at varying valuation levels. The solid marginal cost line (labeled S) and the dotted marginal revenue line (labeled MR) cross at a quantity of five units, yielding a monopoly price of $1.10. The "competitive" price at which marginal cost and demand intersect is $.80. These sessions were conducted under conditions of private, incomplete information. The top chart shows the sequence of transactions prices for twenty four-minute periods of double auction trading; notice that there is a downward trend and that the prices are about midway between the competitive and monopoly levels in the last half of the session. The index of monopoly effectiveness, defined in equation (1) below, is approximately .6 in the final periods of the session.

$$(1) \qquad M = \frac{(\text{actual profit} - \text{competitive profit})}{(\text{monopoly profit} - \text{competitive profit})}$$

Other double auction monopolies that fail to yield monopoly prices are reported in Smith and Williams (1989). In contrast, the monopolist in the posted-offer session shown in the bottom chart of Figure 5.5 achieves a monopoly outcome with five units sold and $M = 1$.

Plott (1989, 1144) notes that the monopolist has trouble exercising power in a double auction because buyers are not behaving as passive price takers, but rather are withholding purchases. This buyer resistance caused M to be negative in one of Smith's other replications of this design. Porter (1991) has questioned this interpretation by noting that, in a static, single-period context, the monopolist has an incentive to lower price at the end of the period in order to sell marginal units. Porter conjectures that the noncooperative equilibrium in this context may involve pricing in the range between competitive and monopoly levels.

One key to the monopolist's success in the posted-offer market can be seen by considering buyers' incentives. Once a buyer is given an option to shop and decides not to purchase all profitable units, there is no chance to recover the lost profits later in the period. In a posted-offer auction, when viewed as a static, single-stage game, it is always a dominant strategy for each buyer to purchase all profitable units; it would only make sense to withhold purchases in a multiperiod posted-offer auction, where such behavior may affect price posting in subsequent periods. This is different from the double auction case in which buyers can hold out in the early part of a period, knowing that if the price is not lowered as a result, they have a chance to make a purchase later in the same period (Harrison, McKee, and Rutstrom 1989, 68).

When the tables are turned and the buyers post bids for the product of a single seller, the monopolist is in a much weaker position. Prices were quite competitive in these sessions, which were also conducted with private incomplete information and the parameters of Figure 5.5 (Smith 1981a). The monopoly effectiveness index, averaged over the final period for all periods for all sessions in each treatment cell revealed this pattern:

> double auction monopoly: $M = 0.36$
> posted-offer monopoly: $M = 1.00$
> posted-bid monopoly: $M = 0.15$

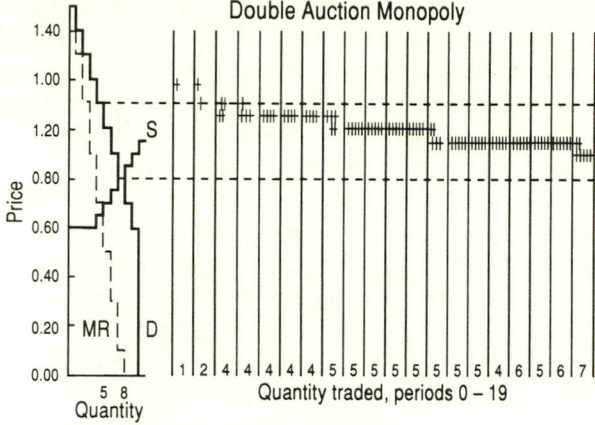

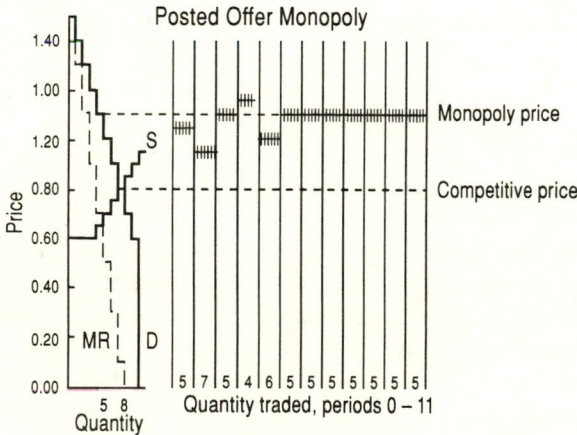

Figure 5.5. Two monopoly sessions: a comparison of double auction and posted-offer outcomes. *Source:* Constructed with data from Smith 1981a.

Smith's (1981a) posted-offer auction is perhaps unusual in that each buyer only has one unit to purchase profitably at the monopoly price, so under-revelation of demand means accepting a profit of zero. This may discourage under-revelation.[64] In PO monopoly sessions with a similar demand structure and with increasing costs, Isaac, Ramey, and Williams (1984) also observed one monopolist who fully exploited the market power, but two of the other three were unsuccessful at maintaining supra-competitive prices. The index of monopoly effectiveness for the final period, averaged across sessions, was only .45, about halfway between the theoretical values for competitive and monopoly outcomes.

Coursey, Isaac, and Smith (1984) also report the results of four monopoly PO sessions, but with decreasing costs up to capacity. The structure is that of a natural monopoly in the sense that, when one seller is producing at minimum average cost (which is also the capacity in this design), demand would be insufficient to enable another with the same cost function to sell any output at a profit. Significant demand withholding by experienced buyers prevented two of the monopolists from sustaining monopoly prices. Again, the index of monopoly effectiveness ended up being rather low: .56, as compared with a theoretical value of 1.0. (In this decreasing-cost, natural-monopoly design, the authors define the competitive quantity to be the largest that can be sold without a loss by at least one seller, and the corresponding "competitive price" is equal to the firm's average cost. This is the price used as the baseline for calculating monopoly M values.)

A number of other papers report monopoly PO experiments under a variety of information and cost conditions.[65] Table 5.3 provides a comparison of final-period monopoly M values (but recall that Coursey, Isaac, and Smith [1984], is not strictly comparable since they based their M value calculations on a condition that price equals average, not marginal cost). The papers just discussed are listed in the first three rows; the three studies listed at the bottom, in contrast, involved simulated buyers, as can be seen from the "buyer type" column. One reason for using simulated buyers is that Coursey, Isaac, and Smith had noted the effect of buyer under-revelation on the relatively low values of M in their monopoly sessions. Harrison and McKee (1985) argued that the use of simulated buyers is an interesting treatment because it is difficult to take the possibility of buyer under-revelation very seriously in many natural monopoly markets (e.g., telephones) in which the buyers are small and dispersed.[66] Harrison and McKee (1985) observed higher values of monopoly effectiveness in their simulated-buyer, monopoly markets, but the participants had design experience with the decreasing-cost design, subject to an additive parametric shift, as indicated in the experience column of the table.[67]

Another interesting issue is the effect of experience. As shown in Table 5.3, Harrison, McKee, and Rutstrom (1989) subsequently found that subjects with design and role experience were much more effective monopolists ($M = .78$) as compared with inexperienced monopolists ($M = .44$), even when buyers were simulated in both experience conditions. They conclude that experience makes subjects into better monopolists, especially experience in a separate, earlier experiment: "Experience in the form of more periods in the initial session is not equivalent to coming back and participating a second time despite having to face new cost and demand conditions in the latter situation" (p. 89). They also observed that the data with experienced subjects are less variable: "This suggests that small sample observations with inexperienced subjects be viewed with some skepticism" (Rutstrom 90). The effects of experience in other contexts will be discussed in detail in section VIII below.

Harrison, McKee, and Rutstrom also evaluate the effects of altering the shape of the cost function. They find that subjects are (1) better monopolists with constant costs than with decreasing costs and (2) better monopolists with decreasing

Table 5.3. The Effects of Restraint Mechanisms on Monopoly Effectiveness in Posted-Offer Auctions

	Subject Experience	Buyer Type	Cost Function	Monopoly M Value	Loeb-Magat M Value	Contested Market M Value
Smith (1981a) (1 session)	?	Human	Increasing	1.00		
Isaac, Ramey, and Williams (1984)[a]	Inexperienced	Human	Increasing	0.45		
Coursey, Isaac, and Smith (1984)	Experienced	Human	Decreasing	0.56[b]		.02[b]
Harrison and McKee (1985)[c]	Design experience	Simulated	Decreasing	0.72	−.36	.09
Harrison, McKee, and Rutstrom (1989)[d]	Inexperienced	Simulated	Decreasing	0.44	−.22	.00
Harrison, McKee, and Rutstrom (1989)[d]	Design and role experience	Simulated	Decreasing	0.78	−.24	.06

Notes: M = (trading profit − CE profit)/(monopoly profit − CE profit), calculated as an average of M values for the final period common to all sessions in a treatment cell. The trading profit does not include regulatory subsidies.

[a] The final-period value of M was estimated from a figure in their paper.

[b] The CE profit used to calculate the M value is determined by a price-equals-average-cost condition.

[c] Data from experiments C2 (with complete demand information) and C4 (with an opportunity for conspiracy) were omitted. The subjects in some sessions were preselected on the basis of a test for risk neutrality. Some of the contested markets involved two sellers, and others involved three sellers.

[d] All subjects were preselected on the basis of a test for risk neutrality, and some of the contested market sessions involved three sellers.

costs than with increasing costs (Mann-Whitney probabilities 1.00 and .90, respectively). But the indexes of monopoly effectiveness for period four, the final period common to cost treatments with experienced subjects, are .77 with constant costs, .76 with decreasing costs, and .09 with increasing costs.[68]

Summary. Pricing in posted-offer monopolies is higher than in double auction monopolies. Posted-offer monopolists are generally able to hold prices well above competitive levels, but on average, profits are significantly below theoretical monopoly levels. Monopoly pricing in posted-offer markets is facilitated by experience and by constant or decreasing costs. The effect of using simulated buyers, as compared with a small number of human buyers, is probably to facilitate monopoly pricing a little. I would conjecture that, under posted-offer rules, natural markets with large numbers of small buyers are best approximated by simulated buyers in the laboratory.

B. Decentralized Regulatory Proposals

Despite the fact that rate-of-return regulation is the most commonly used procedure in natural-monopoly situations, it is known to create incentives for inflating
both costs and the rate base. Even if an astute regulator can avoid these abuses,
this system does not allow for subsidies, so rate-of-return regulation would, at
best, result in average-cost pricing. Given the heavy informational requirements
of rate-of-return regulation, there is considerable interest in alternatives, especially alternatives with subsidies that may generate efficient marginal-cost pricing
outcomes.

Loeb and Magat (1979) proposed a mechanism in which the regulator promises
to pay a subsidy that equals the Marshallian consumer surplus at the price selected
by the monopolist. Since the regulated monopolists' profit would then include all
surplus, the efficient, marginal-cost price would result if the regulator knows the
demand curve and the monopolist knows the cost curve. When these information
conditions are implemented in the laboratory, the Loeb-Magat mechanism works
nicely; prices are driven down to competitive (marginal cost) levels, as indicated
by the low numbers in the "Loeb-Magat M value" column of Table 5.3.[69] Harrison
and McKee (1985) found that the large subsidies generated by this mechanism
could be eliminated by having prospective monopolists bid for the right to be a
monopolist. They used a second-price auction designed to induce demand revelation with risk-neutral subjects, and they preselected their subjects on the basis of
a test for risk neutrality.

The most significant drawbacks of the Loeb-Magat mechanism are the magnitudes of the subsidies and the requirement that the regulatory agency be able to
calculate surplus-based subsidies accurately. Finsinger and Vogelsang (1981)
proposed a modification in which the subsidy is an approximation of Marshallian
surplus that is calculated on the basis of observed prices and quantities. Let p_0 and
q_0 denote the initial (supra-competitive) price and quantity before the regulation
is implemented, and let p_t and q_t denote the prices and quantities demanded in
period $t = 1, 2, \ldots$. Then the subsidy in the first period is $q_0[p_0 - p_1]$, which
generates a penalty if price is increased. The subsidy in each subsequent period is
the previous period's subsidy plus a term that represents the quantity-weighted
value of the price reduction, so in period two the subsidy is $q_0(p_0 - p_1) + q_1(p_1 -
p_2)$, and so forth. With a uniformly decreasing price sequence, these subsidies
generate a step-function approximation of the gain in consumer surplus, which
provides the intuition for the theoretical attractiveness of the mechanism. This
mechanism does not require knowledge of the demand curve, and the subsidies
can be much lower than those of the Loeb-Magat mechanism.

One problem is that a price increase results in a penalty that must be paid in all
future periods. Since the penalty is calculated on the last period's high demand at
the lower price, a price increase followed by an equal decrease will result in a
negative increment to surplus forever after.[70] This unforgiving aspect of the
mechanism caused bankruptcies in three of the four sessions in which it was used
in Cox and Isaac (1986). Bankruptcies occurred whether or not the monopolist

was given complete information about the demand curve. Cox and Isaac (1987) developed a modification of the Finsinger-Vogelsang subsidy calculation for the case of a price increase. This modification avoids the penalties that are generated by price cycles; there is a permanent penalty for permanent price increases, but not for price increases that are reversed. All ten sessions using this new mechanism converged to the optimal (marginal cost) price outcome.

Summary. Although there is a monopoly pricing problem in laboratory PO experiments, it can be alleviated with decentralized regulation. With demand information, the Loeb-Magat mechanism works very well, and an auction can be used to reduce subsidy payments. In the absence of demand information, the Cox-Smith modification of the Finsinger-Vogelsang mechanism has yielded good results, at least in one decreasing-cost environment.

C. Potential Competition as a Regulator: Market Contestability

It has been about a hundred years since Clark (1887) emphasized the role of latent competition and raised the question of whether it would be as effective as actual competition in restraining monopoly pricing. More recently, the theory of contestable markets has formalized the effects of potential entry in a way that highlights the importance of the absence of sunk costs. In order to evaluate the design conditions of alternative experimental studies of contestability theory, it is necessary to review the requirements of the theory for the special case of homogenous-product markets used in the laboratory tests to date.

Baumol, Panzar, and Willig (1982, 6) characterize a *contestable market* as one in which (1) there is at least one potential rival with the same cost structure, (2) "potential entrants evaluate the profitability of entry at the incumbent firm's prices," and (3) there are no barriers to entry or exit, and, in particular, there is a possibility of hit-and-run entry: "Such entrants need not fear changes in prices by the incumbent firms for, if and when such reactions do occur, . . . that firm need only exit." Therefore, there can be no sunk costs. The fundamental result is that a contestable market can only be in equilibrium if the prices and quantities of the incumbent firm are *sustainable*, which in turn requires that no new firm with the same cost function as the incumbent can earn a profit by charging a lower price and earning a profit by selling all or part of the demand at that lower price. For the decreasing cost, natural-monopoly environment found in laboratory tests, any equilibrium must involve the incumbent choosing the price and quantity for which demand equals average cost.

The formal statement of the contestable markets theory does not predict that the average-cost pricing outcome will be always observed, but this seems to be the position taken by the theory's proponents: "Even if it is run by a monopoly, a contestable market will yield only zero profits and offer inducements for the adoption of Ramsey-optimal prices . . ." (Baumol, Panzar, and Willig 1982, 292). In particular, the assertion is that potential competition in the absence of sunk costs is as good as actual competition and that even horizontal mergers among potential entrants that do not alter contestability will not have harmful effects.

Coursey, Isaac, and Smith (1984) conducted an experiment designed to evaluate the effects of contestability under the same decreasing-cost, natural monopoly conditions described above for their posted-offer monopoly markets, which were used as a basis of comparison. Sellers chose prices independently in a standard posted-offer environment. In this context, a "competitive price" is the Ramsey-optimal price, the lowest price that yields nonnegative earnings for the incumbent; that is, this is an average-cost price for the incumbent. In the contested experimental markets, four of the duopolies yielded competitive price outcomes, and the other two exhibited downward trends in price, with price deviations from the CE level being less than 50 percent of the monopoly price deviation. Average final-period market efficiency increased from 49 percent in the monopoly experiments to 86 percent in the contested markets. The final-period value of the monopoly effectiveness parameter, averaged across experiments, was .02, which is significantly lower than the M value of .56 for the baseline monopoly sessions.[71] Harrison and McKee (1985) and Harrison, McKee, and Rutstrom (1989) observed similar, low values of the monopoly effectiveness parameter in contested markets, even though the buyers in their experiments were simulated; see the right-hand column of Table 5.3 to make comparisons with monopoly M values.

One interesting feature of summary data in Table 5.3 is that monopoly effectiveness is lower in the Loeb-Magat regulated markets than is the case in contested markets. This observation is consistent with the theory: price is supposed to fall to average cost (the Ramsey-optimal level) in contested markets, but the Loeb-Magat mechanism should drive price down to marginal cost, which is below average cost under decreasing cost conditions.[72] Contestability does not demand that a regulator have demand information, however, nor does it involve subsidies.

Contestable market theory would have little practical value for policy makers if the theory were sensitive to "small" sunk cost imperfections. Coursey, Isaac, Luke, and Smith (1984) take the same decreasing-cost structure from the Coursey, Isaac, and Smith paper and introduce a sunk cost in the nature of a five-period operating license. This license had a price of $2, which is less than the theoretical monopoly profit. The "incumbent" was required to purchase this license once for periods 1–5 and again for periods 6–10. The other seller stayed out and earned a "normal rate of return" for the first five periods, but could enter by purchasing a license after period five. Beginning in period 10, both sellers made license purchase decisions independently. The prices supported the "weak contestable markets hypothesis," in the sense that prices were closer to the competitive (Ramsey-optimal) level than to the natural-monopoly level, in all twelve sessions, six with simulated buyers and six with human buyers. But prices actually converged to the competitive level in only about half of the sessions, as compared with the two-thirds that had converged without sunk costs in Coursey, Isaac, and Smith (1984). Moreover, no single-seller, competitive natural-monopoly was observed; the entrant entered in all twelve sessions in period 6, and all sellers who exited later reentered the market if given the chance, that is, if the market did not terminate.

Gilbert (1989) has argued the Coursey, Isaac, Luke, and Smith (1984) results with sunk costs do not justify a claim that contestable markets theory can be extended to cover situations with sunk costs. In particular, the entry observed in laboratory markets generates inefficient duplication if the license fee represents a real cost.

It is important to distinguish between the predictions of contestable markets theory and the predictions of the relevant noncooperative game theory. I would expect that an increase in the number of price-setting competitors from one to two would improve market performance in a noncooperative equilibrium in most market structures, although it is possible to construct Cournot examples with inefficiently high levels of entry. It would be nice to see an experiment that could distinguish the implications of contestability from those of the noncooperative theories that IO economists commonly use.[73] Certainly, it is easier to check the necessary conditions for contestability than it is to calculate noncooperative equilibria in all but the simplest environments, and, in this sense, contestability would be a convenient crutch if it works.

A key behavioral assumption of the contestable-markets theory is that the entrant evaluate the profitability of entry given the incumbent's current prices. Harrison (1986) reports an experiment in which this restriction is "hard-wired" into the institution by forcing the incumbent to post a price first, which the entrant can observe before deciding on a price for that period. As Gilbert (1989) notes, Harrison thereby provides a test of the theory under the most favorable condition, in which a critical behavioral assumption is satisfied. But the timing assumptions in Harrison's design do not correspond to the setup in most unregulated markets, where the incumbent can respond quickly to an entrant's price cut. In contrast, a regulated monopoly, such as AT&T in the 1970s, may have operated with the first-mover disadvantage that is hard-wired into the Harrison setup.

Using a continuous-time flow market described in section V, Millner, Pratt, and Reilly (1990a) were able to implement a condition that, in my view, implements the possibility of hit-and-run entry in an interesting and relevant manner, thereby providing a useful "stress test" for contestable-markets theory. At any instant, the seller with the lowest price in their design generally makes all sales and, in this sense, is the incumbent. The other seller can observe the price and decide whether to undercut it at any moment. Since the probability of an incumbent's price change is essentially zero on a sufficiently short time interval, the entrant can be very sure that a price cut will initially capture the market. In addition, exit can be almost instantaneous. The flow-market experiments involved decreasing costs, up to capacity, and simulated, continuous-time buyers. Market efficiencies were quite low, and efficiencies with experienced subjects were not much different from the theoretical efficiency in a monopoly, which is a direct contradiction of contestable markets theory.[74] See Table 5.4 for comparisons. What Millner, Pratt, and Reilly do not observe is any stable pricing behavior; when the prices fall too

Table 5.4. Effects of Monopoly Restraint Mechanisms on Market Efficiency in Posted-Offer Auctions

	Design			Efficiency (E)		
	Experience	Buyer Type	Cost	Theoretical Monopoly	Observed Monopoly	Contested Market
Isaac, Ramey, and Williams (1984)[a]	Inexperienced	Human	Increasing	85%	85%	—
Coursey, Isaac, and Smith (1984)	Role experience	Human	Decreasing	60	49	86%
Millner, Pratt, and Reilly (1990a)	Inexperienced	Simulated	Decreasing	50–60	55	67
Millner, Pratt, and Reilly (1990a)	Design, role experience	Simulated	Decreasing	50–60	—	62

Notes: E = (actual surplus/CE surplus) × 100, calculated as an average of the E values for the final period (or time interval) common to all sessions in a treatment. For the sessions with decreasing costs, the CE surplus is determined by a price-equals-average-cost condition.
[a] The final-period efficiency value was estimated from the authors' figure 16.

low, one seller will often exit, at which time the other will raise price dramatically. I suspect that the unstable price cycles could eventually lead to some continuous-time analogue of noncooperative randomization in the presence of small adjustment costs or perceptual delays.[75] In one of their sessions, however, the price cycle switched to a very slow and disciplined decline as each seller undercut the other by pennies every several seconds in a successful attempt to share the market at near-monopoly prices.[76]

Future experimental work should make more effort to distinguish the predictions of noncooperative game theory from those of contestable markets theory. In addition, experimenters should provide an alternative for the potential entrants that is more interesting than simply earning nothing or a deterministic normal rate of return in a dummy alternate market. Subjects probably feel a desire to be "in" rather than "out," and the construction of an interesting, market-like alternative to entry into the incumbent's market would make the results more convincing. Since contestable markets theory seems to work well in some environments and not in others (e.g., flow markets), experiments that deal directly with the policy implications of contestable markets theory would be most valuable. For example, is it really irrelevant that a horizontal merger wave among potential entrants will have no effect on performance in a contestable market?

Summary. The simultaneous-choice, discrete-time PO experiments show that the addition of an equally efficient potential competitor can reduce monopoly effectiveness to competitive levels. The discipline of potential competition is not as effective when the no-sunk-cost assumption of contestable markets theory is violated. More damaging to contestable markets theory is the poor performance of contested flow markets with no sunk costs and a continuous-time structure that, in my opinion, provides the best implementation of the hit-and-run entry condition assumed by the theory.

D. Predatory Pricing and Antitrust Remedies

The existence of predatory pricing is one of the more controversial issues in industrial organization. Most, but not all, would agree that companies such as Standard Oil of New Jersey engaged in predatory pricing, a pattern of behavior that reduces the predator's current profits in a manner that can only be justified by the prospect of subsequent monopoly profits. Predatory behavior is thought to be less common today; my colleague Kenneth Elzinga once characterized the issue as being whether it is rare like an old stamp or rare like a unicorn. Since it is usually difficult to document predatory intent and since even a perfectly competitive firm would never price below marginal cost, antitrust scholars have proposed the use of cost-based tests, and the arguments in predation cases often center on cost and profit/loss measurements. In contrast, there is no problem with the measurement of costs in the laboratory, so it is possible for the experimenter to spot behavior that cannot be optimal except as an attempt to exclude competitors.

Recall that the contestable-markets experiments involved sellers with identical technologies, and even though profits were driven down to low levels, market dominance by one seller was not observed. Isaac and Smith (1985) conducted a series of posted-offer sessions in which they modified earlier contestable-markets designs by introducing asymmetries to provide the incumbent, seller A, with an advantage over the other, seller B. The incumbent had a higher capacity, lower costs, and a larger initial cash endowment to cover losses. Importantly, the PLATO posted-offer program was altered to permit price and quantity choices that yielded losses.

The relevant parts of the Isaac and Smith cost and demand structure are shown in Figure 5.6. In order to construct the market supply function, consider the average costs for sellers A and B, shown on the right side of the figure. Since the minimum of seller A's average variable cost function, AVC_A, is at $2.50, the low-cost seller A would supply zero units at lower prices, and the (thick) market supply function follows the vertical axis up to $2.50. At this price, seller A would supply the seven units that are arrayed with decreasing costs on the left side of the figure (each unit cost for seller A has an "A" underneath the corresponding step on the left). Seller B would not supply any units until the price rises to $2.66, the minimum of its average cost, so the thick market supply curve is vertical at seven units between $2.50 and $2.66, a price at which seller B provides the three units with decreasing costs shown on the left side of the figure. The supply overlaps the market demand function in the vertical range from $2.66 to $2.76, which is la-

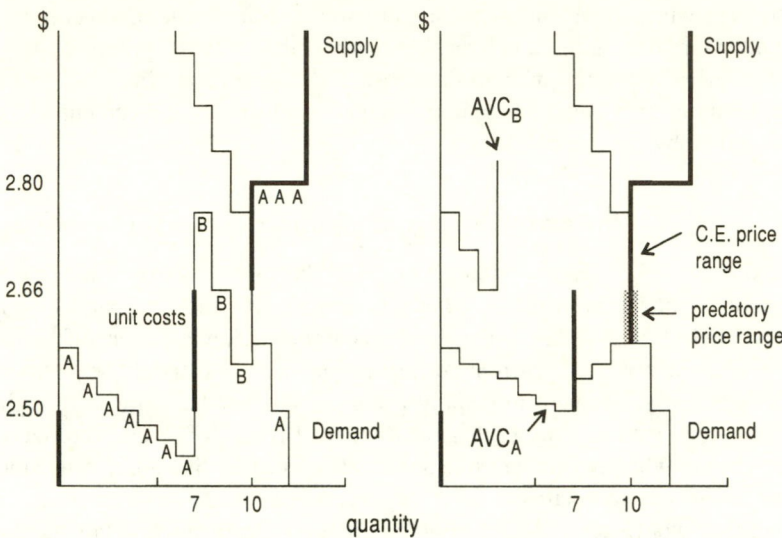

Figure 5.6. The Isaac-Smith design for predatory pricing. *Source:* Isaac and Smith 1985.

beled the "C.E. price range." Seller A has three extra-marginal units shown at costs of $2.80, just above the competitive price range, and seller B has other units with even higher costs (not shown).

Now consider the ability of seller A to engage in predatory pricing. There are various types of predatory behavior, but one possibility is for seller A to choose a price below the minimum of AVC_B (to keep B out), and therefore, below the marginal cost of meeting demand at that price. Pricing below marginal cost in this predatory manner need not result in a loss for seller A if the price is above AVC_A, as would be the case for a price in the "predatory range" of the demand curve, shown on the right side of the figure, with a quantity limit of ten.[77] This action will leave no room for profitable entry by seller B, and seller A will earn a small profit since price exceeds average cost at ten units. This action is predatory in the sense that prices in the predatory range are below the $2.80 marginal cost of the tenth unit for seller A. An outcome in which A sells all ten units is inefficient, since this seller's three extra-marginal units are more costly than the three infra-marginal units of seller B. Therefore, this design permits an inefficient predatory outcome that does not require the predator to sustain losses, although profits during the predation phase are lower than would be the case in a competitive equilibrium. A predatory action that drives the other seller out *may* allow seller A to earn much higher, monopoly profits.

Predatory pricing was not observed in any session, even after introducing several other design variations (e.g., sunk costs) intended to be progressively more favorable to such pricing, and hence the provocative title "In Search of Predatory Pricing." Anyone who has witnessed subjects' enthusiasm for being in the market trading process will wonder if the lack of predation is due to the absence of a reasonable alternative activity for the "prey." In particular, will a low-cost seller forego predation because of common knowledge that even a high-cost seller would suffer some losses rather than stay out of the market? Rutstrom (1985) modified the Isaac and Smith design by introducing an "alternate market" with fixed earnings of twenty-five cents per period, but this modification did not produce predatory pricing either.

Harrison (1988) modified the Isaac and Smith design in a clever manner; he conducted a posted-offer session with five markets and eleven sellers, each of whom could only enter one market at a time. Seven of the sellers were given the Isaac and Smith "seller B" cost function, shown in Figure 5.6, regardless of which market they entered. Each of the other four sellers had a preferred market in the sense that they could be a low-cost "seller A" in that market, but they would have seller-B costs if they entered any other market. There was only one potential seller A in each of four markets; in this sense, each potential low-cost seller had its own market. The efficient entry pattern required each of the four potential low-cost sellers to go to their "own" market and share it with a high-cost seller, and for the remaining high-cost sellers to congregate in the only market for which no seller can have low costs. Demand in each market was simulated and corresponded to the demand in Isaac and Smith.

Harrison reports one session with this multimarket version of the Isaac and Smith design. There are instances of predatory pricing. The outcomes for one of these markets, market I, are reproduced in Table 5.5. In period 1, three sellers enter, sellers 1 and 7 with high costs and seller 4 with a seller-A cost function for this market. As can be seen from the table, seller 7 posts the highest price, sells no units, and leaves for one of the other four markets in period 2. Sellers 1 and 4 remain, and this market reaches an efficient outcome in period 3, with seven units for the low-cost seller and three units for the other, as was seen from the earlier analysis of Figure 5.6. The outcome is efficient again in period 4, and both prices are in the competitive range. In period five, seller 4 offers ten units at a price of $2.64, which is below seller 1's lowest average cost, in a clear instance of predatory pricing. This behavior is intensified in the next period, after which seller 1 switches to another market. Seller 4 takes advantage of the resulting monopoly position by raising price in the following periods, which were quite profitable. Prices for all markets were posted on the blackboard after each period, and seller 4 offers a predatory price/quantity combination in period 10, perhaps in an attempt to counter or deter entry, which occurs anyway in the next period. There were cases of predatory pricing in several of the other markets; there was even one instance of a small seller pricing below the average cost of the larger, more efficient seller.[78]

Jung, Kagel, and Levin (1990) followed a different approach in their search for predatory pricing; they structured an experiment on the basis of a simple signaling game in which predatory pricing is an equilibrium outcome. Each session involves a subject monopolist who encounters a different potential entrant in a series of eight periods. In each period, the potential entrant for that period decides to enter or stay out, and the monopolist decides to fight or accommodate, which is observed by the prospective entrants. An entrant's preferences are such that

Table 5.5. Market I of Multimarket Predatory Pricing Session

Period	Seller ID	Posted Price	Quantity Limit	Quantity Sold	Characterization of Outcome
1	1	$2.90	3	2	
	4	2.51	7	7	
	7	3.49	3	0	
2	1	2.85	4	0	
	4	2.69	10	10	
3	1	2.60	3	3	Efficient
	4	2.69	10	7	
4	1	2.70	3	3	Efficient, competitive
	4	2.69	7	7	
5	1	2.70	3	0	Predatory
	4	2.64	10	10	
6	1	2.66	3	0	Predatory
	4	2.60	10	10	
7	4	2.65	7	7	
8	4	2.85	7	7	Supra-competitive
9	4	3.15	7	7	Supra-competitive
10	4	2.60	10	10	Predatory
11	4	3.10	7	7	Fortunate
	7	3.14	3	0	
12	4	3.15	7	3	
	10	2.99	3	3	

Source: Harrison 1988.
Note: Asterisk indicates

entry is only worthwhile if the monopolist accommodates. The monopolist is one of two "types": a strong monopolist prefers to fight, and a weak monopolist prefers to accommodate in a single period. The monopolist knows his own type, which was determined randomly at the start of the eight-period sequence, but the entrant can only try to infer the monopolist's type on the basis of observed responses to previous entrants. There is a sequential equilibrium in which a weak monopolist will fight entry in early periods in order to deter subsequent entry. This "predatory" fight response by weak monopolists was commonly observed. The sessions were conducted in an abstract setting; for example, the monopolist was called a "type-B player," and there was no mention of prices, quantities, entry, etc.[79]

Since predation is so difficult to diagnose in legal proceedings, a number of more-or-less mechanical rules have been proposed to prevent predation. Isaac and Smith (1985) ran several sessions that implemented two restrictions on predatory pricing that had been proposed in the antitrust literature: a prohibition of quantity expansion by the incumbent for two periods after entry, and a prohibition of temporary price cuts; that is, price cuts by the incumbent after entry had to be maintained for five periods. The effect of this policy was to raise prices and to reduce efficiency.[80] These experimental results are important since the implementation of antipredation policies with perverse effects would be unfortunate if predatory pricing is rare. One might object that antipredation policies should be evaluated in a context where predation occurs, but remember that these policies would restrict an incumbent's price and/or production responses to entry in any market, not just those where predation is thought to occur. Therefore, we should be careful about advocating a policy that has unwanted side effects in otherwise healthy markets.

Summary. Predatory pricing is not observed in simple posted-offer market environments that, in some respects, are quite favorable to predatory behavior. Moreover, some prominent antipredation proposals for limiting the price and quantity responses of an incumbent can have perverse effects in laboratory markets that were relatively efficient before the implementation of the antipredation policy. But the provision of an interesting alternative market to serve as the home base for the prey can yield predatory outcomes. In abstract experimental games with asymmetric information, subjects make decisions that correspond to the predation interpretation of the game. The interesting policy issue is not whether predatory pricing can be observed in the laboratory, but rather, it is whether and under what conditions predatory pricing is likely to occur in natural markets. The issue then is to what extent laboratory results will carry over into markets of antitrust concern. I believe that the home-market cost advantage in the Harrison design and the signaling opportunities in the Jung, Kagel, and Levin design are present in a variety of naturally occurring markets. But the observations of predatory pricing in the laboratory would be more convincing if there were more replication in multimarket design, and if the signaling design had more market-like details.

VII. Market Structure and Market Power

Market power exists when a seller has the ability to raise price above competitive levels, and to do so profitably. One of the central issues in industrial organization is the manner in which market power can be created, exercised, and extended. In laboratory experiments, even a monopolist may have considerable difficulties if the demand function is unknown and if human buyers can resist price increases, as indicated by the wide range of observed values of the monopoly effectiveness index in Table 5.3.

The addition of competitors may mitigate the market power of a monopolist. But observation of prices that converge to competitive levels in an experiment cannot be interpreted as the failure to exercise market power if this power does not exist for the multiseller environment being considered. The degree of market power is usually not considered explicitly in discussions of the competitive tendencies of nonmonopolized PO and DA experiments. Despite the fact that supra-competitive pricing usually involves quantity reductions, such reductions are typically discussed in the context of the efforts of buyers to under-reveal demand in an effort to "counter-speculate" against an explicit or implicit seller conspiracy.[81]

A. Definitions of Market Power

As was the case with simple monopolies, it is necessary to distinguish between the existence of market power as a theoretical matter and the exercise of such power in a multiseller situation. Market power can exist on either side of the market, but the discussion that follows will pertain to sellers' market power.

Holt (1989) suggests two alternative definitions. *Equilibrium market power* exists if there is a noncooperative equilibrium that results in supra-competitive prices. When buyers are major players in the market, such an equilibrium must include their behavior. Since it is difficult to calculate noncooperative equilibria in many trading institutions—e.g., double auctions—it is useful to have an alternative, non-game-theoretic definition.[82] This second definition is based on the 1984 Department of Justice horizontal merger guidelines. A seller is said to have *unilateral market power* if a unilateral deviation from a competitive equilibrium is profitable for that seller, given that all other traders continue to use the strategies that generated the competitive equilibrium. The class of deviations that can be considered in this test depends on the nature of the decision variables in the laboratory market institution, such as quantity in a Cournot quantity-choice experiment.[83] One drawback of this definition is that a seller with unilateral market power may not be able to exercise it if one or more buyers also have unilateral market power. Both definitions of market power are sensitive to the nature of the feasible messages and decisions for traders in a particular laboratory trading institution. This sensitivity is desirable, given the documented effects of institutional variations on prices in experiments.

Since experiments typically consist of a series of repeated market periods, it is natural to distinguish between static market power, obtained by applying one of the definitions to the single-period market game and dynamic market power that may exist in the supergame. With an infinite horizon, it is well known that, in theory, collusive outcomes can be supported by noncooperative behavior with appropriate threats to revert to the noncooperative outcome in stage games that follow deviations. Cooperation can be an equilibrium strategy if the expected gain from defecting in the current period is outweighed by the reduction in expected future profits when both players defect in all subsequent periods until the randomly determined termination.[84] In this manner, equilibrium market power can exist in a dynamic sense, even when it does not exist in a static sense.

When subjects are not permitted to communicate directly, I will use the term *tacit collusion* to refer to outcomes in which prices exceed the levels determined by static noncooperative equilibria in the market-period stage games. Tacit collusion of this type can result from the fear of punishments in a dynamic, noncooperative equilibrium, as noted above. Tacit collusion can also result from the altruism and mutual respect that can develop in multiperiod interactions.

B. Market Power in Double Auctions

One reason that the double auction is widely used in experimental research is that it is reliable; competitive outcomes are almost always obtained in non-monopolized DA markets with private incomplete information and stationary supply and demand conditions. But this convergence to the competitive price would not be surprising if traders did not have the power to manipulate price in their favor. Consider, for example, the DA design used for the last five periods in Figure 5.5. Recall that each of the four sellers has a capacity of four units at a cost of $5.70 and that the quantity demanded is eleven. If all sellers offer to sell at $5.70 and buyers divide their purchases randomly, the sellers will obtain 5¢ commissions on the units sold. A unilateral increase in a seller's offer will result in no sales, since the others' residual supply exceeds the market demand quantity. In other words, excess supply at supra-competitive prices exceeds each seller's capacity.[85]

Although the lack of market power in the Figure 5.4 design (periods 6–10) is extreme, it is not common in experimental designs for sellers to have enough low-profit marginal units to make it worthwhile to attempt to manipulate price. In contrast, there is no market power when sellers have only a single unit that is traded in a competitive equilibrium, since it is not profitable to refuse to sell this unit in order to alter price, unless the seller anticipates that the effect would endure until a subsequent period.[86]

When I first started to think about double auctions about ten years ago, I was surprised that the conventional wisdom then (and now) seemed to be that prices in a nonmonopolized double auction are not affected by most of the structural market characteristics that are the focus of a standard course in industrial organization: demand elasticity, concentration, capacity constraints, entry barriers, and so on. So I decided to try to design a double auction treatment that would not yield competitive prices, even with multiple sellers. The resulting design, developed in collaboration with Anne Villamil and Loren Langan, involves five buyers and five sellers, with values and costs that generate the supply and demand structure shown at the left side of Figure 5.7. Three of the sellers have one to three inframarginal units that could be traded in a competitive equilibrium, but the other two sellers (S1 and S2) have five inframarginal units, most of which are located on the horizontal step at the competitive price of $2.60. If one of these large sellers were to refuse to sell two units and if all other traders behaved competitively, then the price would rise by 25¢ to $2.85. Since the two marginal units withheld were at a cost of $2.60 and would be traded at $2.60 in a competitive equilibrium, the only loss is the 5¢ commission on each. The price increase yields a gain of 25¢

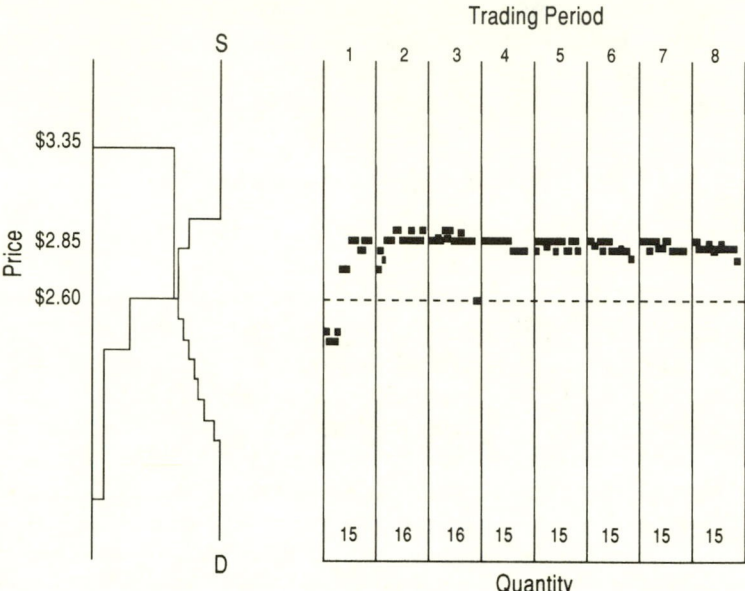

Figure 5.7. Double auction with seller market power. *Source:* Holt, Langan, and Villamil 1986.

on each of the other units, so the unilateral refusal to sell is profitable.[87] The buyers in this design were given three high-value units at $3.35 in an attempt to make any effort to counter-speculate unprofitable, since each unit is so profitable that the loss from under-revealing demand is not justified by the possibility of driving the price back toward the competitive level.

This design was used in our very first double auction (Holt, Langan, and Villamil, hereafter HLV 1986), with inexperienced subjects and inexperienced experimenters! The prices did not converge to the competitive level. The sequence of transactions data for one of these markets is shown on the right side of Figure 5.7. The prices start low, probably as a result of the very low costs on the first five units, but afterwards prices pass through the CE price and do not return. The transactions quantity was at fifteen after the fourth period, so the price/quantity combinations can be thought of as falling on the vertical region of the demand curve between $2.60 and $2.85.[88] As long as the price does not reach the $2.85 level, there is no substitution of a high-cost extra-marginal unit, and hence, no efficiency loss. Prices in about half of the other sessions stayed above the CE level in this manner, but surprisingly, price converged to within pennies of the CE level in the other sessions. This indicates just how competitive the DA institution is.

Davis and Williams (1991) replicated this experiment with the PLATO network, and they also found supra-competitive pricing, but with less bimodality in the data. In Figure 5.8 the vertical axis measures penny deviations from the competitive price, so 0 and 25 correspond to the competitive price of $2.60 and the

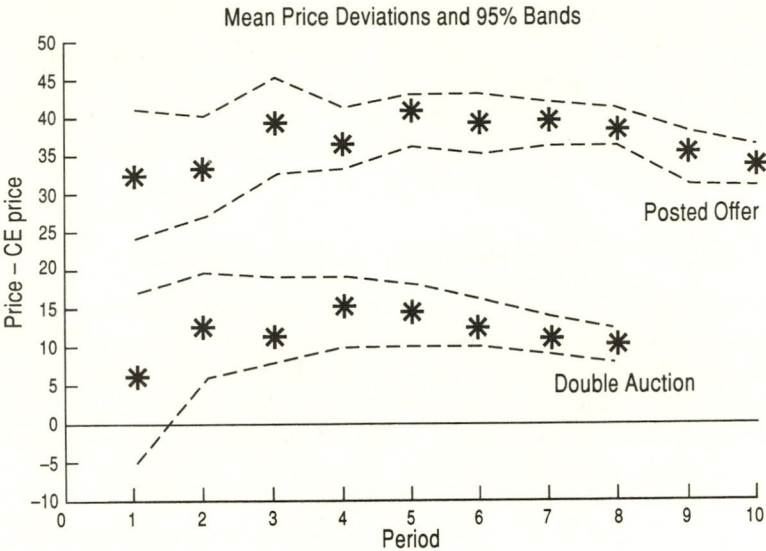

Figure 5.8. Double auction and posted-offer prices for the HLV seller market power design. *Source:* Constructed with data from Davis and Holt (1991).

supply step at $2.85, respectively. For the double auction results in the lower part of the figure, the eight asterisks show the average prices (across four sessions) in each of eight periods. The bands of dotted lines show the range in which 95 percent of the prices lie. Davis and Williams ran a parallel series of four posted-offer sessions with this HLV seller-market-power design using simulated buyers, and the shaded band with 95 percent of the data is much higher, with average prices ending up at a level of about $0.35 above the competitive price. The double auction is still more efficient in this environment, as can be seen from row 4 of Table 5.2. The passive role of simulated buyers in a posted offer auction is probably a factor in the less competitive nature of this institution, as the analysis of the next subsection indicates.

How significant is the exercise of market power with the HLV design? Davis and Williams stress that they see little evidence of quantity withholding by sellers with market power in double auctions, and that the outcomes are very efficient. These results are consistent with Porter's (1991) observation that a seller would never want to leave profitable units unsold in the final moments of trading in a Nash equilibrium for that period. Plott (1989, 1125) argues that results with the HLV design should be interpreted with caution. Plott notes that excess supply is only one unit at prices just above the competitive equilibrium in this design, and that the Easley and Ledyard (1988) (non-game-theoretic) model of double auction pricing, which predicts convergence to the CE price in other cases, does not necessarily predict convergence in the special case of one unit of excess supply. In a different design, Friedman and Ostroy (1989) do not observe the exercise of market power in either double auctions or clearinghouse auctions. The question is if the exercise of market power in double auctions is a "boundary" result for a particular parameter choice, without much general significance; this is Vernon Smith's view, as expressed in private correspondence. A related issue is whether market power will ever have any efficiency effects in nonmonopolized double auctions.[89]

C. Market Power in Posted-Offer Auctions

Plott (1986, 735) comments that "the posted-price institution induces an upward pressure on prices. . . . The relative effect of the posted prices was first demonstrated by Plott and Smith in comparison experiments. . . . Even now no theory about the relative influence of the posted-price institution has been published to my knowledge, but the effect has persisted under a variety of parametric situations . . ." (footnotes omitted).

In posted-offer auctions, capacity constraints arise naturally from the finite numbers of units provided to sellers. In such contexts, the competitive equilibrium may not be a noncooperative equilibrium if excess supply at supra-competitive prices is so small that sellers have a unilateral incentive to raise price above competitive levels, that is, if a lower quantity at a higher price is more profitable than a higher quantity at the competitive price. The critical factor is not the absolute amount of excess supply, but rather, the residual demand that remains after other sellers make all sales at the lower price.

By reassigning units of capacity from one seller to another, there is no change in either market supply or excess supply at supra-competitive prices, yet market power can change. I attended a conference two years in a row in which a researcher reported that this type of unit reallocation had an unanticipated and unexplained effect on average prices. As a consequence, Davis and I decided to design a reallocation that would have a clear and easily calculated effect on market power. Consider the design shown on the left side of Figure 5.9, where the identity number of one of the five sellers is listed below each unit on the supply curve. Sellers 1, 2, and 3 each have three units, and sellers 4 and 5 each have a single unit. Notice that all units for all sellers can be sold at a common price of $3.09, which is the highest competitive price. At this price, any seller who raised price unilaterally would make no sales, since the excess supply is three units at supra-competitive prices. Conversely, a unilateral price cut from a common price of $3.09 would not increase a seller's sales quantity and, hence, would be unprofitable. The highest competitive price is, therefore, a Nash equilibrium in the market stage game, and there is no market power by either definition given at the beginning of this section.

Next suppose that the two (boldfaced) high-cost units for seller 3 are given to sellers 1 and 2. This does not alter supply, demand, or the excess supply, but it does increase the residual demand should either of these sellers raise price unilaterally. Sellers 1 and 2 now have four units, and a unilateral price increase from $3.09 to the limit, $5.39, will increase the seller's profit (since the $2.30 increase

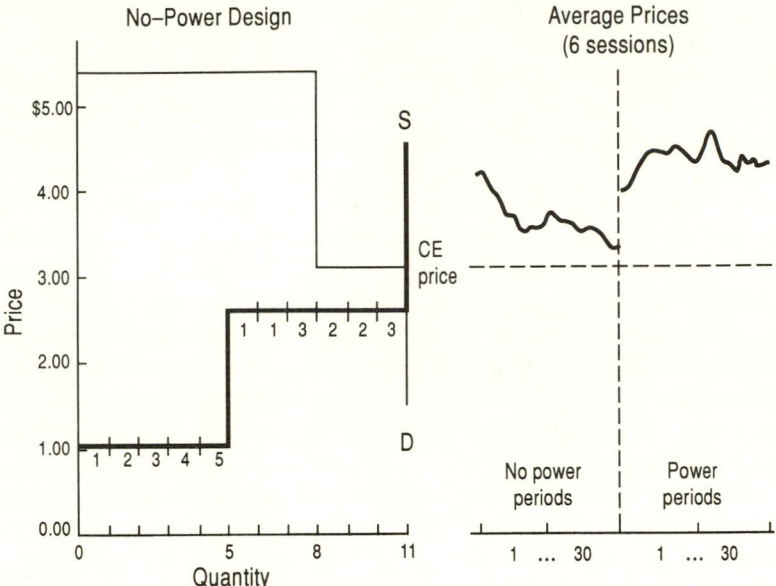

Figure 5.9. The effects of market power in posted-offer auctions. *Source:* Constructed with data from Davis and Holt (1994b).

in the price obtained for the first unit exceeds the loss of $0.50 on each of the three marginal units). After obtaining the additional unit, sellers 1 and 2 have market power, and the Nash equilibrium for the market stage-game involves randomization on the range from $3.29 to $5.39.[90]

Davis and Holt (1994b) report the results of six PO sessions, each with thirty periods under the no-power treatment and thirty periods under the power treatment that results from the reallocation of seller 3's marginal units. The order of treatments was reversed in every other sequence. Subjects were experienced, and buyers were simulated. In the no-power periods, prices begin high and fall to near-competitive levels, as shown in Figure 5.9 to the left of the dotted vertical line. In the periods with the power treatment, prices initially rose and then stayed high and variable, as shown to the right of the dotted vertical line in the figure. Prices were higher under the power treatment in all six sessions. Prices in the power design are well up into the range of randomization that is applicable for this design. In both designs, there is some evidence of tacit collusion in the sense that prices are above the levels predicted by static, noncooperative theory. This type of tacit collusion in posted-offer markets with seller market power is also reported by Davis, Holt, and Villamil (1990) for a different design in which the stage-game equilibrium also involves randomization. Besides the fact that prices are too high relative to the mixed-strategy equilibrium, there is considerable autocorrelation in the price series for most subjects, which is inconsistent with randomization. This autocorrelation is also reported by Kruse, Rassenti, Reynolds, and Smith (1994), who nevertheless conclude that the theoretical mixed-strategy equilibrium tracks some of the qualitative features of the equilibrium price patterns as excess capacity is altered.

Grether, Schwartz, and Wilde (1988) review several equilibrium shopping models in which seller market power could result from the presence of a shopping cost or an exogenous limitation on buyers' information about posted prices. Pricing behavior in posted-offer sessions tended to conform to the (Nash equilibrium) prediction for the informational and structural conditions used in the session. When the prediction involved supra-competitive pricing, it was always observed. One of the treatments involved a setup in which the prediction is the monopoly price. In this treatment, sellers' posted prices were written on the blackboard, but without their identification numbers. Buyers, who each had a single unit with a reservation value of L, were able to observe the exact price distribution before shopping. Each buyer could either pick a single seller at random from this distribution or pay for a sample of two prices and buy a unit from the seller with the lowest price in the sample. No buyer would wish to purchase the sample if its cost is greater than the spread between high and low prices. Therefore, the equilibrium cannot involve sellers choosing a common price below L, since a small unilateral price increase by one seller will not cause any buyer to purchase a sample. Consequently, a small price increase will not reduce the number of buyers who randomly arrive to make purchases. It follows that each seller has a unilateral incentive to raise price at any common price below L, and model parameters were selected so that the noncooperative equilibrium is the monopoly price of L.[91] Prices converged to L in three of the four times that this treatment was implemented.

Summary. It would be very misleading to conclude that laboratory evidence largely supports the notion that competitive, Walrasian outcomes are resilient to changes in institutional and structural conditions. Market power that results from capacity constraints or shopping costs can produce supra-competitive prices reliably in posted-offer auctions. Changes in market power that leave the shapes of supply and demand unchanged can also affect prices significantly. Sellers are sometimes able to exercise market power in double auctions, but the influence of seller market power is much weaker because of the incentives to offer last-minute price concessions and the more active role that buyers have in this institution. I have yet to see a design in which efficiency is significantly reduced by market power in a nonmonopolized double auction.[92]

VIII. Plus Factors That Facilitate Collusion

After measuring concentration and the changes that would be caused by a proposed horizontal merger, a standard procedure in antitrust analysis is to consider "plus factors," or market conditions that may make collusion (either tacit or explicit) more likely. Some of the most important plus factors, such as the absence of potential entry, have been covered in earlier sections. This section covers repe-

Output of Column Player

		5	6	7	8	9	10	11	12
	5	80,80	77,84	75,87	72,89	70,90	67,90	65,89	62,87
	6	84,77	81,81	78,83	75,85	72,85	69,85	66,83	63,81
	7	87,75	83,78	80,80	76,81	73,81	69,80	66,78	62,75
Output of Row Player	8	89,72	85,75	81,76	77,77	73,76	69,75	65,72	61,69
	9	90,70	85,72	81,73	76,73	72,72	67,70	63,67	58,63
	10	90,67	85,69	80,69	75,69	70,67	65,65	60,61	55,57
	11	89,65	83,66	78,66	72,65	67,73	61,60	56,56	50,51
	12	87,62	81,63	75,62	69,61	63,58	57,55	51,50	45,45

Figure 5.10. A bimatrix Cournot duopoly game (payoff for row, payoff for column). *Source:* Holt 1991.

tition, communication, numbers, and contracts. Many other interesting factors that come up in antitrust cases have not been evaluated in the laboratory, and this is an important area for further work.[93]

Very simple laboratory environments are especially useful for isolating the effects of communication, repetition, payoff symmetry, and other factors that may enhance or retard cooperation. Therefore, much of the work to be surveyed in this section involves situations in which the payoffs are presented in a simple matrix form, such as prisoner's dilemma and matrix oligopoly games. To understand better the strategic situation that subjects face in this type of game, consider the payoff matrix in Figure 5.10, which is a truncated version of the Cournot duopoly payoff table used in Holt (1985).[94] Subjects could choose any output quantity between 4 and 22, but the part of the table reproduced here only shows the penny payoffs for outputs from five to twelve, with the payoff of the row player listed first. Looking down the diagonal from the upper left to the lower right, it is apparent that the symmetric perfectly collusive output is 6, which yields profits of 81 for each. Looking down the "8" column, it is apparent that row's best response to an output of 8 for column is to choose an output of 8, and vice versa, so (8,8) is a symmetric Cournot-Nash equilibrium.[95] These payoffs were generated with a linear demand, constant marginal cost, and a normal profit (negative fixed cost) to ensure that profits were 45¢ at the competitive outcome. For the demand and cost functions used, the competitive outcome, where price equals marginal cost, occurs with outputs of 12 for each person.

The competitive output of 12 is also the output predicted by the "consistent conjectures equilibrium" (CCE) proposed by Bresnahan (1981). Early oligopoly theory was long plagued by the indeterminacy of "conjectural variations," and the CCE is a method of determining which of many possible conjectural variations is consistent with actual responses. Mechanically, the consistent conjecture is found by taking the total differentials of sellers' first-order conditions (when they contain conjectured responses) and then imposing a consistency requirement that the actual response to others' decisions be equal to the conjectured responses. I was initially interested in a new equilibrium concept with an intriguing title and with the ability to explain most of the tacit price collusion observed by Dolbear et al. (1968) in simultaneous-price-choice matrix games.[96] But I was skeptical of the CCE prediction that a duopoly market with a homogenous product, linear demand, and constant cost would yield a competitive price. These structural assumptions were satisfied in the Fouraker and Siegel (1963) experiment to be discussed below; and to my surprise, they had observed very competitive outcomes, especially in triopoly sessions.

The Fouraker and Siegel experiment did not clearly distinguish the Cournot and CCE (in this context competitive) outcomes, in part because the profits at the CCE/competitive outcome were zero in the Fouraker and Siegel design. Subjects are always led to believe that they may earn a significant amount of money in a laboratory session, so behavior is less likely to stabilize around the predictions of an equilibrium that yields zero earnings. To give the CCE a reasonable chance, I added 45¢ to all earnings amounts to obtain the payoffs shown in Figure 5.10, and the payoff of (45,45) for outputs of 12 was thought to be sufficient to keep subjects motivated.

Several series of complete-information duopoly markets were conducted with this design. In one session, twelve subjects were successively rematched with different partners in a series of ten single-period games (Holt 1985, section IV). Subjects were separated into two groups of six and were seated in two adjoining rooms at a distance that made it impossible to see others' decision sheets. Participants were given ID numbers that were written on their decision sheets, and they were shown the sequence of numbers of the other subjects with whom they would be matched. Subjects could see that they were matched with a different person in each period. At the start of a period, they were given several minutes to choose and record a quantity decision. Then the decision sheets were collected and matched. The "other seller's quantity" and the subject's own earnings were recorded on each decision sheet, which was then returned.

The data for every third matching (matchings 1, 4, 7, and 10) are plotted as frequency distributions in Figure 5.11. Initially, the output choices were fairly uniformly distributed from five to eleven, as indicated by the flatness of the "ribbon" for the first matching or period ("pd. 1") at the front of the figure. In the fourth matching, two of the twelve subjects were still trying to cooperate, but there is a prominent hump around the outputs of 8 and 9. The modal output choice in the seventh matching is 9, and some of the subjects making this choice were writing rivalistic comments about relative earnings on their "Comment Sheets" for this period.[97] For example, one subject who chose an output of 9 in the sixth period remarked: "only a 1 cent 'loss' occurs producing at 9 instead of 8. This keeps the other firm's profits down." This seller chose 8 in the final matching, and most other output decisions shifted back to the Cournot level, as shown by the

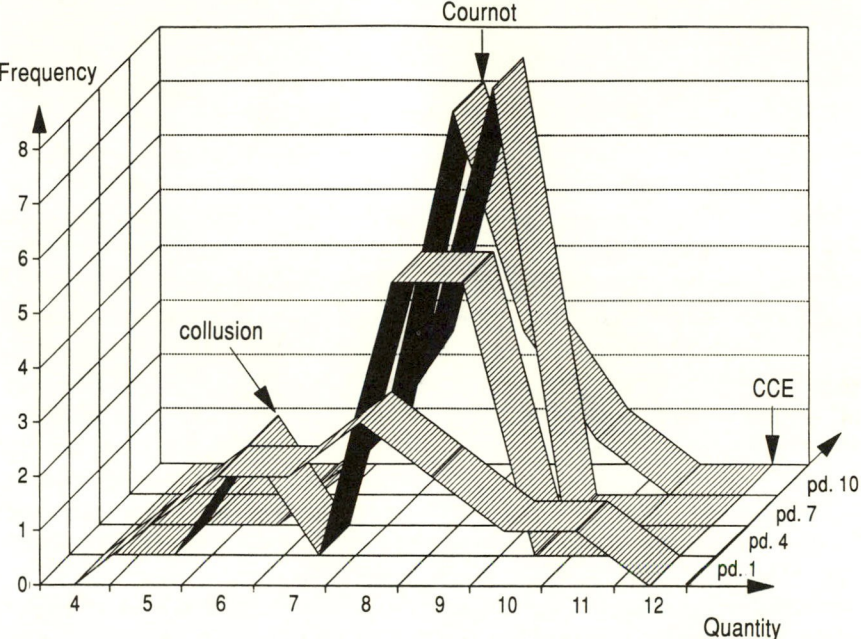

Figure 5.11. Frequency of quantity choices for the first, fourth, seventh, and tenth matchings in a Sequence of ten single-period Cournot duopoly games. *Source:* Holt 1985, section IV.

ribbon at the back of the figure. This session has not been replicated with other groups of subjects, and, given what I now know about group effects, I am hesitant to conclude that Cournot behavior will result from sequences of one-period matchings in quantity-choice games.[98] The session does provide a counterexample to the predictions of the CCE concept. In separate sessions with the same payoff matrix, subjects were matched with the same duopolist partner for a sequence of periods, with a random stopping rule, and about one-fourth of the pairs were able to reach the collusive outcome (see below). There was no support for the CCE concept under either treatment; this is an example of an experiment that is used for theory rejection.

A. Repetition with Different Cohorts: Experience

Two issues arise with repetition: the effects of repetition with the same cohort, and the effects of previous experience with other cohorts. Repetition with the same cohort in a series of market periods could increase cooperation if it takes time to establish trust and/or a reputation for punishing defections. Repetition with different cohorts may increase cooperation, for example, if it is hard to repair a breakdown of trust, and the switch to a new cohort allows people to start over in their attempts to cooperate. These are intuitive, non-game-theoretic observations; in theory, the effects of repetition depend on the stopping rule and the structure of the payoffs.

First consider experience with different cohorts. In the *single-period*, quantity-choice duopolies discussed above, Holt (1985, section IV) found that initial attempts to cooperate vanished after successive rematchings with different partners in a deterministic rotation pattern. Cooper, DeJong, Forsythe, and Ross (1991) observed that players made cooperative decisions about 30 percent of the time in single-period prisoner's dilemma games with rematching.[99] The incidence of cooperation was higher in initial matchings (43 percent) than in later matchings (20 percent). Therefore, repetition of single-period encounters has been observed to reduce cooperation, which in theory should not exist in these single-period encounters.

Repetition with previous cohorts has been observed to increase cooperation in multistage games. Stoecker (1980) matched subjects in a sequence of ten-period price-choice duopoly games with a tabular payoff function that simulated demand. The ability to switch partners every ten periods probably allows subjects to break out of deadlocks, and the ten periods of repetition provides some inducement to cooperate, even though the unique subgame-perfect outcome in this finite-horizon structure is to defect and price competitively in all periods. After a number of rematchings of this type, Stoecker found that the rates of cooperative behavior were very high until the last several periods of the ten-period sequences. In a later paper with sequences of ten-period prisoner's dilemma games, Selten and Stoecker (1986) observe some decay in cooperation rates ("unraveling") in later matchings.

Davis and Holt (1989) also observed that subjects with previous experience in two-stage matrix games were more cooperative and were more likely to use decisions in the second stage that punish defection and reward cooperation in the first stage. This was a relatively complicated game in which cooperation in the first stage can be an equilibrium outcome, which may explain the importance of experience. Benson and Faminow (1988) report an experiment that was designed explicitly to compare the behavior of experienced and inexperienced subjects (in duopoly price-choice markets with product differentiation and incomplete information). The experienced subjects had participated in similar, but not identical sessions. They observe significantly more tacit cooperation among subjects with such experience. The authors do not consider the alternative hypothesis that people who cooperated more successfully in earlier sessions were more likely to sign up again for the experienced sessions. It is a possibility that the effect of experience would be overstated as a result. Nevertheless, it is reasonably safe to conclude that experience with previous cohorts in multiperiod encounters can increase cooperation, whether or not such cooperation is an equilibrium outcome for the multiperiod game.

One relevant distinction may be whether or not the change in cohort occurred in the same session or between sessions on different days. In the multiperiod duopoly markets in Holt (1985), subjects were rematched after the random termination of the first pairing, and the levels of cooperation for the second pairing were no higher than for the first. In contrast, the increased cooperation observed by Davis and Holt (1989) and Benson and Faminow (1988) was for changes in cohorts on different days. If this difference is relevant, then it provides support for the standard practice of using "experience" to mean participation in the same type of game or institution in a previous session.

B. Multiperiod Repetition with the Same Cohort

Fouraker and Siegel (1963) matched subjects in groups of two or three for a sequence of identical market periods. The number of periods was unknown to subjects until the end. Subjects chose quantity levels simultaneously, and each person's payoff was calculated with a table that was determined by a linear demand function for a homogeneous product, with constant costs of production. Fouraker and Siegel report outputs for the twenty-first period. In the complete-information duopoly markets, outputs were approximately uniformly distributed in the range from the collusive industry output of 30 to the competitive (price-equals-common-marginal-cost) industry output of 60.[100] Industry outputs were often below the static Cournot level of 40–44 for a duopoly, which indicates that some tacit collusion developed in these repeated Cournot games.[101] In the complete-information, three-seller markets, about two-thirds of the industry outputs were *above* the Cournot triopoly output of 45–48; that is, most of the triopoly participants exhibited rivalistic rather than tacitly collusive behavior. About half of the complete information, triopoly outcomes were very close to the competitive output prediction of 60, despite the fact that this yielded zero profits.[102] With incomplete information about others' payoffs (and only information about the sum of others' quantity decisions), triopoly outcomes were closer to the Cournot outcomes that correspond to the static noncooperative equilibrium for the stage game.

Carlson (1967) used a variant of this nonmatrix setup, with incomplete demand information.[103] In two sessions, he used a steep demand function that should yield explosive price oscillations under the cobweb theory in which sellers base current production decisions on the assumption that price will be the same as it was in the previous period. In two other sessions, the demand was flatter, and the market should converge under static cobweb expectations. The observed price patterns for the sessions with the explosive design were no more unstable than for the other sessions.[104] In Carlson's sessions, the output quantities converged to near competitive levels in all sessions, but this result must be interpreted with caution since the sessions involved twenty to twenty-five sellers and the author does not calculate the Cournot equilibria. Subjects in the Holt and Villamil (1986) four-seller session were given no demand information, and the mean and median price was near the competitive level, and nowhere near the Cournot level. Binger et al. (1990) report the results of forty-period Cournot markets with complete demand information. Averaging across sessions and periods, the market quantities approximate the Cournot levels for the two-seller no-communication sessions, and quantities are about midway between competitive and Cournot levels for the five-seller no-communication sessions. Wellford (1990) reports outcomes in the range between the Cournot and competitive predictions for multiperiod sessions, with either five or eleven sellers and complete demand information. Beil (1988), who used a payoff matrix to simulate demand, also finds that the quantity decisions typically exceed the static Cournot levels in four-seller markets. There is more tacit collusion with only two sellers; Holt (1985) and Mason, Phillips, and Redington (1991) report that quantities in multiperiod duopoly games are between the Cournot and collusive levels.

The overall pattern of results in multiperiod, Cournot quantity-choice experiments is summarized: (1) with Cournot duopolies, outcomes fall on both sides of the Cournot prediction, and some cases of near perfect collusion occur, and (2) with more than two sellers, outcomes are often more competitive than the Cournot prediction.

Next consider the effects of repetition in price-choice experiments. Fouraker and Siegel observed a downward price trend in price-choice experiments with a very competitive setup: a homogeneous product and no capacity constraint (the seller with the lowest price sells all).[105] The price decline was more abrupt for triopolists than for duopolists. Murphy (1966) used a modification of the basic Fouraker and Siegel (1963) incomplete-information design for price-setting duopolists, and he ran the sessions for more periods. He found that an initial downward trend was reversed later.[106] Very extensive repetition has sometimes resulted in high levels of cooperation. Alger (1986, 1987) also reports significant amounts of cooperative pricing behavior in duopoly posted-offer markets (with no-power designs) that sometimes lasted for more than 100 periods. The stopping rule for these markets was not announced to the subjects. Harrison, McKee, and Rutstrom (1989, 89) note one potential problem with Alger's markets:

> One would want to ensure that the rewards to subjects after so many periods dominated the subjective costs of participating in a meaningful way (one of us observed some of these experiments in progress, and was struck by the widespread boredom of the subjects as well as their relief at the end of the session). It is not obvious that statistically-significant differences of prices of a few pennies implies statistically-significant differences of expected income to subjects.

This raises an important methodological issue; for most purposes, incentives should not be diluted to keep earnings constant when the number of market periods is increased.

The way in which cooperation can change over time is critical for many applications. Experimentalists usually do not want to truncate treatment sequences before behavior stabilizes, but unnecessarily long sequences can limit the ability of the experimenter to switch treatment conditions. My own experience in current work with Doug Davis is that prices in the first ten to twenty periods of a posted-offer auction can be misleading. Some of our (to date, unreported) posted-offer sessions involve five sellers in a no-power design with simulated demand and a preannounced stopping point of sixty periods. Prices can rise significantly above competitive levels between periods 10 and 20, and there is no predominant pattern after that point in most sessions. In a bimatrix quantity-choice setting with four sellers and no information about the stopping point, Beil (1988) reports two seventy-period markets in which the outcomes reached the approximate Cournot level by period 5 and did not change significantly thereafter.[107] Mason, Phillips, and Nowell (1991) report that the adjustment is slower in Cournot duopoly matrix games when the payoffs are asymmetric than is the case with symmetric payoffs. Moreover, subjects in the asymmetric games were less cooperative.

Although the studies just discussed involved repetition for a sequence of periods with the same cohort, none provided a specific control, that is, a matched treatment with no repetition. Using the same payoff table that generated the non-cooperative outcomes by period 10 in the single period games reported in Figure 5.11, Holt (1985) conducted multiperiod sessions with a random stopping rule. In particular, subjects were told that they would continue to be matched with the same partner until the throw of a die yielded a six, so the probability of continuation was 1/6.[108] As is well known, this introduces a type of discounting that gives more weight to current earnings. By the end of the multiperiod markets (determined by the throw of a die), about 40 percent of the subjects were selecting output decisions below the static Cournot level, that is, more cooperative than Cournot behavior. Overall, about one-fourth of the duopoly pairs were able to reach the symmetric, joint-payoff-maximizing outputs. This is reassuring, since the joint-maximizing outcome can, in this infinite-horizon context, be supported by the threat of reversion to the static Cournot decisions in all periods following a defection.[109] But perhaps more important than the threat of this "trigger" punishment is the opportunity to establish trust in duopoly situations with repetitions; a number of pairs were able to coordinate joint incremental movements toward the joint-maximizing levels by simultaneously choosing outputs of (8,8), followed by (7,7) and (6,6). In several cases, large, seemingly punitive output expansions were used by subjects who had been choosing outputs below the Cournot level while their partners had been earning higher payoffs by using higher outputs.

Feinberg and Husted (1993) investigate the effects of the rate of discount on collusion in quantity-choice games by (1) having a random termination probability of one-sixth and (2) by having payoffs decline over time at either a fast rate or a slow rate. They find that collusive duopoly outcomes are less likely with high discount rates.

Palfrey and Rosenthal (1992) provide another direct study of the effects of repetition. Their experiment involves a comparison of (1) repeated one-shot games with different cohorts and (2) nonrepeated multistage games with the same cohort, where a random device was used to determine the final period. Although this is a public goods game with a complicated private information structure, the basic incentive structure is similar to that of a prisoner's dilemma, with a noncooperative equilibrium for the stage game that yields earnings that are far below earnings that would result from cooperative decisions. In the repeated treatment, the authors show that a cooperative outcome with rotation of contributions could be supported by "trigger strategy" threats to revert to the noncooperative equilibrium for the stage game. In the experiments, repetition raises contributions rates by an amount that is statistically significant but not particularly large relative to the cooperative outcome. Palfrey and Rosenthal (1992, 4) conclude that these results are "not encouraging news for those who might wish to interpret as gospel the oftspoken suggestion that repeated play with discount rates close to one leads to more cooperative behavior." Sell and Wilson (1991) also find little support for the use of trigger strategies to support cooperation in repeated, four person public goods games with a random termination device. Of course, the effects of repetition may be more pronounced in simpler games. In particular, punishments are more likely to be effective when there are only two players, so that a punishment can be targeted to the defector without harming third parties (see the discussion of numbers effects below). Nonbinding communications can also increase the likelihood of observing the more efficient outcomes supported by trigger strategies (see the discussion of Brown-Kruse, Cronshaw, and Schenk [1993] in the next section).

Summary. Repetition has been observed to decrease cooperation in single-period market games. In multiperiod games, repetition with the same cohort and with previous cohorts has been observed to increase cooperation. The amount of experience needed before behavior stabilizes is an open and important question, and the answer may be design and institution specific. Posted-offer markets probably ought to be run for at least fifteen periods, unless pilot sessions indicate otherwise. Very long sequences of market periods, however, do not necessarily generate perfect collusion. Moreover, there is no direct evidence to support the view that trigger strategies will result in cooperative outcomes in multistage games with random termination rules and no communications.

C. Pure-Numbers Effects and the Ability to Punish

The possibility of direct punishment is a factor that facilitates cooperation. In a duopoly market, either seller can send a direct message by reducing price or expanding quantity. Davis, Holt, and Villamil (1990) found a fair amount of tacitly collusive pricing in posted-offer duopolies, even in their no-power design. But there was much less supra-competitive pricing in triopoly markets with the no-power design. The authors conjectured that this difference was due to the inability of triopolists to punish one noncooperative rival without harming the other. The subjects in Stoecker's (1980) sequence of ten-period duopoly experiments were unable to maintain collusive prices when they were subsequently matched as triopolists. Fouraker and Siegel (1963) also found more competitive behavior with three sellers than with two. Binger et al. (1990) observe (1) high levels of cooperation in quantity-setting duopolies and (2) near-competitive behavior with five quantity-setting subjects (in the later periods of parallel sessions).

Isaac and Reynolds (1989) survey the state of general opinion and advice about workable competition in antitrust settings and find considerable support for the notion that two firms are too few and four may be sufficient for good performance. A change in the number of sellers may alter the price predictions of standard oligopoly models, but it was Chamberlin (1962) who first suggested that the underlying nature of the equilibrium concept may differ between small group and large group situations.[110] Nevertheless, I am skeptical that there will be a magic number of sellers that ensures competitive outcomes; institutional and structural details cannot be ignored. For example, posted prices are way above competitive levels in the five-seller power design of Davis and Holt (1994b) that is reproduced in Figure 5.9.

It is useful to distinguish between two possible effects of increasing the number of sellers beyond two: it is harder to monitor the specific decisions of the others, and it is harder to punish a specific rival. On rereading Fouraker and Siegel (1963) for this survey, I noticed that their incomplete information treatments were altering both payoff and monitoring information. In the quantity-choice sessions with incomplete information, each seller was only told the sum of others' quantity choices, so a duopolist could monitor the other's output, and a triopolist could not do so with the same precision. Was the more competitive behavior in the Cournot triopolies due to the increase in the number of sellers or to the change in the ability to monitor?

Beil (1988) reports some preliminary research designed to address the importance of firm-specific monitoring and punishment. In four-seller Cournot sessions, the ability to monitor the previous periods' outputs of each of the other three sellers did not increase observed cooperation beyond that observed in sessions without monitoring. A second treatment involved the ability to punish a specific rival; this was implemented by giving each seller the ability to direct a payoff penalty toward one specific rival in each period. The penalty was fixed and ranged from 10 to 50¢. Observed cooperation increased dramatically in periods with the targeted-penalty option, and joint-maximizing outcomes were often observed. Although this penalty was costless to the sender and perhaps unrealistically precise, its dramatic effect can help us understand why there is less tacit collusion with more sellers in markets with no specific penalty.[111] If two sellers are showing a lot of restraint and a third is cutting price (or expanding output), then neither of the two cooperative sellers can punish the deviant with a price cut without also affecting the earnings of the other cooperative seller, which may trigger a price war.

One feature of all of these analyses is that an increase in the number of sellers typically changes the incentive structure of the game in a variety of ways. For example, increasing the number of price-setting sellers of a homogeneous product from two to three will reduce the profit for each if they share the demand at a common price, but correcting this by increasing demand will increase the incentive that each has to undercut the others' common price. One interesting issue is whether the numbers effect on prices is only due to the change in the individual's own incentive structure and has nothing to do with the number of sellers. A pure-numbers effect could be investigated by altering the number of sellers, holding the incentive structure constant. Such a pure-numbers effect could be due to a number of factors, including the reduced ability to punish a deviant competitor in a large-numbers situation.

Dolbear et al. (1968) used a clever design that isolated a pure-numbers effect, holding constant the incentives to collude tacitly. This was done by using a bimatrix-game payoff table with the row determined by the subject's own price decision and the column determined by the average price of competitors.[112, 113] In the duopoly sessions, the column was determined by the other seller's price, but using the same table in the four-seller and sixteen-seller designs was the way in which the authors were able to change the number of competitors without altering the incentives to raise prices above static noncooperative equilibrium common to all treatments. Subjects always knew the number of other sellers, and that the stage game would be repeated an indeterminate number of times with the same group of competitors. Some sessions were conducted with complete information about payoffs but incomplete information about the termination point, which was undisclosed but which turned out to be at the end of period 15. Prices in the twelve duopoly markets with complete payoff information ranged from being lower than the noncooperative level up to the collusive level. But four out of six of the four-seller markets with complete information yielded noncooperative prices.[114] The same pattern was observed in a parallel series of markets with private incomplete information; all four-seller markets and a sixteen-seller market converged to the noncooperative price level, but prices in five of six incomplete-information duopolies were above the noncooperative levels.[115] Therefore, an increase in the number of sellers produces a reduction in prices that cannot be attributed to changes in the incentive structure.

A surprisingly small pure-numbers effect is reported by Davis and Holt (1994b) in a design in which a merger reduces the number of sellers from five to three. The authors use as a baseline a "power design," which is the design in Figure 5.9 after reallocating the boldfaced units from seller 3 to sellers 1 and 2. This power-design baseline is then altered by merging sellers 3, 4, and 5, a merger that reduces the number of sellers, but as they show, does not alter the noncooperative equilibrium mixed price distribution. The merger increases prices in five of six sessions with paired pre-merger and post-merger treatments; the effect is small but statistically significant. Similarly, Isaac and Reynolds (1989) find a "marginally significant" increase in efficiency when a fixed industry capacity is equally divided among four sellers instead of two sellers, in posted-offer sessions with identical simulated demand functions. The plots of average prices, however, reveal a clear pure-numbers effect on price.

In contrast, Isaac and Walker (1988) find no clear pure-numbers effect in a public goods experiment in which the size of the group is changed from four to ten without altering the marginal per capita return of a contribution to the public good. They discuss two other studies of pure-numbers effects in the literature on prisoner's dilemma games, with group sizes ranging from three to nine; in one study, the effect was not significant, and in the other the effect was for larger groups to cooperate more (when the payoffs were altered with group size to hold constant the marginal incentive to cooperate).[116] The primary difference that I detect between studies that find no pure-numbers effects and those that do not is whether duopoly is the basis of comparison. For example, there would be no clear numbers effect in the Dolbear et al. data if one were only to compare their four-seller sessions with the single sixteen-seller session.

Summary. Increases in the numbers of sellers result in more competitive behavior, both in absolute terms and (with two sellers as a baseline) in relation to the static, noncooperative equilibrium (which itself typically changes with the number of sellers). But with more than three participants, there seems to be little or no evidence for a pure-numbers effect that is measured by changing the number of sellers in a way that does not alter the incentive structure. With two sellers, a defector can be punished directly without harming a cooperative third party, and there is some evidence that the possibility of direct punishment enhances cooperation.

D. Communication

The simplest form of communication is indirect; it involves sending "signals" with price and quantity decisions. Fouraker and Siegel (1963) limited this type of signaling in their incomplete-information, price-choice sessions; the subjects were only told whether their price was low, tied, or high. The others' prices were observed in the complete-information sessions, which generated more tacit cooperation, especially with two sellers. Is the more competitive behavior in their incomplete information treatment due to the inability of a high-price seller to communicate a signal by going all of the way up to the joint-maximizing price, instead of inching up timidly? Signaling of this nature precedes collusive phases of the Davis and Holt (1994b) sessions with publicly posted prices. My guess is that the Fouraker and Siegel data present a biased impression of the likelihood of obtaining noncooperative outcomes under incomplete payoff information.

Most of the experimental work on communication pertains to explicit, verbal discussions. Nonbinding communications generally improve cooperation in prisoners' dilemma games (Dawes, MacTavish, and Shaklee 1977) and in sealed bid auctions (Isaac and Walker 1985).[117] Daughety and Forsythe (1987a, 1987b) and Binger et al. (1990) report that face-to-face nonbinding group discussions are effective in raising price in repeated Cournot games in which the quantity decisions are made privately after the preperiod discussion. Moreover, Daughety and Forsythe (1987a) report that the opportunity to collude in initial periods of a session had a carryover effect in subsequent periods in which discussion was not permitted. Similarly, Isaac, Ramey, and Williams (1984) find that posted-offer prices are increased when sellers are given a chance to meet face to face and discuss collusion in a nonbinding manner prior to each trading period. Indeed, PO conspiracies generate high prices as reliably as PO monopolies, but the index of monopoly effectiveness is lower for PO conspiracies, as is apparent from Table 5.6.

Table 5.6. The Effects of Conspiracies

	Price (deviation from CE)	Efficiency	Monopoly Effectiveness
Theoretical CE	.00	100	0
DA with conspiracy	.15	92	38
PO without conspiracy	.03	90	−15
PO with conspiracy	.27	85	17
PO monopoly	.28	85	45
Theoretical monopoly	.60	85	100

Source: Isaac, Ramey, and Williams (1984). The data are for the final period of
treatment, averaged across all sessions in each treatment cell. The data were
obtained by interpolation from their figure 16.

In contrast, nonbinding group communications did not appear to increase the
incidence of cooperation in a parallel series of double auctions conducted by
Isaac, Ramey, and Williams (1984). This observation is consistent with the results of attempts to conspire in double auctions reported earlier by Isaac and Plott
(1981). The failures of conspiracies are probably due to the strong temptation that
sellers have to cut price during double auction trading.[118, 119] Another case of
ineffective (nonbinding group) collusion is reported by Harrison and McKee
(1985, 64) for decreasing-cost, posted-offer experiments with simulated buyers.
I would conjecture that the breakdown of collusion here is due to the strong
incentive to expand sales in a decreasing cost environment (recall that Isaac,
Ramey, and Williams observed effective collusion in PO markets with increasing
costs).

Cooper et al. (1991) implement a tightly controlled amount of communication
that involves a written suggested decision in a prisoner's dilemma game. There is
one-way communication when only one person can send such a message, and
there is two-way communication when both players can send such messages simultaneously. In both cases, the communication is just the label of a decision, and
there is no opportunity for response. Neither form of communication increases
cooperation in their single-period prisoner's dilemma games, with rematchings.[120]

Holt and Davis (1990) introduced a similar type of controlled communication
into posted-offer triopoly markets with simulated demand, but with an opportunity for response. Prior to posting prices, a randomly determined seller could fill
in the blank in the following sentence: "_____ is an appropriate price for the
market in this period." The other sellers could indicate a general response: *A* for
agreement, *L* for too low, or *H* for too high. We began by adding a couple of
periods of this treatment onto the end of some sessions being run for a different
purpose, and the results were immediate jumps of prices to near-collusive levels.
We thought that we knew what to expect when we later started to run sessions that

began with an initial fifteen periods of ordinary posted-offer trading, and with ten subsequent periods of posted-offer trading preceded by the nonbinding announcements. The general pattern without announcements was for prices to start high and decline gradually over the initial fifteen periods. The first several price announcements were at the joint-maximizing level, but the seller making the announcement would often price a little below the suggested price, and others sellers would tend to do the same. The incentive to reduce price slightly is large in these posted-offer markets with a homogeneous product. As a result, prices declined again, with a level and slope that almost matched the initial decline without announcements. The nonbinding announcements had a transitory effect in both designs used (with market power and without it). This episode illustrates the importance of letting a treatment condition run more than several periods.

Friedman's (1967) classic study of collusion also involved a message from one duopolist and a response by the other. These communications were written in prose on pieces of paper. The trading institution was a simultaneous-price-choice matrix game, with essentially complete information, which was repeated between five and twenty-five times. The payoff matrix incorporated a significant amount of product differentiation, which reduced the incentive to make small price reductions from a common, collusive price. In over three-fourths of the periods, the proposal transmitted was accepted in the response, and these agreements were honored in nine-tenths of the periods in which they were reached. In another paper with product differentiation (along a spatial dimension), Brown-Kruse, Cronshaw, and Schenk (1990) find that the introduction of nonbinding communication changes the predominant outcome from an inefficient Nash equilibrium for the stage game to an efficient, joint-maximizing pattern of locations. I would conjecture that the effectiveness of the communication activity in these differentiated-product environments is due to the reduced incentive to make small price cuts, as compared with the Holt and Davis (1990) markets with a homogeneous product.

Summary. The effectiveness of nonbinding communication in inducing cooperation seems to be sensitive to the trading institution and the incentives to defect at the margin; the effect is greatest with posted prices and differentiated products, and the effect is less in double auctions. Other factors, such as decreasing costs and the nature and timing of messages, are probably important. Therefore, future work on communication could be usefully focused on designs that parallel specific environments that may come up in antitrust cases, for example, the trade press announcements of price changes, posting of future prices in computerized listings, and sellers' ability to confirm buyer-specific price quotes with each other.

E. Contractual Provisions

Market institutions and contractual practices are like organisms that compete for survival in an environment in which efficiency is rewarded. In evaluating the effects of institutions and contractual practices, I generally take a position of "innocent until proven guilty," unless the practice is being imposed by government agencies or industry trade associations. Even in the latter case, it is essential to keep in mind what the alternative would be in the absence of the proposed practice. The focus in this subsection is on contractual provisions that may facilitate supra-competitive pricing; contracts that have other, efficiency-enhancing effects are discussed in section IX.

An important type of contractual restriction is one in which sellers are forced to post prices and to sell at the posted price, as opposed to a situation in which negotiations are decentralized and bilateral. Recall that Chamberlin (1948) observed a tendency for the transactions quantity to be inefficiently high under decentralized trading. In contrast, Joyce (1983) did not observe much difference between symmetric double auction markets of the type that Smith (1962) had used and markets with decentralized trading among subjects walking around a room ("Chamberlin markets").[121] But a closer examination of the Joyce structure suggests to me that, if anything, his experiment provides *support* for the excess-quantity hypothesis described above. This is because the supply and demand functions used are such that there is only one extra-marginal unit that could have traded; that is, the competitive equilibrium quantity is just one unit less than the total number of units that sellers have to sell and buyers have to buy. The Joyce design would be quite similar to the design in Figure 5.2 if one were to truncate the supply and demand curves to the right of a vertical line at a quantity of 8 (by removing the second, high-cost units for sellers S3–S6 and the second, low-value units for buyers B3–B6). Then, at most, the excess quantity could be one unit, and the resulting efficiency loss would be small if the difference between cost and value of the extra-marginal units were small, as was the case in his design.

Hong and Plott (1982) also consider the effects of decentralized trading. This paper represents an innovative laboratory study of a proposal to require shippers on U.S. inland water routes to file rates with the ICC, with changes to be filed in advance (a fifteen-day period was discussed). This proposal really involves at least two aspects: centralized price posting ("announcements") and advance notice of price increases. Hong and Plott consider the announcement aspect by comparing two telephone negotiation sessions with two parallel posted-offer sessions. The decentralized nature of telephone trading corresponded to the status quo in which contracts were negotiated bilaterally, with the terms only being known to the participants. The posted offer was implemented in a parallel manner by letting buyers call sellers in any order (no restrictions other than those resulting from busy phone lines) to make purchases at the posted prices; discounts were not permitted. To prevent collusion, sellers were not given the phone numbers of other sellers.

All four sessions involved the same group of thirty-three subjects, which makes the notion of independent observations a little fuzzy; therefore, I will only discuss the first sessions under each treatment. The demand and supply configurations, shown on the left side of Figure 5.12, were carefully motivated by a study of the structure of the U.S. barge industry, and demand shifted to the right in period 5. As can be seen from the diamond symbols that mark the mean prices in the PO markets, prices are a little above the competitive equilibrium in the first four periods, as would be expected from previous PO results. The mean negotiated prices, represented by asterisks, are approximately competitive. Recall that

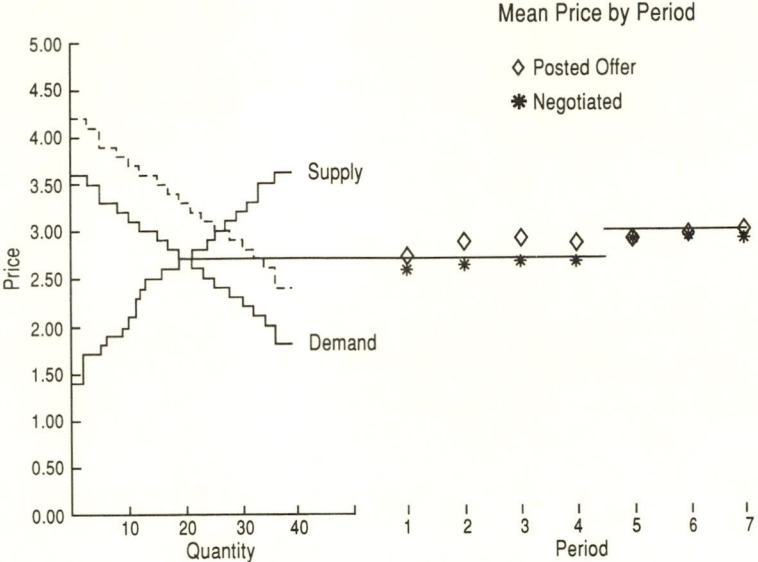

Figure 5.12. A comparison of mean negotiated prices and posted prices. *Source:* Constructed with data from Hong and Plott (1982, sessions 1 and 2).

posted prices do not respond quickly to demand shifts (Davis, Harrison, and Williams 1989). In Figure 5.12, the posted prices that are above the competitive level before the demand shift are approximately competitive after the shift. Negotiated prices respond immediately to the shift.

The supply and demand functions have been redrawn in Figure 5.13 with quantity on the vertical axis, and here we see the Chamberlinian tendency for trading volume to be a little too high under decentralized trading, as the asterisks are above the dashed lines that track the competitive quantity predictions. Interestingly, the PO volume, which is "too low" before the demand shift is approximately competitive after the posted prices are slow to adjust to the shift. In sessions 3 and 4, not shown, demand shifts back to its original position in period 8, and negotiated prices adjust downward more quickly. Over all four sessions, the efficiency is 92 percent under negotiations and 87 percent under posted pricing (see Table 5.2 for comparisons with other studies). The reduced trading volume in the PO treatment falls most heavily on small sellers. Projecting the results back to the structure of the U.S. barge industry, Hong and Plott conclude that the rate-filing proposals would reduce efficiency and force many small operators out of business.

Although the excess-quantity results in Hong and Plott (1982) are consistent with earlier experiments and with Chamberlin's simulations, I am a little uneasy about classifying the excess-quantity outcome with negotiated prices as a confirmed empirical pattern. Chamberlin's subjects had no financial motivation, and Hong and Plott (1982) only report two sessions, done in the same week with the same group of subjects. In addition, Grether and Plott (1984), to be discussed next, also contains results for markets with decentralized telephone communica-

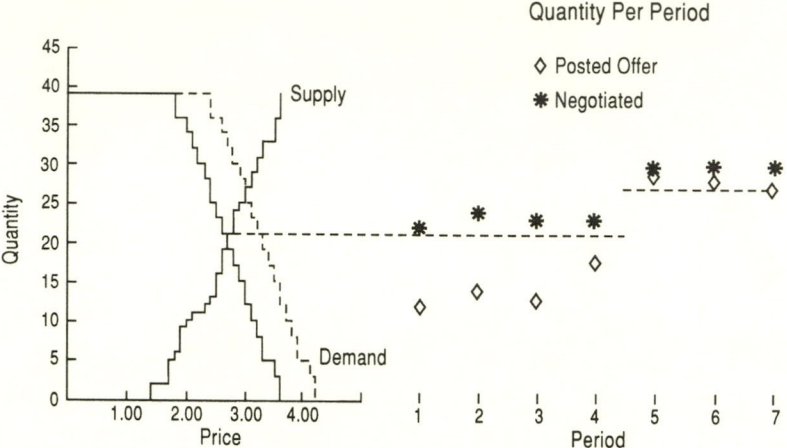

Figure 5.13. Transactions quantities for negotiated-price and posted-price sessions. *Source:* Constructed with data from Hong and Plott (1982, sessions 1 and 2).

tions (their N–NN treatment). They report that prices are somewhat above the competitive level, and that efficiencies are near 100 percent, which leads me to doubt that trading volume exceeded competitive levels.

A second innovative analysis of facilitating practices is the Grether and Plott (1984) paper, which was motivated by the Federal Trade Commission litigation of the *Ethyl* case. The practices involved (1) uniform delivered pricing, (2) advance notice of price increases, and (3) "most-favored-customer" contracts, which specify that the buyer is entitled to a discount if the seller offers a discount to another buyer. Advance notice lets sellers post price increases on a trial basis and rescind them if others do not follow; this ability to communicate may facilitate coordinated price increases. But high posted prices may have little meaning if sellers engage in aggressive discounting, and the theory of the FTC case was that the most-favored-customer contracts deter discounting. To understand how the contract may affect discount decisions, imagine a seller saying to a buyer: "If I give you this discount, I'm required by contract to give a matching discount to all other buyers with whom I have sales contracts, and I cannot afford to do this."[122]

Grether and Plott implement treatments that correspond to a number of variations of these practices, and two to three treatments were used in each of the eleven sessions. The treatments usually ran for three to fifteen periods before being changed. Figure 5.14 shows the supply and demand structure, which was selected on the basis of industry-specific information that came out in the FTC investigation. In particular, there were nine buyers and four sellers, two of which were dominant and had most of the marginal units on the flat part of the supply curve as it crossed demand at a price of 54¢. These sellers would have market power in a quantity-choice setting, and the price that would result from a Cournot equilibrium (in quantities) would be $1.05, as shown by the upper horizontal dotted line in the figure. The noncooperative equilibrium (in the actual price/

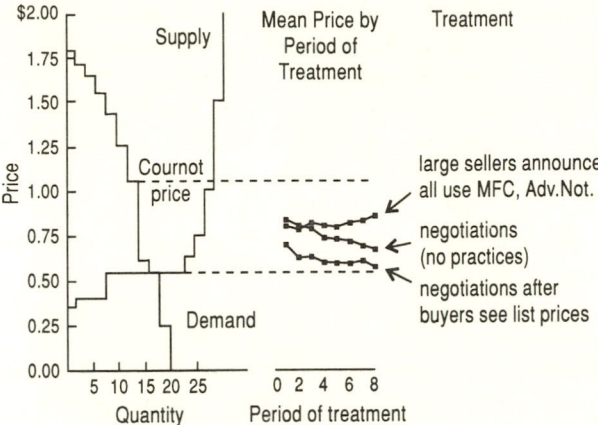

Figure 5.14. The effects of facilitating practices litigated in *Ethyl*. *Source:* Calculated with data from Grether and Plott (1984).

discount decisions) was not provided; this equilibrium could, of course, be affected by the practices.

The connected dots on the right show the mean prices by period number after the start of a treatment condition. With telephone negotiations (with no restrictive practices), prices start midway between competitive and Cournot levels and fall toward the competitive level. The failure of mean prices to reach competitive levels quickly may be due to the concentration of units in the hands of the two dominant sellers, which contrasts with the less concentrated structure used by Hong and Plott.

One other treatment seemed to be even more competitive than decentralized negotiations, this involved only large sellers making price announcements to buyers, with no restrictions on subsequent telephone negotiations, that is, no MFC or advanced notice. In this treatment (ABNN), the prices fall to competitive levels, as shown by the line labeled "negotiations after buyers see list prices" in Figure 5.14. The essential difference between this treatment and the posted-price treatment used by Hong and Plott is that discounts from list were not permitted in the latter case.

The least competitive treatment involved all practices, with large sellers announcing their prices to all buyers and sellers, with advance notice and MFC restrictions imposed. Under this treatment (LAYY), prices are about midway between Cournot and competitive levels. Grether and Plott consider other combinations of practices, but none of the other treatments was implemented enough times to isolate the effects of specific practices with precision. Nevertheless, the overall pattern is that the practices raise prices. This latter finding is consistent with the subsequent analysis of facilitating practices in Holt and Scheffman (1987), a theoretical paper that was largely stimulated by the earlier experimental results.

One methodological issue raised by the Grether and Plott study is the extent to which the laboratory market structure should mimic the structure of markets that motivated the study. It is impractical to incorporate the complexity of naturally occurring markets into a design that subjects will comprehend in a two-hour session. Moreover, it is usually preferable to use very simple designs so that equilibria for competing theories can be explicitly calculated. The key is to simplify in a way that allows one to focus on the issue at hand. In this case, the defense in the *Ethyl* case conceded that prices were probably above competitive levels in the market for lead-based additives, but they argued that this was a result of the concentrated structure, not of the contractual practices being litigated. Consequently, Grether and Plott used a design that incorporated structural factors thought to facilitate supra-competitive prices: inelastic demand, two dominant sellers, and no entry.

There are many other ways in which contracts, regulations, and industry practices can alter firms' incentive structures. If the number of possible decisions that can be made is institutionally restricted, the effect may be to facilitate cooperation. For example, Dolbear et al. (1969) used a two-person price-choice matrix game that was repeated for thirty-two periods with the same pairings. One treatment involved a large 35×35 matrix, and the other involved a 2×2 prisoner's dilemma payoff matrix that results from extracting the noncooperative and joint-maximizing points embedded in the larger matrix. Cooperation was more difficult to coordinate and maintain with the larger matrix, and payoffs were lower. Brown-Kruse (1991) observes some cases of reasonably effective tacit cooperation in PO markets in which price is restricted to be in multiples of $0.25. Overall, the average price was not significantly different from the average price for markets with no such restriction. Since restrictions of this type are unlikely to arise in naturally occurring markets, these results are perhaps of most interest to experimentalists who must decide how many gradations to introduce in a laboratory setup. Finally, note that contractual practices in unregulated markets are endogenous, so the effects of exogenously imposed laboratory rules should be interpreted with care.[123]

Summary. Contractual provisions can have a price-increasing effect that cannot be attributed to concentration or other factors. As compared with unrestricted and decentralized telephone negotiations, prices are higher with publicly posted list prices, provided that either (1) discounts are not permitted or (2) discounts trigger MFC clauses that reduce the price for other buyers, and increases in list prices are restricted by an advance notice requirement. This is a useful area for experimentation, despite the fact that few innovative facilitating-practice cases are being pursued at present.

IX. Product Differentiation and Multiple Markets

A common reaction that nonexperimentalists have to many of the results reviewed here is that the theories work remarkably well, but that this may not be the case in complex, multimarket situations. One case in which multiple markets may matter is the Harrison (1988) study in which predatory pricing, which had been the object of a search, appeared when sellers could choose between a number of markets in which to sell.[124] This section reviews some other applications involving related markets that are distinguished spatially, vertically, or in terms of product quality.

A. Product Quality, Asymmetric Information, and Market Failures

Lynch, Miller, Plott, and Porter (1986) conducted sessions in which sellers would first choose one of two quality levels. Quality could not be directly observed by buyers. Both sellers' costs and buyers' values depended on quality, and the high-quality "supers" yielded a greater surplus of value over cost than the lower-quality "regulars." The product was sold in a variation of a oral double auction, where each bid or offer had to specify the quality to which it allegedly pertained. When sellers were forced to advertise the true quality of the product, the result was an efficient provision of the high-quality product, the quality that provided the most surplus. Removing the identities of sellers and providing only post-purchase quality information led to inefficient "lemons" outcomes in which low-quality products were produced and sold at correspondingly low prices (96 percent of the units sold in sessions with unknown seller identities were of low quality). The overall proportion of efficient, high-quality units sold increased if sellers' identities were observed, thereby permitting some development of reputations. But lemons outcomes were frequently observed in sessions with known seller identities. Efficiency was increased dramatically by giving sellers the opportunity of offering a warranty that would force the seller to compensate a buyer if the advertised quality did not match the delivered quality.[125] Holt and Sherman (1990) also observed lemons outcomes in posted-offer auctions with a large number of quality "grades."

DeJong, Forsythe, and Lundholm (1985) investigate a similar multigrade structure, with the clever twist that higher quality means a lower probability that the buyer will suffer a fixed monetary loss. But there is some chance that a loss will occur even with the higher grades; therefore, the buyer is unable to distinguish a "rip off" from bad luck, ex post. Sellers propose a price and a quality level independently, and these decisions are posted as in a posted-offer auction. Then buyers select sellers. Finally, sellers decide on the actual quality level to deliver, which determines their costs. A lemons outcome (low quality, low price) is only observed in about half of the cases. Sellers' ID codes are observed by buyers, and there is some evidence of reputation building; sellers who deliver high quality are, on average, able to obtain higher prices. But it was common for sellers to "rip off" buyers who had trustingly paid a high price in anticipation of high quality.[126]

The importance of repeated interaction in establishing efficient outcomes is indicated by the results of three-person games reported in Davis and Holt (1994c). These games were presented in matrix form, where one person, who can be thought of as a buyer, decides which of the other two to "do business with." The person selected, who can be thought of as a seller, would then choose between two quality levels. The seller not selected would earn nothing, and the seller selected would earn more with the decision that can be interpreted as low quality. The decision to provide high quality maximizes joint payoffs. Sellers tended to provide low quality in single-stage games. Low quality was also prevalent in two-period matchings, despite the tendency for buyers to punish a low-quality decision by switching sellers after the first period. This switching by buyers in the final stage is not irrational, non-Nash behavior, since all sellers have the incentive to provide low quality in the final stage, whether or not the buyer switches. Therefore, the threat to switch (if low quality is delivered in the first stage) is credible, and this possibility can (at least in theory) support a subgame-perfect equilibrium in which the seller selected in the first stage provides high quality, the buyer does not switch, and the same seller provides low quality in the second and final stage.[127] Similarly, the buyer strategy of rewarding high quality by not switching and punishing low quality by switching can support cooperative, high-quality outcomes in non-terminal periods of longer games. When the same buyer and sellers were matched for ten periods, such cooperative outcomes were much more common than was the case in the two-period matchings. Even though quality was not observed prior to purchase, the ability to switch provided a strong incentive to develop reputations in the ten-period treatment.

One way around problems of "moral hazard" that arise with asymmetric information is to allow sellers to invest in costly, observable signals. If the cost of signaling is lower for a high-quality product, then it is often the case that there is a separating equilibrium in which the buyers can infer the unobserved quality from equilibrium signals. Miller and Plott (1985) designed and conducted an experiment with these features. Sellers were endowed with units that were exogenously designated as having high or low quality (regulars or supers). The value of a unit for the buyer consisted of two parts; one part that depended on intrinsic quality and another that depended on the seller's signal, which added value in the same way that a warranty can both serve as a signal and make a product more valuable to buyers. Buyers could not observe the product's intrinsic quality prior to purchase, but they could observe the signal. Trades were made via oral double auctions, with simultaneous markets going for different signal levels. For example, a buyer could announce a bid price for a product with a signal of 30, and a seller could announce an asking price for a product with a signal of 20, etc. Although there was considerable variation across sessions, about half of the sessions were best characterized by significant signaling behavior. A typical pattern of adjustment was for signaling to occur in excessive amounts, that is, in greater amounts than was needed for separation, and then for the amount of signaling with supers to be reduced downward toward the efficient level that just deters the sale of regulars with positive signals. Efficient signaling outcomes were more likely to occur when the difference in signaling costs for supers and regulars was large.[128]

One case of a reasonably efficient outcome, despite informational asymmetries, is provided by Plott and Wilde (1982) in a study of the operation of markets for expert advice. In these markets, buyers could either buy product X or product Y, and the product with the highest value was determined by the unobserved value of a random variable. In one state, the buyer was better off with product X, and in the other state, the buyer was better off with product Y. Each buyer was given a card with probabilistic information about the buyer's own state. Under the diagnosis treatment, only the sellers could observe this information and recommend a product. Sellers had an incentive to recommend product Y to all buyers, as it was more profitable at the near-competitive prices determined by double auction trading. Buyers could consult with different sellers, and the competition among sellers resulted in a common diagnosis pattern that did depend on the information on the buyer's card. The temptation to deviate and recommend the most profitable product in all cases was restrained by the apparent reluctance of buyers to purchase from sellers who offered a diagnosis that differed from the norm. Pitchik and Schotter (1984) also report relatively high levels of honest diagnoses in an experiment in which consumers could search sequentially for expert advice, at a cost.

Another way in which sellers can differentiate their products is in the terms of the contracts that they offer. Wiggans, Hackett, and Battalio (1990) set up a variation of one-sided offer markets in which sellers compete in the dimension of the fixed payment components of contracts. One market involves fixed-price contracts, where the fixed payment is the only payment. The other market involves cost-plus contracts, where the cost "report" made by the seller is added to the fixed payment. For the structure used, the cost-plus contract provides the seller with the incentive to make an optimal "effort" decision, but it also provides the seller with an incentive to overstate cost, ex post. This paper is innovative in that simultaneous, one-sided offer markets endogenize the choice of contract. When buyers have enough ex post information to detect and switch from sellers who overstate costs, the (subgame perfect) equilibrium involves the use of efficient cost-plus contracts, which is what is uniformly observed in the high-information sessions after an initial adjustment phase. With less information, there is more overreporting of cost, and consequently, a higher proportion of inefficient fixed-price contracts.

B. Spatial Competition

The most interesting implication of Hotelling's theory of spatial competition is that there will be too little product differentiation in terms of firms' locations. For example, suppose that consumers are located uniformly along a line of unit length, and that each consumer's demand is a decreasing function of the full price, that is, monetary (F.O.B.) price plus the product of travel cost and distance traveled. If all firms have constant costs and are forced to charge a common price that exceeds this cost, then a consumer who makes a purchase will choose the closest seller. In this context, the efficient outcome is the one that minimizes the sum of consumer's travel costs, by having firms be equally spaced. But if two sellers are equally spaced at locations of .25 and .75 on the line, both have a unilateral incentive to increase sales by moving toward the center. The Nash equilibrium for the single-period game is for them to locate in the center, and in this sense there is too little differentiation.

Brown-Kruse, Cronshaw, and Schenk (1993) conducted a duopoly experiment with this structure. The random stopping rule was to terminate the market if a red ball was drawn (with replacement) from an urn for which ⅛ of the balls are red. The resulting probability of continuation (⅞) is high enough to support the efficient outcome (locations at .25 and .75) as a Nash equilibrium, with trigger strategies that specify a punishment location of .5 following any deviation. The overwhelming tendency was for subjects to locate at the center (.5), which is another example of the noncooperative stage-game equilibrium outperforming a trigger-strategy equilibrium. But there was a second series of sessions with nonbinding communication via message boxes on the subjects' terminal displays, and in this case the predominant locations are at .25 and .75, which corresponds to the efficient outcome supported by trigger strategies.[129]

Besides generating a type of product differentiation, geographic distance can result in separate markets. One plus factor that is sometimes mentioned in antitrust cases is a situation in which two competitors face each other in a number of geographic or product markets. The argument is that this multimarket exposure gives each seller an incentive to exercise restraint or "mutual forbearance," since opportunistic behavior in one market may invoke a price war in other markets. It is also possible to tailor market-specific punishments for a rival's competitive behavior in that market. Feinberg and Sherman (1985, 1988) evaluate this conjecture in both quantity-choice and price-choice matrix game experiments. Under one condition, subjects are paired with a different person in each of two or three duopoly markets for a sequence of periods with no announced endpoint. The other condition is identical except that each subject meets the same rival in all markets. More cooperation was observed under the multimarket condition in both studies, but the test statistics indicate that the effect is marginal and, in my opinion, too small to have antitrust implications. Phillips and Mason (1992) also find somewhat mixed results; when Cournot duopolists compete simultaneously in two markets with different payoff matrixes, cooperation is higher in one market and lower in the other, as compared with control treatments in which subjects compete in a single market.

C. Vertically Related Markets

Another category of experiments with multiple markets involves vertical relationships. If a product can be purchased in one market and sold in a second that is separated in space or time, then the product can be thought of as an input that is transformed into output in the second market on a one-to-one basis. Experiments with this general setup have been reported by Miller, Plott, and Smith (1977), Williams (1979), Plott and Uhl (1981), Hoffman and Plott (1981), and Williams and Smith (1984). With double auction trading, speculators generally increase efficiency and reduce intermarket or intertemporal price fluctuations due to demand shifts. More recently, Goodfellow and Plott (1990) report the results of simultaneous double auction trading in a setup in which the production function for the output is nonlinear. There were six suppliers of the input who traded only in the input market, and six consumers who traded only in the output market. In addition, there were four producers who could buy input and transform it, at a cost, into output to be sold in the output market. The parametric structure is simple, but the simultaneous determination of two market prices and quantities would probably require a lot more calculation time for most of us than the fifteen to twenty minutes that it took most of the laboratory markets to adjust to the competitive equilibrium.

There is a series of experimental papers on vertical issues that arise in the transportation of natural gas through pipeline networks. In these applications, there are two levels of input markets, the wellhead markets for gas and the space on interconnected pipelines. Markups over cost at each level ("double marginalization") can compound monopoly problems unless the system is vertically integrated. Each link in the pipeline network can be priced separately, and therefore, coordination problems are severe. Pipelines have traditionally been viewed as natural monopolies to be regulated, but there is recent interest in whether competition can improve performance. Plott (1988) shows that the network coordination problem cannot be solved with a multimarket version of a Walrasian tatonnement mechanism. McCabe, Rassenti, and Smith (1989) discuss an experiment in which a multimarket variation of a uniform-price clearinghouse auction was used to determine prices, and the resulting outcomes were substantially competitive. Rassenti, Reynolds, and Smith (1988) show that, in this uniform-price auction framework, the replacement of monopolized pipeline links with joint ownership (cotenancy) increases efficiency.

Summary. When quality is not observed by buyers prior to purchase, the result is often a lemons outcome in which units of inefficiently low quality dominate the trading at low prices. Efficiency is improved by warranties, signals, and competition among sellers for the trust of buyers. When products differ in a linear, spatial dimension, differentiation can be excessive (locations at the center). Speculation tends to increase efficiency in double auction markets that are separated spatially or temporally. Competitive price theory has generally worked well in multimarket trading under double auction rules. I would like to see more work in vertical antitrust issues, for example, vertical foreclosure, using trading institutions that are appropriate for producer goods markets.

X. Conclusion

This section does not contain a summary for skimmers or bewildered readers; the summary paragraphs at the ends of subsections are written for this purpose. Instead, this conclusion consists of a number of comments and suggestions.

Beginning with Cournot's (1838) original theoretical analysis of structures ranging from monopoly to pure competition, there has been relatively little emphasis on the effects of market institutions and contractual practices. Perhaps the most interesting outcome of the experimental work on IO issues is the surprisingly large effect of institutional changes on trading outcomes. Indeed, a casual reader of the experimental economics literature may wonder what happened to all of those structural variables, (concentration, demand elasticity, etc.). But structural variables can have important effects. For example, potential competition can have a dramatic effect in contested markets, an effect that is mitigated by the introduction of sunk costs. Also, price levels can be sensitive to market power that is derived from monopoly, oligopoly with capacity constraints, and restrictions that contracts and trading institutions place on flexible price concessions. In particular, supra-competitive prices are regularly observed in laboratory institutions that approximate conditions found in many retail and producer goods markets. It would be seriously misleading to sweep the literature on market experiments under the rug of competitive Walrasian outcomes for double auctions and to ignore the prevalence of supra-competitive prices in many oligopoly experiments.

There is, however, a wide range of laboratory settings that seem to generate reasonably efficient, competitive outcomes. One of the ongoing embarrassments in this area is the lack of a convincing theory of why such competitive outcomes are observed in complex real-time markets such as double auctions. One research agenda would involve a series of interactive modifications of theory and experimental designs that span the gap between the rather rigid, no-discount structure of a posted-offer auction, the more interactive double auction, and the free-for-all nature of decentralized Chamberlinian bargaining markets.

One common pattern is for theorists and antitrust economists to begin an analysis by choosing an oligopoly model such as Cournot or Bertrand. It is natural, therefore, to encounter curiosity about whether one's favorite model outperforms others in the laboratory. Werden (1991, 18) recently concluded his review of the experimental evidence on structure and performance: "The experimental literature generally indicates that the competitive outcome does not occur with a small number of players. There is support for the Cournot model, but it is not overwhelming." Most experimentalists would probably disagree with this conclusion; competitive outcomes can occur with small numbers of sellers, even with monopolists, when they face human buyers in double auctions or decentralized negotiations. Werden (1991, 19) explicitly notes that double auctions do not match the trading institutions used in most industrial markets, a view that I share. But decentralized (e.g., telephone) negotiations are relevant to the study of producer goods markets and have been observed to generate reasonably competitive outcomes (Grether and Plott 1984; Hong and Plott 1982). In addition, the Cournot model doesn't even work particularly well when its controversial assumptions (quantity-choice and market-clearing-price) are imposed by the experimenter; quantities are too high with three or more sellers interacting in a series of market periods (Binger et al. 1990; Wellford 1990; Beil 1988). Moreover, at this time there is very little support for the Cournot model if sellers make quantity decisions before price negotiations with human buyers (see section V above).

To a theorist, a behavioral assumption such as subgame perfectness should apply in all noncooperative games if it applies in one such game. In contrast, Chamberlin's (1962) distinction between large groups and small groups is based on the view that the appropriate equilibrium concept for one situation may not be appropriate for another. The experimental economics literature indicates that one should be cautious about arguments that extend behavioral assumptions to new environments. It is apparent from the literature on experimental bargaining (see chapter 4) that perceptions and notions of fairness and focalness can be important, especially in contexts in which the nature of the equilibria depends on beliefs off of the equilibrium path. Moreover, some principles of rationality such as backward induction are difficult for subjects to discover in the absence of experience in the subgames, which is a tall order in complicated dynamic situations. Just because a behavioral assumption, such as subgame perfectness, yields good predictions in a particular game does not mean that we should accept the implications of a theoretical model that relies on this assumption in another context. This is also an argument in favor of designing experimental environments to more closely approximate markets of interest in the study of industrial organization.

Plott (1989, 1170) also discussed the issue of when a model applies:

> Three models do well in predicting market prices and quantity: the competitive equilibrium, the Cournot model, and the monopoly (joint maximization) model. Experiments help define the conditions under which each of these alternative models apply. Some tendency exists for the error of a model when applied to data to be sensitive to structural and institutional variables (e.g. posted prices tend to be higher than prices under oral double auctions) but, generally speaking, when a model applies, it does so with reasonable accuracy.

This point of view is disconcerting for theorists, who as Camerer has commented, search for the Holy Grail, a general principle that applies in all situations. The approach of experimentalists seems to be to try to find a theory that is good for a specific situation, or as John Ledyard remarked, "theory with a dummy variable," and only then look for unifying principles.[130]

My own opinion is that noncooperative game theory, which is the dominant paradigm in IO, should play a larger role as the unifying principle in the analysis of laboratory market data. Why was the competitive outcome observed in the no-power treatment and not in the power treatment variation of Figure 5.9? Because it is a noncooperative equilibrium for the market-period stage game in one case and not in the other. Why is a monopoly seller unable to establish monopoly prices in a double auction? Porter's (1991) answer is that the noncooperative equilibrium probably involves making price concessions late in the market period. There are many instances in which noncooperative equilibria in the market period stage games provide biased predictions, but I think that we should begin with these predictions and, as experimentalists, try to explain the direction of the bias. For example, if tacit collusion causes prices to be above noncooperative levels in price-choice environments, then why do quantities tend to be above noncooperative, Cournot levels; that is, why do we often see the reverse of tacit collusion in quantity-choice environments with more than two or three sellers? The answers to questions such as these may aid in the refinement of dynamic theories.

Several warnings are appropriate at this point:

1. *It is not true that a design is always better if it replicates more of the key assumptions of some theory, nor, conversely, is it always best to make experimental conditions as "realistic" as possible.*

Recall that experiments can serve a variety of purposes, such as testing the behavioral assumptions of a theory, testing the sensitivity of the accuracy of the theory to violations of "unrealistic" structural assumptions, and searching for stylized facts in complex market processes. It is not always the case that a theory has more predictive power in the laboratory if all of its assumptions are strictly implemented; there is some evidence that static, noncooperative equilibria for complete information games may have just as much predictive power under conditions of private incomplete information. The appropriate degree of conformity between the laboratory environment and related naturally occurring markets, or between the laboratory environment and relevant theoretical constructs, depends on the purpose of the experiment.

2. *Sometimes it is appropriate to design with theory in mind.*

It would be nice to know what are the stage-game noncooperative equilibria in market experiments, even if subjects are not given complete information. To do this may require using simpler market structures and running the risk that referees will criticize you, either for not fully implementing the conditions of the (in this case, noncooperative game) theory, or for not being able to find all of the dynamic equilibria that involve interperiod punishments and rewards. Noncooperative equilibrium predictions can be useful even under conditions of private incomplete information, just as competitive predictions can be useful with a finite number of sellers and as monopoly predictions can be useful when the seller initially has no demand information. For example, consider the observation that prices are lower and more variable in a contested PO market than in an uncontested monopoly PO market. Is the presence of contestability anything more than the game-theoretic addition of a second competitor? To answer this, we need to calculate the (possibly mixed) equilibrium for the contested market. And the monopoly outcome is a useful standard of comparison in such experiments, even under private incomplete information.

3. *Generalize with caution.*[131]

Researchers should be careful in comparing results with previous work when both experience conditions and market cost/demand conditions are different. The ground rule here is to replicate first and then compare. Trader experience with the same institution and market structure can reduce variability and increase the accuracy of theoretical predictions. Experience in a previous session with different subjects is especially important. Experiments with inexperienced subjects are often appropriate and interesting, but comparisons across experience levels can be risky, and more data may be needed to establish results with inexperienced subjects. The shapes of supply and demand curves can also matter. (The subjects in the Harrison, McKee, and Rutstrom [1989] sessions were better monopolists when costs were constant or decreasing than when costs were increasing.) It is especially risky to claim that a single experiment confirms a general theory or establishes a stylized fact, as the Walker and Williams (1988) reconsideration of the effects of one-sided bid or offer auctions indicates. A theory that is consistent with the data from a series of experiments can be used to project the results to other environments.

4. *Choose research topics with care.*

To focus on important IO issues requires keeping up with the theoretical and antitrust literatures and maintaining a curiosity for understanding the mechanics of how markets function. Comparisons of trading institutions should be well motivated by questions of theory or policy. We must continue to refine and develop laboratory trading institutions. New hardware and software technologies make it possible, when appropriate, to alter trading institutions (e.g., PO markets with discounting, PO flow markets).

Notes

*This work was supported in part by grants from the University of Virginia Bankard Fund and the National Science Foundation (SES 9012694). I wish to acknowledge the influence that coauthors and colleagues have had on the views expressed in this survey, in particular, Jordi Brandts, Doug Davis, John Kagel, Charles Plott, Stan Reynolds, Al Roth, Roger Sherman, Vernon Smith, Fernando Solis-Soberon, and Anne Villamil. Research assistance was provided by Lisa Anderson and Anne Gulati. I accept responsibility and offer apologies for any errors and misrepresentations that remain.

1. Chamberlin's (1948) paper is also discussed in Roth (chapter 1).
2. Chamberlin barely mentioned his own 1948 paper in a short footnote in the 8th edition of *The Theory of Monopolistic Competition.*
3. Smith is currently the director of the Economic Science Laboratory at the University of Arizona, where some of the most interesting experimental research in industrial organization is being done.
4. See chapter 1 of this volume for more details.
5. Friedman's (1969) somewhat critical review notes that Hoggatt (1959) is the first oligopoly experiment to be reported.
6. Incidentally, much of this early work was done in Pittsburgh, the site of the 1990 conference for authors of this handbook.
7. In the most recent edition, Scherer and Ross (1990), Smith is mentioned in a footnote, as is Charles Plott and several other experimentalists.
8. When I started thinking about experiments, one of my dissertation advisors (Ed Prescott) warned me that "it was a dead end in the 60s and it will be a dead end in the 80s."
9. In *Econometrica*, there were only two or three empirical papers on standard IO issues between 1980 and 1985, one of which was the Miller and Plott (1985) laboratory study of signaling.

10. The discussion of methodology that follows is strongly influenced by the work of others, as noted in the footnotes and references. Also see Davis and Holt (1993, chap. 9) for a consideration of the relationship between types of experiments, experimental designs, and nonparametric statistical tests.

11. See Schwartz and Reynolds (1983) and Gilbert (1989) for discussions of timing assumptions in the contestable markets literature.

12. Plott (1989) is an updated version of Plott (1982).

13. DeJong, Forsythe, and Uecker (1988), for example, report that average performance was the same for businessmen and students, but that the market with businessmen subjects showed greater variance. Dyer, Kagel, and Levin (1989) and Burns (1985) find that businessmen sometimes attempt to transfer experience from naturally occurring markets by the use of rule-of-thumb decision procedures in the laboratory. These rules, which may be well adapted for dealing with uncertainties or sales quotas in the field, were sometimes unprofitable in the laboratory environment. Ball and Cech (1991) survey the existing work on subject pool effects.

14. Coursey, Isaac, Luke, and Smith (1984) suggest that it is natural to test behavioral assumptions before exploring the sensitivity of the theory to violations of its structural assumptions.

15. See, for example, just about any issue of the *Rand Journal of Economics*.

16. This point of view is elaborated in Smith (1989, 161).

17. Roth (1986) presents a categorization of types of experiments that includes searching for stylized facts.

18. The nature and extent of pilot sessions should be reported. The use of pilot sessions to debug instructions and procedures is less controversial than the use of pilots to refine a treatment structure. It is quite possible that a treatment effect is more apparent in some designs than others, but if one fiddles around until the treatment effect shows up clearly several times in a row, then the interpretation of statistical tests is misleading.

19. Instructions for this program are reprinted in Davis and Holt (1993, appendix A4.2).

20. Such commissions, which were paid to induce the trade of marginal units, are no longer used (Plott 1989). Prohibitions against trading at a loss may help subjects avoid misunderstandings and keystroke errors, but warnings built into computerized market programs serve the same purpose, without a strict prohibition. Even warnings may be inappropriate in an experiment with the possibility of speculation or predatory pricing.

21. *Specific Instructions to Sellers:*

> During each market period you are free to sell to any buyer or buyers as many units as you might want. For the first unit that you sell *during a trading period* you will incur the cost listed in row (2) of your decision sheet, marked *cost of 1st unit*. If you sell a second unit, you will incur the cost listed in row (5) marked *cost of 2nd unit*, etc. (For illustrative purposes, we only consider the two-unit case.) The earnings on each sale, which are yours to keep, are computed by taking the difference between the selling price and the cost of the unit sold.
>
> Suppose, for example, that the cost of your 1st unit is $140, as shown in row (2) of the first column on the decision sheet, and suppose that the cost of your 2nd unit is $160, as shown in row (5). If you sell your first unit for $200, you would enter this amount in row (1), and your earnings would be $200 - 140 = 60$ on the 1st unit, as shown by the entry in row (3). Similarly, suppose that you sell a second unit at $190, which is recorded in row (4). Then your earnings for this unit would be $190 - 160 = 30$, as shown by the entry in row (6). Your total earnings for the period would be 60 (on the first unit) + 30 (on the second unit), which equals 90, to be entered in row (7).
>
> The blanks in the table will help you keep track of your earnings. Regardless of whether or not others have already sold units during the period, the selling price for the first unit that *you* sell *in a trading period* should be entered in row (1) at the time of sale. You should then record the earnings on this sale, as directed in row (3). The sale of your

2nd unit during the period would be recorded similarly in rows (4)–(6) of the column for the period. At the end of the period, record the total earnings on all units for the period in row (7). Subsequent periods will be recorded similarly, but at the beginning of each new period, you will start at the top of the column for that period and work downward. You cannot start selling units in the next column until that period begins. You may keep track of your cumulative earnings in the bottom row of the table.

22. To induce decreasing marginal costs, the opposite convention could be imposed.

23. In particular, complete information requires subjects to know the utility functions that others use to make choices between uncertain prospects.

24. The reader should be alerted to the fact that some of the Fouraker and Siegel incomplete information treatments had the property that a seller was unable to observe the exact value of the other(s) decision(s), ex post. I will only use incomplete information with reference to payoffs.

25. I was tempted to refer to the two cases more simply as "private information" and "incomplete information," but besides being inconsistent with Fouraker and Siegel, this would be inaccurate, since game theorists refer to *any* situation with less than complete information about the extensive form of the game as one of incomplete information.

26. Blocking is a term that was first used in agricultural experiments where there are many nuisance variables (moisture, exposure, soil) that differ from one plot of land to another. One solution is to divide each plot of land into two parts and apply one treatment (e.g., seed type) to each part, that is, to each combination of nuisance variables. Besides sequence order, common nuisance variables in economics experiments are subject experience levels and the university location from which subjects are drawn. A complete, balanced block in this context would be to run each experimental treatment the same number of times for each possible configuration of nuisance variables, for example, at each location, in each sequence order, and with each experience level. It is not feasible to block every possible nuisance variable. For example, it would be tedious to replicate sessions with every possible permutation of the relation between order of arrival to the experiment and role assignment (large buyer, monopolist, etc.) in a market. In such cases, the nuisance variable can be controlled with a randomized block, for example, assigning experiment roles randomly. Blocking and other design issues are discussed in more detail in Davis and Holt (1993, chap. 9).

27. The treatment of trading institutions in the first edition of Scherer's text, although limited, was more detailed than in most theoretical analysis that preceded. In the diagram of the Structure/Conduct/Performance paradigm, one of the "basic conditions" listed was institutional: "the methods employed by buyers in purchasing (e.g., acceptance of list prices as given vs. solicitation of sealed bids vs. haggling)" (Scherer 1970, 4).

28. This point is discussed in Smith (1982b), who provides relevant citations.

29. Eckel and Goldberg (1984) describe such a regulation in the Canadian brewing industry.

30. With simulated buyers, one way to present the payoffs for a duopoly price-choice experiment is to provide a payoff matrix, where the two sellers' prices determine a row and column, and the matrix entry consists of a payoff for each seller. One problem with matrix-payoff experiments is that the matrixes become large and cumbersome in markets with asymmetries and multiple agents or multidimensional decisions. As a consequence, most posted-offer experiments are implemented by explaining payoffs in terms of cost and revenue functions, not matrices.

31. The Plott and Smith (1978) instructions are for a posted-bid institution (described below), and the change to a posted-offer required the obvious changes. I also made some minor modifications, mostly to avoid the exclusive use of the male pronoun. This is a Plott and Smith product that has been tampered with; I am to blame for any errors.

32. A posted-offer with one seller and one buyer, each with a single unit, is an example of an "ultimatum bargaining game" in the sense that the seller's nonnegotiable price offer is essentially a proposed split of the surplus that equals the difference between the buyer's value and

the seller's cost. The buyer must either accept the proposed split or reject, in which case both earn nothing. A posted-bid auction with a single seller and buyer also implements an ultimatum game. This type of bilateral bargaining game is discussed in detail in chapter 4.

33. The calculation of this equilibrium is a little more complicated than the discussion here would indicate, since the arrival patterns of buyers must be considered.

34. The single seller in a discriminative auction has a passive role and is usually simulated in auction experiments, which are discussed in chapter 7.

35. In a competitive auction with a single prize, the winner pays the second-highest price, and this is called a "second-price auction," to distinguish it from a "first-price auction," that is, a discriminative auction with a single prize that is sold at the highest bid price.

36. One feature of the Grether, Isaac, and Plott proposal was for the primary uniform-price auction to be followed by a secondary aftermarket in which airlines could adjust their portfolios of slots, for example, to match takeoffs and landings, etc. Rassenti, Smith, and Bulfin (1982) developed and tested a "smart" computer-assisted auction program that was designed to optimize allocations without an aftermarket. Their program yielded higher efficiencies than a comparison set of sessions with the uniform price auction followed by a double auction aftermarket.

37. Friedman and Ostroy (1989) also report surprisingly competitive results for the clearinghouse auctions in environments in which agents have unilateral incentives to try to manipulate the price outcome.

38. See Davis and Holt (1993, chap. 5) for a discussion of recent experimental work on variations of call market procedures.

39. For example, Johnson and Plott (1989) use the terms "posted price" and "passive one price," which are not so bad, to describe markets in which sellers chose quantities simultaneously. I suppose the rationale is that sellers make simultaneous decisions in both quantity-choice and price-choice institutions and that the main difference is in the slopes of the reaction functions.

40. One difference, however, is that all traders in a laboratory offer auction observe each trade that is made.

41. Note that a one-sided bid auction with a single seller of a single unit is similar to an English auction, but it is the bidders, not the auctioneer, who raise the price until excess demand falls to zero. The same comparison can be made between a Dutch auction and an offer auction with a single seller of a single unit who lowers the offer sequentially until one of the buyers indicates an acceptance.

42. Hess (1972) uses a somewhat different procedure in an early experiment in which buyers were seated on one side of the room and sellers on the other. Negotiations were public because traders had to speak loudly enough to be heard on the other side of the room.

43. Subjects in a double auction typically make bids and offers for a single unit. Competitive outcomes have also been observed with multiple-unit trading, for example, Plott and Gray (1989). Friedman and Ostroy (1989) implement a double auction in which subjects make bids and offers for continuously divisible units.

44. I have changed the Plott and Smith oral bid institution to an oral double auction. I have also added some warnings that avoid common errors that subjects make in recording contracts. As before, I am to blame for any problems that are due to the modifications.

45. For more discussion of the competitive tendencies of the double auction, see Smith (1982a).

46. Williams (1980) and Smith and Williams (1981, 1983) describe the details of a popular mainframe implementation of the double auction on a PLATO (now "NovaNet") network. A double auction program for networked personal computers is documented in Johnson, Lee, and Plott (1988), and their program is available from the authors on request. The latter program permits subjects to trade in up to twenty double auction markets simultaneously. There are a number of other PC-based programs for double auctions; these differ in the amount of graphical feedback that traders receive during and between periods. This diversity is good since there is some benefit from being able to check results with different implementations.

47. Smith and Williams (1983) studied the effects of these institutional features. The simplest baseline is a temporal queue in which the last bid and offer submitted are displayed to the

market for a minimum period of time, and bids and offers that arrive are queued by time of arrival. The variability of prices is reduced and the speed of convergence is increased if this temporal queue is changed to a rank-order queue. Although only the best standing bid and offer are displayed under a rank-order queue, the ranking of nondisplayed bids and offers induces a type of competitive jockeying for position that seems to enhance the competitiveness of a double auction. The rank-ordered queue is an electronic version of a "specialist's book."

48. See Holt, Langan, and Villamil (1986) for a discussion of the slight procedural differences between their session and that of Smith and Williams.

49. Following Smith and Williams, a 5¢ "commission" was paid to each trader for each unit transacted. Since sellers (buyers) were prohibited from selling at a price below cost (buying at a price above value), the effect of the commissions was not precisely equivalent to raising buyers' values and reducing sellers' costs by five cents. Until recently, such commissions were commonly used in double auction experiments; the effect of small commissions is to induce the trading of marginal units. The incentive effect of the commission, together with the no-loss trading rule, is not exactly analogous to that of commissions paid in actual auction markets; therefore, the commissions are now used less frequently.

50. See chapter 7 for a discussion of auction experiments with zero intelligence traders.

51. The efficiencies for Davis and Williams (1986) and (1991) are as reported by the authors. In the other cases, the overall efficiencies in Table 5.2 had to be calculated from numbers given in the papers. For each session, I averaged the efficiencies for all periods, and for each treatment, I averaged the efficiencies for all sessions. Exceptions, noted in the footnotes in the table, were motivated by a desire to make a balanced comparison.

52. Mestelman and Welland (1988) compare the outcomes of double auctions and posted-offer auctions when production decisions are made in advance of the trading activity, with no inventory. For their design, the double auction is more efficient, but the prices in the posted-offer institution are not significantly higher than in the double auction (unlike the usual case). This is because prices in an oral double auction with advance production are no higher than with production to demand, but prices in the posted-offer institution are reduced by the requirement to produce in advance. See Mestelman and Welland (1987) for a description of the market structure for which these conclusions apply. The possibility of inventory carryover with advance production is introduced in Mestelman and Welland (1991). Subjects have trouble keeping inventory costs down, as was also the case in Friedman and Hoggatt (1980).

53. Chamberlin (1948) conjectured that asymmetries in the valuations and costs of infra-marginal units would have a stronger effect on price than asymmetries for extra-marginal units.

54. Davis and Williams (1986) use the Smith and Williams (1982) design in a series of posted-offer sessions, and report that the distribution of the surplus has no significant effect on the direction of convergence in these PO markets.

55. Note the difference between an experiment with human traders and a simulation with artificial agents that use exogenously specified trading rules.

56. *Ethyl Corporation, E.I. du Pont de Nemours and Company, PPG Corporation and Nalco Chemical Corporation*, Docket no. 9128. Federal Trade Commission. This case will be discussed in more detail in section VIII.

57. The computer program that controls the experiments was written by Doug Davis of Virginia Commonwealth University.

58. In some sense, it is surprising that nonbinding list prices would have any effect, since, for example, buyers seem to ignore nonbinding, false advertising in other contexts (Lynch et al. 1986, conclusion 14). One relevant difference may be that Davis and Holt use a restriction that buyers cannot visit a seller twice in the same period, which introduces a type of search cost.

59. See Davidson and Deneckere (1986).

60. This reversal may seem curious, since both Cournot and Bertrand games can be represented in matrix form as prisoner's dilemmas, with a Nash equilibrium that is Pareto dominated by a collusive outcome. The reversal of comparative statics effects is caused by the fact that the

reaction functions have positive slopes in price choice models (one should raise price if competitors do so) and negative slopes in quantity choice models (one should expand quantity if others restrict their quantities, and thereby shift your residual demand outward).

61. The first experimental and theoretical analysis of capacity choice decisions can be found in several papers, including Sherman (1969, 1971), which are collected in Sherman (1972, part II). The emphasis is on risk attitudes and psychological factors that affect the propensity to cooperate when capacity decisions precede price competition.

62. I assumed that price is determined by the midpoint of the vertical overlap of demand and supply functions.

63. These two aspects of the monopoly problem are related, but not perfectly. For example, monopoly pricing in the box design of Figure 5.5 yields high profits, but no welfare loss. Other aspects of monopoly performance, such as the possibility of a reduced incentive to innovate, are more controversial and have been generally ignored in the experimental economics literature, with the exception of Isaac and Reynolds (1988, 1992).

64. This observation does not affect the validity of the comparisons of the DA and PO trading institutions; it merely suggests that prices may be unusually high in all of the sessions with this design.

65. In addition, see Palfrey (1983, 1985) for an experimental analysis of pricing when a multi-product monopolist can sell products jointly in a "bundle."

66. Vernon Smith has told me that this conjecture has never been tested formally. The use of human buyers may make a difference even in a large-numbers situation, since buyers may withhold demand out of a dislike for monopolies. And the monopolist may fear that human buyers will resist a price increase after a decrease has occurred. Smith (1981b) speculates on the importance of using human buyers, as opposed to simulated buyers.

67. The observation that posted prices are higher with simulated buyers is consistent with the results of Brown-Kruse (1991) in nonmonopolized, contested markets; she reports that pricing is more competitive with human buyers.

68. The effect of demand characteristics on monopoly posted-offer pricing has not been explored systematically, with the exception of the Reynolds (1991) ongoing experimental study of the effects of durability. This experiment is designed to evaluate the "Coase conjecture" that the power of a monopoly producer will be diminished or eliminated if the good is durable and can be resold. Preliminary results provide some support for the Coase conjecture under private information conditions.

69. The negative Loeb-Magat M values are due to the fact that the marginal cost curve overlaps demand on a 25 cent vertical region for the designs being reported, and the highest competitive price was used to calculate the CE profit, so $M = 0$ at this highest competitive price. The M value becomes negative as the monopolist lowers price below the highest competitive price, but the reduced trading profit is exactly matched by increased subsidy payments.

70. Suppose that price is raised in period 1 and reduced again in period two, so that $p_2 = p_0$, and therefore $p_1 - p_0 = p_1 - p_2 > 0$. Then the usual formula for the subsidy in period two, $q_0(p_0 - p_1) + q_1(p_1 - p_2)$, will be negative since demand in period 0 is higher at the lower price: $q_0 > q_1$.

71. Brown-Kruse (1991) modified the Coursey, Isaac, and Smith (1984) design by introducing an "alternate market" that was selected by choosing a 0 quantity limit in the contested posted-offer market. The purpose was to find out whether previous competitive outcomes were the result of competition that was forced artificially by not providing an alternative activity. The price patterns for sessions with the alternate market were not noticeably different from price paths in control sessions without the safe haven. The sessions with human buyers yielded prices that appeared to be heading for a level that equates profits in the two markets, which is roughly consistent with the Coursey, Isaac, and Smith results for a case of a zero profit for a seller who makes no sales in the contested market.

72. As indicated above, under the Loeb-Magat mechanism, prices were driven below the highest competitive price, which generated negative M values.

73. I would guess that the equilibria involve randomization for the step-function environments used in the experiments discussed here, and such equilibria are difficult to calculate.

74. As is usually the case in reporting the results of a contestable market experiment with decreasing costs, the competitive equilibrium baseline used in efficiency calculations is the allocation that maximizes total surplus, *subject to the constraint that no firm earn a loss.* Therefore, the competitive equilibrium in this context involves a price-equals-average-cost condition for the incumbent.

75. In a very narrow and uninteresting sense, this unstable behavior is consistent with the formal "fundamental result" of contestability theory, that is, that any equilibrium must be sustainable, at least as long as the concept of equilibrium precludes unstable behavior.

76. This type of tight, almost disciplined price decline was also observed by Davis and Holt (1994b) in some of their relatively long (60 period) posted-offer sessions with five sellers.

77. Recall that each seller in a posted-offer market chooses a price and a quantity limit, which is the maximum number of units offered for sale at the posted price.

78. Although it is unusual to report only one session, the purpose of the paper was to demonstrate the possibility of predatory pricing. One other unusual aspect of this session is that all subjects had experience in three somewhat related PO experiments, and all subjects were also students in Harrison's class. It would be worthwhile to replicate these important results in a more standard environment.

79. Garvin and Kagel (1989) work with a design that has somewhat more of a market-like appearance. Here the monopolist is either a high-cost or low-cost type, determined randomly. The monopolist begins by choosing an integer, which can be interpreted as an output. This decision (but not the monopolist's type) is observed by the other player, who then chooses between two decisions that can be interpreted as entry or no entry. This is a matrix game, with post-entry profits that equal those in the theoretical Cournot duopoly equilibrium. For some parameter variations of this game, experienced subjects settle into a pooling equilibrium in which monopolists who draw a high cost expand output and deter entry. In this sense, there is limit pricing on the part of the high-cost monopolists.

80. Holt and Solis-Soberon (1990) analyze the theoretical effects of quantity and price-based antipredation policies in posted-offer environments. The antipredation policies alter the equilibrium mixed distribution of prices in a very simple, finite horizon model.

81. Of course, experimentalists are aware of the possible effects of market power, as is apparent from a comment made by Smith (1976, 44): "None of the experiments to be summarized in this report have systematically varied market structure except insofar as changes in the conditions of supply and demand have been affected by changes in the number of sellers and buyers. But in each case reported here numbers are large enough and economic power sufficiently dispersed to yield competitive price behavior."

82. The existing analyses of noncooperative equilibria in continuous-time double auctions are dependent on restrictive structural and/or behavioral assumptions. In a recent survey of auction theory, Wilson (1990, 36) notes the strong tendency of double auctions to converge to the perfectly competitive outcome, but he adds that this "striking finding is quite robust, but its conformity to the predictions of game theory is mute due to the dearth of theoretical results." See Gode and Sunder (1991) for a non-game-theoretic analysis of adjustment in double auctions. Easley and Ledyard (1988) and Friedman (1991) have also made progress in modeling behavior in double auctions. Cason and Friedman (1991) discuss the degree to which some of these models are able to explain observed patterns in bids, asks, and transactions in double auctions. This latter paper is reviewed in chapter 7.

83. Although easier to use in practice, the unilateral market power test is not as straightforward as it may seem. First it is necessary to specify a configuration of traders' strategies that generated a competitive outcome (and some ambiguity is present if there are many such configurations). The resulting strategy vector is typically not a noncooperative equilibrium, and it is only necessary to evaluate the profitability of unilateral deviations from this vector; it is not necessary to calculate such an equilibrium. Moreover, the deviation that turns out to

be profitable when unilateral market power exists does not have to be an element in a noncooperative equilibrium strategy vector. For example, consider a Bertrand price-choice duopoly game with common, constant average costs of zero. Capacity constraints may make it profitable for a seller to raise price above the competitive level of zero, yet this increase is typically not an element in an equilibrium price vector; and it may not even be in the range of prices selected in a mixed-strategy equilibrium.

84. In practice, Roth and Murnighan (1978) seem to have been the first economists to attempt to induce an infinite horizon by using a random mechanism to terminate the session. Murnighan and Roth (1983) observed that an increase in the probability of continued interaction resulted in greater cooperation in prisoner's dilemma games (in which subjects were, unknowingly, playing against simulated opponents).

85. A relatively minor variant of this box design (with five units of excess supply) was used by Kachelmeier and Shehata (1990) in a comparison of double auction trading in the United States, Canada, and the People's Republic of China. Subject-pool differences, if they exist, may be easier to spot in a design with more latitude for efforts to manipulate price.

86. Interestingly, some theoretical proofs of the convergence of DA prices to competitive levels involve assumptions that preclude the exercise of market power. For example, Friedman (1984) and Wilson (1987) assume that each trader has only one unit to buy or sell.

87. Recall that the deviation need not be an element of a noncooperative equilibrium. As noted by Porter (1991), noncooperative equilibrium behavior in the single market period could not involve quantity withholding, since it is always optimal to sell inframarginal units at the last instant if there is an outstanding offer that is no lower than the CE price.

88. The absence of quantity withholding is consistent with Porter's (1991) observation in the previous note.

89. Van Boening and Wilcox (1992) have shown that double auctions may not produce high efficiencies when sellers face fixed costs that preclude the existence of a competitive equilibrium.

90. Holt and Solis-Soberon (1992) discuss the various methods of calculating mixed-strategy equilibria in posted-offer markets with step-function structures that arise naturally in the laboratory from the provision of discrete units.

91. Buyers were not permitted to pay a price above L, and they were paid a 10¢ "commission" on each unit purchased in order to induce purchases at the price of L.

92. I suspect that, if efficiency is to be reduced in stationary double auction trading, one would need a large number of buyers, each with only one infra-marginal unit. This single infra-marginal unit would give the buyers a strong incentive to make purchases and no incentive to behave strategically (within a period). The number of sellers would have to be low enough so that sellers have numerous units that are inframarginal and marginally profitable at the competitive price. Excess capacity at supra-competitive prices would have to be small enough so that a small minority of sellers could not expand production and negate other sellers' efforts to restrain production and force prices up. The inefficiency might arise when some sellers give in to the temptation to sell high-cost extra-marginal units to the market as the price rises.

93. Scherer and Ross (1990) contains a broad discussion of factors that are thought to facilitate or to limit oligopolistic coordination. See Jacquemin and Slade (1989) for a more theoretical treatment of this topic.

94. The layout of the payoff table used in Holt (1985) has been altered so that the basic features will be more easily recognized by the reader who is familiar with the prisoner's dilemma game. The game in the table is not, strictly speaking, a prisoner's dilemma, since the decision to "cooperate" with an output of 6 is not a dominated strategy.

95. Because payoffs were rounded off to the nearest penny amount, there are asymmetric joint-profit-maximizing outcomes, but always with a market output of 12. There are also asymmetric Cournot/Nash equilibria, but the outputs sum to 16 in each case.

96. See the discussion in Holt (1985, section II).

97. The use of comment sheets is not common, and for good reason. First, the comments are generally worthless remarks, at least in terms of their economic content. Second, as econo-

mists, we mostly care about what people do, not what they say, although the rivalistic comments in the bimatrix experiment did help me understand how subjects could be moving in the "wrong" direction away from tacit collusion. Finally, there is some concern that behavior may be affected if subjects are put in a situation in which they may feel like they have to rationalize their actions. This potential bias can be avoided by asking for comments at the end of the session, and not using the same subjects in a later session.

98. Notice that each subject has been matched with each other subject by the final matching, so the six duopoly choices in the final period will not be independent observations if behavior is affected by outcomes of previous matchings. In other words, the behavior of a subset of participants in early matchings may affect the behavior of others in later matchings. Clearly, more independent observations with different cohorts are needed to make any statistical claims.

99. There are many related papers that report results of public goods experiments, which typically have a structure that is similar to a prisoner's dilemma; there is a joint-payoff-maximizing outcome that is not a noncooperative equilibrium. The rate of cooperative contributions to the public good is relatively high (50–60%) in a single-period public goods game, but cooperation declines with repetition, whether or not the repetition involves being re-matched with different groups of potential contributors. These results are discussed in chapter 2.

100. In one sense, there was never complete information, since subjects were not told the number of periods in advance.

101. For sixteen complete information duopoly markets, the industry outputs for period 21 were 25, 30, 30, 32, 33, 38, 39, *40, 40, 44*, 45, 49, 50, 55, 59, and 60, where outputs in the Cournot range are in italics.

102. The period 21 outputs for eleven complete-information triopoly markets were 40, 44, *46, 47*, 51, 58, 59, 59, 62, 63, and 70, where outputs in the Cournot triopoly range are in italics.

103. In two of the sessions, subjects were told that price is a decreasing function of the market quantity. But some demand information was provided by suggestive examples in the instructions. For example, subjects were all instructed to choose a common quantity in a no-pay practice period, which revealed a single point on the demand curve, but in a manner that was highly suggestive since the resulting market quantity was lower than the competitive quantity. Even worse, the suggested output decisions yielded different market prices for the two demand-slope treatments. In the other two sessions, subjects were told that the price in the previous period had been 0.12, which is also suggestive since this price is 0.05 below the competitive price.

104. Wellford (1989) and Johnson and Plott (1989) also report stable results for parameterizations that would be explosive in a cobweb model. A partial exception to this pattern is a four-seller session described in Holt and Villamil (1986) in which the market price and quantity followed a nearly square, counterclockwise cobweb path for about seven periods. Even here, the elicited pre-period price expectations indicate that only one seller was basing quantity choice on a static expectation that price would not change. Johnson and Plott (1989) observed several damped cobweb-like cycles in their Cournot, quantity-choice sessions.

105. The payoffs were presented as a column of earnings numbers that correspond to each possible of the lowest posted price.

106. The reader should be warned that the figure in Murphy's paper that summarizes his data is incorrectly labeled as Fouraker and Siegel data, and vice versa.

107. In this design, the quantity-choice behavior in these relatively long sessions did differ from behavior in shorter, twenty-period treatment sequences, but the small number of independent observations makes it difficult to infer much from this difference.

108. The die was not thrown in the presence of the subjects, which is unfortunate since the credibility of the stopping rule is enhanced if subjects can monitor procedure.

109. From Figure 5.10, we see that subjects earn 81 each in the cooperative (6,6) outcome and only 77 in the Cournot (8,8) outcome. Starting in a cooperative outcome, a subject can raise earnings from 81 to 85 by expanding output from six to eight, for a one-period gain of 4¢. But if the other seller expands output to the Cournot level of eight in subsequent periods, each

seller will earn 77. Thus the sure one-period gain of 4¢ from defection in the current period must be compared with the 5/6 probability of having earnings reduced by 4¢ in the next period, and in every subsequent period until the experiment is terminated. It is straightforward to show that the 4¢ gain from the initial defection is less than the expected value of the reduction in earnings that occurs in the punishment phase.

110. There is at least one well-documented case of the absence of a numbers effect in laboratory markets. In a constant cost, repeated Cournot game, Wellford (1990) found no statistically significant price effect of a merger that reduced the number of sellers from five to four or from eleven to ten. Recall from the earlier discussion that quantity-choice markets with more than two sellers tend to be more competitive than the Cournot prediction, and this fact would dilute the price effect of a merger in a constant-cost environment. Moreover, the data in these Cournot markets was quite variable from period to period, which may mask any treatment effect.

111. One simple way in which a punishment can be very direct is the ability of a buyer to switch to another seller. This type of punishment is implemented in Wiggins, Hackett, and Battalio (1990) and Davis and Holt (1994c), both of which will be discussed in section IX.

112. The use of words such as "competitors" is undesirable, since such words may induce rivalistic behavior. It is not clear from the description of the procedures whether the table used in the experiments was labeled in the same manner as the table that was published in the article.

113. This payoff structure was generated from a demand function that involved some product differentiation; that is, the seller with the highest price did not necessarily have zero sales. The underlying demand function was linearly increasing in the average of others' prices, and linearly decreasing in the seller's own price.

114. The authors state that the noncooperative equilibrium price is 18, which is true, but the restriction on the use of integer prices in the payoff table results in a second symmetric equilibrium at 17. My summary of their data reflects this fact.

115. In fact, average prices for each treatment were essentially the same (within two-tenths of a penny) in the two information conditions. This is interesting and perhaps surprising, since the good performance of the noncooperative equilibrium in the four seller case is not negated by incomplete information. Conversely, the average tendency to cooperate tacitly in duopoly markets is not facilitated by complete information.

116. See chapter 2 of this handbook for more discussion of the Isaac and Walker results.

117. Dawes et al. (1977) point out that communication is a complex variable, and they attempt to isolate the element of communication that increases cooperation in prisoner's dilemma situations. Discussion of an unrelated problem (humanization) does not increase cooperation, but discussion of the dilemma at hand (humanization plus relevant discussion) does raise cooperation rates from 1 percent to 72 percent. Allowing participants to make a nonbinding commitment after the discussion has no additional effect beyond discussion with no commitment.

118. Kirkwood (1981) suggested that the failure of explicit conspiracies in double auction markets may be either due to the lack of seller market power or to the tendency for buyer market power to neutralize any power that sellers possess. I would be curious to see what happens with a seller conspiracy in a double auction using the HLV seller market-power design that was discussed in the previous section.

119. The results reported in Clauser and Plott (1991) also highlight the importance of the temptation to offer sequential price reductions in a double auction that follows a conversation among sellers.

120. The effects of cheap talk in games is reviewed in chapter 3.

121. Unlike Chamberlin, Joyce allowed the same group of subjects to interact in a series of market periods.

122. Also present in many contracts, but not explicitly litigated, were "meet-or-release" provisions that release a buyer from a purchase contract if a seller does not meet a lower price offered by a competitor.

123. Laboratory studies with endogenously determined contractual practices are rare. One ex-

ception is Berg, Coursey, and Dickhaut (1988). These authors conducted sessions in which traders could choose between two trading institutions, a stylized, auctionlike mechanism and a bargaining mechanism. Efficiency was increased when a third-party "market provider," who earned a fixed percentage of the trading profits, was allowed to decide which institution(s) to offer.

124. Another recent study of entry is that of Meyer et al. (1992), which can be interpreted as a two-market Cournot competition in which each subject must choose only one of the markets in which to offer the subject's single unit of output.

125. DeJong, Forsythe, Lundholm, and Uecker (1985) also find that a liability rule, which forces compensation for the delivery of a low-quality item, will eliminate the effects of moral hazard in their laboratory environment. Palfrey and Romer (1986) report an experiment in which sellers can choose between different types of warranties.

126. DeJong, Forsythe, and Uecker (1988) report similar results when businessmen are used as subjects.

127. This equilibrium is a weak Nash equilibrium, since the buyer is indifferent between sellers in the second stage, as both will provide low quality.

128. Since nobody has been able to analyze the equilibrium of the double auction as a noncooperative game, the standard game-theoretic concepts cannot be applied to evaluate the Miller and Plott data. Other theories can be applied. For signalling experiments in simpler matrix game situations, see Garvin and Kagel (1989), Brandts and Holt (1992), and Banks, Camerer, and Porter (1994).

129. In a separate study with a qualitatively similar demand structure, Brown-Kruse (1989) fixed the locations of two sellers symmetrically around the midpoint of a line and let them choose prices simultaneously. Prices tended to be below the Nash equilibrium prices. In some location treatments, the price is close to the price that maximizes the minimum payoff.

130. Camerer's and Ledyard's comments were made in the 1990 conference for handbook authors in Pittsburgh.

131. Vernon Smith suggested "Summarize, Don't Generalize" as an alternative title for this section.

Bibliography

Alger, Dan. 1986. *Investigating oligopolies within the laboratory*. Washington D.C.: Bureau of Economics, Federal Trade Commission.

———. 1987. Laboratory tests of equilibrium predictions with disequilibrium data. *Review of Economic Studies* 54: 105–45.

Ashenfelter, Orley. 1989. How auctions work for wine and art. *Journal of Economic Perspectives* 3(3): 23–36.

Ball, Sheryl B., and Paula A. Cech. 1991. The what, when and why of picking a subject pool. Working paper. Indiana University.

Banks, Jeffrey S., Colin F. Camerer, and David Porter. 1994. An experimental analysis of Nash refinements in signaling games. *Games and Economic Behavior* 6:1–31.

Baumol, William J., John C. Panzar, and Robert D. Willig. 1982. *Contestable markets and the theory of industry structure*. New York: Harcourt Brace Jovanovich.

Beil, Richard O. 1988. Collusive behavior in experimental oligopoly markets. Working paper. Texas A&M.

Bellman, R., C. E. Clark, D. G. Malcom, C. J. Craft, and F. M. Riccardi. 1957. On the construction of a multistage multiperson business game. *Journal of Operations Research*. 5:469–503.

Benson, Bruce L., and M. D. Faminow. 1988. The impact of experience on prices and profits in experimental duopoly markets. *Journal of Economic Behavior and Organization*. 9:345–65.

Berg, Joyce E., Don L. Coursey, and John W. Dickhaut. 1988. Market mechanism as an object of choice: Experimental evidence. Draft. Olin School of Business, Washington University of St. Louis.

Binger, Brian R., Elizabeth Hoffman, and Gary D. Libecap. 1988. Experimental methods to advance historical investigation: An examination of cartel compliance by large and small firms. Forthcoming in *The Vital one: Essays in honor of Jonathan R. T. Hughes*. Joel Makyr, editor, Greenwich, Conn.: JAI Press.

Binger, Brian R., Elizabeth Hoffman, Gary D. Libecap, and Keith M. Shachat. 1990. An experimetric study of the Cournot theory of firm behavior. Working paper. University of Arizona.

Brandts, Jordi, and Charles A. Holt. 1992. An experimental test of equilibrium dominance in signaling games. *American Economic Review* 82:1350–65.

Bresnahan, Timothy F. 1981. Duopoly models with consistent conjectures. *American Economic Review* 71:934–45.

Brown-Kruse, Jamie L. 1989. Hotelling's model of spatial product differentiation and Nash equilibrium theory. Working paper. University of Colorado.

———. 1991. Contestability in the presence of an alternate market: An experimental examination. *Rand Journal of Economics* 22:136–47.

Brown-Kruse, Jamie L., Mark B. Cronshaw, and David J. Schenk. 1993. Theory and experiments on spatial competition. *Economic Inquiry* 31:139–65.

Burns, Penny. 1985. Experience and decision making: A comparison of students and businessmen in a simulated progressive auction. In *Research in experimental economics, vol. 3*, V. L. Smith, editor, Greenwich, Conn.: JAI Press. 139–57.

Carlson, John. 1967. The stability of an experimental market with a supply-response lag. *Southern Economic Journal*. 33:305–21.

Cason, Timothy N., and Daniel Friedman. 1991. An empirical analysis of price formation in double auction markets. Working paper. University of California at Santa Cruz.

Chamberlin, Edward H. 1948. An experimental imperfect market. *Journal of Political Economy* 56:95–108.

———. 1962. *The theory of monopolistic competition (A re-orientation of the theory of value)*, 8th edition, Cambridge, Mass.: Harvard University Press.

Clark, John Bates. 1887. The limits of competition. *Political Science Quarterly*. 2:45–61.

Clauser, Laura, and Charles R. Plott. 1991. On the anatomy of the 'nonfacilitating' features of the double auction institution in conspiratorial markets. Forthcoming in *Double Auction Market: Institutions, Theories, and Laboratory Evidence*, D. Friedman, S. Genakopolos, D. Lave, and J. Rust, editors. Reading, Mass.: Addison-Wesley.

Cooper, Russell, Douglas V. DeJong, Robert Forsythe, and Thomas W. Ross. 1991. Cooperation without reputation. Working paper. University of Iowa.

Cournot, Agustin A. 1929 (originally 1838). *Researches into the mathematical principles of the theory of wealth*. With essay and bibliography by Irving Fisher, New York: Macmillan.

Coursey, Don, R. Mark Isaac, and Vernon L. Smith. 1984. Natural monopoly and the contested markets: Some experimental results. *Journal of Law and Economics*. 27:91–113.

Coursey, Don, R. Mark Isaac, Margaret Luke, and Vernon L. Smith. 1984. Market contestability in the presence of sunk (entry) costs. *Rand Journal of Economics*. 15:69–84.

Cox, James C., and R. Mark Isaac. 1986. Incentive regulation: A case study in the use of laboratory experimental analysis in economics. In *Laboratory Market Research*, S. Moriarity, editor, Norman, Okla.: University of Oklahoma Center for Economic and Management Research. 121–45.

———. 1987. Mechanisms for incentive regulation: Theory and experiment. *Rand Journal of Economics* 18:348–59.

Cyert, Richard M., and Lester B. Lave. 1965. Collusion, conflit et science economique. *Economie Appliquee* 18:385–406.

Daughety, Andrew F., and Robert Forsythe. 1987a. Industrywide regulation and the formation of reputations: A laboratory analysis. In *Public regulation: New perspectives on institutions and policies*, E. Bailey, editor, Cambridge, Mass.: MIT Press 347–98.

―――. 1987b. Regulatory-induced industrial organization. *Journal of Law, Economics, and Industrial Organization* 3:397–434.

Davidson, Carl, and Raymond Deneckere. 1986. Long-run competition in capacity, short-run competition in price, and the Cournot model. *Rand Journal of Economics.* 17:404–15.

Davis, Douglas D., and Charles A. Holt. 1989. Equilibrium cooperation in two-stage games: Experimental evidence. Working paper. University of Virginia.

―――. 1993. *Experimental economics.* Princeton, N.J.: Princeton University Press.

―――. 1994a. The effects of discounts in laboratory posted-offer markets. *Economics Letters* 44:249–53.

―――. 1994b. Market power, and mergers in laboratory markets with posted prices. *RAND Journal of Economics20* 25:467–487.

―――. 1994c. Equilibrium cooperation in three-person, choice-of-partner games. *Games and Economic Behavior* 7:39–53.

Davis, Douglas D. and Arlington W. Williams. 1986. The effects of rent asymmetries in posted offer markets. *Journal of Economic Behavior and Organization.* 7:303–16.

―――. 1991. The Hayek hypothesis in experimental auctions: Institutional effects and market power. *Economic Inquiry* 29:261–74.

Davis, Douglas D., Glenn W. Harrison, and Arlington W. Williams. 1993. Convergence to nonstationary competitive equilibria: An experimental analysis. *Journal of Economic Behavior and Organization* 20:1–22.

Davis, Douglas D., Charles A. Holt, and Anne P. Villamil. 1990. Supracompetitive prices and market power in posted-offer experiments. University of Illinois BBER Faculty Working Paper No. 90–1648.

Dawes, Robyn M., J. MacTavish, and H. Shaklee. 1977. Behavior, communication and assumptions about other people's behavior in a commons dilemma situation. *Journal of Personality and Social Psychology* 35:1–11.

DeJong, Douglas V., Robert Forsythe, and Russell J. Lundholm. 1985. Ripoffs, lemons, and reputation formation in agency relationships: A laboratory market study. *Journal of Finance* 40:809–20.

DeJong, Douglas V., Robert Forsythe, and Wilfred C. Uecker. 1988. A note on the use of businessmen as subjects in sealed offer markets. *Journal of Economic Behavior and Organization* 9:87–100.

DeJong, Douglas V., Robert Forsythe, Russell J. Lundholm, and W. C. Uecker. 1985. A laboratory investigation of the moral hazard problem in an agency relationship. *Journal of Accounting Research* (23) (supp.): 81–120.

Dolbear, F. T., L. B. Lave, G. Bowman, A. Lieberman, E. Prescott, F. Rueter, and R. Sherman. 1968. Collusion in oligopoly: An experiment on the effect of numbers and information. *Quarterly Journal of Economics* 82:240–59.

―――. 1969. Collusion in the prisoner's dilemma: Number of strategies. *Journal of Conflict Resolution* 13:252–61.

Dyer, Douglas, John H. Kagel, and Dan Levin. 1989. A comparison of naive and experienced bidders in common value offer auctions: A laboratory analysis. *Economic Journal* 99:108–15.

Easley, David, and John O. Ledyard. 1988. Theories of price formation and exchange in double oral auctions. Social Science working paper 611. California Institute of Technology.

Eckel, Catherine C., and Michael A. Goldberg. 1984. Regulation and deregulation in the brewing industry: The British Columbia example. *Canadian Public Policy* 10:316–27.

Feinberg, Robert M., and Thomas A. Husted. 1993. An experimental test of discount-rate effects on collusive behavior in duopoly markets. *Journal of Industrial Economics* 41 (2):153–60.

Feinberg, Robert M., and Roger Sherman. 1985. An experimental investigation of mutual forbearance by conglomerate firms. In *Industry structure and performance*, J. Schwalbach, editor, Berlin: Sigma Rainer Bohn Verlag. 139–66.

―――. 1988. Mutual forbearance under experimental conditions. *Southern Economic Journal* 54:985–93.

Finsinger, J., and I. Vogelsang. 1981. Alternative institutional frameworks for price incentive mechanisms. *Kyklos* 34:388–404.

Fouraker, Lawrence E., and Sidney Siegel. 1963. *Bargaining behavior.* New York: McGraw-Hill.

Friedman, Daniel. 1984. On the efficiency of experimental double auction markets. *American Economic Review* 74:60–72.

———. 1991. A simple testable model of double auction markets. *Journal of Economic Behavior and Organization* 16:47–70.

Friedman, Daniel, and Joseph Ostroy. 1989. Competitivity in auction markets: An experimental and theoretical investigation. Working paper 202. University of California at Santa Cruz.

Friedman, James W. 1963. Individual behavior in oligopolistic markets: An experimental study. *Yale Economic Essays* 3:359–417.

———. 1967. An experimental study of cooperative duopoly. *Econometrica* 35:379–97.

———. 1969. On experimental research in oligopoly. *Review of Economic Studies* 36:399–415.

Friedman, James W., and A. C. Hoggatt. 1980. *An experiment in noncooperative oligopoly.* Supplement 1 to *Research in experimental economics*, V. L. Smith, editor, Greenwich, Conn.: JAI Press.

Garvin, Susan, and John Kagel. 1989. An experimental investigation of limit entry pricing. Working paper. University of Pittsburgh.

Gilbert, Richard J. 1989. The role of potential competition in industrial organization. *The Journal of Economic Perspectives.* 3(3): 107–27.

Gode, Dhananjay K., and Shyam Sunder. 1989. Human and artificially intelligent traders in computer double auctions. Working paper. Carnegie Mellon University.

———. 1991. Allocative efficiency of markets with zero intelligence (ZI) traders: Market as a partial substitute for individual rationality. Working paper. Carnegie Mellon University.

Goodfellow, Jessica, and Charles R. Plott. 1990. An experimental examination of the simultaneous determination of input prices and output prices. *Southern Economic Journal* 56:969–83.

Grether, David M., and Charles R. Plott. 1984. The effects of market practices in oligopolistic markets: An experimental examination of the *Ethyl* case. *Economic Inquiry* 24:479–507.

Giether, David M., R. Mark Isaac, and Charles R. Plott. 1981. The allocation of landing rights by unanimity among competitors. *American Economic Review* 71:166–71.

———. Forthcoming. *The allocation of scarce resources: Experimental economics and the problem of allocating airport slots, underground classics in economics.* Boulder, Colo.: Westview Press.

Grether, David M., Alan Schwartz, and Louis L. Wilde. 1988. Uncertainty and shopping behavior: An experimental study. *Review of Economic Studies* 55:323–42.

Harrison, Glenn W. 1986. Experimental evaluation of the contestable markets hypothesis. In *Public regulation*, E. Bailey, editor Cambridge, Mass.: MIT Press.

———. 1988. Predatory pricing in a multiple-market experiment: A note. *Journal of Economic Behavior and Organization* 9:405–17.

Harrison, Glenn W., and Michael McKee. 1985. Monopoly behavior, decentralized regulation, and contestable markets: An experimental evaluation. *Rand Journal of Economics* 16:51–69.

Harrison, Glenn W., Michael McKee, and E. E. Rutstrom. 1989. Experimental evaluation of institutions of monopoly restraint. Chapter 3 in *Advances in behavioral economics, vol. 2,* L. Green and J. Kagel, editors, Norwood, N.J.: Ablex Press, 54–94.

Hart, Oliver D. 1979. Monopolistic competition in a large economy with differentiated commodities. *Review of Economic Studies* 46:1–30.

Hess, Alan C. 1972. Experimental evidence on price formation in competitive markets. *Journal of Political Economy* 80:375–85.

Hoffman, Elizabeth, and Charles R. Plott. 1981. The effect of intertemporal speculation on the outcomes in seller posted offer auction markets. *Quarterly Journal of Economics* 96:223–41.

Hoggatt, Austin. 1959. An experimental business game. *Behavioral Science* 4:192–203.

Holt, Charles A. 1985. An experimental test of the consistent-conjectures hypothesis *American Economic Review* 75:314–25.

———. 1989. The exercise of market power in laboratory experiments. *Journal of Law and Economics* 32 (pt.2): S107–S131.

Holt, Charles A., and Douglas D. Davis. 1990. The effects of non-binding price announcements in posted-offer markets. *Economics Letters* 34:307–10.

Holt, Charles A., and David Scheffman. 1987. Facilitating practices: The effects of advance notice and best-price policies. *Rand Journal of Economics* 18:187–97.

Holt, Charles A., and Roger Sherman. 1990. Advertising and product quality in posted-offer experiments. *Economic Inquiry* 28:39–56.

Holt, Charles A., and Fernando Solis-Soberon. 1990. Antitrust restrictions on predatory pricing: Possible side effects. Working paper. University of Virginia.

———. 1992. The calculation of equilibrium mixed strategies in posted-offer auctions. In *Research in experimental economics, vol. 5*, M. Isaac, editor, Greenwich, Conn.: JAI Press. 189–229.

Holt, Charles A., and Anne Villamil. 1986. A laboratory experiment with a single-person cobweb. *Atlantic Economic Journal* 14:51–4.

———. 1990. The direction of price convergence in oral double auctions. Working paper. University of Illinois.

Holt, Charles A., Loren Langan, and Anne Villamil. 1986. Market power in oral double auctions. *Economic Inquiry* 24:107–23.

Hong, James T., and Charles R. Plott. 1982. Rate filing policies for inland water transportation: An experimental approach. *Bell Journal of Economics* 13:1–19.

Isaac, R. Mark, and Charles R. Plott. 1981. The opportunity for conspiracy in restraint of trade. *Journal of Economic Behavior and Organization* 2:1–30.

Isaac, R. Mark, and Stanley S. Reynolds. 1988. Appropriability and market structure in a stochastic invention model. *Quarterly Journal of Economics* 103:647–71.

———. 1989. Two or four firms: Does it matter? Draft. University of Arizona.

———. 1992. Schumpeterian competition in experimental markets. *Journal of Economic Behavior and Organization* 17:59–100.

Isaac, R. Mark, and Vernon L. Smith. 1985. In search of predatory pricing. *Journal of Political Economy* 93:320–45.

Isaac, R. Mark, and James Walker. 1985. Information and conspiracy in sealed bid auctions. *Journal of Economic Behavior and Organization* 6:139–59.

———. 1988. Group size hypotheses of public goods provision: An experimental examination. *Quarterly Journal of Economics* 103:179–200.

Isaac, R. Mark, Valerie Ramey, and Arlington W. Williams. 1984. The effects of market organization on conspiracies in restraint of trade. *Journal of Economic Behavior and Organization* 5:191–222.

Jacquemin, Alexis, and Margaret E. Slade. 1989. Cartels, collusion, and horizontal merger. In *Handbook of industrial organization, vol. I*, R. Schmalensee and R. D. Willig, editors, New York: Elsevier Science Publishers. 415–73.

Johnson, Michael, and Charles R. Plott. 1989. The effect of two trading institutions on price expectations and the stability of supply-response lag markets. *Journal of Economic Psychology* 10:189–216.

Johnson, Alonzo, Hsing Yang Lee, and Charles R. Plott. 1988. Multiple unit double auction user's manual. Social Science Working Paper 676. California Institute of Technology.

Joyce, Patrick. 1983. Information and behavior in experimental markets. *Journal of Economic Behavior and Organization* 4:411–24.

———. 1984. The Walrasian *Tatonnement* mechanism and information. *Rand Journal of Economics* 15:416–25.

Jung, Yun Joo, John H. Kagel, and Dan Levin. 1990. On the existence of predatory pricing: An experimental study of reputation and entry deterrence in the chain-store game. Working paper. University of Houston.

Kachelmeier, Steven J., and Mohamed Shehata. 1990. The cultural and informational boundaries of economic competition: Laboratory markets in the People's Republic of China, Canada, and the United States. Working paper presented at the ESA Meetings in Tucson, Arizona.

Ketcham, Jon, Vernon L. Smith, and Arlington W. Williams. 1984. A comparison of posted-offer and double-auction pricing institutions. *Review of Economic Studies* 51:595–614.

Kirkwood, John B. 1981. Antitrust implications of the recent experimental literature on collusion. In *Strategy, predation, and antitrust analysis*, S. Salop, editor, Washington, D.C.: Federal Trade Commission, Bureau of Economics. 605–21.

Kreps, David, and Jose Scheinkman. 1983. Quantity precommitment and Bertrand competition yield Cournot outcomes. *Bell Journal of Economics* 14:326–37.

Kruse, Jamie Brown, Steven Rassenti, Stanley S. Reynolds, and Vernon L. Smith. 1994. Bertrand-Edgeworth competition in experimental markets. *Econometrica* 62 (2): 343–71.

Lave, Lester B. 1962. An empirical approach to the prisoner's dilemma. *Quarterly Journal of Economics* 76:424–36.

———. 1965. Factors affecting cooperation in the prisoner's dilemma. *Behavioral Science* 10:26–38.

Loeb, M., and W. Magat. 1979. A decentralized method for utility regulation, *Journal of Law and Economics* 12:399–404.

Lynch, M., R. M. Miller, C. R. Plott, and R. Porter. 1986. Product quality, consumer information and 'lemons' in experimental markets. In *Empirical approaches to consumer protection economics*, P. M. Ippolito and D. T. Scheffman, editors, Washington D.C.: FTC Bureau of Economics. 251–306.

Mason, Charles F., and Owen R. Phillips. 1991. An experimental analysis of the effects of vertical integration. Working paper. University of Wyoming.

Mason, Charles F., Owen R. Phillips, and Clifford Nowell. 1991. Duopoly behavior in asymmetric markets: An experimental evaluation. Working paper. University of Wyoming.

Mason, Charles F., Owen R. Phillips, and Douglas B. Redington. 1991. The role of gender in a non-cooperative game. *Journal of Economic Behavior and Organization* 15:215–35.

McCabe, Kevin, Steven Rassenti, and Vernon L. Smith. 1989. Designing 'smart' computer assisted markets in an experimental auction for gas networks. *European Journal of Political Economy* 5:259–83.

Mestelman, Stuart, and Douglas Welland. 1987. Advance production in oral double auction markets. *Economics Letters* 23:43–48.

———. 1988. Advance production in experimental markets. *Review of Economic Studies* 55:641–54.

———. 1991. Inventory carryover and the performance of alternative market institutions. *Southern Economic Journal* 57:1024–42.

———. 1992. Inventory carryover, experience, and clearance sales: A comparison of posted offer and double auction trading institutions. Working paper. McMaster University.

Mestelman, Stuart, Deborah Welland, and Douglas Welland. 1987. Advance production in posted offer markets. *Journal of Economic Behavior and Organization* 8:249–64.

Meyer, Donald J., John B. Van Huyck, Raymond C. Battalio, and Thomas R. Saving. 1992. History's role in coordinating decentralized allocation decisions. *Journal of Political Economy* 100:292–316.

Miller, Ross M., and Charles R. Plott. 1985. Product quality signaling in experimental markets. *Econometrica* 53:837–72.

Miller, Ross M., Charles R. Plott, and Vernon L. Smith. 1977. Intertemporal competitive equilibrium: An empirical study of speculation. *Quarterly Journal of Economics* 91:599–624.

Millner, Edward L., Michael D. Pratt, and Robert J. Reilly. 1990a. Contestability in real-time experimental flow markets. *Rand Journal of Economics* 21:584–99.

———. 1990b. An experimental investigation of real-time posted-offer markets for flows. Working paper. Virginia Commonwealth University.

Murnighan, J. Keith, and Alvin E. Roth. 1983. Expecting continued play in prisoner's dilemma games. *Journal of Conflict Resolution* 27:279–300.

Murphy, James L. 1966. Effects of the threat of losses on duopoly bargaining. *Quarterly Journal of Economics*. 80:296–313.

Palfrey, Thomas R. 1983. Bundling decisions by a multiproduct monopolist with incomplete information. *Econometrica* 51:463–83.

———. 1985. Buyer behavior and welfare effects of bundling by a multiproduct monopolist: A laboratory investigation. In *Research in experimental economics, vol. 3*, V. L. Smith, editor, Greenwich, Conn.: JAI Press. 73–104.

Palfrey, Thomas R., and T. Romer. 1986. An experimental study of warranty coverage and dispute resolution in competitive markets. In *Empirical approaches to consumer protection economics* P. Ippolito and D. Scheffman, editors, Washington D.C.: Federal Trade Commission, 307–72.

Palfrey, Thomas R., and Howard Rosenthal. 1992. Repeated play, cooperation, and coordination: An experimental study. Working paper. California Institute of Technology.

Phillips, Owen R., and Charles F. Mason. 1991. Mutual forbearance in experimental conglomerate markets. *Rand Journal of Economics* 23:395–414.

Pitchik, Carolyn, and Andrew Schotter. 1984. Regulating markets with asymmetric information: An experimental study. R.R. #84–12. C.V. Starr Center for Applied Economics, New York University.

Plott, Charles R. 1982. Industrial organization theory and experimental economics. *Journal of Economic Literature* 20:1485–1587.

———. 1986. Laboratory experiments in economics: The implications of posted price institutions. *Science* 232:732–8.

———. 1988. Research on pricing in a gas transportation network. Technical report 88–2. Federal Energy Regulatory Commission.

———. 1989. An updated review of industrial organization: Applications of experimental methods. In *Handbook of industrial organization, vol. II*, R. Schmalensee and R. D. Willig, editors, Amsterdam: North Holland, 1109–76.

Plott, Charles R., and Peter Gray. 1990. The multiple unit double auction. *Journal of Economic Behavior and Organization* 13:245–58.

Plott, Charles R., and Vernon L. Smith. 1978. An experimental examination of two exchange institutions. *Review of Economic Studies* 45:133–53.

Plott, Charles R., and Jonathan T. Uhl. 1981. Competitive equilibrium with middlemen: An empirical study. *Southern Economic Journal* 47:1063–71.

Plott, Charles R., and Louis Wilde. 1982. Professional diagnosis vs. self-diagnosis: An experimental examination of some special features of markets with uncertainty. In *Research in experimental economics, vol. 2*, V. Smith, editor, Greenwich, Conn.: JAI Press. 63–112.

Porter, Robert H. 1991. A review essay on *Handbook of industrial organization, Journal of Economic Literature* 29:553–72.

Rapoport, Anatol, and Albert M. Chammah. 1965. *Prisoner's dilemma: A study in conflict and cooperation*. Ann Arbor: University of Michigan Press.

Rassenti, Stephen J., Stanley S. Reynolds, and Vernon L. Smith. 1988. Cotenancy and competition in an experimental double auction market for natural gas pipeline networks. Working paper. University of Arizona.

Rassenti, Stephen J., Vernon L. Smith, and R. Bulfin. 1982. A combinatorial auction for airport time slot allocation. *Bell Journal of Economics*. 13:402–17.

Reynolds, Stanley S. 1991. An experimental investigation of Coase's conjecture on durable-goods monopoly pricing. Working paper. University of Arizona.

Roth, Alvin E. 1986. Laboratory experimentation in economics. In *Advances in economic theory*, T. Bewley, editor, Fifth World Congress, Cambridge: Cambridge University Press. 269–99.

Roth, Alvin E., and J. Keith Murnighan. 1978. Equilibrium behavior and repeated play of the prisoner's dilemma. *Journal of Mathematical Psychology* 17:189–98.

Rutstrom, E. E. 1985. In search of a reconciliation of results in predatory pricing experiments. Working Paper. University of Western Ontario.

Sauermann, Heinz, and Reinhard Selten. 1959. Ein Oligolpolexperiment. *Zeischreft fur die Gesante Staatswissenschaft* 115:427–71.

Scherer, F. M. 1970. *Industrial market structure and economic performance.* Chicago: Rand McNally.

Scherer, F. M., and David Ross. 1990. *Industrial market structure and economic performance.* Boston: Houghton Mifflin.

Schwartz, Marius, and Robert J. Reynolds. 1983. Contestable markets: An uprising in the theory of industry structure: Comment. *American Economic Review* 73:488–90.

Sell, Jane, and Rick K. Wilson. 1991. Trigger strategies in repeated-play public goods games: Forgiving, non-forgiving, or non-existent? Working paper. Rice University.

Selten, Reinhard, and Rolf Stoecker. 1986. End behavior in sequences of finite prisoner's dilemma supergames: A learning theory approach. *Journal of Economic Behavior and Organization* 7:47–70.

Sherman, Roger. 1966. Capacity choice in duopoly. Unpublished doctoral dissertation. Pittsburgh: Graduate School of Industrial Administration, Carnegie-Mellon University.

———. 1969. Risk attitude and cost variability in a capacity choice experiment. *Review of Economic Studies* 36:453–66.

———. 1971. An experiment on the persistence of price collusion. *Southern Economic Journal* 37:489–95.

———. 1972. *Oligopoly, an empirical approach.* Lexington, Mass.: Lexington Books.

Siegel, Sidney, and Lawrence E. Fouraker. 1960. *Bargaining and group decision making.* New York: McGraw-Hill.

Smith, Vernon L. 1962. An experimental study of competitive market behavior. *Journal of Political Economy* 70:111–37.

———. 1964. The effect of market organization on competitive equilibrium. *Quarterly Journal of Economics* 78:181–201.

———. 1965. Experimental auction markets and the Walrasian hypothesis. *Journal of Political Economy* 73:387–93.

———. 1976. Bidding and auctioning institutions: Experimental results. In *Bidding and auctioning for procurement and allocation,* Y. Amihud, editor, New York: New York University Press. 43–64.

———. 1981a. An empirical study of decentralized institutions of monopoly restraint. In *Essays in contemporary fields of economics in honor of E. T. Weiler (1914–1979),* J. Quirk and G. Horwich, editors, West Lafayette: Purdue University Press. 83–106.

———. 1981b. Theory, experiment and antitrust policy. In *Strategy, predation, and antitrust analysis,* S. Salop, editor, Washington, D.C.: Federal Trade Commission, Bureau of Economics. 579–603.

———. 1982a. Markets as economizers of information: Experimental examination of the 'Hayek Hypothesis.' *Economic Inquiry* 20:165–79.

———. 1982b. Reflections on some experimental market mechanisms for classical environments. In *Choice models for buyer behavior, research in marketing,* Supplement 1, Leigh McAlister, editor, Greenwich, Conn.: JAI Press. 13–47.

———. 1989. Theory, experiment and economics. *Journal of Economic Perspectives,* 3(1):151–69.

Smith, Yernon L., and Arlington W. Williams. 1981. On nonbinding price controls in a competitive market. *American Economic Review* 71:467–74.

———. 1982. The effects of rent asymmetries in experimental auction markets. *Journal of Economic Behavior and Organization* 3:99–116.

———. 1983. An experimental comparison of alternative rules for competitive market exchange. In *Auctions, bidding, and contracting: Uses and theory,* R. Englebrecht-Wiggans et al., editors, New York: New York University Press. 307–34.

———. 1989. The boundaries of competitive price theory: Convergence, expectations, and transactions costs. In *Advances in behavioral economics, vol. 2,* Leonard Green and John Kagel, editors, Norwood, N.J.: Ablex Publishing.

Smith, Vernon L., Arlington W. Williams, W. Kenneth Bratton, and Michael G. Vannoni. 1982. Competitive market institutions: Double auctions vs. sealed bid-offer auctions. *American Economic Review*, 72:58–77.

Spence, A. Michael. 1976. Product selection, fixed costs, and monopolistic competition. *Review of Economic Studies* 43:217–35.

Stoecker, Rolf. 1980. *Experimentelle Untersuchung des Entscheidungsverhaltens im Bertrand-Oligopol*, vol. 4 of *Wirtshaftstheoretische Entscheidungsforschung*, Universitat Bielefeld, Bielefeld: Pfeffersche Buchhandlung.

Tirole, Jean. 1988. *The theory of industrial organization*. Cambridge, Mass.: MIT Press.

Van Boening, Mark V., and Nathaniel T. Wilcox. 1992. A fixed cost exception to the Hayek hypothesis. Working Paper. University of Mississipi.

Vickrey, William. 1961. Counterspeculation, auctions, and competitive sealed tenders. *Journal of Finance*. 16:8–37.

Walker, James, and Arlington Williams. 1988. Market behavior in bid, offer, and double auctions: A reexamination. *Journal of Economic Behavior and Organization* 9:301–14.

Wellford, Charissa P. 1989. A laboratory analysis of price dynamics and expectations in the cobweb model. Discussion Paper 89–15. University of Arizona.

———. 1990. Horizontal mergers: Concentration and performance. In *Takeovers and horizontal mergers: Policy and performance*, Ph.D. dissertation, University of Arizona.

Werden, Gregory J. 1991. A review of the empirical and experimental evidence on the relationship between market structure and performance. Economic Analysis Group Discussion Paper EAG 91–3. U.S. Department of Justice.

Wiggans, Steven N., Steven C. Hackett, and Raymond C. Battalio. 1990. An experimental study of contractual choice under variable reputational enforcement. Draft. Indiana University.

Williams, Arlington. 1979. Intertemporal competitive equilibrium: On further experimental results. In *Research in experimental economics, vol. 1*, V. L. Smith, editor, Greenwich, Conn.: J.A.I. Press. 255–78.

———. 1980. Computerized double-auction markets: Some initial experimental results. *Journal of Business* 53:235–58.

Williams, Arlington, and Vernon L. Smith. 1984. Cyclical double-auction markets with and without speculators. *Journal of Business* 57:1–33.

Williams, Fred E. 1973. The effect of market organization on competitive equilibrium: The multi-unit case. *Review of Economic Studies* 40:97–113.

Wilson, Robert. 1987. On equilibria in bid-ask markets. In *Arrow and the ascent of modern economic theory*, G. Feiwel, editor, Houndmills, U.K.: Macmillan.

———. 1990. Strategic analysis of auctions. Working paper. Stanford Business School.

6

Experimental Asset Markets: A Survey

Shyam Sunder

Capital or asset markets are distinguished from other markets by the informational role of prices and by the duality of the traders' role: each trader may buy *and* sell asset(s) in exchange for money or some other numeraire commodity.* Although prices in other markets may inform the participants in the sense of making them aware of their opportunity sets, prices in capital markets inform the traders substantively as determinants of their endogenously formed demand and supply. Asymmetry of information among the traders is an essential ingredient for prices to have an informational role, and I use this as the defining characteristic of capital or asset markets research covered in this review.

Information dissemination and aggregation *can* occur, but does not occur under all conditions. When it does occur, it is rarely instantaneous or perfect. Although such lags and imperfections often annoy the theorists, they can be surprisingly small when we consider the complexity of task facing the traders, and the documented limitations of human information processing (see Camerer, chapter 8 in this volume). These lags and imperfections also provide a more convincing basis for noisy rational expectations models than the exogenous noises (e.g., supply noise) artificially introduced in the theoretical models to construct such equilibria. While theoretical models focus on transaction price as the vehicle for information transmission in markets, experiments reveal the presence and importance of other parallel channels of communication such as bids, offers, identity of traders and timing, and so on. Experiments have also made it possible to develop more refined theories of the precise role of various vehicles (such as arbitrage and logical inference) in information transmission in markets.

The first asset market experiments were not conducted until the early 1980s. They have, however, already yielded a number of key results. The Hayekian hypothesis about the importance of the informational role of prices in markets has received consistent support. Dissemination of information, from informed to the uninformed, and aggregation of individual traders' diverse bits of information through the market process alone have been shown to be concrete, verifiable phenomena, bringing abstract theory into empirical domain.

As the experimental camera focused on information processing in asset markets, the theoretical line drawing has been filled in by details, shadows, color, and warts. This finer grain portrait of asset markets confirms the rough outline of the extant theory but is considerably more complex, providing guidance and challenges for further theoretical investigation of the role of information in markets.

Perhaps the most important finding to emerge from a decade of experimentation is that statistical efficiency of a market *does not* imply that it is allocatively or informationally efficient. In econometric studies of field data from asset markets, absence of profitable filter rules or other arbitrage opportunities is assumed to imply informational efficiency of the market. Experiments have shown that markets we know to be informationally inefficient can be quite efficient by these statistical criteria.

The first section of this chapter reviews evidence on informational efficiency of markets. The second section concerns the behavior of markets for derivative claims (e.g., futures, options, and contingent claims) and their effect on the market for the primary asset. The third section focuses on bubbles and false equilibria—a topic for which laboratory modeling is especially useful because it is difficult to address with field data. The fourth section concerns learning in competitive markets. The fifth section compares econometric analyses of data from the field and the data gathered in the laboratory, and the sixth section addresses several investment and public policy issues to which these results are pertinent. The seventh section discusses laboratory modeling of asset markets, followed by a summary and some concluding remarks in the eighth section.

I. Informational Efficiency of Markets

Informational efficiency of capital markets is a central theme in modern finance. Empirical observations about the brownian motion-like statistical properties of prices were made by Bachelier (1900), Kendall (1953), Roberts (1959), Alexander (1961), Cootner (1964), Fama (1965), and others. Samuelson (1965) applied the no-arbitrage condition to prove that properly anticipated prices must behave like a random walk. The logic of arbitrage suggests that when the informed traders move to take advantage of their information, the price will move by an amount and in the direction that eliminates this advantage. Neutral observers of such a market would observe an association between the unanticipated information obtained by the informed traders and the consequent movement of market prices.

Knowledge of this association would enable even the uninformed traders to infer from an observed price increase that some traders in the market have favorable information about the asset. Lucas (1972) used this inverse inference from observed price to the state of nature in rational expectations environments (see Muth 1961) where the price is the consequence of optimal actions of traders. Information is not wasted; in equilibrium, price summarizes and reveals (i.e., is a sufficient statistic for) all the relevant information in possession of all the traders (see Hayek 1945; Grossman 1976). The idea that prices in stock markets promptly and unbiasedly (though not precisely) adjust to reflect information came to be labeled as the efficient market theory (see Fama 1970).

A. Field Data from Financial Markets

Price data gathered from stock and commodity exchanges provided the initial impetus for development of the random walk theory and made it possible for researchers to test this statistical theory. Several difficult problems arose in testing the efficient market theory with field data. Strictly speaking, empirical testing of the theory requires that the observed prices be compared against the correct theoretical prices after taking into account the prevalent information conditions that produce the observed prices. It is difficult for a researcher to know these private information conditions in markets in which thousands of traders participate. Even if these private information conditions were somehow known, how could one determine the correct theoretical stock price of, say, General Motors on June 1, 1993, to serve as a benchmark of comparison to evaluate the efficiency of prices observed in the market?

Empirical testing of market efficiency therefore centered on *changes* in stock prices associated with private or public events that become observable to the researcher. If it is known a priori that an event represents "good news" for the stockholders of a firm and the price of its stock is found to increase upon its occurrence, one could conclude that the market price adjusts to reflect the information represented by that event. In spite of supportive results from a large number of such studies (and many ambiguous or contradictory results; see Fama 1990, for a recent survey) this incremental approach could not erase the suspicion that even if the market is efficient in small changes, it may yet be grossly mispriced in the large. Further, efficiency of price *changes* does not rule out the inefficiency of price levels.

The general principle that it is possible for market prices to reflect information so the uninformed traders are able to act as if they are informed cannot be conclusively tested with the field data. There are two major obstacles to such field testing: prices change due to information arrival as well as other events, and identification of the informed traders in the field is no mean task. Rational expectations equilibrium models, on the other hand, have merely shown the feasibility of the principle. Since the analytical models used to characterize the equilibrium are concerned with the end point of the process of equilibration, and not with the process itself, existence of the equilibrium provides no guarantee that it would be reached. Further, the analytical models, typically stripped of institutional details, do not tell us much about the market structure and environment in which this general principle may hold.

B. Designing Experimental Asset Markets

Experimental studies of informational efficiency of asset markets can be divided into three groups. The first group of studies focuses on dissemination of information from a group of identically informed insiders to a group of identically uninformed traders. The second set of studies is concerned with the more difficult task of market aggregation of diverse information in possession of individual traders and the dissemination of this information across all traders. The third group of studies endogenizes the production of information and focus on simultaneous equilibrium in both the asset and the information markets. Details of designing asset markets can be found in Sunder (1991) and Friedman and Sunder (1994).

Endogenous modification of demand and supply based on within-market experience and learning is a key feature of asset market studies. The stage for the experimental examination of this phenomenon was set by three prior studies of learning *across* markets. Miller, Plott, and Smith (1977) and Plott and Uhl (1981) examined formation of derived demand by introducing arbitrage opportunities across markets. Forsythe, Palfrey, and Plott (1982) allowed each participant to be a buyer as well as a seller in the same market, thus creating opportunities for derived demand as well as supply.

The upper panel of Figure 6.1 reproduces figure 2 of Forsythe, Palfrey, and Plott's (1982) paper that reports the result of their first market labeled "Experiment 1." The market consisted of eight consecutive trials, labeled "Years" 1 through 8, each consisting of two periods, A and B. Certificates traded in these markets had no uncertainty of dividends and, therefore, no chance for information asymmetry across traders. This study focused on determining whether, over replication of trials, learning of equilibrium in period 2 market seeps back into period 1 market and alters the behavior of that market from naive to perfect foresight equilibrium.

Each trader in these markets was given an endowment of two identical assets and an interest-free loan of cash (to serve as working capital) at the beginning of each trial. Each asset paid a dividend to its holder at the end of period A as well as period B. Dividends were private and different across three classes of traders, creating gains from trade. For example in Market 1, period A and B dividends were 300 and 50 for type I traders, 50 and 300 for type II traders, and 150 and 250 for type III traders. The horizontal lines for period B indicate the unique equilibrium price of 300. For period A, the broken horizontal line indicates the naive equilibrium price of 400. However, the perfect foresight equilibrium price for period A, based on the knowledge of the market value of assets in period B, is higher by 200; the solid horizontal line indicates this perfect foresight equilibrium price of 600. Each dot represents an observed transaction for one asset in chronological order. The average of transaction prices for each period is shown at the bottom.

This experiment revealed that the initial behavior of the market in period A is well described by the naive equilibrium (400 in the top panel of Figure 6.1). However, over repeated trials under a stationary environment, convergence toward the perfect foresight equilibrium (600 in top panel of Figure 6.1) takes place, as more and more of the traders learn to exploit the market opportunities available to them in period B, and to appreciate the implications of this opportunity for their strategy in period A. Frank (1988) repeated the Forsythe, Palfrey, and Plott (1982) experiment on economics undergraduates using computer (instead of oral) double auction by adding once-for-all shifts as well as trended shifts in economic

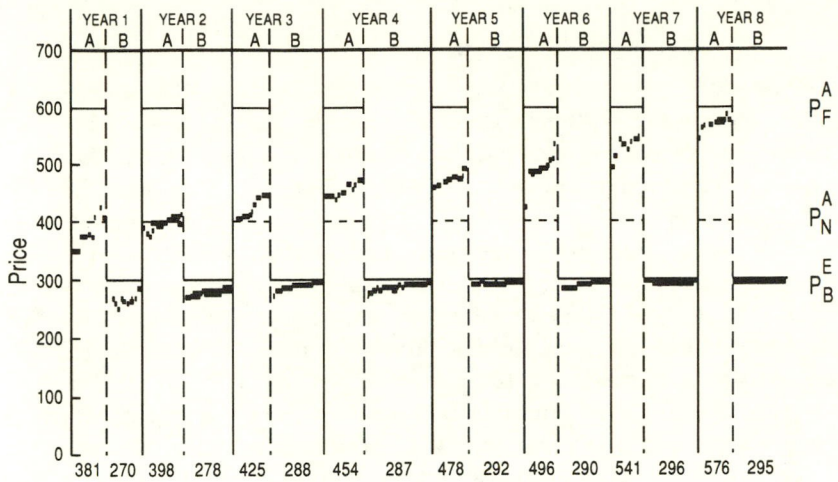

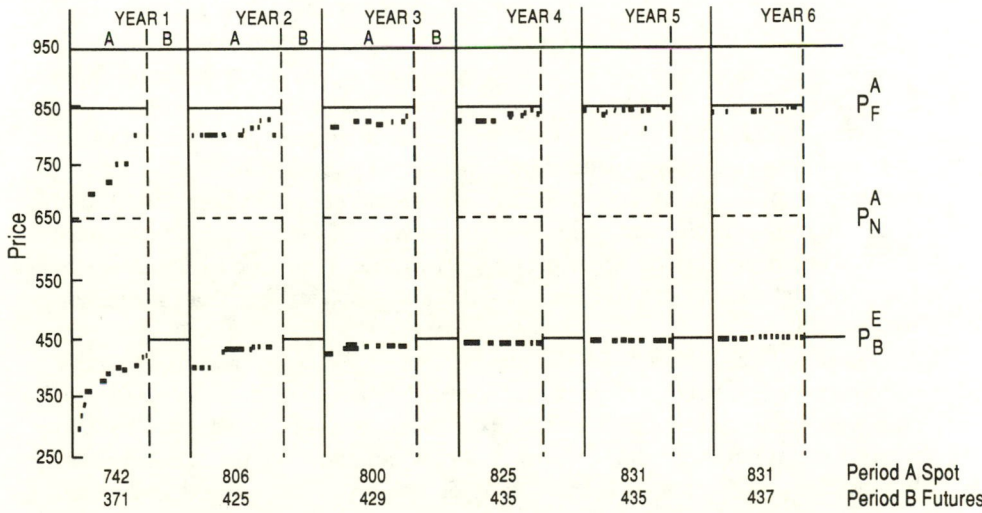

Figure 6.1. Transmission of information across markets. Top: sequence of contract and average prices for Experiment 1. Bottom: sequence for Experiment 5. *Source:* Forsythe, Palfrey, and Plott 1982, figures 2 and 6.

fundamentals. The perfect foresight model "does a remarkably good job of predicting where these markets will go," even though the explanatory power is diminished somewhat in shifting environments.

Dissemination of information from period B to period A markets created derived demand and supply in period A and set the stage for experimental examination of endogenous creation of demand and supply due to information aggregation and dissemination *within* markets.

C. Dissemination of Information

Plott and Sunder (1982) designed a market in which traders could trade units of a single-period asset, one unit at a time, in a double auction. The market had three types of traders, and for each type of trader the dividend could take one of two possible values, depending on the exogenously realized state of the world with known probabilities (see Table 6.1). In effect, they simplified Forsythe, Palfrey, and Plott's (1982) assets from two to one period and added uncertainty to dividends. Information about the realized state of the world was given to six traders (two of each dividend type), while the other six traders (two of each type) remained uninformed. The fact that half of the traders in the market had the information was common knowledge, but the identity of the informed traders remained private. Dividends and probabilities were chosen so the price and allocation predictions of the rational expectations and prior information competitive equilibria were distinct in one of the two states of the world.

For example when state Y was realized, informed traders of type I, II, and III knew that their dividend from holding the asset in that period would be 100, 150, and 175, respectively. Traders who do not learn the state might attribute a value of 220, 210, or 155 to the asset, depending on whether they are of type I, II, or III (see the last column of Table 6.1), if we assume that they are risk neutral. Supply of assets is limited to the aggregate initial endowment of 24 (2 for each of the twelve traders). The large working capital loan to traders means that each type of trader has a large flat demand for the asset at a price equal to its value to him or her. The market supply and demand configuration is shown in Figure 6.2. The competitive equilibrium price is the maximum of the six individual values listed above, which is 220. Since the uninformed traders of type I value the asset the most, they are the predicted holders of the asset under the prior information equilibrium.

The rational expectations model, on the other hand, suggests that this prior information equilibrium will not be sustained. The uninformed traders of type I, who pay a price as high as 220 with the expectation of receiving a dividend of 400 with 40 percent chance, soon discover that they never receive the high dividend. Whenever state X is realized, informed traders of type I pay more than 220 and shut the uninformed traders of type I out of the market. On the other hand, whenever an uninformed trader of type I is able to buy the assets at or below 220, the dividend turns out to be only 100 in state Y. If the uninformed traders refuse to be fooled all the time and learn from the market behavior whether the state is X or Y, the price under state Y would be the maximum of 100, 150, and 175, which is 175. Thus in rational expectations equilibrium, price in state Y is 175 and the assets will be held by type III traders. Furthermore, since those who are initially uninformed learn the state from observing the market behavior, type III holders will include such traders along with those who are initially informed. This market was designed so the prior information and rational expectations equilibrium price and allocation predictions under state Y were distinct. The empirical question is

Table 6.1. Parameters and Equilibria for a Simple Asset Market

	Dividends in States of the World		
	State X Probability = 0.4	State Y Probability = 0.6	Expected Dividend
Trader type			
I	400	100	220
II	300	150	210
III	125	175	155
RE equilibrium			
Price	400	175	
Asset holders	Trader type I	Trader type III	
PI equilibrium			
Price	400	220	
Asset holders	Trader type I, informed	Trader type I, uninformed	

Source: Extracted from Plott and Sunder (1982, tables 2 and 3).

whether these (or some other) equilibria will organize the data. Existence of the theoretical equilibria provide no assurance that such equilibria will be attained under any specific trading mechanisms.

Plott and Sunder (1982) found that, given experience with replications, the behavior of these markets converges to close proximity of the predictions of the rational expectations theory that assumes that traders are able to infer the state of the world from the observed market phenomena.

Figure 6.3 plots the individual transaction prices of the twelve periods of this market in chronological order. The rational expectations price (400 for state X, 175 for state Y) is shown in solid horizontal line, while the prior information price for state Y is shown in a broken horizontal line (prior information price for state X is 400). The first two periods of the session were procedural warm ups when no information was distributed to the traders. In X-state periods (4, 7, and 9) price converged close to 400, the common prediction of both models. In Y-state periods (3, 5, 6, 8, and 10) prices converged close to the rational expectations prediction of 175 instead of the prior information prediction of 220. End-of-period asset holdings shown at the top of Figure 6.3 show that Y-state asset allocations were more consistent with the prior information predictions in early periods; however, as traders gained experience, asset allocations became more consistent with the predictions of the rational expectations model. In period 3, eighteen of twenty-four units of assets were allocated to type I traders as predicted by the prior

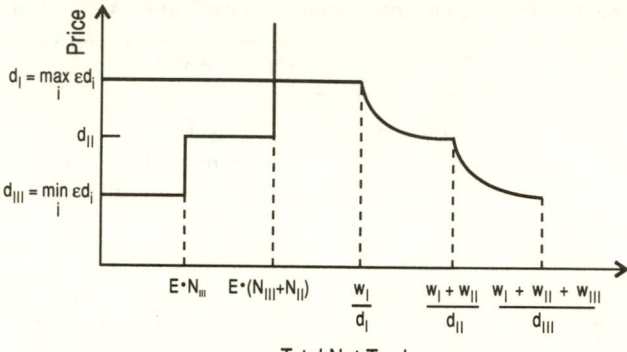

Figure 6.2. Market supply and demand functions. W_i = initial working capital of investors of type i; N_i = number of agents in the market of dividend type i; E = initial endowment of securities per agent; d_i = dividend of agents of dividend type i; ε = mathematical expectation with respect to the prior probability distribution of the states of nature. *Source:* Plott and Sunder 1982, figure 1.

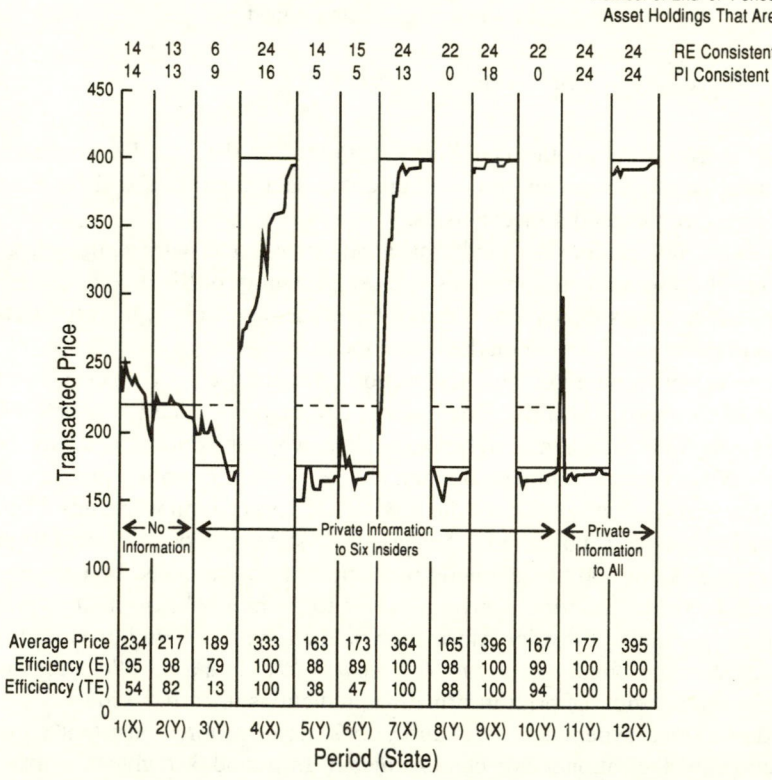

Figure 6.3. Dissemination of information in an asset market. *Source:* Plott and Sunder 1982, figure 4.

Table 6.2. Direction of Asset Transfers When the Rational Expectations and Prior Information Models Made Contradictory Predictions

	Period and State							
	3 Y	4 X	5 Y	6 Y	7 X	8 Y	9 X	10 Y
Certificates sold per uninformed agent when RE model predicts sales and PI model predicts purchases (agent types I and II)	–2.5		–0.5	–0.25		2		2
Certificates bought per informed agent when RE model predicts purchases and PI model predicts sales (agent type III)	–1.5		0.5	1.5		5		4.5

Source: Extracted from table 15 of the working version of Plott and Sunder (1982).
Note: Positive numbers are consistent with RE predictions.

information model; only six were allocated to type III traders according to the prediction of the RE model. By period 10, only two assets were allocated to type I while twenty-two were in the hands of type III traders.

Finally, it is the behavior of the uninformed traders of type I and type III under state Y that is critical in distinguishing between the rational expectations and prior information models. The rational expectations model predicts that uninformed traders of types I and II will learn from the market and thus refuse to buy at 175 assets that have a prior information expected value of 220 or 210 for them. It also predicts that the uninformed traders of type III will learn from the market and be willing to pay prices as high as 175 for assets that have a prior information expected value of only 155 in Y periods. Row 1 of Table 6.2 shows that the uninformed agent of types I and II started out buying assets in period 3, gradually decreased their buying in periods 5 and 6 and then sold all their assets (2 per trader) in periods 8 and 9. Row 2 shows that the uninformed agents of type III started out selling an average of 1.5 assets per trader in period 3 and started buying beginning period 5. In periods 8 and 10, these initially uninformed traders became so confident of the information they had learned from observing the market that they bought, on average, more assets per capita than the informed traders of type III did.

Experience with replications is necessary, and instantaneous convergence to equilibrium is not observed. Of course, Smith (1962) discovered that convergence to equilibrium needs replication even in the simpler environments of his early experiments (spot markets for non-durables without uncertainty in private costs or values). It would have been surprising if more experience were not needed for convergence to rational expectations equilibrium in environments where subjects face state uncertainty and have so much more learning to do. Once the traders have been exposed to the range of exchange possibilities available to them, the market can disseminate information about the realized state of the world for a particular period in a surprisingly economical fashion—by the first few bids and asks.

The approximate nature of convergence is the second important qualification to these results. Again, even in the simpler environments of Smith's (1962) experiments, convergence to equilibrium was noisy and approximate. Increased complexity is accompanied by increased noise.

However, establishing the empirical existence of such a market does not establish that all, or even most, market structures and environments converge to rational expectations equilibrium upon replication. A number of studies have explored the boundaries of the market structures and environments in which such results hold. In their fifth market, Plott and Sunder (1982) added a third state of nature to their two-state design discussed above, without noticeably delaying or weakening the convergence of prices, allocations, and efficiency to the rational expectation predictions. Banks' (1985) experiments also used three-state assets and yielded comparable results.

Only a few experiments with assets with four or more discrete states, or a continuum of states, have been attempted in the laboratory so far. As the number of states is increased, it takes more periods of trading to experience and learn the market consequences of each state. Moreover, as the number of states increase, the average distance between the equilibrium prices of any pair of states decreases. For any given level of price noise, traders are less certain of the state-price correspondence they may conjecture on the basis of their observations. Increase in the number of states to be learned and the crowding of equilibrium prices should delay and dilute the convergence to rational expectations equilibria. In an alternative treatment, Plott and Sunder (1982) introduced eleven subjective states of nature by distributing to the insiders an imperfect signal about which of the two possible states of nature prevailed.[1] The eleven periods of replication in this experiment proved to be insufficient for the traders to disentangle the equilibria for each of the eleven signals. Given the inherent noise levels, such a market may not reach rational expectations equilibrium even after a few dozen repetitions. If eleven discrete states are too many, what is likely to happen in a continuum of states? Similar caution is appropriate in interpreting theoretical and experimental results obtained from stationary environments to naturally occurring markets where conditions relevant to their equilibrium behavior are subject to continual change. The boundaries of the applicability of rational expectations models in such markets need further exploration.

Copeland and Friedman (1987) experimented with sequential distribution of information among traders. They divided each five-minute period into four equal segments of seventy-five seconds each. A randomly chosen subset of traders received information at the end of the first, second, and the third time segment, respectively. Once informed, a trader knew for sure which of the two possible states of nature had occurred in that period. Copeland's (1975) and Jennings, Fellingham, and Starks' (1981) models, based on the assumption that traders do not learn about the state of nature from observing the market phenomena, predict that trading volume under sequential arrival of information would be higher than under simultaneous arrival of information. Instead, the actual trading volume was significantly higher in markets where information was given to traders simultaneously. Sequential arrival of information presents the uninformed with a choice between trading against possibly better-informed opponents, or simply refusing to trade for a few minutes until information arrives. Reluctance to trade against better-informed opponents is also reflected in their analysis of bid-ask spreads. Wider bid-ask spreads were observed in early periods, in early parts of periods, and in seconds immediately following the arrival of information. In these markets, every trader knew that he or she would receive perfect information about the state of nature no less than seventy-five seconds before the end of the trading period. One interpretation of these results is that it is not necessarily advantageous to trade early in a period before the information arrives. This interpretation is also supported by Frank's (1988) and Friedman's (1993a) subsequent experiments where traders preferred to transact in the later part of a trading period.

How widely must the distribution of information be to ensure its dissemination in the market? This is a question about measurement of a market parameter, and parameters measured in the laboratory cannot easily, or meaningfully, be translated to the field environments. It is more useful to ask the qualitative question: does the increase in the number of insiders increase the speed or precision of information dissemination in the market?

Plott and Sunder (1982) kept the number as well as the identity of the informed traders fixed at six out of a total of twelve. Sunder (1992) observed information dissemination when as few as one out of twelve traders was informed. However, dissemination with one, two, or even three informed traders cannot be relied upon; such informationally-thin markets are prone to serious malfunctioning, especially when traders have some confidence in their ability to extract information from the market phenomena.[2] Von Borries and Friedman (1989) compared the performance of a two-state, single-period, eight-trader asset market in which the number of the informed was fixed at four, against the performance of a similar market in which the number of the informed traders was randomly chosen each period to be either one or zero. The identity of the informed trader, when there was one, also was randomly chosen each period. Information is disseminated in the market with four informed traders, but not in the second market. This result suggests that as the market becomes thinner in information, dissemination of information becomes more chancy. Watts (1993) examined Plott and Sunder's (1982) markets by making the presence of informed traders a random variable; there was 50–50 chance that zero or six out of twelve traders in the market had received perfect information about the realized state of the world before the market opened for trading. Her results confirmed that the uncertainty about the presence of informed traders in the market weakens the reliability and precision of rational expectations predictions, especially in the state corresponding to the lower price.

Is it possible to detect the presence of insiders in a market by applying statistical techniques to data collected in the laboratory? Lundholm (1986) compared Plott and Sunder's (1982) data for initial periods when no trader was informed against later periods in which 50 percent of the traders were informed and reached an affirmative conclusion. Markets with asymmetric information have a higher volume, and this volume is attributable to activities of the insiders. In markets with asymmetric information, a price change is more likely to be followed by another of the same sign. He developed a logistic response model that could predict the presence of insiders in a market with about 75 percent accuracy. Whether these results would hold in data obtained from markets in which the existence of informed traders is *not* common knowledge is an open question. Camerer and Weigelt's (1990a, 1990b) experiments (discussed in the section on bubbles and false equilibria) suggest that it takes many replications to learn to recognize the presence or absence of information from market characteristics.

The number of insiders in these experiments was relatively large, and the number as well as the identity of insiders was exogenously determined. Once these variables are endogenized (in experiments reported in the section on costly information) it may be more difficult to detect the presence of insiders. Further, the uninformed would like to learn not only whether, and how many, insiders are present, but also what the insiders know about the state of nature.

Few researchers have explored the possibility of drawing ex post statistical inference from experimental data gathered by other researchers. Such techniques are frequently applied to data gathered from stock and commodity exchanges, and their application in the laboratory would be an illuminating linkage between these two types of empirical research. It is interesting that Lundholm's own analysis was motivated by Morse's (1980) efforts to use field data to test his own model about the effect of the presence of insiders on market behavior. Lundholm recognized that, in spite of other advantages of using the field data, Morse's tests were deficient in one critical respect—unobservability of the presence of insiders, the treatment variable. The laboratory allows exact measurement of the treatment variable.

D. Aggregation of Information

The studies reviewed above demonstrate that it is possible for markets to disseminate information from perfectly informed insiders to the uninformed. Is it also possible for a market to perform the more subtle and difficult task of aggregating the less-than-perfect, diverse information in possession of individual traders, and disseminating it to all traders? If this were to happen, such a market would function as if every individual trader has access to all the information in possession of all the individuals. Hayek's (1945) critique of central planning suggested that he believed that markets are able to accomplish this feat. Grossman (1981) proved that such information aggregation would lead to allocations that cannot be Pareto dominated by a planner who had access to all of the economy's information. Do there exist markets that will aggregate and disseminate private information in possession of egoistic individuals?

Plott and Sunder (1988) modeled information aggregation in the laboratory by using three discrete dividend states. Traders were endowed with two or more units each of a single-period asset. The dividends of this asset depended on which one of the three possible states of nature with known probabilities (X, Y, or Z), was realized in that period. Every trader received diverse, but imperfect information about the state of nature before trading by a oral double auction began: if the realized state was X, one half of the participating traders, randomly chosen, were privately informed that the state was "not Y," while the others were similarly informed "not Z." This system of distributing information was common knowledge among the traders. Dividends and probabilities were chosen so the equilibrium predictions of the rational expectations model were distinct from the predictions of the prior information or Walrasian equilibrium in which traders extracted no information about the state of nature from observing the market.

This experiment consisted of three series of markets. In series A, consisting of five market sessions, a single-period, three-state asset was traded among traders who received diverse information about the realized state of the world and received different dividends from the same asset depending on the class of traders they belonged to. These markets did not converge to rational expectations equilibrium. Two markets of series B were created by unbundling the single asset of series A markets so traders could trade a complete set of three different state-contingent claims. Three markets of series C were created by modifying series A design so all traders belonged to the same dividend class. Series B and series C markets converged to rational expectations equilibrium.

When dividends varied across traders, the markets could not aggregate information by trading the single, three-state asset described above. In such environments, the task of extracting information about the realized state of nature from others' bids and asks is more complicated. Plott and Sunder (1988) experimented with two alternative treatments. In one treatment (series C), dividends of all traders were made identical. With the common knowledge of identical dividends, traders were able to interpret others' bids and asks in an unambiguous manner and extract information to revise their own beliefs about the realized state of nature.

In the second treatment (series B), they replaced the market for a single three-state asset by a simultaneous market for three single-state-contingent assets. X-contingent asset paid dividend x_i to trader i if state X was realized and trader i held the asset at the end of trading. Y-contingent and Z-contingent assets were similarly defined.

For example, Table 6.3 shows that X-contingent asset paid dividends of 70, 230, and 100 to traders of type I, II, and III, respectively, if state X was realized and nothing otherwise. Under state X, two traders of each type knew that the state was "not Y" while two traders of each type knew that it was "not Z." Thus, there was no aggregate uncertainty. Rational expectations equilibrium aggregates the diverse information available to individuals and yields prices of 230, 0, and 0 for X-, Y-, and Z-contingent assets respectively in state X. Prior information equilibrium, on the other hand, assumes that no aggregation of information occurs. This market, with simultaneous trading in three different assets, is considerably more

Table 6.3. Parameters and Equilibria for a Complete Market

	X-Asset Dividend in State			Y-Asset Dividend in State			Z-Asset Dividend in State		
	X	Y	Z	X	Y	Z	X	Y	Z
Trader type and number									
I (4)	70	0	0	0	130	0	0	0	300
II (4)	230	0	0	0	90	0	0	0	60
III (4)	100	0	0	0	160	0	0	0	200
RE equilibrium									
State	X	Y	Z	X	Y	Z	X	Y	Z
Price	230	0	0	0	160	0	0	0	300
Asset holders (trader type)	II	—	—	—	III	—	—	—	I
PI equilibrium									
State	X	Y	Z	X	Y	Z	X	Y	Z
Price	146	146	101	58	58	49	169	208	208
Asset holders (trader type with information)	II (not Z)	II (not Z)	II (not Y)	III (not Z)	III (not Z)	III (not Y)	I (not Y)	I (not Y)	I (not X)

Source: Extracted from Plott and Sunder (1988, tables 1 and 2).
Note: Prob (X) = Prob (Y) = Prob (Z) = 1/3.

complex than single asset markets. Yet, as can be seen from Figure 6.4, it was able to aggregate information. Transaction prices for X-, Y-, and Z-contingent assets in periods 1–9 are plotted against time in three panels of Figure 6.4. Each dot represents one transaction. When two consecutive transactions occur in the same market, the two dots representing these transactions are joined by a line. The realized state of nature for each period is shown at the bottom. In each panel, a solid horizontal line indicates the price prediction of the rational expectations equilibrium (e.g., 0 for X- and Y- and 300 for Z-contingent markets in period 1). Average transaction price for each market and overall allocative efficiency is shown at the top by period. Within a few periods, all three asset prices, as well as allocations (not shown here) converge close to the predictions of the rational expectations equilibrium.

Periods 10–13 in Figure 6.4 show that, when the three state-contingent assets of periods 1–9 were bundled together and traded as single assets, the market was unable to aggregate information. By experimenting with several other markets, Plott and Sunder (1988) found that a market that trades a single three-state asset is unable to aggregate information when dividends vary across traders.

These experiments are a good example of potential for productive interplay

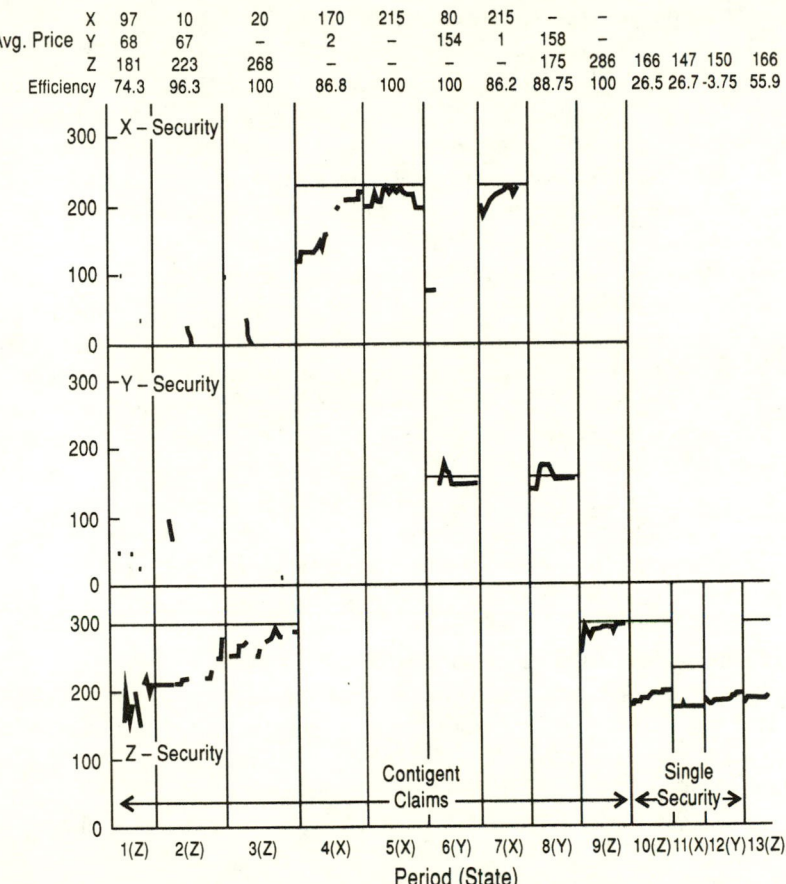

Figure 6.4. Aggregation and dissemination of information in complete markets with state-contingent securities. *Source:* Plott and Sunder 1988, figure 4.

between theory and experimental data. The first three markets of the experiment were motivated by a curiosity to find out if the ability of double auctions to *disseminate* information, documented in Plott and Sunder's (1982) experiment, extends to *aggregation* of diverse information. In order to test the information aggregation hypothesis, the market for a single two-state asset used in Plott and Sunder (1982) was modified to a single three-state asset market. When this market failed to aggregate information, the authors searched for explanations of this failure. They realized that this market was incomplete (because a single asset cannot span the three-state space). The rational expectations equilibrium in both complete as well as incomplete markets would be identical, and there had been no theoretical work to suggest either that incomplete markets would have difficulty in arriving at this equilibrium or that a more complete set of trading instruments would facilitate information aggregation and efficiency. Yet, in observing the process of trading in incomplete markets and the difficulty traders had in extracting information from market data, it became clear that expanding the message set available to traders (i.e., prices of different assets in this case) until it spanned the state space may enable traders to distinguish the realized state from other states on the basis of observable market data. This conjecture led to the design and testing of a second set of markets (series B) in which a complete state-spanning set of assets was traded. The conjecture turned out to be correct, and markets of this series aggregated information. The experimental work now needs to be followed by theoretical analyses of conditions that promote informational efficiency (see section on learning sequences for further discussion).

Besides empirical demonstration that aggregation of diverse information can take place through certain market processes, Plott and Sunder (1988) yielded a second important result about the relationship between statistical and allocative efficiency of a market. All eight single-security, heterogenous-preference markets failed to aggregate information. In other words, all these markets were allocatively and informationally quite inefficient; the potential gains from trading actually exploited in these markets varied from a minimum of 8 percent to a maximum of 78 percent. However, in spite of this gross informational inefficiency, the price data revealed no obvious opportunities that could be exploited advantageously by the traders. Application of hypothetical filter trading rules to the price data generated from these experiments revealed that such rules are dominated by a naive buy-and-hold strategy. Had these data been generated in the field, we may well have concluded, on the basis of such statistical tests, that these markets are efficient. But, possessing the knowledge of information and dividend conditions, the experimenter *knows* that these markets are, allocatively and informationally, quite inefficient. Statistical efficiency of markets and lack of arbitrage opportunities would appear to be a necessary condition for informational efficiency; it is not sufficient.

Forsythe and Lundholm (1990) conducted detailed experiments to search for conditions that would allow information aggregation in incomplete markets in spite of heterogeneous preferences. They observed aggregation of information when the entire table of dividends was common knowledge among traders *and* the subjects were given additional sessions of trading experience. On the other hand, O'Brien and Srivastava (1991b) showed that even with uniform, common-knowledge dividends (across traders), addition of sufficient complexity (e.g., multiple, multiperiod assets, correlation of dividends across assets and across periods, absence of common knowledge about distribution of information) can render aggregation of information difficult or unlikely. Which of these market characteristics are crucial to its information aggregation ability remains to be explored.

O'Brien (1990) examined the effect of withholding the ex post revelation of the state of nature on market behavior. Instead of announcing the realized state of nature at the end of each period, he withheld the announcement until the end of the last period of the market. Withholding this information prevented a market that could otherwise aggregate information from doing so. Ex post revelation of the state would allow individual traders to recursively modify their rules of infer-

ence about the state of nature from observation of the market. The results suggest that such recursive modification is crucial to convergence of markets to rational expectations equilibrium. When states of nature are not revealed—and it is not unusual to have years of delays in markets for corporate equity—one must be careful in interpreting the behavior of natural markets in terms of rational expectation models.

Kruse and Sunder (1988) and Eberwein (1990) are experimenting with the common knowledge of information distribution as a treatment variable. Plott and Sunder (1982) suggest that the behavior of markets with asymmetric information may be sensitive to common knowledge conditions. Ang and Schwarz (1985) report an experiment in which common knowledge about information distribution is manipulated. Since their manipulations were conducted sequentially over various subsets of periods in a single market session, more detailed work is needed to obtain definitive results. The Kruse and Sunder design seeks to compare the performance of markets in which absence of information is common knowledge against markets in which it is not. This research design differs from Camerer and Weigelt's (1990b) in which the number of informed traders is randomly set to zero or six each period; when information is absent, this absence is not common knowledge. Experimental designs described in this paragraph seem to push experimental complexity close to its limits, yielding only a few noisy observations from a large amount of time and money spent on experimentation.

Results of these experiments suggest that aggregation of information in markets depends on features of markets—rules, information distribution, common knowledge, experience of traders, number, nature and relationship of assets traded, etc. Specific empirical relationships between these features and the performance characteristics of markets identified in these experiments may help incorporate such features into analytical models of markets. Some markets aggregate information, all of them do not. The difficult work lies ahead in establishing more precise understanding of factors that facilitate or retard information aggregation.

E. Market for Information

Studies of information aggregation and dissemination in markets revealed that it is unrealistic to expect this process to be complete or instantaneous, even in simple laboratory settings. Even in the absence of exogenous noise, laboratory prices are necessarily noisy, relative to the predictions of formal models. If markets instantaneously and completely reveal information produced or purchased by the informed at positive cost, there would be no incentives to produce information. How do we reconcile costly information production with the revelation of information in markets?

Noisy rational expectations models addressed this problem by deriving equilibria in which asset markets reveal some information, but noise disguises just the right amount of information to allow the informed traders to recover the cost of information (see Grossman and Stiglitz 1980; Hellwig 1980; and Verrecchia 1982). Sunder (1992) allowed traders in his single-period, two-state asset market

to buy perfect information about the realized state of nature before trading opened in the asset market.[3] The informed traders' gross profits exceeded the gross profits of the uninformed. However, when the cost of information was netted out, these profits were statistically indistinguishable. Noisy revelation of information in asset market was just enough to compensate the informed for the cost of buying information.

Two sets of markets in Sunder (1992) provide insights into the equilibrating process. When information was auctioned off to the four (out of twelve) highest bidders in a uniform price sealed bid auction (at the fifth highest bid price), the price of information was relatively high in the early periods (see Figure 6.5, top of the upper panel). However, with a few periods of experience, traders learned to infer the state of nature from market observations in the asset market (Figure 6.5, bottom of the upper panel), and they lowered the amounts they were willing to pay for information, creating a steep fall in the price of information. In later periods of these experiments, the price of information was just enough to be recovered from small deviations between the transaction and full revelation rational expectations equilibrium prices in the asset market.

In a second set of markets, the price of information was fixed and each trader had to choose each period if she wished to be informed about the state of nature by paying this price. The number of buyers of information did not stabilize (see Figure 6.5, upper part of the bottom panel). All traders in this market are in an essentially symmetric position and the double auction does not allow them a mechanism to coordinate or communicate their information-buying decisions. The result was that the number of informed traders varies widely over a range. When many traders buy information, information is promptly revealed through the prices (see Figure 6.5, lower part of the bottom panel), depriving the buyers of information of the opportunity to recover their information costs. In other periods, when only a few buy information, the market occasionally fails to reveal information, allowing the informed to reap large profits. On the average across many periods, however, the net profits of the informed and the uninformed tend towards equality.

Copeland and Friedman (1991, 1992) examined the behavior of asset markets with sequential arrival of information, with the provision of costly purchase of information early in each period. In the simplest cell of their four-cell experimental design, they obtained results similar to those reported by Sunder (1992) in simpler environments.[4] When they used more complex settings, revelation of information in asset markets becomes less than complete, allowing higher gross profits for the buyers of information and higher price of information. Von Borries and Friedman (1989) used an environment similar to Copeland and Friedman's (1992) with uncertain presence of a single informed trader who received information at zero cost. In the absence of common knowledge about distribution of information, the asset markets are not able to reveal information when the monopolist insider is present, allowing the insider to earn large net profits. It is likely that the price of the right to be the monopolist insider would have reduced his net profits to the level of the other traders if the right to be the insider had been

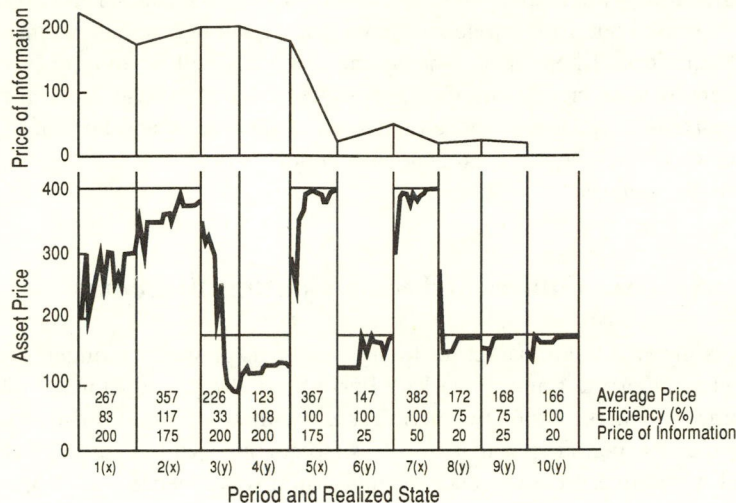

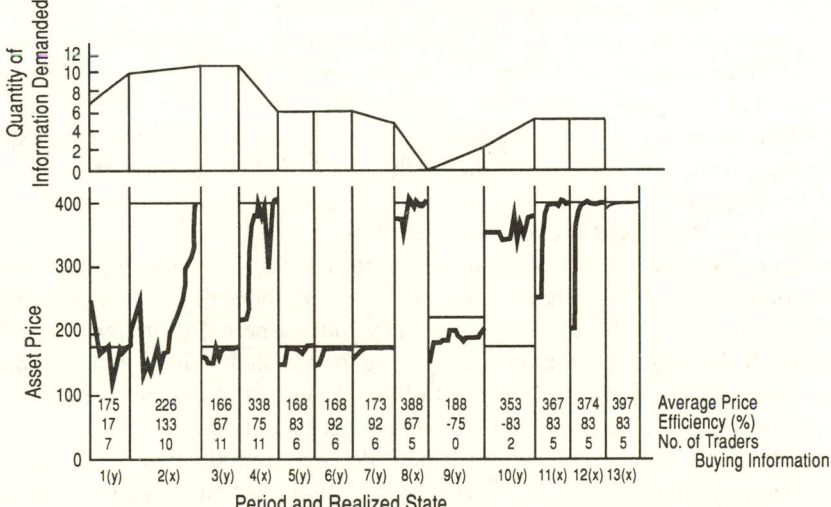

Figure 6.5. Asset and information market equilibria with costly information. Top: information price and asset price for market 1. Bottom: information demand and asset price for market 2. Information prices are for sealed-bid auction with fixed supply; asset prices are for double oral auction; information demand is the number of traders who bought information at a price fixed by the experimenters. *Source:* Redrawn from Sunder (1992, figures 1 and 2).

auctioned off. As long as entry into the information market remains free, the behavior of asset and information markets is consistent with the theory. Theoretical models of noisy rational expectations equilibrium use exogenous sources of noise (e.g., supply noise in Grossman and Stiglitz [1980]). King (1987) modelled his experimental markets with such exogenous supply noise. However, it is clear, from the data gathered to date, that noise is an inherent characteristic of experimental markets. It is also inherent in natural markets (see Black 1986). Analytical models started out using exogenous noise arising out of state uncertainty to construct equilibria. I hope that someday these models will develop to incorporate endogenous noise arising out of *behavioral* uncertainty instead. Since the behavioral noise is ever present, indeed inherent, in laboratory and field markets, the advantage of incorporating exogenous, state-of-nature noise into laboratory experiments is unclear.

II. Futures and State-Contingent Claims

What is the effect of a market for futures contracts or state-contingent claims on the behavior of the primary market? Forsythe, Palfrey, and Plott (1982, 1984) examined the markets for a two-period asset (without uncertainty) and found that when the first period spot market was supplemented with a futures market for period two delivery, convergence to equilibrium was speeded up. Theirs was the first laboratory evidence to provide qualitative support to Hicks' (1939), Danthine's (1978) and Grossman's (1977) idea that futures markets help disseminate the private information about the future plans and price expectations of various agents in an economy, thus increasing the informational and allocative efficiency of the spot market.

While there was no payoff uncertainty in the Forsythe, Palfrey, and Plott experiments, perfect foresight equilibrium in the first period of the asset life could not be reached until the traders learned the equilibrium price in the second (and the last) period of the asset life. Even with subjects who had participated in previous asset double auctions, it took eight replications for the transaction prices in the first period to enter the neighborhood of the perfect foresight equilibrium prediction (see top panel of Figure 6.1). Then they added a period A futures market for period B delivery. The bottom panel of Figure 6.1 shows the transaction price data from this session. The higher set of dots represent transactions in period A spot market while the lower set of dots represent transactions that occurred in period A for a futures contract for period B delivery. Introduction of futures trading had two effects. First, as indicated by the absence of any dots in period B in the lower panel of Figure 6.1, spot market trading in period B dried up completely. Second, the period A spot price converged close to the perfect foresight equilibrium level of 845 by the end of the first trial itself (instead of the eighth trial in the upper panel). Existence of the side-by-side futures and asset markets made it easier for each trader to estimate the perfect foresight value of the asset.

Forsythe, Palfrey, and Plott (1984) reported that the variance of spot prices increases in the presence of futures markets. This result is consistent with the notion that futures prices enable more information to be promptly incorporated into prices, and greater volatility of spot prices in the presence of futures is simply reflective of this faster adjustment process. Like cholesterol, there seems to be good and bad volatility—good if it is caused by more precise tracking of rational expectations equilibrium and bad if it arises for any other reason.[5] They also found that the allocative efficiency of the market is higher with futures markets than without.

Friedman, Harrison, and Salmon (1983) extended the Forsythe, Palfrey, and Plott (1982, 1984) experiments by adding a third period to the life of their assets. Subject experience and existence of a futures market in the first and the second period for the third period delivery were the two treatment variables in their experiment. They confirmed that the presence of a futures market speeds up convergence to perfect foresight equilibrium price. However, contrary to prior results, they also found that the presence of a futures market reduces allocative efficiency as well as price volatility in the spot market.[6] The authors attribute the lower efficiency of their futures markets to aberrant behavior of a single trader (out of a total of nine). Addition of a third period to asset lives made these markets considerably more complex, and the reported results are based on six sessions of only three to five replications of three period cycles. With computerized auctions, it should be possible to run many more replications. Resolution of these paradoxical results remains open.

In their second study, Friedman, Harrison, and Salmon (1984) added state uncertainty by using two-state, three-period assets and introduced information asymmetry by giving perfect information about the realized state of nature to three traders (one of each dividend type). In Figure 6.6, x's in the upper panel show that the transaction prices in a spot market without concurrent futures markets have difficulty converging to the perfect foresight equilibrium prices corresponding to the realized state (shown by solid horizontal lines). Introduction of futures trading in periods A and B (for period C delivery) promoted dissemination of information given to insiders. This can be seen in the lower panel of Figure 6.6 where spot market transaction prices (x's) in periods A and B are closer to their respective perfect foresight equilibrium prices (indicated by solid horizontal lines) in the presence of futures transactions (indicated by o's). Consistent with their previous paper, they could not find evidence that the futures markets induce higher allocative efficiency in spot markets. The presence of futures markets stabilizes transaction prices (lower coefficient of variation), especially in the presence of event uncertainty. This finding is consistent with some, but not all of the field studies of price volatility reviewed by Cox (1976). For example, Working (1960) and Gray (1977) in onion futures, Tomek (1971) in wheat futures, and Powers (1970) in pork belly futures found that price volatility is lower in the presence of concurrent futures markets in the field. On the other hand, on the basis of laboratory experiments, Forsythe, Palfrey, and Plott (1984) reached the opposite conclusions on price stability as well as efficiency and gave some plausible reasons why such might be the case.

In summary, experimental studies agree on the positive effects futures trading has on speeding the convergence of price to an informationally efficient equilibrium and do not support Svensson's (1976) predictions to the contrary about price. On price stability and allocative efficiency, the laboratory results seem to be no more consistent than the field studies so far.

Three other derivative securities—state-contingent options, call options, and

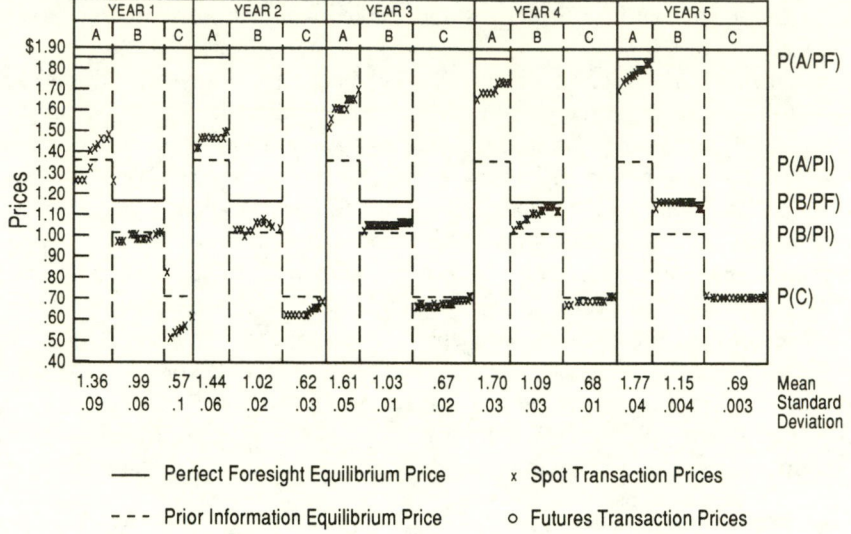

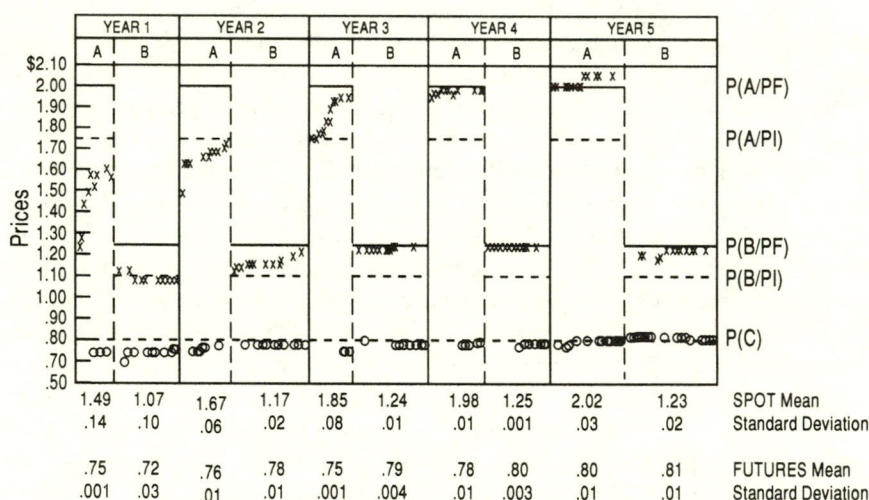

Figure 6.6. Effect of futures trading on asset markets. Top: Experiment 1. Bottom: Experiment 2. *Source:* Friedman, Harrison and Salmon 1984, figures 5 and 6, enhanced for clarity of exposition.

put options—have been examined for their effect on market behavior in laboratory settings. Derivative securities expand traders' message space and render the market less incomplete. Plott and Sunder (1988) found that when they introduced Arrow-Debreu state-contingent options, information and allocational efficiency of markets increased dramatically (see Figure 6.3 and its discussion in the section on information aggregation above). Kluger and Wyatt (1990) introduced a call option to a two-state, single-period asset environment and found that the presence of call options in the market speeded up the convergence of price to the informa-

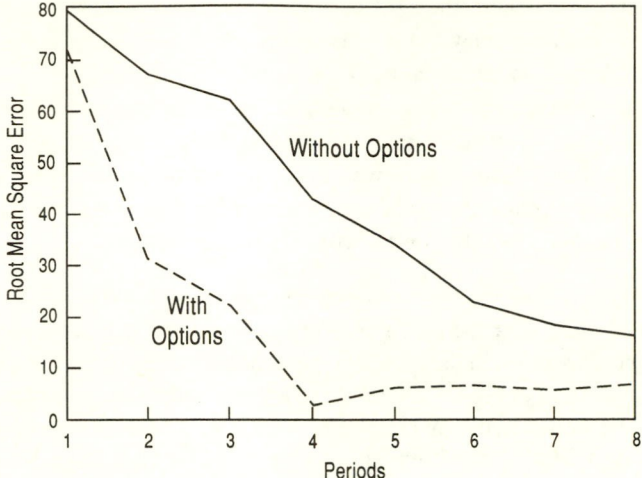

Figure 6.7. Mean squared error of asset prices with and without options traded. *Source:* Drawn by the author on the basis of data from Kluger and Wyatt (1990, appendix A).

tionally efficient equilibrium level (see Figure 6.7). Allocative efficiency of these markets also increased.

Kluger and Wyatt (1990) also used the observed option and asset prices to estimate the implied volatility of asset prices and compared these estimates to the volatility of full information aggregation asset prices. The results suggest that traders used option prices to estimate the variability of asset prices across states. O'Brien and Srivastava are currently experimenting with call and put options in two-period, three-state asset markets with diverse information. The laboratory evidence to date lends support to the idea that the presence of option type derivative securities increases the informational efficiency of asset markets. The theory (see Ross 1976), the field data (see Manaster and Rendleman 1982; Jennings and Starks 1986), and the laboratory evidence seem to converge to the same conclusion.

III. Bubbles and False Equilibria

Can market value of assets become unhinged from its "fundamentals" and become dependent solely on free-floating expectations? Is Keynes's (1936, 156) oft-quoted description of stock markets accurate?

> Or, to change the metaphor slightly, professional investment may be likened to those newspaper competitions in which the competitors have to pick out the six prettiest faces from a hundred photographs, the prize being awarded to the competitor whose choice most nearly corresponds to the average preferences of the competitors as a whole; so that each competitor has to pick,

not those faces which he himself finds the prettiest, but those which he thinks likeliest to catch the fancy of the other competitors, all of whom are looking at the problem from the same point of view. It is not the case of choosing those which, to the best of one's judgment, are really the prettiest, nor even those which the average opinion genuinely thinks the prettiest. We have reached the third degree where we devote our intelligences to anticipating what average opinion expects the average opinion to be. And there are some, I believe, who practice the fourth, fifth and higher degrees.

Of course, if each competitor believed his own opinion to be the best estimate of the opinion of the others, the outcome of the competition will not come unhinged from the fundamentals—in this case, the personal opinions of the individual competitors. Answers to questions about the existence and formation of bubbles and false equilibria depend on how people form their beliefs and expectations.

In a world of uncertainty, "fundamentals" get replaced by expectations about the fundamentals. Mutual dependence of current prices and current expectations about the future yields two types of bubble theories. First, deviation of asset price from its intrinsic value can be compounded over time in rational expectations equilibrium to form a bubble (see Tirole 1982). When individuals have finite decision horizons and markets are incomplete, one cannot guarantee that asset prices will not create such a bubble. Second, "sunspot" equilibria arise when agents form certain arbitrary beliefs that alter the fundamentals of the economy in such a way that such beliefs become self-fulfilling (see Evans 1989).

Formal models either rely on a consistency condition such as rational expectations or use Bayesian revision with some ad hoc prior and likelihood function, or use some ad hoc adaptive process. Given the key role of assumptions about belief formation in economics, surprisingly little work has been done in modeling and testing the theories of belief formation within environments where market discipline prevails. It is difficult to gather reliable data on beliefs and expectations from the field. It is almost never possible to rule out the chance that the apparent generation and bursting of bubbles in the field data is due to some information unknown to the researchers.[7] Laboratory testing of bubbles phenomena has the advantage that the researcher has access to and control of the information structure of such markets. Consequently, experimental methods are now being applied to study bubbles.

Many interesting experiments on formation of expectations have concerned inflation. Daniels and Plott (1988), Lim, Prescott, and Sunder (1994), Marimon and Sunder (1993, 1994), Marimon, Spear, and Sunder (1993), and McCabe (1989) are examples of this work. However, the substantive matter of these papers will take us on a digression from asset markets, the main concerns of this review. Jack Ochs's "Coordination Problems" in this volume reviews this literature. I shall therefore limit attention on the study of bubbles and false equilibria in asset markets.[8]

Sunder (1992) reported observations of false equilibria in markets for single-period, two-state assets with insider information (see period 10 in lower panel of Figure 6.4). Each trader had to decide each period whether to buy perfect information about the state at a fixed price (see the section on market for information above for further details of the design). In early periods of these markets, six or more out of twelve traders chose to pay the price of being informed, and the asset markets converged to rational expectations equilibrium revealing the state of nature to those who did not buy information. As the advantages of free riding became apparent, the number of traders willing to pay the fixed price of information dropped. False equilibria were observed only in the later periods of markets when at least one trader was informed, the number but not the identity of the informed traders was common knowledge, short sale restrictions were in place, and no more than one trader was informed on the buyer side of the market. By later periods, most, if not all, traders had acquired some confidence in their ability to infer the state of nature from observing the market. Common knowledge about the positive number of informed traders gave them reason to think that the market does have the information about the state. The short sale restriction prevented the informed traders on the sell side of the asset market from exploiting their information to the fullest extent, thus preventing its revelation through the price. The information monopolist on the buy side of the asset market had the ability to maintain a false equilibrium at a low price without fear of competition from other informed buyers.[9] The combination of these circumstances created opportunities for false equilibria to develop in five (out of twenty-one) periods; such equilibria were actually observed in three periods.

Theoretical predictions about such false equilibria were made by Beja (1976), Grossman (1976) and Milgrom (1981). When traders know the state-price correspondence and have reasons to believe that the market provides them with information better than their own private information, they may have reasons to discard their private information and rely entirely on the market to inform them. Under these circumstances, market variables can become self-fulfilling, and any price from the state-price correspondence is sustainable. False equilibrium is observed when price is sustained at a level that does not correspond to the realized state of nature. These conditions seem to have been approximated in some periods of Sunder's (1992) markets described above.

Having discovered that inferring state from price can sometimes lead them astray, traders may be less confident in repeating such behavior in subsequent periods. Verifying if, and when, this higher order of learning takes place will take even longer and require more experiments and replications. Virtually all stories of stock manipulation depend, at least in part, on the willingness and tendency of some traders to infer the state of nature from observable market actions of others, while the manipulators exploit this tendency by also engaging in non-observable actions at the same time.[10]

Short sale restriction is an exogenously imposed rule of the market. Removal of short sale restriction permits informed traders to exploit their information to the maximum possible extent until price adjusts to eliminate such opportunity to profit. It is therefore possible that false equilibria could be eliminated simply by removing the short sale restriction. The rationale for imposing the short sale restrictions in laboratory economies is essentially the same as in the stock exchanges—to reduce the chances of bankruptcy among traders. If short sale restriction turns out to be the cause of such inefficient equilibria, it would be the collective price paid by the market participants to reduce the welfare losses associated with the possibility and actual occurrences of bankruptcy.

Camerer and Weigelt (1990b) searched for false equilibria (which they refer to as "mirages") in markets similar to Sunder's (1992). During each period the number of informed traders was chosen to be either zero or six (out of twelve). However, unlike Sunder (1992), the number of informed traders in their experiments was not announced. The absence of knowledge about the number of informed traders in any given period created a possibility that some traders may incorrectly believe that the information is present. Such beliefs may induce actions that help bring the observed market variables close to equilibrium values for one of the two states of nature. They reported observing four false equilibria out of a possible forty-seven periods when the number of informed traders was zero.

For example, consider the transaction price data for period 6 in Figure 6.8. The three types of horizontal lines mark the three different types of equilibrium price predictions for the information conditions prevailing in the respective periods. The price of individual transactions is plotted on the vertical scale against transaction sequence number on the horizontal scale. The period number is followed by a code for information condition and the mean of transaction prices for the period. Code W (warmup) means that the state was not determined; X(Y) means that half the traders in the market were informed that X(Y) dividend will be paid while the other half were uninformed about the state; N means that no trader knew the state, though this lack of information was not common knowledge.

In period 6, code N indicates that nobody knew the state of the world. The no-information equilibrium price of 265 is shown by a horizontal line. Had the information condition been X or Y, rational expectations equilibrium price would have been 375 or 175, respectively. As can be seen from Figure 6.8, the market opened with a transaction at 350 and closed at 365 with a maximum price of 370. It is clear from transaction prices (as well as from asset allocations not shown here) that in period 6 the traders behaved as if they were virtually certain that this was an X period, even though, in fact, nobody had any information. A few temporary "mirages" that did not last for a whole period were also observed. Several other periods in Figure 6.8 indicate prices far in excess of the equilibrium level; these were not classified as mirages because the asset allocations did not match with the rational expectations equilibrium allocations for the observed price. Watts (1993) independently conducted experiments with a similar research design and observed only one period of false equilibrium out of a possible thirty-one.

There is an important difference between the false equilibria reported by Sunder and by Camerer and Weigelt. In the former, false equilibria occurred in the

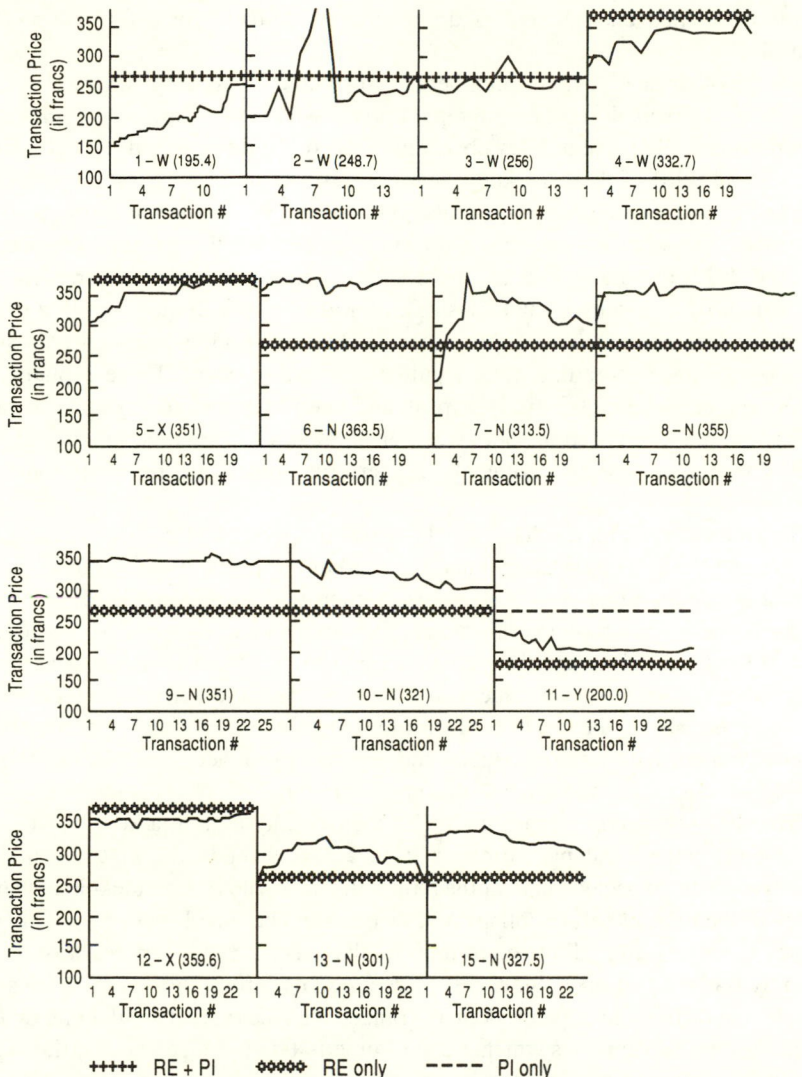

+++++ RE + PI   ◆◆◆◆◆ RE only   ---- PI only

Figure 6.8. Formation of an information mirage in a market: time series of transaction prices. *Source:* Camerer and Weigelt 1990, figure 2.

second half of the experiments after the traders had learned the state-price correspondence and had discovered that they could free ride on market information as long as they knew that other trader(s) in the market were informed. After the first half a dozen or so periods, convergence of the asset market to rational expectations equilibrium became plainly obvious to many traders. Establishment of rational expectations equilibrium in the asset market led more and more traders to realize that they did not have to buy information in order to become informed. When enough traders dropped their demand for information, false equilibria arose.

On the other hand, with the number of informed traders being either zero or six, Camerer and Weigelt report more rapid trading with fewer unaccepted bids/offers when insiders are present. They observed false equilibria in periods that constitute the second third of their markets because, they explain, by then the traders had learned the state-price correspondence, but had not yet learned to distinguish between the presence or absence of informed traders on the basis of the pace of trading. It is possible to attribute these false equilibria to traders' overreaction to the similarity of the first few trades of a period to trades in the preceding period in which insiders happened to be present.[11] Once the traders learned to discriminate by the pace of trading, false equilibria ceased to occur. These explanations from both papers are essentially ex post, and need to be verified by more detailed investigation. The question about whether the behavior observed in these experiments represents the end point of the learning process in these environments remains open.

The most surprising results to date have been reported by Smith, Suchanek, and Williams (1988) using a double auction market for a fifteen-period asset which paid a dividend, either zero or x_1, x_2, or x_3, each with probability 0.25, at the end of each period. For risk-neutral traders, the asset had an expected value of $15 \Sigma x_i/4$ in the first period, and this value declined by $\Sigma x_i/4$ each period. The values of x_i were the same for all traders, and the structure, including zero redemption value of the asset at the end of the fifteenth period, was common knowledge. Risk neutral traders with rational beliefs, and common knowledge of rational beliefs, would have no reason to trade in this environment.

Yet, they observed vigorous trading in their twenty-eight markets, as well as a persistent tendency of prices to rise from a low level in the first few periods (relative to the expected value of the remaining dividends) to an inexplicable high level in the middle before collapsing towards the end (see Figure 6.9). This tendency to engage in trading and to transact the asset at bubble prices was attenuated by trader experience. Since this market had no information asymmetries, the results are difficult to explain. Perhaps traders start the markets with quite diverse home-grown expectations which are not immediately homogenized by the experimenter's instructions. Common knowledge may not be easily imparted. It is also possible that individual traders have very different ways of adapting their beliefs to market observations, and the model they use to adapt their own beliefs is not necessarily consistent with the model used to adapt their beliefs about others' beliefs. Thus, a trader who believes that a "greater fool" would buy the asset at an even higher price in the future, may buy it now at a price that exceeds its fundamental value.

King et al. (1990) conducted further experiments to determine if the frequency or size of bubbles might be reduced by short selling, availability of credit to buy assets on margin, brokerage fees, limits on price changes, subjects familiar with the results of prior bubble experiments, and subjects drawn from the world of business. Their results, discussed in more detail in the section on public

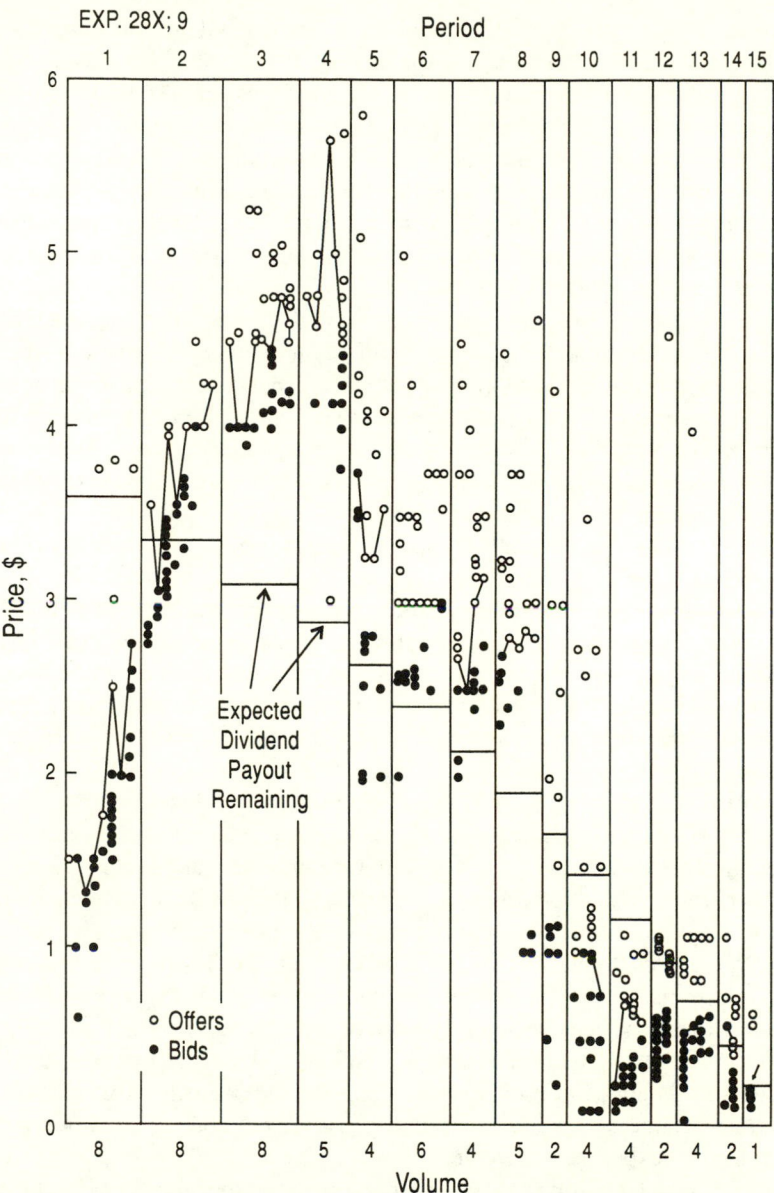

Figure 6.9. Formation and bursting of a bubble. *Source:* Smith, Suchanek, and Williams 1988, figure 9.

policy, suggest that none of these treatments have any significant impact on the occurrence of bubbles. Of all the factors they tested, repeat experience in trading in this specific environment is the only one that reduces bubbles. Porter and Smith (1989) found that neither the elimination of dividend uncertainty nor the introduction of futures markets eliminates price bubbles in this setting; existence of futures markets does reduce the amplitude of the bubble significantly. Given Porter and Smith's result, it is not surprising that, when King (1990) sold perfect information about the dividend to three or four of the nine traders in his markets, it had little effect on the incidence of bubbles.

Current work to generate a consistent explanation of Smith, Suchanek, and Williams' (1988) results focuses on careful examination of instructions, increasing the depth of markets, and making subjects responsible for paying any losses they may incur out of their pockets, and introduction of cross-market arbitrage opportunities. At the time of this review, lack of repeat experience alone seems to be the simplest and most likely explanation of Smith, Suchanek, and Williams' results. Few asset markets with uncertainty get close to equilibrium in less than four or five replications or trials. In case of a single-period asset, each period is a trial. However, for a fifteen-period asset, one cycle of 15 periods is a single trial, two cycles are two trials, and so on. Since a single experimental session may have time enough for only one trial of a fifteen-period asset, several sessions are needed to impart the same level of experience to subjects as could be imparted in a few periods of a single-period asset market. If this explanation holds up, the Smith, Suchanek, and Williams results may not turn out to be so surprising after all.

Camerer and Weigelt (1990a) experimented with an indefinitely-lived asset that had probability 0.15 of being extinguished at the end of any period. The dividends were diverse across subject and were privately and perfectly known to them. Since the probability of extinguishment is analytically equivalent to a discount rate on an infinitely lived asset, they examined such markets for occurrences of bubbles. In eleven out of twelve markets, bubbles failed to materialize, and subjects in the twelfth market had participated in an experiment in which price inflation had been exogenously induced. Camerer and Weigelt's experiment failed to support the bubbles observed in Smith et al.'s fifteen-period asset markets. Given indefinite life of asset in Camerer and Weigelt's experiment, one might have expected a greater chance of generating bubbles. This difference between the two experiments remains to be explained.

Perhaps a useful distinction can be drawn between the sources of bubbles and the false equilibria. The false equilibria arise when some traders *incorrectly* believe that the state of nature is, say, X, when in fact it is Y (as in Sunder 1984, 1992) or when it is, in fact, unknown (as in Camerer and Weigelt 1985). The bubbles, on the other hand, arise when some traders believe that other traders, for whatever reasons, would be willing to pay more than the asset was worth and decide to pay a high price themselves in the hope of extracting some capital gains. In bubbles experiments, there is market or strategic uncertainty, even though there is no state uncertainty.

IV. Learning and Dynamics

How is information aggregated and disseminated in asset markets? In these markets, traders must not only learn about the trading opportunities made available to them by the market, but they must also infer the state of the world from market data. In simpler commodity double auctions only the first of these two issues is present. In spite of some progress, (Wilson 1982; Friedman 1984; Easley and Ledyard 1986; and Gode and Sunder 1993a, 1993b, 1994), convergence in these simple double auctions is not well understood. Dynamics of information aggregation and dissemination is even more complex because the knowledge of trading opportunities affects prices, prices are used to infer the state, and this inference about the state itself affects the prices and alters the trading opportunities.

A. Adjustment Path

It is not clear that an obvious learning sequence exists to disseminate and aggregate information in asset markets. Jordan (1983) and Kobayashi (1977) examined a model of tâtonnement adjustment in which agents first use their private information to express their demands and supplies, so the market converges to a temporary private information equilibrium. The knowledge of this temporary equilibrium is included in the traders' information set that determines their demands in the next iteration of tatonnement. These iterations continue until no trader chooses to revise her demand. This process generally converges to rational expectations equilibrium. This iterative tatonnement imposes a synchronized sequence of alternate steps of generating market data from information sets and generating information sets from market data across all traders. Nontatonnement processes such as double auctions have no mechanism for enforcing such a synchronized sequence *within* a trading period. Whether convergence would actually occur in such processes is a matter for empirical observation and more detailed modeling of dynamics.

Experimental studies reveal that learning of rational expectations equilibrium does not always occur successfully in double auctions. Plott and Sunder (1982, 1988), Forsythe and Lundholm (1990), and O'Brien and Srivastava (1991b, 1991c) show some evidence that, as suggested by Jordan and Kobayashi models, private information equilibrium provides a better description of data from early periods of an auction; the performance of rational expectations equilibrium as a description of data improves in later periods, even when it fails to dominate the prior information equilibrium. However, this process does not capture many observed aspects of information aggregation.

B. Variables That Transmit Information

Several attempts have been made to form and test conjectures about the nature of the learning process in asset markets on the basis of experimental data. Though formal models of equilibrium rely largely, if not exclusively, on price as the vehicle for transmission of information in markets, traders also observe many other variables such as bids, asks, identity of traders, timing, intensity and volume of bids, asks, and transactions. In oral auctions, eye contact, voice, laughter or side remarks provide additional vehicles for communication. It is not unusual to observe that, after some experience with replications, the very first transaction of a period occurs at a price close to the rational expectations equilibrium and away from the prior information equilibrium (see, for example, period 8 in Figure 6.3). On the basis of such observations, it is easy to reject the proposition that transaction prices are the sole vehicles for transmission of information in markets. Unaccepted bids and offers that precede the transactions play an important role.

DeJong et al. (1991) conducted a computerized replication of two of Plott and Sunder's (1982) oral double auctions by restricting the information available to each trader. These traders could only learn, in real time, the current bid, the current ask, and the price of their own transactions; the computer masked the price of others' transactions, and the identities of traders associated with bids, asks, or transactions. These markets did disseminate information from the insiders to the uninformed and converged to rational expectations equilibrium, though the speed of dissemination indicated by the extra profits was slower. Bids, asks, trader's own transaction prices and their timing seem sufficient for information dissemination. In the context of a double auction, it is difficult to see how the information available to the traders could be cut any further.

The identity of traders is salient in oral auctions but not in computer auctions. Plott and Sunder (1982) used a fixed set of insiders across all periods of each market and conjectured that the ability of the uninformed to identify the informed traders might be important. A questionnaire survey of the traders failed to support this conjecture. Banks (1985) also conjectured that the fixed identity of the insiders might be a key to rational expectations convergence, possibly by making it easier for their identity to be revealed. However, the performance of his markets in which the identity of the informed was changed each period was substantially unchanged. Identification of the insiders does not appear to be a necessary condition for rational expectations convergence. Whether such identification facilitates convergence remains unverified.

The availability of various market variables and the timing of their availability to various market participants are important features of the rules of most markets. For example, information on the outstanding bids and asks in the specialist's book in the New York Stock Exchange is not available to people who are not on the Exchange floor. In addition, a specialist may hold working orders from traders that may not be entered in the book at all, and revealed selectively to traders on the floor at the specialist's discretion. Communication among traders in computerized trading systems is both limited and more detailed, as compared to the information available in oral auctions. Designing the rules of an asset market may be facilitated by better understanding the role of each element of communication among traders.

C. Learning Sequences

At least two kinds of learning are identifiable in asset markets: (1) about the realized state of the world, and (2) about the state-equilibrium correspondence. At the beginning of the first period of a market, the uninformed agents do not know the state of the world for that period, and due to heterogeneity of preferences or dividends that are private, no agent knows what the price would be under any given state. Formal models of learning in markets usually focus on learning about the state. However, learning about the state cannot occur unless traders learn the equilibrium price and net trade correspondence associated with each state. Applied to experimental markets, this reasoning suggests that traders must first learn about prices associated with various states before they can hope to infer the state from prices.

Profit data can be used to distinguish these two types of learning in a market. Given the flat demand and vertical supply in the Plott and Sunder (1982) markets (see Figure 6.2), transactions at equilibrium price award the entire surplus to the equilibrium sellers and none to the equilibrium buyers. Transactions at equilibrium price distribute the total payoff equally among equilibrium buyers and sellers. If information is evenly distributed among the equilibrium buyers and sellers, equality of payoffs earned by the two groups of traders indicates that the equilibrium price correspondence has been revealed to the traders and understood by them.

Even if the equilibrium price correspondence were known to all traders, uninformed traders may fail to arrive at the correct inference about the realized state for a particular period and, therefore, receive a smaller payoff than the informed traders. Equality of payoff between informed and the uninformed traders is, therefore, an indication of learning about the state.

Plott and Sunder (1982) used convergence of equilibrium buyers' and sellers' profits as a measure of learning the price for a given state, and convergence of the period profits of the informed and the uninformed traders as a measure of learning the state given the market price. Figure 6.10 shows the ratio of profits of equilibrium buyers/sellers and of informed/uninformed traders for the market shown in Figure 6.3. By these measures, it appears that these two kinds of learning occur simultaneously, not sequentially as suggested by comparative static models. However, since profit data are measured by period, they do not rule out the possibility that sequential learning occurs *within* the trading periods.

Forsythe, Palfrey, and Plott (1982) noted that in their markets for two-period assets, convergence to equilibrium in period B *preceded* the convergence in period A in the sense that it took fewer replications (see upper panel of Figure 6.1). This "swingback" phenomenon suggests that learning in markets is sequential. Since all the data needed to arrive at perfect foresight equilibrium in period B was immediately available to the traders, period B markets converged early. Perfect foresight demands, supplies, and, therefore, the equilibrium for period A depended on the knowledge of period B market value of the asset. Equilibrium in

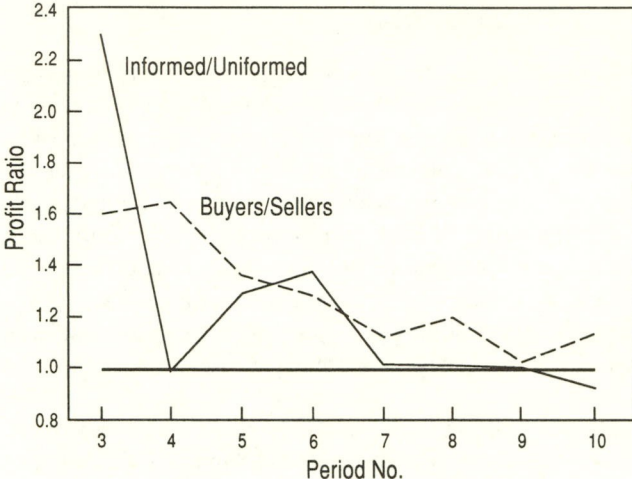

Figure 6.10. Ratio of profits of buyers/sellers and Ratio of profits of informed/uniformed. *Source:* Drawn by the author on the basis of data given in the working paper version of Plott and Sunder (1982).

period A, therefore, followed the period B equilibrium. Introduction of period A futures market for period B delivery speeded up the process by speeding up the availability of information about period B equilibrium. In any case, perfect foresight, when it is observed in market behavior, must be *acquired* through historical observation and experience.

Anderson, Johnston, Walker, and Williams (1991) examined computerized markets for three-period assets similar to the oral markets of Friedman, Harrison and Salmon (1983) and found that the convergence to perfect foresight equilibrium takes place only after the subjects acquire a great deal of experience:

> Although it is not clear how these very subtle institutional and procedural differences can explain the behavior discrepancy between our experiments and the two reported by FHS, it is clear that there is more driving these markets than is captured by either the simple perfect foresight or prior information models. Our interpretation is that trading based on capital gains expectations is quite common. This is most readily apparent when we observe prices in excess of the PF equilibrium prediction in the first year of trading. It is unclear why subjects have such expectations in the absence of prior relevant market information. Speculative trading at prices well above a level supported by an asset's intrinsic dividend value is, however, quite consistent with results reported by Smith, Suchanek and Williams (1988) in PLATO double auction asset markets with a 15-period time horizon. The repetitive stationarity of market years appears to be a critical factor leading to the deterioration of these expectations. In the experiments using experienced subjects, the improvement in the predictive ability of the PF model is at least in part due to subjects "learning" to have common expectations that are supported by the exogenous dividend structure.

Bronfman (1990) estimated the decision functions of traders by replicating Smith, Suchanek, and Williams (1988) experiments modified to yield one-period-ahead price forecasts from each trader. She concludes that the trader behavior of the type reported by Smith, Suchanek, and Williams is more consistent with their extrapolating market trends than with their use of intrinsic values. Following intraperiod price movements as trends explains an important part of the data gathered in these experiments. Obviously intrinsic values must play a role too, especially in the behavior of experienced traders. This role has not been isolated in Bronfman's study.

D. Aggregate Uncertainty

Dynamics of information aggregation seem to be affected by aggregate uncertainty and the number of trades. There are empirical suggestions in several studies that the observed behavior of asset markets corresponds more closely to equilibrium predictions when there is no aggregate uncertainty in the market about the state of the world (Plott and Sunder 1982; O'Brien and Srivastava 1991b). Lundholm (1991) subjected this proposition to formal tests. He modified Plott and Sunder's (1988) asset market design (single, three-state asset with single period life, identical dividends across all traders; see the section on aggregation of information above) by adding a fourth state and by making dividends common knowledge among the traders. In markets *without* aggregate uncertainty, he distributed imperfect information signals to individuals in such a way as to eliminate aggregate uncertainty. For example, when state X was realized, one third of the traders in the market learned that the state was "not Y," another third learned that it was "not Z" and "not W," respectively. The markets *with* aggregate uncertainty were created by withholding one of the three "not" signals from the traders. He found that efficiency of asset markets increases when aggregate uncertainty is eliminated. He also found that, contrary to general belief, an increase in the number of traders does not necessarily increase the speed or precision of information aggregation. Both these effects are consistent with individual differences in risk attitudes and information processing. These individual differences become more important in the presence of aggregate uncertainty. As the number of traders increases, so does the range between the extremes, making it more difficult for traders to draw consistent inferences from observed data.

E. Role of Arbitrage

The preceding discussion suggests that dissemination of information in asset markets is a complex process involving many observables and trader inferences. As a first cut, it is useful to find out how much of the information dissemination or aggregation can be understood in terms of arbitrage behavior alone, that is, by traders' attempts to make profits on the basis of the private information in their possession without exposing themselves to any risk.

For example, consider series B markets reported by Plott and Sunder (1988) (see the section on information aggregation above) in which a complete set of single-state-contingent claims are traded in an environment with no aggregate uncertainty. Since every trader was given information to rule out one of the three possible states of nature, competition in the markets for claims corresponding to the two "not states" drove the prices of these claims to zero; any price other than zero would have offered opportunity for riskless arbitrage to more than one trader. Once these prices went to zero, rational expectations equilibrium in the market for claim corresponding to the realized state could be arrived at by either the arbitrage argument, or by simple inference of the third state when the remaining two have been ruled out on the basis of the market phenomena observable to all. Such opportunities were not available to traders in the incomplete markets (e.g., the last four periods in Figure 6.4) when a single compound asset was traded; these markets failed to aggregate information.

O'Brien and Srivastava (1991c) developed a formal theory using the arbitrage arguments. They identify a set of "separating portfolios" whose price must go to zero, based on private information of traders, if the markets in which they trade are free of arbitrage, liquid, and perfectly competitive. Complete markets always have sufficient number of separating portfolios, so the full exploitation of arbitrage opportunities in these markets implies full aggregation of information. However, full aggregation of information does not always require the markets to be complete in the traditional sense of that term; O'Brien and Srivastava define "informationally complete" markets that have enough separating portfolios to ensure that the absence of unexploited arbitrage opportunities implies information aggregation. They suggest that even redundant securities can play a useful role in information aggregation.

This theory only says that if an informationally complete market is perfectly liquid and if traders do not leave any arbitrage opportunities unexploited, then the market must be at rational expectations equilibrium. Whether a market that is designed to be informationally complete is actually observed to be liquid and arbitrage free depends on the depth of competition, trading institution, trader incentives, and their behavioral characteristics. O'Brien and Srivastava present empirical evidence from 16-trader double auction markets that (1) zero arbitrage and liquidity (and therefore information aggregation) are observed, but not always; (2) competition reduces arbitrage; and (3) availability of separating portfolios facilitates information aggregation. These empirical results are consistent with the results reported in Plott and Sunder (1988).

F. Generation of Bids and Asks

In their "bubble" experiments, Smith, Suchanek, and Williams (1988) show that price change from period t to $t + 1$ follows excess number of bids over offers (or offers over bids) in period t. They suggest that the large number of unaccepted bids in period t generate the capital gain expectation in period $t + 1$. Why excess bids or offers arise in the first place remains open.

O'Brien and Srivastava (1991b) proposed a simple rule for constructing a range for bids and asks submitted by individual traders based on the prior information in their possession at the beginning of the period and the price of completed transactions since the beginning of the period. After n transactions have been completed in a period at prices $p_1, p_2, \ldots p_n$, range for the next bid is given by

$$p_{n+1}^b < \text{Min } \{(n\, p_n^b + p_n) / (n + 1), \text{Max dividend}\},$$

where p_0^b is the bidder's expected dividend given his initial information at the beginning of the period. The ask range for offers is analogously defined as

$$p_{n+1}^a > \text{Max } \{(n\, p_n^a + p_n) / (n + 1), \text{Min dividend}\},$$

where p_0^a is the asker's expected dividend given his initial information. They reported that only some 5 to 18% of actual bids and asks fell outside these ranges. This explanatory power is high, especially when one notes that these ranges are constructed after each transaction without any strategic considerations. On the other hand, these ranges are open on the safe side (low bids and high offers) and cannot be violated in that direction.

This brief review suggests that the experimental literature on asset markets has so far been focused on discovering conditions under which market data may or may not be well described by various static models of equilibrium. Explorations of learning and dynamics has been carried out mostly as an afterthought. Experiments have, however, produced valuable data to support efforts for building dynamic theories.

V. Econometric Comparisons of Field and Laboratory Data

A. Variance Bound Tests

LeRoy and Porter (1981) argued that if securities are efficiently priced in a market, variance of security prices should not exceed the variance of the discounted present value of dividends. Shiller (1981) has shown that the variance of realized stock prices significantly exceeds the variance of discounted present value of dividends *actually realized* in the subsequent years. Since researchers have no way of knowing the ex ante distribution of future dividends, or discount rates, field tests of this idea must necessarily be based on some assumption about this distribution (e.g., it is identical to the realized distribution in the subsequent periods).

This difficulty of testing the theory on field data has given rise to a lengthy and inconclusive debate (see Camerer 1989). Those who believe in market rationality claim that their null hypothesis remains to be rejected, while others claim that the null hypothesis of excess volatility stands (see Marsh and Merton 1986; Shiller 1986). In laboratory environments, ex ante distribution of dividends is known to the researcher, making it possible to conduct more powerful tests of the excess volatility hypothesis. O'Brien and Srivastava (1991b) have reported some preliminary tests of this type on laboratory data on two-period securities. But they did not utilize the fact that ex ante distribution of dividends is known in laboratory data. Variance bound tests that utilize this advantage of laboratory data on long-lived assets should make a useful contribution to this open debate.

B. Arbitrage Relationships

In a great deal of efficient markets literature in finance, it has been held that the absence of arbitrage opportunities in the market implies that the price reflects all information available to the market participants. If the price at any time does not reflect the information, the argument goes, it would be possible for traders to make money through riskless arbitrage until the no-arbitrage condition holds. An important contribution of experimental work to finance has been a demonstration that the absence of arbitrage opportunities in a market *does not* imply informational efficiency.

Plott and Sunder (1982) subjected their transaction price data to three kinds of statistical tests—mechanical filter tests, serial correlation of log price changes, and frequency distribution of log price changes. All tests were applied to within-period transaction data. They found that certain statistical characteristics of field data are shared with the data generated in laboratory.

Tests on transaction price data from stock exchanges suggest that it is difficult to devise mechanical trading rules that consistently yield abnormally high returns (see Alexander 1964; Fama and Blume 1966). Plott and Sunder (1982) compared the performance of three trading rules: (1) Buy and hold: buy one certificate at the opening transaction price of each period and liquidate at the closing transaction price of the period; (2) Trend filter: Observe transaction price trend from opening to current price; if positive, buy if necessary to hold one certificate; if negative, sell if necessary to maintain a short position of one certificate; liquidate at the closing transaction price; (3) y-unit filter: If the transaction price goes up by y or more units, buy if necessary to hold one certificate until the price goes down by y or more units, at which time sell if necessary to maintain a short position of one certificate until the price goes up again by y or more units; liquidate at closing price. Three different filter sizes ($y = 1, 5,$ and 25) were used in these tests.[12]

For the single-period security used in these markets, equilibrium return over time is zero. However, the naive buy-and-hold strategy yields a positive return in early periods that declines to zero as the asset markets converge to rational expectations equilibrium. Trend, one franc, and five franc filters perform almost as well as the naive buy-and-hold strategy, and the twenty-five franc filter performs worse. However, all returns approach zero as the market converges to rational expectations equilibrium. Trading strategy based on the knowledge of the rational expectations equilibrium price yields positive returns.

Plott and Sunder (1982) found that the first order serial correlation of log price relatives $\log(P_t/P_{t-1})$ is insignificantly different from zero. The magnitude of serial correlation does not seem to be affected by the presence of disequilibrium trades. All these tests suggest that serial dependence in price changes in data gathered from stock exchanges are shared by laboratory data for asset markets that converge to rational expectations equilibrium.

Plott and Sunder (1988) reported a surprising result when they applied similar filter tests to examine the transaction prices from series A markets that failed to converge to rational expectations equilibrium.[13] They found that the filter rules fail to generate abnormal profits, even though we know that these markets failed to aggregate information and did not converge to rational expectations equilibrium. Even more important, a trading strategy based on full knowledge of rational expectations equilibrium price, when applied ex post to the data generated in the laboratory, fails to beat the naive buy and hold strategy. This paradoxical result obtains because these markets consistently failed to converge to rational expectations price. Trading on the assumption that the price will reach the rational expectations level is not profitable if the price never gets there. The data from series B and C markets (that converged to rational expectations equilibrium) also did not permit filter rules to earn abnormal returns, but yielded superior returns to strategies based on the knowledge of rational expectations equilibrium price. These results led them to conclude that statistical independence of security price changes or absence of arbitrage opportunities in the market is not a sufficient condition for informational efficiency of the markets that generate such data.

These results and conclusions about the lack of one-to-one mapping between absence of arbitrage profits and informational efficiency of asset markets were confirmed and strengthened by O'Brien and Srivastava (1991b) who applied three separate statistical tests to their data. First, they applied ex post filter tests to bids and asks available in the market (instead of applying them to transaction prices actually observed). Mechanical trading rules could not make money in these informationally inefficient markets. Second, they applied Dickey and Fuller's (1981) unit root test to their price series obtained from markets that failed to aggregate information. They could not reject the unit root hypothesis in informationally inefficient markets. Third, they showed that in one of their multisecurity markets, there existed a portfolio whose value in periods 1 and 2 would differ by a constant amount, independent of information about the realized state of the world. They presented evidence that these riskless arbitrage relationships held reasonably well in their data, even though the asset markets did not always aggregate information.

Empirical foundations of efficient market theory were built on the assumption that statistical testing of price data from markets would reveal any inefficiencies. Validity of this assumption has gone largely unchallenged; since we do not know the equilibrium price in a naturally occurring market at any given time, no serious challenge based on data gathered from the field was possible. With all their other limitations, laboratory markets allow the economist to gather data with the knowledge of equilibrium price under various theories and make comparisons that are impossible to make with the field data. Now that such comparisons are possible and being made, serious doubts have arisen about the assumed equation between statistical efficiency and informational or allocative efficiency of markets.

VI. Investment and Public Policy

When proposals are made to effect changes in existing trading mechanisms or to introduce new mechanisms, government and private policymakers must assess their possible consequences. Novelty of proposals precludes the use of historical data as a basis of forming an opinion in most cases. Market microstructure literature has developed in recent years to use analytical techniques to address such questions (see Gorman 1976; Mendelson 1982; Ho and Stoll 1983; Glosten and Milgrom 1983; Amihud et al. 1985; Kyle 1985; Cohen et al. 1986; Schwartz 1988, for examples). However, as games of incomplete information, even simple trading mechanisms are extraordinarily complex to analyze. Study of alternative designs and performance characteristics of trading institutions is a promising niche for experimental economics in finance. Experimental studies have revealed several results that are important not only for investment policy but also for the design of trading mechanisms, and the manner in which they are regulated. A few studies on these lines are reviewed below.

A. Trading Suspensions and Price Change Limits

Coursey and Dyl (1990) explored the effects of trading suspension and price change limits on price, volume, and efficiency of two-state asset markets similar to those used by Plott and Sunder (1982). After allowing normal trading for five periods, they suspended trading for the next five periods after shifting the probabilities of the two states by a degree unknown to the traders. During trading suspension, traders continued to observe the realized state and receive the resulting dividends. In Figure 6.11, period-wise median of transaction prices has been plotted. Results of the first market, which had no trading suspension, are shown by a solid line. In contrast, results for the market with trading suspension are shown with a dotted line. Both can be compared against the equilibrium bench marks before and after the change in probabilities shown in a solid horizontal line. When trading resumed after suspension, transaction prices in these markets moved toward the new equilibrium level. However, adjustment of prices in markets without trading suspension was faster and more precise. Higher allocative efficiency was achieved in markets without trading suspension. Since the trading process itself is a part of the mechanism by which prices adjust to information, trading suspension does not promote such adjustment. Trading suspensions are often defended on the basis of their distributive consequences, to reduce the informational disadvantage of those who do not actively participate in the trading mechanism. This aspect of the consequences of trading suspensions remains to be explored.

Coursey and Dyl (1990) also examined the effect of imposing limits on the amount by which price could change in any single trading period. Again, they found that the imposition of a limit of 4 percent on the magnitude of price change

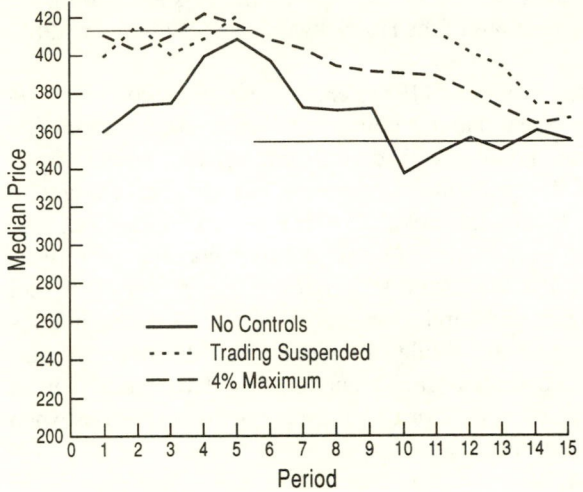

Figure 6.11. Effect of price change limits and trading suspensions in markets. *Source:* Coursey and Dyl 1990, figure 1.

from one period to the next slows down the process of adjustment of prices to information (unknown change in probabilities associated with dividends discussed in the previous paragraph) and reduces allocative efficiency (see dashed line in Figure 6.11). Other features of environments that may create demand for such limits (bankruptcy and default by margin traders, preferential access to information among geographically distributed traders) were absent in their research design and remain to be investigated.

B. Double Auction versus Call Market

Friedman (1993a) compared the performance of continuous double auction market and call market for Copeland and Friedman's (1993a) asset markets with uncertain dividends and asymmetric information. In a continuous double auction, a transaction is completed when an outstanding bid or ask is accepted by another trader; each period therefore consists of multiple bids, asks, and transactions, typically at different prices. In a call market, bids and asks are accumulated until some predetermined condition is fulfilled and the maximum possible number of transactions are simultaneously cleared at a single price per clearing.

Friedman (1993a) found that trading volume is higher in double auction, perhaps because the double auction allows each trader to be a gross buyer as well as a gross seller in the same period. Friedman (1993a) used three measures of efficiency to compare double auction and call markets. Actual transaction prices in a call market are closer (in root mean squared deviations) to the rational expectations price, than in a double auction. Call markets generate narrower bid/ask spreads, and their allocative efficiency is indistinguishable from the allocative efficiency of double auctions. Since most of the past work in asset markets has been done using only double auctions, these results may come as a surprise to

some experimentalists. Narrower bid/ask spreads of call markets are also inconsistent with the theoretical predictions of the Ho, Schwartz, and Whitcomb (1985)
model.

Liu (1992) repeated Plott and Sunder (1988) experiments with computerized
continuous and call auctions. She found that continuous double auctions are more
efficient when all traders are endowed with diverse information; however, call
auctions dominate when uninformed traders are present in the market along with
diversely informed insiders. Van Boening et al. (1992) repeated Smith, Sucharek,
and Williams' (1988) experiment in closed-book call markets and found little
change in results. Williams and Walker (1993) conducted one open-book call
market wth 300 subjects, again with similar results. This line of research holds
promise for further interesting results. While call markets may discover the equilibrium price more precisely, continuous double auctions may have the advantage
of faster (albeit less precise) discovery of price during the inter-call periods when
the call market leaves the price undefined.

C. Specialist Privileges and Book Display

Friedman (1993b) experimented with a variety of special privileges granted to
one or more traders in double auctions or call markets. All privileges bring significant extra profits to their beneficiaries. The privileges tested in double auctions
included (a) earlier receipt of order flow information, (b) ability to arbitrage cross-
ing bids and asks submitted by the traders who receive order flow information
with a time delay,[14] and (c) ability to submit bids and asks while other traders are
restricted to accept others' bids or offers. Allocative efficiency of the market as a
whole increases slightly under (a) and (b) but declines under (c). In call markets,
(a) last mover and (b) order flow access privileges are both modestly profitable and neither impairs allocative efficiency of the market. He also found that
where timely order flow information was distributed to *all* traders in a call market;
allocative efficiency of the market declined, probably due to strategic bidding
behavior.

D. Control of Speculative Bubbles

King et al. (1990) examined the effect of several institutional factors on the propensity of the market to generate price bubbles in an environment that is known
to generate bubbles. Nine to twelve traders have the opportunity to buy or sell a
fifteen-period asset in each period of its life. The asset yields to its holder a
dividend of 0, 8, 28, or 60¢ with equal probability each period. Equilibrium price
of the asset starts at $3.60 in the first period and declines each period in steps of
$0.24 to $0.24 in the last period. Equilibrium trading volume is zero; all dividend
information is common knowledge and there are no gains from trading. Yet this
environment generates bubbles in the middle third of the trading periods (see
discussion of Smith et al. [1988] in the section on bubbles above).

It might be argued that bubbles are created by over-optimistic traders, and

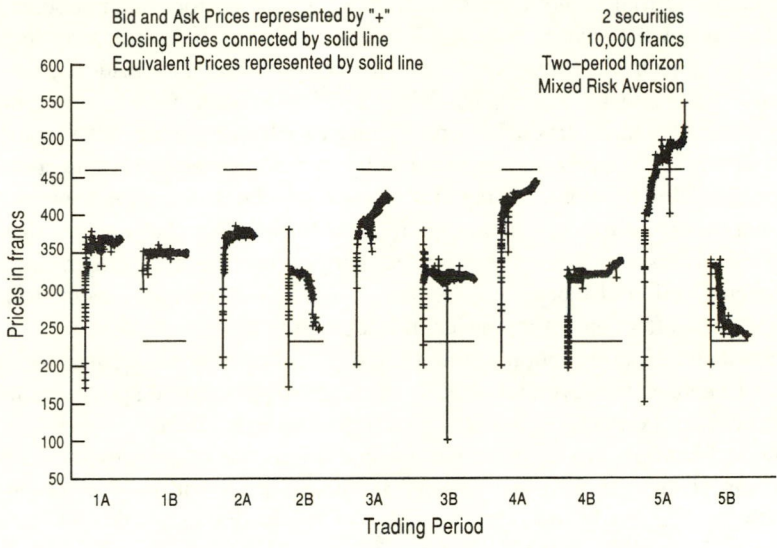

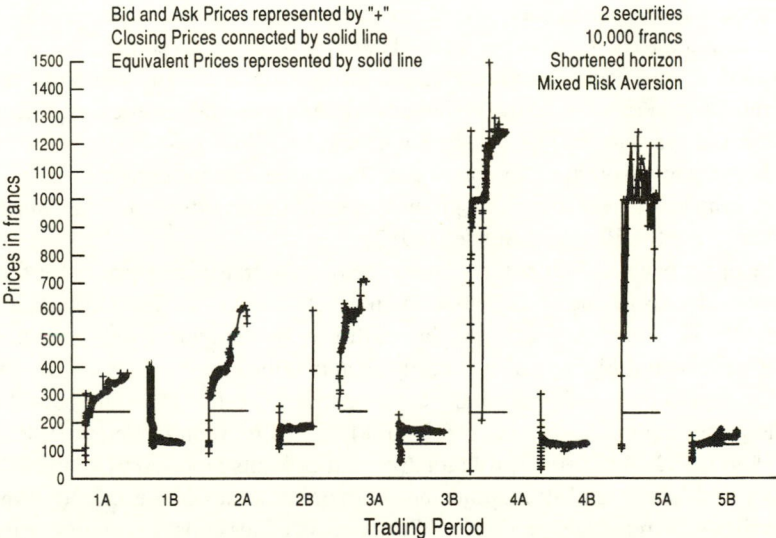

Figure 6.12. Bid, ask, close and equilibrium prices. *Source:* Ang and Schwarz 1992, figures 3 and 4.

introducing an opportunity to short sell would allow the better-informed traders to make money at the expense of the over-optimistic traders, and thus discipline them. Such disciplining won't occur if there were no traders who are better informed or willing to subject themselves to the higher risks of short sales.[15] Further, depending on the timing of the short sale and cover trading, it is plausible that a scramble to cover at the last moment may create its own bubble.

Allowing traders to sell short (up to two units beyond their initial endowment of two units each) does not reduce the number of periods for which bubbles last, nor does it cut the size of bubbles. Trading volume is increased even higher, further away from the equilibrium level of zero. Neither this evidence nor the evidence presented by Kluger and Wyatt (1991) or Rietz (1991) supports the widely-held idea that introducing opportunity to sell short reduces the incidence of bubbles in asset markets. The opportunity to buy on margin is conjectured to reduce formation of bubbles. King et al.'s experimental data does not support the idea that opportunity to buy on margin reduces bubbles. On the contrary, the size of bubbles in markets with inexperienced margin traders is even larger. Simultaneous introduction of margin buying and short sale opportunities seems to have no significant effect on the incidence of bubbles.

Transaction costs discourage trading and presumably work against the incidence of bubbles. However, when King et al. (1990) introduced significant transaction costs to their design, this treatment also had little effect.

Ang and Schwarz (1992) examined the conditions that may promote or inhibit formation of bubbles in asset markets. In their experiment, they modified the Forsythe, Palfrey, and Plott (1982) market for two-period assets (see the discussion of designing experimental asset markets above). They replaced certain dividends by uncertain dividends that depended on which of the two possible states of nature was realized in each period, and rotated the dividend types of individual subjects after each two-period trial. Their two-period asset life, being much shorter than the fifteen-period asset life in Smith, Suchanek, and Williams' (1988) and related experiments, allowed them to conduct five trials in each experimental session (versus only one in Smith, Suchanek, and Williams). Diversity of dividends and gains from trading meant that the traders had to learn the equilibrium prices from the market, even though their design had no information asymmetries like those used in Plott and Sunder (1982).

The upper panel of Figure 6.12 shows the bid/ask/transaction prices for the five two-period trials of one of their baseline markets (market 3). The horizontal lines show the risk neutral perfect foresight equilibria. By comparing these results with the upper panel of Figure 6.1, it is easily seen that the uncertainties introduced by randomness of dividends caused the convergence to perfect foresight equilibrium in their baseline markets to be slower and less precise than in Forsythe, Palfrey, and Plott (1982). The same is true relative to the results reported by Frank (1988).

Ang and Schwarz (1992) subjected their baseline design described above to three different treatments in three additional sets of sessions. In the first set, they offered significantly large additional bonus payments to subjects based on relative ranking of the sum of net change in their cash position plus the market value of their asset portfolio at the end of period A trading. This treatment was designed to shorten the investment horizon of traders along the lines of portfolio managers in the investment world. As can be seen in the lower panel of Figure 6.12, introduction of this extra incentive launched a wild bubble in period A that increased progressively over the five trials, even though period B prices converged close to risk neutral equilibrium. The size of such bubbles was only partially restrained when subjects were asked to play with twenty dollars of their own money. Willingness to play with their own money raises the possibility that these subjects might be more risk-loving, or at least less risk averse, than others.

Ang and Schwarz (1992) conjectured that such bubbles may arise from the imbalance between buying and selling powers of subjects in laboratory experiments. Such imbalance is represented in the real world by short-sale restrictions and high costs, as well as by availability of credit to leverage long positions. In their second treatment, they modified their baseline design to equate the buying and selling power by increasing the asset endowment of traders and reducing the cash endowment until it is approximately equal to the market value of assets. In addition, they retained the short-term horizon bonus of the first treatment described above. In spite of this bonus, bubbles disappeared, and the asset was traded at a discount from risk neutral equilibrium in period A.

In their third treatment, Ang and Schwarz (1992) used Jackson Personality Inventory (1976) and Jackson, Houraney, and Vidmar (1972) tests to pre-screen subjects who were more averse to monetary risk (conservatives) from those who were less averse (speculators). They compared separate baseline sessions of conservatives and speculators against their performance when short-term horizon bonus was introduced. In baseline experiments, speculators traded in period A at a smaller discount than the conservatives did. Introduction of a short-term horizon bonus created a period A bubble in the speculator markets but not in the conservative market.

On the basis of these experiments, Ang and Schwarz (1992) conclude that short-term decision horizons of traders, market power imbalance in favor of buyers, and presence of traders who are inclined to take monetary risks promote formation of bubbles in asset markets. Removal of the short-term bonuses and the market power imbalance seems to be sufficient to eliminate them. They suggest that modifying regulatory environment so buyers as well as sellers face similar costs in implementing their ideas will reduce unnecessary volatility.

Rietz (1991) designed an experiment to test general equilibrium predictions for two-asset market in which each asset pays a simple dividend contingent on one of the two states with known probabilities. Aggregate payoff is identical across the states and all subjects can always eliminate their risk entirely, yielding an equilibrium price ratio of two assets equal to their ratio of the probabilities of states in which they yield a dividend. No-arbitrage restrictions give precise predictions about absolute prices, their sum, and asset allocations. The main advantage of this design is that in spite of aggregate uncertainty, absolute price levels—and, therefore, price bubbles—are well defined without need to specify traders' attitudes toward risk.

Rietz (1991) found that, on average, trading does facilitate risk sharing to the extent of about 60 percent of ideal, and relative price ratio generally corresponds to the ratio of the corresponding probabilities. However, absolute asset prices, and their sum, consistently exceed the predictions to form bubbles. These single-period asset market bubbles are persistent and cannot be explained if all subjects are expected utility maximizers. Bubbles create arbitrage opportunities that are seldom exploited, even after they are explained and pointed out to subjects. The

author explains the results in terms of decision regret. However, as Ang and
Schwarz's (1992) and O'Brien and Srivastava's (1991a) experiments suggest,
understanding and exploiting arbitrage trading opportunities may not come naturally from one or two sessions of trading experience.

E. Bid-Ask Spread

In theoretical models, bid-ask spread is shown to be increasing in uncertainty
(Copeland and Galai 1983) and decreasing in trading volume (Glosten and Harris
1988). Both these hypotheses have been subjected to laboratory tests.

Copeland and Friedman (1987) compared the behavior of bid-ask spreads
across periods, within periods, and across the moment of information arrival.
They found that (1) the bid-ask spread narrows in later periods as subjects gain
experience, (2) spreads narrow in the later part of trading periods as more traders
receive information and prices converge to equilibrium, and (3) spreads widen
immediately upon distribution of new information to subsets of traders creating
information asymmetry. Overall, they concluded that their data support a positive
relationship between uncertainty and bid-ask spreads.

Campbell et al. (1991) examined the effect of increasing uncertainty about the
equilibrium price in perishable goods double auctions by adding a different random number to individual supply and demand schedules for each trading period.
They found that, compared to markets in which supply and demand conditions
remained stationary over periods, randomness increased the bid-ask spread.

O'Brien and Srivastava (1991b) compared the bid-ask spreads across the two
period lives of their securities in which traders faced greater uncertainty in period
1 than in period 2. They found the spreads to be greater and, therefore, consistent
with the uncertainty hypothesis. Bid-ask spreads are also found to be positively
correlated with the mean absolute deviation of transaction prices from rational
expectations equilibrium. Given the greater complexity of information structure,
period 1 markets have greater difficulty in converging to rational expectations
equilibrium, leaving the traders less certain about the state. They found no correlation between trading volume and bid-ask spread.

F. Off-Floor and Block Trading

In their experiment cited above, Campbell et al. (1991) also introduced the opportunity to conduct off-floor trades (that did not show as public data to the other
traders) and block trades (three units or more per transaction, as compared to one
unit per transaction for other traders). They observed a greater off-floor volume in
markets that also exhibited wider bid-ask spreads, probably because of greater
uncertainty in the environment. Introduction of opportunity to transact in blocks
also caused off-floor trading to increase. Since most off-floor trades took place
within the bid-ask spread, their data support "the hypothesis that a motive for
such trades is to split privately the gain represented by the bid-ask spread without
revealing publicly a willingness to make price concessions" (1).

VII. Laboratory Modeling of Asset Markets

In designing a laboratory economy, it is tempting to make it as similar as possible to the naturally occurring empirical phenomenon that the experimentalist wishes to explore. On the other hand, the experimentalist is attracted to making the laboratory economy resemble the formal or informal *models* of that phenomena. Reproducing the field environment inside the lab, or implementing the exact details of a formal model of that phenomena, is difficult, often impossible. Moreover, increasing the resemblance of the laboratory economy to the formal model may make it less similar to the field environment, and vice versa. What should an experimentalist do? Should he try to get as close to one, or the other, or should he try to strike a balance between the two? If so, how?

Let us consider the purpose and usefulness of modeling, the relationship between a phenomenon of substantive interest and its models, and the relationship among various models of the same phenomenon. If realism were to be the dominant criterion for judging a model, each phenomena would be its own best model. There is only one real thing. The New York Stock Exchange is its own best model. Yet we *build* models. The Stock Exchange has been modeled in reporters' language, in regulators' rules, in statisticians' numbers, in mathematicians' equations, in artists' canvas and paint, in architects' drawings, in masons' bricks and stone, in scientists' computer programs, in photographers' film and video, and in economists' laboratories. Why do we build these models of the Exchange that we know do not capture all the reality of this complex entity? Why do we use so many different media for making "important" models of the real thing?

The demand for models arises from the finiteness of our own capacity either to perceive or to comprehend all aspects of the infinitely complex reality. A few sentences on the evening television news, a few columns in the morning newspaper, or an equation or a graph in a book of economics abstract the infinite details of the day's events into a comprehensible model of these events. Mapping from reality to model is not necessarily unique, even for a given modeling medium. For any given purpose, we choose or build a model that serves us satisfactorily.

The value of a model is judged by how well it captures the chosen aspect of the reality *and* by how completely it discards all other aspects of reality as unwanted details. Its value lies in simplicity, not in complexity. What is an essential factor in a model built for one purpose, is unessential detail in another model of the same reality.

The choice of the modeling medium depends on what aspect of the reality is considered essential to the purpose of building the model. Different media are able to capture different aspects of the reality well. Mathematics and laboratory are two of the media used in economics, just as paint and marble are two of the media used by artists to model a person. While paint on canvas can capture the color better, marble has the advantage of capturing the space. While a sculptor may use a painting or photograph for help or inspiration, her art will still be seen in relation to its principal subject.

Similarly, mathematics and a laboratory populated by human subjects have different advantages, and disadvantages, in modeling different aspects of economic reality. While laboratory modeling is often assisted, even inspired by the great deal of mathematical models already available, evaluating laboratory work in terms of its fidelity to the mathematical model is just as sterile as evaluating a sculpture in relation to a photograph. Laboratory work can and does yield insights into economic phenomena that cannot be obtained analytically. The reverse is also true. Potential to yield such insights is a suitable evaluation criterion.

Limitations of each modeling medium force the development of standard operating procedures or routine assumptions in each field. This is certainly true of formal analytical modeling and laboratory modeling in economics. Identification of these limitations becomes especially important when one takes an analytical model and "tests" it with data in the laboratory or field. It is essential that the experimentalist, in seeking guidance from an analytical model, separate methodological conveniences from the essential aspects of the economic field environment that he wishes to explore, and discard the former before setting out to construct the laboratory model.

Laboratory modeling of asset markets differs from equity and commodity futures markets in the field in three important respects. First, most laboratory markets use one- or two-period assets, and re-endow the traders at the end of each one or two-period cycle. This design enables subjects to learn through repetition over periods; it also reduces, without eliminating, the possibility of developing speculative bubbles in asset markets. Second, the traders are typically divided into two or more types of investors, and a different set of dividend values is assigned to each type of trader in order to create gains from trading under perfect information and to make it possible to define and measure allocative efficiency of these markets in a meaningful way.

Heterogenous redemption values have a natural interpretation in commodity spot markets; a car manufacturer may get a different value from a sheet of steel than a furniture manufacturer does. In laboratory models of asset markets this heterogeneity is frequently justified by the possibility of different tax rates, consumption patterns, or attitudes toward risk for different traders. However, a great deal of trading in capital markets is driven by differences in the traders' beliefs and information about the investment and production processes that underlie the capital markets. After all, the allocative efficiency of capital markets can only be judged relative to the allocation of capital among competing investments. Assignment of heterogenous dividends to traders in laboratory asset markets is a convenient modeling technique that encapsulates the traders' beliefs and information about this investment and production process.

The third, and perhaps the most important, abstraction in laboratory models of capital markets is the use of a small number of discrete states of the world to create uncertain environments. A small number of discrete states permit the traders to observe and learn the state-price correspondence within some ten or twenty replications of a typical laboratory session. Learning this correspondence for a larger number of discrete states, or for a continuum of states, may require more experience than is possible within the laboratory environment. This abstraction raises some thorny problems about some generalizations.

Unlike commodity markets where each trader is assigned the role of a buyer or a seller, asset markets permit traders to transact in both directions. Three implications follow from the duality of traders' role. First, traders' profits include capital gains and losses in addition to the usual margin on the units sold (relative to their cost) and on the units bought (relative to their redemption value, usually labeled "dividends" in asset markets). Second, the opportunity to speculate is accompanied by the possibility of bankruptcy, creating the problem of enforceable and credible payoffs to the participating subjects. Third, unless the costs, redemption values, or information are varied across traders, these markets have no gains from trading and their allocative efficiency is undefined.

VIII. Concluding Remarks

What has been learned from the experimental work with asset markets?

First, dissemination and aggregation of information through the trading mechanism alone (as opposed to conversations among traders, or news) is possible. Rational expectations equilibrium, requiring the seemingly impossible bootstrap operation of learning from one's own creation, is an observable, reproducible phenomena of regular empirical characteristics. One may still argue that such phenomena cannot occur in a specific market environment, but it is no longer possible to dispute its existence in general.

Second, it is no longer defensible to argue that rational expectations can be achieved instantaneously, or precisely, or without replication. Nor is it defensible to argue that such equilibria are achieved in all market environments.

Third, the absence of arbitrage opportunities in the market is not a *sufficient* condition for informational or allocative efficiency of a market. From the predicate—if a market were not allocatively and informationally efficient, some participant would have incentive to exploit this inefficiency—one cannot deduce that all markets must be efficient. A trader may have the information and the incentives but not the means of doing so. Conditions under which the rational expectations bootstrap works remain to be fully understood. Dimensionality of market signals in relation to the size of the state space, ex post observability of realized states, and stationarity of the market environment seem to be important features that promote efficiency.

Fourth, formation of individual expectations and beliefs in economically rich environments of asset markets is a complex, diverse, perhaps even unstable, phenomenon. Statistical laws that may capture the important systematic features of expectation formation in market settings remain to be identified.

Finally, the experimental method has already been shown to be a valuable tool that helps refine our understanding of asset markets. Using this tool in judicious conjunction with theoretical analysis and field data will yield insights into poorly understood aspects of asset market behavior such as formation of bubbles, stability of markets, impact of insider trading, and of alternative regulatory policies and trading institutions.

Notes

*Comments from Colin Camerer, Robyn Dawes, John Kagel, Alvin Roth, Vernon L. Smith, Charles R. Plott, Brian Kluger, Edward Dyl, Dan Friedman, Ron King, and Russ Lundholm on earlier versions of this chapter are gratefully acknowledged. Financial support for this research was provided by Margaret and Richard M. Cyert Family Funds and by the National Science Foundation under Contract SES-8912552.

1. If the realized state was X (prior probability 1/3), the subjects saw a string of ten binary digits drawn with replacement from an urn which contained 4 zeros and 1 one. If the realization was Y (prior probability 2/3), the string of ten binary digits was drawn from an urn containing 3 zeros and 2 ones. Thus, the string presented to subjects could contain anywhere from 0 to 11 ones, yielding eleven distinct Bayesian posterior probabilities of X ranging from .90 (for 0 ones) to 0.0005 (for 10 ones), and eleven distinct rational expectations equilibrium prices ranging from 262 to 350. Also see Liu (1992).
2. I return to this topic in the section on bubbles and false equilibria.
3. The design of asset markets used in this experiment was identical to the Plott and Sunder (1982) design described in the section on information dissemination and Table 6.1. Plott and Sunder (1982) gave information about the realized state of the world to some traders for free before trading opened in the asset market; in contrast, Sunder (1992) sold this information to traders. In the first set of markets, the four highest bidders bought information at the fifth highest bid price through a sealed bid auction. In the second set of markets, all those who wished to could buy information a price announced in advance by the experimenter.
4. Copeland and Friedman's experiment was subdivided into four equal subperiods of 60 seconds each. Under "*Sim*ultaneous" treatment, all traders received information simultaneously at the beginning of one of the subperiods; under "*Seq*uential" treatment, different traders received information at the beginning of different subperiods. All traders in a market were divided into three groups of "clones." Under "*Hom*ogenous" treatment, the realized state of the world for each period (i.e., the good/bad dividend payout from the asset) was identical across the three groups; under "*Het*erogenous" treatment, the dividend payout for each group was independent of the other groups. Thus, they used a 2×2 experimental design (*Sim* vs. *Seq* and *Hom* vs. *Het*). The first cell of this design (the *Sim/Hom* treatment) is the simple design comparable to Sunder's (1992). The other three cells represent more complex settings.
5. Ang and Schwarz (1985, 840) also reached a similar conclusion on the basis of their laboratory experiment: "Thus, the role of speculators may not be entirely dysfunctional, nor is greater price volatility necessarily harmful."
6. Since allocative efficiency of a market depends not on price but on the identity of the buyers and sellers, faster convergence to perfect foresight equilibrium price is not necessarily inconsistent with reduced efficiency.
7. See Flood and Garber (1980), Hamilton and Whiteman (1988), and Flood and Hoderick (1990).
8. See Camerer (1989) for a survey of bubbles and fads literature, as well as its relationship with some of the early experimental work. Also, the Spring 1990 (Vol. 4, No. 2) issue of the *Journal of Economic Perspectives* carried a symposium on bubbles, including a brief overview by Joseph G. Stiglitz.
9. Given the finite number of traders in the market, this information monopolist (unlike Kyle's

1985) had no incentive to reveal the information through his trading activity by the end of the period.

10. See Friedman (1984, 64) for the famous anecdote concerning stock manipulation in London by Nathan Rothschild at the time of the Battle of Waterloo.

11. See Duh and Sunder (1986, 1994), Camerer (1990), and Anderson and Sunder (1995) for a discussion of the use of representativeness heuristic in experimental markets.

12. As is the practice with applications of filter rules in research studies with field data, Plott and Sunder (1982) also applied the filter tests to the data ex post. Buying and selling (including short selling) is assumed to have no effect on the market. Thus, the fact that taking short positions is constrained under rules of the market does not preclude researchers from testing the filter rules that generate short sales.

13. See the section on aggregation of information above for description of markets in series A, B, and C.

14. When traders do not have up-to-the-second information on the inside spread, the specialist may receive a bid that exceeds the inside ask or an ask that is below the inside bid.

15. The short sellers were required to cover their shorts before the end of the last period of the asset life, and failure to cover carried a substantial fine.

Bibliography

Alexander, Sidney. S. 1961. Price movements in speculative markets: Trends or random walks. *Industrial Management Review* 2:7–26.

———. 1964. Price movements in speculative markets: Trends or random walks, no. 2. *Industrial Management Review* 5:25–46.

Amihud, Y., Thomas S. Y. Ho, and Robert A. Schwartz, editors. 1985. *Market making and the changing structure of the securities industry*. New York: Lexington Books.

Anderson, Matthew J., and Shyam Sunder. 1995. Professional Traders as Intuitive Bayesians. *Organizational Behavior and Human Development Processes* (forthcoming).

Anderson, Scott, David Johnston, James Walker, and Arlington Williams. 1991. The efficiency of experimental asset markets: Empirical robustness and subject sophistication. In *Research in experimental economics, vol. 4*, Mark Isaac, editor, Greenwich, Conn.: JAI Press. 107–90.

Ang, James S., and Thomas Schwarz. 1985. Risk aversion and information structure: An experimental study of price volatility in the security markets. *Journal of Finance* 40:824–44.

———. 1992. The formation and control of asset bubbles: An experimental study. Working paper. Southern Illinois University and Florida State University. November.

Bachelier, M. L. 1900. *Theorie de la speculation*. Paris: Gauthier-Villars.

Banks, Jeffrey S. 1985. Price-conveyed information versus observed insider behavior: A note on rational expectations convergence. *Journal of Political Economy* 93:807–15.

Beja, A. 1976. The limited information efficiency of market processes. Working paper. University of California.

Black, Fischer. 1986. Noise. *Journal of Finance* 41 (July): 529–43.

Bronfman, Corinne. 1990. Expectation formation and price fluctuations in laboratory asset markets. Working paper. University of Arizona. June.

Camerer, Colin. 1989. Bubbles and fads in asset prices. *Journal of Economic Surveys* 3:3–41.

———. 1990. Do markets correct biases in probability judgment? Evidence from market experiments. In *Advances in behavioral economics, vol. 2*, John Kagel and L. Green, editors, Norwood, N.J.: Ablex. 126–172.

Camerer, Colin, and Keith Weigelt. 1985. Non-price information in the rational expectations of asset traders: Some experimental results. Working paper. University of Pennsylvania.

———. 1990a. Bubbles and convergence in experimental markets for infinitely-lived assets. Working paper. University of Pennsylvania.

Camerer, Colin, and Keith Weigelt. 1990b. Information mirages in experimental asset markets. Working paper. University of Pennsylvania.

Campbell, Joseph, Shawn LaMaster, Vernon L. Smith, and Mark Van Boening. 1991. Off-floor trading, disintegration, and the bid-ask spread in experimental markets. Forthcoming in *Journal of Business.*

Cohen, Kalman J., Steven F. Maier, Robert A. Schwartz, and David K. Whitcomb. 1986. *The microstructure of securities markets.* Englewood Cliffs, N.J.: Prentice-Hall.

Cootner, Paul A., editor. 1964. *The random character of stock market prices.* Cambridge, Mass.: MIT Press.

Copeland, Thomas E. 1975. A model of asset trading under sequential information arrival. *Journal of Finance* 30:1149–68.

Copeland, Thomas E. and Daniel Friedman. 1987. The effect of sequential information arrival on asset prices: An experimental study. *Journal of Finance* 42:763–98.

———. 1991. Partial revelation of information in experimental asset markets. *Journal of Finance* 46:265–81.

———. 1992. The market value of information: Some experimental results. *Journal of Business* 65:241–66.

Copeland, Thomas E., and Dan Galai. 1983. Information effects of the bid-ask spread. *Journal of Finance* 38:1457–69.

Coursey, Don L., and Edward A. Dyl. 1990. Price limits, trading suspensions, and the adjustment of prices to new information. *Review of Futures Markets* 9:343–60.

Cox, C. C. 1976. Futures trading and market information. *Journal of Political Economy* 84:1215–37.

Daniels, Brian P. and Charles R. Plott. 1988. Inflation and expectations in experimental markets. Working paper. California Institute of Technology.

Danthine, Jean-Pierre. 1978. Information, futures prices, and stabilizing speculation. *Journal of Economic Theory* 17:79–98.

DeJong, D., R. Forsythe, R. Lundholm, and S. Watts. 1991. Do prices convey information: Further experimental evidence. In *Research in experimental economics*, Mark Isaac, editor, Greenwich, Conn. JAI Press.

Dickey, D. A., and W. A. Fuller. 1981. Likelihood ratio statistics for autoregressive time series with a unit root. *Econometrica* 49:1057–71.

Duh, Rong Ruey, and Shyam Sunder. 1986. Incentives, learning, and processing of information in a market environment: An examination of the base-rate fallacy. In *Laboratory market research*, Shane Moriarty, editor, University of Oklahoma, Center for Economic and Management Research.

Duh, Rong-Ruey, and Shyam Sunder. 1994. El agente económico como un Bayesiano intuitivo: Evidentia expreimental (Economic agents as intuitive bayesians: Experimental evidence). *Cuadernos Economicos De ICE* 54 (1993–1992): 101–28.

Easley, David, and John O. Ledyard. 1992. Theories of price formation and exchange in oral auctions. In *The double auction market: Institutions, theories, and evidence*, D. Friedman and J. Rust, editors, Santa Fe Institute Series in the Sciences of the Complexity, Proceedings vol. XV, New York: Addison-Wesley.

Eberwein, Curtis J. 1990. Information aggregation under differing information structures: Some preliminary results. Working paper. University of Pittsburgh.

Evans, G. W. 1989. On the fragility of sunspots and bubbles. *Journal of Monetary Economics* 23:297–317.

Fama, Eugene F. 1965. The behavior of stock market prices. *Journal of Business* 38:34–105.

———. 1970. Efficient capital markets: A review of theory and empirical work. *Journal of Finance* 25:383–417.

———. 1990. Efficient capital markets: II. CRSP Working paper 303. University of Chicago. December.

Fama, E. F., and Marshall E. Blume. 1966. Filter rules and stock-market trading. *Journal of Business* 39:226–41.

Flood, Robert P., and Peter M. Garber. 1980. Market fundamentals versus price-level bubbles: The first tests. *Journal of Political Economy* 88:745–70.

Flood, Robert P., and Robert J. Hoderick. 1990. On testing for speculative bubbles. *Journal of Economic Perspectives* 4:85–101.

Forsythe, Robert, and Russell Lundholm, 1990. Information aggregation in an experimental market. *Econometrica* 58:309–47.

Forsythe, Robert, Thomas R. Palfrey, and Charles R. Plott. 1982. Asset valuation in an experimental market. *Econometrica* 50:537–68.

————. 1984. Futures markets and informational efficiency: A laboratory examination. *Journal of Finance* 39:955–81.

Frank, Murray. 1988. Asset trading in computerized experimental markets. Working paper. University of British Columbia. June.

Friedman, Daniel. 1984. On the efficiency of experimental double auction markets. *American Economic Review* 74:60–72.

————. 1993a. How trading institutions affect financial market performance: Some laboratory evidence. Forthcoming in *Economic Inquiry*.

————. 1993b. Privileged Traders and asset market efficiency: A laboratory study. Forthcoming in *Journal Financial & Quantitative Analysis*.

Friedman, Daniel, Glenn Harrison, and J. Salmon. 1983. Informational role of futures markets and learning behavior—Some experimental evidence. In *Futures markets—modelling, managing and monitoring futures trading*, M. E. Streit, editor, Oxford: Basil Blackwell.

————. 1984. The informational efficiency of experimental asset markets. *Journal of Political Economy* 92:349–408.

Friedman, Daniel, and Shyam Sunder. 1994. *Experimental methods: A primer for Economists.* Cambridge, U.K., and New York: Cambridge University Press.

Glosten, L., and L. Harris. 1988. Estimating the components of the bid-ask spread. *Journal of Financial Economics* 21:123–42.

Glosten, Lawrence, and Paul Milgrom. 1983. Bid, ask and transaction prices in a specialist market with heterogeneously informed traders. *Journal of Financial Economics* 9:71–100.

Gode, Dhananjay K., and Shyam Sunder. 1993a. Lower bounds for efficiency of surplus extraction in double auctions. In *The double auction market: Institutions, theories, and evidence*, D. Friedman and J. Rust, editors, Santa Fe Institute Series in the Sciences of the Complexity, Proceedings vol. 15, New York: Addison-Wesley. 199–219.

————. 1993b. Allocative efficiency of markets with zero intelligence traders: Markets as a partial substitute for individual rationality. *Journal of Political Economy* 101:119–37.

————. 1994. Human and artificially intelligent traders in a double auction market: Experimental evidence. In *Computational organization theory*, Kathleen Carley and Michael Prietula, editors, Hillsdale, N.J.: Lawrence Erlbaum Associates. 241–62.

Gorman, Mark B. 1976. Market microstructure. *Journal of Financial Economics* 3 (June).

Gray, Roger W. 1977. Onions revisited. *Journal of Farm Economics* 65:273–76.

Grossman, S. J. 1976. On the efficiency of competitive stock markets where traders have diverse information. *Journal of Finance* 31:573–85.

————. 1977. The existence of futures markets, noisy rational expectations, and informational externalities. *Review of Economic Studies* 44:431–49.

————. 1981. An introduction to the theory of rational expectations under asymmetric information. *Review of Economic Studies* 48:541–59.

Grossman, S., and J. Stiglitz. 1980. On the impossibility of informationally efficient markets. *American Economic Review* 70:393–408.

Hamilton, James D., and Charles H. Whiteman. 1988. The observable implications of self-fulfilling expectations. *Journal of Monetary Economics* 16:353–74.

Hayek, F. A. 1945. The use of knowledge in society. *American Economic Review* 35:519–30.

Hellwig, M. F. 1980. On the aggregation of information in competitive markets. *Journal of Economic Theory* 22:477–98.

Hicks, John R. 1939. *Value and capital.* Oxford: Oxford University Press.

Ho, Thomas S. Y., and Hans Stoll. 1983. The dynamics of dealers markets under competition. *Journal of Finance* 38:1053–74.

Ho, Thomas S. Y., Robert A. Schwartz, and David K. Whitcomb. 1985. The trading decision and market clearing under transaction price uncertainty. *Journal of Finance* 40:21–42.

Jackson, Douglas. 1976. *Jackson personality inventory manual.* Goshen, N.Y.: Research Psychologists Press.

Jackson, Douglas, D. Hourney, and N. Vidmar. 1972. A four-dimensional interpretation of risk taking. *Journal of Personality* 40:433–501.

Jennings, R., John Fellingham, and L. Starks. 1981. An equilibrium model of asset trading with sequential information arrival. *Journal of Finance* 36:143–161.

Jennings, R., and L. Starks. 1986. Earnings announcements, stock price adjustment, and the existence of option markets. *Journal of Finance* 41:107–25.

Jordan, James S. 1982. A dynamic model of expectations equilibrium. *Journal of Economic Theory* 28:235–54.

Kendall, M. G. 1953. The analysis of economic time series—Part I: Prices. *Journal of the Royal Statistical Society* (Series A) 96:11–25.

Keynes, John Maynard. 1936. *The general theory of employment, interest and money.* New York: Harcourt Brace.

King, Ronald R. 1987. Noisy rational expectations equilibrium in experimental markets. Working paper. Washington University. October.

———. 1990. Private information acquisition in experimental markets prone to bubble and crash. Working paper. Washington University.

King, Ronald R., Vernon L. Smith, Arlington W. Williams, and Mark Van Boening. 1990. The robustness of bubbles and crashes in experimental stock markets. Forthcoming in *Journal of Economic Behavior and Organization.*

Kluger, Brian D., and Steve B. Wyatt. 1990. Options and efficiency: Some experimental evidence. Working paper. University of Cincinnati.

———. 1991. Noise and the information aggregation process. Working paper. University of Cincinnati. December.

Kobayashi, Takao. 1977. A convergence theorem of rational expectations equilibrium with price information. Working paper No. 79, IMSSS. Stanford University.

Kruse, Jamie, and Shyam Sunder. 1988. Common knowledge and information dissemination. Carnegie Mellon University.

Kyle, Albert. 1985. Continuous auctions and insider trading. *Econometrica* 1315–35.

LeRoy, Stephen F., and R. Porter. 1981. The present value relation: Tests based on implied variance bounds. *Econometrica* 49:555–74.

Lim, Suk S., Edward C. Prescott, and Shyam Sunder. 1994. Stationary solution to the overlapping generations model of fiat money: Experimental evidence. *Empirical Economics* 19 (No. 2):255–77.

Liu, Yu-Jane. 1992. Auction mechanisms and information structure: An experimental study of information aggregation in security markets. Mimeo. National Chung Cheng University (Taiwan).

Lundholm, Russell J. 1986. Information asymmetry and capital market behavior: Some evidence from a laboratory market setting. In *Laboratory Market Research*, Shane Moriarty, editor, Norman, Okla.: University of Oklahoma Press.

———. 1991. What affects the efficiency of the market? Some answers from the laboratory. *The Accounting Review* 66:486–515.

Lucas, Robert E. 1972. Expectations and the neutrality of money. *Journal of Economic Theory* 4:103–24.

Manaster, S., and R. Rendleman. 1982. Option prices as predictors of equilibrium stock prices. *Journal of Finance* 37:1043–57.

Marimon, Ramon, Stephen E. Spear, and Shyam Sunder. 1993. Expectationally-driven market volatility: An experimental study. *Journal of Economic Theory* 61 (No. 1): 74–103.

Marimon, Ramon, and Shyam Sunder. 1993. Indeterminacy of equilibria in a hyperinflationary world: Experimental evidence. *Econometrica* 61 (No. 5): 1073–1108.

———. 1994. Expectations and learning under alternative monetary regimes: An experimental approach. *Economic Theory* 4:131–62.

Marsh, Terry A., and Robert C. Merton. 1986. Dividend variability and variance bounds tests for rationality of stock market prices. *American Economic Review* 76:483–98.

McCabe, Kevin A. 1989. Fiat money as a store of value in an experimental trading game. *Journal of Economic Behavior and Organization* 12:215–31.

Mendelson, Haim. 1982. Market behavior in a clearing house. *Econometrica* 50:1505–24.

Milgrom, Paul. 1981. Rational expectations, information acquisition, and competitive bidding. *Econometrica* 49:921–44.

Miller, R. M., Charles R. Plott, and Vernon L. Smith. 1977. Intertemporal competitive equilibrium: An empirical study of speculation. *Quarterly Journal of Economics* 91:599–624.

Morse, Dale. 1980. Asymmetrical information in security markets and trading volume. *Journal of Finance and Quantitative Analysis* 15:1129–48.

Muth, John. 1961. Rational expectations and the theory of price movements. *Econometrica* 29:315–35.

O'Brien, John. 1990. The formation of expectations and periodic ex post reporting: An experimental study. Working paper. Carnegie Mellon University.

O'Brien, John, and Sanjay Srivastava. 1991a. Liquidity and persistence of Arbitrage in experimental options markets. In *The double auction market: Institutions, theories, and evidence*, D. Friedman and J. Rust, editors, Santa Fe Institute Series in the Sciences of the Complexity, Proceedings Vol. XV New York: Addison-Wesley.

———. 1991b. Dynamic stock markets with multiple assets: An experimental analysis. *Journal of Finance* 46:1811–38.

———. 1991c. Arbitrage and informational efficiency: Theory and experimental evidence. Working paper. Carnegie Mellon University. March.

Plott, Charles R., and Shyam Sunder. 1982. Efficiency of experimental security markets with insider information: An application of rational-expectations models. *Journal of Political Economy* 90:663–98.

———. 1988. Rational expectations and the aggregation of diverse information in laboratory security markets. *Econometrica* 56:1085–1118.

Plott, Charles R., and Jonathan T. Uhl. 1981. Competitive equilibrium with middlemen: An empirical study. *Southern Economic Journal* 47:1063–71.

Porter, David, and Vernon L. Smith. 1989. Stock market bubbles in the laboratory. Working paper. University of Arizona.

Powers, Mark J. 1970. Does futures trading reduce fluctuations in the cash markets? *American Economic Review* 60:460–64.

Rietz, Thomas A. 1991. Arbitrage, asset prices and risk allocation in experimental markets. Working papers. Northwestern University. November.

Roberts, Harry V. 1959. Stock market patterns and financial analysis: Methodological suggestions. *Journal of Finance* 14:1–10.

Ross, Stephen. 1976. Options and efficiency. *Quarterly Journal of Economics* 90:75–89.

Samuelson, Paul A. 1965. Proof that properly anticipated prices fluctuate randomly. *Industrial Management Review* 6:41–50.

Schwartz, Robert A. 1988, *Equity markets: Structure, trading and performance*. New York: Harper & Row.

Shiller, Robert. 1981. Do stock prices move too much to be justified by subsequent changes in dividends? *American Economic Review* 71:421–36.

———. 1986, Comments on Miller and on Kleidon. *Journal of Business* 59:S501–S505.

Smith, Vernon L. 1962. An experimental study of competitive market behavior. *Journal of Political Economy* 70:111–37.

Smith, Vernon L., Gerry L. Suchanek, and Arlington W. Williams. 1988. Bubbles, crashes, and endogenous expectations in experimental spot asset markets. *Econometrica* 56(6):1119–52.

Sunder, Shyam. 1984. Rational expectations equilibrium in asset markets with costly information. Working paper. University of Minnesota.

———. 1991. An introduction to design, planning and conduct of asset market experiments. Working paper, Carnegie Mellon University, February 1991.

———. 1992. Market for information: Experimental evidence. *Econometrica* 60:667–95.

Svensson, L.E.O. 1976. Sequences of Temporary Equilibria, Stationary Point Expectations, and Pareto Efficiency. *Journal of Economic Theory* 13:169–83.

Tirole, Jean. 1982. On the possibility of speculation under rational expectations. *Econometrica* 50:1163–81.

Tomek, William G. 1971. A note on historical wheat prices and futures trading. *Food Research Institute Studies* 10:109–13.

Van Boening, Mark, Arlington W. Williams, and Shawn LaMaster. 1992. Price bubbles and crashes in experimental call markets. Working paper. Indiana University.

Verrecchia, Robert. 1982. Information acquisition in a noisy rational expectations economy. *Econometrica* 50:1415–30.

Von Borries, Alexander, and Daniel Friedman. 1989. Monopolist insiders in computerized asset markets: A note on some experimental results. Working paper. University of California at Santa Cruz.

Watts, Susan. 1993. Private information, prices, asset allocation and profits: Further experimental evidence. In *Research in experimental economics, vol. 5*, Mark Isaac, editor, Greenwich, Conn.: JAI Press.

Williams, Arlington W., and James M. Walker. 1993. Computerized laboratory exercises for microeconomic education: Three applications motivated by the methodology of experimental economics. Forthcoming in *The Journal of Economic Education*.

Wilson, Robert. 1982. Double auctions. Unpublished manuscript. Stanford University.

Working, Holbrook. 1960. Price effects of futures trading. *Food Research Institute Studies* 1:3–31.

7

Auctions: A Survey of Experimental Research

John H. Kagel

Introduction

Auctions are of considerable practical as well as theoretical importance. In practical terms, the value of goods exchanged each year by auctions is huge. In theoretical terms, auctions play a prominent role in the theory of exchange as they remain one of the simplest and most familiar means of price determination in the absence of intermediate market makers. In addition, auctions serve as valuable illustrations of games of incomplete information as bidders' private information is the main factor affecting strategic behavior (Wilson 1992).

In organizing this survey I have relied heavily on Wilson's (1992) and McAfee and McMillan's (1987a) surveys of auction theory. That is, I have chosen to review series of auction experiments that deal with theoretical issues, along with follow-on experiments designed to sort out between competing explanations of the behavior observed. This serves to circumscribe greatly the literature reviewed.

There are two main strands to the literature: private value auctions, where bidders know the value of the item to themselves with certainty, and common value auctions, where the value of the item is the same to everyone, but different bidders have different information about the underlying value. This review is almost exclusively concerned with one-sided auctions, auctions in which there are many buyers and one seller or many sellers and one buyer. Two-sided auctions with many sellers and many buyers are not nearly as well understood theoretically and for this reason have not received the same kind of attention in terms of theory testing as one-sided auctions. (However, see Holt, chapter 5, and Sunder, chapter 6, for the many uses of two-sided auctions in industrial organization experiments and asset market experiments, respectively.)

Part I reviews private value auction experiments. The experimental procedures employed are characterized in section I.A. Section I.B focuses on the Revenue-Equivalence Theorem: In auctions with independently distributed private values,

first-price and Dutch auctions and second-price and English auctions are strategically equivalent, so that prices should be the same in first-price and Dutch auctions and in second-price and English auctions. The revenue equivalence theorem
fails as slightly higher average prices are found in first-price compared to Dutch
auctions and in second-price compared to English auctions. Experiments aimed at
identifying the behavioral basis for these breakdowns are reviewed. Experiments
exploring comparative static implications of auction theory—increased bidding
in response to increased competition, increased revenue resulting from uncertainty about the number of rival bidders, and increased revenue in response to
public information in auctions with affiliated private values—are reported in sections I.C and I.D. Nash equilibrium bidding theory does remarkably well in predicting the sign of these comparative static manipulations. Sections I.E and I.F
explore the effect of different types of information feedback on bidding and adjustments in bidding over time (learning) in experimental auction markets. Section I.G evaluates rival interpretations of bidding above the risk neutral Nash
equilibrium in first-price auctions, an outcome that is commonly accounted for in
terms of risk aversion. The size of this section, a little over a third of section I, is
out of proportion to the substantive issue at stake (are bidders really risk averse
or does something else underlie bidding above the point predictions of the theory), but this question has sparked considerable controversy among experimentalists. As such it provides a case study in the kind of dialogue and successive
interaction that heightens our understanding of behavior.

Part II reviews common value auction experiments. The overriding issue here
concerns the existence and persistence of the "winner's curse," when the high
bidder ignores the adverse selection problem inherent in winning the auction and
winds up paying "too much." Roth, chapter 1, reviews the early experimental
work on this topic, which is taken as the starting point for this review. Section
II.A reviews studies of the winner's curse in sealed bid auctions with symmetric
information. These studies show the winner's curse to be alive and well, at least
for inexperienced and moderately experienced bidders. Further, unlike private
value auctions, Nash equilibrium bidding theory fails to predict the directional
effect of increased numbers of bidders and public information about the value of
the item. The winner's curse in English auctions and auctions with asymmetri-
cally informed bidders is explored in section II.B. Experiments investigating the
winner's curse in other market settings—bilateral bargaining games with asymmetric information, "blind bid" auctions, and two-sided auction markets where
quality is endogenously determined—are reported in section II.C. Section II.D
reports on learning and adjustment processes in settings with a winner's curse.

Section III covers "other topics," those that do not fit squarely under sections
I and II. Section III.A looks at collusion in auction experiments. Comparisons
between field studies and experimental data are offered in section III.B. Sections
III.C and III.D conclude with a brief review of two-sided auctions and other applications of auction market experiments.

A brief concluding section summarizes what has been learned to date. I call
attention to open research issues in the course of the review.

I. The Symmetric Independent Private-Values Model

The independent private values (IPV) model corresponds to the case where each bidder knows his valuation of the item with certainty and bidders' valuations are drawn independently from each other. Although bidders do not know their rivals' valuations, they know the distribution from which they are drawn. Experimental research has been largely restricted to the case in which valuations, x, are drawn from a uniform distribution $[\underline{x}, \bar{x}]$.

Vickrey (1961) was the first to solve the independent private-values model using a game theoretic formulation. Assuming risk neutral bidders, in a first-price sealed bid auction (in which the high bidder pays the price she bids) the unique risk neutral Nash equilibrium (RNNE) bid function given the uniform distribution $[\underline{x}, \bar{x}]$ is

(1)
$$b(x) = x + \frac{(n-1)}{n}(x - \underline{x})$$

where n is the number of bidders in the auction.

The first-price auction is theoretically isomorphic to the Dutch auction where the auctioneer starts with a high initial price and then lowers the price until a bidder accepts the current price. In theory these two institutions yield the same expected price since the situation facing a bidder is the same in both auctions: each bidder must choose how high to bid without knowing the others' decisions and, if she wins, the price she pays is equal to her bid.

In an English auction the price is increased until only one bidder remains. This can be done by having an auctioneer announce prices or having bidders call the bids themselves. The essential feature of the English auction is that bidders always know the level of the current best bid. Here bidders have a dominant strategy of bidding up to their private valuation, x. To bid less than x sacrifices opportunities for winning the item and making a positive profit, no matter how small, while bidding above x and winning results in certain losses. In a second-price sealed bid auction (sometimes referred to as a Vickrey auction) the high bidder wins the item and pays a price equal to the second-highest bid. The bid function here is

(2) $b(x) = x.$

This too is a dominant strategy as (i) bidding below x reduces the chance of winning the item with no increase in profit since the second-highest price is paid, and (ii) bidding above x and winning *as a result* of the higher bid results in losses. Note that the dominant bidding strategy in both these auctions does not depend on the number of bidders, risk attitudes, or the distribution from which private values are drawn.

With risk neutral bidders, the *expected* price paid under all four auctions is the same (Vickrey 1961, Meyerson 1981, Riley and Samuelson 1981). This is referred to as the revenue-equivalence theorem. The mechanism underlying this result is that bids in the first-price auction equal the expected maximum of the distribution of others' valuations (Wilson 1992). The latter corresponds to the predicted dominant strategy price in second-price and English auctions. With risk aversion, the revenue-equivalence theorem breaks down as first-price and Dutch auctions generate greater expected revenue than English or second-price auctions. This follows from the fact that risk aversion promotes bidding above the RNNE in the first-price and Dutch auctions, while the dominant bidding strategy remains unaffected in English and second-price auctions.

Properties of single unit first-price and English auctions extend to multiple unit auctions in which each bidder demands at most one unit of the item and $n > q$, where q is the number of (identical) units of the commodity offered for sale.[1] Uniform price (competitive) auctions in which the k successful bidders pay the highest rejected bid (the k + 1 highest bid) correspond to second-price/English auctions in the sense that each bidder has a dominant strategy of bidding her private valuation. Discriminatory auctions, in which each successful bidder pays the price bid, correspond to first-price auctions in the sense that (i) with risk neutrality, *expected* revenue is the same as the uniform price auction (Milgrom and Weber 1982, Weber 1983) and (ii) with risk aversion, bids will be above the RNNE prediction, yielding greater expected revenue than in the competitive auction (Harris and Raviv 1981).

In what follows I will also have occasion to discuss third-price sealed-bid auctions, auctions in which the high bidder wins the item but pays the third-highest bid price. The third-price auction is a completely synthetic institution, one that does not (and will likely never) exist outside the laboratory. However, to be faithful to Nash equilibrium bidding theory in third-price auctions requires a number of strategic responses quite different from those required in first-price and second-price auctions, examination of which can provide insight into the behavioral processes at work in private value auctions. With bidders' valuations drawn from a uniform distribution, the symmetric RNNE bid function for a third-price auction is

$$(3) \qquad b(x) = \underline{x} \, \frac{n-1}{n-2} \, (x - \underline{x})$$

Note that in the third-price auction $b(x) > x$ for all $x > \underline{x}$ and (somewhat counterintuitively) $b(x)$ *decreases* for *increases* in n (Kagel and Levin 1993). Further, with constant absolute risk aversion, bidders continue to bid above their private valuations but *below* the RNNE line (and the more risk averse bidders are, the more they bid below the RNNE), the exact opposite of the bidding pattern, relative to the RNNE reference point, in first-price auctions.

A. Experimental Procedures

An experimental session typically consists of several auction periods in each of which a number of subjects bid for a single unit of a commodity under a given pricing rule. The item is often referred to as a "fictitious commodity" or simply as a "commodity," in an effort to keep the terminology as neutral as possible and *not* to relate the auction to any particular market for fear that this may induce subjects to bid in ways they think appropriate to that market (a loss of experimental control). Usually the number of subjects matches the number of active bidders, so that a given set of bidders compete with each other across the different auction periods. This opens up the possibility of super-game effects and bidding rings, issues that are addressed in section III.A below.

Subjects' valuations are determined randomly prior to each auction period and are private information. Valuations are typically independent and identical (iid) draws from a uniform distribution $[\underline{x}, \bar{x}]$, where $\underline{x}$ and $\bar{x}$ are common knowledge. In each period the high bidder earns a profit equal to the value of the item less the price; other bidders earn zero profit for that auction period.[2] Bids are commonly restricted to be nonnegative and rounded to the nearest penny. Some auction experiments, particularly some of the earlier ones, restricted bids to be at or below private valuations (Cox, Roberson, and Smith 1982); the first-price auction series reported in Kagel, Harstad, and Levin (1987). In sealed bid auctions, after all bids have been collected, the winning bid is announced. Some researchers provide additional information: for example Kagel et al. (1987) reported all bids, listed from highest to lowest, along with the underlying resale values and profits of the high bidder (subject identification numbers are suppressed, however), whereas Cox, Smith, and Walker (1988) reported only the high bid. There have been only limited inquiries into the effects of these different information treatments on outcomes (see section I.E below).

English auctions have been implemented using (i) an open outcry procedure where the bidding stops when no one indicates a willingness to increase the price any further (Coppinger, Smith, and Titus 1980) and (ii) an English clock procedure, where prices start at some minimal value and increase automatically, with bidders indicating the point at which they choose to drop out of the auction (which is irrevocable for that period), and the last bidder wins the item at the next-to-last dropout price (Kagel et al. 1987).

In implementing these auctions subjects are sometimes provided with examples of valuations and bids along with profit calculations to illustrate how the auction works (Cox et al. 1985a). Sometimes reliance is placed exclusively on dry runs, with no money at stake, to familiarize subjects with the auction procedures (Kagel et al. 1987). Sometimes both examples and dry runs are employed (Battalio, Kogut, and Meyer 1990). Although there have been no explicit studies of the effects of these alternative training procedures, examples carry with them the danger of implicitly telling subjects how the experimenter expects/wants them to bid, as they provide models which subjects may try to mimic. Dry runs have their problems as well, as subjects may use the opportunity to send signals to their rivals at no cost to themselves.

B. Tests of the Revenue-Equivalence Theorem

Tests of the revenue-equivalence theorem involve two separate issues. The more basic issue concerns the strategic equivalence of first-price and Dutch auctions and of second-price and English auctions. Given the strategic equivalence of these different auctions, average prices (revenue) are predicted to be the same, irrespective of bidders' risk attitudes. Assuming that strategic equivalence is satisfied, a second issue concerns revenue equivalence between first-price/Dutch auctions and second-price/English auctions. As noted, revenue equivalence here depends on risk neutrality in the first-price/Dutch auctions. However, risk preferences have typically not been controlled for (see, however, section I.G.4 below).

The experimental data show that subjects do not behave in strategically equivalent ways in first-price and Dutch auctions (Coppinger et al. 1980, Cox et al. 1982) or in English and second-price auctions (Kagel et al. 1987). Further, bids in single unit first-price and Dutch auctions are commonly above the RNNE, consistent with risk aversion (section I.G explores the question of risk aversion in some detail). Prices are also commonly above the equilibrium (dominant) strategy prediction in second-price auctions, although here bidding is independent of risk attitudes. In English auctions bidding typically converges to the dominant strategy prediction after a few auction periods.

1. Tests of the Strategic Equivalence of First-Price and Dutch Auctions

Coppinger et al. (1980) and Cox et al. (1982) report higher prices in first-price compared to Dutch auctions, with these higher prices holding across auctions with different numbers of bidders (it is important to explore the effects of varying numbers of bidders here as the bid function depends on n).[3] These results are summarized in Table 7.1. Price differences averaged \$0.31 per auction period, with Dutch prices approximately 5 percent lower, on average, than in first-price auctions. To minimize the effects of between auction variation in prices, which can be sizable, Cox et al. (1982) emphasized paired-comparison designs, auction series in which the underlying distribution of private valuations is the same while the auction institution varies.

Efficiency in private value auctions can be measured in terms of the percentage of auctions where the high value holder wins the item, auctions with Pareto efficient outcomes.[4] First-price and Dutch auctions varied systematically with respect to efficiency levels, with 88 percent of the first-price auctions being Pareto efficient, compared to 80 percent of the Dutch auctions (Cox et al. 1982).

Bidding was significantly above the RNNE in first-price auctions for all $n > 3$, with mean prices in auctions with three bidders being only slightly above the RNNE. Dutch auction prices, while lower than in first-price auctions, were above the RNNE price for all $n > 3$ as well, with Dutch prices in auctions with three bidders somewhat below the RNNE price. Cox et al. (1982) conclude that

> In first-price auctions for groups of size N = 4, 5, 6 and 9, but not for N = 3, we reject the null hypothesis of risk-neutral Nash equilibrium bidding behavior in favor of our version of the Ledyard risk-averse model (where bidders have constant relative risk aversion) of Nash bidding behavior. (33)

Table 7.1. Price Differences: Dutch versus
First-Price Auctions

n	First Price	Dutch Price	Difference
3	2.36	1.98	.38
	2.60	2.57	.03
4	5.42	4.98	.44
	5.86	5.68	.18
5	9.15	8.72	.43
	9.13	8.84	.29
6	13.35	13.25	.10
	13.09	12.89	.20
9	31.02	30.32	.70

Source: Cox, Roberson, and Smith 1982, table 7.
Note: Means for paired-comparison auction sequences. Two entries
indicate two paired-comparison sequences for that value of n.

In addition, Cox et al. (1982) conjectured that pricing at the RNNE in first-price auctions with three bidders might reflect a breakdown in the noncooperative behavior which underlies the Nash bidding model. However, subsequent experiments report bidding which is substantially, and significantly, above the RNNE in first-price auctions with three bidders (Cox, Smith, and Walker 1988; Dyer, Kagel, and Levin 1989a). Two explanations for these differences immediately suggest themselves. First, Cox et al. (1982) employed a cross-over design with subjects bidding in sequences of Dutch and first-price auctions so that the lower bidding in Dutch auctions may have carried over to lower prices in first-price auctions (see Harstad 1990, reported in section I.B.2, and Rietz (1993), reported in section I.G.4, for reports of hysteresis effects in IPV auctions). Second, expected profit conditional on winning the auction was substantially higher in the later studies, and there is evidence that with higher expected profit bidders act as if they are more risk averse (section I.G.1).[5]

Understanding the Failure of the Isomorphism between
Dutch and First-Price Auctions

Cox et al. (1982) offer two alternative explanations for the lower bidding in Dutch versus first-price auctions. One model is based on the assumption that there is a positive utility of "suspense" associated with playing the "waiting game" in the Dutch auction which is additive with respect to the expected utility of income from the auction. The other is a real time model of the Dutch auction in which bidders update their estimates of their rivals' valuations, mistakenly assuming them to be lower than they initially anticipated as a consequence of no one having taken the item as the clock ticks down (what they refer to as the probability miscalculation model).

These alternative formulations are elaborated on and tested in Cox et al. 1983a. The test procedure consisted of tripling the conversion rate from experimental to U.S. dollars in a series of Dutch auctions. Assuming that the utility of money income function has the constant relative risk averse (CRRA) form, and that the utility of suspense associated with the Dutch auction is *independent* of the amount of money involved, tripling the conversion rate will increase the suspense component of the game resulting in higher prices. Contrary to the suspense model's prediction, Cox et al. (1983a) are unable to reject a null hypothesis of no difference in auction prices as a result of tripling the conversion rate.

These results rule out the suspense model specified and are consistent with the probability miscalculation model which predicts no response to the change in conversion rates. However, as Cox et al. (1983a) point out, these no-change results are consistent with a number of other model specifications as well. For example, the suspense model prediction rests critically on the assumption that the utility of suspense is *independent* of the amount of money at stake in the auction. If, as seems plausible, the utility of suspense is a positive function of the amount of money at stake, then whether and how prices will change in the Dutch auction as the conversion rate increases depend on the rate at which the utility of suspense increases with increases in the conversion rate.[6] Further, subsequent research suggests problems with the adequacy of CRRA as a maintained hypothesis and the efficacy of using changes in conversion rates as a treatment variable for determining the effects of incentives on behavior (see section I.G.1 below). Tests based on alternative model specifications, as well as experimental manipulations for which the probability miscalculation model predicts a *change* in behavior, have yet to be conducted. The latter is important since, in general, it is preferable to employ manipulations requiring changes in behavior with respect to a preferred hypothesis in order to feel really comfortable with the validity of that hypothesis.

2. Tests of the Strategic Equivalence of Second-Price and English Auctions

Kagel et al. (1987) report failures of strategic equivalence in second-price and English auctions with affiliated private values. For now we ignore the affiliation issue since the dominant strategy is unaffected by affiliation (affiliation is defined in section I.D along with an analysis of first-price auctions with affiliated private values, in which case affiliation does affect the Nash equilibrium). The results of Kagel et al. for second-price auctions are shown in Figure 7.1. In these auctions prices averaged $2.00 (11%) *above* the dominant strategy price. These results have since been replicated in independent private value auctions with both experienced and inexperienced bidders (Harstad 1990, Kagel and Levin 1993), so that bidding above the dominant strategy cannot be attributed to affiliation or to subject inexperience. Bidding above the dominant strategy in second-price auctions is relatively wide spread. For example, Kagel and Levin (1993) report that 30 percent of all bids were essentially at the dominant strategy price (within 5 cents of it), 62 percent of all bids were above the dominant strategy price, and only 8

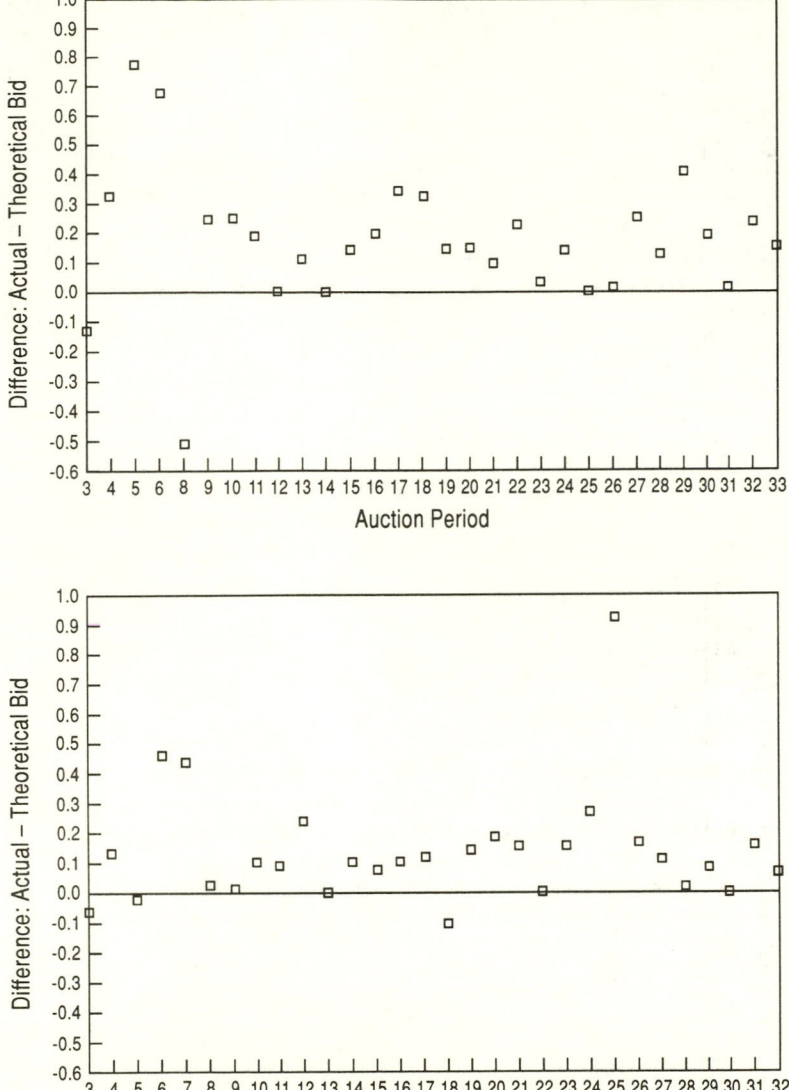

Figure 7.1. Second-price auctions: deviations from dominant strategy price (deviations are normalized by dividing through by the domain from which private valuations are drawn). Top panel, session 1; bottom panel, session 2. *Source:* Kagel, Harstad, and Levin 1987.

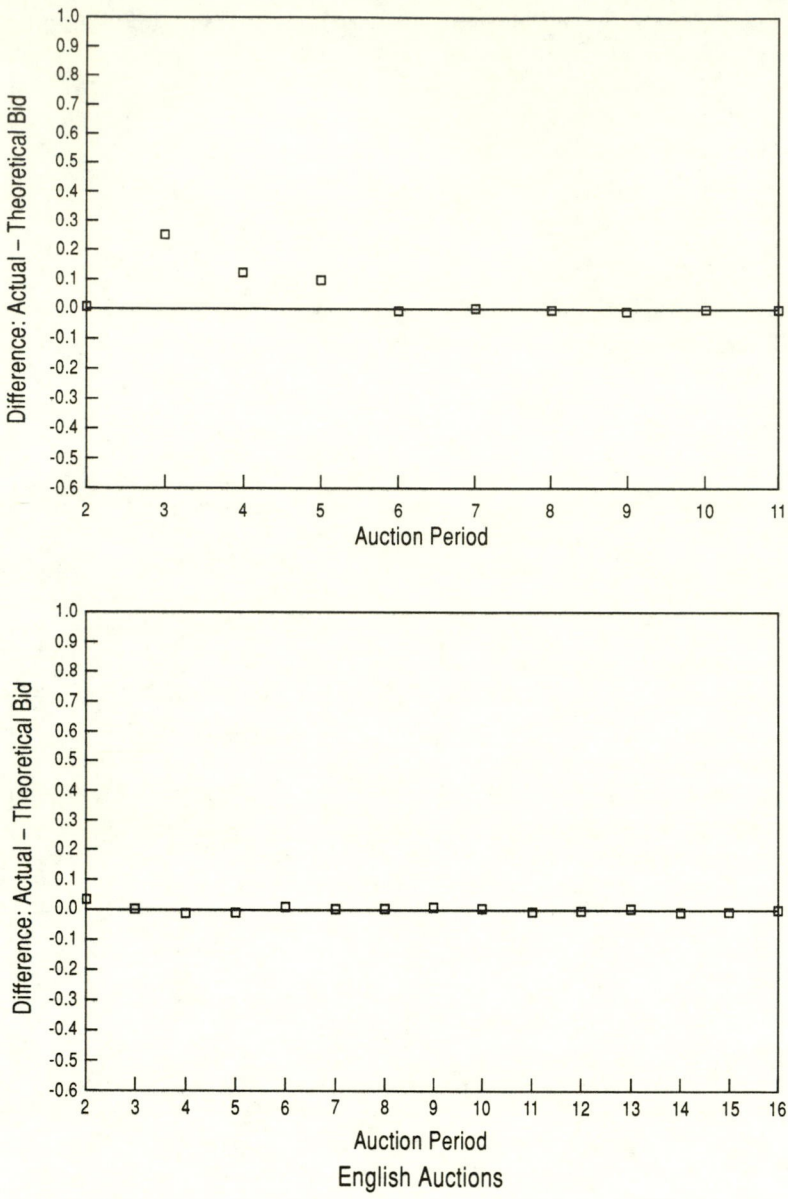

Figure 7.2. English auctions: deviations from dominant strategy price (deviations are normalized by dividing through by the domain from which private valuations are drawn). Top panel, session 1; bottom panel, session 2. *Source:* Kagel, Harstad, and Levin 1987.

percent of all bids were below it.[7] In contrast, as shown in Figure 7.2, in English clock auctions market prices rapidly converged to the dominant strategy price.

Convergence to the dominant strategy price in English auctions is also reported in Coppinger et al. (1980) for single unit IPV auctions and in Van Huyck, Battalio, and Beil (1993) and McCabe, Rassenti, and Smith (1990) for multiple unit IPV English clock auctions (the seller offers multiple units, but each buyer can purchase at most a single unit).[8] Cox et al. (1985a) report that subjects failed to follow their dominant bidding strategy in multiple unit, uniform price, sealed bid auctions. However, unlike the single unit auctions, only a minority of the bids (33 percent for inexperienced subjects, 15 percent for experienced subjects) were above their private valuations, while a majority of the bids were below valuations.[9] Smith and his associates (Smith 1980, Coppinger et al. 1980, Cox et al. 1982) report single unit second-price auctions in which prices converge to the dominant strategy price from below. However, in at least one of these experiments (Cox et al. 1982) subjects were explicitly *prohibited from bidding above their valuations.*

Harstad (1990) reports a variant of the second-price auction (referred to as a "price list" auction) in which subjects indicate whether each of 101 prices (uniformly distributed over the range of conceivable market prices) is acceptable or not, with the bidder with the highest acceptable price winning the item and paying a price equal to the highest of any rival's acceptable price. Although mean prices in these auctions are below the dominant strategy price, these differences are dwarfed by the standard error, indicating a substantial amount of bidding above and below the dominant strategy price. Finally, Harstad (1990) also observed subjects in standard second-priced auctions who had fourteen to sixteen periods of experience in first-price auctions. Mean bids were slightly below the dominant strategy prediction in these second-price auctions, indicating that prior experience in first-price auctions is sufficient to eliminate the average overbidding reported.[10] However, Harstad does note a core of subjects who continuously overbid in the second-price auctions, as if no significant lesson was carried over from the first-price auctions.

The frequency of Pareto efficient outcomes in second-price auctions is quite comparable to first-price auctions. For example, 82 percent of the first-price auctions and 79 percent of the second-price auctions reported in Kagel and Levin (1993) were Pareto efficient.

Understanding the Failure of the Isomorphism between
English and Second-Price Auctions

Bidding above the dominant strategy price in second-price auctions would have to be labeled a mistake, since bidding at value is a dominant strategy, irrespective of risk attitudes, the number of rival bidders, the distribution of resale values, and so on. Kagel et al. conjecture that bidding above x is based on the illusion that it improves the probability of winning with little cost as the second-highest bid price is paid. The overbidding observed is sustainable in the sense that average profits are positive. Further, the idea that bidding modestly above x only increases the chances of winning in cases where you don't want to win is far from obvious. Finally, to the extent that more precise conformity with the dominant bidding strategy results from negative feedback as a consequence of deviating from it, this feedback is weak. For example, for second-price symmetric bid functions of the sort $x + k$, with k equal to the average overbid observed for the high bidders by Kagel et al., the probability of losing money conditional on winning the auction was .36, while the unconditional probability of losing money averaged .06.[11] These punishment probabilities are relatively small, particularly if bidders start with the illusion that modest bidding over valuation increases the probability of winning without materially affecting the price paid; this presumption is usually correct. One straightforward way to test this conjecture is to see what happens to such overbidding when punishment is more likely, as when the number of bidders increase (data reported in section I.C.1 provide somewhat equivocal support for this prediction.)

The structure of the English auction would seem to make it relatively transparent to bidders that they should not bid above their valuations. First, in contrast to second-price auctions, any time you win and bid above your valuation in an English auction, you necessarily lose money. This element of the English auction would appear to play some role because Kagel et al. observed some early overbidding, which collapsed immediately after losses or when losses would have been earned in the dry-run period. Second, the "real time" nature of the English auction would seem ideal for producing observational learning, learning without actually having to lose money, since in comparing the going price with their private value, subjects are likely to see that they will lose money, should they win, whenever the price exceeds their private value. This interpretation is supported by the results of Harstad's (1990) "price list" auctions described in the previous section. Unlike the English auction, in the price list auction you do not necessarily lose money should you win and bid above your private valuation. However, like the English auction, the price list auction focuses attention on whether each price is acceptable or not, which tends to raise the question of whether you want to win with such a bid, much as in the English auction. The net effect is that the difference between bids and values is not significantly different from zero in the price list auction, although there remain a core of bidders who consistently bid above their valuations.

3. Summing Up

The behavioral breakdown of the strategic equivalence of first-price and Dutch auctions and of second-price and English auctions is analogous to the preference reversal phenomenon, where theoretically equivalent ways of eliciting individual preferences do not produce the same preference ordering (see the Introduction, section III.F.1 and Camerer, chapter 8, section III.I).[12] Psychologists attribute the preference reversal phenomenon to a breakdown in procedural invariance principles so that the weight attached to different dimensions of a problem varies systematically with the response mode employed.[13] In the auctions, prices are higher when bidders must specify a price, as in the first and second-price auctions, compared to the open auctions where the decision is essentially to accept or reject the price that the auctioneer announces. Like the P(rice)-bets in the preference reversal phenomenon, the sealed bid auctions focus attention on the price dimension of the problem, and, like the P-bets, generates somewhat higher prices. On the other hand, the accept/reject decisions involved in the Dutch and English auctions focus attention on profitability, generating somewhat lower prices.

A number of economists have expressed surprise and/or concern regarding subjects' failure to follow consistently the dominant strategy in second-price auctions. The first thing to remember is that the dominant strategy is far from transparent to the uninitiated in second-price auctions (second-price auctions are rarely employed in practice, and Vickrey's seminal paper characterizing the dominant strategy was published in 1961, although economists had, presumably, studied auctions for a number of years prior to this). Note also that there is a small literature by psychologists showing that dominance is often violated in individual choice settings when it is not transparent (Tversky and Kahneman 1986).[14] Further, there is little doubt that if presented with Vickrey's argument, or clear enough examples embodying that argument, subjects would follow the dominant strategy. The latter is, however, quite beside the point in terms of understanding the behavioral forces underlying dominance violations.

In spite of the bidding above valuations observed in second-price auctions, my colleagues and I have argued that the dominant bidding strategy does have some drawing power in explaining behavior. First, one might ask why we don't see even greater deviations from the dominant bidding strategy in second-price auctions? We can only presume that bidders are responding, to some extent, to the forces underlying the dominant strategy: if they bid even higher, the likelihood of winning when they don't want to increases. Second, Kagel and Levin (1993) note that if we declare a bid within $0.05 of a player's private valuation as, for all practical purposes, corresponding to the dominant bidding strategy, then approximately 30 percent of all bids are at the dominant strategy. This is well above the frequency of bidding within $0.05 of private valuations in first-price sealed bid auctions and in third-price auctions, which average less than 3 percent in both cases. Finally, increasing the number of bidders from five to ten, while holding the distribution of resale values constant, does result in higher (more aggressive) bidding in first-price auctions, yet produces no change, or a possible modest reduction, in bids in second-price auctions, which is what the theory predicts (see section I.C.1). (The reduction in bids may result from the increased probability of losing money as a consequence of overbidding with increased n.) Thus, what we are seeing in second-price auctions is relatively stable and modest (in terms of expected cost) bidding above valuations, rather than a complete collapse of the theory. We attribute this overbidding to perceptual errors (response mode effects), given that it does not occur in the English auction, which has the same dominant bidding strategy.

C. Effects of Varying and Uncertain Numbers of Bidders

A basic prediction of first-price IPV auctions is that increasing the number of bidders results in higher (more aggressive) bidding. Somewhat counter-intuitively the same treatment effect reduces bids in third-price IPV auctions. Further, if bidders have constant or decreasing absolute risk aversion (which includes CRRA bidders), and there is uncertainty about the number of bidders (numbers uncertainty), this uncertainty raises revenue, on average, compared to revealing information about the number of bidders (McAfee and McMillan 1987b, Matthews 1987). Experiments exploring these comparative static predictions are reported here. In all cases, on average, behavior changes in the way the theory predicts.

1. Effects of Changing Numbers of Bidders

Battalio, Kogut, and Meyer (1990) report a series of first-price IPV auctions in which they exogenously varied the number of bidders while holding the underlying distribution of private valuations constant. Primarily relying on the dual market bidding technique,[15] the large majority of individual subjects (86 percent) increased their bids, on average, when the market size increased from five to ten bidders, with the majority of these increases (60 percent) being statistically significant. Further, none of the subjects who decreased their bids, on average, did so by a statistically significant amount.

Dyer et al. (1989a) report auctions in which bidders made contingent bids, one in a market of size 3 and another in a market of size 6 (in contingent bidding there is uncertainty about the number of bidders in the market so that bids are made conditional on the number of bidders actually present in the market). Seventy-four percent of all contingent bids were higher in the market of size 6 than in the market of size 3. Further, only 3 percent of the bids were in the wrong direction, a larger bid in the market of size 3. For the remaining 23 percent of the observations, the two contingent bids were equal. One reason for the high frequency of equal bids was that subjects did not always change their bids when their valuations were relatively low. These bidders had little chance of winning the auction and therefore little to gain from making the "proper" changes. Discarding the lowest one third of resale values reduced the proportion of equal bids to 12 percent, of the remaining two thirds of the bids, while the error rate associated with bidding more in the small market remained at 3 percent (see section I.G.2 for further discussion of the effects of low expected profit on bidder behavior).

Cox et al. (1988) studied the effects of varying numbers of bidders on the coefficient estimates of individual subject bid functions in IPV first-price auctions. From equation (1) it is clear that the slope of the bid function is increasing in n. The assumption of constant relative risk aversion (CRRA) offered in Cox et al. modifies the bid function as follows

(4)
$$b(x) = \underline{x} + \frac{n-1}{n-r} (x - \underline{x})$$

where r is the coefficient of relative risk aversion (with $r = 0$ corresponding to risk neutrality and $r \leq 1$ required for individual rationality), so that the slope of the bid function is increasing for all $r < 1$. Average sample means of individual subject slope coefficients were increasing for group sizes 3, 4, 5, and 9, with the sample mean for group size 6 below that of group size 4 and 5. Although no pair of means for $n = 4$, 5, or 6 were significantly different from each other, the mean slope coefficient for $n = 3$ was significantly less than the rest, and the slope coefficient for $n = 9$ was significantly more than the rest.

Although it is clear from these first-price auction results that, in general, subjects respond correctly to increased numbers of rivals, it is possible that this is simply a reflex reaction rather than a response to the strategic forces inherent in IPV auctions, since in market settings increased numbers of rivals typically calls for more aggressive behavior. Further, as shown in Kagel et al (1987), there exist relatively simple ad hoc bidding models which predict more aggressive bidding with increased n in first-price auctions. For example, consider the following ad hoc bidding model: Individual i discounts her bid relative to her value by some constant proportion, $\alpha > 0$, of the difference between her value and the lowest possible value, with some accounting for the probable location of rivals in that interval; that is, she uses a discount factor $\alpha(x - \underline{x})/n$. The resulting bid function is

$$(5) \qquad b(x) = x - \frac{\alpha(x - \underline{x})}{n} = x + \frac{n - \alpha}{n}(x - \underline{x})$$

which has all of the qualitative characteristics of the CRRA bid function (4).

The third-price IPV auction provides a more stringent test of the equilibrium prediction of the effects of increased numbers of bidders since it predicts lower (less aggressive) bidding in response to more rivals, contrary to the reflex reaction hypothesis and the ad hoc bidding model's predictions. Kagel and Levin (1993) test this prediction for auctions with five versus ten bidders, with the results reported in Table 7.2. In first-price auctions all bidders increased their average bids, with bids *increasing* an average of $0.65 per auction period (significant at the 1 percent level). In contrast, in second-price auctions the majority of bidders did not change their bids, with the average change in bids being −$0.04 (not significantly different from zero). However, in third-price auctions 46 percent of all subjects *decreased* their bids, on average, for an average decrease of $0.40 per auction period (significant at the 5 percent level). Further, even stronger qualitative results are reported when the calculations are restricted to valuations lying in the top half of the distribution: the average increase in bids in first-price auctions is $1.22, and 59 percent of all subjects decrease their bids, on average, in third-price auctions, with an average decrease of $0.86 per auction period. Although a number of bidders in third-price auctions clearly err in response to increased numbers of rivals by increasing, or not changing, their bids, the change in pricing rules has relatively large and statistically significant effects on bidder's responses in the *direction* that Nash equilibrium bidding theory predicts.

Table 7.2. Effects of Changes in Number of Rivals on Bids

	All Private Valuations				Top Half of Private Valuations			
	Changes in Average Bids by Individual Subjects (auctions with $n = 5$ vs. $n = 10$)			Average Dollar Change in Bids (standard error mean)	Changes in Average Bids by Individual Subjects (auctions with $n = 5$ vs. $n = 10$)			Average Dollar Change in Bids (standard error)
Auction	Increased	Decreased	No Change[a]		Increased	Decreased	No Change[a]	
First price	10	0	0	0.65[b] (0.11)	10	0	0	1.22[b] (0.12)
Second price	2	3	5	−0.04 (0.08)	3	1	6	0.02 (0.04)
Third price	16	18	5	−0.40[c] (0.17)	11	23	5	−0.86[b] (0.26)

Source: Kagel and Levin 1993.
[a]Average absolute difference is less than or equal to $0.05.
[b]Significantly different from 0 at 1% level.
[c]Significantly different from 0 at 5% level.

2. Uncertainty Regarding the Number of Bidders

In most theoretical auction models the number of competing bidders is assumed to be fixed and known to all bidders. McAfee and McMillan (1987b) and Matthews (1987) generalize auction theory to allow uncertainty regarding the number of bidders (numbers uncertainty). They show that in IPV first-price auctions if the number of bidders is unknown and bidders have constant or decreasing absolute risk aversion—a belief that most economists hold as a working hypothesis (Arrow 1970, Machina 1983) and which includes CRRA—then expected revenue is greater if the actual number of bidders is concealed rather than revealed.[16] In contrast, if bidders are risk neutral, expected revenue is the same whether the actual number of bidders is revealed or concealed. Examining the effects of numbers uncertainty provides an internal consistency test of the hypothesis that bidding above the RNNE in first-price auctions reflects, at least in part, elements of risk aversion.

Dyer et al. (1989a) compared a contingent versus a noncontingent bidding procedure. The contingent bidding procedure served to reveal the number of bidders by permitting each bidder to submit a vector of bids, with each bid in the vector corresponding to a specific number of rivals, and with that bid binding when the realized number of rivals matched the number of the contingent bid. In the noncontingent bidding procedure only a single bid was permitted and had to be made prior to the random draw determining the number of active bidders in the market, thereby concealing information about the number of rivals. The market revenue predictions of the theory were clearly satisfied as the noncontingent bidding procedure raised more revenue than the contingent procedure, with a mean difference of $0.31 (which is significant at the 1 percent level) on an average revenue base of $20.67. Although the revenue predictions of the theory were satisfied, examination of individual bids showed that (i) narrowly interpreted, the Nash equilibrium bidding theory underlying the market predictions was rejected, as less than 50 percent of all bids satisfied the strict inequality requirements of the theory, but (ii) a majority of the deviations from these inequality requirements favored the revenue-raising predictions of the Nash model, and, in a large number of cases, involved marginal violations of the theory.

Dyer et al. (1989a) score these results as a partial success for the theory and the argument that bidding above the RNNE in private value auctions is, at least in part, a result of risk aversion. This evaluation is based on the evidence reported and on the fact that the theory assumes symmetry (identical bid functions) and that all bidders, no matter how small the expected gain, will find it worthwhile to adjust their bids, assumptions which are unlikely to be strictly satisfied, so that it is probably asking too much to expect the point predictions of the theory to be exactly satisfied. I return to the question of risk aversion in private value auctions in section I.G.

3. Summing Up

Examining the effects of varying numbers of bidders tests one of the basic comparative static implications of auction theory. Increased numbers of rivals almost always results in higher (more aggressive) bidding in first-price auctions, at least for bidders who perceive themselves as having a realistic chance of winning the auction. This is not just a reflex reaction to increased competition, as the same treatment effect has essentially no impact on bidding in second-price auctions and results in lower bids in third-price auctions, as Nash equilibrium bidding theory predicts. With numbers uncertainty, concealing (as opposed to revealing) information about the number of rivals raises average market prices, as predicted if bidders exhibit constant or decreasing absolute risk aversion. This last result serves as qualified support for the idea that bidding above the RNNE in first-price auctions results, in part, from risk aversion.

D. Auctions with Affiliated Private Values

In auctions with affiliated private values, bidders know the value of the item to themselves with certainty, but a higher value of the item for one bidder makes higher values for other bidders more likely (private values are positively correlated relative to the set of possible valuations).[17] Auctions with affiliated private values have a number of comparative static implications with interesting behavioral and normative implications. In particular, the effects of public information about rivals' valuations should, on average, increase revenue assuming risk neutral bidders (the impact of public information about item valuation is particularly prominent in common value/mineral rights auctions and will be discussed in detail in section II.A). There are clear predictions regarding individual responses to such information which can be readily tested as well.

Kagel et al. (1987) used a two step procedure to generate affiliated private values: First, a random number x_0 was drawn from a uniform distribution on $[\underline{x}, \bar{x}]$. Second, once x_0 was determined, private values x were determined, one for each bidder, randomly drawn from a uniform distribution $[x_0 - \epsilon, x_0 + \epsilon]$, where ϵ was common knowledge. Announcing x_0 provides maximum public information about the distribution of rivals' private valuations, reducing the auction to one with IPVs.

For private valuations in the interval $\underline{x} + \epsilon \le x \le \bar{x} - \epsilon$, the RNNE bid function when x_0 is not known is

$$(6) \qquad\qquad b(x) = x - \frac{2\epsilon}{n} + \frac{Y}{n}$$

where Y is a negative exponential which becomes negligible rapidly as x moves beyond $\underline{x} + \epsilon$. With x_0 announced, this reduces to the following IPV bid function:

$$(7) \qquad\qquad b(x, x_0) = (x_0 - \epsilon) + \frac{n-1}{n}\, [x - (x_0 - \epsilon)]$$

(the lower bound of the interval, $x_0 - \epsilon$, serves the role of $\underline{x}$ in the standard IPV auction design—recall equation (1)). Under the RNNE, revealing x_0 raises individual bids unless x is very close to $x_0 + \epsilon$. The intuition here is straightforward: In symmetric bidding models each agent bids as if she has the high signal value since this is when she wins, the only event that counts. As such, bidders with relatively low valuations are, on average, surprised following the announcement of x_0, realizing that they had lower valuations than they had assumed prior to the announcement, and raise their bids in efforts to win the item. This in turn puts pressure on bidders with higher valuations to raise their bids, resulting in increased prices and more revenue.

With affiliated private values and risk aversion, bids are above the RNNE model prediction. Further, with risk aversion, the release of public information, even large amounts of public information, such as announcing x_0, may not result in increased revenue (Milgrom and Weber 1982, Kagel et al. 1987).[18] However, assuming symmetry in bidding, Kagel, Harstad, and Levin demonstrate that for any concave utility function, all bidders whose private valuations lie below $C(x_0)$ $= x_0 + [(n - 2)/n]\epsilon$ will raise their bids following the announcement of x_0. This prediction has considerable bite since on average the highest valuation lies just above $C(x_0)$.

Kagel et al. (1987) contrast the Nash equilibrium bidding model's predictions with two ad hoc bidding models. In the ad hoc models bidders do not consider the best response to their rivals' behavior, but simply discount their bids taking account of rudimentary strategic forces inherent in varying ϵ and n. One might justify bidding schemes of this sort with reference to the strong informational and cognitive requirements inherent in calculating a best response to rivals' behavior. As such, the ad hoc models serve as benchmarks against which to evaluate bidders' responsiveness to the strategic forces underlying the more sophisticated Nash equilibrium bidding theory.

The ad hoc bidding models can readily account for bidding above the RNNE in auctions with affiliated or independent private values, and predict linear bid functions (section I.C.1, equation (5), formulates one such model for the IPV case). But the ad hoc models also predict that revealing x_0 will result in no change, or a decrease, in average winning bids. Further, in the ad hoc models for all $x >$ $C(x_0)$ bids will be lowered following the announcement of x_0, in contrast to the Nash model's prediction that bids are likely to increase in this interval.

Bidding was studied under several values of ϵ. With $\epsilon = \$6$, the smallest ϵ value employed, high bids (prices) averaged \$0.29 *below* the RNNE prediction (these deviations are significant at the 10 percent level).[19] In contrast, with $\epsilon = \$12$ and \$24, prices were significantly *above* the RNNE prediction (averaging \$1.40 and \$3.34 above it). Both the ad hoc and the Nash bidding model with risk aversion can account for these data, but to do so the markdown coefficient in the ad hoc model would have to vary with ϵ and the utility function underlying the Nash model would have to exhibit increasing, as opposed to constant, relative risk aversion.[20]

Public information about rivals' valuations (announcing x_0) increased prices an average of \$0.22 per auction, which is about 30 percent of the increase predicted under the RNNE and is not significantly different from zero. Further, these changes in revenue were quite variable across auctions (substantially more so than equilibrium predictions), with most of the increase being accounted for by one of five auction series. However, public information announcements were only implemented with $\epsilon = \$12$ and \$24, when bidding under private information conditions was well above the RNNE. As such, the results are closer to the predictions of a risk averse Nash equilibrium bidding model that permits some increase in revenue, than the ad hoc models which predict no change or a decrease in prices with the release of public information.

Table 7.3 shows how individual subjects altered their bids following the announcement of x_0. In cases where $x < x_0$ (the first column in Table 7.3), both the ad hoc and the Nash equilibrium bidding models predict that subjects will raise their bids. This happened 67 percent of the time, with the large majority of the deviations from this prediction involving no change in bids. Undoubtedly, a partial explanation for the relatively large numbers of unchanged bids here is, as one subject remarked, a result of the slim chances of winning the auction, so that it did not pay to bother calculating a bid increment (similar results were reported for bidders with low resale values in auctions with varying numbers of bidders, section I.C.1).

For bidders with resale values in the interval $x_0 < x < C(x_0)$, both the sophisticated ad hoc bidding model and the Nash equilibrium bidding model predict that

**Table 7.3. Effects of Public Information on Individual Bids
with Affiliated Private Values**

Bids	Private Values Relative to x_0		
	$x < x_0$	$x_0 \leq x \leq C(x_0)$	$x > C(x_0)$
$b(x,x_0) > b(x)$	66.8%	67.0%	38.2%
$b(x,x_0) = b(x)$	27.3%	17.0%	18.2%
$b(x,x_0) < b(x)$	5.9%	16.0%	43.6%
Total number of bids	187	106	55

Source: Kagel, Harstad, and Levin 1987.
Notes: Each entry is the percentage of the values drawn, relative to x_0, as in
   the column heading, for which the subject responded as in the row head-
   ing. Analyses restricted to $\underline{x} + \varepsilon \leq x \leq \bar{x} - \varepsilon$. $C(x_0) = x_0 + (n-2)\varepsilon/n$.

bids will increase with the release of public information. This happened in 67
percent of the cases, well above the frequency expected by chance factors alone.
Attempts to rationalize the failure to change bids here on grounds of subjective
transactions costs, in conjunction with a low probability of winning the auction,
are on substantially weaker footing than when $x < x_0$, and should be counted as
violations of both the ad hoc and the Nash equilibrium bidding models.

The last column in Table 7.3 shows what happens to bids when $x > C(x_0)$. Nash
equilibrium bidding theory, accounting for risk aversion, calls for increasing or
decreasing bids here, depending on the degree of risk aversion and the location of
private values in the interval $[C(x_0), x_0 + \varepsilon]$. In contrast, even the most sophisticated of the ad hoc bidding models calls for *all* bidders reducing their bids here.
Instead, a sizable proportion increase their bids, consistent with the Nash bidding
model's prediction.

Summing Up

In first-price auctions with affiliated private values, Nash equilibrium bidding
theory organizes the data better than either of two ad hoc bidding models. Public
information about others' valuations increases average market prices, but the increase is smaller and less reliable than predicted under RNNE bidding. Lower
average revenue might be attributed to risk aversion, and the high variability may
be attributed to the sizable frequency of individual subject bidding errors relative
to the theory.

E. Effects of Price Information in Private Value Auctions

There is considerable diversity in price information feedback following submission of sealed bids in field environments and between different research groups in
the laboratory. For example, government agencies typically report back the full
set of bids, along with bidders' names, as they are required to do so by law, but
the private sector typically does not report any prices to losing bidders, just that

they were not successful. Although a persistent bidder can often obtain fairly complete price information on a private sector job, most do not, and for those who do the data are less precise than on public sector bids.[21]

Isaac and Walker (1985) have studied the effect of price information feedback in IPV auctions. Under their full information condition subjects were provided with all bids from the previous period and the bidder's identification number. In the limited information condition subjects were given only the winning bid from the previous period and the identification number of the winner. In first-price auctions with four bidders, prices under the limited information condition were consistently higher than under the full information condition, but there were no significant differences in efficiency between the two information conditions.

Standard noncooperative game theoretic models of auctions make no mention of the effects of price information following bid submission since most theory relates to single period auctions where such feedback would be irrelevant.[22] It is interesting to speculate as to how price feedback impacts on bidding. In the auction experiments, unlike the single-period theory, a fixed number of players bid in a series of twenty-five auction periods. This suggests two possibilities (which are not mutually exclusive): First, the full information condition may provide bidders with a chance to signal their intentions not to bid very aggressively when they have low valuations. That is, the added information promotes tacit collusion to some extent (although winning bids are still above the RNNE prediction). Second, bidders are unlikely to determine immediately what their best strategy is and to have to go through a trial and error learning period as they explore the effects of different bidding strategies. In this case the price information may provide them with a better sense of what their rivals' bids are likely to be and to help correct for overly pessimistic, or overly optimistic, initial expectations. (Section I.F briefly examines adjustment/learning patterns in private value auctions.)

Cox, Smith, and Walker (1984) examined the effects of suppressing information about the highest accepted and highest rejected price (their standard price information feedback) in multiple unit discriminatory price auctions. They found no effect on bidding. Battalio et al. (1990) examined the effect of reporting the winning bid versus the highest three bids in auctions with five and ten bidders. They found no systematic response to the increased information. The suggestion is that relatively minor variations in price information, compared to the major variation implemented in Isaac and Walker (1985), have little effect on bidding.

Finally, Isaac and Walker also studied the effects of information in auctions where bidders were permitted to discuss strategy prior to bidding and to form cartels. These results will be reported in section III.A, which deals with collusion in auctions.

F. Learning, Adjustment Processes, and Cash Balance Effects in First-Price Private Value Auctions

There has been very little study of learning and adjustment processes in private value auctions as, eyeballing the data, investigators typically observe no pronounced trends in bids relative to resale values.[23] There is, however, increasing

**Table 7.4. Time Trend and Cash Balance Effects in
Private Value Auctions**

Isaac and Walker (1985)[a]

Full Information:
$\quad$ 0.826 x − 0.246 peri + 0.003 bal$_{t-1}$ $\qquad\qquad$ $R^2 = .954$
$\quad$ (0.006)[b]   (0.102)[c]   (0.008)

Limited Information:
$\quad$ 0.858 x − 0.530 peri + 0.012 bal$_{t-1}$ $\qquad\qquad$ $R^2 = .938$
$\quad$ (0.007)[b]   (0.122)[b]   (0.014)

Battalio, Kogut, and Meyer (1990)[d]

$\quad$ 0.936 x + 0.026 dx + 0.022 peri + 0.008 bal$_{t-1}$ $\quad$ $R^2 = .979$
$\quad$ (0.004)[b]   (0.003)[b]   (1.04)   (0.013)

Kagel, Harstad, and Levin (1987)[e]

$\quad$ 0.984 x − 0.063ε − 2.50 peri − 0.031 bal$_{t-1}$ $\qquad$ $R^2 = .996$
$\quad$ (0.002)[b]   (0.014)[b]   (0.635)[b]   (0.023)

Notes: peri = 1/(auction period); bal$_{t-1}$ = cash balance at the time of the bid;
$\quad$ dx = change in slope coefficient for $n = 10$. Numbers in parentheses are
$\quad$ standard errors.
[a] $(n = 4, \bar{x} = \$10, \text{IPV})$.
[b] Significantly different from 0 at 1% level, two-tailed t-test.
[c] Significantly different from 0 at 5% level, two-tailed t-test.
[d] $(n = 5 \,\&\, 10, \bar{x} = 29–59, \text{IPV})$.
[e] $(n = 6, \text{affiliated private values})$.

evidence of systematic adjustments in bidding over time in first-price auctions.
Smith and Walker (1993), using mean deviations from RNNE bidding as the
dependent variable, report that more experienced bidders (those participating in
their second, third and fourth auction series) bid significantly higher, as if they are
more risk averse, than inexperienced bidders in auctions with four bidders.

Dyer (personal communication) in a limited inquiry, used a fixed effect regression model to identify relatively large, systematic reductions in bids over time for
inexperienced bidders in auctions with three bidders.[24] Dyer found further reductions in bids when these subjects participated in a second and third auction series,
with the adjustment process essentially completed by the end of the second auction series. These results, in conjunction with Smith and Walker's, suggest that
the most pronounced adjustments in bids will occur for inexperienced bidders and
that a nonlinear time trend will provide a better fit to the data than a linear adjustment process. Finally, in Dyer's experiment adjustments in bids were sufficiently
strong that the coefficient value for the resale variable (x) dropped from 0.764 for
inexperienced bidders to just barely above the RNNE prediction of 0.666 for
experienced bidders.

Further exploration of adjustments in bidding over time are reported in Table 7.4

where fixed effect regression estimates of time trends in bidding are shown for several different private value auction experiments.[25] In each case the time trend variable is the inverse of the auction period, involving a nonlinear time trend specification. In the Isaac and Walker experiment the time trend coefficient is significant under both full and limited information conditions, with the negative coefficient value indicating *higher* bidding over time. Interestingly, the data suggest a more pronounced increase in bids under limited, as compared to full, information conditions. The time trend coefficient is not significant in the Battalio et al. experiment. Finally, the Kagel et al. experiment, with affiliated private values, shows a pronounced increase in bidding over time as well.

Specifying a nonlinear, as compared to a linear adjustment process seems superior on theoretical grounds as it allows more rapid learning initially and permits the adjustment process to converge to some steady state behavior rather than continuing forever at the same rate. It also tends to generate more significant results, as a linear time trend specification fails to achieve statistical significance at conventional levels for the Kagel et al. data and for the Isaac and Walker data under full information conditions and is only marginally significant (at the 10 percent level) in the Isaac and Walker data under limited information conditions. Taken together with Dyer's results, these data suggest that, more often than not, there is some initial adjustment in bids in private value auction experiments, and that the speed and size of adjustment (and even its direction) may be sensitive to the number of competing bidders.

In an effort to capture the impact, if any, of prior earnings on bids, the lagged value of subjects' cash balances (bal_{t-1}) are also included in the regressions reported in Table 7.4. With constant absolute risk aversion, or with subjects evaluating outcomes in terms of deviations from the current status quo in each auction period (as in prospect theory, Kahneman and Tversky 1979), bids should be independent of cash balances. This is a necessary condition for treating these auction series as a collection of single shot auctions. Consistent with this requirement, the cash balance variable does not achieve statistical significance at anything approaching conventional levels in any of these experiments.

G. Risk Aversion, CRRA, the Flat Maximum Critique, and the Binary Lottery Procedure for Controlling Risk Preferences

Bidding above the RNNE outcome is the most common outcome in single unit first-price private value auctions. (Figure 7.3 provides representative data on this score for high bidders in auctions with $n = 3$ and 6.) Bidding above the RNNE outcome can be rationalized in terms of risk aversion. This insight has generated a number of research results, as well as considerable controversy among experimentalists. This section reviews these results and the controversies surrounding them in some detail, as it provides a case study in the give and take of experimental inquiry that results in increased understanding of behavior.

In response to the observation that bidding is typically above the RNNE in

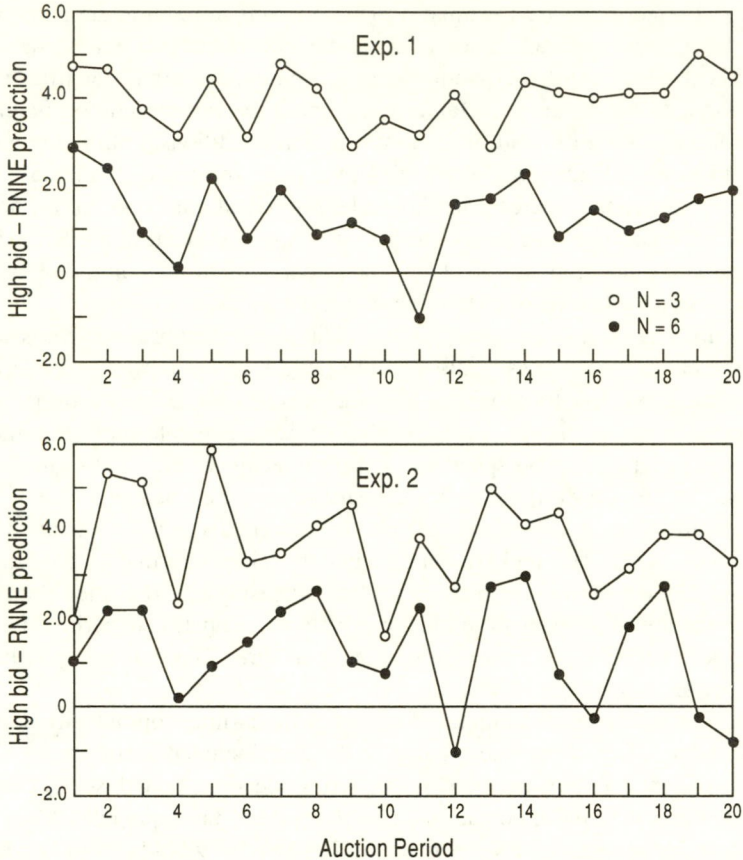

Figure 7.3. First-price auctions: deviations from RNNE price. *Source:* Dyer, Kagel, and Levin 1989a.

single unit first-price auctions, Cox, Smith, and Walker developed a model of heterogeneous bidders with constant relative risk averse (CRRA) utility functions (hereafter referred to as CRRAM; see Cox et al. (1988) for a summary of their model and results). CRRAM provides a focus for much of what follows since Cox, Smith, and Walker have vigorously pursued its development and actively defended it against alternative explanations. The objective of CRRAM is to provide a unified account of bidding above the RNNE in first-price private value auctions in terms of the maintained hypotheses of risk aversion and equilibrium bidding. This has led to a number of criticisms.

First, CRRAM fails as a maintained hypothesis even in terms of characterizing risk aversion in first-price auctions. Second, Harrison (1989) has argued that Cox, Smith, and Walker's conclusions regarding risk aversion are not well supported, as the expected cost of deviating from RNNE bidding is quite small (less than $0.05 at the median), so that in terms of expected monetary payoffs ("payoff space") many subjects had little to lose from such deviations (the flat maximum critique). This has set off a vigorous debate among experimentalists (see the September 1992 issue of the *American Economic Review*).[26] Third, although risk aversion organizes bidding in some private value auction environments, it fails in others. This casts doubt on risk aversion as the primary causal factor behind bidding above the RNNE in first-price auctions. Fourth, the failure of the binary lottery technique (Roth and Malouf 1979) to eliminate higher than predicted bids in first-price private value auctions calls into question the joint hypotheses of risk aversion *and* equilibrium bidding (however, results here are sensitive to the way the technique is introduced and the statistical procedures used to evaluate it).

Results of this dialogue suggest that with respect to the primary issue, the role of risk aversion in first-price auctions, it is probably safe to say that risk aversion is one element, but far from the only element, generating bidding above the RNNE. This is not to say that there is no longer any debate regarding the relative importance of risk aversion versus other factors, or in terms of what these other factors are.

1. Risk Aversion and CRRAM As Applied to Single Unit First-Price Auctions

Market prices from first-price private value auctions generally exceed the RNNE prediction irrespective of the number of bidders in the auction or the research group conducting the investigation (sections I.B.1 and I.C). Examining individual subject bidding data from their own auctions, Cox et al. (1988) measure deviations from the RNNE outcome. Applying a Wilcoxon signed ranks test to these deviations, for 91.1 percent of the subjects the deviations lie above the RNNE (in 75 percent of these cases the deviations are significant at the 5 percent level using a two-tailed test). Thus, the direction of deviations from the RNNE are overwhelmingly on the side predicted for risk averse bidders. Employing a second nonparametric test to these deviations, for 60 percent of the auction series (twenty-eight out of forty-seven), a null hypothesis of identical bid functions is rejected. Cox et al. (1988, 73) conclude, "Bid diversity is a prominent, but not extreme, characteristic of our subject pool."

The CRRAM hypothesis implies that each agent's bids will be a homogeneous linear function of resale values for bids that do not exceed an upper bound, defined as the maximum bid that would be entered by the least risk averse bidder in the population (b^*).[27] This leads to the regression specification

$$(8) \qquad b_i = \alpha_i + \beta_i x_i \quad \text{for } x_i \leq \frac{n - r_i}{n - 1} b^*$$

where we have suppressed the random error term, all bids and valuations are measured relative to $\underline{x}$, and the subscript *i* refers to the fact that α, β, and *r* have subject specific values. CRRAM implies that $\alpha_i = 0$ and $\beta_i = (n - 1)/(n - r_i)$, where r_i is the coefficient of relative risk aversion for bidder i (see equation (4), section I.C). Fits of (8) to individual subject data yield uniformly high R^2 values of 0.96 or better for 80 percent of the individual subjects (Cox et al. 1988). However, for

22 percent of these bid functions, the intercept term, α, is significantly different from zero. Further, α is not randomly distributed around zero, with 63 percent of $\alpha < 0$, more than would be expected on the basis of chance factors alone. These significant intercept values indicate that "some bidders bid zero or a smaller fraction of value at low values or that other bidders bid consciously and deliberately in excess of value." (Cox et al. 1988, 79–80).[28] Cox et al. (1988) have also tested CRRAM against a general log-concave model by adding squared and cubed values of x_i to (8). For 38 percent of the individual subject data tested, they reject the null hypothesis that the bid functions are strictly linear. These results indicate that CRRAM forms a good, but far from perfect, characterization of Cox et al.'s (1988) individual subject bidding data. See, however, Rietz (1993, section I.G.4) who argues that failure to account for heteroskedastic errors and censoring of bids biases the standard errors of the regression coefficients downward, resulting in larger type I errors than the assumed value.

Tests of CRRAM

A unique implication of CRRAM is that multiplying the profit of a winning bid by any factor $\lambda > 0$ affects only the utility scale, but has no effect on the equilibrium bid (Cox et al. 1983b, 1988). To test this prediction Cox et al. (1983b) compared market prices from first-price auctions with a one-to-one conversion rate of experimental to U.S. dollars to auctions with a three-to-one conversion rate. Cox et al. (1988) later compared mean coefficient estimates of α_i and β_i from individual subject bid functions for these same data. In both cases they fail to reject a null hypothesis of no change, consistent with the CRRAM model.

In contrast, other tests yield less favorable outcomes for CRRAM. Kagel et al. (1987) (section I.D) found that as expected profit conditional on winning the auction increased, bidders increased their bids proportionately more, earning a smaller share of profits compared to the RNNE prediction, a result that is inconsistent with constant relative risk aversion, but which is consistent with increasing relative risk aversion.[29] Since, within the context of CRRAM, these results could possibly be explained by the nonlinear component of the CRRAM bid function that characterizes high bids, Kagel and Levin (1985) looked at individual subject bid functions, truncating the data set consistent with the requirements of CRRAM and testing whether CRRAM's restrictions held as expected profits conditional on winning the auction varied. Kagel and Levin (1985) reject the null hypothesis that the bid coefficients satisfy CRRAM's restrictions for 40 percent of their subjects.[30]

Further evidence that subjects increase their bids proportionately more as expected profit increases is reported in Kagel and Roth (1992), in this case for auctions with varying numbers of bidders. In these auctions, the underlying support from which valuations were drawn remained constant as n decreased, so that the expected profit conditional on winning the auction increased. Actual profit as a percentage of the predicted RNNE profit decreased in eight out of eight auction series. In contrast, according to CRRAM, profit earned as a percentage of RNNE profit should increase with decreases in n.[31]

These results stand in marked contrast to the tripling of payoff values reported by Cox et al. (1983b, 1988) which resulted in no significant differences in mean intercept values or slopes of individual subject bid functions and no significant changes in market prices. These differences in outcomes may reflect the fact that: (i) in Cox et al.'s experiment profits were tripled by increasing the conversion rate from experimental dollars to U.S. currency, so that the distribution of private values and all other variables over which bidders were choosing remained unchanged, requiring no changes in behavior to remain faithful to CRRAM, while (ii) the experiments reported in Kagel and Roth and Kagel et al. (1987) required substantial adjustments in bidding patterns if behavior was to satisfy CRRAM, thereby providing a much more demanding test of the null hypothesis. That is, Cox et al. (1983b, 1988) implemented an experimental manipulation for which their hypothesis predicted no change in subjects' behavior, and they detected no change and concluded that this supports their hypothesis. But if bidding above the RNNE were due to factors *not* accounted for by their CRRAM model, their experimental manipulation (which left unchanged virtually all of the experimental environment) was unlikely to change these factors either. In contrast, the manipulations reported in Kagel et al. (1987) and Kagel and Roth require a *change* in behavior to be faithful to CRRAM, and the predicted pattern of behavior was not observed.

Finally, Smith and Walker (1993) test for CRRA in a series of auctions with changes in conversion rates from experimental to U.S. dollars ranging between 0 and 20, and find that "all three regressions for risk aversion show that there is some tendency for individuals to bid higher (more risk averse) as payoff level is increased after correcting for the effect of experience" (242). Thus, at this stage, there is a growing consensus that, contrary to the CRRAM hypothesis, as expected profit conditional on winning the auction increases, subjects act as if they are relatively more risk averse.[32]

2. The Flat Maximum Critique

Harrison (1989) presents a methodological critique of the evidence Cox, Smith, and Walker employ to reject RNNE bidding theory. Harrison argues that under the typical payoff values employed the expected cost of deviations from the RNNE is quite small (less than $0.05 at the median), so that in terms of expected monetary payoffs ("payoff space") many subjects had little to lose from deviating from the RNNE strategy (i.e., the payoff function around the maximum is flat). Harrison argues the significance of the differences reported between bids and the RNNE (deviations in the "message space") need to be reexamined.

In replying to Harrison, Cox et al. (1989a, 1989b, 1992) focus on Harrison's contention that "it is more natural to evaluate subject behavior in expected payoff space" (Harrison 1989, 749), and they interpret his cost of deviation measure as attaching cardinal value to expected utility differences. In arguing that it is more natural to evaluate behavior in payoff space, Harrison has overstated his case. However, as a diagnostic tool, evaluating outcomes in payoff space reflects the common sense observation that when financial incentives are "small" (i.e., there are "low" expected costs to deviating from a particular outcome) the experimenter *may* have lost control, other arguments in subject's utility function *may* guide behavior, and this *may* result in systematic deviations from the theory. The suggestion is that bidding above the RNNE, and the differences in individual subject bid functions observed, *may* be characteristic of such systematic deviations.

Harrison's criticism applies with special force to Cox, Smith, and Walker's efforts to develop CRRAM since there is no known analytic solution for the CRRAM equilibrium bid function for bids above b^*, the maximum bid of the most risk loving subject in the auctions (Cox et al. 1988). Since the expected cost of deviating from the RNNE, or CRRAM, equilibrium bid function increases with bidder's private valuations (as the likelihood of winning the auction is higher for those with higher valuations), Cox, Smith, and Walker's investigation of CRRAM is based on private valuations for which the expected cost of deviating from equilibrium is the lowest. Kagel and Roth (1992) have examined this implication of Harrison's critique, computing the simple correlation coefficient between private values and the absolute value of the size of the deviation from RNNE bidding relative to the underlying private valuation ([actual bid − RNNE predicted bid]/ private valuation). They report statistically significant negative correlations within each auction series, demonstrating that with lower valuations (and lower probability of winning the auction), the absolute size of the deviation from the RNNE is proportionately larger. Further, the average absolute size of these deviations is 2–3 times larger in cases where bids are made on the basis of the lowest 20 percent of the distribution of private values compared to the highest 20 percent of the distribution. That is, the greatest proportionate deviations from the RNNE predictions are made by bidders who draw the lowest valuations, bidders who have the smallest chance of winning the auction.[33] For these bidders the expected cost of deviating from the Nash equilibrium (even if they are risk neutral) is lowest.

The natural response to the flat maximum critique is to increase the marginal expected cost of deviations from the RNNE and see if they persist. Alternatively, one can implement experimental treatments designed to provide stern tests of the comparative static implications of the risk aversion hypothesis and see if it continues to organize behavior. Sections I.C.2 and I.D have already described two tests of the comparative static implications of risk aversion; additional tests are reported in sections I.G.3–I.G.4. The remainder of this section focuses on the effect of increasing the marginal cost of deviations from RNNE bidding.

Kagel and Roth (1992) report results from first-price auctions in which the expected profit conditional on winning the auction (assuming RNNE bidding) is substantially higher than in the experiments reported in Harrison (1989) or those typically conducted by Cox, Smith, and Walker. Looking at these experiments, median foregone expected income averages a little over $0.18 in each auction period, with a high of $0.31 and a low of $0.05.[34] This is substantially higher than the median foregone expected income reported in Harrison (1989), which averages $0.04, with a high of $0.06 and a low of $0.02. In addition, Smith and Walker (1993) have conducted auctions in which experimental dollars are transformed into U.S. dollars at rates of 10 and 20 to 1. The impact of this manipulation, evaluated in terms of its effect on individual subject bid functions, has been to reduce the mean square residual error as payoffs increase, so that subjects adhere closer to a given bidding strategy as payoffs increase, and for subjects to bid as if they are somewhat more risk averse. The median foregone expected income in auctions with the highest dollar transformations in Smith and Walker (1993) are substantially greater than those reported in Cox et al. (1988) or in the Harrison (1989) paper. Of course it is not possible to determine if these higher levels of foregone expected income, or any level of foregone expected income for that matter, are sufficiently large to be salient for subjects. But scaling up the expected loss function, to these levels at least, does not eliminate bidding above the RNNE.

In contrast to the relatively small median foregone expected income for all bidders, high value holders forego substantially more in expected income terms as a consequence of bidding above the RNNE, averaging $1.34 for the auctions reviewed in Kagel and Roth (1992), compared to $0.18 for all bidders. The difference in foregone expected income between the high private value holders and all bidders results from the fact that bidders with lower resale values have substantially smaller chances of winning the auction, which drives down foregone expected income substantially. The net effect is that bidders with relatively low resale values have sharply reduced financial incentives to behave in accordance with the theory. This is the primary point of Harrison's paper as I see it, a point which has been reflected in the data at several other places; for example, in the responses to varying numbers of bidders (section I.C) and the effects of public information in auctions with affiliated private values (section I.D).

In replying to his critics Harrison (1992) implicitly rejects the notion that increasing the expected cost of deviating from the RNNE and determining that the behavior persists (or gets stronger) is sufficient to overcome the flat maximum critique:

> An alternative class (of priors about decision making costs) that might be appropriate is the *percent* foregone income, with this *percentage* calculated relative to some reference decision. . . . Moreover, if subjects do follow a decision rule of this kind one could not eradicate a lack of payoff dominance by simply scaling up the payoff function (such procedures would work if we replaced "α %" with "α cents" in the decision rule). (Harrison 1992, 1441, italics added)

This idea of replacing an α cents rule with an α percent rule is simply not tenable for profit maximizing economic agents, the null hypothesis underlying Harrison's original argument and much of economic theory. Further, Harrison (1992) belittles the usefulness of comparative static tests of the internal consistency of proposed explanations for behavioral anomalies. This methodological position provides overly strong protection for the null hypothesis since many times economic models have inherently flat maxima. Therefore, tests of behavioral consistency across a variety of treatment conditions provide a basis for investigating such anomalies. To dismiss such anomalies strictly because the null hypothesis has a relatively flat maximum simply affords the null hypothesis too much protection, particularly in the absence of any hard data that the theory works as predicted. (Tests of the internal consistency of the risk aversion hypothesis across private value auction environments are reported in the next section.)

3. Risk Aversion and Overbidding in Related Environments

Bidding above the RNNE in first-price auctions can be explained in terms of risk aversion. Empirically, in fitting bid functions to the data, what risk aversion does is add an extra degree of freedom. Accounting for diversity in bidder's risk preferences adds even more degrees of freedom, which is bound to result in an even closer fit to the data. The question remains though whether risk aversion and bidder heterogeneity provide a coherent explanation of deviations from RNNE bidding theory across a variety of auction institutions and experimental manipulations. To the extent that it does, there is added support for the argument that risk aversion is the mechanism underlying bidding above the RNNE in first-price auctions. To the extent that it does not, it is doubtful that risk aversion is the basic causal factor behind such overbidding. Note, in raising the issue of how well risk aversion does in related auction environments I am not denying the utility of exploring CRRAM (or any other model for that matter) in efforts to organize deviations from risk neutral bidding in first-price auctions. What I am arguing, however, is that risk aversion has implications outside the domain of first-price auctions, and it is incumbent on experimenters to explore these implications before feeling too comfortable with the risk aversion argument, no matter how good the fit to data from first-price auctions.

Sections I.C.2 (the case of numbers uncertainty) and I.D (the effects of public information in auctions with affiliated private values) provide two instances in which risk aversion serves to account, reasonably well, for comparative static responses to novel treatment conditions. Further, Chen and Plott (1991) investigate first-price auctions where valuations are drawn from nonuniform distributions and where the Nash equilibrium bidding function is nonlinear. Here too CRRAM exhibits good fits to the data. These results—in conjunction with the fact that bidding above the RNNE tends to be most pronounced in auctions with higher expected profit conditional on winning the auction, conditions under which risk aversion would be expected to be most prominent in the data—provide evidence that risk aversion has some explanatory power in private value auctions. However, there are several settings where bid patterns directly contradict the risk aversion hypothesis or raise questions about the role of risk aversion in bidding above the RNNE in first-price auctions.

The persistent bidding above the dominant strategy in second-price auctions (section II.A.2) can't help but raise the question of whether similar perceptual errors might be responsible for bidding above the RNNE in first-price auctions. Note that bidding the dominant strategy in second-priced auctions is *independent* of attitudes towards risk. Nevertheless, subjects persistently bid above their private valuations when they are permitted to do so. In light of this, it is natural to entertain the hypothesis that related perceptual errors may help explain systematic deviations from the RNNE in first-price auctions (see the discussion in section I.B.3c).[35] In fact Cox et al. (1985b) suggest one such model in a footnote, although they do not pursue it relative to the CRRAM alternative.

In Cox et al. (1984) multiple unit discriminatory auctions were conducted under several different values of n (the number of bidders) and q (the quantity offered for sale), with data being reported for experienced bidders (in discriminatory auctions the winning bidders each pay the price bid). In four of the ten treatment conditions studied, average revenue was consistently *lower* (usually significantly lower) than predicted under the RNNE bidding model, contrary to the risk aversion hypothesis. In the other six treatment conditions revenue was consistently greater (usually significantly greater) than predicted under RNNE, consistent with the risk aversion hypothesis.

Cox et al. (1984) explore a number of potential explanations for these differences. They are unable to find any explanation that works consistently across treatment conditions:

> But at this juncture in the research program we have no explanation of the Group I experiments in Figure 12 that are inconsistent with both the CRRA and the VHR models (models of risk averse Nash equilibrium bidding). The group I experiments are characterized by a pronounced tendency of individuals to bid below the risk neutral Vickrey bid function. It is natural to conjecture that this is due either to cooperative behavior as suggested in [Cox, Robertson, and Smith 1982] in single unit auctions when there are only three bidders, or to strictly convex (risk preferring) preferences for monetary outcome. (Cox, Smith, and Walker 1984, 1008).

Note that the cooperative behavior referred to in single unit auctions with three bidders has since been resolved (the results do not replicate with higher expected profits and/or somewhat different procedures—section I.B.1). The anomalous findings relative to risk aversion for multiple unit auctions have never been resolved.

In third-price IPV auctions risk aversion involves bidding *below* the RNNE prediction, the exact opposite of the pattern implied in first-price auctions (Kagel and Levin 1993). In auctions with five active bidders this prediction is supported, as the majority (61 percent) of bids lie below the RNNE prediction. However, in auctions with ten bidders, the majority of bids (60 percent) lie *above* the RNNE line. In going from five to ten bidders subjects first act as if they are predominantly risk averse, then as if they are predominantly risk loving! The suggestion is that something other than risk attitudes, as specified in conventional expected utility theory, is guiding behavior here.

Cason (1992) studied an auction in which several buyers bid for a single item whose price is fixed by a random draw from a known distribution. The value bidders place on the item is known at the time they bid, but the randomly determined sale price is unknown. The high bidder wins the item and pays the randomly determined sale price, provided his bid is at or above it. In this set-up the symmetric RNNE calls for bidding above resale values (as bids only determine whether or not a buyer wins the item, not the price paid). With either constant absolute or constant relative, risk aversion equilibrium bids are *below* the symmetric RNNE (as in a third-price auction). Nevertheless Cason reports bidding significantly above the RNNE in auctions with both 3 and 6 bidders and with both inexperienced and experienced bidders.

Harrison (1990) attacks the issue of risk aversion directly. Using the Becker, DeGroot, Marschak (1964) procedure (see Roth, chapter 1, section III.F.4.a) to test directly for risk aversion over small gambles, he determines the distribution of risk preferences for a group of undergraduate students, not unlike those used in typical first-price auction experiments. Using Bayesian econometric techniques and data from Cox et al. (1982, 1983a, 1983b), he finds far too much risk loving in his sample population to be consistent with the degree of risk aversion implied by the CRRAM hypothesis using the first-price auction data.[36] Note that Harrison's conclusions are restricted to the CRRAM specification as it is not possible, in general, to recover risk preferences from bidding since this reflects bidders' own risk preferences *and* their reaction to the behavior (risk preferences) of others, unlike the gambles which strictly measure own risk preferences. CRRAM however has the special property that the linear portion of the bid function depends exclusively on bidders' own risk preferences, being independent of the distribution of risk preferences in the sample population. For more general specifications of risk aversion, consistency tests would require playing against programmed bidders who played according to the RNNE. To be most relevant tests of this sort should use reference gambles that are fully comparable to those faced in the auctions, along with using the same subjects in both the gambles and the auctions.

4. Using the Binary Lottery Procedure to Control for Risk Aversion

Assuming that subjects maximize expected utility, experimenters can, at least in theory, use a binary lottery procedure to induce risk preferences of their choosing (Roth and Malouf 1979, Berg, Daley, Dickhout, and O'Brien 1986). Under the lottery procedure, participants in the auction earn points (rather than income) which are used to determine their chances of winning the larger of two monetary prizes in a lottery following the auction (see the discussion in section III.F.4 of the Introduction).[37] Since according to expected utility theory preferences are linear in the probabilities and bidders' earnings are in probability points, as long as there is a one-to-one relationship between points and lottery tickets, the lottery procedure must lead expected utility maximizers to bid as if they are risk neutral.

There are at least three different ways of looking at efforts to employ the binary lottery procedure to control bidders' risk preferences in auctions. First, these efforts may be viewed as an additional comparative static test of the CRRAM hypothesis, and of risk aversion in general, since if bidders are indeed expected utility maximizers, then it follows as a matter of logic that the binary lottery procedure is capable of controlling risk preferences (Kagel and Roth 1992, express this point of view). Second, directly contrary to this point of view, auctions may be viewed as a vehicle for testing the binary lottery procedure, so that failure to control risk preferences in auctions would result in questioning the general effectiveness of the lottery procedure. This application involves a joint test of Nash equilibrium bidding theory and the lottery procedure, so that the validity of the test depends critically on one's priors regarding the ability of Nash equilibrium bidding theory to organize precisely behavior in private value auctions (Cox et al. [1985b] and Walker, Smith, and Cox [1990] express this point of view). Third, applications of the binary lottery procedure may be viewed on strictly practical grounds as efforts to develop another tool to help with theory testing; for example, if the binary lottery procedure can be used to move bidders closer to risk neutral bidding, more precise tests of the revenue raising effects of public information in auctions with affiliated private value can be conducted since increased revenue depends critically on the existence of risk neutral bidders (recall section I.D).

Cox et al. (1985b) and Walker et al. (1990) report results from a series of first-price private value auctions designed to test whether the lottery procedure does in fact induce risk neutral bidding.[38] The criteria for determining risk neutrality is whether the slope coefficient in the linear regression specification (equation (10)) is significantly different from the risk neutral prediction using ordinary least squares (OLS) regressions. Their primary conclusion is that the lottery procedure can *not* be used reliably to induce risk neutral bidding as the large majority of slope coefficients remain significantly above the RNNE prediction. There is some suggestion of prior conditioning effects in their data, as bidding under the lottery procedure moves subjects with no prior experience in first-price auctions in the direction of risk neutrality, compared to inexperienced subjects without the lottery procedure (although here too the average value of β is significantly above the risk neutral prediction; Walker et al. 1990, conclusion 6).[39]

Walker et al. (1990) rationalize the failure of the lottery procedure to induce risk neutral bidding and of their maintained hypothesis of CRRAM, which assumes expected utility maximization, by arguing that the failure of the lottery procedure is due to the failure of the compound lottery axiom.

> Our tests of the lottery procedure are based on the hypothesis that the CRRAM bidding model of first-price auctions is a successful predictor of bidding behavior. We chose the environment of the first-price auction because of the success of earlier direct tests of the CRRAM for that market institution. Given the lack of success of the lottery procedure in this environment, we feel our results have important implications for future research. First, it can be conjectured that our results provide indirect evidence of the failure of the compound lottery axiom of expected utility theory in the sense that there is an explicit compounding of the lottery and the auction procedure (in the tests of the compound lottery axiom). (23)

Walker et al. recognize that derivation of the CRRAM bidding function makes use of the compound lottery axiom so that they also argue

> In suggesting below that the failure of the lottery procedure to induce risk neutral behavior may be due to the failure of the compound lottery axiom we do not suggest that the axiom need fail in all contexts. In fact, within the context of CRRAM there is no evidence this axiom fails. (23, note 1)

Since Walker et al. provide no references to any independent experiments designed to isolate tests of the compound lottery axiom within the context of CRRAM, to this reviewer, at least, the results of Walker et al. might better be viewed as further evidence that risk aversion is not the sole, or even the primary, factor underlying bidding above the RNNE in first-price auctions (recall section I.G.3).

Rietz (1993) raises questions about the conclusions of Cox et al. (1985b) and Walker et al. from another perspective and reaches quite different conclusions regarding the ability of the lottery technique to control bidders' risk preferences. A potentially important procedural difference between Rietz and Walker et al. (1990), (as well as Cox et al. 1985a), is that Walker et al. always quoted values, bids, and profits in monetary units, which then serve to determine the probability of winning the large prize. In contrast, Rietz quotes all values, bids, and profits directly in terms of points. In addition, Rietz examines the effects of three different types of prior experience: (1) bidders start out in (standard) first-price dollar auctions, (2) the first-price lottery procedure is used throughout, and (3) the lottery procedure is first employed in second-price auctions, to familiarize subjects with the procedure when there is a "simple dominant strategy" (Rietz did not permit subjects to bid above their private value in the second-price auctions, simplifying the decision problem considerably).

Rietz finds that prior experience is important. Bidders who start out in standard first-price dollar auctions move closer to the RNNE prediction following the cross-over to the lottery procedure. But a null hypothesis of risk neutrality can still be rejected under the lottery technique.[40] In auction series employing the first-price lottery procedure from the start, the price distribution is even closer to the RNNE prediction. In this case the price distribution in one of two auction series does not differ significantly from the RNNE prediction. Finally, for bidders who start out in second-price lottery auctions, none differed from the RNNE prediction following the cross-over to first-price lottery auctions. With this kind of prior training the lottery procedure was successful in inducing the desired preferences. Unfortunately Rietz reports no control condition using second-price dollar auctions that were then crossed over to first-price dollar auctions to determine if the second-price training itself would produce closer conformity to the RNNE outcome. However, barring a hysteresis effect of this sort, which seems unlikely (see note 11 for evidence supporting this presumption), his results suggest that successful implementation of the lottery procedure rests on subjects first becoming familiar with the procedure in a fairly simple context and then placing them in more complicated settings like the first-price auction.

Rietz also looks at individual subject bid functions. He compares tests of the RNNE hypothesis using OLS estimators with least absolute deviation (LAD) estimators (Powell 1984). Rietz argues that censoring (it is individually irrational for subjects to bid above their resale values in first-price auctions) and heteroskedastic errors result in artificially high rejection rates of the null hypothesis of risk neutrality using OLS estimators. The LAD estimators correct these biases. The differences can be quite dramatic. Using OLS estimators, Rietz rejects the null hypothesis that the binary lottery procedure controlled subjects' preferences, as intended, for seven of eight subjects in series that began with dollar auctions, for four of eight subjects in series that always employed first-price lottery auctions, and for seven of sixteen subjects in auctions that began with the second-price lottery procedure. The corresponding rejection rates using the LAD estimators are 1 of 8, 0 of 8 and 0 of 16. Although Rietz's LAD tests are based on asymptotic properties of the estimators rather than their small sample properties, which may understate the rejection rate, he argues that the results indicate that OLS estimates, like those employed in Cox et al. (1985b) and Walker et al. (1990), may overstate the rejection rate. The econometric biases Rietz identifies in estimating individual subject bid functions are likely to apply to other tests of auction theory using OLS estimates as well.

5. Summing Up

This section started by noting that there was considerable debate among experimenters regarding the role of risk aversion in bidding above the RNNE outcome in first-price private value auctions. The debate has pushed research in a number of directions. Cox, Smith, and Walker's initial work demonstrated that a model of heterogeneous risk averse bidders provided a better fit to the experimental data than homogeneous risk neutral, or risk averse, bidding models. At the same time CRRAM has some notable inadequacies even in first-price private value auctions: there are (mild) nonlinearities in individual subject bid functions, intercepts of individual subject bid functions are often significantly different from the CRRAM prediction of zero, and in a number of cases bidders act as if they become more risk averse as the expected profit conditional on winning the auction increases. There is some suggestion that minimum income thresholds from winning the auction may be responsible for these last two effects.

The flat maximum critique argues that deviations from risk neutrality observed in first-price private value auctions may be a consequence of low expected costs of deviation from RNNE, so that the resulting loss of experimental control permits other arguments in subject's utility function to guide behavior. While a number of experimenters have taken the flat maximum critique as a frontal attack on auction experiments (and in some cases on the entire field of experimental economics), to this reviewer it serves as a useful diagnostic tool that *may* indicate when control of subjects' behavior is likely to be lost. Results from a number of first-price auction experiments involving considerably greater expected cost of deviating from the RNNE than in Harrison's study or the typical Cox, Smith, and

Walker experiment show subjects continuing to bid above the RNNE at considerably greater expected cost to themselves. Thus, scaling up the expected loss function, to these levels at least, does not eliminate bidding above the RNNE.

Looking at bidding in other auction settings, there are several instances in which the risk aversion hypothesis fails, most notably in third-price auctions and in multiple unit discriminatory auctions. These results, in conjunction with bidding above the dominant strategy in second-price auctions, raise serious questions regarding the role of risk aversion as the mechanism underlying bidding above the RNNE in single unit first-price auctions. One response to these contrary data is to point out that they come from considerably more complicated settings than first-price auctions, so that to some extent these breakdowns are not surprising and should not be counted too heavily against the risk aversion explanation.[41] To this reviewer, this response is inadequate since it fails to account for the fact that the very simplicity of first-price auctions means that bidders can develop reasonable ad hoc rules of thumb that result in "as if" risk averse Nash equilibrium bidding, when in fact the underlying behavioral process bears little relationship to Nash equilibrium bidding theory (see equation (5) in section I.C.1). Consequently, it requires examining behavior in more complicated environments to distinguish between risk aversion and such ad hoc bidding rules. The bottom line to all of this is that despite its failures, the risk aversion explanation has its successes too, so that it probably has some role to play in explaining bidding in private value auctions.

Applications of the binary lottery procedure to induce risk neutral bidding in first-price auctions has met with mixed results. Rietz (1993) reports considerably more success than Cox et al. (1985b) or Walker et al. (1990) in inducing risk neutral preferences as judged by the equilibrium predictions for risk neutral bidders. There are differences between the two experiments both in terms of underlying procedures and statistical tests used to evaluate the success of the technique.

II. Common Value Auctions

In common value auctions the value of the auctioned item is the same to all bidders. What makes the auction interesting is that bidders do not know the value at the time they bid. Instead they receive signal values that are related to (affiliated with) the value of the item.[42] Mineral lease auctions, particularly the Federal government's outer continental shelf (OCS) oil lease auctions, are common value auctions. There is a common value element to most auctions. Bidders for an oil painting may purchase for their own pleasure, a private value element, but they may also bid for investment and eventual resale, reflecting the common value element.

Judgmental failures in common value auctions are known as the "winner's curse." Although all bidders obtain unbiased estimates of the item's value, assuming homogeneous bid functions, they only win in cases where they have the highest signal value. Unless this adverse selection problem is accounted for in the bidding, it will result in winning bids that produce below normal or even negative profits. The systematic failure to account for this adverse selection problem is referred to as the "winner's curse."

Oil companies claim they fell prey to the winner's curse in early OCS lease sales (Capen, Clapp, and Campbell 1971; Lorenz and Dougherty 1983, and references cited there-in). Similar claims have been made in auctions for book publication rights (Dessauer 1981), professional baseball's free agency market (Cassing and Douglas 1980), corporate takeover battles (Roll 1986), and real estate (Ashenfelter and Genesore 1992). Economists typically treat such claims with caution as they imply that bidders repeatedly err, in violation of basic notions of economic rationality (see the exchange between Cox and Isaac [1984, 1986] and Brown [1986], for example). Further, a number of studies question the oil companies claims regarding losses in early OCS sales (see Wilson [1992] for a brief review of the literature; see also section III.B below).

Laboratory experiments show that inexperienced bidders are quite susceptible to the winner's curse (Bazerman and Samuelson 1983; Kagel and Levin 1986; Kagel, et al. 1989; reviewed in Roth 1988; chapter 1, section III.E of this volume). In fact, the winner's curse has been such a pervasive phenomenon that most of the initial experimentation in the area has focused on its robustness and the features of the environment that might attenuate its effects. Secondary issues concern the role of public information and different auction institutions on revenue. Public information concerning the value of the item should raise prices, assuming risk neutral bidders and no winner's curse (Milgrom and Weber 1982). Further, second-price auctions should raise more revenue than first-price auctions, and English auctions should raise more revenue than second-price auctions, assuming risk neutral bidders, no winner's curse, and a symmetric Nash equilibrium (Milgrom and Weber 1982).

Section II.A looks at the winner's curse in sealed bid common value auctions. Experimental procedures are first characterized, followed by a summary of results in first-price auctions, including the effects of public information on revenue. The impact of limited-liability for losses is discussed and results are reported from second-price auctions. Section II.B looks at the winner's curse in English auctions and in auctions with asymmetric information, where one bidder knows the value of the item with certainty. Experimental work on the winner's curse in other market settings—in bilateral bargaining games with uncertainty, in "blind bid" auctions, and in two-sided auction markets with a lemon's problem—are reviewed in section III.C. What little is known about whether and how bidders learn to overcome the winner's curse is reported in section II.D.

A. The Winner's Curse in Sealed Bid Common Value Auctions

Procedures employed in common value auction experiments are similar to auctions with affiliated private values (section I.D). The common value, x_o, is chosen randomly each period from a uniform distribution on $(\underline{x}, \bar{x})$. Under symmetric information conditions each bidder is given a private information signal, x, drawn from a uniform distribution on $[x_0 - \epsilon, x_0 + \epsilon]$, where ϵ is known (thus private information signals are positively affiliated). In first-price auctions the high bidder earns $x_0 - b$, where b is the high bid. Losing bidders earn zero profits.

Under this design bidders have a risk free strategy of bidding max $[x - \epsilon, \underline{x}]$, which is computed for them in the form of a lower bound estimate of x_0, along with an upper bound estimate of x_0 (min $[x + \epsilon, \bar{x}]$). Bidders are provided with illustrative distributions of signal values relative to x_0 and several dry runs before playing for cash. Following each auction period they are provided with the complete set of bids, listed from highest to lowest, along with the corresponding signal values, the value of x_0 and the earnings of the high bidder (subject identification numbers are, however, suppressed).

Bidders are provided with a starting cash balance and have the opportunity to bid in a series of auctions. Should a subject exhaust her cash balance, she is declared bankrupt and no longer allowed to bid. Surviving bidders are paid their end of experiment balances in cash. To hold the number of bidders fixed while controlling for bankruptcies, $m > n$ subjects are often recruited, with only n bidding at any given time (who bids in each period is determined randomly or by a fixed rotation rule). As bankruptcies occur m shrinks, but (hopefully) remains greater than or equal to the target value n. Alternative solutions to the bankruptcy problem are discussed below.

1. First-Price Sealed Bid Auctions

Wilson (1977) was the first to develop a Nash equilibrium solution for first-price common value auctions, while Milgrom and Weber (1982) provide some significant extensions and generalizations of the Wilson model. For risk neutral bidders and signals in the interval $\underline{x} + \epsilon \leq x \leq \bar{x} - \epsilon$, the Nash equilibrium bid function is

$$(9) \qquad\qquad b(x) = x - \epsilon + Y$$

where Y is a negative exponential, which becomes negligible rapidly as x moves beyond $\underline{x} + \epsilon$.[43]

In common value auctions bidders usually win the item when they have the highest, or one of the highest, estimates of value. Define $E[x_0 \mid X = x_1]$ to be the expected value of the item conditional on having the highest signal value.[44] The latter provides a convenient measure of the extent to which bidders suffer from the winner's curse since in auctions in which the high signal holder always wins the item, bidding above $E[x_0 \mid X = x_1]$ results in negative expected profit. Further, even with zero correlation between bids and signal values, if everyone else bids above $E[x_0 \mid X = x_1]$, bidding above $E[x_0 \mid X = x_1]$ results in negative expected profit as well. As such, if the high signal holder frequently wins the auction and a reasonably large number of rivals are bidding above $E[x_0 \mid X = x_1]$, individuals bidding above $E[x_0 \mid X = x_1]$ are likely to earn negative expected profit.

Auctions with inexperienced bidders show a pervasive winner's curse that results in numerous bankruptcies. Table 7.5 provides illustrative data on this point. For the first nine auction periods profits averaged $-\$2.57$ compared to the RNNE

Table 7.5.
Profits and Bidding in First Nine Auction Periods for Inexperienced Bidders

Experi-ment	Percentage of Auctions with Positive Profits	Average Actual Profits (t-statistic)	Average Predicted Profiits under RNNE $(S_M)^a$	Percentage of All Bids with $b > E[x_0 \| X = x_1]$	Percentage of Auctions Won by High Signal Holder	Percentage of High Bids with $b_1 > E[x_0 \| X = x_1]$	Percentage of Subjects Going Bankrupt[b]
1	0.0	−4.83 (−3.62)[c]	0.72 (0.21)	63.4	55.6	100.0	50.0
2	33.3	−2.19 (−1.66)	2.18 (1.02)	51.9	33.3	88.9	16.7
3	11.1	−6.57 (−2.80)[d]	1.12 (1.19)	74.6	44.4	88.9	62.5
4	11.1	−2.26 (−3.04)[c]	0.85 (0.43)	41.8	55.6	55.6	16.7
5	33.3	−0.84 (−1.00)	3.60 (1.29)	48.1	44.4	88.9	50.0
6	22.2	−2.65 (−1.53)	2.55 (1.17)	67.3	66.7	100.0	33.3
7	11.1	−2.04 (−2.75)[d]	0.57 (0.25)	58.5	88.9	66.7	50.0
8	11.1	−1.40 (−2.43)[d]	1.59 (0.34)	51.9	55.6	55.6	16.7
9	44.4	0.32 (0.30)	2.37 (0.76)	35.2	88.6	66.7	16.7
10	0.0	−2.78 (−3.65)[c]	3.53 (0.74)	77.2	66.7	100.0	20.0
11	11.1	−3.05 (−3.53)[c]	1.82 (0.29)	81.5	55.6	88.9	37.5
Average	17.2	−2.57	1.90	59.4	59.6	81.8	41.1

Source: Kagel, Levin, Battalio, and Meyer 1989.
[a] S_M = standard error of mean.
[b] For all auction periods.
[c] Statistically significant at the 1 percent level, two-tailed test.
[d] Statistically significant at the 5 percent level, two-tailed test.

prediction of $1.90, with only 17 percent of all auction periods having positive profits. This is not a simple matter of bad luck either, as 59 percent of all bids and 82 percent of the high bids were above $E[x_o \mid X = x_1]$. Further, 40 percent of all subjects starting these auctions went bankrupt. The winner's curse for inexperienced bidders is a genuinely pervasive problem which has been reported under a variety of treatment conditions (Kagel et al., 1989, Lind and Plott 1991) and for different subject populations, including professional bidders from the commercial construction industry (Dyer, Kagel, and Levin 1989b, discussed in section III.B below).[45]

Kagel and Levin (1986) report auctions for moderately experienced bidders (those who had participated in at least one prior first-price common value auction experiment). Treatment variables of interest were the number of rival bidders and the effects of public information about x_o on revenue. Table 7.6 reports some of their results. For small groups (auctions with three or four bidders), the general pattern was one of positive average profits which, although well below the RNNE prediction, were clearly closer to the RNNE than the zero/negative profit levels of the winner's curse (profits averaged $4.68 per period, about 65 percent of the RNNE prediction). In contrast, larger groups (auctions with six or seven bidders) had average profits of −$.88, compared to the RNNE prediction of $4.65 per period. Although profits earned were substantially better than predicted under a naive bidding model, indicating considerable adjustment to the adverse-selection problem, these adjustments were far from complete.[46] Further, comparing large and small group auctions, actual profit decreased substantially more than profit opportunities as measured by the RNNE criteria. This implies that subjects were bidding more aggressively, rather than less aggressively, as the number of rivals increased, contrary to the RNNE prediction.

Public information was provided to bidders in the form of announcing x_L, the lowest signal value (and announcing that x_L was announced). For the RNNE, public information about the value of the item raises expected revenue. The mechanism here is similar to the one operating in auctions with affiliated private values: Each bidder bids as if she has the highest signal value since this is when she wins, the only event that counts. For bidders whose private information signals are less than x_1, public information about the value of the item will, ex post, raise the expected value of the item. This results in an upward revision of these bids, which in turn puts pressure on the highest signal holder to bid more.

These strategic considerations hold for a wide variety of public information signals (Milgrom and Weber 1982). There are, however, several methodological advantages to using x_L. First, the RNNE bid function is readily solved for x_L, so that the experimenter continues to have a benchmark model of fully rational behavior against which to compare actual bidding. Second, x_L provides a substantial amount of public information about x_o (it cuts expected profit in half), while still maintaining an interesting auction. As such it should have a substantial impact on prices, regardless of any inherent noise in behavior. And the experimenter can always implement finer, more subtle probes of public information after seeing what happens with such a strong treatment effect.

Table 7.6. Profits and Bidding by Experiment and Number of Active Bidders: Private Information Conditions (profits measured in dollars)

Auction Series (Number of Periods)	Number of Active Bidders	Average Actual Profit (t-Statistics[a])	Average Profit under RNNE (Standard Error of Mean)	Percentage of Auctions Won by High Signal Holder	Percentage of High Bids with $b_1 > E[x_0 \mid X = x_1]$
6 (31)	3–4	3.73 (2.70)[b]	9.51 (1.70)	67.7	22.6
2 (18)	4	4.61 (4.35)[c]	4.99 (1.03)	88.9	0.0
3 small (14)	4	7.53 (2.07)	6.51 (2.65)	78.6	14.3
7 small (19)	4	5.83 (3.35)[c]	8.56 (2.07)	63.2	10.5
8 small (23)	4	1.70 (1.56)	6.38 (1.21)	84.6	39.1
1 (18)	5	2.89 (3.14)[c]	5.19 (0.86)	72.2	27.8
3 large (11)	5–7	−2.92 (−1.49)	3.65 (0.62)	81.8	63.6
7 large (18)	6	1.89 (1.67)	4.70 (1.03)	72.2	22.2
4 (25)	6–7	−0.23 (−0.15)	4.78 (0.92)	69.2	46.2
5 (26)	7	−0.41 (−0.44)	5.25 (1.03)	42.3	65.4
8 large (14)	7	−2.74 (−2.04)	5.03 (1.40)	78.6	71.4

Source: Kagel and Levin 1986.
[a] Tests null hypothesis that mean is different from 0.0.
[b] Significant at 5 percent level, two-tailed t-test.
[c] Significant at 1 percent level, two-tailed t-test.

Kagel and Levin (1986) found that in auctions with small numbers of bidders (three or four), public information resulted in statistically significant increases in revenue that averaged 38 percent of the RNNE model's prediction. However, in auctions with larger numbers of bidders (six or seven), public information significantly *reduced* average revenue. Kagel and Levin attribute this reduction in revenue to the presence of a relatively strong winner's curse in auctions with large numbers of bidders. If bidders suffer from a winner's curse, the high bidder consistently overestimates the item's value, and announcing x_L is likely to result in a downward revision of the most optimistic bidder's estimate. This introduces a potentially powerful offset to any strategic forces tending to raise bids and will result in reduced revenue if the winner's curse is strong enough. Kagel and Levin relate this result to anomalous findings from OCS auctions with field data (this relationship is summarized in Roth 1988; Introduction, section III.E and section III.B below).

Finally, looking at market outcomes with x_L announced, average profits were positive in all auction sessions, with no systematic differences in realized profits relative to predictions between auctions with small and large numbers of bidders. Further, although there was considerable variation in profits relative to the RNNE model's predictions across auction series, on average profits were only slightly less than predicted. These two characteristics suggest that with the large dose of public information involved in announcing x_L, the winner's curse had largely been eliminated.

2. Limited Liability and "Safe Havens"

In the Kagel and Levin (1986) design subjects enjoyed limited liability as they could not lose more than their starting cash balances. Hansen and Lott (1991) have argued that the overly aggressive bidding reported in Kagel and Levin *may* not have resulted from the winner's curse, but could instead be a rational response to this limited liability. In a single-shot auction, if a bidder's cash balance is zero, so that they are not liable for losses, it indeed pays to overbid relative to the Nash equilibrium. With downside losses eliminated the only constraint on more aggressive bidding is the opportunity cost of bidding more than is necessary to win the item. In exchange, higher bids increase the probability of winning the item and making positive profits. The net effect, in the case of zero or very small cash balances, is an incentive to bid more than the Nash equilibrium prediction.

Hansen and Lott's argument provides a possible alternative explanation to the overly aggressive bidding reported in Kagel and Levin and Kagel et al. (1989). It also serves as a warning to experimenters not to overlook potential limited-liability problems in designing their experiments. For example, research on bubbles in asset markets indicates that limited liability for losses may be at least partially responsible for the size and persistence of the bubbles reported (Bronfman 1990).

Responses to the limited-liability argument in common value auctions have been twofold. First, Kagel and Levin (1991) have revaluated their design and their data in light of Hansen and Lott's arguments. They show that their design protects against limited-liability problems and that for almost all bidders cash balances were *always* large enough that it *never* paid to deviate from the Nash equilibrium bidding strategy in a single-shot auction. Second, Lind and Plott (1991) replicated Kagel and Levin's experiment in a design that eliminated limited-liability problems and reproduced Kagel and Levin's (1986) primary results. This provides experimental verification that limited-liability forces do not account for the overly aggressive bidding reported.

Kagel and Levin's design protects against limited liability for losses since bidding $x - \epsilon$ insures against all losses and is close to the predicted RNNE bid function (recall equation (9)). For example, consider a bidder with a private information signal of $80 in an auction where the value of the item is $50, the bidder has a cash balance of $10, and $\epsilon = \$30$. In this example the RNNE bid is $52.27 in a market with four bidders, or $50.41 in a market with seven bidders, so that the bidder is fully liable for all losses (and a good deal more) relative to the Nash equilibrium bid.[47] And as long as bidders have sufficient cash balances to cover their maximum losses relative to the Nash equilibrium bid, overbidding *cannot* be rationalized in terms of a Nash equilibrium.[48] Rather, overbidding in this case must be explained on some other grounds, such as the judgmental error underlying the winner's curse.[49]

Lind and Plott (1991) replicated Kagel and Levin's (1986) results for buyers' and sellers' auctions in which bankruptcy problems were eliminated. To get around the bankruptcy problem in buyers' markets, private value auctions where subjects were sure to make money were conducted simultaneously, thereby providing a source of funds which reduced the likelihood of bankruptcy in the common value auction. In addition, subjects agreed that if they wound up with losses they would work them off doing work-study type duties (photocopying, running departmental errands, etc.) at the prevailing market wage rate.[50] In sellers' markets, bidders tendered offers to sell an item of unknown value. Each bidder was given one item with the option to keep it and collect its value or to sell it. In this auction, all subjects earned positive profits, including the winner, but the winner could suffer an opportunity cost by selling the item for less than its true value.[51]

Lind and Plott's results largely confirm those reported by Kagel and Levin and their associates. First, a winner's curse exists, and although the magnitude and frequency of losses decline with experience, it persists (see Table 7.7). Second, the winner's curse does not result from a few "irrational" bidders, but almost all agents experience the curse and bid consistent with curse behavior. Finally, Lind and Plott test between alternative models of bidder behavior—comparing the RNNE bidding model with the naive bidding model offered in Kagel and Levin (1986). Since these models imply different sets of parameter restrictions on a common functional form, Lind and Plott compute F-statistics comparing the sum of squared errors of the unrestricted model with the restricted model, using the F-statistic as a measure of the relative goodness of fit of the competing models.

Table 7.7. Frequency of Losses for Winners in All Experiments

	Experiment				
	1. Buyers	2. Buyers	3. Sellers	4. Sellers	5. Sellers
Periods 1–10					
Number of periods of loss	8/10	8/10	5/10	6/10	5/10
Average profit per period	−7.90	−8.31	−0.075	−0.048	0.001
	(−7.90)	(−8.31)	(−29.80)	(−48.20)	(1.10)
Average RNNE profit per period	4.53	5.70	0.177	0.060	0.048
	(4.53)	(5.70)	(70.96)	(60.44)	(68.71)
Periods 11–20					
Number of periods of loss	4/10	2/7	3/7	2/10	7/10
Average profit per period	4.57	3.12	0.053	0.032	−0.016
	(4.57)	(3.12)	(21.00)	(31.60)	(−22.40)
Average RNNE profit per period	18.47	13.58	0.212	0.048	0.037
	(18.47)	(13.58)	(84.85)	(48.15)	(52.68)
Periods 21–30					
Number of periods of loss				3/10	5/10
Average profit per period				0.058	−0.004
				(58.40)	(−6.10)
Average RNNE profit per period				0.104	0.090
				(104.02)	(128.91)
Periods 31–40					
Number of periods of loss				2/5	8/10
Average profit per period				0.063	−0.033
				(62.80)	(−46.80)
Average RNNE profit per period				0.065	0.024
				(65.34)	(33.72)

Source: Lind and Plott 1991.

Notes: Profits are measured in dollars and francs; numbers in parentheses are francs. $N = 7$ in all auctions; $\epsilon = \$30$ and 200 francs in buyers and sellers auctions respectively. The RNNE was calculated only in cases where $\underline{x} + \epsilon \le x_i \le \bar{x} - \epsilon$. Some of the winners' signals were not in this range, in which case no prediction was made for the RNNE.

They find that neither model organizes the data, but that the RNNE provides a better fit. This last result, in conjunction with the negative average profits reported, indicate that there was partial but incomplete adjustment to the adverse selection forces in Lind and Plott's auctions.

    Cox and Smith (1992) have conducted common value auctions with a "safe haven"—bidders have a choice between participating in the auction or obtaining a certain payoff from a "safe haven." The safe haven payoff is an independent private value draw from a uniform distribution with each potential bidder learning their safe haven value before deciding whether or not to participate in the auction. One idea behind the safe haven is that it may alleviate the winner's curse through eliminating experimenter demand effects: Without the safe haven, bidders who have not learned to bid profitably may continue to make suboptimal decisions in response to implicit experimenter demands that they continue to bid and try to win the item. With a safe haven this implicit demand to win the item is eliminated, as the experimenter has provided subjects with an alternative, sanctioned activity.

To test for a safe haven effect, Cox and Smith conduct auctions with a zero income safe haven and with a positive income safe haven employing Kagel and Levin's (1986) design. They find substantially more bankruptcies and more winner's curse (bidding above $E[x_0 \mid X = x_1]$) with the zero income safe haven. They interpret these results as "providing strong support for the importance of including a positive-income safe haven in common value bidding theory and experiments. Without the positive-income safe haven, the winner's curse is rampant and the theory fails dramatically to predict the behavior of inexperienced subjects" (Cox and Smith, 1992, 26).

There are a number of problems with this conclusion. First, with respect to the question of whether demand induced effects underlie the winner's curse, Kagel and Levin's design offers a considerably better option than the zero income safe haven: bid $x - \epsilon$, a sanctioned activity that provides bidders with a positive probability of winning the auction and completely protects them from losses. That is, the Kagel and Levin design has built into it a "safe haven" option that is both sanctioned and offers considerably higher expected earnings than the zero income safe haven. Second, to the extent that bidders do not have the wherewithal to identify this safe haven, as Cox and Smith implicitly assume, explicit provision of a zero income safe haven should be sufficient to eliminate any experimenter demand effects. Nevertheless, the winner's curse is rampant in Cox and Smith's zero-income safe haven sessions, producing an average bankruptcy rate of 75 percent for inexperienced bidders, compared to an average bankruptcy rate of 41 percent for inexperienced bidders in the no safe haven experiment in Kagel et al. (1989).[52] Third, differences in bankruptcy rates and the size of the winner's curse between positive income and zero income safe havens fail to control for large differences in the number of active bidders between the two treatments (for example, in Cox and Smith's Group II sessions with inexperienced bidders, there are 3.4 active bidders on average with the positive income safe haven versus 5.6 bidders in the zero income treatment). It is well established, both in theory and experimentally, that in auctions with fewer bidders the adverse selection problem is less severe, hence less room for bankruptcies and bidding above $E[x_0 \mid X = x_1]$. (Indeed, under the naive bidding model offered in Kagel and Levin [1986] and Lind and Plott [1991], expected profits are positive as long as there are three or fewer bidders). As to the broader question this study implicitly poses, whether naturally occurring auction markets adjust to the winner's curse by causing bidders to exit the market, or whether some other adjustment mechanism(s) are at work (like the ones characterized in sections II.C.2, II.C.3, and III.B.2 below), this remains an open empirical question the resolution of which will require careful field studies of auction markets.

3. Second-Price Sealed Bid Auctions

Lind and Plott (1991) are puzzled by their finding that although there is a winner's curse, the RNNE model provides the best fit to the data: "A major puzzle remains: of the models studied, the best is the risk-neutral Nash-equilibrium model, but that model predicts that the curse will not exist" (344). They go on to comment, "Part of the difficulty with further study stems from the lack of theory about (first-price) common value auctions with risk aversion. . . . If the effect of risk aversion is to raise the bidding function as it does in private (value) auctions, then risk-aversion . . . might resolve the puzzle; but, of course, this remains only a conjecture" (344). Second-price auctions provide an ideal vehicle for exploring these conjectures.

In contrast to first-price auctions, behavior of risk averse bidders is well understood in second-price auctions with both *symmetric* risk averse bidders and with *asymmetric* risk averse bidders.[53] Overly aggressive bidding in second-price common value auctions cannot be rationalized in terms of bidders' risk aversion. Rather, best responses involve less aggressive bids for risk averse than for risk neutral bidders. Further, this comparative static implication of the theory holds for both risk averse symmetric and asymmetric Nash equilibria and even extends to auctions where the strategy profile is not an equilibrium (corresponding predictions in first-price auctions require symmetry and are conditional on risk attitudes and the underlying distribution of information at bidders' disposal).[54]

Kagel, Levin, and Harstad (1994) investigate these comparative static predictions along with the effects of public information in second-price common value auctions. Using a fixed effect regression model, and comparing auctions with four and five bidders to auctions with six and seven bidders, they find no response to increasing numbers of rivals for moderately experienced bidders. This directly contradicts the Nash equilibrium prediction. However, it is consistent with a naive bidding model in which bidders fail to account for the adverse selection problems inherent in winning the auction.

In auctions with four or five bidders public information in the form of announcing x_L raises average revenue some 16 percent of the symmetric RNNE model's prediction (but the increase is not significant at conventional levels). In contrast, in auctions with 6 or 7 bidders announcing x_L *reduces* average revenue by $4.00 per auction period (which is significant at conventional levels), compared to the predicted increase of $1.80 per period under the symmetric RNNE. As in the first-price auctions, the ability of public information to increase revenue appears to be conditional on eliminating the worst effects of the winner's curse as bidders earned positive average profits in private information auctions with four or five bidders and substantial negative profits in auctions with six or seven bidders.

4. Summing Up

A strong winner's curse is reported for inexperienced bidders in sealed bid common value auctions as high bidders earn negative average profits and consistently bid above the expected value of the item conditional on having the high signal value. Similar results are reported for both student subjects and professional bidders from the construction industry (Dyer et al. 1989b). Arguments that these results can be accounted for on the basis of bidders' limited-liability for losses have been shown to be incorrect (Kagel and Levin 1991; Lind and Plott 1991). Safe haven treatments have yet to identify any experimenter demand effects underlying the winner's curse.

In the absence of a winner's curse, public information tends to raise revenue as the theory predicts. However, with a winner's curse, public information reduces revenue as the additional information helps bidders to correct for overly optimistic estimates of the item's worth. These results are found in both first and second-price auctions. Finally, increased numbers of bidders produces no change in bidding in second-price auctions, contrary to the robust Nash equilibrium prediction that bids will decrease.

B. More Winner's Curse: English Auctions and First-Price Auctions with Asymmetric Information

Dan Levin and I have investigated the winner's curse in two other common value auction settings—English auctions and first-price auctions with asymmetric information—in efforts to identify conditions where it might be eliminated for inexperienced bidders. In both settings the winner's curse is alive and well, although it is clearly less severe in English than in first-price auctions.

1. English Auctions

In a symmetric RNNE of an English auction, the bidder with the low signal value (x_L) drops out of the auction once the price reaches his signal value.[55] The intuition here is roughly as follows: Given symmetry, the low signal holder knows that those remaining in the auction have higher signal values. But the low signal holder can't profit from this additional information since it is only revealed once price is greater than these remaining signal values; that is, price is already greater than the expected value of the item to the low signal holder.

The price at which the low bidder drops out of the auction reveals his signal value to the remaining bidders. Since with symmetry you only win when you have the high signal value, given the uniform distribution of signal values around x_o, $(x_L + x)/2$ provides a sufficient statistic for x_o (where x is the bidder's own signal). This sufficient statistic is the equilibrium bid in the symmetric RNNE, with the high bidder paying the price at which the next-to-last bidder dropped out. Expected profits in the English auction are roughly half the level predicted in first-price auctions (as long as $n > 2$).

Table 7.8. English versus First-Price Auctions: Inexperienced Bidders

	$\varepsilon = 6$		$\varepsilon = 12$	
	Actual Profit	Predicted Profit	Actual Profit	Predicted Profit
English auction	−1.87	0.89	−1.80	1.68
	(0.51)	(0.29)	(0.77)	(0.40)
First-price auction	−3.85	0.99	−3.75	2.76
	(0.71)	(0.19)	(0.89)	(0.53)
Difference: first-price less English	−1.98	0.10	−1.95	1.08
	(0.87)	(0.34)	(1.19)	(0.65)

Source: Kagel and Levin 1992.

Notes: $n = 7$. Actual and predicted profits are mean values, with standard error of the mean in parentheses.

The information dissemination process in English auctions has much in common with first and second-price auctions when the lowest private information signal is announced—the primary difference is that in the English auction information revelation is endogenous rather than exogenous. In sealed bid auctions with public information, bidders consistently earned positive average profits, even though these same bidders lost money under private information conditions (Kagel and Levin 1986; Kagel et al. 1992). This suggests the possibility that the winner's curse will be attenuated or even eliminated in English auctions, even with inexperienced bidders.

However, this is not the case (Kagel and Levin 1992). Table 7.8 reports actual profit and predicted profit under the symmetric RNNE from a series of English auctions with inexperienced bidders, along with data from a series of first-price auctions using the same subject population. Bidders in the English auctions failed to avoid the winner's curse, earning profits which were, on average, significantly below zero. However, profits were higher in the English auctions compared to profits for inexperienced bidders in first-price auctions who suffered from an even stronger winner's curse.[56] Higher profits translate into lower revenue, so these results directly contradict the symmetric RNNE model's prediction that English auctions will raise more revenue than first-price auctions. Lower revenues from "public" information (other bidders drop out prices) is, however, consistent with the effect of announcing the lowest private information signal in sealed-bid auctions when bidders suffer from a winner's curse (Kagel and Levin 1986; Kagel et al. 1992; see section II.A above). However, unlike the sealed bid auctions, in the English auctions this correction effect of "public" information does not completely eliminate the winner's curse as bidders continue to earn negative average profits.

Inexperienced bidders are unable to avoid the winner's curse in the English auctions for two related reasons. First, contrary to the theory's prediction, the low signal holder does not drop out of the bidding when the price reaches his signal value. Rather, the lowest drop-out price is typically above the lowest signal value, averaging $2.69 per auction period for the data in Table 7.6 (with a standard error of the mean of 1.00). Second, high bidders fail to compensate for the overly optimistic estimate of x_0 inherent in these drop-out prices. In fact they exacerbate it somewhat, as the average difference between the high bid and the symmetric RNNE bid was $3.30 per auction period. The level of overoptimism involved in the low drop-out price and the level of overbidding relative to the symmetric RNNE prediction are positively correlated ($r = .63$), indicating that the more optimistic the estimate of the item's value inherent in the low drop-out price, the higher the winning bid. This suggests that announcing the low signal value in English auctions would further attenuate the winner's curse, for which there is some limited experimental evidence (Kagel, unpublished data).

2. Auctions with Asymmetric Information

In auctions with asymmetric information some bidders are better informed than others about x_0. Dan Levin and I have implemented an extreme form of asymmetric information where one bidder (the insider), chosen at random in each auction period, knows the value of the item with certainty, and this is common knowledge. All remaining bidders (the outsiders) receive private information signals as in the symmetric information design. The bidder with inside information faces a pure strategic problem in the sense that the lower he bids the greater his profits will be should he win the item, but the less likely he is to win assuming that the others enter minimally competitive bids (i.e., never bid below $x - \epsilon$). The outsiders still have the problem of avoiding the winner's curse, only now they are competing against a bidder who knows the value of the item with certainty. In implementing this experimental design we conjectured that the existence of an insider might induce outsiders to bid more conservatively, thereby reducing or even eliminating the winner's curse. If the latter were correct, it would provide a possible insight into how adverse selection problems are avoided outside the laboratory, since many markets with a strong common value element (such as the used car market) have asymmetric information structures.

Table 7.9 reports data for high bidders from a series of asymmetric information auctions with inexperienced bidders, along with data from symmetric information auctions using the same subject population.[57] Data reported from the asymmetric information auctions are restricted to outsiders (the less informed) bidders. Profits for the outsiders are negative and significantly below zero for both values of ϵ, indicating that the winner's curse is alive and well in auctions with asymmetric information. Further, bids commonly exceed the expected value of the item conditional on winning the auction, indicating that these negative profits were not a result of unusually bad realizations of x_0.[58] Finally, it does not appear that the

Table 7.9. Asymmetric Information versus Symmetric Information in First-Price Auctions: Inexperienced Bidders

	$\varepsilon = 6$				$\varepsilon = 12$			
	Actual Profit[a]	Dis-count $(x-b)^a$	Percentage of Auctions Won by High Signal Holder[a]	Frequency of $b_1 >$ $E[x_0 \mid X = x_1]^b$	Actual Profit	Dis-count $(x-b)^a$	Percentage of Auctions Won by High Signal Holders[b]	Frequency of $b_1 >$ $E[x_0 \mid X = x_1]^b$
Asymmetric Information[c]	−3.67 (0.46)	−0.46 (0.53)	61.5 (8/13)	100.0 (12/12)	−2.71 (0.98)	−4.72 (0.89)	70.8 (17/24)	87.5 (21/24)
Symmetric Information	−3.38 (0.91)	−0.89 (0.780)	33.3 (5/15)	80.0 (12/15)	−0.61 (0.85)	−6.67 (0.65)	63.6 (28/44)	65.9 (29/44)
Difference: Asymmetric Information less Symmetric Information	−0.29 (1.07)	0.43 (0.99)	28.2	20.0	−2.10 (1.32)	1.95 (1.10)	7.20	21.6

Notes: $n = 7$. All data are for high bidders only.
[a] Mean value, with standard error of the mean in parentheses. Average profit in asymmetric information auctions is conditional on outsiders' winning the auction.
[b] Mean value, with number of auctions in parentheses.
[c] Data for less informed bidders only.

existence of insiders materially reduces the aggressiveness of outsiders' bids, as the average difference between outsiders' signal values and bids (the bid discount) is somewhat smaller, and the average losses somewhat larger, than in the corresponding symmetric information auctions.[59]

C. The Winner's Curse in Other Market Settings

The potential for a winner's curse is not limited to common value auctions. Anytime items of varying quality are sold, and there is asymmetric information between buyers and sellers, there is an adverse selection problem with a potential winner's curse. This section reviews experiments dealing with three different markets of this sort: bilateral bargaining games with asymmetric information, "blind bid" auctions, and two-sided auctions where product quality is endogenously determined. Although inexperienced subjects suffer from a winner's curse in all three settings, the strength of the winner's curse varies considerably, being quite persistent in the bilateral bargaining game and being eliminated after a few replications when product quality is endogenously determined. The latter outcome results from the strong incentive sellers have to dilute quality, which creates such a strong adverse selection problem that the market quickly unravels to the point that only "lemons" are sold, with buyers paying lemon's prices.

1. The Winner's Curse in Bilateral Bargaining Games with Asymmetric Information

Samuelson and Bazerman (1985) explored the winner's curse in a bilateral bargaining game with asymmetric information. This game adapted Akerlof's (1970) example of adverse selection in a market with lemons. Buyers (the acquiring firm) know that the target's value (v) is uniformly distributed in the interval [0, $100], with the value to the buyer being $1.5v$. Buyers do not know v at the time they bid, but sellers do. Under this design, with sellers following the dominant strategy of only accepting offers that are greater than or equal to v, expected profit to the buyer for any *accepted* bid is negative, so the optimal bid is zero.[60]

The original Samuelson and Bazerman study consisted of a game where buyers bid one time only, and the experimenter acted as the seller. Comparing games with and without monetary incentives, the overwhelming number of subjects (92 percent and 93 percent, respectively) fell prey to the winner's curse, bidding positive amounts for the target firm.[61] The majority of subjects (59 percent with monetary incentives, 73 percent without) followed the naive strategy of bidding somewhere between the expected value of the target ($50) and the expected value of the target in the hands of the acquiring firm ($75), with most others bidding less. Samuelson and Bazerman attribute the modest downward shift in the bid distribution under monetary incentives to risk aversion.[62]

Ball, Bazerman, and Carroll (1991) extended Samuelson and Bazerman's design to allow for learning from repeated play. Each subject played a total of twenty trials, and players received feedback regarding the value of the company and how much money was made or lost following each trial. Players were given starting cash balances that were more than sufficient to cover any expected losses and were paid their net, end of experiment balance in cash. Figure 7.4 shows their results. There is virtually no downward adjustment in mean bids from the beginning to the end of the twenty trials, with bids over the first three trials averaging $57 compared to $55 over the last three trials. Only 7 percent of the subjects (five out of sixty-nine) learned to avoid the winner's curse during the experiment, defined as bidding either $0 or $1.00. Students with quantitative backgrounds (e.g., engineering degrees) did no better in avoiding the winner's curse than those with nonquantitative backgrounds (e.g., English degrees).

The Ball et al. experiment, like the Samuelson and Bazerman study, employed "realistic" instructions, subjects being told the following:

> In the following exercise you will represent Company A (the acquirer), which is currently considering acquiring Company T (the target) by means of a tender offer. (Ball et al. 1991, Appendix 1)

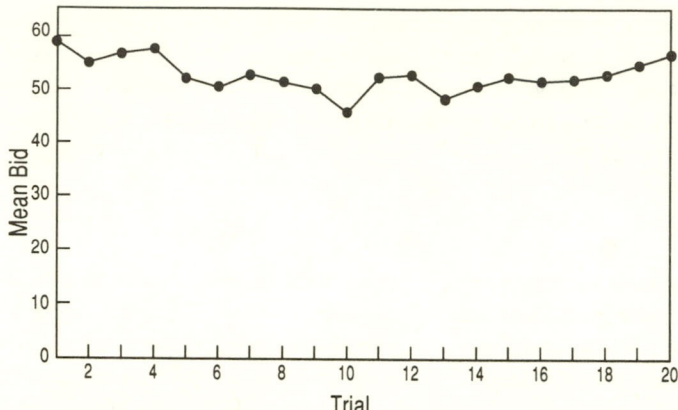

Figure 7.4. Average bids in bilateral bargaining game. *Source:* Ball, Bazerman, and Carroll 1991.

Further, subjects were explicitly told that the target company was expected to accept any offer greater than or equal to its value, but that

> acquiring a company is a neutral event—your performance will be judged only on the value of your assets at the end of this exercise. (1991, Appendix 1)

Nevertheless, for many experimentalists (myself included), embedding the game in a takeover context, particularly with MBA students, might be expected to generate overly aggressive bidding as a result of demand induced experimenter effects (see Rosenthal, 1976, chap. 11, for example). In response to this criticism, Ball (1991) has replicated the twenty-period design using value-free instructions, with no difference in the outcome: 5 percent of the subjects (two out of thirty-seven) avoided the winner's curse.

Cifuentes and Sunder (1991) have independently replicated the Ball et al. results using value-free instructions and forty trials in a session. In addition, under one treatment condition, v was distributed uniformly on the interval [$10, $100]. Since the value to the buyer was $1.5v$, this creates nonnegative expected profit (hence no winner's curse) for bids between $10 and $30, with an optimal bid of $19 to $20, generating an expected profit of $0.28 per trial. Thus, buyers did not have to withdraw from active bidding to avoid the winner's curse. This is important since it might be argued that subjects bid positive amounts in the Ball et al. design out of boredom.[63] Nevertheless, Cifuentes and Sunder found few subjects avoiding the winner's curse: only two out of thirteen learned to bid 0 consistently with $v \in$ [$0, $100], and only 7 percent of all bids were between $10 and $30 for $v \in$ [$10, $100]. Overall, bids averaged well above the equilibrium prediction.

A Loser's Curse

Holt and Sherman (1994) conjecture that "Other possible influences, such as the thrill of winning, can lead to the same effect in bidding for objects of unknown value as the winner's curse." To test this conjecture, they modified the parameters of the bilateral bargaining game to produce a "loser's curse," parameter values under which a naive bidder, who ignores the seller's incentive, bids *less* than is optimal and, consequently, wins less often than he should. This is done as follows: Let the value of the item to the owner be $v = 0.5 + V$ where V is uniformly distributed on the interval $[0, 0.5]$. As in Ball et al., the value to the acquiring firm is $1.5v$, and the owner only sells when the bid $b \geq v$. Under these parameters the optimal naive bid, the bid which maximizes expected value ignoring the seller's acceptance rule, is *less* than the optimal bid that conditions on the seller's acceptance rule, thereby generating a "loser's curse". In contrast let $v = 1.5 + V$ where V is uniformly distributed on the interval $[0, 4.5]$. This produces a standard winner's curse with the optimal naive bid greater than the optimal bid which conditions on the seller's acceptance rule.[64] Further, the expected loss from overbidding here exactly matches the expected loss from underbidding in the loser's curse.[65]

If the winner's curse is a result of the thrill of winning rather than a failure to account for the seller's acceptance rule, than underbidding will not materialize in the loser's curse, or if underbidding does occur, it will be substantially weaker than overbidding in the winner's curse. Results from this experiment show that average actual bids are remarkably close to the naive bid under both sets of parameter values. As such, Holt and Sherman's data indicate that the thrill of winning does not explain the winner's curse.

2. The Winner's Curse in "Blind Bid" Auctions

Consider the following extension of the bilateral bargaining game. Several buyers compete to purchase an item whose value (v) is common to all buyers and is uniformly distributed on some known interval. The seller receives no value from retaining the item and sells it in a first-price sealed bid auction. Further, the seller, who knows the exact value of the item, has an option, prior to the sale, of revealing the value of the item or concealing it (in which case the item is said to be "blind bid"). Buyers have no information other than what the seller provides them and the distribution of v.

If none of the sellers reveals the value of the item, buyers should bid the expected value, earning negative profits on low valued items and positive profits on high valued items. However, sellers have an incentive to reveal information on high valued items in order to receive full value for them. In this case buyers face an adverse selection problem for items that are blind bid. If buyers adjust to this adverse selection problem, the only sequential equilibrium is one in which the game completely unravels, with sellers revealing information on all but the lowest valued items and being indifferent between revealing or concealing information on the low valued items (Milgrom and Roberts 1986; Forsythe, Isaac, and Palfrey 1989). Failure to recognize this adverse selection problem results in a winner's curse, with buyers earning negative average profit on the blind bid items.

Forsythe, Isaac, and Palfrey (1989) report an experiment investigating blind bid auctions of this type.[66] Each experimental session consisted of a series of auctions, so there was time for feedback and learning. Sellers were required to reveal truthfully the value of items that were not blind bid. Values of blind bid items were publicly announced at the end of each auction period.

Under these procedures, Forsythe et al. report clear evidence of a winner's curse in early auction periods. First, there was an adverse selection problem as seller's blind bid lower valued items right from the start.[67] Second, the winning bid was greater than the value of the item for 69 percent (59/85) of all blind bid items. This winner's curse was present in later auction periods as well, with buyers suffering losses on two thirds of the blind bid items. Further, sellers took advantage of the winner's curse as almost all low valued items (96 percent) were blind bid, although the theory predicts that sellers will be indifferent between blind bidding or revealing information on these low valued items.

More important, however, than the existence of a winner's curse in this experiment is the unraveling reported within each auction series as fewer and fewer items were blind bid over time: 44.2 percent of all items in the first ten periods compared to 28.1 percent from the eleventh period on. In addition, the value of blind bid items decreased monotonically over time, as the unraveling argument predicts, as did the prices paid for the items and the average losses on blind bid items.[68] These results are illustrated in Figure 7.5, which shows the value of the blind bid items and the amounts bid, by auction period, from two of Forsythe et al.'s markets.

These results lead Forsythe et al. (230) to conclude that

> the practice of blind bidding causes no difficulties once an equilibrium is obtained. After sufficient market experience, sellers only blind bid low quality items, and buyers, bids indicate that they had adjusted their beliefs properly.

In other words, most of the excess profit sellers earned on low valued items occurred in the initial auction periods prior to the unraveling (equilibrium) outcome. The relatively rapid reduction in bids and losses on blind bid items stand in marked contrast to the persistence of the winner's curse in the bilateral bargaining game. What seems partly, if not entirely, responsible for these differences is the role that sellers play. In the blind bid auctions sellers must sell the item to make any profit, and it is in their best interest to respond to buyers' naive bidding strategies by revealing information about higher valued items. This in turn creates an adverse selection problem on the blind bid items for which buyers do not fully compensate in their bidding (as they continue to suffer losses on two thirds of all blind bid items), but to which they partially adjust by lowering their bids. And this process repeats itself, as sellers now have incentives to reveal information on even lower quality items. Consequently, the market structure, with sellers having the opportunity and incentive to reveal information on lower valued items, speeds up the unraveling, which naturally limits the extent of the winner's curse in these markets. As will be shown in the next section, similar forces are at work in markets where quality is endogenously determined.

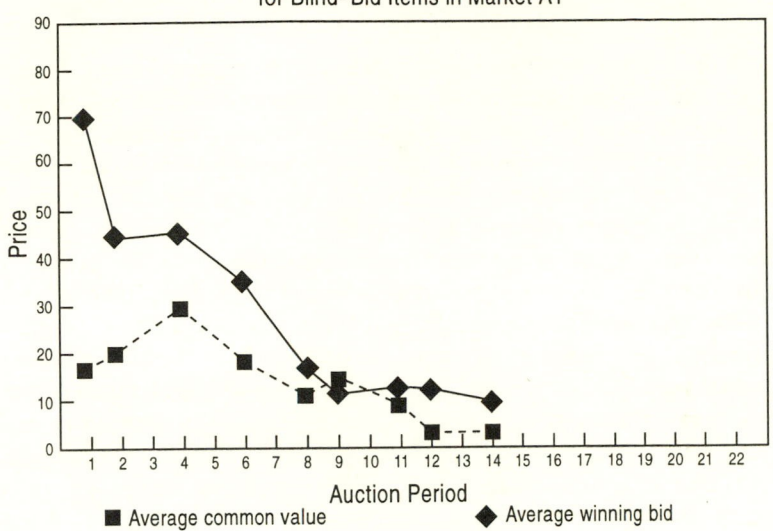

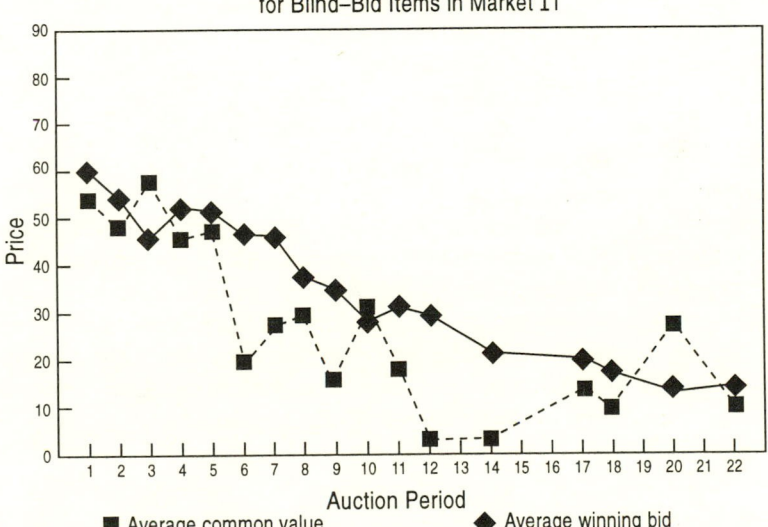

Figure 7.5. Common values and winning bids for blind bid items. Gaps in data points indicate that no items were blind bid that period. *Source:* Forsythe, Isaac, and Palfrey 1989.

3. Lemons and Ripoffs: The Winner's Curse in Markets
with Quality Endogenously Determined

Lynch, Miller, Plott, and Porter (1986, 1991) study markets in which product quality is endogenously determined and cannot be observed by buyers prior to purchase (in all other experiments reviewed so far value has been exogenously determined). Sellers chose between producing a high or a low quality product where the marginal cost of producing the high quality product was greater than the low quality product. Buyers obtained greater value for the high quality product. It was common knowledge that it cost sellers more to produce "supers" (the high quality product) compared to "regulars." Markets were organized as continuous double auctions (see section III.C and Holt, chapter 5, section V) with several buyers and several sellers on either side of the market.

In markets where there were no enforceable warranties and sellers' identities were anonymous, so that they could not develop reputations for product quality, there is a potential "lemons" problem with sellers producing only low quality products. This in turn creates an adverse selection problem that, if not correctly anticipated, can result in large losses for buyers as a result of paying premium prices for what turn out to be low quality products (the winner's curse). As Lynch et al. (1986, 1991) demonstrate, inexperienced buyers fell prey to the winner's curse, even in this simplified setting, as sellers almost always produced a low quality product and buyers almost always paid prices greater than the highest possible redemption value for these low quality products, at least in the first market period. However, these large losses, in conjunction with sellers' continued delivery of low quality products, generated rapid adjustments on buyers' part so that prices were within 5 francs of those predicted by the lemons model by the fourth period in virtually all markets.[69]

Lynch et al. go on to explore the effects of warranties and sellers' reputations for correcting the lemons problem (warranties are effective, but reputation effects do not necessarily guarantee efficient market performance—see chapter 5, section IX). However, the relevant point to note here is that even in this simplified setting buyers initially fell prey to the winner's curse and that sellers' behavior, almost always supplying low quality products, appears to have been largely responsible for the rapid elimination of the problem.

4. Summing Up

In the bilateral bargaining game with asymmetric information buyers repeatedly suffer from a winner's curse as they fail to account for the adverse selection problem inherent in the seller's strategy of rejecting bids below the value of the item. It is clear at this point that the buyer behavior reported in the original Samuelson and Bazerman (1985) paper is robust and remarkably resistant to the feedback associated with repeated losses. (Factors that promote learning in this environment, and in common value auctions, are discussed in section II.D below.)

In both the blind bid auction experiment of Forsythe et al. and the lemons market of Lynch et al. there are potential adverse selection problems, which are realized. But the worst of the winner's curse effect is relatively short lived as the market unravels. In both cases the rather rapid elimination of the winner's curse is directly attributable to the market structure, in particular the actions sellers take in pursuit of their own self interest. This exacerbates the adverse selection problem and buyers' losses unless they make some adjustment in the right direction. In other words, in these markets the active role that sellers play seems largely responsible for the market unraveling and with it the elimination of the winner's curse. Further, new entrants, or infrequent participants, in markets such as this are likely to be protected from the strong winner's curse found in the start-up phase of the market by the fact that they unravel so quickly and are likely to stay unraveled with any sizable group of experienced bidders staying in the market.

D. Learning and Adjustment Processes in Markets with a Winner's Curse

This section is concerned with adjustments in bidding when sellers' actions do not contribute to eliminating the winner's curse—common value auction experiments and bilateral bargaining experiments with asymmetric information. Learning and adjustment over time are important phenomena in many experimental situations. Learning processes are of growing interest to theorists as well since it is clear that Nash equilibria are not established instantaneously, but rather are likely to evolve out of some sort of learning and adjustment process. In what follows, we report on what little is known about factors underlying subjects' adjustments to the winner's curse in these games.

Ball et al. (1991) and Cifuentes and Sunder (1991) report virtually no adjustment to the winner's curse in repeated bilateral bargaining trials (recall Figure 7.4). Indeed, the absence of any noticeable within session adjustments in both these studies is quite remarkable, at least to this reviewer. However, as Ball et al. show, behavior does adjust in response to (i) buyers playing the part of sellers and (ii) buyers returning for a second night of play.

To determine the effect of experience as sellers (the informed player) on performance as buyers (the uninformed player), Ball et al.'s subjects participated in two experimental sessions. The first session consisted of two parts: twenty trials in which subjects acted as buyers, followed by twenty trials in which they acted as sellers. In their role as sellers, subjects were told the value of the company they were trying to sell, given an offer and asked to accept or reject it (offers were taken from a representative subject's behavior as a buyer in an earlier experiment). Following each period, the computer calculated the sellers' earnings for that period and the period earnings for their imaginary buyer opponent. In the second experimental session, conducted several days following the first, subjects again played the role of buyers for twenty trials. As a control condition another group of subjects acted as buyers in an initial experimental session (of twenty trials), returning as buyers for a second experimental session several days later.

In the case where subjects acted as both buyers and sellers, the percentage of learners (defined as subjects bidding zero from any particular trial until the end of the experimental session) jumped from 9 percent (four out of forty-four) to 37 percent (fifteen out of forty-one) between sessions 1 and 2 (a statistically significant increase).[70] Further, the mean bid for the non-learners changed from $51 to $34, suggesting that, although they had not learned to avoid bids with negative expected profit, they had learned to reduce their chances of losing money in any given trial and to reduce their losses conditional on the event of winning. It is interesting to note that these bidding adjustments took place at the beginning of the second experimental session, and that there was virtually no adjustment over time within the second session.

BBC report some adjustments in the control group as well. The percentage of learners increased from 6 percent (two of thirty-four) to 12 percent (four of thirty-four), although this difference is not significant at conventional levels. Further, the mean bid of nonlearners dropped from $50 to $34, almost the same as the reduction in bidding reported for the nonlearners who had played as sellers. Here, too, almost all the learning took place between the two experimental sessions, with minimal adjustments within the second session.

The fact that playing as sellers dramatically affected buyers' behavior squares nicely with one's intuition. The role reversal from buyer to seller literally forces buyers to act out the behavior of sellers, which should promote incorporating the informed party's (seller's) decisions into their bids after the experience. In other words, to the extent that the winner's curse results from buyer's failure to account for the adverse selection problem inherent in the seller's decision rule, playing the role of sellers promotes buyers accounting for this fact.

In common value auctions there are two distinctly different vehicles for bids adjusting over time. First, there is the possibility of "market learning" as bankruptcies drive out the more aggressive bidders and more aggressive bidders earn lower than average profits, self-selecting out of further experimental sessions. Second, there is the possibility for individual learning as subjects respond to repeated losses by bidding less. There is evidence that both factors are at work in common value auctions.

In Lind and Plott (1991), both the number of bidders and the size of ϵ were held constant throughout. Lind and Plott conclude that "the winner's curse persists with experience but the magnitude and frequency of losses decline with experience" (Conclusion 2). Clear evidence for this is found in Table 7.7, reported earlier. There, both loss frequencies and average profits are divided into ten period quartiles for each experimental session. As can be seen, with the notable exception of session 5, both the frequency and magnitude of losses decrease after the first ten trials.[71] To the extent that these adjustments are real rather than spurious, they must be the result of individual learning as no bankruptcies occurred in these sessions.[72]

Garvin and Kagel (1991) identify substantial adjustments in bidding in first-price auctions between inexperienced and experienced bidders (subjects who have participated in one previous first-price auction series). Table 7.10 reports some of their results. For example, with $n = 4$, the winning bid is *greater* than

Table 7.10. Effects of Experience on Bidding in First-Price Common Value Auctions

		Percentage of Auctions Won with x_1^a	High Bidders: Percentage of $b_1 >$ $E[x_0 \mid X=x_1]^a$	All Bidders: Percentage of $b_1 >$ $E[x_0 \mid X=x_1]^a$	Percentage of Auctions with Positive Profit[a]	Average Actual Profit[b]	Average Predicted RNNE Profit[b]	Average Discount $(x-b)^{b,c}$
$n=4$	Inexperienced	73.2	75.6	64.6	43.9	−1.32	5.01	4.60
		(30/41)	(31/41)	(106/164)	(18/41)	(0.79)	(0.60)	(0.69)
	Experienced	66.3	34.8	29.5	58.4	1.37	4.32	8.07
		(59/89)	(31/89)	(105/356)	(52/89)	(0.49)	(0.41)	(0.36)
$n=6$ or 7	Inexperienced	56.7	76.7	58.2	30.0	−3.75	2.76	3.56
		(17/30)	(23/30)	(121/208)	(9/30)	(0.89)	(0.53)	(0.97)
	Experienced	47.4	68.4	33.8	31.6	−0.32	2.93	5.53
		(9/19)	(13/19)	(45/133)	(6/19)	(0.56)	(0.54)	(1.10)

Source: Garvin and Kagel 1991.

Note: $\varepsilon = \$12$.

[a] Numbers in parentheses are raw data.

[b] Numbers in parentheses are the standard error of the mean.

[c] Data for $x \geq \underline{x} + \varepsilon$.

$E[x_0 \mid X = x_1]$ in 75.6 percent of all auctions with inexperienced bidders compared to 34.8 percent with experienced bidders. Or, looking at the same behavior from a different point of view, for inexperienced subjects the average discount $(x - b)$ for winning bidders was $4.42, well below what is required to avoid the winner's curse (a discount of $7.20 with $\epsilon = \$12$), compared to an average discount of $7.44 for experienced bidders. This overly aggressive bidding translates into negative average profits for inexperienced bidders of $1.32 per auction period and losses in over 50 percent of all auction periods, compared to positive average profits of $1.37 and profits in 58.4 percent of all auctions for experienced bidders.

Garvin and Kagel (1991) identify two mechanisms behind the changes reported. First, a kind of market learning/self-selection effect is at work as bankrupt subjects were much less likely to return for the second auction series: 27 percent of bankrupt bidders (four out of fifteen) returned, while 86 percent of the solvent bidders (thirty-two out of thirty-seven) returned.[73] Further, subjects who failed to return for further experimental sessions (which includes bankrupt bidders), bid more aggressively, on average, as measured by differences in the average discount rate (the discount rate is defined as a bidder's signal value minus their bid, divided by ϵ).[74] Second, there were clear individual subject learning effects as inexperienced bidders bid less in response to actually losing money (experiential learning) and in response to potentially losing money had they applied their bidding strategy to the high bidder's signal (observational learning). Under some conditions responses to these "hypothetical" losses were almost as large as the response to actually losing money. In some cases losing bidders who would have made money had their bid won the auction bid higher following auctions in which the high bidder made a positive profit. Although these "hypothetical" gain effects retard convergence to the RNNE (since bidding was above the equilibrium to begin with), they are smaller and less frequent in magnitude than the hypothetical losses, so the net effect of observational learning is to move bidding closer to the RNNE.

One noticeable difference between the common value auctions and the bilateral bargaining experiments is the within session adjustments to the winner's curse reported for inexperienced subjects: in the bilateral bargaining experiments there is virtually no adjustment, while reasonably large reductions in bids are found in the auctions. It is interesting to conjecture as to the basis for these differences. Ball et al. (1991) argue that there is a higher frequency of earning positive profits conditional on winning in the bargaining game (this happens 1/3 of the time with a naive bidding strategy) than in the auctions, so that the message, "bid less," comes through much more clearly in the auctions. Although this observation is true of the studies reported in Kagel et al. (1989), inexperienced bidders earned positive profits in 30 percent or more of the auction periods in Garvin and Kagel (Table 7.10) and in the first ten auction periods in Lind and Plott (Table 7.7). So this explanation appears suspect. A second factor to consider is that actual losses are often considerably larger in the auctions—they average around −$1.30 in Table 7.10 and around −$8.00 in the first ten periods in Lind and Plott—compared to −$0.06 per period in Ball et al. and Cifuentes and Sunder (experimental dollars were converted into cash at the rate of 1 cent to the dollar in the bilateral bargaining studies). Perhaps subjects are more sensitive to these larger losses (recall section I.G).[75] Third, the observational learning reported by Garvin and Kagel in common value auctions is not available in the bilateral bargaining game where bidders only get to see the outcome of their own choices.[76] It remains to sort out carefully between these alternative explanations.

III. Additional Topics

Several additional topics are reviewed here. Section III.A reports the limited evidence on collusion in experimental auction markets. Section III.B relates the experimental findings to results reported from field studies. Sections III.C and III.D conclude with a brief discussion of two-sided (double) auctions and some other uses of auction market experiments reported in the literature.

A. Collusion

Most of the auction theory literature assumes that bidders act noncooperatively. This assumption may not be appropriate under some conditions, to the point that in field settings there is constant concern with the possibility of overt or tactic collusion (Cassady 1967, Graham and Marshall, 1987). With the notable exception of one auction series reported in Lind and Plott (1991), outright collusion among bidders has not been reported under standard experimental procedures. (The collusion reported in Lind and Plott was short lived and, apparently, unsuccessful, as there was always at least one defector.)

A number of significant obstacles must be overcome to mount a successful conspiracy in laboratory auction markets. Communication among bidders is typically not allowed, and subjects are usually brought together for a single auction session or, in the case of repeated sessions, group composition typically changes between sessions. As such, although there may be occasional signalling of a willingness to cooperate by an individual subject through, for example, submitting an unusually low bid, there is little chance for successful conspiracies to develop.

Isaac and Walker (1985) studied conspiracies through allowing bidders to discuss and coordinate bidding strategies. Discussions were allowed after bidders received their private resale values, but before they were required to bid. Isaac and Walker's announcement read as follows:

> Sometimes in previous experiments, participants have found it useful, when the opportunity arose, to communicate with one another. We are going to allow you this opportunity while we reset the computer between periods.
>
> There will be some restrictions.
>
> You are free to discuss any aspect of the experiment (or the market) that you wish, except that:
>
> (1) You may not discuss any aspect of the quantitative information on your screen.
> (2) You are not allowed to discuss side payments or physical threats.

A monitor was present to insure these restrictions were satisfied. A first-price (discriminatory) private value sealed bid auction was employed with four bidders and either one or three units of the commodity offered for sale, with feedback on auction outcomes consisting of either the winning bid (and that bidder's subject number) or all bids (with the associated subject numbers).

Isaac and Walker (1985) report active conspiracies developing in seven of twelve auction series, where a conspiracy is defined as all four bidders actively attempting to formulate and implement a collusive bidding scheme. Of the five remaining auction series, in two of them some bidders actively attempted to conspire, but at least one bidder openly refused to cooperate, and in the remainder the discussion never proceeded as far as an explicit conspiratorial scheme. Auction series with active conspiracies typically evolved to the point where the player(s) with the highest resale value(s) won the item with a minimum bid, with their co-conspirators bidding zero. Auction series with active conspiracies were stable, there being only three apparent cases of cheating. The results were ambiguous regarding Isaac and Walker's conjecture that conspiracies would be less successful if losing bids were not announced.

Dyer (personal communication) investigated tacit collusion in first-price private value auctions with three bidders. His treatment variable involved bidding in auctions with a fixed number of other bidders whose identity was known compared to bidding in groups whose composition was randomly determined between auctions (the length of time these treatments were in effect was not announced, but they lasted a minimum of nine auction periods). The same set of subjects participated in three auction series, which took place over a two week period. Using a fixed effects regression model to analyze the data, his results are sensitive to both the regression specification and the data set employed. Fitting separate regressions to each auction series, he identifies a statistically significant effect in the expected direction (lower bidding with fixed identity) in the first auction series using a nonlinear time trend specification (some sort of time trend specification is necessary since bids as a proportion of resale values drift down over time—see section I.F above). But a linear time trend yields the opposite sign for this auction series (and is not statistically significant) and there are no significant treatment effects in the second and third auction series (the signs of the treatment variables are not consistent either). Fitting a single regression to the entire data set, a linear time trend specification shows a statistically significant effect in the expected direction, but the nonlinear time trend specification yields the opposite sign (which is not statistically significant). Adjustments in bidding reported across experimental sessions suggests that the nonlinear specification provides a more faithful representation of the data (see section I.F). Given these mixed results and the importance of the issue (is there a supergame effect when employing the same group of subjects within a given auction series) there is a clear need for more study.

My students and I have studied the effects of explicit opportunities for collusion in first-price common value auctions, implementing a variant of Isaac and Walker's procedures.[77] In common value auctions the experimenter faces the obvious problem of potentially large losses since x_0 varies over reasonably wide intervals (see section II.A). To solve this problem, a reserve price rule was established by drawing another signal at random from the interval $[x_0 - \epsilon, x_0 + \epsilon]$ and subtracting ϵ from it. A winning bid had to meet or beat the reserve price for the item to be sold. Two different information conditions were implemented, one in which both the reserve price rule and its realization was announced prior to bidding, and one in which only the price rule, but not its realization, was common knowledge. Two auction series were conducted, both beginning with five periods using the procedures described in section II.A, but with the addition of the reserve price rule. Subjects were then provided with an opportunity to communicate using an announcement similar to Isaac and Walker (1985), except that bidders *were* allowed to discuss and compare their private information signals. After ten auction periods, information conditions were changed from announcing the reserve price realization to no announcement in series 1, and from no announcement to announcing the reserve price realization in series 2.[78] These conditions were maintained for an additional ten auction periods.

Table 7.11 reports the results of these two auction series. In both cases, bidders suffered from the winner's curse under the no communication condition, which is not surprising as subjects had no prior experience with common value auctions. Collusion was active in both auction series when it was permitted, with a rotation

Table 7.11. Mean Profits in Common Value Auctions with Conspiracy

Auction Series	No Discussions		Discussions			
			Reservation Price Announced		Reservation Price Not Announced	
	Actual	Predicted[a]	Actual	Maximum Possible[b]	Actual	Predicted[c]
1	−2.54 (0.88)	1.66 (0.63)	4.85 (1.16)	4.86 (1.16)	1.21 (0.54)	2.05 (0.85)
2	−1.06 (0.50)	1.37 (0.52)	3.71 (1.06)	3.79 (1.06)	−0.07 (0.58)	0.00 (0.00)

Note: Numbers in parentheses are the standard error of the mean.
[a] Assuming RNNE bidding with no bid floor.
[b] Assuming bid floor provides focal point for conspiracy.
[c] Assuming optimal information pooling and risk neutrality in setting conspiracy price (see text).

rule (phases of the moon rule) used to determine the winning bidder (there was only one apparent break from the collusive arrangement, and that lasted for a single period). When the reserve price was announced it served as a focal point for the collusive price, with the winning bid being at or a few cents above it.

In cases where the reserve price was not announced, but where the rule was known, risk neutral bidders could maximize expected profit by pooling their information to establish an estimate of x_o, with the winner bidding $E[x_o] - \epsilon$. (Optimal pooling of information here requires averaging the low and high signal values to estimate $E[x_o]$.) In fact, the winning bid was well above $E[x_o] - \epsilon$, averaging \$1.56 (0.703) and \$1.95 (1.18) above it in the two auctions (standard errors of the mean are in parentheses).[79] From the information at hand it is not possible to tell if bidding above $E[x_o] - \epsilon$ resulted from a failure to properly pool information or from efforts to increase the chances of coming in above the unannounced reservation price (as might be expected if bidders are risk averse).[80] The net result was that actual profits were about half of what they would have been had the winner bid $E[x_o] - \epsilon$.

One interesting side product of this study is the realization that the reserve price, when announced, provides a focal point for collusive pricing should it exist. In contrast, announcing the price rule, but not its realization, results in risk neutral conspirators failing to purchase a number of items (half of them, on average, in our design) and possibly raising average prices on account of risk aversion. Although it is a robust prediction of auction theory that reserve prices will be used and announced, reserve prices, when they exist in practice, are typically not announced. Several elegant explanations of this apparent discrepancy between theory and practice have been offered in terms of noncooperative game theory

(McAfee and McMillan 1987c, Graham, Marshall, and Richard 1990). As seen here, an alternative explanation for this practice is the tendency for bidders to collude in auctions, a problem of considerable concern in practice (Cassady 1967), and the fact that when a reservation price is announced, it serves as a focal point for the collusive outcome.

B. Comparing Results from Field Studies with Experiments

There are important tradeoffs in studying auction theory using field as compared to experimental data. In an experiment, the researcher has full control of the auction structure so that, for example, a pure common value or private value auction can be constructed and the private information signals/valuations underlying bids are known. Failure to control these factors can make interpretation of field data problematic, as most actual auctions contain important private as well as common value elements, and the investigator must construct proxies for the private information signals/valuations underlying bids. Laboratory control also permits quite precise and demanding tests of the theory and facilitates identifying the causal factors underlying the behavior reported. On the other hand, field data have the advantage that they involve experienced professionals, with substantially larger amounts of money at stake than in the typical auction experiment, which may result in fundamentally different behavior. Wilson (1992, 261–62) summarizes the differences between field studies and laboratory experiments nicely:

> Empirical (field) studies must contend with less complete data, and few controls in the auction environment are possible. On the other hand, they have the advantage that the data pertain to practical situations in which the stakes are often large and the participants are skilled and experienced.

Despite these differences, results from field studies and experiments are complimentary in the sense that they both deal with the same phenomena, auction behavior. As such, both similarities and differences in behavior need to be identified (and, in the case of differences, hopefully reconciled) in order to enhance understanding. One purpose of this section is to make these comparisons.

A middle ground between field studies and experiments is to bring experienced professionals into the laboratory to participate in an experiment. Here, one presumably has the best of both worlds, strict control over the structure of the auction and experienced professionals to behave in it. Dyer et al. (1989b) did this in an experiment comparing the behavior of student subjects with construction industry executives in a common value offer auction. Behavior was found to be qualitatively similar as both subject populations fell prey to the winner's curse. This raises the puzzling issue of why presumably successful executives from the construction industry, an industry in which the competitive bidding process is often characterized as essentially a common value auction, could do so poorly in the laboratory.[81] The second purpose of this section is to provide summary results from a field study of the construction industry designed to answer this question.

1. Direct Comparisons between Laboratory and Field Data

In comparing empirical results from field studies with experiments, I rely heavily on the summaries of field work provided in McAfee and McMillan (1987a) and Wilson (1992). McAfee and McMillan note two unsurprising predictions of auction theory that have been confirmed using field data (primary sources underlying these conclusions are reported in parenthesis): (i) other things equal, a bidder with a higher valuation will submit a higher bid (in the case of offer auctions, a firm with lower costs submits a lower bid) (Gaver and Zimmerman 1977), and (ii) competition matters, so that the winning bid increases as the number of bidders increases (in the case of offer auctions, the winning bid falls) (Gaver and Zimmerman 1977; Brannman, Klein, and Weiss 1984). A third unsurprising prediction confirmed in field data is that in common value auctions better informed bidders make a higher rate of return than less informed bidders (Mead, Moseidjord, and Sorensen 1984; Hendricks and Porter 1988). All three of these predictions have also been confirmed in experimental data: (1) Bid functions estimated from private value auction experiments are strongly increasing in bidders' private valuations (Cox et al. 1988; section I.F, Table 7.4, above), while those for common value auctions are increasing in the buyers' signal values (Kagel and Levin 1986; Kagel et al. 1989). (2) Bid functions in first-price private value auctions are increasing in the number of bidders so that the winning bid must be increasing (section I.C), while bidders' profits are decreasing in common value auctions as n increases, so that the winning bid must be increasing as well (Kagel and Levin 1986). (3) In common value auctions with asymmetric information, less informed bidders' profits average around 25 percent of the informed bidders' profits (Kagel and Levin, unpublished data).

Considerable field work has been devoted to the study of outer continental shelf (OCS) oil lease auctions in the Gulf of Mexico for the period from 1954 to 1969. (OCS leases are often cited as the canonical form of the common value auction). Much of the research here, as in common value auction experiments, has focused on the existence and consequences of the winner's curse. Initial studies by petroleum geologists, who coined the term "winner's curse," claimed that winning bidders earned less than the market rate of return on their investments (Capen, Clapp, and Campbell 1971). Subsequent, more careful studies by economists yield more mixed results. Mead, Moseidjord, and Sorensen (1983) found after-tax rates of return to be somewhat less than average returns on equity for U.S. manufacturing corporations, concluding that

> they [the lessees] have historically received no risk premium and may have paid too much for the right to explore for and produce oil and gas on federal offshore lands. (43)

Note that different authors interpret the same results quite differently. Although Kagel and Levin (1986) argue that these results provide qualified support for Capen, Clapp, and Campbell's position, McAfee and McMillan (1987a) argue that they overturn these conclusions. Part of the difference in interpretation has to do with whether investors require a risk premium for investing in oil and gas leases, with Mead et al. (1983) suggesting that they do. Others contend that large oil companies with access to capital markets and a diversified portfolio of leases would not be expected to earn risk premiums.

Hendricks, Porter, and Boudreau (1987) independently examined rates of return for OCS leases during the period from 1954 to 1969. Using somewhat different accounting procedures from Mead et al. (1983) they concluded that average realized profits were negative for auctions with more than six bidders, a conclusion remarkably similar to that reported in Kagel and Levin (1986). Hendricks et al. point out that these negative profits can be explained by nonoptimal bidding strategies that fail to account for the winner's curse, or equally, by adverse selection effects in estimating the number of bidders. That is, since most tracts receive less than six bids, and assuming that firms expect this, *ex post* profits will be less on tracts receiving more bids. Overall, Hendricks et al. conclude that "the data are consistent with both the assumptions and predictions of the [common value] model," allowing for bidders' uncertainty about the number of active bidders on each tract. As Wilson (1992) points out, however, this conclusion is stronger than in previous studies, where mixed results regarding profitability are often reported (Gilley, Karels, and Leone 1986).

Given the inconclusive nature of rate of return studies for OCS leases, Kagel and Levin (1986) use an anomalous finding reported in Mead et al. (1983, 1984) comparing rates of return on drainage with wildcat leases as suggesting important similarities between field and laboratory studies. A wildcat lease is one for which no positive drilling data are available, so that bidders have symmetric information. On a drainage lease hydrocarbons have been located on an adjacent tract so that there is asymmetric information, with companies who lease the adjacent tract(s) (neighbor(s)) having superior information to other companies (nonneighbors). The anomaly reported by Mead et al. is that *both* neighbors and nonneighbors earned a higher rate of return on drainage compared to wildcat leases. In other words, with asymmetric information, even the less informed bidders (nonneighbors) received a higher rate of return on drainage leases than on leases with symmetric information (wildcat tracts). Kagel and Levin (1986) rationalize this result by arguing that there is an important public information component to drainage tracts, and the public information may have corrected for a winner's curse that depressed rates of return on wildcat tracts. Details of this argument are outlined in chapter 1, section III.E and will not be repeated here.

A subsequent study of drainage lease auctions by Hendricks and Porter (1988), for this same time period, does not yield this anomalous result. Rather, Hendricks and Porter (1988) report the more conventional outcome that nonneighbors (those with inferior information) bidding on drainage tracts earned lower rates of return than firms bidding on wildcat tracts. However, updating their analysis to include production data from the 1980's, and more reliable production estimates prior to 1980, Hendricks and Porter (1992) obtain net rate of return estimates quite similar to Mead et al. (1984): *both* neighbors and nonneighbors earned a higher rate of return on drainage leases than the rate of return on wildcat leases.[82]

Anomalous results also emerge from field studies involving U.S. timber lease sales which have been conducted using both English and first-price auctions. Some have used these auctions to test the revenue-equivalence theorem: Do the two methods yield the same price on average? Using ordinary-least-squares regressions, Mead (1967) reports that sealed bid auctions had significantly higher prices than English auctions. Further study by Hansen (1985, 1986), who noted a selection bias caused by the way the Forest Service chose which auction to use, and corrected for it using a simultaneous equations model, found that although sealed bid auctions had slightly higher prices than the English auctions, the difference was not statistically significant, so that revenue equivalence could not be rejected. The puzzling part about these results is that there are strong common value (or at least correlated private value) elements to timber lease sales which should, in theory, result in English auctions raising more revenue. McAfee and McMillan (1987a) note this puzzle and go on to add

> The puzzle could be resolved by appealing to risk aversion of the bidders, but this remains an open empirical question. Given the sensitivity of the Revenue-Equivalence Theorem to its underlying assumptions, the theorem cannot be meaningfully tested until some way is found to test for independent private values against affiliated values. (727)

Experimental studies offer a possible alternative resolution to this anomaly. Common value auction experiments comparing sealed bid with English auctions show that English auctions do not consistently generate higher prices. In auctions where bidders commonly suffer from a winner's curse, as occurs with inexperienced bidders, sealed bid auctions consistently yield higher prices than English auctions (recall Table 7.8 from section II.B). Further, in auctions where bidders consistently earn positive profits, but still exhibit relatively strong traces of the winner's curse, as with moderately experienced bidders, the two auctions yield roughly the same prices (Kagel and Levin 1992). That is, in auctions where bidders suffer from traces of the winner's curse, the public information inherent in low bidders' drop-out prices tends to reduce rather than raise revenue (just as experimenter announced public information produces the same effect when bidders suffer from the winner's curse—see sections II.A and II.B above). Of course, to use this mechanism to resolve the anomaly in the timber sales field data requires postulating that bidders suffer from elements of the winner's curse.

It is worth adding here that in affiliated private value auction experiments, public information did not raise nearly as much revenue as predicted under risk neutrality (Kagel et al. 1987, reviewed in section I.D). Although risk aversion may partially explain these results, the data also show a sizable frequency of individual subject bidding errors associated with the release of public information, and these bidding errors inhibit the revenue raising mechanism underlying the theory. In short, the experimental evidence indicates that the revenue raising possibilities associated with affiliated value auctions are not nearly as robust as symmetric auction theory would lead one to expect, and the timber sale results are consistent with this fact.

2. Differences in Structure between Laboratory and Field Auctions

Dyer and Kagel (1992) address the question of why experienced construction industry executives fell prey to the winner's curse in laboratory offer auctions, as reported in Dyer et al. (1989b). They focus on two possibilities, which are not necessarily mutually exclusive. One is that the executives had learned a set of situation specific rules of thumb which permit them to avoid the winner's curse in the field, but which could not be applied in the laboratory. The second is that the bidding environment created in the experiment, which is based on theoretical work, is not representative of the environment encountered in the field.

Evidence supporting this first possibility emerges from interviews with contractors. In these interviews it is clear that an important determinant of the risk associated with bidding a job involves the architect/owner. The architect/owner's reputation for admitting mistakes, or ambiguities, in construction plans, and their willingness to implement functionally equivalent construction outcomes using alternative, and cheaper, construction techniques than originally specified, play an important role in the cost estimates assigned to specific job components, as well as the markup assigned to the total cost estimate.[83] In addition, firms tend to specialize in different types of construction projects (or at least their estimators do). Experienced contractors pride themselves on their familiarity with building different types of structures and figure their estimates to lie within a rather narrow band of the true value. This familiarity is based on past experience, to the point that in one bidding session I sat in on, the firm had just completed a similar building designed by the same architect. At one point, when in doubt on the cost estimate to assign to a particular component of the job they were bidding on, the bid team simply pulled up records from the recently completed job and filled in the missing numbers.[84] Needless to say, the contractors did not have these situation specific rules to rely on when bidding in the laboratory.

Evidence that the field environment differs in important ways from theoretical specifications operationalized in the laboratory is summarized in Table 7.12, which shows the distribution of bids on a particular job, measured in terms of deviations from the low winning bid. The first thing the reader will note is that the low bid is some $30,000 *below the low winning bid*. This was the result of a bidding "error" which resulted in the original low bidder withdrawing his bid without penalty after the bids were announced.[85] Standard auction theory does not account for such possibilities.[86] The second thing to note is the small difference between the winning low bid and the second lowest bid ("money left on the table"), less than 1 percent of the low bid. This difference is minuscule and indicative of the relatively small differences between the low bid and the second lowest bid characteristic of much of the industry, which averaged around 5 percent for the sample of jobs analyzed in Dyer and Kagel. By way of contrast, Hendricks et al. (1987) report money left on the table from OCS leases averages around 50 percent of the winning bid.[87] This implies that there is much smaller scope for the winner's curse to express itself in the branch of the construction

Table 7.12. Bids by Firm Measured in Terms of Deviation
from Low Winning Bid

Firm	Deviaton from Low Bid (dollars)	Deviation as a Percentage of Low Bid	Firm	Deviaton from Low Bid (dollars)	Deviation as a Percentage of Low Bid
1	−30,000[a]	−0.71	8	105,000	2.47
2	0	0.00	9	142,000	3.33
3	32,000	0.75	10	144,000	3.38
4	64,000	1.50	11	155,000	3.64
5	74,600	1.75	12	166,000	3.90
6	87,679	2.06	13	183,000	4.30
7	90,000	2.12	14	564,000	13.25

[a] Mistake in bid and let out of bid. Second-highest bidder got the job. Mean bid $4.38 million.

industry in which these executives worked. As such, private value elements, such as the firm's overhead and the amount of idle resources anticipated, often play an important role in determining the low bidder.[88]

3. Summing Up

Unsurprising predictions of auction theory regarding higher winning bids with more bidders, and higher profits for bidders with superior information in common value auctions with asymmetric information, are confirmed in both field and laboratory studies. There were reports of a winner's curse in early OCS oil lease auctions, but these findings have been subject to considerable dispute, as have other citings of the phenomenon. Anomalies identified in laboratory experiments have parallels in field data, but alternative explanations for the field data are available as well. Professional bidders from the construction industry fell prey to the winner's curse in a laboratory offer auction. Reasons suggested for this are that (i) learning tends to be situation specific, and the experiment stripped away many of the contextual clues the professionals employ in field settings and (ii) the construction industry has private value and repeated play elements that were not present in the experiment, which mitigate the winner's curse.

C. Two-Sided Auctions

Experimental investigations of two-sided (double) auctions have commonly employed stationary aggregate supply and demand schedules (schedules that remain constant across auction periods). This is in contrast to one-sided auction experiments where buyers' valuations/information signals are randomly drawn each auction period. Two-sided auctions, particularly continuous double auctions, have been used in this way to investigate questions in industrial organization theory (see chapter 5) and in price formation in asset markets (see chapter 6). They have typically not been used to investigate theories of double auction markets in the same way that one-sided auction experiments have. The primary culprit here is that, until recently, there have been no clearly articulated theories of double auction markets in terms of Bayesian Nash equilibria of games with incomplete information (see Wilson [1992] for a review of recent research along these lines), in large measure because of the difficulties in modeling strategic behavior on both sides of the market.[89] Two preliminary experimental studies have, however, investigated recently developed Bayesian Nash equilibrium models of double auction markets. Both involve private value auctions with buyers' valuations and sellers' costs drawn randomly each auction period from known distributions and with buyers and sellers limited to trading a single unit.

Cason and Friedman (1993) study continuous double auction (CDA) markets. A continuous double auction (CDA) market permits trade at any time in a trading period, with buyers and sellers free to continuously update their bids and offers. Cason and Friedman test three CDA models concerned with price formation *within* trading periods. In order of decreasing rationality, these are Wilson's (1987) waiting game/Dutch auction model (a sequential equilibrium model in which transactions occur between the highest valued buyer and lowest cost seller remaining in the market), Friedman's (1991) Bayesian game against nature (where traders ignore the impact of their own current bids and asks on subsequent offers by others but employ Bayes' law in updating bids and offers), and Gode and Sunder's (1993) budget constrained zero intelligence (ZI) trading model (buyers bid randomly between their valuation and zero, and sellers offer randomly between their cost and the upper bound of the cost distribution).[90] The contrasting predictions looked at concern serial correlation between successive transaction prices, the nature of successive bid and ask sequences culminating in a transaction, the extent to which early transactions occur between high value buyers and low cost sellers, and the extent to which gains from trade are exhausted (efficiency).

Two data sets are used to test these predictions, only one of which strictly satisfies the theoretical requirements of all the models (buyers and sellers trade single units with new random valuations in each trading period). This one data set consists of three experimental sessions with four buyers and four sellers and inexperienced traders. Tests for serial correlation in transaction prices can not reject the null hypothesis of zero correlation, consistent with Wilson's (1987) waiting game model. However, the few traders involved result in only two or three transactions within each market period, so that the power of this test is quite low. Changes in successive bids and offers favors Friedman's Bayesian game against nature as successive improvements in bids (offers) culminating in a trade are most often made by different buyers (sellers) rather than the same buyer (seller) as the waiting game model predicts (ZI traders exhibit no consistent pattern with respect to this characteristic). Higher valued buyers and lower cost sellers tend to trade sooner, but the rank order correlations between buyer (seller) valuation and transaction order are weak and fall within the range predicted by the ZI algorithm. Efficiency levels are uniformly high, averaging 93 percent, which is a little lower than found in ZI simulations. Cason and Friedman are keenly aware of the data limitations underlying their analysis, calling for more experiments, particularly those with experienced traders, so that the common knowledge assumptions underlying Wilson's waiting game model are more likely to be satisfied.

Kagel and Vogt (1993) provide some initial data for Satterthwaite and Williams (1989a, 1989b, 1993) buyers' bid double auction (BBDA) markets.[91] The BBDA is a clearing house trading mechanism in which buyers and sellers submit a single bid and offer each trading period on the basis of which the market clears. The BBDA is a particularly attractive model to investigate since it makes a number of strong predictions: sellers have a (nontransparent) dominant strategy of offering at cost, given a uniform distributions for costs and valuations symmetric risk neutral buyers bid a simple proportion of their valuation which is increasing in the number of traders, and Satterthwaite and Williams have computed the exact increase in the expected gains from trade as the number of traders increase, assuming a symmetric RNNE. The latter provides the focus for Kagel and Vogt's experiment, as efficiency is predicted to increase from 93 percent in auctions with two buyers and two sellers, to near 100 percent in auctions with as few as eight buyers and eight sellers.

Two data sets were used to test these predictions, only one of which strictly satisfies the structural requirements of the theory. This one data set consists of two auction sessions with inexperienced bidders and one with experienced bidders. Against the benchmark of the symmetric RNNE model's predictions there were a number of shortcomings. Sellers did not adhere to the dominant strategy of offering at cost, which was not unexpected given results reported for the simpler one-sided second-price auctions and multiple unit uniform price auctions (see section I.B.2). Buyers bid well above the symmetric RNNE, much like the overbidding reported in one-sided first-price auctions (section I.G). Efficiency failed to increase significantly as the number of traders increased; rather, it increased modestly on average and the direction of change was erratic across experimental sessions. The fact that efficiency failed to increase can be largely attributed to buyers bidding substantially more than predicted in auctions with few traders and to there being practical upper bounds on how much bids can increase without exceeding buyers' valuations. However, efficiency measures were uniformly high, averaging 88 percent in markets with two buyers and two sellers and 90 percent in markets with eight buyers and eight sellers. This is substantially higher than predicted for ZI traders under the BBDA and consistently higher than predicted under a fixed price rule.[92] Kagel and Vogt conclude by noting the need for further research exploring the effects of instructions designed to better explain the somewhat complicated trading rules underlying the BBDA and the effects of computerized sellers, which may make for a more stable environment for learning to take place. There is certain to be considerably more research investigating the properties of two-sided auctions in terms of games with incomplete information in the future.

D. Other Auction Studies

Experimentalists have used auctions to investigate a variety of topics, not all of which could be covered in detail here: Cech et al. (1987) and Guler and Plott (1988) have used auctions to study incentive contract issues of the sort involved in military procurement contracts, Palfrey (1985) has used auctions to investigate the efficiency and distributional consequences of the common practice of selling a variety of different items in "bundles," and Pitchik and Schotter (1988) have investigated a budget-constrained, sequential auction with the primary purpose of testing the predictive power of trembling hand perfect equilibria. Auction markets serve as an ideal vehicle for experimental studies of these and a variety of other issues. As Wilson (1992) notes, auctions are apt subjects for applications of game theory because they present explicit trading rules that largely fix the "rules of the game." These well-specified rules of the game serve to fix the rules and design of an experiment. In addition, the strategic behavior that can be modeled using auctions is, more often than not, of practical importance as well. This promises to spur a number of new experimental applications in the future.

IV. Conclusions

Studies of experimental auction markets have been going on for over ten years now, paralleling the profession's interest in the theoretical properties of these markets. This research has established several facts about behavior relative to the theory.

In private value auctions the revenue-equivalence theorem fails. Bids in first-price auctions are higher than in Dutch auctions, and bids in second-price auctions are higher than in English auctions. This failure of the revenue-equivalence theorem may result from response mode effects with the sealed bid auctions focusing attention on the price dimension, and the open auctions focusing attention on earnings, thereby generating small but consistent differences in bids. This failure of the revenue-equivalence theorem appears to represent a simple bid level effect rather than a more fundamental breakdown in Nash equilibrium bidding theory as the theory correctly predicts the directional relationship between bids and valuations, and the directional effects of changing numbers of bidders, under different bid price rules. In addition, the Nash equilibrium bidding model performs better than sophisticated ad hoc bidding models in first-price auctions with affiliated private values. Still unresolved is the debate regarding the relative importance of risk aversion versus bidding errors in organizing deviations from the RNNE model's point predictions in first-price auctions.

Nash equilibrium bidding theory performs much worse in common value auctions. Common value auctions are substantially more complicated than private value auctions as they incorporate a difficult item estimation problem in addition to the strategic problems involved in competitive bidding. In common value auctions inexperienced bidders suffer from a winner's curse, falling prey to the adverse selection problem inherent in these auctions. Overbidding here does not just involve a bid level effect but represents a more fundamental breakdown in the theory resulting in reversal of a number of important comparative static predictions: bidding does not decrease in response to increased numbers of bidders in second-price auctions as the theory predicts, and public information about the value of the item reduces, rather than raises, revenue in the presence of the winner's curse. This perverse effect of public information in the presence of a winner's curse extends to English common value auctions as well. Experienced bidders eventually adjust to the adverse selection forces inherent in common value auctions, but this largely reflects situation specific learning and market selection effects rather than theory absorption, so the ability of the theory to correctly predict bidding in field settings remains an open question.

The winner's curse extends to other market settings as well, being particularly robust in bilateral bargaining games with asymmetric information. However, blind bid auctions and markets where quality is endogenously determined unravel rather quickly, largely eliminating the winner's curse. What these markets add that the auctions and bilateral bargaining games lack is the dynamic interaction between sellers pursuing their own self interest, which exacerbates the adverse selection problem, and bidders adjusting in the right direction to the adverse selection effect. This process repeats itself until the market unravels, resulting in only lemons being sold or only low valued items being blind bid and with buyers largely adjusting to these extreme adverse selection effects.

Notes

Research support from the Economics and Information, Science and Technology Divisions of NSF, the Sloan Foundation and the Russell Sage Foundation are gratefully acknowledged. Special thanks to my coauthors Dan Levin and Ron Harstad for the many enlightening discussions on auction theory. Helpful comments on earlier drafts of this paper were received from Sheryl Ball, Raymond Battalio, Mark Isaac, John Ledyard, Dan Levin, Jack Ochs, Charles Plott, Rob Porter, Alvin Roth, Vernon Smith, James Walker, Elmar Wolfstetter, and participants at the Conference on the *Handbook of Experimental Economics*. Susan Garvin provided valuable research assistance throughout. I alone am responsible for errors and omissions.

1. There has been some experimental interest in one-sided auctions where bidders demand more than one unit of the good (Smith 1967, Belovicz 1979, Miller and Plott 1985; Grether, Isaac, and Plott 1989). There are limited theoretical results for such multiple unit auctions (see Forsythe and Isaac [1982] and Maskin and Riley [1989] for theory developments) and these have yet to be subject to systematic experimental investigation.

2. In the case of tied high bids, the winner is selected using a random tie breaking device.

3. These papers represent the first experimental studies of the IPV model with a clear theoretical focus. Frahm and Schrader (1970) conducted an earlier experimental study but employed a multiple unit sequential auction in which bidders did not know the number of units to be auctioned off (the latter was a stochastic variable whose mean and distribution was unknown). Frahm and Schrader offer no theoretical solution for their design.

4. Assuming some bidder heterogeneity, or random errors in bidding, efficiency measures will be sensitive to the support from which resale values are drawn and the number of bidders: other things equal, the larger the difference in $(\bar{x} - \underline{x})$ and/or the smaller n is, the higher the

average efficiency levels reported. Comparative efficiency measures are most meaningful when measured across auctions holding these variables constant.

5. Expected profits conditional on winning the auction were \$1.20 (Cox et al. 1982), \$1.50 (Cox et al. 1988) and \$7.50 (Dyer et al. 1989a).

6. I am grateful to my colleague Dan Levin for pointing this out to me. Cox et al. (1983a, 217) acknowledge this point as well.

7. Kagel and Levin (1993) report minimal learning on bidders' part as well, even following the occasional out-of-pocket losses that result from overbidding.

8. The Van Huyck, Battalio, and Beil results are part of a training exercise prior to participation in a more elaborate two stage game. The results in question have not been published, but they find some initial bidding above the dominant strategy price, similar to Kagel et al. (1987), with rapid convergence to the dominant strategy price (personal communication).

9. Several auction series with experienced subjects screened bidders to exclude those with the greatest absolute deviations from the dominant bidding strategy in the uniform price auctions, so the data from these auctions, must be treated with some caution.

10. A similar hysteresis effect is reported in Cox et al. (1985a) for multiple unit auctions. Bidding in an initial sequence of discriminatory auctions produced significantly lower bidding in subsequent uniform price auctions compared to bidding in an initial sequence of uniform price auctions. However, Harstad (1990) finds that prior experience need not necessarily affect bidding. In auction series involving several first-price auctions, followed by several second-price auctions, followed by several first-price auctions, bidding in the second series of first-price auctions is indistinguishable from the first series.

11. The expected cost of typical deviations from the RNNE found in first-price auctions is discussed in Harrison (1989) and section I.G.2 below.

12. My views on this issue have been heavily influenced by my colleague Dan Levin.

13. According to this literature the weight attached to a dimension increases when the dimension is psychologically more "compatible" with the response mode. Unfortunately, compatibility is not usually defined in advance, but is considered datum to be extracted from the problem. This does not obviate the apparent robustness of the effect. Tversky, Slovic, and Kahneman (1990) provide strong evidence for response mode effects underlying preference reversals. However, the exact cause of the phenomena is still a hotly debated topic (see the Introduction, section III.F.1, and Camerer, chapter 8, section III.I).

14. The crucial question subjects must pose to recognize the dominant strategy is do I want to win *as a result of* increasing my bid? The claim is that this question does not immediately leap to mind when bidding in a second-price auction.

15. Under the dual market technique each subject places two bids based on the same resale value (x), one in a market of size 5 and one in a market of size 10, with the market from which payment is made determined randomly after both bids are made. The dual market technique is as close as one can come to operationalizing the *ceteris paribus* conditions underlying the comparative static implications of economic theory. It has the advantage of controlling for extraneous variability in outcomes resulting from variations in private valuations across market conditions, as well as controlling for between subject variability, as the same bidder has the same valuation for the item in both markets. Assuming expected utility maximization on bidders' part, and randomly determining which market to pay off in, the optimal strategy in each market is independent of the other markets. The first extensive applications of this technique are reported in Smith (1980) and Palfrey (1985), but they did not investigate its properties relative to alternative procedures. Battalio et al. (1990) report extensive tests of whether the technique distorted bids in markets with changing numbers of bidders. They found no effects. Kagel et al. (1987) report less extensive tests of the technique in auctions with affiliated private values. They report no distortive effects as well.

16. In these models the number of bidders is determined exogenously and is not a function of resale values or the underlying support of the private values. This sort of situation would hold if, for example, auction participation were by invitation only, with the seller choosing to reveal or conceal the number of invitees.

17. See Milgrom and Weber (1982) for a formal definition and properties of affiliation.

18. Again, the intuition here is straightforward: Consider an extremely risk averse bidder who, under private information conditions, bids very close to his valuation out of fear of losing the object to rivals. Announcement of x_o will, on average, assuage his fears, resulting in lower bidding and lower average prices.

19. Allowing for bidders learning about the experiment by throwing out the first three auction periods, high bids still averaged $0.10 *below* the RNNE with $\epsilon = \$6$, but the null hypothesis of risk neutrality can no longer be rejected at conventional significance levels.

20. Bidders also show increasing relative risk aversion in the corresponding IPV auctions with x_o announced.

21. Examination of bid tabulation data for construction contractors shows considerable diversity in the zeal with which different contractors obtain these data (Dyer and Kagel 1992). Records from at least one firm in our sample routinely show fairly complete information on bids from private sector jobs, with this information obtained from the architect and/or rival bidders. Many firms simply report "not known" for the distribution of bids on such projects. Section I.A characterizes the diversity in laboratory practices regarding price information feedback.

22. Stigler (1964), in a well known article, discusses the role this information can play in policing bid rings. For more on this see section 3.1 below.

23. On a more formal level, Cox et al. (1988) examined individual subject regressions in which they included a linear time trend variable. For 20% of the subjects the time trend coefficient is significant, with the significant subjects evenly split between increasing and decreasing their bids over time, suggesting no systematic within experiment learning effect.

24. The fixed effects regression model employs a different intercept coefficient for each subject to capture between subject variability in the data, but assumes identical coefficient estimates for the independent variables employed in the regression. Dyer also tested for tacit collusion in groups whose composition remained fixed between auction periods compared to groups whose composition was randomly determined in each auction period. These results are reported in section III.A.

25. The regression results reported here are new. I thank the authors of the original studies for providing me with access to their data.

26. The exchange in the *American Economic Review* fails to capture the intensity of the passions raised by this issue as the editors toned down the language on all sides for the published commentaries.

27. Cox et al. (1982, 1988) were unable to obtain an analytic solution for the bid function in cases where x would produce bids above b^*.

28. Cox et al. (1988) offer an extended version of CRRAM to account for the large number of bid functions with significant intercept values. The model incorporates a utility of winning the auction and a minimal income level (threshold) bidders aim for in winning the auction. When the utility of winning exceeds the income threshold, the bid function has a positive intercept; when the income threshold exceeds the utility of winning, the bid function has a negative intercept. To test this model Cox, Smith, and Walker conducted auctions with lump sum payments and lump sum charges for winning the auction. The prediction is that lump sum payments should produce higher intercepts than no payments and no payments should yield higher intercepts than lump sum charges. The intercepts line up as predicted for 78% of the pairwise comparisons reported. These experimental manipulations are of inherent interest, irrespective of any issues regarding CRRAM, since lump sum payments or charges should produce an intercept shift under RNNE bidding, as well as a variety of other model specifications, regardless of the existence of an income threshold for winning the auction or a utility of winning.

29. This result was obtained both in auctions with affiliated private values as well as in auctions with x_o announced.

30. Kagel and Levin's (1985) tests were confined to IPV auctions (auctions with x_o announced, see section I.D). This rejection rate is well above the 22% frequency with which Cox et al. (1988) report statistically significant intercept values in their regressions, but only slightly above the 38% frequency of nonlinear bid functions reported. Cox et al. (1992, 1407–8)

object to these results citing a working paper by Cox and Oaxaca (1992) in which they reanalyzed Kagel and Levin's data, introducing a time trend to account for possible changes in bidding over time. The Cox and Oaxaca analysis shows that 54% of the bidders violate the restrictions implied by CRRAM (which is within the range of rejections reported in Kagel and Levin under various assumptions regarding b^*). Cox and Oaxaca also develop and apply a spline-function technique that uses all the data in Cox et al. (1988) for $n = 4$ to estimate both parts of the CRRAM bid function. Nearly 50% (nineteen out of forty) of the individual subject regressions violate the CRRAM restrictions (at the 10% significance level or better; Cox and Oaxaca table 2). Nevertheless, Cox et al. (1992, 1401) claim that "the results [from Cox and Oaxaca] indicate that CRRAM organizes all of the data quite well."

31. This can be seen as follows. Normalizing $x = 0$, profit for the high bidder under the RNNE is $x_i - [(n - 1)/n]x_i$, while under CRRAM profits for the high bidder are $x_i - [(n - 1)/(n - r_i)]x_i$. Assuming that bidders with the high resale value win the auction, as happens in over 80% of the auction periods, profits for CRRAM bidders as a percentage of the RNNE are $[1 - (n - 1)/(n - r_i)]/(1 - (n - 1)/n]$, which for positive r_i is increasing for decreases in n. Cox et al. (1992, 406) object to these tests on the grounds that (i) the "analysis is based entirely on the use of a linear bid function" but the data include observations from the upper part of the bid function (the non-linear portion according to CRRAM) and (ii) that the simple formula used here "has no valid implication for this question" since "correct expected profit calculations for these bid functions involve the use of order statistics." Objection (i) has not stopped Cox, Smith, and Walker from using *only* winning bids in testing CRRAM (for example Cox et al. 1983b). In fact, one of the motivations for the tests reported in Kagel and Levin (1985) was the weakness of the test reported in Cox et al. (1983b) which used only winning bids. Cox et al. (1992) have provided no counter example or details underlying objection (ii), which seems misdirected in this case.

32. In spite of misgivings about CRRA, my colleagues and I have had occasion to employ it when working with risk averse Nash bidding models. The reason for this is quite simple: CRRA provides one of the few closed form solutions available for characterizing risk averse Nash bidding in first-price auctions; hence it can be useful in providing some idea of the impact of risk aversion on auction outcomes. See Kagel et al. (1987) for just such an application.

33. Cox et al. (1992, footnote 14) argue that these negative correlations are to be expected in the context of an effort cost model of decision making: "This is because, in the model, the higher expected utility when values are higher results in increased opportunity cost of a nonoptimal decision; thus more decision effort is expended." This observation correctly captures the spirit of our argument and the main message, as I understand it, of Harrison's (1989) original argument.

34. Cox et al. (1992) object to these calculations on the grounds that since part of the data come from experiments using dual markets forgone earnings should be determined by multiplying through by the probability of being paid in a market. Kagel and Roth (1992) did not do this, noting that similar results are found independent of the number of dual markets employed. What the data appear to be telling us is that payoffs matter, but that there may be a threshold or context effect. In other words, bidders with high valuations put more effort and care into formulating bids in (all) dual markets (since they know there is a high probability of winning in one of the markets) than the effort and care expended with a low valuation in a single market with a comparable overall probability of winning.

35. Cox et al. (1992, 1401) argue, "Again, as in first-price auctions, this anomaly could be addressed with a utility of winning model (or a decision-cost model as in Smith and Walker)." It is hard to see how a utility for winning can organize this anomaly given that overbidding does *not* occur in English auctions (recall section I.B.2 above).

36. As Harrison (1992) points out, the payoff function under the Becker et al. procedure is quite flat, probably flatter than in Cox, Smith, and Walker's first-price auctions. Nevertheless, this is a nice example of the kind of internal consistency test that can be applied in the presence of inherently flat payoff functions.

37. For example, instead of paying $[x - b(x)]$ dollars to the winning bidder, the winner is paid $[x - b(x)]$ lottery tickets. The winner then participates in a post auction lottery in which she receives y_1 dollars with probability $[x - b(x)]/x$ and y_2 dollars ($y_1 > y_2$) with probability $1 - [x - b(x)]/x$. Losing bidders in the auction all receive y_2 dollars as well.

38. Harrison (1989) reports experimental treatments using a similar design with similar results.

39. Walker et al. note that they brought twelve of these inexperienced bidders back to play again without observing any further movement toward risk neutral bidding.

40. Using nonparametric test statistics applied to market prices, Rietz's first-price dollar auctions all resulted in price distributions lying significantly above the RNNE prediction, thereby demonstrating that in the absence of controls for risk aversion, subjects bid as if they were risk averse under his procedures.

41. Although this response may apply to multiple unit discriminatory and third-price auctions, it is of questionable relevance to second-price auctions.

42. Prasnikar and Roth (1992) (see Roth, chapter 4 in this text) report a common value auction in which there is no uncertainty about the value of the item. Prices converge to the value of the item within a few auction periods.

43. See Kagel and Levin (1986) for signals outside the interval $\underline{x} + \epsilon \le x \le \bar{x} - \epsilon$.

44. $E[x_0 \mid X = x_1] = x - \epsilon(n - 1)/(n + 1)$ for $\underline{x} + \epsilon \le x \le \bar{x} - \epsilon$

45. Roth (1988; chapter 1, section III.E) reviews earlier experimental work on the winner's curse where bidders were required to come up with their own estimates of the value of the item.

46. In the naive bidding model subjects act as if they are in an auction with affiliated private values, as they ignore the adverse selection problem but discount their bids relative to their signal values out of strategic considerations (following the dictates of equation (6) in section I.D). The naive bidding model insures negative expected profit whenever $n > 3$.

47. These calculations rely on the fact that $Y = [2\epsilon/(n + 1)] \exp[-(n/2\epsilon)(x - (\underline{x} + \epsilon)]$ in equation (9) and assumes $\underline{x}$ is \$25. For RNNE bidding, the maximum possible losses occur when $x = \underline{x} + \epsilon$ and are equal to Y (Kagel and Levin 1991).

48. Literally, this is only a local result. However, in the simulations reported in Kagel and Levin (1991), in auctions with four or seven bidders, with $\epsilon = \$30$ and cash balances of \$4.50 (which forty-eight out of the fifty bidders always had), unilateral deviations from the RNNE bid function were not profitable.

49. Hansen and Lott go further, however, arguing that even if there were sufficiently large starting cash balances to cover all potential losses, there might still be a limited-liability problem in the initial auction periods due to multiperiod effects. This part of their argument does not apply to the Kagel and Levin design however (see Kagel and Levin 1991).

50. Lind and Plott report only one subject having to work off an \$8 loss, which he actually did. Obviously it may be difficult to enforce subjects working off losses. However, this can be dealt with by holding the participation fee in escrow and, when there are a number of different experiments taking place on a regular basis, the subject can be denied participation in these experiments until the debt is paid off.

51. To keep costs down the seller's auctions were conducted in francs as opposed to dollars. The conversion rate from francs to dollars reduced the cost of the experiment, but meant that losses due to departures from Nash behavior were substantially smaller in the selling experiment. Lind and Plott note that should otherwise inexplicable differences in behavior be observed across the two designs, these incentive differences would be an obvious line of research to pursue.

52. I conjecture that one factor underlying the higher bankruptcy rates reported in Cox and Smith results from the limited feedback bidders have regarding auction outcomes (only winning bids) versus the much more extensive feedback offered in Kagel and Levin (1986) and Lind and Plott (all bids and the corresponding signal values). The latter permits observational learning (determining the outcome of your bidding strategy conditional on having one of the higher, winning signal values) which helps bidders to adjust to the adverse selection problem underlying the winner's curse (Garvin and Kagel 1991; section II.D below).

53. The symmetric Nash equilibrium bidding function for second-price auctions was first reported in Matthews (1977). Milgrom and Weber (1982) extend Matthews' analysis to consider the effects of public information. Levin and Harstad (1986) showed that this function is the unique symmetric Nash equilibrium. Harstad (1991) extends the analysis to asymmetric Nash equilibria where the source of asymmetry is differences in bidders' risk preferences.

54. The intuition with respect to this strong result about the number of bidders is that as long as bidders rely on their private signal values to determine their bids (so that bid profiles are strictly increasing in x), then as n increases the expected value of the item conditional on winning decreases. And since this is a second-price auction, many of the strategic considerations that complicate the first-price auction are not present.

55. Milgrom and Weber (1982) develop this symmetric RNNE for the English clock auction. There are other symmetric equilibria as well, but all symmetric equilibria yield the same expected revenue (Bikhchandani and Riley 1991). This is the most plausible of the symmetric equilibria. Bikhchandani and Riley also discuss the existence of asymmetric RNNE for the English auction. The experiments reported here use an English clock procedure similar to the one described in section 1.2b. I assume $\underline{x} + \epsilon \le x_L \le \bar{x} - \epsilon$.

56. T-statistics here are 2.27 with $\epsilon = \$6$, significant at the 5% level (two-tailed t-test) and 1.98 with $\epsilon = \$12$, significant at the 10% level (two-tailed t-test).

57. The control group differs from Table 7.8. The latter auctions used senior undergraduates and night MBA students from the University of Houston. The data in Table 7.9 used primarily day MBA students from the University of Pittsburgh and some senior undergraduate economics majors.

58. For the asymmetric information auctions, $E(x_o \mid X = x_1)$ is calculated strictly on the basis of the outsider's signal values. With symmetry this provides a lower bound on the expected value of the item conditional on winning.

59. Actually, for $\epsilon = \$12$ the bid discount for the symmetric information auctions is significantly greater, at the 10% level. However, the control condition consists of two auction series, one of which exhibited unusually rapid adjustment to the winner's curse, with substantially higher average bid discounts than observed in any other symmetric information series. Further, the last twelve auctions in this session (with $\epsilon = \$12$) employed a dual market technique with subjects first bidding in a symmetric information market and then bidding in the asymmetric information market. In these auction periods the average difference in the bid discount across information conditions was substantially smaller than in Table 7.9 and was not significantly different from zero at conventional levels. This suggests that the differences reported in Table 7.9 resulted from a subject group effect rather than a treatment effect.

60. Expected profit here is $(b/200)(wb - 200)$, which for $b \le 100$ is negative for all $w < 2$.

61. In the case of monetary incentives, subjects were responsible for losses out of their own pockets. The decision to play in this case was voluntary. Subjects were MBA students drawn from managerial economics classes, with the experiment serving as an introduction to decision making under uncertainty. Nineteen of 131 students chose *not* to participate with monetary incentives.

62. See Carroll, Bazerman, and Maury (1988) for a closely related study that uses verbal protocols in efforts to understand better the cognitive processes underlying buyers' decisions.

63. Samuelson and Bazerman (1985) had designs that addressed this issue as well. But they used one-shot trials with no allowance for learning.

64. Let p_A be the probability the seller accepts the bid b, let $v = c + V$, where c is the constant in the owner's valuation function, and let $V \in [0, R]$. Then the expected value of the item to the naive bidder is $E(G_N) = p_A [1.5(c + R/2) - b]$ and the expected gain to a rational bidder is $E(G_R) = p_A [1.5(c + b)/2 - b]$. The optimal naive bid maximizes $E(G_N)$ while the optimal rational bid maximizes $E(G_R)$. In the loser's curse $b_N < b_R$ and $E G \mid b_R) > E G \mid b_N)$. These inequalities are reversed with the winner's curse. See Holt and Sherman (1994) for further details.

65. Differences in the expected value of the naive bid and the rational bid are very small here—less than 2 cents. If anything this might be expected to bias the results in favor of the thrill of winning as the expected cost of deviating from the rational bid is quite small.

66. My analysis concentrates on the three pure common value auction series. The other three auction series combine common and private value elements, which complicates any evaluation of the winner's curse.

67. The average value of blind bid items in period 1 was 41.8 (with a standard error of the mean of 12.4) compared to an average value of 91.7 (with a standard error of the mean of 0.33) on those items that were not blind bid.

68. Average losses were 10¢ per item in the first ten periods compared to 4¢ per item from period eleven on. Excluding the positive profits made on one very high valued item that was blind bid out of seller's ignorance, or seller's error, mean profits averaged −6.6¢ with a standard error of the mean of 2.72, for period 11 on, so that buyers' profits on these blind bid items were significantly below zero. Including this one outlier, losses averaged −3.6¢ with a standard error of the mean of 4.0, which is not significantly below zero. Detailed reporting of the data in the *Rand Journal* facilitated these calculations. The *Journal* and the authors are to be applauded for this.

69. Information about product quality was delivered privately to buyers after their purchases. Public delivery of this information would undoubtedly speed up the adjustment process.

70. Mean earnings for the three subjects who did not return were slightly higher than those that did.

71. A Z statistic comparing the first quartile with the second quartile shows a statistically significant reduction in the proportion of auctions with losses from 64% to 41% ($Z = 2.24$, $p < .05$).

72. In the two buyer sessions reported in Table 2.7 there is a noticeable and unexplained increase in average predicted profits from playing the RNNE in the second quartile. This confounds any explanation of increases in actual profits in terms of individual learning.

73. A chi-square test indicates that this difference is significant at better than the .01 level.

74. The relevance of this market learning outside of laboratory markets is problematic. Entry conditions were closed in the experiment—subjects were recruited back exclusively from those who had participated in earlier auction market sessions. In field settings, open entry conditions permit new, inexperienced bidders (firms) to join the bidding. And it is not clear if these new players must undergo their own self-selection process and, if so, what the market impact would be since they would presumably make up a minority of active bidders.

75. Lind and Plott contain auctions with large monetary losses (the high price auctions) and with small losses (the offer auctions, which use an artificial currency, see Table 7.7). Their results are not sufficiently clear cut to reach a firm conclusion on this point. The threat of bankruptcy might also carry with it some embarrassment which would heighten subjects' sensitivity to losses.

76. Lind and Plott reported all bids and signal values to subjects as well.

77. These auctions were carried out as a research project in an undergraduate class in experimental economics. The undergraduate students involved were Robert Van Winkle, Danielle Rondelez, and Matt Zander.

78. In series 1 the reserve price realization was announced in the initial auction periods that did not permit communication. In series 2 the reserve price realization was not announced in the first five periods.

79. Pooling the data across auction series, a t-test shows these differences to be significant at better than the .01 level.

80. Minimal rationality requires the winning bid to be less than or equal to $E[x_0]$. With the notable exception of one period in auction series 2, this minimum rationality requirement was satisfied.

81. Dyer et al. (1989b) address the issue of whether the executives may not have taken the experiment seriously.

82. This despite some potentially important differences in rate of return methodology and drainage lease samples between the two studies. Although differences in rate of return between nonneighbor drainage leases and wildcat leases are not statistically significant ($t = 0.80$), neither are the differences in rates of return between neighbors and nonneighbors on drainage leases ($t = 1.13$).

83. In the experiment, one of the executives jokingly inquired "Who is the architect associated with this job?"

84. It is my understanding that different oil companies specialize in different geological formations so that they can better apply accumulated past knowledge to interpret seismic records.

85. For publicly owned projects, there are laws explicitly recognizing the possibility of "arithmetic" errors in bids, permitting the contractor to withdraw his bid without penalty. What constitutes an arithmetic error is often loosely interpreted. In this case, the low bidder used a plumbing subcontractor's bid which the subcontractor withdrew. However, the subcontractor was unable to reach all general contractors, the original low bidder included, in time to adjust their bids. What is clear in the construction industry is that no one wants a builder, or subcontractor, working for them who is terribly unhappy with their bid, as this affects the speed, quality, and "headaches" associated with the construction. Owners requiring that such bids be lived up to are likely to suffer from a winner's curse of their own. In OCS bidding, where the winner's curse expresses itself in terms of an inflated bonus bid, there are no corresponding considerations since the bonus bid is a sunk cost.

86. The ability to withdraw bids without penalty opens up additional strategic possibilities. However, in field settings, owners and contractors are involved in a game with two-sided reputations, so that too frequent withdrawal of bids may result in being left off future invited bid lists.

87. There are fewer bidders on average for OCS leases (3.5 versus 7.5 in the construction data). Limiting analysis of the construction data to jobs with 4 bidders or less results in auctions with an average of 3.4 bidders and average money left on the table of 6.7% (with a standard error of 8.8%) (Dyer and Kagel 1992).

88. In a frequently cited study, Thiel (1988) models highway construction bidding as a pure common value auction completely ignoring the important private value elements underlying bids in this industry. He finds no evidence of a winner's curse which may result from either this specification error or the modeling errors identified in Levin and Smith (1991).

89. Models developed to date deal with auctions in which buyers and sellers have a single unit to trade. In contrast, much of the experimental literature deals with two-sided auctions in which buyers and sellers each have several units available for trade.

90. ZI traders achieve remarkably high efficiency levels in continuous double auctions. Gode and Sunder (1993) conclude that the high efficiency levels commonly reported in CDA's probably has more to do with the structure of the institution than any particular skill on traders' part. The ZI model provides a zero rationality benchmark against which to compare outcomes.

91. This is a special case of what Satterthwaite and Williams refer to as the k-th price auction— the case of $k = 1$.

92. ZI traders achieve average efficiencies of 29% in markets with two buyers and two sellers and 36% in markets with eight buyers and eight sellers. In contrast, for the continuous double auction lower bounds on efficiency are around 90%. The main difference between ZI traders under a clearing house mechanism and the CDA is that the clearing house is completely unforgiving with respect to bids and offers that fail to achieve mutually beneficial trades, while the ability to make repeated bids and offers forgives such mistakes in the CDA.

Bibliography

Akerlof, G. 1970. The market for lemons: Qualitative uncertainty and the market mechanism. *Quarterly Journal of Economics* 89:488–500.

Arrow, K. J. 1970. *Essays in the theory of risk bearing.* Amsterdam: North Holland.

Ashenfelter, O., and D. Genesore. 1992. Testing for price anomalies in real estate auctions. *American Economic Review: Papers and Proceedings* 82:501–5.

Ball, S. B. 1991. Experimental evidence on the winner's curse in negotiations. Diss., Evanston, IL: Northwestern University.

Ball, S. B., M. H. Bazerman, and J. S. Carroll. 1991. An evaluation of learning in the bilateral winner's curse. *Organizational Behavior and Human Decision Processes* 48:1–22.

Battalio, R. C., C. A. Kogut, and D. J. Meyer. 1990. The effect of varying number of bidders in first-price private value auctions: An application of a dual market bidding technique. In *Advances in behavioral economics*, Vol. 2, L. Green and J. H. Kagel, eds., Norwood, N.J.: Ablex Publishing.

Bazerman, M. H., and W. F. Samuelson. 1983. I won the auction but don't want the prize. *Journal of Conflict Resolution* 27:618–34.

Becker, G. M., M. H. DeGroot, and J. Marschak. 1964. Measuring utility by a single-response sequential method. *Behavioral Science* 9:226–32.

Belovicz, M. W. 1979. Sealed-bid auctions: experimental results and applications. In *Research in experimental economics*, V. L. Smith, ed., Greenwich, Conn.: JAI Press.

Berg, J. E., L. A. Daley, J. W. Dickhout, and J. R. O'Brien. 1986. Controlling preferences for lotteries on units of experimental exchange. *Quarterly Journal of Economics* 101:281–306.

Bikhchandani, S., and J. G. Riley. 1991. Equilibria in open common value auctions. *Journal of Economics Theory* 53:101–30.

Brannman, L., J. D. Klein, and L. Weiss. 1984. Concentration and winning bids in auctions. *Antitrust Bulletin* 29:27–31.

Bronfman, C. 1990. Expectations, trade behavior and price fluctuations in laboratory asset markets. Paper presented at Econometric Society Winter Meeting, Washington, D.C.

Brown, K. C. 1986. In search of the winner's curse: comment. *Economic Inquiry* 24:513–16.

Capen, E. C., R. V. Clapp, and W. M. Campbell. 1971. Competitive bidding in high-risk situations. *Journal of Petroleum Technology* 23:641–53.

Carroll, J. S., M. H. Bazerman, and R. Maury. 1988. Negotiator cognitions: A descriptive approach to negotiators' understanding of their opponents. *Organizational Behavior and Human Decision Processes* 41:352–70.

Cason, T. N. 1992. An experimental investigation of the seller incentives in EPA's emmission trading auction. Mimeograph. University of Southern California.

Cason, T. N., and D. Friedman. 1993. An empirical analysis of price formation in double auction markets. In *The double auction market: Institutions, theory and evidence*, D. Friedman and J. Rust, eds., Redwood City, Cal.: Addison-Wesley.

Cassady, R. 1967. *Auctions and auctioneering*. Berkeley and Los Angeles: University of California Press.

Cassing, J., and R. W. Douglas. 1980. Implications of the auction mechanism in baseballs' free agent draft. *Southern Economic Journal* 47:110–21.

Cech, P., D. Conn, J. C. Cox, and R. M. Isaac. 1987. An experimental study of competitive bidding incentive contracts in procurement. Discussion Paper 87–8. University of Arizona.

Chen, K.-Y., and C. R. Plott. 1991. Nonlinear behavior in sealed bid first price auctions. Social Science Working Paper 774. California Institute of Technology.

Cifuentes, L. A., and S. Sunder. 1991. Some further evidence of the winner's curse. Mimeograph. Carnegie Mellon U.

Coppinger, V. M., V. L. Smith, and J. A. Titus. 1980. Incentives and behavior in English, Dutch and sealed-bid auctions. *Economic Inquiry* 43:1–22.

Cox, J. C., and R. M. Isaac. 1984. In search of the winner's curse. *Economic Inquiry* 22:579–92.

———. 1986. In search of the winner's curse: Reply. *Economic Inquiry* 24:517–20.

Cox, J. C., and R. L. Oaxaca. 1992. Empirical bid functions and auction theory. Mimeograph. University of Arizona.

Cox, J. C., and V. L. Smith. 1992. Endogenous entry and exit in common value auctions. Mimeograph. University of Arizona.

Cox, J. C., B. Roberson, and V. L. Smith. 1982. Theory and behavior of single object auctions. In *Research in experimental economics*, Vernon L. Smith, ed., Greenwich, Conn.: JAI Press.

Cox, J. C., V. L. Smith, and J. M. Walker. 1983a. A test that discriminates between two models of the Dutch-first auction non-isomorphism. *Journal of Economic Behavior and Organization* 14:205–19.

Cox, J. C., V. L. Smith, and J. M. Walker. 1983b. Tests of a heterogeneous bidder's theory of first price auctions. *Economics Letters* 12:207–12.

———. 1984. Theory and behavior of multiple unit discriminative auctions. *Journal of Finance* 39:983–1010.

———. 1985a. Expected revenue in discriminative and uniform price sealed bid auctions. In *Research in experimental economics*, vol. 3, V. L. Smith, ed., Greenwich, Conn.: JAI Press.

———. 1985b. Experimental development of sealed-bid auction theory: Calibrating controls for risk aversion. *American Economic Review: Papers and Proceedings.* 75:160–65.

———. 1988. Theory and individual behavior of first-price auctions. *Journal of Risk and Uncertainty* 1:61–99.

———. 1989a. Theory and misbehavior, in first-price auctions: Comment. Paper presented at the Economic Science Association Meeting, Tucson.

———. 1989b. A comment on laboratory experimentation in economics: A methodological overview. Mimeograph. University of Arizona.

———. 1992. Theory and misbehavior in first price auctions: Comment. *American Economic Review* 82:1392–412.

Dessauer, J. P. 1981. *Book publishing*. New York: Bowker.

Dyer, D., and J. H. Kagel. 1992. Experienced bidders in common value auctions: Behavior in the laboratory vs the natural habitat. Mimeograph. University of Pittsburgh.

Dyer, D., J. H. Kagel, and D. Levin. 1989a. Resolving uncertainty about the number of bidders in independent private-value auctions: An experimental analysis. *Rand Journal of Economics* 20:268–79.

———. 1989b. A comparison of naive and experienced bidders in common value offer auctions: A laboratory analysis. *Economic Journal* 99:108–15.

Forsythe, R., and R. M. Isaac. 1982. Demand-revealing mechanisms for private good auctions. In *Research in experimental economics*, vol. 2, V. L. Smith, ed., Greenwich, Conn.: JAI Press.

Forsythe, R., R. M. Isaac, and T. R. Palfrey. 1989. Theories and tests of "blind bidding" in sealed-bid auctions. *Rand Journal of Economics* 20:214–38.

Frahm, D., and L. Schrader. 1970. An experimental comparison of pricing in two auction systems. *American Journal of Agricultural Economics* 52:528–34.

Friedman, D. 1991. A simple testable model of double auction markets. *Journal of Economic Behavior and Organization* 16:47–70.

Garvin, S., and J. H. Kagel. 1995. Learning in common value auctions: Some initial observations. Mimeograph. University of Pittsburgh. Forthcoming in *Journal of Economic Behavior and Organization*.

Gaver, K. M., and J. L. Zimmerman. 1977. An analysis of competitive bidding on BART contracts. *Journal of Business* 50:279–95.

Gilley, O. W., G. V. Karels, and R. P. Leone. 1986. Uncertainty, experience and the "winner's curse" in OCS lease bidding. *Management Science* 32:673–82.

Gode, D. K., and S. Sunder. 1993. Allocative efficiency of markets with zero intelligence traders. *Journal of Political Economy* 101:119–37.

Graham, D. A., and R. C. Marshall. 1987. Collusive bidder behavior at single object second price and English auctions. *Journal of Political Economy* 95:1217–37.

Graham, D. A., R. C. Marshall, and J. Richard. 1990. Phantom bidding against heterogeneous bidder. *Economics Letters* 32:13–17.

Grether, D. M., R. M. Isaac, and C. R. Plott. 1989. *The allocation of scarce resources: Experimental economics and the problem of allocating airport shots. Underground classics in economics*. Boulder, Col.: Westview Press.

Guler, K., and C. R. Plott. 1988. Private R&D and second sourcing in procurement: An experimental study. Social Science Working Paper 684. California Institute of Technology.

Hansen, R. G. 1985. Empirical testing of auction theory. *American Economic Review* 75:156–9.

———. 1986. Sealed-bid versus open auctions: The evidence. *Economic Inquiry* 24:125–42.

Hansen, R. G., and J. R. Lott, Jr. 1991. The winner's curse and public information in common value auctions: Comment. *American Economic Review* 81:347–61.

Harris, M., and A. Raviv. 1981. Allocation mechanisms and the design of auctions. *Econometrica* 49:1477–99.

Harrison, G. W. 1989. Theory and misbehavior of first-price auctions. *American Economic Review*. 79:749–62.

———. 1990. Risk attitudes in first-price auction experiments: A Bayesian analysis. *Review of Economics and Statistics* 72:542–46.

———. 1992. Theory and misbehavior of first-price auctions: Reply. *American Economic Review* 82:1426–43.

Harstad, R. M. 1990. Dominant strategy adoption, efficiency, and bidders' experience with pricing rules. Mimeograph. Virginia Commonwealth U.

———. 1991. Asymmetric bidding in second-price, common-value auctions. *Economic Letters* 35:249–52.

Hendricks, K., and R. H. Porter. 1988. An empirical study of an auction with asymmetric information. *American Economic Review* 76:865–83.

——— 1992. Bidding behavior in OCS drainage auctions: Theory and evidence. Paper presented at the 1992 European Economics Association Meetings.

Hendricks, K., R. H. Porter, and B. Boudreau. 1987. Information, returns, and bidding behavior in OCS auctions: 1954–1969. *Journal of Industrial Economics* 35:517–42.

Holt, C. A., Jr., and R. Sherman. 1994. The loser's curse and bidder's bias. *American Economic Review* 84:642–52.

Isaac, R. M., and J. M. Walker. 1985. Information and conspiracy in sealed bid auctions. *Journal of Economic Behavior and Organization* 6:139–59.

Kagel, J. H., R. M. Harstad, and D. Levin. 1987. Information impact and allocation rules in auctions with affiliated private values: A laboratory study. *Econometrica* 55:1275–1304.

Kagel, J. H., and D. Levin. 1985. Individual bidder behavior in first-price private value auctions. *Economics Letters* 19:125–28.

———. 1986. The winner's curse and public information in common value auctions. *American Economic Review* 76:894–920.

———. 1991. The winner's curse and public information in common value auctions: Reply. *American Economic Review* 81:362–9.

———. 1992. Revenue raising and information processing in English common value auctions. Mimeograph. University of Pittsburgh.

———. 1993. Independent private value auctions: Bidder behavior in first-, second- and third-price auctions with varying numbers of bidders. *Economic Journal* 103:868–79.

Kagel, J. H., D. Levin, R. Battalio, and D. J. Meyer. 1989. First-price common value auctions: Bidder behavior and the winner's curse. *Economic Inquiry* 27:241–58.

Kagel, J. H., D. Levin, and R. M. Harstad. 1994. Comparative static effects of number of bidders and public information on behavior in second-price common value auctions. *International Journal of Game Theory* 23.

Kagel, J. H., and A. E. Roth. 1992. Comment on Harrison versus Cox, Smith and Walker: Theory and misbehavior in first-price auctions. *American Economic Review* 82:1379–91.

Kagel, J. H., and W. Vogt. 1993. Buyer's bid double auctions: Preliminary experimental results. In *The double auction market: Institutions, theory and evidence*, D. Friedman and J. Rust, eds., Redwood City, Cal.: Addison-Wesley.

Kahneman, D., and A. Tversky. 1979. Prospect theory: An analysis of decision under risk. *Econometrica* 47:263–91.

Levin, D., and R. Harstad. 1986. Symmetric bidding in second price common value auctions. *Economics Letters* 20:315–19.

Levin, D. S., and J.L. Smith. 1991. Some evidence on the winner's curse: Comment. *American Economic Review* 81:370–75.

Lind, B., and C. R. Plott. 1991. The winner's curse: Experiments with buyers and with sellers. *American Economic Review* 81:335–46.

Lorenz, J., and E. L. Dougherty. 1983. Bonus bidding and bottom lines: Federal off-shore oil and gas. SPE 12024. 58th Annual Fall Technical Conference, Society of Petroleum Engineers.

Lynch, M., R. M. Miller, C. R. Plott, and R. Porter. 1986. Product quality, consumer information and "lemons" in experimental markets. In *Empirical approaches to consumer protection economics*, P. M. Ippolito and D. T. Scheffman, eds., Washington D.C.: FTC Bureau of Economics. 251–306.

———. 1991. Product quality, informational efficiency, and regulations in experimental markets. In *Research in experimental economics*, R. Mark Isaac, ed., Greenwich, Conn.: JAI Press.

Machina, M. J. 1983. The economic theory of individual behavior toward risk: Theory, evidence and new directions. Technical Report No. 433. Center for Research on Organization Efficiency. Stanford University.

Maskin, E. S., and J. G. Riley. 1989. Optimal multi-unit auctions. In *The economics of missing markets and information*, F. Hahn, ed., Oxford, England: Oxford University Press.

Matthews, S. A, 1977. Information acquisition in competitive bidding processes. Working Paper. California Institute of Technology.

———. 1987. Comparing auctions for risk-averse buyers: A Buyer's Point of View. *Econometrica* 55:633–46.

McAfee, R. P., and J. McMillan. 1987a. Auctions and bidding. *Journal of Economic Literature* 25:699–738.

———. 1987b. Auctions with a stochastic number of bidders. *Journal of Economic Theory* 43:1–19.

———. 1987c. Auctions with entry. *Economics Letters* 23:343–47.

McCabe, K. A., S. J. Rassenti, and V. L. Smith. 1990. Auction institutional design: Theory and behavior of simultaneous multiple-unit generalizations of the Dutch and English auctions. *American Economic Review* 80:1276–83.

Mead, W. J. 1967. Natural resource disposal policy: Oral auction versus sealed bids. *Natural Resources Journal* 7:195–224.

Mead, W. J., A. Moseidjord, and P. E. Sorensen. 1983. The rate of return earned by leases under cash bonus bidding in OCS oil and gas leases. *Energy Journal* 4:37–52.

———. 1984. Competitive bidding under asymmetrical information: Behavior and performance in Gulf of Mexico drainage lease sales, 1954–1969. *Review of Economics and Statistics* 66:505–8.

Meyerson, R. 1981. Optimal auction design. *Mathematics of Operations Research* 6:58–73.

Milgrom, P., and R. J. Weber. 1982. A theory of auctions and competitive bidding. *Econometrica* 50:1485–527.

Milgrom, P., and J. Roberts. 1986. Relying on the information of interested parties. *RAND Journal of Economics* 17:18–22.

Miller, G. J., and C. R. Plott. 1985. Revenue-generating properties of sealed-bid auctions: An experimental analysis of one-price and discriminative processes. In *Research in experimental economics*, vol. 3, V. L. Smith, ed., Greenwich, Conn.: JAI Press.

Palfrey, T. R. 1985. Buyer behavior and the welfare effects of bundling by a multiproduct monopolist: A laboratory investigation. In *Research in experimental economics*, vol. 3, V. L. Smith, ed., Greenwich, Conn., JAI Press.

Pitchik, C., and A. Schotter. 1988. Perfect equilibria in budget-constrained sequential auctions: An experimental study. *RAND Journal of Economics* 19:363–88.

Powell, J. L. 1984. Least absolute deviations estimation for the censored regression model. *Journal of Econometrics* 25:303–25.

Prasnikar, Vesna, and A. E. Roth. 1992. Considerations of fairness and strategy: Experimental data from sequential games. *Quarterly Journal of Economics* 107:865–88.

Rietz, T. A. 1993. Implementing and testing risk-preference-induction mechanisms in experimental sealed-bid auctions. *Journal of Risk and Uncertainty* 7:199–213.

Riley, J. G., and W. F. Samuelson. 1981. Optimal auctions. *American Economic Review* 71:381–92.

Roll, R. 1986. The hubris hypothesis of corporate takeovers. *Journal of Business* 59:197–216.

Rosenthal, R. 1976. *Experimenter effects in behavioral research*. New York: Irvington Publishers.

Roth, A. E. 1988. Laboratory experimentation in economics: A methodological overview. *Economic Journal*. 98:974–1031.

Roth, A. E., and M. W. K. Malouf. 1979. Game theoretic models and the role of information in bargaining: An experimental study. *Psychological Review* 86:574–94.

Samuelson, W. F., and M. H. Bazerman. 1985. The winner's curse in bilateral negotiations. In *Research in experimental economics*, vol. 3, V. L. Smith, ed., Greenwich, Conn.: JAI Press.

Satterthwaite, M. A., and S. R. Williams. 1989a. The rate of convergence to efficiency in buyer's bid double auction as the market becomes large. *Review of Economic Studies* 56:477–98.

———. 1989b. Bilateral trade with the sealed bid k-double auction: Existence and efficiency. *Journal of Economic Theory* 48:107–33.

———. 1993. Theories of price formation and exchange in *k*-double auctions. In *The double auction market: Institutions, theory and evidence*, D. Freidman and J. Rust, eds., SFI Studies in Sciences of Complexity. Redwood City, Cal.: Addison-Wesley.

Smith, V. L. 1967. Experimental studies of discrimination versus competition in sealed-bid auction markets. *Journal of Business* 40:56–84.

———. 1980. Relevance of laboratory experiments to testing resource allocation theory. In *Evaluation of econometric models*, J. Kinsata and J. Ramsey, eds., New York: Academic Press.

Smith, V. L., and J. M. Walker. 1993. Rewards, experience and decision costs in first price auctions. *Economic Inquiry* 31:237–44.

Stigler, G. J. 1964. A theory of oligopoly. *Journal of Political Economy* 72:44–61.

Thiel, S. E. 1988. Some evidence on the winner's curse. *American Economic Review* 78:884–95.

Tversky, A., and D. Kahneman. 1986. Rational choice and the framing of decisions. *Journal of Business* 59:S251–78.

Tversky, A., P. Slovic, and D. Kahneman. 1990. The causes of preference reversals. *American Economic Review* 80:204–17.

Van Huyck, J. B., R. C. Battalio, and R. O. Beil. 1993. Coordination failure, game form auctions, and tacit communication. *Games and Economic Behavior* 5:485–504.

Vickrey, W. 1961. Counterspeculation, auctions, and competitive sealed tenders. *Journal of Finance* 16:8–37.

Walker, J. M., V. L. Smith, and J. C. Cox. 1990. Inducing risk neutral preferences: An examination in a controlled market environment. *Journal of Risk and Uncertainty* 3:5–24.

Weber, R. J. 1983. Multiple-object auctions. In *Auctions, bidding and contracting: Uses and theory*, Richard Engelbrecht-Wiggans, Martin Shubic, and Robert M. Stark, eds., New York: New York University Press.

Wilson, R. 1977. A bidding model of perfect competition. *Review of Economic Studies* 44: 511–18.

———. 1987. On equilibria of bid-ask markets. In *Arrow and the ascent of modern economic theory*, G. Feiwel, ed., Houndmills, U.K.: MacMillan Press. 375–414.

———. 1992. Strategic analysis of auctions. In *Handbook of game theory with economic applications*, vol. 1., R. J. Aumann and S. Hart, eds., Amsterdam: Elsevier Science Publishers.

8

Individual Decision Making

Colin Camerer

I. Introduction

I will review recent experimental studies of individual decision making, with their implications for economics in mind.[*] Decision making is increasingly important for economics for at least two reasons.

First, in many economic settings individuals make decisions by and among themselves: consumers save, sell their labor, buy houses and durable goods, form economic and social relationships, and bargain. In these cases the institutional veils separating people from others are thin. A couple decides whether to buy a house from another couple; Mario hires a college student to work in the grocery store he owns; a daughter borrows money from her mother. (In other settings the institutional veil separating individuals doing business is thick—Monique lends money to the shareholders of General Motors through the concrete veil of Citibank, where she has a savings account and GM has a line of credit.)

The thickness of institutional veils is important because there is a strong intuition that institutional forces correct errors people make; the more directly people trade with each other, that intuition implies, the more likely their errors are to persist. Economic analysis has increasingly reached into settings with thin veils recently. Judges are presumed to make law as if they had economic efficiency in mind; there are models in which people optimize marriages, sleep, suicide, and extramarital affairs; the household is modeled as a unit of production; and so forth. In these settings systematic errors by individuals may not be corrected by institutional forces. Studies of individual decision making can help predict when market prices may be wrong and allocations inefficient and suggest ways to improve efficiency.

Second, economic analysis has also reached into increasingly complicated domains recently. Until thirty years ago there were few formal models with any uncertainties. Weak assumptions about agent rationality were adequate to generate strong market level results (e.g., Pareto optimality). Now many models presume agents can make choices under risk and uncertainty, over time, keeping in mind subtle game-theoretic effects. As the models grow more and more complicated, agents are assumed to have more and more rationality. Then it is more likely individual agents violate the models; studies like the ones I describe may tell us how and why.

A. Limited Rationality and Decision Research

For the last thirty years or so, most research on individual decision making has taken normative theories of judgment and choice (typically probability rules and utility theories) as null hypotheses about behavior, and tested those hypotheses in psychology experiments. Much of this work is called "behavioral decision research" (a term coined by Edwards [1961a]) or, sometimes, "cognitive illusions," or "cognitive misperceptions." The goal is to test whether normative rules are *systematically* violated and to propose alternative theories to explain any observed violations.

The most fruitful, popular alternative theories spring from the idea that limits on computational ability force people to use simplified procedures or "heuristics" that cause systematic mistakes (biases) in problem solving, judgment, and choice. The roots of this approach are in Simon's (1955) distinction between *substantive* rationality (the result of normative maximizing models) and *procedural* rationality—people behave coherently by following reasonable procedures but sometimes make suboptimal decisions as a result.

1. Why Study Errors in Decision Making?

Cataloguing systematic violations of rational models was not always the theme of the psychologists' efforts. In 1967, Peterson and Beach wrote a review of research on intuitive statistical judgment and concluded that people obeyed normative laws rather well. Psychologists began focusing on judgment errors in the 1970s because they thought judgment errors might reveal how people generally make judgments, just as optimal illusions tell us about perception and forgetting tells us about memory (Kahneman and Tversky 1982). The same scientific heuristic is used in other fields. The Great Depression, the stock market crash of 1987, and the savings-and-loan crisis are carefully studied for clues about the general behavior of economies and markets. Engineers study bridge collapses and airplane crashes to learn how to build sturdier bridges and planes.

Whether people make judgment errors frequently or not is difficult to judge and—to most psychologists—beside the point. Psychologists study errors because if people use simplified procedures to judge and choose, those procedures may be seen most clearly through the errors they cause. For economists, the frequency of errors is important because errors might affect economic efficiency, and methods for removing errors could be useful policy tools.

B. Two Controversies: Methods and Implications

Since many of the psychologists' studies can be seen as direct attacks on assumptions of individual rationality,[1] the studies are sometimes hotly debated. There are two kinds of debates: methodology and implications.

The conventional *methods* used in psychological studies of decision making are often different than the conventions established by experimental economists (detailed throughout this handbook). In the psychology experiments, subjects are often not paid according to their performance, or are paid small amounts; stimuli have natural labels that may induce nonmonetary utilities; subjects do not always make repeated choices under stationary replication; treatments are sometimes created by deceiving subjects; and so forth. As a result, many economists discount evidence from the psychologists' studies. Replication of findings using the methods of experimental economics is therefore popular and tests robustness of results.

The *implication* of evidence of irrationality is another source of controversy. Despite the psychological evidence, economists have been cautious about reconsidering the presumption in their work that agents maximize choices based on well-informed preferences. Their caution is often defended by a tenet of "positive economics" (Friedman 1953): the market-level predictions may be approximately right even if the model of individuals from which the predictions are derived is wrong. Thus, better models of individual decision making *may not* improve market level prediction; whether they do is fundamentally an empirical question that economics experiments help answer (e.g., Plott 1986). Experiments are helpful because they naturally give simultaneous observations of individual and aggregate activity, which are the best raw material for judging whether individual errors are present and important for aggregate behavior. There are a few studies of this sort, comparing individual and aggregate behavior within an experiment. They are reviewed below, in sections II (C,D,F.2) and III (I.3, J.1).

C. A Map and Guidebook

The chapter is organized in two sections, judgment (II) and choice (III). The study of judgments is almost purely psychological, except for a few replications and market studies by experimental economists. Studies of choice have had more interplay between axiomatic theories (mostly, though not exclusively, generated by economists) and experimental data gathered by economists and psychologists alike.

I have tried to weave the many studies by psychologists and the relatively few by experimental economists into whole cloth depicting classes of systematic mistakes and the procedures people use that seem to create the mistakes. I say the most about ongoing debates in which several studies have cumulated knowledge—aggregation of Bayesian errors in markets, utility theory, preference reversals, buying-selling price gaps. But in many places, economists have not joined the debate because they are not familiar with psychological results, do not appreciate their impact on economics, or think the results are unlikely to replicate. I try to remedy unfamiliarity by discussing a broad array of results in minimal detail, to encourage appreciation by providing recipes for expressing psychological findings in theoretical terms familiar to economists, and to provoke replication with numerous suggestions for further research.

The methodological range of studies summarized in this chapter is perhaps as wide as in any chapter in the handbook. I sprinkled brief digressions about methodology throughout the chapter, at points where they illuminate debate and where the debate provides a context that adds flavor to an otherwise bland discussion.

Other sources include Thaler (1987), who presents much of the same evidence organized as a critique of economic tenets (and see his *Journal of Economic Perspectives* columns, collected in Thaler [1992]). Edited collections of important articles in behavioral decision theory are Kahneman, Slovic, and Tversky (1982), Arkes and Hammond (1987) and Bell, Raiffa, and Tversky (1988). There are graduate level textbooks by Dawes (1988) and Hogarth (1987). Texts by Bazerman (1990) and Russo and Schoemaker (1989) are easier, Yates (1990) harder. A series of articles in the *Annual Review of Psychology* (most recently Payne, Bettman, and Johnson [1992]) provide an authoritative chronicle of psychological decision research. The chapter by Abelson and Levi (1985) is a rough equivalent of this chapter, aimed at psychologists. New work on models of choice is reviewed by Machina (1987), Fishburn (1988), Weber and Camerer (1987), and Camerer and Weber (1992).

The psychology-economic nexus is covered by the book edited by Hogarth and Reder (1987) (reprinting a 1986 *Journal of Business* special issue), critically reviewed by Smith (1991). Cox and Isaac (1986) cover a small patch of similar ground.

II. Judgment

A. Calibration

Good probability judgments should match actual relative frequencies. The match is shown in a "calibration curve."[2] For example, in 1965 the National Weather Service began requiring its meteorologists to announce numerical judgments of the probability of precipitation. Figure 8.1 shows a calibration curve for one forecaster, using actual forecasts from several days. On the Y axis is the relative frequency of events (proportion of days with precipitation) for each category of probability forecast shown on the X axis. The number of events in each forecast category is indicated by the size of each point (and written alongside it). The forecaster shown in Figure 8.1 said there was a 30 percent chance of rain on 160 days; it actually rained slightly more than 30 percent of those days.

Accuracy of probability judgments has two distinct components, calibration and resolution (sometimes called "calibration-in-the-small" and "calibration-in-the-large"). Calibration is how well the event forecast in a particular category (all events with .3 probability) matches the actual relative frequency of those events (50 of 160 occurred). In a calibration curve like the one shown in Figure 8.1, calibration is measured by how close points are to the identity line (adjusting for

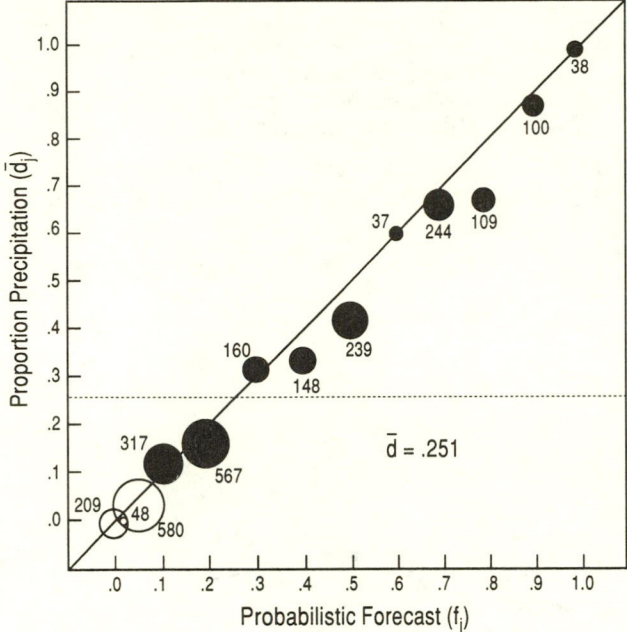

Figure 8.1. Calibration graph for forecaster A's probabilistic forecasts of precipitation for the Chicago area. Numbers are case frequencies. *Source:* Murphy and Winkler 1977.

sampling error). Resolution (also called "discrimination") is how well probabilities enable one to discriminate between likely and unlikely events. A high-resolution forecaster will have many forecasts in the extreme categories near zero and one. When making predictions is difficult—in long-term economic forecasting, for example—resolution may only be achieved at the expense of calibration, by confidently making high and low guesses that are only partly right.

The judgments of the weather forecaster in Figure 8.1 show terrific calibration (the points are close to the line) and good resolution (most of the observations are between zero and .2). Calibration as good as the weather forecasters' seems to be rare (see Lichtenstein, Fischhoff, and Phillips 1982). Some empirical calibration curves based on students' judgments are shown in Figure 8.2. These are "half-range" curves: from two possible answers to a general interest question—did potatoes come from Ireland or Peru?—subjects pick the more likely answer and judge its probability (which must be at least .5).

In general subjects are overconfident. They are insufficiently regressive in judging the likelihood of events. Events they say are certain happen only 80 percent of the time. "Full range" curves, with subjective probabilities from zero to one, show overconfidence too. (Events judged to be impossible happen 20 percent of the time.) However, subjects are often *under*confident when questions are easy (i.e., when the percentage of people answering the questions correctly is high).

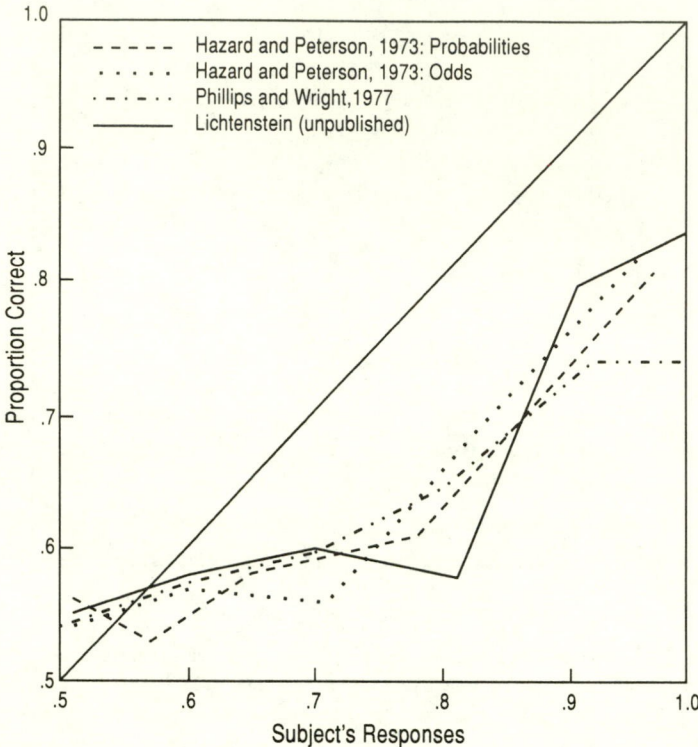

Figure 8.2. Calibration for half-range, general-knowledge items. Reprinted from Lichtenstein, Fischhoff, and Phillips (1992) with permission of Cambridge University Press. For sources cited in figure, see ibid.

1. Scoring Rules

In most of the studies above, subjects were not directly rewarded according to the accuracy of their probabilities. "A proper scoring rule" is a scheme that rewards probability judgments, depending on the judgment and the outcome of the event being forecasted, in a way that induces truthful revelation of probabilities. An example is the quadratic scoring rule: If the subject reports a probability p, pay her $\$(2p - p^2)$ if the event occurs and $\$(1 - p^2)$ if the event doesn't occur.[3] (Or define $I = 1$ if the event occurs and $I = 0$ if not, and pay $\$(1 - (p - 1)^2)$.) For example, a subject who reports $p = .10$ earns either $\$.19$ if the event occurs or $\$.99$ if not; a report $p = .20$ earns $\$.36$ or $\$.96$. If the subject thinks the true probability is .20, then the $p = .20$ bet earns an expected value of .2 ($\$.36$) + .8 ($\$.96$) = $\$.84$ and the $p = .10$ bet earns $\$.83$, so the subject should report $p = .20$.

Besides being incentive-compatible, scoring rules enable judgments of probability to be elicited without mentioning the word "probability" or defining it.

Instead, a subject expresses a probability judgment implicitly, by choosing among various bets. (Scoring rules are sometimes used to grade students for probabilistic answers to multiple-choice questions.)

However, scoring rules assume risk neutrality; if a subject is risk averse her expressed probabilities will be biased toward .5. (Allen [1987], suggests paying subjects in lottery tickets; cf. the discussion of the binary lottery procedure in chapter 1.) And the payoff function has a flat maximum around the true subjective probability p, as the example above indicates, so subjects are not penalized much for misreporting.[4]

The calibration studies described in this section did *not* use proper scoring rules. However, there seems to be little difference between judgments motivated by scoring rules and unmotivated judgments (Beach and Phillips 1967; Jensen and Peterson 1973). The main difference is that when subjects use extreme probabilities too frequently (and inappropriately), scoring rules punish their mistakes severely and reduce them (Fischer 1982). When rewarded with "improper" scoring rules that do not penalize misreports, subjects learn to misreport probabilities (Nelson and Bessler 1989). For example, suppose subjects who report an event probability p are paid p if the event occurs and $1 - p$ otherwise. Then subjects quickly learn to exaggerate their beliefs, reporting $p = 1$ if their true belief is above .5 and reporting 0 otherwise.

Scoring rules could be useful in a wide range of economics experiments to measure probabilistic beliefs in an incentive-compatible way. For example, game theories often make sharp predictions about beliefs that are difficult to test indirectly (e.g., beliefs after "out-of-equilibrium" events that should never occur and that actually occur only rarely). Some researchers have used scoring rules to elicit beliefs of subjects in games. The only published economics experiment that use them, that I know of, is McKelvey and Page (1990).

2. Confidence Intervals

Other studies have elicited confidence intervals for *quantities* (the length of the Amazon river, next month's spot oil price), instead of probabilities for *events*. In these studies confidence intervals are typically too narrow; subjects seem to anchor on a point estimate, then adjust upward and downward by too little. Fifty-percent intervals included the true quantity only about 30 percent of the time; 98 percent intervals, only 60 percent of the time (Alpert and Raiffa 1982). Subjects can learn to spread their intervals out with intensive feedback and training, but they never get high-probability intervals quite wide enough.

Many studies have examined the effects of expertise on overconfidence. A lot of these studies were motivated by the impressive performance of weather forecasters, shown in Figure 8.1. Researchers then became curious whether other experts were equally well calibrated. Professional accountants' intervals around estimated account balances of client firms are good (Tomassini et al. 1982). Weather forecasters' intervals of high and low temperatures are precisely the right width (Murphy and Winkler 1974). But intervals around estimates of physical constants, published in physics journals, are systematically too narrow (Henrion and Fischhoff 1984).[5]

There are mixed effects of expertise in studies of event-probability calibration too. Students and professionals forecasting outcomes of basketball and baseball games are poorly calibrated (Yates 1982; Ronis and Yates 1987). Novices, statistical experts, and blackjack dealers are equally well calibrated (Keren 1988) and expert bridge players are better calibrated than novices (Keren 1987) at judging the probability of winning a hand given certain cards. Physicians are accurate in some settings and poor in others, especially diagnosing rare diseases (Yates 1990, table 4.1; cf. the discussion of base-rate fallacy in section I.C.1 later). Betting odds at horseracing tracks are well calibrated, with a slight but persistent tendency to overestimate the chance that longshots will win and underestimate the chances of favorites (Ziemba and Hausch 1986). (Curiously, the opposite betting pattern occurs at Hong Kong racetracks; see Busche and Hall 1988.) Forecasts by professional economists of the chance of economic downturn are pretty well calibrated one quarter ahead, but the calibration gets much worse as the forecast horizon extends out to four quarters (Braun and Yaniv 1992).

There are a few cross-cultural studies of calibration. Asians seem to have high resolution—they use extreme probabilities a lot—but are very badly calibrated (Wright et al. 1978; Yates et al. 1989). Some psychologists think differences in the role of chance and bravado in Asian and Western philosophies and culture might account for the differences.

Recent studies found an important difference between "local confidence," the appropriateness of a single confidence interval for a single quantity, and "global confidence," the fraction of several intervals that contain their true quantities. Subjects were university employees and students who were asked ten questions about local operations (e.g., what is the current value of the university's land holdings?). The subjects' 90 percent confidence intervals were too narrow (as usual) but their global confidence was not bad: they guessed that about five of ten intervals contained true quantities, when only three of ten actually did (Sniezek and Buckley 1991; see also May 1986). These results suggest an important difference between the psychological process of constructing a judgment about a *single* quantity (or event) and making a collective guess about several such judgments. Most of us are probably overconfident about the chance of publishing our next article in a leading journal or teaching a brilliant class tomorrow, but are more level-headed about how many of our next ten articles or ten classes will be similarly successful.

The pervasive finding that subjects are (locally) overconfident may have important economic implications. If people underestimate the width of distributions of future quantities, they will underinvest in flexibility and insurance, which might have implications for equilibrium models of rental and ownership of housing, choices of mortgage terms (adjustable vs. fixed-rate), marriage and divorce rates, managerial investments in manufacturing flexibility, and so on. Underestimation of variation might help explain why so many small businesses fail because of insufficient cash flow (stemming from overly narrow planning, perhaps; cf. Kahneman and Lovallo 1993).

Recent studies of calibration and confidence have rekindled debate along three lines. The first idea is that part of the apparent overconfidence could be caused by probability judgments that are correct on average but contain error (Erev, Wallsten, and Budescu 1992; Soll 1993). The second claim is that calibration researchers may have selected sample questions nonrandomly, oversampling "tricky" questions in which natural cues yield the wrong answer (such as the Peru-Ireland potato question), and hence producing more overconfidence than is present in natural settings (Gigerenzer, Hoffrage, and Kleinbolting 1991; Juslin, in press). Some new studies sample questions differently and reduce apparent overconfidence, but Griffin and Tversky (1992) and Soll (1993) sampled randomly and still observe overconfidence.

Third, Griffin and Tversky (1992) suggest a framework to organize many empirical results on confidence results. They point out that evidence has both strength (or extremeness) and *weight*. In several studies they find that judgments of confidence overemphasize the strength of evidence (compared to a Bayesian probability benchmark) and underemphasize its weight. Their framework can explain the observed difference in calibration for hard and easy questions (people underweigh the strong weight of evidence in easy questions), conflicting results on expert calibration (experts will be highly overconfident in unpredictable environments, when they overweight weak evidence), and predicts some other phenomena.

B. Perception and Memory Biases

Machines are natural metaphors and benchmarks for human perception and thinking. The metaphor of man as an information-processor now dominates cognitive psychology (e.g., Lachman, Lachman, and Butterfield 1979). It has proved fruitful by suggesting coherent theory and many empirical tests. Can people record events as cameras do? Are memories stored like films in a library? Does information-processing proceed in steps like a computer program?

However, much evidence suggests that human perception deviates systematically from the camera benchmark and memory deviates from the computer benchmark. (My goal in this very brief section is to inform readers about some shreds of evidence, to whet their appetites, and to suggest ways the data might matter for economics.) For example, Bruner, Postman, and Rodrigues (1951) showed subjects glimpses of playing cards in which colors and shapes were deliberately mismatched—hearts were black instead of the familiar red. Subjects thought they saw the familiar cards (red hearts). Errors of this sort are systematic, not random: people more often err by mistaking unfamiliar patterns for familiar ones than vice versa. Put more formally, errors in absorbing information appear to be correlated with how unusual the information is. Misperception of surprising events implies that agents will misperceive outliers that signal regime switches or turning points in a time series. Their expectations will not be rational (in the sense of efficiently using available information) because the processing of new information depends on the stock of old information, or familiar images.[6]

There are many biases in memory too. When guessing which cancer claims more lives or which journal to submit an article to, people sample their memories. Sampling memories is a natural and reasonable heuristic because our memories are a sample of life. But even if our life sample is random, the sample we retrieve from memory will not be random because memories are not equally retrievable or "available" (Tversky and Kahneman 1973). For example, the most pleasant and least pleasant memories are more easily remembered, which creates illusory nostalgia (Holmes 1970). Personal and concrete experiences are often overweighed (Nisbett et al. 1976). For example, Kunreuther et al. (1978) found that the purchase of earthquake insurance *rose* after a quake (though the probability of a subsequent large quake actually falls, because stress on the fault line is relieved). The availability of personal experiences is thought to create "egocentric" biases in judgments of fault (both spouses think they are responsible for more than half of their household chores, or arguments [Ross and Sicoly 1982]; or two sides in an experimental dispute both think a judge's settlement with favor them [see Babcock et al. in press]). Memorable media reports cause biases in judgments because media coverage is not random[7] (e.g., Greenberg et al. 1989). For example, Combs and Slovic (1979) found that newspapers vastly overreport accidents compared to diseases, and people think deaths from disease and accidents are equally common. (In fact, deaths from diseases are 15 times more common.)

Availability can limit imagination and make theories, lists of words, or "fault trees" appear more complete than they really are. In a study by Fischhoff, Slovic, and Lichtenstein (1978), students and automechanics underestimated the probability of "other causes" in an incomplete fault tree listing reasons why a car would not start. Similar biases in imagining contract contingencies might lead contracts to appear overly incomplete.

C. Bayesian Updating and Representativeness

When the probabilities people judge are conditional, as in updating belief in X after learning M, they should follow the prescription of Bayes' rule:

$$P(X|M) = \frac{P(M|X)P(X)}{P(M)}$$

Computing probabilities using Bayes' rule is complicated. People seem to use simple heuristics instead: they anchor on $P(X)$ and adjust it to reflect M; or they judge $P(X|M)$ by how "representative" X is of M (Tversky and Kahneman 1982).

Representativeness will be a useful heuristic because representative values are generally more common than unrepresentative ones. (Eagles are less representative of the set of birds than robins, and less common.) But judging likelihoods according to representativeness neglects some features that are normatively important according to Bayes' rule—including the base rates $P(X)$ and $P(M)$, sampling properties, and regression effects. Other features that are *not* normatively important loom large in representativeness-based thinking. Representativeness therefore creates several systematic departures from Bayesian judgment, or biases.

1. Underweighting of Base Rates

A famous problem used to study Bayesian judgment was introduced by Kahneman and Tversky (1972):

> A cab was involved in a hit and run accident at night. Two cab companies, the Green and the Blue, operate in the city. You are given the following data:
>
> (a) 85 percent of the cabs in the city are Green and 15 percent are Blue.
> (b) a witness identified the cab as Blue.
>
> The court tested reliability of the witness under the same circumstances that existed on the night of the accident and concluded that the witness correctly identified each one of the two colors 80% of the time and failed 20% of the time. What is the probability that the cab involved in the accident was Blue rather than Green?

In the experiments, subjects are given the problem exactly as written above, often as part of a package of problems. Their probability judgments are recorded, and they are paid a small sum for participating (or course credit, in some cases).

The median and modal response is .80. It appears that subjects think the witness' judgment is representative of the actual color of the cab, and its representativeness leads them to confuse $P(\text{identify Blue} \mid \text{Blue}) = .8$ (from the court's test) with the probability that is asked for, $P(\text{Blue} \mid \text{identify Blue})$. According to Bayes rule, the posterior probability that is asked for, $P(\text{Blue/identify Blue})$, should reflect the base rate $P(\text{Blue}) = .15$ also; but the base rate plays no role in the logic of representativeness. When the base rate is included the correct posterior probability is .41.[8]

In these problems, and others like them, base rates are usually underweighted and often entirely neglected. Studies show that when attention is drawn to base rates, by varying the base rate in several versions of the problem or presenting them in causal forms (15 percent of the cab *accidents* in the city involve Blue cabs), subjects take base rates into account but still underweigh them (Ajzen 1977; Bar-Hillel 1980a; cf. Koehler 1989).

The cab question is typical of stimuli used by psychologists to study judgment. Word problems describing natural events are used to *escape* from the limits of earlier traditions that emphasized more abstract stimuli,[9] on the sensible presumption that psychological processes people use in everyday life could be better understood by asking people questions drawn from everyday life. The use of the word problems raises some methodological concerns for both economists and psychologists. For example, economists might wonder whether base rate neglect affects asset prices in a market; some studies answering this question are reported in section II.G below. We return to the methodological concerns after describing a replication of the base rate studies.

Grether (1980) studied base rate neglect in an abstract setting with three bingo cages. A draw from the first cage (whose contents were known) determined whether state A or state B had occurred. The state A cage had four N balls and two Gs; the B cage had three Ns and three Gs. Subjects observed a sample of six draws from whichever cage had been chosen (A or B) and were asked to decide which cage was more likely. For example, a subject might observe a sample of one N and five Gs, then choose whether to bet that the draws came from the A or B cage. The process was repeated several times, with fresh samples each time. At the end of the experiment, one trial was picked and a subject earned $10 if they had picked the right cage on that trial.

Using logit estimation, Grether found that subjects weighted the base rates $P(A)$ and $P(B)$ less than the likelihoods $P(\text{sample} \mid A)$ and $P(\text{sample} \mid B)$, as representativeness predicts, but they did not ignore the base rates entirely. Subjects also thought $P(A \mid \text{sample})$ was especially high when the sample was four Ns and two Gs, exactly matching the contents of the A cage (and similarly for the sample matching the B cage). Previous experience with a particular sample, or experience combined with monetary incentives for accuracy, reduced representativeness bias slightly but did not eliminate it. Concerned that Grether's subjects were not properly motivated, Harrison (1989b) replicated Grether's experiment with a variety of financial incentives. He found little evidence of representativeness among subjects with experience or financial incentive. There is no obvious way to reconcile the disagreement between his results and Grether's.

Grether (1991) extended his earlier work in three ways. In one experiment he was able to bound the degrees of belief in random events by having subjects choose between a bet on the most-likely cage and a bet on a chance device (so that choices revealed whether beliefs were higher [>.75] and lower [<.25]). In a second experiment he elicited probability judgments with a variant of the incentive-compatible Becker, DeGroot, and Marschak (1964) procedure (see chapter 1 for a description). Choices in both experiments *were* affected by representativeness. Probabilities elicited with the BDM procedure in the second experiment were often far too low or too high, but on average they were fairly close to Bayesian (within .05 to .10).

In a third experiment the A and B cages each had ten balls and samples of four balls were drawn. Assuming four ball samples cannot be representative of ten ball cages, representativeness should not affect judgments. In this experiment, judgments were quite different than in the first two experiments—sample information was *under*weighted rather than overweighted (see the next section on conservatism). Grether concluded: "This [difference] suggests that in making judgments under uncertainty individuals use different decision rules in different decision situations," a "contingent-judgment" hypothesis espoused by many psychologists, (e.g., Payne, Bettman, and Johnson 1992).

A Digression on Methodology: Psychology and Economics

Grether's experiments are designed to address many criticisms some economists have of methods used by some psychologists. The Bayesian judgment problem was operationalized using physical devices (bingo cages) rather than a vignette like the cab problem. Subjects made choices rather than simply reporting probabilities; they were paid $10 if one of their choices, randomly selected, was correct. (In Grether [1991], a typical error cost 5 to 20¢.) Subjects made repeated choices, with an opportunity to learn; in the psychology studies, subjects often answer each question once because the purpose of the experiment is to study initial intuitions, not learning. The existence of *some* errors was reasonably robust to all these changes in conditions in Grether's data, but not in Harrison's. Incentives also reduced the number of incoherent and outlying responses (Grether 1981; cf. Smith and Walker 1993).

The difference between psychological and economic experiments should not be overstated. In the 1960s, long before Grether's work, psychologists and others used random devices to study judgment (Edwards 1968) and used the BDM procedure to study valuations (Lichtenstein and Slovic 1971). Even recently, there is substantial overlap across disciplines in methods, and substantial variation within disciplines. However, the typical differences in methods are worth analyzing because they usually follow from different background presumptions about human nature and different target domains investigators hope to generalize to. It is presumptuous to argue that either general method is superior.

For example, many psychologists are curious whether people can recognize and apply statistical rules to everyday situations, like the cab problem in which statistical structure is not transparent. They often use vignettes or problems drawn from natural settings (rather than problems based exclusively on random devices) because (1) they want to learn how people reason about natural events and (2) they think people may reason differently about events and about random devices. Given these interests and presumptions, word problems are well suited to doing their research and bingo cages are not. Economists are interested in different questions (not how people reason but whether people violate Bayes's rule) and are also more inclined to presume that reasoning about bingo cages and taxicabs is similar. For these purposes, cages and dice are better because they lay bare the statistical structure (making detection of a Bayesian error clear) and are presumed to be good substitutes for word problems.

Another area of typical difference is financial motivation of subjects. Psychologists do not always motivate subjects financially—though many have and a few are adamant about doing so—because incentives usually complicate instructions and psychologists presume subjects are cooperative and intrinsically motivated to perform well. (Natural stimuli are also thought to keep subjects mentally involved and raise their instrinsic motivation, which substitutes for financial motivation.)

Repetition is another area of typical difference. The psychologists' tasks are often not repeated, with stationary replication, because psychologists are often most curious about *initial* behavior in a complicated environment. In addition, many psychologists think stationary replication overstates the frequency, speed, and clarity of feedback the world actually provides. Economists tend to think oppositely: they are mostly curious about equilibrium behavior—the last period, not the first—and they think extensive laboratory feedback is the best time-compressed imitation of the strong learning forces present in natural settings.

To reiterate, there is substantial overlap in the way psychologists and economists do experiments. When their methods do differ, very roughly speaking, psychologists use natural stimuli, do not pay subjects, and do not repeat tasks. Economists pay subjects, prefer blandly labeled random devices as stimuli, and insist on repeating tasks. My view is that these different methods are preferred by different investigators because they effectively produce answers to different questions. Broad-minded students of individual decision making should have a healthy tolerance for variety in methods. (And variation in methods is essential to gathering data, to determine whether different methods do affect behavior substantially.)

It is worth noting that judgment errors, like those revealed in the cab problem, have been a lively topic of research within psychology too (e.g., Cohen 1981). Many of the arguments made in that literature are like those economists have made about methods or interpretations of results. For example, Gigerenzer, Hell, and Blank (1988) used physical devices to operationalize base rates and found some reduction in base rate neglect (though Grether, and others mentioned later, also found substantial base rate neglect using physical devices).

A more interesting argument is that some apparent biases might occur because the specific words used, or linguistic convention subjects assume the experimenter is following, convey more information than the experimenter intends.[10] An example is the famous "Linda problem" (Tversky and Kahneman 1983). Subjects are told the following:

> Linda is 31 years old, single, outspoken, and very bright. She majored in philosophy. As a student, she was deeply concerned with issues of discrimination and social justice, and also participated in anti-nuclear demonstrations.

> Then they are asked to rank several statements about Linda by their probability:

> Linda is a teacher in elementary school.
> Linda works in a bookstore and takes Yoga classes.
> Linda is active in the feminist movement (F).
> Linda is a psychiatric social worker.
> Linda is a member of the League of Women Voters.
> Linda is a bank teller (T).
> Linda is an insurance salesperson.
> Linda is a bank teller and is active in the feminist movement (F&T).

Any ranking of probability should satisfy the conjunction law: Linda is less likely to be a feminist bank teller (marked F&T), than to be a bank teller (T) or a feminist (F), since the event F&T is a conjunction of the events F and T. In fact, about 90 percent of subjects exhibit a conjunction fallacy, ranking the event F&T as more likely than one (or both) of the events F and T, usually T. (In a sample of well-trained Stanford decision sciences doctoral students, 85 percent made the same mistake.) The standard psychological explanation is that the description of Linda is more *representative* of a feminist bank teller than of a bank teller; subjects mistakenly think it is therefore more *likely* that Linda is a feminist bank teller.

The potential linguistic problem is this: in the presence of the statement "Linda is a feminist bank teller," subjects might think that the statement "Linda is a bank teller" tacitly excludes feminists; they might think it actually means "Linda is a bank teller (and is not a feminist)." If subjects interpret the wording this way, none of the statements are conjunctions of others and no probability rankings are wrong.

The linguistic interpretation can be tested in several ways. For example, use a between-subjects design in which some subjects rate the T statement without seeing the F&T statement (and vice versa); or replace "Linda is a bank teller" with the clearly comprehensive "Linda is a bank teller, who may or may not be a feminist," or with the more specific "Linda is a bank teller (and is not a feminist)" and see whether conjunction errors persist.

In fact, the purely linguistic interpretation appears to be wrong. Tversky and Kahneman (1983) tried both the between-subjects and the clearly-comprehensive variations and still found persistent conjunction fallacies. Others manipulated subtle details of wording and found no substantial changes in some conjunction problems (Morier and Borgida 1984) and some error reduction in others (Krosnick, Fan, and Lehman 1990).

2. Underweighting of Likelihood Information (Conservatism)

A second bias is underweighting of likelihood information, or "conservatism." Conservatism has been observed in Bayesian updating tasks like the one Grether studied. Consider two bingo cages, A and B. Bingo cage A contains seven red and three blue balls; B contains three red and seven blues. Suppose each cage is equally likely. Suppose a sample of eight reds and four blues is drawn (with replacement, of course), which clearly favors the A cage. What is $P(A \mid 8$ red, 4 blue)? The typical response is between .7 and .8 but the Bayesian posterior is actually .97. Subjects are far too conservative in drawing conclusions from samples like these. One estimate derived from experimental data suggests that it takes two to five observations to produce a perceived diagnostic impact equal to the Bayesian impact of one observation (Edwards 1968).

McKelvey and Page (1990) ran a study in which subjects observed different parts of a full sample, then reported probability estimates to each other. After hearing the estimates of others, people reported new estimates (taking into account the estimates of others), and so on for several rounds. (This iterative process resembles the aggregation of information through polls and other processes; see McKelvey and Ordeshook [1985]). They observed some conservatism in updating of probabilities. Eger and Dickhaut (1982) found some conservatism when accounting students simply reported probabilities, but the effects were substantially reduced when stimuli were described an accounting context. The conservatism also disappeared when subjects revealed probabilities by betting against an experimenter in a way that penalized Bayesian errors. By contrast, Sanders (1968) found conservatism using a proper scoring rule with no financial incentives.

At first glance, the conflict between evidence of base rate neglect (reviewed in the last section) and conservatism seems to indicate that people use Bayes's rule on average, but sometimes they weigh base rates too little and sometimes too much. This is a weak justification for adhering to Bayes's rule as a descriptive principle in all circumstances, if one can predict the situations in which the two errors occur. (By analogy, a light jacket is the wrong thing to wear on a trip with stops in Alaska and Taipei, even if it is appropriate for the average temperature of the two places). Whether errors are predictable across situations is then the crucial empirical question.

There seem to be several reasons why base rates are underweighted in some settings (the taxicab problem) but sample information is underweighted in others (conservatism experiments). Base rates *are* incorporated when they are salient or interpreted causally, as they are likely to be in the conservatism experiments (partly because judgments are repeated). Also, sample information may be underweighted in the conservatism tasks because it is *not* highly representative (as witness accuracy is in the taxicab problem); for instance, no sample of draws exactly matches the contents of the bingo cages. Furthermore, Griffin and Tversky (1992) argue that conservatism and base rate neglect are opposite sides of the same coin. They argue that both phenomena result from people overweighting the strength of evidence and underemphasizing its weight. Conservatism is a kind of underconfidence that results when people underemphasize the large size (or weight) of a sample of weak evidence. Base rate neglect occurs because people overemphasize strong evidence.

3. The Law of Small Numbers and Misperceptions of Randomness

In the logic of the representativeness, there is no place for sample size: a small sample can represent the population or process that generates it as well as a large sample can (for example, a sample of two coin flips, one head and one tail, represents the Bernoulli trial very nicely). The belief that all samples will closely resemble the processes or populations that generated them is an intuitive extension of the law of large numbers to small samples, facetiously called "the law of small numbers" (Tversky and Kahneman 1971). The law of small numbers predicts that agents will gather too little data and will overgeneralize from small samples to distributions. In economic applications, they will search too little (see the evidence in section III.K) and learn too quickly, compared to models of optimal sampling and inference.

The law of small numbers also causes biases like the "gambler's fallacy": when people are asked to generate or identify random sequences their sequences often have negative autocorrelation (Wagenaar 1972), because the prototypical representative random series repeatedly self-corrects to keep the sample proportion close to the population proportion (see Bar-Hillel and Wagenaar [in press] for a recent review). For example, lottery betting on a given number actually drops off sharply—by nearly half—in the several days after that number wins (Clotfelter and Cook 1993).

Mathematically sophisticated subjects are better at generating truly random numbers, but so are children who have not yet learned the law of small numbers (Ross and Levy 1958; Chapanis 1953). People can also be taught to choose randomly after several hours of training with excellent feedback (e.g., several measures of the randomness in the previous block of responses, Neuringer [1986], and see Edwards [1961b]). These training data suggest that experienced agents in some settings might be able to learn to choose randomly. Whether they do in other settings, under natural conditions, is an empirical question.

Truly random sequences will show no negative autocorrelation. Observers who expect negative autocorrelation in a random series will be surprised by the number of long runs they see and will come to believe the series is positively autocorrelated. This misconception appears to be the origin of the unshakable belief among basketball fans and players that outcomes of shots are positively autocorrelated—players have "hot hands"—even though both field data and experiments show hits and misses are remarkably close to independent (Gilovich, Vallone, and Tversky 1985). Camerer (1989b) found that mistaken belief in winning streaks—team-wide hot hands—created errors in betting odds on professional basketball games of about one point. (The error is small because professional teams score roughly 100 points a game.) And Brown and Sauer (1993) question whether streak beliefs are mistakes, but their tests are inconclusive. Regardless, betting markets are active and patterns like the perceived hot hand are very easy to observe and profit from; such markets might be the *worst* place to find biases. The modest one point error suggests that larger effects might exist in markets that are less well policed.[11]

Misperceptions of random sequences are important in game theory because mixed strategy play in repeated games assumes subjects can generate independent random draws (or appeal to independent privately-observed hunches that others do not observe). O'Neill (1987) reported that average play corresponded to mixed strategy proportions in a zero-sum game with a unique mixed strategy equilibrium. Skeptical of the strength of O'Neill's conclusions, Brown and Rosenthal (1990) reanalyzed his data. Their reanalysis and subsequent work by others are a good case study illustrating how careful critique of an imaginative experiment can lead to further designs and a cumulation of knowledge. Brown and Rosenthal first pointed out that some test statistics O'Neill used, like the percentage of times the row player won, had little statistical power to distinguish equilibrium mixed strategy play from various disequilibrium alternatives (like random choices with equal probabilities for all strategies). Then they showed that despite the lack of power to detect deviations from mixed strategy predictions, about a third of the players did deviate significantly, in different directions.

Furthermore, choices were *not* independent across plays; choices often depended on one's own previous plays and on the opponent's previous play (and sometimes on the interaction).

The work on randomization is now extensive and suggests an area of genuine collaboration and cross-fertilization between economists and psychologists. The conclusions of O'Neill, and Brown and Rosenthal, have been largely replicated by Rapoport and Boebel (1992) and Mookherjee and Sopher (1994). In these games, many players seemed to believe in the law of small numbers: after they won by making a particular choice, they were less likely to try the same choice. Whether players can detect the predictable nonrandomness that other players exhibit is an interesting open question.

Rapoport and Budescu (1992) compared the randomness of sequences subjects generated in two conditions: (1) a *game* condition in which they played a two strategy game with a unique mixed strategy equilibrium (with each strategy equally likely) 150 times and were paid for each choice according to the outcomes; and (2) a *choice* condition in which the subjects were simply told to choose randomly 150 times (and were not paid for their choices). Formally the two tasks are the same. But in the game condition, subjects created sequences that were more random than those they produced by random choices; for example, subjects reversed their previous choice 59.1 percent of the time in the choice condition (exhibiting "negative recency"), but they only reversed 53.4 percent of the time in the game condition. (A true randomizer would reverse 50 percent of the time.) One explanation for the difference is that subjects played the game more seriously because money was at stake. Rapoport and Budescu suggest a second, psychological explanation: remembering previous choices is essential for choosing nonrandomly; perhaps playing the more complex game inhibited memory of previous choices, making it more difficult not to randomize.

Mookherjee and Sopher (1994) compared behavior in two conditions, in which subjects learned their own payoffs but the choices and payoffs of others were either known or unknown. In many "routine-learning" models, knowing the choices or payoffs of others is inessential because players are assumed to simply choose strategies that yielded high payoffs in the past. These models predict that behavior in the known and unknown conditions should be the same. Behavior was not the same: convergence toward equilibrium mixtures was more rapid when the other players' choices and payoffs were known, suggesting a sophistication the routine-learning models do not capture.

Methodological Digression: Training

Several psychologists have tried to train subjects to avoid judgment errors ("debiasing"). Fischhoff (1982) reports some successful training exercises, mostly using large amounts of well-structured feedback. For example, overconfidence and hindsight bias (discussed in section II.F below) can be reduced by having people generate reasons why their predictions or recollections might be wrong. (Groups and organizations might debias individual judgment if several people

generate such reasons, questioning each others' judgment. But the opposite could occur too—groups could *inflame* bias—if groups generate supporting arguments or if overconfidence is taken as a signal of knowledge.)

Extensive studies suggest reasons to be pessimistic about how well training transfers across time or tasks. When subjects adapt to a setting and optimize in it, it is often the case that they have *not* learned a general rule they can recognize to apply to a structurally identical task that has different surface features. For example, Kagel and Levin's (1986) subjects learned to avoid the winner's curse in three bidder markets, but overbid when three bidders were added; compare with chapter 7.

Nisbett et al. (1987) and Larrick, Morgan, and Nisbett (1990) trained subjects to use simple statistical rules and ignore sunk costs. For example, 45 percent of their trained subjects gave a correct response on a sunk cost problem, compared to 29 percent of untrained subjects. A month later, the trained subjects reported they had bought and *not* used 1.14 objects or activities—e.g., they returned a rented videotape without watching it—compared to 0.84 by untrained subjects. These are modest victories for training, but the breadth of the rules people have learned to use is subject to debate.

4. Market Level Tests of Representativeness

A central question for economics is whether individual judgment errors aggregate to create errors in market prices, allocations, and effficiencies (and whether errors aggregate in groups,[12] firms, and societies). The aggregation question has been addressed theoretically by Haltiwanger and Waldman (1985), Russell and Thaler (1985), Akerlof and Yellen (1985), and many others. Whether individual errors affect market behavior depends on the answers to many deep questions (see Camerer 1992b): do rational agents have more impact than irrational agents? (Do the more rational agents know who they are? Can they get more capital? Is it always optimal to behave rationally when others are not?) Do irrational agents learn from others? Can they buy advice? Can they go bankrupt? (Will they be replaced by other irrational agents if they do?).

The answers to these questions will undoubtedly vary across markets (cf. Zeckhauser 1986, table 1). They are fundamentally empirical questions. To answer them, some evidence of judgment error in market behavior has been gathered (see Thaler 1992). But the evidence is inevitably controversial because it is easy to construct rationalizations of apparent market anomalies based on risk aversion, transaction costs, unobserved variables, or—the current fashion—information asymmetries. To test whether individual errors affect markets, it is therefore helpful to conduct market experiments in which competing explanations can be ruled out. The next section describes some studies of whether errors in Bayesian judgment, caused by representativeness, affect prices and allocations in markets.

Duh and Sunder (1986) published the first market study. They tested whether underweighting of base rates (see section II.D.1 above) affected prices in a market

for one-period assets. Their design and those used by me (Camerer 1987,1990) were both inspired by Grether (1980). I will describe my own design in some detail.

Asset values depended on which of two states, X and Y, occurred. States were physically represented by bingo cage draws. If X had occurred ($P=.6$) three balls were drawn with replacement from an X bingo cage, hidden in a box, containing one red ball and two black balls. If Y occurred the cage had two reds and one black.

Subjects were given two shares of an asset and loaned experimental currency (francs) each period. Subjects earned a state-dependent dividend for each share they held at the end of the period. (There were two dividend schedules, creating type I and type II traders.) The value of the assets to subjects therefore depended on their subjective probabilities of X and Y, which depended on the sample of balls drawn from the X or Y bingo cage. A sample of one red (and two blacks) indicates the state is likely to be X. A Bayesian subject would calculate

$$P(X \mid 1 \text{ red}) = \frac{P(1 \text{ red} \mid X)P(X)}{P(1 \text{ red} \mid X)P(X) + P(1 \text{ red} \mid Y)P(Y)} = .75$$

The judgment literature suggests several alternative hypotheses about how subjects estimate $P(X \mid 1 \text{ red})$. One could interpret representativeness to imply $P(X \mid 1 \text{ red}) = 1$ (Duh and Sunder's NBR1 model). An interpretation more faithful to representativeness is $P(X \mid 1 \text{ red}) = P(Y \mid 2 \text{ red})$, which follows if the base rates $P(X)$ and $P(Y)$ are ignored. Both of those theories are rejected by the data. An hypothesis that fits better is "exact representativeness," in which $P(X \mid 1 \text{ red}) > .75$ because a sample of one red and two blacks exactly matches the contents of the X bingo cage. Given any such assumption about $P(X \mid \text{sample})$, predictions about prices and allocations can be derived by assuming risk neutrality and competitive equilibrium.

Each experiment had thirty to forty trading periods with stationary replication, using different samples each period. Since the equilibrium price varied among four possible prices from period to period (one price for each different sample), prices were volatile and convergence was slow. Camerer (1990) reports the time series of mean prices in all sessions. Camerer (1987) condenses the data in a compact way, shown in Figure 8.3, giving a time series of confidence intervals around the mean price *across* several sessions with the same parameters.[13] Bayesian predictions for each sample are shown by horizontal lines.

Figure 8.3 shows that mean prices vary across sessions (the confidence intervals are wide). Across periods with the same sample, prices converge roughly to the Bayesian predictions. An "R" denotes the direction of price deviations expected by (exact) representativeness. Prices in zero-red and three-red periods are remarkably close to Bayesian (though the Bayesian probabilities are also close to 0 and 1 in those cases, so there is less room for error). Prices in the one-red and two-red periods begin well below the Bayesian prediction, and converge above it in the direction of representativeness.

Dividend parameters were carefully chosen in the experiment so that final allo-

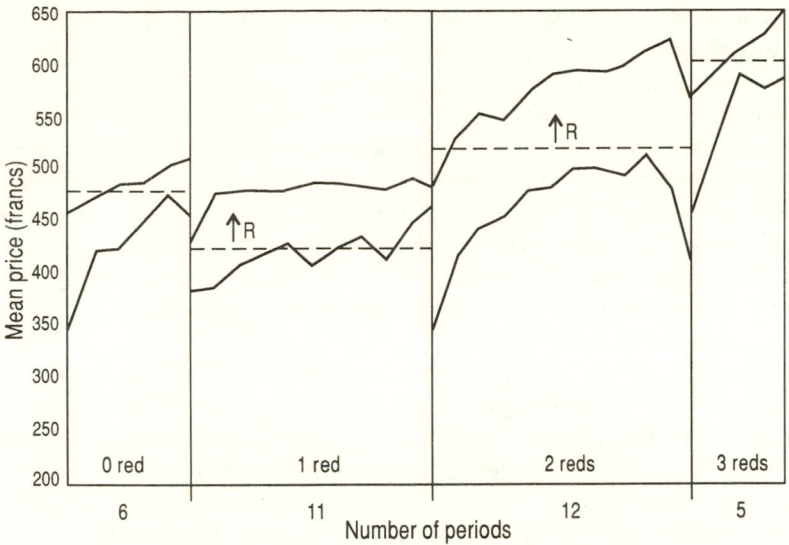

Figure 8.3. Confidence intervals around average prices in market experiments on representatives. "R" denotes direction of predicted judgment bias. *Source:* Camerer 1987.

cations of shares, as well as prices, would distinguish the Bayesian and representativeness explanations. When the sample had one-red, the Bayesian expected values were equal for type I and type II traders, so the Bayesian theory predicts an equal allocation of shares among the two types (even if subjects are risk averse or risk preferring). The representativeness theory predicts that type I traders will hold more shares. In fact, about 80 percent of the shares were held by type I traders (90 percent after traders were once-experienced), supporting the representativeness theory.

The price biases are modest in probability terms[14] but small in cost—about a nickel per trade, or a couple of dollars over an experiment. However, paying subjects five times as much made little difference.

Experience reduces price bias but does not eliminate it. Experience also reduces noise in prices and trading, which makes biases more statistically significant and causes allocations to reject the Bayesian assumption even more strongly.

Duh and Sunder (1986) ran similar experiments using a design with several interesting variations (including a wider range of prior state probabilities and a labeling difference). Their results are similar. Subjects were close to Bayesian, but they erred in the direction of an extreme representativeness theory that predicts that a sample of one draw is taken as perfectly diagnostic. Allocations were strongly supportive of representativeness.

Anderson and Sunder (1989) report four experimental sessions comparing students with professional securities and commodity traders, in a design similar to Duh and Sunder (1986) and Camerer (1987). In three of the four sessions, the prices predicted by the Bayesian theory were below the prices predicted by representativeness theories. Prices were far from Bayesian in the student sessions, and closer to Bayesian in the sessions with traders. (However, in their design representativeness pushes prices below Bayesian levels, just as risk aversion does. It is possible the professionals are simply less risk averse, and therefore *appear* more Bayesian.) Allocations did not favor either the Bayesian or representativeness theories, though there is some movement toward Bayesian allocations in the professional trader sessions. The professional traders also showed less underweighting of base rates in a word problem similar to the cab problem discussed in section II.C.1. While these data are limited, they do suggest professional traders are less prone to neglect base rates, and more likely to trade assets closer to Bayesian prices, than students.

Ganguly, Kagel, and Moser (in press) ran market experiments using an asset whose value depended on the success of a hypothetical firm. A base rate of success and likelihood information were given, making the firm's success isomorphic to the cab problem, which elicits large underweighting of base rates. Their study has two innovations: a word problem is used to test for representativeness (the studies above used bingo cages); and both individual judgments and market prices are measured each period, so one can measure whether market prices reduce individual error. In two sessions, judgments and prices were much closer to the base rate neglect prediction than to the Bayesian prediction. There is no apparent convergence to Bayesian price levels across sixteen periods.

Plott and Wilde (1982) studied product markets in which agents give advice to buyers about product quality, based on samples of data that agents can see but buyers cannot. They report some evidence that agents used representativeness, rather than Bayes's rule, in drawing inferences from the samples.

This small collection of work on market level effects of Bayesian judgment errors suggests that errors caused by representativeness are the rule, not the exception, in experimental market prices and allocations. The errors are relatively small when uncertainty is generated by chance devices (bingo cages). Errors are quite large when uncertainty is generated by word problems like the taxicab problem. Market experience appears to reduce error, though not eliminate it (Camerer 1987); professional trading experience does appear, tentatively, to reduce error (Anderson and Sunder 1990). Future research could profitably continue to map out the boundaries of the influence of judgment error, compare individuals and their market behavior more carefully, and replicate whether experience and education reduce error (as they appear to, in some studies). Studies should also begin to disentangle the influences of incentives, competition, task repetition, learning from outcome feedback, and learning from actions of others, which are currently confounded in market treatments.

D. Confirmation Bias and Obstacles to Learning

An important source of disagreement between psychologists and economists concerns learning. Psychologists often suspect that the immediate, frequent, clear, exogenous feedback subjects receive in economics experiments overstates how well people learn in natural economic settings. Economists, in contrast, think that experiments understate the rate of natural learning because context, access to advice, higher incentives, and added time to reflect or calculate are absent from experiments, and probably improve performance in natural settings.

Much of the psychologists' pessimism arises from evidence of heuristic tendencies in judgment that present obstacles to learning (e.g., Einhorn and Hogarth 1978). I mention only two obstacles here. One tendency is called "confirmation bias." A tricky problem due to Wason (1968) can be used to illustrate this:

You are shown four cards, marked E, K, 4, and 7. Each card has a letter on one side and a number on the other. You are given the following rule: Every card with a vowel on one side has an even number on the other side. Which cards must you turn over to test whether the rule is true or false?

In the four-card problem, most subjects answer that E must be turned over, or E and 4. They think you should check the one card with a vowel (E)—you should—and perhaps check the even-number card (4) too. The correct answer is E and 7. Few subjects think to turn over the 7, but they should because the rule is falsified if the 7 card has a vowel on the other side. The four-card problem suggests that in testing an hypothesis, people instinctively seek evidence that could confirm the hypothesis: for example, finding a vowel on the other side of 4 would provide support for the rule, but that evidence could actually never test whether the rule is always true (as turning over the 7 can). Confirmation bias is one force that may inhibit learning.

A related problem is the production of treatment effects (or self-fulfilling prophecies). When people believe an hypothesis is true, their actions often produce a biased sample of evidence that reinforces their belief.[15] A busy waiter who thinks poorly-dressed patrons tip badly will give them poor service and receive a bad tip, reinforcing his theory. Treatment effects inhibit learning whether one's underlying belief is false. (The only way to test the belief is by experimenting, giving good service to a poorly-dressed patron.) Expectations of a bank run, or a bubble in asset prices, can be self-fulfilling in a similar way.

E. Expectations Formation

There is a large literature on expectations formation, and a smaller literature about expectations people form about variables generated endogenously by their own collective activity—future prices, for instance.

There are many studies of whether price expectations are rational. Most of the studies use published forecasts by consumers, businessmen, or professional economists (see Lovell [1986], and Williams [1987], for reviews). Generally, they find that forecasts are biased: forecast errors (forecasts minus actual results) have a nonzero mean. Forecasts usually violate rationality of expectations: they are correlated with observable variables (typically past forecast errors and current forecast levels), implying that some available information is ignored when forecasts are made. Forecasts also usually follow an adaptive process in which forecast changes are related to past forecast errors (Nerlove 1958, and see below).

Apparent violations of rationality of naturally-occuring forecasts could be due to Bayesian learning in an economy where the statistical process generating outcomes keeps changing (Caskey 1985; Lewis 1989). For example, the surveys show that businessmen were consistently surprised by the persistence of price inflation in the 1970s (their forecast errors had a negative mean). It could be argued that their forecasts were rational, ex ante, but the stochastic inflation process changed during the period and it took forecasters some time to learn whether the change was temporary or permanent.

To control for changes in the statistical process generating outcomes, several experiments examined forecasts of outcomes of a statistical process that is unknown to subjects but fixed throughout the experiment, and known to be fixed (Schmalansee 1976; Garner 1982; Bölle 1988). Their results are generally inconsistent with rationality of expectations too, but suggest some learning and rationality in special settings (a random walk with no drift, in Dwyer et al. [1993][16]).

Several researchers have gathered forecasts that subjects in an experimental market make of the future prices that they themselves generate (Carlson 1967; Knez, Smith, and Williams 1985; Williams 1987; Daniels and Plott 1988; Smith, Suchanek, and Williams 1988; Wellford 1989; Camerer and Weigelt 1990; Peterson 1993). I will describe the Williams (1987) study in detail. He conducted experiments with a series of five double auctions for single period goods. Starting after the first period, subjects forecasted the mean price in the next period. The person with the lowest cumulative absolute forecast error earned $1. The forecasts were generally remarkably accurate, but the small deviations from rationality were statistically significant. Nearly half the forecast errors were zero (the mode), but on average prices were about a penny too high. (Since goods cost about $5, a penny deviation is tiny.) Forecast errors were modestly autocorrelated ($r = .15$, $p < .01$). Expectations were estimated to be adaptive[17] if the adaptation coefficient b was positive in the specification:

$$(1) \qquad E(P_t) - E(P_{t-1}) = b[P_{t-1} - E(P_{t-1})] + e_t,$$

(where $E(P_1)$ denotes the forecast of prices in period t and P_{t-1} is the actual price in period $t - 1$). Williams estimated $b = .86$. Forecasts of experienced subjects, who had participated in other auction experiments, were less biased and less error prone, but not by much. Peterson (in press) found that the estimated b in equation (1) converged to one across periods of an experiment, and changes were largest for the least experienced subjects.

Besides contributing to the debate about rationality of forecasts, the studies by Williams and others allayed methodological fears that simply gathering forecasts might affect market behavior. One concern was that asking subjects to forecast prices before each period might increase or decrease their attention to market behavior and affect convergence. But patterns of convergence looked like those in previous double auction experiments (see chapter 5 for examples), suggesting there was no such effect. Another concern is that subjects who are rewarded for making accurate forecasts may sacrifice trading profit to collect the best-forecaster bonus. There was no evidence of such an effect either.

Williams's methods and results are typical of most other studies. Forecasts are usually slightly biased (too low if prices are rising; too high if prices are falling).

Forecast errors are autocorrelated and correlated with some observables (previous price changes or current forecast levels). And forecasts are generally adaptive; estimates of the adaptiveness coefficient b are remarkably constant across a wide variety of studies, between .6 and .8.

A notable exception is Daniels and Plott (1988). They studied forecasts in goods markets with price inflation that was induced by shifting supply and demand curves upward by 15 percent each period (until the last few periods). Prices adjusted to the inflation a bit sluggishly. Graphs of average forecasts and prices suggest that forecasts were biased and autocorrelated (they were too low during inflation, and overshot when the inflation stopped). But regressions indicated that subjects' forecasts were rational rather than adaptive. It is not clear why the expectations of their subjects (Cal Tech students) are not adaptive, as they are in most other studies.

Price forecasts are easy to gather. Perhaps experimenters should collect them routinely. So far, the forecasts have not generally been put to much use to inform either psychology or economics, but they could be. A good example is Smith, Suchanek, and Williams (1988) who use evidence of systematic forecast error to explain why price bubbles persist in experimental asset markets (see chapter 6).

Psychological Studies of Expectations

Psychologists have done two kinds of studies germane to understanding rationality of expectations. One kind is studies of "multi-cue probability learning" (MCPL) (e.g., Castellan 1977). In MCPL studies subjects try to predict a dependent variable from given values of predictor variables, in a series of 100 or so trials. The studies indicate that learning is very difficult except in simple, deterministic situations (e.g., when dependent variables are a linear combination of independent variables; Brehmer 1980). Learning stochastic rules is especially difficult.

A second body of literature concerns judgments made repeatedly by people (many of them experts) in natural settings where stochastic outcomes depend on some observable predictors (e.g., test scores) and some unobservables. Examples include medical or psychiatric diagnosis (severity of Hodgkins' disease, schizophrenia), predictions of recidivism or parole violation by criminals, ratings of marital happiness, and bankruptcy of firms. About 100 careful studies have been documented so far. The remarkable finding in almost all these studies is that weighted[18] linear combinations of observables predict outcomes better than individual experts can (Meehl 1954; Dawes, Faust, and Meehl 1989). In a typical study (Dawes 1971), it was discovered that academic success of doctoral students could be predicted better by a sum of three measures—GRE scores, a rating of the quality of the student's undergraduate school, and her undergraduate grades— than by ratings of a faculty admissions committee. (Put bluntly, the faculty's deliberation just added noise to the three measure index.) The *only* documented exceptions to the general conclusion that models outpredict experts are a few kinds of esoteric medical diagnosis.

In these studies, experts routinely violate rational expectations by using observable information inefficiently (worse than simple models do). The violations have two common forms: (1) experts often add error to predictions by using complicated interactions of variables (weighting grades from low-quality schools more heavily, for example), rather than more robust linear combinations of variables; (2) experts pay attention to observable variables that they should ignore because the variables are not highly predictive of outcomes (personal interviews, for example). These psychological tendencies can be traced to some of the judgment biases discussed above (e.g., Camerer and Johnson 1991).

F. Iterated Expectations and the Curse of Knowledge

In many economic settings, agents must guess what others think. These guesses are "iterated expectations," or expectations of expectations. We can express these formally as follows: suppose agent i and j have information sets I_i and I_j and agent i is guessing j's expectation about a variable X. Then j forms the expectation $E(X|I_j)$ and i forms an iterated expectation, $E(E(X|I_j)|I_i)$.

Most asymmetric-information settings are modeled by assuming one agent knows strictly more than another ($I_{less} \subseteq 1_{more}$). These models usually revolve around the less-informed agent's attempt to learn what the more-informed agent knows, perhaps by observing a signal (cf. the asset market examples in chapter 6). A hidden assumption in the models is that the more-informed agent has an accurate mental model of the less-informed. The psychology of memory and imagination suggests that assumption may be wrong: it is hard for the more-informed agent to forget what she knows and imagine what the less-informed agent is thinking, because her extra information is available in memory.

Normatively, $E(E(X|I_{less}|I_{more})$ should equal $E(X|I_{less})$. If the extra information in I_{more} is hard to forget, empirical estimates of $E(E(X|I_{less}|I_{more})$ will be biased away from $E(X|I_{less})$ toward $E(X|I_{more})$. This bias is called the "curse of knowledge" (Camerer, Loewenstein, and Weber 1989). It seems common: teaching is made difficult by knowing too much; after solving a problem it seems obvious that others should see the solution too[19] (Nickerson, Baddeley, and Freeman 1987); and what writer of computer manuals—an expert, usually—has ever written one that novices can understand?[20]

1. False Consensus and Hindsight Bias

Two brands of curse of knowledge have been studied in some depth. One brand is called "false consensus" (an unfortunate misnomer): people use their own tastes and beliefs as information in guessing what others like and believe (Ross, Greene, and House 1977). In one study, students were asked whether they would walk around a campus for thirty minutes wearing a sign saying "Eat At Joe's." Some did, others refused. The interesting finding is that both kinds of subjects thought others were likely to make the same choice they made. Those who wore the sign estimated 62 percent of others would; those who refused thought 67 percent would refuse. Using one's own tastes or beliefs as information is not a mistake unless that information is overweighted. (It is reasonable to use one's own tastes as a single draw from the population distribution of tastes. Then two Bayesians with different tastes will have different posterior beliefs about the population—as the two groups of sign-wearers and refusers did—but a difference in posterior beliefs is not necessarily an error. See Dawes [1990].) I suspect overweighting one's own tastes might contribute to the high failure rate of small businesses: owners think more consumers share their tastes than actually do and either under-invest in market research or ignore its result.

A second kind of curse of knowledge is "hindsight bias": current recollections of past judgments tend to be biased by what actually happened since then (see Fischhoff 1975; Hawkins and Hastie 1990; Christensen-Szalanski and Willham 1991). Fischhoff and Beyth (1975) asked subjects about the likelihood of various events occurring before Nixon's historic trip to China (Will Nixon meet Mao?). Several months later, after the trip was over, subjects were asked to recall what probabilities they gave before the trip. They remembered having given higher probabilities than they actually had for events that happened, and lower probabilities for events that didn't happen. Subjects were not paid for accurate recollection but I bet the hindsight bias persists even with financial reward (assuming subjects cannot record their initial answers and look them up afterwards). Hindsight bias is often modest in magnitude but robust, and affects events with low ex ante probabilities most strongly. Hindsight bias appears to create second-guessing in firms, courts, and political institutions, which may create added employment risk when good ex ante decisions results in bad ex post outcomes (cf. Baron and Hershey 1988).

2. Market Level Tests of Curse of Knowledge

Camerer, Loewenstein, and Weber (1989) tested whether the curse of knowledge affected prices in experimental markets.

Before the markets began, one group of "uninformed" subjects guessed the 1980 earnings-per-share (EPS) of several actual companies, based on accounting data from 1970–1979 and a Value Line profile of the firm's 1980 prospects. Call the uninformed subjects' average estimate $E(\text{EPS} \mid \text{data})$.

Traders in asset markets then traded a one period asset that paid a dividend equal to the average estimate of uninformed subjects, $E(\text{EPS} \mid \text{data})$. To value the asset correctly, market traders had to make the best possible guess of what uninformed subjects thought 1980 earnings would be. Market subjects knew the *actual* 1980 earnings per share. Their guess about the uninformed subjects' average estimate is therefore an iterated expectation, $E[E(\text{EPS} \mid \text{data}) \mid \text{data} + \text{EPS}]$. If market subjects suffer from the curse of knowledge, asset prices will be closer to true EPS than they should be. (It will be hard for traders to imagine that subjects could not have guessed the true EPS.) A separate control group of subjects did not trade in any markets, but simply made judgments about what the asset value would be (knowing the 1980 EPS); they were rewarded for accurate forecasts just as market traders were.

This setting is similar to underwriting, in which a group of expert buyers must purchase goods that are resold to a group of less-expert consumers. The consumers' opinions establish the value of the goods, which the expert buyers must anticipate. Financial underwriting or buying of clothes, art, or wine for retail sale are examples. The empirical question is whether the experts will let their extra knowledge get in the way when figuring out what nonexperts will buy.

Traders traded assets based on eight different companies, for two trading periods each. (We used two trading periods to measure the change in forecasts and prices between periods. We used only two periods so we would have time to trade several companies because we suspected—correctly, as it turned out—that there might be inherent variation in the degree of curse of knowledge across companies, which we hoped to average out by using eight companies.) The degree of curse of knowledge, or hindsight bias, was estimated by having traders give forecasts of the asset value three times, before each of the two trading periods and after the last period. We compared their forecasts to the actual asset value (0 percent bias) and the true 1980 earnings (100 percent bias). Figure 8.4 illustrates the degree of bias across the eight companies. The mean degree of bias in the forecasts of market subjects after two trading periods is shown by a regular line. The mean bias in the control-group individual judgments is shown in Figure 8.4 with a dotted line.

The market traders' forecasts exhibited roughly 30 percent bias, whereas the individual subjects' forecasts exhibited roughly 60 percent bias. Thus, market forces reduced the curse of knowledge in traders' judgments by about half, compared to the control group subjects, but did not eliminate the curse entirely.

A closer look at individual behavior suggests why market forces had an effect. Less biased traders were slightly more active in the markets (56 percent of bids, offers, and acceptances) than more biased traders (44 percent). Prices generally began between the 0 percent bias and 100 percent bias levels. Of the price changes that moved toward one benchmark and away from the other, 63 percent of the changes were toward the 0 percent bias benchmark. In these experiments, the market is actually a bundle of forces that could be separated in future work. Compared to the individual-subject control group, traders in the market made three forecasts (rather than one); spent more chronological time thinking about each company; and had the opportunity to learn from bids, asks, and acceptances by others. We suspect the third force is most important. The double auction market is a specialized communication mechanism that allows people to express their opinions, and learn from others, in a limited form. It could be usefully compared to other opinion-aggregation schemes (e.g., open group discussion) and other exchange institutions for bias-reducing properties.

The curse of knowledge implies that more information might hurt those who are trying to guess what people without the information think. If a harmful good is freely disposable—toxic waste, or curse producing information—it should have a price of zero; but information is *not* freely disposable if it is hard to forget or ignore. We ran two market experiments, with eight traders in each, to see whether traders would bid zero for curse-producing information (Camerer

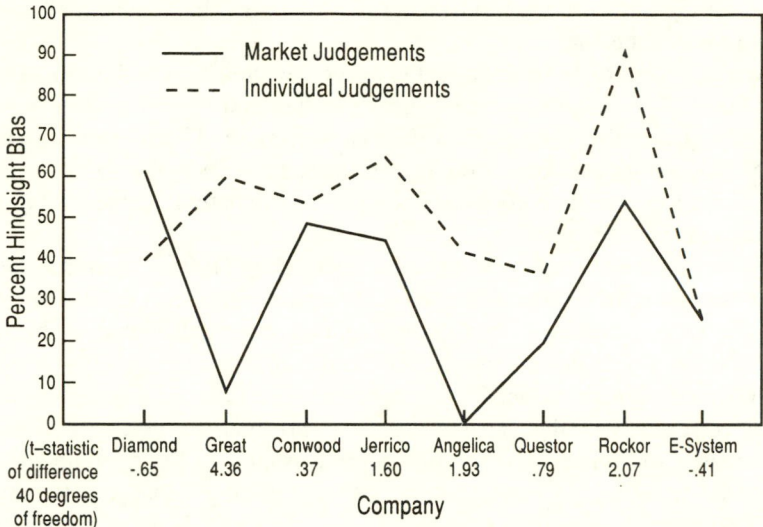

Figure 8.4. Degree of hindsight bias (or curse of knowledge) in individuals (dotted line) and market traders (solid line). *Source:* Camerer, Lowenstein, and Weber 1989.

1992b). We auctioned off the actual 1980 EPS to four traders in a uniform price auction where the price was determined by the fifth highest bidder (cf. chapter 7). Information was auctioned off once for each of the eight companies.

Bids began at very high levels, close to the asset value itself (around $3), probably because some subjects had no idea what the information was worth. Others bid zero immediately. After two or three company auctions, the market price converged to zero. Some subjects even made small negative bids—they wanted to be *paid* to know something worthless, perhaps because they knew it was not freely disposable and might hurt their judgments.

G. *The Illusion of Control*

People sometimes act as if tasks that involve only chance have an element of skill too. Psychologists call this belief the "illusion of control." Gamblers throw dice hard to produce high numbers. Lottery bettors buy "dream books" that explain what numbers to bet after a certain dream. People wait longer or pay more for specific numbers in a lottery than for randomly-assigned numbers (Langer 1975).

The illusion of control is one kind of "magical thinking," a misunderstanding of causal relation, akin to rain dances and superstitions.[21] There is some remarkable evidence that control illusion improves mental health. In one experiment, subjects were allowed to bet varying amounts of money, with varying expressions of confidence, on a chance device. Subjects who *did not* suffer from the illusion of control—they bet less money, less confidently—were more likely to be clinically depressed than others. (They are "sadder but wiser," Alloy and Abramson 1979.) Taylor and Brown (1988) review a wide range of evidence that suggests that unrealistic illusions of optimism and control, rather than realism, are associated with mental health.

Control illusion might be important in agency relationships and compensation. In the standard economic model of agency, output is assumed to be a function $v(e, \theta)$ of an agent's effort e and a random variable θ. The illusion of control implies that agents and employers overestimate the effect of effort (dv/de). In equilibrium, they will tie compensation too closely to output, and reward or punish more than is optimal.

In an experimental study of agency contracts, Berg (1995) found that control appears to matter in an interesting way. In her setting, agents choose an effort level. Output is correlated with effort and with an observable signal. In the "control" condition agents have control over the signal because their effort is correlated with the signal's value. In the "no-control" condition, their effort is not directly correlated with the signal (so they have no control over it); but the signal is informative to principals because the *joint* distribution of output and signal *is* correlated with effort.[22] Optimal contracts should use the signal to determine an agent's compensation in both conditions, since the signal is always informative about the agent's effort (when coupled with observed output).

Subjects did use the signal in the control condition, but not in the no-control condition. They acted as if penalizing an agent for outcomes (signal values) beyond her control was pointless or unfair. The result jibes with evidence from natural settings that shared-housing contracts and executive compensation does not depend strongly on variables that are uncontrollable but informative, as it should (Wolfson 1985; Antle and Smith 1986).

H. Judgment: Summary and New Directions

The studies reviewed in this section suggest a variety of heuristic rules people use to make complex judgments: they rely on what's available in memory, and similarity, to judge likelihoods and correlations; they are overconfident when they state probabilities of events or forecast numbers; their expectations are adaptive, responding to observed marketwide behavior rather than expressing a rational understanding of the market (but see Lucas 1986); iterated expectations—expectations about the expectations of others—are incorrectly influenced by memory; and people overestimate the influence of personal control.

Only a few of these findings have been replicated with the methods of experimental economists. More replications would test robustness of the findings.

Only a few of the replications took place within economic institutions (markets). The market experiments, on errors in Bayesian updating and iterated expectations, suggest markets reduce simple judgment errors but do not eliminate them. (Experience and expertise seem to reduce errors too.) More tests in which individual errors might be manifested in economic settings, including games or markets, would be useful. Tests could introduce institutional features such as overlapping generations, bankruptcy, access to capital, and advice markets, to carefully dissect precisely how markets reduce error.

III. Choice under Risk and Uncertainty

Most economists are familiar with theories that represent choices by numerical functions (e.g., a utility function). Sometimes functional forms are simply posited, but usually theorists search for primitive axioms on preferences that imply a specific functional form (e.g., expected utility). A less familiar form of choice theory is a process model that expresses the procedure a person uses to make choices, in an algorithm. (Expected utility maximization is an example of an algorithm.) Process models will generally not obey the axioms of utility theory, so the preferences they generate cannot be neatly summarized by a utility function.

Within economics there is a vast amount of work on axiomatic utility representations and a little work on process models. I will try to summarize both.

A. Expected Utility

During the development of statistical reasoning, it was taken for granted that proper choice meant maximizing expected monetary value. Provoked by the St. Petersburg paradox, in 1738 Daniel Bernoulli proposed maximizing some concave function of money (he suggested logarithmic), to reflect diminishing marginal value of dollars. Expected utility was born.

Almost two hundred years later von Neumann and Morgenstern (1944) showed, en route to game theory, that if preferences obeyed a particular set of axioms then those preferences could be represented by the expectation of some utility function.

The discovery of underlying axioms was important because it is easier to judge the intuitive plausibility of specific axioms than to judge the appeal of the utility representation they imply. (Establishing the axioms also laid the groundwork for modern theorists to weaken specific axioms and generate surprising alternative theories.) The utility representation can also discipline preferences by pointing out inconsistencies and violations of appealing properties (Strotz [1953, 392] gives an example). Expected utility also provided a natural way to establish "measurable utility" (cf. Zeuthen 1937), which was in great demand at the time.

1. Notation and a Diagram

Some notation is useful. Denote lotteries by X, Y, Z, and probabilistic mixtures of lotteries by $pX + (1 - p)Y$. (Specific outcomes are just degenerate lotteries with an outcome probability of one.) Denote X preferred to Y by $X > Y$, and X indifferent to Y by $X \sim Y$.

Predictions and data can be usefully displayed in the triangle diagram developed by Marschak (1950) and put to good use by Machina (1982) and others.[23] Fix three gambles X_L, X_M, X_H (the subscripts represent *low*, *medium*, *high*) such that $X_H > X_M$, $X_M > X_L$, and $X_H > X_L$. (In most experiments, the gambles are

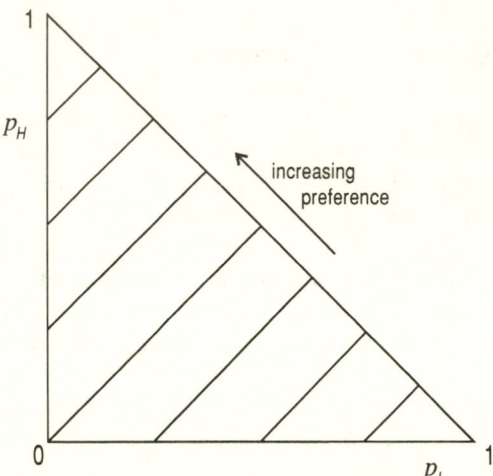

Figure 8.5. The Marschak-Machina triangle diagram (showing EU indifference curves). *Sources:* Marschak 1950; Machina 1982.

degenerate gambles with certain outcomes, such as 0, \$5, or \$10). Take the set of compound gambles which are probability mixtures in which each of the three gambles occurs with (objective) probabilities P_L, P_M, P_H. If we assume that two stage compound lotteries are equally preferred to single stage gambles with the two stage probabilities multiplied together (an important assumption we return to later) then this set of gambles can be represented in two dimensions, in $P_L - P_H$ space, as in Figure 8.5. (The third dimension, P_M, is implicit in the graph because $P_M = 1 - P_L - P_H$.) Since the sum of the probabilities cannot be greater than one, the set of feasible probabilities is a triangle bounded by the lines $P_L = 0$ (the left edge), $p_M = 0$ (the hypotenuse), and $p_H = 0$ (the lower edge). A utility theory makes a specific prediction about the shape of indifference curves that connect equally preferred gambles in the triangle diagrams.

2. The Axioms

The axiom system von Neumann and Morgenstern used to derive EU got refined by others (e.g., Marschak 1950; Herstein and Milnor 1953). The crucial axioms are as follows:

1. Ordering. Preferences are complete (either $X > Y$, $Y > X$, or $X \sim Y$) and transitive ($X > Y$, $Y > Z \Rightarrow X > Z$). Graphically, completeness guarantees that any two points in the triangle are either on the same indifference curve or on two different curves; transitivity guarantees that indifference curves do not cross *within* the triangle (e.g., Fishburn 1984).
2. Continuity. For all $X > Y > Z$, there exists a unique p such that $pX + (1 - p)Z \sim Y$. Continuity guarantees that there are no open spaces in the indifference map; uniqueness of p guarantees that indifference curves are not "thick."
3. Independence. If $X > Y$, then $pX + (1 - p)Z > pY + (1 - p)Z$ for all Z and $p \in (0, 1)$. Independence implies indifference curves are parallel straight lines.

The axioms imply that preferences can be represented by a numerical utility index, and the utility of a gamble is the expected utility of its possible outcomes. For a discrete lottery with several outcomes x_i, each with a p_i chance (denoted $\Sigma \, p_i X_i$) the functional form for EU is:

$$(2) \qquad\qquad U(\Sigma \, p_i X_i) = \Sigma \, p_i u(x_i)$$

In expected utility, probabilities of outcomes are assumed to be objective and known; choices are made under "risk." But in most natural settings probabilities are not well known or agreed upon; choices are made under "uncertainty." In subjective expected utility (SEU) (Ramsey 1931; Savage 1954), people take acts that yield consequences in uncertain states (see section III.F later). If act preferences obey several axioms like those in EU, preferences can be represented by an expected utility of consequences weighted by beliefs about states (their subjective, or "personal" probabilities). Anscombe and Aumann (1963) fused EU and SEU by allowing outcomes with objective probabilities ("roulette lotteries") *and* uncertain states with subjective probabilities ("horse lotteries"). Since most of the debate about EU holds for SEU too, and most experiments test only EU, I defer further discussion of SEU until below.

B. *Some History and Early Evidence*

The publication of von Neumann and Morgenstern's book in 1944 caused quite a stir. Economists had just become satisfied with ordinal utilities, unique only up to monotone transformations, and knew how much analysis could be done using preferences that reveal only ordinal utility (Hicks and Allen 1934[24]). Then, just as economists became convinced that cardinal utility was unnecessary, von Neumann and Morgenstern discovered a simple way to derive utility cardinally: $u(X) = p$ when X is judged to be indifferent to $pH + (1p)L$ (and $u(H) = 1$, $u(L) = 0$ arbitrarily).

1. Three Controversies

The first of three immediate controversies was mathematical. In their book, von Neumann and Morgenstern said nothing about an outcome set, indifference, or an independence axiom. In brief symposium papers in *Econometrica*, Samuelson (1952) and Malinvaud (1952) solved these mysteries and showed how the now-familiar independence axiom followed from von Neumann and Morgenstern's axioms. The second controversy was confusion over whether a von Neumann–Morgenstern utility function was a riskless value function too (à la Bernoulli), and could either be derived from preferences over lotteries *or* by directly comparing differences in lottery outcomes (Ellsberg 1954).[25] It's *not* a riskless value function.

The third, and greatest controversy came at a symposium in Paris in 1952, where Maurice Allais presented two papers[26] critical of the descriptive power of the theory of the "American school" (including Friedman, Savage, de Finetti,

Marschak, and others cited above) and introduced his famous paradoxes (Allais 1953). (More about them below.)

After von Neumann and Morgenstern's book was published, empirical tests began to trickle in. Excellent reviews of early work are Edwards (1954c, 1961a) and Luce and Suppes (1965). The collection edited by Thrall, Coombs, and Davis (1954) reflects the spirit of groping with the new models in an historically fascinating way.

2. Initial Tests

Preston and Baratta (1948) did the first test. They auctioned off chances to win x points with probability p, for 42 (x, p) pairs.[27] Bids were approximately linear in outcome x and nonlinear in probability p: Low-probability gambles ($p = .01, .05$) were sold for several times expected value, high-probability gambles for slightly less than expected value. (Indeed, the probability weight function they estimated, shown in Figure 8.6, looks strikingly like the "decision weight" function hypothesized thirty years later by Kahneman and Tversky [1979], but the interpretation is a bit different.[28]) The modern reader will suspect the quality of their evidence because the methods are casual and unorthodox, the sample is small, and hypotheses are not tested. But similar findings of nonlinear probability weights were reported by Griffith (1949) using racetrack betting (later, McGlothlin 1956), Attneave (1953) using guessing games, and Yaari (1965) using indifference judgments.

Mosteller and Nogee (1951) estimated utility curves by offering subjects complicated bets on three-die outcomes. Subjects played all bets they chose, and earned about $1 per hour. Since the same bets were offered repeatedly, certainty-equivalents were estimated by observing which bets subjects took half the time they were offered.

Student subjects were slightly risk averse; National Guardsmen were rather risk seeking.[29] Using utilities estimated from one sample to predict fresh choices, EU got about 70 percent right (compared to 50 percent right for expected value). There was strong evidence of nonlinear probability weighting by National Guardsmen (much as in Preston and Baratta's study) but not by students, as shown in Figure 8.6.

There were several complaints about Mosteller and Nogee's design. One was that the bets had complicated probabilities. Edwards began to test EU with an eye toward measuring subjective weights of probabilities, using simpler stimuli.[30] In choices among gambles that were played out he discovered consistent "probability preferences" (overweighting of specific probabilities), notably a preference for .5 (Edwards 1953, 1954a). Replication in a military context (hypothetical choices of attack targets) yielded slightly different results (Edwards 1954b). Nobody has found quite these probability preferences since. Edwards's data also show that probability weights for potential gains and losses differ, indicating a kind of "wishful thinking" (cf. Irwin 1953[31]).

In the early 1950s the psychologist Clyde Coombs began trying to measure subjective probability and utility simultaneously. (Edwards showed that this was

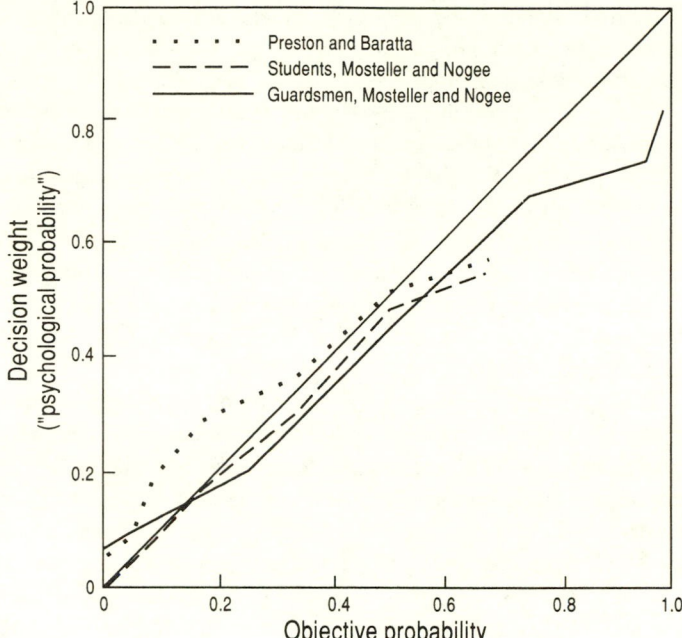

Figure 8.6. Empirical decision weights derived from two early studies. *Sources:* Preston and Baratta (1948); Mosteller and Nogee (1951).

important to do, since nonlinearities in subjective probability were observed when utility was assumed to be linear, but he did not show precisely how to do it.) Some of Coombs's early results were supportive of expected utility. But Coombs initially scorned gambles over money (thinking subjects could not avoid responding to numerical money values rather than psychological utilities), so it is impossible to compare the predictive accuracy of EU to the natural benchmark, expected value. Using money, Coombs and Komorita (1958) found that utilities did satisfy a kind of additivity.[32] Hurst and Siegel (1956) found that an "ordered metric" utility model outpredicted expected value, in an experiment where prisoners chose bets over cigarettes (a common setting for early psychology experiments).

Davidson, Suppes, and Siegel (1957) untangled probability weights and utility most carefully.[33] Their technique depends on finding an event that is perceived to be exactly as attractive to bet on as to bet against. After rejecting coins and regular dice, they chose a six-sided die with two nonsense syllables (ZEV and ZOV, shown by others to have few almost no mental associations) on three sides each. Since subjects did not care whether bets paid off on ZEV or ZOV, their subjective probabilities could be taken to equal .5. Using choices over bets on the special die, bounds on utilities could be determined while holding subjective probability fixed.[34]

The estimated utility functions were remarkably consistent across sessions. Twelve of fifteen subjects had nonlinear curves, typically showing risk preference for gains and risk aversion for losses. An experiment betting on one side of a four-sided die showed that people gave an event with objective probability .25 a decision weight of about .25.

In later studies Tversky (1967a,1967b) and others were able to operationalize the independence of probability and utility (the crucial feature of EU) as a kind of additivity that was easy to check experimentally. Tversky experimented with prisoners, playing gambles for money, candy, and cigarettes using the Becker, DeGroot, and Marschak (1964) procedure. Their choices generally obeyed additivity—i.e., independence—but showed either a utility for gambling (when riskless value functions and risky utility functions were compared) or subadditive weighted probabilities (see also Edwards 1962). Experiments by Wallsten (1971) supported independence too.

In the 1950s people also began exploring stochastic choice models (Debreu 1958; Luce 1958, 1959; Luce and Suppes 1965), which allow subjects to choose differently when facing the same choice several times. In these models a gamble's *probability* of being chosen out of a pair increases with its utility[35] (in EU, the probability increases in a step, from 0 to 1). Many experiments (e.g., Mosteller and Nogee 1951) were designed with stochastic choice models in mind, which meant long repeated sessions in which subjects made the same choice many times. (Wallsten [1971] had four subjects, each making choices for thirty hours.) This technique is largely out of fashion now except in some domains of mathematical and experimental psychology.

C. Mounting Evidence of EU Violation (1965–1986)

Except for some evidence that probabilities were weighted nonlinearly, and the simmering impact of Allais's paradoxes, EU emerged relatively unscathed from the first waves of tests. Elicitation yielded reasonable utility functions; expected utility predicted choices better than expected value did; independence of probability and utility was generally satisfied. Then evidence of paradox began to mount.

1. The Allais Paradoxes

Many felt Allais's examples used such extreme sums that they did little damage to everyday application of EU. But the examples were provocative and were replicated repeatedly in the 1960s and later with smaller sums (and paid subjects).

The most famous Allais example illustrates a "common consequence effect." Subjects choose between $A1$ and $A2$, where $A1 = (1$ million francs$)$ and $A2 = .10$ chance of 5 million francs, .89 chance of 1 million francs, and .01 chance of 0, denoted $A2 = (.10, 5$ million francs; $.89, 1$ million francs; $.01, 0)$. They also choose between $B1 = (.11, 1$ million francs; $.89, 0)$ and $B2 = (.10, 5$ million francs; $.90, 0)$. It is easy to show that the frequent choice pattern $A1 > A2$ and $B2 > B1$ violates expected utility. The choices are shown in a triangle diagram in Figure 8.7. EU requires that indifference curves be parallel lines. Since the chords connecting the choices $A1$-$A2$ and the choices $B1$-$B2$ are parallel, subjects with parallel indifference curves must choose either $A1$ and $B1$, or $A2$ and $B2$.

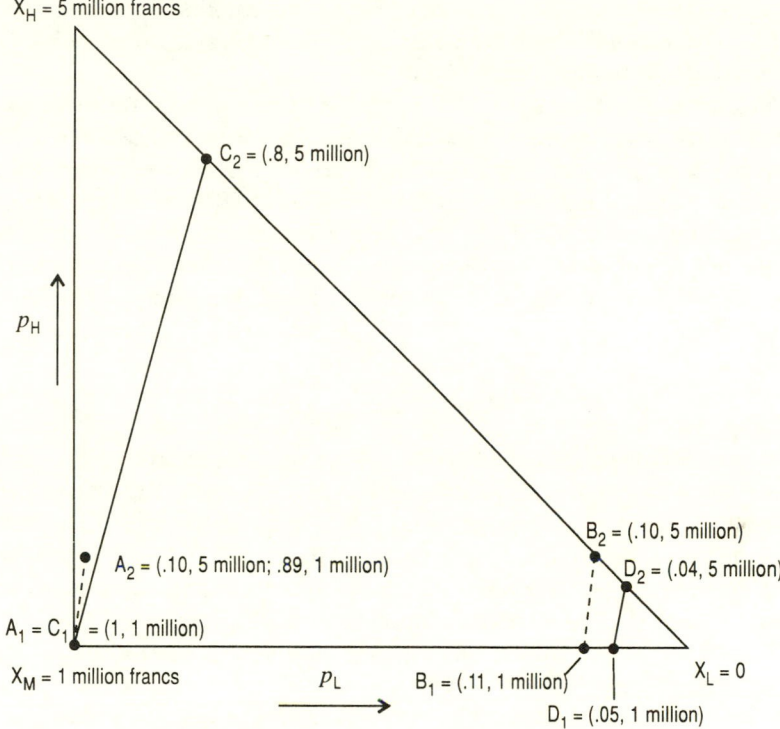

Figure 8.7. Allais's common consequence ($A_1 > A_2$, $B_2 > B_1$) and common ratio ($C_1 > C_2$, $D_2 > D_1$) effects.

The Allais paradox attacked EU in a fundamentally different way than the painstaking empirical tests of the 1950s did. The paradox circumvents elicitation of utilities and directly tests consistency required by the axioms, using two pairwise choices. Most recent tests have followed this route too. An important drawback is that the *degree* of inconsistency and differences among individuals are hard to measure with this method.

The first Allais replication, in a dissertation by MacCrimmon (1965), reported about 40 percent EU violations. Morrison (1967) used gambles over actual grade points, and found 30 percent violation. (Open discussion among subjects improved consistency with EU slightly.) Slovic and Tversky (1974) found 60 percent violation and presented subjects with written arguments pro and con EU. After reading both arguments, slightly *more* subjects switched their choices to become inconsistent with EU than became consistent.

MacCrimmon and Larsson (1979) reviewed several axiom systems and some empirical evidence, and reported new data testing robustness of the paradoxes. They found fairly robust common consequence effects with different parameters (though the effects are strongest for extreme payoffs and probabilities). They also studied a second "common ratio" problem due to Allais (see Figure 8.7): choose either $C1 = (1$ million francs) or $C2 = (.80, 5$ million francs; .20,0), and either $D1 = (.05, 1$ million francs; .95,0) or $D2 = (.04, 5$ million francs; .96,0). Notice that the payoffs in $C1$ and $C2$ have the same ratio of probabilities, $1/.8$, as in $D1$ and $D2$ ($.05/.04$); hence the term "common ratio effect." People often choose $C1 >$ $C2$ and $D2 > D1$, violating EU.

MacCrimmon and Larsson (1979) found the common ratio effect was less robust than the common consequence effect: A majority violated it with large amounts when the winning probabilities in the C gambles were much different than those in the D gambles, but the rate of violation fell to a third or less as the stakes and probability differential fell. Their evidence was the broadest indication that the proportion of subjects violating EU might vary dramatically with choice parameters, suggesting a direction for further tests and ripe opportunity for alternative theories.

2. Process Violations

As Allais's paradoxes continued to provoke debate, a second wave of psychological evidence began to rise, even more deeply critical of EU as a descriptive theory. In experiment after experiment, subjects appeared to use procedures or processes which were much simpler than EU (or even EV). For instance, in one study the value of gambles was better predicted by an *additive* combination of probability and outcomes ("risk dimensions") than by their product (Slovic and Lichtenstein 1968), even when subjects were told the gambles' expected values (Lichtenstein, Slovic, and Zink 1969).

In some experiments subjects compared the probabilities of winning in two lotteries, and their outcomes, in a way that led to intransitive cycles (Tversky 1969). Loomes, Starmer, and Sugden (1991) give a recent illustration. In their study, many subjects chose $(.6, £8) > (.3, £18)$ and $(1, £4) > (.6, £8)$ but also chose $(.3, £18) > (1, £4)$. (These cycles accounted for about 17 percent of the patterns resulting from the three pairwise choices.) An intuitive explanation is that these subjects chose the gamble with the larger probability as long as the payoffs were close, but chose $(.3, £18) > (1, £4)$ because the payoff £18 is sufficiently greater than £4.[36] In some experiments on multiattribute choice under certainty (finding an apartment), subjects were not told the attribute values for each choice, like the rent on apartment 1 or the size of apartment 3, unless they asked to see those values. (Forcing subjects to ask for information is a primitive way to measure their information search and draw inferences about their thinking processes.) Utility-maximizing subjects should ask to see all the information but most subjects did not (Payne 1976). Instead, subjects often chose a single attribute, such as rent, then eliminated all apartments with rent above some threshold and never asked to see the other attribute values for those eliminated apartments.[37]

3. Prospect Theory

Sweeping evidence and an alternative "prospect theory" was offered by Kahneman and Tversky (1979). They replicated Allais's common ratio paradox and introduced others. Prospect theory has four important elements: an editing stage in which rules either dictate choices or transform gambles before they are evaluated; choice of a reference point (from which gains and losses are measured); a riskless value function over gains and losses; and a function that weights probabilities nonlinearly and applies the resulting "decision weights" to outcomes, to evaluate gambles. Each element in the theory is derived from experimental evidence.

The idea that people value changes from a reference point, rather than wealth positions, is an old one (e.g., Markowitz 1952). It extends to the financial domain the widespread evidence that in making psychophysical judgments, like brightness and heat, people are more sensitive to changes from adapted levels than to absolute levels (Helson 1964).[38] As many people have noted, there is no axiom in EU implying that wealth positions are valued rather than changes in wealth, but it follows from the integration of assets and could be viewed as a basic principle of rational choice (like "description-invariance" and some other principles described later). Furthermore, it is easy to construct examples in which an EU maximizer will make consecutive choices which are suboptimal (compared to simultaneous choices) if she values changes rather than wealth positions (e.g., Tversky and Kahneman 1986, S255–256).

Kahneman and Tversky presented new data suggesting the value function has two important properties: (1) it is steeper around the reference point for losses than for gains ("loss-aversion")[39]; and (2) risk attitudes "reflect" around the reference point—the value function is concave for gains (risk averse) and convex for losses (risk seeking). Fishburn and Kochenberger (1979) also reviewed published studies showing reflection. Like the existence of a reference point, reflection can be interpreted as a psychophysical phenomenon, diminishing marginal sensitivity (marginal gains feel less and less good, marginal losses feel less and less bad).

The decision weight function in prospect theory is akin to earlier measurements of subjective weights of probabilities, by Edwards, Preston, Baratta, Mosteller, and Nogee, et al. The data suggest low probabilities are overweighted and high probabilities are underweighted, as shown in Figure 8.6, with a crossover point roughly between .1 and .3. Underweighting of high probabilities implies a "certainty effect," in which special weight is given to certain outcomes compared to slightly uncertain ones (i.e., the decision weight function is convex and steep near one).

4. Elicitation Biases

Many researchers discovered systematic biases in elicitation of utility functions. In the chained certainty-equivalence technique, a value of p is chosen and people are asked for X'. such that $X' \sim pH + (1 - p)L$ (H and L are high and low amounts), X'' such that $X'' \sim pH + (1 - p)X'$, etc. Karmarkar (1974) and McCord and de Neufville (1983) found that using higher values of p in a chained procedure yielded more concave utility functions. Hershey and Schoemaker (1980) found that substantially more subjects preferred a loss of $10 to a gamble (.01, −$1,000) when it was called an insurance premium than when it was unlabeled. (Lypny

[1991] corroborated this finding in an interesting experimental study of hedging.) Hershey and Schoemaker (1985) also found that utility functions elicited using probability and certainty equivalents were systematically different (cf. Johnson and Schkade 1989), violating the presumption that utility is invariant to the procedure used to elicit it (see section III.I later). Hershey, Kunreuther, and Schoemaker (1982) summarized many of these elicitation biases and others.

Wolf and Pohlman (1983) elicited parameters of a specific kind of utility function from a Treasury bill dealer, by eliciting certainty equivalents for several hypothetical gambles over his wealth. Then they estimated the same parameters using the dealer's actual bids (combined with the dealer's forecasts of the resale price of the bids). The utility functions derived in these two ways were similar in form (decreasing absolute, roughly constant proportional risk aversion) but the degree of risk aversion evident in bids was much larger than in the hypothetical choices. (His bids would have been four times as large as they actually were if he had bid according to the utility function derived from hypothetical choices.) The study is not conclusive evidence of a hypothetical-real difference, because that difference was confounded with the method by which utility was elicited (certainty-equivalents vs. actual bids). However, the difference suggests caution in extrapolating from a utility function measured one way, to its application in another domain.

D. Generalizations of Expected Utility and Recent Tests

By the mid-1970s or so, several developments had convinced many researchers that it was time to take alternatives to EU seriously. Important milestones were grudging acceptance of the power of Allais's examples; the ubiquity of EU violations in choices, process data, and elicitation procedures; the elegance of Kahneman and Tversky's batch of new paradoxes; and Machina's (1982) assimilation of some of the empirical evidence against EU and introduction of sophisticated tools for doing economic theory without the independence axiom.[40]

The anomalies motivated theorists to propose generalizations of expected utility in which axioms are weakened or replaced. Most of the theories weaken independence, but theorists have explored generalizations of other axioms too.[41]

Several recent empirical studies test these generalizations of EU. I will first describe some of the theories, then describe tests of various theories in some detail (see also Camerer 1992a). Table 8.1 summarizes several theories and their predictions about the shape of indifference curves in the Marschak-Machina triangle diagram.

Before reviewing the various theories, a note about the modern influence of Allais and his European colleagues is appropriate (see Hagen 1991). Allais (1979) himself felt there were two main sources of EU violations: a certainty effect, and the fact that EU expressed aversion to risk only indirectly, through curvature of the utility function. He proposed a "neo-Bernoullian" model that presumes a cardinal utility function of outcomes, obeys stochastic dominance, and assumes people choose gambles according to both the expectation *and* the variance of the gamble's utilities. (Higher expectation, and lower variance, are preferred.) Hagen (1969) proposed a similar model in which positive skewness of utility is preferred as well.

These contributions got relatively little attention in the United States and England, for both sociological and scientific reasons. Their articles are bluntly critical of EU (and of some other alternative theories); I suspect many American readers are put off by the critical tone. Most of the work is published in book chapters or in journals like *Theory and Decision* and *Journal of Economic Psychology*, which are more widely read in Europe than in the United States. Most importantly, the Allais and Hagen formulations have free functions that seem to be especially difficult to measure and test. For example, one cannot easily concoct a paradox like Allais's to test Allais's own theory, by using pairwise choices that hold constant the influence of statistical moments of the *utility* of gambles, without knowing the underlying utility function. (And the utility function cannot be easily measured using certainty-equivalents, as in EU, because choices are assumed to depend on expectation *and* on higher moments.)

1. Predictions of Generalized EU Theories

Weighted utility theory (Chew and MacCrimmon 1979a; Chew 1983) assumes a weakened form of independence. As above, denote gambles by capital letters (X, Y, Z), compound gambles by $pX + (1 - p)Z$, and preference for X over Y by $X >$. Their axiom is:

Weak Independence. If $X > Y$, then for all p in $(0, 1)$ there exists a unique q in $(0, 1)$ such that $pX + (1 - p)Z > qY + (1 - q)Z$ for all Z.

Weak independence in combination with the other EU axioms implies a representation of the form

$$(3) \qquad U(\Sigma p_i x_i) = \frac{\Sigma p_i w(x_i) u(x_i)}{\Sigma p_i w(x_i)}$$

In weighted utility, indifference curves are straight lines that meet at a point outside the triangle. (If $w(X_M) < 1$, for instance, in the domain of three outcome gambles where X_M denotes the middle outcome, then the curves will look like those in Figure 8.8.)

There is a generalization of weighted utility called "skew-symmetric bilinear" (SSB) utility theory (Fishburn 1982, 1983, 1988). In SSB utility, preferences are represented by a function of *both* lotteries, $\phi(X, Y)$. $X > Y$ if and only if $\phi(X, Y) > 0$; $\phi(X, Y) = 0$ implies $X \sim Y$.

SSB results from replacing EU with a weakened form of independence called "symmetry," adding a betweenness axiom (see below), retaining completeness and continuity, and abandoning transitivity. When transitivity is added back in, surprisingly, SSB reduces to weighted utility.

Regret theory (Bell 1982; Loomes and Sugden 1982, 1987a) generalizes SSB further by extending it to choices between lotteries with correlated outcomes

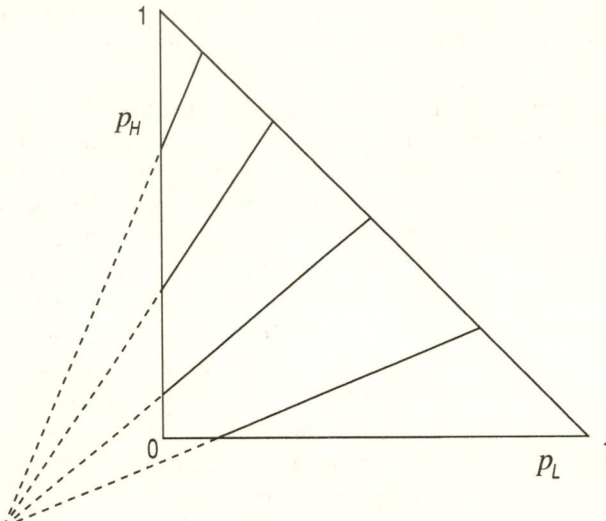

Figure 8.8. Indifference
curves that fan out.

(i.e., where the outcome from one lottery depends statistically on what the other lottery's outcome was). Some tests are described in section III.H.2 below.

Implicit EU. A weakened form of SSB or weighted utility, called "implicit weighted utility" by Chew (1989), or "implicit EU" by Dekel (1986), depends on a weakened form of independence called "betweenness."

> Betweenness. If $X > Y$, then $X > pX + (1 - p)Y > Y$ for all p in (0, 1) (or $X \sim Y$ implies $X \sim pX + (1 - p)Y \sim Y$ for all p in [0, 1]).

Betweenness implies neutrality toward randomization among equally-good outcomes. It yields an implicit utility representation of the form

$$(4) \qquad\qquad U^* = U(\Sigma\, p_i x_i) = \Sigma\, p_i u(x_i, U^*)$$

The utility function $u(x_i, U^*)$ denotes the utility of an outcome x_i, but the utility function used to value x_i depends on U^*. (Utility is therefore defined implicitly: U^* is an expected utility that is calculated using a utility function that depends on U^*.) In implicit utility, indifference curves are straight lines (which are positively-sloped, and don't cross over), but they are not necessarily parallel as in EU.

Betweenness can be violated in either of two ways. If preferences are strictly "quasi-convex," then $X \sim Y$ implies $X > pX + (1 - p)Y$ (people are averse to randomization). If preferences are strictly "quasi-concave," then $X \sim Y$ implies $pX + (1 - p)Y > X$ (people prefer randomization). In the triangle diagram, quasi-convex (-concave) preferences imply concave (convex) indifference curves.

Chew, Epstein, and Segal (1991) propose a weakened form of betweenness, called "mixture symmetry": If $X \sim Y$ then $pX + (1 - p)Y \sim (1 - p)X + pY$. Together with other axioms, mixture symmetry implies that preferences switch from quasi-convex to quasi-concave, or vice versa, as gambles improve (in the sense of stochastic dominance). (Curves then switch from concave to convex, or vice versa, as one moves northwest in the triangle diagram.)

In weighted utility theory, indifference curves may "fan out," getting steeper as one moves from the lower right-hand corner (or southeast) to the upper left-hand corner (or northwest), as in Figure 8.8. (They can also "fan in," getting less steep to the northwest.) Steeper indifference curves correspond to more risk averse behavior: the steeper the curve, the more p_H a person demands in order to accept a unit increase in p_L. Therefore, fanning out occurs if people are more risk averse toward gambles that are better (in the sense of stochastic dominance).[42] Machina (1982) showed that several empirical anomalies could be explained by the *fanning out* hypothesis (without requiring the further assumptions of weighted utility theory).

Gul (1991) proposes a theory incorporating *disappointment*. The intuition is that the probabilities of outcomes below and above a gamble's certainty-equivalent are weighted differently to reflect the additional satisfaction from having "beaten the odds," or unhappiness from having lost to them. His theory is a special case of implicit EU that satisfies betweenness and allows curves to fan in for better gambles (in the northwest part of the triangle) and fan out for worse gambles (in the southeast).

In *expected utility with rank-dependent probability weights* cumulative probabilities are weighted, and the utilities of outcomes are weighted by the differential in the weighted cumulative probability (Quiggin 1982; Segal 1987b, 1989; Yaari 1987; Green and Jullien 1988). (This procedure ensures that stochastic dominance is never violated, which can happen if probabilities are weighted separately.) The weight of an outcome depends on its probability and its rank order in the set of possible outcomes. Suppose we rank outcomes from high to low, $x_1 > x_2 > \ldots > x_n$. Then the functional form for rank-dependent utility is

$$(5) \qquad U(\Sigma p_i x_i) = \sum_{i=1}^{n} u(x_i) \left[g(p_1 + p_2 + \ldots p_i) - g(p_1 + p_2 + \ldots p_{i-1}) \right]$$

Note that if $g(p) = p$, the bracketed expression reduces to p_i, and equation (5) reduces to EU. In rank-dependent theory, indifference curves will not be straight lines unless the probability transformation function $g(p) = p$; otherwise, they are curved in a way which depends on $g(p)$ (Roell 1987; Camerer 1989a). A convex $g(p)$ expresses risk aversion in a novel way, by underweighting the probabilities of the highest-ranked outcomes and (since weights sum to one) overweighting the lowest-ranked outcomes; similarly, concave $g(p)$ expresses risk preference.

Lottery-dependent utility theory (Becker and Sarin 1987) assumes only stochastic dominance, ordering, and continuity. The theory is quite general:

$$(6) \qquad U(\Sigma p_i x_i) = \Sigma p_i u(x_i, c_F)$$

where $c_F = \Sigma h(x_i) p_i$. Becker and Sarin (1987) suggest an exponential form for the utility function $u(x_i, c_F)$ which makes the theory more precise and useful. Indifference curves fan out in the exponential form and lottery-dependent preferences are quasi-convex (curves are concave) if $h(x)$ is concave (Camerer 1989a, 73).

In *prospect theory* (Kahneman and Tversky 1979), indifference curves may vary with the choice of reference point, but for testing purposes it is useful to consider a variant of prospect theory which assumes that the reference point is current wealth. Then the value of a gamble is simply

$$(7) \qquad\qquad V(p_1 x_1 + p_2 x_2) = \pi(p_1)v(x_1) + \pi(p_2)v(x_2)$$

In general, $p_1 + p_2 \le 1$ (and $1 - p_1 - p_2$ is the probability of getting nothing). If $p_1 + p_2 = 1$ and both x_i have the same sign, then the value is

$$(7') \quad V(p_1 x_1 + p_2 x_2) = v(x_1) + \pi(p_2)(v(x_2) - v(x_1)) = (1 - \pi(p_2))v(x_1) + \pi(p_2)v(x_2)$$

The shape of the indifference curves determined by equations (7) and (7') depends on $\pi(p)$, but they will certainly be nonlinear unless $\pi(p) = p$. If $\pi(p)$ is most nonlinear near 0 and 1 (as originally proposed by Kahneman and Tversky) the curves will change slope and shape dramatically at the edges. As a result, choices between gambles inside the triangle will violate EU less than choices involving gambles on the edges.

Prospect theory was originally restricted to gambles with one or two nonzero outcomes. In "cumulative prospect theory," Tversky and Kahneman (1992) extend the theory to gambles with many outcomes (including continuous distributions) using a rank dependent form like equation (5) (cf. Starmer and Sugden 1989a, 99–100). The difference is that, in their formulation, probabilities of gains and losses can be weighted differently. They also suggest a parsimonious, one parameter probability weighting function[43]:

$$(8) \qquad\qquad g(p) = p^\gamma/(p^\gamma + (1 - p)^\gamma)^{1/\gamma}$$

Other Theories

Handa (1977) proposed a precursor to prospect theory in which probabilities were weighted nonlinearly (see, much earlier, Edwards 1954c). Karmarkar (1978) and Viscusi (1989) propose specific functional forms for probability weights $\pi(p)$. Leland (1991) suggests an "approximate" EU in which people lump outcomes (and possibly probabilities) into discrete categories, making their utility functions discontinuous (cf. Rubinstein 1988). One special feature of this approach is that it allows convergence to EU with experience, since experience permits finer-grained categorization of outcomes (cf. Friedman 1989).

2. Empirical Studies Using Pairwise Choices

There are many recent studies using pairs of choices to test EU and its generalizations. Each of the theories described above predicts different indifference curve shapes in some part of the triangle. The predictions are summarized in Table 8.1. By choosing pairs carefully from throughout the triangle, each theory can be tested against the others. The first study of this kind was done by Chew and Waller (1986). I will describe their design because it is typical and raises basic methodological questions.

Table 8.1. Predictions of Competing Theories about Properties of Indifference Curves

Theory	Functional Form for U*		Restrictions	Properties of Curves			
	Continuous, $U^*(F(x))$	Discrete, $U^*(\Sigma p_i x_i)$		Straight Lines?	Fanning Out?	Fanning In?	Miscellaneous
Expected utility	$\int u(x)dF(x)$	$\Sigma p_i u(x_i)$		Yes	No	No	Curves parallel
Weighted utility	$\dfrac{\int u(x)w(x)dF(x)}{\int w(x)dF(x)}$	$\dfrac{\Sigma p_i w(x_i)u(x_i)}{\Sigma p_i w(x_i)}$	$w(X_m)<1$ $w(X_m)>1$	Yes Yes	Yes No	No Yes	Curves meet in a point
Implicit expected utility	$\int u(x,U^*)dF(x)$	$\Sigma p_i u(x_i,U^*)$		Yes	Maybe	Maybe	Only testable property is betweenness
Fanning-out hypothesis	$\dfrac{-U''(x;F)}{U'(x;F)} \geq \dfrac{-U''(x;G)}{U'(x;G)}$ if $F(x) \leq G(x)$ for all x			Maybe	Yes	No	Movements to northwest cause steeper slopes
Lottery-dependent utility	$\int u(x,c_F)dF(x)$ $c_F = \int h(x)dF(x)$	$\Sigma p_i u(x_i,c_F)$ $c_F = \Sigma h(x_i)p_i$	h concave h convex	No No	Yes Yes	No No	Curves concave Curves convex
Prospect		$\pi(p_x)v(x) + \pi(p_y)v(y)$ $p_x + p_y < 1$ or $x < 0 < y$ $(1 - \pi(p_y))v(x) + \pi(p_y)v(y)$ $p_x + p_y = 1$ and $0 < x < y$ or $y < x < 0$		No	Lower edge	Left edge, hypotenuse	Parallel along $P_H = (1 - P_L)/2$
Rank-dependent utility	$\int u(x)d[g(F(x))]$	$\displaystyle\sum_{i=1}^{n} u(x_i)[g(\sum_{j=1}^{i} p_j) - g(\sum_{j=1}^{i-1} p_j)]$	g concave g convex	No No	Lower edge Left edge	Left edge Lower edge	Parallel along hypotenuse

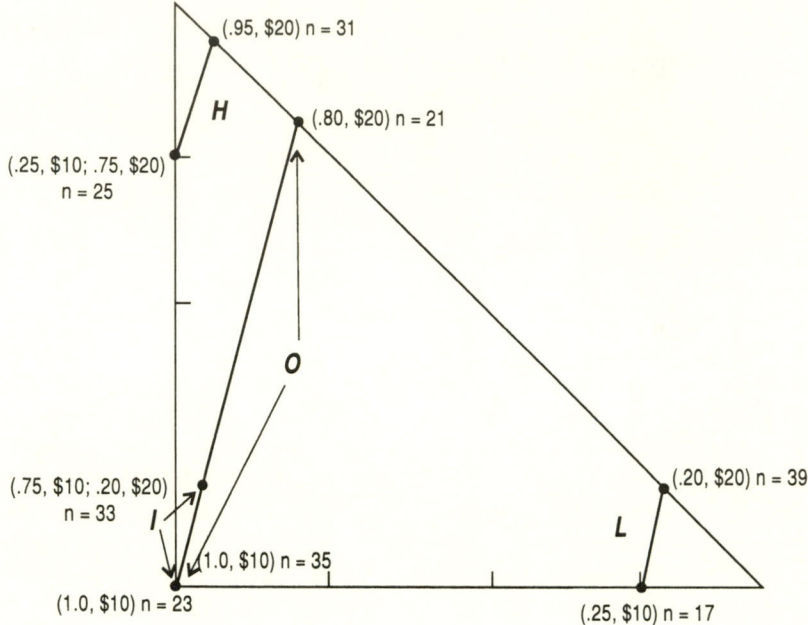

Figure 8.9. Chew and Waller's *HILO* structure and results. *O, I, L,* and *H* denote the four gamble pairs used in their experiment. The number of subjects (total 56) choosing each gamble in each pair is shown in parentheses. Dollar amounts are in thousands. *Source:* Chew and Waller 1986.

Chew and Waller used an ingenious, compact set of choices (originally developed by Chew and MacCrimmon 1979b) called the "*HILO* structure." Figure 8.9 shows one set of four *HILO* pairs they used (their context 2b), drawn in a triangle diagram. The three outcomes in the gambles, in thousands, are X_H = \$20, X_M = \$10, and X_L = 0. Every subject chose one gamble from each of the four pairs, four choices in all.

The pairs were picked to efficiently detect several different effects with only four choices: the common ratio effect (pairs *O-L* and *O-H*), the common consequence effect (*I-L* and *I-H*), and a test of the betweenness axiom (*I-O*). Figure 8.9 shows the number of subjects (out of fifty-six) who chose the gambles in each pair. Subjects were not allowed to express indifference and didn't play any gambles.

The common ratio effect occurred because thirty-five subjects chose risk-aversely in the *O* pair (thirty-five picked (1.0,\$10) and twenty-one picked (.80,\$20)) but only seventeen did so in the *L* pair. A weak common consequence effect occurs because twenty-three subjects chose risk aversely in the *I* pair and seventeen did in the *L* pair.

The fanning out hypothesis predicts that people become more risk averse, and indifference curves fan out, with movement toward the northwest corner. The prediction appears false in the Chew and Waller data: fewer subjects chose risk aversely in the H pair (twenty-five) than in the O pair (thirty-five),[44] and about the same number chose risk aversely in the I pair (twenty-three).

Pairs I and O test whether the betweenness axiom holds (since the inner gamble (.75,$10; .20,$20) in pair I is a probability mixture of the outer gambles (1.0,$10) and (.80,$20).) Betweenness is violated because 35 subjects chose (1.0,$10) in the O pair but only 23 chose it in the I pair.

A Methodological Digression:
Between- vs. Within-Subjects Analysis

Psychologists call the sort of analysis expressed by Figure 8.9 "between subjects": the fractions of subjects behaving in a particular way in two different settings are compared (but the subjects may be different in the two settings). In a "within subjects" analysis, the fact that a single subject made choices in two or more settings is exploited. Within-subjects tests are always more statistically powerful, but they run a certain risk: presenting several stimuli to a single subject could conceivably induce her to behave more consistently than she would if she saw the stimuli one at a time. For example, in tests of whether two different descriptions of an equivalent problem elicit the same choices ("framing effects"), presenting the two problems one after the other might cause a subject who recognizes the equivalence to guess that the experiment tests for consistency, and respond accordingly. (The same issue arises in some of the judgment research reported in section II above.[45])

Many people think within-subjects analysis is the only proper analysis in choice experiments, because EU requires consistency of individual preferences. But, of course, between-subjects tests are equally legitimate (though less powerful) if the subjects in different groups can be presumed to have the same distribution of tastes, up to sampling error, because they were drawn from a single population.

Chew and Waller (1986) did a within-subjects analysis by counting how many subjects exhibited a particular pattern across choices. For instance, in the O and L pairs (the common ratio test) twelve subjects chose the less risky gamble in both pairs and sixteen subjects chose the more risky gamble in both pairs, so twenty-eight of the fifty-six subjects satisfied EU. Of the twenty-eight who chose *incon*-sistently, twenty-three (82 percent) chose risk aversely in O and risk preferringly in L, manifesting the standard common-ratio pattern.

Another Methodological Digression:
Judging Violation Rates

Is a 50 percent rate of EU violation (twenty-eight of fifty-six chose inconsistently) large or small? If we allow random error in expression of preferences, then the appropriate benchmark for violation rates should be the fraction of people who switch their choices when making *the same choice* twice (called "reliability" in psychometrics).[46] Chew and Waller did not measure the fraction of random switching but other studies suggest that percentage is about 25 to 35 percent for choices like these (Starmer and Sugden 1987b; Camerer 1989a). Using that benchmark, a z-test shows that the fraction of inconsistent subjects in the O-L pairs (28/56) is much too high to be a chance deviation from random switching. Another way to test whether violations are systematic is to compare the fraction of inconsistencies in both directions. In the O-L pairs, twenty-three of twenty-eight switched in one direction and five in another, an asymmetry unlikely to occur by chance.

Of course, the violation rate is likely to be sensitive to the gamble pair chosen. Two similar gambles will have a violation rate close to 50 percent. That simply means that if your goal is to reject theories, using such a pair of gambles will require a large sample to detect true systematic violation statistically.

A Third Methodological Digression: Incentives

In Chew and Waller's study, choices were entirely hypothetical. In most other studies subjects played one of the gambles they chose.[47] The common procedure of randomly choosing one of several gambles to play has been tested by Camerer (1989a, 82) and Starmer and Sugden (1991a): it elicits roughly the same preferences as when subjects make only one choice (and play the gamble they picked).

Several studies have compared hypothetical choices with real choices (in which one choice was played). They found either no effect or a slight tendency for playing gambles to yield more risk aversion (Edwards 1953; Becker, DeGroot, and Marschak 1963; Camerer 1989a; Battalio, Kagel, and Jiranyakul 1990; Hogarth and Einhorn 1990; Schoemaker 1990; cf. Slovic 1969).

Harrison (1990) reported the only evidence that actually playing a gamble substantially reduced the rate of EU violations (Battalio et al. [1990] and Camerer [1989a] report no such effects). In his common-ratio experiment, seven of twenty subjects violated EU when choices were hypothetical and three of twenty (different) subjects violated EU when choices were real. The difference is not significant at conventional levels ($p = .15$).

In a contrasting study, Kachelmeier and Shehata (1992) elicited certainty-equivalents from Chinese students (using the BDM procedure), for gambles with high or low outcomes. Subjects played every gamble, and payoffs ranged from 1 to 10 yuan, which are substantial amounts for students who spend about 60 yuan per month. Certainty-equivalents exhibited dramatic overweighting of low probabilities at both high and low payoff levels (e.g., the certainty equivalent of (p, X) was about twice pX for $p = .05$ or $.10$); similar patterns were observed with Canadian students playing hypothetical gambles. Risk aversion among the Chinese students was also greater for high payoffs than for low payoffs. Thus, the overweighting of low probability observed in so many experiments (which leads to many EU violations) is present when very large payoffs are used, but large payoffs also induce some differences in risk aversion.

In experiments where gambles are played, the amount of expected value (EV) subjects lose by violating EU is usually small. Unfortunately, there is no simple way to design experiments that have large expected value penalties for violating

EU but that can also sharply distinguish EU from competing theories (including EV). Since the effect of dominant payments is difficult to determine empirically, a pragmatic way to approach the problem is to spell out and test whatever theory or intuition underlies the claim that higher payoffs would reduce EU violations (such as Smith and Walker's [1993] analysis of "decision cost"). The intuition seems to be that subjects will calculate more, think harder, or somehow see the appeal of axioms when they are faced with larger stakes. But in experiments where subjects were told expected values (Lichtenstein, Slovic, and Zink 1969) or given written arguments explaining the independence axiom—making it easy for them to think harder—EU violations were not reduced (Slovic and Tversky 1974). Indeed, some studies suggest that the main effect of paying subjects is a reduction in variance of their responses, which *increases* the statistical significance of EU violations (Harless and Camerer 1994).

The effect of paying subjects is likely to depend on the task they perform. In many domains, paid subjects probably *do* exert extra mental effort, which improves their performance, but in my view choice over money gambles is *not* likely to be a domain in which effort will improve adherence to rational axioms. Subjects with well-formed preferences are likely to express them truthfully, whether they are paid or not. If their preferences are not well formed, it seems unlikely that subjects would be both sophisticated and lazy enough to make an expected utility calculation when they are paid, but not when choices are hypothetical. (Furthermore, if payment does induce more formal reasoning, it is likely to be expected *value* maximization, not EU maximization.)

Other Studies of Common Consequence and Common Ratio Effects

Chew and Waller's data replicate the common ratio and common consequence effects in the southeast corner, but they show little fanning out in the northwest corner. Camerer (1989a) found the same general pattern. In a replication using the Allais payoffs, Conlisk (1989) found fanning *in* in the northwest corner and Prelec (1990) found dramatic fanning *in* (55 percent of subjects) close to the lower edge and southeast corner. (Their subjects did not play gambles.)

Starmer and Sugden (1989a,1989b) studied a wide variety of common ratio problems. The rate of EU violations was only significant in three of fifteen pairs. They found strong fanning out along the lower edge, and some fanning in along the left edge. Starmer (in press) found common consequence effects, showing fanning *in* rather than the more typical fanning out, especially along the lower edge.

Battalio, Kagel, and Jiranyakul (1990) observed fanning in along the lower edge, in common ratio problems where gambles had strictly positive payoffs. Fanning in also appeared in the northwest corner with gains and the southeast corner with losses.

The patterns in these studies are complicated. Most of the differences in results can probably be traced to small differences in the particular gambles being studied. It would be useful to have a composite picture of the indifference curves revealed by all the studies, but nobody knows how to create such a composite (but see Harless and Camerer 1994, discussed below). It does seem that any composite picture is likely to cast doubt on the generality of fanning out. For example, the fanning out that is observed in the Allais problems along the lower edge of the triangle is generally reduced or reversed—sometimes fanning in occurs—along the left edge. The fanning out hypothesis was suggested by Machina (1982) to explain evidence that had come primarily from the lower right corner of the triangle (e.g., the Allais paradoxes illustrated in Figure 8.7). His inference from those data to the entire triangle was ingenious, but apparently not quite right.

Two classes of theories can account for most of the mixed fanning evidence from common ratio and common consequence studies. One class of theories posits mixtures of fanning in and fanning out (Neilson in press) or derives them from axioms (Gul [1991], which adds only one parameter to EU). Another class weights probabilities nonlinearly, which generates indifference curves that fan out or in depending on the weighting function.

Evidence of Betweenness Violation

Camerer and Ho (1994) reviewed nine studies in which the betweenness axiom was tested. (Tests of betweenness efficiently test several theories that assume it— weighted and implicit EU, disappointment, SSB, and regret—in one fell swoop.) In these studies, betweenness is frequently violated but the pattern of violations is complicated. Gambles with gains generally show quasi-convexity (concave indifference curves) except close to the lower and left edges (cf. Bernasconi 1994); loss gambles show the opposite. The fact that curvature reflects for gains and losses implies people seem to weight gain and loss probabilities differently (see Tversky and Kahneman 1992). Evans (1992) found comparable degrees of betweenness violation when gamble valuations were elicited with the BDM procedure, and with second- and fifth-price sealed-bid auctions (see chapter 7).

We fitted data from all the studies to a variant of EU with nonlinear rank-dependent probability weights (using the weighting function (8)). The maximum-likelihood coefficient estimates were around $\gamma = .60$, which implies a nonlinear weighting roughly like that pictured in Figure 8.6, with probabilities under .30 overweighted and probabilities above .30 underweighted. The data therefore reject betweenness (which requires $\gamma = 1$) and corroborate both guesses from the earliest studies from the 1940s and sharper estimates from studies almost fifty years later (e.g., Tversky and Kahneman [1992] estimate $\gamma = .61$ for gains and $\gamma = .69$ for losses). But the very latest evidence (Wu 1994) shows some violations of the rank-dependent approach which should renew interest in prechoice "editing" rules.

The most prominent theory that can account for the mixed fanning reported in the last section, Gul's (1991) disappointment theory, assumes betweenness. The fact that betweenness is often violated casts doubt on Gul's theory and leaves the nonlinear-weighting theories as the best available account of *both* complex fanning out patterns and betweenness violation.

Evidence of Better Conformity to EU Inside the Triangle

One of the most interesting and robust effects in the new wave of tests is that EU violations are much smaller (though still statistically significant) when subjects choose between gambles that all lie inside the triangle. Conlisk (1989), Gigliotti and Sopher (1990), Camerer (1992b), and Harless (1992b) all discovered this phenomenon independently.

The shrinkage of EU violations inside the triangle does not vindicate EU. Inside gambles have probabilities p_L, p_M, and p_H which are all nonzero; edge gambles have at least one of the three probabilities equal to zero. The fact that violations disappear when moving from the edge of the triangle inside suggests they are probably due to nonlinear weighting of probabilities near zero (as the rank-dependent weighting theories and prospect theory predict).[48] Much as Newtonian mechanics is an adequate approximation at low velocities, but relativistic mechanisms is accurate at all velocities, the linear weighting of probabilities imposed by EU may be an adequate approximation when outcome probabilities are not too low or high. Morgenstern (1979) drew the analogy with mechanics, and anticipated such a conclusion: "[T]he domain of our axioms on utility theory is also restricted. . . . For example, the probabilities used must be within certain plausible ranges and not go to .01 or even less to .001, then be compared to other equally tiny numbers such as .02, etc." (178).

Whether nonlinear weighting of low probabilities affect choices among natural gambles with many outcomes is a fundamental empirical question. In any case, theories that assume nonlinear probability weights are here to stay: they are the only theories that can explain evidence of mixed fanning, violation of betweenness, *and* approximate EU maximization inside the triangle.

Informal and Formal Summaries of Evidence

There are at least two ways to summarize all this evidence on experimental testing of various utility theories. Camerer (1992a) summarizes the evidence informally in a list of "stylized facts." Many of the facts can be expressed as shapes of indifference curves in the Marschak-Machina triangle. The crucial facts appear to be that indifference curves vary in (local) slope from risk averse to risk seeking; indifference curves fan in and out in a systematic, complex pattern (strict fanning out can be rejected); betweeness violations imply that indifference curves are not straight; indifference curves are more nearly parallel inside the triangle than on the interior; and curves for gains and losses reflect around a 45 degree line.

The right kind of nonlinear probability weighting function can have all these properties. Figure 8.10 shows curves plotted by Tversky and Kahneman (1992), for gambles over gains and losses, for cumulative prospect theory using their one parameter weighting function. The dotted line shows pairs with equal expected value. The plotted indifference curves have all the properties mentioned in the previous paragraph: They are sometimes flatter (more risk preferring) and sometimes steeper (more risk averse); they both fan in and out; they are not straight; they are most curved near the triangle boundaries; and they reflect from gains (panel a of Figure 8.10) to losses (panel b).

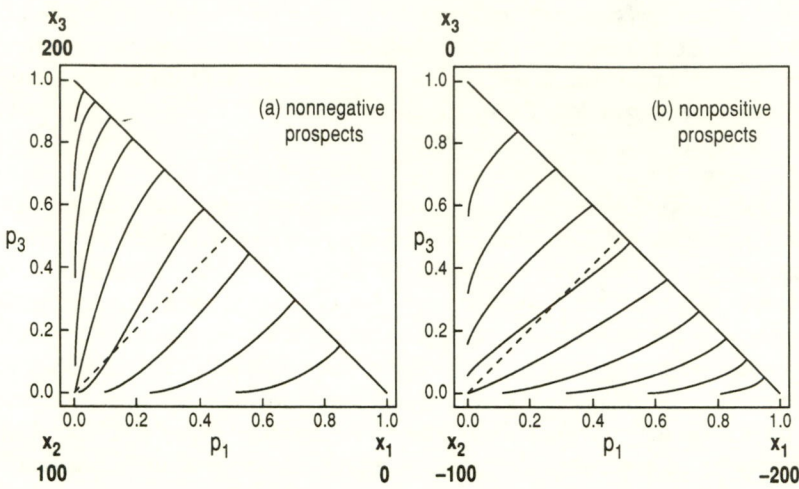

Figure 8.10. Empirically derived indifference curves of cumulative prospect theory for gambles over (a) gains and (b) losses. *Sources:* Tversky and Kahneman 1992.

A Statistical Summary

Harless and Camerer (1994) summarize the evidence more formally. In studies with several pairwise choices, like those discussed above, theories are usually judged by what fraction of the choice patterns they predict correctly. For example, in the Chew and Waller (1986) study people made one choice from each of four pairs. There are $2^4 = 16$ possible patterns of choices. EU predicts only two of those patterns, and excludes fourteen of them. Most statistical tests compare the percentage of patterns that are predicted—two of sixteen in the EU example, or 12.5 percent—with the percentage of subjects actually choosing those patterns (25 percent in their data) and perform some hypothesis test. Harless and I show that this method ignores useful information. If one adds the possibility that people choose erroneously with some probability, then EU predicts that some of the fourteen excluded patterns are more likely than others. Considering all fourteen patterns equally likely mistakes ignores information in the relative frequency of the fourteen patterns that could be used to judge the theory.

We developed a method that uses all the data and generates a chi-squared statistic testing each of several alternative theories. Since chi-squared statistics can be added across independent experiments, the results of several studies can be easily aggregated using our method. The result is an "efficient frontier" of theories that are most accurate (best-fitting), given the number of patterns they allow (most parsimonious). A compilation of twenty-three data sets, from a total of 2,000 subjects making 8,000 choices, shows that the following theories are on the efficient frontier: mixed fanning, prospect theory, EU, and EV.

The difference between boundary gambles and interior gambles emerges strikingly from the compiled data. For interior gambles, there is a broad range of parsimony-accuracy tradeoffs for which EU is the best theory. But for boundary gambles, EU is *never* preferred. (If one is willing to trade off enormous predictive accuracy for parsimony, preferring EU to a generalization, then one should go even further and choose EV over EU.)

A Field Observation and Experiment

Marshall, Richard, and Zarkin (1992) studied an interesting field situation. They begin with a fact: in 1983 in the United States, twice as many accidents (per trip) occurred during evening rush hours (4–7 P.M.) than occurred during morning rush hours (7–10 A.M.). The choice of whether to wear a seat belt is a choice between two risky accident distributions: wearing a seat belt is, roughly speaking, a risk-averse choice: it reduces the probability of having a serious accident but, curiously, slightly *raises* the probability of having *some* kind of accident. Since accident rates are lower in the morning, the safer morning choice is a better pair of gambles than the evening choice (in the sense of stochastic dominance), so the fanning out hypothesis predicts that people will behave more risk-aversely—wearing their seat belts—in the morning than in the evening. They do: more people wear seat belts in the morning than in the afternoon (15.4 percent vs. 13.9 percent). Marshall et al. show that observations of increased seat belt use in the morning, when accident rates are lower, reject the EU hypothesis and support fanning out.

Their conclusion is debatable because strong, unrealistic assumptions must be made to conduct the statistical tests and an experiment with students, in which choices and accident rates were presented abstractly, did not corroborate the field observation. (Students overwhelmingly made the choice corresponding to wearing seat belts in both time periods.) Nonetheless, their method is a unique illustration of how field data could test alternative choice theories.

Cicchetti and Dubin (1994) did a similar study (but with no experimental component): they fit an EU model to consumer decisions to buy insurance against the cost of repairing wires in their phones. The EU model fits reasonably well. They cannot reject the hypothesis that consumers estimate repair probability accurately, but the data also show some modest support for nonlinear weighting of probabilities.[49]

3. Empirical Studies Measuring Indifference Curves

The most direct approach to testing generalized utility theories through their predictions about the shape of indifference curves, is by directly assessing indifference curves. Hey and Strazzera (1989) estimated curves by eliciting a set of equally good gambles, using a series of "lottery-equivalent" (McCord and De Neufville 1986) indifference judgments.[50] Some curves crossed (reflecting intransitivity) or had negative slopes (reflecting stochastic dominance violations). Lines fit to the elicited curves generally obeyed EU (parallelism could not be rejected), but the statistical power to reject EU was limited by the number of curves and the number of points on each curve.

Abdellaoui and Munier (1994) did a similar curve-fitting exercise. They found evidence of fanning out using common-ratio type choices, and some fanning out along the lower and left edges of the triangle. Curves were roughly parallel in the triangle interior.

Hey and Di Cagno (1990) used choices scattered throughout the triangle, rather than indifference judgments, then fitted probit models to the choices. They strongly reject a special form of regret theory, but accept a more general form.

4. Empirical Studies Fitting Functions to Individuals

A few researchers have estimated functional forms or parameter values for individual subjects (Currim and Sarin [1989] for prospect theory, and Currim and Sarin [1990] and Daniels and Keller [1990] for lottery-dependent utility). In a typical experiment, a subject makes a series of choices or states certainty-equivalents for several gambles. To fit EU, for example, a particular form of utility function is assumed, such as $u(x) = 1 - e^{-cx}$, and a best-fitting value of c is estimated (by minimizing squared deviations from the stated certainty-equivalents, for example). Alternative theories have more degrees of freedom and require estimation of more parameters. Then the fitted parameter values are used to predict choices in a hold-out sample of fresh choices. The method in Hey and Orme (1994) is similar except goodness-of-fit tests are used (EU is tested as a restriction on non-EU theories) instead of making predictions for a hold-out sample.

The results of these studies are somewhat discouraging for new theories. Alternative theories always fit initial choices better than EU, since they have extra degrees of freedom, but they do equally as poorly as EU predicting *new* choices, getting only about 60 percent right. (In the Hey and Orme study, the EU restrictions cannot be rejected for about half the subjects; for the other half, prospective reference theory or the one-parameter version of cumulative prospect theory appear to fit best.) These early results serve as a reminder that many subjects obey EU, and the lean functional form in EU is more statistically robust to estimation error than more complex functional forms are (e.g., Carbone and Hey [1994]). Of course, these are initial efforts. Refined techniques and larger samples might work better and enable more precise estimation of non-EU functions and parameters, and better predictions of hold-out sample choices.

Lattimore, Baker, and Witte (1992) also fit variants of EU with nonlinear probability weights to choices by students and prisoners (involving gambles over crimes and sentences). They assumed a power utility function $u(x) = x^\gamma$, and a two-parameter probability weighting function of the form:

$$(9) \qquad \pi(p_i) = \frac{\alpha p_i^\beta}{(\alpha p_i^\beta + \sum\limits_{j \neq i}^{n} p_j^\beta)}$$

The parameter α expresses additivity of weights (weights add to one if $\alpha = 1$) and β expresses the degree of overweighting of certain probabilities.

Lattimore et al. found reflection effects between gain and loss gambles, and nonlinear weighting of probabilities (roughly similar to Figure 8.6; Camerer and

Ho [1994]; and Tversky and Kahneman [1992]). Their data indicate weighting of losses and gains are slightly different: loss weights are more likely to be subadditive. They did *not* fit parameters to one set of choices then predict new choices.

5. Cross-Species Robustness: Experiments with Animals

Besides the many animal experiments studying risk aversion, "consumer" choice, optimal foraging, etc., there are a few experiments testing whether animals obey expected utility. Rats exhibit the common ratio effect like people do (Battalio, Kagel, and MacDonald 1985). (The cross-species replication is especially notable because the rats respond only sluggishly to incentives—e.g., they only choose a stochastically dominant lever 55 to 90 percent of the time.) Rats also fan out and fan in, just as people do, in the northwest and southeast corners of the triangle, when they choose between levers that give "losses" (delays in dispensing food) (Kagel, MacDonald, Battalio 1990). Rats also fan in over gains (cups of water) in some parts of the triangle, and violate the betweenness axiom (MacDonald, Kagel, and Battalio 1991), though no attempt has been made to check whether people exhibit those patterns for comparable gambles.

So *all* the available evidence to date indicates rats exhibit the same EU violations people do.[51] This cross-species generalizability is profound; it encourages the search for theories that can explain both human and non-human behavior in one fell swoop. My own view (which may be biologically naive), is that rats and humans are more likely to share misperceptions of probabilities than to share feelings of regret and disappointment. So if one prefers a common theory across species, the animal data shifts a bit more support to theories with nonlinear probability weights.

6. Some Conclusions from Recent Studies

The evidence collected in the last five years is as voluminous as the evidence gathered at any stage of testing EU. There are important lessons in the data.

Common ratio and common consequence effects are easy to replicate, but their strength varies across probabilities and outcomes. Fanning out is systematically violated for several kinds of gambles. Risk attitudes, and weighting of probabilities, appear to reflect around a reference point. There is an interaction between the degree of EU violations and the size and sign of outcomes (cf. Edwards 1954a)—i.e., violations are more frequent when outcomes are larger. Some models can account for the interaction by abandoning separability of outcomes and probability weights (e.g., Hogarth and Einhorn 1990; Becker and Sarin 1987), but the loss in parsimony may be too high a price to pay for better fit.

Many studies (beginning with Preston and Baratta 1948) are consistent with overweighting of low probabilities (below .2 or so) and underweighting of higher probabilities. Mixed fanning, betweenness violations, disappearance of EU violations inside the triangle, and replication of human results with animal subjects, might all be accounted for by nonlinear weighting. Some other studies, not mentioned above, also found evidence that probabilities between .3 and .8 are underweighted (Cohen, Jaffray, and Said 1985; Cohen and Jaffray 1988; de Neufville and Delquie 1988).

The few attempts to fit models for individual subjects suggest that more general theories *fit* better than EU (since they have more degrees of freedom) but are no better in *predicting* new choices. More studies of this sort are crucial for establishing whether the new theories can actually make better predictions than EU.

Among classes of theories, we can declare a few winners and losers in the empirical sweepstakes. Theories that incorporate nonlinearity in probability—such as the rank-dependent approaches, particularly, and cumulative prospect theory—appear to have the necessary empirical properties (Figure 8.10) and will, I think, prove relatively easy to work with formally. Betweenness-based theories (including implicit and weighted EU, and disappointment theory) have elegant formal properties but cannot accomodate apparent nonlinearity in probability adequately.

Finally, the continued use of EU can only be justified in two fairly narrow ways: first, EU is not so badly violated in choosing over gambles with the same set of possible outcomes (triangle interior), or with probabilities well above 0 and below 1—though it is still statistically rejectable. Second, EU might be preferred in an application where parsimony is *very* highly valued compared to predictive accuracy (but even then, EV is often just as good).

7. Investments in Risky Assets

Loomes (1991a) conducted a novel experiment. He gave subjects lotteries over three events, denoted A, B, and 0 (a zero payoff), which occurred with probabilities p_A, p_B, and $1 - p_A - p_B$. (A was always more likely than B.) Subjects could allocate £20 between the events A and B, in any proportion they liked. If an event occurred, they earned the amount of money they allocated to that event. (Subjects played one lottery.) For example, suppose $p_A = .6$ and $p_B = .4$. A person who is risk averse might allocate $A^* = £10$ and $B^* = £10$ (then he is certain to earn £10); a risk seeker might allocate $A^* = £20$, creating a .6 chance of winning £20. The money-splitting task resembles allocation of wealth in a portfolio of risky assets: making A^* and B^* close to £10 is like buying bonds; making A^* close to £20 is like buying stocks.

An EU maximizer will divide the money to solve $u'(A^*)/u'(£20 - A^*) = p_B/p_A$. A risk neutral or risk-preferring person will put all £20 in the more likely outcome, A. A sufficiently risk averse person will put less than £20 in A.

This simple problem provides a remarkably powerful test of several alternative choice theories. Under EU, as p_A and p_B fall, the amount A^* should stay the same if the ratio p_B/p_A is held constant. (Regret should not affect A^* either, in the display that was used.) Fanning out predicts the amount A^* will rise, and a restricted form of rank-dependent EU predicts it will fall.[52] When $p_A = .6$ and $p_B = .4$ subjects put £13.15 in A^* on average. Half the subjects chose amounts proportional to the probabilities ($A^* = 12$, $B^* = 8$). As p_B and p_A fell, to .2 and .3, a third chose $A^* = £10$, and the average A^* fell to £11.58. The drop in A^* violates EU and fanning out.

No current theory explains all the observed behavior. Current theories assume the choices of A^* and B^* are induced from underlying preferences between gambles— i.e., a person chooses $A^* = 12$ and $B^* = 8$ if and only if $(p_A, 12; p_B, 8) > (p_A, A'; p_B, 20 - A')$ for all other values of A'. Maybe subjects do not induce divisions from preferences; instead, they regard money-splitting as akin to problem-solving and use a simple heuristic (such as $A^*/B^* = p_A/p_B$) that generates allocations that are inconsistent with complete pairwise preferences.

The money-splitting task vaguely resembles investment in risky assets. Kroll, Levy, and Rapoport (1988a,1988b) studied asset portfolio problems more directly. Their experimental design operationalizes portfolio theory (Tobin 1958; Markowitz 1959): Subjects can invest in two risky stocks with normally-distributed returns (one has a higher mean and variance than the other). They can also invest in risk free bonds or borrow, up to a limit, by issuing bonds. Portfolio theory makes a remarkably counterintuitive prediction, called "portfolio separation": differences in risk tastes determine how much is invested in riskless bonds (or is borrowed) and how much is invested in stocks, but everyone will hold the same proportions of the two stocks in their stock portfolio, regardless of risk tastes. (For example, an optimal portfolio might place 60 percent of the stock investment in stock 1 and 40 percent in stock 2; those proportions should be the same for all investors, regardless of the overall amount they have invested in stocks instead of bonds.)

Relative to the theoretical prediction, subjects invested too heavily in the high-return, high-variance stock and did not issue enough bonds. (About a quarter of their portfolio choices were stochastically dominated by portfolios in which more funds are borrowed and invested in the low-return stock.) Since different subjects chose different stock mixtures, portfolio separation was badly violated.

Kroll et al. paid some subjects ten times as much money, to see how behavior would change. Highly paid subjects invested more heavily in the low-return, low-variance stock, bringing their portfolios closer to the optimal mixture. (They also searched more for information about stock returns in previous periods, even though they were told returns were independent each period.) However, my guess is that the increased incentive brought their portfolios closer to the optimum simply by increasing risk aversion and reducing investment in the high-variance stock, which coincidentally moved allocations toward the optimum predicted by portfolio theory.

A third study by Kroll and Levy (1992) varied several features of the earlier studies: MBA students participated in weekly sessions over a semester, competed for grade points in a tournament structure, and could see the publicly posted decisions and performance of others. The students' portfolios were much closer to those predicted by portfolio theory than in the two earlier studies; however, they did not reallocate portfolios in response to changes in between-stock intercorrelation as sharply as the theory prescribes (but subjects in the earlier studies did not respond at all). Students also tended to mimic the decisions of high-performing students, and the tournament payment structure appeared to create a borrowing frenzy at the end of the experiment.

E. Subjective Expected Utility

In "subjective expected utility" (SEU), probabilities are *not* objectively known as they are assumed to be in EU. The events over which people have subjective (or "personal") probabilities are called "states." Decision makers choose acts X which yield consequences $x(s)$ that depend on which of several states ($s \in S$) occurs. The SEU axioms show when preferences can be represented by subjective expected utility, with utilities $u(x(s))$ and (subjective) state probabilities $p(s)$ *both* derived from preferences, as follows:

$$(10) \qquad\qquad \text{SEU}(X) = \sum_{s \in S} p(s)u(x(s))$$

SEU was inspired by Ramsey (1931) but made clear by Savage (1954), who combined the von Neumann and Morgenstern (1944) EU approach with de Finetti's (1937) calculus of subjective probabilities. Since probabilities in SEU are derived from preferences, rather than assumed (as in EU), SEU applies more widely. See Fishburn (1988, 1989) and Karni and Schmeidler (1990) for technical reviews, or Camerer and Weber (1992).

Most of the empirical evidence specifically critical of SEU concerns precisely the distinction between whether probability is known or unknown. This basic distinction goes by many names: risk versus uncertainty (Knight 1921); unambiguous versus ambiguous probability (Ellsberg 1961); precise or sharp versus vague or fuzzy probabilities. In SEU the distinction between known and unknown probability is pointless because subjective probabilities are never unknown—they are always known to decision makers (and inferrable from choices). But empirical evidence suggests people do make such a distinction.

1. The Ellsberg Paradox

The first serious challenge to SEU was posed by the paradoxes of Ellsberg (1961). Two similar problems were posed in his remarkable paper. Here is one of them:

A decision maker chooses from an urn that contains thirty red balls and sixty balls in some combination of black and yellow. There are two pairs of acts, X and Y, and X' and Y'. Acts have consequences of W or 0, defined in Table 8.2. For example, the act X pays W if a red ball is drawn; Y pays W if a black ball is drawn.

Many people choose $X > Y$ and $Y' > X'$. The number of black balls that yield a win if act Y is chosen is unknown (or ambiguous); people prefer the less ambiguous act X. The same principle, applied to the second choice, favors Y' because exactly sixty balls yield W. (The same is true for losses, $W < 0$.) In this example, people prefer acts with a known probability of winning. That is, they take confidence in estimates of subjective probability into account when making choices.

Such a pattern is inconsistent with the sure-thing principle of SEU. Suppose $p(r)$, $p(b)$, and $p(y)$ are the subjective probabilities of drawing a red, black, or yellow ball. Under SEU, $X > Y$ if and only if $p(r)u(W) > p(b)u(W)$ (setting $u(0) = 0$), or $p(r) > p(b)$. Similarly, $Y' > X'$ implies $p(b \cup y) > p(r \cup y)$. If we assume probabilities are additive, then $p(b \cup y) = p(b) + p(y)$ (since $p(b \cap y) = 0$). Then $Y' > X'$ implies $p(b) > p(r)$, which conflicts with the earlier inequality.

Table 8.2. The Ellsberg Paradox

Act	30 Balls Red	60 Balls Black	Yellow
X	W	0	0
Y	0	W	0
X'	W	0	W
Y'	0	W	W

Source: Ellsberg 1961.

There are several reactions to the paradox. One is to deny it (e.g., de Finetti 1977; Howard 1992)—whether there are thirty balls, or some number between zero and sixty, *shouldn't* matter—but denial does not explain the evidence. Another reaction is reductionist (Marschak 1975): even if probability is not sharply known, there may be a sharp "second order" distribution of probability (SOP), or probability of various probabilities, that restores the usefulness of SEU. For example, in the Ellsberg case a person might not know the number of black balls, but might think that each possible number of balls from zero to sixty is equally likely (i.e., $p[k$ black balls$] = 1/61$ for $0 \leq k \leq 60$). But there is no guarantee that a sharp second-order probability exists, or that it captures subjects' intuitions about ambiguity. A more constructive reaction is to study the paradox empirically.

2. Conceptions of Ambiguity

Defining ambiguity is a popular pastime in decision theory. Ellsberg's (1961, 657) definition is typical, if messy: ambiguity is the "quality depending on the amount, type, reliability, and 'unanimity' of information, giving rise to one's degree of 'confidence' in an estimate of relative likelihoods." I favor a slightly pithier definition: ambiguity is *known-to-be-missing information*, or not knowing relevant information that could be known (Frisch and Baron 1988; cf. Heath and Tversky 1991).

The missing information definition includes other kinds of ambiguity as special cases. The composition of the ambiguous Ellsberg urn is missing information, which is relevant and could be known but is not. Doubts about the credibility of sources and disagreements among experts create missing information (namely, whether a source or expert can be believed). Keynes (1921) proposed that the *weight* of evidence be taken into account along with its implications. For instance, in Scottish law there are three verdicts: guilty, innocent, and unproven. While evidence might imply guilt, if there is too little evidence it has low weight and the verdict will be "unproven." If the weight of evidence is defined as the fraction of available information, then missing information lowers evidential weight.

3. Empirical Tests

Ellsberg did not run any formal experiments,[53] but his thought experiments were frequently replicated and extended. Becker and Brownson (1964) did the first careful study. Their subjects chose between urns containing 100 red and black balls. Drawing a red ball[54] paid $1. The number of red balls fell within a different range for each urn. For example, one urn had exactly fifty red balls; another had between fifteen and eighty-five balls. The urns with unknown contents were covered; they did not report how many balls were actually used in each. Subjects chose between pairs of urns, differing in the range of red balls, and said how much they would pay to draw from their preferred urn.

Subjects always picked the less ambiguous urn and paid high amounts to avoid ambiguity (which increased with the degree of ambiguity). For example, they paid an average of $.36 to choose from an urn with 50 red balls instead of an ambiguous urn with 0 to 100 red balls. (The expected value of a draw was $.50!)

There were several other studies in the 1970s and 1980s, all using similar paradigms. In *most* of the studies one choice was picked randomly and played for money. Some stylized facts emerged from these studies.

Ambiguity aversion is found consistently in variants of the Ellsberg problems (many of them using small actual payoffs). Ambiguity averters are typically immune to written arguments against their paradoxical choices (e.g., Slovic and Tversky 1974), and pay substantial premiums to avoid ambiguity—around 10 to 20 percent of expected value or probability (MacCrimmon and Larsson 1979; Curley and Yates 1989; Bernasconi and Loomes, 1992). Risk attitudes and ambiguity attitudes are uncorrelated (Cohen, Jaffray, and Said 1985; Hogarth and Einhorn 1990). Subjects would rather bet on known probabilities p than on known probability distributions of probability (compound lotteries) with a mean of p (Yates and Zukowski 1979; Larson 1980). Increasing the range of possible probabilities increases ambiguity aversion (Curley and Yates 1985). There is some evidence of ambiguity *preference* for betting on gains with low ambiguous probability, or betting on losses with high probability (e.g., Kahn and Sarin 1988). (This may be due to perceived skewness in ambiguous distributions of low and high probability, which makes their means higher and lower than is assumed.)

Curley, Yates, and Abrams (1986) tested several psychological explanations for ambiguity aversion. Subjects who said the urn could not be biased against them were ambiguity averse too, suggesting ambiguity aversion is not due to an expressed belief in "hostile" generation of outcomes. Subjects were ambiguity averse when indifference was allowed (cf. Roberts 1963). Subjects were more ambiguity averse when they knew the contents of the ambiguous urn would be revealed afterward to others.

Competence

Ambiguity aversion implies there may be a gap between subjects' beliefs about an event's likelihood and their willingness to bet on the event. (In SEU there can be no such gap, since beliefs are *derived* from betting preferences.) Heath and

Tversky (1991) suggest that competence—knowledge, skill, comprehension—is what causes the gap. They ran one set of experiments in which subjects gave probability assessments for natural events they knew a little or a lot about. (They were rewarded with a scoring rule.) The subjects were then asked whether they would like to bet on the event, or on a chance device constructed to have the same probability as the event. If people are ambiguity averse they should always prefer to bet on chance devices since events are inherently ambiguous. But subjects who knew a lot about a domain of events preferred betting on events; those who knew little preferred betting on chance. People preferred betting on events they knew a lot about *holding beliefs constant.*

The competence hypothesis broadens the study of choice anomalies in SEU by suggesting that ambiguity about probability is just one of many forces that makes people reluctant to bet, by undermining competence. Heath and Tversky suggest that competence influences betting because personal and social assignments of credit and blame are asymmetric: competent people can take credit for winning in a way that incompetent people cannot, and incompetent people may suffer more blame.

Ambiguity in Markets

Camerer and Kunreuther (1988) studied ambiguity in an experimental market for hazards that incurred a loss; subjects could pay "insurance" to get rid of them. A second-order probability distribution was used to induce ambiguity in loss probability (i.e., the probability had three possible values, which were equally likely). Ambiguity had little effect on market prices or volume, but it did increase the variance in the distribution of sales across sellers (i.e., some sellers sold more insurance policies and others sold none).

Sarin and Weber (1993) studied ambiguity in market settings. They auctioned off ambiguous and unambiguous lotteries in double-oral and sealed bid auctions with German subjects. An unambiguous lottery was a draw of a ball from an open urn with five winning and five losing balls (a winning draw paid 10 marks). An ambiguous lottery was a draw from a hidden urn with an unknown composition of balls. They found persistent ambiguity aversion around $p = .5$ (but not around $p = .05$), even under stationary replication, and even when the ambiguous and unambiguous lottery markets operated simultaneously.

While these two studies *explicitly* tested the effect of ambiguity in an experimental market, other studies may provide indirect evidence of ambiguity effects. In most market experiments subjects are not fully informed about the market's structure (they know only their own valuations), so they face some ambiguity due to missing information. In games, they usually know the entire structure, but their opponent's rationality is ambiguous. Anomalous behavior in markets and games might therefore be explained by ambiguity aversion (Camerer and Karjalainen, 1994). For example, subjects in market experiments often behave very conservatively early in the experiment (e.g., failing to trade when it is optimal); their behavior is usually labelled "risk aversion" or "confusion." The apparent confusion may be a manifestation of ambiguity aversion: subjects would rather do nothing, foregoing profits, than take action in an ambiguous environment where information is missing and they feel incompetent. As the experiment progresses, subjects learn and the amount of missing information shrinks, reducing their ambiguity aversion and conservative behavior. Thus, notions like competence, missing information, and ambiguity aversion might help us make sense of disequilibrium behavior early in experiments, which we currently call "confusion" and largely ignore.

4. Formal Models

Several kinds of formal models have been proposed to accomodate ambiguity effects. Some of the models are axiomatic generalizations of SEU. Others invoke psychological principles or propose ad hoc decision rules. I mention just a few (see Camerer and Weber 1992, for details).

There are several ways of modifying SEU without abandoning the expectations principle. Utilities can depend directly on ambiguity (Smith 1969; Sarin and Winkler 1989). Expected probabilities can be underweighted (Fellner 1961; Einhorn and Hogarth 1985), or possible probabilities in a second order distribution can be weighted nonlinearly before taking their expectation (Segal 1987a; Kahn and Sarin 1988; Becker and Sarin 1990). The nonlinear weights might depend on outcomes (Hazen 1987).

Another way to modify SEU is to replace the expectation principle with more general decision rules that combine expected SEU with the minimum SEU over a set of possible probabilities (this was Ellsberg's proposal; cf. Hodges and Lehmann 1952, and Gärdenfors and Sahlin 1982). A special case of the combined model is maximizing the minimum SEU over some set of possible probabilities (Gilboa and Schmeidler 1989), perhaps weighting possible probabilities by a person's willingess to bet on them (Nau 1989). (Allowing preferences over ambiguous acts to be incomplete can yield a constrained maximin representation too; Bewley 1986.)

More radically, subjective probabilities may be precise but nonadditive: that is, $p(A \cup B) \neq p(A) + p(B) - p(A \cap B)$ (Luce and Narens 1985; Gilboa 1987; Schmeidler 1989; Wakker 1989; Tversky and Kahneman 1992). The idea is that unwillingness to bet on ambiguous states can be expressed by attaching lower subjective probability to those states. Nonadditive SEU must be calculated with a special summation or integral, first discovered by Choquet (1955). If states are ranked by the utilities of their consequences $f(s_i)$ for a particular act f, from $u(f(s_1)) > \ldots > u(f(s_n))$, then the finite Choquet integral is

(11)
$$u(f(s_1))p(s_1) + \sum_{i=2}^{n} u(f(s_i)) \left[p(\bigcup_{j=1}^{i} s_j) - p(\bigcup_{j=1}^{i-1} s_j) \right]$$

Note that if $p(.)$ is additive and the states s_j are mutually exclusive, then the term in brackets reduces to $p(s_i)$ and equation (11) reduces to SEU. There is obviously a close kinship between nonadditive probability in SEU and rank-dependent probability weights in EU (compare equations (11) and (5)).

5. Applications to Economics

Theoretical and applied work on variants of SEU is several years behind the work on EU reviewed in section III.D. For example, there are virtually no empirical tests pitting the formal models against each other.

There are several applications to economics. Dow and Werlang (1992) apply SEU with nonadditive probability to financial markets. They show that in theory increased ambiguity creates wider bid-ask spreads. Blank (1991) reports a large *American Economic Review* experiment comparing single-blind refereeing, when a paper's author is known to the referee, with double-blind refereeing, when the author is unknown. (Not knowing the author of a paper, and knowing that you could, creates ambiguity.) Incoming papers were randomly allocated to the two reviewing conditions. Single-blind papers are rated more highly by referees (3.47 vs. 3.37, on a five-point scale), and accepted more frequently (14.1 percent vs. 10.6 percent) than double-blind papers; one could ascribe the difference to ambiguity aversion. French and Poterba (1991) document a global preference for home-country investments, which costs investors the equivalent of about 3 percent in annual returns in foregone diversification. The preference for home-country investment and the revealed preference for publishing known-author papers are consistent with the Heath and Tversky (1991) finding that people prefer to bet on events they know more about (holding likelihood constant).

In surveys using hypothetical vignettes (based on naturally occurring risks), Hogarth and Kunreuther (1985, 1989) found that pricing decisions by professional actuaries and insurance underwriters reflect ambiguity aversion. (Indeed, ambiguity premiums are *required* by many of the pricing rules used in insurance companies; see Hogarth and Kunreuther 1990.) Knight (1921) and Bewley (1986) suggest entrepreneurship can be understood as ambiguity neutrality. Bewley also sketched some applications of his theory to labor contracting.

The idea that missing information creates uncomfortable ambiguity implies that agents will demand information simply to reduce ambiguity (and discomfort), even if the information does not help them make better decisions. (Demand for information could then be modeled as a primitive, instead of deriving it from preferences over outcomes that result from informed decisions.) Demand for ambiguity-reducing information may help explain potential anomalies like uninformative advertising and alleged medical overtesting.

F. Choice over Time

In traditional models of choice over time, simple axioms imply that preferences over consumption streams $X = (x(1), x(2), \ldots, x(n), \ldots)$ can be represented by an additive discounted utility representation (e.g., Fishburn and Rubinstein 1982):

$$(12) \qquad X > Y \leftrightarrow \Sigma\, d(t)x(t) > \Sigma\, d(t)y(t)$$

where $d(t)$ represents the present value of consumption at time t. Further axioms imply the familiar exponential forms $d(t) = d^t$ and $d(t) = e^{-dt}$.

Considering the importance of intertemporal choice in economic theory, there have been relatively few experimental tests of choices over time. The tests conducted so far indicate several systematic violations that are remarkably similar to violations of EU. (1) Implicit discount rates, derived from choices over income or consumption streams, decline with time horizon: people are much more impatient about immediate delays than about future delays of the same length. Put formally, discount rates seem to be hyperbolic, $d(t) = (1 + \alpha t)^{-\beta/\alpha}$, rather than exponential ($d(t) = e^{-\alpha t}$). (The exponential form is the limit of the hyperbolic form as α goes to zero.) (2) Discount rates are larger for smaller amounts of income or consumption, and are larger for gains than for losses of equal magnitude. (3) People demand more to delay consumption than they will pay to speed it up. Loewenstein and Prelec (1992) give a generalization of discounted utility, using a value function akin to the one in prospect theory, which can explain all these anomalies.

Some of these findings, especially hyperbolic discounting, have been replicated by Thaler (1981), Loewenstein (1988), Benzion, Rapoport, and Yagil (1989), and Shelley (in press). Hyperbolic discount rates are also commonly observed in experiments with animals (e.g., Ainslie 1975).

Human subjects were not financially rewarded in many of these experiments. Indeed, economic experiments on choices over time are extremely difficult to run because subjects cannot be paid immediately. Even if experimenters intend to pay, subjects may not trust them. Making subjects return to collect their money also imposes a cost that must be accounted for. A few experimenters have used monetary payments and observed the same anomalies observed in hypothetical choices (Loewenstein 1988; Holcomb and Nelson 1989; Horowitz 1991; Carlson and Johnson 1992).

Time affects choices in some other interesting ways (see Loewenstein and Elster 1992). Temptation arises if immediate discount rates are too high, creating a problem of self-control (examples include smoking, overeating, procrastination, and using credit cards; see Ausubel 1991). Many people have modeled self-control as a neo-Freudian conflict between multiple selves: a myopic self greedily consumes immediately while a foresightful self tries to restrict the myopic self's binges (Thaler and Shefrin 1981; Schelling 1984; Laibson 1994). The neo-Freudian view helps explain the existence of institutions that make self-control easier—Christmas clubs, "forced saving" by overwithholding income taxes from wages, voluntary diet plans that ration food, and so on.

Ex ante anticipation of consumption, or cherishing of ex post memories of consumption, may affect timing of choices too. Loewenstein (1987) asked college students when they would prefer to kiss their favorite movie star. (Kisses were hypothetical.) The median subject preferred to wait three days, exhibiting a negative discount rate, to savor the consumption before it occurred. Savoring and its negative counterpart, dread, are probably important parts of the explanation for why people buy insurance and gamble.

Varey and Kahneman (1992) explore judgments of the overall quality of temporally extended episodes (such as watching a movie or taking a week-long vacation). A natural model is that people judge overall utility by cumulating or integrating momentary utilities experienced across the episode. This model appears to be wrong in interesting ways. For example, the cumulation model predicts that episode length will be correlated with overall quality, but in experiments using short and long films, length is only a weak correlate. People also appear to dramatically overweigh the momentary utilities at the peak and end of the episode (Fredrickson and Kahneman in press). It is easy to generate dominance violations as a result of this overweighting: in one study, subjects preferred long, mildly painful colonoscopies that ended with a gradual easing of pain to shorter ones that had less overall discomfort but ended painfully (Redelmeier and Kahneman 1993).

G. Process Theories and Tests

There is a large body of work, mostly by psychologists, spelling out procedures people use to make choices. I will mention only a few germane contributions.

When the number of alternatives is large, people often use conjunctive and disjunctive rules to reject alternatives, especially in complicated settings with many alternatives having several dimensions or attributes (e.g., Einhorn 1970). These rules specify cutoff levels for all attributes. With a conjunctive rule, if an alternative falls below *any* cutoff it is rejected. In a disjunctive rule, an alternative that satisfies any cutoff is not rejected. Tversky (1972) proposed and tested a related rule called "elimination by aspects" (EBA): subjects pick one attribute with a probability that depends on its importance, eliminate alternatives without the attribute (or below a cutoff level), then choose another attribute and repeat the procedure.

Grether and Wilde (1984) studied conjunctive rules experimentally. Subjects were forced to use conjunctive rules to make choices. "Inspecting" an attribute had a cost; subjects could choose cutoffs and the order of inspection. Subjects tended to inspect the lowest-inspection-cost attributes. They often violated normative predictions of optimal cutoffs and inspection order (Wilde 1982) because they ignored the influence that a drop in cost of inspecting one attribute should have on inspection order and the level of other attributes' cutoffs. (Roughly speaking, subjects used a partial-equilibrium mental model and ignored important general equilibrium effects.)

Using simulations, Johnson and Payne (1985) showed that in some choice settings simple decision rules, like conjunctive rules, are almost as accurate as more complex rules, like EV-maximization, and take much less effort. (Estimates of effort come from psychological studies of how long it takes to perform various mental operations such as adding, remembering, multiplying.) Johnson and Payne's simulations give an underpinning to the "labor theory of cognition" proposed by Smith and Walker (1993) (cf. Marschak 1968; Wilcox, in press). In the labor theory of cognition, mental effort is like manual labor: People dislike thinking hard; more effort is supplied in response to higher incentives (except when constrained at computational limits); and greater effort reduces the variance of responses around an optimum.

The labor theory is a natural way for economists to comprehend thinking, but in some ways it represents a psychological step backward. Some history is needed to explain my point. From about 1930 to 1960, psychology was dominated by "behaviorism," the study of the response of animals (including people) to stimulus. Behaviorism ignored the details of cognitive process and treated the brain as a black box. In the 1960s a new way to model cognition came around—the brain is like a computer—and the information processing paradigm was born. Behaviorism was largely abandoned (except for some domains of animal learning) because the computer metaphor was so appealing and because of mounting evidence, such as transfer of learning across tasks, which was anomalous for behaviorism and cried out for a cognitive explanation.

The labor theory of cognition is a partial return to behaviorism because it concentrates on the relationship of stimulus (incentives) to response (choices), compressing the details of cognitive processing into the catch-all category, "effort." The empirical question is whether research that incorporates more detail of thinking processes, like that discussed in section II and in parts of this section, generates better predictions than the labor theory. I think it does in many cases. However, the simpler labor theory may still be useful in some economic applications (especially in formal theorizing) because of its parsimony and rough accuracy.

H. Description Invariance

Utility theories makes several invisible background assumptions that are usually considered too innocuous to spell out. Two crucial assumptions are "description invariance" and "procedure invariance": different representations of the same choice problem, and different elicitation procedures, should yield the same preference (Tversky and Kahneman 1986).[55] Money illusion is an example: doubling all wages and prices, or denominating them in Irish pounds rather than dollars, shouldn't make anyone feel richer.

Both principles are sometimes violated. Invariance violations are especially troublesome for utility theories (including generalizations of EU and SEU) and provide the strongest indications that preferences are constructed from procedural rules.

Luce and von Winterfeldt (1994) offer a similar decomposition of axioms. They distinguish between axioms of "structural rationality" (or "accounting equivalences"), which prescribe indifference between formally equivalent descriptions of a gamble, axioms of "preference rationality" (like independence), and axioms of "quasi-rationality," which prescribe how consequences are coded as gains and losses.

1. Framing Effects

The most famous violations of description invariance are "framing effects," reversals of preference induced by changes in reference points. For example, McNeil, Pauker, and Tversky (1988) gave some American doctors and Israeli medical students data on survival rates after treatment for lung cancer by radiation therapy and surgery, as shown in Table 8.3. (Survival rates are the percentage of

Table 8.3. Survival and Mortality Framing of Lung Cancer Treatments

	Survival Frame (% alive)		Mortality Frame (% dead)		Both Frames Presented	
	Radiation	Surgery	Radiation	Surgery	Radiation	Surgery
After treatment	100	90	0	10		
After one year	77	68	23	32		
After five years	22	34	78	66		
Percentage choosing each:						
American doctors and medical students	16	84 (87)	50	50 (80)	44	56 (223)
Israeli medical and science students	20	80 (126)	45	56 (132)	34	66 (144)

Source: McNeil et al. 1988.
Note: Numbers in parentheses are *ns*.

patients surviving a given length of time.) Others were given the same data, phrased as mortality rates (percentage of patients who died before a given length of time). A third group got both frames. In the survival frame, 16 to 20 percent favored radiation therapy, since surgery only reduces immediate survival from 100 to 90 percent and keeps more patients alive in the long-run. But in the mortality frame the 10 percent death rate after surgery looms large; then nearly half favored radiation. Given both frames, 40 percent favored radiation (suggesting the mortality frame is more natural or potent).

The most pressing question is whether framing effects are systematic and predictable. The evidence is mixed. Fischhoff (1983) used a simple pairwise choice that could be framed several ways. Subjects' ratings of which frames seemed most natural were uncorrelated with the frames they appeared to use in making choices. Van Schie and Van Der Pligt (1990) found similar results: expressed frame preferences were only weakly correlated with risk aversion in choices (replicating Fischhoff's discouraging result), but the initial description of the choice *did* affect risk aversion. (If the problem was initally posed in terms of losses, rather than neutrally, frames emphasizing losses were preferred and choices were more risk seeking.)

Gertner (1993) reports an interesting framing finding using data from actual bets (averaging $3,200) on a television game show. He reports that when the cash stake available for betting increased by $1, bets increased by about $.60 (cf. the "house money" effect in Thaler and Johnson [1990]). But when the amount of cash winnings that couldn't be bet increased (or when a contestant had won a car) by $1, bets increased by only a penny. The data are clearly inconsistent with the theory that contestants integrate assets (bettable cash, unbettable cash, and cars) then bet based on their integrated assets.

Thaler (1985) proposed a "hedonic editing" rule for choosing reference points. For example, people should segregate two $50 gains (resetting their reference point to absorb the first gain before valuing the second one) because $v(50) + v(50) > v(100)$ if $v(.)$ is concave for gains. But Thaler and Johnson (1990) found that hedonic editing did not explain choices in two-stage settings where a prior gain or loss was followed by a choice. People use a variety of rules instead.

Consider a prior loss of −$7.50 followed by a second-stage choice between $0 and (.5,$2.25; .5,−$2.25). If subjects integrate the loss and the choice (and obey prospect theory), they choose between −$7.50 and (.5,−$5.25; .5,−$9.75), and take the gamble, because they are risk seeking over losses. But if subjects segregate the loss they will take $0 over the gamble (which is unappealing because of loss aversion). Sixty percent of subjects rejected the gamble, which suggests they are *segregating* the prior loss.

Now consider a prior loss of −$7.50 followed by a choice between $2.50 and (.33,$7.50; .67,$0). Under integration, the choice is between −$5.00 and (.33,0; .67,−$7.50); subjects should gamble. Under segregation, subjects should take the sure $2.50. In fact, 71 percent of the subjects preferred the gamble, which suggests they are *integrating* the prior loss. Integrating the loss is appealing because the integrated gamble gives a .33 chance of breaking even by winning $7.50 and recouping the prior loss.

In the first situation, the prior loss appears to be segregated from the gamble choice. In the second situation the loss appears to be integrated (when breaking even is possible). Framing principles appear to be a long list of rules like these dictating whether people integrate or segregate depending on contextual details (cf. Luce and von Winterfeldt's, [1994] discussion of "joint receipt").

2. Lottery Correlation, Regret, and Display Effects

The correlation between outcomes of two lotteries is an element of choice description which, according to EU, should not affect preferences. Consider the top two choices in Table 8.4 (see Loomes 1988a). The probability distributions of A and B outcomes are the same in both choices—A is (.3,10) and B is (.7,5)—but their correlation is different. In choice 1, the payoffs are negatively correlated and in choice 2 they are positively correlated.[56] Under any utility theory that assigns a number to outcome distributions, $u(A)$ and $u(B)$ should be the same in both choices. But regret theories assign a number to $u(A, B)$, so the correlation between A and B outcomes can matter.

Loomes and Sugden (1987a) suggest a "convexity" (or "regret aversion") hypothesis to make the theory testable. Convexity implies that the comparative utility from getting 0 and foregoing 10 is worse than the sum of comparative utilities from getting 0 instead of 5, and getting 5 instead of 10. (That is, $u(0,10) < u(0,5) + u(5,10)$.) Then people might switch preference from $A1 > B1$ in choice 1 to $B2 > A2$ in choice 2 (but they should not switch the opposite way).

In experiments with choices displayed graphically such as the top two choices in Table 8.4 (with one gamble actually played), about a third of subjects switch

Table 8.4. Choices in Regret Experiments

		Probability of State			
		.3		.7	
Choice 1	A1	10		0	
	B1	0		5	
		.3	.4		.3
Choice 2	A2	10	0		0
	B2	5	5		0
		.3		.7	
Choice 3 (collapsed table)	A3	10		0	
			.7		.3
	B3		5		0

preferences between the two displays, 80 percent of them in the direction predicted by convexity (Loomes 1988a,1988b, 1989a; Loomes and Sugden 1987b; Starmer and Sugden 1989c). Regret-aversion also predicts that if payoffs are juxtaposed properly people will choose a stochastically dominated lottery (e.g., (.38,$3; .2,$10) will be preferred to (.42,$3; .2,$10)). About half of subjects *did* violate dominance in this way in studies by Tversky and Kahneman (1986) and Loomes, Starmer, and Sugden (1992).

Battalio, Kagel, and Jiranyakul (1990) found much less switching when the *A* and *B* payoffs were shown horizontally, rather than vertically as in Table 8.4. In tests with several different displays, Harless (1992a) only found systematic regret effects—switching in the direction predicted by regret aversion—in the vertically aligned Table 8.4 display. He also experimented with displays in which states yielding the same payoff were collapsed for each act, as shown in choice 3 in Table 8.4. Regret effects presumably arise from comparing two acts' outcomes in the same state (i.e., comparing two row entries within a column). The choice 3 display might weaken regret effects by making it more difficult to compare outcomes within a column. Indeed, Harless found no regret effects when choice 3 displays were used.

Starmer and Sugden (1993b) found no regret effects using choice 3 displays ("strip displays") either. They discovered something else even more subtle, and astonishing: Compare choice *B*2, (.3,5; .4,5; .3,0), with choice *B*3, (.7,5; .3,0). Both describe the same lottery (a 70 percent chance of winning 5), but the *B*2 choice has two states that yield the prize of 5, one with .3 probability and one with .4 probability, while choice *B*3 has a single winning state, with probability .7. Yet they found that about 10 percent more subjects preferred the two state choice *B*2 over a third gamble than preferred the one state choice over the third gamble.

Simply splitting one state into two states with the same outcome, and the same total probability, increased preference for an act noticeably. (A similar preference-for-splitting can occur in theories with nonlinear weights, since $w(.1) + w(.1)$ can be greater than $w(.2)$. Indeed, Tversky and Kahneman [1986] exploited this property to construct violations of stochastic dominance in "opaque" choices.)

The regret studies show the interplay of experimental studies, and the cumulation of discoveries, at its best. Several studies by Loomes, Starmer, and Sugden established an important anomaly, the effect of lottery correlation on choices, which violated description invariance but could be neatly explained by regret aversion. Then a small test by Battalio et al. hinted that regret aversion could be sensitive to display effects. Harless landed a second, harder blow. Then Starmer and Sugden confirmed that regret aversion largely disappeared when displays were altered. In so doing, they (re)discovered the remarkable fact that splitting states made an act substantially more attractive. This is a story of successful detective work. The effects are small in magnitude. The studies used large samples of subjects (40–200 or so) for statistical power and a wide variety of gambles for robustness. Less methodical investigators might have falsely accepted the null hypothesis that there were no regret effects in the first place or underestimated their sensitivity to display.

Earlier studies tested the effect of using different lottery displays—trees, matrices, verbal descriptions—on the rate of Allais paradox choices (Moskowitz 1974; Keller 1985a). Display effects were generally too small to eliminate violations, but large enough that more work on display effects could prove fruitful.

3. Compound Lottery Reduction

Most utility theories contain an explicit or implicit reduction axiom stating that whether a lottery is described as a compound gamble with several probabilistic stages or as a single-stage gamble should not affect preference.

The reduction axiom has great normative appeal but is often violated in direct comparisons between one-stage choices and multiple-stage choices (Bar-Hillel 1973; Ronen 1973; Kahneman and Tversky 1979; Keller 1985b; Bernasconi and Loomes, 1992; Conlisk 1989). Most violations seem to be caused by the tendency to "isolate" the uncommon elements of two gambles, by cancelling common first-stage probabilities or common final-stage payoffs. For example (Kahneman and Tversky 1979), gamble 1 is a two-stage gamble in which there is a .75 chance of winning nothing at the first stage and a .25 chance of moving to a second stage gamble that pays a certain 3000. Denote gamble 1 by (.75,0;.25[1,3000]). Gamble 2 is a .75 chance of winning nothing at the first stage and a .25 chance of moving to a second-stage gamble that pays 4000 with probability .8, or nothing with probability .2. Gamble 2 is denoted (.75,0;.25[.8,4000;.2,0]). In reduced form, these compound lotteries are equivalent to (.25,3000) and (.2,4000); most people pick the riskier gamble 2, (.2,4000). The isolation effect refers to the tendency to ignore the common (.75,0) stage and choose gamble 1 or gamble 2 by isolating their uncommon second-stage elements. Then people usually choose gamble 1 because they prefer (1,3000) to (.8,4000;.2,0).

This cloud of violation has a silver lining, however. Since isolation is simply an application of the independence axiom, the independence axiom (and the betweenness axiom) is less often violated when gambles are presented in compound form (see Conlisk 1989; Segal 1990; Luce 1990; Brothers 1990; Camerer and Ho 1994; Bernasconi 1992; cf. von Winterfeldt, Chung, Luce, and Cho 1992). In the example above, if people prefer (1,3000) to (.8,4000;.2,0), then they will prefer the compound gamble (.75,0;.25[1,3000]) to (.75,0;.25[.8,4000;.2,0]).

Reduction is important for some procedures that are widely used in experimental economics. An example is the "random lottery" procedure, in which subjects make many choices but only one choice is picked, at random, and played out for money. If subjects violate independence and the random lottery procedure is used, then if they obey reduction they will *not* always choose as if they made only one choice. (Whether they will do so depends on the set of choices and the nature of their independence violations.) But suppose subjects isolate each pair while they are choosing, rather than multiplying its probabilities by the chance of that pair being randomly picked.[57] Then they will choose as if they were making only one choice, even if they violate independence. In fact, people *do* seem to isolate each pair (Starmer and Sugden 1991a; cf. Camerer 1989a).

Reduction plays a similar role in the Becker, DeGroot and Marschak (1964) procedure for revealing preferences and in the Vickrey auction for gambles (see chapter 1). If subjects obey reduction and violate independence, these mechanisms will not be preference-revealing for gambles (Chew 1985; Karni and Safra 1987). But if subjects violate reduction by isolating, both techniques *are* preference-revealing. Ironically, the violation of reduction that is implied by the isolation effect works to the experimenter's advantage, *ensuring* the usefulness of the random-lottery procedure and the BDM procedure.

Reduction is also assumed in attempts to induce risk neutrality by paying subjects in lottery tickets (Smith 1961; Roth and Malouf 1979; Berg et al. 1986). Evidence on the effect of the ticket procedure is mixed (see chapter 1 and chapter 7). In the ticket mechanism, reduction violations work against the experimenter.

I. Procedure Invariance

Elicited preferences should be invariant to the procedures used to elicit them, but they seem not to be. The elicitation biases mentioned above in section III.C.4, such as differences in utility functions derived by probability- and certainty-equivalence, violate procedure invariance.

Shafir (1991) discovered a violation of procedure invariance that is both illustrative and startling. Consider two lotteries, (.5, $50) and (.8, $150; .2, −$10). Asked which lottery they would choose if they had neither, 75 percent of subjects ($n = 279$) picked the riskier one, (.8, $150; .2, −$10). Asked which they would give up if they had both, 50 percent preferred to give up (.8, $150; .2, −$10). The pattern is surprising because complete preferences, and invariance of expressed preference to whether the choice is an acceptance or a rejection, imply that the two percentages should add to 100 percent. Shafir's explanation is that the second gamble is "enriched"—there is a good reason to pick it (it has a higher winning payoff) *and* a good reason to reject it (it has a chance of losing).[58] If people choose gambles with more positive features, and reject gambles with more negative features, then enriched gambles with both kinds of features will both be chosen and rejected more often, a dramatic violation of the principle that the procedure for eliciting choice should not affect choices. Notice that this violation, while not substantively rational, seems to have a clear procedural explanation that is amenable to formal modeling.

Another violation of procedure invariance with a long history is preference reversal (e.g., Tversky and Thaler 1990; Loomes forthcoming). The reversal literature began when Slovic and Lichtenstein (1968) noticed that the prices subjects gave for bets were highly correlated with bet payoffs, but choices were more highly correlated with probabilities. They conjectured that if subjects were offered two bets, one with a high probability and low payoff (a "*P*-bet") and another with a low probability and high payoff (a "$-bet"), they might choose the high-probability *P*-bet but price the high-payoff $-bet higher.

They were right. Lichtenstein and Slovic (1971, 1973) observed systematic, widespread preference reversals (see also Lindman 1971). The reversals attracted relatively little attention in psychology; perhaps there were plenty of other demonstrations that how a question is asked influences its answer (cf. opinion polls), and psychologists were busy discovering other anomalies. Then Grether and Plott (1979) replicated the earlier findings, using the Becker, DeGroot, and Marschak (BDM) (1964) procedure to elicit incentive-compatible selling prices. Their replication attracted much attention within economics. The early debate is described in chapter 1.

1. New Evidence of Preference Reversal

Recent evidence has established some new facts. Reversals disappear when choosing over portfolios of gambles played repeatedly (Wedell and Bockenholt forthcoming); this is unsurprising because repeated play reduces the difference in probabilities and payoffs of the two bets that generate reversals. Irwin et al. (1993) established large reversals in choosing vs. pricing consumer goods and environmental values (such as cleaner air). In gambles over real losses from a cash endowment, subjects exhibited reversals in the opposite direction—when they chose $-bets they usually priced *P*-bets higher (less negatively) (McDonald, Huth, and Taube 1991). Casey (1991) also found opposite reversals using buying prices and high-stakes gambles (replicated with real payoffs in Casey [1994]).

Most other recent evidence addresses three general explanations for reversals (laid out by Tversky, Slovic, and Kahneman 1990). Reversals are either (1) an artifact of the method used to elicit bet prices; (2) violations of transitivity; or (3) violations of procedure invariance.

The artifact explanation (1) has attracted by far the most attention from economists. The idea is that the Becker, DeGroot, and Marschak (BDM) (1964) procedure does *not* elicit truthful selling if the independence axiom is violated and reduction is obeyed (see Holt 1986; Karni and Safra 1987; Segal 1988). Apparent reversals might then be due to systematic misreports of true selling prices.

Cox and Epstein (1989) avoided problems with the BDM procedure by using a different method. They asked subjects to value a P-bet and $-bet concurrently, then compared the *rank* of the valuations with subjects' pairwise choices. Subjects were somewhat motivated to give accurately ranked valuations because the higher-ranked gamble in one randomly chosen pair was played for money (but they were not penalized for inaccurate valuations so long as the preferred gamble had a higher valuation). Since the BDM procedure was not used, any reversals in preference could not be due to BDM distortions. They observed fewer asymmetric reversals (P-bet $>$ $-bet, $-bet priced higher), but many symmetric reversals. The rate of symmetric reversals is roughly similar to the 15 to 25 percent rate of reversal observed in some studies cited earlier, in section III.D.2, but is substantially lower than would be expected from purely random switching.

There are strong theoretical, philosophical, and empirical counterarguments to the artifactual explanation, which blames the BDM procedure for apparent reversals. First, the BDM procedure only fails if independence is violated *and* reduction is obeyed. If subjects exhibit an isolation effect and violate reduction (as they appear to do; see section III.H.3) then the BDM procedure works properly.

Second, virtually identical patterns of reversals are observed when prices were elicited *without* the BDM procedure (in earlier studies); so how can the BDM procedure be blamed for those reversals? (Are they a coincidence?)

Third, Safra, Segal, and Spivak (1990a,1990b) showed that the artifactual explanation has two testable implications: (1) reversing preference goes hand in hand with violating independence by fanning out; and (2) a gamble's selling price SP (derived using BDM) and certainty-equivalent CE (derived from introspection by subjects) need not be equal, but SP and CE should lie on the same side of the gamble's expected value. New experiments suggest both implications are false. McDonald, Huth, and Taube (1991) discovered that implication (1) is false—subjects who exhibited fanning out were no more likely to reverse preferences than others who did not fan out. Keller, Segal, and Wang (1993) discovered that implication (2) appears to be false too—although SP and CE lie on the same side of EV nearly two-thirds of the time, the violations of this same-side property are strikingly asymmetric: 22 percent of subjects show SP $>$ EV $>$ CE while only 9 percent show CE $>$ EV $>$ SP. (If SP-CE differences are due to independence violations in the BDM procedure, the two patterns are random errors and should be roughly equal in number.)

Given the strength of these counterarguments—the second one of which has been known for twenty years—it appears that the artifactual explanation may have received too much attention from talented researchers with better things to do.

Tversky, Slovic, and Kahneman (1990) conducted an experiment to separate the transitivity (2) and procedure invariance explanations (3) of reversals.[59] Consider a P-bet (35/36,$4) and a $-bet (11/36,$16). If a subject chose the P-bet, then stated prices of $3.50 for the P-bet and $5.00 for the $-bet, she reversed preference in the usual way. Subjects then chose between the P-bet and a predetermined certain amount ($3.85, in this case) and between the $-bet and $3.85. Choosing $3.85 instead of the $-bet (for which the subject stated a price of $5) would indicate the $-bet was overpriced in the pricing task compared to its value in choice, indicating that choice-based preference and value-based preference are different (i.e., procedure invariance is violated). If procedure invariance holds but transitivity is violated, then P-bet $>$ $-bet but P-bet $<$ $3.85 and $3.85 $<$ $-bet. In their data, most reversals (66 percent) were due solely to overpricing of $-bets. Only 10 percent reflected intransitivity. Cox and Grether (1991) closely replicated this result (10.5 percent intransitivity).

Loomes, Starmer, and Sugden (1989, 1991) disputed these results (see also Loomes 1991b). They think the method understates the degree of intransitivity and overstates the importance of mispricing. They used a similar design and found more evidence of intransitivity. In one experiment, they compared the frequency of reversals measured two ways. First, subjects stated valuations and then chose between certain amounts and gambles (as in Tversky et al.). For example, a subject who said the P-bet was worth $3.50 would later be asked to choose between the P-bet and $4.00. Second, a subject's preferences in the choice between the P-bet and $4.00 were automatically determined ("imputed") from their earlier valuation. (In the example, the subject would be forced to choose the $4.00, since she said the P-bet was worth $3.50.) The second method (imputed-choice) forces valuations and choices to be consistent; the first method (actual-choice) does not. If choice valuation discrepancies generate reversals there should be substantially more reversals with the actual-choice method (because the imputed-choice method does not allow discrepancies). In fact, there were slightly more reversals using actual choices (11.75 vs. 14). In another experiment using only choices, Loomes, Starmer, and Sugden (1991) got about 20 percent intransitive cycles. Loomes and Taylor (1992) got 25 percent cycles using gambles over losses. These data show about twice as many intransitivities (in a pure-choice setting) as were reported by Tversky et al. and Cox and Grether. Regardless of the precise "market share" of intransitivity, it seems clear that both intransitivity and procedural variance play a role in explaining reversals. Both phenomena are well worth studying further.

Bostic, Herrnstein, and Luce (1990) and Loomes (1991c) elicited prices using an iterated choice procedure in which subjects made choices between a bet and a series of certain amounts that varied up and down until indifference was reached, establishing a price. Replacing pricing (a judgment task) with iterated choice should reduce the number of reversals if they are caused by procedure variance. Reversals *were* reduced.

Recent process evidence is informative too. Schkade and Johnson (1989) used a computer display, with probability and payoff information hidden in boxes that opened when the subject moved a cursor into them, to trace what information a subject was looking at (and for how long). Subjects looked at payoffs a larger fraction of the time when setting prices (55 percent) than when choosing (45 percent).

Johnson, Payne, and Bettman (1988) made probabilities more difficult to process simply by multiplying them (e.g., 9/10 became 513/570). The change made expectation-based strategies more computationally difficult and doubled the number of reversals.

Much of the new evidence corroborates the original Slovic and Lichtenstein interpretation of the cause of reversals. Their interpretation is now known as "contingent weighting": the weight attached to a dimension increases when the dimension is psychologically "compatible" with the response mode (payoffs and price-setting, for instance). When no dimension is psychologically compatible, the most "prominent" dimension is weighted more highly (e.g., probability is weighted highly in choosing). Tversky, Sattath, and Slovic (1988) showed contingent weighting effects in several settings, of which preference reversals are just one example. Contingent weighting can also explain the opposite patterns of reversals for gambles over losses (loss amount is weighted more highly in forming valuations than in choosing, leading people to prefer $-bets but price them more negatively). However, explaining opposite reversals using buying prices with high-stakes gambles (Casey 1991) requires a more complicated theory with framing features.

2. Arbitrage and Incentives

Several experimental economists have studied the effects of arbitrage and incentives on preference reversals.

Chu and Chu (1990) money-pumped Chinese students who exhibited reversals (as did Berg et al. 1985). Their subjects stated prices for two gambles and picked one of the gambles. If they exhibited a reversal, choosing the P-bet but pricing the $-bet higher (denoted $c(\$) > c(P)$), an experimenter would sell the subject the $-bet (collecting $c[\$]$), make her switch the $-bet for the P-bet (in accord with her choice), then buy back the P-bet for the price $c(P)$. The subject ended where she began, with no bets, but was $c(P) - c(\$)$ poorer.

For most subjects who expressed reversals, it took roughly two arbitrage cycles to eliminate the reversals. Money-pumping a subject on the first of three gamble pairs reduced reversals in the second and third pair too. Berg et al. (1985) found that the magnitude of reversals, but not their frequency, was reduced by a similar money-pump procedure. These results suggest that in an environment where preference reversal is a recognizable, costly mistake that outsiders can spot and exploit, then people can learn to switch their expressed preferences (or reduce the size of any discrepancy). But there is no evidence of whether subjects who are disciplined this way then learn to express preferences more consistently in the future, or whether reversals actually persist in natural settings.

Bohm (1990) conducted a highly original experiment, recruiting twenty-six Swedish students to choose between and bid for two used cars, a Volvo and an Opel. (The cars were actually sold!) His goal was to test for reversals of prefer-

ence in a high-stakes, natural setting with eager (self-selected) consumers. Most
subjects chose the Volvo, and bid higher for it too. *No* subjects reversed preference (although four reversed weakly, choosing one car but making equal bids).
Bohm concluded that reversals of the usual kind may be uncommon in natural
settings. The problem is that there is no strong a priori reason to expect reversals
in a choice between a Volvo and Opel. So it is difficult to tell whether reversals
disappeared because of the extraordinary incentive in a natural setting with eager
consumers, or because of the poor correspondence between the car choice and the
P-bet/$-bet paradigm.[60]

Harrison (1990) criticized preference reversal experiments for providing inadequate incentive, because small misreports of prices cost subjects very little when
the BDM mechanism is used. He showed that making the scale of price reports
more coarse (e.g., forcing prices to be rounded the nearest $.25 or $.50), or increasing the difference in expected values of the P- and $-bet, reduced the number
of reversals substantially. The effect of coarseness is not surprising (in the reduc-
tio ad absurdum case, if subjects could report only one price then no reversals
would occur). Increasing the expected value, like the effect of money-pumping,
makes expressed reversals more costly and does reduce them. The results point
out that large differences in expression of preference are less frequent than small
ones, but they do little to answer the pressing question of how large such differences are likely to be in natural settings.

Berg and Dickhaut (1990) studied incentives too. Their work uses the two-
error-rate model (Lichtenstein and Slovic 1971). That model assumes a fraction
q of subjects are truly risk averse and prefer the *P*-bet. Subjects make errors in
expressing choices with probability *r*, and rank the prices of the two bets backwards with probability *s*. Certain values of *q*, *r*, and *s* lead to certain fractions of
subjects choosing *P*- or $-bets and setting higher prices for *P*-bets or $-bets. The
observed fraction of reversals can therefore be used to estimate *q*, *r*, and *s*. The
error rate model provides a clearer view of how subjects respond to incentives
than overall reversal rates, because incentives can reduce error but *increase* the
number of reversals.[61]

Berg and Dickhaut showed that experiments that used hypothetical choices or
interdeterminate incentives were best fit by a *three*-error-rate model in which
pricing errors by risk averters (who prefer *P*-bets) were more common than pricing errors by risk seekers. Experiments with incentives for truthful revelation of
prices (using the BDM procedure) were best fit by the two-error-rate model. Experiments with arbitrage (Berg et al. 1985) reduced error rates substantially. Curiously, the error rates *r* and *s* inferred from the data were mostly greater than .5.
This casts doubt on their interpretation as errors in expression of preference, and
poses an important puzzle for work using the error rate models.

Berg and Dickhaut also ran experiments in which subjects earned payoffs in
points that were convertible into lottery tickets, rather than in dollars. Risk aversion and preference were induced by converting points into tickets with concave
and convex functions (a la Berg et al. 1986). Since prices were stated in points,
just as payoffs were, the contingent weighting explanation of Tversky et al.

(1990) predicts the same rate of reversals as in experiments with dollars (unless compatability of a familiar dimension like money is different than an unfamiliar dimension like points). But reversal rates (and error rates) were actually much lower using points, and most reversals occurred when risk-seeking subjects chose the $-bet but priced the P-bet higher. Their paper suggests error rates are sensitive to incentives and raises a new puzzle, since opposite reversals were observed with point payoffs (as in Casey's reverse reversals with buying prices for high-stakes gambles).

3. Reversals and Markets

Knez and Smith (1987) studied market trading and preference reversal. In their experiments, subjects hypothetically chose between a P-bet and $-bet and hypothetically valued both bets (giving selling or buying prices) four times. Between each choice-pricing iteration, they traded the bets in a separate trading period for each bet. The market trading experience reduced the incidence of preference reversal across the four hypothetical choice-pricing iterations, from about 60 to 40 percent. Subjects also sold or offered below their stated minimum selling price, or bid or bought above their maximum buying price, about a third of the time. (The average violation was substantial, about $1 in bets with expected values of $3.85.)

Cox and Grether (1991) studied the influence of markets more thoroughly. They compared selling prices elicited three ways: with the BDM procedure, with sealed bid second-price auctions (see chapter 7), and with an English clock auction in which prices fell steadily until only one person remained willing to sell. Notice that the sealed bid auction requires subjects to state prices directly, while the English clock auction requires a series of choices (i.e., whether to sell at the current price or not). The two markets therefore compare the choice and pricing modes of expressing preference.

Cox and Grether observed a typical rate of predicted reversals (around 60 percent) in the BDM and sealed bid conditions. Reversals in the English auction were much more symmetric; pricing the P-bet higher while choosing the $-bet was more common than the opposite, familiar reversal. Since the English auction is like a series of choices, disappearance of asymmetric reversals is strong evidence that choice-pricing discrepancy underlies reversals. When all three tasks were repeated the rate of predicted reversals declined slightly using BDM (though here they have few data) and both declined substantially and became more symmetric in the two markets. In the markets, bids were highly correlated with the last market price, which suggests that markets reduce reversals by giving traders an observable price to anchor on when generating bids.

Cox and Grether varied incentives too. Some subjects earned a fixed payment of $10 while others played all their choices and earned large amounts (an average of $59) or small amounts ($36). Incentives made little difference in the BDM procedure. In the market tasks, however, fixed-payment subjects behaved in the opposite way to the others, exhibiting no systematic reversals in sealed bid auctions and strong reversals in English auctions. Their data provide a striking example of how incentive effects can vary in predictable ways across domains. In the English auction, watching the price fall is dull. (The fall is larger for the high-payoff $-bet, since the clock starts at each bet's maximum payoff.) Fixed-payment subjects often dropped out of the auction quickly so they could ignore the computer screen and read newspapers or daydream, thereby establishing high selling prices—especially for $-bets, because the fall is slower and more boring—and a high reversal rate.

4. Social Comparison and Reversals

Loewenstein, Blount, and Bazerman (in press) report a novel type of reversal that springs from the tendency of people to compare their outcomes with others'. They went to a class to recruit subjects for experiments. They recruited students in one of three conditions. In one condition, subjects could earn $7 for forty minutes of work; 72 percent of the students ($n = 39$) agreed to participate. In another condition, subjects could earn either $8 or $10, depending randomly on the last digit of their social security number. (No convincing explanation was given for the disparity in wages, a weak point in the study.) Of the students who would have earned $8, only 54 percent ($n = 44$) agreed to participate. In a third condition, students could choose to participate in either experiment. Of those who chose to participate at all, 22 percent chose the $7 experiment and 78 percent chose the $8 to $10 experiment (when they would earn $8). A preference reversal occurs because *fewer* students participated for $8 than participated for $7 when they considered the experiments separately (54 percent versus 72 percent), but many more students elected the better-paying $8 experiment over the $7 experiment (78 percent versus 22 percent) in a direct choice between the two. Students appear to compare their wages with others when rating any one activity (see also Bazerman, Loewenstein, and White 1992), but weight their own wage more highly when choosing among different jobs. This intriguing finding (which is only marginally significant) deserves further exploration.

5. Some Conclusions about Preference Reversals

The discovery of systematic preference reversals is now about twenty-five years old. Economists have concentrated on the role of incentives and incentive mechanisms used to elicit preference. Increased incentive appears to lower implicit error rates, though reversal rates are not always lowered (Berg and Dickhaut 1990; Harrison 1990). Arbitrage reduces the magnitude of reversals, and sometimes their frequency (Berg et al. 1985; Chu and Chu 1990). Experience trading bets in markets appears to reduce reversals, perhaps by giving subjects a way to establish a gamble's worth (Knez and Smith 1987; Cox and Grether 1991). Two studies in new domains—repeated gambles (Wedell and Bockenholt forthcoming) and used car auctions (Bohm 1990)—did not find reversals, which simply shows that not all pairs of choice objects are prone to systematic reversals. Perhaps the clearest result from the last five years of research by economists is that theories that trace reversals solely to problems using the Becker, DeGroot and Marschak mechanism are wrong (see Cox and Epstein 1988; McDonald, Huth, and Taube 1989; Berg and Dickhaut 1990).

Psychologists have been less interested in the roles of incentive and experience, since the replication with casino gamblers by Lichtenstein and Slovic (1973) suggested neither variable was important. Instead, they suspect reversals are caused by a difference in revealed preference that results from different procedures used to elicit preference (Tversky, Slovic and Kahneman 1990; Mellers, Ordóñez, and Birnbaum 1992). Intransitivity appears to play some role too (Loomes, Starmer, and Sugden 1989, 1991).

There are at least three obvious directions for further research. First, since errors underlying reversals, and the dollar size of reversals, can be pounded down by enough incentive and arbitrage, an open question is how much discipline economic settings actually provide. (Knez and Smith [1987] start in this direction.)

It would also be useful to take the psychologists' explanation for reversals—that preferences are procedure-dependent—more seriously. One direction aims at the individual level: for example, Luce, Mellers, and Chang (1993) give a theory for how certainty-equivalents could be constructed for a set of gambles, and yield a preference order systematically different than would be observed in pairwise choices.

Another direction is the market level. (A start down this path is long overdue.) Two examples spring to mind. First, in choice among commodity bundles, if one commodity is the numeraire then the marginal rates of substitution will value that commodity more highly, ceteris paribus. Similarly, in negotiations over alternative multi-attribute settlements, the attributes being adjusted to make a settlement acceptable will seem most valuable (cf. Tversky, Sattath, and Slovic 1990). Second, different exchange institutions correspond to different response modes or procedures for eliciting preference (Machina 1987, 140–41). Buyers in posted-offer markets make choices; bidders set prices. If preferences depend on response modes, prices and allocations should differ systematically across institutions (familiar territory for experimental economists; see Cox and Grether 1991). Chapter 7 offers a related interpretation of the discrepancy between sealed bid and open outcry auctions.

J. Endowment Effects and Buying-Selling Price Gaps

Economic theory predicts that the prices a person will pay to buy and sell an object should be about the same. But a wide variety of studies indicate a large gap between buying prices (measuring "willingness to pay," or WTP) and selling prices ("willingness to accept," or WTA). See Kahneman, Knetsch, and Thaler (1991) and Hoffman and Spitzer (1993) for reviews.

The buying-selling price gap, or WTA-WTP gap, was discovered by environmental economists in the 1970s. For example, Hammack and Brown (1974) found that duck hunters would pay $247 each to maintain a wetland suitable for ducks, but asked $1,044 to give up the wetland. Many other studies reported similar large gaps (see Cummings, Brookshire and Schulze 1986), ratios of median WTA-WTP around two or more. "Contingent valuations" like these[62] are useful for doing cost-benefit analyses to make governmental allocations of non-market goods, and the gap between buying and selling prices raises the difficult question of which price is more appopriate. Knetsch and Sinden (1984) studied price gaps for lottery tickets (with cash or a gift certificate as the prize). In a typical experiment, nineteen of thirty-eight subjects would pay $2 for a ticket, but only nine of thirty-eight would sell at that price.

1. Market Experiments

An immediate concern was whether these gaps would persist in repeated market settings. Coursey, Hovis, and Schulze (1987) studied an unusual "bad," the obligation to hold a harmless bitter-tasting liquid called SOA in one's mouth for twenty seconds. The buying (selling) price was the amount one would pay (accept) to get rid of (assume) the obligation. Prices were bids in a uniform price Vickrey auction in which the four high bidders paid the fifth-highest price. There were large gaps in hypothetical valuations made before the series of auctions, but repeated auctions reduced the gap substantially, to a ratio of 1.5/2.5. However, their conclusions have been disputed (Knetsch and Sinden 1987; Gregory and Furby 1987) because they are especially sensitive to outliers and skewness in WTA values.[63]

Boyce et al. (1992) auctioned off houseplants that resemble pine trees (called Norfolk Island pines). They used the BDM procedure to elicit prices. The prices were then used as bids in an auction among subjects. (Their procedure adds an intermediate step to the usual procedure of having subjects bid directly.) Mean buying and selling prices were $4.81 and $8.00. Prices were substantially higher, $7.81 and $18.43, when subjects knew that any trees they did not keep or buy would be destroyed by the experimenters. (One subject was drafted as a witness, for credibility; some squeamish ones refused.) They suggest the increase in prices captures the "existence value" people place on mere existence of the trees.

Kahneman, Knetsch, and Thaler (1990) ran several market experiments. They first conducted a choice-based sealed offer-bid auction[64] with tokens of known value, to test whether subjects bid their true values. (They did.) The token market established confidence that the auction mechanism elicited good approximations to true values. Then they conducted auctions with coffee mugs, pens, and other consumer goods. The median selling price for a mug was $7.12; the median buying price was $2.87. Prices did not converge much across four trials (one of which was chosen and played afterward). Since mugs were randomly allocated to begin with, if buying and selling prices were the same roughly half the mugs should be traded, but only about a quarter were.

Franciosi et al. (1993) replicated these experiments by changing the instructions to remove terms such as "buyer" and "seller" which, they thought, might be overstating the buying-selling price gap. They observed significantly lower selling-price values ($5.36 versus a mean of $6.89 in the KKT data) but the gap between buying and selling prices was still large. They also replicated the finding of mug-undertrading using a uniform-price double auction (in contrast to the sealed bid mechism used by Kahneman et al.).

Several experiments studied markets for lottery tickets with money prizes. P. Knez, Smith, and Williams (1985) and M. Knez and Smith (1987) compared hypothetical buying-selling prices with actual trading in markets. Subjects routinely paid more in the market than their stated buying price, or sold for less than their stated minimum selling price. Trading volume was only slightly lower than expected if WTA = WTP.

McClelland, Schulze, and Coursey (1991) ran Vickrey auctions for lottery tickets over gains and losses. Elicited buying and selling prices were close together for gain tickets, but selling prices for insurance on loss tickets were roughly bimodal (either zero or several times expected value) and were larger than buying prices.

Harless (1989) measured buying and selling prices using a uniform price Vickrey auction with a within-subjects design. Each subject gave a buying price, immediately followed by a selling price (or vice versa), and paid or received money immediately after each lottery. The within-subjects design enables a buying-selling price ratio to be calculated for each subject. The modal ratio was one, but several ratios were very large. The median and mean of the ratios were 1.3 and 2.7. The low ratios Harless observed show the greater consistency that can sometimes result from a within-subjects design, especially when two tasks follow immediately in time.[65] Kachelmeier and Shehata (1992) also measured buying and selling prices within-subjects. The ratio of median prices in their study was about two, and the difference in prices was highly significant.

Overall, the data suggest that competition or learning in markets reduces the buying-selling price gap somewhat, in some settings, but does not eliminate it. The gap is large for environmental and consumer goods (like wetlands and mugs) and small for lottery tickets. Predispositions of the investigators may also play a role, perhaps through subtle differences in the designs or domains of application they choose.

2. Explanations Based on Experimental Artifacts

The experiments have been careful to eliminate several artifactual explanations for the buying-selling price gap. First, it is possible that subjects do not make hypothetical valuations of duck wetlands or pine trees very carefully, or strategically state high selling prices and low buying prices. Direct comparisons indicate there is some misrepresentation, especially in hypothetical selling prices (e.g., P. Knez, Smith, and Williams 1985; M. Knez and Smith 1987). But in most of the experiments subjects were paid, or got to keep goods they bought or didn't sell, and price gaps persisted.

Second, sellers are wealthier than buyers because they own the object being sold. Wealth effects cause a legitimate buying-selling price gap that can be large under very special conditions.[66] Studies show that wealth effects explain essentially none of the observed price gap. Coursey et al. (1987) controlled for wealth effects by endowing buyers with $10 (but see Knetsch and Sinden 1987). Franciosi et al. (1992) regressed prices given by a subject against the wealth accumulated by that subject earlier in the experiment and found no apparent wealth effect. Kahneman et al. (1990) controlled for wealth effects by allowing some subjects to choose between a mug and a sum of money, for several possible sums of money. These "choosers" are in exactly the same wealth position as sellers endowed with mugs, but their median valuation was only $3.12, close to the median buying price ($2.87) and much lower than the median selling price of $7.12.

3. Endowment Effects: Some Psychology and Implications

The leading psychological explanation for the buying-selling price gap is called the "endowment effect": people prefer the things they own, ceteris paribus. Endowment effects are thought to arise from the "loss aversion" assumption in prospect theory—losses are more painful than equally sized gains are pleasurable (see Tversky and Kahneman 1991). The stylized fact that buying-selling price gaps are larger for environmental and consumer goods than for lottery tickets (in most experiments) suggests that the gap is larger for goods bought for use, and smaller for goods, gambles, or securities that are routinely sold or easily valued.

Endowment effects are related to at least five other psychological effects. These phenomena are conceptually distinct, in principle, but are empirically entangled ("confounded") in some experiments. All of them follow from two principles: valuation relative to a reference point, and loss aversion (Tversky and Kahneman 1991).

1. "Status quo bias" is an endowment effect in which having a current choice, or default option, enhances preference for it (see Samuelson and Zeckhauser 1988; Knetsch 1989; Hartman, Doane, and Woo 1991). For example, New Jersey drivers now get cheaper insurance, restricting their right to sue, unless they pay extra. Only 17 percent of drivers paid extra in 1988. Pennsylvania drivers make the same choice, but their default option is the more expensive, unrestricted insurance. More of them chose the default option, paying extra for the right to sue, than in New Jersey (Johnson et al. 1993). (Part of the difference could be due to transactions cost, of course—the cost of filling out a form and sending it in—but experiments in which subjects *must* choose, forcing them to pay the transaction cost, show a comparable status quo bias.)

2. Buying-selling price gaps can result if people are more sensitive to overpaying (which incurs an out-of-pocket cost) than to selling too cheaply (an opportunity cost), as they appear to be in other domains (Thaler 1980).

3. Ritov and Baron (1991) show that people treat errors of commission, or action, as more blameworthy than errors of omission, or inaction. The reluctance to pay too much is an action error; passing up opportunities to sell is an inaction error. Greater fear of action errors will make buying prices too low; ignorance of inaction errors will keep selling prices too high. Schweitzer (in press) showed that

status quo bias is largely due to a bias in favor of inaction. (Subjects preferred a default option, which would be chosen if no action was taken, even if it differed from the current status quo option.)

4. There is some evidence that the purchase price of assets matters in financial decisions, creating a "disposition effect," because people are reluctant to take actions that create an irreversible loss and are eager to take actions that create gains. For example, trading volume is lower for stocks that have fallen in price (Ferris, Haugen, and Makhija 1988; Weber and Camerer 1992). Casual observation suggests the volume of houses sold falls when housing prices fall. In experimental asset markets, volume appears to thin when bubbles burst (Smith, Suchanek and Williams 1988, see chapter 6).

5. Marshall, Knetsch, and Sinden (1986) asked people whether they would buy or sell objects at certain prices, and how they would advise others. The advice people gave others revealed no buying-selling price gap—the gap disappeared because they urged buyers to pay more—which suggests endowment effects are not recognized or encouraged in giving advice.

An important question is how endowment effects change economic predictions. Tversky and Kahneman (1991) show how theories of choice and exchange can be altered to accomodate endowment effects (which they call "reference-dependence"). Bowman, Minehart, and Rabin (1993) showed how a prospect-theoretic kind of loss aversion could explain empirical anomalies (and predict some new surprises) in economic theories of optimal consumption, savings, and asset pricing. Hardie, Johnson, and Fader (1993) found that an expanded logit choice model, incorporating reference-dependence, fit within-household time series data on orange juice purchases better than a conventional model.[67] Kahneman, Knetsch, and Thaler (1990) showed that trading volume in goods markets was substantially reduced by endowment effects. Hoffman and Spitzer (1993) point out that if marginal buyers and sellers in a market have no endowment effects—if sellers are firms, for instance—then market prices and volumes may not be affected. Endowment effects are therefore likely to have their largest impact when individuals buy and sell on both sides of the market—residential housing, for instance, or some kinds of labor.

Rietz (1991) conducted market experiments that exhibit a surprising endowment effect[68] (and deserves further study). His subjects trade state-dependent contingent claims which pay 1,000 francs (= \$.50). A Blue ticket pays off if the Blue state ($p = .3$) occurs. A Green ticket pays off if the Green state ($p = .7$) occurs. The states are mutually exclusive and exhaustive, so a portfolio of one Blue ticket and one Green ticket pays 1,000 francs with certainty. Subjects are initially endowed with at least two portfolios of tickets (i.e., two Blues and two Greens) in each period. In addition, each subject was endowed, in alternating periods, with either four extra Blue tickets or four extra Green tickets.

Behavior in the double auction markets for tickets tests various theories of prices and allocations. After sixteen trading periods, mean prices were around 350 for Blues, and 850 for Greens, well above the expected values of 300 and 700. The sum of the two prices was often 1,200 or more. Prices this high are bizarre because subjects always began with at least two pairs of Blue and Green tickets. They could sell a pair of tickets, which are worth exactly 1,000 together, for more than 1,000, but they did not do so frequently enough to drive prices down. Furthermore, rational subjects should end a trading period with an allocation of tickets that depends on their risk tastes, but does not depend on their initial endowment. They did not: in periods when they start with four extra Blues they ended the period with more Blues than when they started with four extra Greens and no extra Blues. (Carlson and Johnson [1992] observe a similar endowment effect in experimental bond auctions.)

The puzzling prices and allocations Rietz observed can both be explained by endowment effects: suppose people value whichever tickets they start with more highly. Then Blue-holders will ask a high price for Blues and Green-holders will ask a high price for Greens, which pushes prices above expected value. Because people cannot sell many tickets at the high prices they ask, their final allocations depend on their initial endowments.

Endowment effects have a natural application to law (Hoffman and Spitzer 1993). The Coase theorem presumes that the valuation of a property right is independent of who owns the right, an assumption that is questioned by observed buying-selling price gaps. Cohen and Knetsch (1990) suggest that the law frequently recognizes the special losses that result from reducing one's endowment, and assigns property rights so as to minimize those losses (though see Hoffman and Spitzer 1993).

K. Search

1. Search for Wages and Prices

One setting in which individual decisions have direct market consequences is search. There is a large theoretical literature on search (e.g., Lippman and McCall 1976). In a typical model, a person looks for work each period. With some probability, she turns up a job offer drawn from a distribution. She can accept the offer or search more. If she decides to take the old offer after searching more, it is available with some probability that depends on how much time has passed. The models can apply to consumer shopping and other settings too.

The optimal strategy is usually to set a reservation wage and accept any job that pays more. The optimal reservation wage comes from a difficult recursion (or a series of recursions, if the time horizon is finite). There is little empirical evidence about whether people search as the models predict. So experimental evidence is useful.

Schotter and Braunstein (1981) and Braunstein and Schotter (1982) studied several variants of the basic model with an "infinite" horizon (i.e., subjects could search as long as they liked). Subjects stated reservation wages but were not bound by them (they could accept lower offers). In a baseline condition mean reservation wages were amazingly close to optimal (134.5 vs. 133) but subjects searched too little (3.7 actual periods when 4.5 was optimal). When parameters were changed—whether rejected offers could be recalled, the cost of search, the dispersion in the offer distribution—stated reservation wages and the actual acceptance of offers changed in the correct direction but differences were not always significant. When risk aversion was induced by paying subjects a concave function of points they earned (anticipating the method of Berg et al. 1986), their reservation wage was much too low (110 when 130 was optimal).

Kogut (1990) studied search in infinite-horizon settings too. Subjects paid a search cost each period (typically $.08) and drew price offers from a known uniform distribution. In each trial they paid the price they accepted, and search costs, and earned a known value. Their reservation price should be the same each period, which implies that optimal searchers should never reject an offer, then go back and accept it later.[69] They *did* accept old offers, about a third of the time. They often stopped searching too early (even assuming a large degree of risk aversion). Most of the early stops occurred just before the *total* search cost was large enough to make their profit negative, suggesting some subjects are sensitive to sunk costs and not to marginal costs and benefits of search.

Cox and Oaxaca (1989) studied search in finite-horizon experiments with twenty periods of search. (They chose finite horizons to establish more control than was exerted in the infinite-horizon setting of Braunstein and Schotter.) Assuming they were risk neutral, subjects quit searching at the optimal point 80 percent of the time. Searches ended an average of half a trial too early. As in the Braunstein and Schotter experiments, search duration responded in the right direction to several parameter changes, including search cost and offer dispersion, but the size and significance of the changes was not optimal.

Cox and Oaxaca (1990) replicated their earlier results but asked subjects to precommit by stating reservation wages that were used to automatically accept or reject offers.[70] (Precommitment made little difference except for a slight increase in risk aversion and some learning effects that disappeared after several trials; Cox and Oaxaca [in press].) Stated reservation wages followed the optimal path reasonably well (optimality under risk aversion could not be rejected), except they were too low at the start and too high at the end; overall, subjects searched too little, compared to a risk neutral benchmark.

Hey (1982) studied search in a shopping setting where the price distribution was unknown. (Subjects were not paid.) Recorded statements subjects made during the experiment ("verbal protocols," to psychologists) suggested six rules of thumb. One rule was a reservation wage strategy. Other rules prescribed stopping points depending on the previous sequences of price offers (e.g., stop if the current price is above the previous price). These rules might be manifestations of judgment biases discussed in section II, since many of them try to capitalize on apparent nonrandomness in the price series. Hey found some subjects using each of the six rules, or mixtures of them.

In Hey (1987) subjects were paid and half of them knew the price distribution. Knowing the distribution increased subjects' use of the optimal reservation price strategy, but financial incentives did not. The ability to recall rejected offers actually *hurt* slightly (reducing overall profits), which is puzzling. And they searched too little (perhaps due to risk aversion).

Moon and Martin (1990) extended Hey's work. They spelled out several more alternative heuristics subjects might use. In their data, cutoff rules such as "wait for a price k standard deviations above the mean" explain decisions roughly as well as the optimal theory. Simulations show that heuristic rules can be very close to optimal (only 1 percent worse).

Harrison and Morgan (1990) studied several search problems. In variable-sample trials their subjects could buy a sample of n_k offers in each period k. In sequential trials subjects could only sample one price at a time ($n_k = 1$). In fixed-sample trials subjects could only sample for one period ($k = 1$). In theory, the extra freedom in the variable-sample method should enable subjects to earn about 10 percent more profits than in the sequential or fixed-sample trials.

Subjects *did* exploit the freedom in variable-sample trials. They chose bigger samples than in the $n_k = 1$ sequential trials and searched longer than in the $k = 1$ fixed-sample trials. They earned substantially higher profits too, but the increases were not significant by nonparametric tests. The direction and raw size of deviations from optimal sampling are not reported (a result of the authors' obsession with the *cost* of deviations), but the fraction of subjects who made errors of a certain cost are reported. Subjects are apparently good at deciding whether to keep searching, but not as good at choosing the number of offers to sample each period (cf. judgment errors in section II above, especially II.D.3).

Since the optimal strategies in these search problems are difficult to derive, the subjects' approximation of them in many of the experiments is generally impressive. But there are some anomalies, especially in responses to parameter changes. And in general people search too little, compared to the amount of search recommended under risk neutrality. It would be useful to induce risk neutrality or measure the degree of risk aversion to test whether the observed undersearch can be rationalized by risk aversion. It would also be helpful to know whether heuristic rules could produce such an impressive approximation to optimality (simulations by Moon and Martin [1990], suggest they can). Heuristic rules might also explain the persistent tendency to undersearch and the relative inability to choose optimal sample sizes.

A natural extension is to experimental markets where sellers choose prices while buyers shop around. Sellers must understand how buyers search to set prices optimally. A variety of theoretical models predict endogenous price dispersion that depends heavily on shopping habits. Grether, Schwartz, and Wilde (1988) report experimental evidence supportive of some models.

Another interesting direction is to reproduce apparent search anomalies from natural settings. For instance, Pratt, Wise, and Zeckhauser (1979) found that across categories of consumer goods, price dispersion (standard deviation) was a roughly linear function of mean price. This finding is rational if search costs are higher for more expensive goods. A competing behavioral explanation is that people calculate the marginal benefit from shopping as a percentage, not a dollar amount; they search longer for a $5 saving on a $20 calculator than for a $50 saving on a $400 washing machine.

2. Search for Information

There are many psychological studies on the purchase of information that is used for making decisions. The results are much like those for search over wages and prices: people are insufficiently sensitive to factors such as accuracy of information and cost, which should affect search, and overly sensitive to factors that should be irrelevant, such as the source of information or the total information available (e.g., Connolly and Gilani [1982] and references they cite). One study found that providing subjects with a decision aid, which converted information into decisions optimally, reduced mistakes in information purchase by about half (Connolly and Thorn 1987).

It would be useful to extend the psychologists' results to economic domains in which the value of information is derived from its use in making decisions, such as information markets coupled with asset markets (e.g., Sunder 1991; Copeland and Friedman 1992; and see chapter 6).

L. Choice: Summary and New Directions

The studies reviewed in this section suggest a variety of broad classes of anomalies of the standard utility theories under risk and uncertainty. Many of the anomalies can be traced to the ideas that values are judged relative to a reference point, probabilities are not weighted linearly, and decision weights are not the same as beliefs. Preferences also seem to depend on the way choice objects are described (creating framing effects), the procedure by which they are elicited (creating preference reversals), and on one's current endowment (creating a buying-selling price gap). These phenomena, and anomalies in portfolio choice and the purchase of information, suggest people use simple procedures to make choices, constructing their preferences from procedural rules rather than maximizing over well-formed preferences.

At the same time, studies of search and market trading of risky assets (cf. chapter 6) suggest that models based on maximization are not badly violated (Plott 1986; Smith 1991). Future research should concentrate on three classes of explanation (and exploration) for the disagreement across studies: (1) experience, incentive, and discipline in markets combine to create stable preferences which are well approximated by normative models (contrary to the individual choice results); (2) anomalies in the models, which loom large in a large sample of individual choices, are too small to see in markets; or (3) studies of markets and search have not looked at the settings in which anomalies are likely to be large and common. (For example, buying-selling price gaps are largest with consumer goods and smallest with money gambles.)

IV. Conclusions, and Research Directions

My perspective in this chapter is unapologetically behavioral. I think the search for systematic deviations from normative models of individual decision making has been extremely fruitful.

Economists have had two reactions to data on individual decision making and have made two kinds of contributions, which might be called "destructive" and "constructive." *Destructive* tests, often motivated by skepticism, are designed to check whether apparent anomalies are replicable, robust across settings, or might be due to flaws in experimental design. My opinion is that *some* occasional tests of this sort are essential, but too much energy has been devoted to destructive testing with very little payoff. Not a single major recent (post-1970) anomaly has been "destroyed" by hostile replication of this sort.

Constructive reactions of economists to decision research have taken at least two forms. One reaction is the construction of alternative theories to explain anomalies. For example, Kanodia, Bushman, and Dickhaut (1989) show that the failure to ignore sunk costs—managers sticking with projects after learning they are bad investments—can be privately rational, for the managers, if there is information asymmetry about their talent. Theories of this sort are easy to construct (probably too easy); most of the theories posit information asymmetries, then show that an apparently irrational action—sticking with bad projects, following the herd (Scharfstein and Stein 1990), sticking with an inefficient status quo (Fernandez and Rodrik 1991)—is actually rational because the action conveys information. The main problem with this class of theories is that most posit a highly stylized economic setting much different than the setting created in the original experiments demonstrating the anomaly: at best they are *sufficient* explanations for an anomaly, but they are hardly necessary. Of course, in principle these explanations can be pitted against behavioral accounts and tested (e.g., Berg, Dickhaut, and Kanodia, in press). (I fear many readers do the opposite, exhibiting a "sufficiency bias" by taking sufficient explanations as *ending* the need to explore a behavioral phenomena further.) Experiments can play a special role because one can test theories of individual behavior directly *and* simultaneously test their implications in markets, rather than testing *only* market implications.

A second constructive reaction is expressed by Plott (1986) and Smith (1991). They frame the basic issue as a puzzle of aggregation: why do models that assume individuals behave rationally perform so well describing behavior in market experiments, if individuals behave irrationally in psychology experiments? There are three possible answers: (1) It does not take much rationality to behave nearly optimally in an experimental market; (2) traders learn in market experiments; and (3) market experiments overstate the degree of rationality in naturally occurring markets.

Gode and Sunder (1993) explore the first answer. They show, using simulations, that double auctions can be highly efficient even when simulated traders have very limited rationality.

Learning is a second answer, and has been insufficiently explored. For example, in Cox and Grether's preference reversal experiments, subjects' bids in a period are highly correlated with the previous period's winning bid. That correlation suggests markets are helping traders *construct* (or "discover") a preference by watching others, rather than simply revealing their well-formed preferences.

The third answer is that experimental markets overstate the ability of natural markets to erase individual irrationality. (The best answer along these lines can only come from further studies of behavioral phenomena in naturally occurring markets, which lie outside the scope of this handbook.) Two experimental approaches have been taken to exploring the boundaries of market magic. One approach begins with individual errors and constructs an experimental market in which they might persist, to search for domains in which experimental markets might fail. The other approach begins with market level anomalies and searches for explanations based on individual errors.

Several studies reviewed above took the first approach, creating experimental settings in which individual errors were likely, and studying whether errors were reduced by market forces (Duh and Sunder 1986; Camerer 1987, 1990, 1992b; Anderson and Sunder 1989; Camerer, Loewenstein, and Weber 1990; Ganguly, Kagel, and Moser, in press). These studies mostly show a tendency for prices to converge toward, but not to, Bayesian predictions. Psychologically predictable deviations persist. The data suggest the market glass is both half-full of deviations and half-empty because some deviations were drained away by learning.

The second approach tests whether anomalies originally observed in aggregate experimental data can be explained by behavioral models of individual choice. I mention three examples. Lind and Plott's (1991) alternative specifications of nonrational bidding behavior in low-bid common cost auctions with "seller's curse" is one. Cox, Smith, and Walker (1983) is another (cf. chapter 7 for a longer discussion): they give two behavioral models to explain the observed difference between Dutch auction and first price auction prices, and run experiments to test the models. A model in which bidders violate Bayes' rule, by underestimating the risk of losing the auction if time passes, appears to be the better of the two. Guler, Plott, and Vuong (1987) is an especially sophisticated example. They ran experiments based on "zero-out" auctions for airport landing slots, in which a government authority rebates all bidding revenue according to a known formula. Because of the rebates, airlines could bid much more than their reservation prices. Indeed, bids increased explosively over repeated auctions in one set of experiments and converged in another set. The data present a puzzle for traditional analysis: competitive equilibrium predicted badly (because the rebate formulas meant that slot valuations depended on the bids of others) and Nash equilibrium predicted badly too. They then considered two classes of alternative models of bidder decision making: game-theoretic models in which decision rules are derived from system equilibrium conditions (e.g., winning bidders bid slightly more than losing bidders); and decision-theoretic models in which bidders form beliefs over important parameters (e.g., what the losing bid will be) and update their beliefs. Models of the latter sort presume no game-theoretic sophistication and

15. Robyn Dawes suggested another example: therapists who believe that child abusers never stop without therapeutic treatment have their beliefs reinforced every time an abuser visits their clinic. The abusers who refute the theory never come to the clinic!

16. The forecasts of a random walk collected by Dwyer et al. (1993) are the most indicative of rationality of expectations. But even their data are mixed: when forecasts are pooled their variance is greater than the variance from a naive forecast (which is an optimal forecast for a random walk); and two-step-ahead forecasts should be *exactly* equal to one-step-ahead forecasts if subjects know the process is a random walk, but they are not.

17. Adaptiveness conflicts with rationality of expectations because it implies that people use information about a previous forecast error to alter their next forecast. But if forecasts are rational to begin with—randomly distributed around the correct price—then the previous forecast error contains no information and should be ignored (leading to b = zero in (1)). Adaptiveness and bias in forecast errors are therefore likely to go hand in hand, but it is possible that forecasts could be unbiased and—not realizing that—forecasters exhibit adaptiveness.

18. It matters little whether weights are derived by regressing past outcomes on observables ("actuarial" models), by standardizing observables for variance and weighting them equally, or by regressing expert judgments on observables ("bootstrapping" models); they improve accuracy by discarding (noisy regression residuals).

19. After discovering their axioms of expected utility, Morgenstern (1976, 809) reports that von Neumann "called out in astonishment, 'But didn't anyone see that?'"

20. Norman (1988) makes a similar point about product design. As technology improves, it is easy to design products with more functions. The tricky part is conveying the functions to consumers so they can be quickly understood and used. My father bought a VCR that can record up to eight programs a year in advance. He cannot figure out how to record even one program one day in advance.

21. Magical thinking is akin to two false "laws" anthropologists study: the law of similarity (similar objects share properties) and the law of contagion (objects transfer properties by touching). For instance, some primitive people, even civilized children, are afraid of photographs or dolls resembling tigers because they think those objects are as dangerous as tigers are. Innate beliefs like these are important even in modern cultures. Many species of animals are endangered—the black rhinoceros, Mexican sea turtles, some bears—because superstitious people desire to eat the animals or wear parts of them, to improve their health or sexual potency (Gilovich 1991, chap. 1).

22. An example of an uncontrollable, informative signal is the performance of other firms in an industry. The effort of company X's managers does not affect other firms' performance (by much), but the performance of other firms is informative about common industry-wide shocks that company X faced, and hence is useful in judging X's performance.

23. E.g., Machina (1982, 1987); Sugden (1986); and Weber and Camerer (1987).

24. As Edwards (1954c, 386) pointed out, the Hicks and Allen paper "was for economics something like the behaviorist revolution in psychology." It sowed the seeds for modern economists' distrust of survey evidence or introspection, and almost exclusive reliance on actual choices as data for constructing theories of behavior.

25. That is, could the certainty equivalent X' that solves X' $pH + (1 - p)L$ also be got by solving for X' in the difference-comparison $u(H) - u(X') = u(X') - u(L)$? If so, then the von Neumann–Morgenstern utility function is a riskless value function (à la Bernoulli) too. While some passages in von Neumann and Morgenstern's book suggested an equivalence, it is strongly denied in other places. See Fishburn (in press) for an exegesis.

26. Allais felt that a "neo-Bernoullian" value function should underly the theory of choice under risk, and risk aversion could be captured by aversion to variance in value or distortion of probability. The last two hundred pages of Allais and Hagen (1979) air his views.

27. They induced value by letting the player with the most points at the end choose candy, cigarettes, or cigars as a prize (!). It is also notable that several subjects were faculty members

("in many cases they were observed making active use of this [probability] theory" [186]); their responses were no different.

28. The Preston-Baratta curve, and those derived by many others, cannot be taken to reflect pure probability weights because they did not control for nonlinearity of *utility* in deriving it. Furthermore, they interpreted their weights as psychological translations with the formal properties of probabilities (satisfying additivity, etc.) which Kahneman and Tversky's decision weights need not satisfy.

29. The Guardsmen were much closer to risk neutral when instructing agents how to bet for them, which suggests some utility for participation masqueraded as risk preference when they made bets themselves.

30. Edwards (1954c) pointed out that both outcomes and probability could be weighted linearly or nonlinearly and combined, resulting in four possible models. Expected value assumed linearity of both, expected utility assumed linearity of probability only, no model assumed linearity of outcomes only (until Handa 1977 and Yaari 1987), and Edwards proposed an extension of expected utility in which both were nonlinear. He used the term "subjective expected utility" to refer to his extension, but I will refer to "nonlinear probability weights" instead since Savage (1954) defined subjective expected utility differently than Edwards.

31. In their inflation experiment, Daniels and Plott (1988) tested whether buyers forecasted lower prices than sellers, reflecting a kind of wishful thinking (or residue of magical belief that forecasting low prices would make prices low). In forty-eight of seventy-eight periods average buyer and seller forecasts *were* different ($p = .02$, one-tailed). This is a good example of the kind of behaviorally provocative finding that emerges by gathering richer kinds of data, and asking more unorthodox questions, than experimental economists often do.

32. That is, suppose a, b, c, and d are all measured utilities. Then $a > b$ and $c > d$ should imply $a + c > b + d$. It did, in twenty-nine of thirty cases.

33. The excruciating care in their techniques is remarkable. Disentangling subjective probability and utility was considered the crucial empirical question in decision making in the 1950s (after Ramsey showed how to do it in principle in 1931) and no effort was spared to do it properly. All choices were operationalized with random devices; subjects played some gambles, for substantial stakes; instructions and a lot of raw data are published in their monograph; subjects were run in up to three repeated sessions; subjects actually played gambles at the end, etc. Their instructions read (52): "These dice have been made especially for us, and they are as fair as dice can be. In fact, they have been ground to specifications accurate to 1/10,000th of an inch."

34. This design addressed another complaint about Mosteller and Nogee, that utility of money was confounded with utility of gambling because subjects compared certain sums (no utility of gambling) with gambles (utility of gambling). In the Davidson et al. design they compared two bets, rather than stating certainty-equivalents, so utility of gambling was held fixed.

35. This approach is fundamentally different than that taken by Machina (1985) and Crawford (1988) who show that with quasi-concave preferences people *prefer* to randomize in choosing between two gambles, generating the appearance of stochastic choice.

36. The data are also consistent with their regret-based theory (see section II.H.2 later) which assumes a different logic than the attribute-comparison process described here. However, the original Tversky (1969) data are inconsistent with regret aversion. Furthermore, those data and the Loomes and Sugden cycles can both be explained by an additive-difference model discussed by Tversky.

37. This behavior is consistent with a multiattribute utility model in which each attribute has a separable utility, and the attribute utilities are added to determine the alternative's overall utility. But eliminating high-rent apartments entirely implies that the disutility from rent above some threshold is negatively infinite.

38. Put your left hand in hot water and your right hand in cold water for a minute. Both will adapt to the temperatures of the water in which they sit. Then put both hands in the same tub of warm water. Since your hands are sensitive to *changes* from the temperature level to which

they have adapted, the hot left hand will feel colder, and the cold left hand will feel warmer, even though the water temperature they both feel is precisely the same. Prospect theory assumes a similar kind of adaption works in judging satisfaction with monetary (and other) outcomes.

39. For example, subjects are roughly indifferent between getting nothing, and accepting a coin flip between −$10 and $X when X is around 25 (Tversky and Kahneman 1991).

40. The breadth of Machina's technical contribution might be questioned on empirical grounds. His 1982 paper, for example, showed that if people integrate assets and are "globally" risk averse—that each of the "local utility functions" used to value different gambles exhibit risk aversion—then many implications of EU models assuming a single risk averse utility function would hold. But the usefulness of his remarkable proof is undercut by empirical evidence that local utility functions are *not* uniformly risk averse or risk seeking (see especially sections III.D and III.H later); so the "if" part of his "if-then" proof appears questionable.

41. The implications of weakening other axioms have been thoroughly worked out too. Aumann (1962) showed that weakening completeness to acyclicity of preferences ($X > Y$, $Y > Z$ implies $Z \not\succ X$—Z is not preferred to X) yields a unidirectional partial order in which $u(X) > u(Y)$ if $X > Y$ (but $u(X) > u(Y)$ does not always imply $X > Y$, because preferences can be incomplete). Hausner (1954) and Chipman (1960) showed that weakening continuity yields a vector utility representation over which preferences are lexicographic, rather than a single real-valued function.

42. Machina (1982) defined fanning out formally as follows: Suppose a gamble X stochastically dominates Y. (Then X lies to the northwest of Y—higher p_H, lower p_L—in a triangle diagram.) Indifference curves fan out if the slope of their tangent line at X is greater than the slope at Y. Fanning in is the opposite: the slope at X is smaller than at Y.

43. In general, weighting functions have two important features, the location of the crossover point where $g(p) = p$, and the degree of curvature. The one parameter form in equation (8) does not allow both features to move independently; the crossover point falls as curvature becomes greater. Adding a second parameter decouples these two graphical properties.

44. The *H-O* comparison does not quite test fanning out, because all the gambles lying along the *O*-pair chord are not stochastically dominated by the *H*-chord gambles. Thus, one can construct an unusual pattern of local utility functions that fan out and generate the observed data. This is a good example of how a very small difference in the design of pairs (pulling the p_H in the riskier *O*-pair gamble down below the p_H in the less-risky *H*-pair gamble) makes a big difference between a clean test of fanning out and an approximate test.

45. Many of the judgment experiments used between-subject designs because they search for inconsistencies in judgments in two settings. The optimal choice of design depends on the need for statistical power (within is more powerful than between), the subjects' tolerance for repeated tasks (high tolerance permits within), and the errors from overstating and understating consistency relative to natural settings (the conventional view is that within overstates, between understates, but I do not know of much evidence on precisely this point).

46. Earlier studies (e.g., Mosteller and Nogee 1951) gathered such data by giving subjects identical choices many times. The danger is that making so many choices may overwhelm subjects and may induce them to use simple rules that masquerade as conformity to theory (as data in Slovic, Lichtenstein, and Edwards [1965] suggest).

47. Whether experimenters have subjects play gambles is not entirely a product of economic background or modern raised consciousness. Siegel, Coombs, Edwards, Slovic, Tversky, and other psychologists often had subjects play gambles in the 1950s and 1960s. Some felt that playing gambles made little difference and quit doing it; others think playing gambles is important.

48. Neilson (1989) suggests a clever alternative theory in which *utilities* rise when gambles have fewer possible outcomes. His theory avoids nonlinear weighting of probabilities entirely. This theory violates continuity, and cannot explain all the empirical data, but deserves further exploration.

49. Their model uses a Taylor series expansion to approximate expected utility by several terms

whose coefficients can be estimated. In the EU approach, the coefficient of the variance of repair probability (in their notation, $(p - p_0)^2$) should be zero. The coefficient appears to be negative (with a modest t-statistic of 1.57), which suggests a weighting function $g(p)$ that is concave around the low repair probability of .005 (as predicted by prospect theory and some other accounts).

50. Subjects were shown an initial gamble on either the left or lower triangle edge then asked to name a gamble on the hypotenuse, where $p_M = 0$, which was equivalent in preference (i.e., a point on the same indifference curve). Subjects then named successive interior points that were equally preferred until three to five points on a single indifference curve were found. (Subjects did not play any gambles.)

51. Real (1991) studied the behavior of bees "visiting" artificial flowers with different probability distributions of nectar (controlled by the experimenter). He discovered that bees appear to underestimate low probabilities of getting rewarded with nectar, and overestimate high probabilities, which hints at an important cross-species difference in probability perception between bees and people.

52. As the two probabilities fall (maintaining a constant ratio), if fanning out is true people will become more risk seeking and choose larger values of A^*.

53. Ellsberg alluded to "a large number of responses, under absolutely nonexperimental conditions" suggesting ambiguity aversion is the majority pattern of choice.

54. The color red was chosen by a coin flip, after "the group was asked if there was any objection to flipping a coin to determine the winning color for the game to be played" (67). In other experiments subjects could choose a color to bet on, or were asked their certainty-equivalents for bets on both colors.

55. A third principle is "context invariance": preference for an object should not depend on the set of choices from which it can be picked. There are some interesting violations of this principle too (Huber, Payne, and Puto 1982; Tversky and Simonson 1993). The lottery correlation effect observed in studies of regret, described in section III.H.2 later, are another example, because they show that preference for a gamble in a pairwise choice depends in a systematic way on the gamble it is paired with.

56. In many choice experiments, the correlation of outcomes is not explicitly fixed. Regret may cause EU violations if subjects have particular correlations in mind.

Battalio, Kagel, and Jiranyakul (1990), Harless (1992a), Camerer (1989a, 1992a), Starmer and Sugden (1987b) used displays that controlled for regret effects and still found EU violations; Tversky and Kahneman (1992) controlled for regret and found SEU violations (using bets on natural events). However, it is true that the most striking EU violations appeared in studies that did not control for regret (e.g., Prelec 1990, and Conlisk 1989). Loomes and Sugden (1987b), Loomes (1988a), and Starmer and Sugden (1989a) found that regret effects account for part of the common ratio and common consequence effects, but not all.

57. Notice that violating reduction in random-gamble settings by isolating each pair economizes on mental effort; to obey reduction requires multiplying probabilities and choosing a portfolio of gambles to maximize the choice of an extremely complicated compound lottery.

58. Similarly, an "enriched" person like the entertainer Madonna is likely to be both married frequently (chosen) and divorced frequently (rejected); a business with many unusual features might be a likely candidate for both acquisition and divestment.

59. Tversky et al. also used a procedure to avoid criticism of BDM, like Cox and Epstein's procedure, in which subjects stated prices that were used only to rank bets. An important difference is that subjects priced each bet in a pair separately (rather than concurrently, as in Cox and Epstein, which appeared to make pricing much more like choice). Tversky et al. also showed a dramatic rate of reversals in a novel intertemporal choice context. People appeared much more impatient when choosing than when pricing: for example, 57 percent of subjects preferred $1,600 in eighteen months to $2,500 in five years, but only 12 percent priced the $1,600 bond higher.

60. Bohm's experiment strikes me as an example of both the best and the worst of experimental economics methods brought to bear on a psychologically-inspired phenomenon. The econo-

mists' intuition that people might behave differently if they are highly motivated drove his extraordinary design, creating a test of robustness to incentives that few psychologists would ever conduct. At the same time, his odd choice of objects (Volvo and Opel) violates the basic recipe for producing reversals that has been well-known since the early 1970s: that is, have people choose between two objects that are high and low on opposite attributes, then "price" both objects (or adjust one to indifference) using a rating scale that matches one of the two attributes. A poor choice of objects meant the ingenuity of his design was largely wasted.

61. A lower value of r implies less error in choosing, so more P-bettors will actually choose the P-bet. Since reversals occur when P-bettors price the \$-bet higher, an increased number of P-bettors can raise the overall reversal rate.

62. Such valuations are often called "contingent valuations" because they are designed to measure how consumers value goods *as if*—or contingent on the assumption that—there is a market for the good.

63. When means are used, WTP = \$3.45 and WTA = \$4.71 in the final auction; when medians are used, WTP = \$1.33 and WTA = \$3.49.

64. In their auction, bids were not stated directly. Instead, buyers (sellers) were asked whether they would prefer to buy (sell) a mug or not, at each price between 0 and \$10 (in \$.25 intervals). Their responses were used to construct demand and supply curves; their intersection determined a market price and who would trade. Thus, subjects' bids were constructed from choices between the good and a series of potential market prices. (In psychological terms, bidding is a choice task rather than a "production" or valuation task.) The procedure seems to make bidding one's true valuation more transparent; conversely, it makes strategic underbidding to affect prices more opaque. (Strategic underbidding can be optimal because the risk of failing to buy at a profitable price, because of underbidding, is offset by the potential gain from being the price-setter and lowering the price.)

65. As discussed in a section III.D methodological digression, the within-subjects design may overstate subjects' consistency (compared to the degree observed in between-subjects designs) if subjects think consistency is demanded of them, or if the equivalence of buying and selling is more transparent and if the buying and selling tasks are conducted right after one another.

66. Hanemann (1991) points out that the wealth effect can be large if income elasticity is high and the cross-elasticity of other goods with the good being valued is low. These conditions might apply to some environmental goods (such as glorious beachfront property or mountaintop views) but they only apply in experiments with more mundane goods such as mugs under the absurd presumptions that (1) there are no good substitutes for mugs and (2) sellers prefer to spend most of their mug-wealth on mugs. (The condition (2) is empirically indistinguishable from the endowment effect, and can be considered a formal restatement of it.)

67. The reference-dependent model also explains the finding that cross-price elasticities appear to be asymmetric: high-quality brands gain more market share from low-quality brands by cutting prices than vice versa (because consumers do not want to give up the high quality 'in their endowment').

68. Kahneman, Knetsch, and Thaler (1990) suggest that endowment effects are *not* particularly common in markets where goods are specifically bought for exchange, but Rietz's results suggest otherwise.

69. Call the optimal reservation price in period t P_t. If an observed price P' is rejected one period, then $P' < P_t$. Since the reservation price should be P in all periods, if $P' < P_t$ in one period it is less than P_t in all periods (since $P_t = P$) and should never be recalled.

70. One motive for eliciting reservation wages directly is that the percentage of searches ending at the right time is a weak test of whether behavior is optimal. Cox and Oaxaca (1990) calculate that a naive subject who used the mean of the offer distribution as a reservation wage would end searches optimally 75 percent of the time. Compared to this benchmark, the fact that 80 percent of searches ended at the right time is unimpressive.

71. I am always surprised that economists do not eagerly or routinely turn to the psychological models as viable alternatives, or at least to psychological facts for theoretical inspiration. Of

course, the psychological ideas usually do not come packaged as economists need them. Psychological models are often parameter-heavy or expressed verbally, since models are not usually constrained by severe analytical or econometric demands. Refitting the models is a chore economists must do for themselves. I do not see how psychologists can offer more help than they have already, in papers such as Tversky and Kahneman (1991).

Bibliography

Abdellaoui, M., and Bertrand Munier. 1992. Experimental estimation of indifference curves in the Marschak-Machina triangle: Can decision models be ranked or risk structure related? Working paper. GRID, ENS de Cachan.

Abelson, Robert P., and A. Levi. 1985. Decision making and decision theory. In *Handbook of social psychology*, 3rd ed., G. Lindzey and E. Aronson, editors, New York: Random House.

Ainslie, G. 1975. Specious reward: A behavioral theory of impulsiveness and impulse control. *Psychological Bulletin* 82:463–509.

Ajzen, I. 1977. Intuitive theories of events and the effects of base-rate information on prediction. *Journal of Personality and Social Psychology* 35:303–14.

Akerlof, G., and J. Yellen. 1985. Can small deviations from rationality make significant differences in economic equilibria? *American Economic Review* 75:708–20.

Allais, M. 1953. Le comportement de l'homme rationel devant le risque, critique des postulates et axiomes de l'ecole Americaine. *Econometrica* 21:503–46.

———. 1979. The so-called Allais paradox and rational decisions under uncertainty. In *The Expected Utility Hypothesis and the Allais Paradox*, M. Allais and O. Hagen, editors, Dordrecht: Reidel.

Allais, M., and Hagen, O. E. editors. 1979. *The expected utility hypothesis and the Allais Paradox*. Dordrecht: Reidel.

Allen, F. 1987. Discovering personal probabilities when utility functions are unknown. *Management Science* 33:542–4.

Alloy, L. B., and L. Y. Abramson. 1979. Judgment of contingency in depressed and non-depressed students: Sadder but wiser? *Journal of Experimental Psychology: General* 108:441–85.

Alpert, M., and H. Raiffa. 1982. A progress report on the training of probability assessors. In *Judgment Under Uncertainty: Heuristics and Biases*, D. Kahneman, P. Slovic, and A. Tversky, editors, Cambridge: Cambridge University Press. 294–305.

Anderson, M. J., and S. Sunder. 1988. Professional traders as intuitive Bayesians. Working paper 88–89–51. Carnegie-Mellon University.

Anscombe, F. J., and R. Aumann. 1963. A definition of subjective probability. *Annals of Mathematical Statistics* 34:199–205.

Antle, R., and A. Smith. 1986. An empirical investigation of the relative performance evaluation of corporate executives. *Journal of Accounting Research* 24:1–39.

Argote, L., R. Devadas, and N. Melone. 1990. The base-rate fallacy: Contrasting processes and outcomes of group and individual judgment. *Organizational Behavior and Human Decision Processes* 46:296–310.

Argote, L., M. A. Seabright, and L. Dyer. 1986. Individual versus group use of base-rate and individuating information. *Organizational Behavior and Human Decision Processes* 38:65–75.

Arkes, H., and Hammond, K. R. 1987. *Judgment and decision making: An interdisciplinary reader*. Cambridge: Cambridge University Press.

Attneave, F. 1953. Psychological probability as a function of experienced frequency. *Journal of Experimental Psychology* 46:81–6.

Aumann, R. J. 1962. Utility theory without the completeness axiom. *Econometrica* 30:445–62; 32 (1964): 210–12.

Ausubel, L. M. 1991. The failure of competition in the credit card market. *American Economic Review* 81:50–81.

Babcock, Linda, George Loewenstein, Samuel Issacharoff, and Colin Camerer. In press. Biased judgments of fairness in bargaining. *American Economic Review*.

Bar-Hillel, M. 1973. On the subjective probability of compound events. *Organizational Behavior and Human Performance* 9:396–406.

———. 1980. The base-rate fallacy in probability judgments. *Acta Psychologica* 44:211–33.

Bar-Hillel, M., and W. A. Wagenaar. In press. Perceptions of randomness. *Advances in Applied Mathematics*.

Baron, Jonathan. In press. Nonconsequentialist decisions. *Behavioral and Brain Sciences*.

Baron, J., and J. C. Hershey. 1988. Outcome bias in decision evaluation. *Journal of Personality and Social Psychology* 54:569–79.

Barro, R., and S. Fischer. 1976. Recent developments in monetary theory. *Journal of Monetary Economics* 2:13–76.

Battalio, R. C., J. H. Kagel, and K. Jiranyakul. 1990. Testing between alternative models of choice under uncertainty: Some initial results. *Journal of Risk and Uncertainty* 3:25–50.

Battalio, R. C., J. H. Kagel, and D. N. MacDonald. 1985. Animals' choices over uncertain outcomes: Some initial experimental evidence. *American Economic Review* 75:597–613.

Bazerman, M. H. 1990. *Judgment in managerial decision making.* New York: Wiley.

Bazerman, M., G. F. Loewenstein, and S. Blount White. 1992. Reversals of preference in allocation decisions: Judging an alternative versus choosing among alternatives. *Administrative Science Quarterly* 37:220–40.

Beach, L. R., and L. D. Phillips. 1967. Subjective probabilities inferred from estimates and bets. *Journal of Experimental Psychology* 75:354–9.

Becker, G. M., M. H. DeGroot, and J. Marschak. 1963. An experimental study of some stochastic models for wagers. *Behavioral Science* 8:41–55.

———. 1964. Measuring utility by a single-response sequential method. *Behavioral Science* 9:226–232.

Becker, J. L. and R. Sarin. 1987. Gamble dependent utility. *Management Science* 33:1367–82.

Becker, J. L., and R. K. Sarin. 1990. Economics of ambiguity in probability. Working paper. UCLA Graduate School of Management.

Becker, S. W., and F. O. Brownson. 1964. What price ambiguity? Or the role of ambiguity in decision-making. *Journal of Political Economy* 72:62–73.

Bell, D. E. 1982. Regret in decision making under uncertainty. *Operations Research* 30:961–81.

Bell, David E., Howard Raiffa, and Amos Tversky. 1988. *Decision making: Descriptive, normative, and prescriptive interactions.* Cambridge: Cambridge University Press.

Benzion, U., A. Rapoport, and J. Yagil. 1989. Discount rates inferred from decisions: An experimental study. *Management Science* 35:270–84.

Berg, J. E. 1995. The impact of controllability and informativeness on the use of public information in contracting: An experimental investigation. Working paper. University of Iowa, College of Business.

Berg, J. E., L. Daley, J. Dickhaut, and J. O'Brien. 1985. Preference reversal and arbitrage. In *Research in experimental economics, vol. 3*, V. L. Smith, editor, Greenwich, Conn.: JAI Press. 31–72.

———. 1986. Controlling preferences for gambles on units of experimental exchange. *Quarterly Journal of Economics* 101:281–306.

Berg, J. E., and J. W. Dickhaut. 1990. Preference reversals: Incentives do matter. Working paper. University of Minnesota Department of Accounting, November.

Berg, J. E., J. W. Dickhaut, and C. Kanodia. In press. The role of information asymmetry in escalation phenomena: Experimental evidence. *Journal of Economic Behavior and Organization*.

Berg, J. E., J. W. Dickhaut, and K. McCabe. 1992. Risk preference instability across institutions: A dilemma. Working paper. University of Minnesota, Department of Accounting.

Bernasconi, Michele. 1992. Different frames for the independence axiom: An experimental investigation in individual decision making under risk. *Journal of Risk and Uncertainty* 5, 159–74.

Bernasconi, M. 1994. Nonlinear preferences and two-stage lotteries: Theories and evidence. *Economic Journal* 104:54–70.

Bernasconi, M., and G. Loomes. 1992. Failures of the reduction principle in an Ellsberg-type problem. *Theory and Decision* 32:77–100.

Bernoulli, Daniel. 1738. Specimen theoriae novae de mensura sortis. *Commentarii Academiae Scientiarum Imperialis Petropolitanae* (for 1730 and 1731) 5:175–92.

Bewley, T. F. 1986. Knightian decision theory: Part I. Cowles Foundation discussion paper no. 807, New Haven, Conn.

Blank, R. M. 1991. The effects of double-blind versus single-blind reviewing: Experimental evidence from American Economic Review. *American Economic Review* 81(5): 1041–67.

Bohm, P. 1990. Behavior under uncertainty without preference reversal: A field experiment. University of Stockholm, Department of Economics.

Bölle, F. 1988. Learning to make good predictions in time series. In *Bounded rational behavior in games and markets*, R. Tietz, W. Albers and R. Selten, editors, Berlin: Springer-Verlag.

Bostic, R., R. J. Herrnstein, and R. D. Luce. 1990. The effect on the preference-reversal phenomenon of using choice indifferences. *Journal of Economic Behavior and Organization* 13:193–212.

Bowman, David, Debby Minehart, and Matthew Rabin. 1993. Modeling loss aversion: Some general issues, and an application to a savings model. Working paper. University of California at Berkeley, Department of Economics.

Boyce, Rebecca R., Thomas C. Brown, Gary H. McClelland, George L. Peterson, and William D. Schulze. 1992. An experimental examination of intrinsic values as a source for the WTA-WTP disparity. *American Economic Review* 82:1366–73.

Braun, Philip A., and Ilan Yaniv. 1992. A case study of expert judgment: Economists' probabilities versus base-rate model forecasts. *Journal of Behavioral Decision Making* 5:217–31.

Braunstein, Y. M., and A. Schotter. 1982. Labor market search: An experimental study. *Economic Inquiry* 20:133–44.

Brehmer, B. 1980. In one word: Not from experience. *Acta Psychologica* 45:223–41.

Brier, G. W. 1950. Verification of forecasts expressed in terms of probability. *Monthly Weather Review* 78:1–3.

Brothers, Alan. 1990. An empirical investigation of some properties that are relevant to generalized expected-utility theory. Unpublished doctoral dissertation. University of California at Irvine.

Brown, J. N., and R. W. Rosenthal. 1990. Testing the minimax hypothesis: A re-examination of O'Neill's game experiment. *Econometrica* 58(5):1065–81.

Brown, William O., and Raymond D. Sauer. 1993. Does the basketball market believe in the hot hand? Comment. *American Economic Review* 83 (5):1377–86.

Bruner, J. S., L. Postman, and J. Rodrigues. 1951. Expectations and the perception of color. *American Journal of Psychology* 64:216–27.

Busche, K., and C. D. Hall. 1988. An exception to the risk preference anomaly. *Journal of Business* 61:337–46.

Camerer, C. F. 1987. Do biases in probability judgment matter in markets? Experimental evidence. *American Economic Review* 77:981–97.

———. 1989a. An experimental test of several generalized utility theories. *Journal of Risk and Uncertainty* 2:61–104.

———. 1989b. Does the basketball market believe in the 'hot hand'? *American Economic Review* 79:1257–61.

———. 1990. Do markets correct biases in probability judgment? Evidence from market experiments. In *Advances in behavioral economics, vol. 2*, L. Green and J. Kagel, editors, Greenwich, Conn.: JAI Press. 126–72.

———. 1992a. Recent tests of generalized utility theories. In *Utility theories: Measurement and applications*, W. Edwards, editor, Cambridge: Cambridge University Press.

Camerer, C. F. 1992b. The rationality of prices and volume in experimental markets. *Organizational Behavior and Human Decision Processes*, 51:237–72.

Camerer, C. F., and T.-H. Ho. 1994. Violations of the betweenness axiom and nonlinearity in probability. *Journal of Risk and Uncertainty* 8:167–96.

Camerer, C. F., and E. J. Johnson. 1991. The process-performance paradox in expert judgment: How can experts know so much and predict so badly? In *Toward a general theory of expertise: Prospects and limits*, K. A. Ericsson and J. Smith, editors, Cambridge: Cambridge University Press.

Camerer, Colin F., and Risto Karjalainen. 1994. Ambiguity and nonadditive probability in non-cooperative game experiments. In *Models and Experiments on Risk and Rationality*, M. Machina and B. Munier editors, Dordrecht: Kluwer Academic Publishers.

Camerer, C. F., and H. C. Kunreuther. 1989. Experimental markets for insurance. *Journal of Risk and Uncertainty* 2:265–300.

Camerer, C. F., G. Loewenstein, and M. Weber. 1989. The curse of knowledge in economic settings: An experimental analysis. *Journal of Political Economy* 97:1232–54.

Camerer, C. F., and M. W. Weber. 1992. Recent developments in modelling preferences: Uncertainty and ambiguity. *Journal of Risk and Uncertainty*, 5:325–70.

Camerer, C. F., and K. Weigelt. 1990. Bubbles and convergence in experimental markets for stochastically-lived assets. Working paper no. 87–09–02. University of Pennsylvania Department of Decision Sciences.

Carbone, Enrica, and John D. Hey. 1994. Discriminating between preference functionals: A preliminary Monte Carlo study. *Journal of Risk and Uncertainty* 8:223–42.

Carlson, J. A. 1967. The stability of an experimental market with a supply-response lag. *Southern Economic Journal* 33:305–21.

Carlson, Cynthia R., and Richard D. Johnson. 1992. Measuring the rate of time preference as a function of delay: An experimental study. Working paper. University of Alberta Department of Marketing and Economic Analysis.

Casey, J. T. 1994. Buyer's pricing behavior for risky alternatives: Encoding processes and preference reversals. *Management Science* 40:730–49.

———. 1991. Reversal of the preference reversal phenomenon. *Organizational Behavior and Human Decision Processes* 48:224–51.

Caskey, J. 1985. Modelling the formation of price expectations: The Bayesian approach. *American Economic Review* 75:768–76.

Castellan, N. J., Jr. 1977. Decision making with multiple probabilistic cues. In *Cognitive theory, vol. 2*, N. J. Castellan, D. Pisoni and G. R. Potts, editors, Hillsdale, N.J.: Lawrence Erlbaum Associates.

Chapanis, A. 1953. Random-number guessing behavior. *American Psychologist* 8:332.

Chew, S. H. 1983. A generalization of the quasilinear mean with applications to the measurement of income inequality and decision theory resolving the Allais Paradox. *Econometrica* 51:1065–92.

———. 1985. Implicit-weighted and semi-weighted utility theories, m-estimators, and non-demand revelation of second-price auctions for an uncertain auctioned object. Working paper 155. Johns Hopkins University Department of Political Economy, June.

———. 1989. Axiomatic utility theories with the betweenness property. *Annals of Operations Research* 19:273–98.

Chew, S. H., L. G. Epstein, and U. Segal. 1991. Mixture symmetry and quadratic utility. *Econometrica* 59:139–63.

Chew, S. H., and K. R. MacCrimmon. 1979a. Alpha-nu choice theory: An axiomatization of expected utility. Working paper 669. University of British Columbia Faculty of Commerce.

———. 1979b. Alpha utility theory, lottery composition and the Allais paradox. Working Paper. No. 686. University of British Columbia, Faculty of Commerce and Business Administration.

Chew, S. H., and W. S. Waller. 1986. Empirical tests of weighted utility theory. *Journal of Mathematical Psychology* 30:55–72.

Chipman, J. S. 1960. The foundations of utility. *Econometrica* 28:193–224.

Choquet, G. 1955. Theory of capacities. *Annales de l'Institut Fourier* 5:131–295.

Christensen-Szalanski, J. J. J., and C. F. Willham. 1991. The hindsight bias: A meta-analysis. *Organizational Behavior and Human Decision Processes* 48:147–68.

Chu, Y.-P., and R.-L. Chu. 1990. The subsidence of preference reversals in simplified and market-like experimental settings: A note. *American Economic Review* 80:902–11.

Cicchetti, Charles J., and Jeffrey A. Dubin. 1994. A micro-econometric analysis of risk-aversion and the decision to self-insure. *Journal of Political Economy* 102:169–86.

Clotfelter, Charles T., and Philip J. Cook. 1993. The "gambler's fallacy" in lottery play. *Management Science* 39:1521–25.

Cohen, D., and J. L. Knetsch. 1990. Judicial choice and disparities between measures of economic values. Working paper. Simon Fraser University.

Cohen, L. J. 1981. Can human irrationality be experimentally demonstrated? *Behavioral and Brain Sciences* 4:317–31.

Cohen, M., Jean-Yves Jaffrey, and T. Said. 1985. Individual behavior under risk and under uncertainty: An experimental study. *Theory and Decision* 18:203–28.

Cohen, M., and J.-Y. Jaffray. 1988. Preponderance of the certainty effect over probability distortion in decision making under risk. In *Risk, decision, and rationality*, B. R. Munier, editor, Dordrecht, Holland: D. Reidel.

Combs, B., and P. Slovic. 1979. Causes of death: Biased newspaper coverage and biased judgments. *Journalism Quarterly* 56:837–43, 849.

Conlisk, J. 1989. Three variants on the Allais example. *American Economic Review* 79:392–407.

Connolly, T., and N. Gilani. 1982. Information search in judgment tasks: A regression model and some preliminary findings. *Organizational Behavior and Human Decision Processes* 30:330–50.

Connolly, T., and B. K. Thorn. 1987. Predecisional information acquisition: Effects of task variables on suboptimal search strategies. *Organizational Behavior and Human Decision Processes* 39:397–416.

Coombs, C. H., and S. S. Komorita. 1958. Measuring utility of money through decisions. *American Journal of Psychology* 71:383–9.

Copeland, T., and D. Friedman. 1987. The market value of information: Some experimental results. *Journal of Business*, 65:241–66.

Coursey, D. L., J. L. Hovis, and W. D. Schulze. 1987. The disparity between willingness to accept and willingness to pay measures of value. *Quarterly Journal of Economics* 102:679–90.

Cox, J. C., and S. Epstein. 1988. Preference reversals without the independence axiom. *American Economic Review* 79:408–26.

Cox, J. C., and D. M. Grether. In press. The preference reversal phenomenon: Response mode, markets and incentives. *Economic Theory*.

Cox, J. C., and R. M. Isaac. 1986. Experimental economics and experimental psychology: Ever the twain shall meet? In *Economic psychology: Intersections in theory and application*, A. J. MacFadyen and H. W. MacFadyen, editors, Amsterdam: North-Holland.

Cox, J. C., and R. L. Oaxaca. 1989. Laboratory experiments with a finite-horizon job-search model. *Journal of Risk and Uncertainty* 2:301–30.

———. 1990. Direct tests of the reservation wage property. Working paper. University of Arizona, Department of Economics.

———. In press. Tests for a reservation wage effect. In *Decision making under risk and uncertainty: New models and empirical findings*, J. Geweke, editors, Dordrecht, Holland: Kluwer Academic Publishers.

Cox, J. C., V. L. Smith, and J. M. Walker. 1983. A test that discriminates between two models of the Dutch-first auction nonisomorphism. *Journal of Economic Behavior and Organization* 4:205–19.

Crawford, V. P. 1988. Stochastic choice with quasiconcave preference functions. Working paper 88–28. University of California, San Diego, Department of Economics.

Cummings, R. G., D. S. Brookshire, and W. D. Schulze, editors, 1986. *Valuing environmental goods*. Totowa, N.J.: Rowman and Allenheld.

Curley, S. P., and J. F. Yates. 1985. The center and range of the probability interval as factors affecting ambiguity preferences. *Organizational Behavior and Human Decision Processes* 36:272–87.

Curley, S. P. and J. F. Yates. 1989. An empirical evaluation of descriptive models of ambiguity reactions in choice situations. *Journal of Mathematical Psychology* 33:397–427.

Curley, S. P., J. F. Yates, and R. A. Abrams. 1986. Psychological sources of ambiguity avoidance. *Organizational Behavior and Human Decision Processes* 38:230–56.

Currim, I., and R. Sarin. 1989. Prospect versus utility. *Management Science* 35:22–41.

Daniels, B. P., and C. R. Plott. 1988. Inflation and expectations in experimental markets. In *Bounded rational behavior in experimental games and markets*, R. Tietz, W. Albers, and R. Selten, editors, Berlin: Springer-Verlag.

Daniels, R. L., and L. R. Keller. 1990. An experimental evaluation of the descriptive validity of lottery-dependent utility theory. *Journal of Risk and Uncertainty* 3:115–34.

Davidson, D., Suppes, P., and Siegel, S. 1957. *Decision-making: An experimental approach*. Stanford, Calif.: Stanford University Press.

Dawes, R. M. 1971. A case study of graduate admissions: Application of three principles of human decision making. *American Psychologist* 26:180–8.

———. 1988. *Rational choice in an uncertain world*. San Francisco: Harcourt, Brace, Jovanovich.

———. 1990. The potential nonfalsity of the false consensus effect. In *Insights in decision making: A tribute to Hillel J. Einhorn*, R. M. Hogarth, editor, Chicago: University of Chicago Press.

Dawes, R. M., Faust D., and P. E. Meehl. 1989. Clinical versus actuarial judgment. *Science* 243:1668–74.

de Finetti, B. 1937. La prevision: Ses lois logiques, ses sources sources subjectives. *Annales de l'Institut Henri Poincare* 7:1–68. English translation in H. E. Kyburg, and H. E. Smokler, editors (1964), *Studies in subjective probability*, New York: Wiley Publisher. 93–158.

———. 1962. Does it make sense to speak of good probability appraisers? In *The scientist speculates*, I.J. Good, editor, New York: Basic Books. 357–64.

de Finetti, B. 1977. Probabilities of probabilities: A real problem or a misunderstanding? In *New directions in the application of Bayesian methods*, A. Aykac and C. Brumat, editors, Amsterdam: North-Holland. 1–10.

De Neufville, R., and P. Delquie. 1988. A model of the influence of certainty and probability "effects" on the measurement of utility. In *Risk, decision, and rationality*, B. R. Munier, editor, Dordrecht, Holland: D. Reidel.

Debreu, G. 1958. Stochastic choice and cardinal utility. *Econometrica* 26:440–4.

Dekel, E. 1986. An axiomatic characterization of preferences under uncertainty: Weakening the independence axiom. *Journal of Economic Theory* 40:304–18.

Dow, J., and S. Ribeiro da Costa Werlang. 1992. Uncertainty aversion and the optimal choice of portfolio. *Econometrica* 60:197–204.

Duh, R. R., and S. Sunder. 1986. Incentives, learning, and processing of information in a market environment: An examination of the base rate fallacy. In *Laboratory market research*, S. Moriarty, editor, Norman, Okla.: University of Oklahoma Press.

Dwyer, G. P. Jr., A. W. Williams, R. C. Battalio, and T. I. Mason. 1993. Tests of rational expectations in a stark setting. *Economic Journal* 103:586–601.

Edwards, W. 1953. Probability preferences in gambling. *American Journal of Psychology* 66:349–64.

———. 1954a. Probability preferences among bets with differing expected values. *American Journal of Psychology* 67:56–67.

———. 1954b. The reliability of probability preferences. *American Journal of Psychology* 67:68–95.

———. 1954c. The theory of decision making. *Psychological Bulletin* 51:380–417.

———. 1961a. Behavioral decision theory. *Annual Review of Psychology* 12:473–98.

———. 1961b. Probability learning in 1000 trials. *Journal of Experimental Psychology* 62:385–94.

———. 1962. Subjective probabilities inferred from decisions. *Psychological Review* 69:109–135.

———. 1968. Conservatism in human information processing. In *Formal representation of human judgment*, B. Kleinmuntz, editor, New York: Wiley. 17–52.

Eger, C., and J. Dickhaut. 1982. An examination of the conservative information processing bias in an accounting framework. *Journal of Accounting Research* 20:711–23.

Einhorn, H. J. 1970. The use of nonlinear, noncompensatory models in decision-making. *Psychological Bulletin* 73:221–30.

Einhorn, H. J., and R. M. Hogarth. 1978. Confidence in judgment: Persistence of the illusion of validity. *Psychological Review* 85:395–416.

———. 1985. Ambiguity and uncertainty in probabilistic inference. *Psychological Review* 92:433–61.

Ellsberg, D. 1954. Classic and current notions of "measurable utility." *Economic Journal* 64:528–56.

———. 1961. Risk, ambiguity, and the Savage axioms. *Quarterly Journal of Economics* 75:643–69.

Epstein, L. G. In press. Behaviour under risk: Recent developments in theory and applications. In *Advances in economic theory: Sixth World Congress of the Econometric Society*, J. J. Laffont, editor, Cambridge: Cambridge University Press.

Erev, Ido, Thomas Wallsten, and David V. Budescu. 1992. Simultaneous overconfidence and conservatism in judgment: Implications for research and practice. Working paper. University of North Carolina, Department of Psychology.

Evans, Dorla A. 1992. Tests of expected utility theory at the individual and market levels. Working paper. University of Alabama at Huntsville, Department of Economics and Finance.

Fellner, W. 1961. Distortion of subjective probabilities as a reaction to uncertainty. *Quarterly Journal of Economics* 75:670–94.

Fernandez, R., and D. Rodrik. 1991. Resistance to reform: Status quo bias in the presence of individual-specific uncertainty. *American Economic Review* 81:1146–55.

Ferris, S. P., R. A. Haugen, and A. K. Makhija. 1988. Predicting contemporary volume with historic volume at differential price levels: Evidence supporting the disposition effect. *Journal of Finance* 43:677–97.

Fischer, G. W. 1982. Scoring-rule feedback and the overconfidence syndrome in subjective probability forecasting. *Organizational Behavior and Human Performance* 29:352–69.

Fischhoff, B. 1975. Hindsight ≠ foresight: The effect of outcome knowledge on judgment under uncertainty. *Journal of Experimental Psychology: Human Perception and Performance* 1:288–99.

———. 1982. Debiasing. In *Judgment under uncertainty: Heuristics and biases*, D. Kahneman, P. Slovic, and A. Tversky, editors, Cambridge: Cambridge University Press. 422–44.

———. 1983. Predicting frames. *Journal of Experimental Psychology: Learning, Memory, and Cognition* 9:103–116.

Fischhoff, B., and R. Beyth. 1975. "I knew it would happen"—Remembered probabilities of once-future things. *Organizational Behavior and Human Performance* 13:1–16.

Fischhoff, B., P. Slovic, and S. Lichtenstein. 1978. Fault trees: Sensitivity of estimated failure probabilities to problem representation. *Journal of Experimental Psychology: Human Perception and Performance* 4:330–4.

Fishburn, P. C. 1982. Nontransitive measurable utility. *Journal of Mathematical Psychology* 26:31–67.

Fishburn, P. C. 1983. Transitive measurable utility. *Journal of Economic Theory* 31: 293–317.

———. 1984. SSB utility theory: An economic perspective. *Mathematical Social Science* 8: 63–94.

———. 1988. *Nonlinear preference and utility theory*. Baltimore: Johns Hopkins Press.

———. 1989. Generalizations of expected utility theories: A survey of recent proposals. *Annals of Operations Research* 19:3–28.

———. 1990. Retrospective on the utility theory of von Neumann and Morgenstern. Working paper. AT&T Bell Labs.

Fishburn, P. C., and G. A. Kochenberger. 1979. Two-piece von Neumann-Morgenstern utility functions. *Decision Sciences* 10:503–18.

Fishburn, P. C., and A. Rubinstein. 1982. Time preference. *International Economic Review* 23:677–94.

Forsythe, Robert, Forrest Nelson, George R. Neumann, and Jack Wright. 1992. Anatomy of a political stock market. *American Economic Review* 82:1142–61.

Franciosi, Robert, Praveen Kujal, Roland Michelitsch, and Vernon Smith. 1993. Experimental tests of the endowment effect. Working paper. University of Arizona, Department of Economics, March.

Fredrickson, Barbara L., and Daniel Kahneman. In press. Duration neglect in retrospective evaluations of affective episodes. *Journal of Personality and Social Psychology.*

French, K. R., and J. M. Poterba. 1991. Investor diversification and international equity markets. *American Economic Review (Papers and Proceedings)* 81:222–6.

Friedman, M. 1953. *Methodology of positive economics*. Chicago: University of Chicago Press.

Friedman, D. 1989. The S-shaped value function as a constrained optimum. *American Economic Review* 79:1243–9.

Frisch, D., and J. Baron. 1988. Ambiguity and rationality. *Journal of Behavioral Decision Making* 1:149–57.

Ganguly, A. R., J. H. Kagel, and D. V. Moser. In press. The effects of biases in probability judgments in asset markets: An experimental examination of the base rate fallacy. *Journal of Economic Behavior and Organization.*

Gärdenfors, P., and N.-E. Sahlin. 1982. Unreliable probabilities, risk taking, and decision making. *Synthese* 53:361–86.

Garner, A. C. 1982. Experimental evidence on the rationality of intuitive forecasters. In *Research in experimental economics, vol. 2*, V. L. Smith, editor, Greenwich, Conn.: JAI Press.

Gertner, Robert. 1993. Game shows and economic behavior: Risk-taking on "Card Sharks." *Quarterly Journal of Economics.* 108:507–21.

Gigerenzer, G., W. Hell, and H. Blank. 1988. Presentation and content: The use of base rates as a continuous variable. *Journal of Experimental Psychology* 14(3):513–25.

Gigerenzer, Gerd, U. Hoffrage, and H. Kleinbölting. 1991. Probabilistic mental models: A Brunswikian theory of confidence. *Psychological Review* 98:506–28.

Gigliotti, G., and B. Sopher. 1990. Testing alternative linear representations of behavior under uncertainty: Expected utility, weighted linear utility, transitive convex and nontransitive convex preferences. Rutgers University, Department of Economics, February.

Gilboa, I. 1987. Expected utility with purely subjective nonadditive probabilities. *Journal of Mathematical Economics* 16:65–88.

Gilboa, I., and D. Schmeidler. 1989. Maxmin expected utility with a non-unique prior. *Journal of Mathematical Economics* 18:141–53.

Gilboa, Itzhak, and David Schmeidler. In press. Case-based decision theory. *Quarterly Journal of Economics.*

Gilovich, T. 1991. *How we know what isn't so: Fallacies of human reasoning*. New York: Free Press.

Gilovich, T., R. Vallone, and A. Tversky. July 1985. The hot hand in basketball: On the misperception of random sequences. *Cognitive Psychology* 17:295–314.

Gode, Dhananjay K., and Shyam Sunder. 1993. Allocative efficiency of markets with zero-intelligence traders: Market as a partial substitute for individual rationality. *Journal of Political Economy* 101:119–37.

Green, J., and B. Jullien. 1988. Ordinal independence in nonlinear utility theory. *Journal of Risk and Uncertainty* 1:355–87. (Erratum, 1989, 2, 119).

Greenberg, M. R., D. B. Sachsman, P. M. Sandman, and K. L. Salomone. 1989. Network evening news coverage of environmental risk. *Risk Analysis* 9:119–26.

Gregory, Robin, and Lita Furby. 1987. Auctions, experiments and contingent valuation. *Public Choice* 55:273–89.

Grether, D. M. 1980. Bayes' rule as a descriptive model: The representativeness heuristic. *Quarterly Journal of Economics* 95:537–57.

———. 1981. Financial incentive effects and individual decision making. Working paper no. 401. California Institute of Technology.

———. 1990. Testing Bayes rule and the representativeness heuristic: Some experimental evidence. *Journal of Economic Behavior and Organization* 17:31–57.

Grether, D., and C. R. Plott. 1979. Economic theory of choice and the preference reversal phenomenon. *American Economic Review* 69:623–38.

Grether, David M., Alan Schwartz, and Louis L. Wilde. 1988. Uncertainty and shopping behaviour: An experimental analysis. *Review of Economic Studies* 60:323–42.

Grether, D., and L. L. Wilde. March 1984. An analysis of conjunctive choice: Theory and experiments. *Journal of Consumer Research* 10:373–85.

Grice, H. P. 1975. Logic and conversation. In *The logic of grammar*, D. Davidson and G. Harman, editors, Encino, Calif.: Dickenson.

Griffin, Dale, and Amos Tversky. 1992. The weighing of evidence and the determinants of confidence. *Cognitive Psychology* 24:411–35.

Griffith, R. M. 1949. Odds adjustments by American horse-race bettors. *American Journal of Psychology* 62:290–4.

Gul, F. 1991. A theory of disappointment in decision making under uncertainty. *Econometrica* 59:667–86.

Guler, K., C. R. Plott, and Q. H. Vuong. 1987. A study of zero-out auctions: Experimental analysis of a process of allocating private rights to the use of public property. Working paper 650. California Institute of Technology, Division of Humanities and Social Sciences, August.

Hagen, O. 1991. Decisions under risk: A descriptive model and a technique for decision making. *European Journal of Political Economy* 7:381–405.

Hagen, O. 1969. Separation on cardinal utility and specific utility of risk in theory of choices under uncertainty. *Statsokonomisk Tidsskrift* 3.

Haltiwanger, J., and M. Waldman. 1985. Rational expectations and the limits of rationality: An analysis of heterogeneity. *American Economic Review* 75:326–40.

Hammack, J., and Brown, G. M., Jr. 1974. *Water fowl and wet lands: Toward bio economic analysis*. Baltimore: Johns Hopkins University Press for Resources for the Future.

Handa, J. 1977. Risk, probabilities and a new theory of cardinal utility. *Journal of Political Economy* 85:97–122.

Hanemann, W. M. June 1991. Willingness to pay and willingness to accept: How much can they differ? *American Economic Review* 81:635–47.

Hardie, B. G. S., E. J. Johnson, and P. S. Fader. 1993. Modeling loss aversion and reference dependence effects on brand choice. *Marketing Science* 12:378–94.

Harless, D. W. 1989. More laboratory evidence on the disparity between willingness to pay and compensation demanded. *Journal of Economic Behavior and Organization* 11:359–79.

———. 1992a. Actions versus prospects: The effect of problem representation on regret. *American Economic Review* 82:634–49.

———. 1992b. Predictions about indifference curves inside the unit triangle: A test of variants of expected utility theory. *Journal of Economic Behavior and Organization* 18:391–414.

Harless, D. W., and C. F. Camerer. 1994. The predictive utility of generalized expected utility theories. *Econometrica* 62:1251–89.

Harrison, G. W. November 1989. The payoff dominance critique of experimental economics. Working paper. University of New Mexico, Department of Economics.

———. 1990. Expected utility theory and the experimentalists. Working paper. University of South Carolina, Department of Economics.

Harrison, G. W., and P. Morgan. June 1990. Search intensity in experiments. *Economic Journal* 100:478–86.

Hartman, R., M. J. Doane, and C.-K. Woo. 1991. Consumer rationality and the status-quo. *Quarterly Journal of Economics* 106:141–62.

Hausner, M. 1954. Multidimensional utilities. In *Decision processes*, R. M. Thrall, C. H. Coombs, and R. L. Davis, editors, New York: Wiley.

Hawkins, S. A., and R. Hastie. 1990. Hindsight-biased judgments of past events after the outcomes are known. *Psychological Bulletin* 107:311–27.

Hazen, G. 1987. Subjectively weighted linear utility. *Theory and Decision* 23:261–82.

Heath, C., and A. Tversky. 1991. Preference and belief: Ambiguity and competence in choice under uncertainty. *Journal of Risk and Uncertainty* 4:5–28.

Helson, H. 1964. *Adaptation level theory: An experimental and systematic approach to behavior*. New York: Harper & Row.

Henrion, M., and B. Fischhoff. 1984. Uncertainty assessments in the estimation of physical constants. Carnegie-Mellon University, Department of Social and Decision Sciences.

Hershey, J. C., H. C. Kunreuther, and P. J. H. Schoemaker. August 1982. Sources of bias in assessment procedures for utility functions. *Management Science* 28:936–54.

Hershey, J. C., and P. Schoemaker. 1980. Prospect theory's reflection hypothesis: A critical examination. *Organizational Behavior and Human Decision Processes* 25:395–418.

———. 1985. Probability versus certainty equivalence methods in utility measurement: Are they equivalent? *Management Science* 31:1213–31.

Herstein, I., and John Milnor. 1953. An axiomatic approach to measurable utility. *Econometrica* 47:291–7.

Hey, J. D. 1982. Search for rules of search. *Journal of Economic Behavior and Organization* 3:65–81.

———. 1987. Still searching. *Journal of Economic Behavior and Organization* 8:137–44.

Hey, J. D., and D. DiCagno. 1990. Circles and triangles: An experimental estimation of indifference lines in the Marschak-Machina triangle. *Journal of Behavioral Decision Making* 3:279–306.

Hey, J. D., and Chris Orme. 1994. Investigating generalizations of expected utility theory using experimental data. *Econometrica* 62:1291–1326.

Hey, J. D., and Elisabetta Strazzera. 1989. Estimation of indifference curves in the Marschak-Machina triangle: A direct test of the 'fanning out' hypothesis. *Journal of Behavioral Decision Making* 2:239–60.

Hicks, J. R., and R. G. D. Allen. 1934. A reconsideration of the theory of value, I; II. *Econometrica* 1:52–75; 196–219.

Hodges, J. L., and E. L. Lehmann. 1952. The use of previous experience in reaching statistical decisions. *Annals of Mathematical Statistics* 23:396–407.

Hoffman, E., and M. L. Spitzer. 1993. Willingness to pay vs. willingness to accept: Legal and economic implications. *Washington University Law Quarterly* 71:59–114.

Hogarth, R. M. 1987. *Judgement and choice*. New York:Wiley.

Hogarth, R. M., and H. J. Einhorn. 1990. Venture theory: A model of decision weights. *Management Science* 36:780–803.

Hogarth, R. M., and H. Kunreuther. 1985. Ambiguity and insurance decisions. *American Economic Review (Papers and Proceedings)* 75:386–90.

———. 1990. Pricing insurance and warranties: Ambiguity and correlated risks. Working paper. University of Chicago, Center for Decision Research.

———. 1989. Risk, ambiguity and insurance. *Journal of Risk and Uncertainty* 2:5–35.

Hogarth, R. M., and M. W. Reder, editors, 1987. *Rational choice: The contrast between economics and psychology*. Chicago: University of Chicago Press.

Holcomb, J. H., and P. S. Nelson. 1989. An experimental investigation of individual time preference. University of Texas-El Paso, Department of Economics.

Holmes, D. S. 1970. Differential change in affective intensity and the forgetting of unpleasant personal experiences. *Journal of Personality and Social Psychology* 15:234–9.

Holt, C. A. June 1986. Preference reversals and the independence axiom. *American Economic Review* 76:508–14.

Horowitz, J. K. 1991. Discounting money payoffs: An experimental analysis. In *Handbook of behavioral economics vol. II*, S. Kaish and B. Gilad, editors, Greenwich, Conn.: JAI Press.

Howard, R. A. 1992. The cogency of decision analysis. In *Utility theories: Measurement and applications*, W. Edwards, editor, Cambridge: Cambridge University Press.

Hurst, P. M., and S. Siegel. 1956. Prediction of decision from a higher-ordered metric scale of utility. *Journal of Experimental Psychology* 52:138–44.

Irwin, F. W. 1953. Stated expectations as functions of probability and desirability of outcomes. *Journal of Personality* 21:329–35.

Irwin, Julie, Paul Slovic, Sarah Lichtenstein, and Gary H. McClelland. 1993. Preference reversals and the measurement of environmental values. *Journal of Risk and Uncertainty* 6:5–18.

Jensen, F. A., and C. R. Peterson. April 1973. Psychological effects of proper scoring rules. *Organizational Behavior and Human Performance* 9:307–17.

Johnson, E., J. Hershey, J. Meszaros, and H. Kunreuther. 1993. Framing, probability distortions, and insurance decisions. *Journal of Risk and Uncertainty* 7:35–51.

Johnson, E. J., and J. W. Payne. 1985. Effort and accuracy in choice. *Management Science* 31:395–414.

Johnson, E. J., J. W. Payne, and J. R. Bettman. 1988. Information displays and preference reversals. *Organizational Behavior and Human Decision Processes* 42:1–21.

Johnson, E. J., and D. A. Schkade. 1989. Bias in utility assessments: Further evidence and explanations. *Management Science* 35:406–24.

Juslin, P. In press. The overconfidence phenomenon as a consequence of informal experimenter-guided selection of almanac items. *Organizational Behavior and Human Decision Processes*.

Kachelmeier, S. J., and Mohamed Shehata. 1992. Examining risk preferences under high monetary incentives: Experimental evidence from the People's Republic of China. *American Economic Review* 82:1120–41.

Kagel, J., and D. Levin. 1986. The winner's curse and public information in common value auctions. *American Economic Review* 76:894–920.

Kagel, J. H., D. McDonald, and R. C. Battalio. 1990. Tests of "fanning out" of indifference curves: Results from animal and human experiments. *American Economic Review* 80:912–21.

Kahn, B. E., and R. K. Sarin. 1988. Modelling ambiguity in decisions under uncertainty. *Journal of Consumer Research* 15:262–72.

Kahneman, D., J. L. Knetsch, and R. H. Thaler. 1991. Anomalies: The endowment effect, loss aversion, and status quo bias. *Journal of Economic Perspectives* 5:193–206.

———. 1990. Experimental tests of the endowment effect and the Coase Theorem. *Journal of Political Economy* 98:1325–48.

Kahneman, D., and D. Lovallo. 1993. Timid choices and bold forecasts: A cognitive perspective on risk-taking. *Management Science* 39:17–31.

Kahneman, D., P. Slovic, and A. Tversky, editors. 1982. *Judgment under uncertainty: Heuristics and biases*. Cambridge: Cambridge University Press.

Kahneman, D., and A. Tversky. 1972. On prediction and judgment. *ORI Research monograph* 12.

———. 1979. Prospect theory: An analysis of decision under risk. *Econometrica* 47:263–91.

———. 1982. On the study of statistical intuitions. *Cognition* 11:123–41.

Kanodia, C., R. Bushman, and J. Dickhaut. 1989. Escalation errors and the sunk cost effect: An explanation based on reputation and information asymmetries. *Journal of Accounting Research* 27:59–77.

Karmarkar, U. D. 1974. The effect of probabilities on the subjective evaluation of lotteries. Working paper no. 698–74. MIT, Sloan School of Management.

———. 1978. Subjectively weighted utility: A descriptive extension of the expected utility model. *Organizational Behavior and Human Performance* 21:61–72.

Karni, E., and Z. Safra. 1987. Preference reversal and the observability of preferences by experimental methods. *Econometrica* 55:675–85.

Karni, E., and D. Schmeidler. 1990. Utility theory with uncertainty. In *Handbook of mathematical economics, vol. 4*, W. Hildenbrand and H. Sonnenschein, editors, Amsterdam: North-Holland.

Keller, L. R. 1985a. The effects of problem representation on the sure-thing and substitution principles. *Management Science* 31:738–51.

———. 1985b. Testing of the "reduction of compound alternatives" principle. *OMEGA International Journal of Management Science* 13:349–58.

Keller, L. R., U. Segal, and T. Wang. 1993. The Becker-DeGroot-Marschak mechanism and generalized utility theories: Theoretical predictions and empirical observations. *Theory and Decision* 34:83–97.

Keren, G. 1987. Facing uncertainty in the game of bridge: A calibration study. *Organizational Behavior and Human Decision Processes* 39:98–114.

———. 1988. On the ability of monitoring non-veridical perceptions and uncertain knowledge: Some calibration studies. *Acta Psychologica* 67:95–119.

Keynes, J. M. 1921. *A treatise on probability*. London: Macmillan.

Knetsch, J. L. 1989. The endowment effect and evidence of nonreversible indifference curves. *American Economic Review* 79:1277–84.

Knetsch, J. L., and J. A. Sinden. 1987. The persistence of evaluation disparities. *Quarterly Journal of Economics* 102:691–5.

———. 1984. Willingness to pay and compensation demanded: Experimental evidence of an unexpected disparity in measures of value. *Quarterly Journal of Economics* 99:507–21.

Knez, M., and V. L. Smith. 1987. Hypothetical valuations and preference reversals in the context of asset trading. In *Laboratory experimentation in economics: Six points of view*, A. E. Roth, editor, Cambridge: Cambridge University Press.

Knez, P., V. L. Smith, and A. W. Williams. 1985. Individual rationality, market rationality, and value estimation. *American Economic Review (Papers and Proceedings)* 75:397–402.

Knight, F. H. 1921. *Risk, uncertainty, and profit*. Boston, New York: Houghton Mifflin.

Koehler, J. J. 1989. The normative status of base rates in probabilistic judgment. Working paper. University of Texas-Austin, Department of Management.

Kogut, C. A. 1990. Consumer search behavior and sunk costs. *Journal of Economic Behavior and Organization* 14:381–92.

Krantz, D., R. D. Luce, P. Suppes, and A. Tversky. 1971. *Foundations of measurement, vol. 1: Additive and polynomial representations*. New Yokr: Academic Press.

Kroll, Y., and H. Levy. 1992. Further tests of the separation theorem and the capital asset pricing model. *American Economic Review* 82:664–70.

Kroll, Y., H. Levy, and A. Rapoport. 1988a. Experimental tests of the separation theorem and the capital asset pricing model. *American Economic Review* 78:500–19.

———. 1988b. Experimental tests of the mean-variance model for portfolio selection. *Organizational Behavior and Human Decision Processes* 42:388–410.

Krosnick, J. A., L. Fan, and D. R. Lehman. 1990. Conversational conventions, order of information acquisition, and the effect of base rates and individuating information on social judgments. *Journal of Personality and Social Psychology* 59:1140–52.

Kuhn, Thomas S. 1970. *The structure of scientific revolutions*. 2nd ed. Chicago: University of Chicago Press.

Kunreuther, H., D. Easterling, W. Desvousges, and P. Slovic. 1990. Public-attitudes toward siting a high-level nuclear waste repository in Nevada. *Risk Analysis* 10:469–84.

Kunreuther, H., R. Ginsberg, L. Miller, P. Sagi, P. Slovic, B. Borkan, and N. Katz. 1978. *Disaster insurance protection: Public policy lessons.* New York: Wiley.

Lachman, R., J. L. Lachman, and E. C. Butterfield. 1979. *Cognitive psychology and information processing.* Hillsdale, N.J.: Lawrence Erlbaum Associates.

Laibson, David I. 1994. Golden eggs and hyperbolic discounting. Working paper. MIT.

Langer, E. J. 1975. The illusion of control. *Journal of Personality and Social Psychology* 32:311–28.

Larrick, R. P., J. N. Morgan, and R. E. Nisbett. 1990. Teaching the use of cost-benefit reasoning in everyday life. *Psychological Science* 1:362–70.

Larson, J. R., Jr. 1980. Exploring the external validity of a subjectively weighted utility model of decision making. *Organizational Behavior and Human Performance* 26:293–304.

Lattimore, P. K., J. R. Baker, and A. D. Witte. 1992. The influence of probability on risky choice: A parametric investigation. *Journal of Economic Behavior and Organization* 17:377–400.

Leland, J. 1991. A theory of approximate expected utility maximization. Carnegie-Mellon University, Department of Social and Decision Sciences.

Lewis, K. K. 1989. Changing beliefs and systematic rational forecast errors with evidence from foreign exchange. *American Economic Review* 79:621–36.

Lichtenstein, S., B. Fischhoff, and L. D. Phillips. 1982. Calibration of probabilities: The state of the art to 1980. In *Judgment under uncertainty: Heuristics and biases*, D. Kahneman, P. Slovic, and A. Tversky, editors, Cambridge: Cambridge University Press. 306–334.

Lichtenstein, S., and P. Slovic. 1971. Reversals of preference between bids and choices in gambling decisions. *Journal of Experimental Psychology* 89:46–55.

———. 1973. Response-induced reversals of preference in gambling: An extended replication in Las Vegas. *Journal of Experimental Psychology* 101:16–20.

Lichtenstein, S., P. Slovic, and D. Zink. 1969. Effect of instruction in expected value on optimality of gambling decisions. *Journal of Experimental Psychology* 79:236–40.

Lightman, A. and O. Gingerich. 1990. When do anomalies begin? *Science* 255:690–95.

Lind, B., and C. Plott. 1991. The winner's curse: Experiments with buyers and with sellers. *American Economic Review* 81:335–46.

Lindman, H. R. 1971. Inconsistent preferences among gambles. *Journal of Experimental Psychology* 89:390–7.

Lippman, S. A., and J. J. McCall. 1976. The economics of job search: A survey (I and II). *Economic Inquiry* 14:155–89; September 1976, 14:347–68.

Loewenstein, G. 1987. Anticipation and the valuation of delayed consumption. *Economic Journal* 97:666–84.

———. 1988. Frames of mind in intertemporal choice. *Management Science* 34:200–14.

Loewenstein, George, and Jon Elster. 1992. *Choice over time.* New York: Russell Sage Foundation Press.

Lowenstein, G., and D. Kahneman. 1991. Explaining the endowment effect. Working paper. Carnegie Mellon University. Department of Social and Decision Sciences.

Loewenstein, G., and D. Prelec. 1992. Anomalies in intertemporal choice: Evidence and an interpretation. *Quarterly Journal of Economics* 107:573–97.

Loewenstein, G., S. Blount, and M. Bazerman. In press. An inconsistency in revealed preference for fairness. *Journal of Economic Behavior and Organization.*

Loomes, G. 1988a. Further evidence of the impact of regret and disappointment in choice under uncertainty. *Economica* 55:47–62.

———. 1988b. When actions speak louder than prospects. *American Economic Review* 78:463–70.

———. 1989. Predicted violations of the invariance principle in choice under uncertainty. *Annals of operations research, vol. 19.*

———. 1991a. Evidence of a new violation of the independence axiom. *Journal of Risk and Uncertainty* 4:91–108.

Loomes, G. 1991b. The causes of preference reversal: Comment. University of York, Centre for Experimental Economics.

———. 1991c. Testing decision theories by using "value equivalences." *Oxford Economic Papers* 43:644–66.

———. In press. Preference reversal: Explanations, evidence and implications. In *Intransitive preference (Annals of operations research, vol. 20)*, Gehrlein, editor.

Loomes, G., C. Starmer, and R. Sugden. 1989. Preference reversal: Information processing effect or rational nontransitive choice? *Economic Journal* 99:140–51.

———. 1991. Observing violations of transitivity by experimental methods. *Econometrica* 59(2):425–39.

———. 1992. Are preferences monotonic? Testing some predictions of regret theory. *Economica* 59:17–33.

Loomes, G., and R. Sugden. 1982. Regret theory: An alternative theory of rational choice under uncertainty. *Economic Journal* 92:805–25.

———. 1987a. Some implications of a more general form of regret theory. *Journal of Economic Theory* 41:270–87.

———. 1987b. Testing for regret and disappointment in choice under uncertainty. *Economic Journal* 97:118–29.

Loomes, Graham, and Caron Taylor. 1992. Non-transitive preferences over gains and losses. *Economic Journal* 102:357–65.

Lovell, M. C. 1986. Tests of the rational expectations hypothesis. *American Economic Review* 76:110–24.

Lucas, R. E., Jr. 1986. Adaptive behavior and economic theory. *Journal of Business* 59:S401-S426.

Luce, R. D. 1958. A probabilistic theory of utility. *Econometrica* 26:193–224.

———. 1959. *Individual choice behavior: A theoretical analysis*. New York: John Wiley and Sons.

———. 1990. Rational versus plausible accounting equivalences in preference judgments. *Psychological Science* 1:225–34.

Luce, R. Duncan, Barbara Mellers, and Shi-jie Chang. 1993. Is choice the correct primitive? On using certainty equivalents and reference levels to predict choices among gambles. *Journal of Risk and Uncertainty* 6:115–43.

Luce, R. D., and L. S. Narens. 1985. Classification of concatenation measurement structures according to scale type. *Journal of Mathematical Psychology* 29:1–72.

Luce, R. D., and P. Suppes. 1965. Preference, utility, and subjective probability. In *Handbook of mathematical psychology, vol. III*, R. D. Luce, R. B. Bush, and E. Galanter, editors, New York: Wiley. 249–410.

Luce, R. Duncan and Detlof von Winterfeldt. 1994. What common ground exists for descriptive, prescriptive, and normative utility theories? *Management Science* 40:263–79.

Lypny, Gregory J. 1991. An experimental study of managerial pay and firm hedging decisions. Working paper. Concordia University, Department of Finance.

MacCrimmon, K. R. 1965. *An experimental study of the decision making behavior of business executives*. Unpublished dissertation. University of California, Los Angeles.

MacCrimmon, K. R., and S. Larsson. 1979. Utility theory: Axioms versus paradoxes. In *The expected utility hypothesis and the Allais Paradox*, M. Allais and O. Hagen, editors, Dordrecht, Holland: D. Riedel. 333–409.

MacDonald, D. N., J. H. Kagel, and R. C. Battalio. 1991. Animals' choices over uncertain outcomes: Further experimental results. *Economic Journal* 103:1067–84.

MacDonald, Don N., William L. Huth, and Paul M. Taube. 1991. Generalized expected utility analysis and preference reversals: Some initial results in the loss domain. *Journal of Economic Behavior and Organization* 17:115–30.

Machina, M. J. 1982. "Expected utility" analysis without the independence axiom. *Econometrica* 50:277–323.

———. 1987. Choice under uncertainty: Problems solved and unsolved. *Journal of Economic Perspectives* 1:121–54.

———. 1989. Comparative statics and non-expected utility preferences. *Journal of Economic Theory* 47:393–405.

———. 1985. Stochastic choice functions generated from deterministic preferences over lotteries. *Economic Journal* 95:575–94.

Malinvaud, E. 1952. Note on von Neumann-Morgenstern's strong independence axiom. *Econometrica* 20:679.

Markowitz, H. 1959. *Portfolio selection: Efficient diversification of investments.* New York: Wiley.

———. 1952. The utility of wealth. *Journal of Political Economy* 60:151–8.

Marschak, J. 1968. Economics of inquiring, communicating, deciding. *American Economic Review* 58:1–18.

———. 1975. Personal probabilities of probabilities. *Theory and decision* 6:121–53.

———. 1950. Rational behavior, uncertain prospects, and measurable utility. *Econometrica* 18:111–41.

Marshall, J. D., J. L. Knetsch, and J. A. Sinden. 1986. Agents' evaluations and the disparity in measures of economic loss. *Journal of Economic Behavior and Organization* 7:115–27.

Marshall, R. C., J.-F. Richard, and G. A. Zarkin. 1992. Posterior probabilities of the independence axiom with non-experimental data. *Journal of Business and Economic Statistics* 10:31–44.

May, K. O. 1954. Intransitivity, utility, and the aggregation of preference patterns. *Econometrica* 22:1–13.

May, R. S. 1986. Inference, subjective probability and frequency of correct answers: A cognitive approach to the overconfidence phenomenon. In *New directions in research on decision making*, B. Brehmer, H. Jungermann, P. Lourens and G. Sevo'n, editors, Amsterdam: North-Holland.

McClelland, G., W. Schulze, and D. Coursey. 1991. The effects of framing and the status quo on compensating and equivalent variation measures of value. University of Colorado at Boulder, Department of Psychology.

McCord, M., and R. De Neufville. 1983. Empirical demonstration that expected utility decision analysis is not operational. In *Foundations of utility and risk theory with applications*, B. P. Stigum and F. Wenstop, editors, Dordrecht, Holland: D. Reidel. 181–99.

———. 1986. Lottery equivalents: Reduction of the certainty effect problem in utility assessment. *Management Science* 32:56–60.

McGlothlin, W. H. 1956. Stability of choices among uncertain alternatives. *American Journal of Psychology* 69:604–15.

McKelvey, R. D., and P. Ordeshook. 1985. Elections with limited information: A fulfilled expectations model using contemporaneous poll and endorsement data as information sources. *Journal of Economic Theory* 35:55–85.

McKelvey, R. D., and T. Page. 1990. Public and private information: An experimental study of information pooling. *Econometrica* 58:1321–39.

McNeil, B. J., S. G. Pauker, and A. Tversky. 1988. On the framing of medical decisions. In *Decision making: Descriptive, normative, and prescriptive interactions*, D. E. Bell, H. Raiffa, and A. Tversky, editors, Cambridge: Cambridge University Press. 562–8.

Meehl, P. E. 1954. *Clinical versus statistical prediction: A theoretical analysis and a review of the evidence.* Minneapolis, Minn.: University of Minnesota Press.

Mellers, B. A., L. D. Ordóñez, and M. H. Birnbaum. 1992. A change of process theory for contextual effects and preference reversals in risky decision making. *Organizational Behavior and Human Decision Processes* 52:331–69.

Mookherjee, D., and B. Sopher. 1994. Learning behavior in an experimental matching pennies game. *Games and Economic Behavior* 7:62–91.

Moon, P. and A. Martin. 1990. Better heuristics for economic search: Experimental and simulation evidence. *Journal of Behavioral Decision Making* 3:175–93.

Morgenstern, O. 1976. The collaboration between Oskar Morgenstern and John von Neumann on the theory of games. *Journal of Economic Literature* 14:805–16.

Morgenstern, O. 1979. Some reflections on utility theory. In *The expected utility hypothesis and the Allais paradox*, M. Allais and O. Hagen, editors, Dordrecht: D. Reidel.

Morier, D. M., and E. Borgida. 1984. The conjunction fallacy: A task specific phenomenon. *Personality and Social Psychology Bulletin* 10:243–52.

Morrison, D. G. 1967. On the consistency of preferences in Allais' paradox. *Behavioral Science* 12:373–83.

Moskowitz, H. 1974. Effects of problem representation and feedback on rational behavior in Allais and Morlat-type problems. *Decision Sciences* 5:225–42.

Mosteller, F., and P. Nogee. 1951. An experimental measurement of utility. *Journal of Political Economy* 59:371–404.

Munier, B. 1989. New models of decision under uncertainty: An interpretive essay. *European Journal of Operational Research* 38:307–17.

Murphy, A. H. 1973. A new vector partition of the probability score. *Journal of Applied Meteorology* 12:595–600.

Murphy, A. H., and R. L. Winkler. 1970. Scoring rules in probability assessment and evaluation. *Acta Psychologica* 34:273–86.

———. 1974. Subjective probability forecasting experiments in meteorology: Some preliminary results. *Bulletin of the American Meteorological Society* 55:1206–16.

Nau, R. F. 1989. Decision analysis with indeterminate or incoherent probabilities. *Annals of Operations Research* 19:375–403.

Neilson, W. 1989. Prospect theory's discontinuities without probability weights. Working paper. Texas A & M, Department of Economics, October.

Neilson, W. S. In press. A mixed fan hypothesis and its implications for behavior towards risk. *Journal of Economic Behavior and Organization*.

Nelson, R. G. and D. A. Bessler. 1989. Subjective probabilities and scoring rules: Experimental evidence. *American Journal of Agricultural Economics* 71:363–9.

Nerlove, M. 1958. Adaptive expectations and cobweb phenomena. *Quarterly Journal of Economics* 73:227–40.

Neuringer, A. 1986. Can people behave "randomly"?: The role of feedback. *Journal of Experimental Psychology: General* 115:62–75.

Nickerson, R. S., A. Baddely, and B. Freeman. 1987. Are people's estimates of what other people know influenced by what they themselves know? *Acta Psychologica* 64:245–59.

Nisbett, R., E. Borgida, R. Crandall, and H. Reed. 1976. Popular induction: Information is not necessarily informative. In *Cognition and social behavior*, J. S. Carroll and J. W. Payne, editors, Hillsdale, N.J.: Erlbaum.

Nisbett, R. E., G. T. Fong, D. R. Lehman, and P. W. Cheng. 1987. Teaching reasoning. *Science* 238:625–31.

Norman, D. 1988. *The psychology of everyday things*. New York: Basic Books.

O'Neill, B. 1987. Nonmetric test of the minimax theory of two-person zerosum games. *Proceedings of the National Academy of Sciences, USA* 84:2106–9.

Payne, J. W. 1976. Task complexity and contingent processing in decision making: An information search and protocol analysis. *Organizational Behavior and Human Performance* 22:17–44.

Payne, J. W., J. Bettman, and E. Johnson. 1992. Behavioral decision research: A constructive processing perspective. *Annual Review of Psychology* 43:87–131.

Peterson, C. R., and L. R. Beach. 1967. Man as an intuitive statistician. *Psychological Bulletin* 68:29–46.

Peterson, S. P. 1993. Forecasting dynamics and convergence to market fundamentals: Evidence from experimental asset markets. *Journal of Economic Behavior and Organization* 22:269–84.

Plott, C. R. 1986. Rational choice in experimental markets. *Journal of Business* 59(4):S301–S327.

Plott, C. R., and L. Wilde. 1982. Professional diagnosis vs. self-diagnosis: An experimental examination of some special features of markets with uncertainty. In *Research in experimental economics*, V. L. Smith, editor, Greenwich, Conn.: JAI Press.

Pratt, J. W., D. A. Wise, and R. Zeckhauser. 1979. Price differences in almost competitive markets. *Quarterly Journal of Economics* 93:189–211.

Prelec, D. 1990. A "pseudo-endowment" effect, and its implications for some recent nonexpected utility models. *Journal of Risk and Uncertainty* 3:247–59.

Preston, M. G., and P. Baratta. 1948. An experimental study of the auction value of an uncertain outcome. *American Journal of Psychology* 61:183–93.

Quiggin, J. 1982. A theory of anticipated utility. *Journal of Economic Behavior and Organization* 3:323–43.

Ramsey, F. 1931. Truth and probability. In *The foundations of mathematics and other logical essays*, F. Ramsey, editor, London: Routledge & Kegan Paul. 156–98. Reprinted in H. E. Kyburg and H. E. Smokler, editors, *Studies in subjective probability*, New York: Wiley, 1964, 61–92.

Rapoport, A., and R. B. Boebel. 1992. Mixed strategies in strictly competitive games: A further test of the minimax hypothesis. *Games and Economic Behavior* 4:261–83.

Rapoport, A., and D. V. Budescu. 1992. Generation of random series in two-person strictly competitive games. *Journal of Experimental Psychology: General* 121:352–63.

Real, Leslie. 1991. Animal choice behavior and the evolution of cognitive architecture. *Science* 253:980–86.

Redelmeier, Don, and Daniel Kahneman. 1993. The pain of an invasive medical procedure: Patients' real time and retrospective evaluations of colonoscopy. Working paper. University of California at Berkeley, Department of Psychology.

Rietz, T. A. 1991. Asset prices and risk allocation in experimental markets. Working paper 109. Northwestern University, Department of Finance, August.

Ritov, I., and J. Baron. 1990. Reluctance to vaccinate: Omission bias and ambiguity. *Journal of Behavioral Decision Making* 3:263–77.

Roberts, H. V. 1963. Risk, ambiguity, and the Savage axioms: Comment. *Quarterly Journal of Economics* 77:327–36.

Roby, T. B. 1965. Belief states: A preliminary empirical study. Decision Sciences Laboratory, L. G. Hascom Field.

Roell, A. 1987. Risk aversion in Quiggin and Yaari's rank-order model of choice under uncertainty. *Economic Journal* 97:143–59.

Ronen, J. 1973. Effects of some probability displays on choices. *Organizational Behavior and Human Performance* 9:1–15.

Ronis, D. L., and J. F. Yates. 1987. Components of probability judgment accuracy: Individual consistency and effects of subject-matter and assessment method. *Organizational Behavior and Human Decision Processes* 40:193–218.

Ross, B. M., and N. Levy. 1958. Patterned predictions of chance events by children and adults. *Psychological Reports* 4:87–124.

Ross, L., D. Greene, and P. House. 1977. The "false consensus effect": An egocentric bias in social perception and attribution processes. *Journal of Experimental Social Psychology* 13:279–301.

Ross, Michael, and Fiore Sicoly. 1982. Egocentric biases in availabilty and attribution. In *Judgment under uncertainty: Heuristics and biases*, D. Kahneman, P. Slovic, and A. Tversky, editors, Cambridge: Cambridge University Press.

Roth, Alvin E., and Michael W. K. Malouf. 1979. Game theoretic models and the role of information in bargaining: An experimental study. *Psychological Review* 86:574–94.

Rubinstein, Ariel. 1988. Similarity and decision-making under risk (Is there a utility theory resolution to the Allais paradox?). *Journal of Economic Theory* 46:145–53.

Russell, T., and R. Thaler. 1985. The relevance of quasi-rationality in markets. *American Economic Review* 75:1071–82.

Russo, J. E., and P. J. H. Schoemaker. 1989. *Decision traps: The ten barriers to brilliant decision-making and how to overcome them.* New York: Doubleday.

Safra, Z., U. Segal, and A. Spivak. September 1990a. Preference reversal and nonexpected utility behavior. *American Economic Review* 80:922–30.

Safra, Z., U. Segal, and A. Spivak. 1990b. The Becker-DeGroot-Marschak mechanism and non-expected utility: A testable approach. *Journal of Risk and Uncertainty* 3:177–90.

Samuelson, P. 1952. Probability, utility, and the independence axiom. *Econometrica* 20: 670–8.

Samuelson, W., and R. Zeckhauser. 1988. Status quo bias in decision making. *Journal of Risk and Uncertainty* 1:7–59.

Sanders, A. F. 1968. Choice among bets and revision of opinion. *Acta Psychologica* 28:76–83.

Sarin, R. K., and M. Weber. 1993. The effect of ambiguity in a market setting. *Management Science* 39:602–15.

Sarin, R. K., and R. L. Winkler. 1992. Ambiguity and decision modeling: A preference-based approach. *Journal of Risk and Uncertainty* 5:389–407.

Savage, L. J. 1954. *The foundations of statistics.* New York: Wiley.

Scharfstein, D. S., and J. Stein. 1990. Herd behavior and investment. *American Economic Review* 80:465–79.

Schelling, T. 1984. Self-command in practice, in policy, and in a theory of rational choice. *American Economic Review* 74:1–11.

Schkade, D. A., and E. J. Johnson. June 1989. Cognitive processes in preference reversals. *Organizational Behavior and Human Decision Processes* 44:203–31.

Schmalansee, R. 1976. An experimental study of expectation formation. *Econometrica* 44:17–41.

Schmeidler, D. 1989. Subjective probability and expected utility without additivity. *Econometrica* 57:571–87.

Schoemaker, P. J. H. 1990. Are risk-attitudes related across domains and response modes? *Management Science* 36:1451–63.

Schotter, A., and Y. M. Braunstein. 1981. Economic search: An experimental study. *Economic Inquiry* 19:1–25.

Schweitzer, Maurice. In press. Disentangling status quo and omission effects: Experimental analysis. *Organization Behavior and Human Decision Processes.*

Segal, U. 1987a. The Ellsberg Paradox and risk aversion: An anticipated utility approach. *International Economic Review* 28:175–202.

———. 1987b. Some remarks on Quiggin's anticipated utility theory. *Journal of Economic Behavior and Organization* 8:145–54.

———. 1988. Does the preference reversal phenomenon necessarily contradict the independence axiom? *American Economic Review* 78:233–36.

———. 1989. Anticipated utility: A measure representation approach. *Annals of Operations Research* 19:359–73.

———. 1990. Two-stage lotteries without the reduction axiom. *Econometrica* 58:349–77.

Shafir, E. In press. Choosing versus rejecting: Why some options are both better and worse than others. *Cognitive Psychology.*

Shelley, M. K. In press. Outcome signs, question frames, and discount rates. *Management Science.*

Simon, H. A. 1955. A behavioral model of rational choice. *Quarterly Journal of Economics* 69:99–118.

Slovic, P. 1969. Manipulating the attractiveness of a gamble without changing its expected value. *Journal of Experimental Psychology* 79:139–45.

Slovic, P., and S. Lichtenstein. 1968. The relative importance of probabilities and payoffs in risk taking. *Journal of Experimental Psychology* 78:1–18.

Slovic, P., S. Lichtenstein, and W. Edwards. 1965. Boredom induced changes in preferences among bets. *American Journal of Psychology* 78:208–17.

Slovic, P., and A. Tversky. 1974. Who accepts Savage's axiom? *Behavioral Science* 19:368–73.

Smith, C. A. B. 1961. Consistency in statistical inference and decision. *Journal of Royal Statistical Society, seriesB* 23:1–37.

Smith, V. L. 1969. Measuring nonmonetary utilities in uncertain choices: The Ellsberg urn. *Quarterly Journal of Economics* 83:324–29.

————. 1991. Rational choice: The contrast between economics and psychology. *Journal of Political Economy* 99:877–97.

Smith, V. L., G. L. Suchanek, and A. W. Williams. 1988. Bubbles, crashes, and endogeneous expectations in experimental spot asset markets. *Econometrica* 56:1119–51.

Smith, V. L., and J. M. Walker. 1993. Monetary rewards and decision costs in experimental economics. University of Arizona, Department of Economics.

Sniezek, J. A., and T. Buckley. 1991. Confidence depends on level of aggregation. *Journal of Behavioral Decision Making* 4:263–72.

Sniezek, J. A., and R. A. Henry. 1989. Accuracy and confidence in group judgment. *Organizational Behavior and Human Decision Processes* 43:1–28.

Soll, Jack B. 1993. Determinants of miscalibration and over/under-confidence: The interaction between random noise and the ecology. Working paper. University of Chicago, Center for Decision Research.

Starmer, C. In press. Testing new theories of choice under uncertainty using the common consequence effect. *Review of Economic Studies*.

Starmer, C., and R. Sugden. 1989a. Violations of the independence axiom in common ratio problems: An experimental test of some competing hypotheses. *Annals of Operations Research* 19:79–102.

————. 1989b. Probability and juxtaposition effects: An experimental investigation of the common ratio effect. *Journal of Risk and Uncertainty* 2:159–78.

————. 1989c. Experimental evidence of the impact of regret on choice under uncertainty. Discussion paper no. 23. University of East Anglia, Economics Research Centre.

————. 1991. Does the random-lottery incentive system elicit true references? An experimental investigation. *American Economic Review* 81(4):971–78.

————. 1993. Testing for juxtaposition and event-splitting effects. *Journal of Risk and Uncertainty* 6:235–54.

Strotz, R. H. 1953. Cardinal utility. *American Economic Review (Papers and Proceedings)* 43:384–405.

Sugden, R. 1986. New developments in the theory of choice under uncertainty. *Bulletin of Economic Research* 38:1–24.

Sunder, S. 1991. Market for information: Experimental evidence. Working paper. Carnegie-Mellon University, GSIA.

Taylor, S. E., and J. D. Brown. 1988. Illusion and well-being: A social psychological perspective on mental health. *Psychological Bulletin* 103:193–210.

Thaler, R. H. 1980. Toward a positive theory of consumer choice. *Journal of Economic Behavior and Organization* 1:39–60.

————. 1981. Some empirical evidence on dynamic inconsistency. *Economics Letters* 8:201–7.

————. 1985. Mental accounting and consumer choice. *Marketing Science* 4:199–214.

————. 1987. The psychology of choice and the assumptions of economics. In *Laboratory experimentation in economics: Six points of view*, A. E. Roth, editor, Cambridge: Cambridge University Press.

————. 1992. *The winner's curse: Anomalies and paradoxes of economic life*. New York: Free Press.

Thaler, R. H., and E. J. Johnson. 1990. Gambling with the house money and trying to break even: The effects of prior outcomes on risky choice. *Management Science* 36:643–60.

Thaler, R. H., and H. M. Shefrin. 1981. An economic theory of self-control. *Journal of Political Economy* 89:392–410.

Thrall, R., C. Coombs, and R. Davis. 1954. *Decision processes*. New York: Wiley.

Tobin, J. 1958. Liquidity preference as behavior toward risk. *Review of Economic Studies* 25:65–86.

Toda, Masanao. 1963. Measurement of subjective probability distribution. Report 3. State College, Pennsylvania, Institute for Research, Division of Mathematical Psychology.

Tomassini, L. A., I. Solomon, M. B. Romney, and J. L. Krogstad. 1982. Calibration of auditors' probabilistic judgments: Some empirical evidence. *Organizational Behavior and Human Performance* 30:391–406.

Tversky, A. 1967a. Utility theory and additivity analysis of risky choices. *Journal of Experimental Psychology* 75:27–36.

———. 1967b. Additivity, utility and subjective probability. *Journal of Mathematical Psychology* 4:175–201.

———. 1969. Intransitivity of preferences. *Psychological Review* 76:31–48.

———. 1972. Elimination by aspects: A theory of choice. *Psychological Review* 79:281–99.

Tversky, A., and D. Kahneman. 1971. The belief in the law of small numbers. *Psychological Bulletin* 76:105–10.

———. 1973. Availability: A heuristic for judging frequency and probability. *Cognitive Psychology* 5:207–32.

———. 1982. Judgments of and by representativeness. In *Judgment under uncertainty: Heuristics and biases*, D. Kahneman, P. Slovic, and A. Tversky, editors, Cambridge: Cambridge University Press. 84–98.

———. 1983. Extensional versus intuitive reasoning: The conjunction fallacy in probability judgment. *Psychological Review* 90:293–315.

———. 1986. Rational choice and the framing of decisions. *Journal of Business* 59:S251–S278. Reprinted in *Rational choice: The contrast between economics and psychology*, R. Hogarth and M. Reder, editors, Chicago: University of Chicago Press, 1987.

———. 1991. Loss aversion in riskless choice: A reference-dependent model. *Quarterly Journal of Economics* 106:1039–61.

———. 1992. Advances in prospect theory: Cumulative representation of uncertainty. *Journal of Risk and Uncertainty* 5:297–323.

Tversky, A., S. Sattath, and P. Slovic. 1988. Contingent weighting in judgment and choice. *Psychological Review* 95:371–384.

Tversky, Amos, and Itamar Simonson. 1993. Context-dependent preferences: The relative advantage model. *Management Science* 39:1179–89.

Tversky, A., P. Slovic, and D. Kahneman. 1990. The causes of preference reversals. *American Economic Review* 80:204–17.

Tversky, A., and R. H. Thaler. 1990. Preference reversals. *Journal of Economic Perspectives* 4:201–11.

Van Naerrsen, R. F. 1962. A scale for the measurement of subjective probability. *Acta Psychologica* 20:159–66.

Van Schie, E. C. M., and J. Van Der Pligt. 1990. Problem representation, frame preference, and risky choice. *Acta Psychologica* 75:243–59.

Varey, Carol, and Daniel Kahneman. 1992. Experiences extended across time: Evaluation of moments and episodes. *Journal of Behavioral Decision Making* 5:169–85.

Viscusi, W. K. 1989. Prospective reference theory: Toward an explanation of the paradoxes. *Journal of Risk and Uncertainty* 2:235–64.

von Neumann, J., and O. Morgenstern. 1944. *Theory of games and economic behavior*. Princeton, N.J.: Princeton University Press.

von Winterfeldt, Detlof, Ngar-Kok Chung, R. Duncan Luce, and Younghee Cho. 1992. Tests of consequence monotonicity in decision making under uncertainty. Working paper. University of California at Irvine, Institute for Behavioral Mathematical Sciences.

Wagenaar, W. A. 1972. Generation of random sequences by human subjects: A critical survey of the literature. *Psychological Bulletin* 77:65–72.

Wakker, P. 1989. Continuous subjective expected utility with non-additive probabilities. *Journal of Mathematical Economics* 18:1–27.

Wason, P. C. 1968. Reasoning about a rule. *Quarterly Journal of Experimental Psychology* 20:273–81.

Weber, M., and C. Camerer. 1987. Recent developments in modelling preferences under risk. *OR Spektrum* 9:129–51.

————. 1992. The disposition effect in securities trading: An experimental analysis. Working paper, University of Chicago Graduate School of Business.

Wedell, D. H., and U. Böckenholt. 1990. Moderation of preference reversals in the long run. *Journal of Experimental Psychology: Human Perception and Performance* 16:429–38.

Wellford, C. 1989. A laboratory analysis of price dynamics and expectations in the cobweb model. Discussion paper 89–15. University of Arizona, Department of Economics.

Wilcox, Nathaniel T. In press. Lottery choice, incentives, complexity and decision time. *Economic Journal*.

Wilde, L. L. 1982. Optimal and nonoptimal satisficing I: A model of "satisfactory" choice. Working paper 363. California Institute of Technology, Division of Social Sciences and Humanities.

Williams, A. W. 1987. The formation of price forecasts in experimental markets. *Journal of Money, Credit, and Banking* 19:1–18.

Wolf, C., and L. Pohlman. 1983. The recovery of risk preferences from actual choices. *Econometrica* 51:843–50.

Wolfson, M. 1985. Tax, incentive, and risk-sharing issues in the allocation of property rights: The generalized lease-or-buy problem. *Journal of Business* 58:159–71.

Wright, G., L. D. Phillips, P. C. Whalley, G. T. G. Choo, K. O. Ng, I. Tan, and A. Wisudha. 1978. Cultural differences in probabilistic thinking. *Journal of Cross-Cultural Psychology* 9:285–99.

Wu, George. 1994. An empirical test of ordinal independence. *Journal of Risk and Uncertainty* 9:39–60.

Yaari, M. E. 1965. Convexity in the theory of choice under risk. *Quarterly Journal of Economics* 79:278–90.

————. 1987. The dual theory of choice under risk. *Econometrica* 55:95–115.

Yates, J. F. 1982. External correspondence: Decompositions of the mean probability score. *Organizational Behavior and Human Performance* 30:132–56.

————. 1990. *Judgment and decision making*. Englewood Cliffs, N.J.: Prentice Hall.

Yates, J. F., M. Toda, D. F. Wang, Y. Zhu, D. L. Ronis, and H. Shinotsuka. 1989. Probability judgment accuracy: China, Japan, and the United States. *Organizational Behavior and Human Decision Processes* 43:145–71.

Yates, J. F., and L. G. Zukowski. 1976. Characterization of ambiguity in decision making. *Behavioral Science* 21:19–25.

Zeckhauser, R. 1986. Comment: Behavioral versus rational economics: What you see is what you conquer. *Journal of Business* 59:S435–S449.

Zeuthen, F. 1937. On the determinateness of the utility function. *Review of Economic Studies* 4:236–39.

Ziemba, W. T., and Hausch, D. B. 1986. *Betting at the racetrack*. Vancouver and Los Angeles: Dr. Z Investments Inc.

Author Index

Subject Index